BITS AND BRIDLES

BITS AND BRIDLES
AN
Encyclopedia

By

Gerhard A. Malm D.V.M.

Grasshopper Publishers
Valley Falls, Kansas

Copyright 1996 by Gerhard A. Malm D.V.M.
All rights reserved. No part of this book may be used
or reproduced in any manner whatsoever without written
permission except in the case of brief quotations embodied
in critical articles or reviews. For information address
Gerhard A. Malm, P.O. Box 36, Valley Falls, KS 66088-0036.

Printed in Topeka, Kansas, by Jostens Inc.

The paper used in this book is acid free 70 pound enamel and
meets the requirements of the American National Standards
for Performance of Paper for Printed Library Materials.
Binding material has been selected for durability.

Library of Congress Cataloging-in-Publicatation Number 96-94493

ISBN: 0-9652818-0-9

CONTENTS

Acknowledgements		Page	VII
Preface			IX
Chapter 1.	Types of Bits		1
2.	Historical Evolution of Bits		7
3.	Anatomy		27
4.	Usage of Various Bits		32
5.	Glossary: Ace to Byers		47
6.	Cahoone to Cutting		76
7.	Daisy to Dressage		101
8.	Driving Bits		110
9.	Driving Bits-Overcheck		135
10.	Drown to Eyes		141
11.	Fabre to Furlong		147
12.	Gag to Guy		156
13.	Hackamore		171
14.	Hackney to Hutton		179
15.	Iceland to Kuehnhold		193
16.	Lady to Liverpool		207
17.	Liverpool		215
18.	Lobdell to Martingale		226
19.	Martingale		235

20.	Mason to Miklar	240
21.	British and Canadian Military and Police Bits	252
22.	German and French Military Bits	262
23.	United States Military Bits and Bridles	270
24.	Millard to Mouth	298
25.	Mouth-piece	305
26.	Mule to Pelham	318
27.	Pelham	333
28.	Pembroke to Purcell	351
29.	Race to Rutledge	359
30.	Sabio to Side	370
31.	Side-pieces	378
32.	Side Plates to Swartzendruber	389
33.	Tails to Typeology	411
34.	Ulrich to Zeller	426
35.	Bridles and Reins	446
36.	Loriners of the Past	466
37.	Contemporary Loriners	531
Bibliography		535
Index		543

ACKNOWLEDGMENTS

Harold Dawley, Dodge City, Kansas

Ralph Emerson Jr., South Glastonbury, Connecticut

Alain Eon, Montrouge, France

Jean Gayle, Aberdeen, Washington

Judy Gourley, Furlong, Pennsylvania

Hilary Harty, Brookline, Massachusetts

Bruce Hundley, Lexington, Kentucky

Dan and Sebie Hutchinson, Santa Fe, New Mexico

Lee Jacobs, Colorado Springs, Colorado

Kentucky Horse Park, Lexington, Kentucky

Bill Mackin, Craig, Colorado

Robert Maclin, Lexington, Kentucky

Ned Martin, Nicasio, California

Hamilton May, Colborne, Ontario, Canada

Lloyd Schultz, Holmen, Wisconsin

U.S. Army Field Artillery and Ft. Sill Museum, Fort Sill, Oklahoma

U. S. Cavalry Museum, Fort Riley, Kansas

Fort Leavenworth Museum, Fort Leavenworth, Kansas

Preface

It is not the intent of this book to make a finished rider out of the reader, but to familiarize the reader with one of the several means of controlling a horse. For other aids to control, the reader should read several of the excellent books on riding written by knowledgeable experts in the field.

My first interest in horses and riding began as a lad during my grade school and later high school years while I stayed with my maternal grandparents. The first horses I remember were a team of dapple gray Percheron geldings weighing about a ton each. I would ride them bareback to the night pasture after their day's work. A team of Wyoming "mustangs" was added about the time of my fifth grade. They were small as draft horses go, probably weighing no more than 1000 pounds each. These were the horses on which I really learned to ride. Since my grandfather did not own a saddle, all oflessons were bareback. Mv favorite was the bran-flecked gray, "Gyp." She could be ridden with only a piece of twine around her lower jaw. On many occasions I rode her with only my legs and body language for control. She was a good teacher.

Horses were a part of my every day routine of chores until I left for college. Although my thoughts were often about horses, the main thrust of my endeavors was to become a veterinarnian. There were two breaks, the summers of 1954 abd i955, which were spent learning and developing my cowboy skills on a ranch near Sheridan, Wyoming. Six dollars a day room and board.

Graduation brought on new challenges: a rural practice, then military service followed by a return to practice. Late one night in 1961 during the process of helping a heifer deliver a calf, I noticed in the faint glow of the kerosene lantern about 50 bridle bits hanging from nails along the top of the wall behind the old horse stall that was being used as a delivery room. The bits were all snaffles, having been used for draft and driving horses. with many variations in the accumulation. Delivery completed, I asked the owner about the bits and the possibility of acquiring a few. His reply, "Take what you want. They have been hanging there for over 25 years and you are the first person to even look at them." The dozen or so bits that I picked were the start of a quest for other bits and knowledge about them. Along the way I found there existed in print several good works on the subject, each with a slightly different slant to its information.

These books are listed in the bibliography of this book under the names of the authors: Carter, Cubitt, Dwyer, Tuke, Latchford, and Taylor. The possession of all these books would be a valuable tool to the serious reader of bits and bitting.

The information gained culminated in *Bible of Bridle Bits,* a photographic display specifically for collectors of bridle bits. This work led me to many individuals who had a similar interest and eventually was instrumental in the formation of the National Bit, Spur and Saddle Collectiors Association headquartered in Colorado Springs, Colorado.

Russel Beatie of Wichita, Kansas, was one of those who shared this mutual interest. He had been working on *Saddles* (University of Oklahoma Press, 1981) and was tying all the loose ends together for publication when we first met. At the same time he was also working on companion books on bridle bits and stirrups. We traded ideas, information and experiences. His untimely death in 1981 left this work unfinished. In early 1990 four boxes of material were delivered to my door with the expression, "Do something with this." The boxes contained the material Mr. Beatie had been working on. The work began in analyzing Mr. Beatie's material along with the mass of material in my stockpile of information.

In all the books, articles and literature available to me, four subjects were not too clearly presented: 1. Familiarizing the reader with the inside of the horse's mouth and how the various types of bits act on the mouth. 2. A list of parts of bits and bridles with a diagram outlining the names of each part. 3. An alphabetical glossary of bits and bridle names and terms. 4. A bibliography on the subject.

This book's way of presenting the material should make it easier for beginners to learn the subject, and for professionals to find the information they may need.

Uniformity of nomenclature is a necessity in any field and is much needed in the area of bridle bits. I have attempted to to do this in the glossary presented in Chapters Five through Thiry-five.

There is hardly a field which is more controlled by personal preference and experience than bitting. When one inquires as to who are the academians in the field, very few names are brought up. Most of the names given are highly respected, knowledgeable trainers with many years of good experience gained by trial and error, which in the final analysis is the end answer. However, for new-comers to the field, the best way to drastically shorten the learning curve time to a good knowledge of bitting is to start by reading the best literature on the subject so that when the time comes for learning by experience, the student will have a basic knowledge of the subject. Experience, combined with academic knowledge is the foundation for making an outstanding rider in the field of bitting.

Horsemen are tradition minded and many of them don't ask "Why."

CHAPTER ONE
Types of Bits

Snaffle Bits:

A snaffle bit is a straight-bar or broken-bar bit with a rein-ring or cheek-piece at each end. It is a two rein, no leverage bit, which usually works on the bars of the horse and/or on the upper corners of the mouth. Its use tends to lift the horse's head higher. If the reins are held low enough, it can work on the horse's bars. There are two types of snaffle bits:

1. The solid-bar snaffle

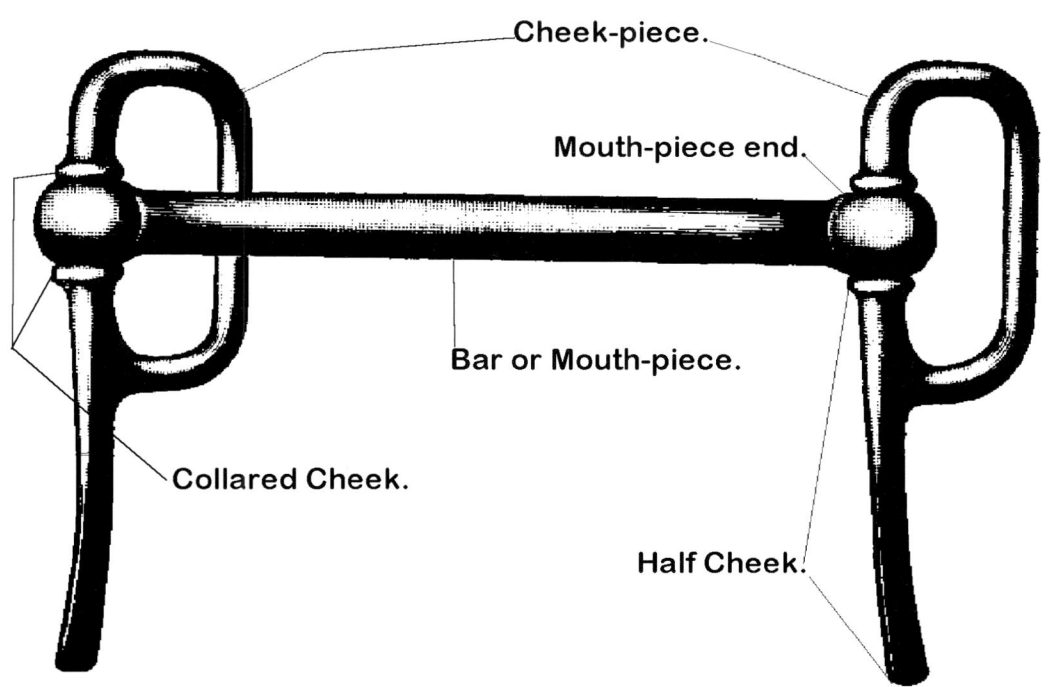

2. Broken Snaffle Bit:

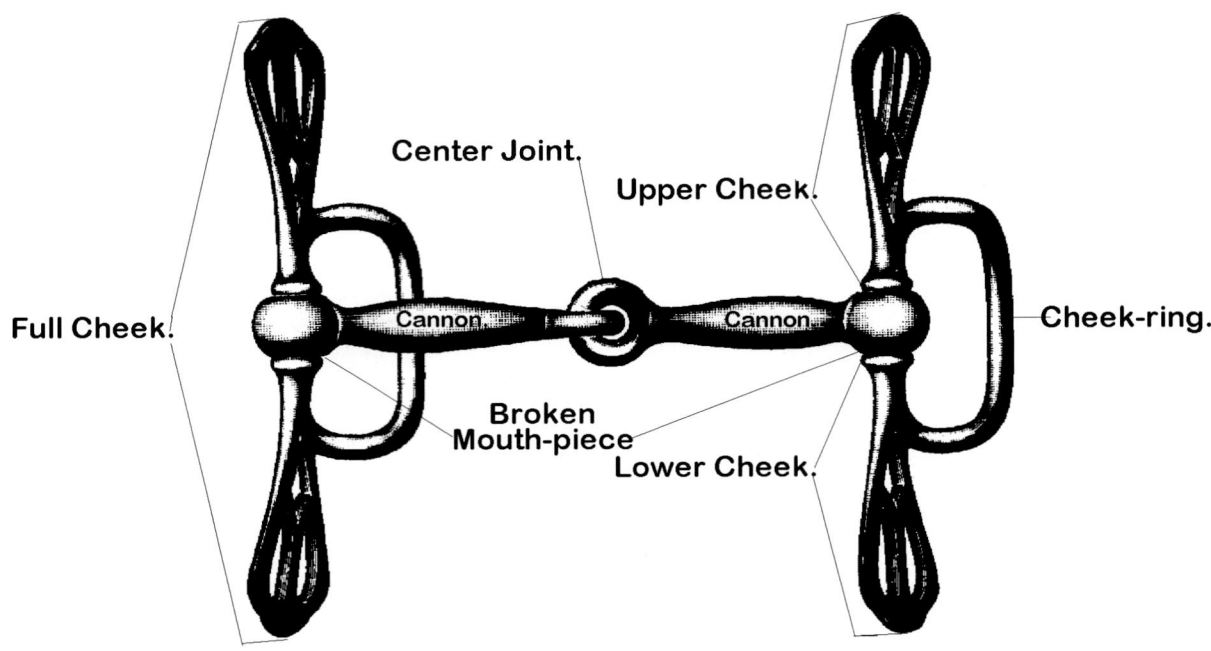

Curb Bit:

The curb bit in conjunction with the curb-chain in the chin groove gives the rider leverage to bend the horse at the poll, pulling its head closer to the chest.

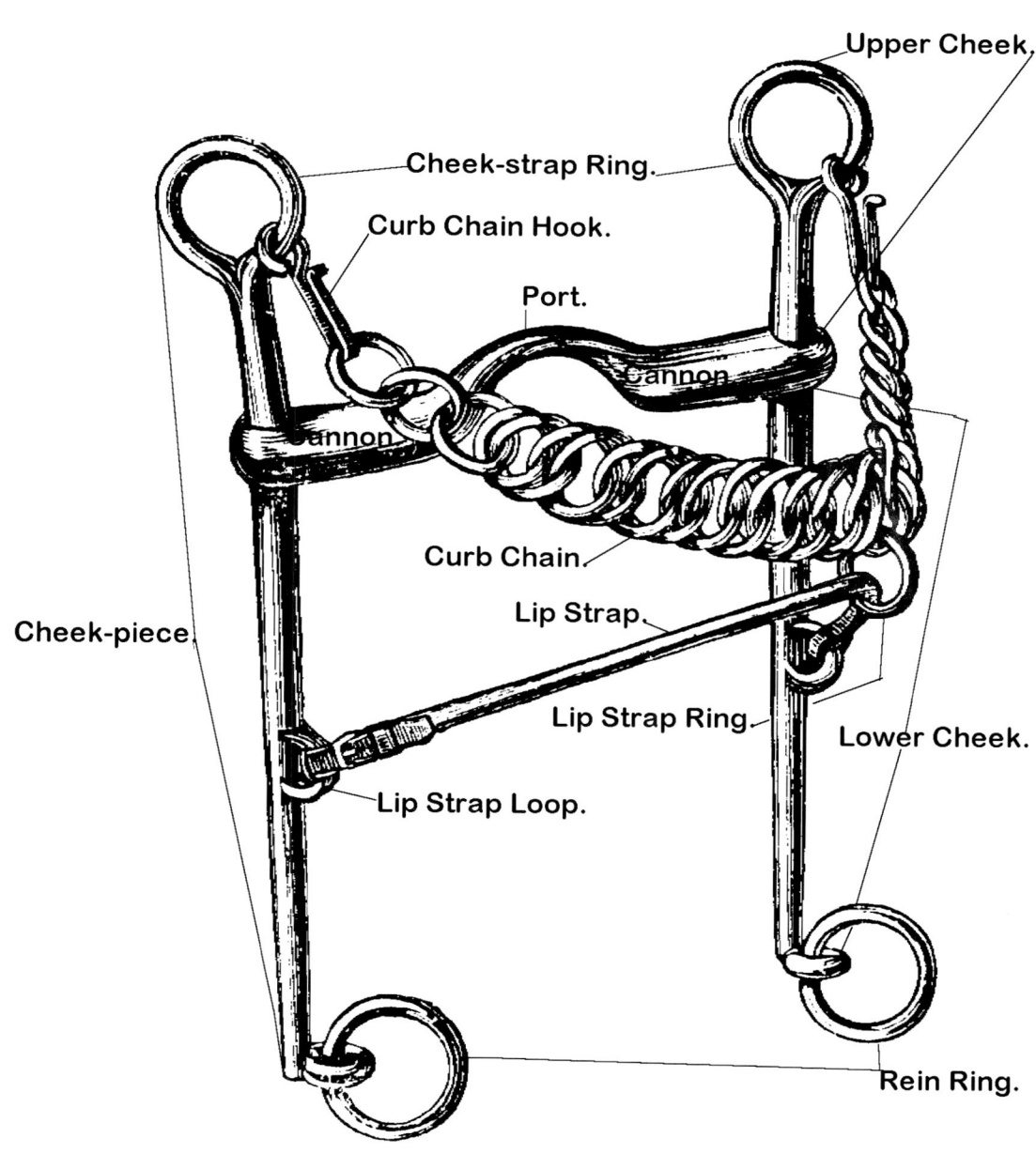

Spade Bit:

The spade bit is a form of curb bit with an exaggerated extension of the port that ends in a curved enlargement in the shape of a spoon. A copper roller may be built into the tip of the spoon. The lip or chin chains may be replaced by a solid bar. The mouth-piece ends (jaw) may be loose or tight.

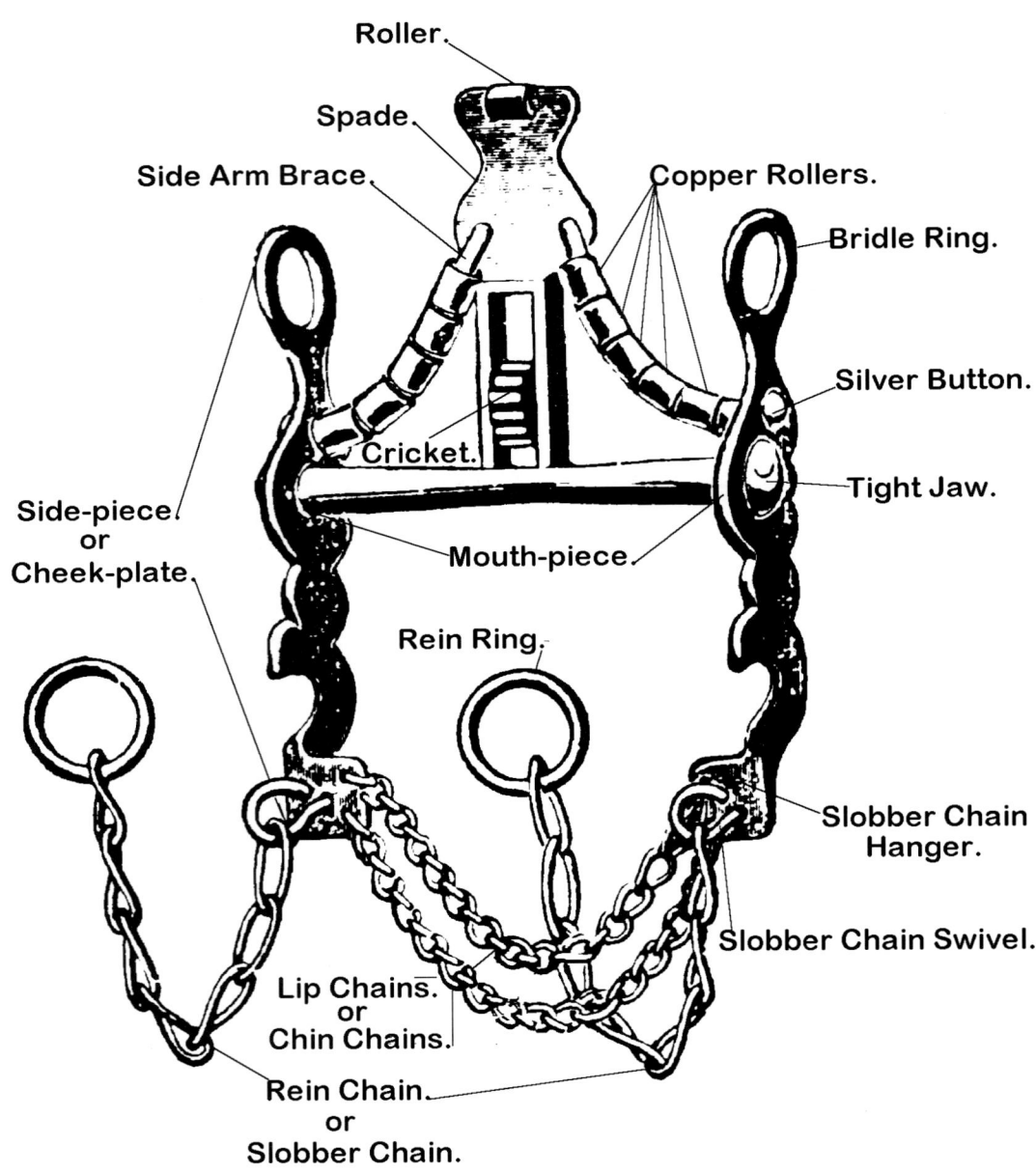

Ring Bit:

The ring bit is a curb bit with a built-on curb in the form of a ring attached to the upper end of the two inch port.

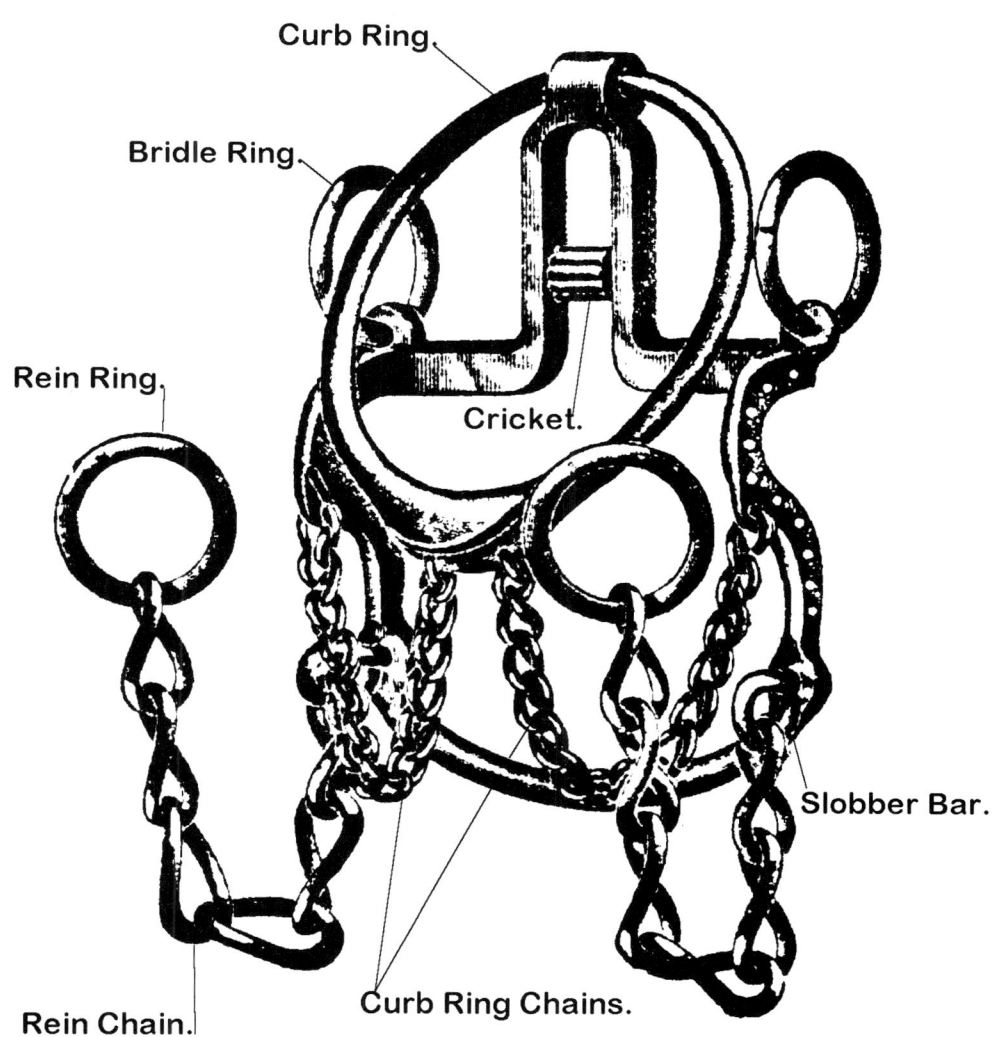

Pelham Bit:

A four ring bit to be used with four reins. The mouth-piece may be a solid bar, jointed or ported. The cheek-pieces may be fixed or loose. This bit attempts to replace in one bit the curb and bridoon bits of the English full bridle.

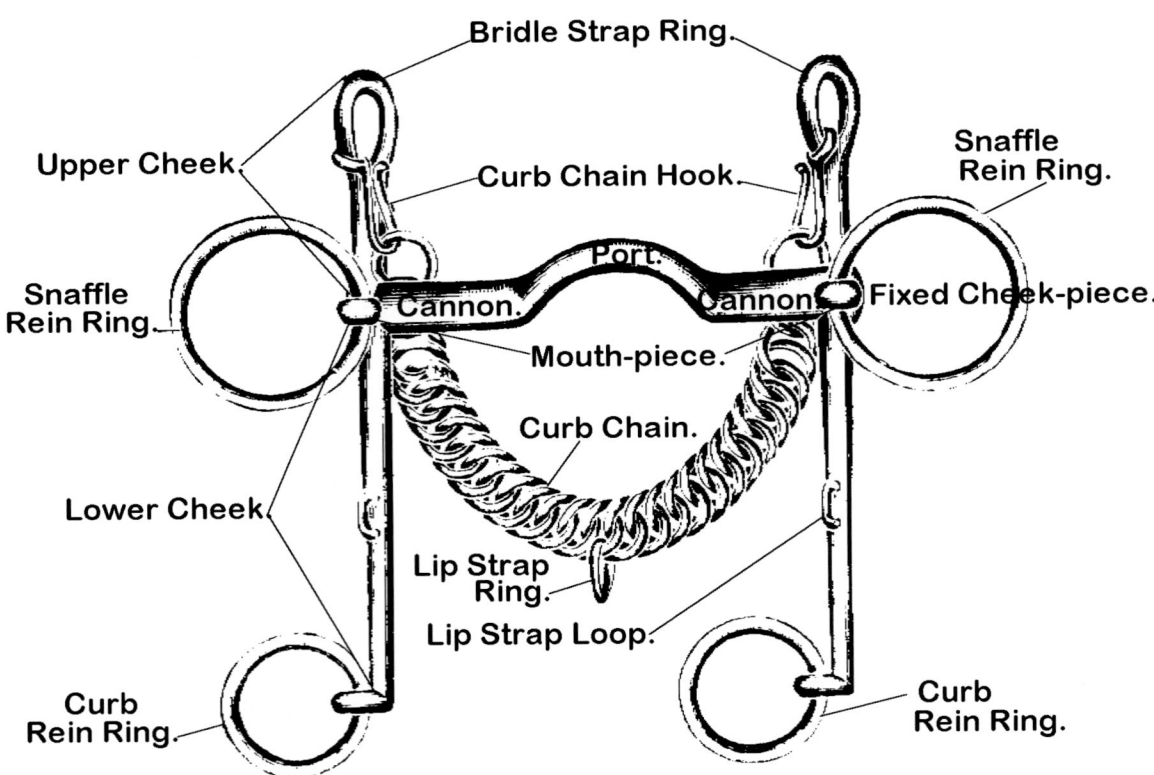

CHAPTER TWO
Historical Evolution of Bits

The evolution of the bridle bit cannot be brought into perspective without a brief overview of the evolution of the horse and how it came to be a servant to mankind. The biographic occurance of horses over the last 60 million years is one of the most frequently cited fossil record interpretations, probably more so than fossil humans and human-like creatures. The best book I found that describes the evolution process of the horse in detail and diagram is *Horses* by George Gaylord Simpson (1951). *The Horse Through the Ages* by Cecil G. Trew (1953) and *The History and the Romance of the Horse* by Arthur Vernon (1946) also merit study. Simpson, a paleontologist, claims that Trew's book is interesting but the chapters on evolution are highly inaccurate, and Vernon's book is romantically treated but the chapters on prehistoric and early historic horses are often inaccurate.

Simpson believes that there were "three-toed" and "single-toed" horses that represented both browsers and grazers on the earth at the same time and in the same general area.

Graphic charts depicting the evolution processes of foot, tooth, skull and height development that are frequently seen in a wide variety of books on horses as representative of orthogenesis are generally believed to be incorrect by most paleontologists. Old notions die hard.

A recent book, *Fossil Horses,* by Bruce J. MacFadden (Cambridge U. Press, 1992), even questions Simpson's interpretation of the evolution process.

The "Great Migration" of Equus from the Western Hemisphere to the landmass of Asia-Europe is the main reason that the horse is present at all today. *Hypohippus miocene,* the preglacial horse of the North American continent, and *Hippidiom neogaem* of the South American pampas became extinct. The only species that survived was the plains horse. This species is thought to be the ancestor of the horses that developed in north-central Asia, because in the Pliocene period, there suddenly appeared species of true horses in several parts of Asia and Europe for which no ancestors can be found in that area. They seem to be typical descendants of the plains horse last seen in America.

The main seat of development appears to be north-central Asia. The several varieties of zebras (Africa) and the wild ass species of Nubia and Somaliland, the onager of the deserts of Asia and the Kiang (Tibet), along with the Asiatic wild horses are all examples of the evolution and migration of Equus.

The only family of original wild horses, not feral or those which have run wild from domesticated herds, known to exist in recent years is the Tarpon or Przevalski. Some writers classify the two as different species; others classify them as one and the same. Those who claim they differ use the criteria of the 40th degree east longitude as the dividing point with the Tarpon (extinct since about 1880) to the west and the Przevalski horse to the east. David P. Willoughby makes a distinct separation of the two species by name and physical criteria. Referring to the Tarpon as South Russian Tarpon *(Equus caballus gmelini)* Willoughby makes character differences in coat color, average wither height, head conformation, face and muzzle shape, mane, dorsal stripe measurements, leg callosities, and tail length.

Fig. 2.0 *Equus caballus gmelini*. The only known drawing of a live South Russian Tarpen by Borisow as it appeared in Col. Hamilton Smith's book *Horses* in *Jardine's Naturalist's Library,* 1841. The animal is immature.

The Przevalski (accepted spelling) horse is named in honor of the Russian explorer Nicolai Mikhailovitch Przhevalski (1839-1888) who is often credited with having "discovered" the wild horse. Considerable confusion attends the history of the animal--so much so, that "rediscover" would perhaps be a more accurate term for Przevalski's part in bringing it to public notice. The English naturalist Col. Hamilton Smith in 1814 obtained a first-hand detailed description of the Mongolian wild horse from some Russian cavalry officers. This description was published by Col. Smith in several editions of *Jazdine's Naturalist's Library,* Vol. 20, *Horses,* starting in 1841.

The brothers Grum-Grshimailo secured four specimen of Przevalski horses in 1889, at the oasis of Gashum, in eastern Dzungaria. According to their report "Przevalski (Americanized spelling) himself, though he crossed the desert of Dzungaria in several directions, never came across any of the wild horses" (Willoughby, p. 129).

Man's first use of the horse was as a food source. The horse was at that time hunted the same as any other wild animal. Even after semidomestication it was often kept solely for its source of meat, blood, hides and possibly at times a supply of milk used to make a type of cheese or yogurt.

Fig. 2.1 *Equus caballus przewalskii*

I have often wondered how the semi-domesticated horse was controlled by the herders. Having tried to drive so-called tame horses on foot a few times, it is hard to imagine how the semi-wild horses could be controlled except that the herder was also mounted at the same time. Historians have not addressed this conflict. I firmly believe that the two occured at about the same time.

When the horse was first used as a beast of burden is lost in antiquity. It is possible that a horse injured or wounded during the hunt was utilized to help carry or drag another kill to the hunter's abode. Or the process may have occured much like Jean M. Auel fictionalized in *The Valley of Horses,* with Ayla's rescue, feeding, training and useful development of "Whinney" (p. 97). Ayla used nothing on "Whinney's" head but learned to steer or guide her friend by shifting her weight and sending messages to her charge by flexing and contracting her legs (p. 167). Ayla later developed a type of harness and then a drag, much like a travois, to help transport large animal kills and supplies to her cave.

A substantial part of the knowledge of man's early history may be credited to graves and grave-goods alone. Even 40,000 years ago, Neanderthal man buried his dead with grave gifts (Lehmann).

Cave drawings and hieroglyphs, tombs, temples and the excavation of ancient cultural centers have all contributed pieces to the puzzle of ancient civilizations. What has remained for us may or may not be the normal equipment of the common man of a specific period being studied. Artifacts from tombs usually represent only the ruling class. Examples we have on friezes, vases, and stelas may reflect the artists' abilities or interpretation. In spite of uncertainty, the information gathered is probably a good representator of the era or time period to which it belongs.

The Grotto (cave) of Montespan in southern Spain has wall engravings that are estimated to be 20,000 years old. One which is deeply engraved depicts two horses lacking heads, but having obese bodies. One of them, whose belly is unusually distended, has carved on its flank a human hand. One may see in this sign a symbol of man's domination over the possibly pregnant animal (*Nat. Geog.* Nov. 1923, p. 146). Another engraving shows the heads of two horses, carved side by side, of such different characteristics that there is no doubt of the artist's intention to represent two widely different types of horses (p. 150). Besides the drawings, bones of horses and other animals were found in the cave (p. 151).

Evidence is available at Stellmoor in North Germany of reindeer being kept in the 8th millennim B. C. (Jankovich, p. 11). Relics excavated in the Kurdish hills of northern Iraq carbon-14 test date the presence of domesticated animals, including horses, as early as 7000 B. C. (Vernam, p. 5).

The tombs of Egypt (especially of King Tutankhamen, ruler from 1347 to 1339 B. C.), the Luristan tombs and village sites of Southwest Asia, the frozen tombs of Siberia (4th century B. C.), and the burial tomb of Chinese ruler Ch'in Shih Huang Ti (3rd century B. C.) have been some of the richest sources of tangible horse equipment in the archeological puzzle.

The Sumerians (a people of ancient Babylonia, the area between the Tigris and Euphrates Rivers, and probably of non-semitic origin) established one of the earliest historical civilizations in the 4th millennium B. C. Their language preserved on clay tablets had no specific word for horse as such. Since the horses originated from the north and northeast they described horses in paraphrases as, "ass of the northeast or mountain ass" (Contenau, p. 55-56).

Herodotus (Greek historian, 5th century B. C.) tells of the high value placed upon the "Nissean horses from Media" (an ancient country in southwest Asia, now the northwest region of Iran) because they were larger than other breeds (Contenau, p. 56).

This may be a good place to pause and take a good look at the information expressed to this point and reflect on several points. Each historian, whether his specialty be Greece (J. K. Anderson), Europe and Western Asia (Jankovich), Babylon and Assyria (Contenau), the Hittites (Lehmann), the Scythians (Rice), the evolution process (Simpson) or any of the authors, such as Dent, Taylor, Vernam, Willoughby or the host of others with tribe or period specialty, has a great deal of information to impart.

The reading, analyzing and interpretation of material often leaves one with the feeling expressed by Socrates, "The more I learn the less I know." The argument for the expression is that the skeleton of historical research is chronology. Each area or land differs from another, and archaeologists may be unable to agree on dates of relics of one area when associated with like relics attributed to a different time in another area or region. One of the keys of period dating much of the area of Southwest Asia (more specifically the Arabian Peninsula) and Egypt is Egyptian archaeology dating back to the earlist Dynastic Period (Protodynastic, 3110-2868 B. C.), although some scholars disagree on the earliest by as much as 200 years (Yadin, p. 28).

In recent years the carbon-14 method of dating has become a guide in determining absolute chronology. The only draw-back is the lack of split-second precision. The method has a range in accuracy of plus or minus 200 years. As a result, it is of little value in recent history, but in some areas it is an invaluable tool. The statement of absolute dating is not always valid for certain periods or populations. Certain societies or people progressed much quicker than others in different parts of the continent--some by as much as several hundred years. Many dates are at best no more than estimates. This is compounded by a lack of absolute uniformity in names and terminology. Added to the confusion is the translation factor, such as from Russian or Hebrew to German or French to English. There is some detail of accuracy lost in the interpretations and translations. Some of this confusion also is the result of the special history of each land and period and the different approaches or methods used by each scholar, as mentioned. Archaeological study is also fraught with the complication of the continuous trading activity between empires and peoples and the ever present warring practices. Maybe that is where the expression "any history is a pack of lies agreed upon," originated.

To further confuse the issue, carbon-14 dating on the remains of a horse found in the fall of 1993 near Dawson City, Yukon Territory, shows that the horse died 26,000 years ago.

"Experts said it is one of the best preserved animals ever discovered in North America."

The dark chestnut hide is complete with a long blond mane and long blond tail. This is in contrast to the dark-coated, dark short mane and tail of that period, depicted by archaeologist, paleontologist and artists. "The remains were so well preserved that intestinal membranes are distinguishable, complete with digested food" (Associated Press, 25 Dec. 1993). Could this be the ancestor of the "Heavenly" horses or hot-blooded horses described by other authors or the ancestor of the present-day Arab type?

The Przevalski horse is sometimes referred to as the Dun horse of the North or the Northern Type. A second type of strong, light-boned, thin-skinned horse tending more toward blacks and bays has been named the Southern or Barb type (Trew, p. 15).

Trew claims one striking difference between the Northern and Southern types is in the gap above the eye in the bones of the skull. This gap is present in the Southern type of horse and in varying degrees in the modern Arab. No trace of the gap is to be seen in the Northern type (Fig. 2.2 and Fig. 2.3). This difference substantiates the descriptions given by Willoughby for the Przevalski and the South Russian Tarpan horses.

Jankovich makes a further distinction by referring to the Northern type as "cold-blooded" and the Southern type as "hot-blooded."

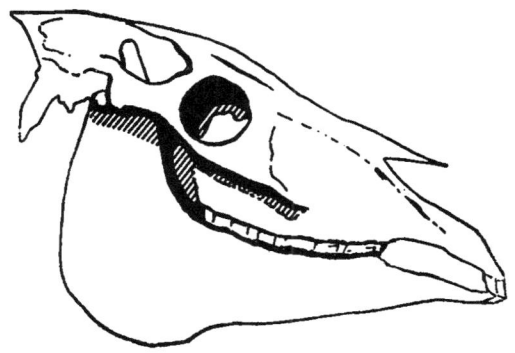

Fig. 2.2 A skull drawing of a modern day Arab with the characteristics of the Southern, or "Hot-blooded" type.

The onager was domesticated perhaps as early as 5000 B.C., but the horse which is not native to western Asia, was first used as a traction animal in the steppes of central Eurasia around 4000 B. C. A thousand years later came the horse-drawn cart, which spread southward to the Antolian Plateau and reached the 'Fertile Crescent' (the semicircle of fertile land encompassing the Tigris and Euphrates valleys and the region of old Palestine and Phoenicia) by the middle of the third millennium B. C. (Bowles, p. 251).

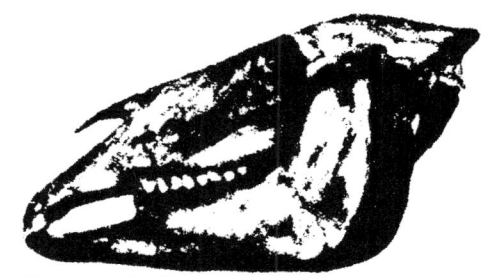

Fig. 2.3 A skull drawing of the Northern or "Cold-blooded" type horse.

The nomadic lifestyle of the tribes (nation or people) involved in the spread and migration of the horse was necessitated by a constant search for water and forage. The gain or loss of grass and water made the diffence between life or death by famine. Increased herd size, not only of horses but of all domestic animals, produced friction between the herd owners. One conflict is recorded in the patriarchial verses of the Old Testament. "And the land was not able to bear them that they may dwell together: for their substance was great. . . And there was strife between the herdsmen of Abram's cattle and herdsmen of Lot's cattle" (Genesis 13:6,7).

More than any other animal, the horse has shaped the course of human history. Without the horse the great chariot empires of the Hittites, Hyksos, Persian, Greek and Romans could never have developed (Bowles, p. 251). The arrival of the steam locomotive ended over 5000 years of the horse as the primary mode of land transportation for mankind, with the exception of the camel and the ass in some areas.

The disbursement of the horse through the Eastern hemisphere and the people or tribes that either followed or contributed to the disbursement in a southernly and westernly direction brought the horse to the people of Europe and Southwest Asia.

The southern limit of wild horse habitat in Asia was approximately the 50th parallel. In this continent that is about the United States-Canadian border. The northern limit is the 65th parallel of latitude or the Arctic Circle. The habitat, as the word implies, developed because of the climatic conditions that influenced the type of food available to the horse. Some believe the lower limit was influenced by diseases, especially those transmitted by insects.

The horse (or onager or ass) became a useful servant when man learned to control the animal. Directing the animal with sticks (in the manner that oxen are driven) while it pulled a mat of brush used as a crude sled, could've been one of the first means of control. Many hundreds of years would lapse before horses would be controlled by a head-stall, halter or bridle.

The advent of the use of metals in the fourth millennium B.C. was a major revolution which led to an improvement in tools, weapons, armor, and eventually equipment for the animals pulling carts. The population of Mesopotamia used two-wheeled carts drawn by oxen, donkeys or onagers (horses were still unknown to the area) as early as 3200 B.C. Copper was still a luxury at that period. The remains found at the ancient city of Susa contained some copper, but most of the tools and equipment were still Neolithic (Grousett, p. 10). The solid-wheeled carts were usually powered by four animals. This was probably necessitated by the small size of the animals, the constrictive style of harness which tended not to utilize the full ability of the animal and the awkwardness and construction of the cart (Fig. 2.4).

The next revolution was the development of the spoked-wheel and the use of the horse as a replacement for the onager or donkey.

Fig. 2.4 A solid-wheel quadragia drawn by four onagers is a portion of the Standard of Ur of the Chalders and is dated ca. 2500 B.C. The rein ring is similar to Fig. 2.8.

During the third and into the second millennium B.C., the nomadic tribes experimented with riding horses. The nomads were not alone in this endeavor; others in southwest Asia had also tried riding horses on hunts and in battles. The practice was not widespread.

The earliest bits were made of horn or bone (Figs. 2.5 and 2.6) with a rawhide or wood mouth-piece. Later copper, bronze and finally iron were the materials used, according to Tozer.

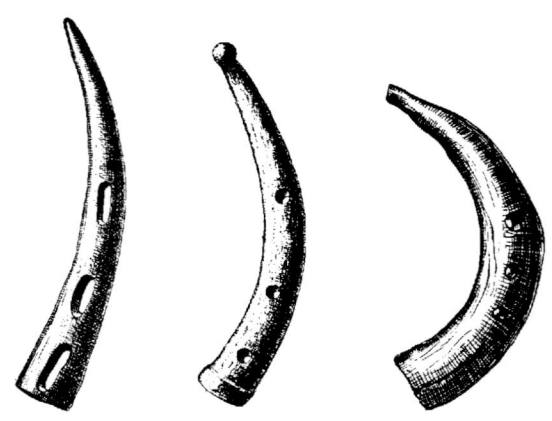

Fig. 2.5 Early bridle bits had bone and antler cheek-pieces and leather or rawhide mouth-pieces.

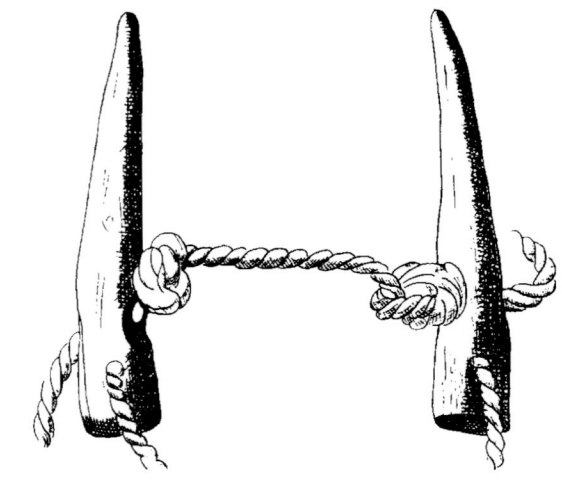

Fig. 2.6 Drawing of a bit made of antlers and connected by a twisted rope or rawhide.

Evacuation of Luristan tombs of Susa (the capitol of ancient Elam in southwestern Iran) yielded the harness and trappings of horses. A tomb contained a bit which consisted of a straight bar with intricate engraved large broad side-pieces attached to strips of leather (Contenau, p. 56). The size of the bit was for a small horse with a narrow mouth. A piece of bone engraved with a bridled and saddled horse resembling the Przevalski type of horse has been found in Susa. The piece has been dated by some to about 3000 B.C. J. K. Anderson disagrees and believes it to be of a much later date.

Some time about 1730 B.C. (Dynastic XV-XVI, 1786-1570 B.C.), the Syrian Hyksos or "Shepherd Kings," brought horses to Egypt (Vernam, p. 6).

Mythology and legendary evidence leads us to believe these Egyptian horses were later brought into Greece. The records from the time of the Hyksos are the first to mention the use of the horse in war, and this in conjuction with chariots. The chariots must have been a fearsome weapon of war to unprotected foot-soldiers (Mertz, p. 142).

Blinders on a bridle were first found in the tomb of the Egyptian Pharaoh, Tutankhamen.

The Greek Homer in *The Iliad* (before or during the 9th century B.C.) alludes to "bits of bronze" placed between the horses' jaws (Tozer, p. 18). A bit found at the Acropolis is said to date back to the early Persian wars of 490-479 B.C. (Tozer, p. 40).

There were no buckles, as we know them, until the time of the Scythians, according to Diane Raddatz (p. 21). The bridles recovered from seventh and sixth century B.C. Scythian tombs had buckles (more like toggles) of bone. Prior to the use of buckles, bridles were tied together with knots, or were sewn and not adjustable.

Prof. J. K. Anderson and Louis Taylor give a more complete history of bits. The source for each is listed in the bibliography under the author's name.

The evolution of bridle and bridle bits can be illustrated by pictorial evidence of what has been preserved and identified. The following photos and drawings are representative of the plainness and intricacy of utility and design that evolved through 5000 years of usage. Time has proven that the simple and original, such as the common broken mouth-piece snaffle, may be the best suited for guiding the horse. The mouth of the horse has not experienced change during this period; only the ideas and concepts of man initiated the radical design changes presented.

Thirty-second Century B.C.

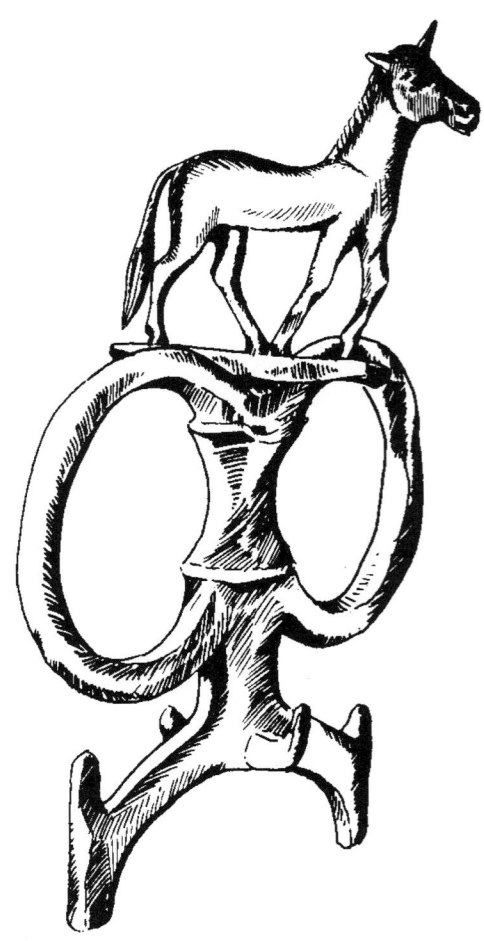

Fig. 2.7 A donkey mascot on a Summerian rein-guide attributed to Queen Shub-ads chariot, 3100 B.C. (Courtesy of The British Musem, London).

Eighteenth Century B.C.

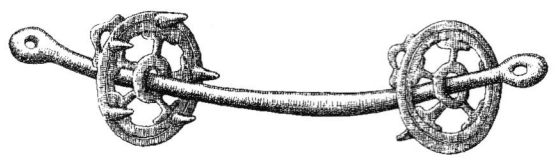

Fig. 2.8 A drawing of a Hyksos bit from Tell el-Ajjal, 18th Century B.C. The loose circular cheek-pieces have inner pronges to affect the sides of the horse's mouth.

Seventeenth Century B.C.

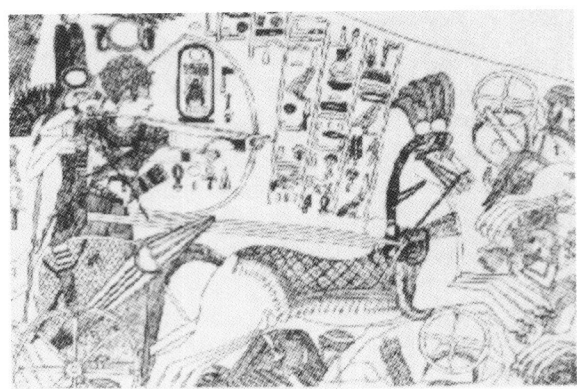

Fig. 2.9 A light Egyptian two-horse war chariot of the 17th Century B.C. The triple cheek-strap of the bridle is representative of the period. The location of the rings on the breast collar gives the appearance of the four reins (two for each horse) acting much like a bearing rein.

Fifteenth Century B.C.

Fig. 2.10 A horse and chariot with driver painted in the tomb of Menna, an official in the government of Thutmose IV, who reigned as pharroh of Egypt from 1412-1402 B.C. The high breast strap and the four reins with a rein to each side of the two horse hitch illustrates the early chariot bridle and harness.

Fourteenth Century B.C.

Fig. 2.11 Heads of chariot horses of Sept-I of Egypt (circa 1321-1300 B.C.). From Ridgeway, *Origin and Influence of the Thoroughbred Horse.* (Fig. 68, on P. 217). The horses are managed by a dropped noseband, with no mouth-piece or bit. Two pair of reins are attached to the noseband: the lower one is controlled by the charioteer; the upper one appears to a bearing rein, fastened to the yoke of the chariot.

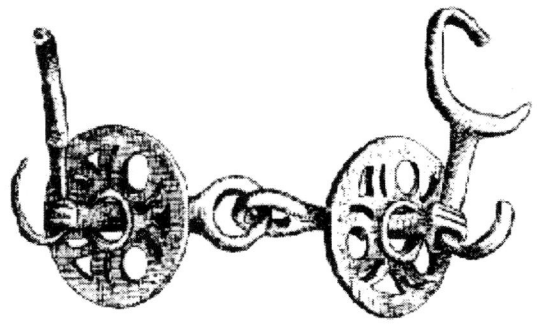

Fig. 2.12 A 14th Century B.C. bit from Luristan (Iran). Many of the snaffle-type bits of this area have the small hands holding the rein-rings.

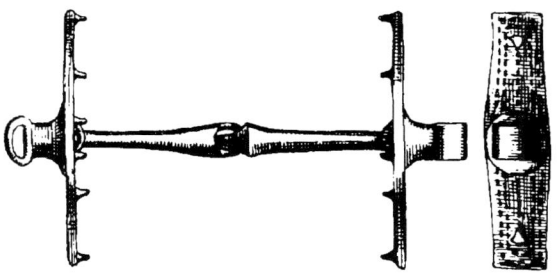

Fig. 2.13 A 14th Century B.C. Egyptian bit with a jointed mouth-piece. Compare the jointed mouth with Fig. 26.19, Chapter 26.

Twelfth Century B.C.

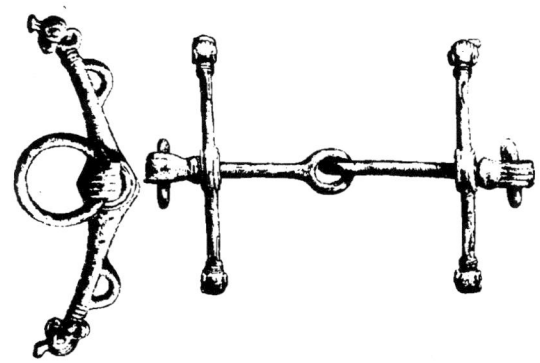

Fig. 2.14 A drawing of the snaffle-type bit from Luristan with the hands holding the rein-rings.

Fig. 2.15 A detail of Ramses III Circa 1204-1172 B.C. on a sculptured pylon at Medinet Habu. The detail represents a bridle with a

15

dropped noseband for control that is held in place by a divided cheek-strap.

Eighth Century B.C.

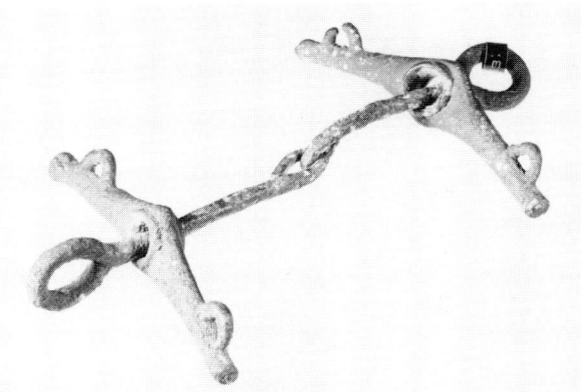

Fig. 2.16 A bronze era bit from the area of Luristan. The metal bit has a blueish and reddish coloration and chips easily. Reference: Museum of Art and History, Geneva, Switzerland. Jean Gayle collection.

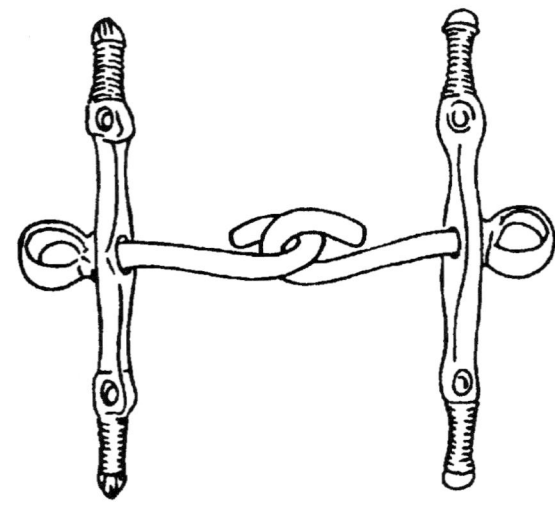

Fig. 2.18 Drawing of a metal 8th Century B.C. bridle bit from the area south of the Caucasus Mountains which is now Georgia (USSR) and Azerbaidzhan.

Ninth Century B.C.

Seventh Century B.C.

Fig. 2.17 A drawing of a cheek-piece from Hungary designed for a split-cheek headstall.

Fig. 2.19 A relief showing a well-developed Syrian bridle of the 7th Century B.C.

Fig. 2.20 A cheek-plate of a Persian bit. This type of cheek-plate is well represented in various museums. The motif has a wide range of variations. Some of the animals included besides the griffons, are horses, cattle, ibex, camels, llamas, panthers (lions), and swine plus others in a variety of combinations and alone. This type of cheek-plate is believed to be from the 7th to the 4th Century B.C.

Sixth Century B.C.

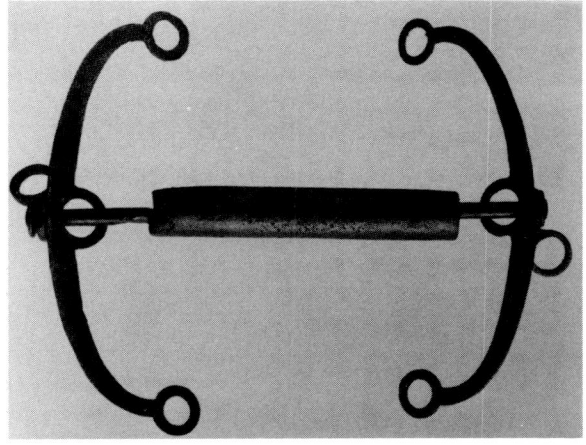

Fig. 2.21 A bit from Olympia (circa 550-490 B.C.) Courtesy of the German Archeological Institute, Athens.

Fig. 2.22 A detail of a relief representing the period of Darius I of Persia (522-486 B.C.). The bridle represents advanced development. The split lower cheek-straps fasten to the bit above and below the mouth-piece to give the bit stability. The bridle has a dropped noseband and the narrow browband is adorned with tassels. A toggle secured the throat-latch; all the other points are secured and cannot be unfastened. Courtesy of The Oriental Institute, University of Chicago.

Fig. 2.23 Drawing of a bit from Greece in the late 6th Century B.C.

Fifth Century B.C.

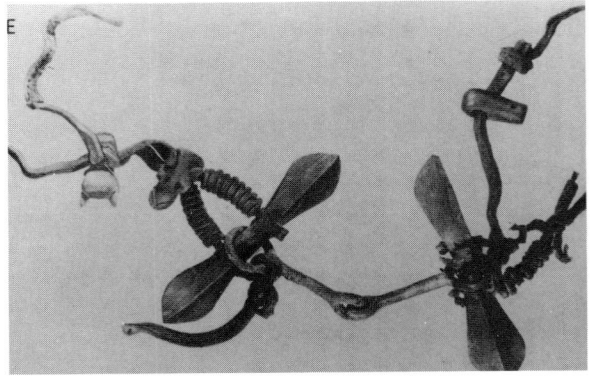

Fig. 2.25 A bronze bit and lower part of a bridle from Pazyryk burial barrow No. 3. *The Frozen Tombs of Siberia,* Sergei Rudenko. Courtesy of The Orion Publishing Groub, Ltd., London.

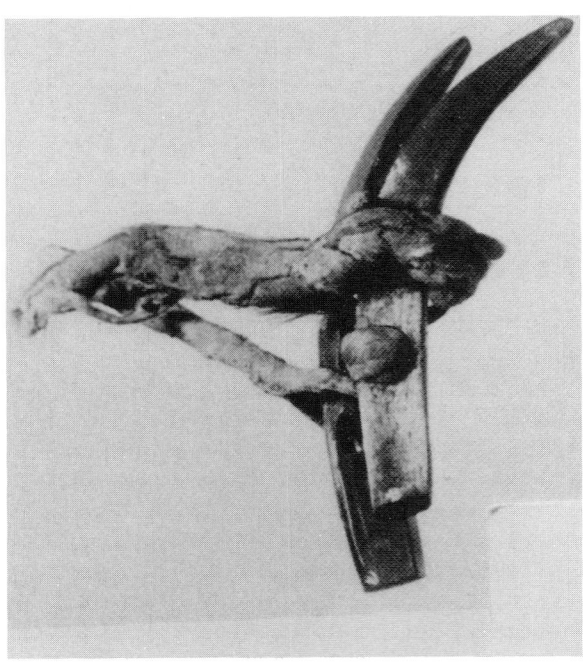

Fig. 2.24 A bit showing the attached cheekpieces from the Pazyryk burial barrow No. 2. *The Frozen Tombs of Siberia,* Sergei Rudenko. Courtesy of The Orion Publishing Group Ltd., London.

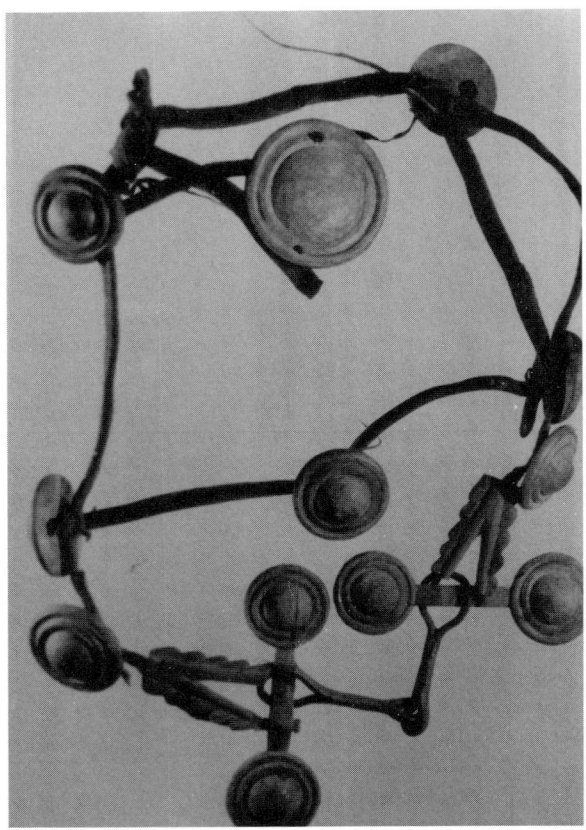

Fig. 2.26 Bridle of a riding outfit from the Pazyryk burial barrow No,. 5. *The Frozen Tombs of Siberia,* Sergei Rudenko. Courtesy of The Orion Publishing Group Ltd., London.

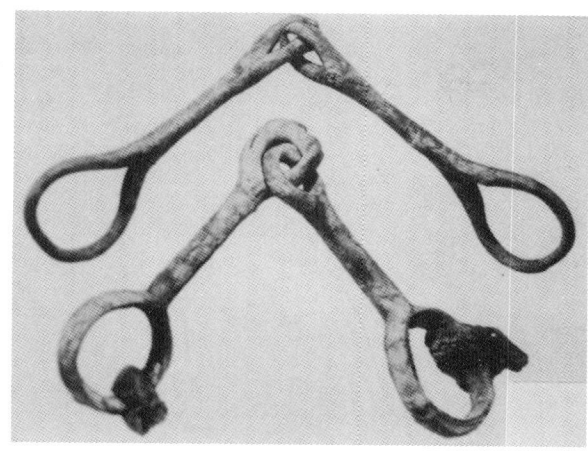

Fig. 2.27 Bronze bits from the Pazyryk burial barrow No. 2. *The Frozen Tombs of Siberia,* Sergei Rudenko. Courtesy of The Orion Publishing Group Ltd., London.

Fig. 2.29 Drawing of a bronze bit from the northern part of the Caucasus Mountains.

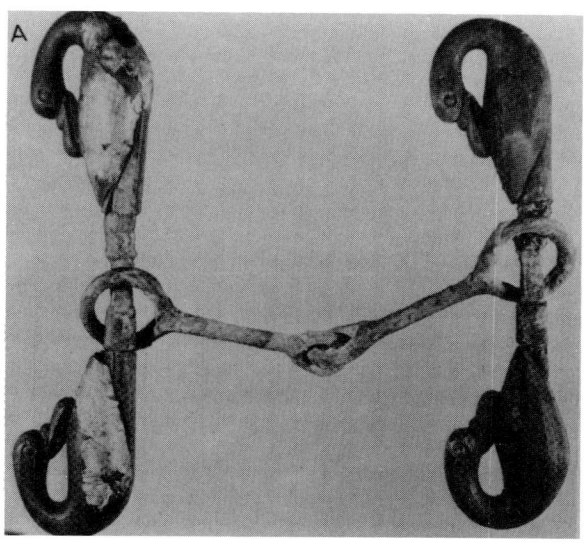

Fig. 2.28 A bronze bit and cheek-pieces with swan terminals from barrow No. 3. *The Frozen Tombs of Siberia,* Sergei Rudenko. Courtesy of The Orion Publishing Group Ltd., London.

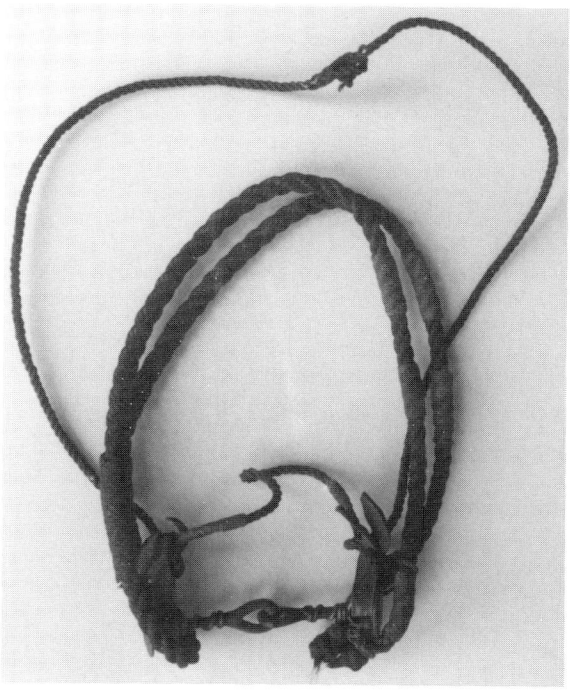

Fig. 2.30 A bridle and bit of the 5th century B.C. The braided hair headstall measures 12 inches from the crown to the bit. The reins and curb-strap are of braided hair.

Fig. 2.31 A detail of the bronze bit in Fig. 2.30. It measure 3 3/4 inches between the curb-strap holes.

Fig. 2.32 A bit from the southwest area of Asia in what is now Iran. The Ibex cheek-pieces are mounted on wood blocks for museum display.

Fig. 2.33 Luristan bit with cheek-pieces in a horse motif. Mounted on wood blocks for Musem display.

Fourth Century B.C.

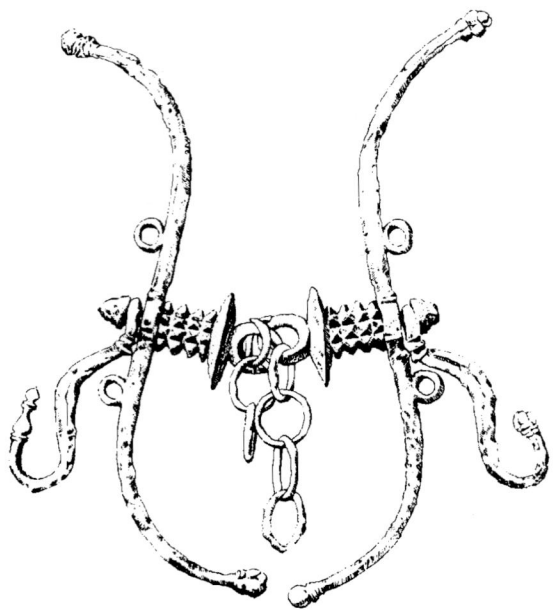

Fig. 2.34

Fig. 2.34 A 4th Century B.C. Grecian bit with echinas and mouthing chains.

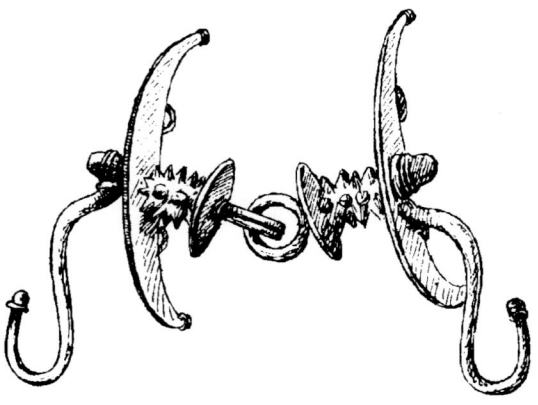

Fig. 2.35 Drawing of a 4th Century B.C. bit from Greece.

Third Century B.C.

Fig. 2.36 A bit from Greece. The notched cannons swivel on the arched center portion. It has a 4 3/4 inch mouth and a 2 inch port. Jean Gayle collection.

Second Century A.D.

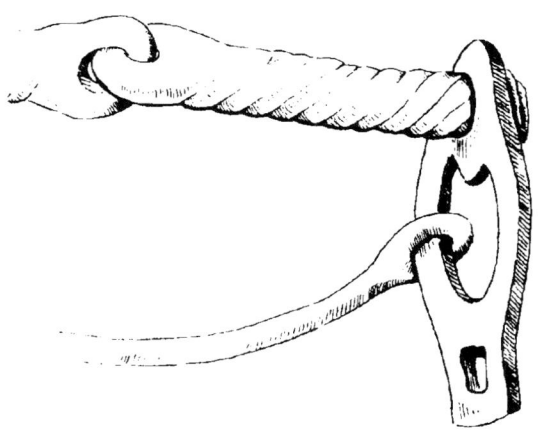

Fig. 2.37 Drawing of a 2nd Century A.D Roman bit.

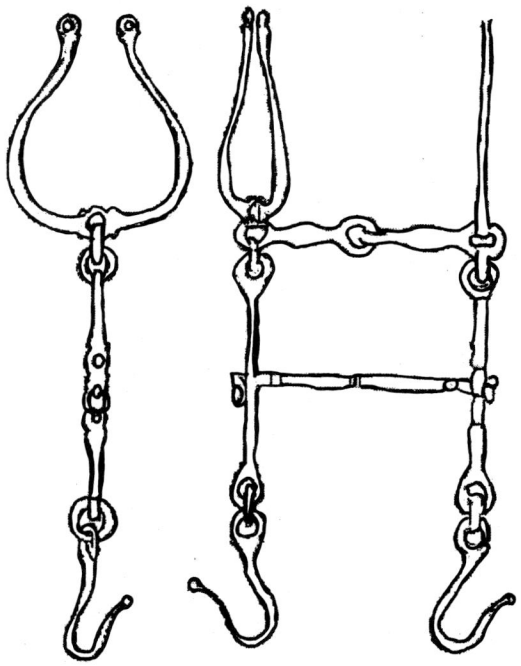

Fig. 2.38 Drawing showing a bridle bit with a side view of the cheek-piece, 2nd Century A.D. Roman.

Fifth Century A.D.

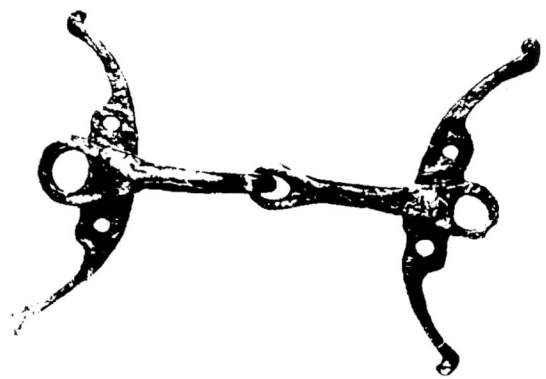

Fig. 2.39 An iron bit from 5th Century A.D. Poland.

Twelfth Century A.D.

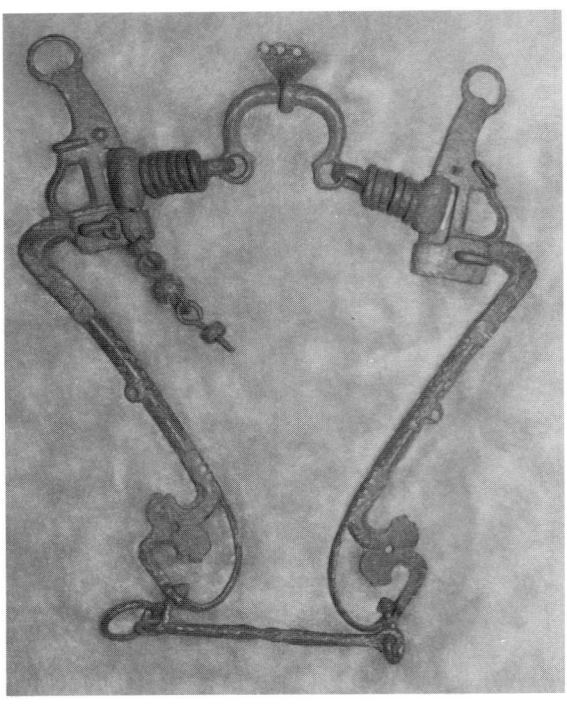

Fig. 2.40 A bit from Egypt in the late 1100's A.D. The bit bears symbols of the countries of the upper Nile (lotus) and the lower Nile (papyrus). Harold Dawley collection.

Fourteenth Century A.D.

Fig. 2.41 Drawing of a snaffle bit from Tannenburg, Prussia, dating in the late 1300's.

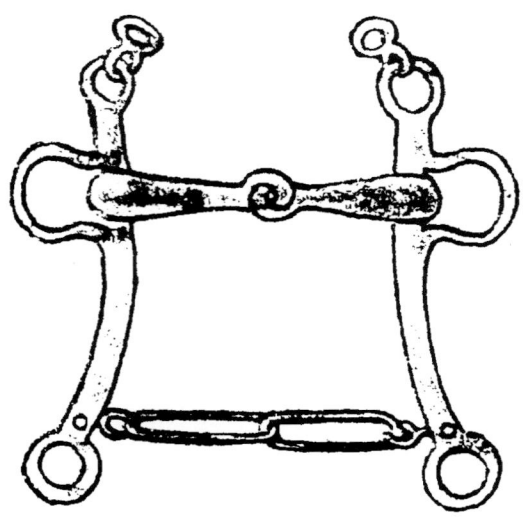

Fig. 2.42 Drawing of a curb bit from Tannenburg, Prussia, dating in the late 1300's A.D.

Fig. 2.43 A drawing of a French bit of the 14th Century A.D.

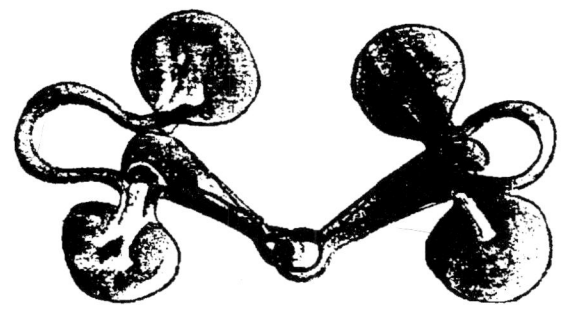

Fig. 2.44 A late 14th Century A.D. snaffle. Similar to a bit in the Prague National Musem.

Fifteenth Century A.D.

Fig. 2.46 A horse muzzle from Germany decorated with odd and unusual animals. William Randolph Hurst collection.

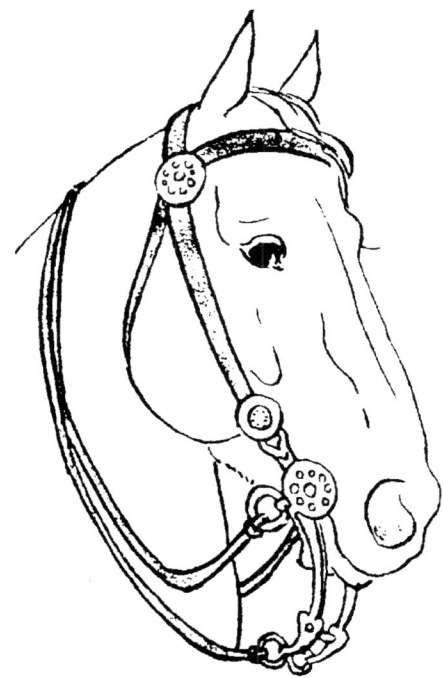

Fig. 2.45 Drawing of a bit and bridle from the painting, "The Adoration of the Magi" by Gentile da Fabrino, 1423 A.D..

Sixteenth Century A.D.

Fig. 2.47 Stag heads decorate the scroll work of this German horse muzzle of 1556 A.D. William Randolph Hurst collection.

Fig. 2.48 Sixteenth Century brass bit from China. Harold Dawley collection.

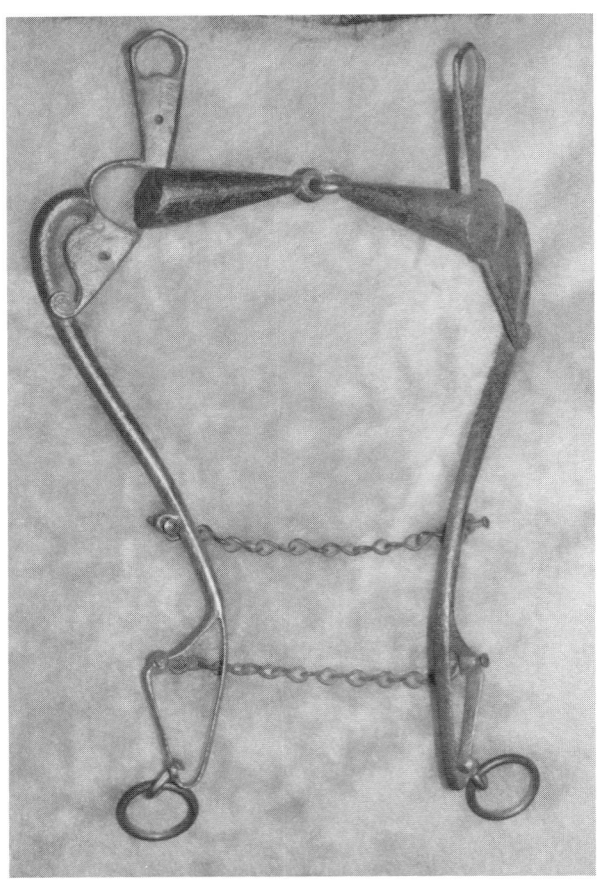

Fig. 2.49 A medieval bit from the 1500's England. Cheek-pieces are 17 1/2 inches long. Harold Dawley collection.

Fig. 2.50 Sixteenth Century A.D. bit with a mix of German and French styles with 13 1/2 inch cheek-pieces, a 4 1/2 inch mouth and hand forged chains. Jean Gayle collection.

Seventeenth Century A.D.

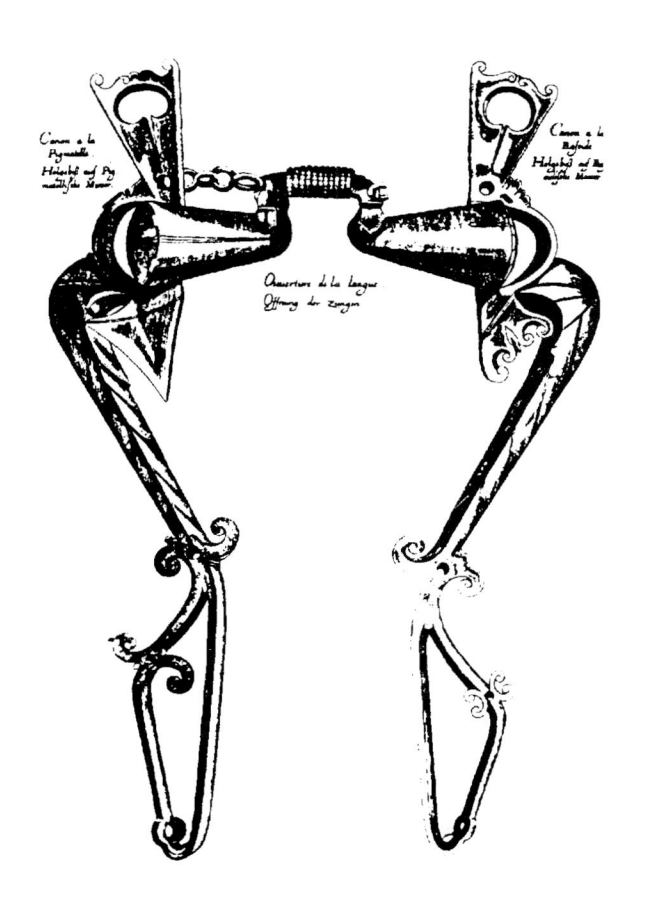

Fig. 2.51 A drawing of a bit from de Pluvinel (1626 A.D.) represented by two different cheek- and mouth-pieces.

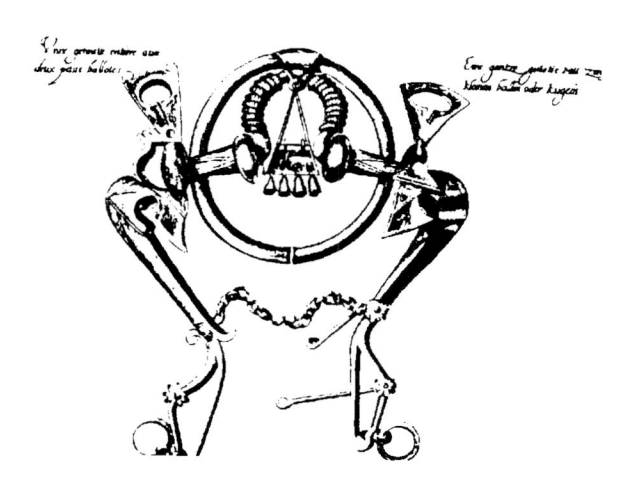

Fig. 2.52 A drawing of a ring bit from de Pluvinael (1626 A.D.) The different cheek-pieces represent two different bits.

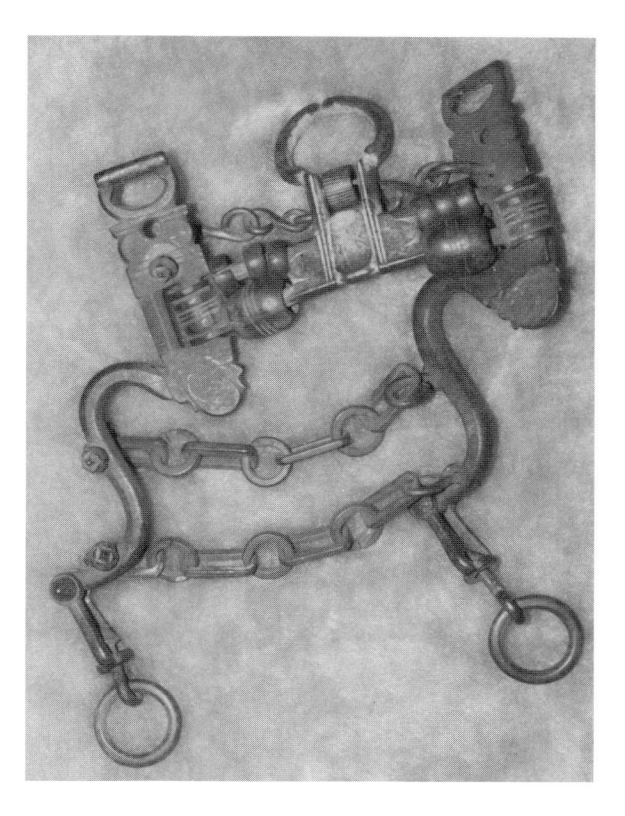

Fig. 2.53 A 17th Century A. D. or earlier bit from Spain. The chain links are of square iron. Harold Dawley collection.

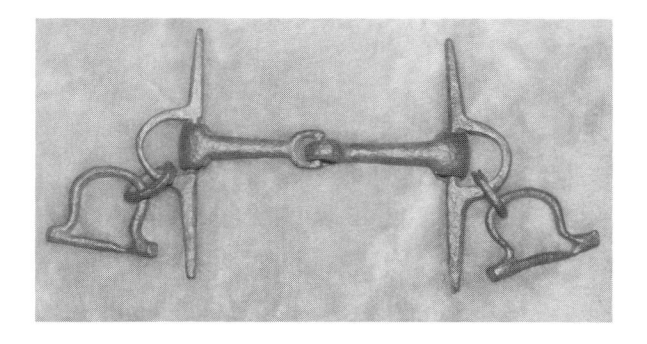

Fig. 2.54 A 17th Century A.D. or eariler bit. Harold Dawley collection.

25

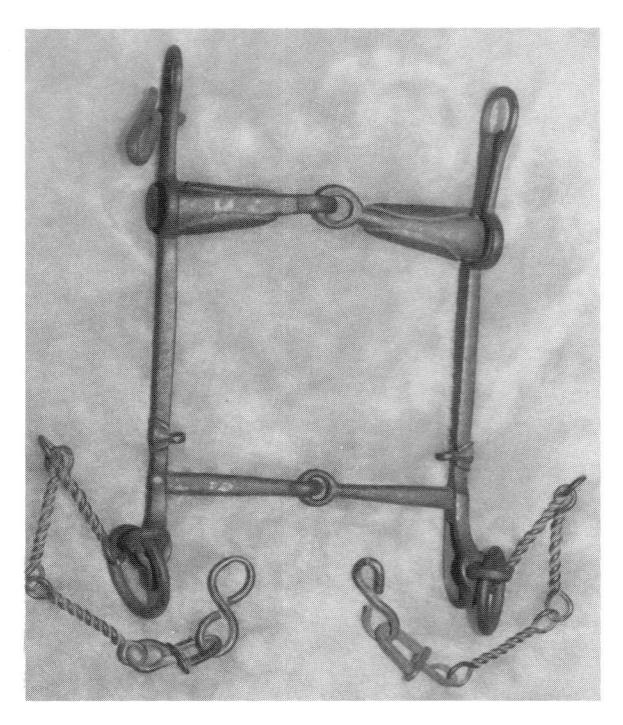

Fig. 2.55 A hollow-mouth bit from France. Harold Dawley collection.

Eighteenth Century A.D.

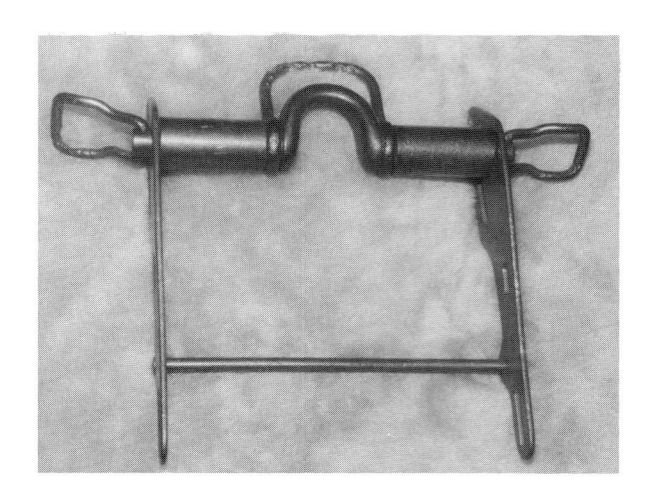

Fig. 2.56 Rollers are placed on each cannon of the mouth-piece. Harold Dawley collection.

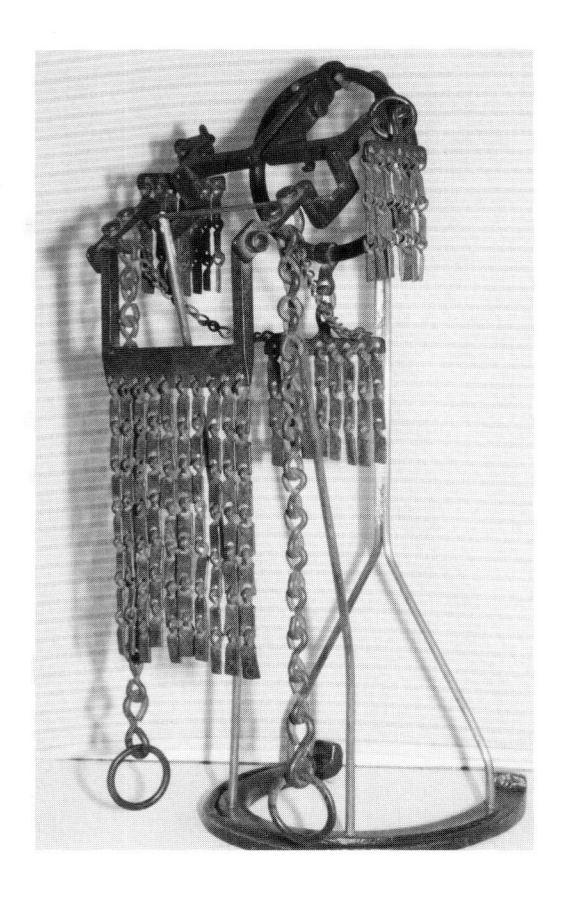

Fig. 2.57 Eighteenth Century A.D. jingle ring bit from Mexico. The bit has 136 jingles in the attachments. Harold Dawley collection.

CHAPTER THREE
Anatomy

A major point to consider before choosing a bit is the conformation of the horse's mouth. No two are quite alike.

Some horses, such as Thoroughbreds and those of like ancestry, have a long thin mouth giving plenty of room for the bit. These horses are suited to either a snaffle (with or without a drop noseband) or a double bridle. The same mouth will be hard to fit with a Pelham or curb bit. A long narrow mouth allows the bit which is properly adjusted and rests lightly and snugly against the corners of the mouth (Fig. 3.7) to ride too high in the mouth. As a result the curb-chain rides up out of the curb or chin groove (Fig. 3.7) and acts on the outer jawbones instead of on the bars of the horse.

Horses with a fatter, shorter mouth are well suited to an ordinary snaffle, a curb or Pelham bit. They have little or no room for the two bits as used in the double or full bridle.

The teeth play an important part in the bitting and comfort of the horse. Stallions, geldings and, in rare cases, a mature mare develop tushes (tusk). Tushes are four spike-like canine teeth (Fig. 3.0), two on each side, one set on the upper jaw (maxilla) and one set on the lower jaw (mandible) directly behind the outside incisors. The canine teeth are present in more mares than is commonly thought and can be felt as small bumps on the lower jaw. They were present in both sexes in Eocene and Miocene (two million to 200,000 years ago) ancestors of existing equidae.

Canine teeth cut down the space available for a bit and in a short mouthed horse can cause a definite bitting problem. The bit will rattle against them and be a distraction to the horse. They are frequently extracted in geldings and sometimes in working stallions by veterinary dental surgeons.

Wolf teeth can also produce the same type of problems. They are rudimentary premolar (P-1, Fig. 3.1) teeth in front of the back teeth (molars) on either side of the jaw, but especially on the top jaw or maxilla. Besides being painful, they also interfer with the bit and can cause a great deal of trouble and fretting.

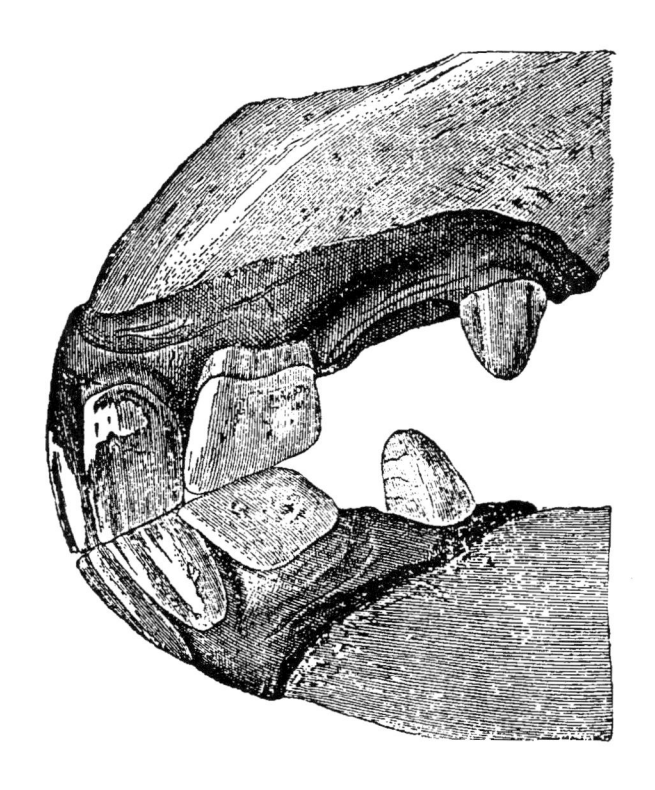

Fig. 3.0 The incisor and canine (tushes) teeth of a horse approximately five years of age.

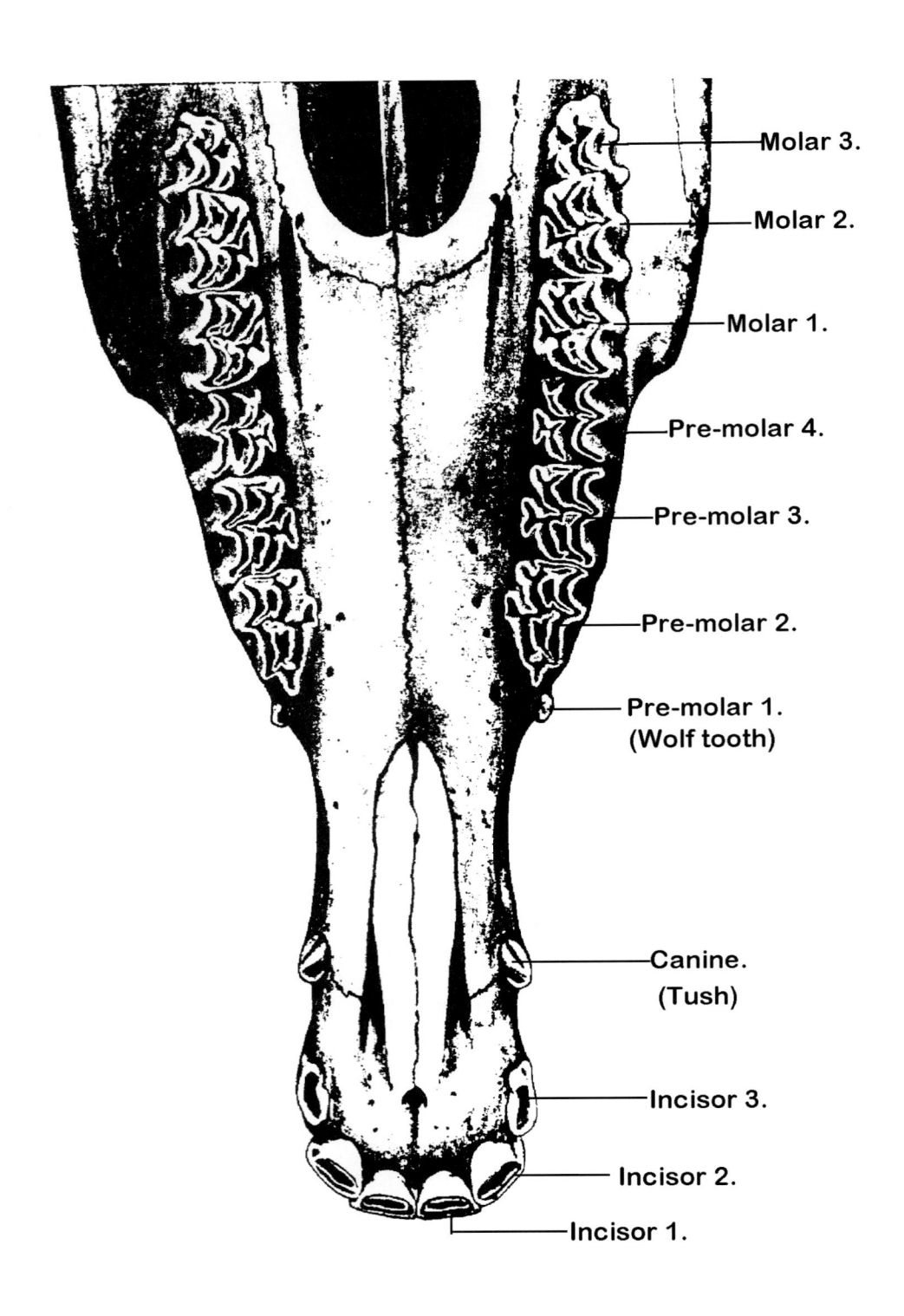

Fig. 3.1 The maxilla or upper jaw with teeth of the horse identified.

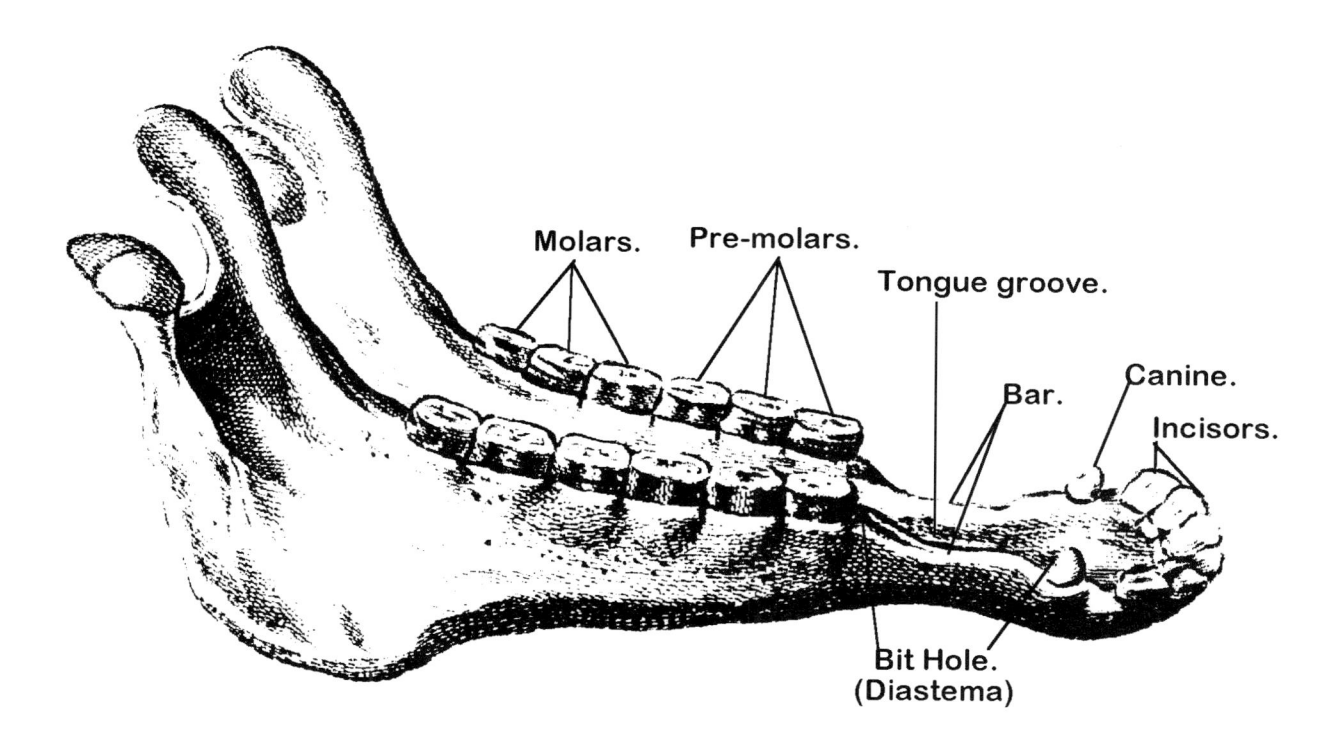

Fig. 3.2 The mandible or lower jaw of the horse.

The common single-jointed snaffle bit is representative of the broken-mouth bit and its action on the horse's mouth. Figure 3.3 represents the position of the joint of the bit bars on the tongue. Pressure is exerted on the lower jaw of the horse by the pinching action when a rein pull is applied to the bit. An examination of the tongue and sides of the mouth will determine if the bit in the pinching process of the single joint has a bad or irritating effect on the tongue or mouth. If no irritation or pinching has occurred, the horse will readily accept the bit.

Because the center of a double-jointed snaffle bit [Fig. 3.4] lies on the tongue, an unequal pull of the reins may have different effects on the horse and each horse may react differently.

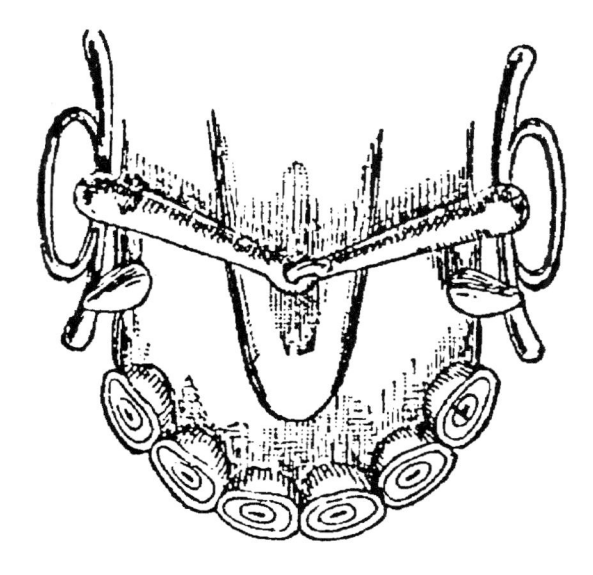

Fig. 3.3 A broken single-mouth snaffle.

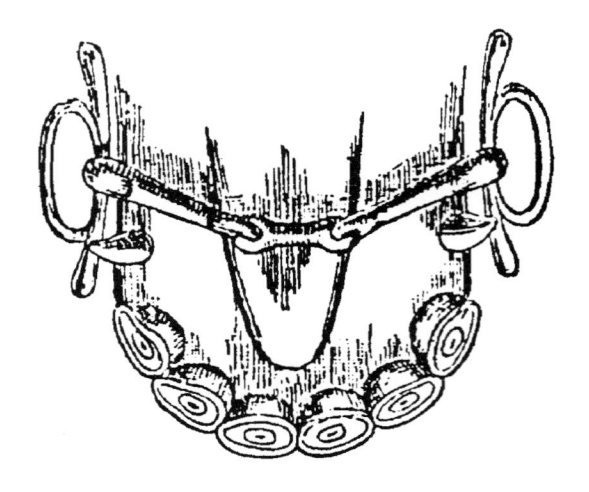

Fig. 3.4 A double-jointed snaffle bit.

The double-barred snaffle bit [Fig. 3.5] is a severe bit designed for a hard-puller or a horse that takes the bit in its mouth and tends to run away. Its severity can be increased by crossing the mouth-pieces [Fig. 3.6]. A pull of the reins causes a pinching process of of the bit as it closes against the bars of the horse. The angles of the bars of the mouth-piece with the double joint to the back teeth reduces the horse's power to hold the bit with its teeth.

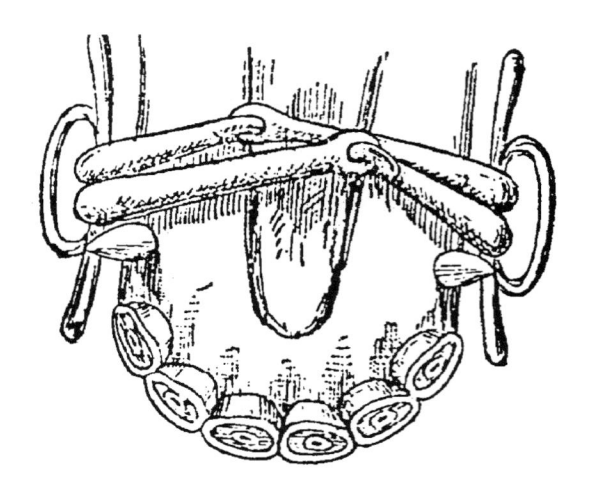

Fig. 3.5 Jointed double-mouth snaffle bit.

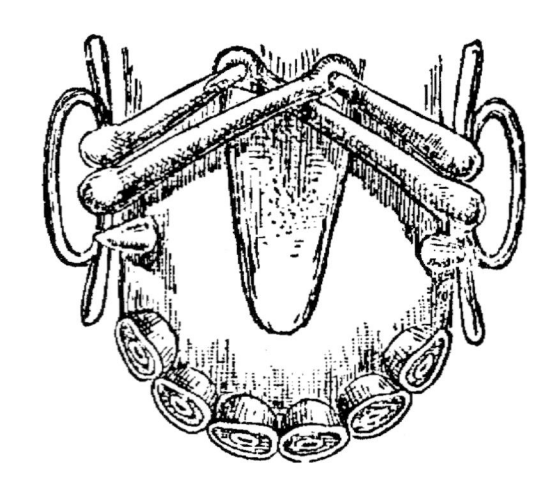

Fig. 3.6 Crossed jointed double-mouth snaffle bit.

When a bridle and bit are fitted to the horse, the noseband of the bridle should be at least one inch below the end of the facial crest [Fig. 3.7]. A noseband that is too close to the facial crest will rub on the end of the crest and irritate or produce an open wound on the face of the horse.

The tongue groove [Fig. 3.2] is the area between the mandibles or lower jaw bones of the horse in which the tongue lies.

The correct position of the curb bit in reference to the teeth and the tongue is illustrated in drawing Fig. 4.8, Chapter 4.

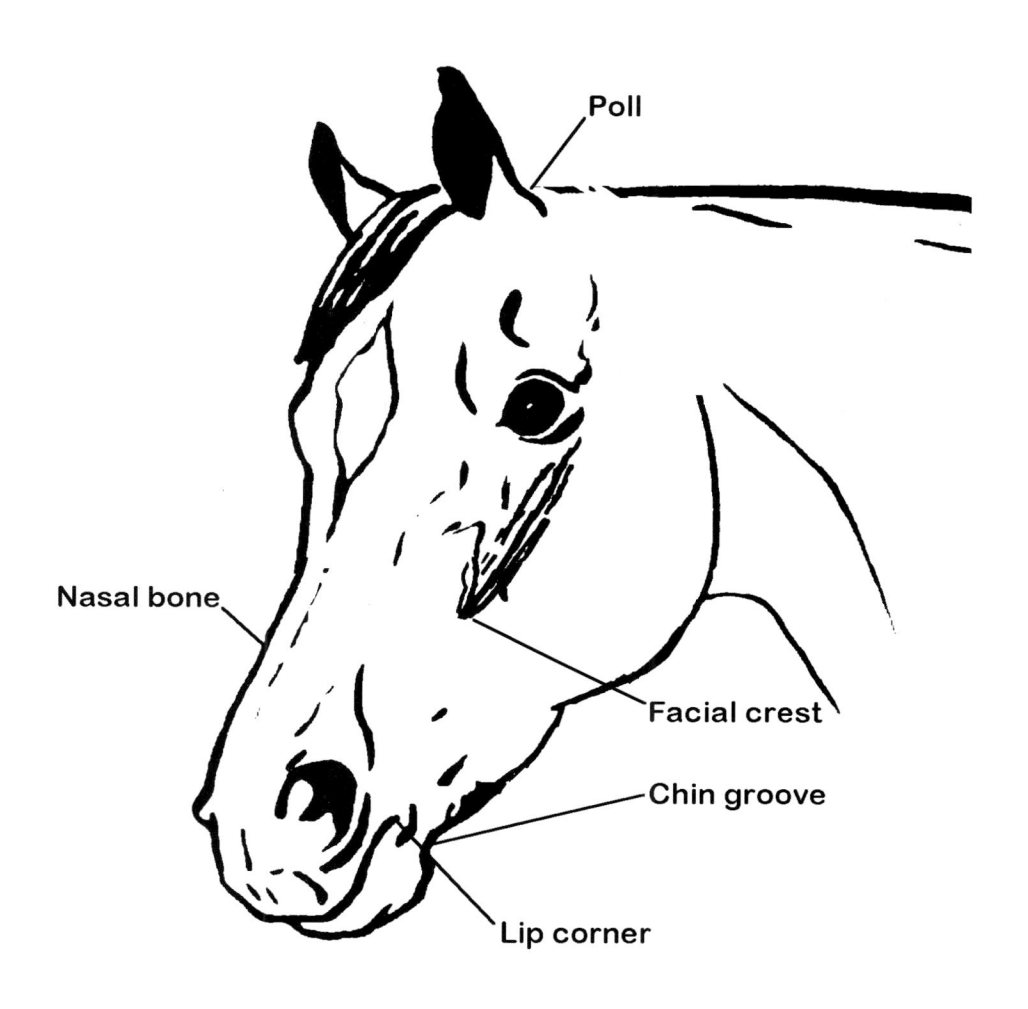

Fig. 3.7 Important areas of the horse's head that affect correct bitting.

CHAPTER FOUR
Usage of Various Bits

Every profession or craft has its own name. The bit maker is called a loriner (or lorimer) by *Webster's International Dictionary*, published in 1927. A book of this title was published in 1871 by Benjamin Latchford, of London. He was the bridle bit, stirrup and spur maker to Her Majesty, Her Royal Highness, The Prince of Wales and others.

E. Hartley Edwards in his excellent book *Saddlery,* states that "for every twenty bits I make, nineteen were for men's heads, and one for the horse's."

Some good horsemen may at first disagree with the statements in this chapter; however, if you will keep in mind that these ideas apply better to bitting in the training of horses than to bits used on already trained horses, many of which mouths have been damaged, then the ideas expressed here will be better understood.

The only author found who approached the art of bitting from an engineering standpoint combined with much experience with horses and a knowledge of its anatomy was Major Francis Dwyer, an Englishman who was Major of Hussars in the Imperial Austrian Service. His book, *Seats and Saddles, Bits and Bitting,* the 4th edition of which was published in 1886, is unique and erudite. This book draws on serious scientific investigation, accompanied by experiments on thousands of horses by distinguished cavalry officers of the Austrian Army of that period, plus Major Dwyer's own experience and engineering background. These combine into a remarkably useful work.

I wish anyone interested in the subject of bits and bitting would take the time to find a copy of his book, especially Part II, "Bits and Bitting," which starts on page 110 and ends on page 198 in the 4th edition. The effort will be worthwhile.

The art of bitting and bridling is a very useful and essential one, because it enables us to avoid the infliction of pain, while it secures to us a perfect control over the horse's movements. It consists in enabling us to exercise the mechanical action of the reins in the proper degree and the right direction, for every horse and for every movement. The rider's balance, his legs and the horse's conformation at any given moment are all part of what we call "control." The word "control" in this reference is addressed only to the use of bits. The statements are associated with horses trained with a tight rein. The principles and techniques used for training and developing loose-reined horses is entirely different and will be presented later in this chapter.

"The influence of good and judicious bitting and bridling on the breaking-in and training of horses is incalculable, while ignorance on these points and abuse of these instruments are a very frequent cause of restiveness, and of the ruin of young animals, especially of highbred ones with their delicate organization." (Reread this paragraph.) "Considering the great number of 'unthinking' riders and drivers that exist in all parts of the world, it seems perfectly miraculous when one looks at the frightful instruments of torture placed, in the absurdest manner, in their horses' mouths, and used in the most wonderful ways, that so few accidents occur. It is only proof of the admirable temperament of our horses" (Dwyer, p. 1 1 0).

"Nothing can be done in the way of bitting for the man that depends for his seat, on his reins or on the stirrups, which comes to the same thing. The rider with a really good, steady seat can jump his horse with precisely the same bitting that suits the school-rider or cavalry soldier" (Dwyer, p.142).

There is scarcely any one expression so common among riders, drivers, grooms and horse-breakers as that a horse's mouth is "hard" or "soft." When asked as to the best method of attaining a soft mouth, which is, of course, that most desired, we find that the exceedingly sensitive gums of the horse are supposed to become soft as a result of being subjected to a greater or lesser amount of pressure from a piece of hard iron. This idea in itself is perfectly monstrous and contrary to fact, inasmuch as long continued pressure, if not too violent in degree, has the tendency to produce a gradual thickening of the membranes, rendering the mouth callous. Pressure so violent in degree as to destroy the tissues and actually involve mechanical softness, produces the reverse of what is understood to be a soft mouth.

There are two ways of expressing what a soft mouth is. We may either say this horse goes well on a light bit, which may be mainly a consequence of good carriage, temper, etc., or we may say, a light bit will probably suit this horse best, because it has a thin tongue, high and sharp bars (gums), a wide tongue-channel and fine lips. But, in truth, the relative thickness or thinness of the tongue is the main point to be considered, because the height of the bars is very nearly the same in all horses, and the width of the tongue-channel always bears a certain proportion to it.

If the horse has been previously trained, then the first information to be obtained is what kind of treatment has it had. Have its bars been flattened or the tissue covering them been scarred by a hard bit and heavy hand?

It will be well to explain here why the perfectly fresh and sensitive mouth of the young horse conveys the sensation of hardness to the hand of the rider, and why the same mouth, after it has really been rendered more or less callous by the application of cold iron to its delicate organization, comes to be called soft.

When a horse is mounted for the first time, the equilibrium of the whole machine is disturbed, which becomes especially remarkable in the neck. The young horse bores (pushes his nose out forward) on his bridle and tries to acquire a new point to lean on, a fifth leg, in fact; he is becoming hard-mouthed. But when the animal has learned how to carry *itself and the rider,* or acquires an artificial equilibrium suited to the altered circumstances, then it no longer seeks this support, and the mouth is called soft. That such is really the case can be very satisfactorily proved. A horse can be brought into perfect equilibrium under the rider without any bridle whatever, merely by using a cavesson instead; and if a snaffle is then put into its mouth, this will be found to be exceedingly sensitive, and it will require some days of riding before it will *"take the bit"* as the phrase is.

From what has been just stated, it will be easy to understand how the seat of the rider comes to exercise so great an influence on the horse's mouth that the horse will go light with one and heavy with another rider. First of all, it is a question of equilibrium. One rider assumes a seat that favors, another one that more or less seriously impedes the efforts of the horse to get into balance, and horses always try to do this. But, secondly, supposing the seats, so far as the distribution of weight is concerned, to be identical, the unsteady rider will seek a support for himself in the reins. The horse immediately bores against this, and becomes a hard puller while the steady seat makes a light hand and a soft mouth (Dwyer 110-117).

S. Sidney, in his *Illustrated Book of the Horse,* said, "One of the most common expressions in speaking of horses is to say that such a one has a hard mouth. It is true that the mouths of some horses are rendered callous on one or both sides from the improper use of a halter used as a bridle for colts, or the abuse of a bit while being broken, or after being broken; but what is called a hard mouth is, as often as not, the result of an improper application of a bit that does not fit the horse, a difficulty which may be removed by changing it" (Sidney, p. 309).

No horse is born with a hard mouth. A hard mouth is made by a heavy handed trainer or improper bitting and handling. "A rider with light hands transmits his wishes gently through the reins to the bit. He also uses other aids: his legs and his position on the horse's back. The better the horseman, the less dependent he is on the shape of his bit," stated Sidney (p 308).

To make the best of a horse's mouth, it is absolutely necessary that a point should be attended to which is almost universally over-looked in this country, *i.e.,* the bit should fit the horse's mouth. The bridle is the instrument of guiding, restraining, and stopping a horse. The most important part of the bridle is the bit. A bit, whether for riding or driving, should be of such a shape and dimensions, and fitted on in such a manner as to control a horse with the least possible effort of the rider or driver. These essentials may be obtained without irritating the animal. Unfortunately, from sheer carelessness and ignorance, a great deal of cruelty is daily practiced on horses in the way of ill-proportioned, ill-shaped, extravagantly large, heavy, and mis-fitting bits, which, drawn tight by the rider, converts them into instruments of torture, cultivates bad habits and creates unsoundness.

One often hears the expression "I use this particular bit to get the horse's attention." The particular bit referred to usually has long lower side-pieces which give too much leverage to the rider, or it has an "unusual" port or mouth-piece which is often a harsh one.

There are five points of control of a horse when a bit and bridle are used. They are:
1. The tongue
2. The bars of the mouth
3. The curb chain groove (chin groove)
4. The poll
5. The nose

The lips are often listed under "points of control;" however, they offer minimal control action, and are easily cut, pinched, or bruised by an ill-fitting bit because they are thin skinned and tender. However, a broken snaffle does act against them as well as against the bars in the horse's mouth. The action of a bit's mouth-piece should be directed against the bars of the mouth, not the lips. Pulling on the lips is of limited value.

The roof of the horse's mouth is also listed by some; however, good bitting precludes its use. The roof of the horse's mouth (hard palate) should never be contacted by the port of the bit, even in any position, but it is often erroneously mentioned in lists of "points of control" by bits. The exception to this is the Spanish spade bit with its long spoon; however, used by a good loose-rein horseman, the spade is practically *never* used to control the horse, but as an occasional reminder to him.

Any bit can be gentle on the horse when used by a "lighthanded," experienced, even-tempered horseman. This should be kept in mind when evaluating the severity potential of any bit.

I don't believe you can be too repetitious by saying over and over how important it should be for the rider to improve himself in order that any bit will be accepted and enjoyed by the horse. You only go backward when you inflict pain by inexperience, and a bad temper. A horse does *not forget.*

This often happens when someone is trying a horse with the possibility of buying. The trainer puts exactly the same bit in the horse's mouth that he has been using, then works the horse for the potential customer (horse does fine). Customer wishes to ride, so gets on the horse with the same bit and the horse acts like a nut. Consequently no sale. If the trainer and customer would take the time to either change to an easier bit or maybe the customer would come back for a couple of riding instructions on an easier bit, this would help. The customer should be able to see what he is going to buy. The customer often gets the horse home to a strange place, strange equipment, strange rider (some are very strange), and the horse is insecure and doesn't know which foot to walk with first, resulting in an unhappy customer. The point is to take the time to teach the rider how to use the bit and set up that horse so the customer and the horse can enjoy life together.

It rarely happens, but a good trainer or owner, when a "broke" horse is sold, will send along with the horse for the new owner the bit that the horse was trained with.

Gentleness or severity of a bit on a horse's mouth is determined by several interacting features of the bit:

1. Size of the mouth-piece: Large in diameter (over 1/2 inch, up to 3/4 inch) mouth-pieces are much gentler on the bars of the horse's mouth. A thin bit (under 1/2 inch) is a harsh bit. The large size allows a greater area for the bit's weight distribution on the bars or tongue.

2. Weight of the mouth-piece: Lightweight steel, hollow mouth-piece, large diameter (viz. German mouth) bits are easier on the horse than a solid mouth, heavy bit. Light aluminum bits tend to rock in the mouth beside having a bitter taste.

3. Shape of the mouth-piece: A large, round, light, smooth shape is gentlest.

4. Width of the mouth-piece of the bit from side-piece to side-piece: If the mouth-piece is too narrow, it will cause a chafing or chapping of the outside of the lips. In the case of a curb with a port, if the mouth-piece is too wide, it will cause the port to rest unevenly on the tongue and bars causing irritation. Bit guards may be used to "shim up" the over-length and reduce its size.

5. Mouth-pieces where they attach to the side-pieces should be gently rounded to prevent chafing of the lips. The mouth-piece should not make a straight 90 degree angle with the side-pieces at this point. Egg-butt ends are good examples of the correct type of rounded corner.

6. The port should not be more or less than 1 1/3 inches in width at the bottom, nor more than 1 1/3 inches high. A narrow port restricts the tongue, and a wide port rests on the bars improperly. A high port hurts the palate on the upper jaw, forcing the horse's mouth open. All the corners of a port should be smoothly rounded, not angular or sharp.

7. The upper side-piece (headstall loop) should be bound outwards slightly. This prevents this part from gouging the cheek of the horse, and also keeps the curb-strap away from the lips, to reduce pinching. A separate loop behind the upper side-piece ring for the curb-chain reduces the chance of pinching the lips.

8. Any bit so designed that in use it can injure, pinch, or cut the horse's tongue or damage the upper jaw palate is a severe bit and it is to be avoided [Fig. 4.0].

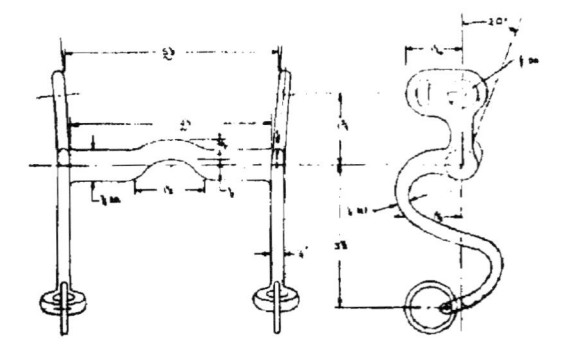

Fig. 4.0 A bit designed correctly according to the suggestions made.

The bars (gums) in a horse's mouth are flat close to the molar teeth, more rounded or pointed farther down, then flatten out when they get near the tusks and incisor teeth, and are covered with soft tissue which must become accustomed to the proper action on them of a correctly handled bit.

Measuring for a Correct Bit:

There are certain dimensions that are necessary to obtain before purchasing a bit. These dimensions are as follows:

1. The width of the mouth from outside of the lips on one side to the outside of the lips on the opposite side.

2. The height of the bars in the horse's mouth measured from the chin groove vertically to the top of the bar (gum).

3. Width of the tongue channel in order to have a proper sized port in the curb.

The mouth gauge and trial bit [Fig. 4.1) invented by Von Weyrother, formerly the Chief of Equitation at Vienna, is an instrument which will produce the dimensions desired.

Von Deynhausen says that the height of the bars is 1 3/4 inches with the majority of horses and that it is very unusual to find it more or less. He says this is a very important dimension, because the upper side-piece should never exceed the height of the bar of the horse's mouth for proper bitting.

If there is very great uniformity in the absolute height of the bars, there is diversity in their shape and texture, some being flat-topped and broad, others presenting a ridge-like surface; some are spongy, soft and comparitively void of feeling, while others appear firmer and more sensitive. All this exercises an immense influence on bitting (Dwyer, p. 136).

There is one essential attended to-- namely, the portion of the mouth-piece destined to rest on the tongue and the bars respectively should keep its proper place, and this can be secured only by making a mouth-piece of precisely the same width as the horse's mouth (Dwyer, p. 174).

The width of the tongue groove or lingual canal as the anatomist would say, is pretty nearly always 3/4 the height of the bars. Since this is very constantly 1 3/4 inches, the tongue groove will be found to be about 1 1/3 inches, which gives us the dimension of the maximum width of the port of a bit, where there is one. Supposing the mouth-piece to have exactly the proper width, if the port be made wider than the lingual canal, its corners will come onto the bars of the horse's mouth and produce pain. This is inconsistent with good bitting and is precisely the reason why it is of great importance that the width of the bit should coincide so accurately with that of the horse's mouth (Dwyer, p.137).

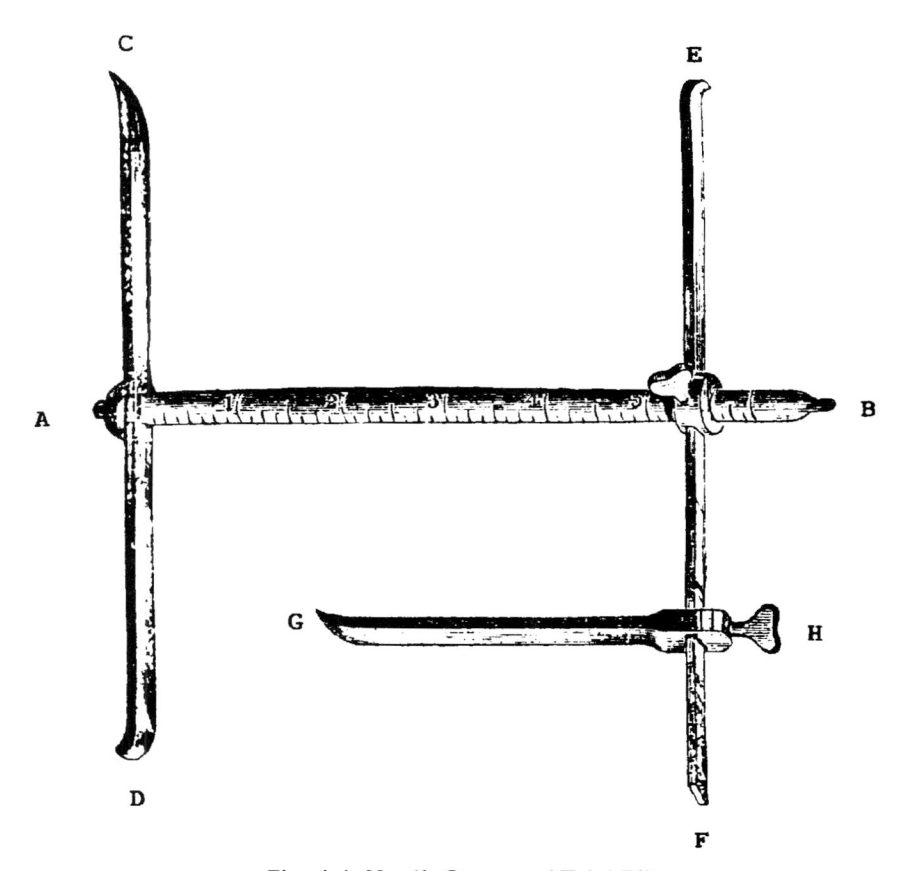

Fig. 4.1 Mouth Gage and Trial Bit.

The mouth-bar or measuring bar (A to B) is six inches or more long and oval in cross section, being almost an inch at the widest axis.

The left cheek-piece (C to D) is fixed at point A, the end of the measuring bar. The right cheek-piece (E to F) slides on the measuring mouth-bar. A set screw is used to secure the sliding cheek-piece after it has been fitted to the proper width of the horse's mouth. The bar G to H is fitted to slide up and down the moveable cheek-piece (E to F) which is graduated into inches by 1/8 inch increments along its lower part. This enables the height of the bars (gums) of the horse's mouth to be measured.

This is done by placing the instrument properly adjusted to the width of the horse's mouth in the mouth with the bar (A to B) directly above the the chin-groove but _under the tongue._ The rod G to H is gently shoved up until it presses lightly into the chin-groove, making sure the gauge stands square at a right angle to the bar of the horse and that the measuring bar (A to B) lies equally on both bars of the horse. The rod G to H is then secured fast, and the screw of cheek-piece (E to F) is loosened so that the cheek-piece can be removed from the mouth-piece without disturbing the rod G to H. Then the height of the bar can be read from the lower limb of the removed cheekpiece.

The first grand rule must be in all cases, to make the mouth-piece precisely so wide that when placed in the mouth, it fits close to the outer surface of the lips without either pressing on these or being subject to lateral displacement (Dwyer, p. 174).

The form and proportions of the mouth-piece must be deduced wholly from the interior conformation of the parts of the mouth on which it is intended to act, and these are the tongue in the center and the bars of the mouth on each side. It has been already pointed out that the relative hardness or softness of the mouth, so far as this depends on the conformation of this organ itself, is a consequence of the greater or lesser thickness of the tongue and the greater or lesser sharpness and sensitivity of the bars. The soft, fleshy tongue is, of course, much less sensitive to pressure than the bony bars, covered only with a very thin membrane (Dwyer, p. 173).

The whole art of bitting consists, so far as the mouth-piece goes, in determining how much of the pressure shall fall on the tongue and how much on the bars.

The correct percentage of weight to rest on the bars as opposed to the correct percentage to rest on the tongue spoken of by Dwyer has been a subject of debate for many centuries, and it certainly can not be settled here.

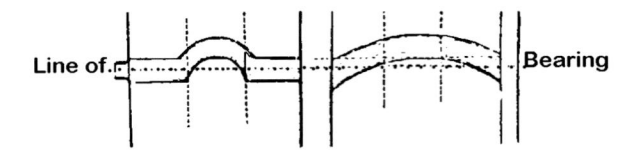

Fig. 4.2 Diagram of the portion of the bit which rests on the bars and that which rests on the tongue with a line of bearing.

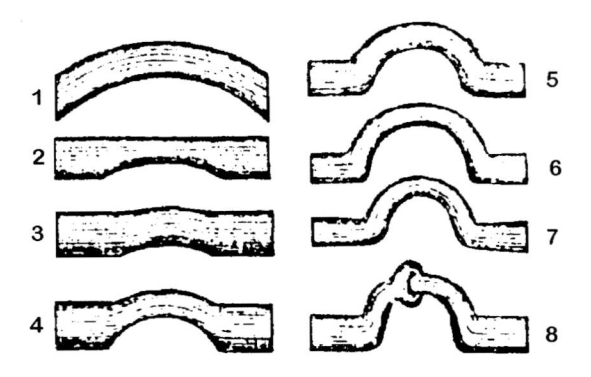

Fig. 4.3 Mouth-piece gradations of tongue freedom.

Figure 4.3 shows a succession of mouth-pieces of the forms generally adapted beginning with the lightest-- that is to say, the one whose pressure is almost entirely exercised on the tongue and proceeding toward increased tongue freedom.

It is difficult to understand how a solid bar mouth-piece, which (to relieve the tongue) curves upward from each side-piece to the center, can rest comfortably on the bars (gums) because it only lays on the outer edge of each gum, not gently across the top of it. There are and have been for a long time, many bits with curved (mullen) mouth-pieces such as this [Fig.4.4].

Flat, narrow (in cross section) bit bars must of necessity be harsher. Serrations (grooves) on a bit are harsher than smooth bits. The Army Reversible (Chapter 21, Fig. 21.7) has serrations on one side and is smooth on the other. Reversing the position of the side-pieces determines which side is acting on the bars of the horse's mouth. The smooth side should be inward next to the lips. A twisted-bar bit (Chapter 15, Fig. 15.6) is serrated over all the mouth-piece. Egg-butt ends (Chapter 25, Fig. 25.47) on a mouth-piece allow a smooth, non-rubbing, chaffing or pinching transition from the mouth-piece to the side-piece. Quite a few horses enjoy playing with a bit. For some horses, it is just nervousness such as when a person chews his lower lip, or grinds his teeth. Rollers on the mouth-piece, or a cricket (roller) in the port of the mouth-piece, entertain the horse.

Wheeled mouth-pieces and ports (Chapter 25) serve the same purpose. Copper-coated mouth-pieces, because of the action of saliva on the copper, give off a taste that the horse appears to like.

When the cricket is not positioned above the horizontal plane of the mouth-piece, that is, it is not up in the port with its lower edge above the mouth-piece, it has a tendency to cut the horse's tongue, sometimes severely. Chain mouth, twisted wire, or saw-tooth bits are in the same category and will also cut the tongue.

A double-jointed (bar-mouth) bit (Fig. 25.10) puts the action of the bit in two places. A double-mouth bit (Fig 4.5) operates in the mouth on the pantograph principle with double converging action. Its severity can be increased by crossing the bars. The true snaffle (ring snaffle) has no curb-chain, therefore it has no lever or fulcrum action on the mouth; a broken snaffle has a nutcracker action on the jaw and lower lips. A broken snaffle with long side-pieces may use a curb-strap or chain. This combines pinching (nutcracker action) with the leverage of a fulcrum. It is now a curb bit.

The nutcracker action on the cannons by the very commonly used broken-snaffle bit adds harshness to its action, but does leave tongue room [Fig. 4.6].

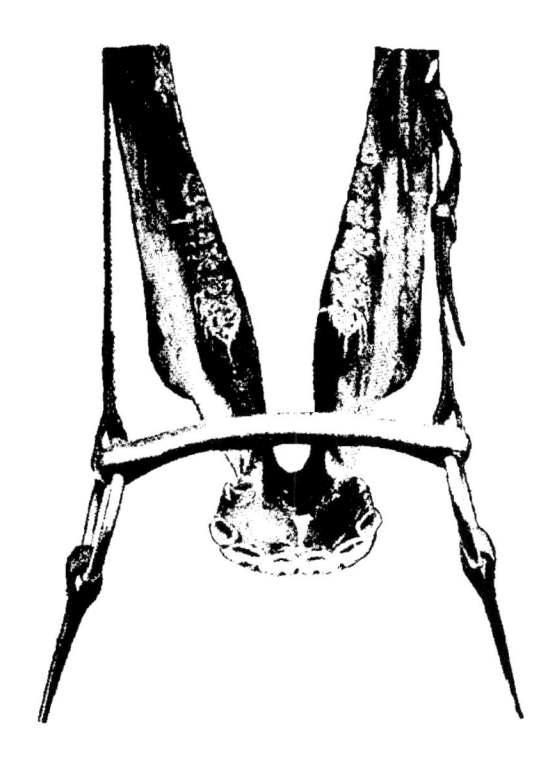

Fig. 4.4 The action of an arched mouth-piece in place on the bars (gums) of a horse's mouth.

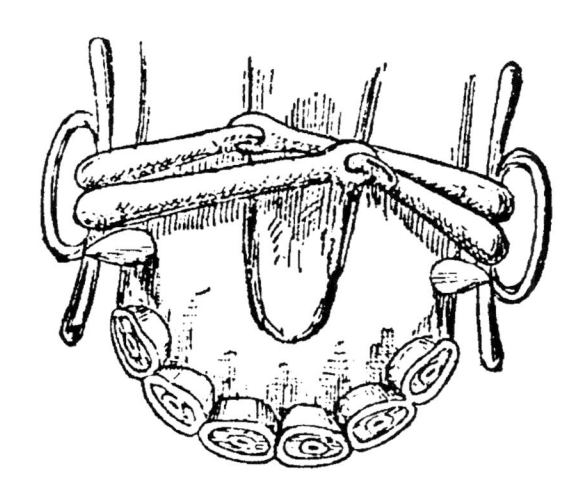

Fig. 4.5 A double-barred snaffle positioned as it is used in the mouth.

The circular rings of a snaffle bit should be large enough in diameter (up to 4 1/2 inches or more) so that they can not be pulled through the horse's mouth from one side. Their method of connection to the ends of the mouth-piece should be such that no pinching of the lips occurs.

Fig. 4.6 Nutcracker action of a broken-snaffle bit.

A broken-snaffle bit with rings acted on by a set of low-held reins works against the bars of the horse's mouth. This snaffle, acted on by the reins held high, works against the lips in the upper corners of the mouth and, as the reins are pulled tighter, raises the horse's head.

A bar snaffle is easy for the horse to get the bit "in his teeth," making him uncontrollable.

A true bridoon is a snaffle bit and only used in conjunction with a curb bit on a full (4-rein) English bridle (Tayler, p. 32).

The Curb Bit:

Many western-style riders use an endless variety of curb bits. They are accumulated from many sources: maybe inherited with the horse, purchased from a catalog or bought at a tack store because the cheek-pieces were ornate or pretty. At some time these and other sources of acquisition have been the folly of most riders, attested to by the wide variety of curb bits found hanging on the walls of tack rooms. Most were not purchased with the idea of using on a particular horse with a special problem (Tollefson, p.42).

The ordinary form of a curb bit consists of two side-pieces and a mouth-piece, with a curve or an inverted U in the center, called the port, and a chain (the curb-chain) attached to the cheeks in such a manner that when the curb-reins are pulled it acts and presses the chin and to some extent on the poll of the horse [Fig. 4.7].

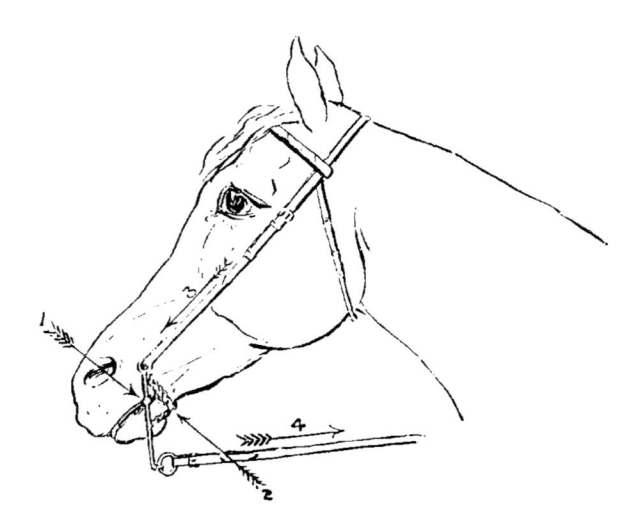

Fig. 4.7 The action of a curb bit as a lever. With a pull on the reins, pressure is placed on the bars of the horse and on the lower jaw by the curb-chain and the poll by the head stall.

The curb bit works by squeezing the lower jaw in a lever and fulcrum action. As the end of the longer lower side-piece is pulled backward by the curb-rein, turning of the mouth-piece in the horse's mouth combined with the compression action of the curb-chain in horse's chin groove on the outside of the lower lip causes the horse some pain to a great amount of pain, depending on the strength of the pull on the curb-reins.

At this point the "light hands" of a good rider are of great value.

The port is the inverted U-shaped or arched portion of a curb bit, intended to make the pressure rest on the bars instead of partly on the tongue. Its purpose is to allow room for the tongue.

When a present day ported curb bit is properly in the horse's mouth, the side-pieces hang in the same plane and parallel to the bridle's cheek-piece or strap [Fig. 4.8] and, as a consequence, until the curb-rein is pulled backwards, the port rests the entire weight of the bit on the tongue, which it should not.

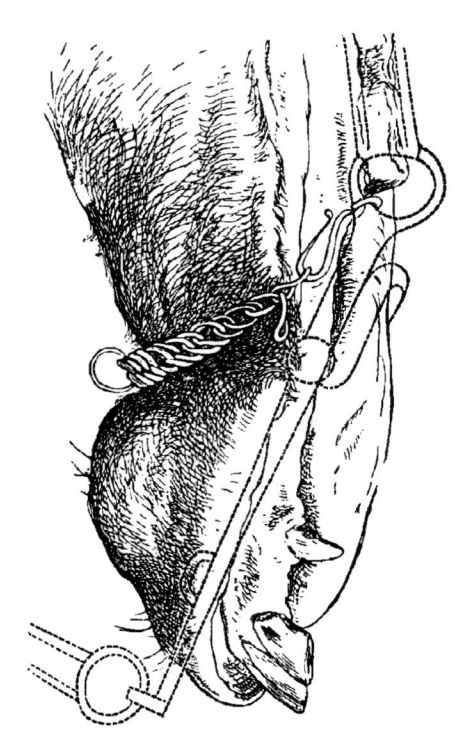

Fig. 4.8 A properly aligned curb bit at rest in the horse's mouth.

It is my belief that, if the mouth-piece were turned slightly so the port leaned somewhat forward when the bit was at rest in the horse's mouth (as in many early French bits), the port would then be just off the tongue and would cause the horse no discomfort. The weight of the bit would then be on the bars of the horse's mouth.

Mouth-pieces which have a low port or a tongue groove, such as a Cambridge mouth or mullen mouth are helpful to the horse. Those mouth-pieces with extremely high ports can be very harsh in the hands of an unskilled rider. A very high-ported curb bit, because of its action between the bars of the lower jaw and pressure on the roof of the mouth, actually pries the horse's mouth open. "The very high ports on bits intended to hold a pulling horse are abominations; a port should be used to give room for the tongue, and for no other purpose" (Sidney, p. 300).

The height of a port is measured from the bottom of the mouth-piece to the very top of the port.

The Curb-chain:

The best fitting curb bit, even when placed in its proper place, will not work unless the curb is of the proper make and length. The curb, whether singular or double, should work flat when twisted to its fullest extent without over twisting. It should be as broad as it can be made without being too broad for the chin groove, which it must not quite fill. If it is too wide, there is always danger of the upper edge rubbing against the bone of the chin. The hooks for attaching the curb should be the same length on both sides of the bit. A bit that produces pain should never be used. A tight curb-chain and powerful bit make the horse poke out its chin, and then an ignorant person pulls harder, tightens the curb and makes the bit more severe.

The proper length for the curb (chain) is about 1/4th more than the width of the bit mouth, the curb-hooks not being included in this. If you take into account the hooks, then the total length of the curb and hooks is one and a half times the width of the bit mouth. Eight-tenths of an inch is usually a proper width for a curb. The fitting process should take place with the mouth-piece placed directly above the chin-groove.

Fig. 4.9 Properly fitted curb-chain.

The Spade Bit:

The Spade bit with its very high spade port is a carryover from the Moorish domination of Spain; however, it should only be used by an expert, light-handed rider on a horse trained to carry a spade bit. In spite of its "macho" attraction for beginners, it should be avoided by them entirely.

In contrast to the definite statements made in the preceeding paragraph against the spade bit, it was for many years the main bit used in the Southwest U. S. The riders of that time were exceptionally capable ones with good hands. Sheila Varian, of Varian Arabians in Arroyo Grande, California, said in a letter to Russel Beatie in March, 1981, that ". . .if it is really a *spade bit horse,* it feels like no other you will ever ride. A softness like cutting smooth butter is a description that fits. A true spade bit horse carries himself with a natural balance I've never gotten with other bits, probably somewhat because of the time spent. However, a good spade horse is WONDERFUL."

Needless to say, Sheila Varian is an accomplished horsewoman, thoroughly capable of making a spade bit horse without damaging its mouth.

Another accomplished horseman and trainer, with many years experience, said that in all his years of training he had only made two spade bit horses and he would not let anyone else ride either of them.

Jo Mora describes the making of a spade bit horse in his own unique manner. In *Trail Dust and Saddle Leather,* he tells of putting flash reins on cowponies that belonged to the era of when people did not punch time clocks and time was measured by calendars. That is why such sweet-reined horses were found in California in the days before the gringo. The amansadores had savvy, patience, with many days or months to work, and a small value on time. A colt may be worked six months or as long as a year with a hackamore, then carry a bit for several months without any reins attached. Then he'd graduate into the two-reined class, when both the hackamore and macate, and the spade bit and reins were used. This would be his thorough and final schooling. When the hackamore was finally discarded, the average colt was a well-reined, sweet-mouthed work pony. The loose-rein trained pony could spin on a two-bit piece, back straight with the least pressure, and from top speed set his tail to the ground and slide to a stop with his back legs tucked neatly under him.

Jo Mora related his experience and education process with the amansadores of the old California school, and came to understand and fully appreciate the "delicate sensitivity" of the spade bit and the hackamore. He knew one old paisano that was snapping and reining broncs when he was 45 or 50. He stated that the paisano would make two or three alterations in the hang of his bosal during the first couple of weeks of breaking a bronc, and he'd often change hackamores two or three times more before the colt was finished. He explained to Mora why he made these changes. He would make the changes to get certain reactions from the physical conformation of the horse and sometimes it was to meet certain *temperamental* qualities. Now that may sound far-fetched to some readers, but that old boy certainly knew his horse flesh and it was all in the day's work with him. When he'd change he would always say to Mora, "No son todos los mismos" (they are not all the same).

Joe Mora rode for several years with a half-breed low port curb. He went into Old Mexico and all through the plateau down to Tierra Caliente and as a rule he used the Chileno or Ring Bit. He said, "everybody seemed to use it."

Robert Hall (Jolon Bits) of King City, California, has been training loose-reined horses and making bridle bits for over 40 years. In his early days of working with paisanos he learned that a horse will not work the "cricket" while the horse is being worked, only when the horse is at rest. If the paisanos did not hear the horse work the cricket after having been worked for 20 minutes or so, they would go back and get a different bit. The process would be repeated until the horse found a bit that was comfortable and would work the "cricket." This process took place before any reins were attached to the bit and the horse was still on the hackamore.

On a horse that's been properly trained and reined with a hackamore, bitted by a good hand, and ridden by a loose-rein stockman who knows what its all about, Hall considers the spade bit tops.

John Richard Young in an article "Calling A Spade A Spade," takes statements like those previously stated to task and goes into great detail as to why the spade bit is an instrument of torture, a relic of the past and belongs in a museum along with brain squeezers and chastity belts. Young explains how a spade bit horse is broken and not trained, in that as the horse is worked and comes to a quick stop, it does not flex its poll or tuck in its nose. The horse instinctively raises its head to alleviate the upward pressure of the spade on the roof of its mouth and opens its mouth in doing so.

Fig.4.10 An example of a spade bit.

Any horse so trained with a spade bit would work just as well or better with a mild curb bit--that is if it was trained and not broken. The spade bit forces the horse to stop or suffer excruciating pain.

I cannot disagree with any of the comments of Mr. Young. The actions he describes are evident in any arena where the spade bit is being used.

The ring bit substitutes a ring around the lower jaw of the horse for the curb chain. The ring is attached inside the mouth to the top of the port [Fig. 4.12]. It too should be avoided by unskilled reinsmen. It can be a harsh cruel bit if the rider is not a good loose-rein horseman.

Any moveable parts of a mouth-piece should be designed so that in its movement it will not pinch the horse's tongue or lips. Worn moving parts should be carefully examined, and the bit discarded when it causes discomfort to the horse.

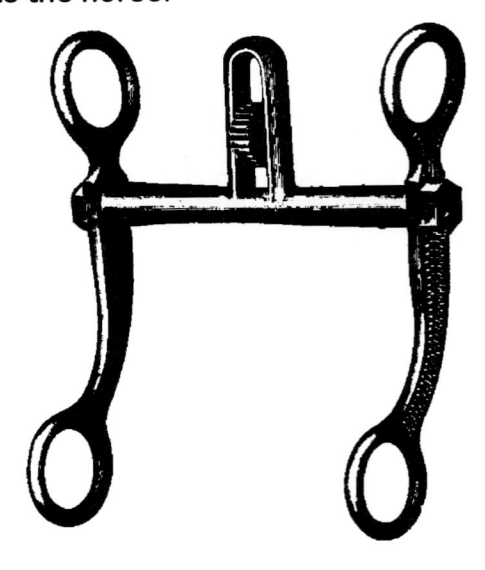

Fig. 4.11 An example of a half-breed bit.

The length and shape of the side-pieces can contribute to the gentleness or severity of the action of the bit. Long ones should not be used. Long lower side-pieces contribute excessive, painful leverage to a curb-chain, and a long upper side-piece tends to allow the mouth-piece to lift, and the curb-chain to be lifted out of the chin groove.

The leverage of a bit is calculated by the number of times greater the lower side-piece (from the bearing line [Fig 4.13] to the center of the rein-ring hole) is than the upper side-piece (from the bearing line to the center of the upper side-piece loop, or if it has a separate curb-chain loop, to the center of this loop). The best ratio is 2 (lower) to 1 (upper), giving a 2 to 1 leverage. The longer the lower side-piece is, the greater the leverage and, in the hands of most riders, the harsher the bit's action on the mouth.

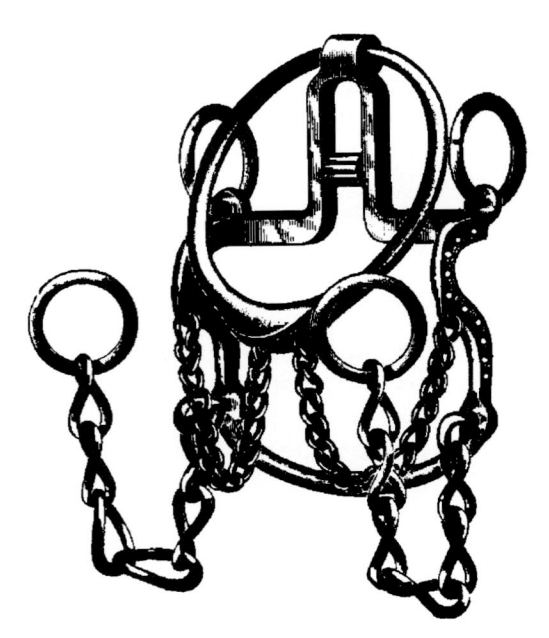

Fig. 4.12 A Chileno or ring bit.

S-shaped, lower side-pieces [Fig. 4.13] were used by many cavalry units because the shape does not easily allow the horse to get the side-piece in its mouth. The lip strap on the lower side of a straight side-piece gives the same beneficial results.

Mrs. Suzanne Norton Jones made an interesting observation in her article (See Bibliography; Articles): "It has been interesting to note why the upper shank of the bit has a circular attachment for the headstall. At one time an elongated slot was used but caused too much pressure on the horse's poll. The circular ring allows a certain amount of swinging action on the bit, thus relieving the pressure from the horse's head."

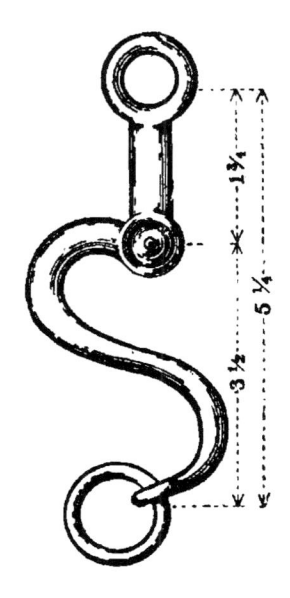

Fig. 4.13 S-shaped side-pieces (a Duke's Cheek) recommended in 1908 by Gen. William H. Carter of the United States Cavalry. The dimensions are the same as those recommended by Major Dwyer.

The Double Bridle:

A double bridle is a two-bitted one with four (two pair) reins. One bit is always a Weymouth curb. The other bit is always a snaffle which is also called a bridoon. A bridoon may also be spelled bradoon. Locale usually determines the spelling.

There are many variations of snaffles used as bridoons: twisted-wire (single or double) snaffle, twisted-bar snaffle, triangle-shaped knife-edged snaffle (fishback), and many others. A Shrewsbury gag can be used, but if it is, it is usually used on a polo horse. The gag snaffle is not permitted by certain breeds in the show ring.

The purpose of the snaffle in a double bridle is to lift the head, while the purpose of the curb is to make the horse's head break at the poll, thus allowing the nose to be tucked toward the rider. It should be understood that in order for the bits to do this, the rider should be squeezing gently with the legs to push the horse into the bridle, as opposed to *pulling* the head into position. The result of these actions is the beautiful collected "set-up" position seen in the show ring.

Fig. 4.14 The Double bridle.

Before you ever move a horse, you should ask for head. You tug gently with first the rein on one side then the other until the horse releases the pressure and is light. Thus the head set. When this is accomplished, then ask the horse to move forward, squeezing with the rider's legs, at a walk, maintaining the same contact with the mouth and the same head set. If the horse begins to resist, then stop. Start again until the horse understands. Do the same thing before going into a trot or canter. It only takes an instant for the horse to change gaits after the horse understands. You will then be able to gently maintain your collection and balance throughout the ride. This is how one moves a horse into the bridle instead of pulling him into it. It takes much patience, but it is easier for the horse to get his hocks under him so that he can work off his hindquarters.

The two bits of a double bridle should normally be used in conjunction with each other. However, in order to correct certain wrong head positions, one bit may be held "as is" and the other bit used to accomplish the correction desired. Under normal circumstances, the rider keeps contact with the horse through the reins at all times.

The Pelham Bit:

"A Pelham bit acts supposedly as a curb and snaffle in one bit," per S. Sidney (p.309). In his *Illustrated Book of the Horse,* published in 1875, Sidney states " . . . it is difficult to see how a mouth-piece with a joint can press a horse's chin and act as a curb, but in practice it is found that light-mouthed horses do bend to the pulling of the curb-rein after being ridden on the snaffle. The value of the Pelham, I myself only use on horses with good snaffle-bridle mouths."

Tuke, in her book *Bits and Bitting*, describes the Pelham as the combining together of a feature or two of the snaffle and curb-style of bits to produce a single mouth-piece which has the combined action of the two bit styles.

Fig. 4.14 A Pelham bit and bridle.

Most of the time two sets of reins are used, but one set is used under some conditions. This results in the *Pelham being a curb with a built-in snaffle.* Many features found in each style of bit will be found in the Pelham, *i.e.*, fixed or sliding mouth-pieces, ported or mullen mouths, jointed eggbutt, which results in a wide variety of bits that carry the title of Pelham. See Chapter 27.

Many books have been written on the use of the different styles of bits described, especially in the training and gaiting of horses for English-style riding and in recent years on Western-style riding. Several of the books are listed in the Bibliography.

CHAPTER FIVE
Glossary: Ace to Byers

The Glossary contains many United States patented bits. The translating of one to seven pages of legal language into comprehensible 50 to 75 word descriptions may leave some questions about a particular bit unanswered. Copies of any United States patent may be obtained by writing to the U. S. Patent Office, Washington, D. C. The current fee (1995) is $3.00 per patent copy.

Ace: An ornate silver concho bit with a spade mouth (Buermann #393) [Fig. 5.0].

Fig. 5.0 Ace, with ornate silver conchos.

Acme: (Buermann No. 42) See Driving, Success, Chapter 8.

Adams, Samuel L., New Britain, CT, Patent No. 428,197, May 20, 1890 [Fig. 5.1]. A curb bit to which is attached a ring through which the lower jaw of the horse passes. The screw by which the ring is attached enables the ring to be set at different lengths.

Agen, O.C. See Over-check, Chapter 9.

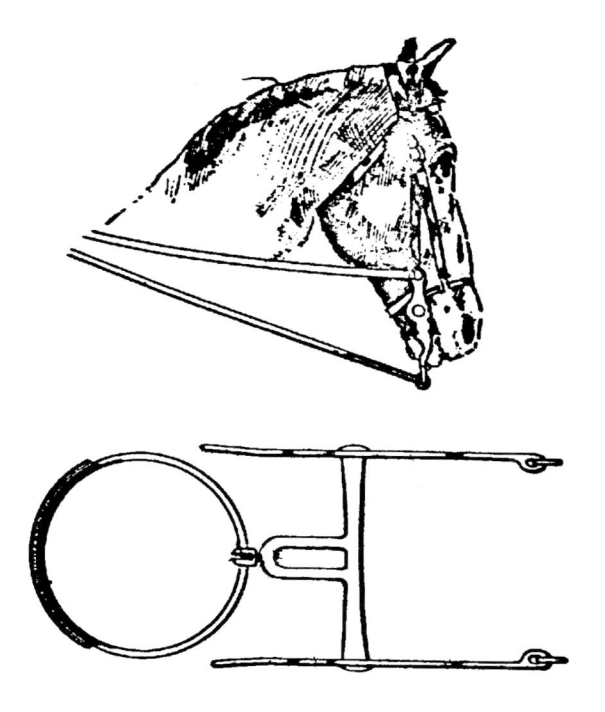

Fig. 5.1 Adams adjustable rein-ring bit.

Alexander, C. M., Washington, D.C., Patent No. 34,343, Feb 11, 1862. Fig. 5.2 shows one of the shanks or side-pieces of the bit to which the headstall and reins are attached. The middle and lower rings on the cheek-piece are for the reins. When easy pressure is applied, the spring will act upon the bit directly, but as soon as a heavy pressure is applied the spring yields and the strap causes the curb to act on the jaw of the horse. The strap may be made longer or shorter, thus the action time of the curb can be changed, or to add more or less pressure. When the strap has more slack there will be greater direct pressure on the bit, and it will take a harder pull on the reins to make the curb act.

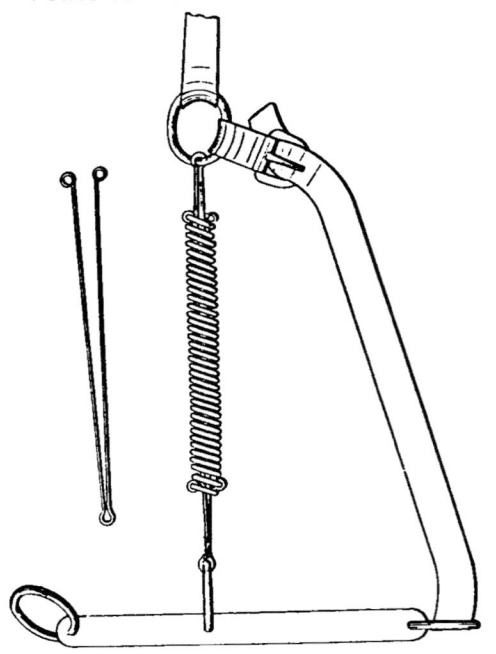

Fig. 5.2 Alexander bit attachment.

Allan, Bona, Jr., Buford, GA, Patent No. 640,619, Jan. 2, 1900 [Fig. 5.3].

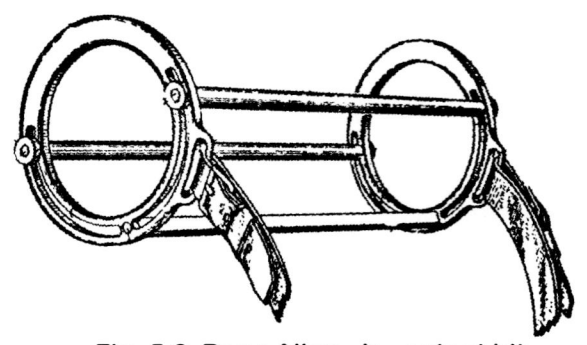

Fig. 5.3 Bona Allan, Jr., patent bit.

Allen, John Hudson, Goldwaite, TX, Patent No. 422,900, Mar. 11, 1890 [Fig. 5.4]. The mouth-bar of the bridle bit is rigidly attached to each end of the inner curb-plates. These curb-plates are curved backward at their upper ends, and are provided with slots for the reception of a curb-strap. The lower ends of the curb-plates are bent outward and provided with transverse slots for the reception of the cheek-pieces.

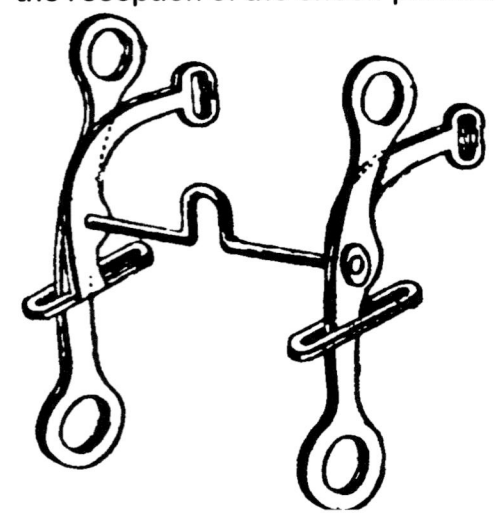

Fig. 5.4 John Allen patent bit.

Alwell, Lee Special bit by W. R. (Wallie) Boone [Fig. 5.5].

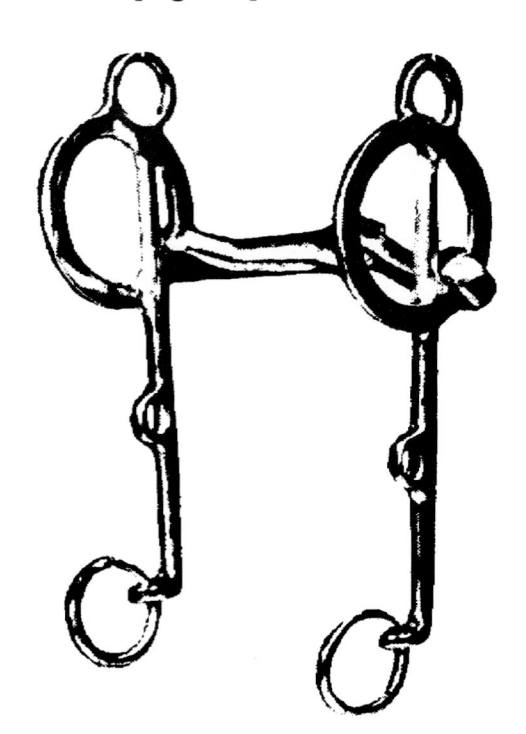

Fig. 5.5 Lee Alwell special bit.

Anderson, Harvey S., Hillsboro, OH, Patent No. 754,632, Mar. 15, 1904

[Fig. 5.6]. A tubular bar or mouth-piece, such as a piece of ordinary galvanized iron pipe, open at both ends to permit air to circulate freely. The cheek-pieces slide on the bar and can be adjusted for width and then locked in place by tightening the screws in the lower knob of the mouth-piece.

Fig.5.6 Anderson tubular bit.

Angle (elbow) Cheek Pelham, See Ashleigh, Fig. 5.11.

Anti-lug Bit; A bit with an extension of the mouth-piece to which an additional ring is attached. Designed to keep the horse from pulling to one side [Fig. 5.7].

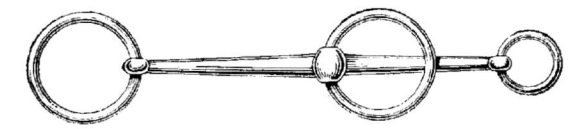

Fig. 5.7 Anti-lug bit or regulator bit.

Anti-rear Bit: See Chiffney bit, Chapter 6.

Appuy (*Loriner,* p. 26); Refers to the quality of a horse's mouth or to whether it is hard-mouthed (poor appuy) or soft-mouthed (good appuy).

Arch: An elevated part of the center of the mouth-piece having unparallel sides. See Mouth-piece, Chapter 25.

Argentine Tom Thumb: See Tom Thumb Bit, Chapter 33.

Arizona: (Buermann No. 422) Silver-mounted Spade Bit [Fig. 5.8].

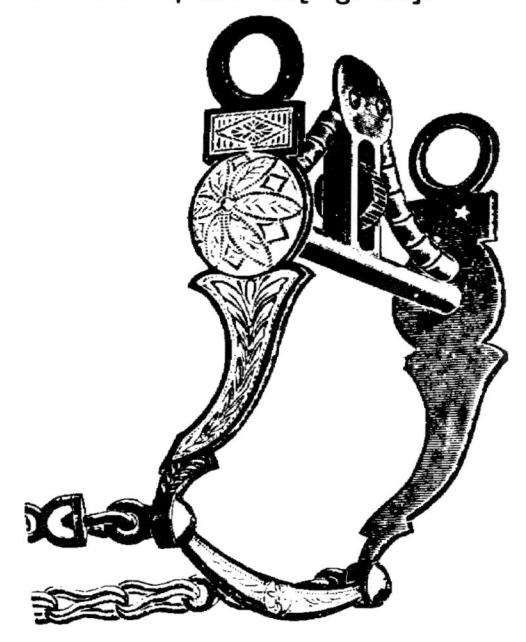

Fig. 5.8 Arizona-style bit by Buermann Mfg. Co.

Arkansaw (Arkansas) Jawbreaker: See Fields, Chapter 11.

Arkwright Curb Bit: English bit design of early 1800's [Fig. 5.9].

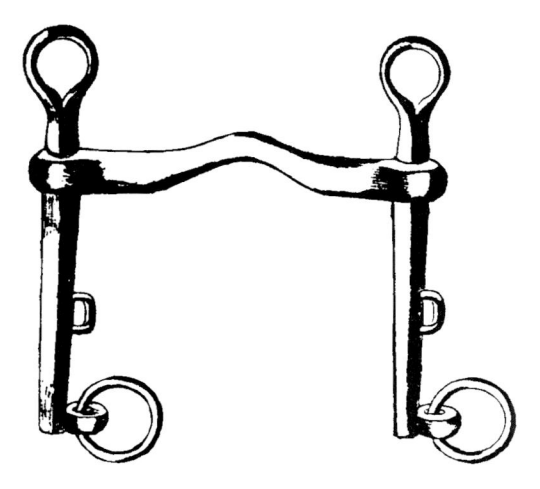

Fig. 5.9 Arkwright curb.

Arnold, Stephen D. and W. F., New Britain, CT, Patent No. 56,872, Aug. 7, 1866 [Fig.5.10]. The mouth-piece is hollow so that its increased size will not add to its weight. Also, the clasp is partially open so as to receive the end of the mouth-piece either by screwing the shank of the clasp or by means of a pin or rivets passing through both the tube and shank.

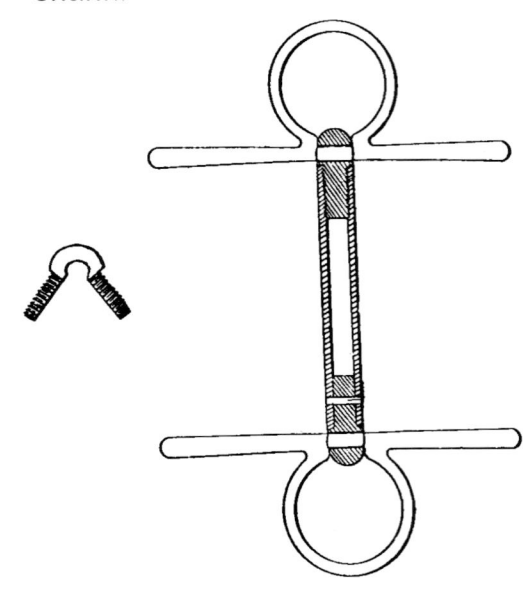

Fig. 5.10 Stephen D. Arnold hollow-mouth bit.

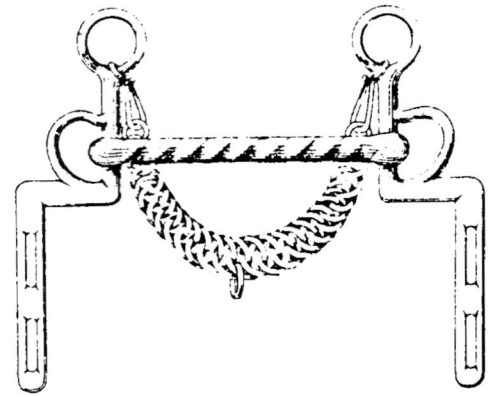

Fig. 5.11 Ashleigh elbow bit.

Artificial Aids: Items such as martingales, spurs and whips used by the rider or driver to convey instruction to the horse.

Ashleigh Elbow Bit: A coach or driving bit, widely used and supplied in a light or heavy pattern [Fig. 5.11]. See Chapter 8.

Askin, Robert. W., Ismay, MT, Patent No. 2,413,426, May 2, 1945 [Fig. 5.12]. A hackamore bit designed to provide a means of exerting pressure on a nose-strap and a jaw strap simultaneously by pulling on the reins.

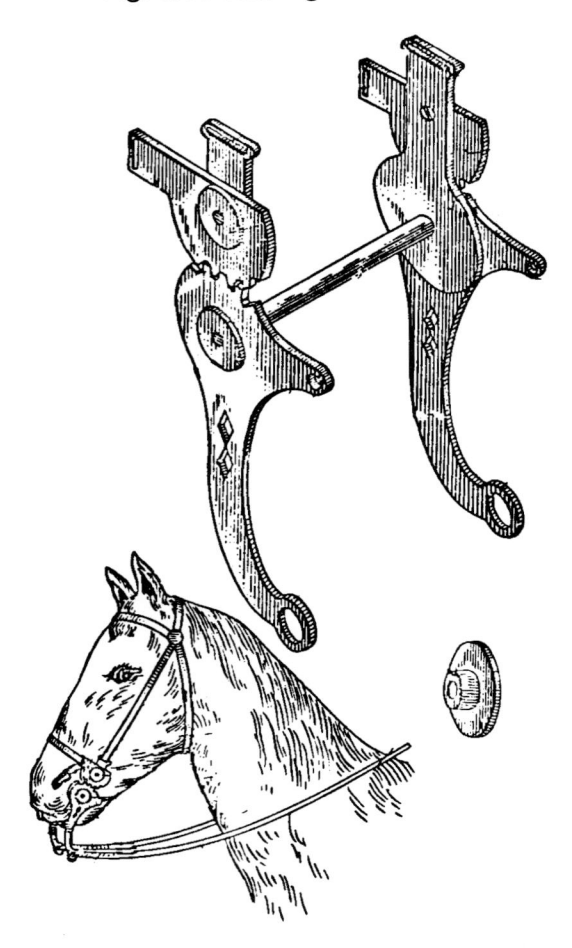

Fig. 5.12 Robert W. Askin hackamore bit.

Atherton, Fisher C., Buffalo, NY, Patent No. 801,436, Oct. 10, 1905 [Fig. 5.13]. When the bit is in its proper position in the horse's mouth, the upper lip and side of the mouth rest upon the horizontal side portions of the check-bar and the arched center is held erect in the mouth by the overcheck line and out of contact with the roof of the mouth by the pressure on the lips on the side portions of the check-bar. When the horse tosses its head or hangs its head, the arched center is thrown against the roof of the mouth. Any slight movement of the main mouth-piece will affect the check bit. The bit also prevents lolling of the tongue.

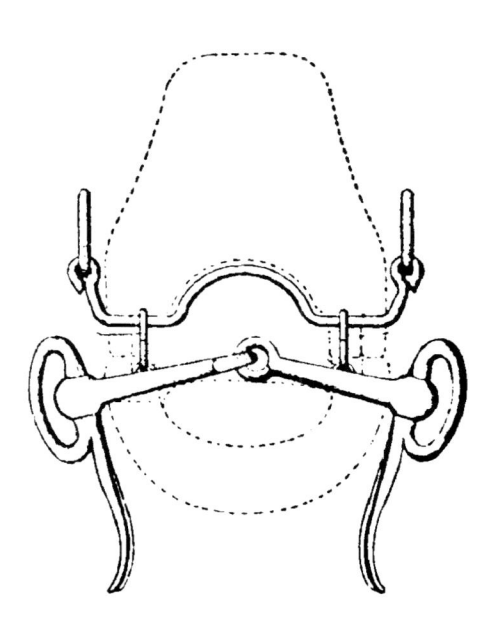

Fig. 5.13 Fisher C. Atherton bit patent.

Aughey, Willaim H., Petroleum Centre, PA, Patent No. 636,099, Oct. 31, 1899 [Fig. 5.14]. The large ring and the large interchangeable port with a roller make this a versatile curb bit. The bit is also called "The Spokane Bit" and was manufactured by The Spokane Bit and Stirrup Co., Billings, Montana.

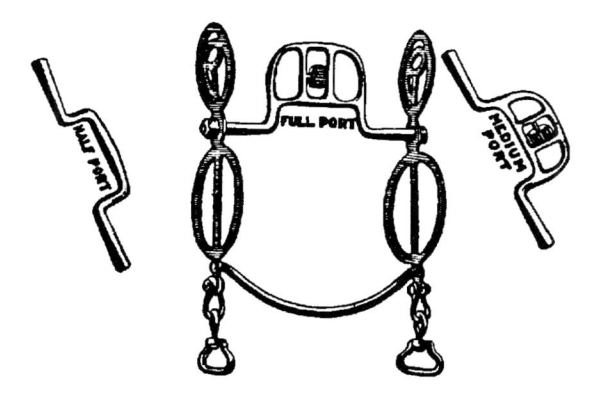

Fig. 5.14 The Aughey or Spokane curb bit with the three sizes of ports.

Austin, Oren and Henry Greek, Painted Post, NY, Patent No. 349,246, Sept. 14, 1886 [Fig. 5.15]. This bit consists of rings formed into curved hooks, into which the rein end-rings may be hooked, taking the place of snaps on the reins.

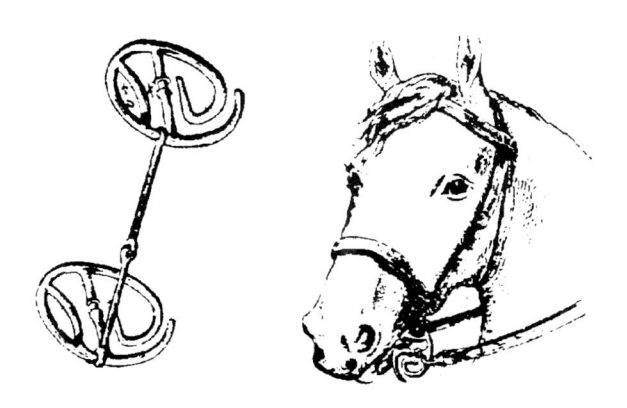

Fig. 5.15 Oren Austin snaffle bit.

Australian loose-ring snaffle: See Fulmer Snaffle, Chapter 11, Fig. 11.35.

Baker, Charles, Minneapolis, MN, Patent No. 325,232, Sept. 1, 1885 [Fig. 5.16]. The bit is adapted for use in a double-rein bridle. When any strain is exerted upon the small inner rings, considerable pressure is brought to bear on the lower jaw of the animal by the clamps, while at the same time the tongue-piece is made to press with a great deal of force on the animal's tongue.

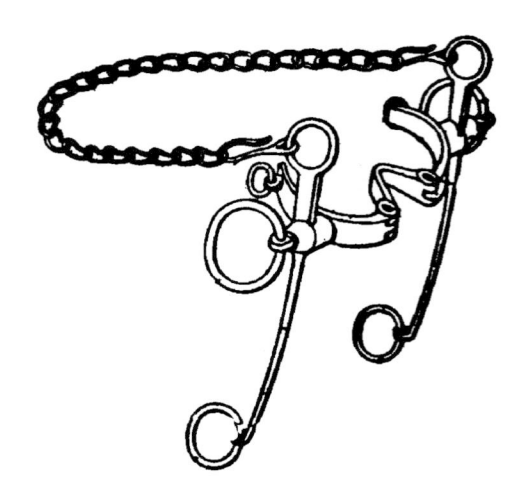

Fig. 5.16 Charles Baker pressure bit.

Baker, Issac L., Prairie City, KS, Patent No. 104,408, June 21, 1870 [Fig. 5.17]. A weaning bit for either colts or calves. The mouth-piece is a round tube with each section slotted or with holes to allow passage of air so that a vaccum cannot be formed in the mouth in the act of sucking.

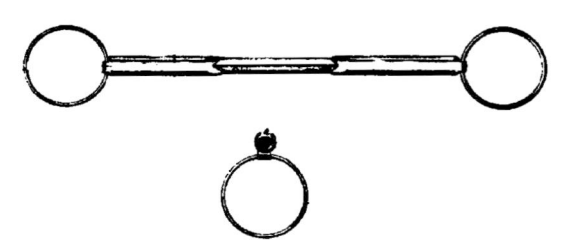

Fig. 5.17 Issac Baker weaning bit.

Baker, John B., Syracuse, NY, Patent No. 24,275, June 7, 1859 [Fig. 5.18]. When a moderate pull is made on the reins, the bit will act only as a snaffle, but when a strong pull is made, the connection between the rein and the bit is drawn downward, causing a change from a snaffle to a curb bit and when the reins are slackened the spring returns the bit to its former position as a snaffle bit.

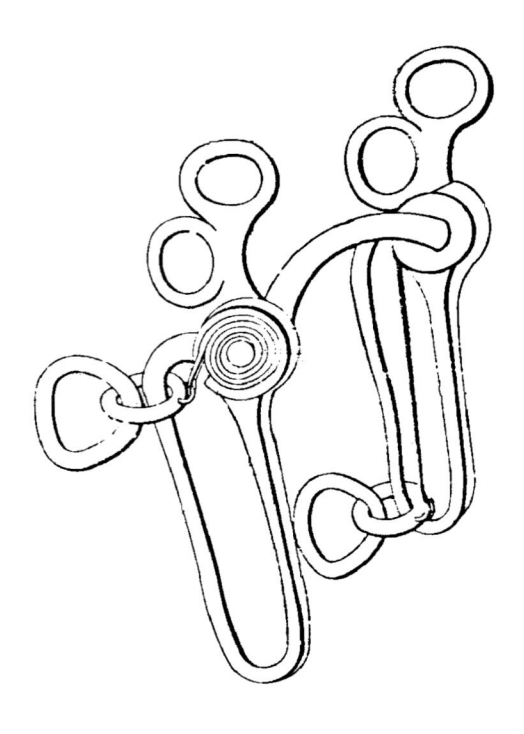

Fig. 5.18 John B. Baker spring-operated snaffle-curb combination bit.

Baker, William C., New York, NY, Patent No. 52,125, January 23, 1866 [Fig. 5.19]. A pull on the reins causes the spiral spring to pull down, putting more pressure on the curb and lengthening the ratio of the pull on the lower cheek-piece.

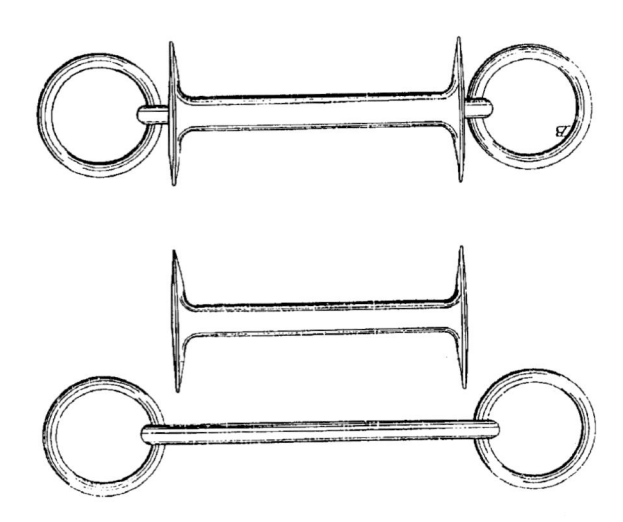

Fig. 5.20 Balch non-chaffing snaffle bit.

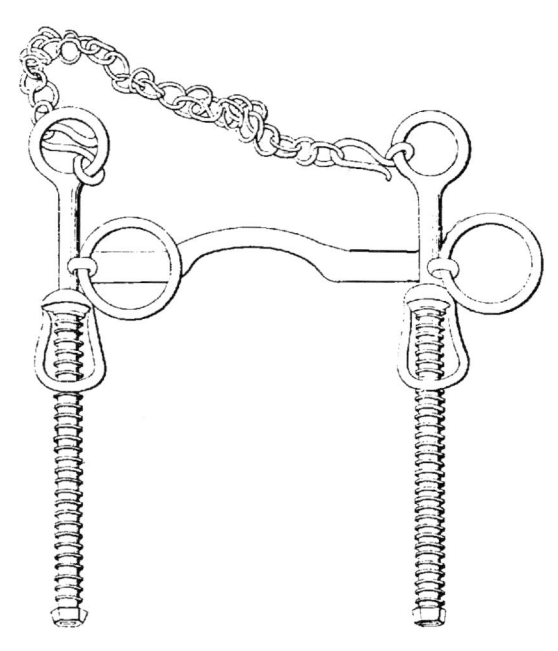

Fig. 5.19 Baker's adjustable curb bit

Balch, Dan Shaw, Bradford, VT, Letter Patent No. 1,299, Aug. 23,1839 [Fig. 5.20]. A bar-snaffle bit with an iron spool that rotates around the mouthpiece, preventing chaffing of the horse's lips.

Balding Gag: See Gag, Balding, Chapter 12.

Baldridge, Herman, Los Angeles, CA, Patent No. 365,958, July 5, 1887 [Figs. 5.21 and 5.21a]. This bit may be used without injury to the tenderest mouth but will be effective in controlling the most fractuous animals. Serves to prevent the horse's tongue from hanging out.

Baldwin, Alexander P., Newark, NJ, Patent No. 84,469, Nov. 21, 1868 [Fig. 5.22]. A bit consisting of a combined upper and lower mouthpiece constructed so that one can vibrate endwise upon or in the other, while together they form but one mouth-piece, the upper piece moving while the lower is stationary.

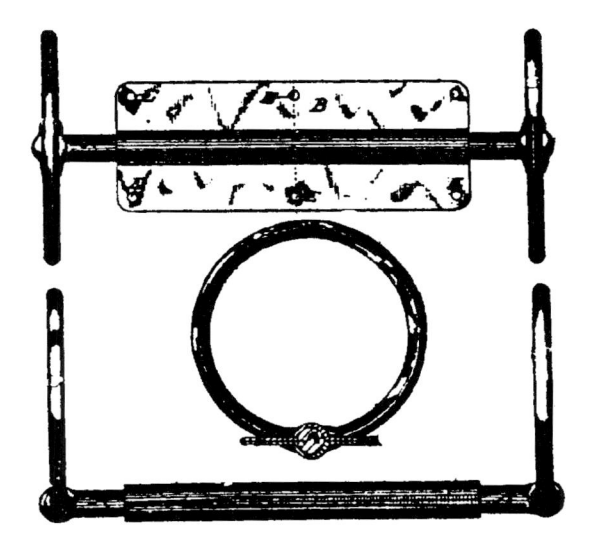

Fig. 5.21 Baldridge bit with a straight mouth and a gag plate.

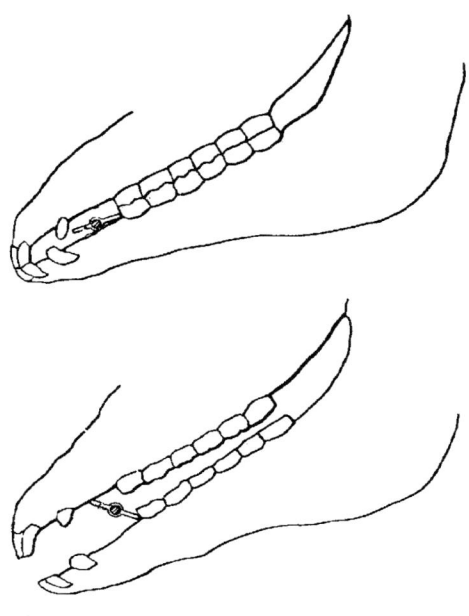

Fig. 5.21a Baldridge bit action on the horse's mouth.

Patent No. 97,022, Nov. 23, 1869 [Fig. 5.23]. A broken-snaffle bit with the joint on a hinge to allow the mouth-piece to bend only in one plain.

Patent No. 326,703, Sep. 22, 1885 [Fig. 5.24]. Construction method of a jointed snaffle bit to provide an inexpensive manufacturing method.

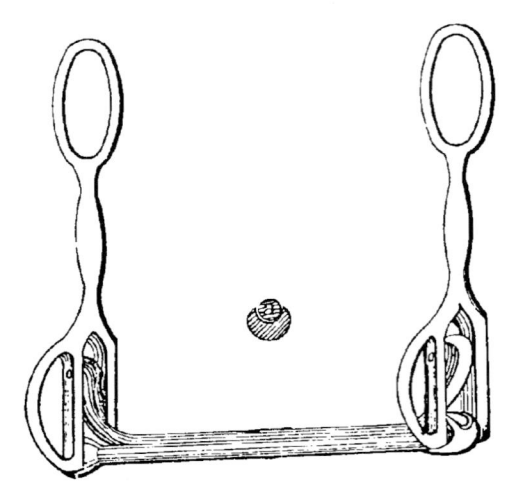

Fig. 5.22 Baldwin double mouth-piece bit.

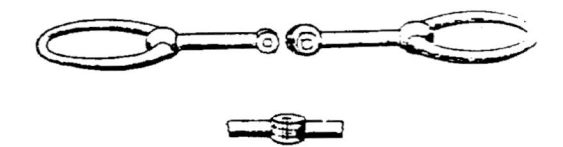

Fig. 5.23 Baldwin construction design.

Fig. 5.24 Baldwin bit construction method.

Baldwin Bit: A universally solid shifting-mouth bit [Figs. 5.25 and 5.25a].

Fig. 5.25 Baldwin shifting-mouth bit.

Fig. 5.25a Cheek-piece detail of Baldwin bit.

Ball Cheek Breaking Bit with players [Fig.5.26]. Enlarged rounded ends are placed on the ends of double or full-cheek snaffle bits.

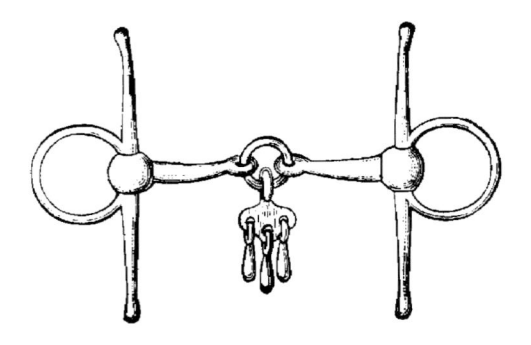

Fig. 5.26 Ball cheek breaking bit.

Ball Cheek Snaffle [Fig. 5.27].

Banbury Polo Bit [Fig.5.28]. An early 19th century English design with a mouth-piece that floats up and down within the slotted cheek-piece. The design of the mouth-piece is often called a "Banbury Mouth."

54

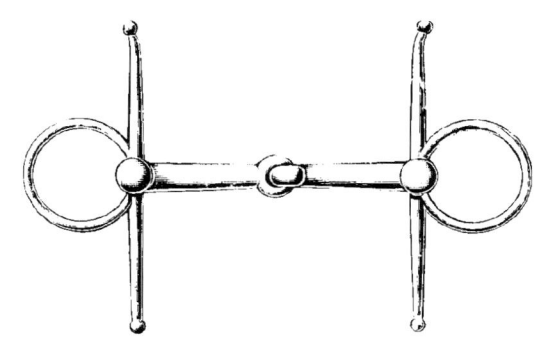

Fig. 5.27 Ball cheek snaffle bit.

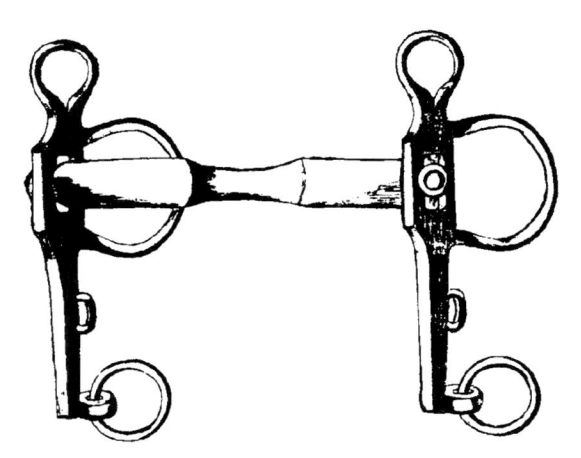

Fig. 5.28 Banbury polo bit. Drawing by W. T. Stone.

Barbour, Pollock, Louisville, KY, Patent No. 319,439, June 9, 1885 [Fig. 5.29]. This patent entails a detachable curb devise that can be added to any ring snaffle bit. The links of the chain can be covered with leather.

Fig. 5.29 Barbour detachable curb.

Barndollar, Winfield J., Pueblo, CO, Patent No. 488,051, Dec. 13, 1892 [Fig. 5.30]. A bridle bit with a bit-bar loosely encircled by a series of unconnected rings whose internal diameter is materially larger than the bit-bar. The outer ring is attached to prevent the loose rings from sliding to the ends of the bar.

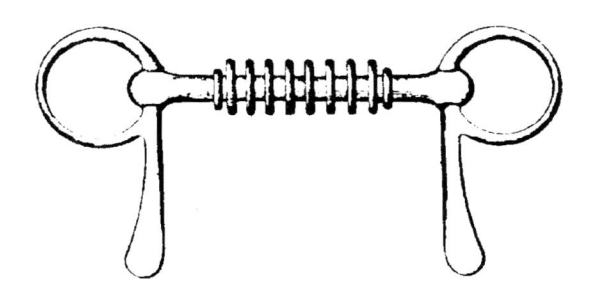

Fig. 5.30 Barndollar bit designed to prevent a horse from protruding its tongue while being used with a bit.

Barnes, Gilbert W., Mount Vernon, NY, Patent No. 124,789, Mar. 19, 1872 [Figs. 5.31, 5.31a, 5.31b and 5.31c]. A pulley bit designed to be used with a check-rein and driving reins.

Fig. 5.31 Barnes pulley bit.

Baron Thornton: See Thornton, Baron, anti-pulling bit, Chapter 33, Fig. 33.12.

Barrel-head (Egg-butt): See Mouth-piece Ends, Chapter 25, Fig. 25.45.

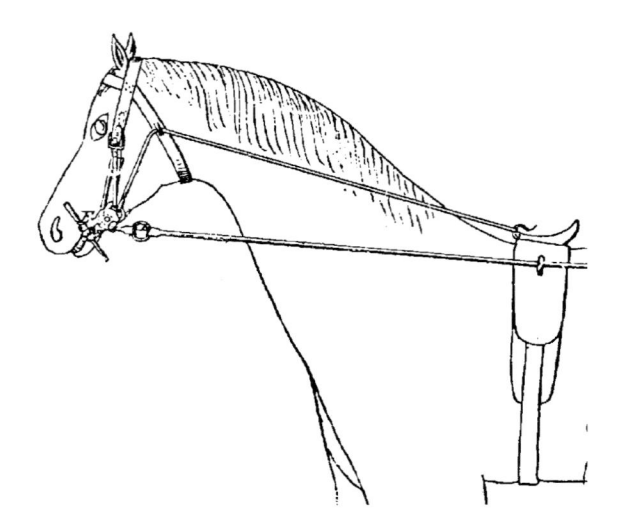

Fig. 5.31a Barnes pulley bit showing rein attachments.

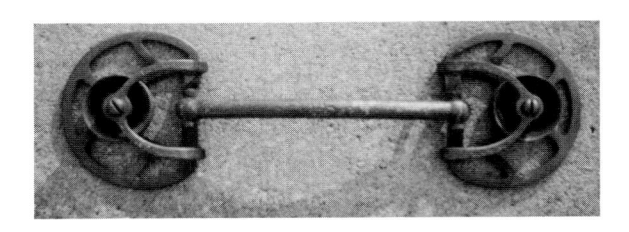

Fig. 31b Barnes production bit.

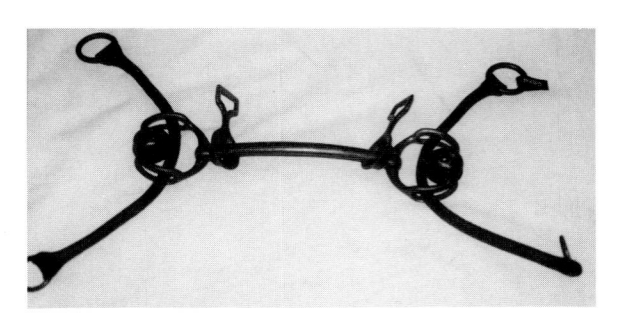

Fig. 5.31c Barnes pully bit with round straps and overcheck loops.

Barrel Racer's Bit: A three-piece gag bit. See Gag Bits, Chapter 12.

Barrel-roller: See Chapter 25, Fig. 25.13.

Barrera, Frank, San Antonio, TX, Patent No. 2,066,087, Dec. 29, 1936 [Fig. 5.32]. A bit with a pair of cheek-pieces, a nose-bar, and an adjustable curb-chain. The cheek-pieces are secured with a bottom lip bar.

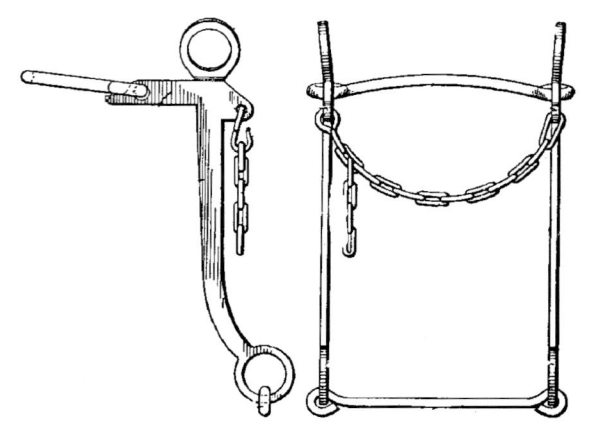

Fig. 5.32 Barrera curb bit that has no mouth-piece.

Bars of a Bit: The portion of the bit that passes through the horse's mouth.

Bartruff, Edwin T., Keokuk, IA, Patent No. 501,987, July 25, 1893 [Fig. 5.33]. A double-barred mouth-piece, with both bars that swivel on the cheek-pieces. A third bar or check bit is attached to the upper mouth-piece by projections with eyes that permit the check bit to move freely.

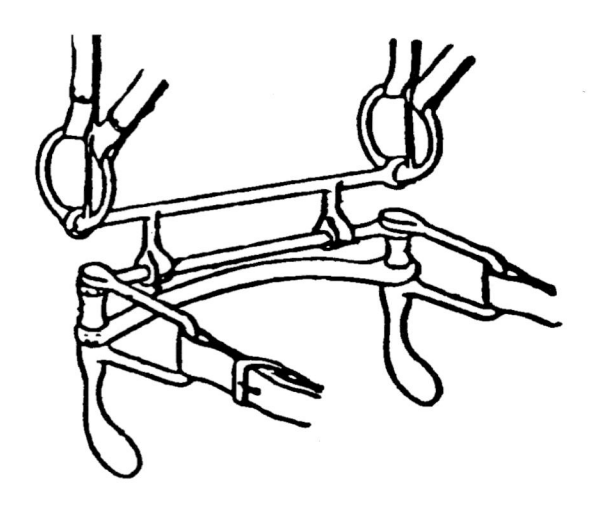

Fig. 5.33 Bartruff double-mouth bit with an over check.

Basket Bit: See Short, Andrew, Chapter 30, Fig. 30.20 and Chapter 2.

Baskin, S. A., Temple, GA, Patent No. 1,113,863, Oct. 13, 1914 [Fig. 5.34].

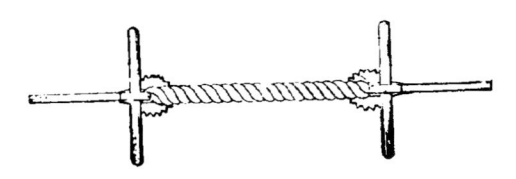

Fig. 5.34 Baskin bit.

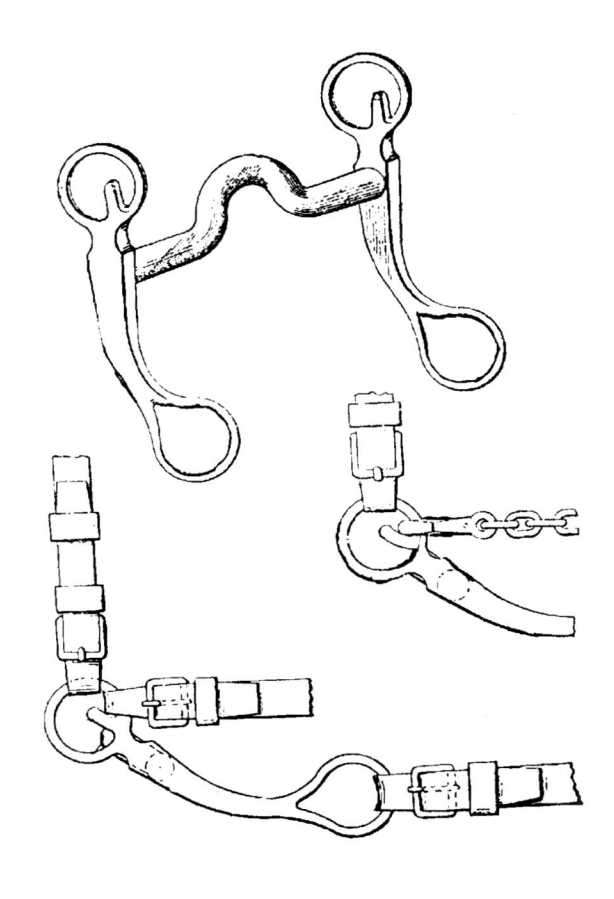

Fig. 5.35 Typical Bass bit.

Bass, James O., Tulia, TX, Patent No. 1,167,541, Jan. 11, 1916 [Fig. 5.35]. The bit has a stop member that extends only part way into the upper side-piece loop. The extension supports the curb-strap and keeps it in an elevated position. This is a trademark of many "Bass" bits.

Bates, Henry H., Washington, D. C., Patent No. 574,058, Dec. 29, 1896 [Fig. 5.36]. A spring-activated bit that produces more tension on the mouth-piece as the reins are pulled and releases tension when the reins are relaxed.

Baucher Bit: A bit that typlifies the correct proportion and size in a curb bit. *(The Saddle-Horse,* Orange Judd Co., New York, 1881) [Fig. 5.37].

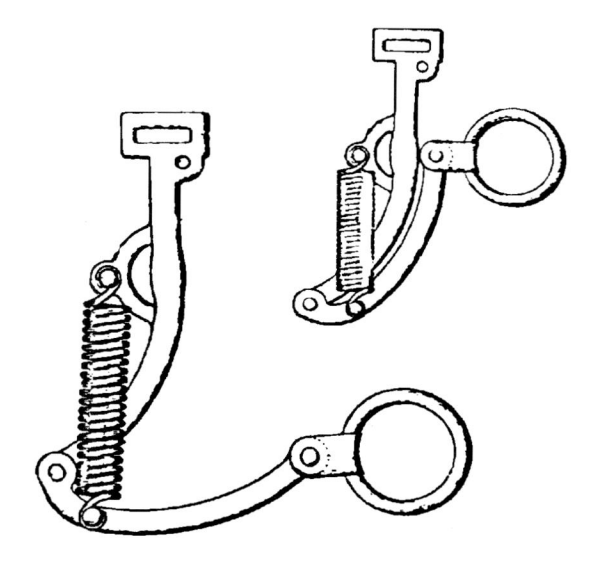

Fig. 5.36 Bates spring-tension bit with the tension of the cheek-piece extended and in the relaxed position.

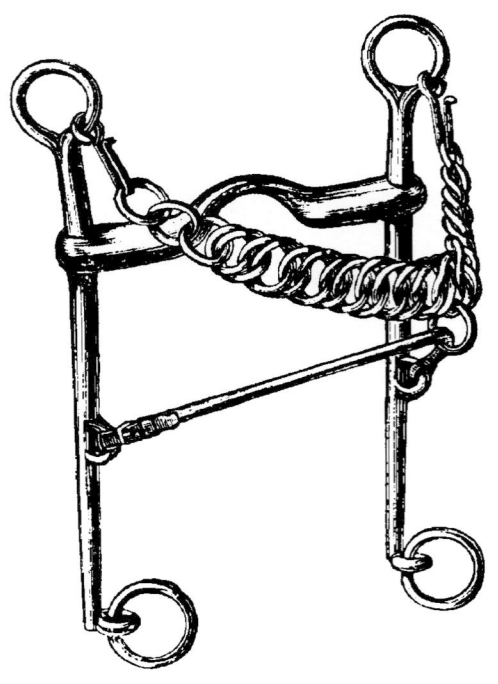

Fig. 5.37 Baucher bit.

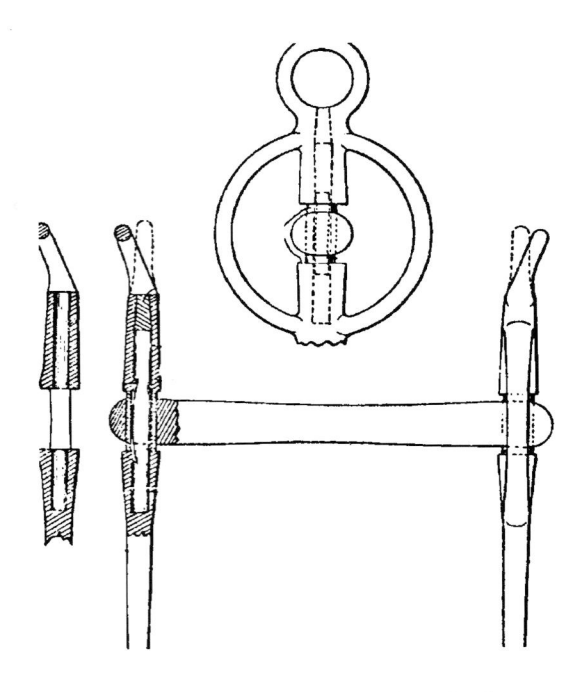

Fig. 5.38 Beard construction design.

Beard, Francis Jean, Bloxwich, England, Patent No. 935,092, Nov. 6, 1906 [Fig. 5.38]. A construction design of the mouth-piece ends made solid as compared to the usual jaw-type ends which close around the cross-bars of the cheek-pieces. The mouth-piece ends are drilled to accept a pin placed down through the top of the cheek-piece, securing the mouth-piece.

Bearing Rein: A term for check-reins frequently used on driving teams to keep their heads at the same height.

Beckeman, John U., and David W. Lukens, St. Louis, MO, Patent No.480,487, Aug. 9, 1892 [Fig. 5.39]. A three-section mouth-piece with the two outer severe sections, larger at the cheek-piece and reduced in size to form the eye links. The curved cheek-pieces are designed for the ends to act like clamping jaws and contact the jaws of the horse when sufficient strength is applied to the reins.

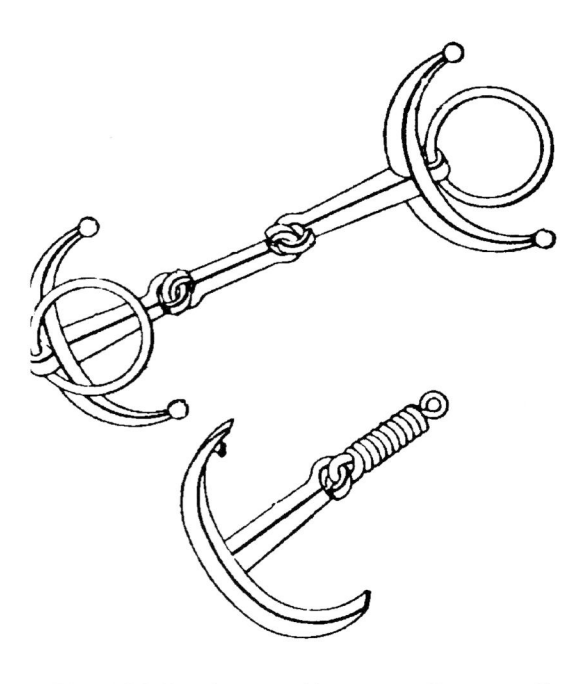

Fig.5.39 Beckeman three-section mouth-piece with clamping cheek-pieces.

Beckwith, Harry W., Omaha, NE, Patent No. 903,351, Nov., 11, 1908 [Fig. 5.40]. A bit with scissor action in which the action pieces of the bit pivot on the mouth-piece.

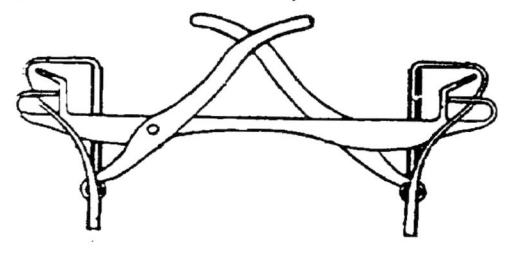

Fig. 5.40 Beckwith scissor bit.

Beery, Jesse, Pleasant Hill, OH, Patent No. 1.078,987, Nov. 18, 1913 [Fig. 5.41]. A combination curb and snaffle bit hung from a single cheek-piece on each side of the bridle. The bit has the freedom of action of two bits hanging on separate cheek-pieces.

Fig. 5.41 Beery combination curb and snaffle bit.

Behind the Bit: A position in which the mouth and bit are behind a vertical plane [Fig. 5.42].

Belknap, Gardner Albert, Beaver Centre, PA, Patent No. 424,258, Mar. 25, 1890 [Fig. 5.43]. A combination bit and bridle with broad mouth-piece ends that have outward flaring tipped perforations to which the headstall is attached and spring-surrounded short rein in the rear to which the driving rein is attached. This provides an elastic attachment to provide a tight rein at all times.

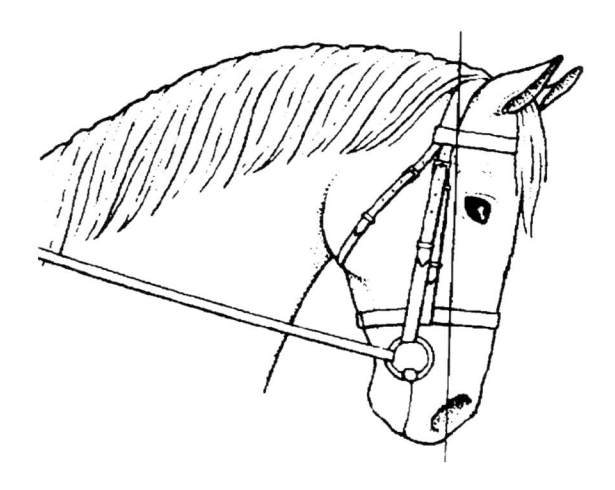

Fig. 5.42 Behind the bit.

Bellringer, James R., New York, NY, Patent No. 169,403, Nov. 2, 1875 [Fig. 5. 44]. The perforated plate that extends four inches or more covers a large area and presses firmly but gently on the tongue. It can be used with a noseband or a curb.

Belmont Polo Bit: See Pelham Bits, Chapter 27, Fig. 27.6.

Ben Morgan Bit: An early style Pelham bit with a reverse arch mouth manufactured by Dewsbury and others [Fig. 5.45].

Bennet, Noah W., Belgrade, MT, Patent No. 930,827, Aug. 10, 1909 [Fig. 5.46]. A bit made for the easy attachment of the curb-strap and check-rein.

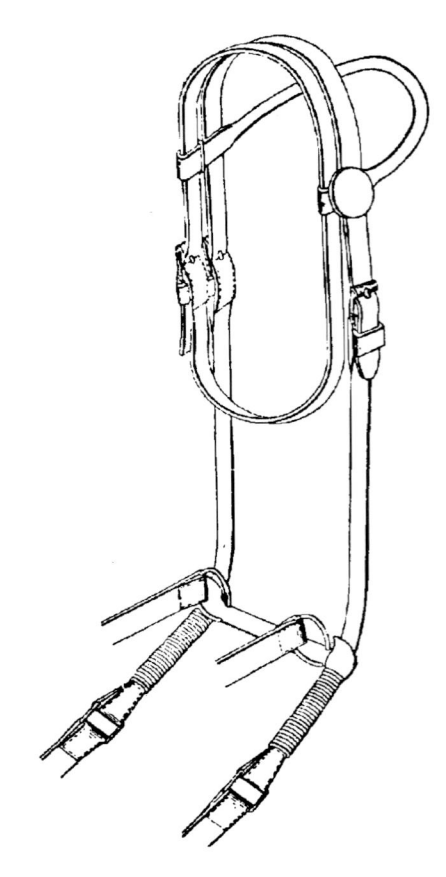

Fig. 5.43 Belknap bit and bridle.

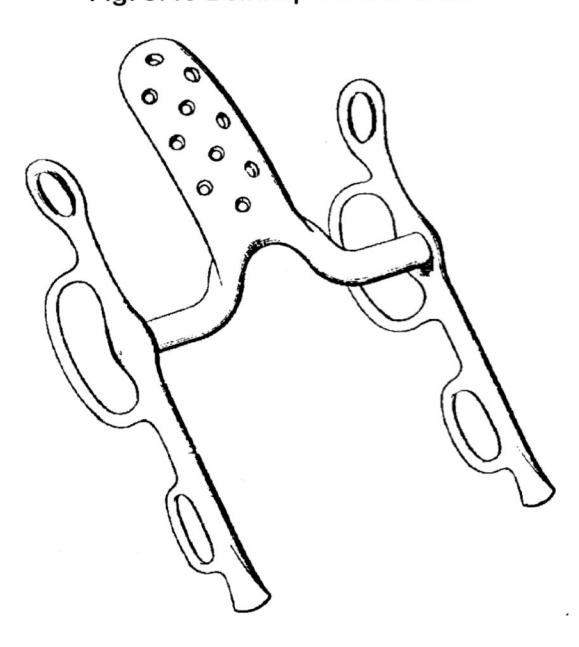

Fig. 5.44 Bellringer perforated-plate curb bit.

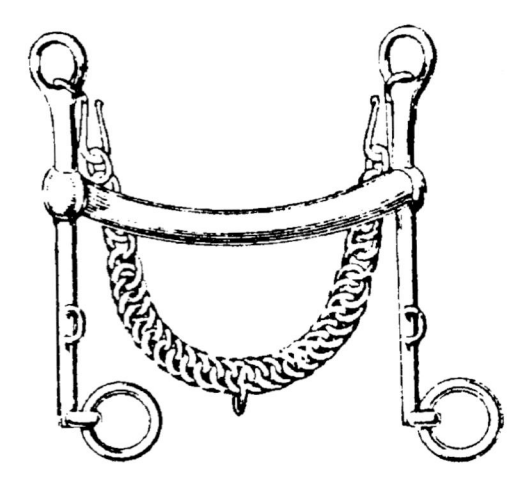

Fig. 5.45 Ben Morgan curb bit.

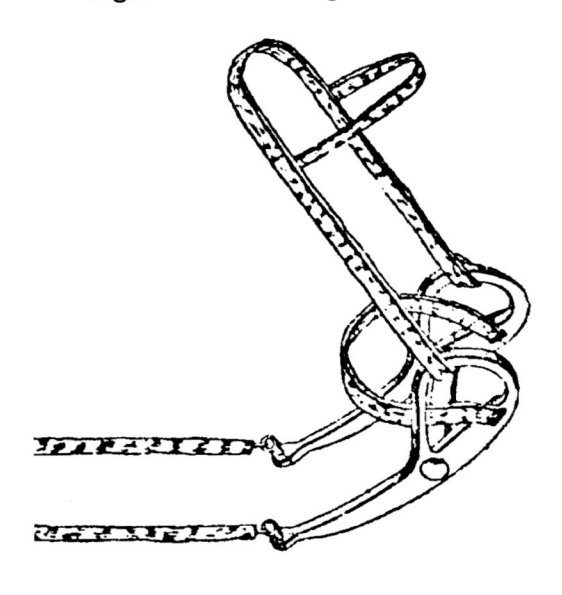

Fig. 5.46 Bennet curb bit.

Bentinck Curb Bit: Eighteenth century bit first manufacured in England [Fig. 5.47].

Bergin, Leland B., Millbrae Highlands, CA, Patent No. 2,012,705, Aug. 27, 1935 [Fig. 5.48]. A bit designed to prevent cutting, pinching or bruising the horse's mouth. The cheekpieces swivel on the ends of the mouth-piece.

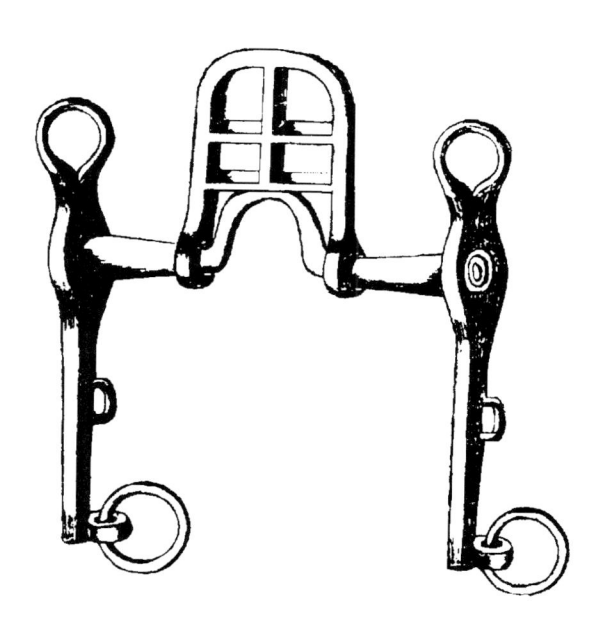

Fig. 5.47 Bentinck curb bit (drawing by W. T. Stone).

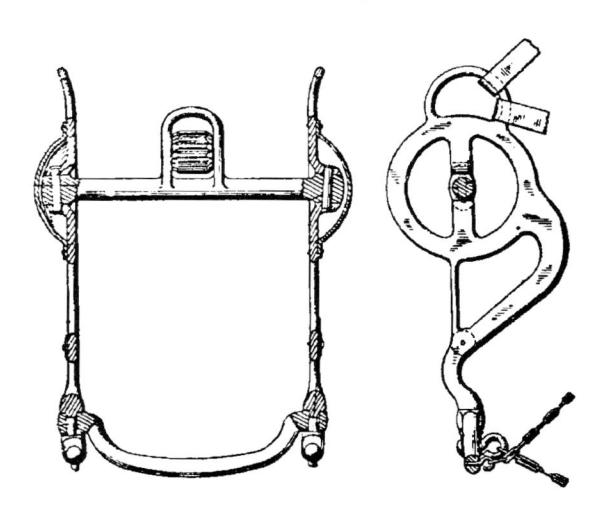

Fig. 5.48 Bergin swivel-cheek curb bit.

Patent No. 2,466,147, Apr 5, 1949 [Fig. 5.49]. An improvement over previous patent.

Berkley Polo Pelham: See Pelham, Chapter 27.

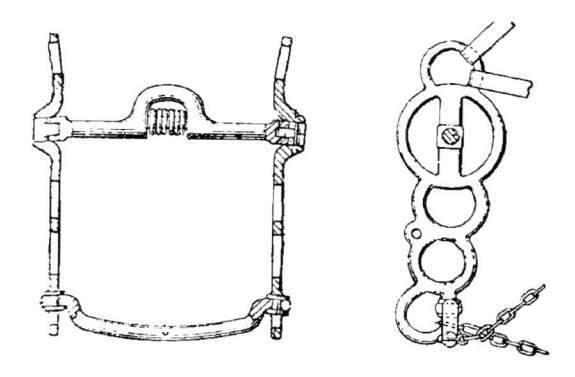

Fig. 5.49 Bergin improved curb bit.

Berry, James W., Huntington, WV, Patent No. 771,226, Oct. 4, 1904 [Fig. 5.50]. A simple burr devise attached to any bridle that will effectively cure the horse of lolling its tongue.

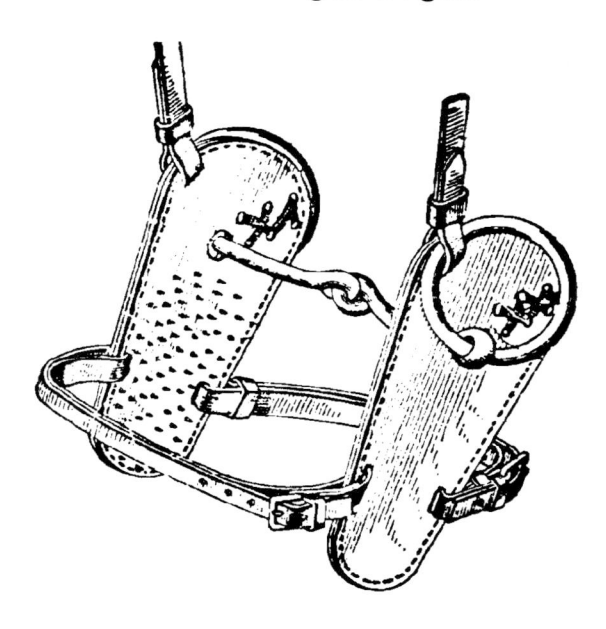

Fig. 5.50 Berry bit cheek burr.

Bersch, Anton, Auburn, NY, Patent No. 422,004, Feb. 25, 1890 [Fig. 5.51]. The pivoting cheek-pieces grip the lower jaw of the horse when the reins are pulled.

Best Out: An overcheck bit. See Overcheck, Chapter 9, Fig. 9.11.

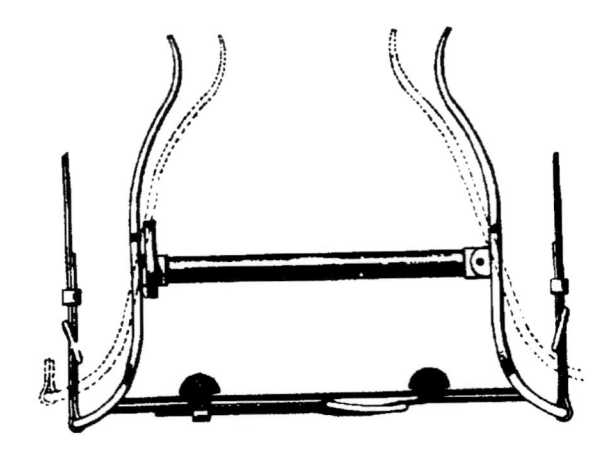

Fig. 5.51 Bersch pressure bit.

Bethe, August L., Hanover, Germany, Patent No. 804,700, Nov. 14, 1905 [Figs. 5.52 & 5.52a]. A bit having jointed sections and a spring activated palate-pressing devise that engages when the bit is rocked. The spring-powered cylinders attached to the side-pieces keep the mouth-piece in a normal position.

Bicycle Chain Snaffle Bit: Jointed mouth with each section having a smooth side and a rough side [Fig. 5.53].

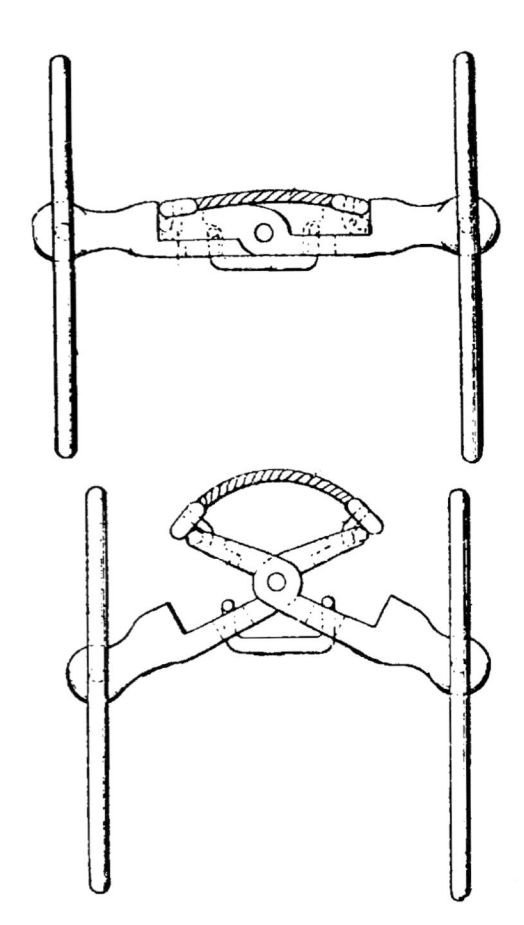

Fig. 5.52 Bethe bit with the mouth in the normal position and the expanded position.

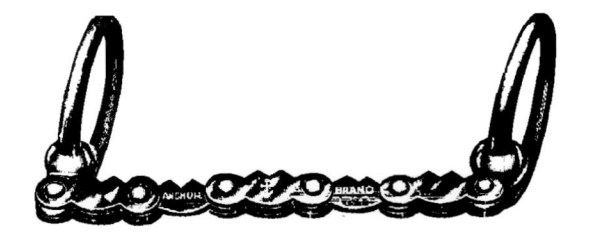

Fig. 5.53 Bicycle chain snaffle bit.

Bigelow, Melvin F., Alden, IA, Patent No. 529,472, Nov. 20, 1894 [Fig. 5.54]. The port in the mouth-piece is covered with a non-abrasive material.

Biggart, George E., Sandy Hill, NY, Patent No. 989,479, Apr. 11, 1911 [Figs. 5.55 and 5.55a]. The side-bars are extended forward and have a bit

Fig. 5.54 Bigelow snaffle and overcheck bit.

in addition to the main bit toward the lower end. The rings in the lower bar are attached to the face straps of the bridle.

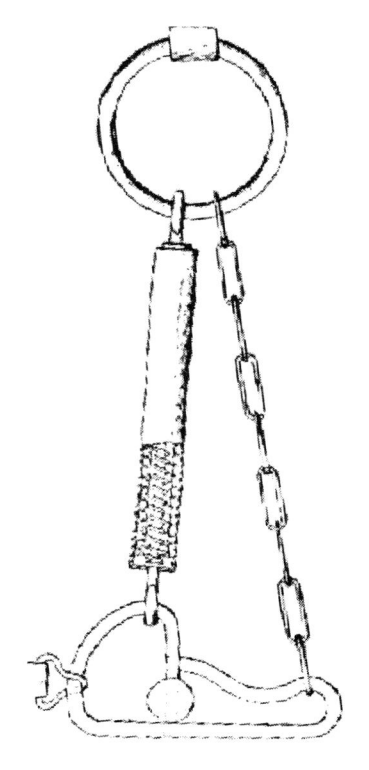

Fig. 5.52a Bethe bit cheek-piece with spring cylinder device.

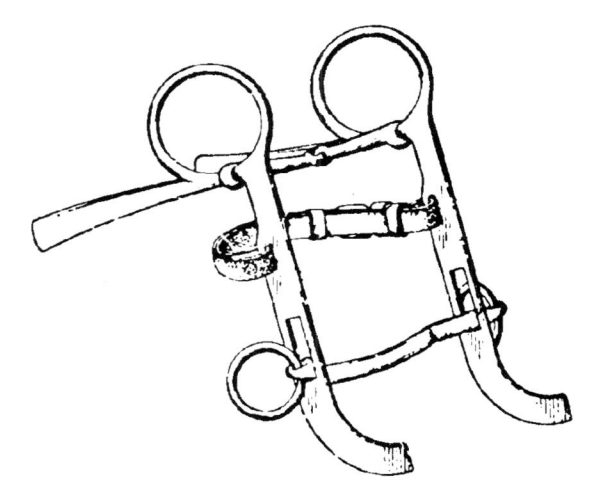

Fig. 5.55 Biggart bridle bit.

Billets: The end of a leather strap that attaches to another piece of tack by a snap, hook, or buckle; a rein-end that attaches to a bit; a headstall end attaching to a bit or to another part of the headstall.

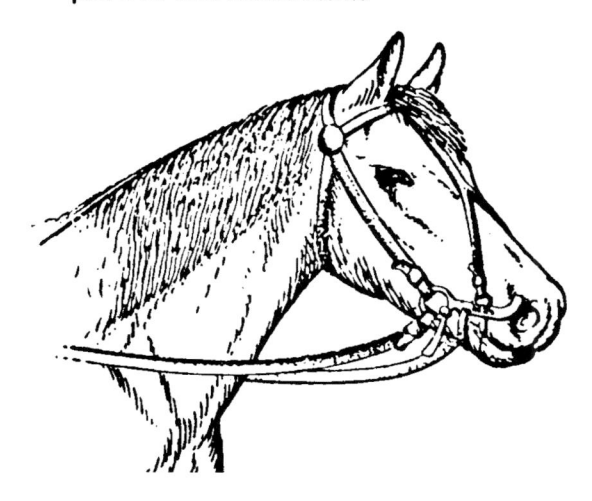

Fig. 5.55a Biggart bit in position showing the method of attachment to bridle.

Binkley, John Siles, Atchison, KS, Patent No. 682,125, Sep. 3, 1901 [Fig. 5.56]. A pulley bit.

Bit: A device inserted in or around the mouth of a horse for control of the horse. Normally attached to a bridle to secure its position in the mouth.

Bit Burr: A piece of leather or rubber to which "burrs" or projections have been added then placed around the mouth-piece of snaffle bits directly inside the cheek-piece or ring [Fig. 5.57].

Fig. 5.57 Bit burr.

63

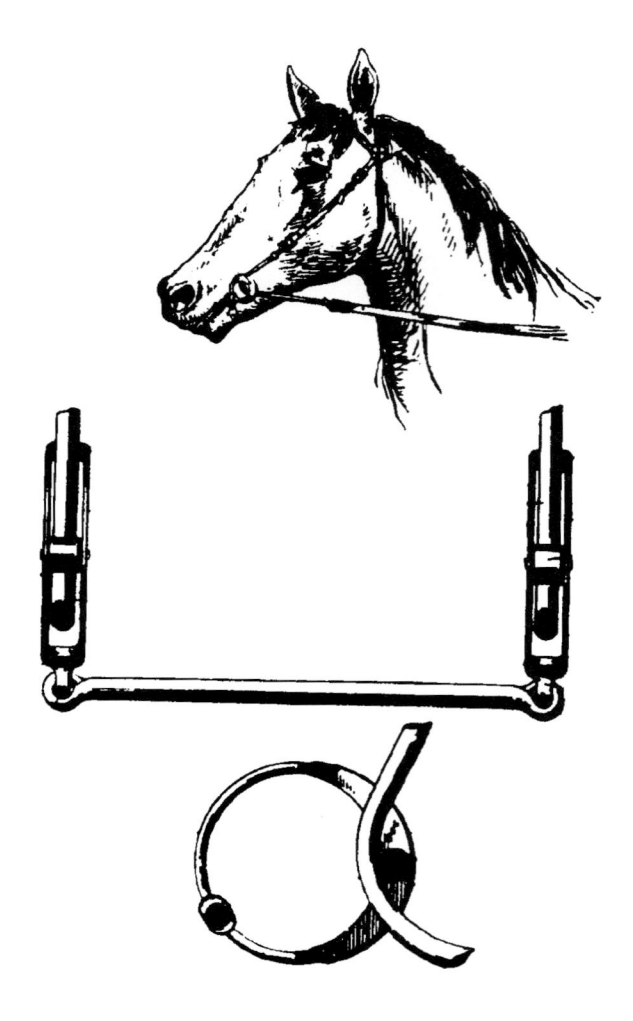

Fig. 5.56 Binkley pulley bit.

Bit-cheek Guard: A circular leather, rubber or similar material, about 3" in diameter with a center hole that is placed inside the cheek-piece and around the mouth-piece to shorten the length of the mouth-piece and/or protect the lips of the horse and keep the horse from pulling the bit through the mouth [Fig. 5.59).

Bit Hole: The area of a horse's mouth between the incisor and molar teeth, where the mouth-piece of the bit lays.

Bit Plate: Refers to the cheek-piece or to the boss on the cheek-piece.

Bit Rod: Another term for the mouth-piece.

Bitless Bridle: Any of a variety of bridles used without bits, the pressure being exerted on the nose and the curb groove instead of in the mouth.

Bitting Rig: A harness or other devise for teaching a horse to obey the commands of the bit [Fig. 5.58].

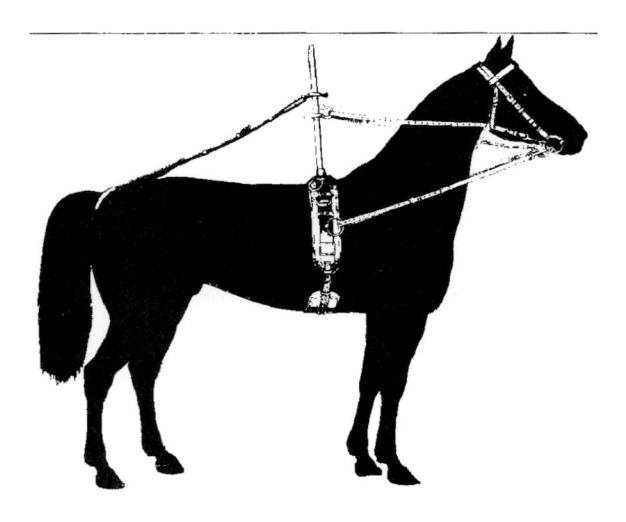

Fig. 5.58 Wright patent developer bitting rig.

Blade Bit: See Fishback Snaffle, Chapter 11, Fig. 11.17.

Blinders: Devices attached to the sides of driving bridles behind the area of the eye to limit the horse to frontal vision only and to keep the horse from looking back to see what the driver is doing. See Chapter 35, Fig. 35.46.

Blinkers: Another term for blinders.

Blyholder, John B., St. Louis, MO, Patent No. 296,815, Apr. 15, 1884 [Fig. 5.60]. A hollow or tubular Tshaped bit used with horses that have the habit of wind-sucking.

Fig. 5.59 A rubber bit-guard.

Fig. 5.60 Blyholder wind-sucking bit.

Boone, W. R. "Wallie": See Chapter 36, Loriners.

Borer: A horse that pulls on the bit by thrusting its head forward and downward.

Bosal: The noseband used with a hackamore. See drawing Chapter 13, Hackamore.

Bosal Hanger: See Hackamore, Chapter 13.

Bosalea: A mechanical hackamore developed for horses with injured mouths or horses whose riders do not have the knowledge, time or desire to train their horses to the bit.

Boss: An ornamental plate, shield or insignia attached to the outer face of the cheek-piece, usually at the juncture of the mouth-piece or above. They may be placed at the juncture of the brow-band and the head stall and are then called ear bosses.

Boucha Bit: See Side-pieces, Chapter 31, Hanging-cheek Bit, Fig. 31.15.

Boughton, S. A., Waterford, NY, Patent No. 118,900, Sep. 12, 1871 [Figs 5.61 and 5.61a]. A double-mouth bit with one end of each mouth-piece secured to one cheek-piece and the opposite end sliding through an opening in the cheek-piece.

Fig. 5.61 Boughton double-mouth bit.

Fig. 5.61a Boughton broken-mouth bit.

Bowles, Zachary T., Hillsborough, TX, Patent No. 403.510, May 21, 1889 [Fig. 5.62]. The rein-eye loops of the cheek-pieces swivel and put extra pressure on the curb.

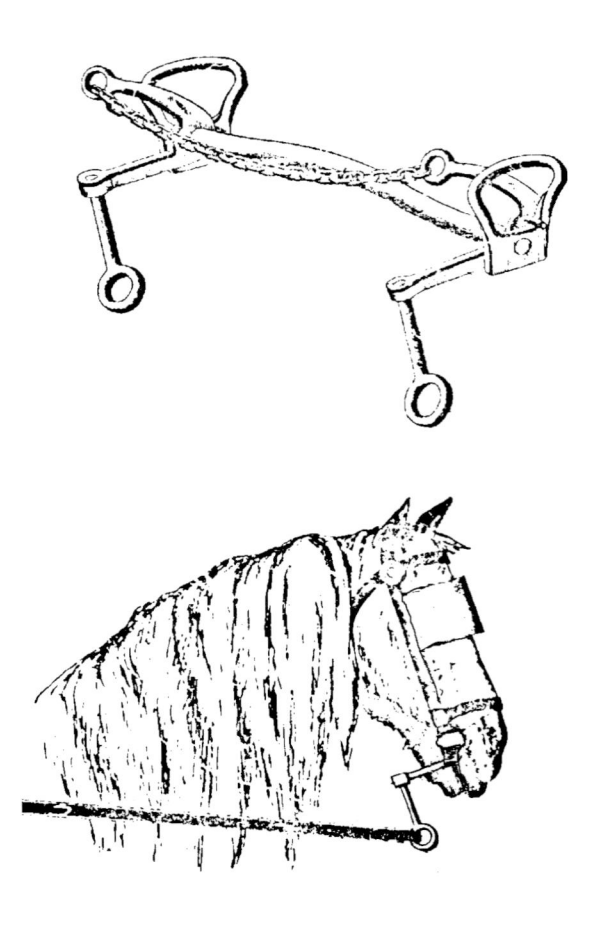

Fig. 5.62 Bowles curb bit.

Bowmaker, John Peter, Okeene, OK, Patent No. 724,791, Apr. 7, 1903 [Fig. 5.63]. The attachment illustrated can be used on any bit of similar type.

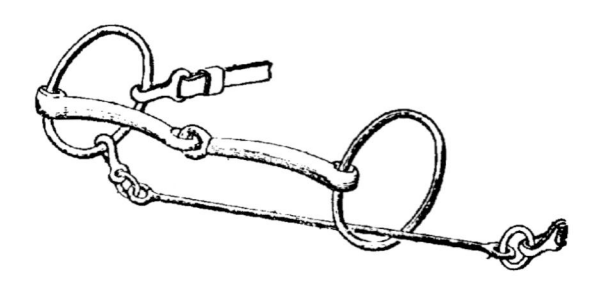

Fig. 5.63 Bowmaker detachable-curb controller.

Boyd, Alonzo, Indianapolis, IN, Patent No. 865,757, Sep. 10, 1907 [Fig. 5.64]. A curb attachment for hitching straps to tie a horse.

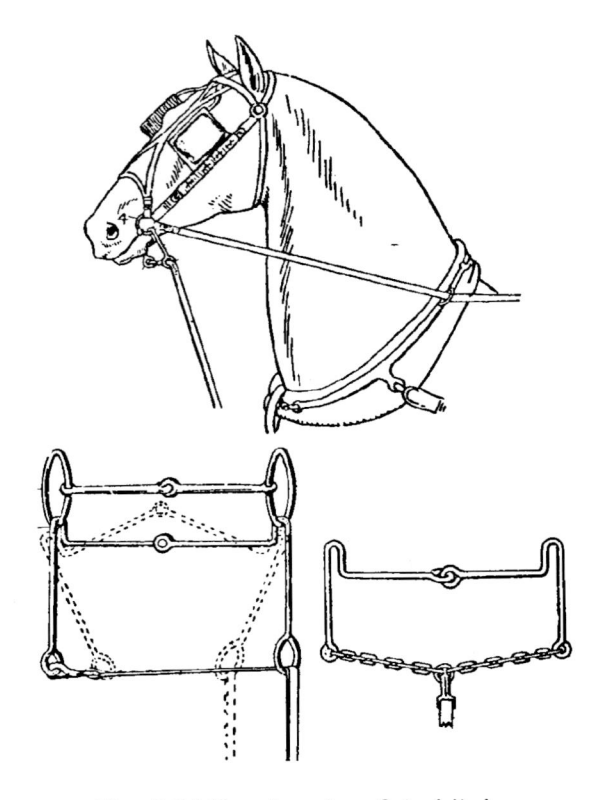

Fig. 5.64 Boyd curb safety-hitch.

Boyer, Frank P., Central City, IA, Patent No. 1,494,884, May 20 1924 [Fig. 5.65]. A mouth-piece with connecting side-rings and rearward extending loops pivoted to the ends of the mouth-piece and connecting curb-levers pivoted back of the mouth-piece.

Boyington, Raymond N., Millford, ME, Patent No. 3,584,437, June 15, 1971 [Figs. 5.66 and 5.66a]. A combination curb and snaffle bit with the claim it can be used to train horses to the bit.

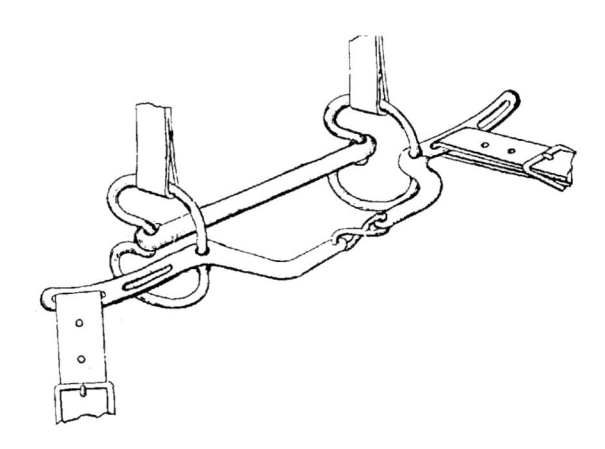

Fig. 5.65 Boyer swivel curb bit.

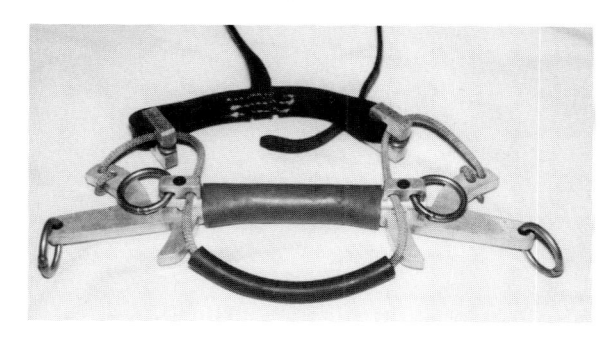

Fig. 5.66 Boyington combination curb and snaffle trainer bit.

Fig. 5.66a Adaptation of Boyington bit patent. Jean Gayle collection.

Brabson, Thomas, Newark, NJ, Patent No. 274,709, Mar. 27, 1883 [Fig. 5.67]. The mouth-piece and cheek-pieces are cast metal. After the holes have been bored in the heads of the mouth-piece and the nipples on the cheek-pieces, the parts can be finished and polished before being joined together.

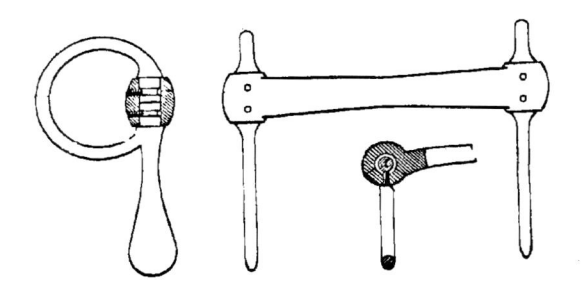

Fig. 5.67 Brabson construction method.

Patent No. 394,454, Dec 11, 1888 [Fig. 5.67a]. Construction method with a chain-type mouth-piece and the entire mouth-piece covered with India rubber.

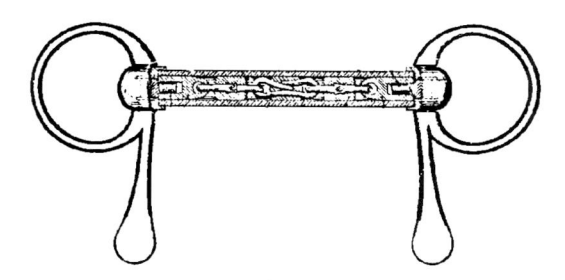

Fig. 5.67a Brabson construction method with rubber vulcanized mouth-piece.

Braced (Reinforced) Cheek-pieces: See Side-pieces, Chapter 31.

Braces: 1) Reinforcement rod for spade bits extending from the cheek-piece on top of the mouth-piece toward and attaching to the spade. See diagram of Spade Bit, Chapter 1.
2) Support for cheek-piece on some curb bits.

Brazilian Bit: A bit manufactured by John Dewsbury and Son, Walsall, England [Fig. 5.68].

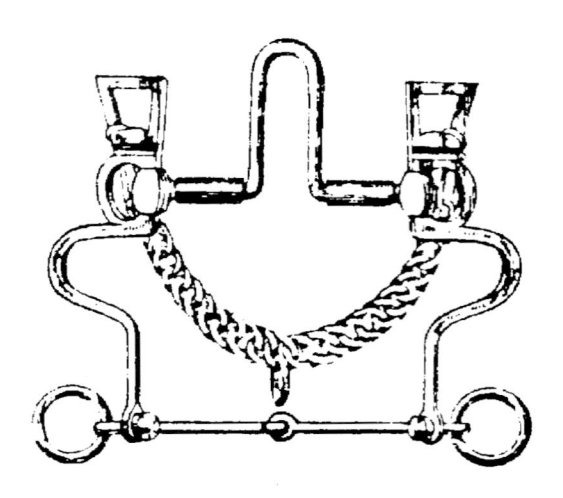

Fig. 5.68 Brazilian bit.

Brazilian Bit: Slobber bar bears inscripton "ESTIDOS UNIDOS DO BRASIL, 15 DE NOVEMBRO, DE 1889." (United States of Brazil, 15 November 1889) Figs. 5.69 and 5.69a.

Fig. 5.69 Brazilian bit.

Breaking Bit with Keys: See Mouthing Bit, Chapter 24.

Breaking (Training Snaffle) Bit: See Training Bit, Chapter 33.

Bridge: A term for a port.

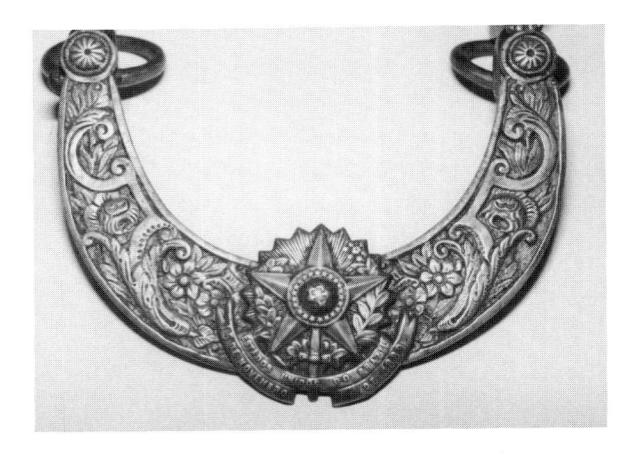

Fig. 5.69a Detail of slobber bar of Brazilian bit.

Bridle: The head gear to which is attached the bit or bits by which the horse is controlled.

Bridle Chain: See Curb-chain, Chapter 6 and Rein Chain, Chapter 35.

Bridle Ring: See Diagram, Chapter 1.

Bridle Teeth: A term for canine teeth or tushes of a horse. See Anatomy, Chapter 3.

Bridle-wise: A horse well-trained to respond to any slight pressure of the rein or on the bit. See Neck-rein, Chapter 26.

Bridoon (Bradoon-English spelling): A light snaffle bit used with a Weymouth bit on a double- or four-rein bridle.

Bridoon, Large Ring: A bit with a four inch or larger diameter cheek-ring.

Briggs, Robert A., Rudd, IA, Patent No. 659,286, Oct. 9, 1900 [Fig. 5.70]. An adjustable bit with many adaptations for headstall attachment and curb attachment. The mouth-piece is composed of three jointed pieces plus an extension of the rein-rings through the cheek-rings.

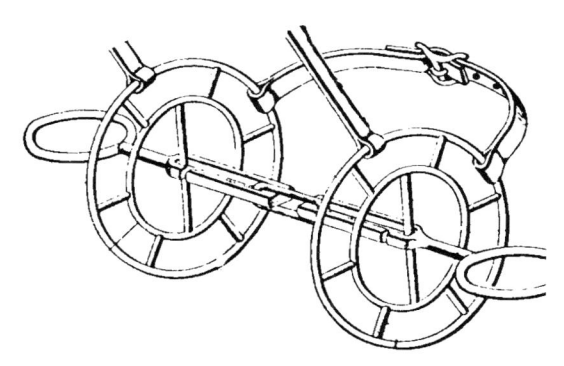

Fig. 5.70 Briggs adjustable flexible-mouth bit.

Brighton Bit: A curb bit of old design from the *Loriner,* No. 68, 1871 [Fig. 5.71].

Fig. 5.72 Britt safety-bridle bit

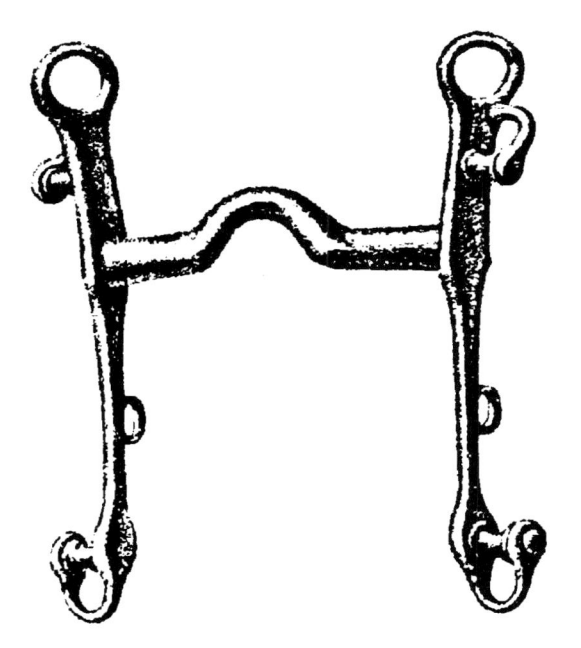

Fig. 5.71 Brighton bit.

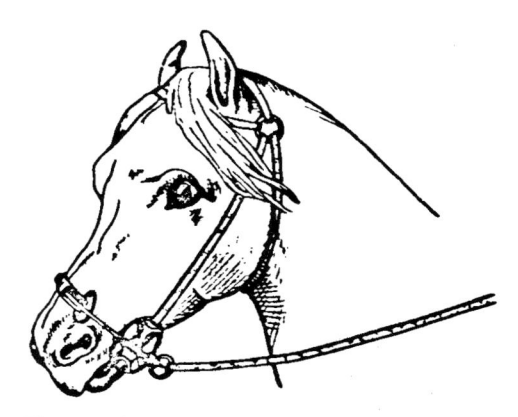

Fig. 5.72a Britt safety bit in position on the horse.

Britt, Lucas P., New York, NY, Patent No. 397,273, Feb. 5, 1889 [Figs. 5.72 and 5.72a]. To be used in combination with the snaffle bit, whereby the horse is controlled by closing his nostrils.

Brockington, George, Newark, NJ, Patent No. 428,767, May 27, 1890 [Fig. 5.73]. Special construction of the core of the mouth-piece and the vulcanized rubber covering of the mouth-piece.

Patent No. 466,485, Jan. 5, 1992 [Fig. 5.74]. Stops added to the ends of the mouth-piece inside the cheek-pieces to prevent the horse from pinching or catching its lips.

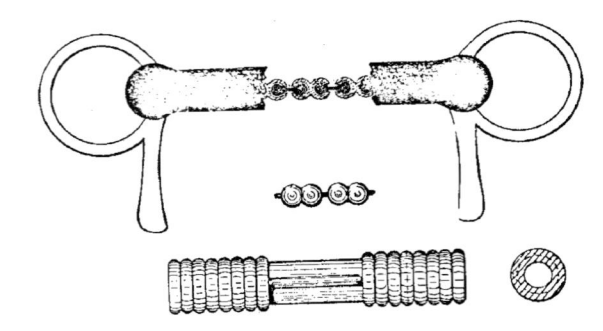

Fig. 5.73 Several details of Brockington bit construction method.

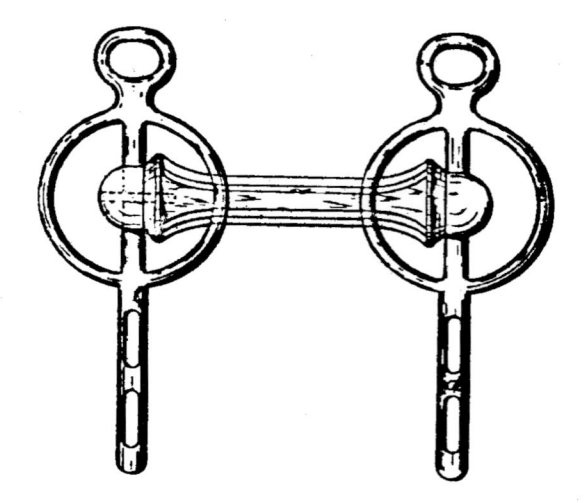

Fig. 5.74 Brockington mouth-piece with enlarged ends.

Broken Mouth-piece: A mouth-piece with a hinge or joint in the center. See Mouth-pieces, Chapter 25.

Bronco Bit: A bit designed by Dick Hill, Sherman, TX, [Fig. 5.75]. Termed a training bit, but by unscrewing the rein-ring on the side of the hollow mouth-piece, the horse can be treated with a medication running from the hole in the center of the mouth-piece.

Brooks, John N., North Java, NY, Patent No. 243,684, July 5, 1881 [Fig. 5.76]. One side of the mouth-piece is smooth and the other provided with sharp angles. The bit can be reversed by alternating the ends of the broad cheek-pieces.

Fig.5.75 Bronco bit.

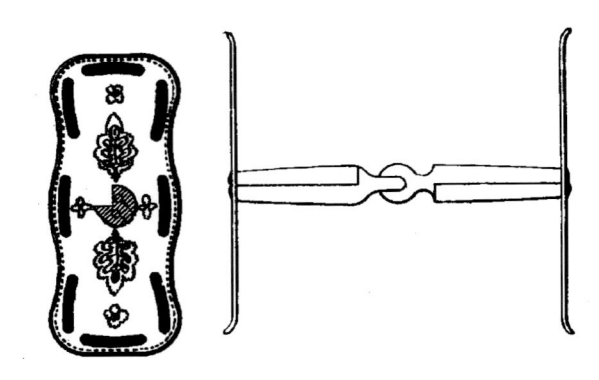

Fig. 5.76 Brooks reversible bit. A cross-section of the mouth-piece can be seen in the center of the broad cheek-piece.

Brott, John R., East Medway and Martin L. Andrews, Melrose, MA, Patent No. 312,182, Feb. 10, 1885 [Fig. 5.77]. Side hooks are used in place of a mouth-piece. The hooks are inserted between the teeth and cheeks. The hooks are connected by a curved bar that passes around the lower jaw of the horse.

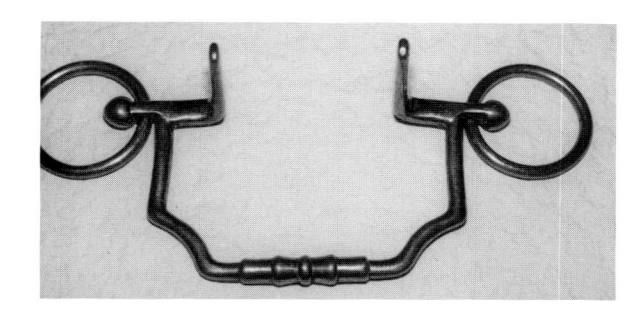

Fig. 5.77 Brott hook bit.

Brow-band: The frontal band of a bridle headstall directly below the ears and above the eyes. See Bridles, Chapter 35.

Brower, William, Baltimore, MD, Patent No. 66,941, July 23, 1867 [Fig. 5.78]. Swivelling pulleys at the ends of the mouth-piece turn to adjust at the pull of the reins, leaving the mouth-piece in a natural position.

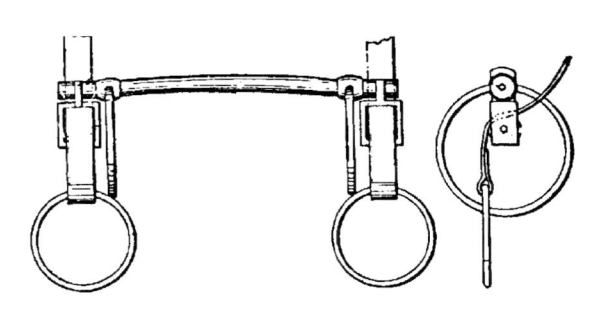

Fig. 5.78 Brower swivel-pulley bit.

Brown, Henry W., Birmingham, AL, Patent No. 1,076,946, Oct. 28, 1913 [Fig. 5.79]. A twisted-mouth snaffle bit with spur on the ends near the inside of the cheek-pieces that come in contact with the lower jaw of the horse when the reins are pulled.

Fig. 5.79 W. H. Brown spurred snaffle bit.

Brown, Lincoln F., Xenia, OH, Patent No. 484,994, Oct. 25, 1892 [Fig. 5.80]. The mouth-bar is provided with a feather or plate, the edge of which may be notched to render its action more effective.

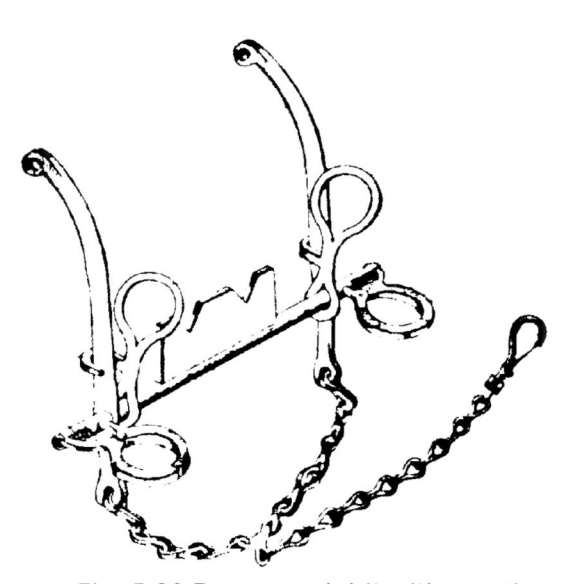

Fig. 5.80 Brown curb bit with mouth-piece plate.

Brown, William P., Racine, WI, Patent No. 632,439, Sep. 5, 1899 [Fig. 5.81]. The sliding springs in the slotted cheek-pieces keep the crossed double mouth-piece in a normal position.

Bryden, Williamson, Chelsea, MA, Patent No. 230,401, July 1880 [Fig.

5.82. A shield of leather that can be attached and sewn to any bar-type mouth-piece.

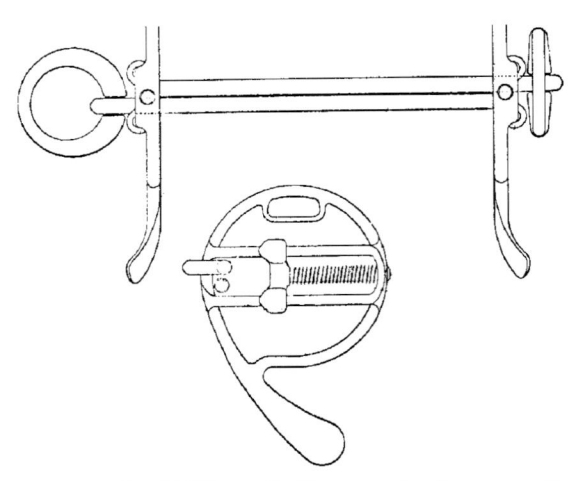

Fig. 5.81 William P. Brown double-mouth scissor bit.

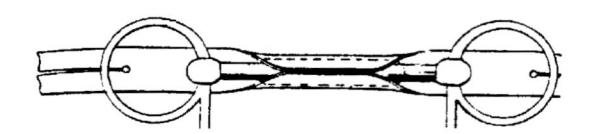

Fig. 5.82 Bryden mouth-piece cover.

Buckeye Safety Bit: See Driving Bits, Chapter 8, Fig. 8.6.

Buck-line: A line used in hitches of multiple teams to keep each horse even with its mate. The line is usually attached to a draw chain.

Buermann, August, Newark, NJ, major manufacturer and owner of many patents. Patent No. 162,348, Apr. 20, 1875 [Fig. 5.83]. The mouth-piece has several small sections and leather spacers held together by a rod passing through the center of the sections and firmly attached to the rein-rings. The circular cheek-pieces are made of leather and held in place by rivets. Not in catalog No. 35 (1922).

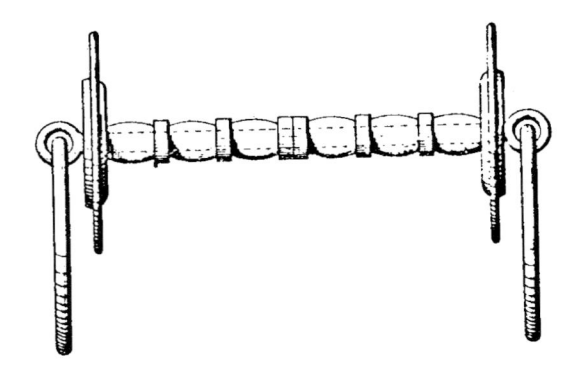

Fig. 5.83 Buermann fixed-ring snaffle bit.

Patent No. 347,225, August 10, 1886 [Fig. 5.84]. A swivel eye-ring for rein attachment used with the half-breed mouth for this curb bit.

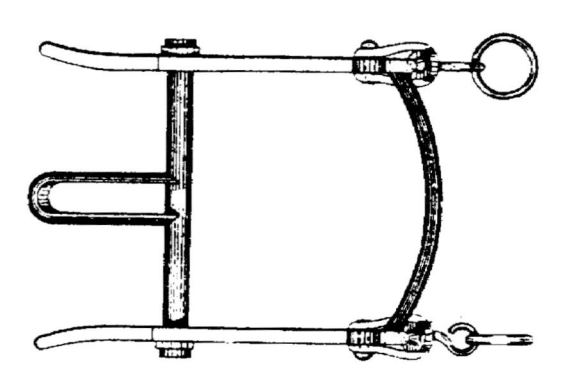

Fig. 5.84 Buermann patent curb bit.

Patent No. 356,918, Feb. 1, 1887, No. 1322 1/2 in Catalog #35 [Fig. 5.85].

Design Patent No. 34,969, August 20, 1901 [Fig. 5.86]. Co-patent with Claude D. Jackson, Amarillo, TX. Bit No. 1909 in Catalog No. 35 features a cowboy astride a bronc on the cheek-piece.

Buggy Snaffles: A term applied to light driving snaffles [Fig. 5.87].

72

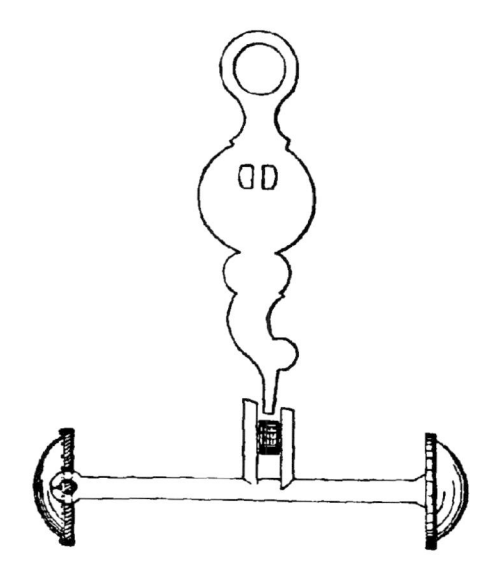

Fig. 5.85 Buermann loose-cheek curb.

Fig. 5.86 Buermann Bronco bit.

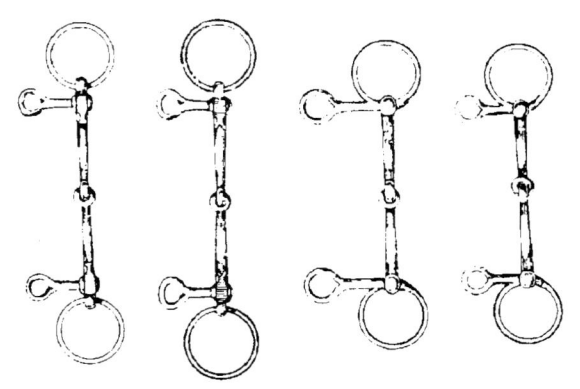

Fig. 5.87 Examples of buggy snaffles from John Dewsbury and Son.

Bulbs: The rounded outer ends of a mouth-piece.

Bumper Bit: A modern extreme curved braced-cheek bit with a mullen-style mouth [Fig. 5.88].

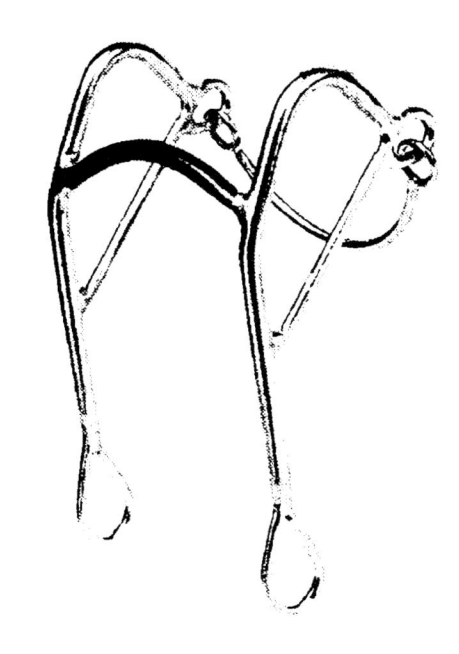

Fig. 5.88 Bumper bit.

Burgess, Richard O., Providence, RI, Patent No. 377,845, Feb. 14, 1888 [Fig. 5.89]. A cross-pull bridle bit employs two mouth-pieces, preferably flexible and crossed in the horse's mouth and secured to the headstall straps and the reins. The bit can be removed from the mouth without removing the bridle or reins.

Burch Check: See Overcheck, Chapter 9.

Burns, James, East Topham, VT, Patent No. 128,532, July 2, 1872 [Fig. 5.90]. Attached to one or more portions of a snaffle bit, a series of two or more small lugs bear against the roots of the tongue or other sensitive parts of the mouth.

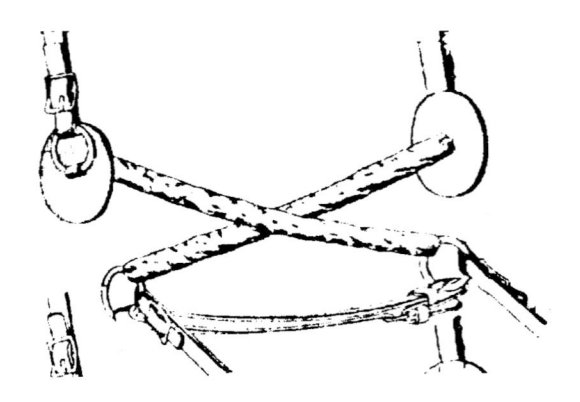

Fig. 5.89 Burgess crossed double-mouth bit.

Fig. 5.90 Burns snaffle bit with lugs attached.

Burr: A rounded piece, usually of leather, about three inches in diameter and faced with bristles. Placed around the mouth-piece inside the cheek-piece. See Figs. 5.50 and 5.57.

Butler, George P., Butter Centre, IA, Patent No. 216,653, June 17, 1879 [Fig. 5.91]. This bit provides a means of preventing the reins and other leather attachments to the bit from becoming twisted.

Fig. 5.91 Butler swivel rein-ring.

Butterfly Bit: A spring-mouth snaffle or saw-mouth bradoon [Fig. 5.92].

Fig. 5.92 Butterfly overcheck bit.

Butterfly Snaffle: See Butterfly Bit.

Butlin, Charles H., Cambridge, England, Patent No. 466,222, Dec. 29, 1891 [Fig. 5.93]. A curb bit that is used on driving horses and used with a driving rein.

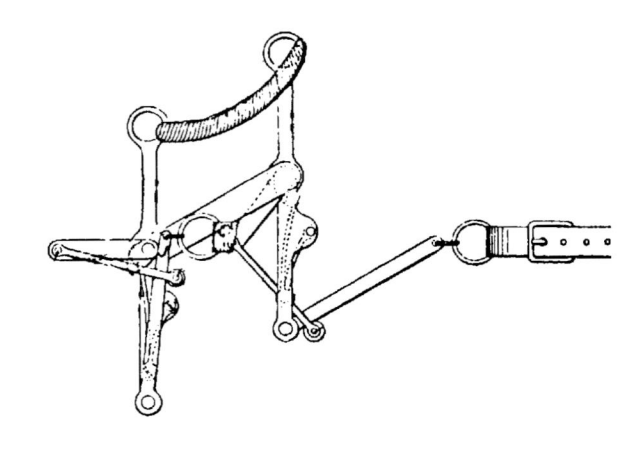

Fig. 5.93 Butlin lever-activated curb driving bit.

Buxton Bit: A curb bit used in a carriage harness--a heavy harness bit [Figs. 5.94 and 5.95].

Byers, Chester Bit: A small roping bit made by W. R. Boone [Fig. 5.96].

74

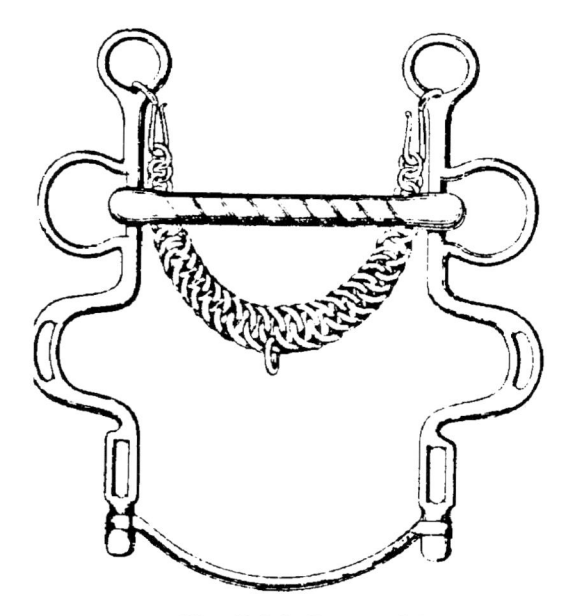

Fig. 5.94 Buxton bit.

Fig. 5.96 Boone's Chester Byers roping bit.

Fig. 5.95 Eighteenth century Buxton-style bit.

CHAPTER SIX
Cahoone to Cutting

Cahoone, Edwin R., Newark, NJ, Patent No. 390,567, Oct. 2, 1888 [Fig. 6.0]. A construction method in which the mouth-piece of the bit consists of a rope of metallic wire encased in a mesh of steel wire, with the mouth-piece and its ends covered by rubber vulcanizing.

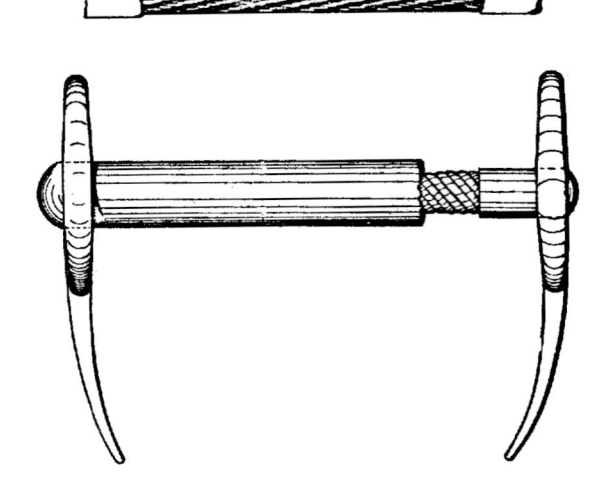

Fig. 6.0 Cahoone construction method, with a cut-away view of the mouth-piece core.

Fig. 6.1 Cain bit with mouth-piece extensions.

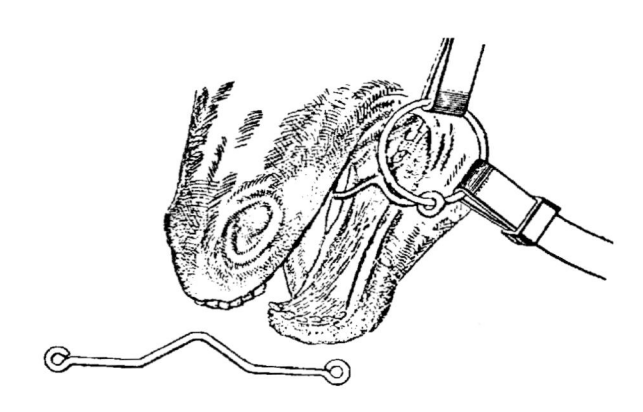

Fig. 6.2 Calhoun loose-ring snaffle bit.

Cain, James Granbury, Memphis, TN, Patent No. 782,216, Feb. 14, 1905 [Fig. 6.1]. Controlling bars are added to the end of the mouth-piece to prevent the bit being pulled through the mouth of the animal.

Calhoun, Andrew J., Rosalia, WA, Patent No. 1,218,053, Mar. 16, 1917 [Fig. 6.2]. The bar or mouth-piece is loosely suspended from a pair of ring cheek-pieces.

California Reins: See Chapter 35.

California Spade Bit: See Spade Bit, Chapters 1 and 31.

Cambridge Mouth: See Mouth-piece, Cambridge, Chapter 25.

Campbell, Alonzo B., Coraopolis, PA, Patent No. 812,112, Feb. 6, 1906 [Fig. 6.3]. It can be termed a lugging, lolling, stumbling and runaway bit. The mouth-piece could be a straight bar or supplied with a port.

Campbell, Hardy W., Columbia, Dakota Terr., Patent No. 387,048, July 31, 1888 [Fig. 6.4]. The bit will prevent horses from lugging or tongue-lolling, and can be used on sore or tender-mouthed horses.

76

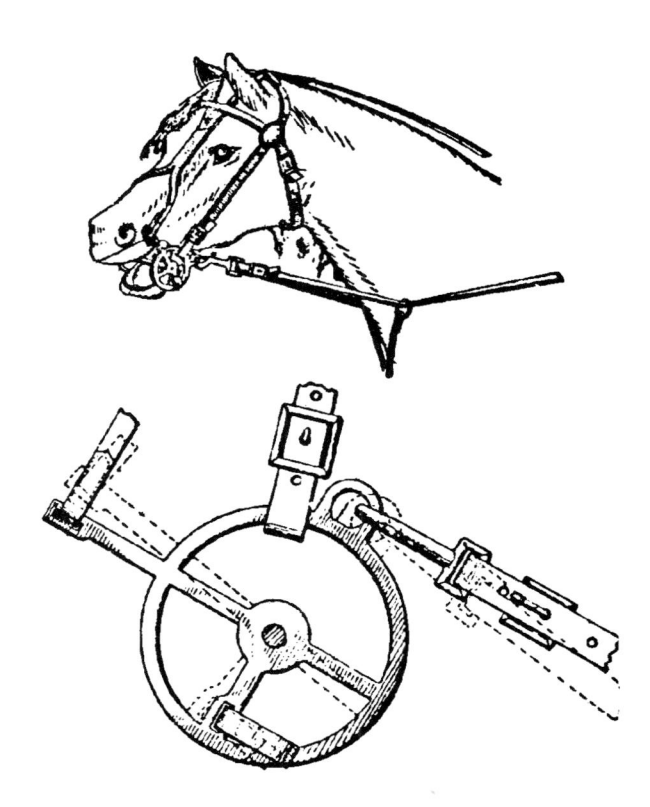

Fig. 6.3 Campbell bit to control vicious hard-mouthed horses.

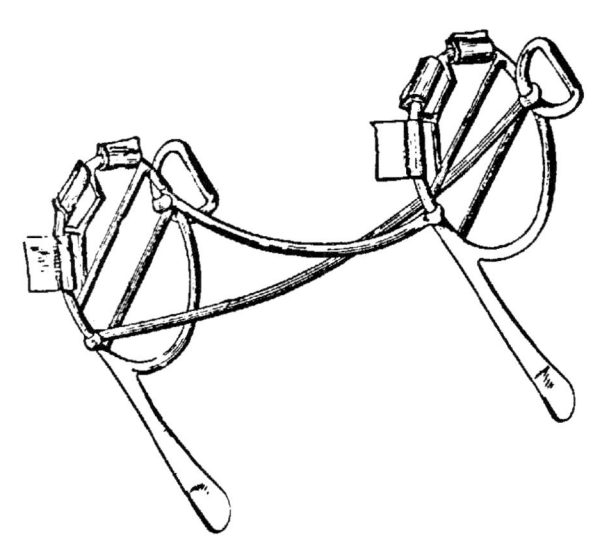

Fig. 6.4 Campbell scissor-mouth bit.

Campbell, John E., Gaines, PA, Patent No. 607,788, July 19, 1896 [Fig. 6.5]. A bridle and bit combination with a pair of pulleys at the brow-band and a pair of pulleys on the bit.

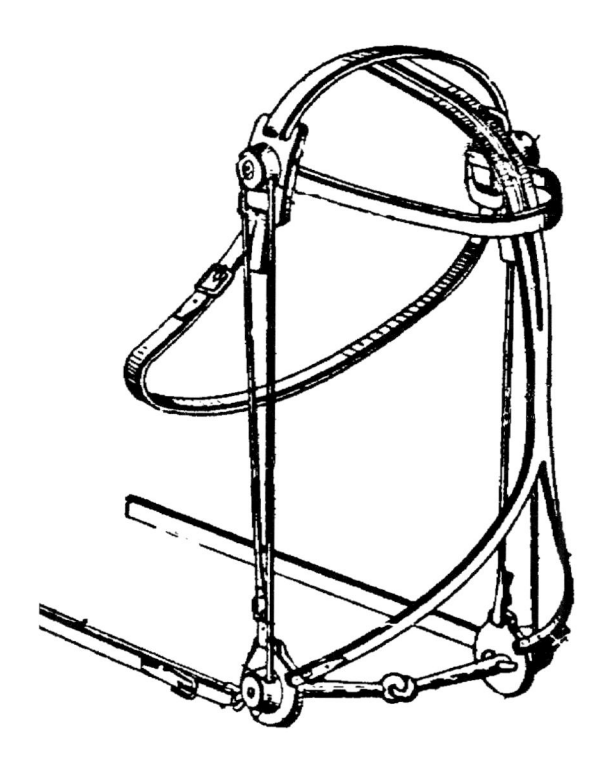

Fig. 6.5 Campbell pulley bit and bridle.

Cannons: The portion of a jointed mouth-piece from the center joint to the cheek-piece. See diagram, Chapter 1.

Canon City Bits: Denotes bits made by prisoners at Colorado State Prison, Canon City, CO., and dates from 1900 or earlier to at least 1950. Some of the bits have a four or five digit number representing the prisoner's number.

Cape Bit: See Pelham, Chapter 27.

Carpenter, Daniel H., Hartford, CT, Patent No. 140,010, June 17, 1873 [Fig. 6.6]. The mouth-piece is flat or rectangular. The face-piece or noseband is constructed of any suitable elastic material.

Carpmill, John F., New Britain, CT, Patent No. 1,267,972, May 28, 1918 [Fig. 6.7]. A bit made of one continuous twisted rod to form the mouth-piece and the cheek-pieces. The patent was assigned to North and Judd Mfg. Co.

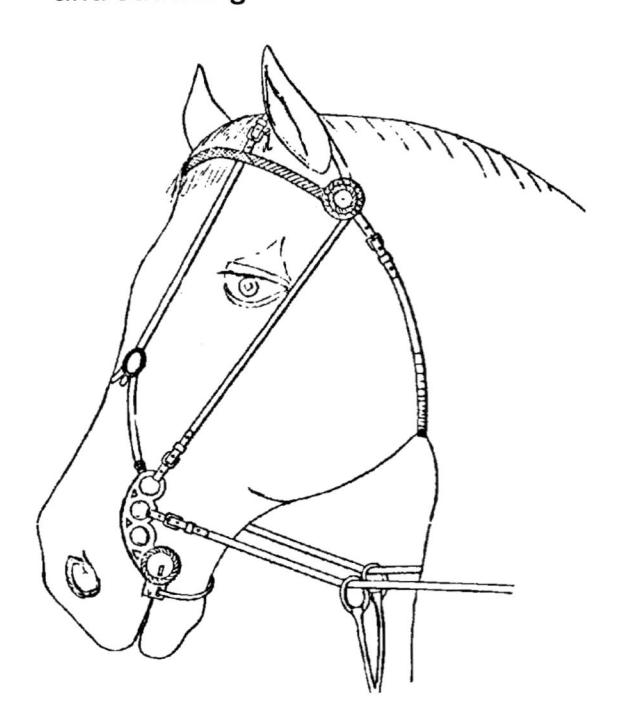

Fig. 6.6 Carpenter tension-control bit.

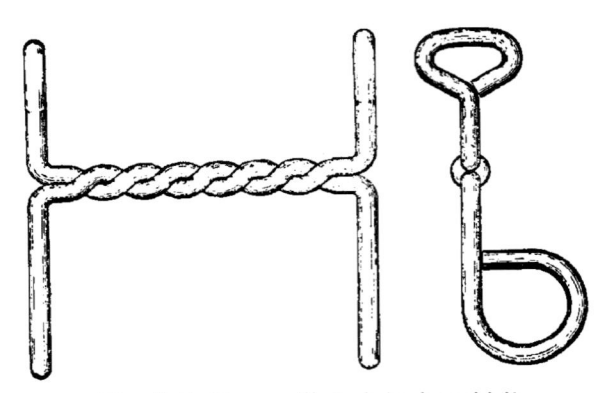

Fig. 6.7 Carpmill twisted-rod bit.

Carson, Robert A., Denver, CO, Patent No. 2,255,704, Feb. 8, 1944 [Fig. 6.8]. A single unitary metal piece combined to form the cheek-pieces and curb (metal) with no mouth-piece. A flexible (leather) mouth-piece consists of a loop and can be inserted or left out. When in place it acts as the primary curb and the metal curb as a reserve for added control. The bit can be used without a bridle.

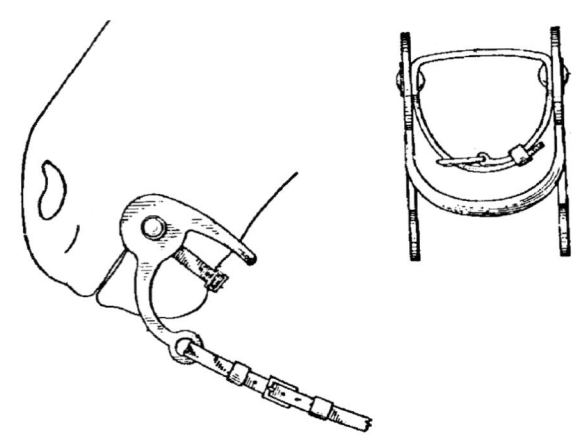

Fig. 6.8 Carson bridleless bit.

Carter, Joseph, Blyth, Ontario, Canada, Patent No. 536,068, Mar. 19, 1895 [Fig. 6.9]. An overdraw bit independent of the driving bit that will stay in the position to which it is placed.

Case, Milton Wendell, Philadelphia, PA, Patent No. 510,158, December 5, 1893 [Fig.6.10]. A check bit with a chin strap that operates like a curb bit.

Casey, Peter, New Port, RI, Patent No. 159,077, Jan. 26, 1875 [Fig. 6.11]. A bit with two mouth-pieces, the top mouth-piece being solid and the lower mouth-piece adjustable to be moved to any of the four holes provided in the cheek-pieces, where it can act as a gag bit.

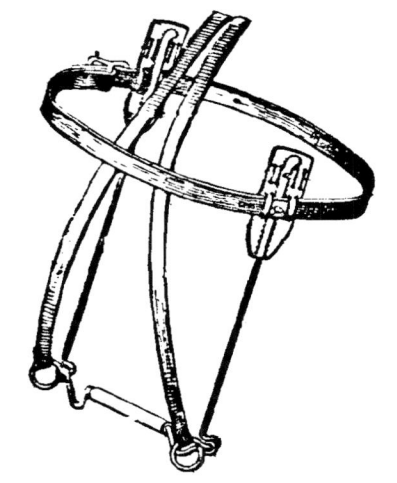

Fig. 6.9. Carter overdraw check bit.

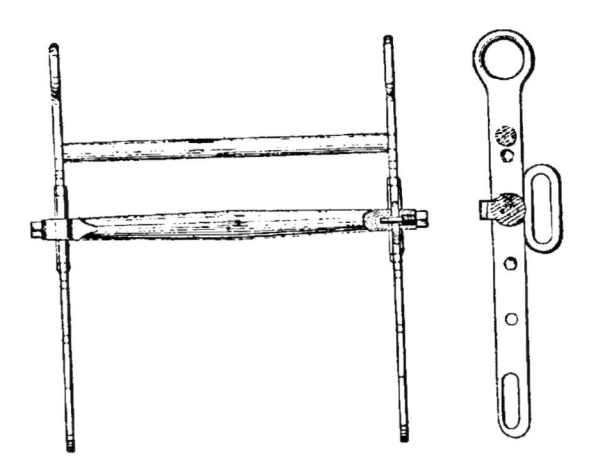

Fig. 6.11 Casey adjustable double mouth.

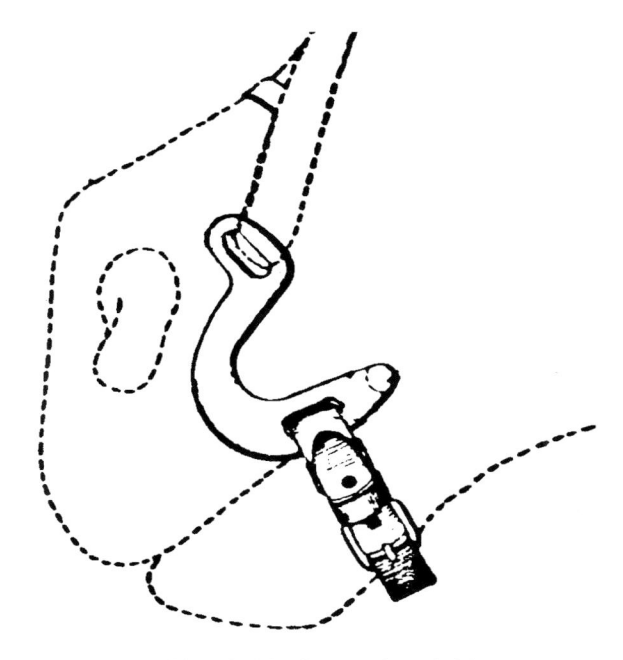

Fig. 6.10 Case check bit.

Catlin, Arthur L., Enid, OK, Patent No. 860,524, July 16, 1907 [Fig. 6.12].

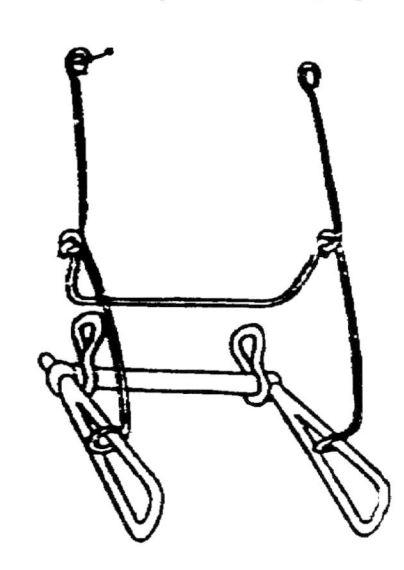

Fig. 6.12 Catlin curb bit with built-in overcheck.

Cavalry: See Military, Chapters 21, 22 and 23.

Caveson (old spelling cavesson): A heavy noseband attached to the headstall or halter, reinforced sometimes with metal. Usually rings are at the top and each side for fastening of lines to a dumb-jockey or to use with a longe line [Figs. 6.13, 6.13a, 6.13b and 6.13c].

Center-piece: Refers to a port or arch.

Cerrata: A noseband with teeth or serrations.

Chain Mouth-piece: See Chapter 25.

Chain Snaffle: See Mouth-piece Chapter 25.

Champing the Bit: The horse makes biting motions at the mouth-piece by snatching at it with the teeth and playing with the mouth-piece. Encouraged in training of colts to increase saliva flow and a moist mouth.

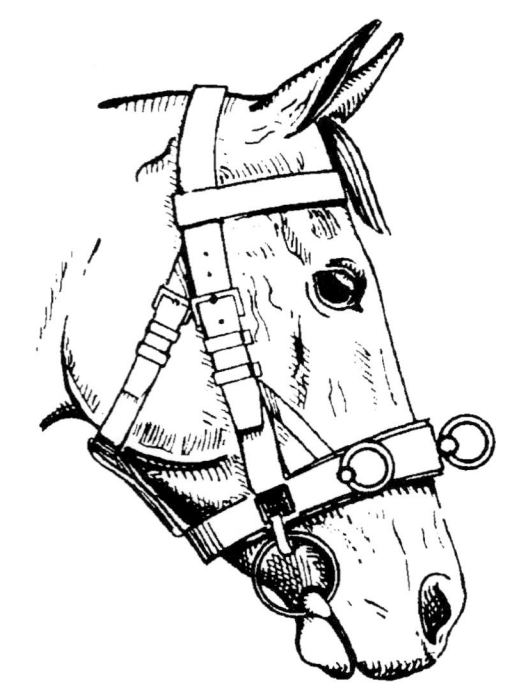

Fig. 6.13a A Caveson and bridle on the head.

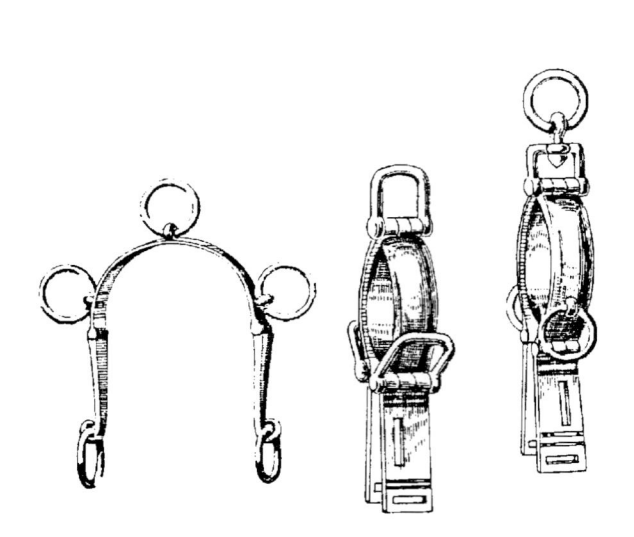

Fig. 6.13 Left to right: French Caveson, Irish Caveson, English Caveson (John Dewsbury & Son).

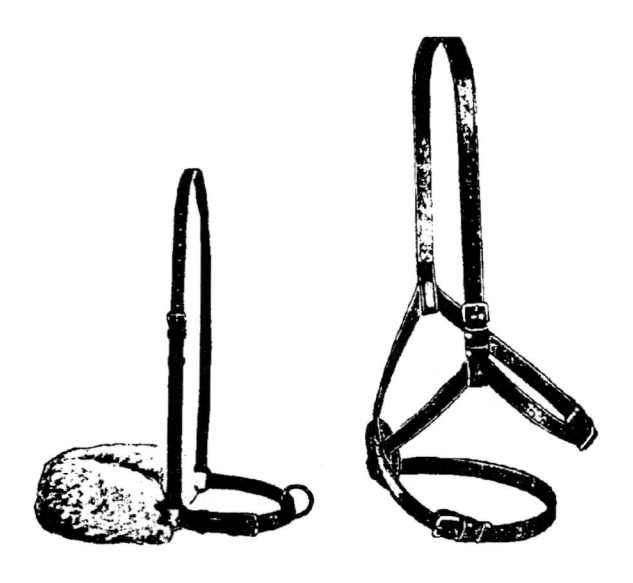

Fig. 6.13b A Shadow Roll Caveson with sheep wool cover and Figure 8 Caveson.

Champ-Neigh Bit: See Driving Bits Chapter 8, Fig. 8.7.

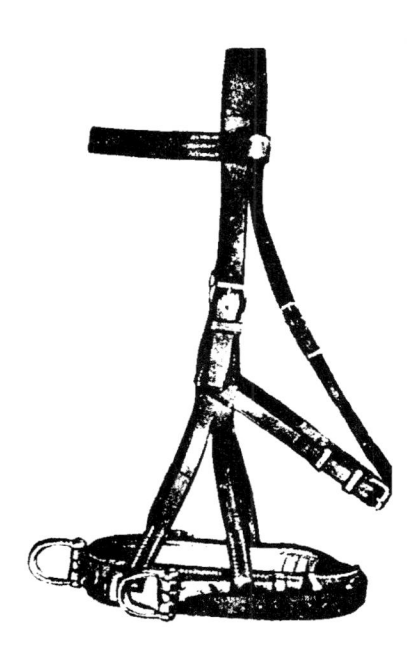

Fig. 13c A lunge Caveson.

Chandler, Clarence A., Bridgeport, MA, Patent No. 290,859, Dec. 25, 1883 [Fig. 6.14]. The coiled spring tends to keep the rein-ring against the cheek-piece. The upper cheek-piece ring accommodates the head-stall and curb-strap or chain. The bit acts as a solid-mouth driving bit or as a curb bit.

Change-mouth Bits: Most of the major bit manufacturing companies produced a bit in which the mouth-piece could be changed. Figure 6.15 illustrates some of the products of the Eldonian Saddlery, Walsall, England.

Chase Bradoon: A simple large ring, jointed mouth-piece snaffle.

Cheats on the Bit: The horse opens its mouth when the bit is pulled upon by the rider.

Check: A shortened term for check-rein or overcheck bit.

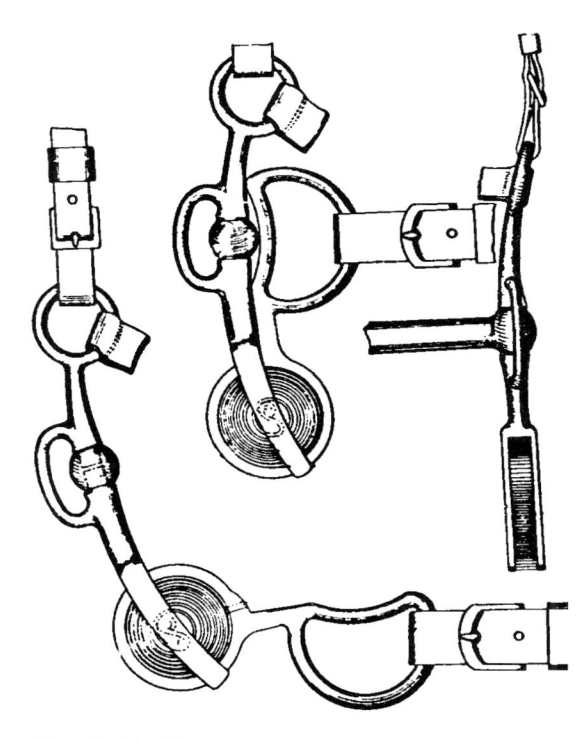

Fig. 6.14 Three views of Chandler's spring-cheek combination bit.

Check-bit: See Overcheck, Chapter 9.

Check-rein Ring: See Pelham drawing, Chapter 1.

Cheek: The portion of a bit outside the mouth to which the mouth-piece is attached. Term used to designate the cheek-strap of a bridle.

Cheek Guards: Shields or circular pieces of leather or other pliable material inserted inside the cheek-piece and attached to the mouth-piece of bits to protect the horse's lips. See Bit Guards, Chapter 5.

Cheek-piece: A plate or ring on the outer end of the mouth-piece of a bit to which the reins and the headstall are attached. See Cheek-piece, Chapter 31.

Cheek-strap: Side-strap of a bridle for attaching the bit.

MOUTHPIECES

PELHAM CHEEKS

WESTERN CHEEKS

WALKING HORSE CHEEKS

WALKING HORSE CHEEKS

CHEEK SELECTION

PELHAM CHEEKS: 4 1/2"   #77286

WESTERN CHEEKS: 10"   #77416

BRACED WALKING HORSE
  CHEEKS: 10"   #77295
                8"   #77302

CIRCLE WALKING HORSE
  CHEEKS: 10"   #77347
                8"   #77348

MOUTHPIECE SELECTION

PORT 1 -77296	PORT 11 -77301
PORT 1C-77421	PORT 11C-77425
PORT 2 -77298	PORT 12 -77310
PORT 3 -77297	PORT 13 -77311
PORT 3C-77422	PORT 14 -77432
PORT 4 -77304	PORT 15 -77427
PORT 5 -77300	PORT 16 -77303
PORT 6 -77305	PORT 17N-77287
PORT 9 -77306	PORT 17R-77288
PORT 10-77307	

HOOKS AND CHAINS

DOUBLE LINK CURB CHAIN   #77240
STANDARD MELTON CURB HOOKS #77241

Mouthpieces: 1, 3, 5, 9, 11, 13, 15, 17, 2, 4, 6, 10, 12, 14, 16

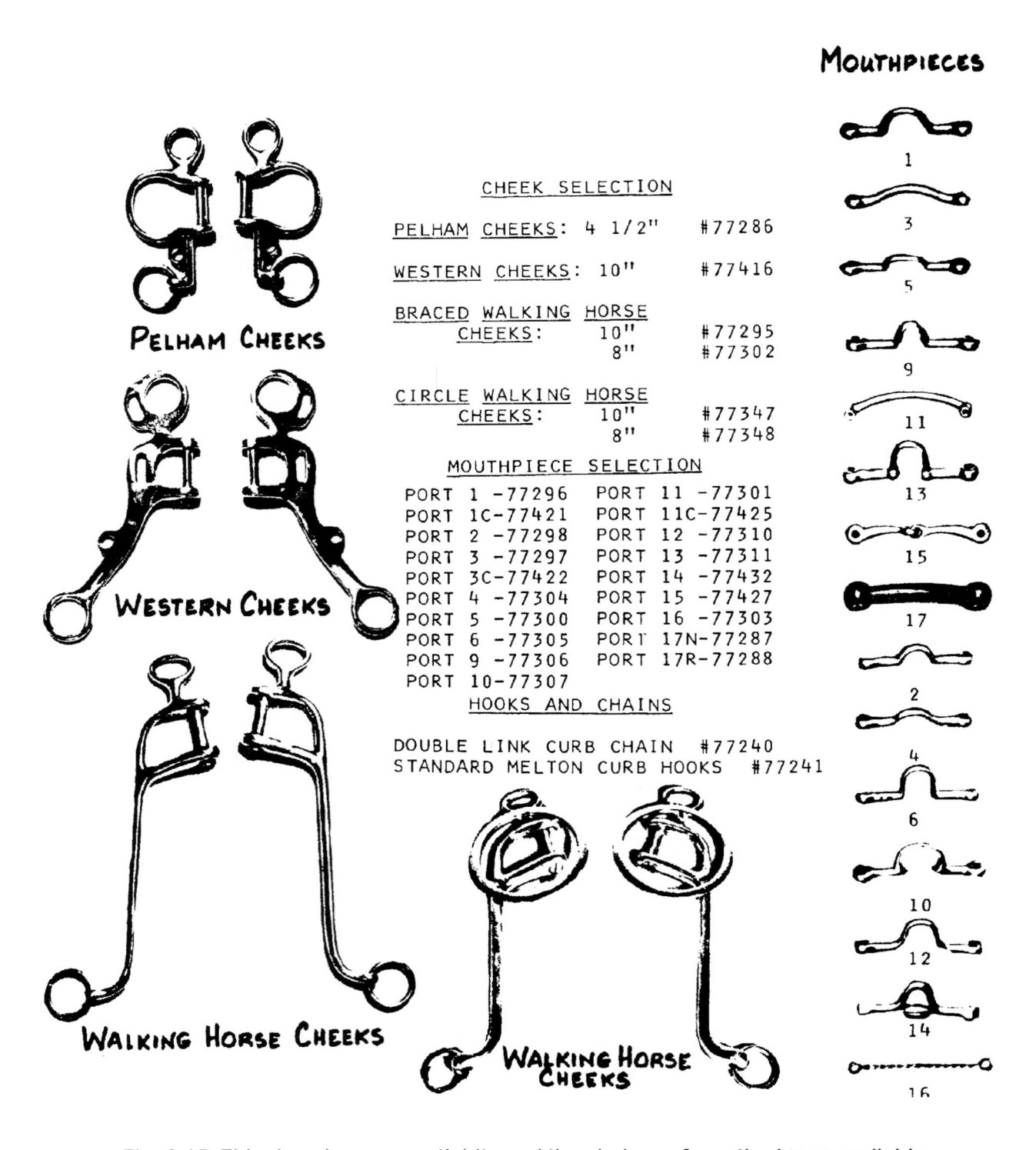

Fig. 6.15 Eldonian change-mouth bits and the choices of mouth-pieces available.

Cheeks: See Cheek-piece.

Cheltenham Gag Bit: See Gags, Chapter 12.

Chenault, John C., Richmond, KY, Patent No. 800,825, Jan. 5, 1915 [Fig. 6.16]. One side or cheek-piece is provided with a spring-held pin in a hollow head to facilitate the removal of the cheek-piece and then the mouth-piece from the horse without opening the teeth.

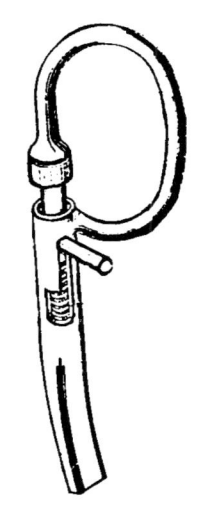

Fig. 6.16 Chenault removeable cheek-piece.

Cherry-roller Bradoon: A bit with a large roller in the center of the mouth-piece.

Chifney: Also called Colt Lead bit [Fig. 6.17]. See also Muscovy Anti-rear Bit, Chapter 26.

Chifney Bit: Early English pattern with a hinged extension of the mouth-piece for attaching reins (*Loriner* No. 46) [Fig. 6.18].

Chihuahua Bit: Buermann bit No. 1312 with a half-breed mouth [Fig. 6.19].

Chileno: Spanish term for a ring bit. See Chapters 1 and 29.

Chin Groove: The groove of the lower jaw just behind the chin. See Anatomy, Chapter 3.

Chin Strap: See Curb Bit diagram, Chapter 1.

Fig. 6.17 Chifney or Colt Lead bit.

Fig. 6.18 A Buxton bit with Chifney action.

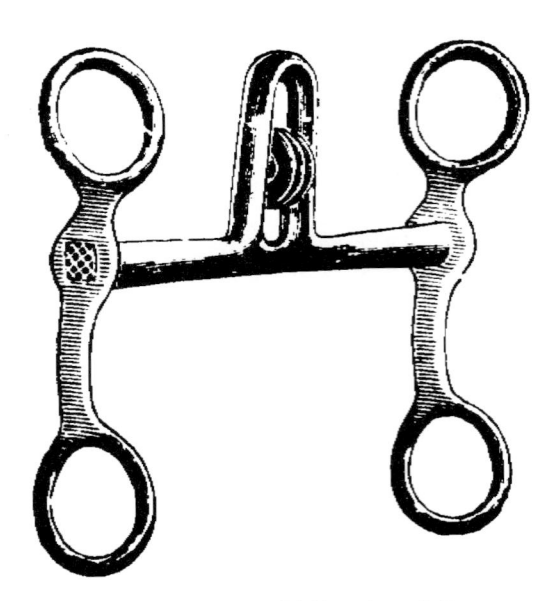

Fig. 6.19 Chihuahua bit.

Christian, Dick Bit: An early 19th century bit made in England [Fig. 6.20]. Often used with a bradoon bit.

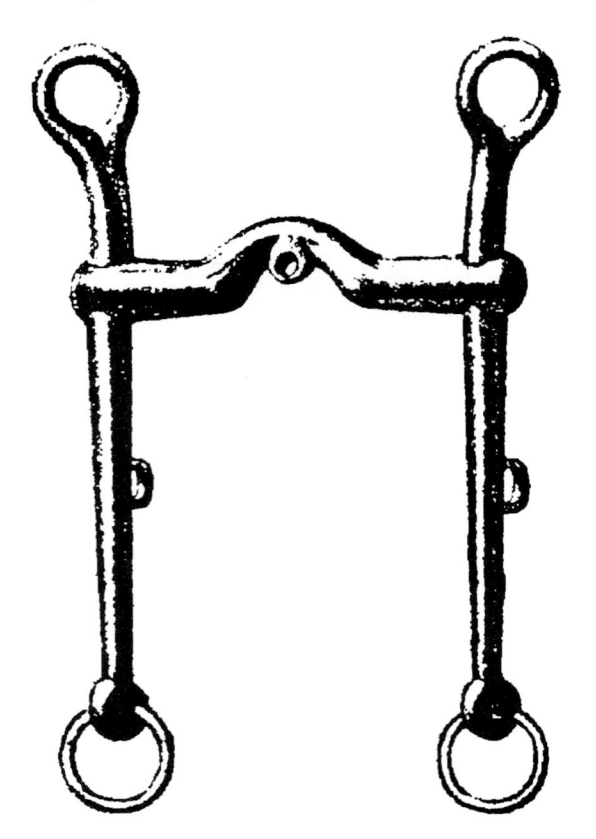

Fig. 6.20 Dick Christian bit.

Ciammaichella, Giovanni, New York, NY, Patent No. 904,682, Nov. 24, 1908 [Fig. 6.21]. A double mouth-piece with the lower smaller one nesting in the underside of the larger upper mouth-piece. The action of the cheek-pieces when the reins are pulled forceably causes the mouth-pieces to separate and act as a gag. Advertised as the Safety-Hygienic Horse Bit and manufactured by the Safety-Hygienic Horse Bit Co. New York, NY.

Fig. 6.21 Ciammaichella bit with view of the cheek-piece action and the size and nesting of the two mouth-pieces. Robert Maclin collection.

Circassian Bit: A broken-mouth snaffle bit with a diamond shape. John Dewsbury No. 222 [Fig.6.22].

Fig. 6.22 Circassian bit.

Citation Bit: A six-ring bit similar to Norton Perfection Bit.

Clamer, John, Lock Haven, PA, Patent No. 574,304, Dec. 29.1896 [Fig. 6.23]. A curb bit with an over-check device.

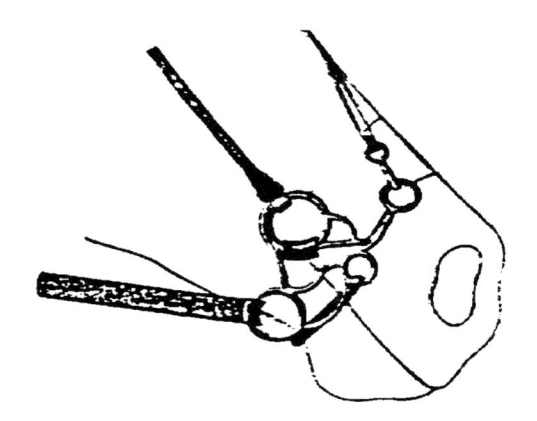

Fig. 6.23 Clamer bit and over-check.

Clamer, Joseph, Trenton, New Jersey, Patent No. 544,563, August 13, 1895 [Figs. 6.24 and 6.24a]. A curved guide bar on the outside of the cheek-rings allows the curb-strap attached to the rings to tighten as the reins are pulled. The bit has a straight-bar mouth.

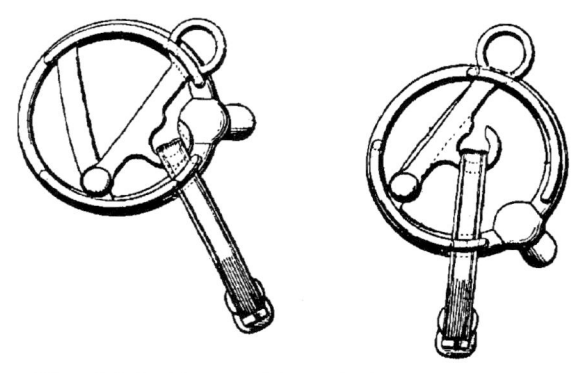

Fig. 6.24 Clamer bit with the reins pulled tight and in the relaxed position.

Clark, Frederic, Portland, ME, Patent No. 565,431, Aug. 11, 1896 [Fig. 6.25]. The broken mouth-piece slides on the two curved cheek-pieces.

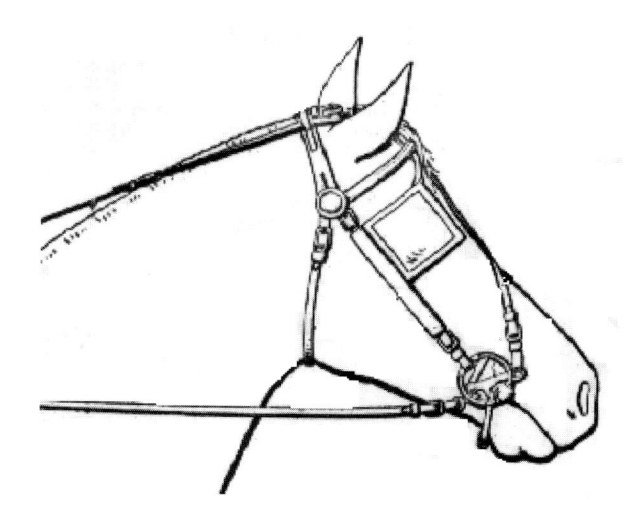

Fig. 6.24a Clamer bit on the horse.

Clark, Wilbur F., Hagaman,, NY, Patent No. 84,170, Nov. 17, 1868 [Fig. 6.26]. A revolving bit having pulleys used in combination with a gag-runner and martingale.

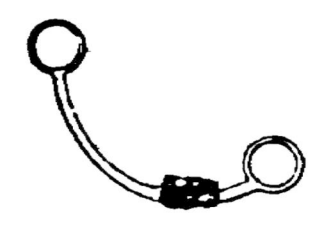

Fig. 6.25 Clark sliding-mouth bit.

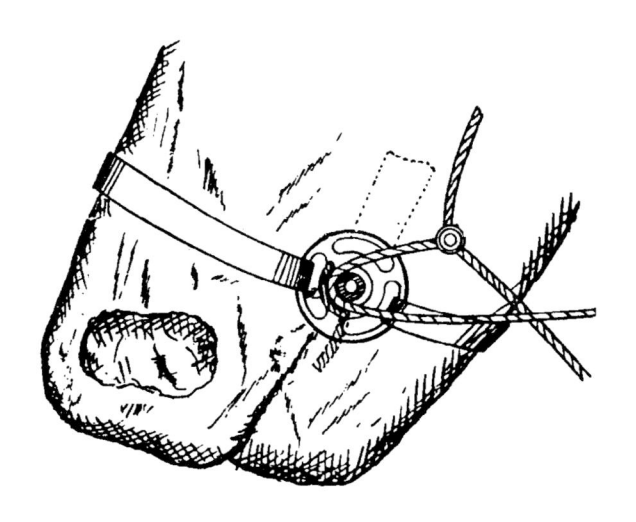

Fig. 6.26 Clark pulley bit.

Clemons, Hiram M., Virginia City, NV, Patent No. 327,139, Sept. 29, 1885 [Fig. 6.27]. The cheek-pieces will retract into the bit and be drawn out by the reins

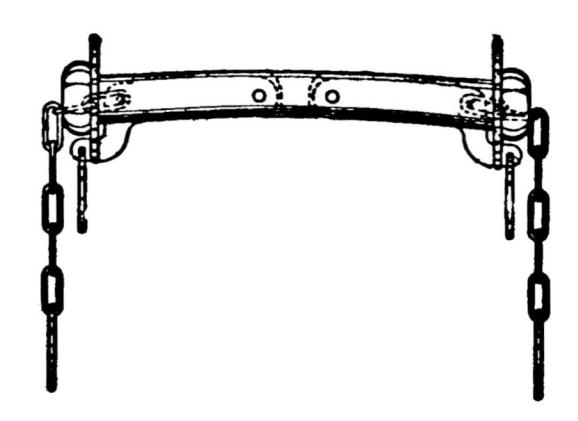

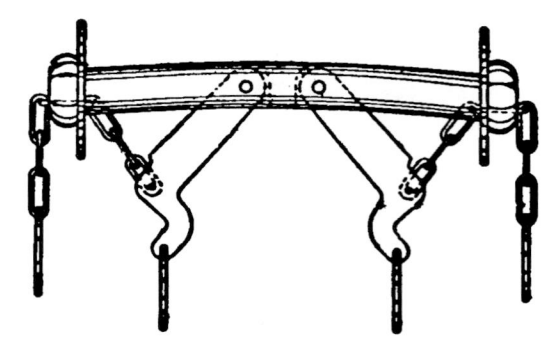

Fig. 6.27 Clemons bridle bit.

Clipper Bit: Early 1800's English bit [Fig. 6.28].

Closed Bit: One without a port or arch in the mouth-piece.

Closed Reins: Reins that are closed or fastened together with a knot. In western riding a whip-like extension is attached to the knot and called a romal.

Coburn, William T., Laramie, WY, Patent No. 498.106, May 23, 1893 [Fig. 6.29]. The mouth-piece terminates in a post extending at a right angle with keepers on the upper and lower ends for the passage of a tubular extension of the bridle cheek-strap and continuing into the rein.

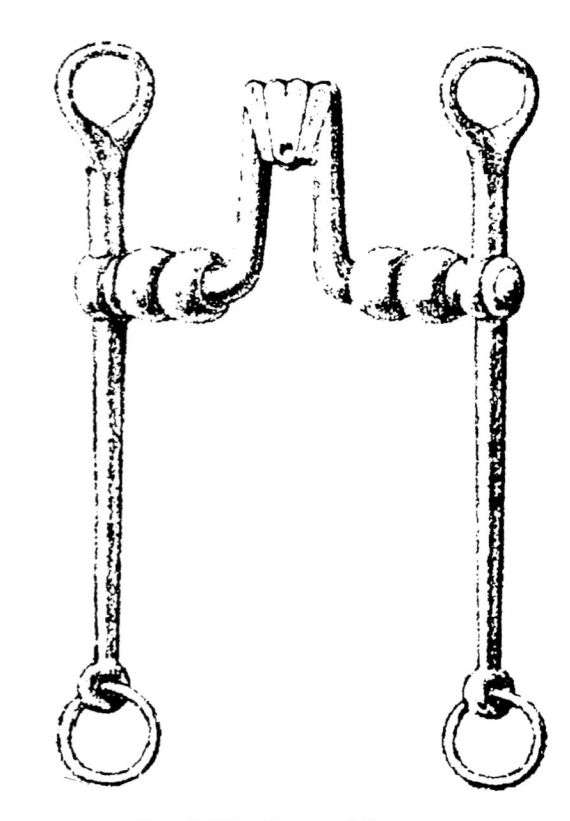

Fig. 6.28 Clipper bit.

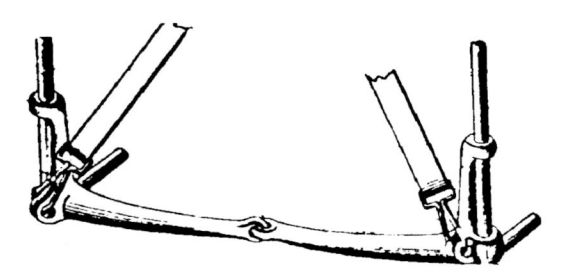

Fig. 6.29 Coburn modified gag bit.

Coe, Emery Miles, Milford City, OH, Patent No. 962,005, Jun. 21, 1910 [Fig.6.30]. The mouth-piece has links that are serrated on one edge and smooth on the opposite edge. The bridle rings and mouth-piece ends prevent the mouth-piece from turning in the mouth.

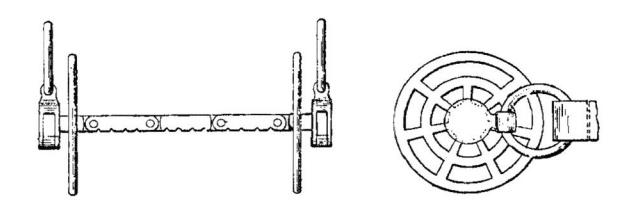

Fig. 6.30 Coe reversible bit.

Cold Jaw: A horse unresponsive to the bit.

Cold Jaw Bit: Refers to a hackamore bit. See Hackamore, T-shaped, Chapter 13.

Cole, Cyrus C., Albion, MI, Patent No. 424,538, Apr. 1, 1890 [Fig. 6.31]. Slots in the outer edge of the cheek-piece rings facilitate the attachment of the reins without snaps or hooks.

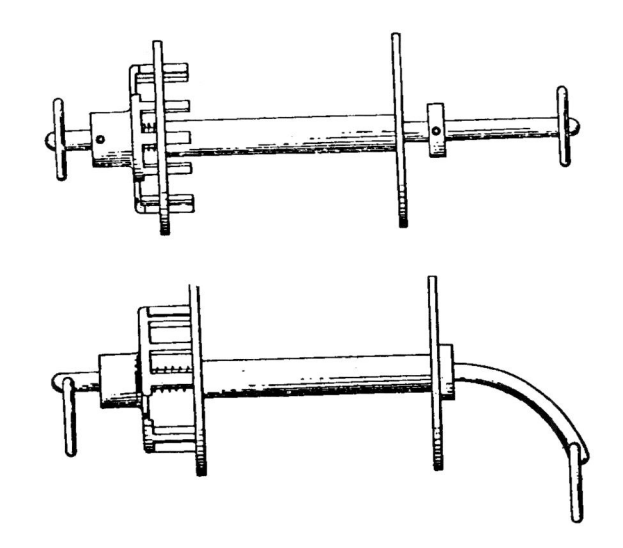

Fig. 6.32 Collins run-out bit.

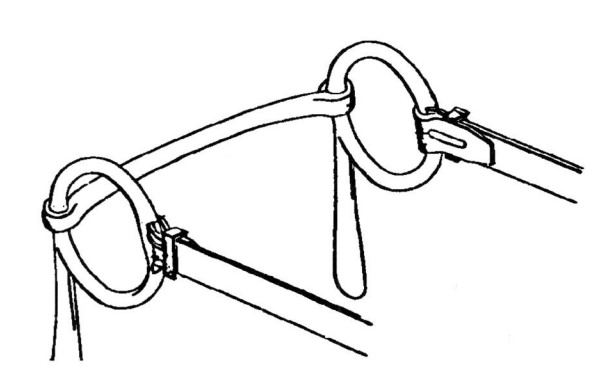

Fig. 6.31 Cole snaffle bit.

Collins, George H., Lynbrook, NY, Design Patent No. 160,249, Sep. 26, 1950 [Fig. 6.32]. A run-out bit.

Collins, William H., Indianapolis, IN, Patent No. 877,296, Jan. 21, 1908 [Fig. 6.33]. A bit attachment to prevent unattended horses from running away. It may be added to any snaffle bit with ring cheeks.

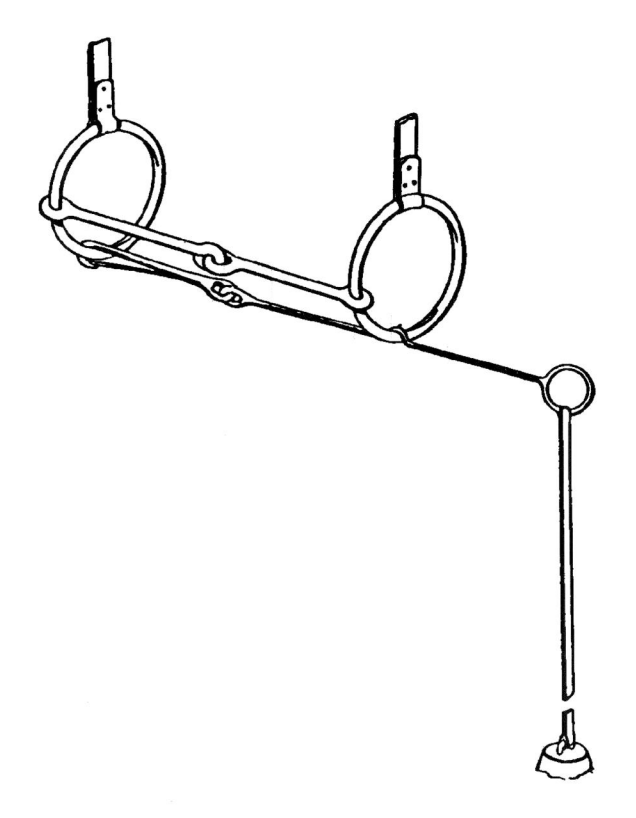

Fig. 6.33 Collins bit-attached ground tie.

Patent No. 879,843, Feb. 18, 1908 [Fig.6.34]. An improvement over Patent No. 877,296.

87

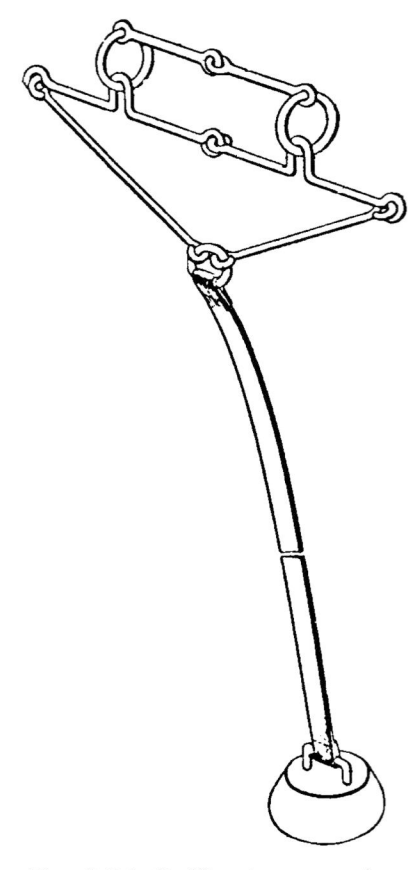

Fig. 6.34 Collins improved ground tie.

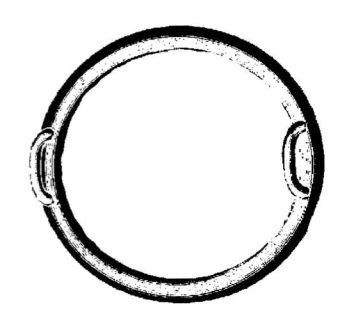

Fig. 6.35 Plain-ring Colt bit.

Fig. 6.36 Colt-breaking bradoon with players.

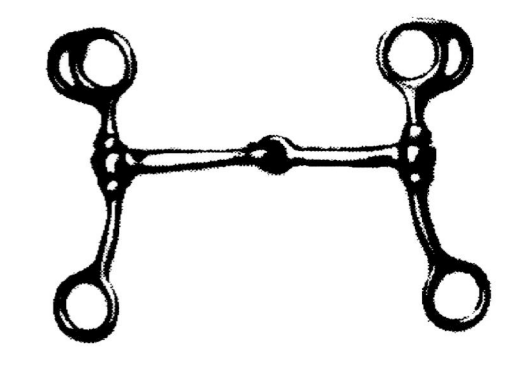

Fig. 6.37 Colt curb bit. Similar to a Tom Thumb bit.

Colorado Bit: A name applied to a western-type of curb bit, including bits by Eldonian Saddlery, Buermann Mfg. Co., Phillips and Gutierrez and Mike Morales. Each had a different design.

Colt Bit: A bit used for training [Fig. 6.35]. See Chifany and Tattersall Bits.

Colt-breaking Bradoon with players [Fig. 6.36].

Colt Curb Bit: Also known as a Jointed Tom Thumb Colt Bit. Similar to a Weymouth bit [Fig.6.37].

Comanche Bit: A bit made by Haydens and Allen in the Texas style [Fig. 6.38].

Combs, Orrin, Walnut Grove, IL, Patent No. 477,102, June 14, 1892 [Fig. 6.39]. When an easy and comfortable bit is desired, the reins are attached to the rear portion of the rings. When a severe bit is desired, the reins are attached to the forward portion of the rings.

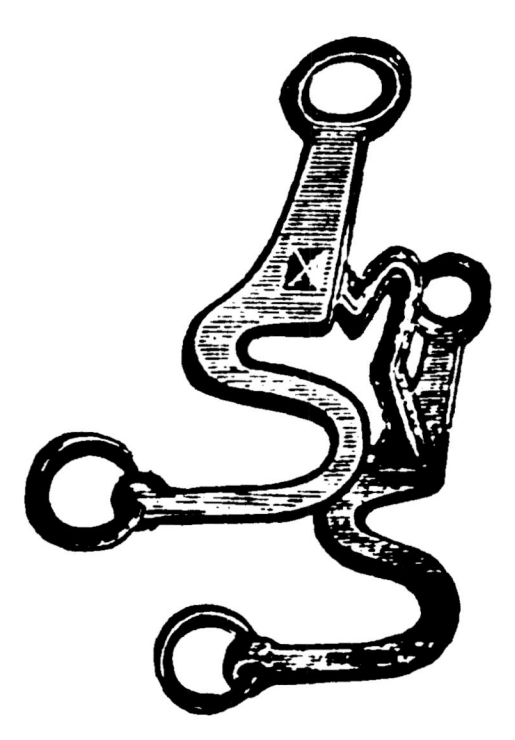

Fig. 6.38 Comanche Texas-style bit.

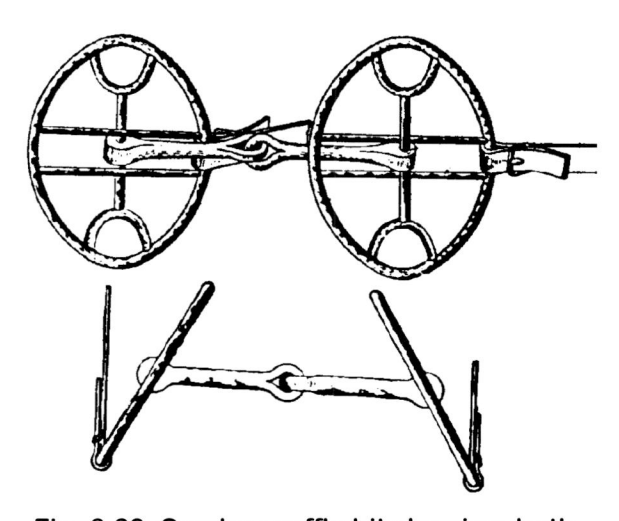

Fig. 6.39 Combs snaffle bit showing both attachment methods.

Conn, Andrew H., Wilton Junction, IA, Patent No. 474,368, May 10, 1892 [Fig. 6.40]. The mouth-piece bearer is inclined outward and upward to allow the mouth-piece to travel up and down as the reins are pulled, putting pressure on the sides of the mouth.

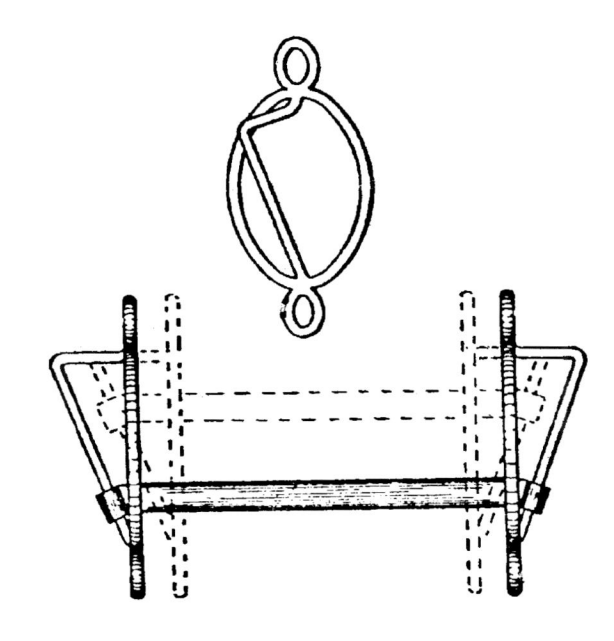

Fig. 6.40 Conn gag bit.

Control Bits: The term is ambiguous. It does not specifiy any type of bit and the name was given to a bit by many manufacturers and each represented a different bit.

Controlling Bit: Name given to Bicycle Chain Bit.

Control Bits for Stallions: See Stallions, Chapter 32.

Converter Straps: Converts a Pelham bit for use on a snaffle bridle by attaching to the top and bottom rings of the cheek-piece. The reins are attached to a ring which slides on the strap.

Cornell, Henry M., Brighton, IL, Patent No. 120,860, Nov. 14, 1871 [Fig. 6.41]. A bar to which the rein-rings are attached passes through the hollow portion of the mouth-piece to which the cheek-pieces are firmly secured.

Fig. 6.41 Cornell snaffle bit.

Cornish Broken Snaffle: See Scorrier Bit, Chapter 30, Fig. 30.11.

Cornish Snaffle: See Scorrier Bit, Chapter 30, Fig. 30.11.

Corpus Christi Bit: A Texas-style bit manufactured by Haydens an Allen [Fig. 6.42].

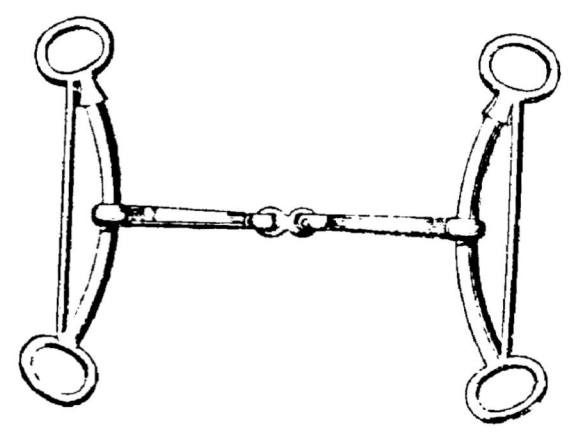

Fig. 6.43 European Cow Bit.

Cow Boy Bit: A Texas-style bit made by Haydens and Allen [Fig. 6.44].

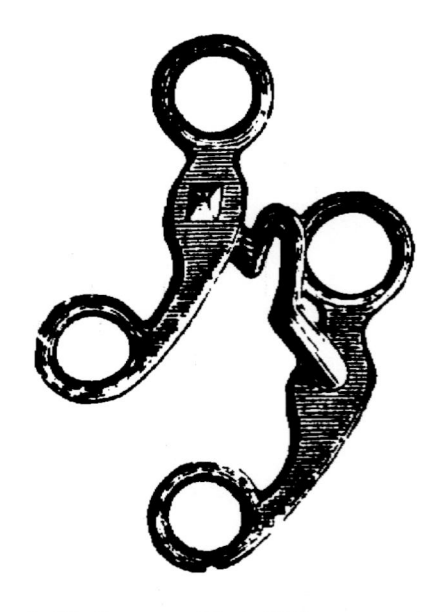

Fig. 6.42 Corpus Christi Texas-style bit.

Cow Bit: A cow bit for north Europe made by Dewsbury and Son [Fig. 6.43]. The mouth-piece slides on the braced cheek-pieces.

Fig. 6.44 Cow Boy bit.

Cowboy Gag Bit: See Gag Bits, Chapter 12.

Cowboy Polo Bit: See Pelham Polo Bits, Chapter 27, Fig. 27.46.

Crab Check Bit: See Over-check Bits, Chapter 9.

Craighead, Samuel, and Henry W. Roberts, Caldwood, MO, Patent No. 690,017, Dec. 31, 1901 [Fig.6.45 and 6.45a]. The upward curved arm of the cheek-piece has a ring to attach the curb-chain. The hinged arms accept the headstall and the reins are affixed to the lower shank rings.

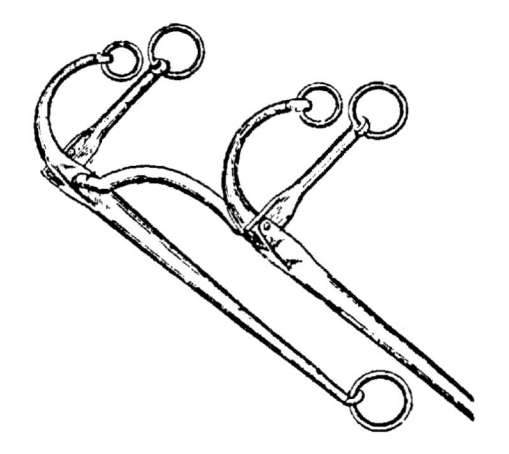

Fig. 6.45 Craighead bit.

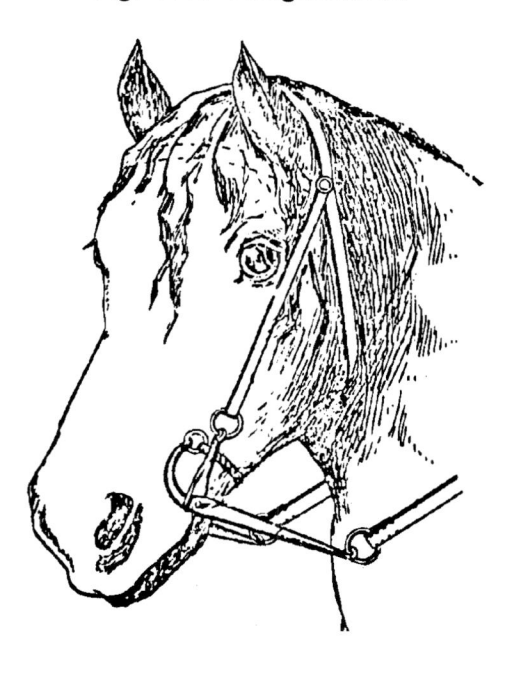

Fig. 6.45a Craighead bit prevents the animal from throwing its head upward.

Crane, Edward N., Newark, NJ, Patent No. 203,001, Apr. 30, 1878 [Fig. 6.46]. A construction method of casting and molding cheek-pieces.

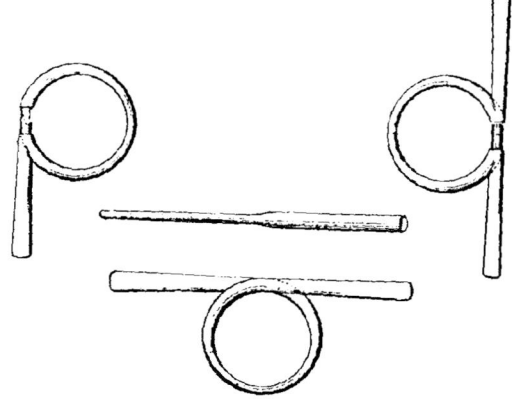

Fig. 6.46 Crane bit construction method.

Patent No. 350348, Oct. 5, 1886 [Fig. 6.47]. The mouth-piece has a central metal chain-type mouth covered with rubber. The check bit is attached by a small ring to the long link to provide for a free movement of the check bit.

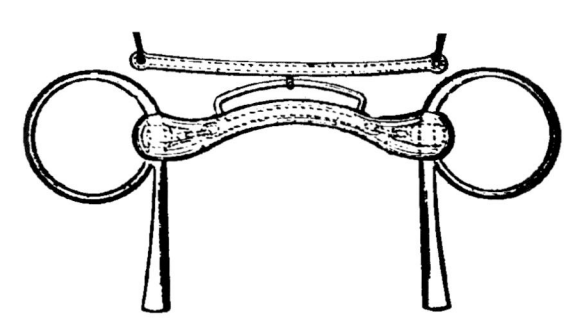

Fig. 6.47 Crane flexible-mouth bit with an overcheck.

Crane, Frederick, Bloomfield, NJ, Patent No. 174,353, Mar. 7, 1876 [Fig. 6.48]. A flexible-mouth snaffle bit with a rubber-covered chain mouth.

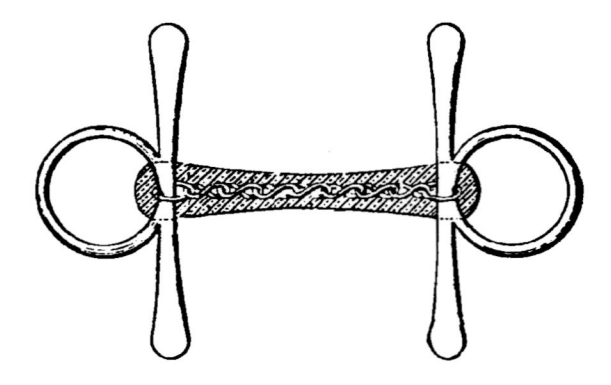

Fig. 6.48 Crane rubber-mouth snaffle bit.

Patent No. 188,726, Mar 27, 1877 [Fig. 6.49]. Construction method for a stronger and safer bridle bit.

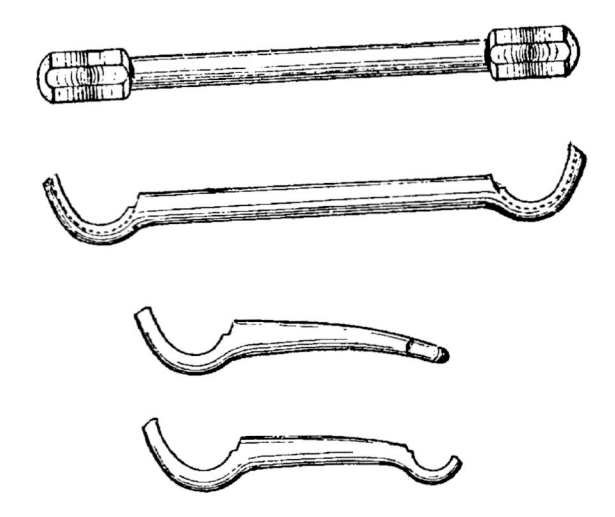

Fig. 6.50 Crane open head mouth construction.

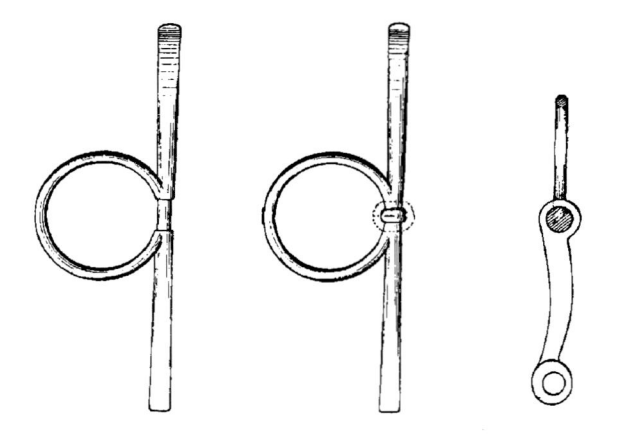

Fig. 6.49 Crane construction method detail.

Patent No. 203002, Apr. 30, 1978 [Fig. 6.50]. Construction method for open head mouth-pieces.

Crane, Henry, New York, NY, Patent No. 28,563, June 5, 1860 [Fig. 6.51]. Supplimental bars are built into the mouth-piece and act on the lower jaw of the horse to prevent the horse from gaining control when it takes the bit in its teeth.

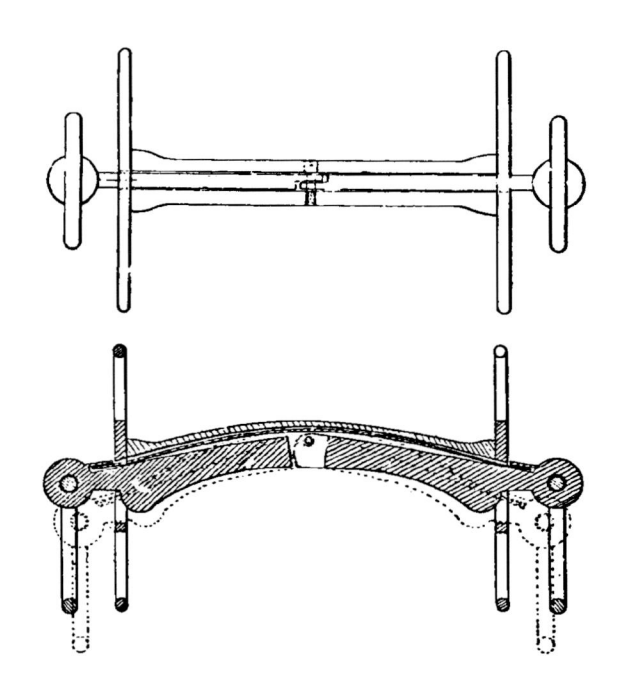

Fig. 6.51 Crane snaffle bit.

Cratty, William, Hialeah, FL, Patent No. 2,555,573, June 5, 1951 [Fig. 6.52]. Convex curved projections from the mouth-piece ends are inside the cheek-pieces and extend above the rings.

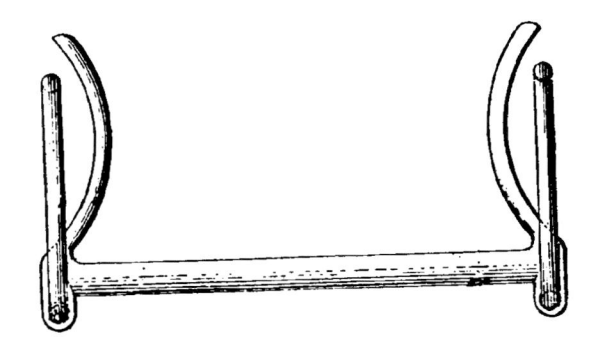

Fig. 6.52 Cratty snaffle bit places pressure on the cheeks.

Crawford, John M., Philadelphia, PA, Patent No. 66,221, July 2, 1867 [Fig. 6.53]. With the bit resting in a normal position, the mouth-piece is at the bottom of the slotted cheek-pieces. A strong pull on the reins causes the mouth-piece to travel up the slots and disengages it from the teeth of the horse.

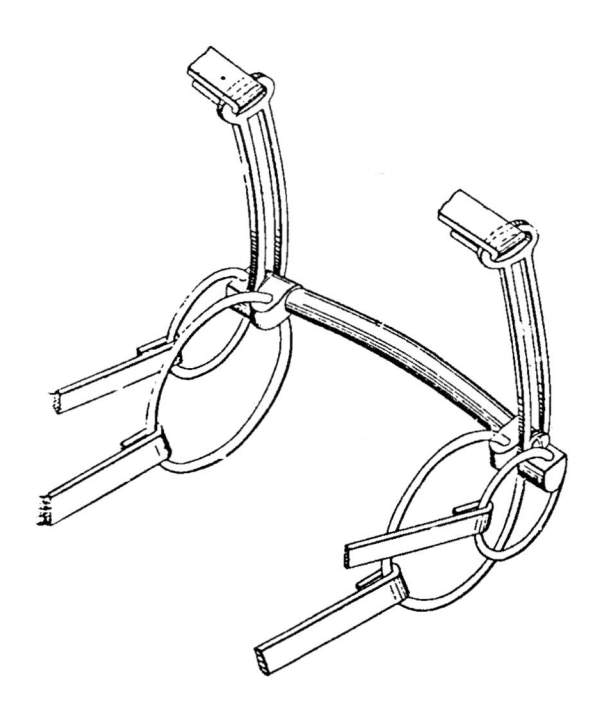

Fig. 6.53 Crawford sliding-mouth bit.

Crescendo Bits: Patented Dec. 26, 1890, by H. Ball, New York [Fig.6.54].

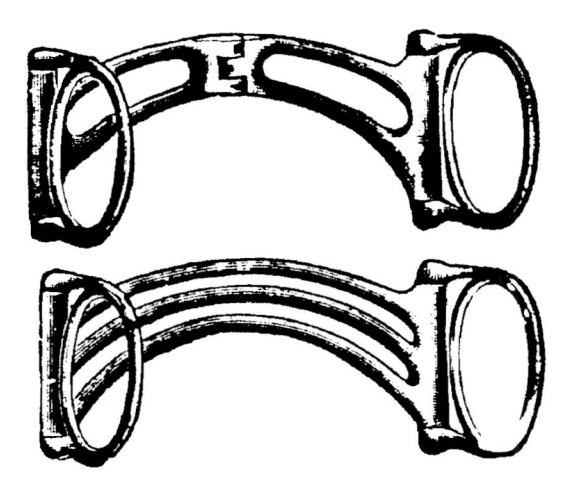

Fig. 6.54 Two types of Crescendo bits.

Crest Strap Bit: A snaffle bit with an attached over-check bit [Fig. 6.55]. Compare with Perfection bit.

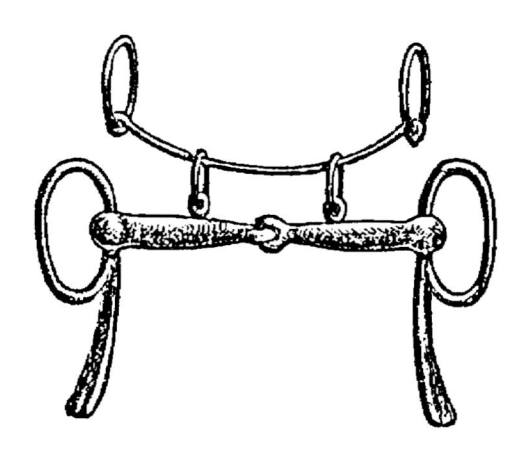

Fig. 6.55 Crest strap bit.

Cricket: A small roller placed in the port of a curb bit and usually made of copper.

Crit Davis: See Over-check Bits, Chapter 9.

Crockett, Oscar, Boulder, CO. Patent No. 2,512,012 Apr. 15, 1948 [Fig. 6.56]. A roping-style bit. See Loriners, Chapter 36.

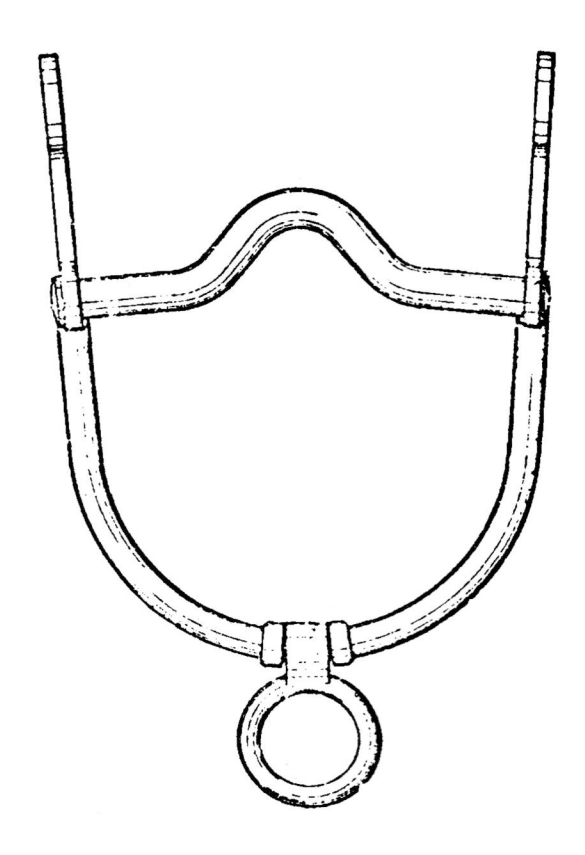

Fig. 6.56 Crockett roping bit.

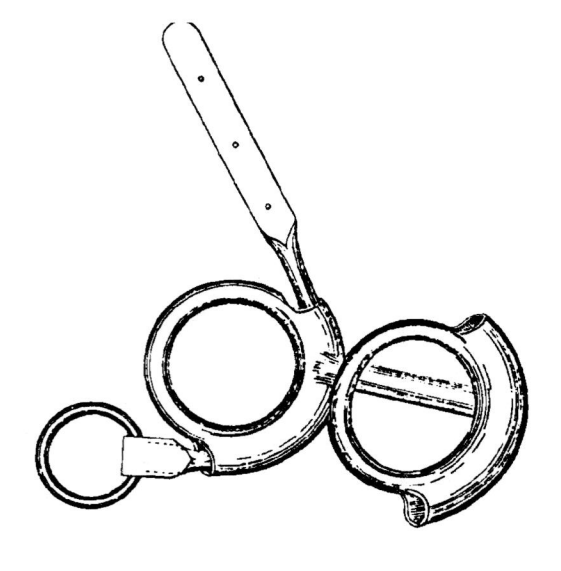

Fig. 6.57 Crook gag bit.

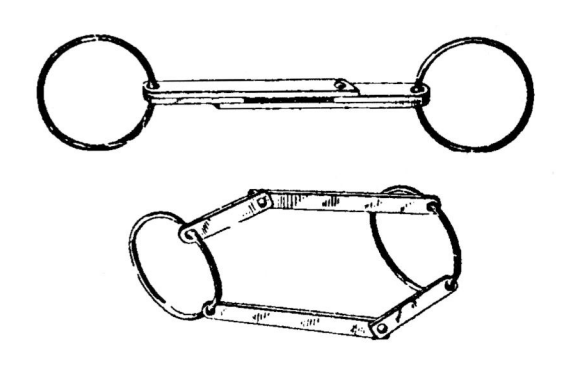

Fig. 6.58 Crose flat-bar bit with two positions displayed.

Crook, Oliver, Dayton, OH, Patent No. 67,509, Aug. 6, 1867 [Fig. 6.57]. A bridle bit with orifices within the front portion of the rings through which rounded straps pass connecting the reins to the headstall.

Crose, Andrew J., Indianapolis, IN, Patent No. 425,212, Apr. 8, 1890 [Fig. 6.58]. Two sets of parallel flat plates with each set having a long and a short plate. The plate-type mouth-pieces are attached to end rings and the plates can be used as a single mouth-piece or separated and used as a more severe bit.

Cross Bar: A term designating the mouth-piece. See Mouth-piece, Chapter 25.

Crown-piece: A strap across the forehead of a bridle connecting the cheek-straps. See Bridle Diagram, Chapter 35.

Cruger, Ernest, London, WI, Patent No. 529.022, Nov. 13,1894 [Fig. 6.59]. A driving bit with a built-in overcheck.

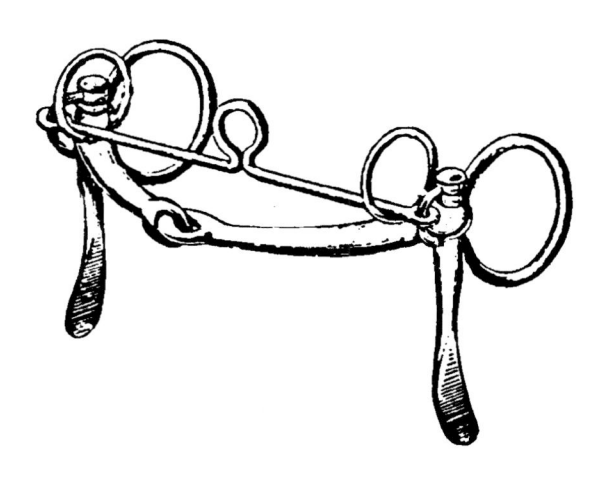

Fig. 6.59 Cruger snaffle and overcheck bit.

Curb: A term: 1) for a chain or strap that is attached to the bit on each side of the cheek-piece near the rein ring of a curb bit, 2) applied to the arched deviation in the center of the mouth-piece of a bit.

Curb Bit: A bit fitted with a piece of chain or strap attached to each cheek-piece near the mouth-piece and fitted into the groove under a horse's chin. See diagram in Chapter 3.

Curb Bit Head: Cheek-piece of a bridle that attaches the bit. See Bridles, Chapter 35.

Curb Chain or Strap: A short chain or strap used with a curb bit [Figs. 6.60 6.60d]. See diagram Bridles, Chapter 35.

Fig. 6.60 Jodhopher flat-link curb chain.

Curb Chain with Chin Strap: Figure 6.61. See diagram Curb Bit, Chapter 1.

Curb Chain Guard: A sleeve of rubber or leather placed over the curb chain to reduce damage to the chin groove [Fig. 6.62].

Fig.6.62 A rubber curb chain guard.

Curb Reins: See Reins, Chapter 35.

Curved Cheek: See Side-pieces, Chapter 31.

Curved Mouth-piece: A Mullen mouth. See Mouth-piece, Chapter 25.

Cutting Horse Bit: A term given to a western-style curb bit with many variations and each manufacturer having its own version.

	No.	Polished.	Nickel-plated.	Extra Best Solid Nickel (Rustless). Registered Trade Mark.
16 Link 8 in. Double Gig Curb	537	1,4	1.8	—
20 ,, 8½in. ,, ,, ,,	346	1.6	1.10	7/-
24 ,, 9 in. ,, ,, ,,	347	1.10	2.2	8/-
26 ,, 9 in. ,, ,, ,,	347½	2.2	2.6	9/-
28 ,, 9 in. Best Double Gig Curb	348	2.6	3/-	10/-
28 ,, 10in. ,, Stout Carriage	534	2.9	3.3	11/-
34 ,, 9 in. ,, Light Buggy ,,	345	2.8	3.3	9/-
		Com. Best	Com Best	
19 ,, 9 in. Stout Single Link Hackney Curb	349	2/- 3 3	2,3 3 9	7/-
19 ,, 9 in. Light ,, ,, ,, ,,	350	1 9 3/-	2/- 3/6	6/-
17 ,, 9½in. Single Link Gig Curb	351	2/3 3/3	2/4 3/8	7/6
17 ,, 11in. Stout Single Link Carriage Curb	352	2/6 3/6	3/- 4/-	8 6
19 ,, 10in. ,, ,, ,, Backband ,,	538	2/6 3/9	3/- 4/3	9/-
15 ,, 9½in. Single Link Curb with Studs on Centre Links	487	18/-	19,-	—
17 ,, Single Link Gig Curb with 10 Oval Links in Centre	759	3/-	3,6	10.6
15 ,, ,, ,, Hackney ,, ,, 9 ,, ,,	486	2.9	3.3	8,6

NICKEL-PLATING GUARANTEED.

Fig. 6.60a Description of curb chains in Fig. 6.60b.

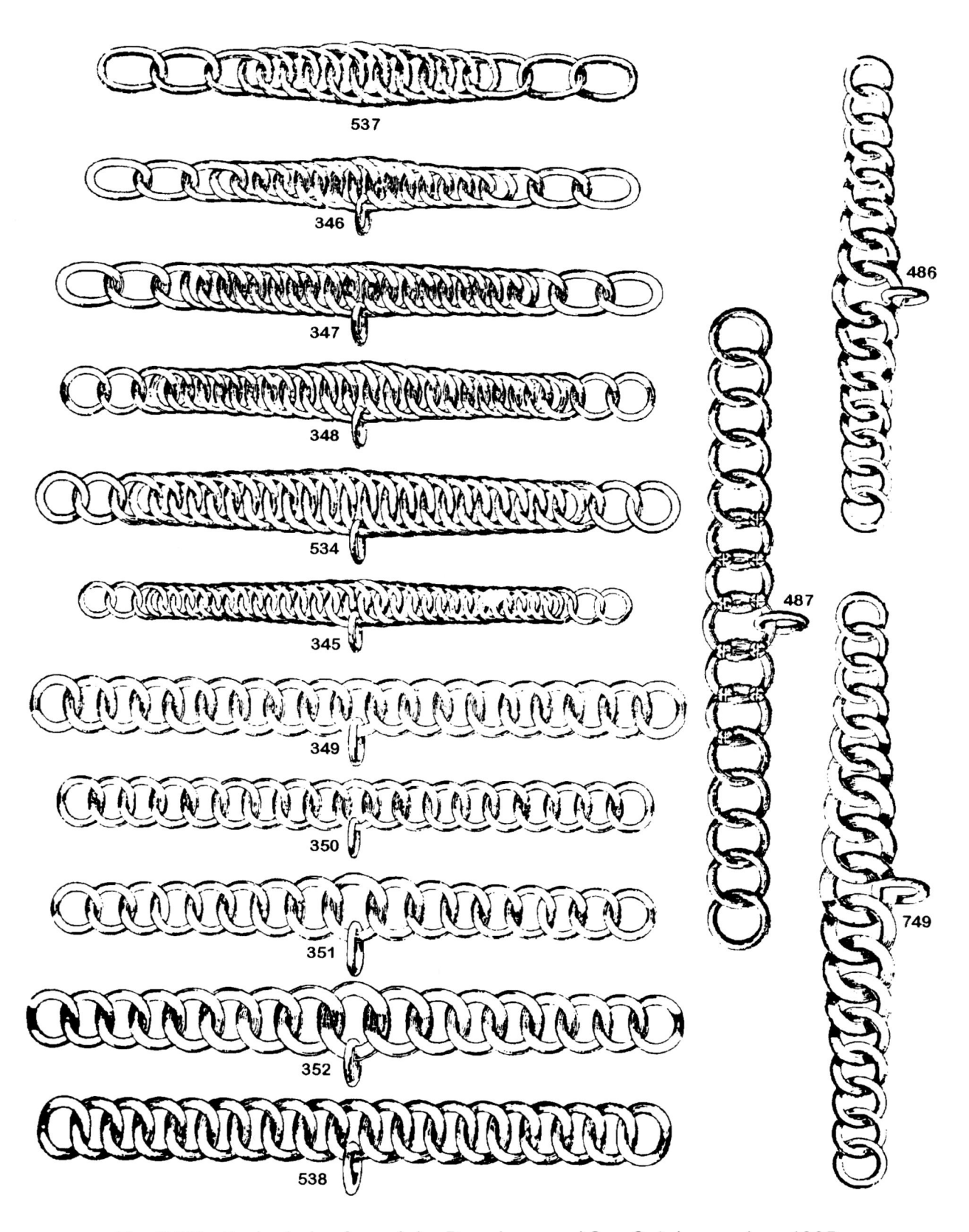

Fig. 6.60b Curb chains from John Dewsbury and Son Catalogue circa 1905.

NICKEL-PLATING GUARANTEED.	No.	Polished.	Nickel-plated.	Extra Best Solid Nickel (Rustless). Registered Trade Marks. V.S NICKEL	Best Solid Nickel (Rustless). Registered Trade Mark. "DEWRALEX"
20 Link Chin Chain, with Hooks complete	531	1/3	1/6	3/6	3/-
30 ,, ,, ,, ,, ,,	336	2/-	2/4	4/-	3/6
11 ,, 8in. Single Hackney Curb	337	9d.	1/-	—	—
16 ,, 7in. Double ,,	338	1/-	1/3	—	—
20 ,, 8in. ,,	339	1/4	1/8	6/-	5/-
22 ,, 8in. ,,	340	1/6	1/10	6/6	5/6
26 ,, 8½in. ,,	341	1/8	2/2	7/6	6/-
30 ,, 8½in. Best Double Hackney Curb	342	2/6	3/-	9/-	7/6
30 ,, 9in. ,, Stout ,,	533	2/9	3/3	10/-	8/6
22 ,, 8in. Double Ladies' Curb	343	1/6	1/10	6/-	5/-
26 ,, 8½in. ,,	536	1/8	2/2	6/6	5/6
34 ,, 8½in. Best Double Ladies' Curb	344	2/9	3/3	8/-	7/-
36 ,, 8½in. ,, ,, ,, Extra Light	535	3/-	3/6	8/6	7/6
		Single gross.	Single gross.	Single gross.	Single gross.
Light Endless Hooks	353	6d.	10d.	—	—
Stout ,,	354	6d.	10d.	—	—
Light Steel	355	1/6	1/10	12/-	—
Stout ,,	356	1/9	2/3	15/-	—
Best Steel Lady's Hook, No. 2	357	4/6	5/6	12/-	—
,, ,, Light Hackney Hook, No. 3	358	4/6	5/6	12/-	—
,, ,, Stout ,, No. 4	359	4/6	5/6	12/-	—
,, ,, Gig ,, No. 5	364	4/6	5/6	15/-	—
Light Steel Liverpool Hook	372	1/8	2/3	12/-	—
Stout ,, ,, ,,	373	2/-	2/3	15/-	—
Best Steel Light Liverpool Hook, No. 3	365	4/6	5/6	12/-	—
,, ,, Stout ,, No. 5	366	4/6	5/6	15/-	—
,, ,, Double ,,	367	10/-	11/6	—	—
,, ,, Patent Circle Curb Hook, Light, Medium or Heavy	623	24/-	30/-	—	—

Fig. 6.60c Description of curb chains and hooks in Fig. 6.60d.

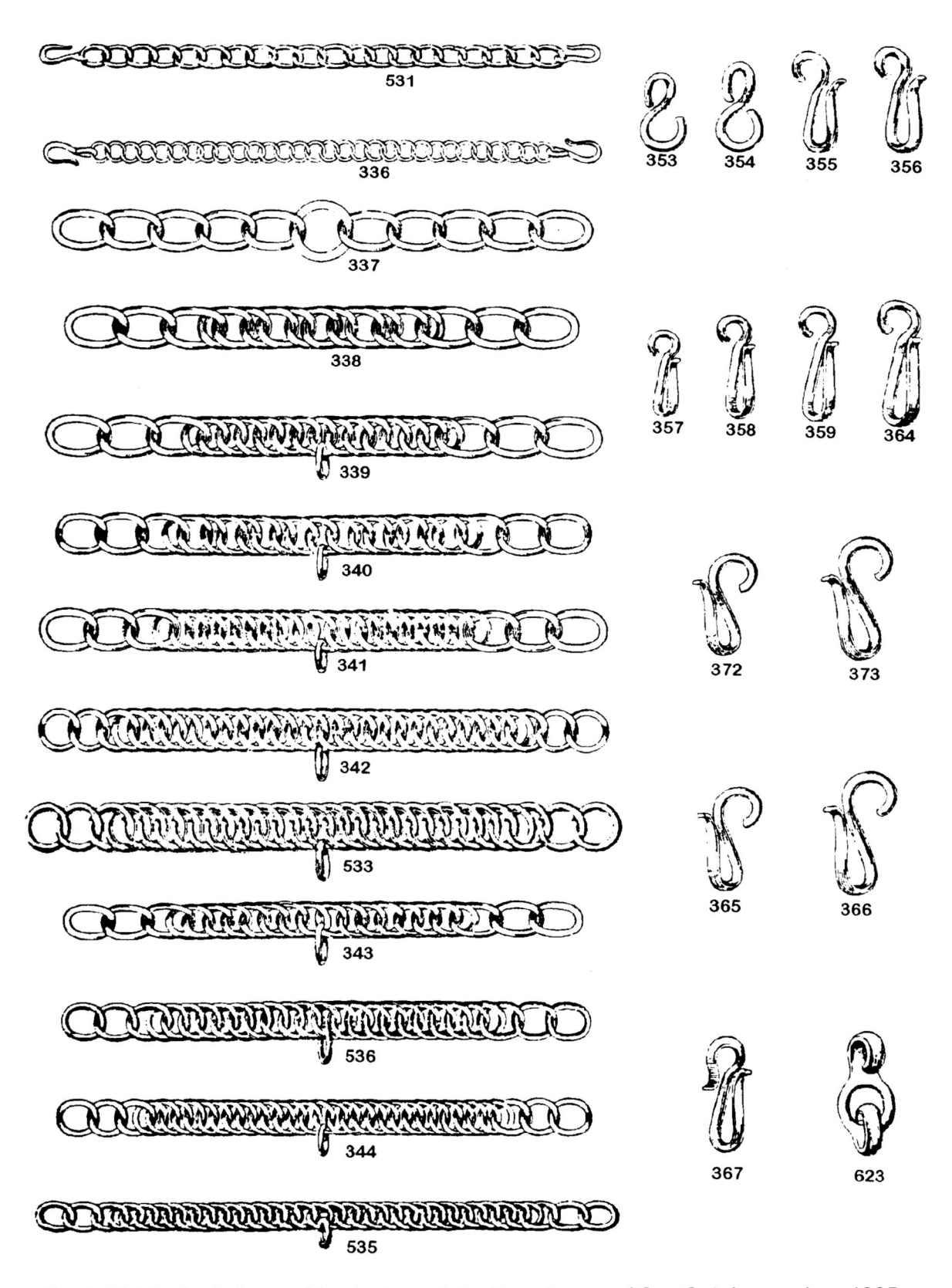

Fig. 6.60d Curb chains and hooks from John Dewsbury and Son Catalogue circa 1905.

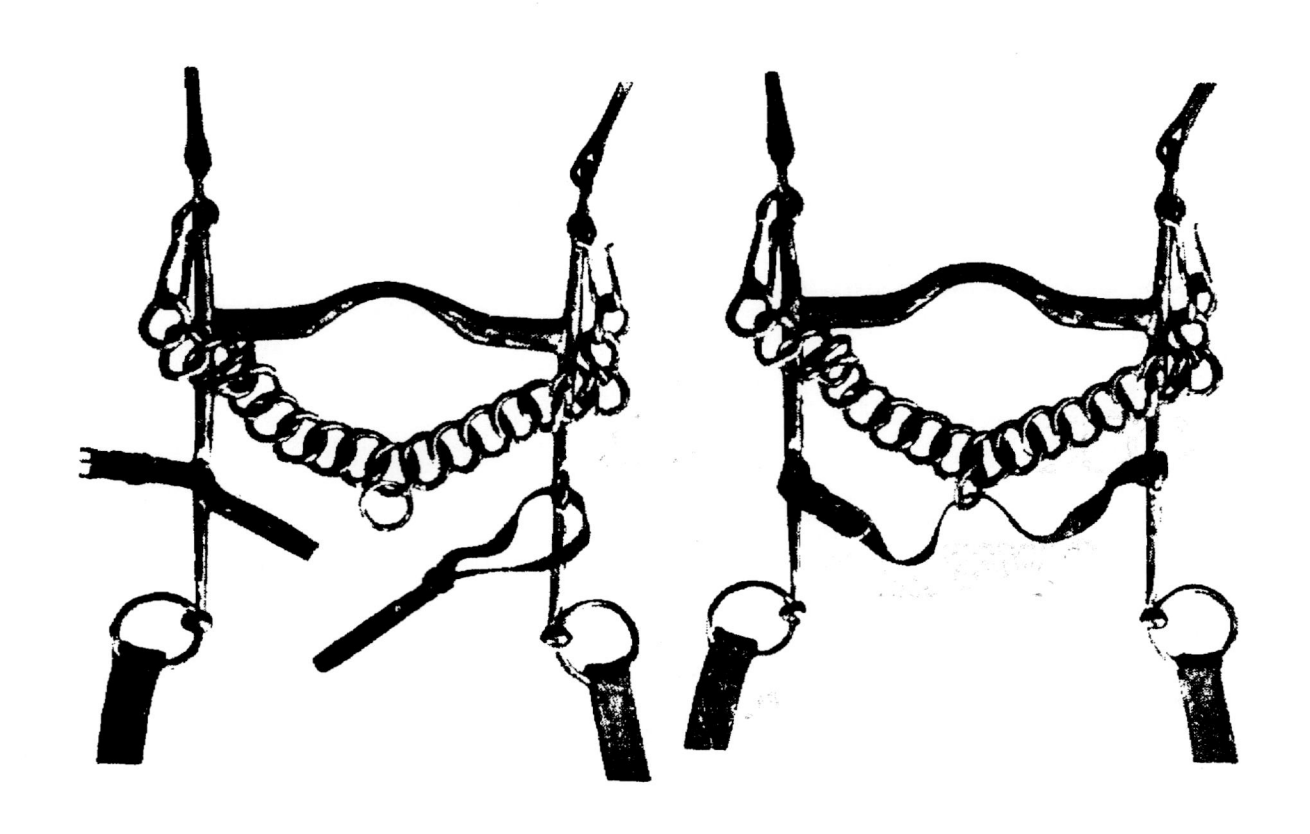

Fig. 6.61 A chin strap unbuckled and a chin strap buckled to the curb chain.

CHAPTER SEVEN
Daisy to Dressage

Daisy Bit: A bit manufactured by several companies with basically the same pattern [Fig. 7.0].

Fig. 7.0 Daisy Bits by Buermann Mfg. Co.

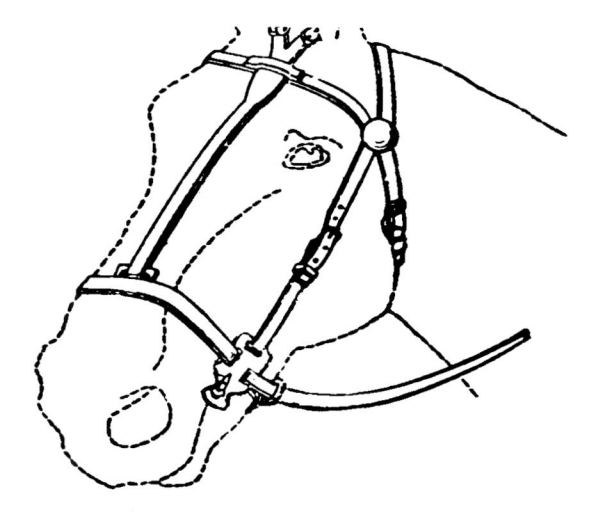

Fig. 7.1 Daly bit and bridle.

Daly, Henry W., Leavenworth, KS, Patent No. 952,610, Mar. 22, 1910 [Fig. 7.1]. A bit with side-plates to which the noseband and draw-rein are connected in a way that a pull on the reins will exert pressure on the nose and also close the horse's mouth.

Daly, Michael J., Granton, NJ, Patent No. 446,944, Feb. 24, 1891 [Fig. 7.2]. The bit with its middle portion formed into a large port or arch and its ends into rings for the headstall and driving reins. The arch is wide enough to allow side-pieces twisted around the outer portion to form rings for the curb-strap.

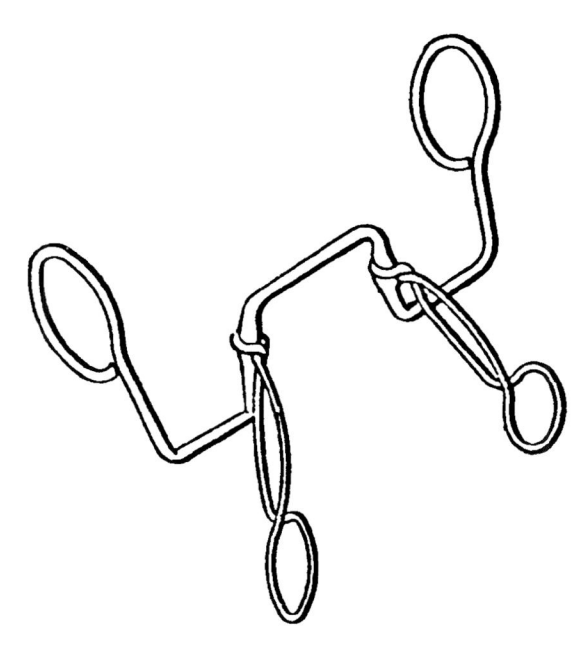

Fig. 7.2 Daly twisted-rod bit.

Dalziel, Ira Barker, Woodside, CA, Patent No. 2,172,501, Sep. 12, 1939 [Fig. 7.3]. A bit constructed with concave cheek-pieces to form a pocket so that when they are brought to bear on the cheeks it will be in an area away from the corners

101

of the mouth. They are made of a soft yielding material.

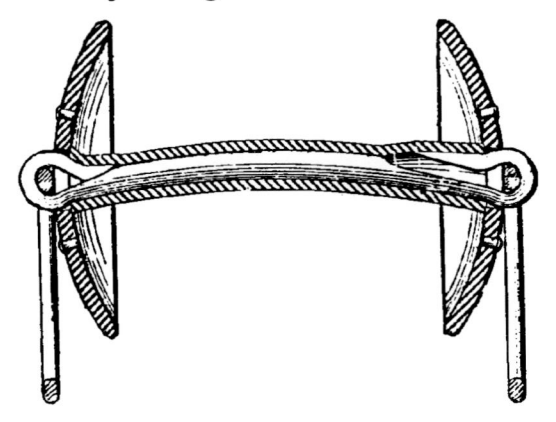

Fig. 7.3 A sectional view of Dalziel soft-cheek bit.

Dan Mace: A snaffle bit sold by Haydens and Allen. The small loops on the half-cheeks provide for a lip strap. Sold with stiff (solid) or jointed mouth. [Fig. 7.5].

Fig. 7.5 Dan Mace snaffle bit.

Daniels Pulley Bradoon: A bit sold by Haydens and Allen, St. Louis, Mo. May have been manufactured by Daniels of England [Figs. 7.4 and 7.4a].

Fig. 7.4 Daniels swivel or pully bradoon.

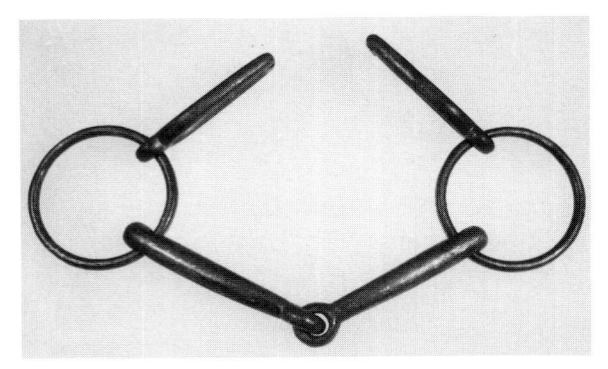

Fig. 7.4a Daniels pully bit.

Darr, Emry Q., Shelbyville, IN, Patent No. 329, 629, Nov. 3, 1885 [Figs. 7.6 and 7.6a]. Composed of two rigid bars of different lengths and placed one above the other which pivot together from a central pin. The upper bar is suspended by the bridle cheek-straps and the lower bar rings accept the driving reins.

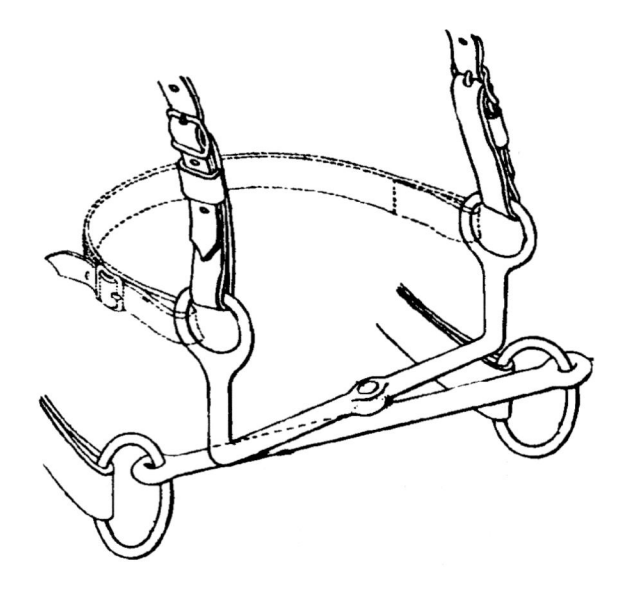

Fig. 7.6 Darr double-swivel-mouth curb bit.

Davis, Crit, Harrodsburg, KY, Patent No. 720,629, Feb. 17, 1903 [Fig. 7.7 and 7.7a]. See Overcheck, Chapter 9.

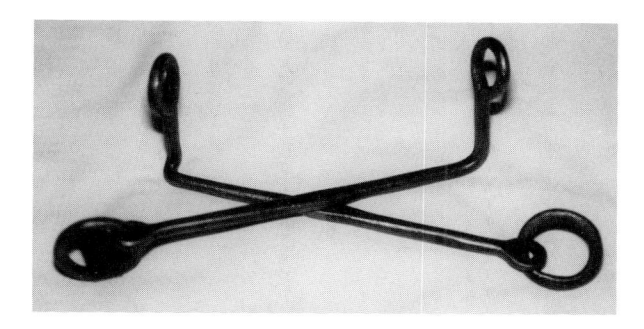

Fig.7.6a Darr production bit. Robert Maclin collection.

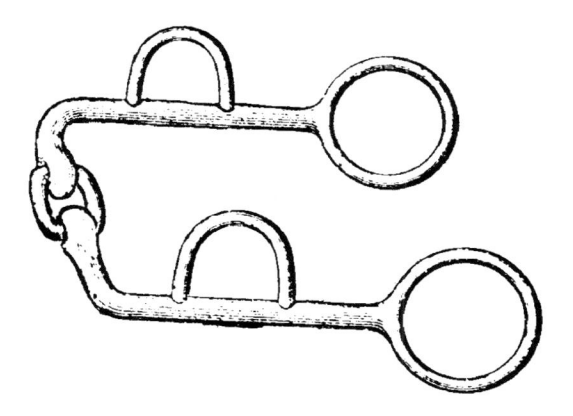

Fig. 7.7 Crit Davis broken-snaffle bit.

Fig. 7.7a Crit Davis production bit. Robert Maclin collection.

Day, Benjamin I., Gibsen County, IN, Patent No. 11,856, May 13, 1856 [Fig. 7.8]. A common curb and lever bit with an attached folding limb to the cheek-piece and kept closed by a spring contained in a boss at the lower end of the levered cheek-piece.

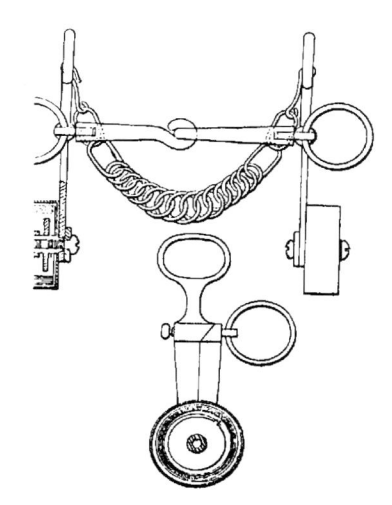

Fig. 7.8 Day spring-tension curb bit.

Day, Edmund, West Springfield, MA, Patent No. 51,151, Nov. 28, 1865 [Fig. 7.9]. The bit uses a substitute for a leather-covered mouth-piece. The mouth-piece is covered with hard India rubber or gutta-percha.

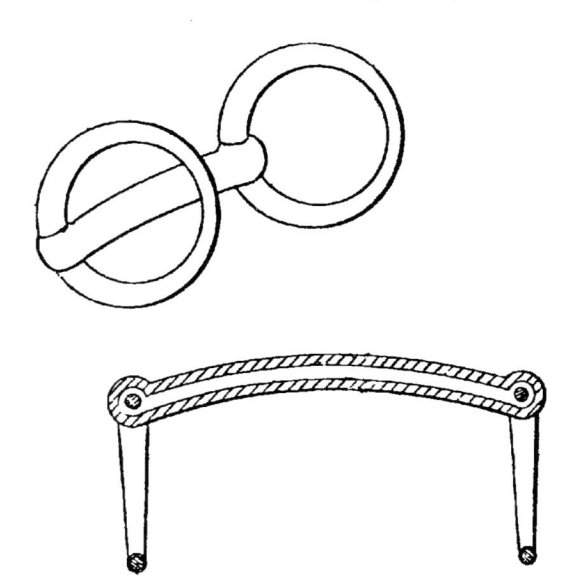

Fig.7.9 Day covered mouth-piece snaffle.

Dean, John, Racine, WI, Patent No. 483,103, Sep. 20, 1892 [Fig. 7.10]. Each cheek-piece is a single wire bent from above the bar to form a single rein-loop and turned around itself below the bar. The non-bent portion of the wire is extended down to form the half-cheek.

Fig. 7.10 John Dean single-wire cheek.

Patent No. 483,104, Sep. 20, 1892, [Fig. 7.11]. A rein pull forces the cheek-pieces inward putting pressure on the side of the mouth.

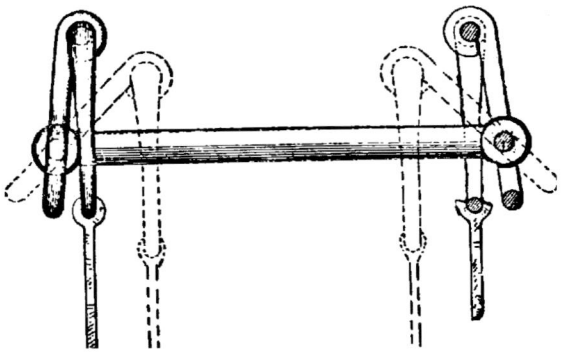

Fig. 7.11 John Dean pressure bit.

Patent No. 657,762, Sep. 11, 1900 [Fig. 7.12]. The mouth-piece is secured to and pivots in the cheek-piece by a pin that is riveted on the lower end. Either a stiff or broken mouth-piece can be used.

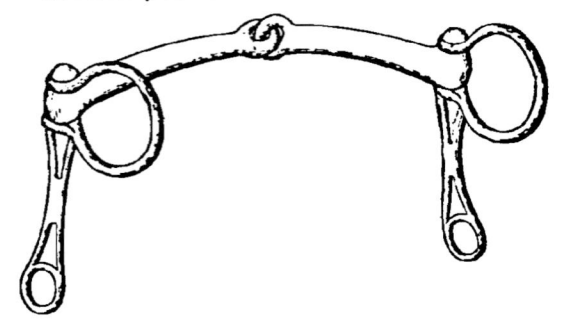

Fig. 7.12 John Dean pivoting-cheek snaffle.

Dean, Levi F., New Milford, PA, Patent No. 374,352, Dec. 6, 1887 [Fig. 7.13]. A solid mouth-piece flattened on the underside to rest easily on the jaws and concave in the center to give room to the tongue. The mouth-piece is set in a frame for bridle and rein attachment that keeps the mouth-piece in a normal position when the horse is quiet. A pull on the reins rotates the mouth-piece to a harsher bit.

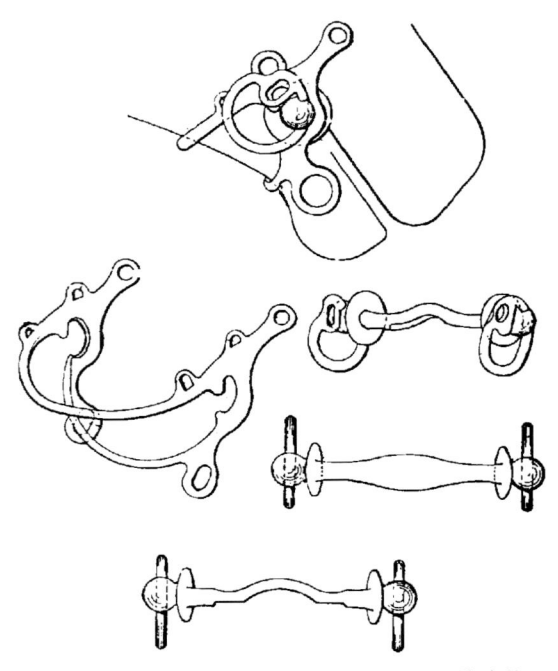

Fig. 7.13 Levi Dean loose-mouth bit.

Dee Cheek: See Side-pieces, Rings, Dee, Chapter 31, Fig. 31.3.

Dee Cheek Race Snaffle: A commonly used snaffle bit with English-style riding [Fig. 7.14].

Fig. 7.14 Dee Ring Race Snaffle.

Dee Rings: See Side-pieces, Rings, Dee Chapter 31, Fig. 31.3

Devereaux, Robert M., Chicago, IL, Patent No. 515,326, Feb. 27. 1894 [Fig. 7.15]. The ends of the bit are rigid cross-bars arranged like cheek-pieces and have snap hooks secured in the upper ends. Designed to be attached to an ordinary halter or headstall.

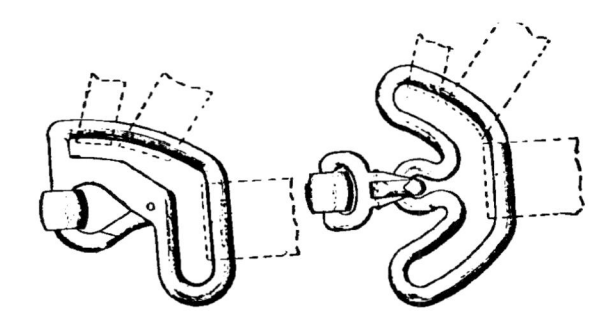

Fig. 7.15 Attachable bridle bit.

De Wolf, David O., Sackett's Harbor, NY, Patent No. 157,470, Dec. 8, 1874 [Fig. 7.16]. The double bars are hinged to bit-rings having the eyes normally lower than but not in line with the bars to limit the tendency to turn the bit in the mouth as the reins are pulled.

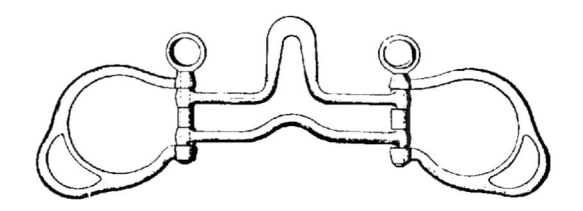

Fig. 7.16 De Wolf double-mouth snaffle bit.

De Wolfe, Harvey A., Costa Mesa, CA, Patent No. 2,510,244, June 20, 1950 [Fig. 7.17]. A rein pull rotates the side-plates and puts pressure on the curb-strap and causes a forward movement of the headstall. Pressure is divided between the noseband and the arched port.

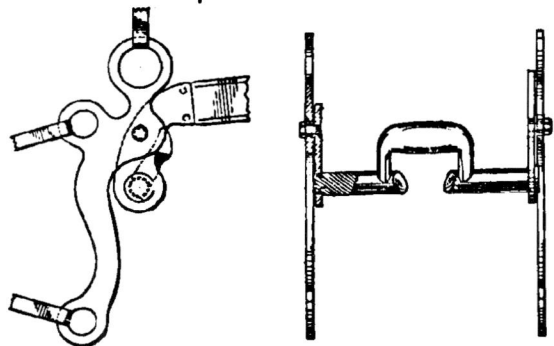

Fig. 7.17 De Wolfe rotating-cheek bit.

Dexter Bits: Refers to the mouth-piece. A bit with a broken mouth and tapered cannons which have ball ends and a variety of cheek-pieces [Fig. 7.18].

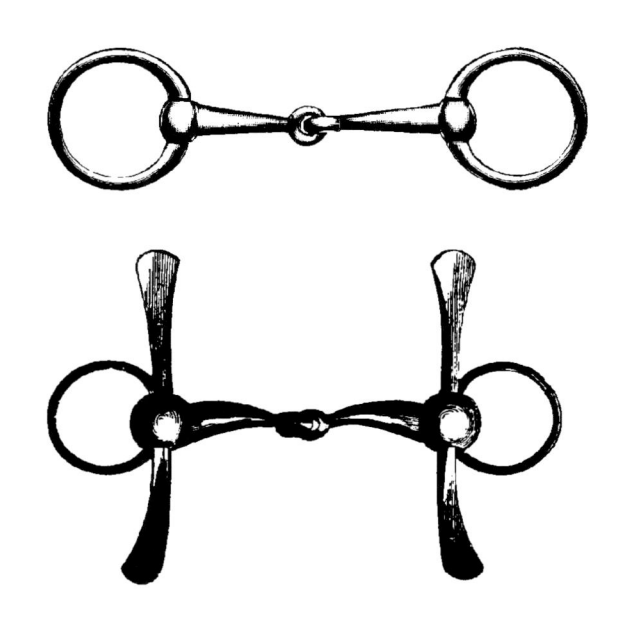

Fig. 7.18 Dexter-mouth snaffle bits.

di Tergolina, Count Vincenzo, Middlesex, England, Patent No. 141,334, July 29, 1873 [Fig. 7.19]. Two joints are placed in the middle of the mouth-piece for the section that lays on the tongue. The mouth-piece is secured to the cheek-pieces which cause the mouth-piece to flex when the reins are pulled.

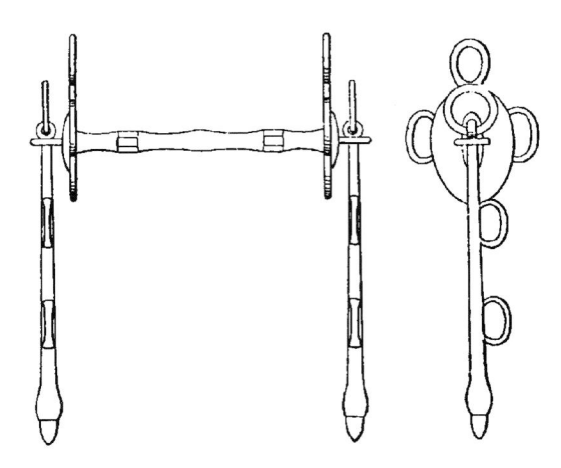

Fig. 7.19 di Tergolina flex-mouth bit.

Diamond Bit: A silver-inlaid bit of the "California Style" by A. Buermann Mfg. Co., with a half-breed mouth-piece [Fig. 7.20].

Fig. 7.20 Buermann Diamond Bit.

Diamond Heel Bit: A bit with a diamond shaped end to the mouth-piece. A Hackney curb bit by Dewsbury and Son [Fig. 7.21].

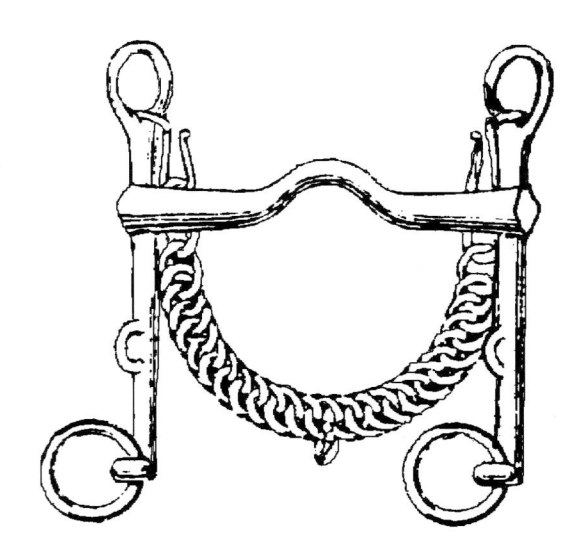

Fig. 7.21 Dewsbury diamond heel bit.

Dick Christian Snaffle Bit: A large ring snaffle bit with a center-link mouth and tapered cannons [Fig. 7.22]. See Figure 6.20.

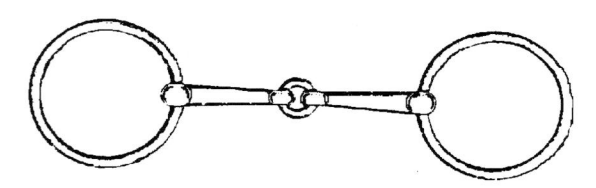

Fig. 7.22 Dick Christian snaffle.

Directum Bit: See Driving, Chapter 8.

Disks: A term applied to some cheek-pieces. Sometimes used to express roller devices on a mouth-piece. See Echini, Hedgehogs, and Rollers.

Doherty, George Albert, Cresent Mills, CA, Patent No. 349,088, Sep. 14, 1886 [Fig. 7.23]. A construction method for snaffle bits. The completed bit is covered with the rubber sleeve.

Dolan, Thomas F., Cando, ND, Patent No. 1,037,878, Sep.10, 1912 [Fig. 7.24]. A bit with the outer ends flattened and slotted for guiding reins. Transverse holes on each end of the mouth-piece receive wire holders to form cheek-pieces for the headstall.

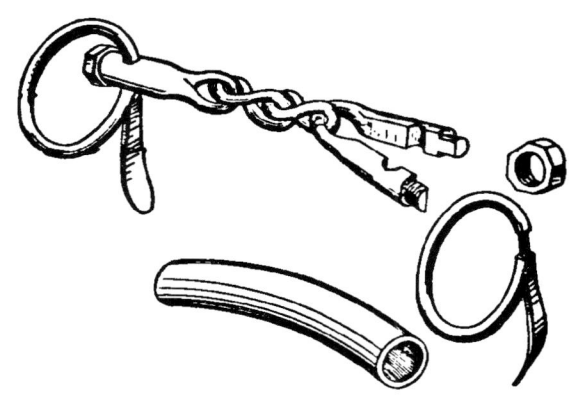

Fig. 7.23 Doherty snaffle construction method.

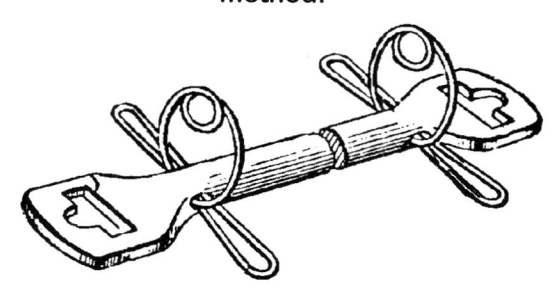

Fig.7.24 Dolan snaffle bit.

Dolphin Bit: A bit dating back to the American Revolutionary War period. An iron bit with 4 3/4 inch mouth and 5 1/8 cheeks.

Donnelly, Daniel Webster, Burlingame, CA, Patent No. 722, 683, Mar. 17, 1903 [Fig. 7.26]. A continuous metal structure to be secured in the horse's mouth by the leather strap and to be used without a bridle. Designed for riding but may be used on driving horses.

Donut: See Bit Guard, Chapter 5, Figure 5.59.

Fig. 7.25 Dolphin Bit. Jean Gayle collection. Photo by Jones Photo Co.

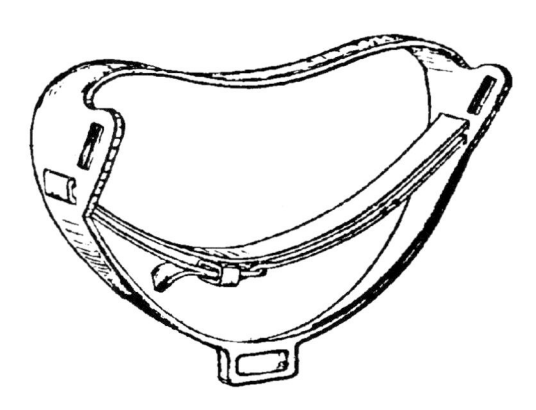

Fig. 7.26 Donnelly bridleless bit.

Double Bridle: A bridle equipped with a curb and a snaffle bit and used with two sets of reins.

Double-jointed Mouth: A bit with two separate broken mouth-pieces close together. See Mouth-pieces, Y or W Mouth Bits, Chapter 25.

Double Twisted Wire Snaffle: A driving bit with a more severe action [Fig. 7.27].

Fig. 7.27 Double-wire broken mouth bit.

Douglas, John, Brooklyn, NY, Patent No. 345,955, July 20, 1886 [Fig. 7.28]. A bit with a flexible mouth-piece of leather or rawhide, with an outer rubber envelope covering.

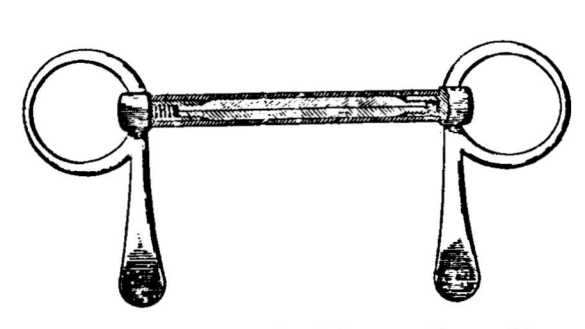

Fig. 7.28 Douglas flexible-mouth snaffle.

Dravelling Snaffle: A double-cheek snaffle with a set of three large mouth-loops which pivot on the mouth-piece. Sometimes referred to as a Tongue-lolling Bit. From the early 1800's [Fig. 7.29].

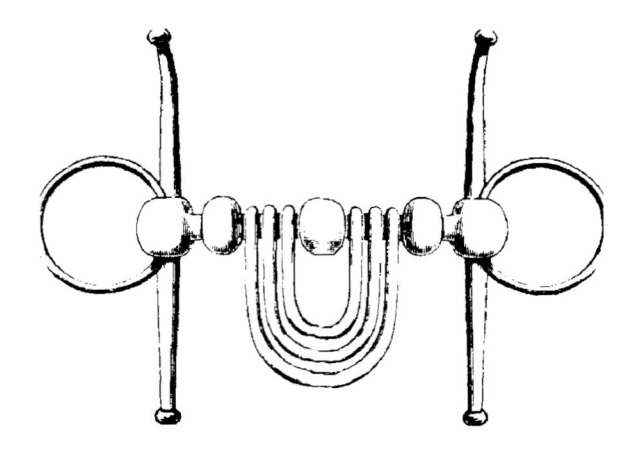

Fig. 7.29 Dravelling snaffle bit.

Dr. Bristol, John S., V. S., Danbury, CT, Patent No. 1,632,589, June 14, 1927 [Figs. 7.30 to 7.30b]. The flat center link acts on the tongue when reins are pulled. Dr. Bristol had over 30 years of practice as an Equine Dentist.

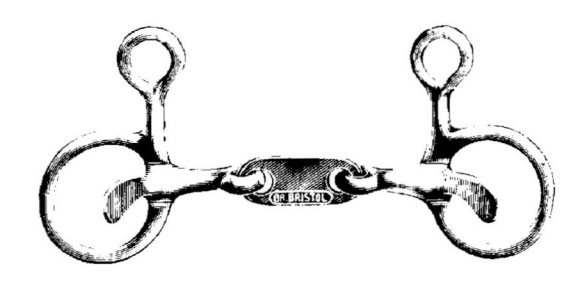

Fig. 7.30 Dr. Bristol hanging-cheek horned bit.

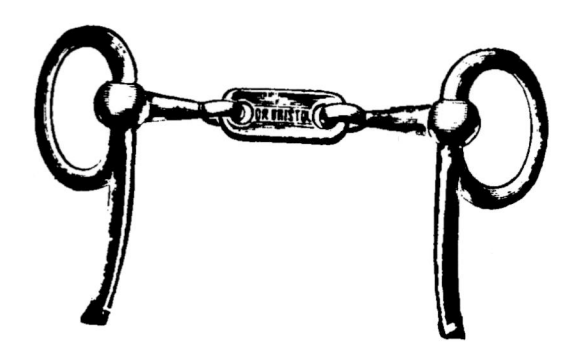

Fig. 7.30a Dr. Bristol half-cheek snaffle.

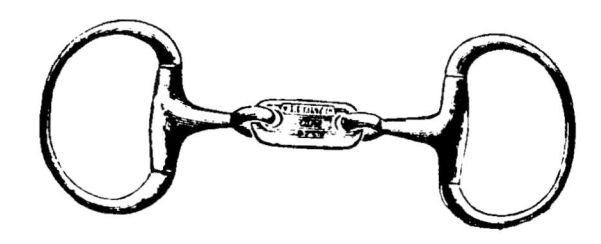

Fig. 7.30b Dr. Bristol barrel head pattern bit.

Dr. Thatcher's Braden Direct Bit: The spoon-shaped side-bars cause pressure on the mouth as the horse tries to turn its head. Used on record breaker Braden-Direct. Supplied in 4 1/4, 4 1/2, 4 3/4 and 5 inch mouths [Fig. 7.31].

Fig. 7.31 Dr. Thatcher's Braden Direct Bit.

Draw Bit: A term for a Gag Bit.

Draw Curb-rein: A rein attached to the saddle girth or breast strap and runs through the bit rings to the rider. Used to train the horse to hold its head down and flex the poll. See Chapter 35.

Draw Rein: Same as Draw Curb-rein.

Dressage Weymouth: See Weymouth, Chapter 34.

Driscoll, James E., St. Paul, MN, Patent No. 492,666, Feb. 28, 1893 [Fig. 7.32]. A bit with adjustment to fit the width of the mouth-bar to the horse. Each outer end of the mouth-piece has a milled collar which enables it and the cheek-pieces to be moved in and out and then secured by a screw cap on the outside of the cheek-piece.

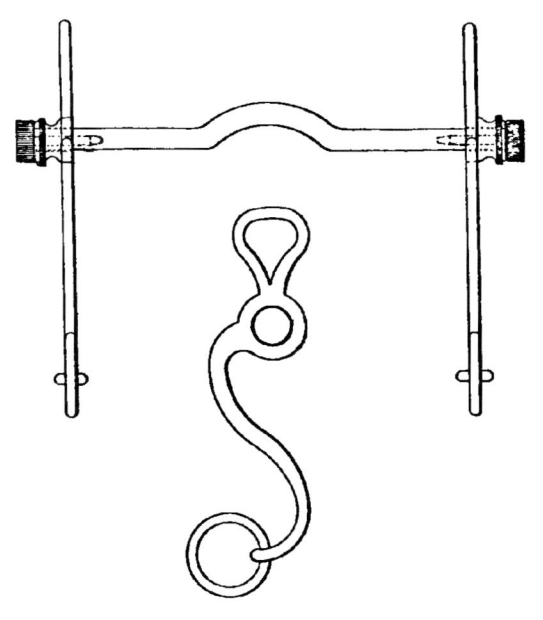

Fig. 7.32 Driscoll adjustable mouth bit.

CHAPTER EIGHT
Driving Bit

Driving Bits: A bit used on a horse that is being driven to a buggy, cart, wagon, or carriage. The term may be used to identify any form of bit, such as a wide variety of snaffle, curb and Pelham bits.

Acme Driving Bit: Patent by Robert Van Arsdale, Racine, WI, No. 422,469, Mar. 4, 1890 [Fig. 8.0]. The bit is also called the "Success" bit.

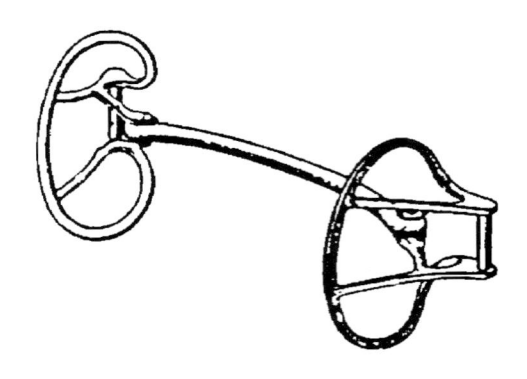

Fig. 8.0 Acme driving bit.

American Half-cheek Bit: Made with a broken or solid mouth-piece [Fig. 8.1].

Fig. 8.1 American half-cheek driving bit.

Ashleigh Elbow Bit: A 19th Century driving bit of common design [Fig. 8.2]. Several variations in size and strength of side-pieces and construction of mouth-piece attachments. A sliding mouth was produced. See Fig. 8.27, Nos. 304 and 305.

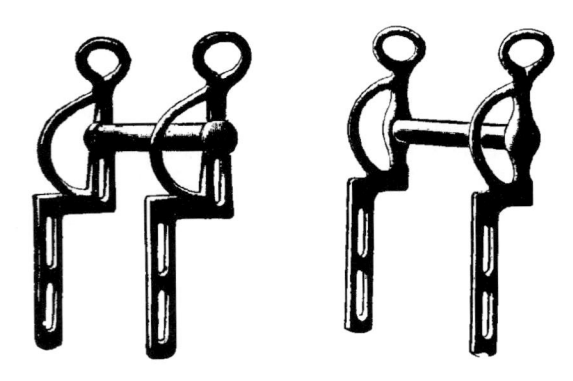

Fig. 8.2 Ashleigh elbow rigid pattern bits with full head pattern (right).

Balancing Bit: The pivoting upper mouth-piece is controlled by round leather reins that function much as a gag when attached to the check-reins [Fig. 8.3].

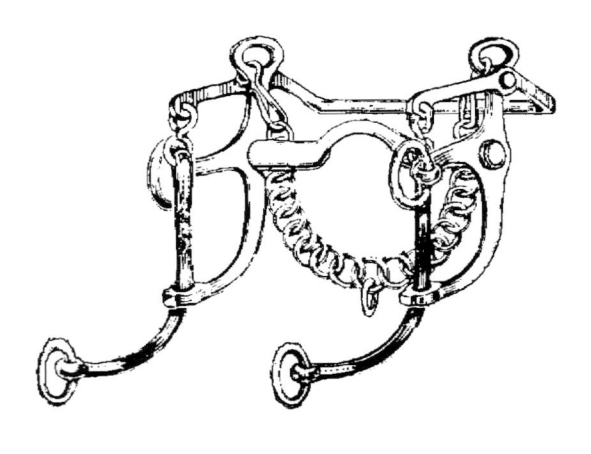

Fig. 8.3 Balancing bit.

Baldwin Driving Bit: See Baldwin Shifting-mouth Bit, Chapter 5, Fig. 5.24.

Beery Driving Bit: A bit patented by Lucius J. Elliot and John Reichert, Racine, WI, No. 774,055, Nov. 1, 1904 [Fig. 8.4].

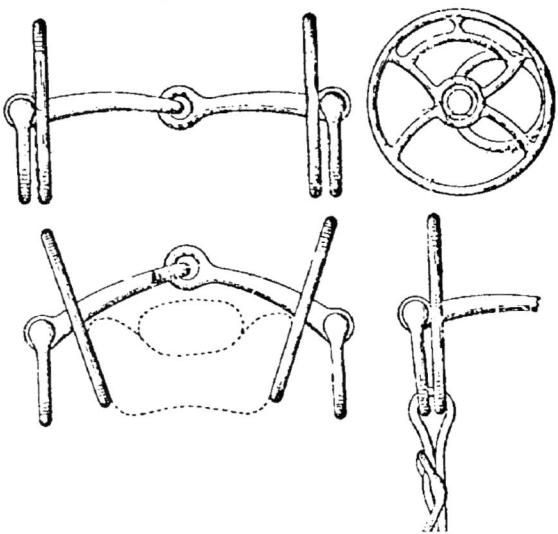

Fig. 8.4 Beery driving bit.

Broken-mouth Bit: A snaffle driving bit with a broken mouth [Fig. 8.5].

Fig. 8.5 A broken-mouth driving bit.

Buckeye Safety Bit: [Fig. 8.6] Patent date of Mar. 15, 1857. Manufactured by several different companies and supplied in a stiff or broken mouth. A few are found with a spoon added to the lower ring.

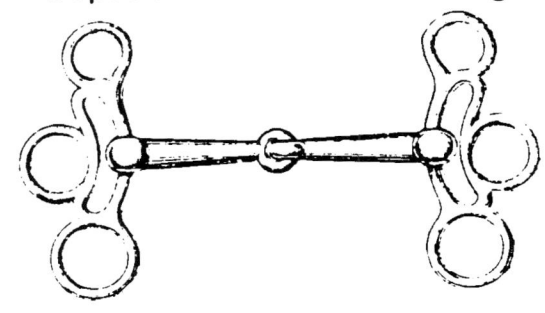

Fig. 8.6 Buckeye Safety bit with a broken mouth.

Buxton Bits: A large bit with S-shaped cheek-pieces used primarily on draft or carrage teams. See Fig. 8.27.

Champ-Neigh Driving Bit: A double bar bit with loose cheek-pieces [Fig. 8.7].

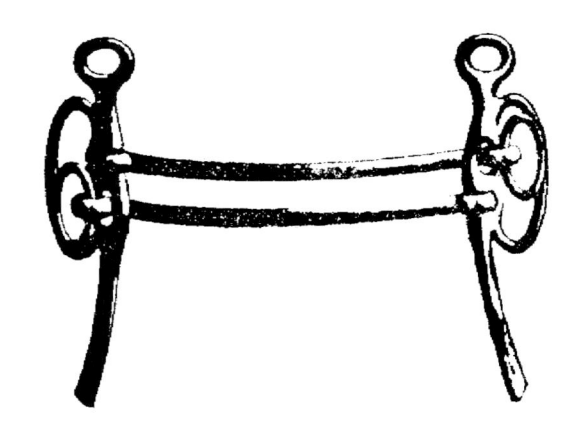

Fig. 8.7 Champ-Neigh driving bit.

Crescendo Bit: See Chapter 6, Fig. 6.54.

Directum Driving Bit: [Fig. 8.8] See John Dean patent Chapter 7, Fig. 7.10.

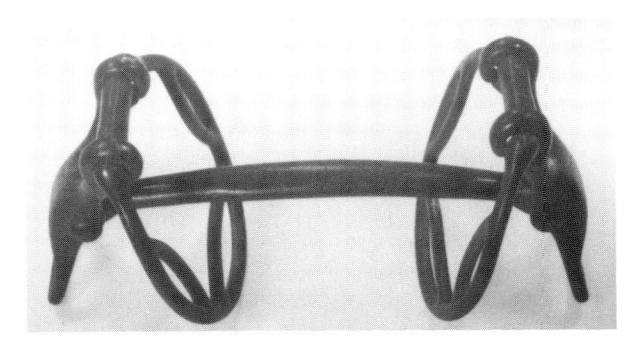

Fig. 8.8 Directum driving bit.

Driving Bits, Fancy and Ornate: See Figs. 8.30 to 8.58.

Duncan, George T., Sr., Seattle, WA, Patent No. 802,375, Oct. 24, 1905 [Figs. 8.9 and 8.10]. Several versions of the bit are illustrated with the Duncan overcheck as a main part of the action of the bit.

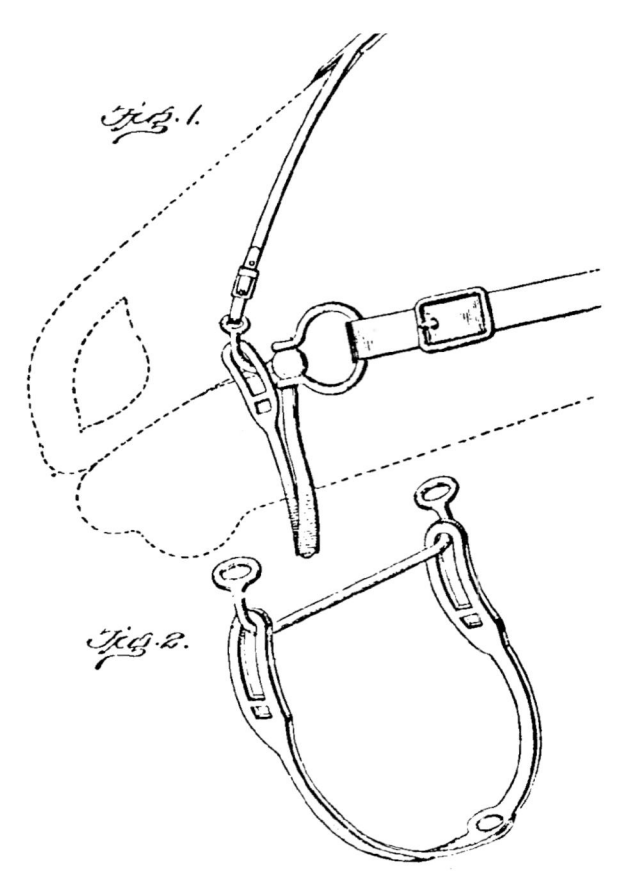

Fig. 8.9 Duncan driving bit and over-check.

Gig: A term used for a light driving bit. The term also applies to a light two-wheeled carriage pulled by one horse.

Gleason, Oscar R., New York, NY, Patent No. 378,305, Feb. 21, 1888 [Fig. 8.11 and 8.11a]. This bit has a square in cross-section mouth-piece and the rings have downward projecting loops for rein attachment.

Gridiron Bit: A bit with a large open mouth-piece [Fig. 8.12].

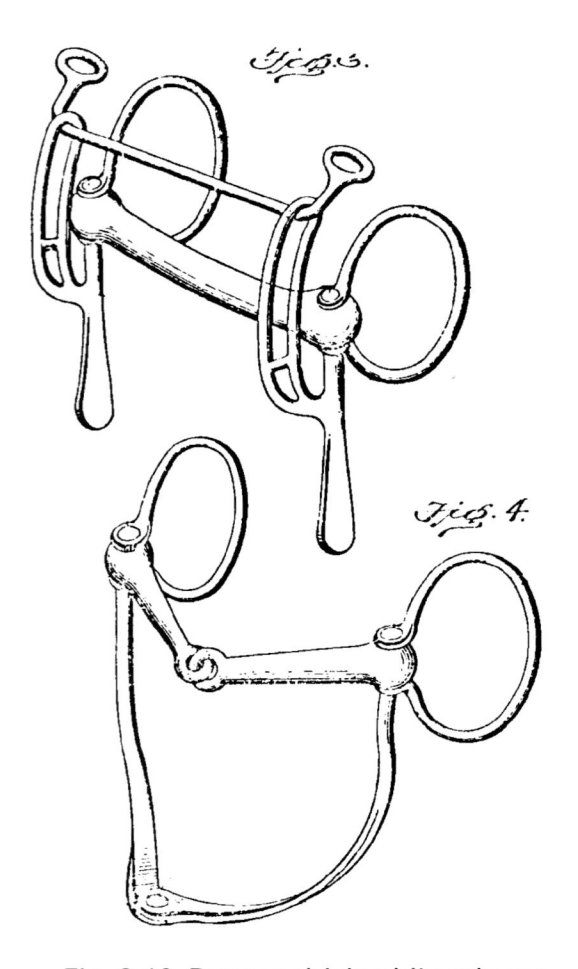

Fig. 8.10 Duncan driving bit and over-check.

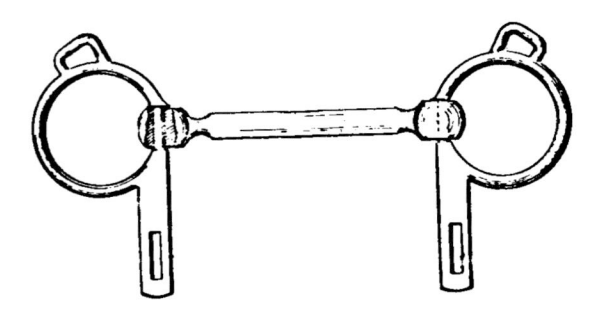

Fig. 8.11 Gleason square-mouth bit.

Half-cheek Driving Bit: See Cheek-pieces, Chapter 31.

112

Fig. 8.11a Gleason bit with a figure-8 link broken mouth and loops added for check-rein attachment. Robert Maclin collection.

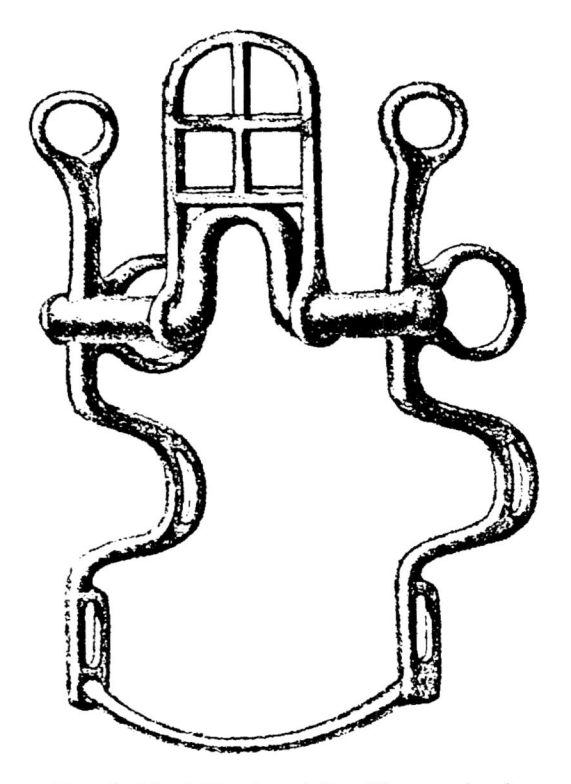

Fig. 8.12 A Buxton bit with a swinging gridiron player.

Fig. 8.12a Swinging gridiron mouth on a curb bit.

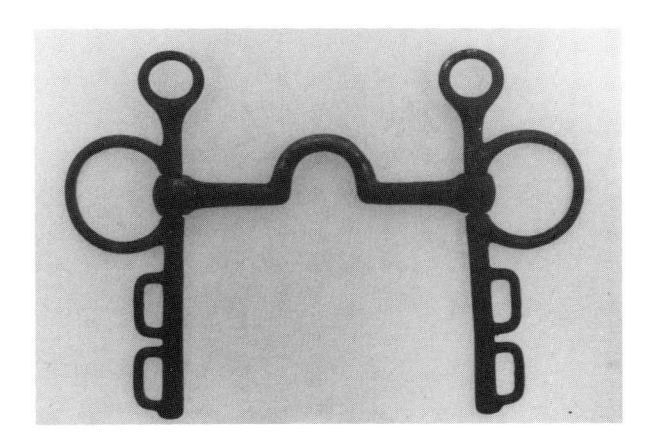

Fig 8.13 Hanoverian ported bit.

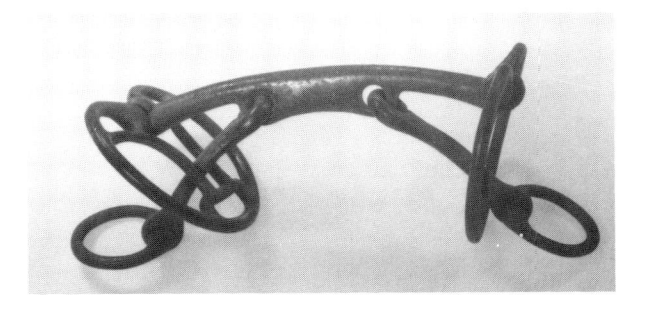

Fig. 8.14 Imperial driving bit.

Hanoverian Bit: A light driving bit with or without a port and fixed or loose cheek-pieces [Fig. 8.13].

Imperial Driving Bit: Patent No. 422,529, Mar. 4, 1890 [Fig. 8.14 and 8.14a], Brent M. Johnson and John Reichart, Racine, WI.

Fig. 8.14a Variation of Imperial driving bit. Robert Maclin collection.

J.I.C. Driving Bit: "Just In Case" a scissor or pantographic mouth bit [Fig. 8.15 and 8.15a]. See patent by Hardy W. Campbell [Fig. 6.4].

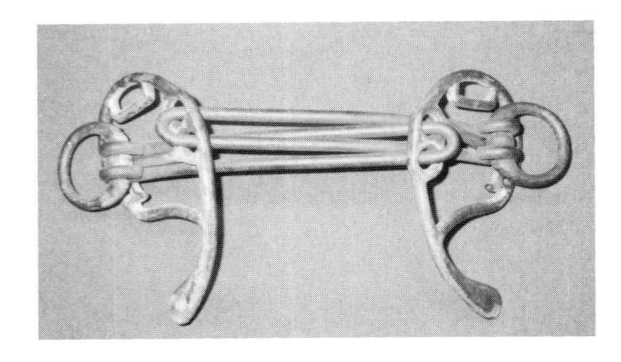

Fig. 8.15b A bit with a double scissor-mouth made in the style of the J.I.C. bit principle. Robert Maclin collection.

Fig. 8.15 J.I.C. driving bit.

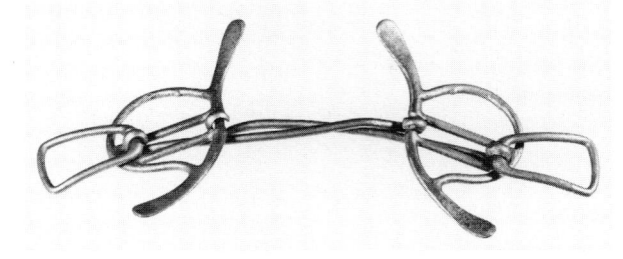

Fig. 8.15a A bit made on the principle of the J.I.C. Jean Gayle collection. Photo by Jones Photo.

Leather: See Mouth-piece, Leather, Chapter 14, Fig. 14.38 and Chapter 25.

LeCompte, George W. Baltimore, MD, Patent No. 582,535, May 11, 1897 [Fig. 8.16].

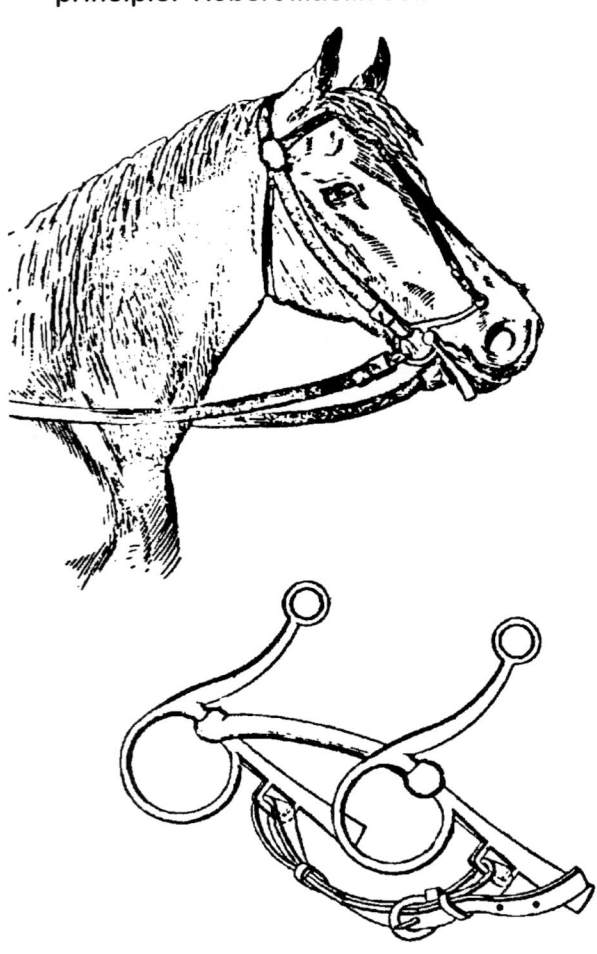

Fig. 8.16 LeCompte driving bit.

Norton Driving Bit: A six-ring bit, Patent No. 313,442, Mar. 3, 1885, by Sylvanus Norton, Sinclairville, NY. The uppermost set of rings in the drawing is for a nose-strap which is

114

hooked to the bridle by a frontal strap. The other rings are for reins and check-reins. If a check-rein is used, the nose-piece may be left off [Fig. 8.17].

Fig. 8.17 Norton six-ring driving bit.

Perfection Driving Bit: [Fig. 8.18]. See Chapter 28 for information.

Fig. 8.18 Perfection driving bit.

Phillips, Charles W. *et al.*, Keokuck, IA, Patent No. 493,339, Mar. 14, 1893 [Fig. 8.19]. A double-bar mouth bit commonly called the "Phillips Safety Bit."

Rockwell, A. H., Harpersville, NY, Patent No. 70,745, Nov. 12, 1867 [Figs. 8.20, 8.20a and 8.20b]. Two sliding bars are connected with a nose- or face-strap. By pulling on the reins, the bars will be forced together and put pressure on the nose of the horse. The original patent called for a three-piece mouth with double links to prevent the bars from sliding through the horse's mouth.

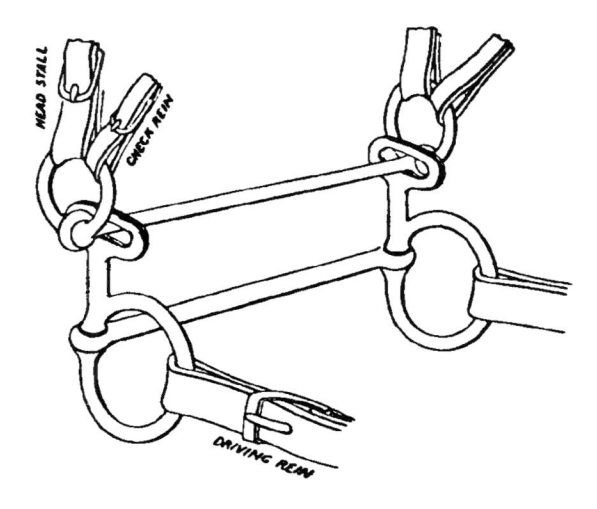

Fig. 8.18 Phillips Safety Bit.

Fig. 8.20 Rockwell production bit.

Fig. 8.20a Imitation Rockwell bit.

Scissor Bit: Any double-mouth bit in which the two mouth-pieces cross and cause a pinching action. An excellent example is the J.I.C. bit [Fig. 8.15].

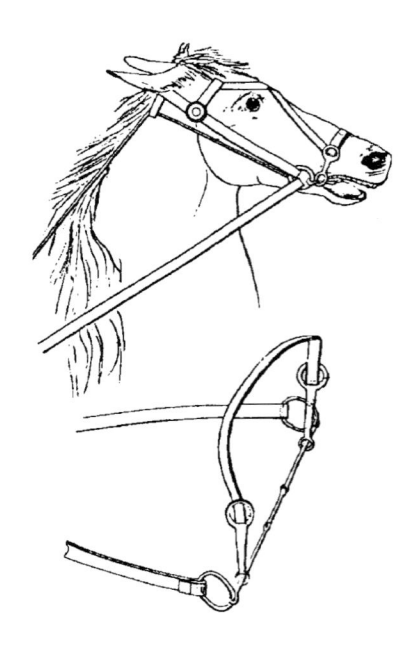

Fig. 8.20b Rockwell patent drawing.

Six-ring Bit: Refers to a snaffle bit with six rings, one set for the headstall, one set for the driving reins and the other set for the check-reins. The Norton bit [Fig. 8.17] is the one most thought of when the term is used [Fig. 8.21].

Fig. 8.21 A six-ring bit with all the rings secured in the 18 inch mouth-piece.

Springstein, Nelson E., Royal Oak, MI, Patent No. 347,209, Aug. 10, 1886 [Fig. 8.22]. A bit with a single-action jointed-mouth in that the bit bends both ways and the spoons can be brought together until they meet. A training bit still popular today.

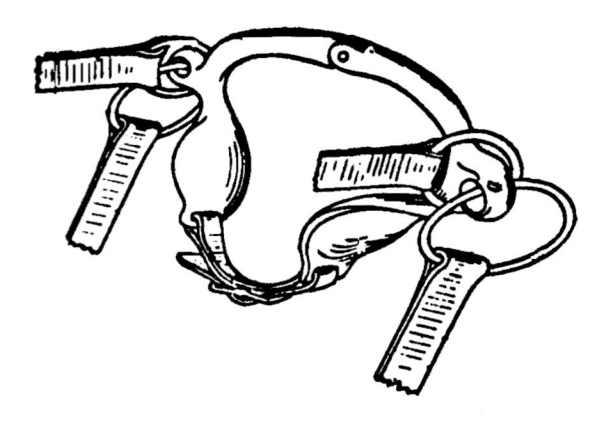

Fig. 8.22 Springstein spoon bit.

Patent No. 371,106, Oct. 4, 1887 [Fig. 8.23]. Similar to Figure 8.22, except the arrangement of the joint is different in that it allows the mouth to bend only one way and the spoons approach each other a given distance.

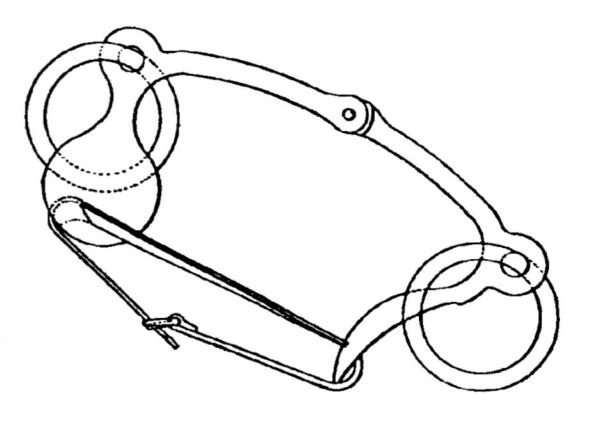

Fig. 8.23 Springstein improved bit.

Success Driving Bit: See Acme driving bit Fig. 8.0.

Swales, Frank, East Sheen, England, Patent No. 898,394, Sep.8,1908 [Fig. 8.24]. The mouth-bar is loosely supported by plain snaffle ring located inside the side-pieces. The top of the side-pieces has a spiral-shaped hook for the attachment of the curb-chain. See Chapter 32.

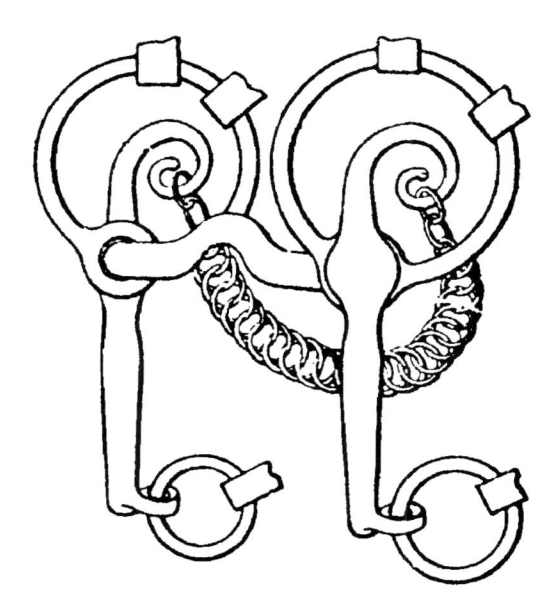

Fig.8.24 Swales 3-in-1 bit.

Swivel-shank Driving Bit: a driving bit with loose cheek-pieces that turn or rotate on the mouth-piece ends.

Triangular Driving Bit: Usually refers to the mouth-piece. See Fishback Snaffle, Chapter 11, Fig. 11.17.

Turton Driving Bit: Refers to the end of the mouth-piece. Similar to an Egg-butt or Barrel-head mouth. See Mouth-piece, Chapter 25 and Chapter 33, Fig. 33.29.

Universal Driving Bit: Term used for Imperial driving bit, Fig. 8.14.

Wilson Driving Bit: See Wilson Bits, Chapter 34.

Wingert, James Leonard, Randolph, NE, Patent No. 822,174 [Fig. 8.25]. The bit utilizes a nose-strap attached to the rings outside the bridle rings. All the rings are secure to prevent sliding on the mouth-piece.

Wright, Jefferson G., Connel, WA, Patent No. 1,375,197, Apr. 19, 1921 [Fig. 8.26]. Two flattened areas at right angles to each other on each end of the mouth-piece, houses the rings. The larger inner rings are for the headstall and the smaller rings for rein attachment.

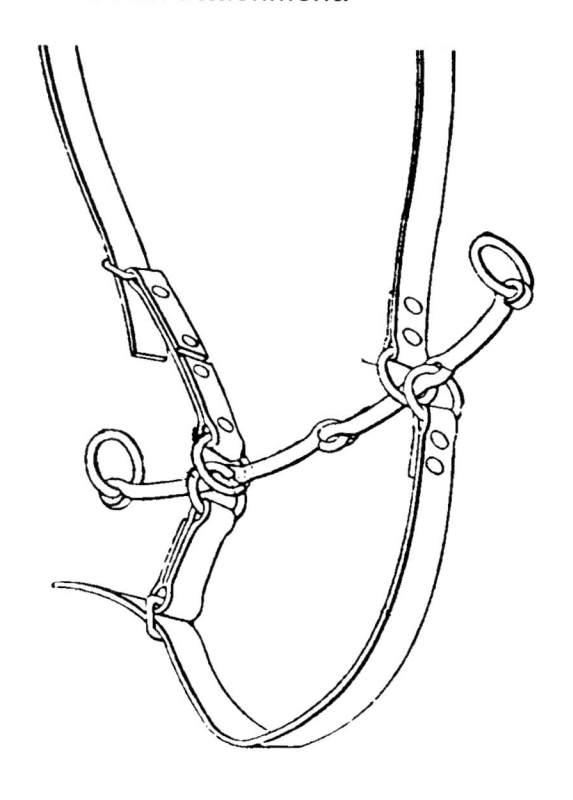

Fig. 8.25 Wingert driving bit.

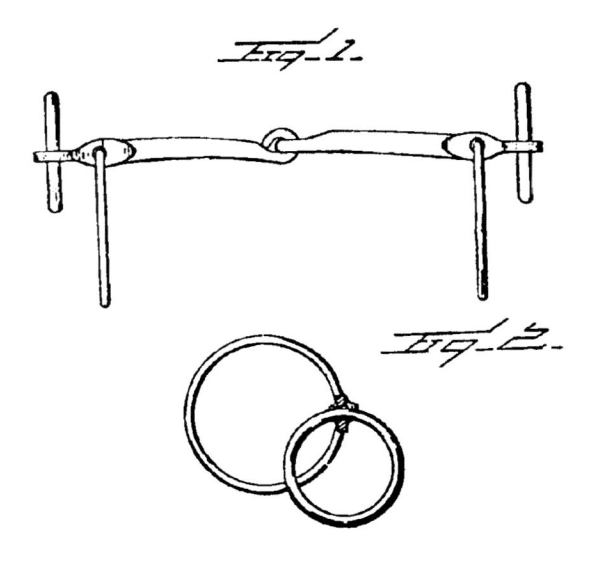

Fig. 8.26 Wright driving bit.

Elbow and Buxton bits [Fig. 8.27] from John Dewsbury and Son catalogue of early 1900's.

304   9 in. Fast-cheek, Half-twisted 5/8 in. mouth, Stout Ashleigh Loop, Elbow Bit and Curb.

462   8 in. Fast-cheek, Half-twisted 1/2 in mouth, Light Ashleigh Loop, Elbow Bit and Curb.

160   9 in. Cheek, 5/8 in. Sliding Half-twisted mouth, Stout Ashleigh Loop, Elbow Bit and Curb.

305   8 in. Cheek, 1/2 in. Sliding Half-twisted mouth, Light Ashleigh Loop, Elbow Bit and Curb.

159   Stout Sliding 9/16 in. Half-twisted mouth, 2 Loop Elbow Coach Bit and Curb.

731   Stout Sliding 9/16 in. Half-twisted mouth, 3 Loop Ashleigh Buxton Bit, with Straight Bottom Bar and Curb.

524   Stout Sliding 9 1/6 in Half-twisted mouth, Buxton Bit, Bent Bottom Bar and Curb.

161   Light Sliding 1/2 in. Half-twisted mouth, Buxton Bit, Bent Bottom bar and Curb.

670   Solid Low Port Mouth Buxton Bit, Solid Bent Bottom Bar and Curb.

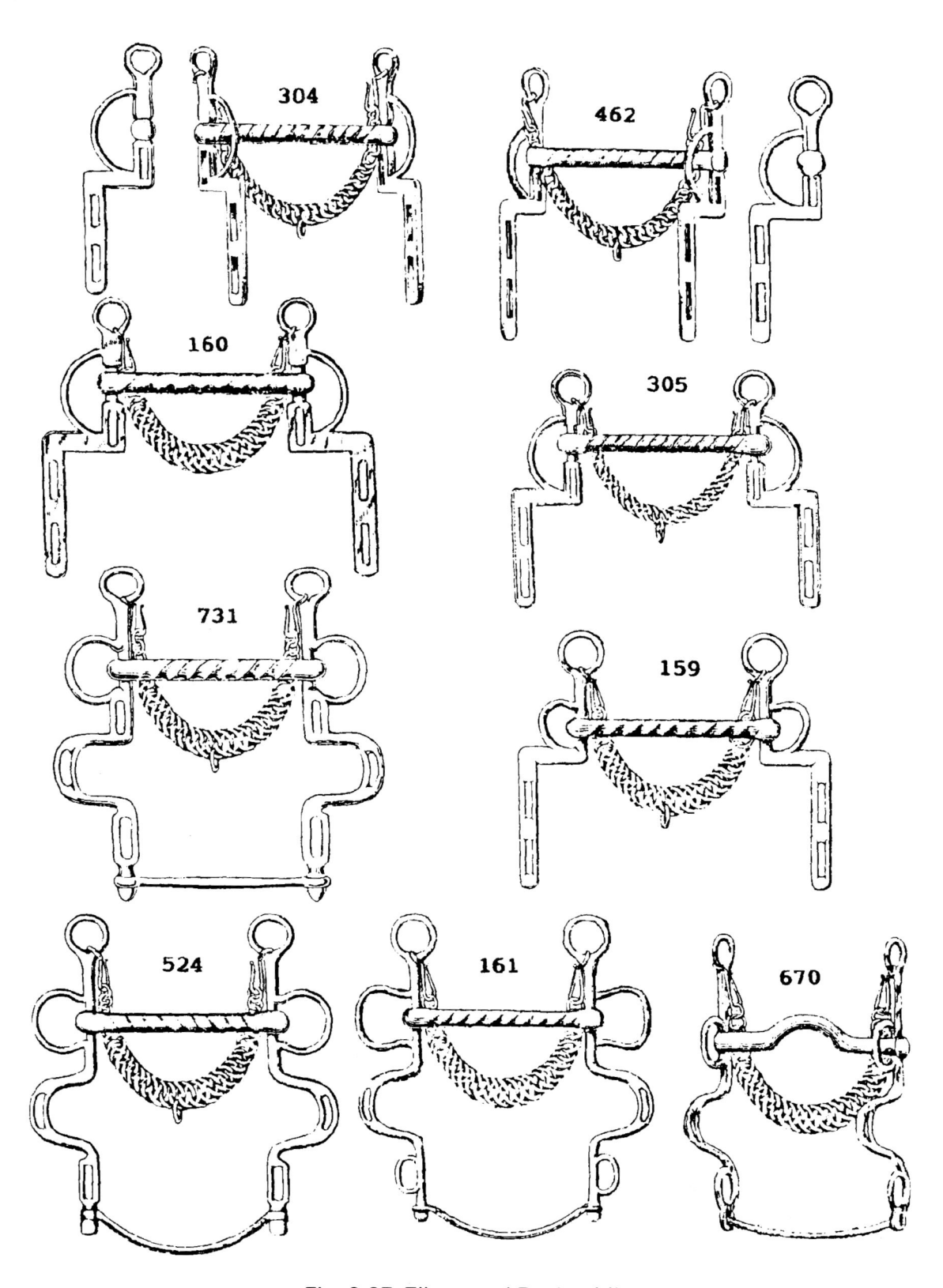

Fig. 8.27 Elbow and Buxton bits.

Elbow and Buxton Bits [Fig. 8.28] from John Dewsbury and Son Catalogue, circa 1905.

473   Extra Stout Ballon Cheek, Jointed Mouth Driving Bit and Curb.

307   Sliding Half-twisted Barmouth Duke of York Driving Bit and Curb.

306   Sliding Mullen Mouth Prince of Wales Driving Bit and Curb.

315   Sliding Half-twisted 1/2 in. Barmouth Connected Ballon Cheek Driving Bit and Curb.

316   Globe Cheek Driving Bit and Curb.

317   Half-twisted 9/16 in. Barmouth Sliding Stout London Cab Bit and Curb. Light Model with 1/2 in. Barmouth.

199   2 Loop Low Port Stage Bit and Curb.

2203   2 Loop Low Port Gig Bit and Curb, Large Eye.

470   Fancy Cheek Sliding Arch 9/16 in. Mouth Driving Bit and Curb.

471   Fancy Cheek Sliding Half-twisted 1/2 in. Mouth Driving Bit and Curb.

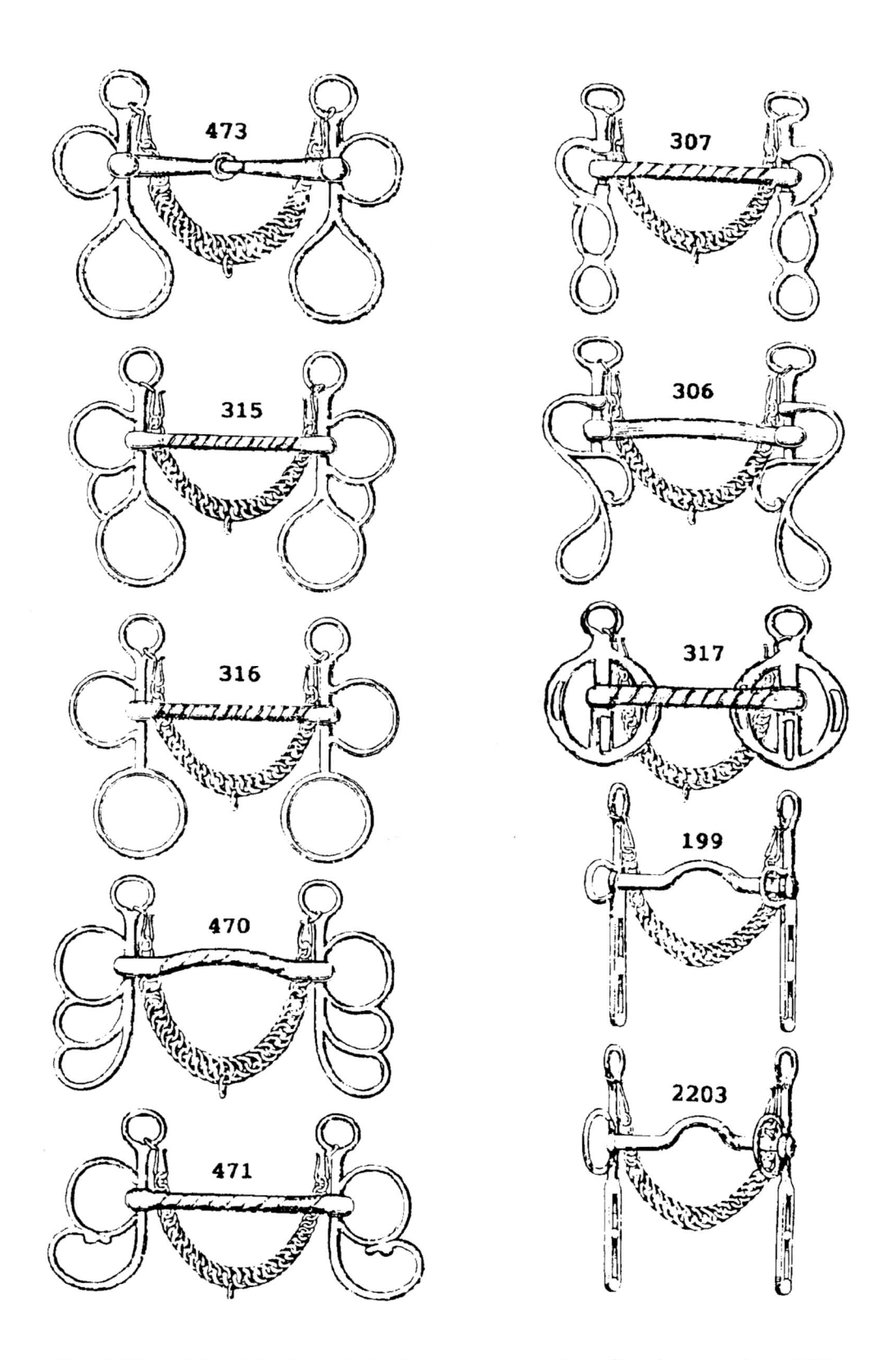

Fig. 8.28 Driving bits from John Dewsbury and Son Catalogue, circa 1905.

Dewsbury Driving Bits continued [Fig. 8.29].

1006	Stout Half-twisted Sliding 9/16 in. Mouth Ballon Cheek Driving Bit and Curb. Made in Light Pattern with 1/2 in Mouth.
6605	Stout 9/16 in. Mouth Fancy Cheek Driving Bit and Curb.
6604	Light 1/2 in. Mouth Fancy Cheek Driving Bit and Curb.
1033	Turn Cheek Mullen Mouth Driving Bit and Curb.
1034	Egg-butt Turn Cheek Mullen Mouth Driving Bit and Curb.
6608	Sliding Mullen Mouth Driving Bit and Curb.
6643	Sliding Mullen Mouth Driving Bit and Curb.
6642	Sliding Mullen Mouth Driving Bit and Curb.
6610	Half-twisted 9/16 in. Barmouth Driving Bit and Curb.
442	Fancy Cheek Low Port Mouth Riding Bit with Noblico Head and Curb.
5052	Fancy Cheek 2 Loop Driving Bit and Curb, with Bent Bottom Bar.
1038	Sliding Mullen Mouth Fancy Cheek Riding Bit and Curb.

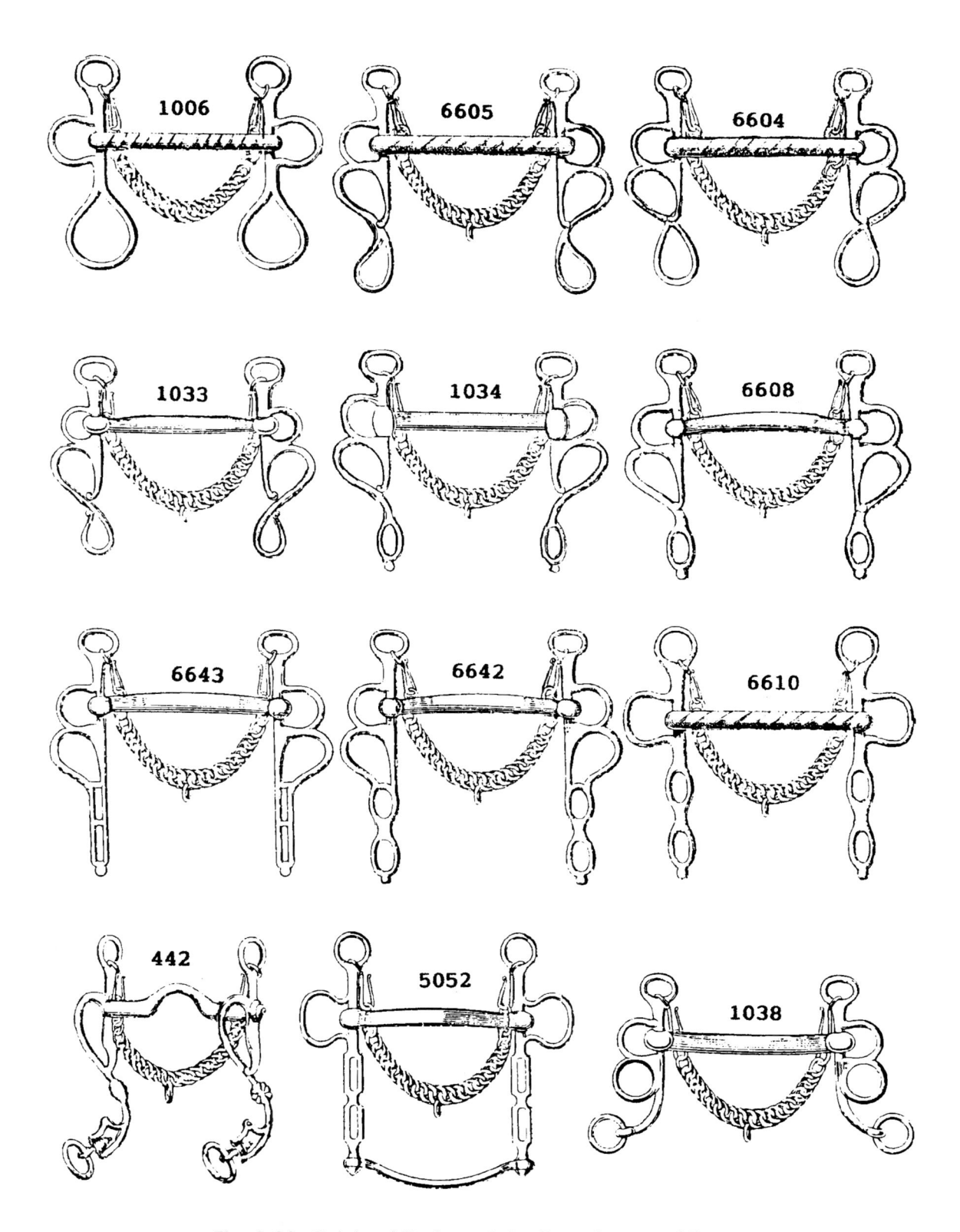

Fig. 8.29 Driving bits from John Dewsbury and Son.

Jointed—*No. 103.* Stiff—*No. 104.*

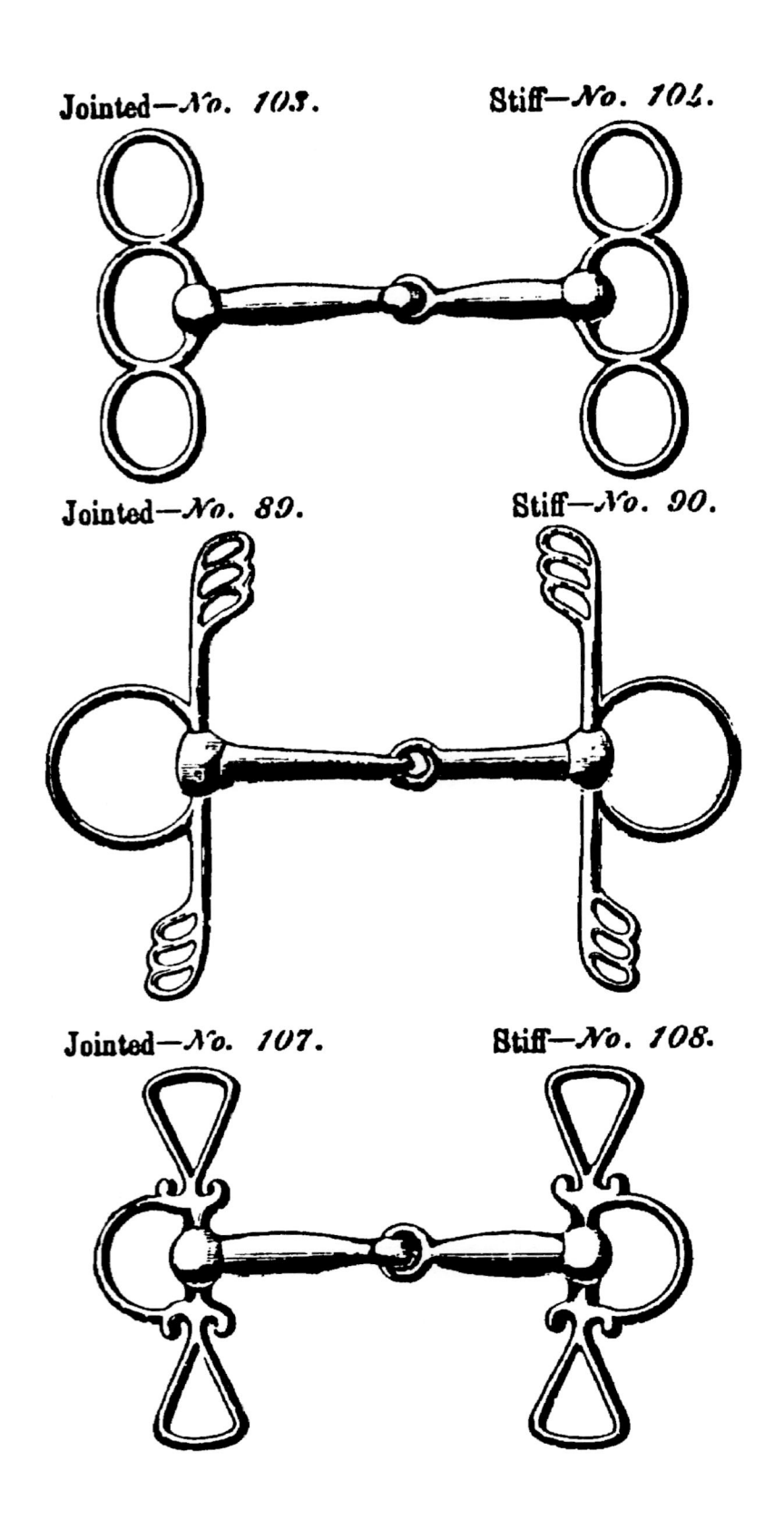

Jointed—*No. 89.* Stiff—*No. 90.*

Jointed—*No. 107.* Stiff—*No. 108.*

Fig. 8.30   Fancy cheek driving bits from O. B. North and Co. Catalogue circa 1885.

Crown
Japanned or Bright-plated

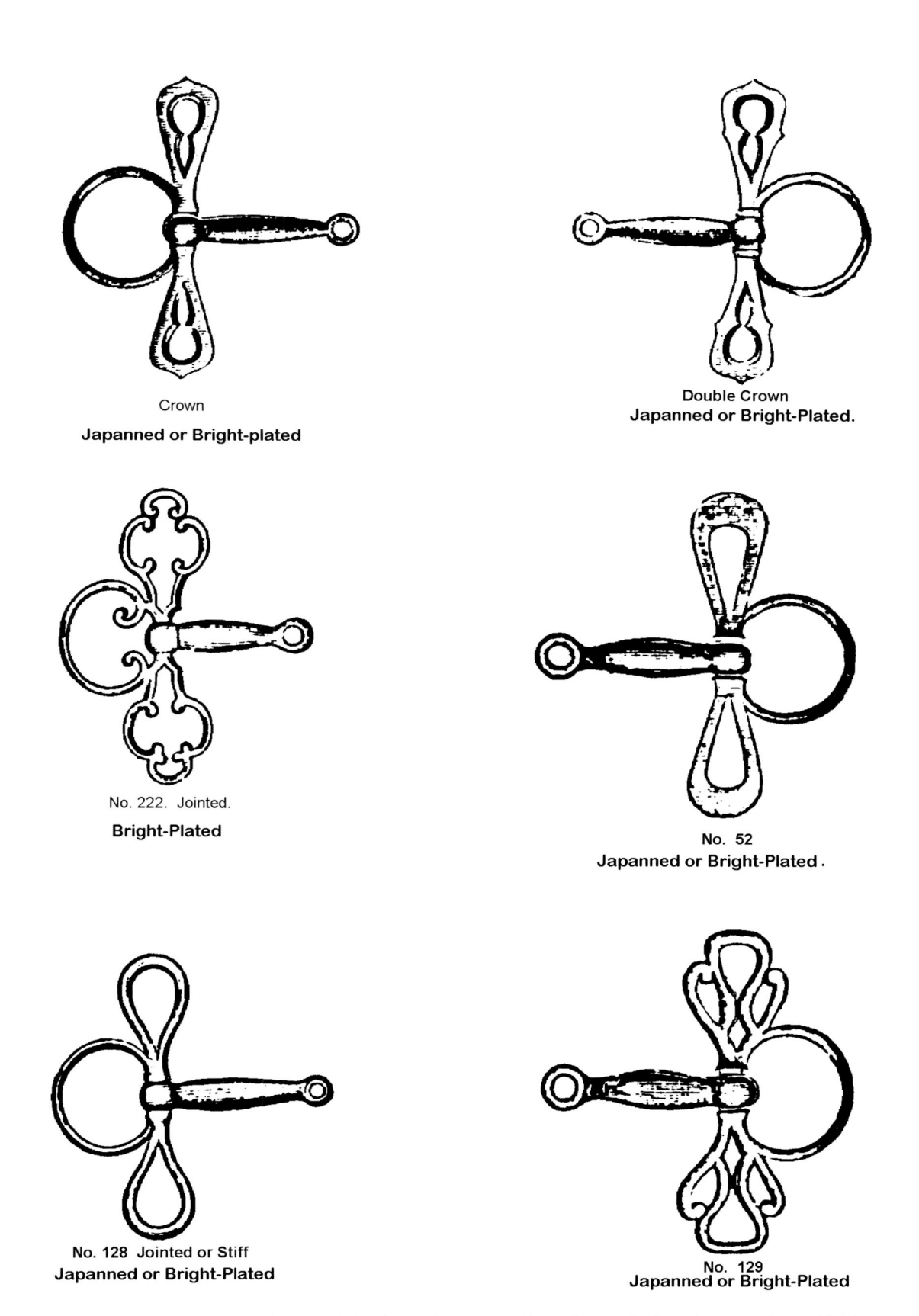

Double Crown
Japanned or Bright-Plated.

No. 222. Jointed.
Bright-Plated

No. 52
Japanned or Bright-Plated.

No. 128 Jointed or Stiff
Japanned or Bright-Plated

No. 129
Japanned or Bright-Plated

Fig. 8.31 Fancy cheek driving bits from Pratt and Letchworth Catalogue circa 1900.

No. 130
Japanned or Bright-Plated.

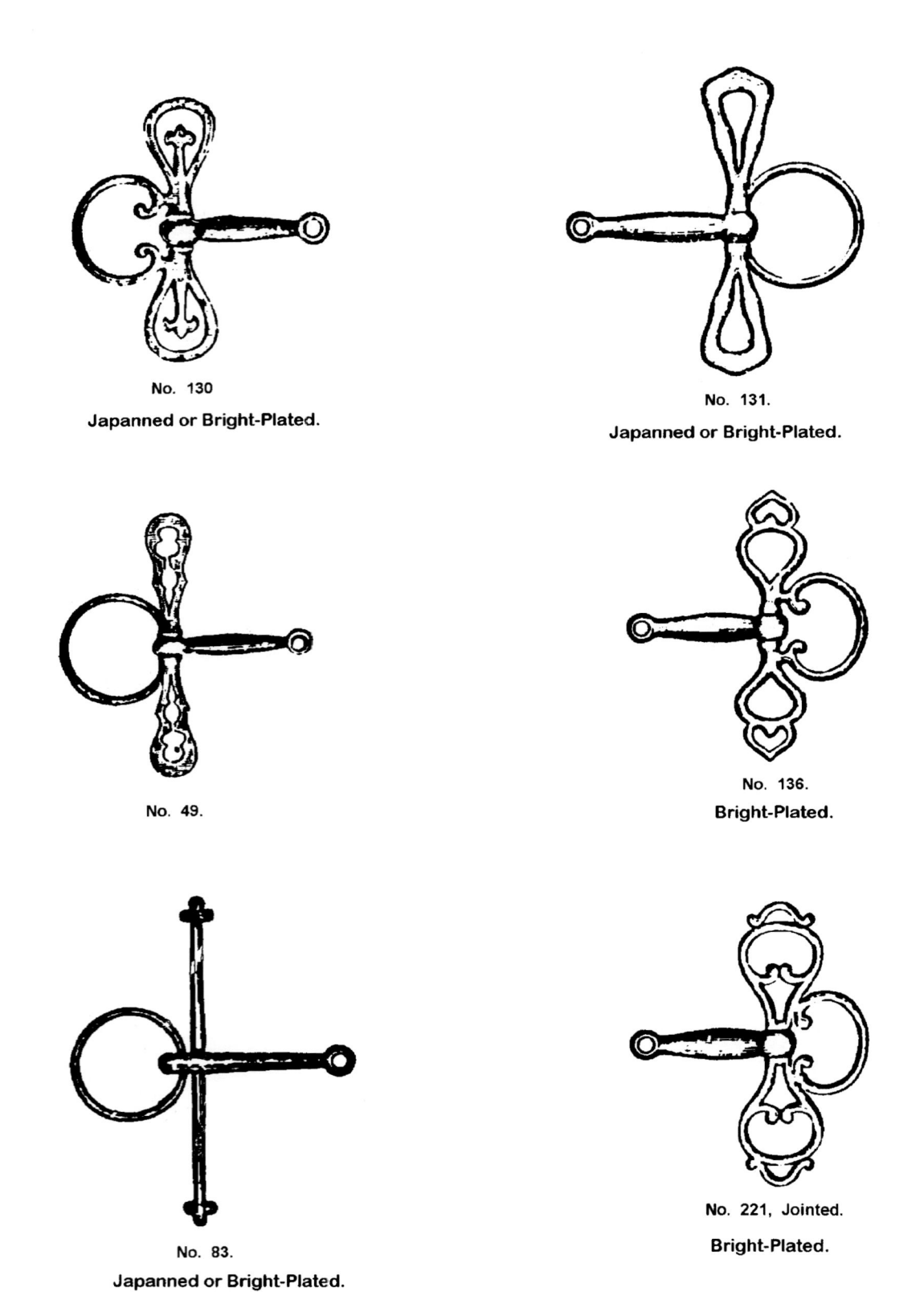

No. 131.
Japanned or Bright-Plated.

No. 49.

No. 136.
Bright-Plated.

No. 83.
Japanned or Bright-Plated.

No. 221, Jointed.
Bright-Plated.

Fig. 8.32 Fancy driving and riding snaffle bits from Pratt and Letchworth's Catalogue circa 1900.

No. 206.

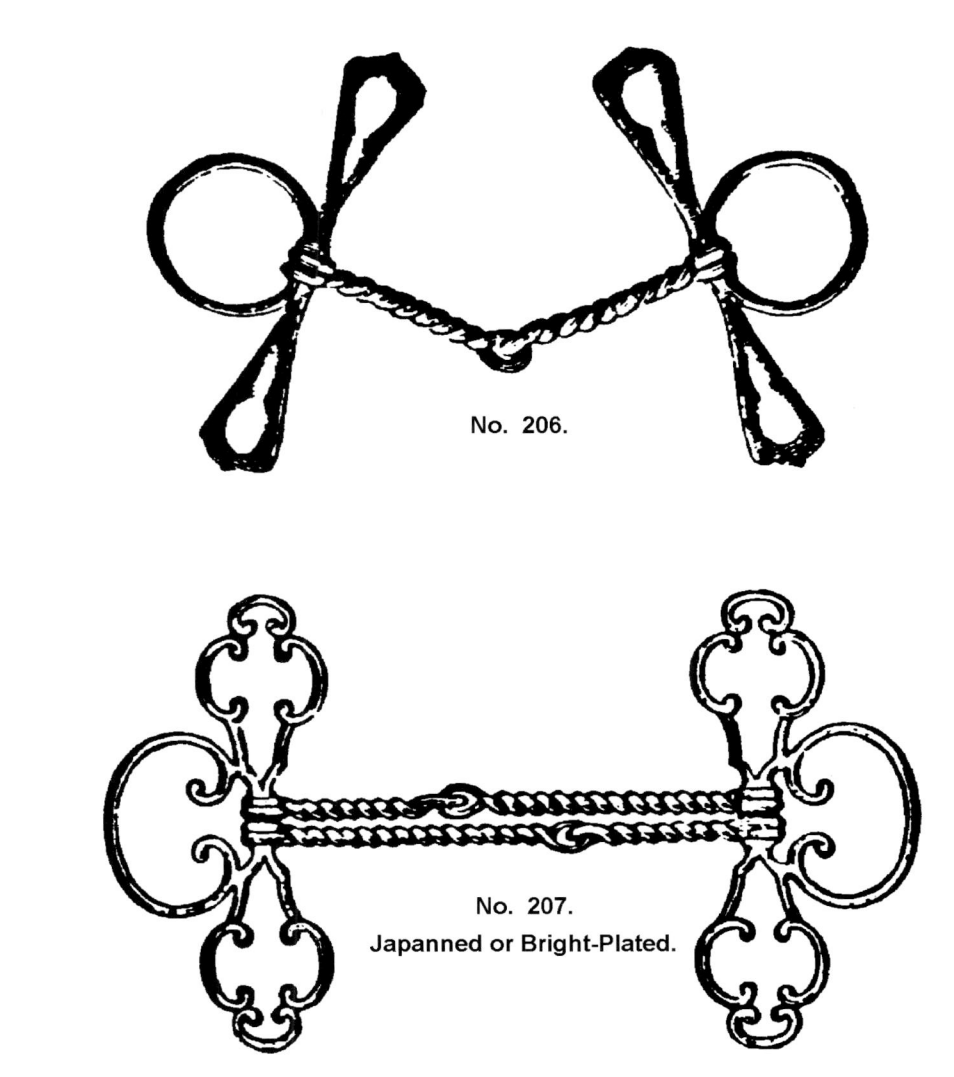

No. 207.
Japanned or Bright-Plated.

Fig. 8. 33 Wire-mouth fancy cheek driving bits.

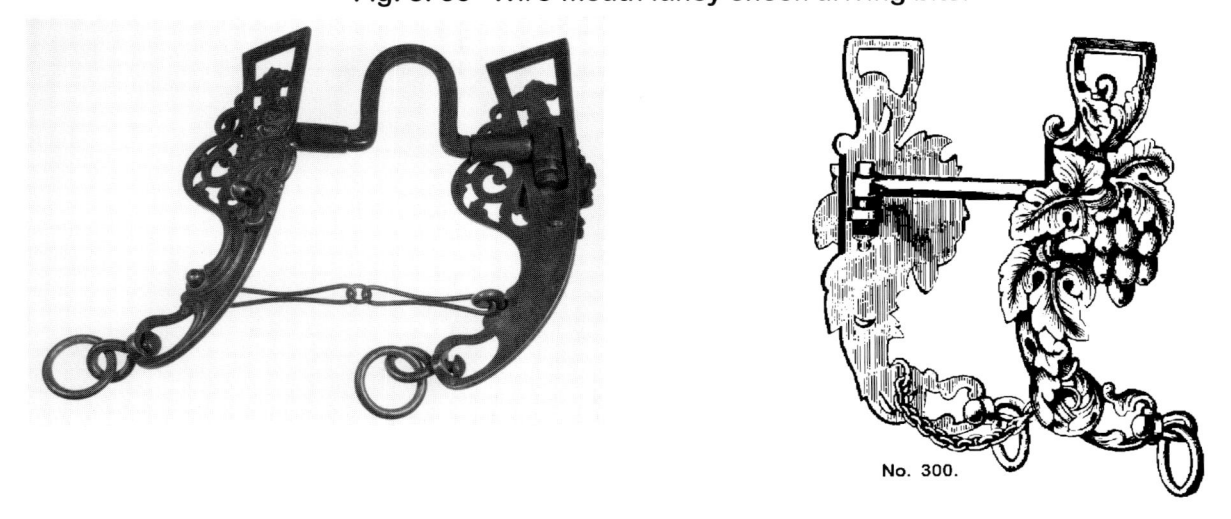

No. 300.

Fig. 8. 34 Ornate cheek bit of the construction style of Linden and Funke, GR.

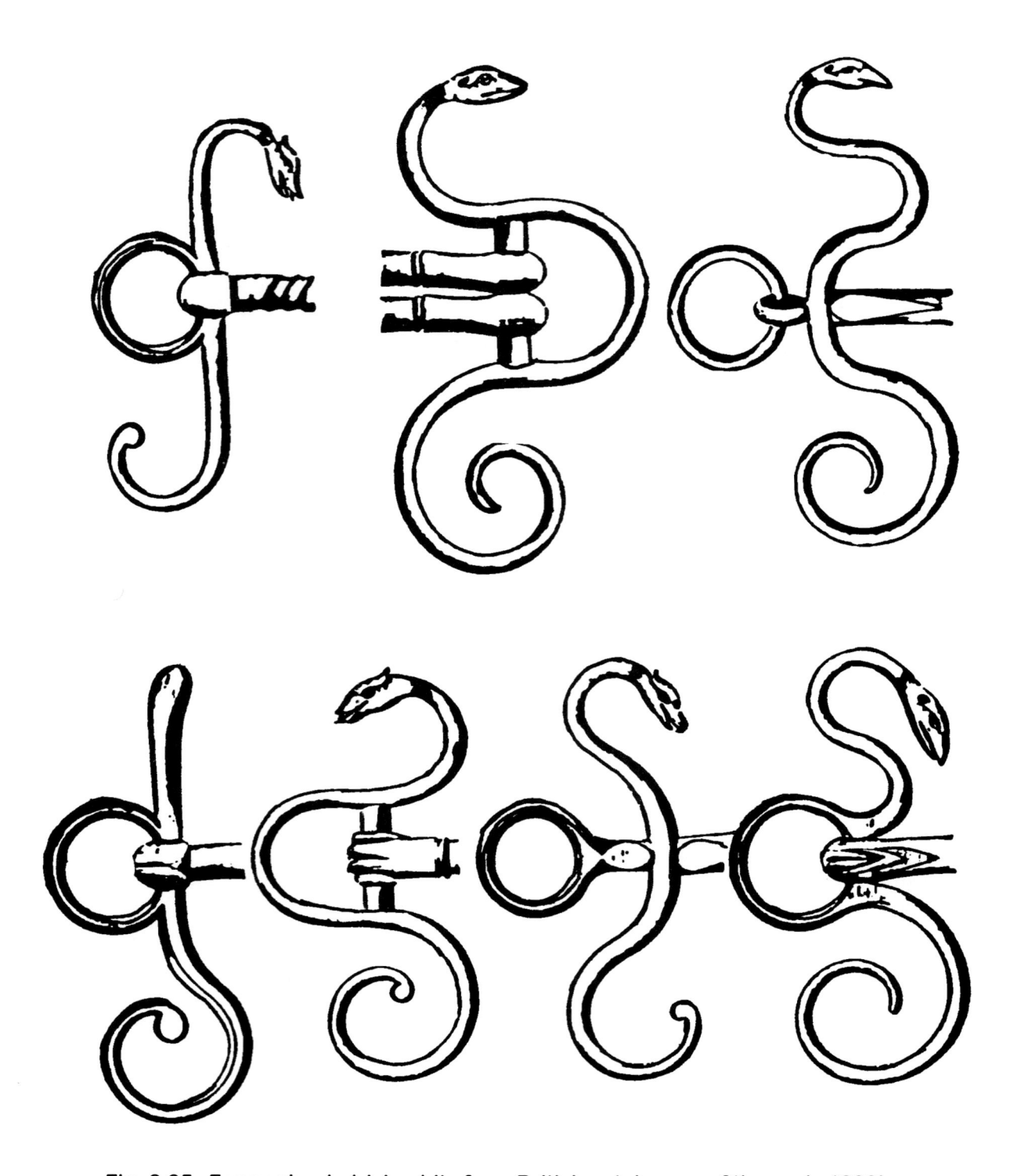

Fig. 8.35 Fancy cheek driving bits from British catalogues of the early 1800's.

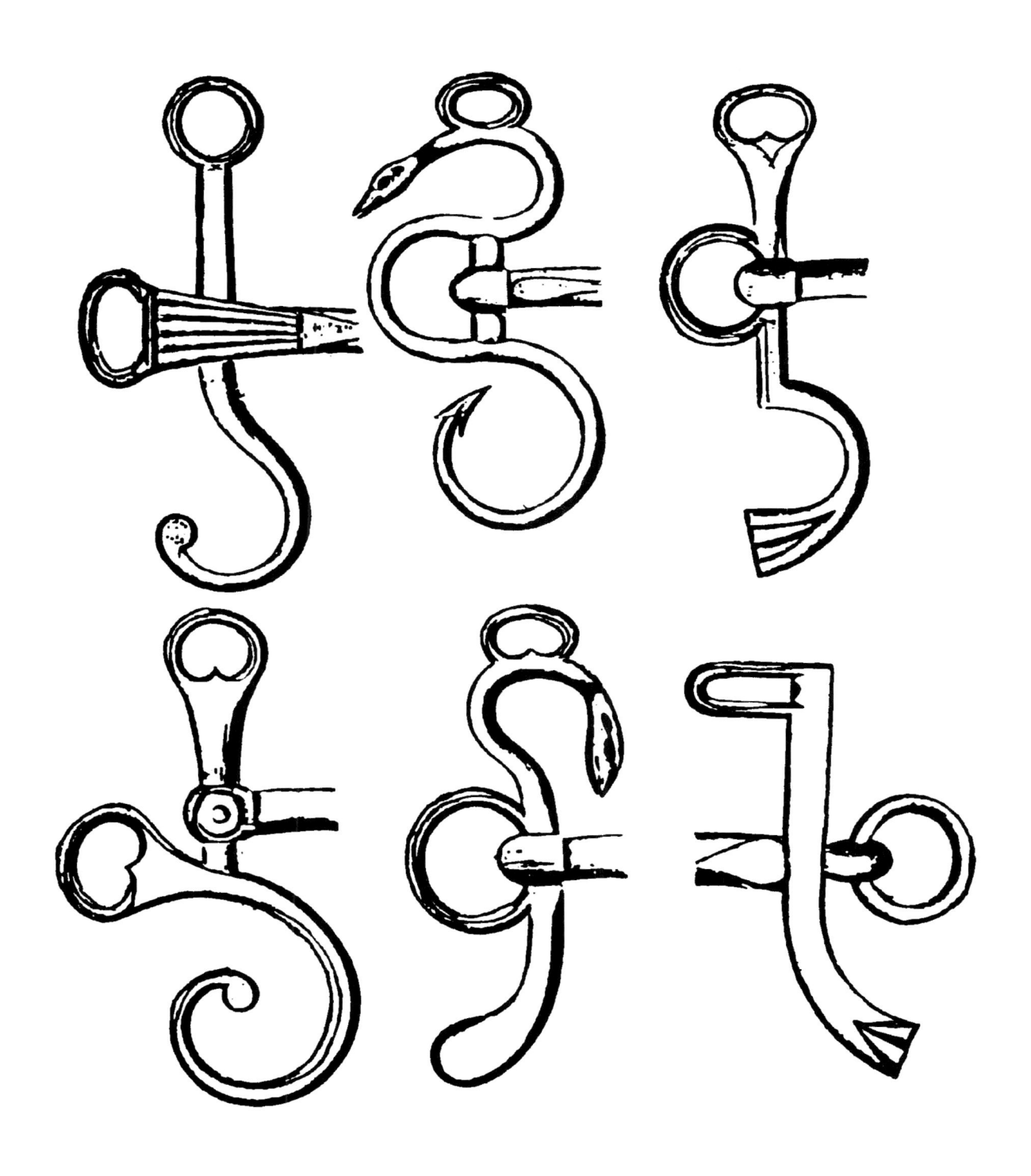

Fig. 8.36 Fancy cheek driving bits from British catalogues of early 1800's.

Jointed No. 101.
Stiff No. 107.

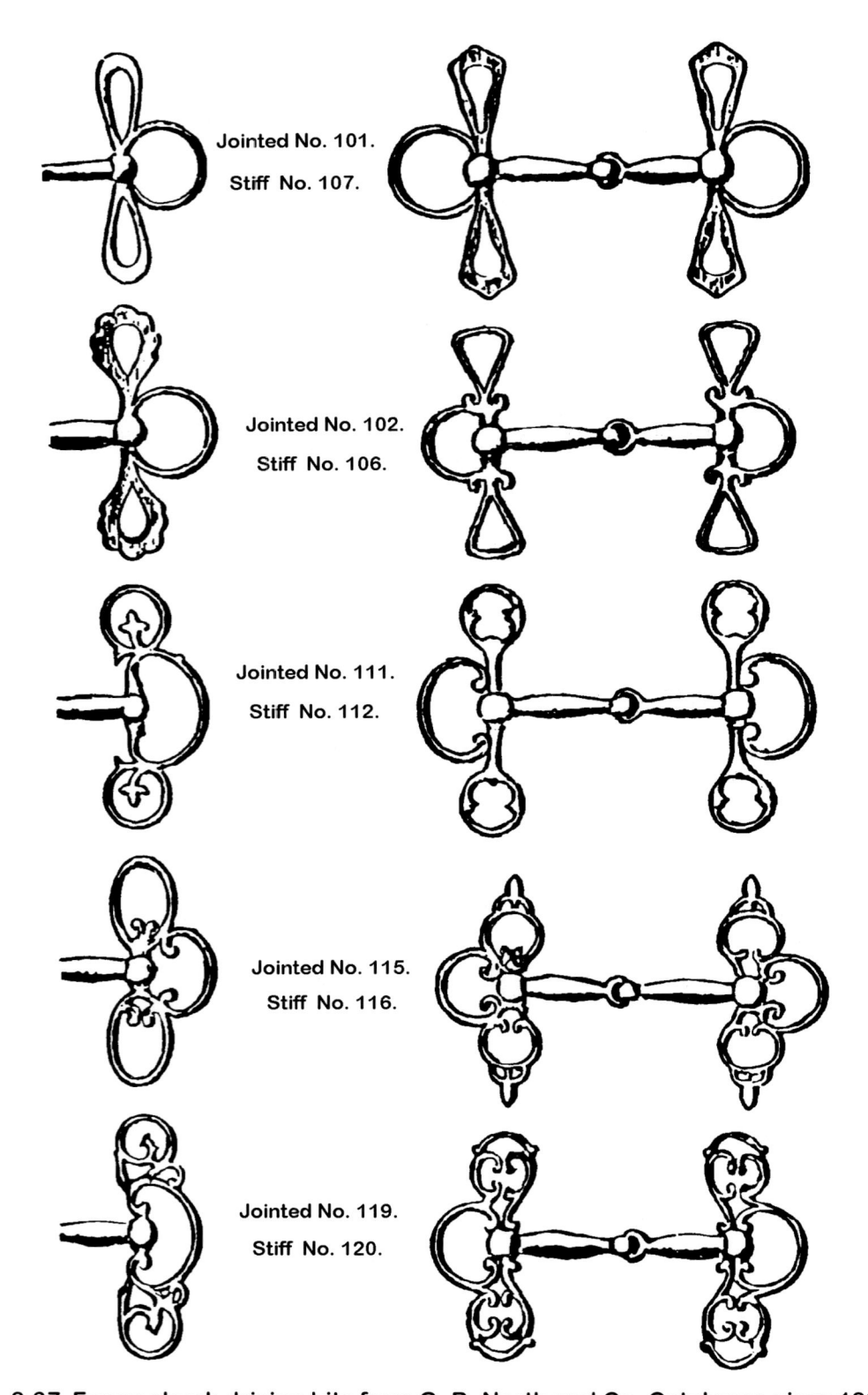

Jointed No. 102.
Stiff No. 106.

Jointed No. 111.
Stiff No. 112.

Jointed No. 115.
Stiff No. 116.

Jointed No. 119.
Stiff No. 120.

Fig. 8.37 Fancy cheek driving bits from O. B. North and Co. Catalogue circa 1885.

Jointed No. 121.

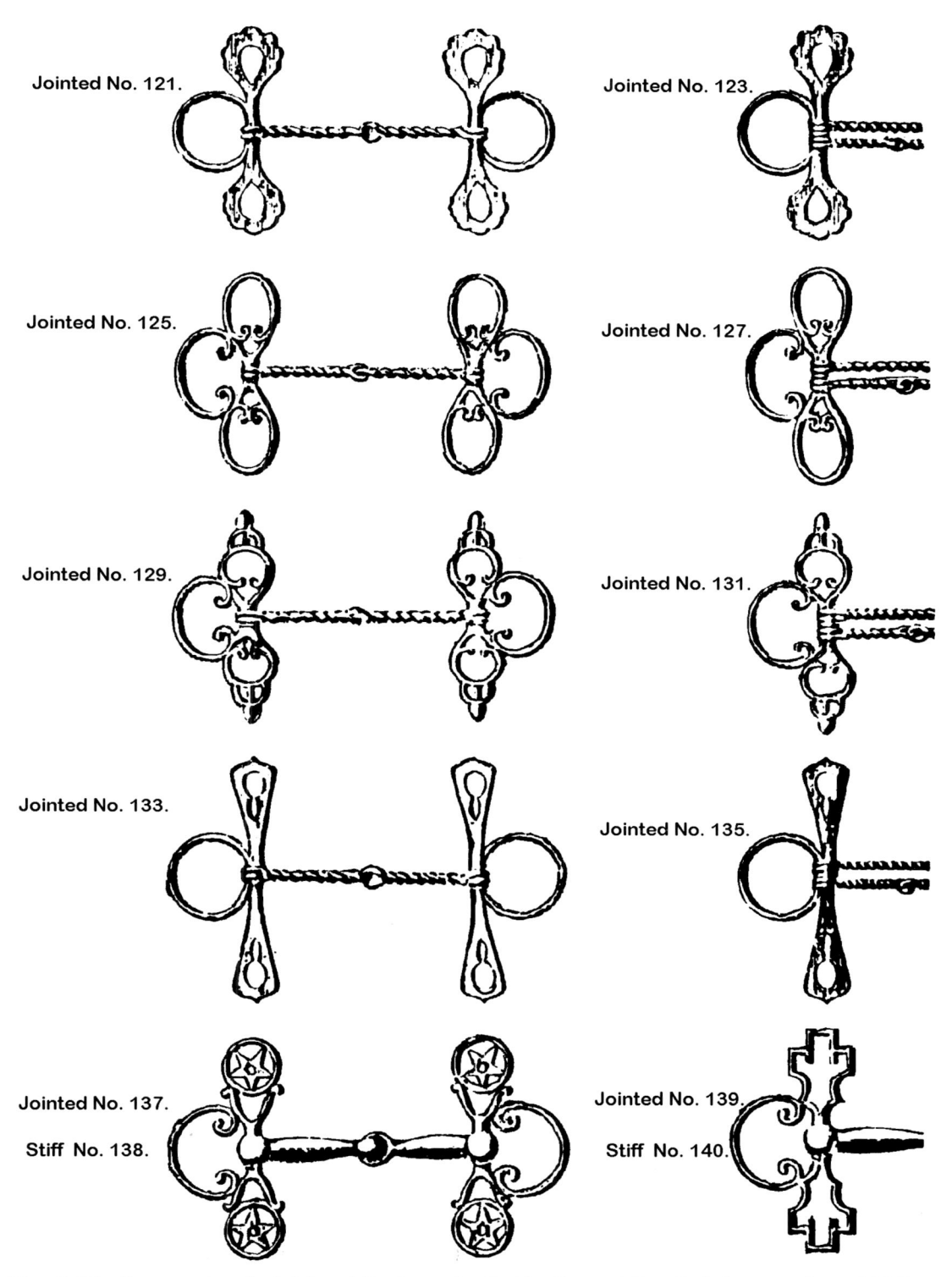

Jointed No. 123.

Jointed No. 125.

Jointed No. 127.

Jointed No. 129.

Jointed No. 131.

Jointed No. 133.

Jointed No. 135.

Jointed No. 137.
Stiff No. 138.

Jointed No. 139.
Stiff No. 140.

Fig. 8.38 Fancy cheek driving bits from O. B. North and Co. Catalogue circa 1885.

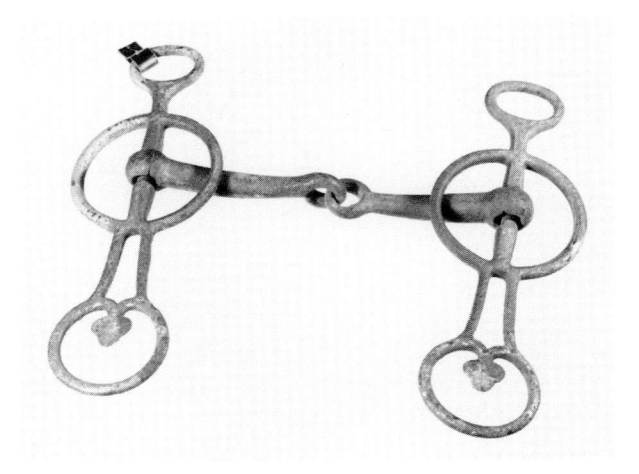

Fig. 8.39 Ornamental cheek bit.

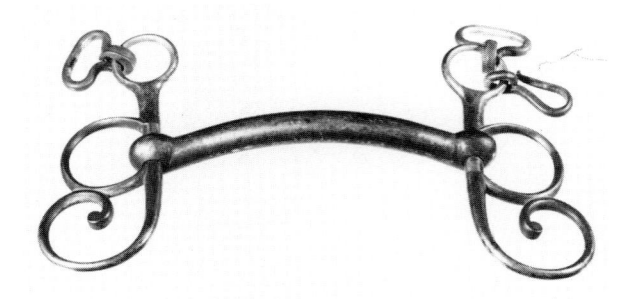

Fig. 8.40 Bit similar to No. 471, Fig. 8.28.

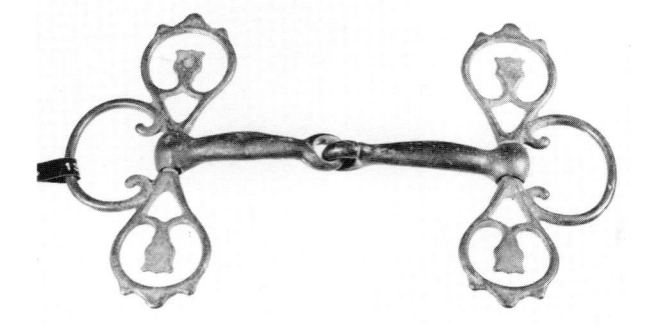

Fig. 8.41 Fancy cheek driving bit.

Fig. 8.42 Six-point star-cheek snaffle bit.

Fig. 8.43 Eagle-cheek snaffle bit.

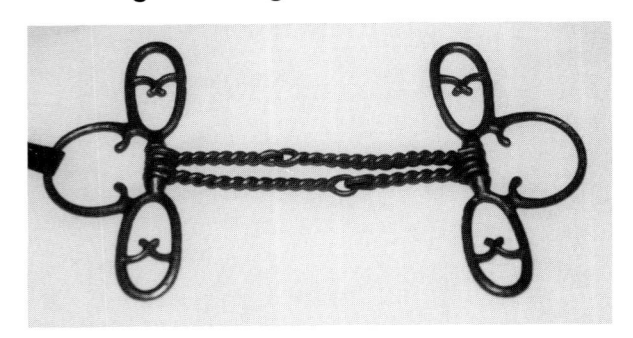

Fig. 8.44 Fancy cheek double twisted-wire snaffle bit.

Fig. 8.45 American shield-cheek snaffle bit.

Fig. 8.46 Fancy cheek snaffle bit.

Fig. 8.47 Snaffle bit with twisted-wire cheeks and mouth-piece.

Fig. 8.48 Fancy cheek snaffle bit.

Fig. 8.49 Fancy half-cheek snaffle bit with twisted-wire mouth-piece.

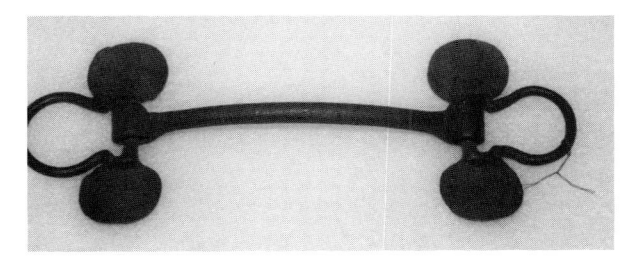

Fig. 8.50 Snaffle bit with paddle cheeks.

Fig. 8.51 Full-cheek snaffle bit. Jean Gayle collection. Photo by Jones Photo.

Fig. 8.52 A fancy cheek snaffle bit.

Fig. 8.53 Fancy cheek snaffle bit.

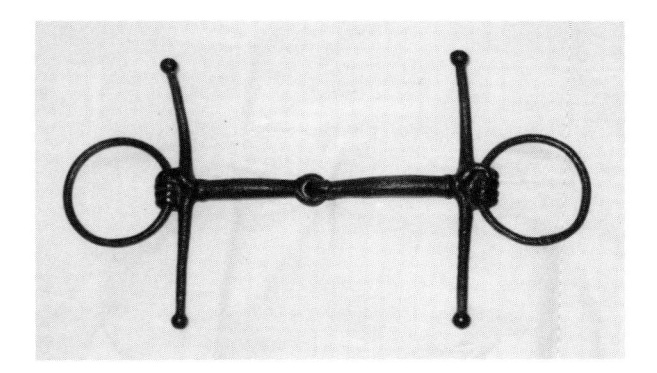

Fig. 8.54 A snaffle bit with the ring holders in the shape of a human hand.

Fig. 8.55 Fancy cheek snaffle bit. Jean Gayle collection. Photo by Jones Photo.

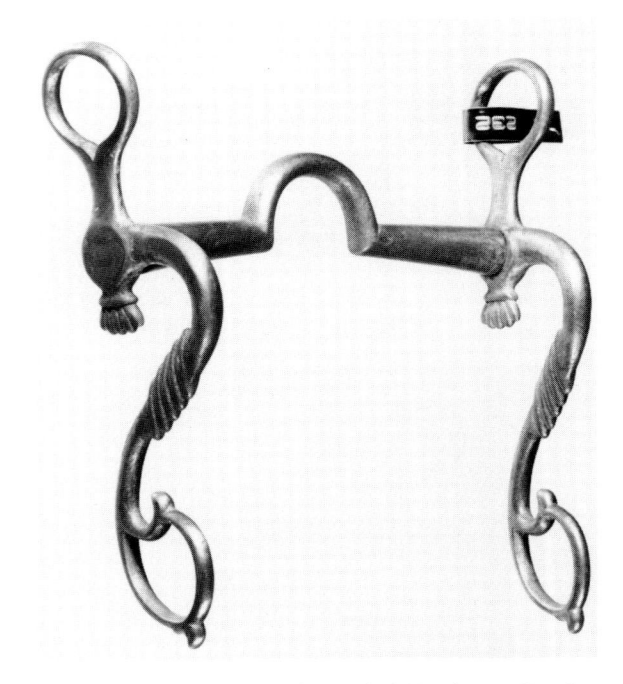

Fig. 8.57 Fancy cheek curb bit. Jean Gayle collection. Photo by Jones Photo.

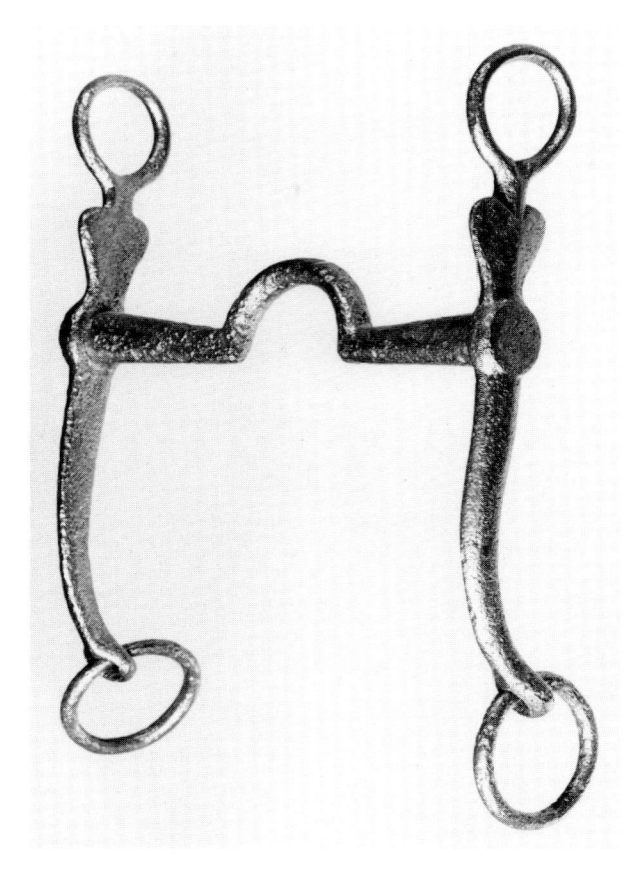

Fig. 8.56 An old curb bit with a heart-shaped upper cheek-piece. Jean Gayle collection. Photo by Jones Photo.

Figures 8.39, 8.40, 8.41, 8.51, 8.55, and 8.58 Jean Gayle collection. Photos by Jones Photo. Figures 8.42, 8.43, 8.44, 8.45 and 8.52 Robert Maclin collection. Figure 8.54 Lloyd Shultz collection. Figures 8.47, 8.48, and 8.50 Kentucky Horse Park archives.

Fig. 8.58 Fancy cheek curb bit. Jean Gayle collection. Photo by Jones Photo.

CHAPTER NINE
Driving Bits-Overcheck

The overcheck bit is an accessory bit, smaller and lighter in weight, and used in association with snaffle bits to maintain head carriage of the horse. They are not commonly used today with the advent of western and pleasure styles of riding and decrease in the use of driving horses. They are still being used primarily on trotting horses and for the most part do not come into the realm of usage by the ordinary horse user. Overcheck bits require knowledgable trainers and users to achieve the results required. As such, overcheck bits should be left alone by most users unless there is a definite necessity and then the user should seek advice from a person skilled in their use.

Agen Overcheck Bit: Name applied to the Grosvenor Overcheck [Fig. 9.5] by A. Buermann Mfg. Co. No. 245, cast steel; No. 1246, "Star Steel Silver;" No. 2460 Non-corrosive Silver or Gold.

Bentmouth Overcheck Bit: See Swales Fig. 9.20.

Best Out Overcheck: Name given to Henry Maxwell Overcheck by Hayden & Allen of St. Louis.

Bicycle Chain Overcheck: An overcheck resembling a bicycle chain [Fig. 9.0].

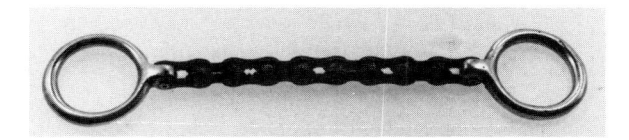

Fig. 9.0 Bicycle chain overcheck.

Burch, Charles H., Copake, NY, Patent No. 986,044, Mar. 7, 1911 [Fig. 9.1].

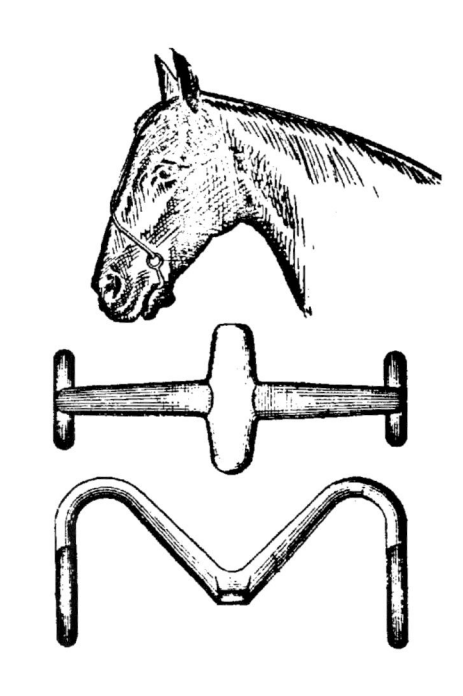

Fig. 9.1 Burch overcheck bit.

Campbell-Alonzo Bit: See Chapter 6, Fig. 6.3.

Carter Overdraw Bit: See Chapter 6, Fig. 6.9.

Case Overcheck: See Chapter 6, Fig. 6.10.

Crabb, Lindsay T., Eminence, KY, Patent No. 434,703, Aug. 19, 1890 [Figs. 9.2 and 9.2a].

Crit Davis, Harrodsburg, KY, Patent Aug. 21, 1888 [Fig. 9.3].

Duncan Overcheck: See Chapter 8, Fig. 8.9.

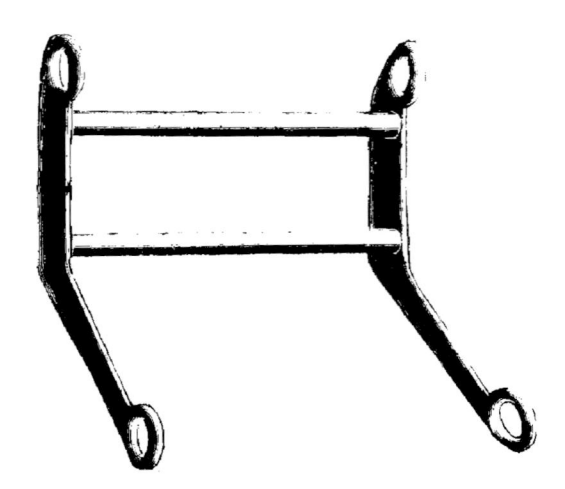

Fig. 9.2 Crabb overcheck bit.

Fig. 9.2a Crabb overcheck with spoon.

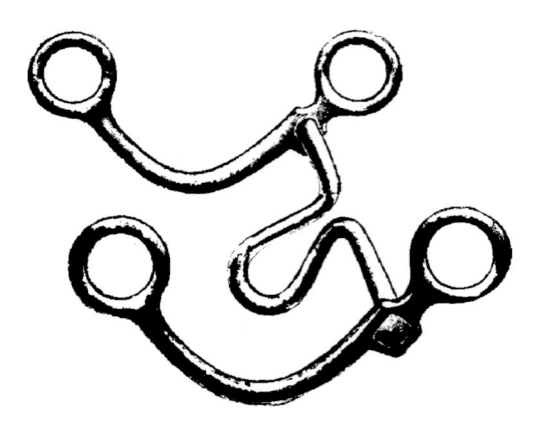

Fig. 9.3 Crit Davis overcheck bit.

English Head Check Bit: Figure 9.4.

Fig. 9.4 English Head check bit.

Gallagher Overcheck: See Chapter 12, Fig. 12.21.

Greenwood Overcheck Bit: See Chapter 12, Fig. 12.42.

Grosvenor Overcheck: Figures 9.5. and 9.5a.

Fig. 9.5 Grosvenor overcheck.

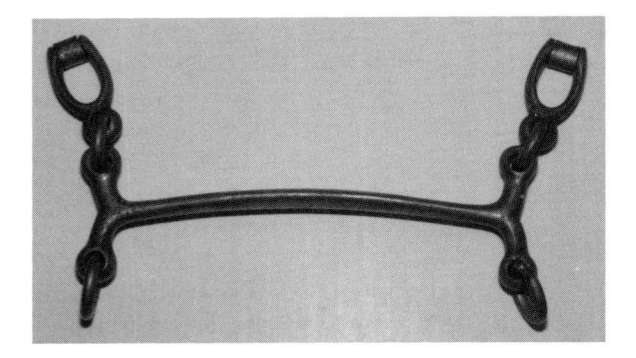

Fig. 9.5a Grosvenor overcheck with pulleys.

Hack Overcheck: A jointed bradoon bit with small rein-rings.

Henry, B. Taylor, New Haven, CT, Patent No. 229-886, July 13, 1880 [Fig. 9.6]. A check bit, sole purpose

136

to check the horse, used together with a reining bit.

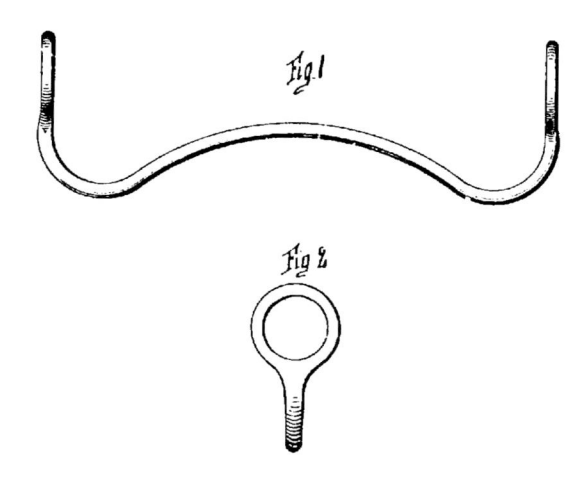

Fig. 9.6 Henry check bit.

Hogan, Dora H. Chicago, IL, Patent No. 1,034,452, Aug. 6, 1912 [Fig. 9.7]. The bit is placed between the upper lip and the teeth of the upper jaw with the bar behind the wolf teeth and in front of the molars of the upper jaw.

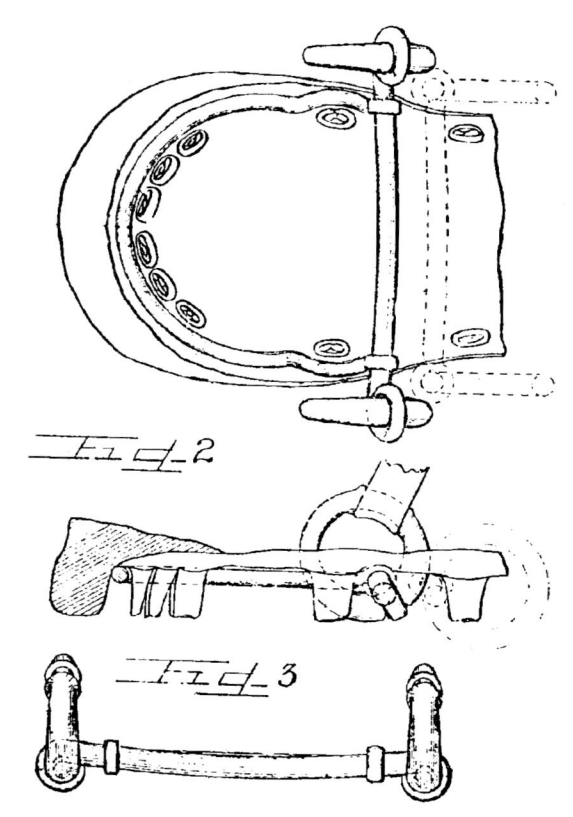

Fig. 9.7 Hogan overcheck.

Hutton Overcheck: Figure 9.8.

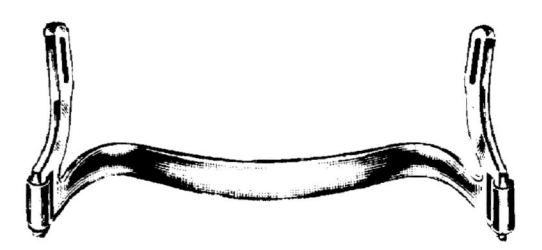

Fig. 9.8 Hutton overcheck.

Jointed Pattern Overcheck: Refers to the jointed mouth-piece.

McKerron Overcheck: Figure 9.9.

Maxwell, Henry C., Rome, NY, Patent No. 269,304, Dec. 19, 1882 [Fig. 9.10]

Fig. 9.9 McKerron overcheck

Maxwell Overcheck Bit: From Haydens & Allen Catalog [Fig. 9.11].

137

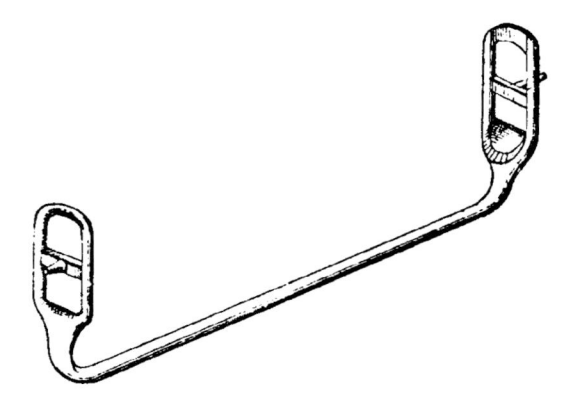

Fig. 9.10 Maxwell overcheck bit.

Fig. 9.11 Maxwell overcheck bit.

Morrey, Edward, Paterson, NJ, Patent No. 1,278,717, Sep. 10, 1918 [Fig. 9.12].

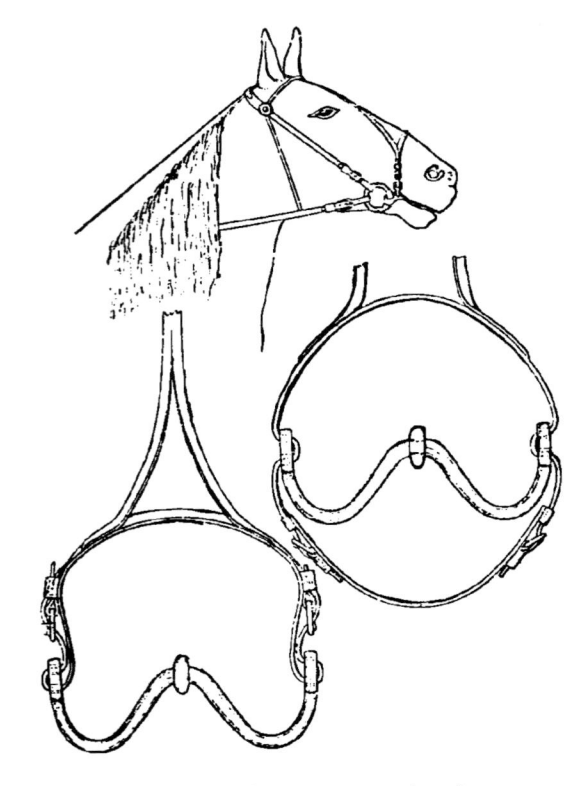

Fig. 9.12 Morrey overcheck.

Raymond Leverage Check: A head controller that works independently of the mouth bit [Fig. 9.13].

Rubber Ball Check: See Swales check, Fig. 9.21.

Rubber Overcheck Bradoon: Flexible rubber 5 1/2 inch mouth [Fig. 9.14].

Fig. 9.14 Rubber overcheck bradoon.

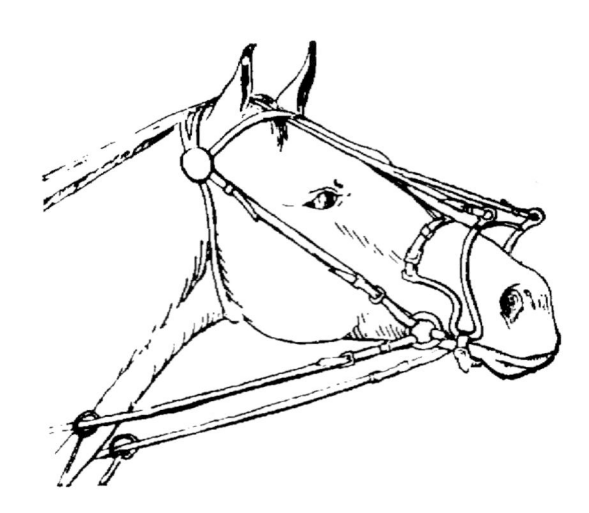

Fig. 9.13 Raymond leveraged check.

Sargeant Overcheck: A double-loop lever-check bit [Fig. 9.15].

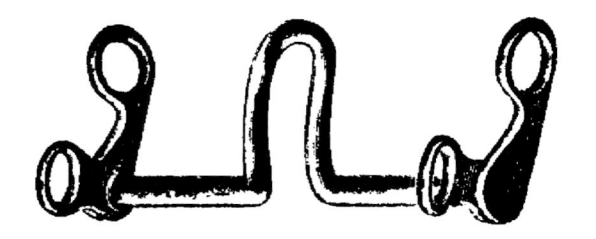

Fig. 9.15 Sargeant overcheck.

Shepard's Overcheck: A patent by Charles Henry Shepard, North Plainfield, NJ [Figs. 9.16, 9.16a and 9.17] No. 506,834, Oct. 17, 1893.

Fig. 9.16 Shepard's overcheck.

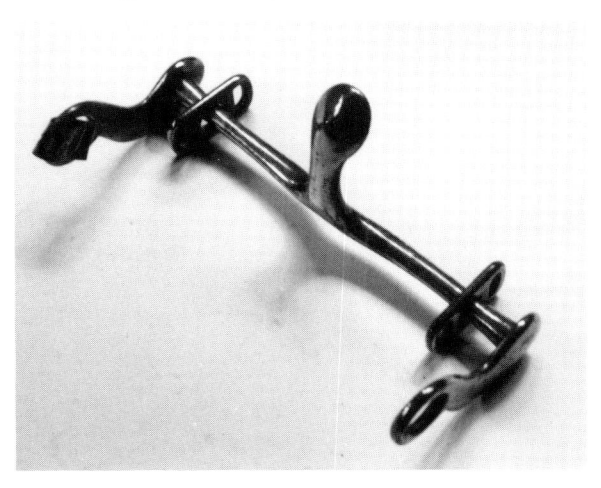

Fig. 9.16a Shepard overcheck production bit. Robert Maclin collection.

Fig. 9.17 Patent drawing of Shepard's overcheck bit.

Shepherd's Overcheck: Advertisers' spelling of Shepard.

Speedway Overcheck: Figure 9.18.

Fig. 9.18 Speedway overcheck.

Stendel Check Bit: Figure 9.19.

Fig. 9.19 Stendel overcheck bit.

Swales, Frank, London, England, Patent No. 531,230, Dec. 18, 1894 [Figs. 9.20, 9.21, 9.22 and 9.23]. A mouthpiece or check bit that can be attached by an India rubber-covered spring to the main mouth-piece of any ordinary liverpool or coach bit.

Fig. 9.20 Swales attachable check bit.

Fig. 9.21 Swales check bit with rubber balls attached.

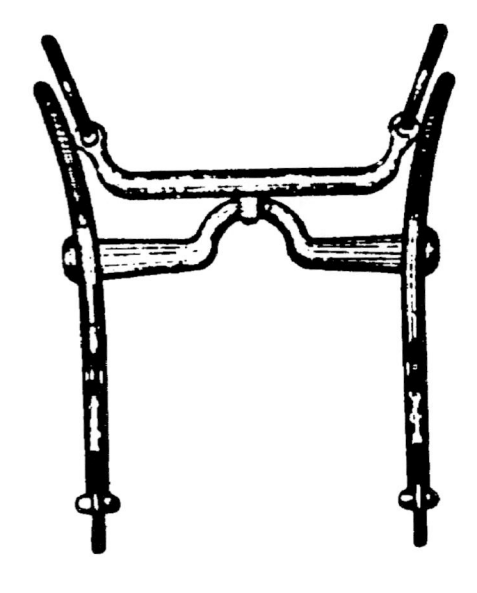

Fig. 9.23 Swales check bit attached to a coach bit.

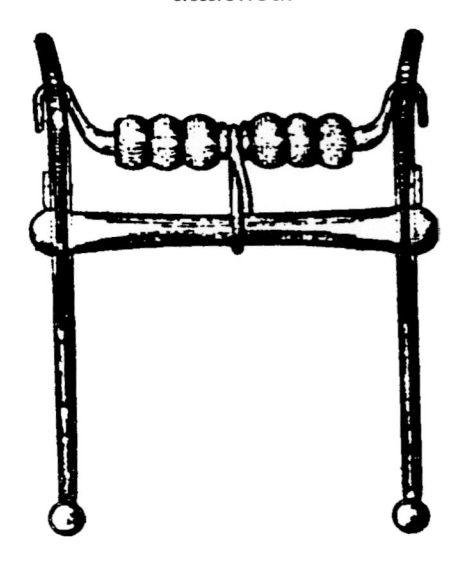

Fig. 9.22 Swales check bit attached to a coach bit.

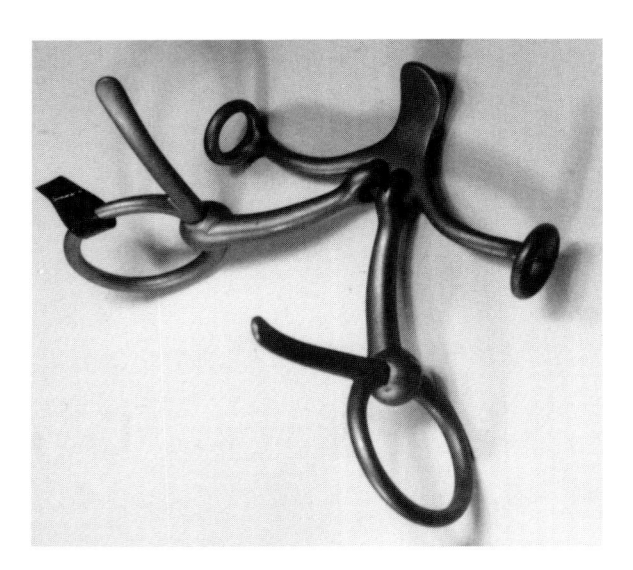

Fig. 9.24 A half-cheek snaffle with an attached overcheck. Robert Maclin collection.

CHAPTER TEN
Drown to Eyes

Drown, Charles W., Brattleboro, VT, Patent No. 709,700, Sep. 23, 1902 [Fig. 10.0]. A jointed bit with a center "bit-roll" which prevents the upward movement of the two cannons. The loose sliding cheek-rings provide for the attachment of the curb-strap, a nose-strap and check-reins if desired.

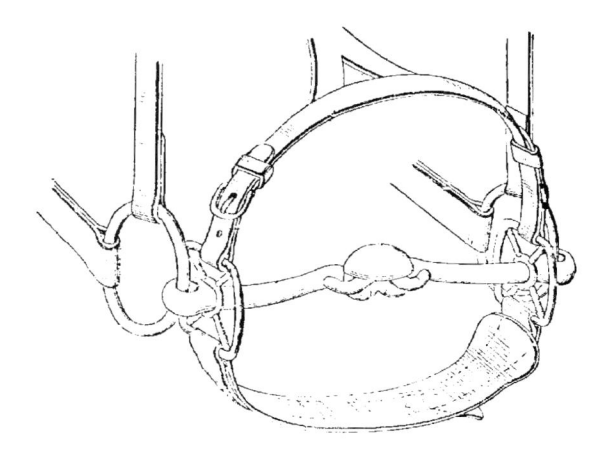

Fig. 10.0 Drown bit with center "bit-roll."

Dudley, George D., Lowell, MA, Patent No. 213,099, Mar. 11, 1879 [Fig. 10.1]. A bit constructed of heavy wire twisted to form the mouth-piece and cheek-pieces in a single unit. The mouth-piece was also made in a continuous twist.

Dumb Jockey: See Bitting Rig, Chapter 5, Fig. 5.58.

Dumpy Curb Bit: See Tom Thumb Curb, Chapter 33, Fig. 33.19.

Duncan Gag: See Gag Bits, Chapter 12.

Duncan, George T., Driving Bit: see Driving Bits, Chapter 8, Fig. 8.9.

Fig. 10.1 Dudley twisted-wire bit.

Dunks, Jesse C., Boulder, MT, Patent No. 856,574, June 11, 1907 [Fig. 10.2]. This bit features a figure-8 center link in the mouth-piece and double curb-chains that are attached to the reins.

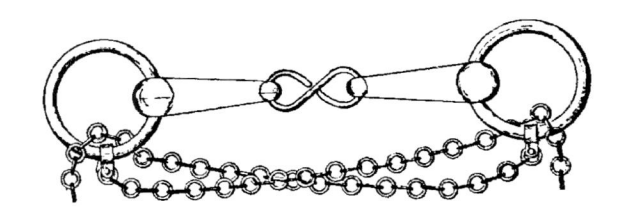

Fig. 10.2 Dunks double curb-chain bit.

Dunn, James M., Kingsville, MO, Patent No. 355,442 [Fig. 10.3]. A gag bit with a ratchetted lever to keep the mouth open when the gag is applied.

Dwyer Curb: A curb bit with the ratio dimensions described by Dwyer of 1:2 upper-cheek to lower-cheek [Fig. 10.4].

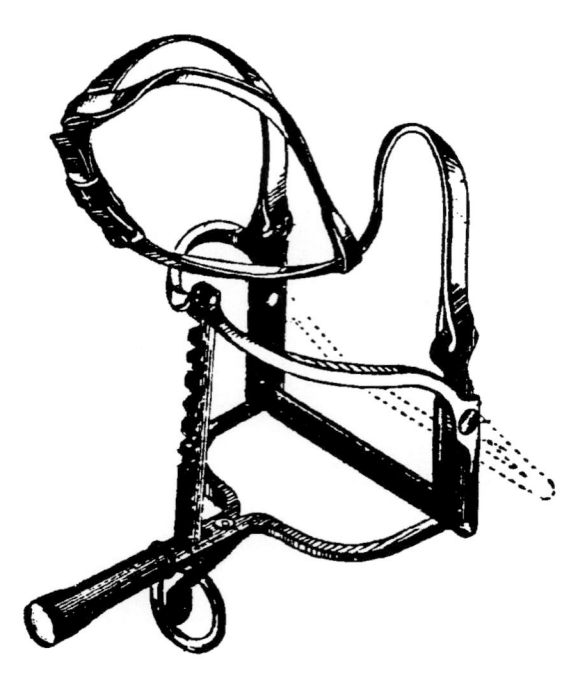

Fig. 10.3 Dunn gag bit.

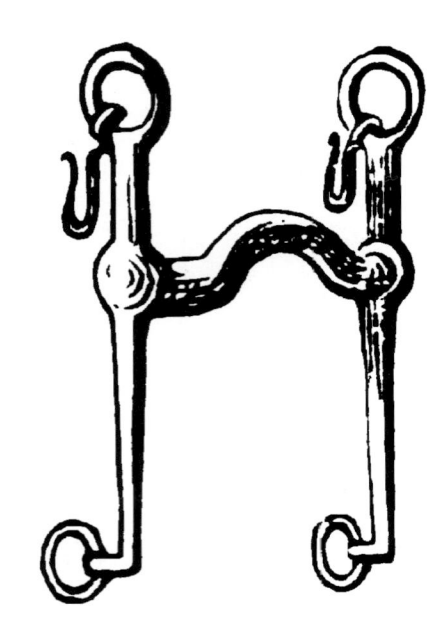

Fig. 10.4 Dwyer's bit.

Ear Bosses: Emblems or bosses attached to the bridle at the juncture of the brow-band and the headstall.

Earhart, Louis, Irwin, IN, Patent No. 177,822, May 23, 1876 [Fig. 10.5]. The three-section mouth-piece has loops in the two outer sections to accommodate snaps on the end of the face-strap.

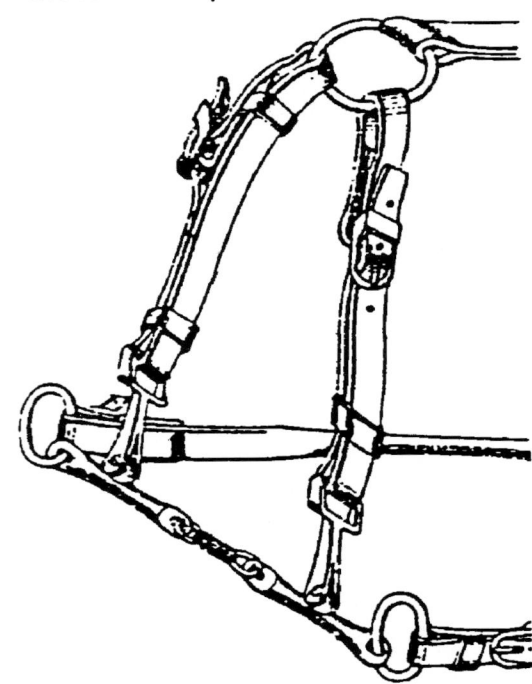

Fig. 10.5 Earhart snaffle bit.

Earl Shaw Special: A curb bit made by Wally Boone [Fig. 10.6]. Similar to the Rugby Pelham.

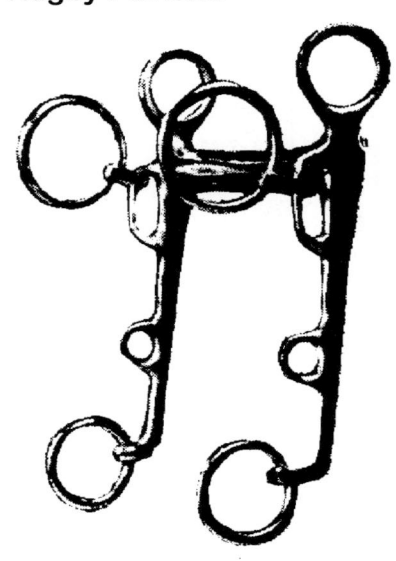

Fig. 10.6 Earl Shaw Special.

Eastwood, Abel, Bucyrus, OH. Patent No. 551,267, Dec. 10, 1895 [Fig.10.7]. A mouth-piece with a central arch and a spindle horizontally through the arch and cheek-pieces secured to the end of the spindle. Coiled springs secured in the cheek-pieces keep the spindle against the central arch until the reins are pulled.

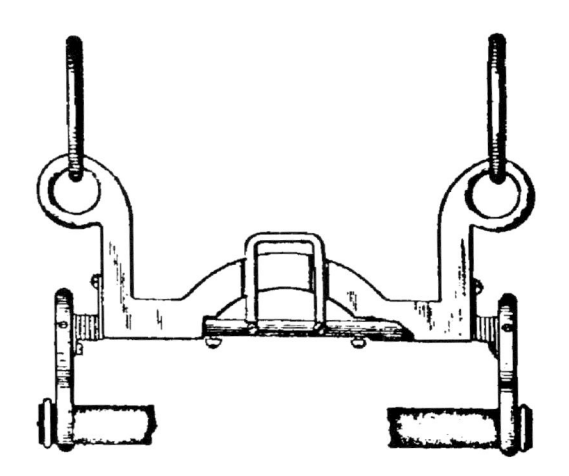

Fig. 10.7 Eastwood bit.

Eberhard, John G., Akron, OH, Patent No. 324,821, Aug. 25, 1885 [Fig. 10.8]. The bit has glass or china inserts lining the loops of the cheek-pieces.

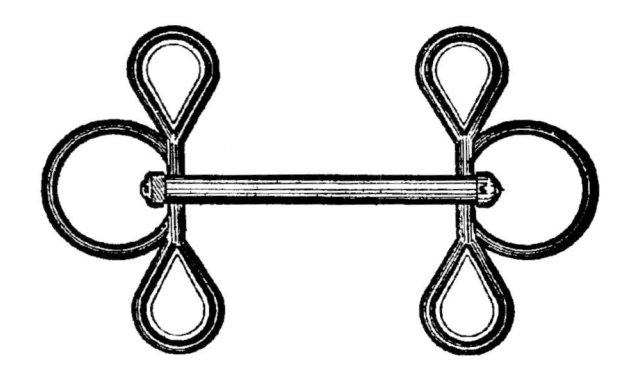

Fig. 10.8 Eberhard glass-enhanced cheek-pieces.

Echini: Or hedgehog, a large rough cannon or mouth-piece [Fig. 10.9].

Fig. 10.9 Bit with echini or hedgehog cannons.

Eddy, George W., Waterford, NY, Patent No. 132,149, Oct. 15, 1872 [Fig. 10.10]. The bit has a pair of arms on the ends of the mouth-piece which press inward against the outer sides of the lower jaw of the horse when the reins are pulled tight.

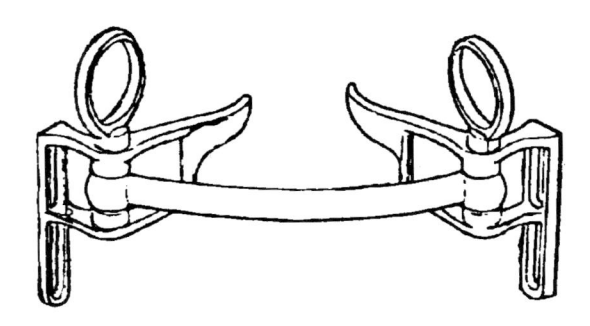

Fig. 10.10 Eddy pressure bit.

Edwards, Cornelius Loren, Newark, NJ, Patent No. 392,998, Nov. 20, 1888 [Fig. 10.11]. The center link of this bit is threaded to receive the screw-bolts from the cannons and the extension of the middle link.

Egg-butt Snaffle: Refers to the mouth-piece ends. See Mouth-pieces, Chapter 25, Fig. 25.48.

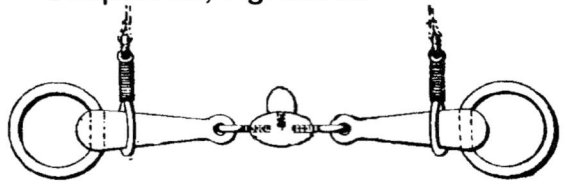

Fig. 10.11 Edwards adjustable-mouth bit.

Egg-link: An oval link in the center of the jointed mouth-piece. See Chapter 25, Fig. 25.12.

Elbow Bit: Figure 10.12 and 10.13. See Driving, Ashleigh, Chapter 8 and Fig. 8.27.

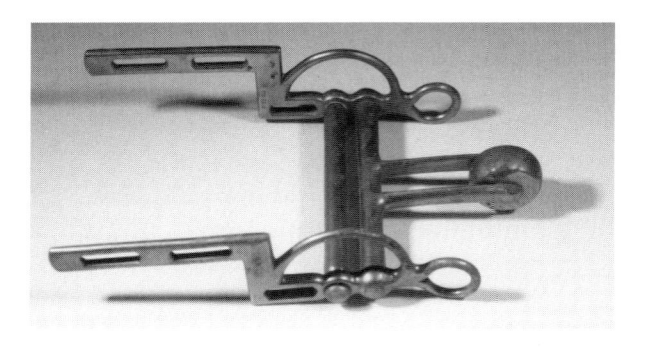

Fig. 10.12 Elbow bit with a double mouth-piece and a three-inch port with a roller in the tip. Kentucky Horse Park archives.

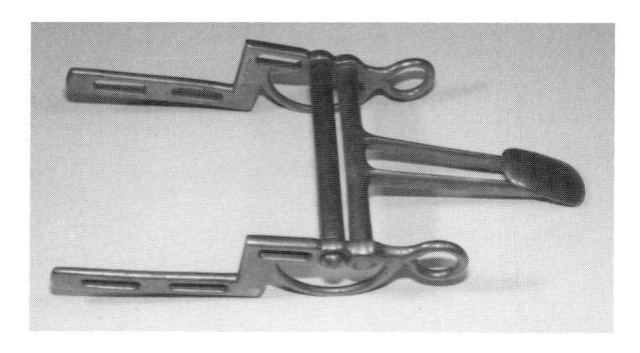

Fig. 10.13 Elbow bit with a double mouth and a four-inch port which has a loose plate that swivels at the port tip. Kentucky Horse Park archives.

Elk Bit: Louis Taylor refers to John S. Rarey driving a team of bull elk with bits in a 4th of July parade in Circleville, OH, sometime during Taylor's teen years. No reference is made as to the type of bit used but he though it was a special one made by Rarey. See Chapter 29.

Elliott and Reichart: Patented the bit commonly termed the Beery Driving Bit. See Chapter 8, Fig. 8.4.

Ely, Alfred B., Newton, MA, Patent No. 88,021, Mar. 23, 1869 [Fig. 10.14]. The spiral or helical spring is applied around the mouth-piece of the bit, between the rings.

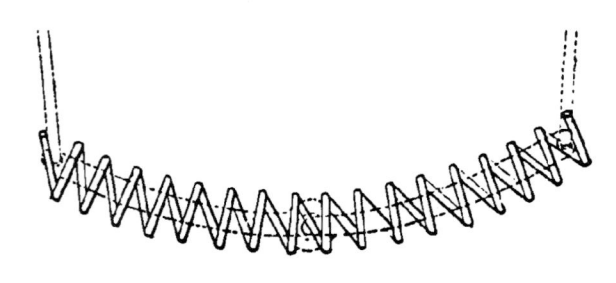

Fig. 10.14 Ely spiral mouth-piece attachment.

Emerson, Richard and William H. Pugh, Racine, WI, Patent No. 444,629, Jan. 13, 1891 [Fig. 10.15]. A strong pull of the reins will cause the sliding, telescoping mouth-piece to shorten its length and the cheek-plates to put pressure on the lower jaw of the horse.

Engle, Washington J., Bloomingdale, IN, Patent No. 962,134, June 21, 1910 [Fig. 10.16]. A pressure bit in that when the reins are pulled the pivoting cheek-pieces apply pressure to the lower jaw.

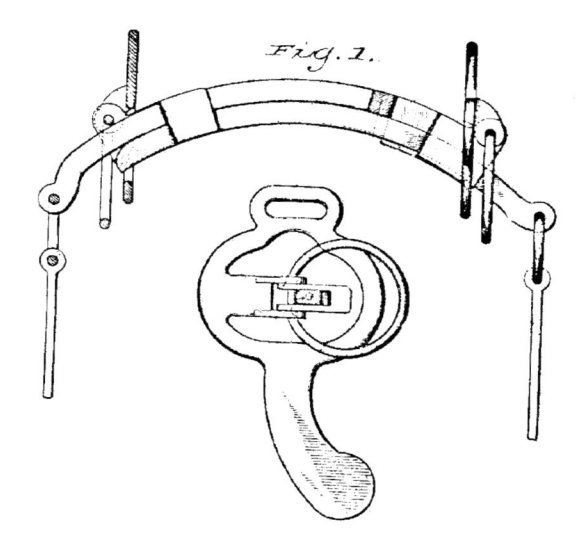

Fig. 10.15 Emerson and Pugh telescoping-mouth bit.

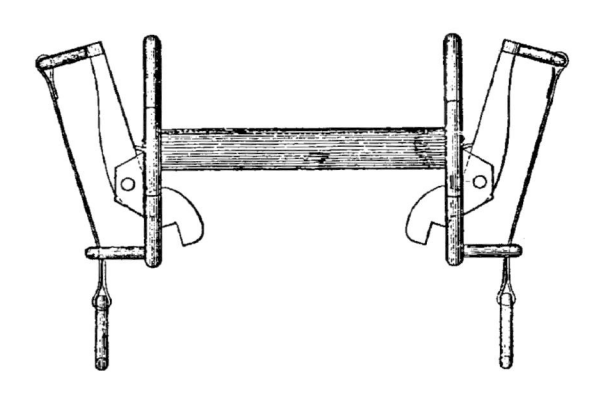

Fig. 10.16 Engle pressure bit.

English Arched Solid Mouth: Term for a mullen-mouth bit. See Chapter 25.

English Bridle: A bridle with a curb and bradoon bit used with two sets of reins. See Chapter 35.

English Hunt: A type of 4-rein bridle. See Chapter 35.

English Pelham: A type of Pelham. See Pelham, Chapter 27.

English Polo: A type of polo bit. See Polo Pelham, Chapter 27.

Erickson, Edor, Philipsburg, MT, Patent No. 1,532,622, Apr. 7, 1925 [Fig. 10.17]. The cheek-pieces of the bit have loops with rollers to accommodate leather straps of a noseband. When the reins are pulled, pressure is applied to the nose as well as the bars of the horse.

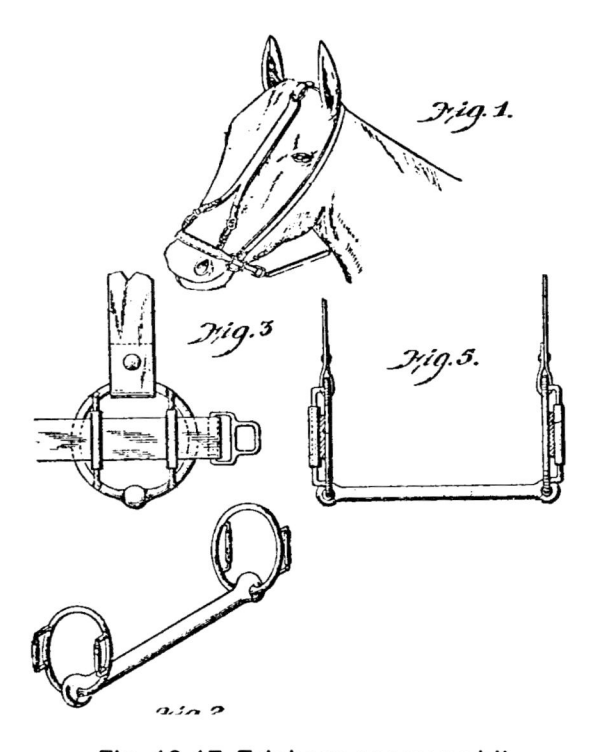

Fig. 10.17 Erickson pressure bit.

Escutcheon: A protective shield such as used around a hole to prevent undue wear and tear on the leather opening.

Espinosa, Jose M., San Francisco, CA, Design Patent No. 16,521, Feb. 16, 1886 [Fig. 10.18]. Rearing-horse pattern sold by Buermann Mfg. Co. and copied by many others.

Fig. 10.18 Espinosa rearing-horse design.

Evans, Frank N., El Cajon, CA, Patent No. 2,745,235, May 15, 1956 [Fig. 10.19]. The noseband applies pressure to the bridge of the horse's nose as the curb applies pressure to the lower jaw.

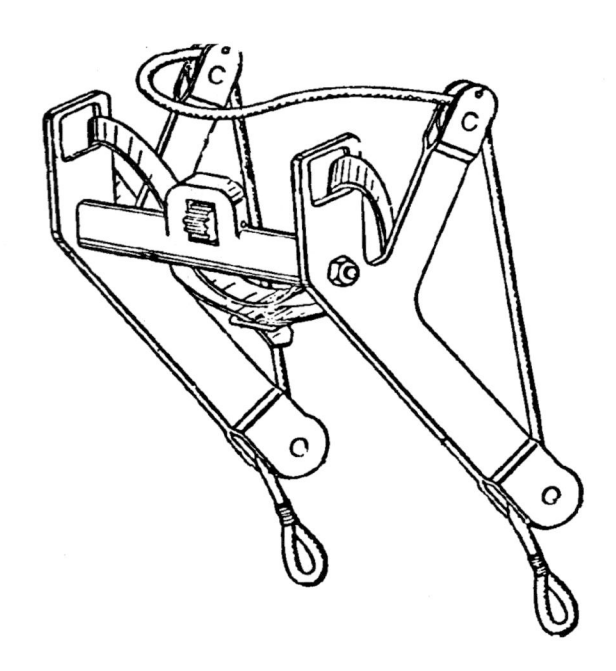

Fig. 10.19 Evens pully-pressure bit.

Eyes: Openings or loops in the cannons of a bit connecting the two sections together as seen in a broken-snaffle bit.

CHAPTER ELEVEN
Fabre to Furlong

Fabre, Jules Maurice, Bordeaux, France, Patent No. 140,023, June 17, 1873 [Fig. 11.0]. The mouth-piece has a revolving or oscillating motion in the side-pieces and is made flat with round edges. Stops limit the extent of the oscillations.

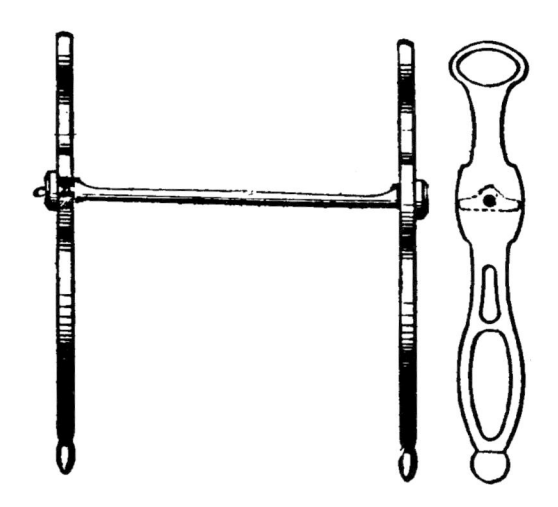

Fig. 11.0 Fabre revolving-mouth bit.

Face-piece: The front or portion of a bridle which crosses or lays on the face of the horse.

Face-strap: Similar to, or sometimes used in place of, a face-piece and most often used with overcheck bits and bridles.

Fairbanks, John A., Cambridgeport, MA, Patent No. 251,424, Dec. 17, 1881 [Fig. 11.1]. A spiral threaded mouth-piece into which a cheek-ring with a threaded screw may be attached.

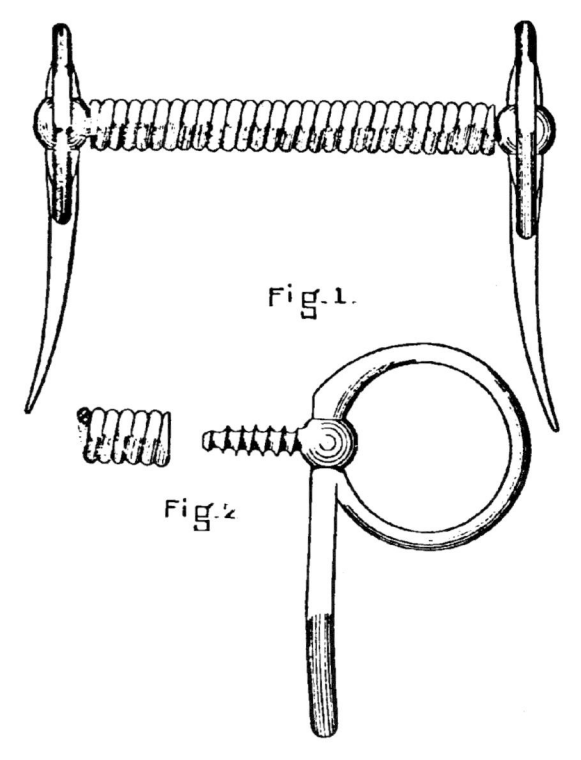

Fig. 11.1 Fairbanks bit-construction method.

Patent No. 348,834, Sep. 7, 1886 [Fig. 11.2]. A construction method in that the mouth-piece is covered with a yielding material such as rubber, leather or other elastic cushion.

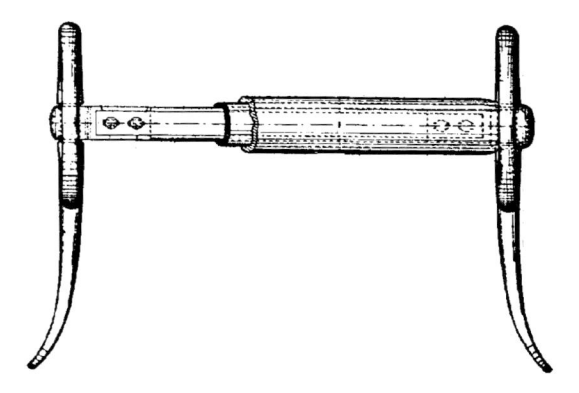

Fig. 11.2 Fairbanks construction method.

Falls, Charles H., Clarksville, IA, Patent No. 559,273, Apr. 28, 1896 [Fig. 11.3]. The hollow tube mouth-piece carries the rod through which the cheek-rings are attached and rotates within the tube.

Fig. 11.3 Falls rotating cheek-pieces.

Patent No. 809,364, Jan. 9, 1906 [Fig. 11.4]. An improvement on Fig. 11.3 in that the lower portion of the free cheek-piece has a cross bar for stabilizing the curb-strap.

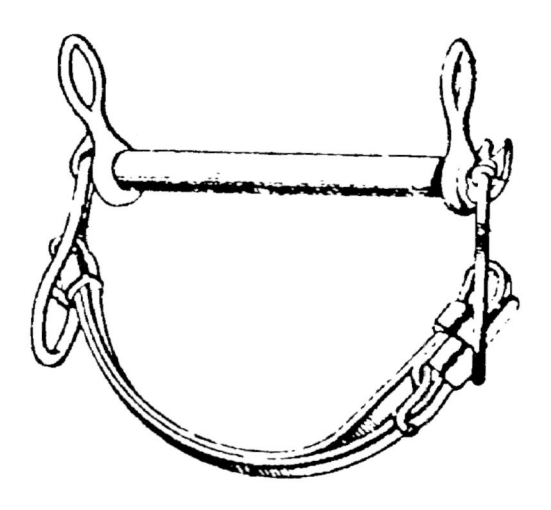

Fig. 11.4 Falls improved bit.

Patent No. 1,060,240, Apr. 29, 1913 [Fig. 11.5]. The flared mouth-piece ends form a continuous attachment to the side-rings. The loose swinging lower portion of the cheek-piece has a hook for attaching the reins directly to the outer ends of the mouth-piece. The cross-link in the lower ring is to affix the curb-strap.

Fig. 11.5 Falls improved bit with flared mouth-piece ends.

Patent No. 1,140,971, May 25, 1915 [Fig. 11.6]. Improvement with a single solid cheek-plate.

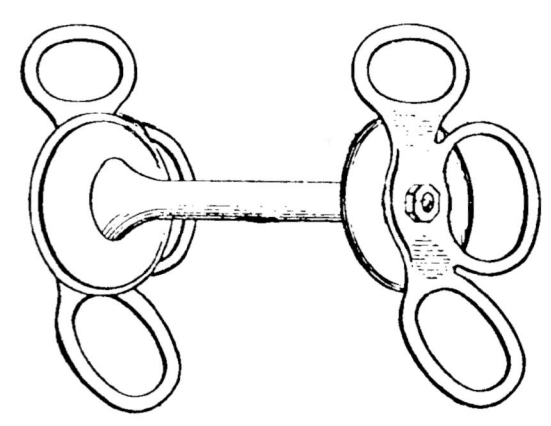

Fig. 11.6 Falls improved bit with solid-plate cheek.

Patent No. 1,178,998, Apr. 11, 1916 [Fig. 11.7]. The side-piece has loops built-in for headstall and curb attachments.

148

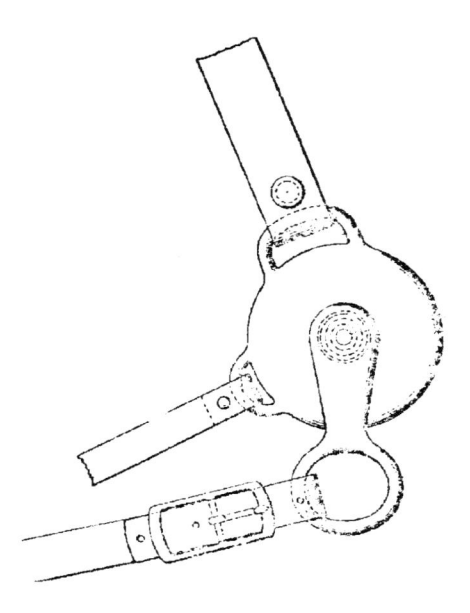

Fig. 11.7 Falls improved bit.

Fast Rein: A horse with a quick response to the rein.

Fate, John Cox, Collegeview, NE, Patent No. 994,732, June 13, 1911 [Fig. 11.8]. The cheek-rings serve as a hub on which the mouth-piece rotates.

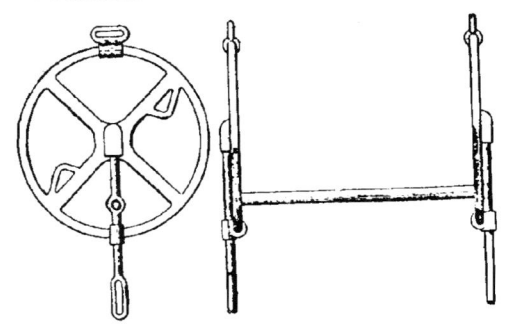

Fig. 11.8 Fate rotating-mouth bit.

Fenner Bit: Early 18th century English bit [Fig. 11.9]. Drawing by W. T. Stone, from Harvey Matthew.

Ferry, E. R., New Haven, CT, Patent No. 79,334, June 30, 1868 [Fig. 11.10]. A pulley bit in that the advantage of pulleys on the bit and bridle are used as a check-rein and the driving reins are attached to the bit-rings.

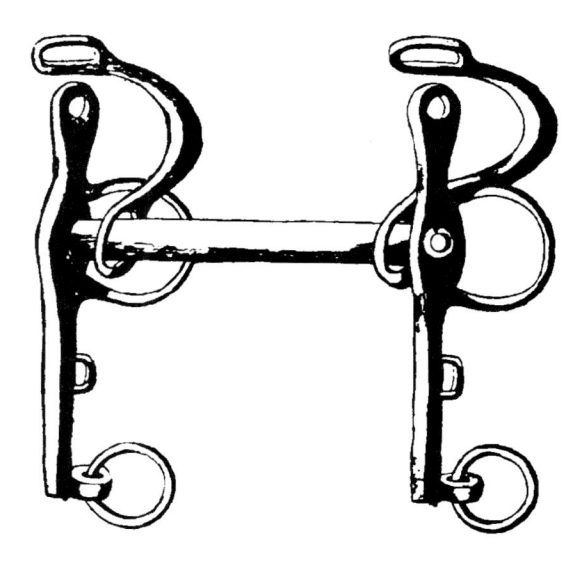

Fig. 11.9 Fenner Bit.

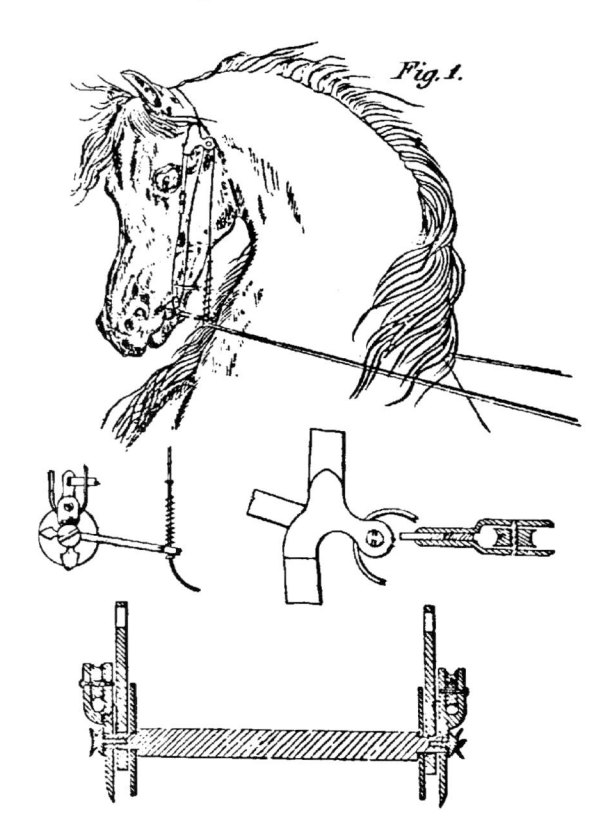

Fig, 11.10 Ferry pulley bit and bridle.

Patent No. 83,055, Oct. 13, 1868 [Fig. 11.11]. An improvement in the cable attachment to the cheek-piece.

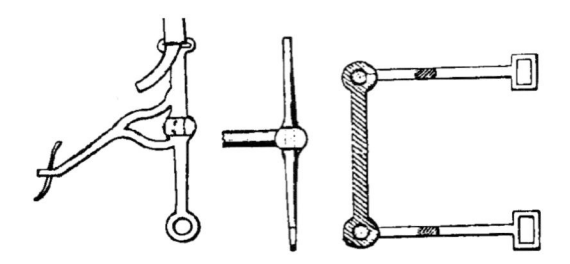

Fig. 11.11 Ferry improved bit.

Fiador: A cord, usually of braided horsehair, used as a safety device or a throat-latch for a hackamore. In more recent years made of cotton cord. See Hackamore, Chapter 13.

Fields, Jesse, Fulton, KY, Patent No. 1,168,617, June 18, 1916 [Fig. 11.12]. A pinching bit which puts pressure on the lower jaw when the reins are pulled. Alias "Arkansas Jaw-breaker" in some areas.

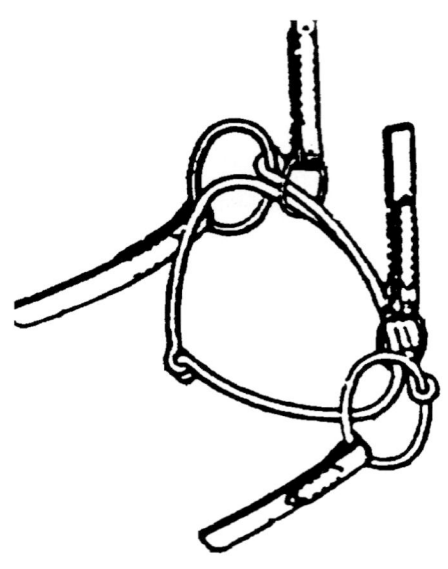

Fig. 11.12 Fields pinching bit.

Fiery, Milton J., Mansfield, OH, Patent Nos. 104,133 and 104,134, June 14, 1870 [Fig. 11.13]. The bit is used with a hitching strap passed through the slotted rings of the cheek-pieces. When the horse tries to leave or attempts to run away when tied the bit clamps on the lower jaw.

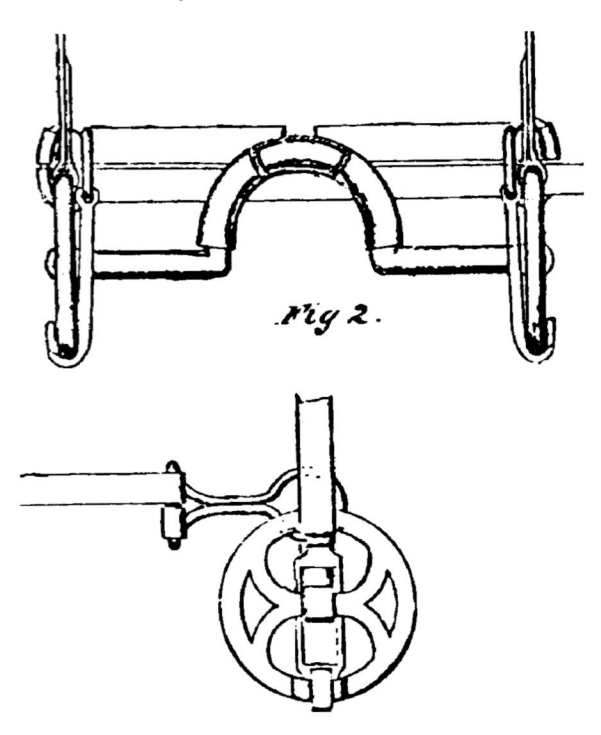

Fig. 11.13 Fiery bit with facilities for a hitching strap.

Fighting-the-bit: A horse that is pressing or pushing its head forward (boring), shaking or throwing its head.

Figure 8 Link: A connecting link in the mouth-piece resembling a figure 8. See Mouth-piece, Chapter 25.

Fillis Bit: A hanging snaffle with a hinged swivelling port in place of a joint [Fig. 11.14].

Fink, Reuben, Lancaster, PA, Patent No. 72,729, Dec. 31, 1867 [Fig. 11.15]. A bit with a checking-ring separate from the driving rein-ring.

Fig. 11.14 Mouth-piece of a Fillis bit.

Fig. 11.15 Fink bit with checking-lever ring.

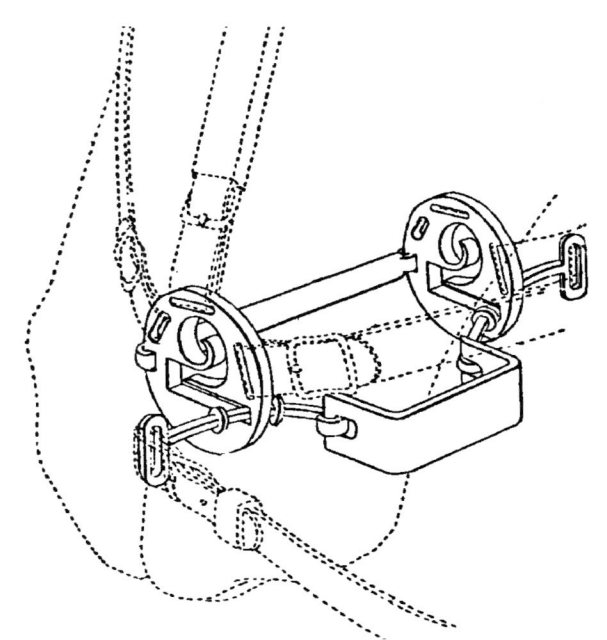

Fig. 11.16 Finnel control bit.

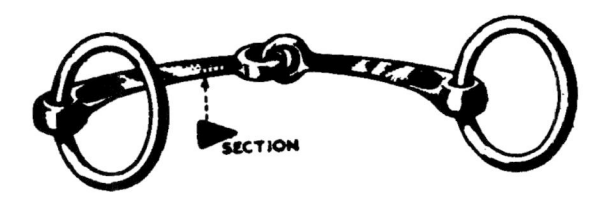

Fig. 11.17 Fishback Snaffle.

Finnel, Oscar and Frank Carson, Boulder, MT, Patent No. 956,063, Apr. 26, 1910 [Fig. 11.16]. A supplemental control device which can be adjusted to fit the horse and condition.

Fishback Snaffle: A severe bit with a small triangular shaped mouth-piece [Fig. 11.17].

Fish Eye Snaffle Cheek: Refers to the end of the mouth-piece and its attachment to the cheek-piece [Fig. 11.18].

Fisher, Charles W., Springfield, OH, Patent No. 532,455, Jan. 15, 1895 [Figs. 11.19 and 11.19a]. A bit with three sections to the mouth-piece. The two outer sections have a built-on collar to keep the bit in the mouth in the proper location.

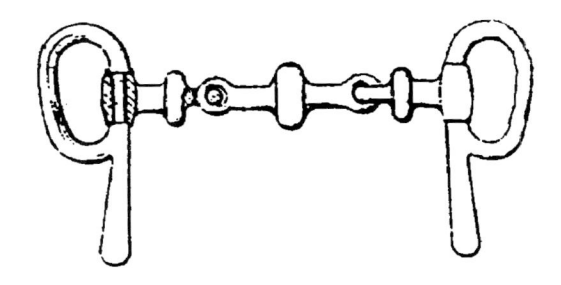

Fig. 11.19 Fisher snaffle bit.

Fig. 11.18 Fish Eye snaffle cheek bit.

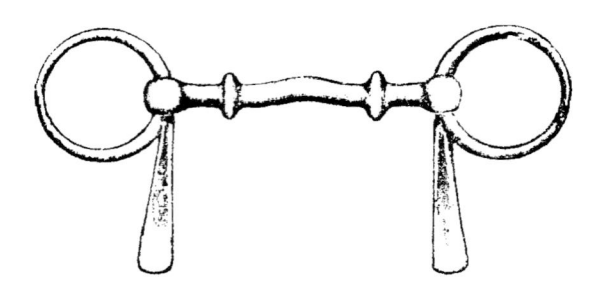

Fig. 11.19a Fisher snaffle variation.

Fisher, Samuel, Mount Washington, MD, Patent No. 398,319, Feb.19. 1889 [Fig. 11.20]. A two-piece hinged bit with snaps on each piece to attach to the rings of a snaffle bit. Sometimes referred to as a "Butterfly" snaffle.

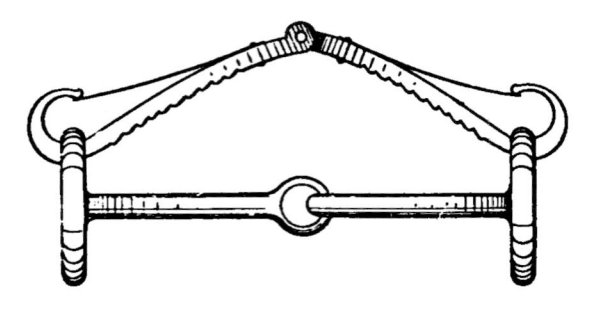

Fig. 11.20 Fisher "Butterfly" snaffle.

FitzGibbon, John, Watkins, NY, Patent No. 782,020, Feb. 7, 1905 [Fig. 11.21]. A large disk in the center of the mouth-piece puts pressure on the tongue and the mouth roof with slight pressure on the reins.

Fig. 11.21 FitzGibbon snaffle bit.

Fixed-cheek: A cheek-piece that is solidly attached to the mouth-piece and does not turn, swivel or rotate.

Flap-reins: A set of reins used as check-reins from the bit and fastened parallel to the saddle. See Bridles and Reins, Chapter 35.

Flat-ring Snaffle: The circular rein-rings are flat in place of being made of round wire. See Wilson Snaffle, Chapter 34.

Flying Trench Bit: An early name given to a thin bradoon bit that is used in a double bridle.

Fogg, Jason T., Garland, ME, Patent No. 584,582, June 15, 1897 [Fig.11.22]. A permanently curved mouth-piece is covered with rubber and the cheek-pieces may or may not be protected by rubber or leather.

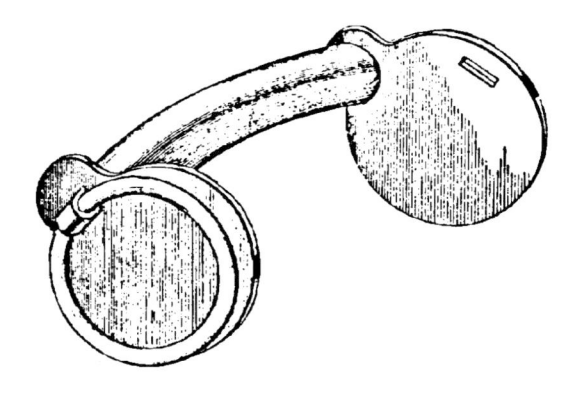

Fig. 11.22 Fogg rubber-covered-mouth bit.

Ford, William S., Clinton, IL, Patent No. 77,810, May 12, 1868 [Fig. 11.23]. A rectangular tube on each end of the mouth-piece allows a flat cheek-strap to pass through and function as a check-rein. The driving reins are attached to the side-ring.

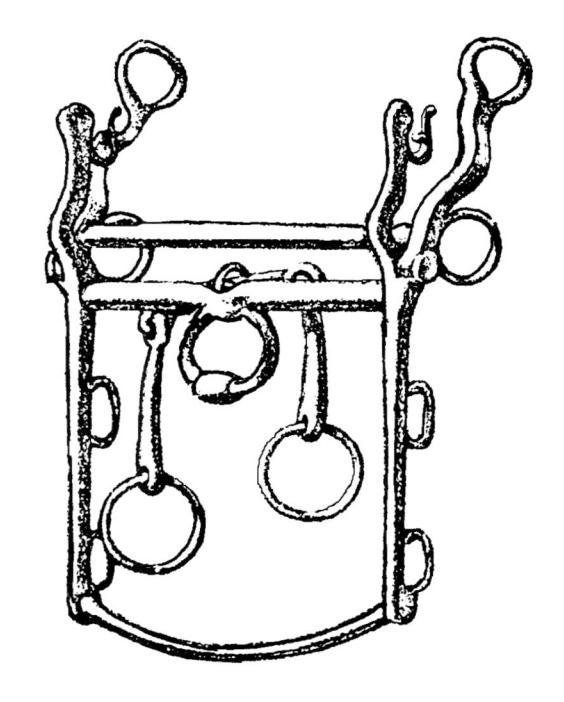

Fig. 11.24 Ford's harness bit.

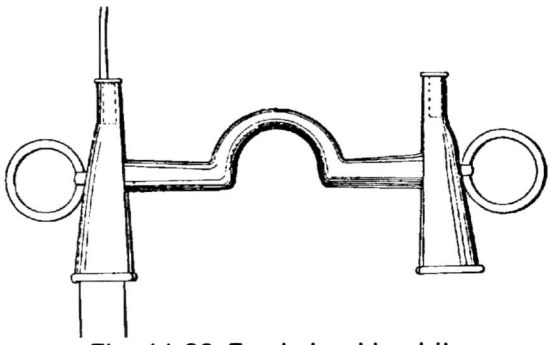

Fig. 11.23 Ford checking bit.

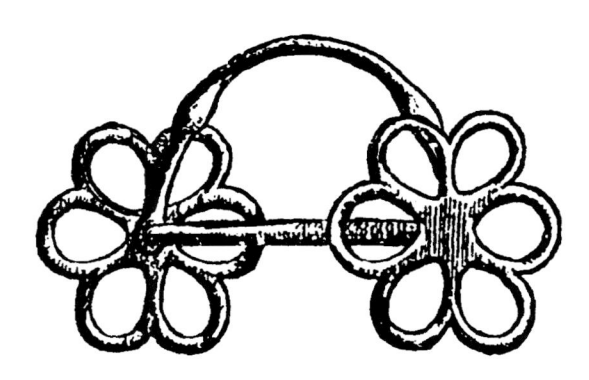

Fig. 11.25 Forget-Me-Not bit.

Ford's Harness Bit: A double-mouth bit shown with an attached bradoon, from *The Loriner*, #88 [Fig. 11.24].

Foreacre Gag Bit: See Gag Bits, Chapter 12.

Forget-Me-Not: Figure 11.25.

Forrest, Bedford W., Memphis, TN, Patent No. 890,419, June 9, 1908 [Figs. 11.26 and 11.27]. The split mouth-piece can be moved and adjusted to lock in several positions. When fully opened, the lower bar acts as a curb and can be adjusted by the knob on the end of the split mouth-piece.

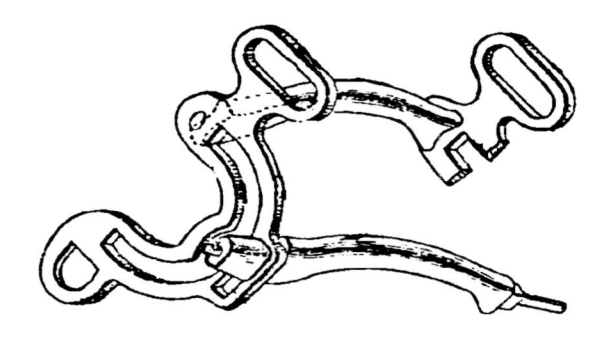

Fig. 11.26 Forrest split-mouth bit patent copy drawing.

Fig. 11.27 Forrest bit photo. Robert Maclin collection.

Four-ring Bit: Refers to a Wilson-type bit [Fig. 11.28, 11.29, and 11.30]. See Chapter 34.

Fig. 11.28 A four-ring bit.

Fig. 11.29 A four-ring bit designed by Dennis Magner, a horse trainer of the late 1800's.

Fig. 11.30 Magner's improved four-ring snaffle with prongs on the mouth-piece to prevent the inner rings from sliding into the center link.

Fowler, Jonathan O., New York, NY, Patent No. 739,163, Sep. 15, 1903 [Fig. 11.31]. A noseband is used to enhance the action of the snaffle bit.

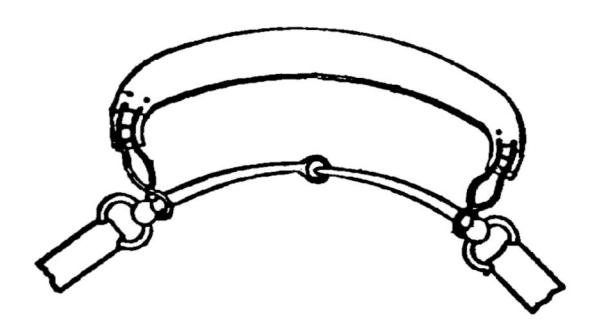

Fig. 11.31 Fowler noseband attachment.

Fowler and LeCompte: See Nosebands, Chapter 26, Fig. 26.26.

French, John M., Chelsea, MA, Patent No. 319,897, June 9, 1885 [Fig. 11.32]. A bit without a mouth-piece. Hooks on the inside of the cheek-pieces hook into the corner of the horse's mouth. They are kept in place by a rigid cross-bar that is placed under the lower jaw of the horse.

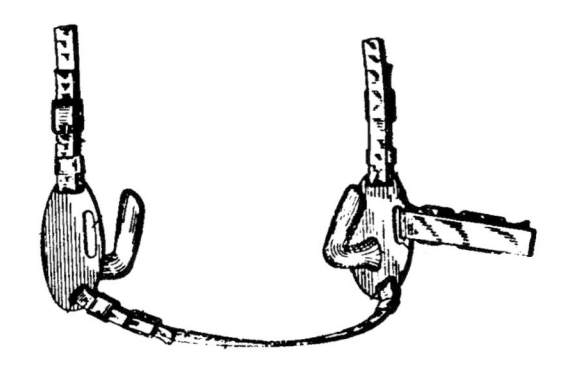

Fig. 11.32 French barless bit.

French-style Liverpool: See Liverpool Bits, Chapter 17.

Front: The brow-band of a bridle. See Bridles, Chapter 35.

Frost, Francis N., New Britain, CT, Patent No. 56,923, Aug. 7, 1866 [Fig. 11.33]. A construction method of a tightly spiraled coil around a chain which holds the cheek-pieces tightly against the the mouth-piece.

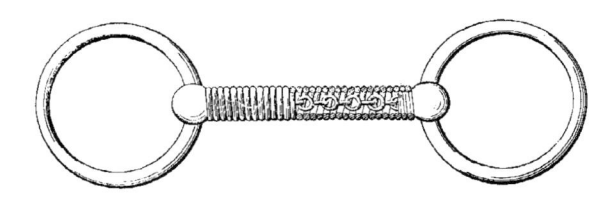

Fig. 11.33 Frost construction detail.

Fryer, Charles M., Piedmont, CA, Patent No. 2,193,451, Mar. 12, 1940 [Fig. 11.34]. The mouth-piece has a ball on each end which fits in a socket of the cheek-piece. Movement of the mouth can be adjusted to fit the horse and the rider.

Full Bridle: Term for a Double Bridle. See Chapter 35.

Full Cheek: Term for a bit with upper and lower extensions of the cheek-piece. See Side-pieces, Chapter 31.

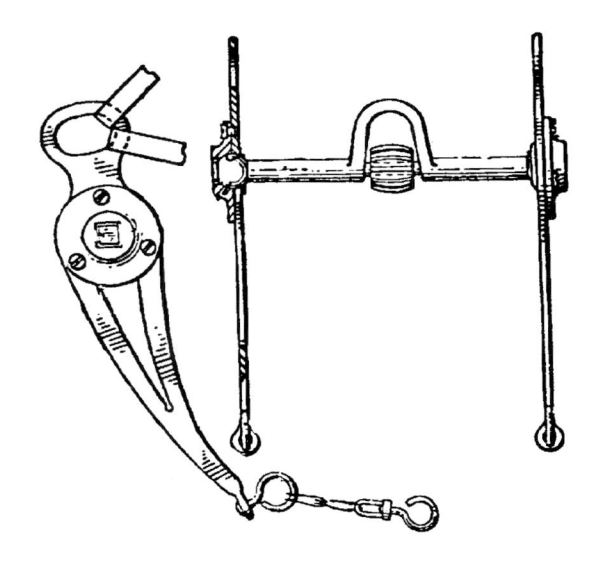

Fig. 11.34 Fryer socket-mouth-end bit.

Fulmer Bit: A full- or double-cheek snaffle with a Turton head [Fig. 11.35]. See Chapter 31.

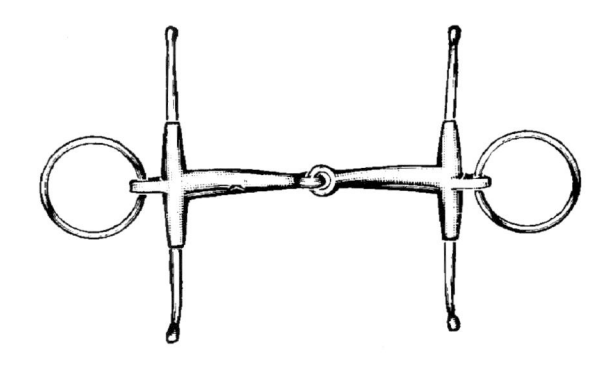

Fig. 11.35 Fulmer snaffle bit.

Furlong, Thomas T., Chicago, IL, Patent No. 225,751, Mar. 23, 1880 [Fig. 11.36]. A mouth-piece with enlarged grooves that adapt to the lips of the horse. Designed to prevent the lips from pressing against the teeth.

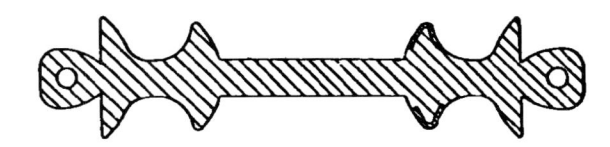

Fig. 11.36 Profile of Furlong mouth-piece design.

155

CHAPTER TWELVE
Gag to Guy

The action of the gag is two fold. As the reins are pulled, pressure is placed upward on the corners of the mouth causing the horse to lift its head while a downward pull is exerted on the poll. This is accomplished by passing the round leather cheek-straps of the bridle through the cheek-rings of the bit or equipping the bit and/or the bridle with pulleys to increase the leverage advantage. Either way causes the results desired in the horse's head carriage.

Ambrose Clark Gag: Figure 12.0.

Fig. 12.0 Ambrose Clark gag.

Balding Gag: Figure 12.1.

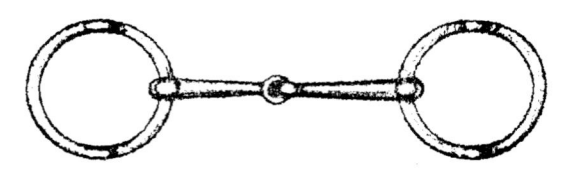

Fig. 12.1 Balding gag bit.

Barnes Pulley Gag: Figure 12.2. See Chapter 5, Fig. 5.31.

Brower Pulley Bit: See Chapter 5, Fig. 5.78.

Brown Gag: See Lincoln Brown Patent, Chapter 5, Fig. 5.80.

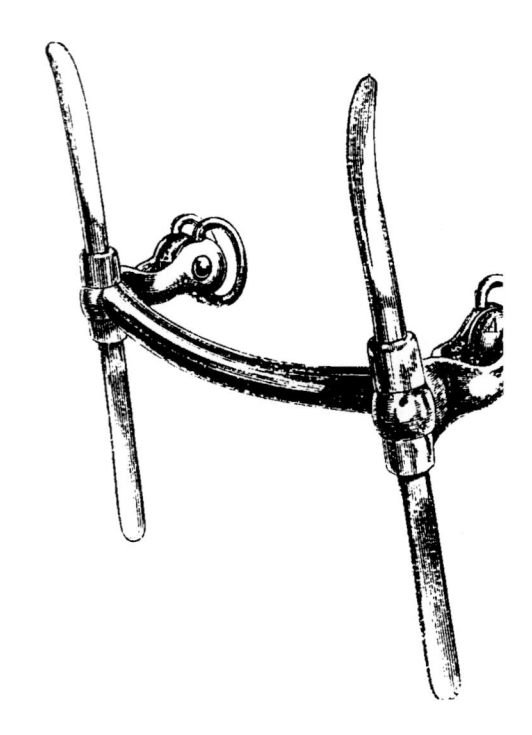

Fig. 12.2 Barnes pulley gag.

Cecil Smith Gag: Now called a Balding Gag or more frequently a Half-Balding Gag [Fig. 12.1a].

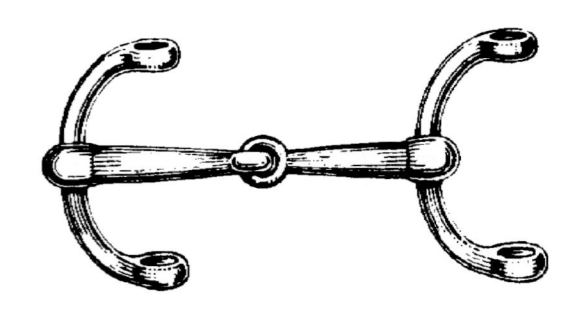

Fig. 12.1a Half-Balding gag bit.

Cheltenham Gag: Cheek-rings are fixed and do not slide on the mouth-piece [Fig. 12.3 and 12.3a].

Fig. 12.3 Cheltenham gag.

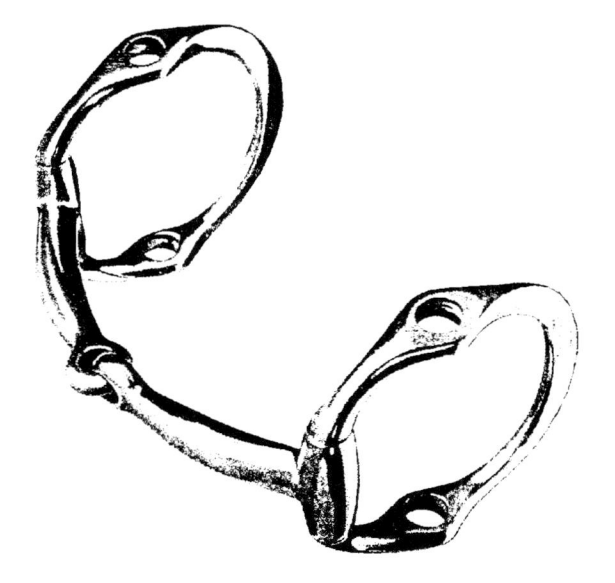

Fig. 12.3a Cheltenham gag, contemporary model.

Citation Bit: Not a true gag bit but often used as a gag. A term for the Norton Perfection Bit [Fig. 12.4]. See Chapter 8, Fig. 8.18.

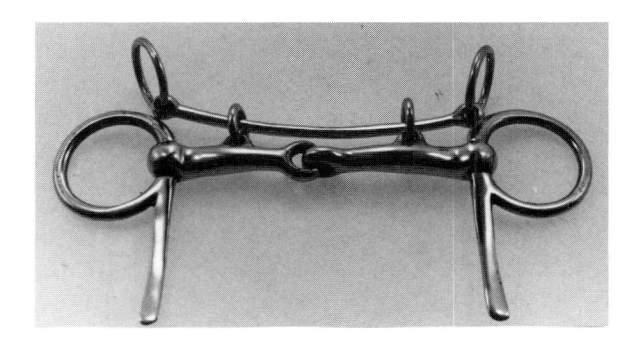

Fig. 12.4 Citation six-ring bit. Robert Maclin collection.

Conn Gag Bit: See Chapter 6, Fig. 6.40.

Cowboy Gag: The bit is produced in several different mouth-pieces by Trammell Bits [Fig. 12.5]. Sliding chain-mouth shown.

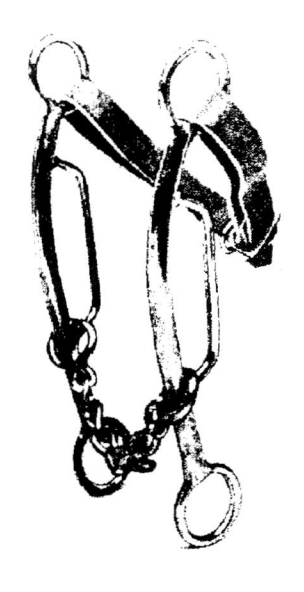

Fig. 12.5 Cowboy gag.

D-Back Gag: A gag bit from *Crockett-Kelly Catalog No. 184* (1984) [Fig. 12.6]. The cannons of the mouth-piece have a slight bend.

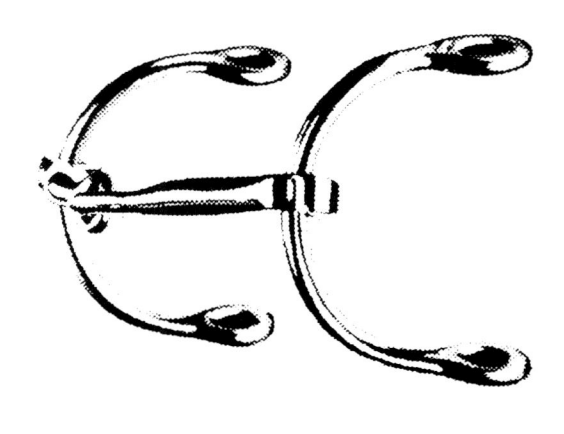

Fig. 12.6 Crockett-Kelly D-back gag.

Duncan Gag: Figure 12.7.

157

Fig. 12.7 Duncan gag.

Egg-butt Gag: A gag bit of basically the same design as the D-gag with an Egg-butt mouth-piece. See Chapter 31.

European Gag Bit: A style of gag bit sold by Libertyville Saddle Shop Inc., Libertyville, IL [Fig. 12.8]. Made in Korea of Kingly Metal Stainless Steel (KMSS) a superior grade of 18/8 stainless steel. Three rein positions on the cheek-pieces allow use as a snaffle or curb bit.

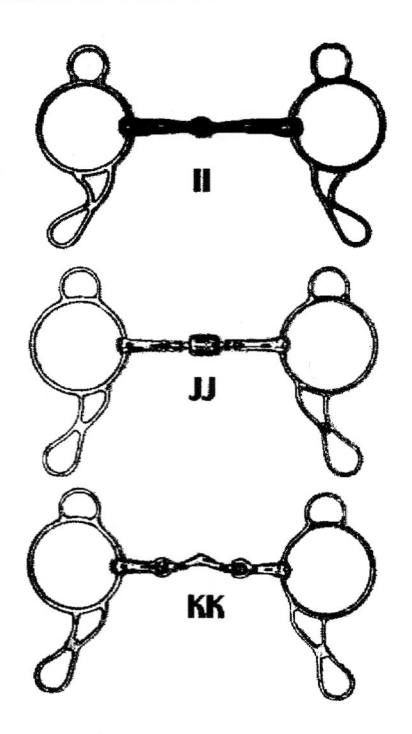

Fig. 12.8 European gag with a variey of mouth-pieces.

Foreacre, Masculine, New Harrisburg, OH, Patent No. 106,044, Aug. 2, 1870 [Fig. 12.9].

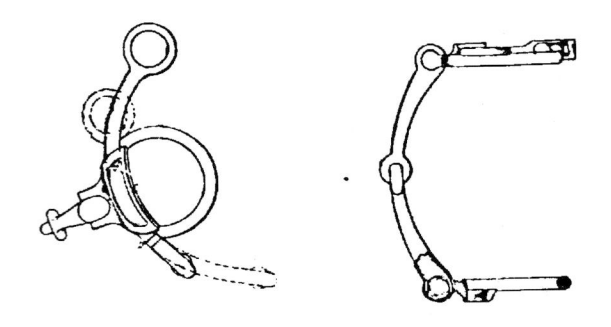

Fig. 12.9 Foreacre gag bit.

Hack Overcheck Gag: See Twisted-mouth Gag, Fig. 12.20.

Harris, James, Kansas, IL, Patent No. 63,886, Apr. 16, 1867 [Fig. 12.10]. The bit consists of a hollow tube on each end of the mouth-piece through which the rounded cheek-straps of the headstall pass and extend as the gag reins. The drive reins are attached to the small ring at the end of the mouth-piece.

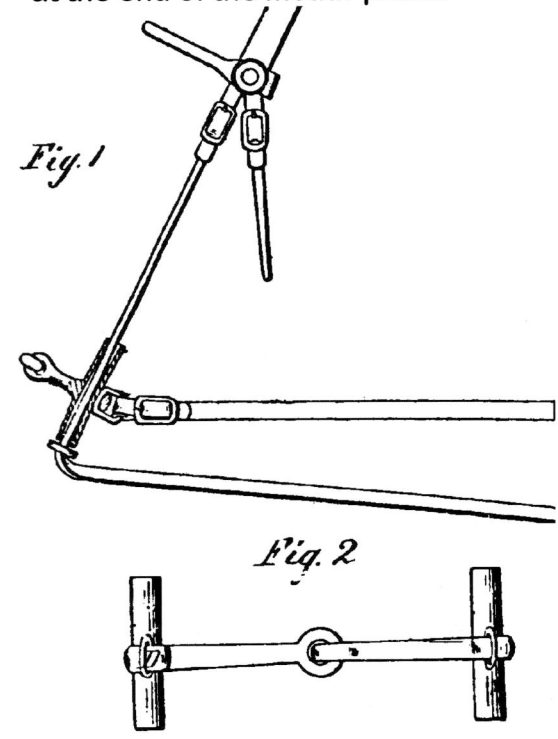

Fig. 12.10 Harris gag bit.

158

Havis, James: A pulley bit with uneven cannons designed for side-pullers and sometimes referred to as a gag bit. See Chapter 15, Fig. 15.10.

Hitchcock Gag: A pulley gag used in combination with a special made bridle [Figs. 12.11 and 12.11a]

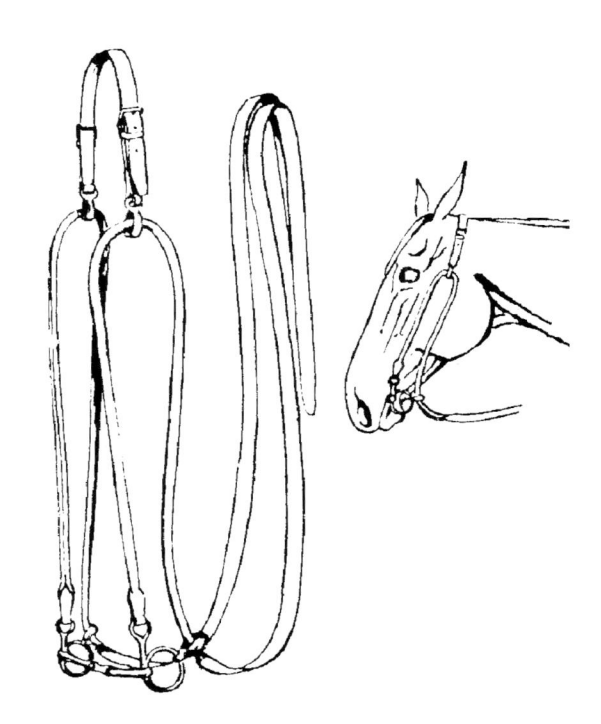

Fig. 12.11 Hitchcock gag and bridle.

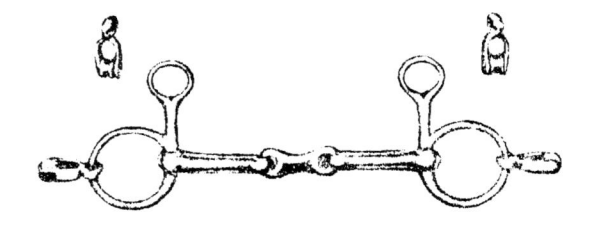

Fig. 12.11a Hitchcock gag and pulleys.

Hunting Gag: See Shrewbury Gag, Fig. 12.18.

Jointed Check Gag: A broken-mouth bradoon or overcheck bit with a half-inch diameter mouth and small side rings.

Nash Bit: See Chapter 26, Fig. 26.9.

Nelson Gag: From *The Loriner* Fig. 12.12.

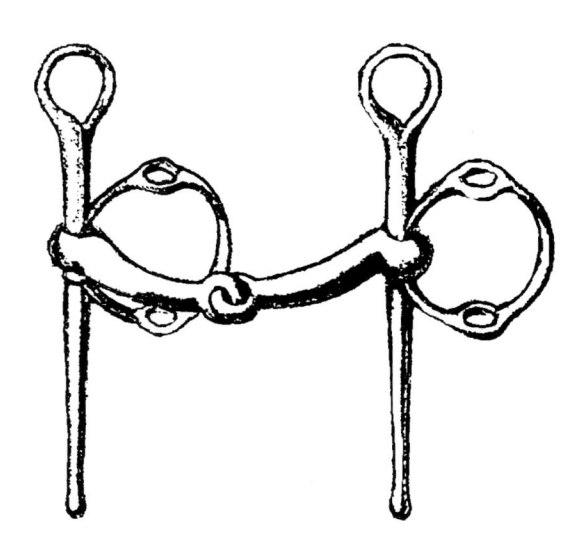

Fig. 12.12 Nelson gag.

Newmarket Gag: Figure 12.13.

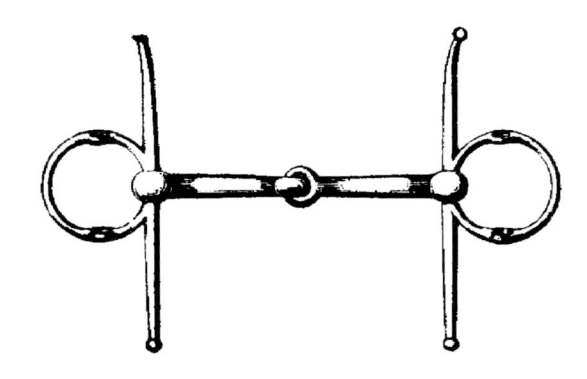

Fig. 12.13 Newmarket gag.

Performance Gag Bit: A style of gag bits sold by Libertyville Saddle Shop Inc., Libertyville, IL [Fig. 12.14]. Made in Korea of Kingly Metal Stainless Steel (KMSS) a superior grade 18/8 stainless steel.

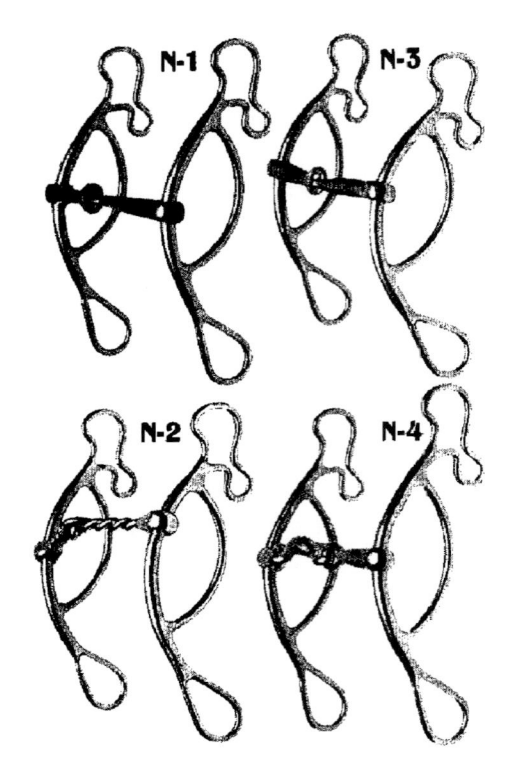

Fig. 12.14 The variations of the Performance Gag Bit with copper or steel mouth-pieces.

Roller Gag: A gag bit with rollers on the mouth-piece [Fig. 12.15].

Fig. 12.15 Roller gag.

Salisbury Gag: A gag bit with holes in the wire rings to accommodate the round cheek-strap of the bridle [Fig. 12.16].

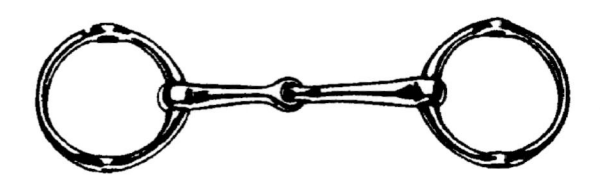

Fig. 12.16 Salisbury gag.

Shrewbury Gag: The mouth-piece is free to slide on the side-ring between the gag line rings [Fig. 12.17].

Fig. 12.17 Shrewbury gag.

Shrewbury Gag, Flat Ring: Figure 12.18.

Fig. 12.18 Flat-ring Shrewbury gag.

Sliding Mouth Gag: See Fig. 12.5.

Swivel Gag: A bit much like an ordinary snaffle bit that has a pulley on the outer end of each cannon. The pulley can swivel within the cheek-ring [Fig. 12.19].

Fig. 12.19 Swivel gag.

Three-piece Gag: Barrel-racers gag. See Fig. 12.8.

Twisted-mouth Gag: Figure 12.20.

Walking Horse Gag: A gag bit much as the Salisbury gag but with small cheek-rings of 2 to 2 1\2 inch diameter.

Fig. 12.20 Twisted-mouth gag.

Weymouth Gag: See Fig. 12.17.

Y or W Mouth Gag: See Chapter 34, Fig. 34.50.

Gag Bridle: A more severe form of bridle, with cheek-pieces made of rounded leather that pass through holes at the top and bottom of the bit-rings, then attach to the reins. See Chapter 35.

Gag Rein: A rein that fastens to the top of the headstall of a bridle and passes through the gag bit to the rider or driver's hand.

Gallagher, Frank, Philadelphia. PA, Patent No. 1,006,203, Oct. 17, 1911 [Fig. 12.21]. An overcheck device that has a leather strap passing over the nose and through a runner or small pully attached to the bridle at the brow-band junction and then attaching to the rein-ring at about the point of the horse's withers.

Gallatin, Daniel S., Dalton, OH, Patent No. 898,637, Sep. 15, 1908 [Fig. 12.22]. A single piece of metal (wire) bent to form loops and rings making the mouth-piece and the side-pieces.

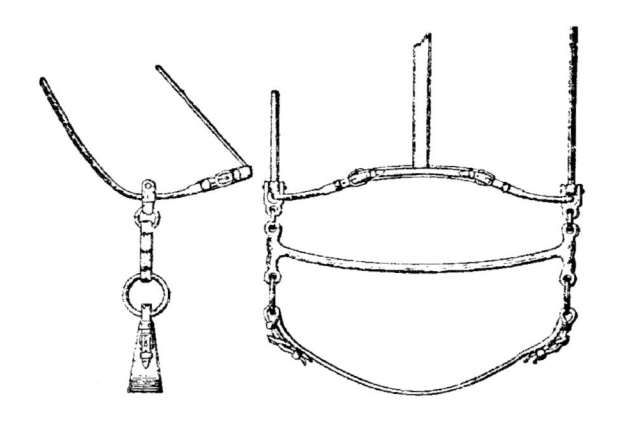

Fig. 12.21 Gallagher checking device.

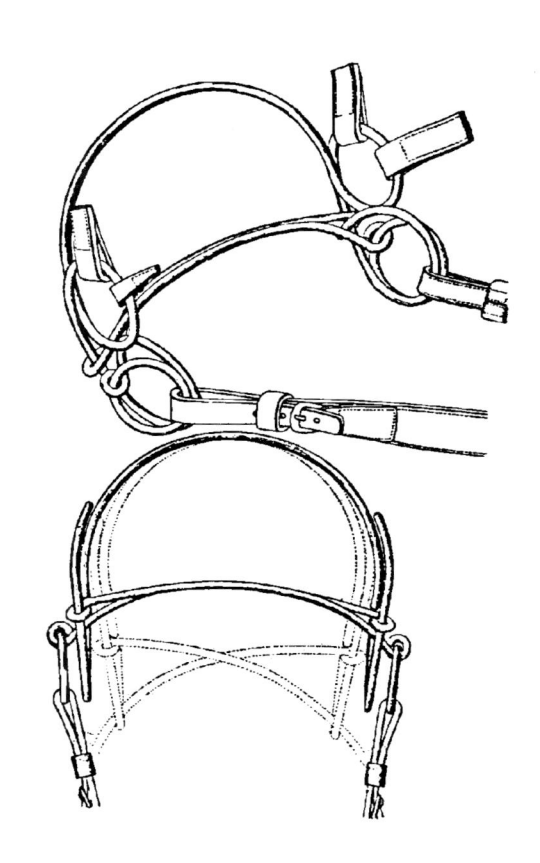

Fig. 12.22 Gallatin bit.

Gallic Bit: An early English term for a curb bit.

Gardner, Walter, Enderby, British Columbia, Canada, Patent No. 830,707, Sep. 11, 1906 [Fig. 12.23]. The mouth-piece continues and is bent around to allow the ends to come close together under the jaw. The cross bars under the jaw are for attachment of a tie-down line. Small rings are placed at what would be the normal end of the mouth-piece for attaching the bridle.

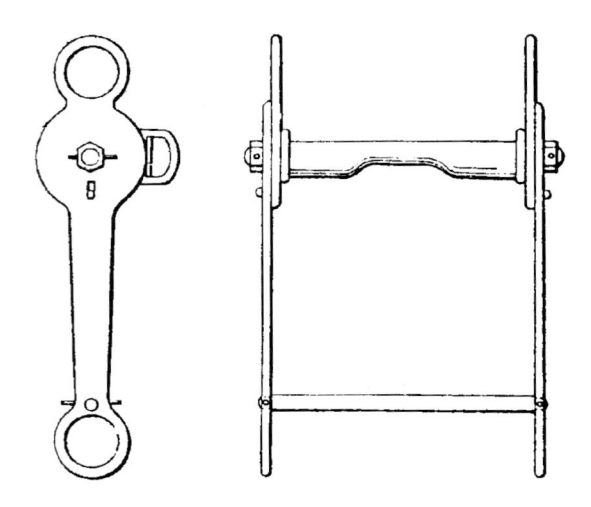

Fig12.24 Gates curb bit.

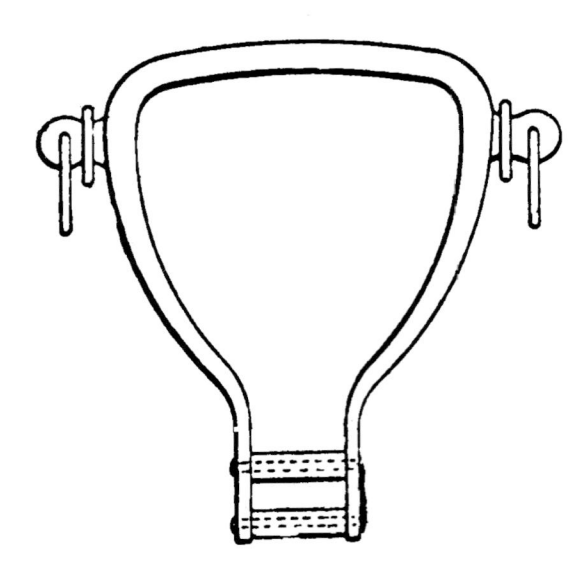

Fig. 12.23 Gardner tie-down bit.

Gates, Joseph, Lincoln, IL, Patent No. 69,910, Oct. 15, 1867 [Fig. 12.24]. The inner ring attached to the mouth-piece is for attachment to the curb and is able to rotate on the mouth-piece. The mouth-piece is round on top and flattened on the bottom. The recessed area of the mouth is for tongue room.

Gentle Broke: A horse trained by gentle methods as opposed to "bronc busting."

George, King III, A State Harness Bit from The Loriner [Fig. 12.25].

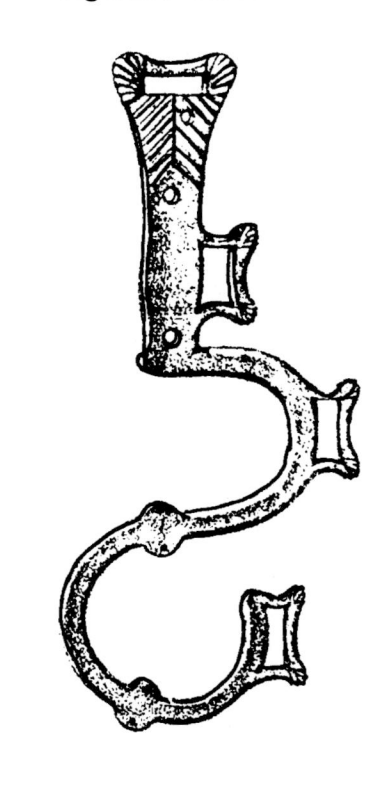

Fig. 12.25 King George III State Harness Bit.

Gerald, Amos F., Fairfield, ME, Patent No. 408,705, Aug. 13, 1889 [Fig. 12.26]. The pivoting pressure levers recess into the bit bar and are activated when the reins are pulled hard.

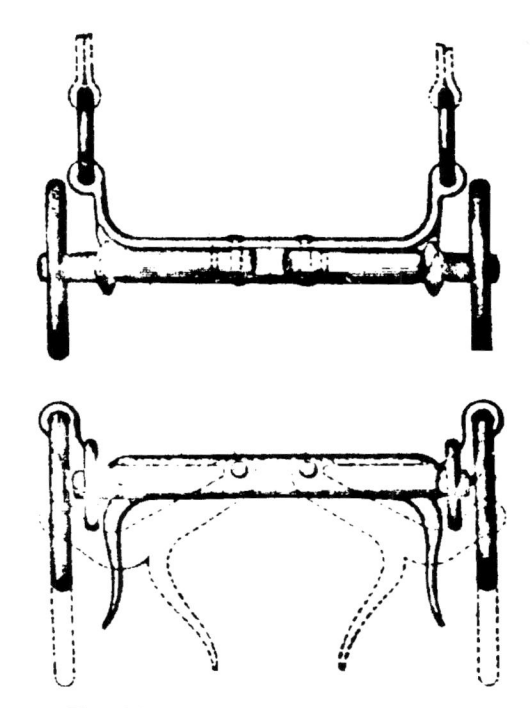

Fig. 12.26 Gerald pressure bit.

Fig. 12.27 Gilbert pressure bit.

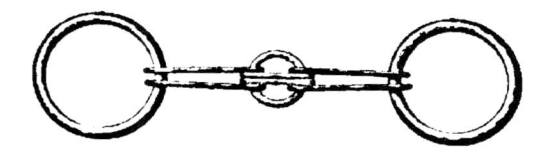

Fig. 12.28 Gillespie snaffle bit.

German Jointed Snaffle: A large diameter hollow-mouth jointed snaffle bit.

Ghost Cord: A small cord that passes around the horse's tongue and lower jaw and extends to the rider's hand.

Gig Bit: A term for a Liverpool or Hackney driving bit. See Chapters 8 and 17.

Gilbert, George A., Milwakee, WI, Patent No. 496,222, Apr. 25, 1893 [Fig. 12.27]. The mouth-piece slides up and down on the slanted inner bars of the cheek-pieces to cause pressure on the sides of the horse's mouth. Compare with the Conn Bit, Chapter 6, Fig. 6.40.

Gillespie, David H., Lockland, OH, Patent No. 498,644, May 30, 1893 [Fig. 12.28]. The cannons of the mouth-piece are connected by two links with a ring placed through the links.

Gilliam, Algernon, Pittsburg, PA, Patent No. 116,945, July 11, 1871 [Fig. 12.29]. Slots in the rear portion of the cheek-pieces allow the mouth-piece to pivot on the attachments to the front of the cheek-pieces.

Ginkinger, Charles L., Sterling, IL, Patent No. 137,913, Apr. 17, 1873 [Fig. 12.30]. The mouth-piece and all the necessary rings or loops are cast in one piece.

Gleason: See Chapter 8, Fig. 8.11.

Gliha, Anthony I., *et.al.*, North Randle, OH, Patent No. 2,500,312, Mar. 15, 1950 [Fig. 12.31]. A run-out bit. When the rein attached to the small ring of the pin that extends through the hollow mouth-piece is pulled, it causes the larger ring on the other end of the mouth-piece to compress and put pressure on the side of the horse's mouth.

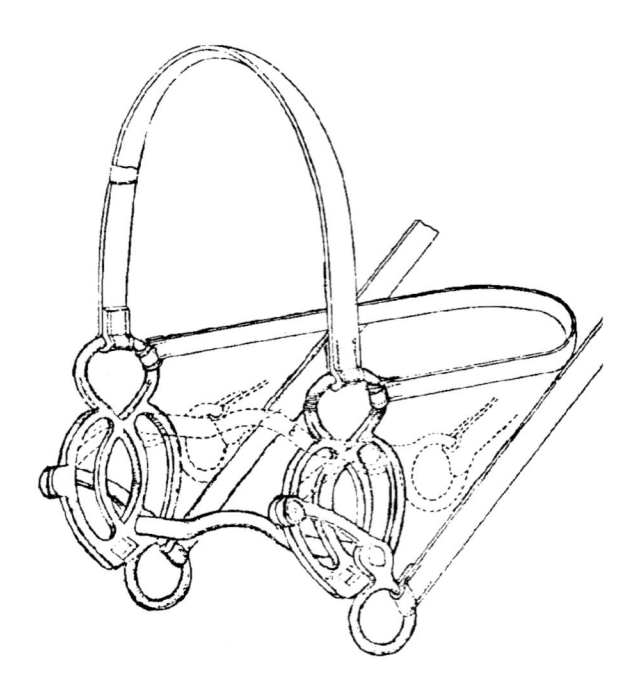

Fig. 12.29 Gilliam rotating-mouth bit.

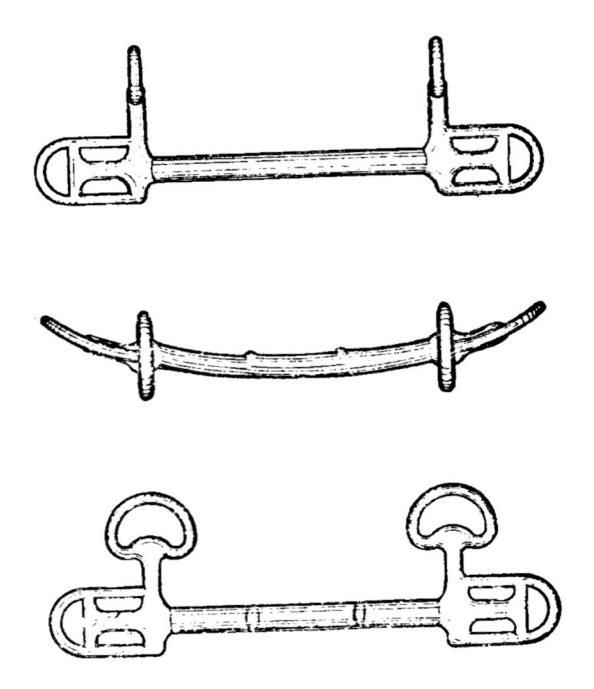

Fig. 12.30 Ginkinger one-piece bit.

Fig. 12.31 Gliha run-out bit.

Globe Bit: A curb bit with enlarged bridle and rein-rings [Fig. 12.32 and 12.32a]. Globe Bits sold by August Buermann and Co.

Globe-cheek Bit: A bit from *The Loriner* with enlarged rings only in the lower portion of the side-piece [Fig. 12.33].

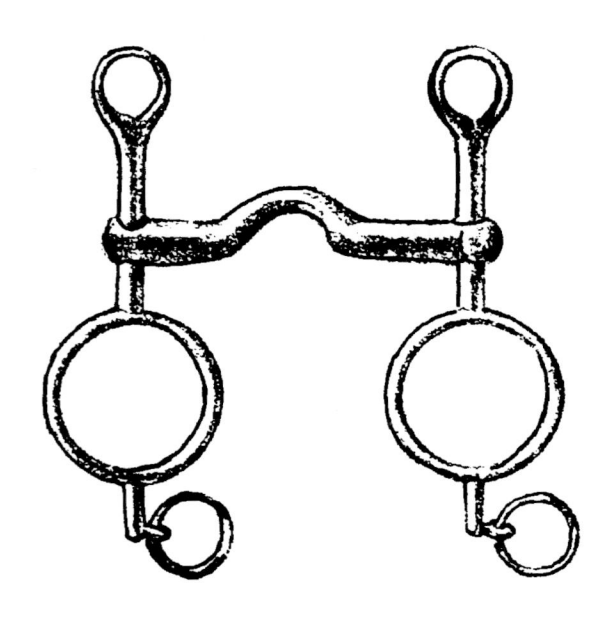

Fig. 12.33 Globe-cheek bit.

Good Mouth: A well trained horse that responds quickly and easily to the slightest call from the rider.

Goodyear, John, Groton, NY, Patent No. 148,293, Mar. 10, 1874 [Fig. 12.34]. A rubber or elastic covering or shield may be used to envelop the mouth at the point where the blades open and close.

164

No. 957½

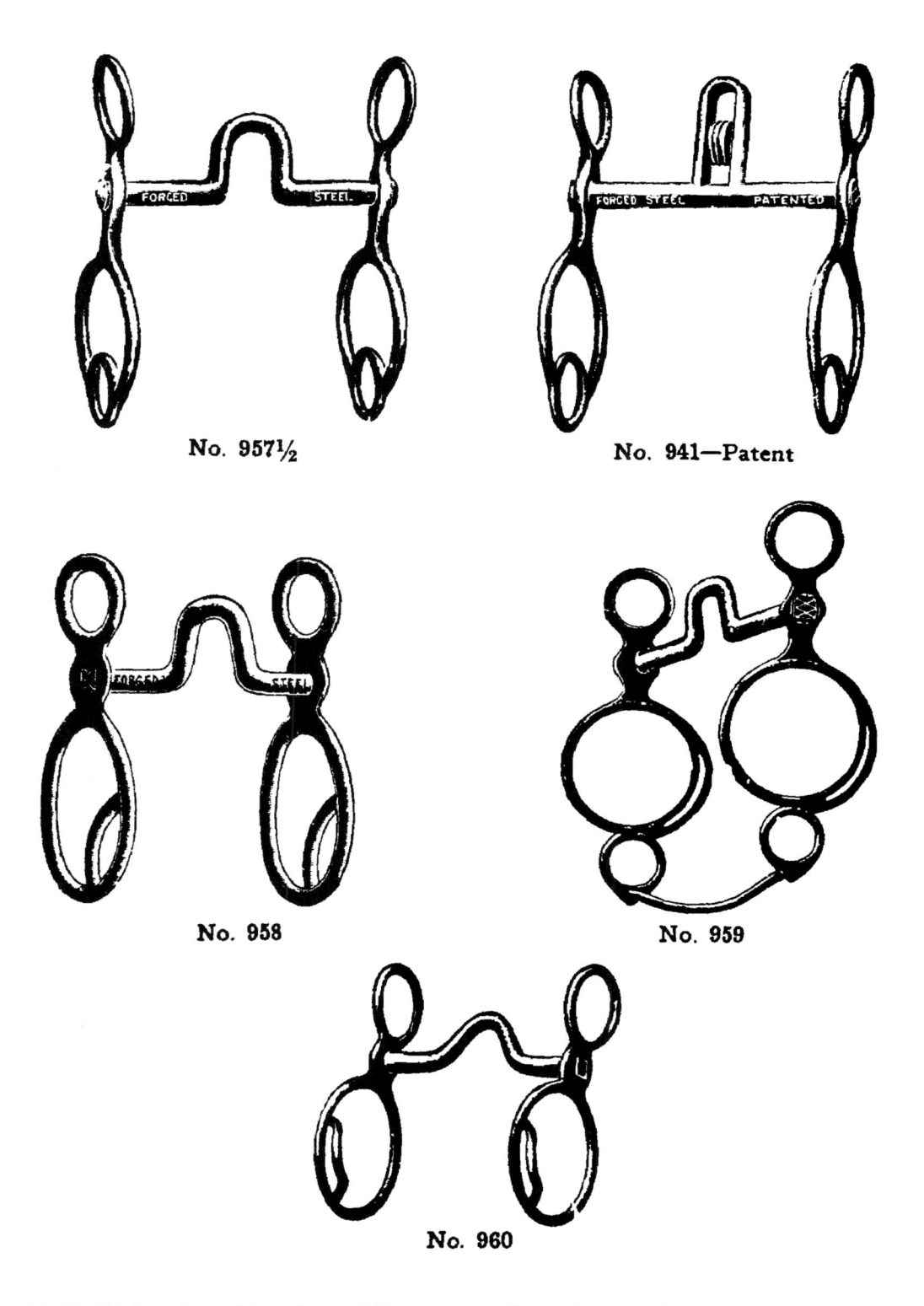

No. 941—Patent

No. 958

No. 959

No. 960

Fig. 12.32 Globe bits sold by August Buermann. From Catalog No. 35, circa 1922. Made in burnished, blued and nickel plated; in hand forged steel and malleable.

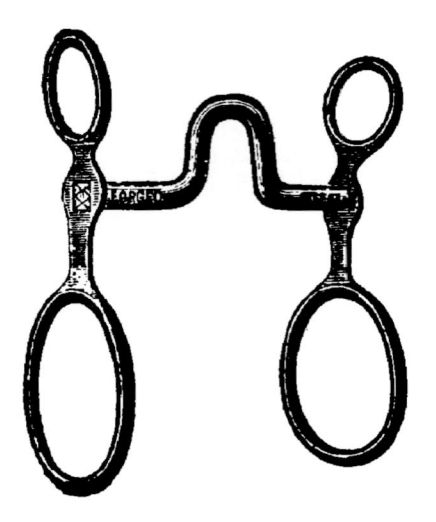

No. 957

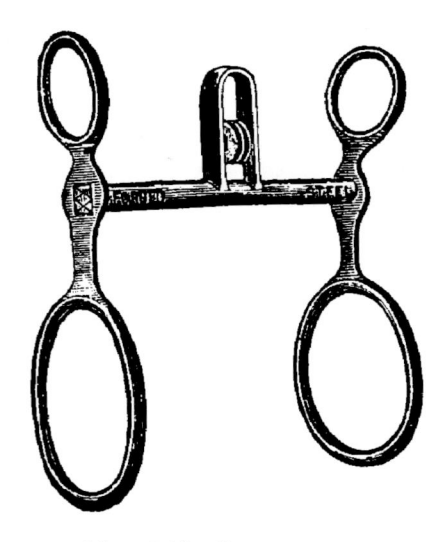

No. 940—Patent

No. 946

No. 948—Patent

Fig, 12.32a Buermann's Cowboy Globe bits. Made in polished, burnished, blued and nickel plated; in hand forged and malleable steel

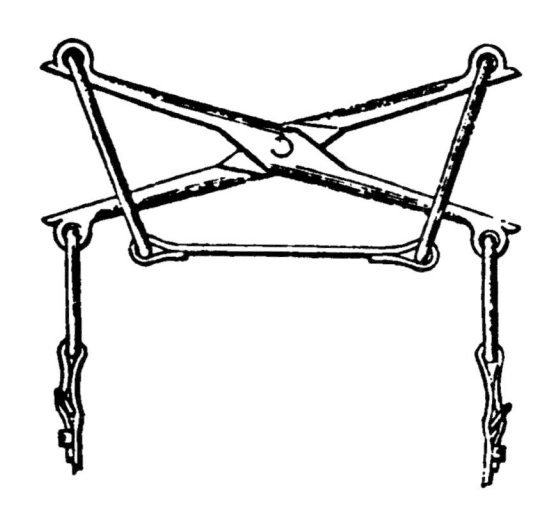

Fig. 12.34 Goodyear scissor bit.

Gordon, Thomas D., Monmouth, IL, Patent No. 519,112, May 1, 1894 [Fig. 12.35]. This is an overdraw bit with the strap placed under the chin rather than to the bit. A tie-down strap is attached to the strap under the chin.

Fig. 12.35 Gordon overdraw strap.

Graham, A. E., Richland, IN, Patent No. 64,970, May 21, 1867 [Fig. 12.37]. A continuous rein passes from the terret or check-hook on the harness backband through the pulleys on the gag bridle and bit cheek-pieces.

Fig. 12.37 Graham checking bit and bridle.

Graham, Absalam, Madison, ME, Patent No. 1,124,888, Jan 12, 1915 [Fig. 12.36]. The chin-bar works well loose and adjusts to the rein pull. The chin-bar can be securely fastened.

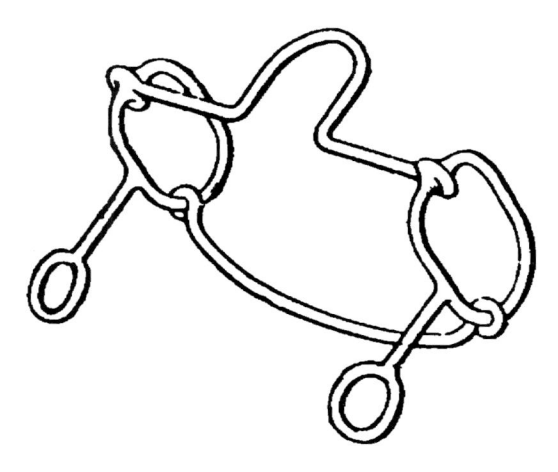

Fig. 12.36 Graham adjustable chin-bar bit.

Grant, Joseph H., Huron, SD, Patent No. 1,211,729, Oct. 2, 1917 [Fig 12.38]. A bridle bit including a tubular bit bar and a guard on each end of the bar consisting of inner and outer concave-convex plates with an intermediate reinforcing plate. The outer edges of the plates have spaced openings for bridle strap connections.

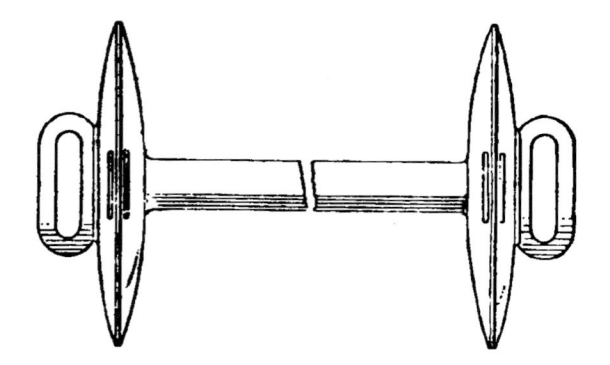

Fig. 12.38 Grant plate-cheek bit.

Graves, George W., Amarillo, TX, Design Patent No. 34,573, May 28, 1901 [Fig. 12.39]. A. Buermann Mfg. Co. No. 1901 "Bronco" bit in catalog No. 35. Cheek-piece displays a cowboy astride a horse with lowered head.

Fig. 12.39 Graves Bronco bit.

Grazing Bit: A bit with an upward curve in the center of the mouth-piece. The width and height of the curve varies. The shanks or cheek-pieces are short or bent backwards to facilitate the horse's grazing with the bit in its mouth [Fig. 12.40].

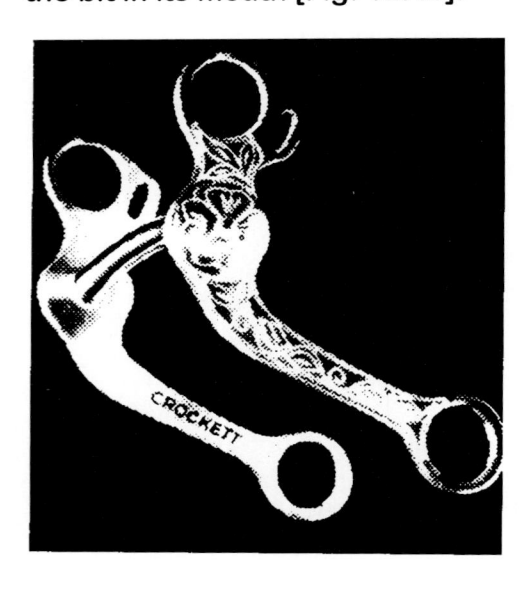

Fig. 12.40 Grazing bit from Crockett.

Green, Clyde W., St. John, WA, Patent No. 1,084,329, Jan 13, 1914 [Fig. 12.41]. The circular cheek-piece has a portion bent outward and provided with a slot for attaching the rein.

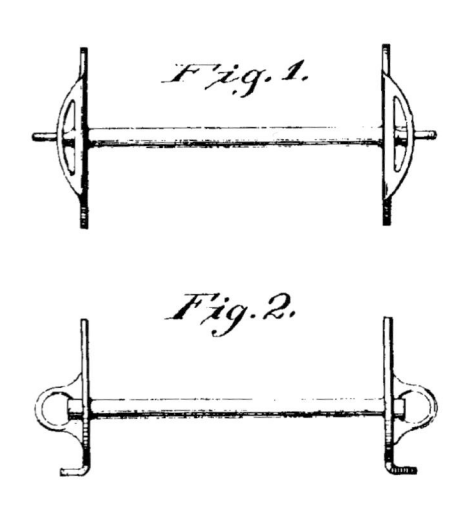

Fig. 12.41 Green snaffle bit.

Greenwood, James W., Springfield, IL, Patent No. 899,298, Sep. 22, 1908 [Fig. 12.42]. An overcheck bit with elongated curved side-bars that extend forward and up.

Fig. 12.42 Greenwood overcheck bit.

Greenwood Port: See Chapter 25.

Gregory, Charles P., Stillwater, MN, Patent No. 444,425, Jan 13, 1891 [Fig. 12.43]. A half-cheek snaffle bit with an overcheck attached to the mid-point of the mouth-piece.

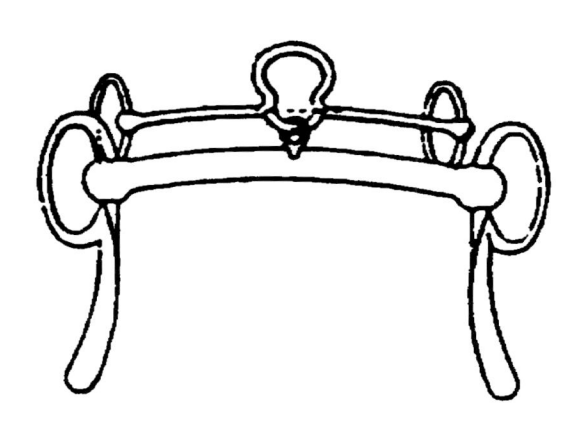

Fig. 12.43 Gregory snaffle bit.

Gridiron Bit: A bit with a mesh or patterned mouth or port. See Bentinek Curb Bit, Chapter 5, Fig. 5.47.

Gripper Bars: Extended projections from the side-pieces of a bit which grab or grip the cheeks or lower jaw of the horse.

Grooved Mouth: A serrated mouth. See Chapter 25.

Grosvenor Check Bit: See Chapter 9.

Ground Tie: A horse trained to stand when the reins are dropped to the ground.

Guard: Term referring to the cheek-piece or a shield placed inside the cheek-piece. See Chapter 5, Bit Guards.

Guedez, Francisco, Caracus, Venezuela, Patent No. 864,641, Aug, 27, 1907 [Fig. 12.44]. The levered side-pieces cause the mouth-piece to slide in the slots of the cheek-pieces.

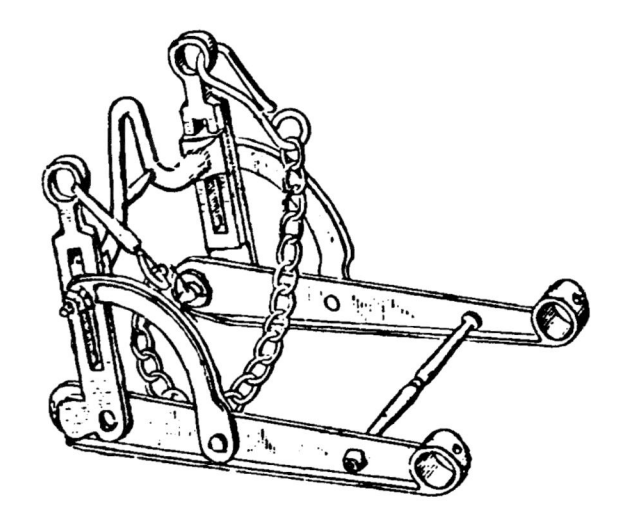

Fig. 12.44 Guedez moveable-mouth curb bit.

Gutta-Percha: A rubber-like gum produced from the latex of various SE Asia trees and used to coat the mouth-pieces of bits as well as other uses.

Guy, Charles E., Racine, WI, Patent No. 418,012, Dec. 12, 1889 [Fig. 12.45]. A modification of the J.I.C. Bit.

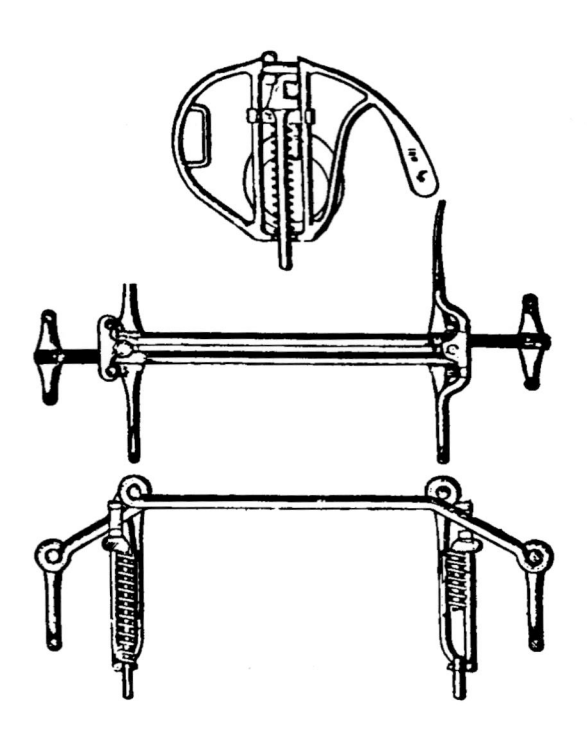

Fig. 12.45 Guy improved scissor bit.

CHAPTER THIRTEEN
Hackamore

The word hackamore is a corruption of the Spanish word *jaquima* which means halter or headstall. The cowboy learned his Spanish by ear and *jaquima* became hackamer and then hackamore. It is basically a halter with reins in place of a lead rope. Many forms or interpretations have been made, each with a specific purpose. In the last 75 years, a metal frame-work called hackamore bit has become popular in many places as a replacement for the bosal.

The hackamore and its name may have originated as early as the 2nd millennium B.C. in the area that is now known as the Arabian countries where the term *Hackma* is still used to describe a halter used on camels. The hackamore as known in this country, is nowhere to be found in Spain today.

The hackamore consists of a headstall, a bosal, a mecate and a fiador. See Diagram, Fig. 13.0.

The headstall is used the same as a bridle headstall and its purpose is to hold the bosal or noseband in position. The fiador's (sometimes pronounced "theodore") purpose is to hold the headstall on the head and support or keep the bosal in position. The mecate is used as the reins and is attached to the heel knot. A mecate is a rope made of horsehair and about 22 feet long. The horsehair rope with its stiff bristles irritates the tender skin of the horse's neck and helps it to learn a little quicker. Modern mecates are often made of cotton rope.

Many people who work with horses have the idea that a horse may be controlled with only a hackamore.

A hackamore is a training device, not a control rig. It is designed and used to train the horse to carry its head properly in preparation for using the bit.

The true hackamore with a bosal and chin knot has little effect on the horse as long as the horse carries its head in the proper position and the rider's hands are in a relaxed position. Only when the rider takes up the reins or the horse drops its head does the learning process begins to take place.

The bosal will drop and the heel knot come up under the chin. The result, in a short time, is two sore spots, one on its nose and one under the chin.

The beginning hackamore training should be done gently and quietly at a slow pace. The purpose of the hackamore is to train the horse to work the commands by itself and get used to having the rider on its back. If the horse is trying to get used to a bit in its mouth, it will take its mind off the training that needs to be done. A trainer needs to let the horse learn the hazards of the hackamore on its own and the training will procede much easier and faster than if the training is forced by sheer hardheadedness on the part of the trainer.

After the horse is trained on the hackamore, then it is ready to begin working with a bit.

Bosal (Bozal): The noseband of a hackamore is used in place of a bit. The most accepted bosal is made of braided rawhide over a twisted rawhide core. In many modern bosals the core is a steel cable covered by rawhide or leather. The diameter varies from pencil size to over an inch [Fig. 13.1, 13.2, 13.3 and 13.4].

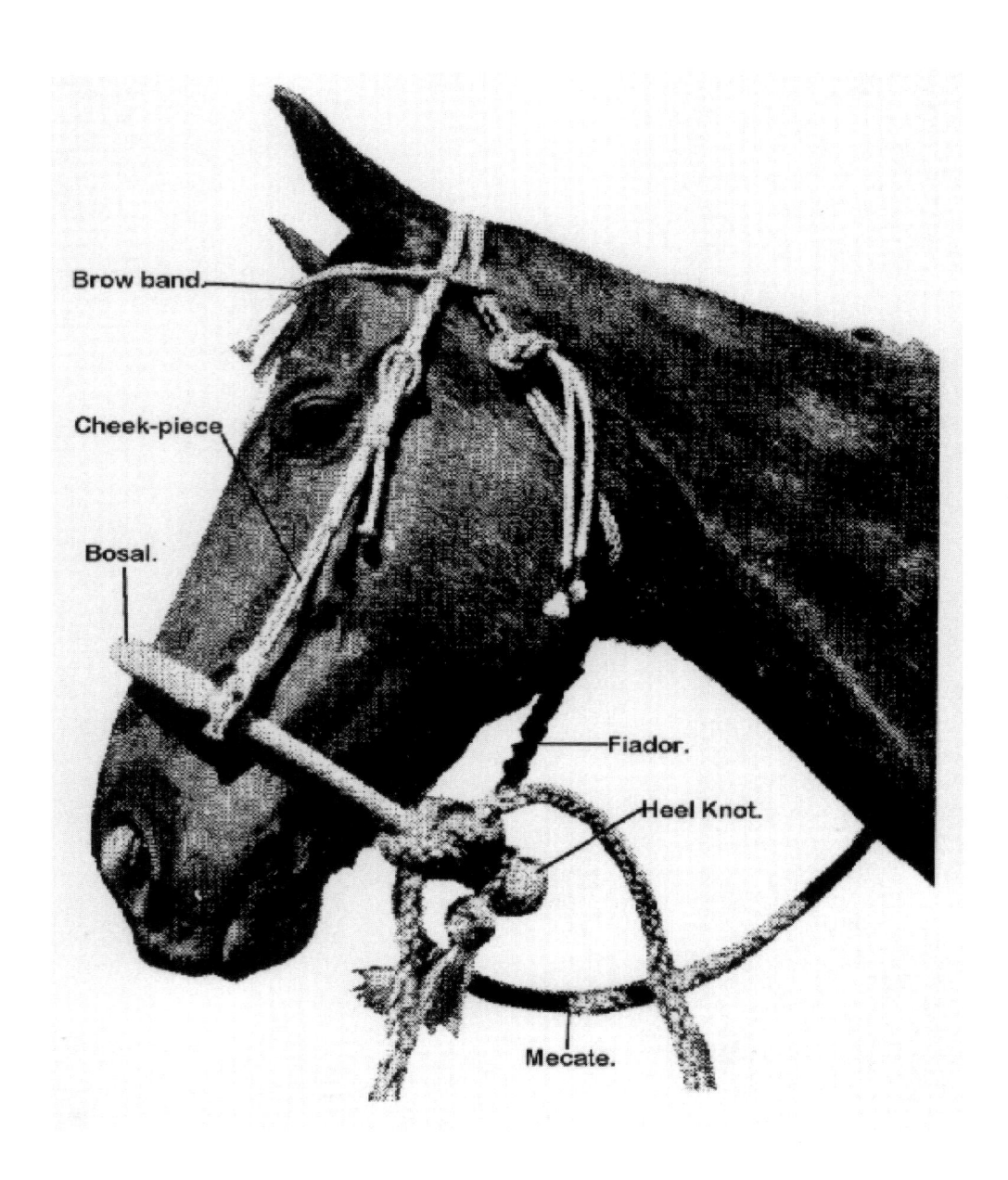

Fig. 13.0 Diagram of the parts of a hackamore.

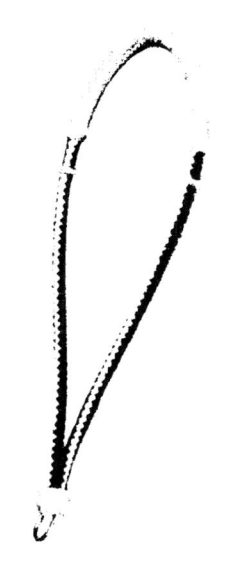

Fig. 13.1 A thin bosal called a pencil bosal.

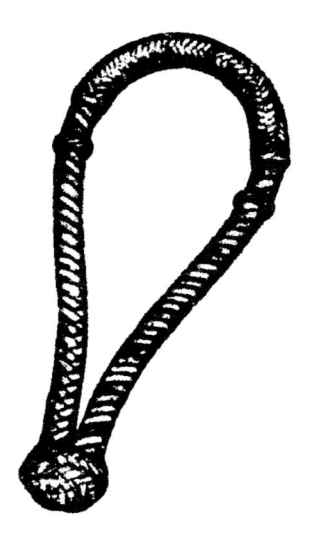

Fig. 13.3 A large-diameter bosal of one inch.

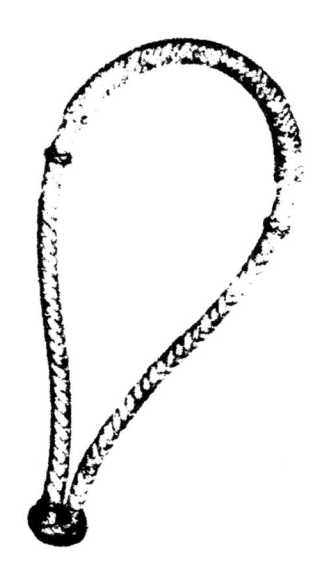

Fig. 13.2 A bosal of average size, about 5/8 inch in diameter.

Fig. 13.4 A bosal with braided knots to restrict the air flow through the nostrils when pressure is applied to the bosal through the mecate.

Bosalea: A Spanish word that is a derivation of *bozal* (muzzle) to designate a riding headstall. The major difference from a hackamore is that the bosalea is for riding only and not for tying. The hackamore with its fiador can be used to tie a horse [Fig. 13.5].

Fig. 13.5 Bosalea. From *The Cowboy at Work* by Fay E. Ward, Courtesy of Universidty of Oklahoma Press, Norman.

Fiador (Feador): A throat-latch or safety devise for the hackamore. It is a small horsehair or cotton sash rope which has been doubled. The fiador passes through the loops of the hackamore brow-band just behind and below the ears. After going around the neck a knot is formed under the throat and an ending second knot is formed around the heel knot or button of the bosal.

Hackalea: A form of hackamore with a single face-strap from the brow-band that divides to give an additional support to the bosal or noseband, much like that of the bosalea.

Hackarees: A term for the combination of metal and leather or rawhide, more commonly referred to as a hackamore bit.

Heel Knot: A knot on the lower end of a bosal to which the mecate is tied. The heel knot acts on the mandibles or lower jaw of the horse in the area of the chin groove. See diagram Fig, 13.0.

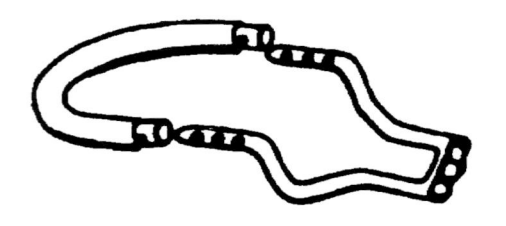

Fig. 13.6 Donal *hackamore bit* made *by* Donal Equipment Co., Sun Valley, CA. The *two*-piece *hackamore bit* can *be* adjusted *by* changing the set of the matched holes. The design and contour allows it to work on the "outside" under the jaw.

Kelly, Pascal M., El paso, TX, Design Patent No. 156,125, Nov. 22, 1949 [Fig. 13.7].

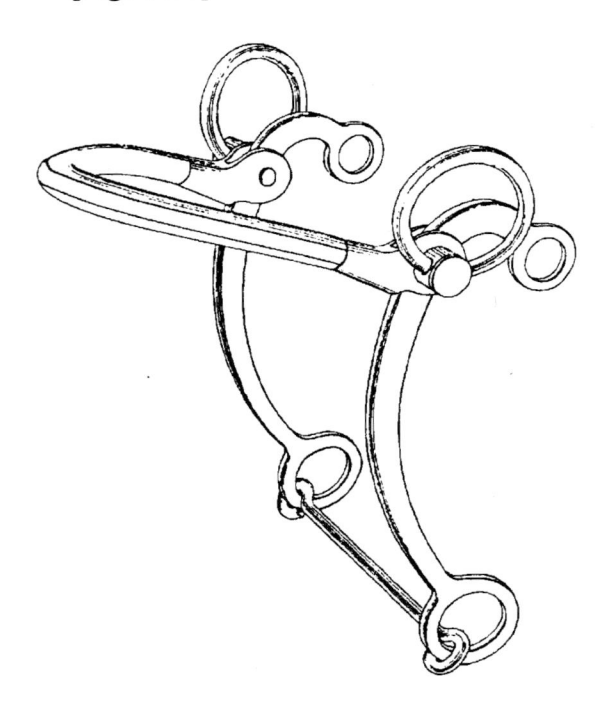

Fig. 13.7 Kelly *hackamore bit* design.

Design Patent No. 177,685, May 15, 1956 [Fig. 13.8].

Design Patent No. 193,351, Aug. 7, 1962 [Fig. 13.9].

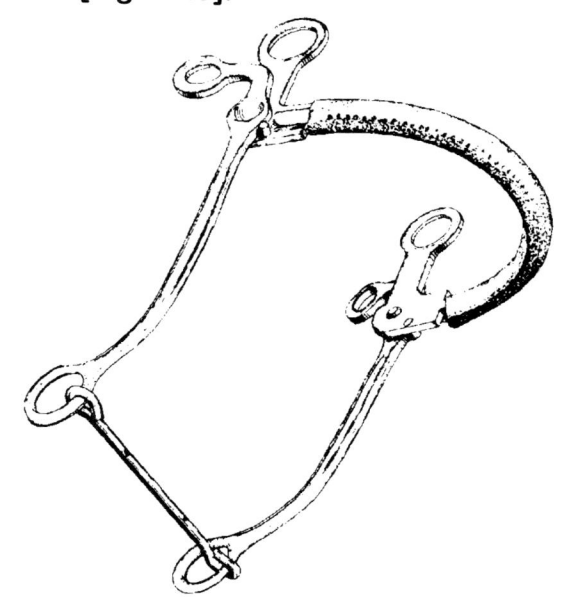

Fig. 13.9 Kelly hackamore design patent.

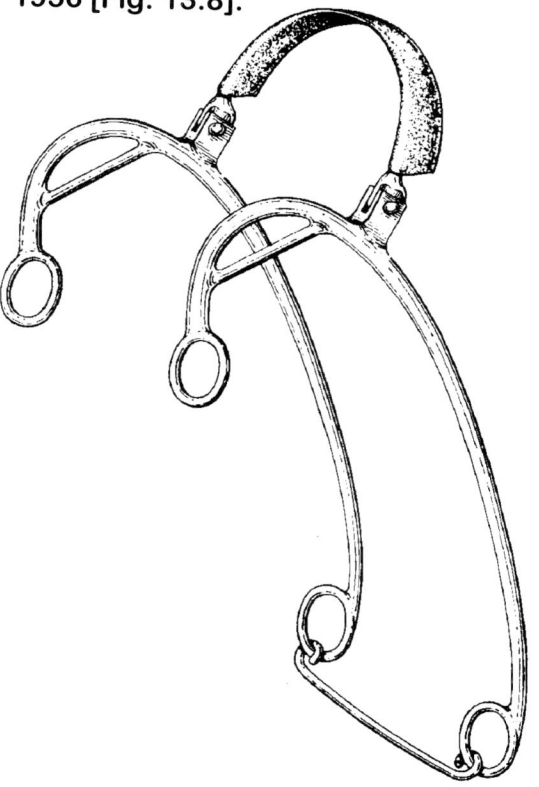

Fig. 13.8 Kelly hackamore design patent.

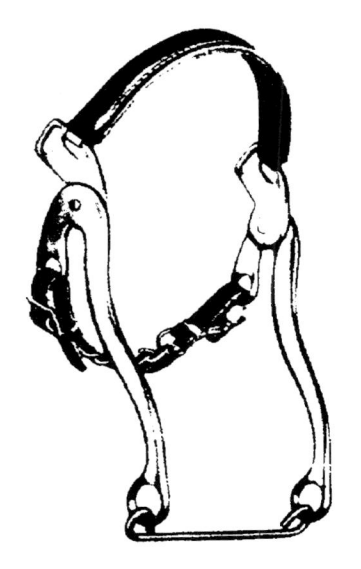

Fig. 13.10 A hackamore bit made by Quick Bits. The curb-chain or strap works in the curb groove with the nose-band on the proper point of the horse's nose bone.

Fig. 13.11 A training hackamore by Quick Bits. Hangs loosely without annoying the horse and with adjustable noseband and headstall.

Ray, Frederick A., Los Angeles, CA, Patent No. 2,225,232, Dec 17, 1940 [Fig. 13.12]. A hackamore bit composed of a flexible chain, circumferentially and inflexible at right angles. It is loosely attached to the cheek-pieces. The bit can be

175

used with or without a mouth-piece and with or without a curb-chain. Designed to start colts and gradually progress in training to only a complete bit.

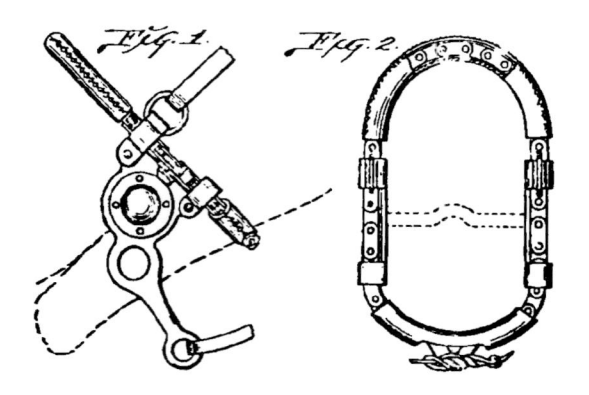

Fig. 13.12 Ray hackamore bit.

Patent No. 2,494,201, Jan. 10, 1950. An improvement over previous patent in that the cheek-pieces pivot on the mouth-piece.

Fig. 13.14 A hackamore bit with control by the noseband, the bit and the curb-chain. From J. C. Sproul, Edmonton, Alberta, Canada.

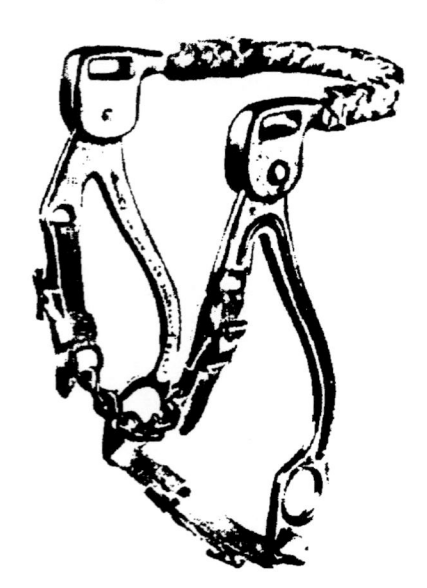

Fig. 13.13 A hackamore bit made by Ruwar Mfg. Co., Denver, CO. Positive lever action without pinching and fits high on the nose. Adjusts to any size horse with the adjustable curb. Made of aluminum alloy.

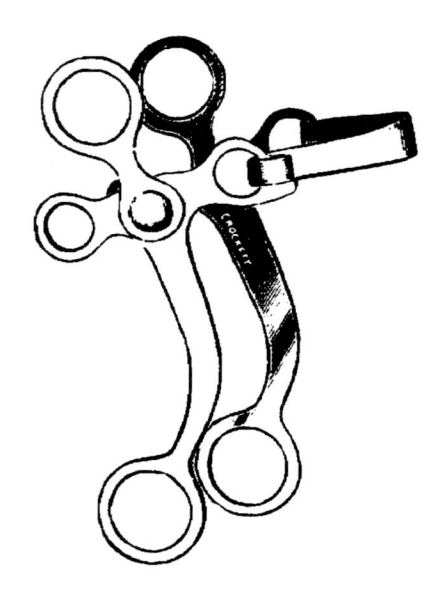

Fig. 13.15 A T-shaped hackamore bit from Crockett.

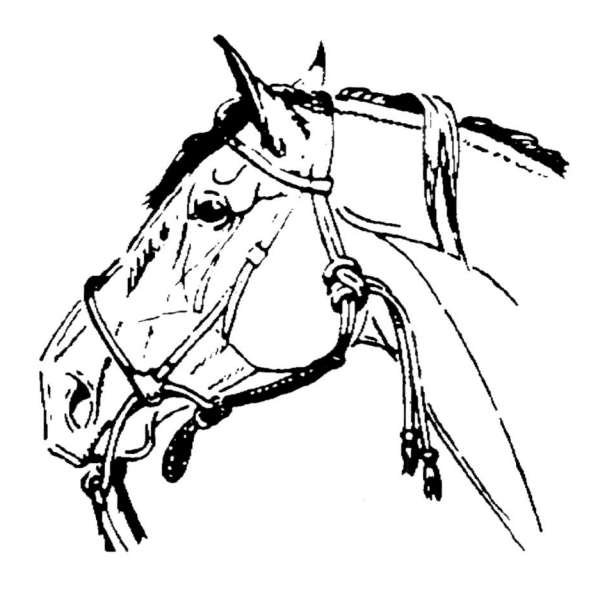

Fig. 13.16 Ward's Stop hackamore with "Combination Hackamore Jaw Cradle." Designed by Fay Ward.

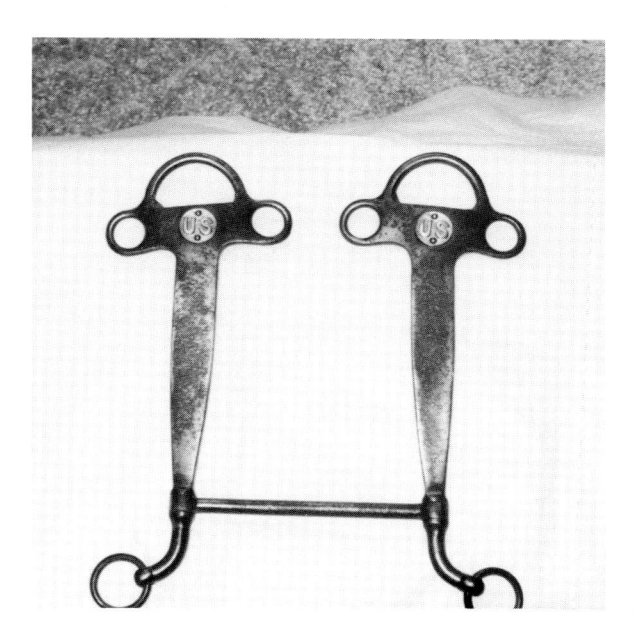

Fig. 13.18 Hackamore bit which has been adorned with U.S. bosses of Shoemaker bit. Lloyd Schultz collection.

Fig. 13.17 Cheek-pieces of a hackamore bit.

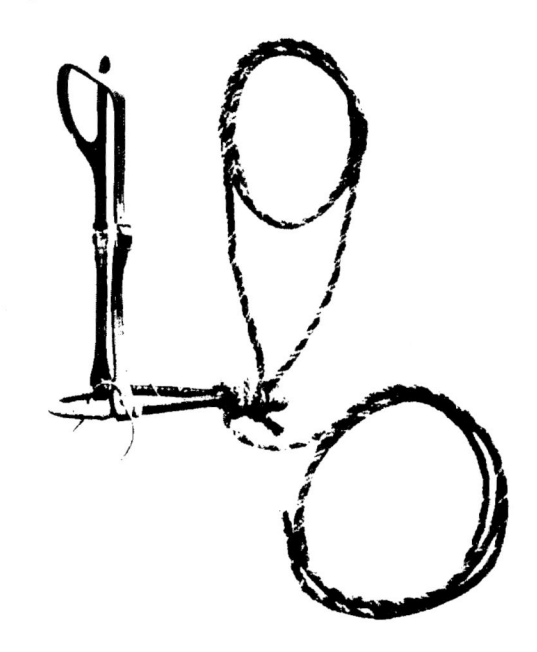

Fig. 13.19 Modern hackamore with a one-ear headstall supplied with a cotton rope mecate and a 5/8 inch bosal.

The Very Best Hackamores

The STRICKLAND
Our new improved combination hackamore bit. Made of lasting durable aluminum. A bit most every rider would like. The new plates have three adjustable slots for the noseband. Removable straight bar mouthpiece, adjustable sheeplined noseband, nickel plated curb chain. 9¼-inch cheeks.

No. 37—Hand engraved. Each $10.00
No. 36—Plain only. Each 7.95

The COLORADO
A streamlined combination hackamore bit. Made of durable aluminum. A fine bit with two adjustments. This bit can be used on the most gentle or rough, hard to control horse. Removable straight bar mouthpiece, adjustable. Sheepskin lined noseband and nickel plated curb chain. 8⅛-inch cheeks.

No. 41—Hand engraved. Each $9.00
No. 40—Plain Each 7.50

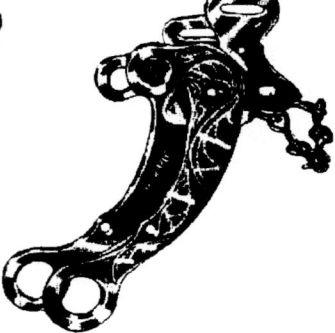

The TEXAS
Ricardo's new hackamore bit, very humane on the mildest horse, 7¾-inch cheeks. Chain noseband will not drop over the horse's nose. Head stall piece fastens to pivot which prevents head stall from tipping forward when pulling reins. Made of airplane aluminum."

No. 65—All hand engraved. Each $8.75
No. 64—Plain. Each .. 6.75

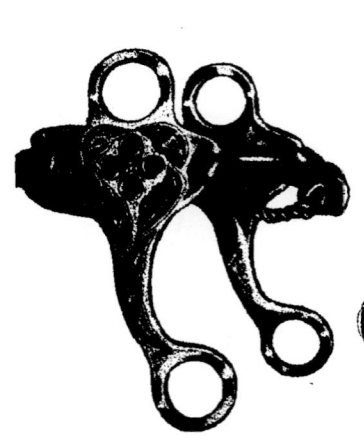

The PHOENIX
The new Ricardo hackamore, adjustable skirting leather sheep lined nose band, combination chain and leather curb strap.

No. 35—Beautifully hand engraved. Each $6.50
No. 34—Plain. Each............ 5.00

The BILLINGS
The Don Ricardo special hackamore, with airplane aluminum nose band, 8-inch cheeks.

No. 31—Beautifully hand engraved. Each $5.50
No. 30—Plain. Each............ 4.00

The CODY
The Texas style long shank hackamore, 9¼-inch cheek. Curved metal noseband covered with sheep skin. Nickel plated curb chain and cross chain. Entire bit made of everlasting aluminum polished to a high lustre and beautifully engraved.
No. 33—Hand engraved. Each $6.75
No. 32—Plain, each............$5.50

Ricardo METAL MANUFACTURERS, 1218 15th ST., DENVER 2, COLO.

Fig. 13.20 Mechanical hackamores or hackamore bits made by Ricardo.

CHAPTER FOURTEEN
Hackney to Hutton

Hackney Bit: A light driving bit made by most major manufacurers of driving bits. Designed for use on hackney horses that weigh today in the range of 700 to 800 pounds. See Fig. 14.0.

Hale, George C., Kansas City, MO, Patent No. 505,762, Sep. 26, 1893 [Fig. 14.1]. A bit and bridle designed for horses pulling fire apparatus, patrol wagons or other vehicles where it is desirable to dispense with the use of a mouth bit.

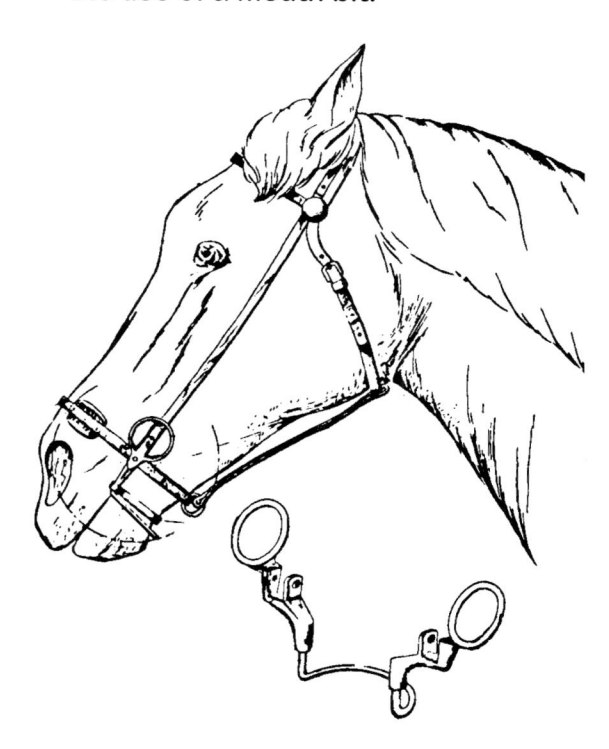

Fig. 14.1 Hale bridle and bit for fire horses.

Half-breed Bit: A western-style bit with a narrow upward extending port which usually has a roller or cricket installed [Fig. 14.2]. See Mouthpieces, Chapter 25.

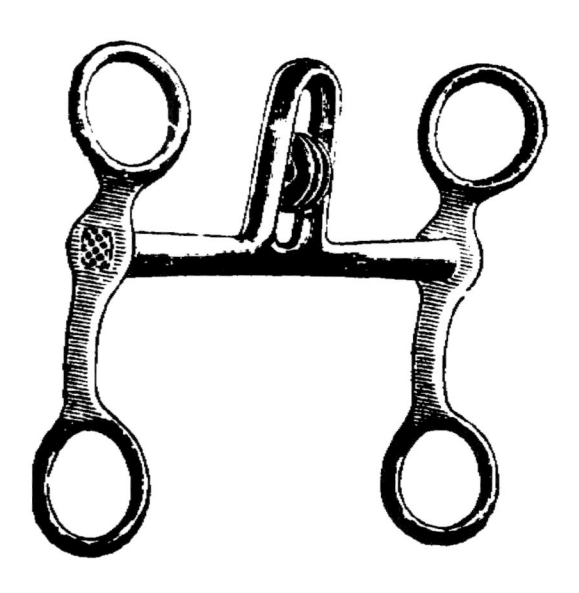

Fig. 14.2 An example of a Half-breed bit.

Half-cheek Bit: A snaffle bit with a projection only one way from the cheek-ring, usually downward. See Side-pieces, Chapter 31.

Half-moon Bit: The lower side of the bit is drawn to a thin edge, but not sharp enough to cut. The edge can be made straight or a little concave. When the small surface is brought against the jaw by a hard pull, sufficient pain is produced to prevent the resistance of the horse [Fig. 14.3].

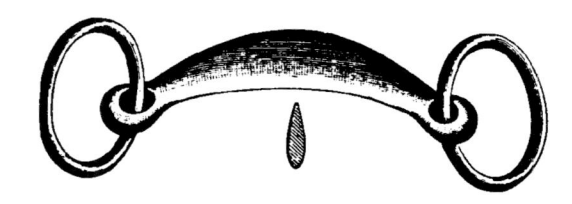

Fig. 14.3 Half-moon Bit.

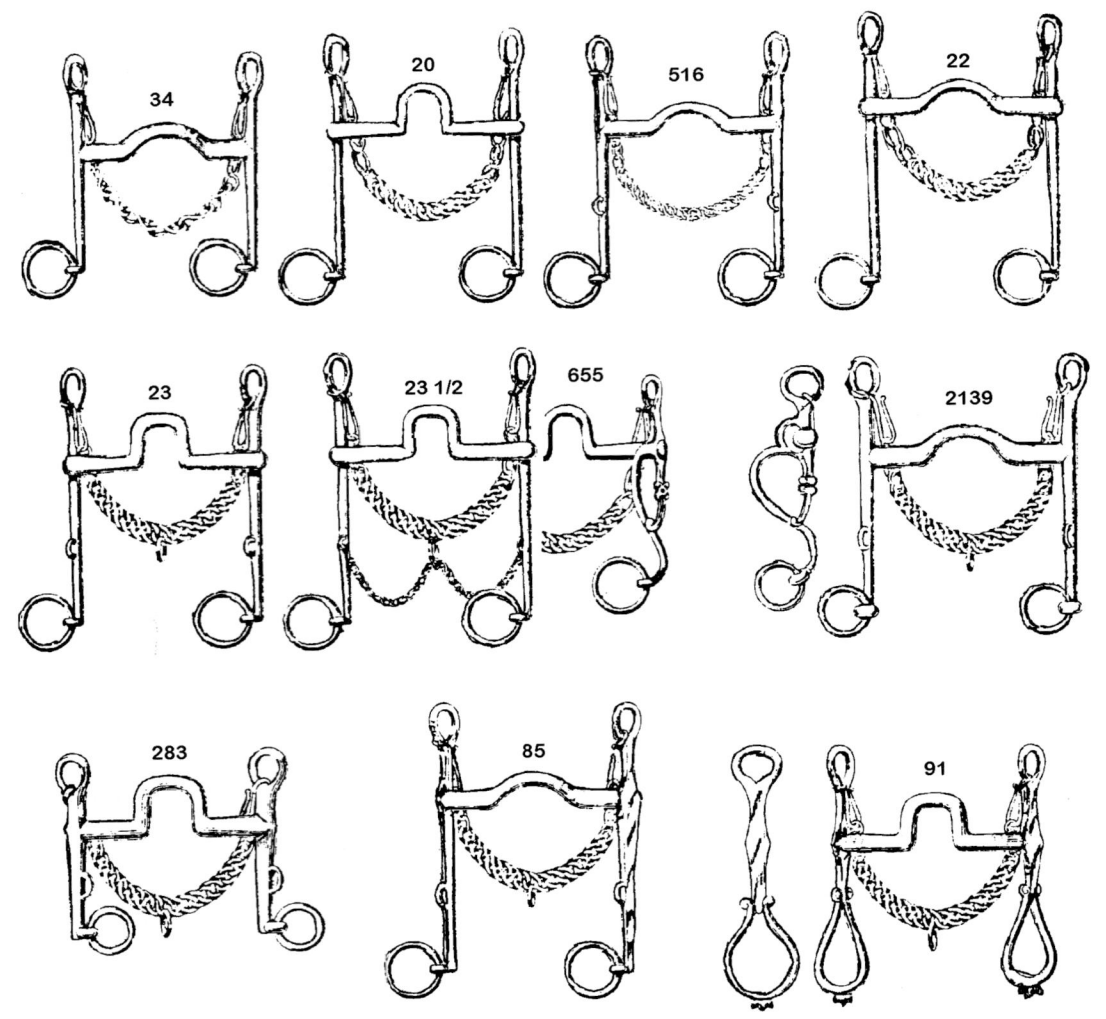

Fig. 14.0 Hackney bits from John Dewsbury and Son. Produced in polished, nickel-plated forged iron, steel and waranteed hard steel, V.S. nickel and solid nickel.

34   Light low port Hackney bit & curb.

20   Light high port Hackney bit and curb.

516   Light chin loop low port Hackney bit and curb.

22   Medium weight low port Hackney bit and curb.

23   Medium weight high port Hackney bit and curb.

23 1/2 Medium weight high port Hackney bit with chin chain and curb.

655   Low port fancy cheek stout pattern bit and curb.

2139   Stout chin loop low port Hackney bit and curb.

283   Stout high port, flat cheek chin loop Hackney bit and curb.

85   Flat cheek low port chin loop Hackney bit and curb.

91   Medium port flat ballon cheek Hackney bit and curb.

Half-moon Pelham: See Pelham, Chapter 27, Fig. 27.1.

Half-spoon Bit: Refers to the cheek-piece. See Side-pieces, Chapter 31.

Hall, Frank P., *et al.*, Pleasanton, KS, Patent No. 720,689, Feb. 17, 1903 [Fig. 14.4]. The cheek-pieces have built in stops to limit the range of the curb action and the internal gag plate.

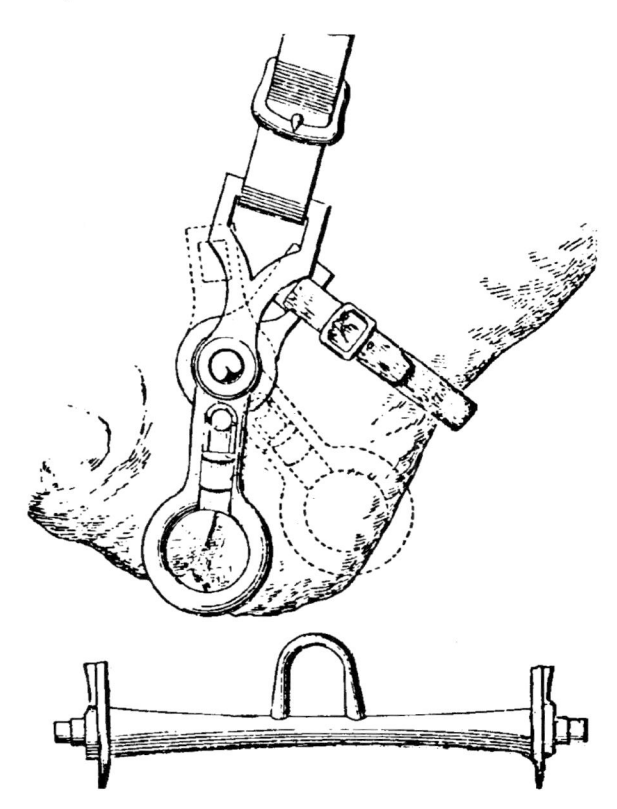

Fig. 14.4 Hall curb bit.

Halter: A head-piece with a lead rope attached for restraining or tying a horse.

Halter Broke: A horse trained to lead by means of a halter and lead rope.

Halter Chain: A chain on the end of a lead rope and attached to the halter. The chain may be attached to the off-side ring of the halter, pass under the chin and through the near-side halter ring. When attached in this manner it can be a more effective control device. Most often used on stallions.

Hancock Curb Bit Mouth-cover: A leather protecting shield placed around mouth-pieces [Fig. 14.5].

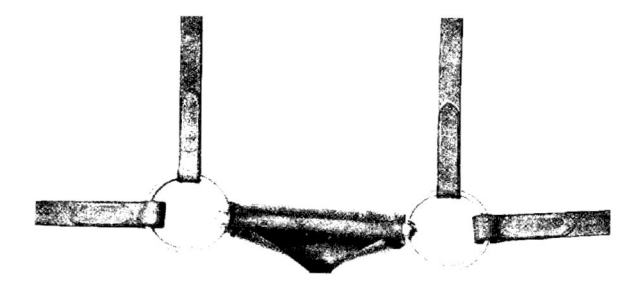

Fig. 14.5 Hancock mouth-piece cover, partially opened.

Hands: Term applied to how a person handles the reins and controls the horse. The term is used in the measurement of horses: one hand equals 4 inches.

Hanging-cheek Snaffle: A bit with the cheek-pieces positioned upward as opposed to the normal method of downward [Fig. 14.6].

Fig. 14.6 Hanging-cheek bit.

Hanging-tongue Bit: A bit for tongue-lolling horses [Fig. 14.7].

Fig. 14.7 Hanging-tongue bit.

Hanovarian Pelham: See Pelham, Chapter 27.

Hanscom, Albert H., Winterport, ME, Patent No. 376.088, Jan. 10, 1888 [Fig. 14.8]. The bit has a metal framework, to connect the cheek-pieces and metal plates, combined with a metal "elliptical" spring that produces a bit that is yielding but will not become set or distorted as rubber-mouth bits are prone to do. The entire mouth-piece is leather-covered.

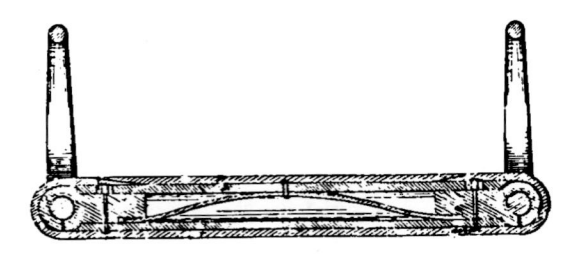

Fig. 14.8 Hanscom flexible-mouth bit.

Hansford, Robert J., Newark, NJ, Patent No. 337,578, Mar. 9, 1886 [Fig. 14.9]. A construction method with the mouth-piece threaded on each end and covered with paper washers treated with zinc chloride. The paper washers can be replaced by removing the cheek-pieces. The paper washers are durable, cheap and the zinc chloride acts medicinally on sore and tender mouths, according to Mr. Hansford.

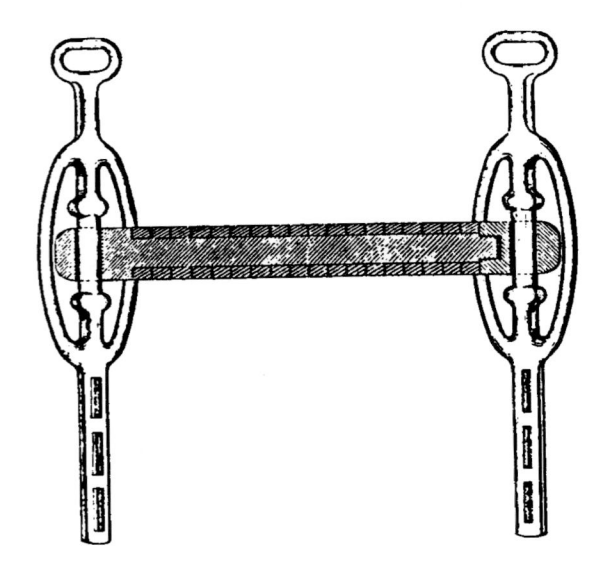

Fig. 14.9 Hansford paper-mouth medicine bit.

Harbec, Charles J., Alma, MT, Patent No. 1,129,126, Feb. 23, 1915 [Fig. 14.10]. The clamping loops of this bit pass over the nose, making the bit a noseband control bit.

Harmanson, Israel, Hopkins, MN, Patent No. 571,563, Nov. 16, 1896 [Fig. 14.11]. The bit has two bars crossed and connected near the center by a loop in the bar. The end of each bar is connected to a noseband. The action is not only on the bars of the horse, but pressure is also exerted on the nostrils of the horse. Two styles of cheek-pieces are shown.

Harness Bit: A term for a bit used on driving horses. See Ford, Frost, Higman, Petersboro, and Thurlow.

Harris, Robert N., Hickory, NC, Patent No. 523,811, July 31, 1894 [Fig. 14.12]. The bit is similar to Warfel's, except that the split mouth-piece is fixed and not adjustable and acts as a mouth-opener and gag.

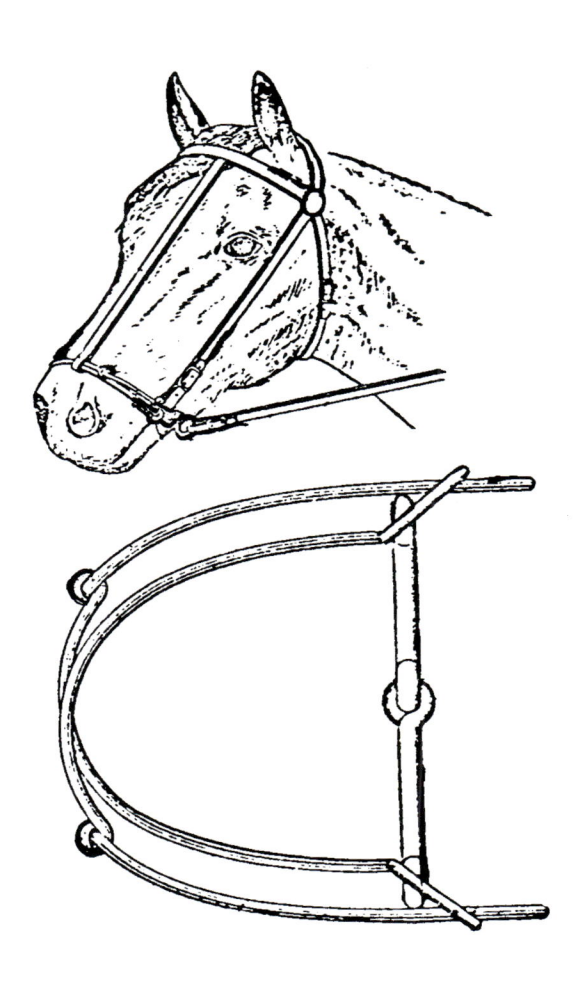

Fig. 14.10 Harbec nose clamp bit.

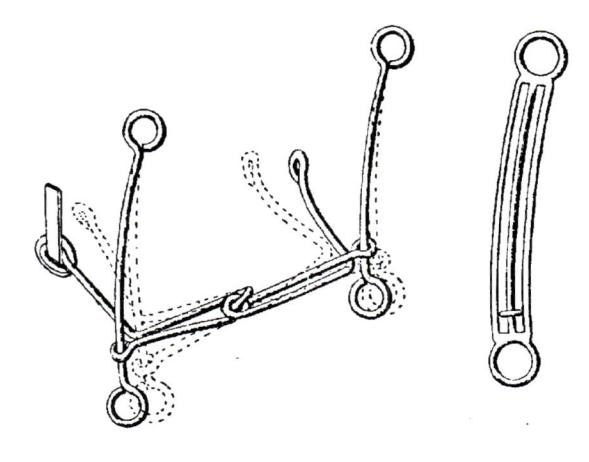

Fig. 14.11 Harmanson double-action bit.

Fig. 14.12 Harris curb bit.

Harry Hightower: A combination curb and bradoon bit with the bradoon attached to the port [Fig.14.13]. An early 18th century bit of England. *Walsall*

*Matthew Harvey
Bath St?
Walsall.*

Fig. 14.13 Harry Hightower Bit. From Harvey Matthew, drawing by W. A. Stone.

Hart, Charles N., Pittsford, VT, Patent No. 544,917, Aug. 20, 1895 [Fig. 14.14]. A combination bit with a built-in overcheck which works loosely in the center link.

Hartman, Henry, Salt Lake City, UT, Patent No. 229,405, June 29, 1880 [Fig. 14.15]. A straight-bar mouthpiece is attached to cheek-pieces with three rings on the upper end plus a hook for the curb-chain. The

183

center ring is for the headstall. The rings closest to the curb-hooks are for the reins and the third set is for the leather frontal piece to go over the nose and attach to the browband of the bridle. The ring at the closed end of the lower cheek-pieces is for the tie-down strap.

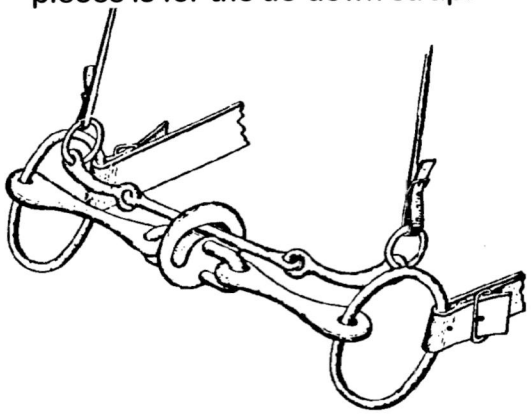

Fig. 14.14 Hart combination snaffle and overcheck bit.

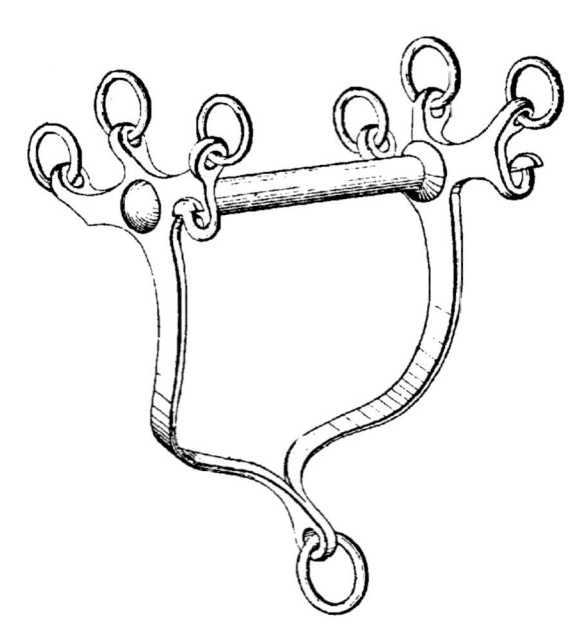

Fig. 14.15 Hartman curb bit.

Harvey, Lindsey, Norris, MS, Patent No. 992,961, May 23, 1911 [Fig. 14.16]. The pivotal cheek-pieces of this bit also have a pivotal curb-strap lever to which the reins are attached. When the reins are pulled, more pressure is placed on the curb groove and mandible of the horse than on the bars of the horse's mouth.

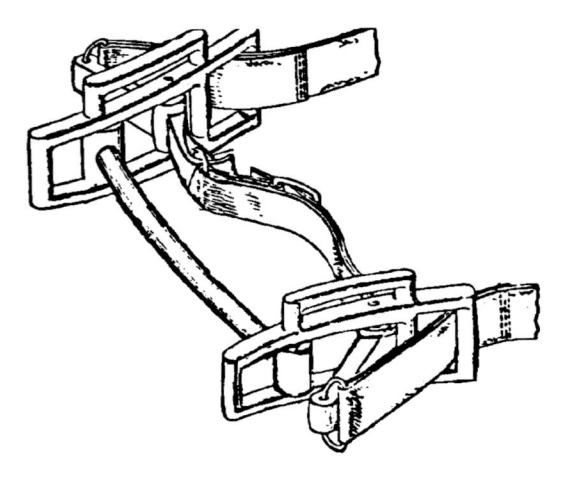

Fig. 14.16 Harvey pressure bit.

Haskell, Franklin L., Leominster, MA, Patent No. 130,994, Sep. 3, 1872 [Fig. 14.17]. This patent combines with the head-stall, a nose-piece or loop to extend around the nose of the animal, the driving-rein and standing martingale, a "toggle check." The "toggle check" has two levered cheek-pieces connected in the center to form the mouth-piece.

Hauser, John Henry, Killam, Alberta, Canada, Patent No. 2,132,469, May 19, 1938 [Fig. 14.18]. A bit with a tubular mouth-piece solidly attached to the plate cheek-pieces. A rod is extended through the hollow mouth-piece and shaped to hold rings for reins. Designed for horses in teams to prevent injury to lips and mouth by the team-mate throwing its head and pulling on the other's bit.

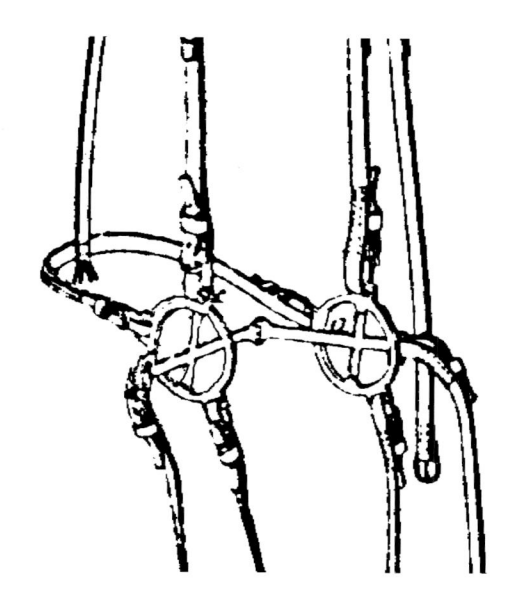

Fig. 14.17 Haskell toggle bit.

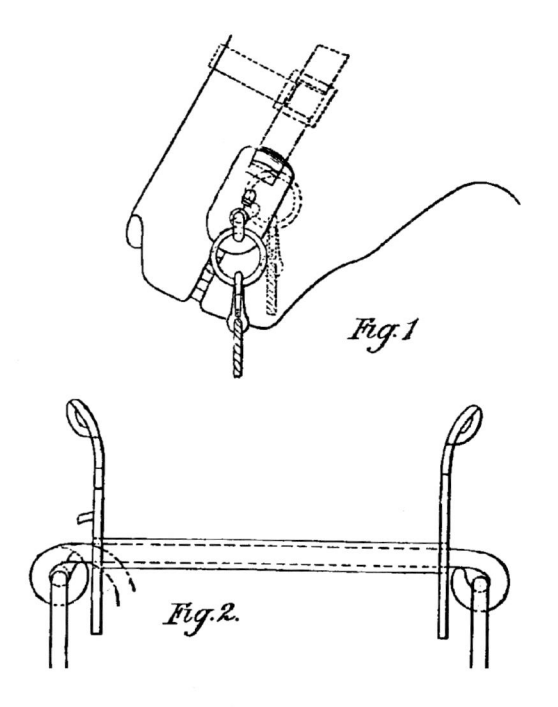

Fig. 14.18 Hauser tubular bit.

Havis, James Bit: See Chapter 15, Fig. 15.10.

Hayden, Peter, New York, NY, Patent No. 243,042, June 14, 1881 [Fig. 14.19]. The curved bar is rigid to the mouth-piece and is passed under the jaw as a bail or loop to be grasped and to hold the animal if necessary. The curved bar is not a curb but is used to control the horse from the ground.

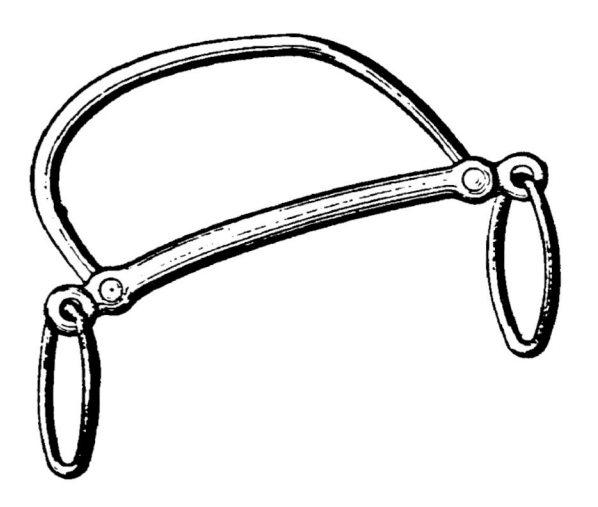

Fig. 14.19 Hayden bail bit.

Hayden, William B., Columbus, OH, Patent No. 63,156, Mar. 26, 1867 [Fig. 14.20]. This patent relates to the construction of the rein-rings, cheek-pieces and jointed mouth-pieces in separate parts and connecting these parts together by passing the cheek-pieces through eyes which are formed on the mouth-pieces and rings. Securing the whole together are bands or collars applied to the cheek-pieces.

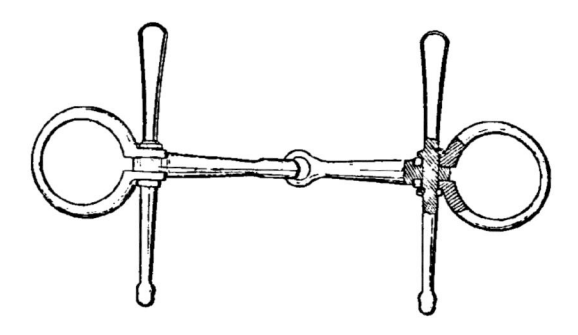

Fig. 14.20 Hayden construction design.

Head Collar: A bitless head-piece with a nose-band similar to a halter.

Head Fighting: A horse that continually throws its head in an effort to loosen the reins or rid itself of the bit.

Head of the Bit: The end of the mouth-piece. See Mouth-pieces, Chapter 25, Figs. 25.45 and 25.49.

Head Rope: A rope attached to the halter for tying a horse.

Headstall: The bridle portion placed on the head of a horse as a holder for the bit.

Hedgehog: A rough attachment to the mouth-piece of a bit. See Echini, Chapter 10.

Heel Knot: The terminal knot of a bosal to which the mecate or reins and lead ropes are attached.

Heinisch, Johann, Belgard, Pomerania, Germany, Patent No. 273,077, Feb. 27, 1883 [Fig. 14.23]. A bit designed to attach to a halter by the hooks on the bit. Two separate designs are presented in Figs. 1 and 2.

Heinze, Charles E., Newark, NJ, Patent No. 326,643, Sep. 22, 1885 [Fig. 14.21]. The mouth-piece is formed of a bundle of flexible wires secured in suitable heads and attached to cheek-pieces. A rubber covering is placed over the wire rope mouth-piece and the mouth-piece ends.

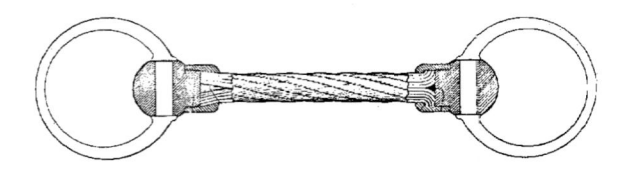

Fig. 14.21 Heinze mouth-piece design.

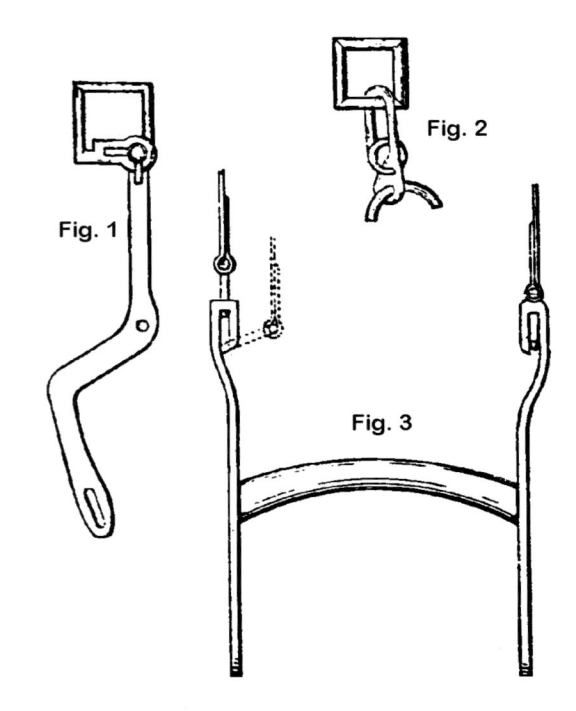

Fig. 14.23 Heinisch bit for attachment to a halter.

Patent No. 481,172, Aug. 23, 1892 [Fig. 14.22]. A construction design in that the mouth-piece ends are cast with an open end. The open end is placed around a center bar in the cheek-piece and closed to secure the mouth-piece.

Fig. 14.22 Heinze mouth-piece end construction design.

Helms, Allen W., Aylesworth, IN, Patent No. 389,809, Sep. 18, 1888 [Fig. 14.24]. The double-barred mouth-piece is secured to one cheek-piece and floats free in the loop of the opposite cheek-piece. The bars cross in the center with a scissor-like action when the reins are pulled.

The serrated inner side of the lower cheek-pieces acts to inflict pain on the lower jaw, especially if a check-rein is attached to the lower rings and the horse does not keep its head up and in.

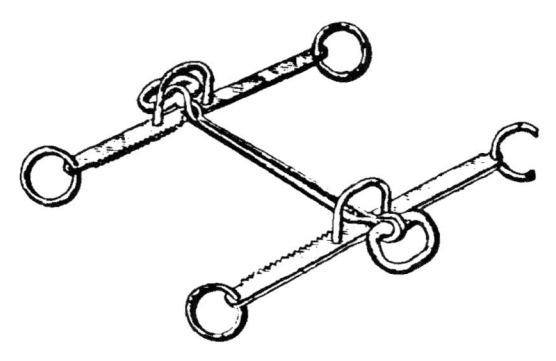

Fig. 14.24 Helms scissor bit.

Patent No. 475,110, May 17, 1892 [Fig. 14.25]. The crossed double mouth-piece is attached to slides that travel up or down the side-bar as pressure is applied to the reins. The padded bar at the top of the bit rests on the nose of the horse.

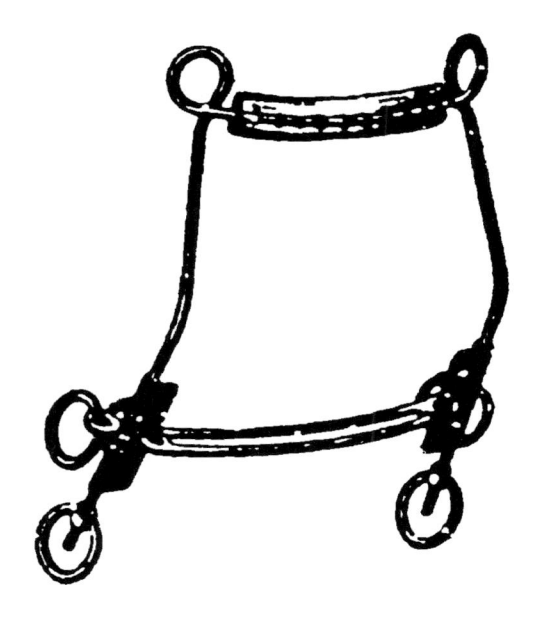

Fig. 14.25 Helms sliding scissor-mouth bit.

Hensley, Bird E., Salem, OR, Patent No. 1,335,964, Apr. 6, 1920 [Fig. 14.26].

A bit that can be used as a snaffle driving bit and with the addition of a curb strap to the upper inner rings, be converted to a curb bit. For use as a snaffle bit, the reins are attached to the loop extending rearward from the mouth-piece. For use as a curb, the reins are attached to the lower cheek-piece loops.

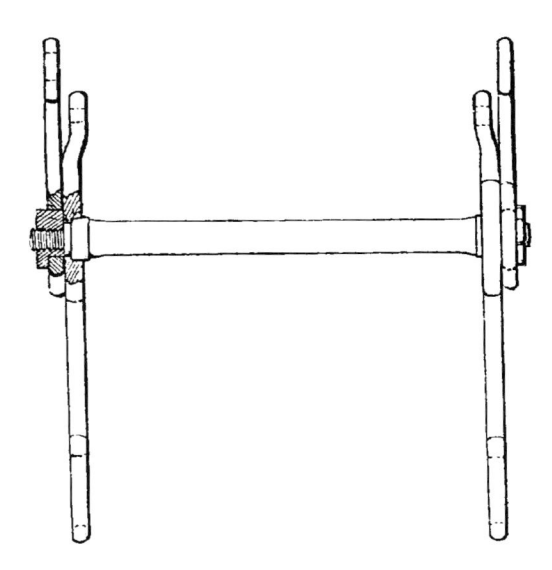

Fig. 14.26 Hensley snaffle-curb-option bit.

Herbert, Joseph Walter, Los Gatos, CA, Patent No. 891,419, June 23, 1908 [Fig. 14.27]. A bit and headstall with a combination of cogs and springs that greatly multiplies the force to push the mouth-piece back into the mouth. The mouth-piece is movable within the cheek-pieces and is pivotal on each side so that each works independently.

Hermosillo Bit: A style of bit loosely jointed at the mouth-piece and cheek-piece, similar to the early Santa Barbara-style bit.

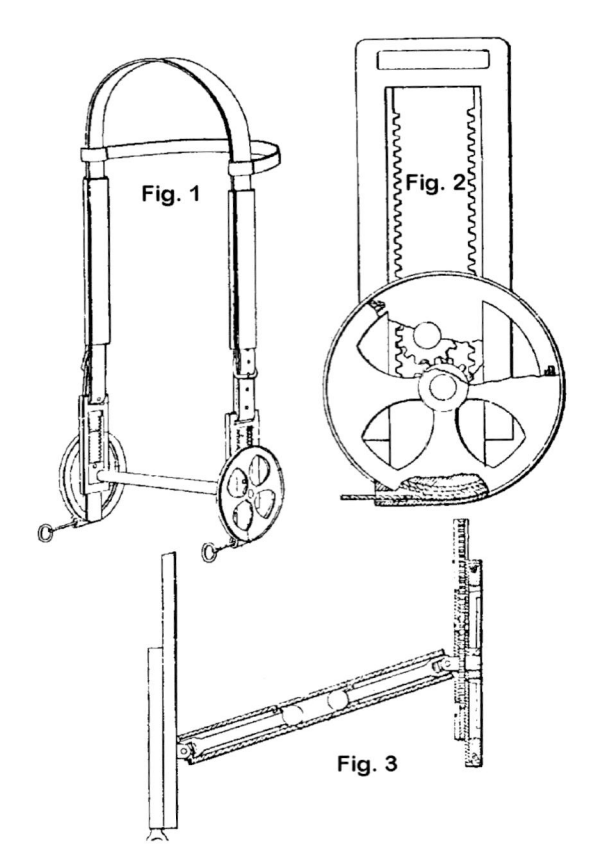

Fig. 14.27 Herbert geared bit.

High Checking: A check-rein usually used on trotters to hold the head checked high.

Hightower, Harry Bit: See Harry Hightower.

Higman's Harness Bit: An early 18th century English bit from *The Loriner* [Fig. 14.28].

Hinged Hunting Snaffle: A Quick Bit with 4-inch flat rings and a 5 1/8 inch width, 3/8 inch diameter snaffle mouth-piece [Fig.14.29]. A copper wire-wrapped mouth is an option.

Hinged-port-mouth Bit: A bit with a port in the mouth-piece and a hinged or loose cheek-piece. See Mouth-pieces, Chapter 25 and Side-pieces, Chapter 31.

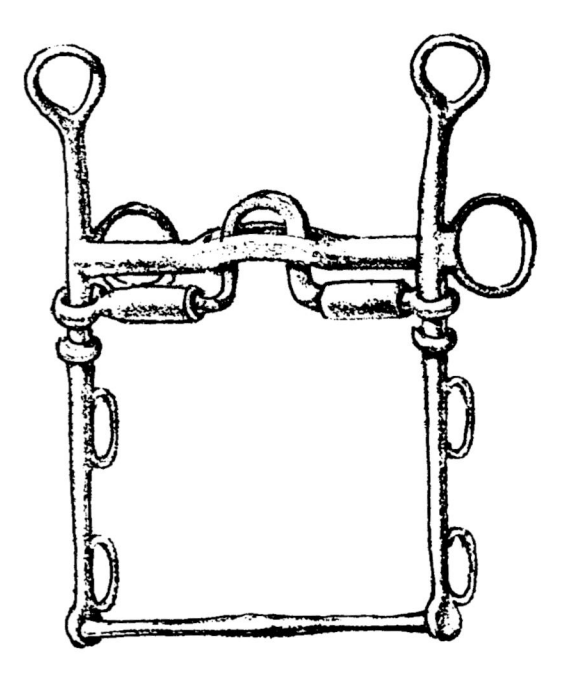

Fig. 14.28 Higman harness bit.

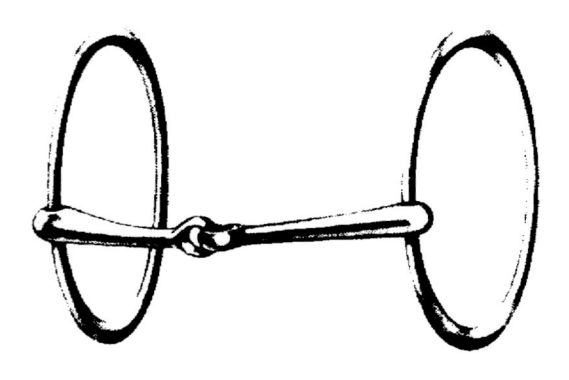

Fig. 14.29 Hinged hunting snaffle.

Hisley, John Peter, Syracuse, NY, Patent No. 160,772, Mar.16, 1875 [Fig. 14.30]. A snap is cast onto a ring-shaped cheek-piece, connected loosely to the mouth-piece.

Fig. 14.30 Hisley bit with snaps built into the check-pieces.

Hitchcock Gag Bit: See Gag Bits, Chapter 12, Fig. 12.11.

Hogan, Dora, Overcheck: See Driving Bits-Overcheck. Chapter 9.

Hogg, Charles B., Boston, MA, Patent No. 41,845, Mar. 8, 1864 [Fig. 14.31]. The bit dispenses with buckles in connecting a rein to the ring or rings of a bit. When the rein is passed through the cheek-piece and looped, a leather on the rein is pushed into place and secures the rein over the two prongs.

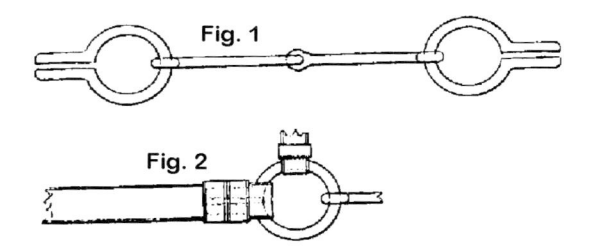

Fig. 14.31 Hogg bridle and bit connection.

Hollow Bar: A hollow mouth bit. See Mouth-piece, German Mouth, Chapter 25.

Hollow-cheek Curb: See Ford's Hollow Cheek, Chapter 11, Fig. 11.23.

Holm, Soren Hansen, San Francisco, CA, Patent No. 167,248, Aug. 31, 1875 [Fig. 14.32]. A bit constructed in two parts to allow easy separation and removal from the mouth of the animal without taking off any portion of the bridle.

Horn Bit: A bit with an extension from the mouth-piece ends. See James patent and Lou Dillon Horn Bit, Chapter 18.

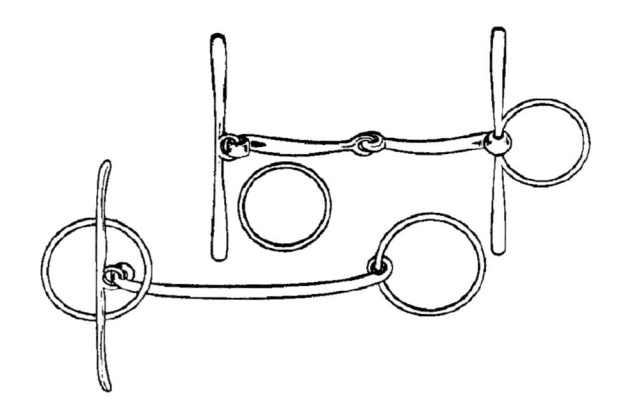

Fig14.32 Holm two-piece detachable bit.

Horner, Charles H., Xenia, OH, Patent No. 442,266, Dec. 9, 1890 [Fig. 14.33]. The mouth-piece travels up and down the cogged cheek-pieces via the geared ends of the mouth-piece.

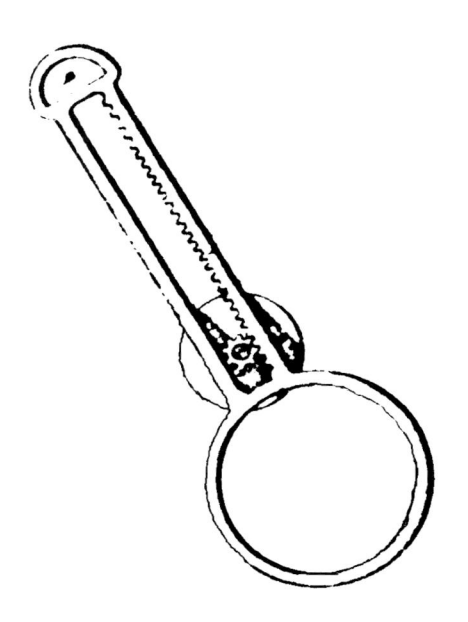

Fig. 14.33 Horner geared-mouth bit.

Horse, Wild Bit: See Espinosa Patent, Chapter 10, Fig. 10.18.

Horseshoe Bit: A bit with cheek-pieces shaped like a horseshoe. See Side-pieces, Chapter 31, Stallion bit.

189

Hourglass Mouth-piece: See Fig. 14.39.

Howlet Mouth: See Chapter 25.

Hubbard, George M., New Haven, CT, Patent No. 332,200, Dec. 8, 1885 [Fig. 14.34]. A construction method in which the mouth-piece is forced into a corresponding opening in the bottom portion of the cheek-piece. When securely in place, a pin is placed through a pre-drilled hole in the cheek-piece, locking it in place.

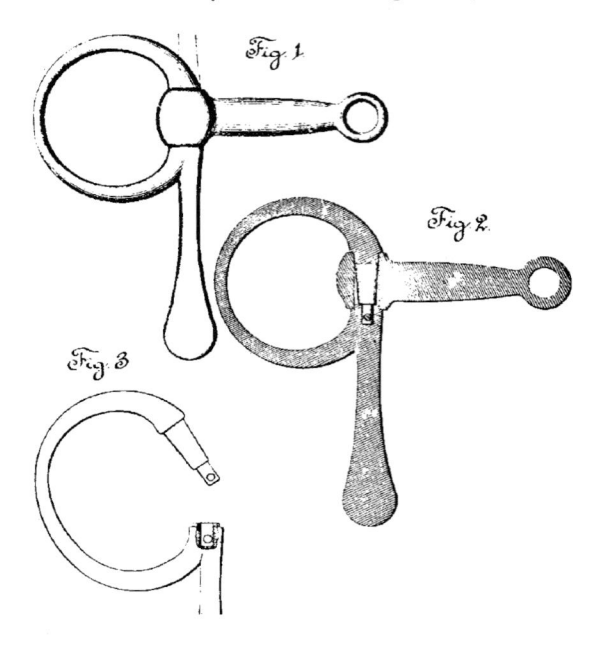

Fig. 14.34 Hubbard construction method.

Patent No. 354,476, Dec. 14, 1886 [Fig.14.35]. A construction method in which the cheek-ring has a coupling that locks in place and is hidden within the barrel-head at the end of the mouth-piece. The cheek-ring has a flange on each side of the barrel-head to prevent the ring from sliding but will allow the mouth-piece to pivot.

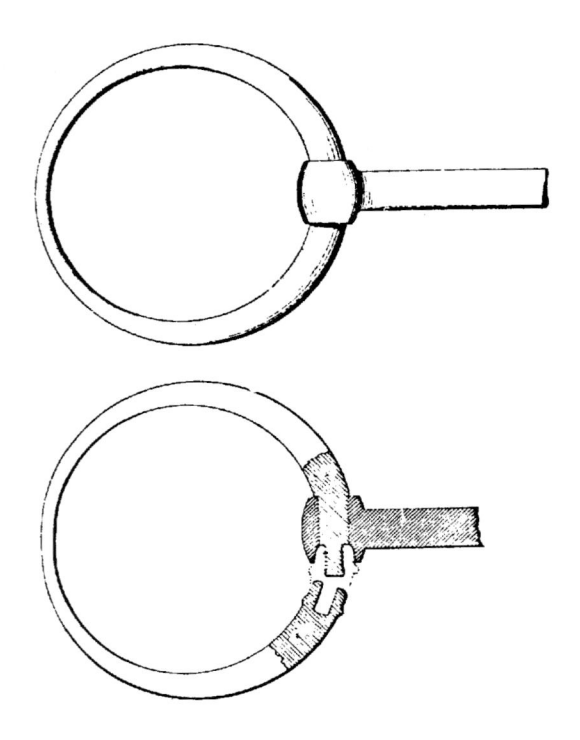

Fig. 14.35 Hubbard construction method.

Hubner, Curt, Berlin, Germany, Patent No. 345,592, July 13, 1886 [Fig. 14.36]. The mouth-piece is chambered and provided with perforations through which a horse may suck the medicines placed in the chambers. The removable caps in the extreme outer ends of the mouth-piece are independent of the cheek-pieces.

Huckins, Chester M., East Topsham, VT, Patent No. 95,801, Oct. 12, 1869 [Figs. 14.37 and 14.37a]. This bit may be used as a straight rigid bit or as a power bit when the toggle-levers are drawn back into position.

Humane Bit: A term applied to any bit that has a soft mouth-piece. The bits are usually of leather or are rubber covered [Fig. 14.38]. See Sears Patent, Chapter 30.

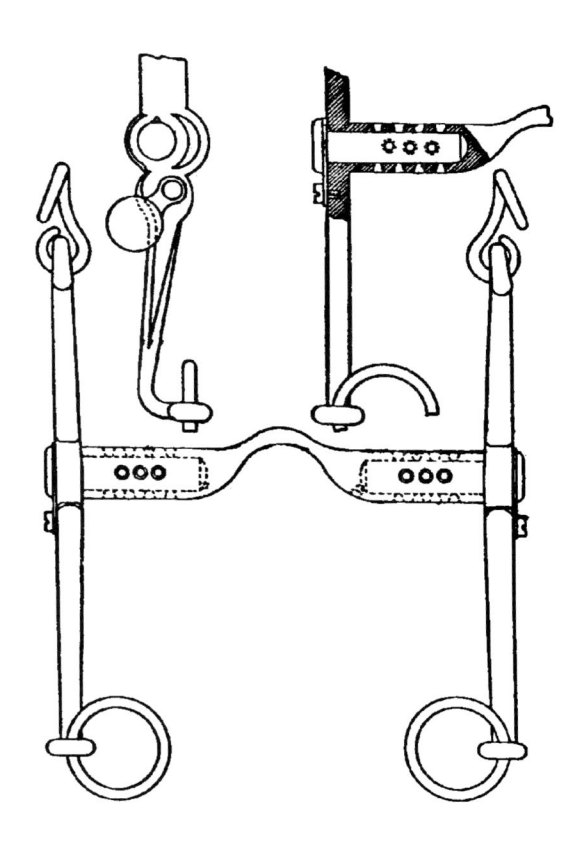

Fig. 14.36 Hubner medicine bit.

Fig. 14.37a Huckins production bit. Robert Maclin collection.

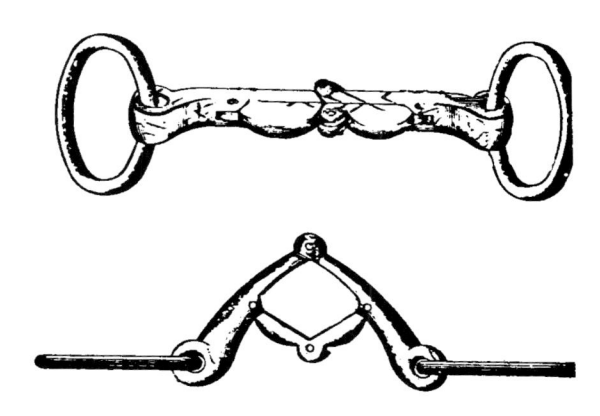

Fig. 14.37 Huckins toggle bit.

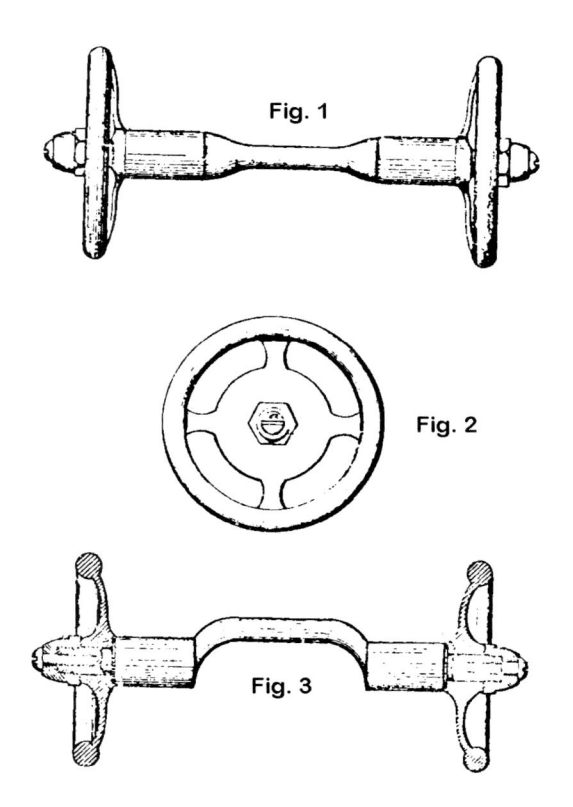

Fig. 14.39 Hutton rotating-mouth bit.

Hutton, Walter M., Patent No. 190,969, May 22, 1877 [Fig. 14.39]. The bar is curved or recessed to allow room for the tongue. The ends of the mouth-piece pass freely through the cheek-pieces to allow the mouth-piece and cheek-pieces to turn independently of each other.

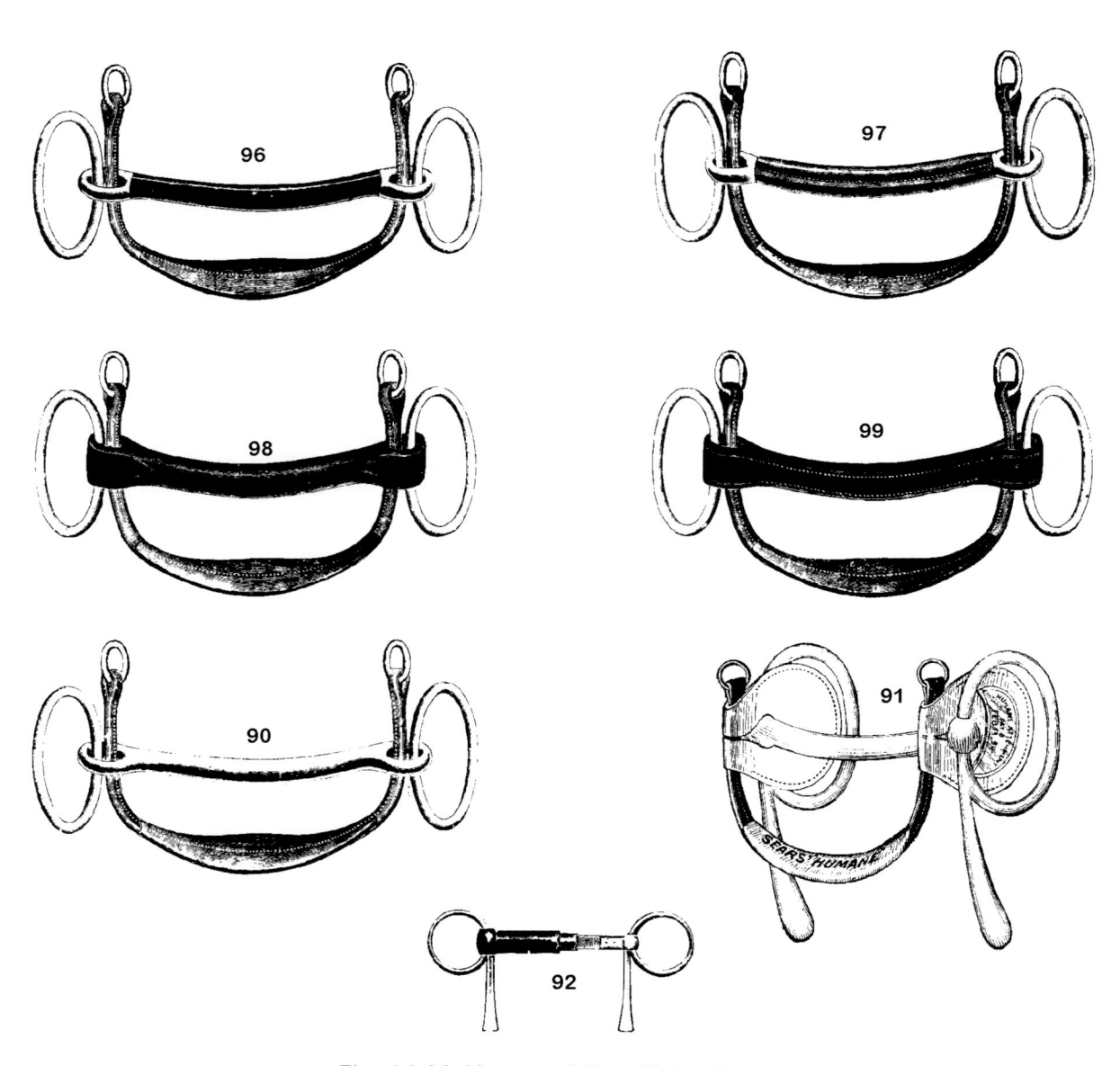

Fig. 14.38 Humane bits with leather or rubber-covered mouth pieces.

CHAPTER FIFTEEN
Iceland to Kuehnhold

Iceland Bit: Figures 15.0 and 15.1.

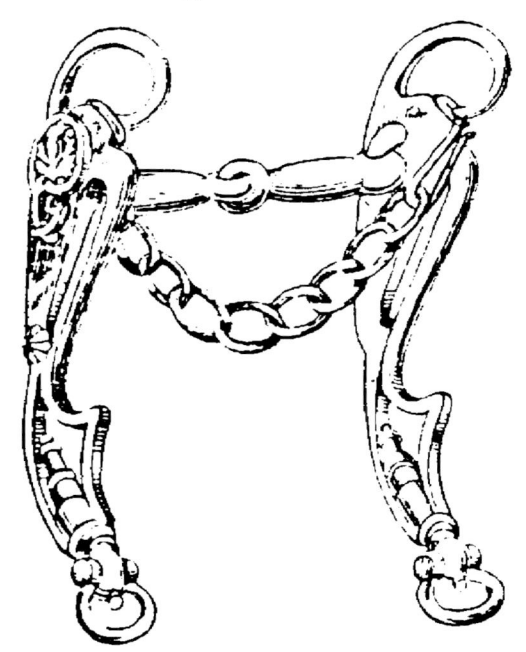

Fig. 15.0 Iceland bit from *John Dewsbury and Son Catalogue*, circa 1905.

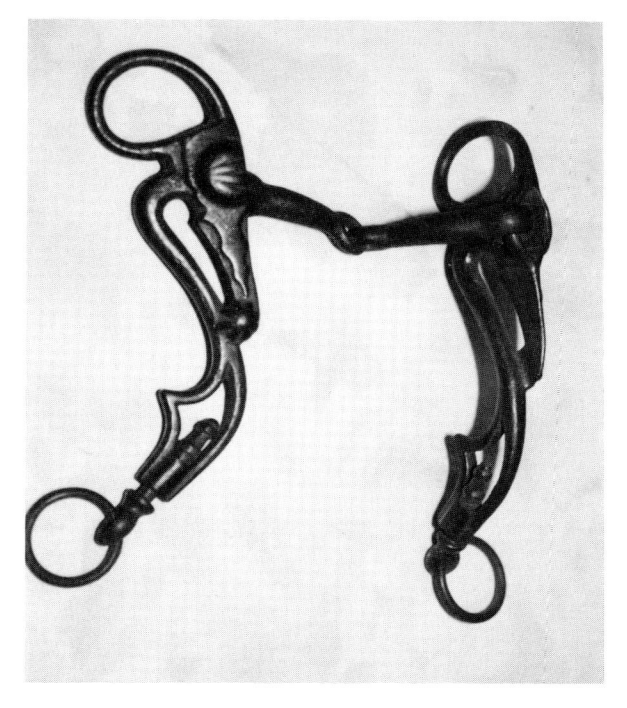

Fig. 15.1 Iceland bit from Harold Dawley collection.

Imperial Snaffle: See Driving, Universal, Chapter 8.

Indian Chief Bit: One of a set of bits that have one of five different bosses on the cheek-pieces. Manufactured by A. Buermann Mfg. Co. and later by North and Judd Mfg. Co. See Buermann, Chapter 36, pages 477 and 478.

Indianola: Name for a Texas-style bit sold by Haydens and Allen, St. Louis, Mo, circa 1900 [Fig. 15.2].

Ingersoll (Bobby) Snaffle: A bit by Quick Bits [Fig. 15.3]. The mouth-piece rotates within the cheek-rings.

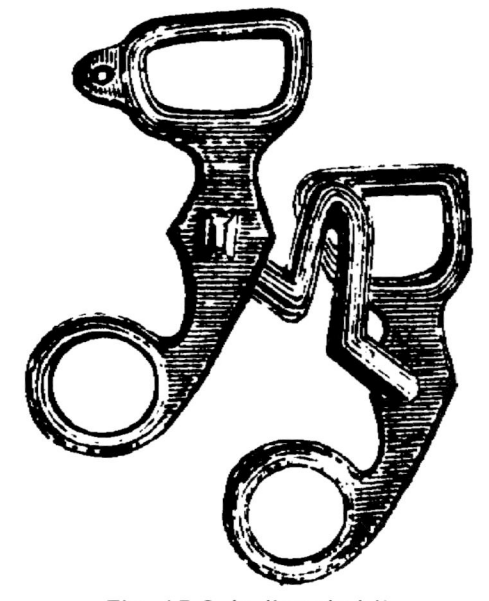

Fig. 15.2 Indianola bit.

Initial Bit: Any bit that has a disk medalion or boss which bears an initial and is attached to the cheekpiece of a bit.

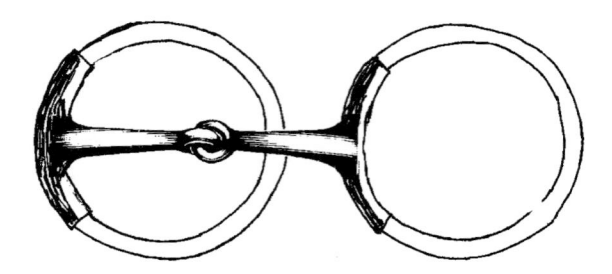

Fig. 15.3 Bobby Ingersoll snaffle.

Irish Flat-ring Snaffle: Figure 15.4.

Fig. 15.4 Irish flat-ring snaffle.

Irish Martingale: See Martingale, Chapter 19.

Iron Duke Bit: An early 18th century bit from England [Fig. 15.5]. From *The Loriner.*

Ives, George W. and Alfred E., Hamden, CT, Patent No. 541,279, June 18, 1895 [Fig. 15.6]. A cord is used to attach the check bit and regular mouth-piece. The amount of separation can be adjusted to produce an easy and pliable bit that will not injure the horse's mouth but will prevent the horse from lolling its tongue over the bit or taking the bit in its teeth.

J.I.C. Bit: "Just In Case" A bit patented by Hardy W. Campbell. See Chapter 8, Fig. 8.15.

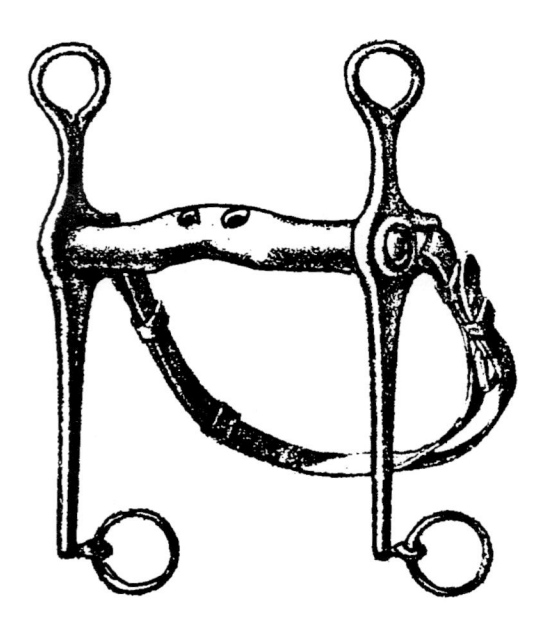

Fig. 15.5 Iron Duke bit

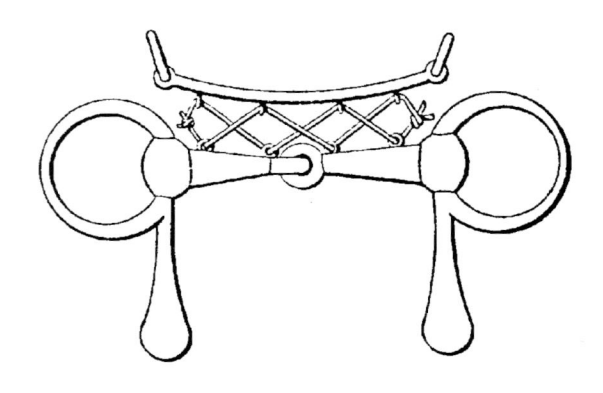

Fig. 15.6 Ives adjustable check bit.

Jackson, Claude D., Amarillo, TX, Design Patent No. 31,040, June 20, 1899 [Fig. 15.7]. A style of globe port bit with the enlarged lower ring egg-shaped and bent to the rear.

Jackson, Edward W., Mount Kisco, NY, Patent No. 328,781, Oct. 20, 1885 [Fig. 15.8]. A combination with the two-part and the three-part snaffle mouth independent of each other.

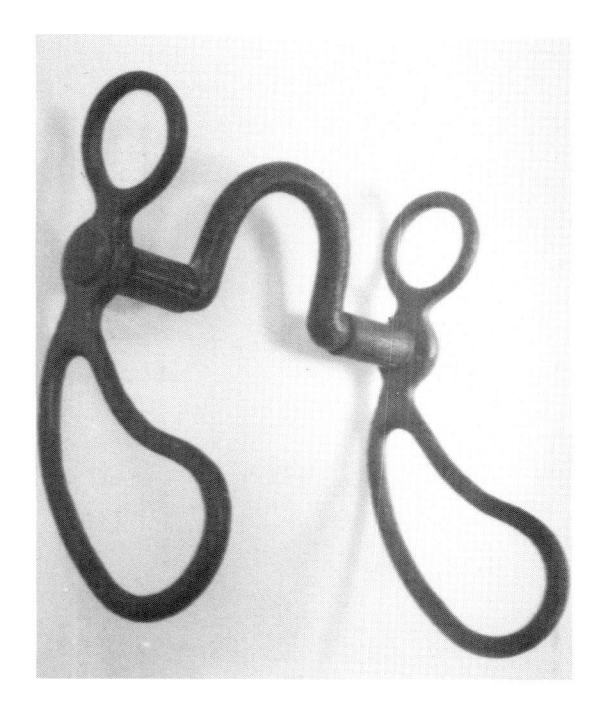

Fig. 15.7 Jackson design patent.

Fig. 15.9 James horn bit.

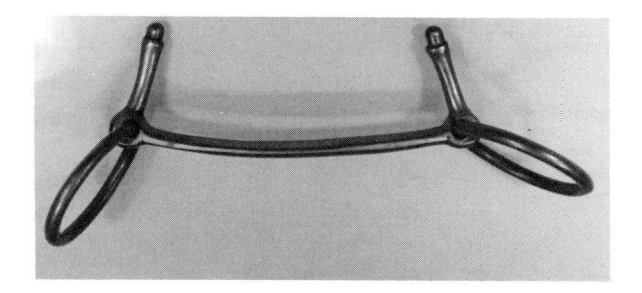

Fig. 15.9a Modern version of James horn bit.

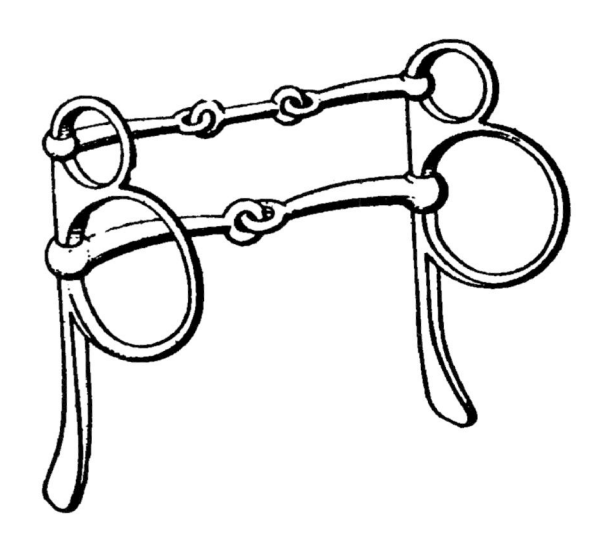

Fig. 15.8 Jackson double-mouth snaffle.

Fig. 15.9b Variation of James horn bit.

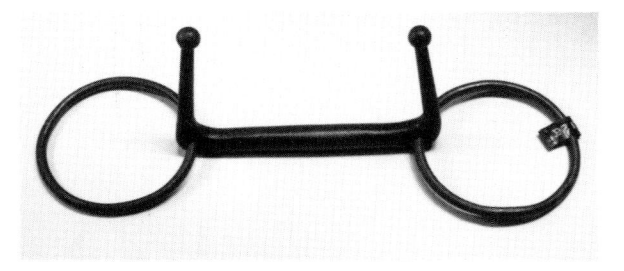

Fig. 15.9c Variation of James horn bit.

James Bit: A horn bit sold by many companies. James Safety Bit is another name for the bit [Figs. 15.9, 15.9a, 15.9b and 15.9c].

James, Henry H., Winnepeg, Canada, Patent No. 1,042,796, Oct. 29, 1912 [Fig. 15.10]. A side-puller bit for horses that want to keep their heads to one side or pull to one side. The

195

bit may be reversed to accommodate either side. Some side-puller bits are made right or left.

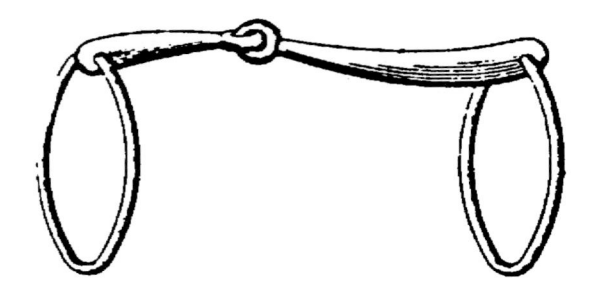

Fig. 15.10 James side-puller bit.

James, Jack Wm., Memphis, TN, Patent No. 478,866, July 12, 1892 [Fig. 15.11]. The rein-rings pivot on the end of the shank. They are made to accommodate a medallion or boss in the outer surface of the ring.

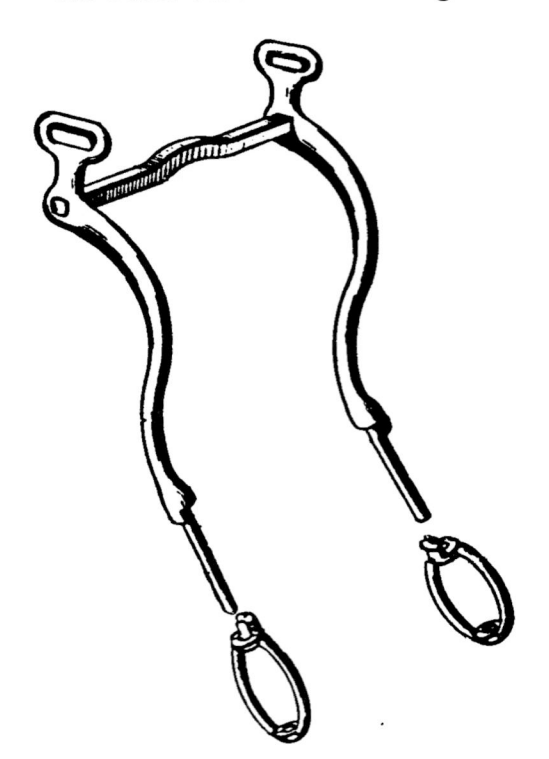

Fig. 15.11 James curb bit with pivoting rein-rings.

Patent No. 478,867, July 12, 1892 [Fig. 15.12]. An improvement in that the rein-rings have stop-lugs to limit the rotary motion and prevent twisting of the reins.

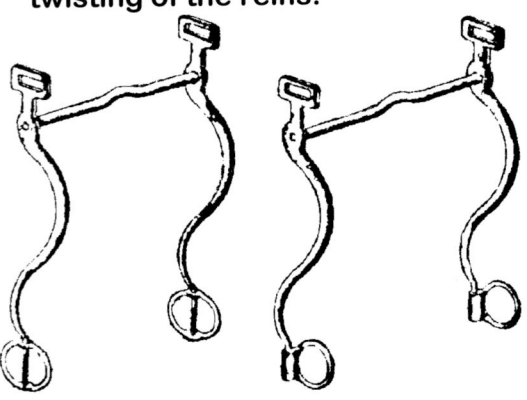

Fig. 15.12 Two variations of James improved curb.

Jandrue, Lewis E., Marlborough, MA, Patent No. 343,585, June 15, 1886 [Fig. 15.13]. A pulley bit with the pully on the head-stall and a friction bar to contain the rein at the ends of the mouth-piece to prevent the bit from being too easily drawn upward in the mouth.

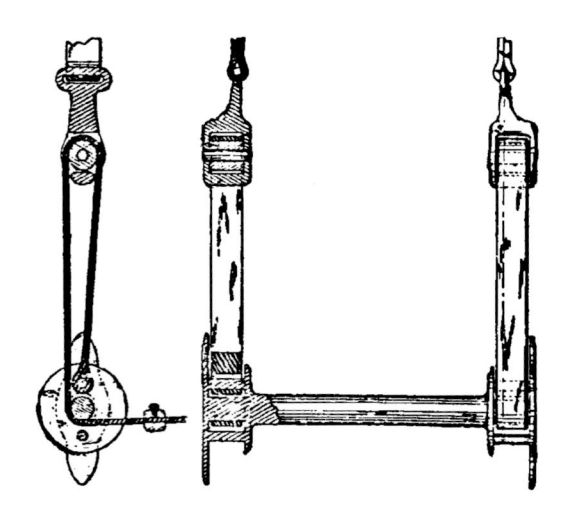

Fig. 15.13 Jandrue pulley bit.

Janes, Lyell Y., Tularose, NM, Patent No. 972,276, Oct. 18, 1910 [Fig. 15.14]. A slight pull upon the bit will cause it to press gently against the mouth of the horse. The mouthpiece is serrated on the lower edge and the ends are designed to slide up and down on the cheek-piece when the reins are pulled.

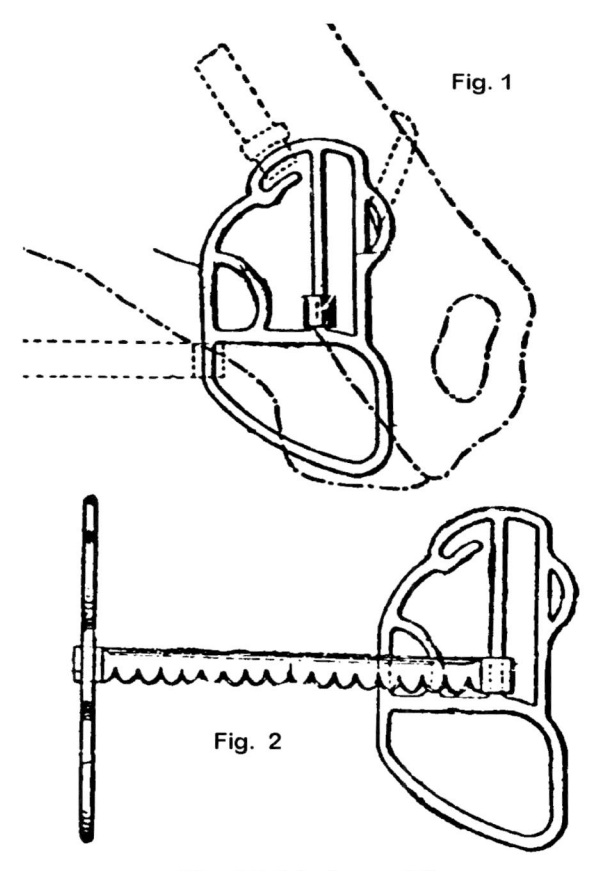

Fig. 1

Fig. 2

Fig. 15.14 Janes bit.

Fig. 15.15 Japanese bit with dragon fly cheek-rings.

Fig. 15.16 Japanese 17th century bit.

Japanese Bit: Seventeenth century origin with unique design of cheek-rings. Almost always with a broken mouth-piece [Figs. 15.15 and 15.16].

Jaquima: Spanish term for hackamore.

Jerk-line: A line attached to only one of the lead horses in a series of teams Hitched to a dray or heavy wagon.

Jimenez, Lino, Baltimore, MD, Patent No. 472, 297, filed Sep. 14, 1891 [Fig. 15.17]. The bit and bridle combination is designed to have a curb strap under the jaw and a second strap over the nose of the horse.

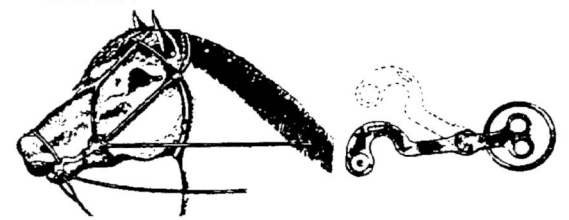

Fig. 15.17 Jimenez double-curb bit and bridle.

Jodhophur Polo Curb-chain: See Polo Pelham, Chapter 6, Fig. 6.60.

Johnson, Bernt, *et al.*, Racine, WI, Patent No. 422,529, Mar. 4, 1890. See Imperial Driving Bit, Chapter 8, Fig. 8.14.

Patent No. 470,051, Mar. 1, 1892 [Fig. 15.18]. The cheek-rings are pivoted to the single mouth-piece and produce pressure on the sides of the lower jaw at the option of the driver.

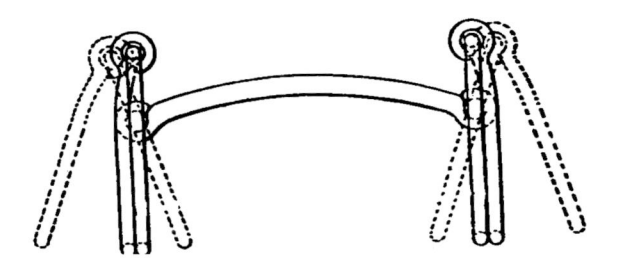

Fig. 15.18 Johnson pressure bit.

Johnson, W. F. and W. R., Wetumpka, AL, Patent No. 29,248, July 24, 1860 [Fig. 15.19]. The jointed crossed mouth-bars have buttons on the outer ends which apply pressure to the nostrils of the horse, effectively checking respiration when the reins are pulled hard.

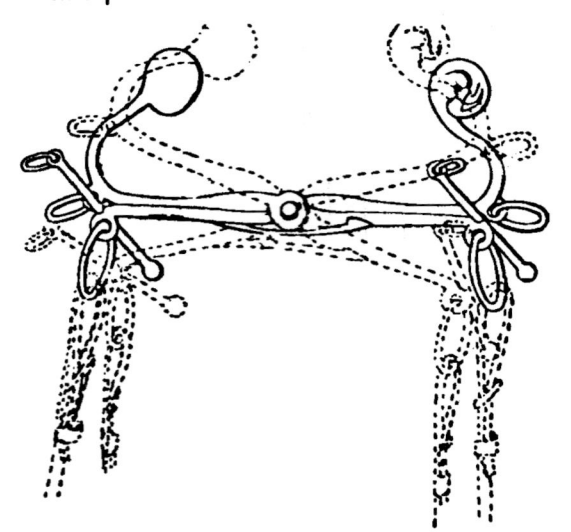

Fig. 15.19 Johnson scissor bit.

Johnson, William C., Oskaloosa, KS, Patent No. 799,602, Sep. 12, 1905 [Fig.15.20]. A bit with a threaded nut on each end of the mouth-piece to change the mouth-piece or the cheek-pieces.

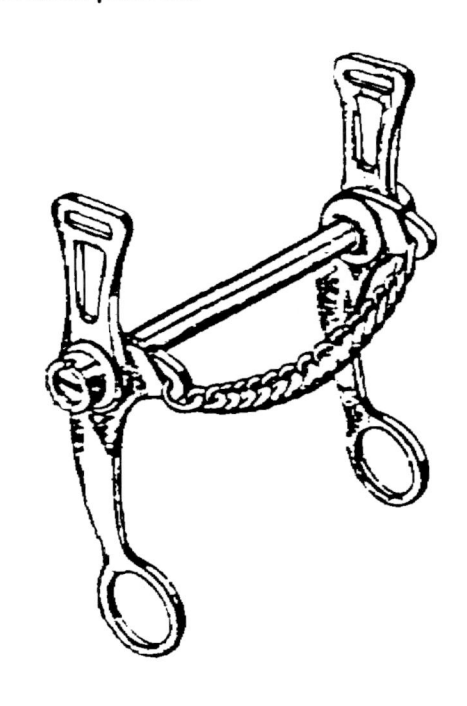

Fig. 15.20 Johnson replaceable-mouth bit.

Johnson, William, *etal.*, Winchester, KS, Patent No. 721,894, Mar. 3, 1903 [Fig. 15.21]. All parts are interchangeable. The mouth-piece is made in both port and straight, narrow, medium and wide. All the pressure is taken from the headstall and applied to the lower jaw. A stop-pin prevents the bit from turning up in the horse's mouth. The curb chain always hangs in the chin groove and is impossible to misplace. Made in nickel-plated or blued. Bits are marked inside the upper cheek-ring "U.S. Bridle Bit Co. Oskaloosa, Ks" or "U.S. Bridle Bit Co., Kansas City Mo."

Johnson Humane-Safety Riding or Driving Bit.

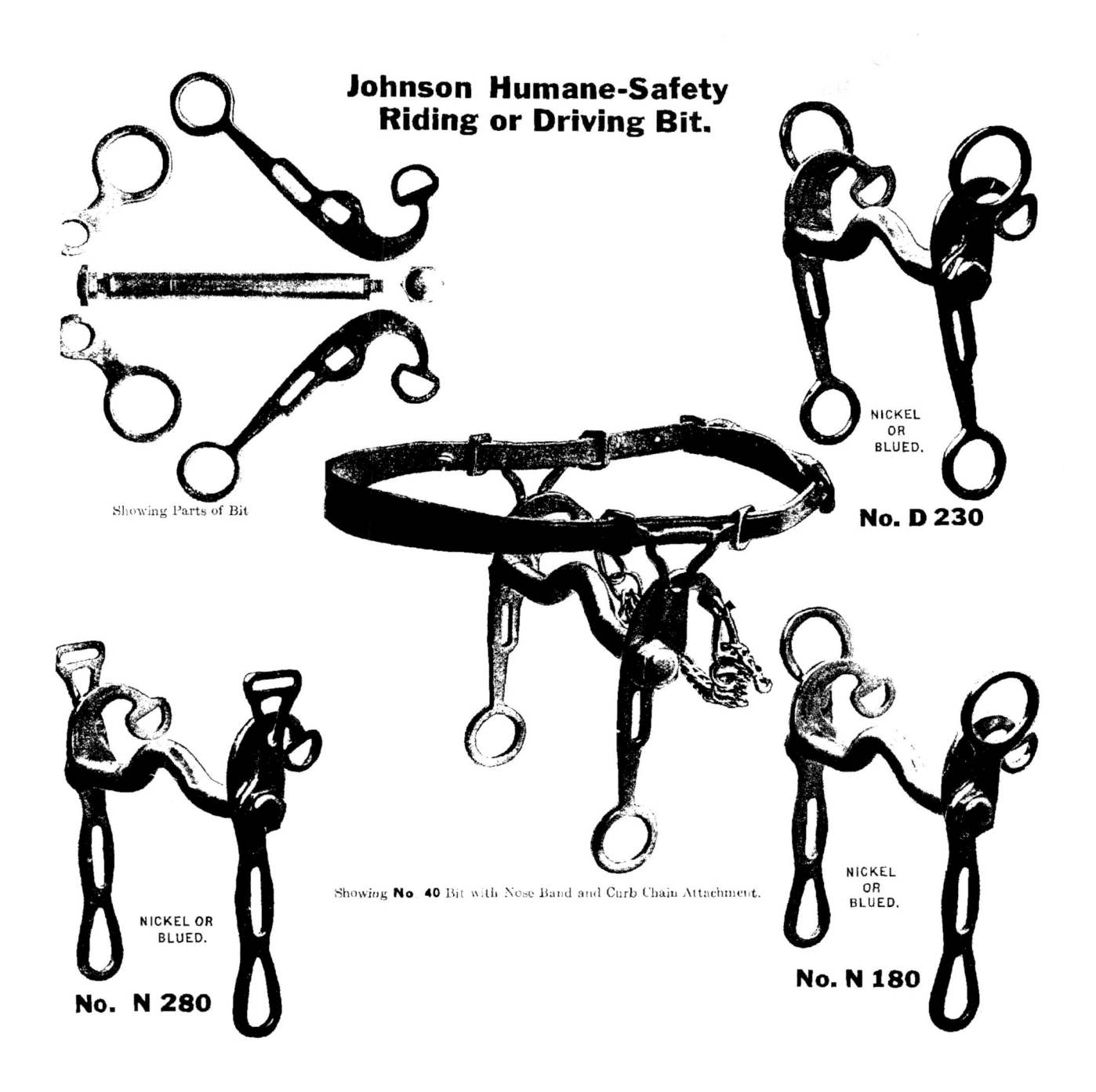

Showing Parts of Bit

Showing **No 40** Bit with Nose Band and Curb Chain Attachment.

No. D 230 — NICKEL OR BLUED.

No. N 280 — NICKEL OR BLUED.

No. N 180 — NICKEL OR BLUED.

Fig. 15.21 Johnson changeable bit.

Johnston, Alva S., Bozeman, Mont. Terr., Patent No. 356,942, Feb. 1, 1887 [Fig. 15.22]. When no strain is placed on the reins, the springs in the cheek-pieces close the parts of the mouth-piece.

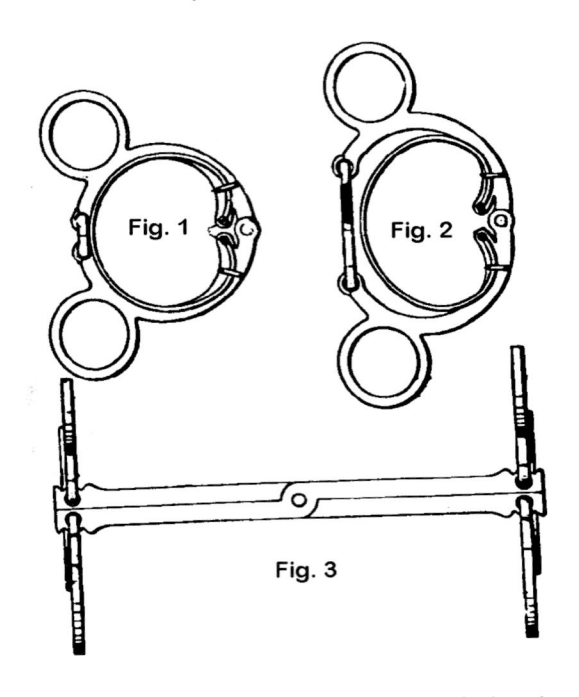

Fig. 15.22 Johnston spring-operated cheek.

Jointed-mouth Bit: A broken mouth-piece or one with a joint. See Chapter 25, Mouth-pieces.

Jones, James H., Lansingburg, NY, Patent No. 248,181, Oct. 11, 1881 [Fig. 15.23]. The mouth-piece is made separate from the cheek-pieces; flat locking buttons on the end of the mouth-piece allow the rapid attachment and removal of the mouth-piece from the bridle.

Jones, Richard W., Syracuse, NY, Patent No. 241,141, May 10, 1881 [Fig,. 15.24]. A piece of half-round metal is bent, shaped and cut to form the mouth-piece of this bit.

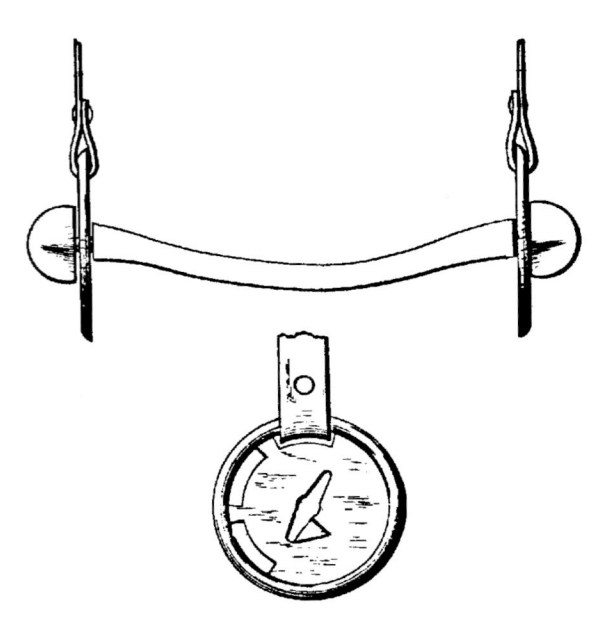

Fig. 15.23 Jones removeable cheek-piece bit.

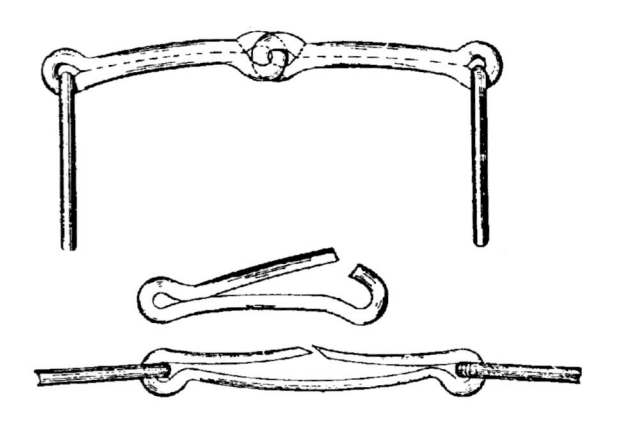

Fig. 15.24 Jones construction design.

Journals: A term applied to the shanks of cheek-pieces.

Judd, Loren F., New Britain, CT, Patent No. 166,615, Aug. 10, 1875 [Fig. 15.25]. When the heads of the mouth-piece are screwed onto the rubber-covered bar, the rims close over the rubber ends preventing a tendency of the rubber to roll up and gradually enlarge.

Fig. 15.25 Judd construction method.

Jungerman, George F., Kansas City, MO, Patent No. 876,461, Jan. 14, 1908 [Fig. 15.26].

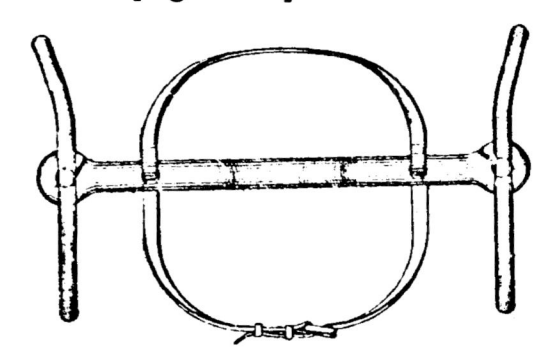

Fig. 15.26 Jungerman curb bit.

Junker Bit: A small Texas-style bit sold by A. Buermann Mfg.Co. [Fig. 15.27].

Fig. 15.27 Junker bit.

Kalkbrenner, Friederick B., Clinton, MO, Patent No. 108,795, Nov. 1, 1870 [Fig. 15.28]. The mouth-piece is split horizontally and one half and the lower portion of the cheek-piece are forged in one piece. The other half is forged in one piece to the upper cheek-pieces. The two pieces are hinged to provide a closed, complete mouth-piece, but when reins are pulled the mouth-pieces separate.

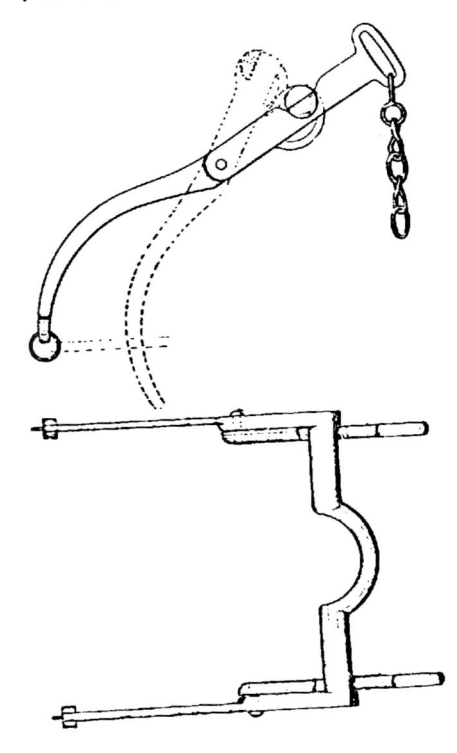

Fig. 15.28 Kalkbrenner split-mouth bit.

Kelly, Louis N., Lancaster, NY, Patent No. 964,917, July 19, 1910 [Fig. 15.29]. The bit has a round hollow mouth-piece with interior grooves and a revolving rod with elongated tongues adapted for intermittent engaging with the grooves on the interior of the outer cylinder mouth-piece.

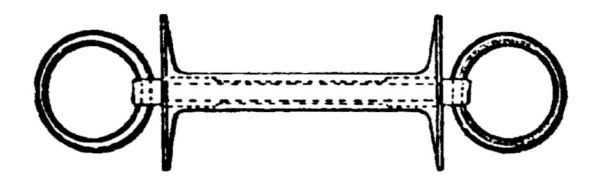

Fig. 15.29 Kelly revolving-mouth bit.

Kelly, Pascal M., El Paso, Texas. Registered several patents. See Crockett-Kelly, Chapter 36, Page 379.

Kerro Pattern: A bit with a wood or rubber interchangeable mouth, supplied with a spanner or wrench [Fig. 15.30].

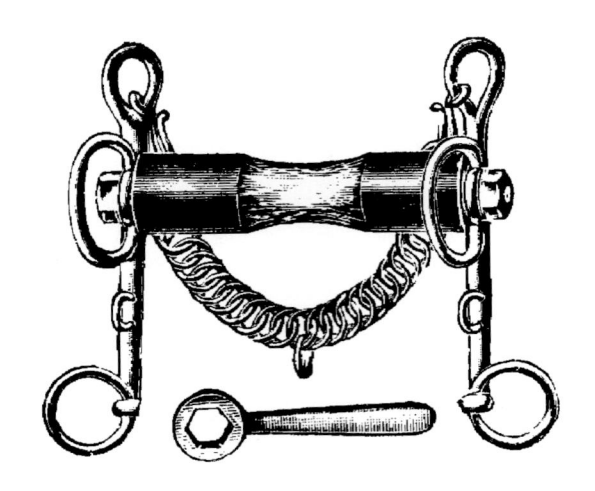

Fig. 15.30 Kerro Pattern.

Kerruish, Ralph J., Littleton, CO, Patent No. 1,792,378, Feb. 10, 1931 [Fig. 15.31]. A bit designed with a curb action for use in sport and gaited horses without injury to the mouth.

Keys: A term for players on a mouthpiece. See Mouthing Bit, Chapter 24.

Kiehl, August F., Norfolk, NE, Patent No. 570,312, Oct. 27, 1896 [Fig. 15.32]. A bridle bit with cheek-pieces arranged in pairs, each carrying a section of the mouth-piece. The divided mouth-piece separates and causes a gag effect when the rein-rings are pulled.

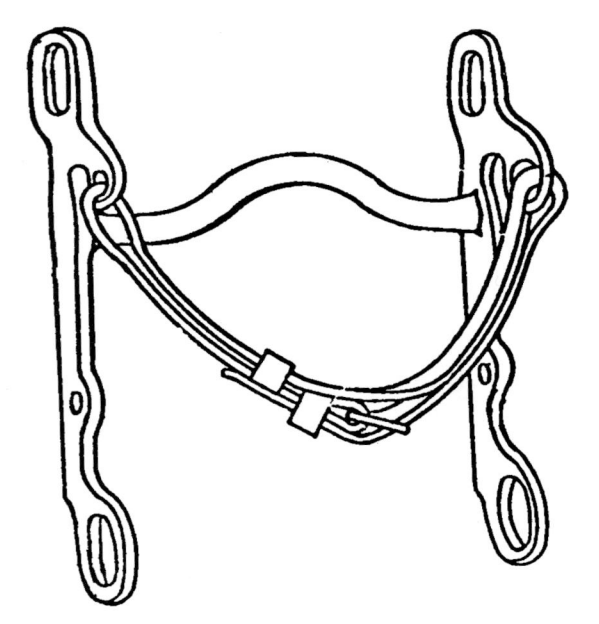

Fig. 15.31 Kerruish curb bit.

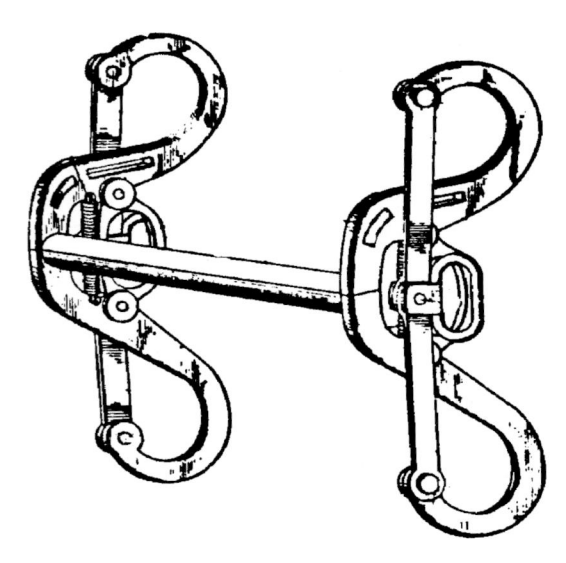

Fig. 15.32 Kiehl split-mouth snaffle bit.

Kimberwick Bit: This bit is an adaptation of a Spanish bit produced for a Mr. Phil Oliver by Lt. Col. F. E. Gibson and named after the village where Mr. Oliver lived. The village is in fact Kimble Wick (two words) which is near Aylesbury in Buckinghamshire, England. It is a type of hanging-snaffle bit with a variety of mouth-pieces, *i.e.*, straight bar, straight-ported, broken-mouth, all of which may be rubber-covered [Fig. 15.33].

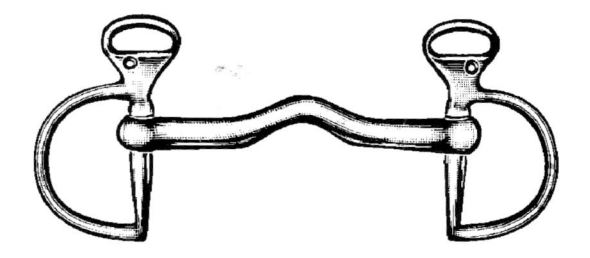

Fig. 15.33 Kimberwick bit with Cambridge mouth.

Kindig, Benjamin W., Jr., York, PA, Patent no. 750,199, Jan. 19, 1904 [Fig. 15.34]. A combined semi-circular line-bit and a straight overcheck bit flexibly connected in the middle of the bits. The overcheck bit is held in place with a ball of greater diameter than the width of the opening in the line-bit.

Fig. 15.34 Kindig flex-mouth overcheck bit.

King, Charles Cooper, Little Rock, AR, Patent No. 768,999, Aug. 30, 1904 [Fig., 15.35]. Extreme tension put on the reins causes the pressure-plates to pinch and close the nostrils of the horse, cutting off its supply of air, "resulting in submission."

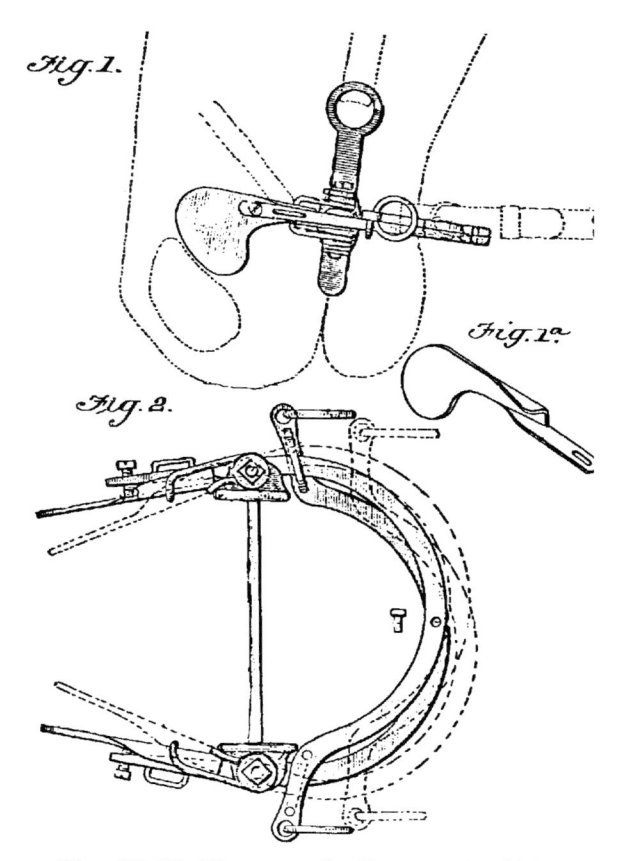

Fig. 15.35 King respiration-control bit.

King, Samuel M., Lancaster, PA, Patent No. 56,762, July 31, 1866 [Fig. 15.36]. Extension of the mouth-piece of a snaffle bit with the outer ends having an opening and grooved roller for a round rein.

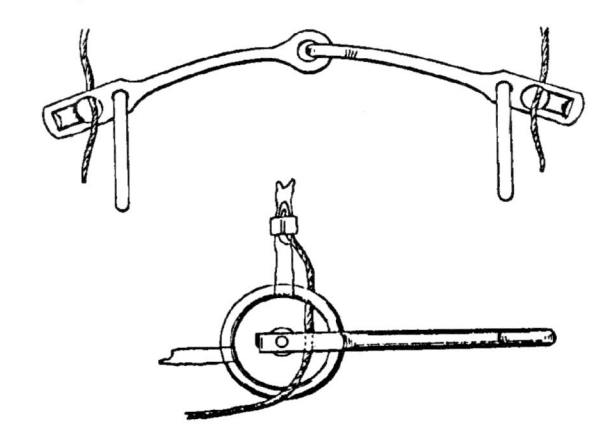

Fig. 15.36 King pulley bit.

Klaus, Caesar, Eureka, IL, Patent No. 907,816, Dec. 29, 1908 [Figs. 15.37, 15.37a, and 15.37b]. A straight-bar bit with springs built into the cheek-pieces which pivot on the ends of the mouth-piece. The action on the reins produces pressure on the horse's jaw.

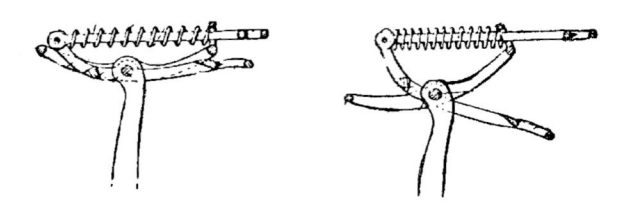

Fig. 15.37 Klaus pressure bit.

Fig. 15.37b Variation of Klaus bit.

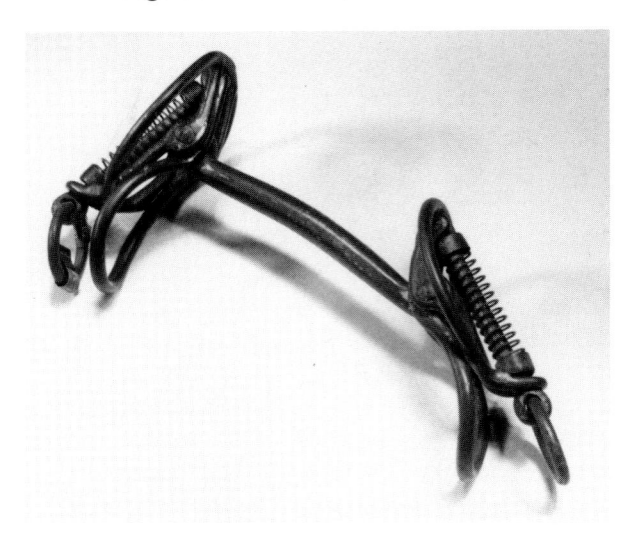

Fig. 15.37a Klaus production bit.

Klein, Frank, Covington, KY, Patent No. 637,802, Nov. 28, 1899 [Fig. 15.38]. A straight-bar bit which employes a noseband and curb-chain in a single action. Designed to have the effects of an overcheck but without the overcheck bit.

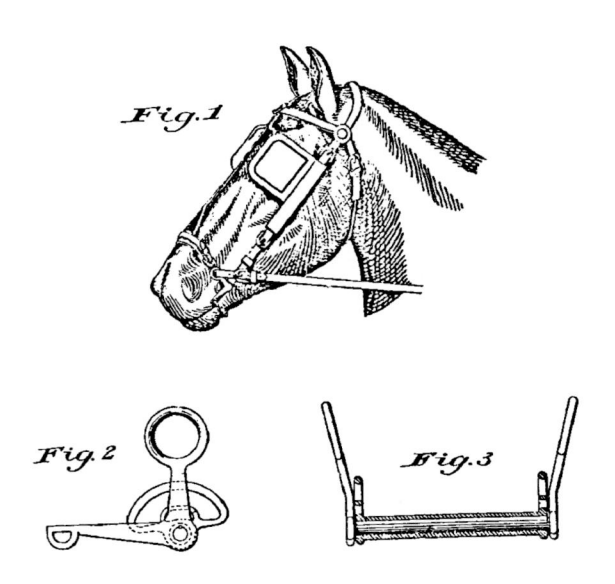

Fig. 15.38 Klein double-curb bit.

Knight, Joseph Price, Philadelphia, PA, Patent No. 615,283, Dec 10, 1898 [Fig. 15.39]. A jointed mouth-piece bit with longitudinal slots in each cannon and a bar passing through the slots to operate as an overcheck.

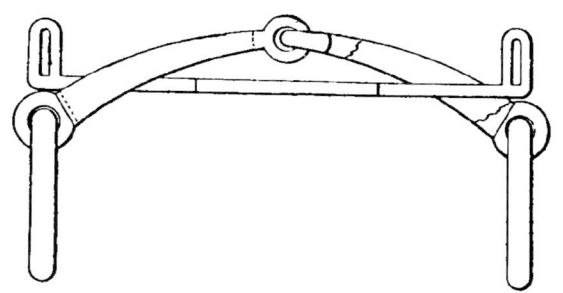

Fig. 15.39 Knight snaffle with built-in overcheck.

Knuckle Bit: An all-brass bit with the cheek-pieces resembling a set of brass knuckles [Fig. 15.40]. One side-piece is marked "Pat'd Mar 14 ?3."

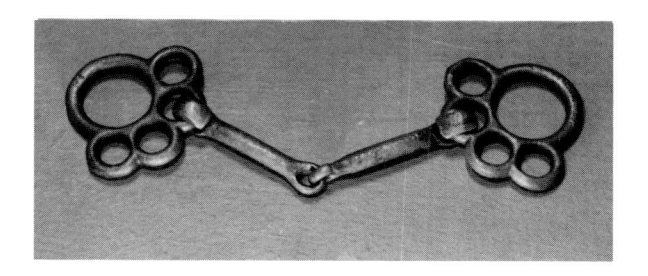

Fig. 15.40 Knuckle bit.

Kochheiser, Phillip B., Bellville, OH, Patent No. 783,966, Feb. 28, 1905 [Fig. 15.41]. The bit is reversible to provide either a smooth edge or a serrated edge mouth-piece. The curved guard passes under the lip of the horse and prevents lateral movement of the bit. The cheek-pieces pivot on the mouth-piece ends to rotate or reverse the mouth-piece.

Kock, William L., Treloar, MO, Patent No. 1,660,490, Feb. 28, 1928 [Fig. 15.42]. The cheek-pieces have elongated slots in which the mouth-piece normally slides. The square mouth-piece ends keep the serrated mouth-piece from rotating in the mouth.

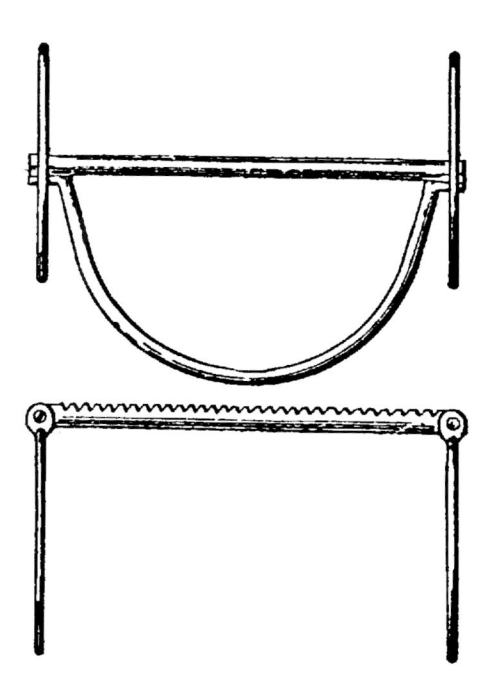

Fig. 15.41 Kochheiser reversible-mouth bit.

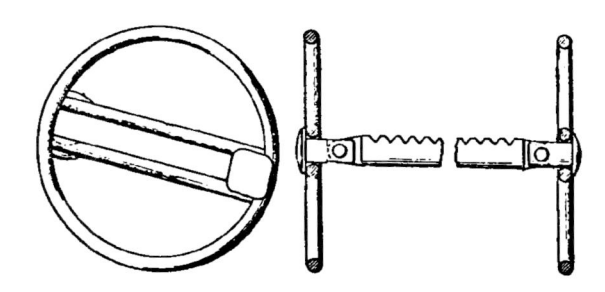

Fig. 15.42 Kock floating-mouth bit.

Kronhein, Wolf, Hamburg, Germany, Patent No. 834,236, Oct. 23, 1906 [Fig. 15.43]. The bit has mounted spring side-bars to which the curb-strap or chain is secured on the upper ring and the rein to lower ring. By pulling on the reins, the curb is gradually pressed against the jaw without the mouth-piece tugging in the mouth.

Kuehnhold, Ferdinand B., Newark, NJ, Patent No. 190,876, May 15, 1877 [Fig. 15.44]. A hook constructed and adapted to be attached to, and detached from, the bit or mouthpiece, instead of being a permanent attachment.

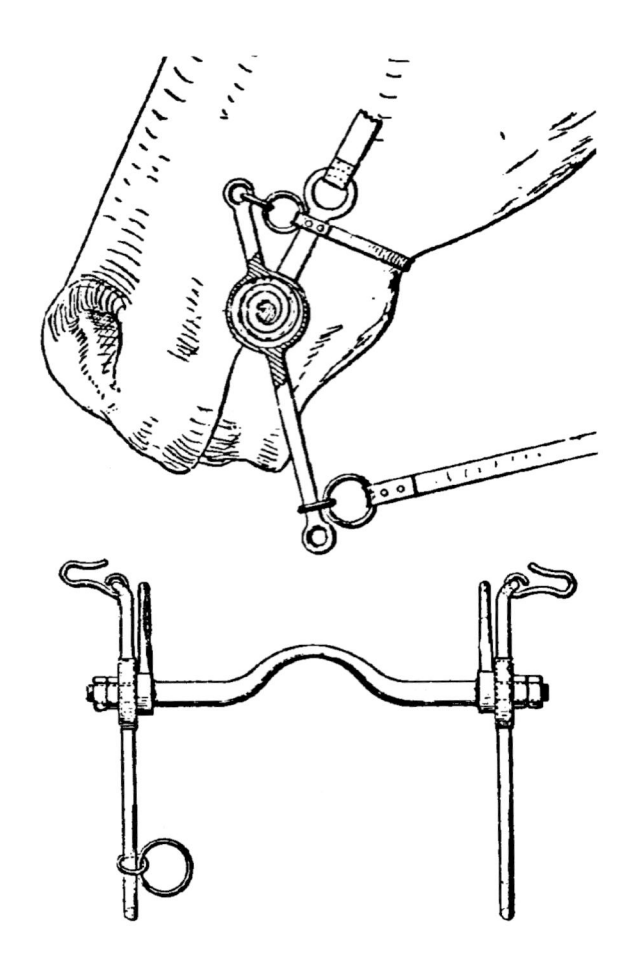

Fig. 15.43 Kronhein spring-controlled curb bit.

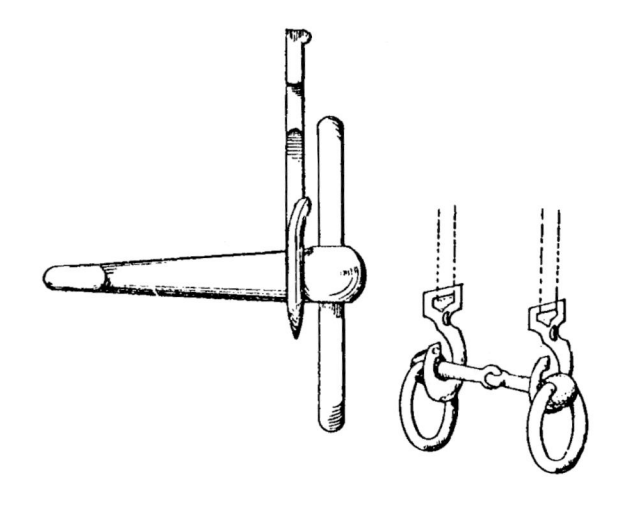

Fig. 15.44 Kuehnhold rein hook.

CHAPTER SIXTEEN
Lady to Liverpool

Lady's Leg Bit: Design Patent No. 17,040, Dec. 28, 1886 [Figs. 16.0 and 16.1] by August Buermann, Newark, NJ and Frank H. Gilham, San Francisco, CA.

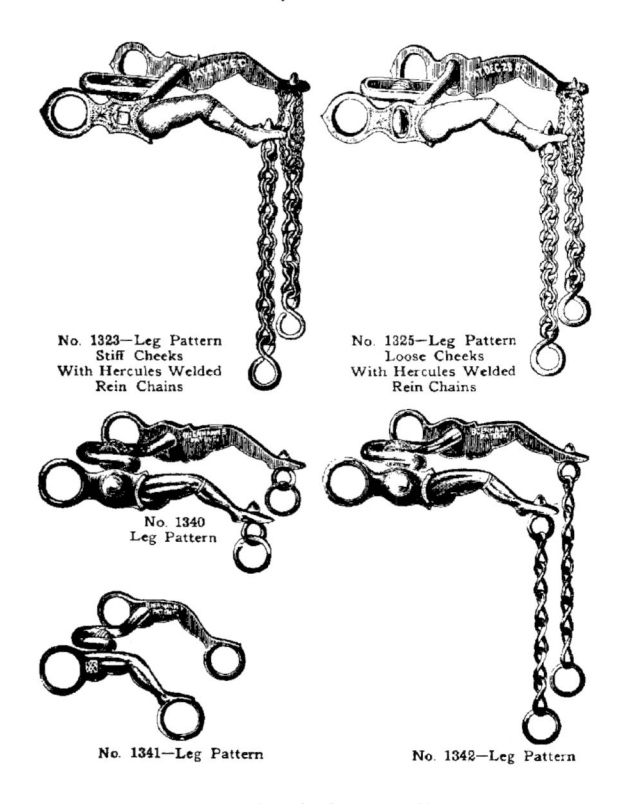

No. 1323—Leg Pattern Stiff Cheeks With Hercules Welded Rein Chains

No. 1325—Leg Pattern Loose Cheeks With Hercules Welded Rein Chains

No. 1340 Leg Pattern

No. 1341—Leg Pattern

No. 1342—Leg Pattern

Fig. 16.0 Lady Leg patterns.

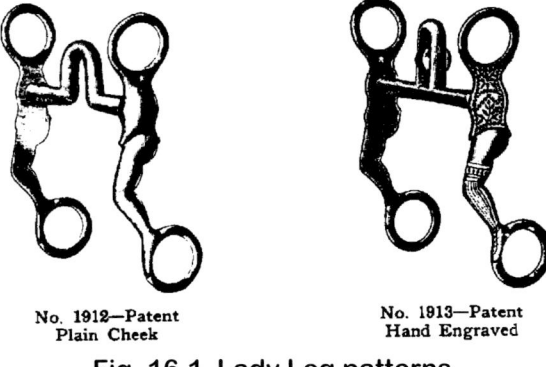

No. 1912—Patent Plain Cheek

No. 1913—Patent Hand Engraved

Fig. 16.1 Lady Leg patterns.

Lamarque, Bernard, Preignac, France, Patent No. 789,742, May 16, 1905 [Fig. 16.2]. An attached bradoon bit is allowed to travel freely by its rings attached to the lower shanks of the curb bit.

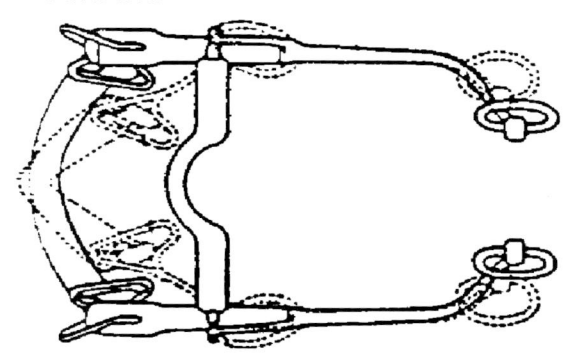

Fig. 16.2 Lamarque curb bit with attached bradoon.

Lancer Polo: Normally referred to as the Ninth Lancer Polo. Rings are sometimes used on this English bit [Fig. 16.3].

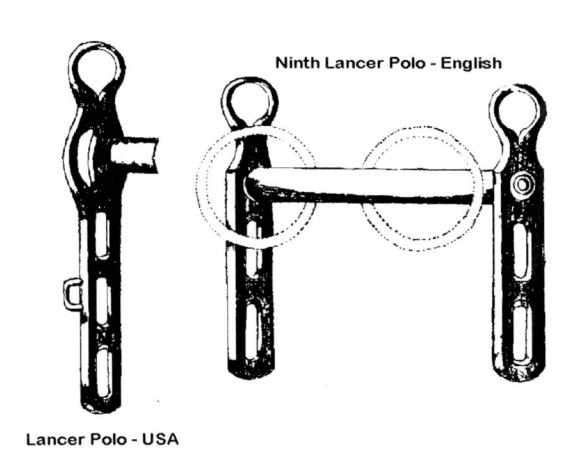

Ninth Lancer Polo - English

Lancer Polo - USA

Fig. 16.3 Ninth Lancer Polo.

207

Langholz, A. H., Chicago, IL, Patent No. 44,002, Aug. 30, 1864 [Fig. 16.4]. The curb hangers swivel on the mouth-piece ends to allow the bit to be reversed without removing the curb. The curb hangers may have a round or slotted aperture.

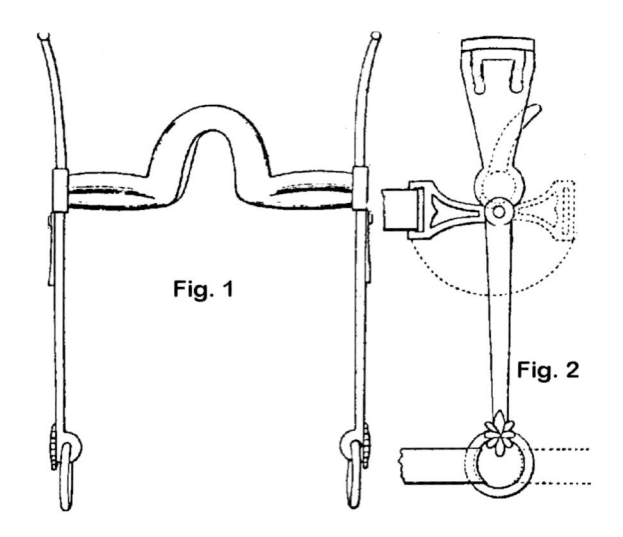

Fig. 16.4 Langholz reversible bit.

Laredo Bit: A small Texas-style curb bit sold by Haydens and Allen, St. Louis, Mo, circa 1900 [Fig. 16.5].

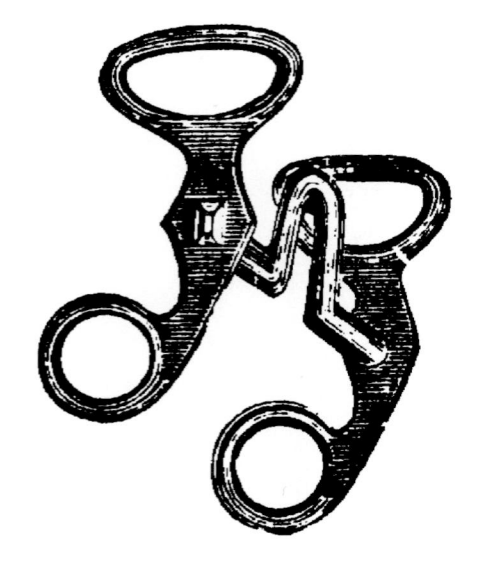

Fig. 16.5 Laredo bit.

Las Cruces Bit: The Cross. A straight-shanked bit of the Southwest U.S. that has its U.S. origin with the early Spaniards. Produced by many companies of the 1800 and early 1900's in a variety of mouth-pieces, but most often with a half-breed mouth [Fig. 16.6].

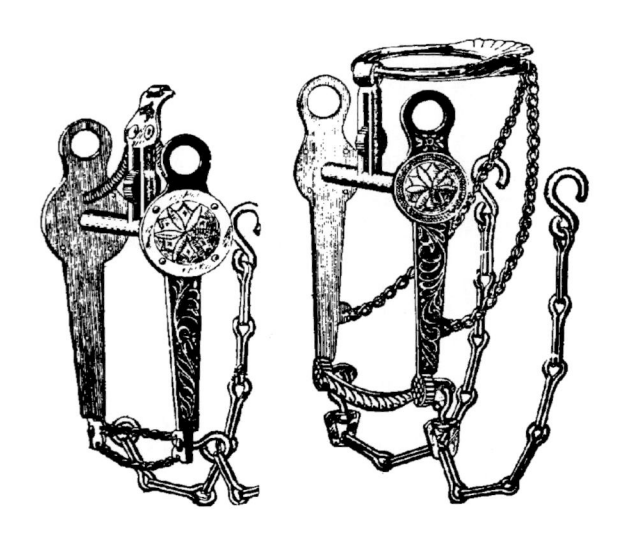

Fig. 16.6 Las Cruces bits with spade and ring mouth-pieces.

Lavaca Bit: A small Texas-style curb bit sold by Haydens and Allen, St. Louis, MO, circa 1900 [Fig. 16.7].

Fig. 16.7 The Lavaca bit.

Lead rein: A rein used to lead another horse, often that of a young child learning to ride.

Le Compte, George W., Baltimore, MD, Patent No. 582,535, May 11, 1897 [Fig. 16.8]. Designed to keep the nose of the horse well out and the mouth closed, giving the horse a "graceful carriage" and preventing "lugging" or "gagging."

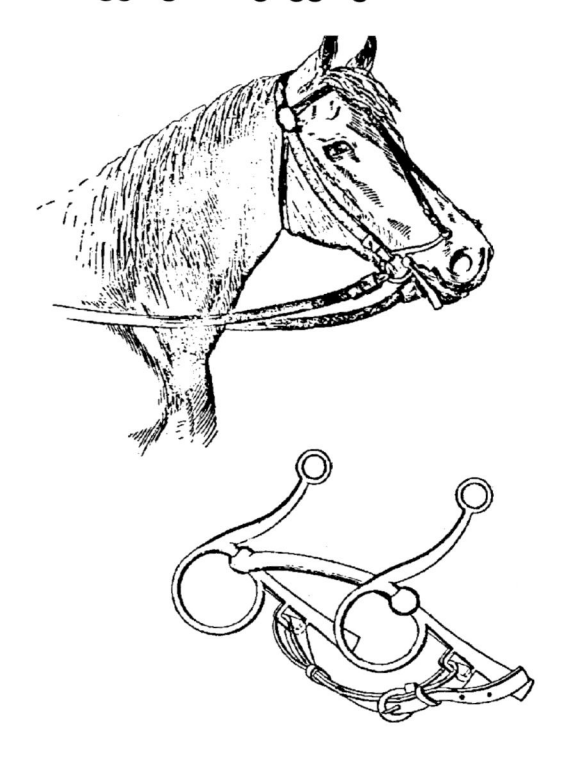

Fig. 16.8 Le Compte driving bit.

Lee Alwell Special Bit: Name given to a bit by W. R. (Wallie) Boone, San Angelo, TX, classified as a polo bit [Fig. 16.9].

Lee, Joseph Loverel, Evant, TX, Patent No. 658,377, Sep. 25, 1900 [Figs. 16.10 and 16.11]. Commonly called "Lee's Patent," a bit with a bar for the mouth, a curb-bar adapted to tie under the lower jaw or lip of the horse and cheek-pieces arranged so that when a pull is exerted it will cause a twisting or turning movement of the bit, bearing down and bringing pressure on the inside and outside of the lower jaw.

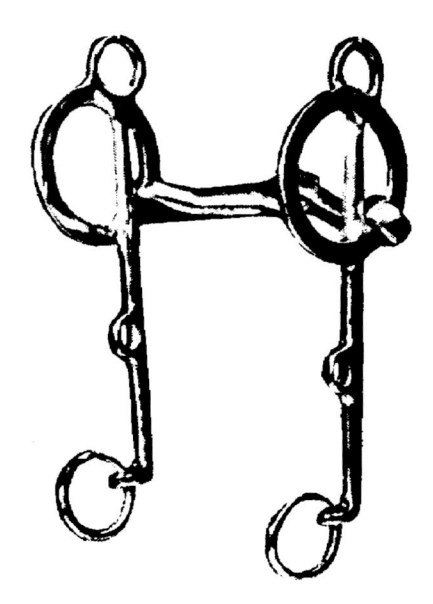

Fig. 16.9 Lee Alwell Special bit.

Fig. 16.10 Lee's Patent on a horse.

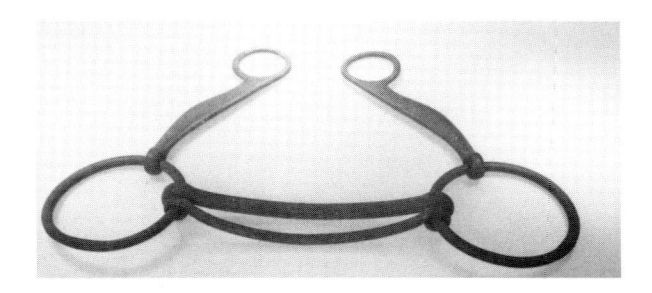

Fig. 16.11 Photo of Lee's Patent. Robert Maclin collection.

Leg Patten Bits: See Figures 16.0 and 16.1.

Leichester Bit and Twisted Bradoon: A set of English bits for a double bridle, of early 1800's from *The Loriner* [Fig. 16.12].

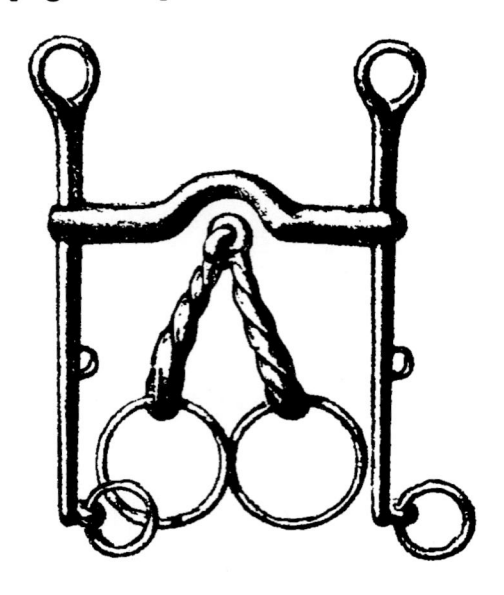

Fig. 16.12 Leichester bit.

Leisenring, Henry G., Wayne, NE, Patent No. 567,033, Sep. 1, 1896 [Fig. 16.13]. An ordinary bit having a second auxillary bit, which is of smaller diameter than the main mouth-piece, and adapted to work backward and forward as well as sideways in the elongated slots of the side-pieces.

Fig. 16.13 Leisenring double-mouth bit. Robert Maclin collection.

Lesser, Max, Duncansby, MS, Patent No. 526,241, Sep. 18, 1894 [Fig. 16.14]. The bit bar has a solid bar with a groove into which lies a concealed ancillary mouth-bar that is controlled and separated from the main bar by a lever system. The bar is operated by a pull on the reins. The ancillary curb is held in a normal concealed position by the curb-strap or chain and the crank and spring system built into the lower end of the levered cheek-piece.

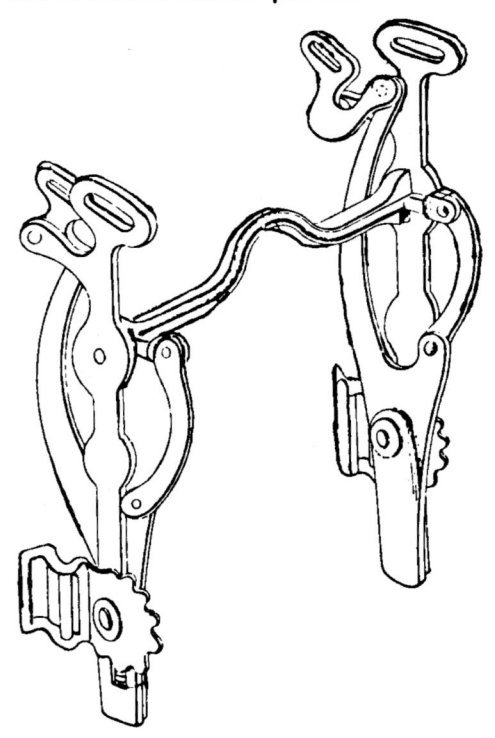

Fig. 16.14 Lesser split-mouth bit.

Letchworth, George J., Buffalo, NY, Patent No. 231,063, Aug. 10, 1880 [Fig. 16.15]. The bit has a compound mouth-piece of two or more members each provided at its ends with independent rein attachments through which the driving reins are drawn. The bits are so arranged that when a breakage occurs the second member comes into play.

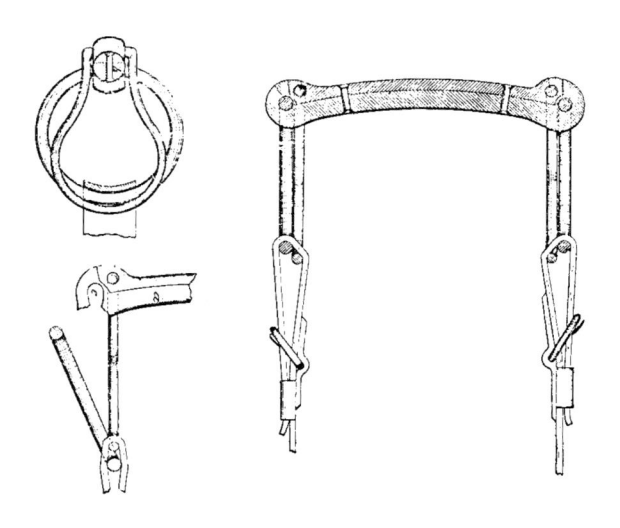

Fig. 16.15 Letchworth double bit.

Patent No. 254,987, Mar. 14, 1882 [Fig. 16.16]. A construction design for molding a jointed-mouth bit.

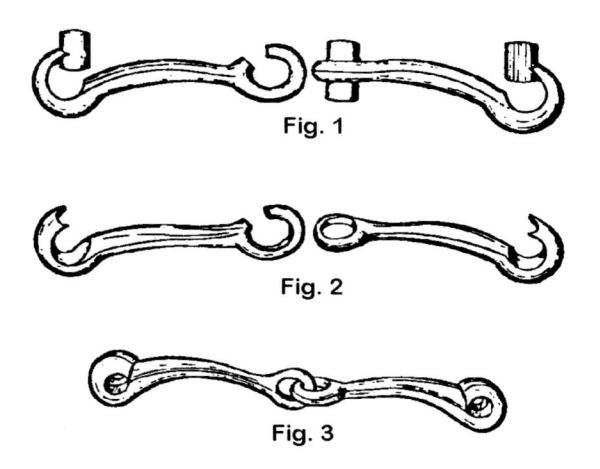

Fig. 16.16 Letchworth construction design.

Letchworth. Josiah, Buffalo, NY, Patent No. 90,857, June 1, 1869 [Fig. 16.17]. This bit has a wrought-iron or wire bit with a smooth cast-iron sleeve or mouth-protector cast around the mouth-piece after the bit is made.

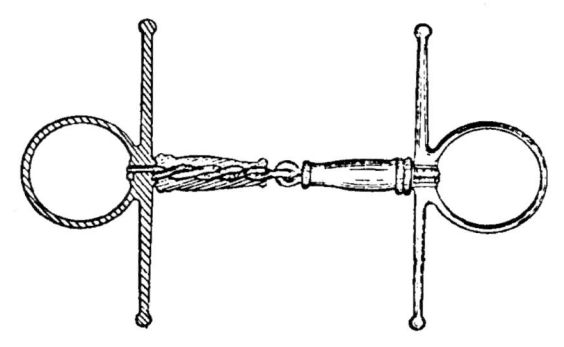

Fig. 16.17 Letchworth manufacturing design.

Patent No. 134,684, Jan. 4, 1873 [Fig. 16.18]. An improvement of No. 90,857.

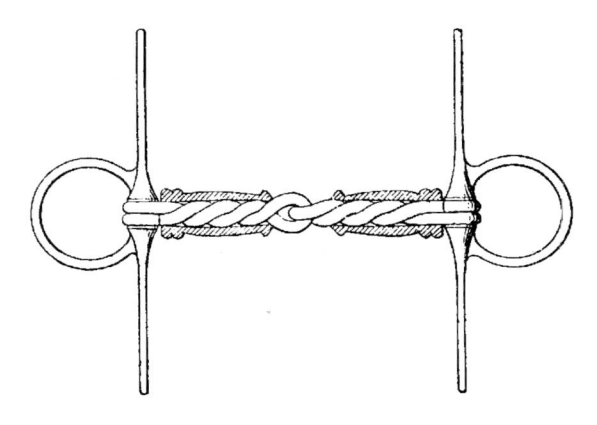

Fig. 16.18 Improved Letchworth design.

Patent No. 178,936, June 20, 1976 [Fig. 16.19]. Rings are attached directly to the mouth-piece so that the rein pull is applied directly to the solid portions of the mouth-piece.

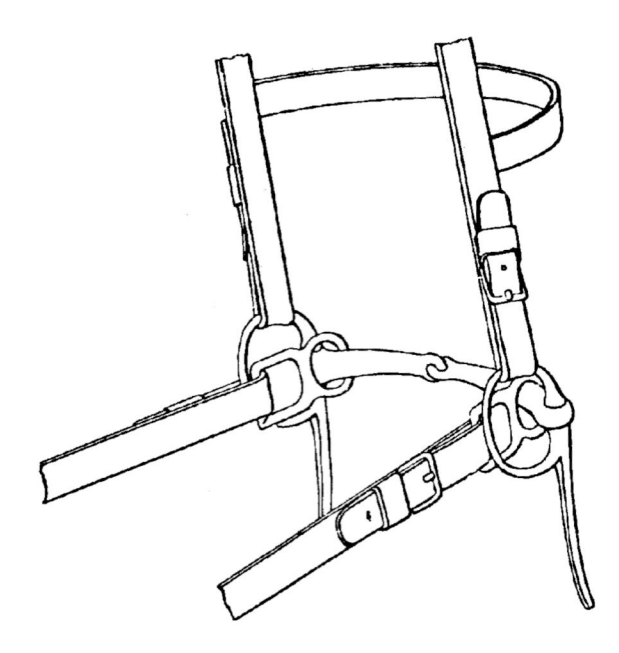

Fig. 16.19 Letchworth loose-ring attachment for snaffle bits.

Letchworth, William P., Buffalo, NY, Patent No. 102,838, May 10, 1870 [Fig. 16.20]. Designed to form the mouth-piece from wrought-iron rods twisted together to form a smooth surface. The collared cheek-rings prevent the mouth-piece from shifting.

Fig. 16.20 Letchworth twisted iron-mouth bit.

Levers: A term for cheek-pieces with an upper and lower extension from the mouth-piece.

Light-mouth: A quality of mouth which requires little or no effort on the bit. A light-mouth cannot be obtained by force but must be made by a light hand from the trainer and patience. A light-mouth must be made.

Lilienthal, Emil, New York, NY, Patent No. 178,013, May 30, 1876 [Fig. 16.21]. A bit with cheek-pieces separated from the mouth-piece by a poor conductor of heat or cold, such as wood, paper, felt, cork or rubber. The idea is to prevent the transfer of heat or cold of the cheek-pieces to the mouth-piece.

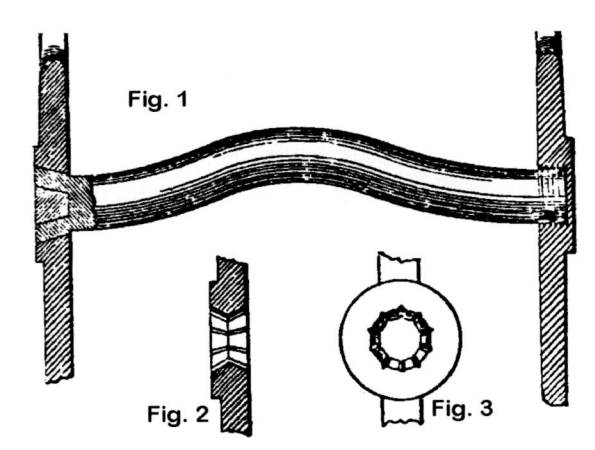

Fig. 16.21 Lilienthal insulated mouth-end bit.

Lilly, Issac, Chicago, IL, Patent No. 367,416, Aug. 2, 1887 [Fig. 16.22]. Removeable clips that can be attached or removed from the mouth-piece of a straight or broken-mouth bit. Prevents tongue lolling of the horse.

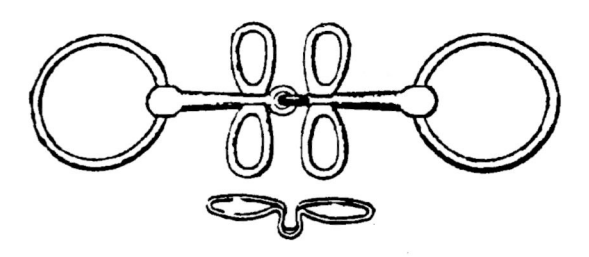

Fig. 16.22 Lilly bit-bar clip.

Line Bit: A regular straight-mouth bit.

Line of the Banquet: A term for how the bit lays within the mouth of a horse.

Link: The connecting piece between the cannons of a broken-mouth bit.

Link "T" Bradoon: A bit with a short chain to which is attached a "T" link. A bit commonly referred to as a watering bit [Fig. 16.23].

Fig. 16.23 A Link "T" bradoon.

Linville, Stephen Archie Miller and Linzy Hicks, Concordia, KS, Patent No. 880,803, Mar. 3, 1908 [Fig. 16.24]. The cheek-pieces are made independent and may rotate around the longitudinal axis of the mouth-piece. The forward projections along with the face straps assist in the control of the horse.

Lipping the Bit: The horse using its lower lip to get the shank of the bit or side-piece of a curb bit in its mouth.

Lip-bar: A bottom bar connecting the two lower side-pieces of some curb bits and Buxton bits. See diagram of curb bit, Chapter 1.

Lip-loop: A small loop mid-way on the reverse side of the lower cheek-piece of some straight-shanked bits. See diagram, Chapter 1.

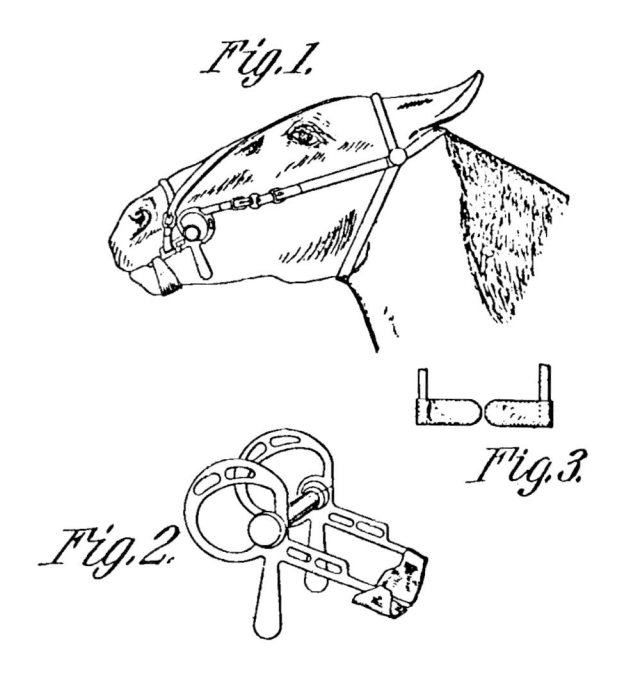

Fig. 16.24 Linville and Hicks control bit.

Lip-strap: A small strap between the lip-loops and often attached to a ring in the lower center of the curb-chain. See diagram, Chapter 1.

Little, Ellis, New York, NY, Patent No. 254,666, Mar. 7, 1882 [Fig. 16.25]. A harness bit made with swinging rein hooks built as part of the cheek-piece and made to be closed by the swinging of the ends of the hooks under the ends of the mouth-piece.

Liverpool Cheeks: Cheek-pieces for a Liverpool bit. See Chapter 17 for different pattern styles.

Liverpool Driving Bit: See Chapter 17.

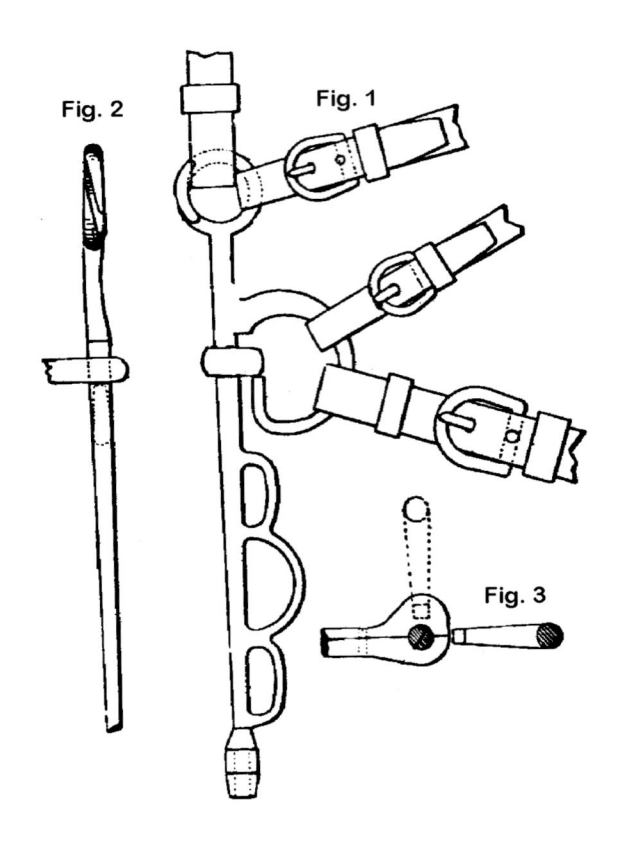

Fig. 16.25 Little harness bit rein attachment.

CHAPTER SEVENTEEN
Liverpool

PATENT UNIVERSAL LIVERPOOL BIT,
With 12 INTERCHANGEABLE MOUTHS and PATENT STEEL SLIDE.

SECTION OF BIT SHEWING STEEL SLIDE

SECTION OF BIT WITHOUT STEEL SLIDE

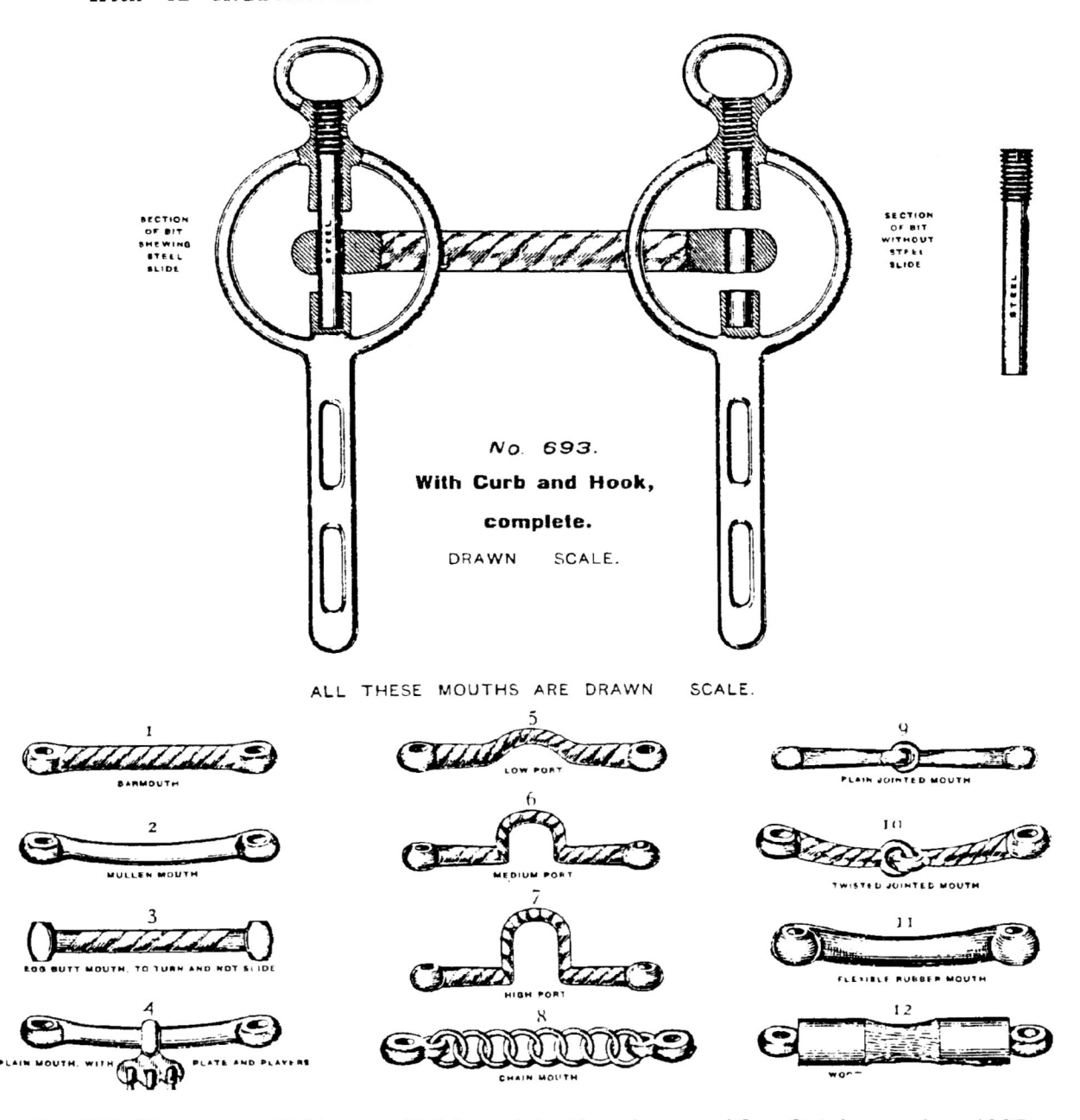

No. 693.
With Curb and Hook, complete.
DRAWN SCALE.

ALL THESE MOUTHS ARE DRAWN SCALE.

1. BARMOUTH
2. MULLEN MOUTH
3. EGG BUTT MOUTH, TO TURN AND NOT SLIDE
4. PLAIN MOUTH, WITH PLATE AND PLAYERS
5. LOW PORT
6. MEDIUM PORT
7. HIGH PORT
8. CHAIN MOUTH
9. PLAIN JOINTED MOUTH
10. TWISTED JOINTED MOUTH
11. FLEXIBLE RUBBER MOUTH
12. WOOD

Fig.17.0 Change-mouth Liverpool bit from John Dewsbury and Son Catalogue circa 1905.

Liverpool bits from John Dewsbury and Son, Walsall, England [Fig. 17.1] circa 1905.

295	2 Loop Half-twisted 9/16 in. Mouth, Solid Liverpool Bit and Curb.
295a	295 with 3 in. Patent Rubber Disks.
295b	295 with Rubber Port.
507	3 Loop Sliding Half-twisted 9/16 in. Mouth, Liverpool Bit and Curb.
84	Loop, Sliding Half-twisted 9/16 in. Mouth, Liverpool Bit and Curb.
2496	Sliding Half-twisted 9/16 in. mouth, Church Window Pattern, Square Guard, Liverpool Bit and Curb.
294	Sliding Half-twisted 9/16 in. Mouth, Fancy Cheek, Liverpool Bit and Curb.
297	Sliding Half-twisted Mouth Horse Shoe Guard. Liverpool Bit and Curb, 1/2 in Mouth.
135	Sliding Mullen Mouth Ballon Shape, Loop in Guard, Liverpool Bit and Curb.
299	Sliding Half-twisted 1/2 in. Mouth Short Cheek Loop Liverpool Bit and Curb.
265	Sliding Half-twisted 1/2 in. Mouth Bar across Guard, Liverpool Bit and Curb.
302	Sliding Half-twisted 1/2 in. Mouth Bar rings in Guard, Liverpool Bit and Curb.

Any of these bits were made in forged iron, steel, warranted hard steel with nickel-plating or solid-nickel. The curbs can be nickel-plated.

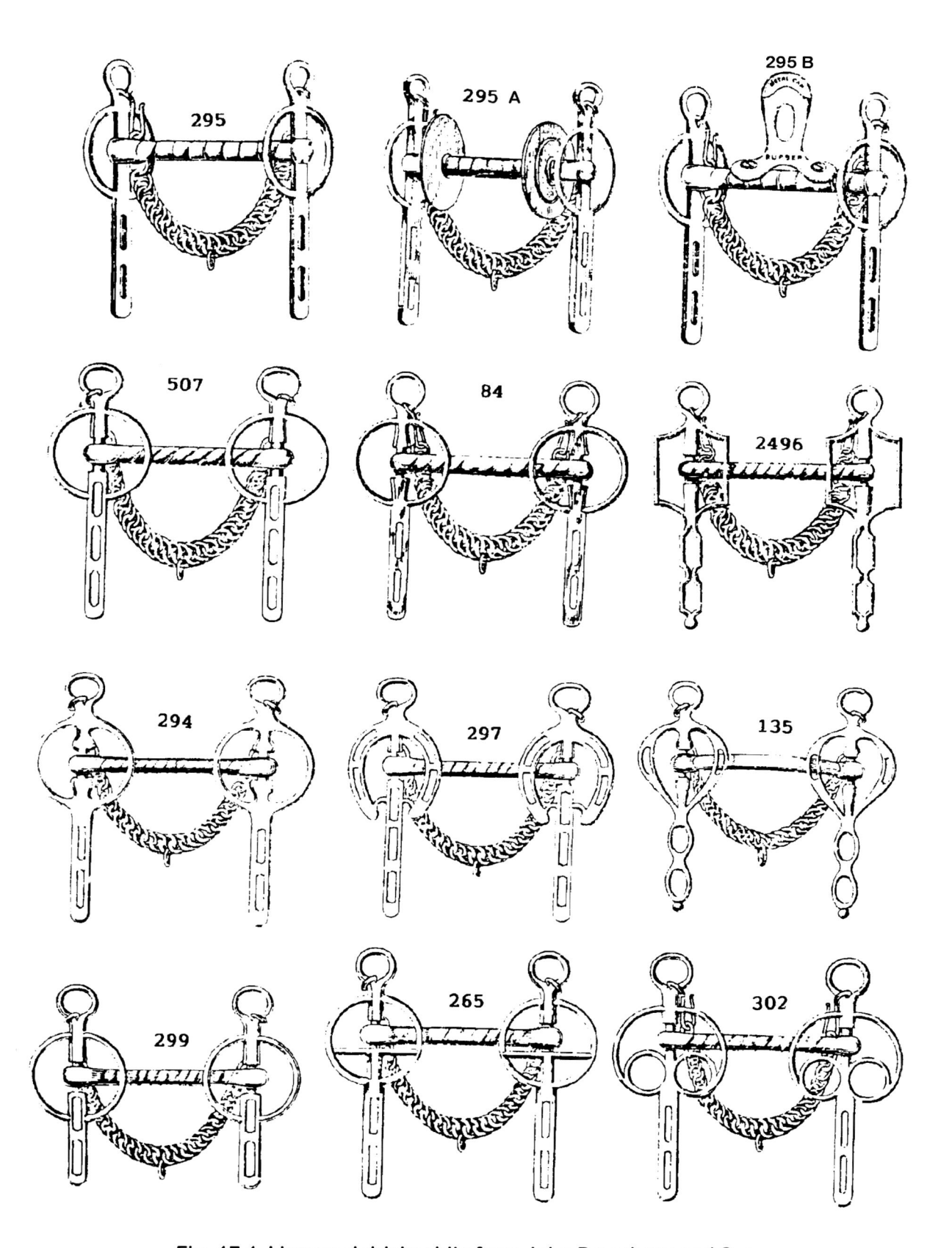

Fig. 17.1 Liverpool driving bits from John Dewsbury and Son.

Liverpool bits from John Dewsbury and Son, Walsall, England [Fig. 17.2] circa 1905.

150   Sliding Half-twisted 1/2 in. Mouth, 2 Egg Loop, Liverpool Bit and Curb.

822   Sliding Half-twisted 7/16 Mouth, Light Buggy Size, Liverpool Bit and Curb.

25   Sliding Half-twisted 1/2 in. Mouth, Gig Size, Liverpool Bit and Curb.

689   Sliding Half-twisted 1/2 in. Mouth, Gig Size, Liverpool Bit and Curb with Patent Steel Slides and Solid Butts.

1046   Hollow Mullen Mouth Liverpool Bit and Curb, Mouth Mullen or Bar-mouth.

763   Sliding Mullen Mouth 2 Loop Liverpool Bit and Curb, with Bent Bottom Bar.

296   Plain Jointed-mouth Liverpool Bit and Curb.

690   Sliding 1/2 in. Bar-mouth, 2 Loop, Egg Butt, Liverpool Bit and Curb.

443   9/16 in. Bar-mouth 2 Loop, Turn Cheek Egg-butt Liverpool Bit and Curb.

416   Light 3 Loop Sliding Half-twisted 7/16 in. Mouth Liverpool Bit and Curb. Available with 2 Loops.

82   Sliding Half-twist 7/16 in. Mouth, 3 Loop Square Pattern, Liverpool Bit and Curb.

153   Sliding Double Jointed-mouth, Liverpool Bit and Curb.

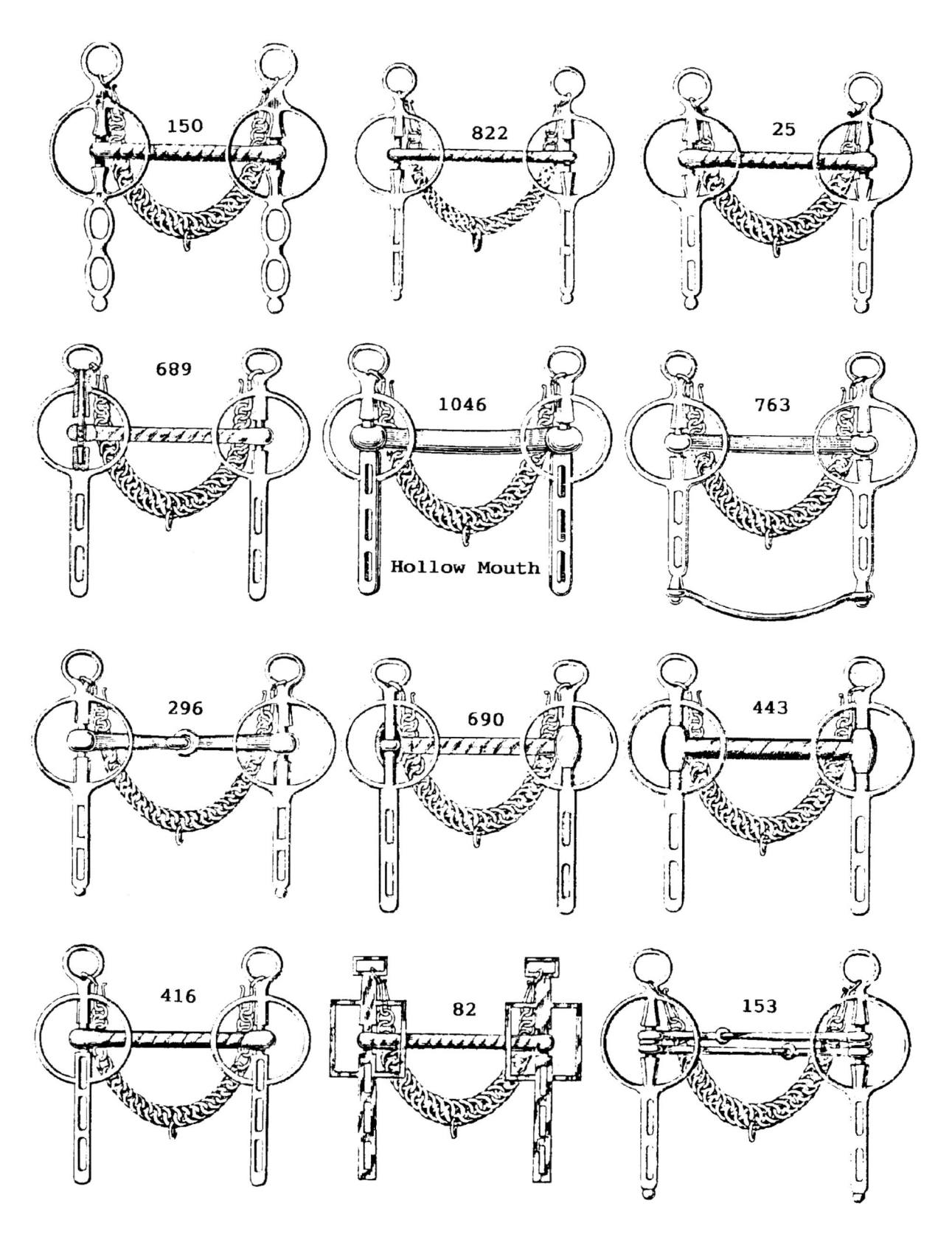

Fig. 17.2 Liverpool driving bits from John Dewsbury and Son.

Liverpool bits from John Dewsbury and Son, Walsall, England [Fig. 17.3] circa 1905.

313	Sliding Half-twisted 1/2 in. Mouth, Elbow, Liverpool Bit and Curb.
417	Sliding Half-twisted 1/2 in. Mouth, Crown Pattern, Liverpool Bit and Curb, Light. Stout Pattern Available.
713	Turn-cheek Mullen Mouth Driving Bit and Curb.
314	Sliding Roller Mouth, 2 Loop, Liverpool Bit and Curb.
762	2 Loop Half-twisted Mouth, Solid Liverpool Bit and Curb with Swing-mouth and Rubber Rollers.
441	3 Loop, Howlet Mouth, Solid Liverpool Bit and Curb.
440	Sliding Half-twisted 9/16 in. Mouth, 2 Loop, 2 Loop in Guard, Liverpool Bit and Curb.
168	Hollow Mouth Liverpool Bit with Holes for Breathing and Removable Ends for Administering Medicine, and Curb.
298	Sliding Half-twisted 1/2 in. Mouth, 2 Loop Fancy Pattern Liverpool Bit and Curb.
169	Universal Liverpool Bit and Curb with 7 interchangeable Mouths and Spanner. See Figure 17.0.

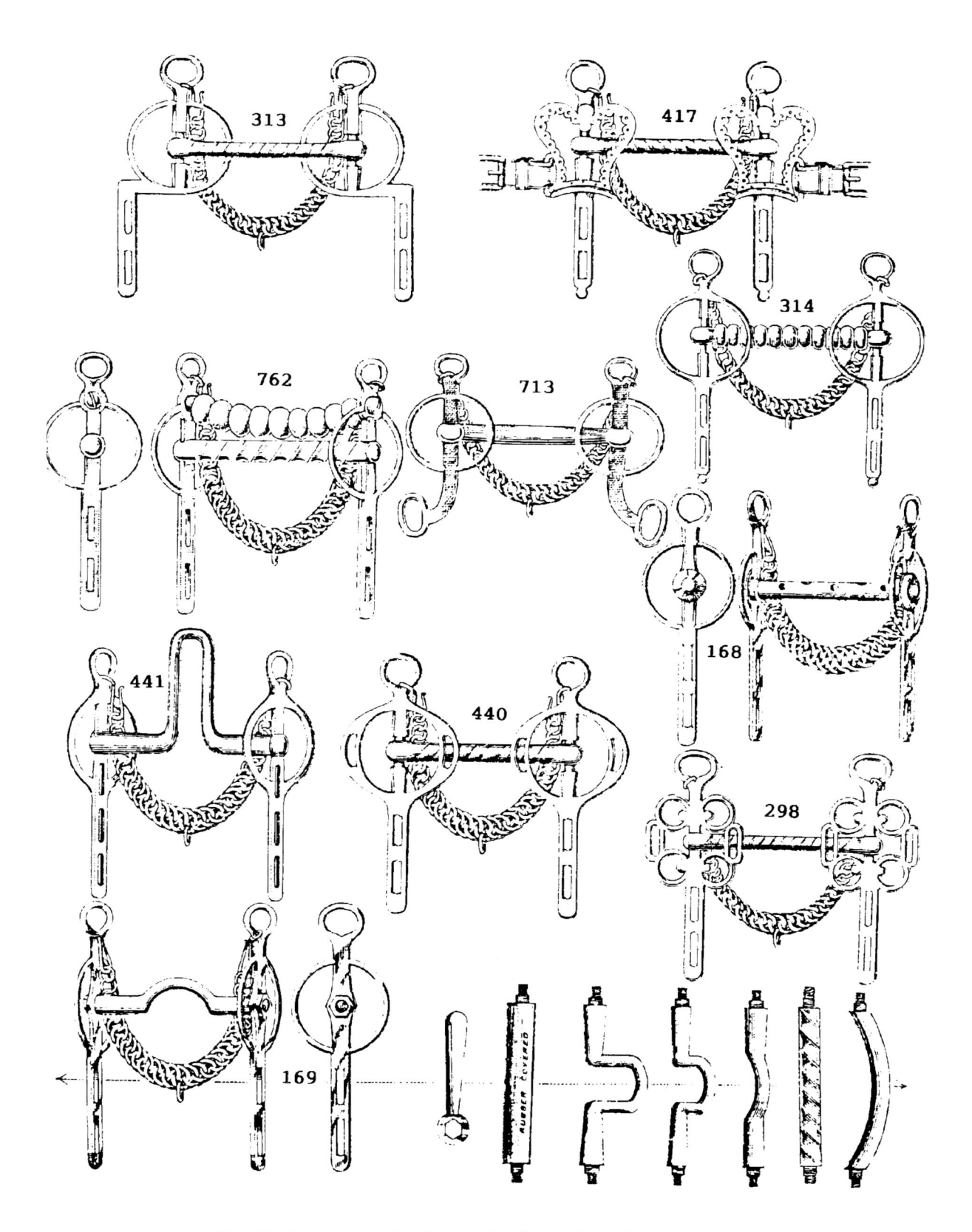

Fig. 17.3 Liverpool driving bits from John Dewsbury and Son.

Liverpool bits from John Dewsbury and Son, Walsall, England [Fig. 17.4] circa 1905.

88   Sliding Half-twisted 9/16 in. Mouth, Square Slide, Liverpool Bit and Curb.

152   Sliding Half-twisted 1/2 in. Mouth, Liverpool Bit and Curb

1056   Sliding Mullen Mouth Square Slide Double Bar Guard Liverpool Bit and Curb.

1066   Solid Low Port Mouth Liverpool Bit and Curb.

439   2 Loop, Turn Cheek, Mullen Mouth, Liverpool Bit and Curb.

151   Sliding Half-twisted 1/2 in. Mouth, Church Window Pattern Loop, Liverpool Bit and Curb.

154   Sliding Plain Revolving Mouth Liverpool Bit and Curb.

251   Sliding Half-twisted 9/16 in. Mouth Double Guard Liverpool Bit and Curb.

444   2 Egg Loop, Sliding Mullen Mouth, Loop in Guard, Balloon Shaped, Bent Bottom Bar, Liverpool Bit and Curb.

445   Fancy Cheek, 1/2 in. Mouth, Square Slide, Liverpool Bit and Curb Solid Bottom Bar.

303   Fancy Cheek Half-twisted 1/2 in. Barmouth, Loops in Guard, Solid Liverpool Bit and Curb.

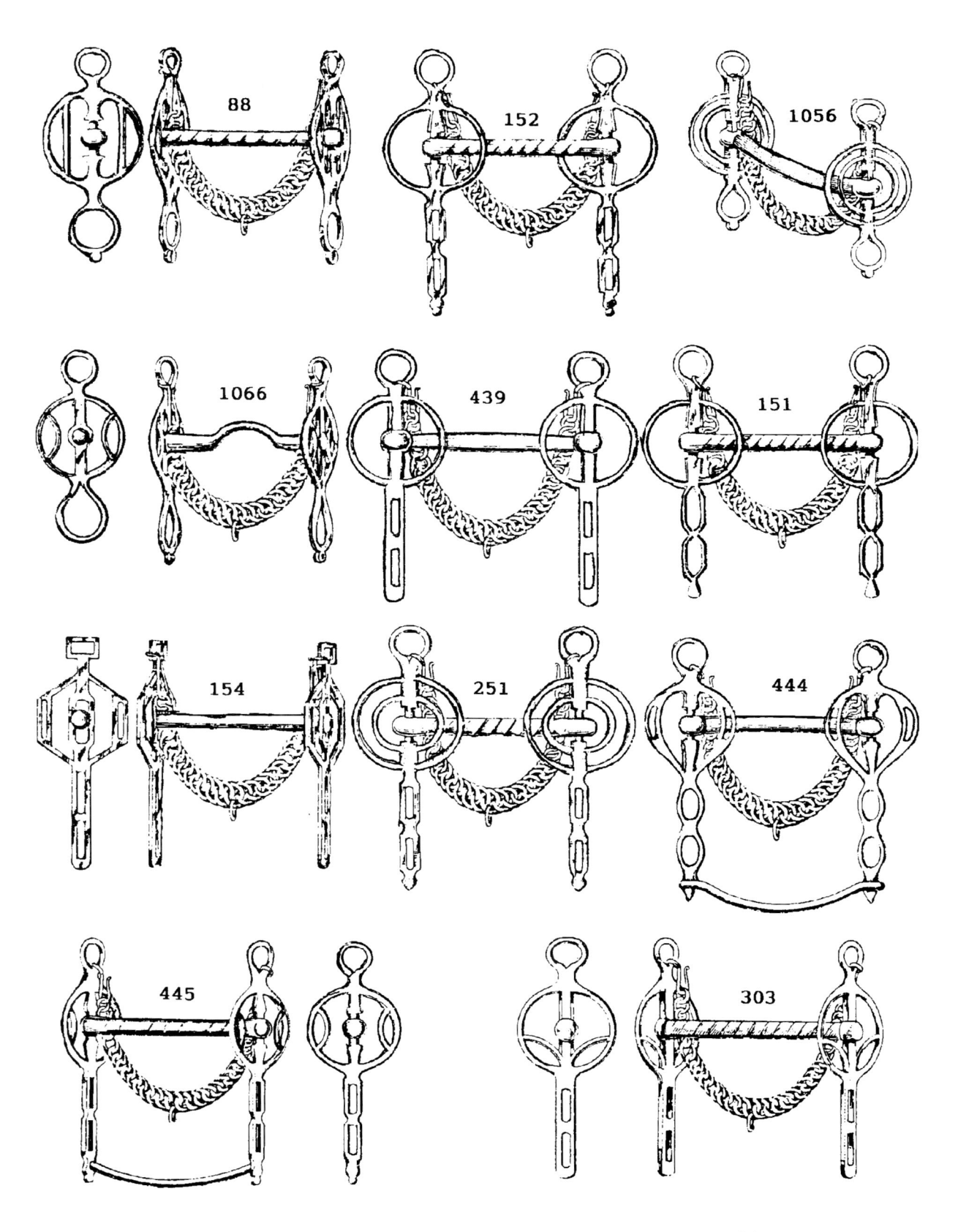

Fig 17.4 Liverpool driving bits from John Dewsbury and Son.

Liverpool bits from John Dewsbury and Son, Walsall, England [Fig. 17.5] circa 1905.

1063	Square Sliding Bar-mouth 1 Loop, Loops in Guard Hexagon Guard, Liverpool Bit and Curb.
1062	Square Sliding Mullen Mouth 3 Loop, Loops in Guard, Square Pattern, Liverpool Bit and Curb.
1061	Square Sliding Mullen Mouth, 2 Loop, Loops in Guard, Crown Pattern Liverpool Bit and Curb.
1059	Square Sliding Mullen Mouth 2 Loop, Loops in Guard, Balloon Shaped, Liverpool Bit and Curb.
1058	Square Sliding Mullen Mouth 2 Loop, Loops in Guard, Ardee Pattern, Liverpool Bit and Curb.
1060	Square Sliding Mullen Mouth 2 Loop, Loops in Guard, Pear Shaped Liverpool Bit and Curb
446	Square Sliding Mullen Mouth 2 Loop, Loops in Guard, Balloon Shape, Liverpool Bit and Curb, with Nut and Ring on Butt.
447	Square Sliding Bar-mouth 1 Loop, Loops in Guard, Balloon Shape, Liverpool Bit and Curb.

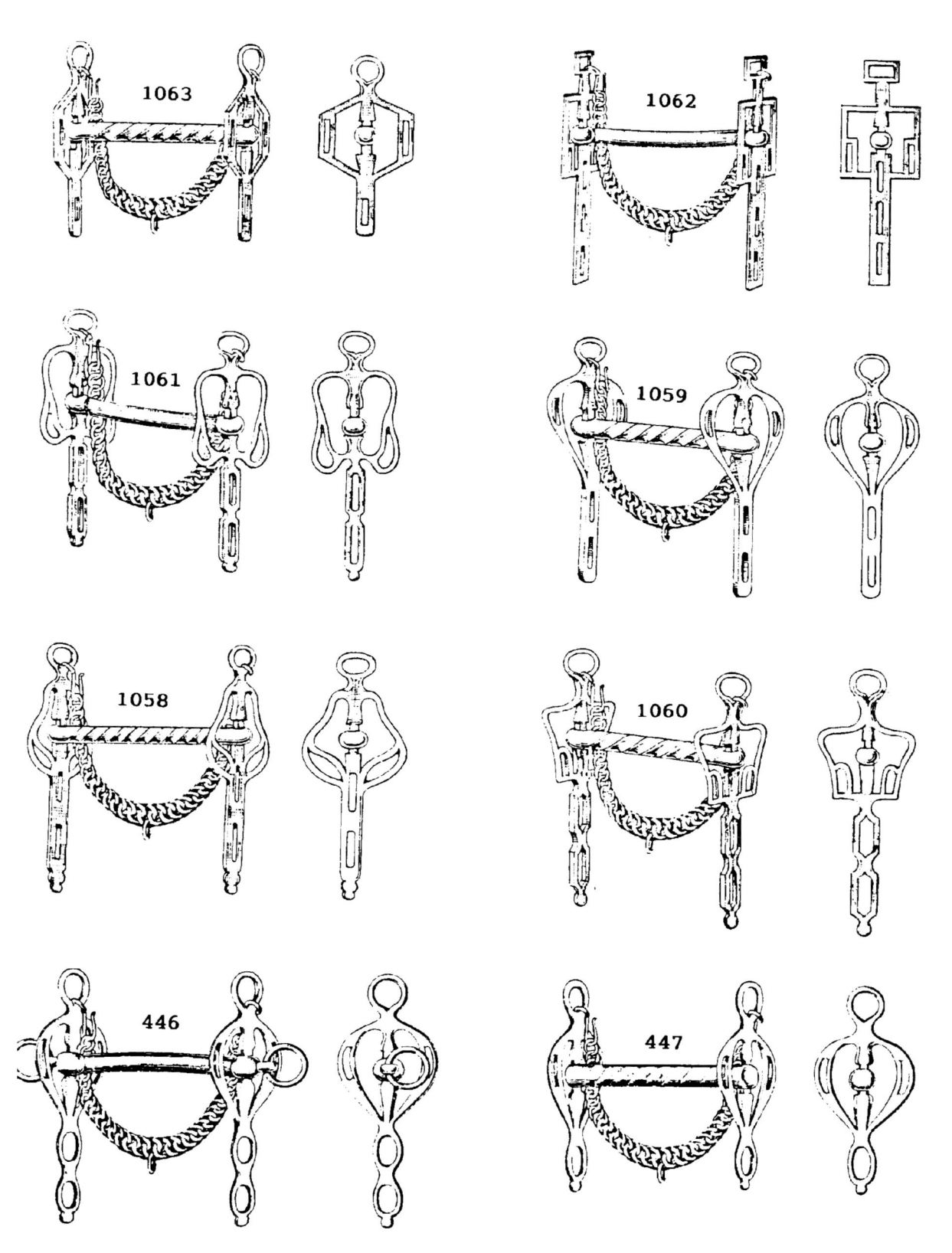

Fig. 17.5 Liverpool driving bits from John Dewsbury and Son.

CHAPTER EIGHTEEN
Lobdell to Martingale

Lobdell, Alonzo, Racine, WI, Patent No. 449,163, Mar. 31, 1891 [Fig. 18.0]. The unique design of the cheek-pieces allows the rein attachment to rotate within the cheek-rings.

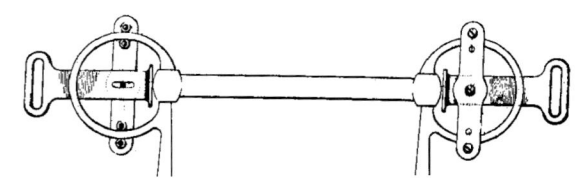

Fig. 18.0 Lobdell rein-attachment.

Lockhard, Hiram: See Chapter 26, Nosebands.

Logan Bit: See Chapter 5, Aughey bit, Fig. 5.14.

Lolling Bit: A bit with a plate or some other device to keep the horse from getting its tongue over the bit or hanging its tongue out the side of its mouth [Figs. 18.1 to 18.3]. See Tongue Bits, Chapter 33.

Fig. 18.1 Lolling bit.

Fig. 18.2 Lolling bit. Robert Maclin collection.

Fig. 18.3 Lolling bit.

Long Cheeks: A bit with longer than normal portion of lower cheek-piece. See Chapter 31, Side-pieces.

Long Reins: A rein or line used in the Longe method of training. The line or rein is 30 feet or longer in length.

Longcor, Leonard C., Belvidere, IL, Patent No. 279,171, June 12, 1883 [Fig. 18.4]. The check bit is attached to the snaffle bit by loose links which provide for some lateral movement. Slots in the forward ends of the links permit the links to operate freely, but prevent the check-bit from turning in the slots.

Longeing: The process of using a long line in conjunction with a cavesson in the training and schooling of a horse. Training takes place in a circular arena.

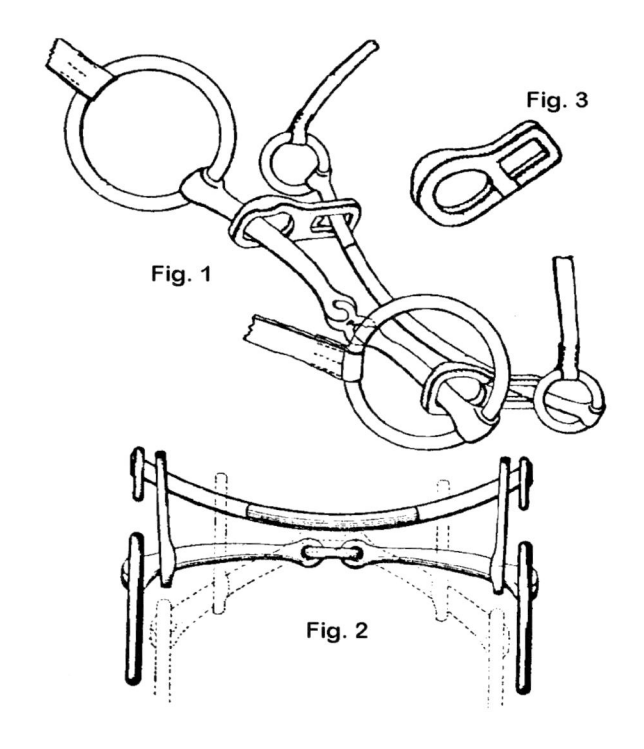

Fig. 18.4 Longcor double bit.

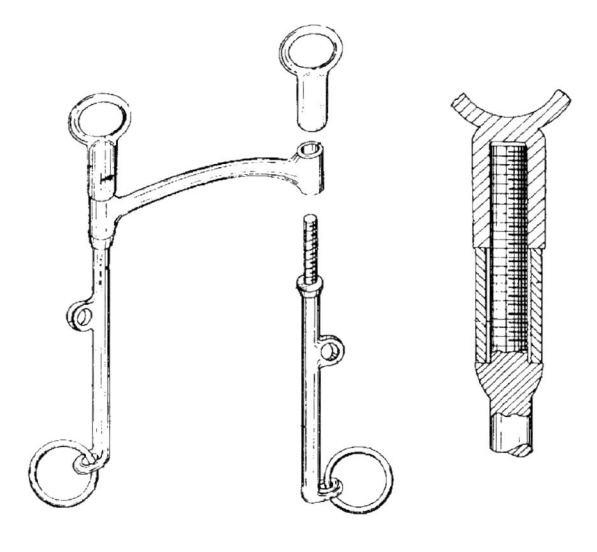

Fig. 18.5 Lovell five-piece bit.

Loose-cheek: A side-piece that moves freely on the mouth-piece end in a vertical plain. See Chapter 31, Side-pieces.

Loose-cheek Pelham: See Chapter 27, Pelham Bits.

Loose Rein Riding: Riding a horse with little or no pressure being applied to the bit. The rider guides the horse by laying the rein against its neck to cue the horse. A style of riding when using spade, ring bit or some curb bits.

Loose-ring Pelham: See Chapter 27.

Loriner: A maker of metal parts used in saddlery, such as bits, stirrups, spurs and curb chains.

Lovell, Cash Alton, Jr., Winston-Salem, NC, Patent No. 3,304,692, Feb 23, 1967 [Fig. 18.5]. A curb bit formed of five parts that can be assembled without welding.

Lowbridge, Jabez, Pittsburg, PA, Patent No. 131,691, Sep.24, 1872 [Fig. 18.6]. A sliding mouth-piece that can move upward or downward in the horse's mouth, attached to a curved bar in the cheek-piece.

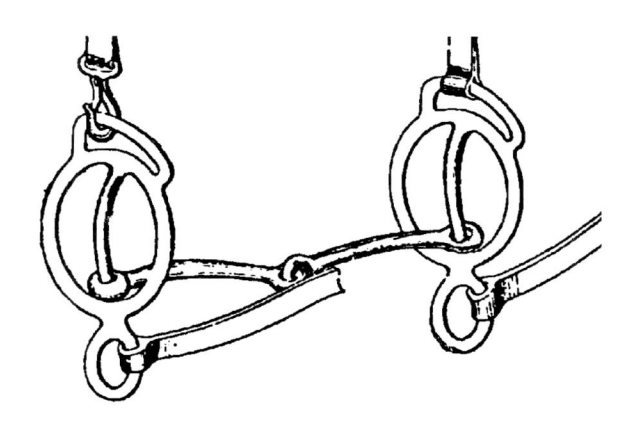

Fig. 18.6 Lowbridge loose-mouth bit.

Lownde's Pelham; See Chapter 27, Pelham bits.

Lunge Rein: See Long rein.

Lungeing: See Longeing.

Lynch, Lawrence, Batavia, NY, Patent No. 311,436, Jan. 27, 1885 [Fig.

18.7]. A hollow tube mouth-piece through which a flexible connection between the rein-rings passes.

Fig. 18.7 Lynch snaffle bit.

Mace, Dan: A half-cheek snaffle bit with loops for a lip-strap, sold by Haydens and Allen, St. Louis, MO [Fig. 18.8].

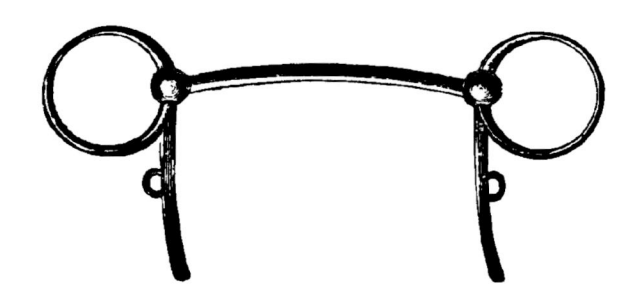

Fig. 18.8 Dan Mace snaffle bit.

Maddox, Jacob, Jr., Auzvasse, MO, Patent No. 485,638, Nov. 8, 1892 [Fig. 18.9]. The oblique angle of the additional arm projecting from the side-piece for the attachment of the curb allows room to prevent chaffing of the lips by the curb.

Magner, Dennis, Brooklyn, NY, Patent No. 233,631, Oct. 26, 1880 [Fig. 18.10]. A pulley curb bit designed for the special bridle.

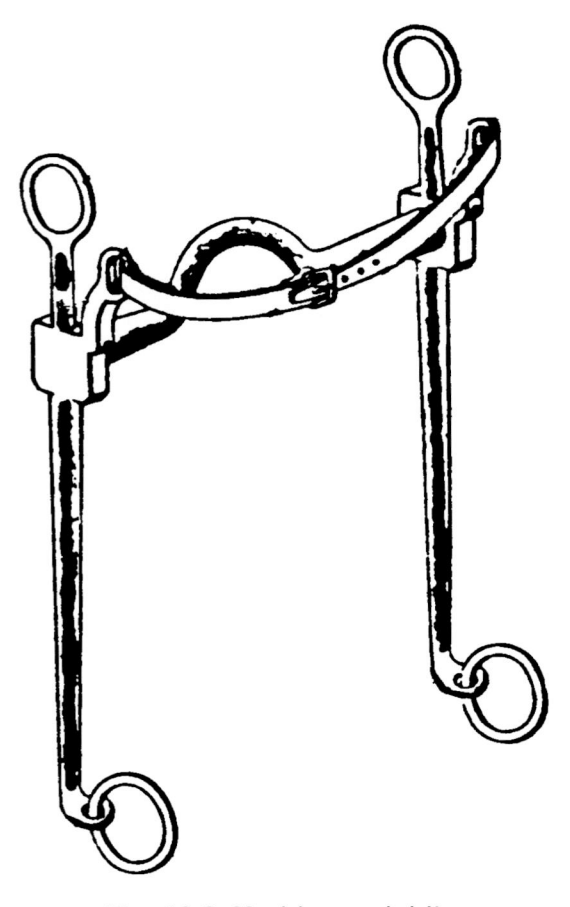

Fig. 18.9 Maddox curb bit.

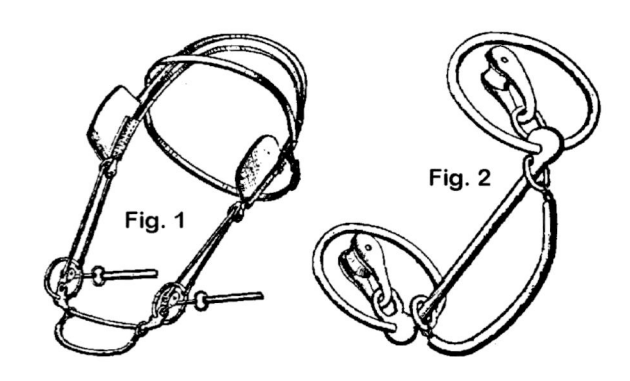

Fig. 18.10 Magner pulley bit.

Mameluke Bit: Moorish reference to a ring bit used by the Mamelukes, an elite cavalry corps of Egyptian soldiers which ruled Egypt from 1250 to 1517 A.D. [Fig. 18.11].

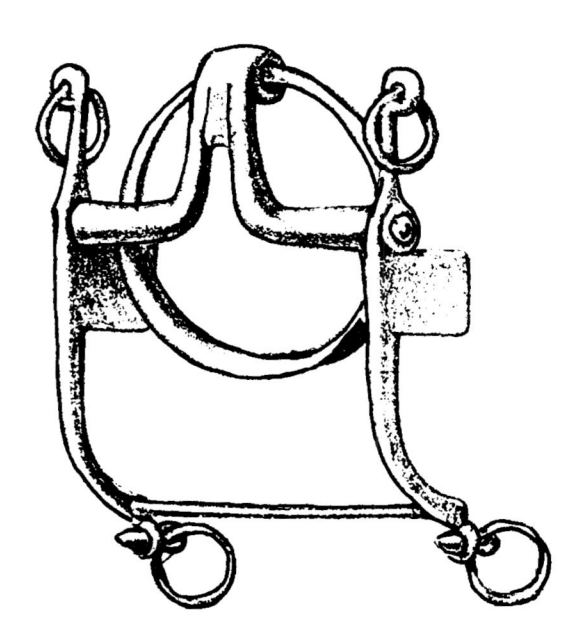

Fig. 18.11 Mameluke bit.

Manning, James A., Danville, IN, Patent No. 368,776, Aug. 23, 1887 [Fig. 18.12]. A spring-controlled concave square smaller-diameter mouthpiece is exposed when the reins are pulled.

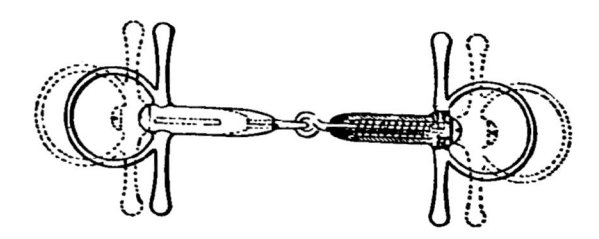

Fig. 18.12 Manning spring-mouth bit.

Martin, William N. and Morgan R. Bellringer, New York, NY, Patent No. 149,497, Apr. 7, 1874 [Fig. 18.13]. An elongated spoon-mouth to prevent the horse from catching and keeping the bit between its teeth.

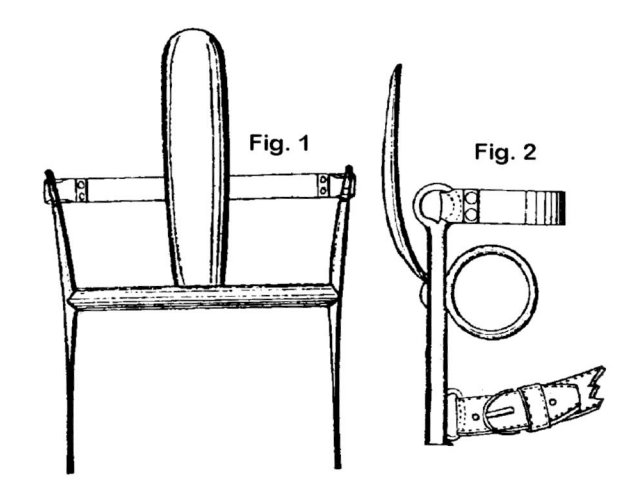

Fig. 18.13 Martin long-spooned bit.

Kentucky Belle

Constance Fenimore Woolson

Summer of 'sixty-three, sir, and Conrad was gone away-
Gone to the country town, sir, to sell our first load of hay:
We lived in the log-house yonder, poor as ever you've seen;
Roschen there was a baby, and I was only nineteen.

Conrad he took the oxen, but he left Kentucky Belle.
How much we thought of Kentucky, I couldn't begin to tell-
Came from the Blue-grass country; my father gave her to me
When I rode north with Conrad, away from the Tennessee.

Conrad lived in Ohio-a German he is, you know
The house stood in broad corn fields, stretching on, row after row,
The old folks made me welcome; they were kind as kind could be;
But I kept longing, longing, for the hills of Tennessee.

Oh for the sight of water, the shadowed slope of a hill!
Clouds that hang on the summit, a wind that never is still!
But the level land went stretching away to meet the sky-
Never a rise, from north to south, to rest the weary eye!

From east to west, no river to shine out under the moon,
Nothing to make a shadow in the yellow afternoon:
Only the breathless sunshine, as I looked out, all forlorn:
Only the "rustle, rustle," as I walked among the corn.

When I fell sick with pining, we didn't wait any more,
But moved away from the corn-lands, out to this river shore
The Tuscarawas it's called, sir-off there's a hill, you see
And now I've grown to like it next best to Tennessee.

*I was at work that morning. Someone came riding like mad
Over the bridge and up the road-Farmer Routh's little lad.
Bareback he rode; he had no hat; he hardly stopped to say:
"Morgan's men are coming, Frau; they're galloping on this way,*

*"I'm sent to warn the neighbors. He isn't a mile behind;
He sweeps up all the horses-every horse that he can find.
Morgan, Morgan the raider, and Morgan's terrible men,
With bowie-knives and pistols, are galloping up the glen!"*

*The lad rode down the valley, and I stood still at the door;
The baby laughed and prattled, playing with spools on the floor;
Kentucky was out in the pasture; Conrad, my man, was gone.
Near, nearer, Morgan's men were galloping, galloping on!*

*Sudden I picked up baby, and ran to the pasture bar.
"Kentucky!" I called-"Kentucky." She knew me ever so far!
I led her down the gully that turns off there just to the right,
and tied her to the bushes: her head was just out of sight.*

*As I ran back to the log-house, at once there came a sound-
The ring of hoofs, galloping hoofs, trembling over the ground-
Coming into the turnpike out from the White-woman Glen-
Morgan, Morgan the raider, and Morgan's terrible men.*

*As near they drew and nearer, my heart beat fast in alarm;
But still I stood in the door-way with baby in my arm.
They came: they passed: with spur and whip in haste they sped along-
Morgan. Morgan the raider, and his band, six hundred strong.*

Weary they looked and jaded, riding through night and through day;
Pushing on east to the river, many long miles away,
To the broad-strip where Virginia runs up into the west,
And fording the Upper Ohio before they could stop to rest.

On like the wind they hurried, and Morgan rode in advance;
Bright were his eyes like live coals, and he gave me a sidewise glance;
And I was breathing freely, after my choking pain,
When the last one of the troops suddenly drew his rein.

Frightened I was to death, sir; I scarce dared look in his face
As he asked for a drink of water, and glanced around the place.
I gave him a cup, and he smiled-'twas only a boy, you see,
Faint and worn, with dim-blue eyes; and he'd sailed on the Tennessee.

Only sixteen he was, sir-a fond mother's only son-
Off and away with Morgan before his life had begun;
The damp drops stood on his temples; drawn was the boyish mouth;
And I thought me of the mother waiting down in the South.

Oh! pluck was he to the backbone, and clear grit through and through;
Boasted and bragged like a trooper; but the big words wouldn't do;
The boy was dying sir, dying, as plain as plain could be,
Worn out by his ride with Morgan up from the Tennessee.

But when I told the laddie that I too was from the South
Water came in his dim eyes, and quivers around his mouth.
"Do you know the Blue-grass country?" he wistfully began to say;
Then swayed like a willow sapling and fainted dead away.

I had him into the log-house and cooked and brought him to;
I fed him, and I coaxed him, as I thought his mother'd do;
And when the lad got better; and the raise in his head was gone,
Morgan's men were miles away, galloping, galloping on.

"Oh, I must go!" he muttered; "I must be up and away:
Morgan-Morgan is waiting for me! Oh! what will Morgan say?"
But I beard a sound of tramping, and kept him back from the door
The ringing sound of horses' hoofs that I had heard before.

And on, on came the soldiers- the Michigan cavalry-
And fast they rode, and black they looked, galloping rapidly:
They had followed hard on Morgan's tracks; they had followed day and night;
But of Morgan and Morgan's raiders they had never caught a sight.

And rich Ohio startled through all those summer days;
For strange, wild men were galloping over her broad highways
Now here, now there, now seen, now gone, now north, now east, now west,
Through river valleys and worn-land farms, sweeping away her last.

A bold ride and a long ride! But they were taken at last.
They almost reached the river by galloping hard and fast;
But the boys in blue were upon them ere ever they gained the ford,
And Morgan, Morgan the raider, laid down his terrible sword.

Well I kept the boy till evening-kept him against his will.
But he was too weak to follow, and sat there pale and still,
When it was cool and dusky-you'll wonder to hear me tell,
But I stole down to the gully and brought up Kentucky Belle.

I kissed the star on her forehead-my pretty, gentle lass
But I knew that she'd be happy back in the old Blue-grass.
A suit of clothes of Conrad's, with all the money I had,
And Kentucky, pretty Kentucky, I gave to the worn out lad.

I guided him to the southward as well as I knew how;
The boy rode off with many thanks and many a backward bow;
And then the glow it faded, and my heart began to swell,
As down the glen away she went, my last Kentucky Belle.

When Conrad came in the evening, the moon was shining high;
Baby and I were both crying-I couldn't tell him why-
But a battered suit of rebel gray was hanging on the wall
And a thin old horse, with a drooping head, stood in Kentucky's stall.

Well, he was kind, and never once said a hard word to me,
He knew I couldn't help it-'twas all for the Tennessee.
But, after the war was over, just think what came to pass
A letter sir; and the two were safe back in the old Blue-grass.

The lad had got across the border, riding Kentucky Belle;
And Kentucky she was thriving, and fat, and hearty and well;
He cared for her, and kept her, nor touched her with whip or spur.
Ah! we've had many horses since, but never a horse like her!

I first became acquainted with the poem "Kentucky Belle" when I was quite small. My grandmother would recite it to me almost in its entirety from memory. She had learned the poem while a schoolgirl about 1892. The poem has kept coming to mind often through the years. It was found in Harper's Fifth Reader of 1889 while doing research in the Kansas Historical Library at Topeka. The poem is an interesting reflection of history. The author.

CHAPTER NINETEEN
Martingale

A martingale is a piece of tack designed to control the carriage of the horse's head. The standing martingale is attached to a noseband on one end and the saddle girth on the other. The running martingale divides after passing through the neck strap. The thought is to give the rider more control on a snaffle bit.

Cheshire Martingale: A running martingale with the neck strap fastened to the saddle [Fig. 19.0].

Fig. 19.0 Cheshire martingale.

False Martingale: A strap attached to the bottom of the harness collar and to the belly band of the harness.

German Martingale: A draw rein, in that the reins are attached to the saddle girth and then pass forward through the rings of the snaffle bit to the rider's hands. Not a true martingale.

Hand-tooled Martingale: Used in combination with a breast collar in western-style riding [Fig. 19.1].

Fig. 19.1 Carved leather martingale and breast collar.

Indian Martingale: A running martingale with the strap continuous and wrapped around the nose to form a noseband [Fig. 19.2].

Irish Martingale: A form of running martingale with the two rings held close by a strap of about 6 inches [Fig. 19.3].

235

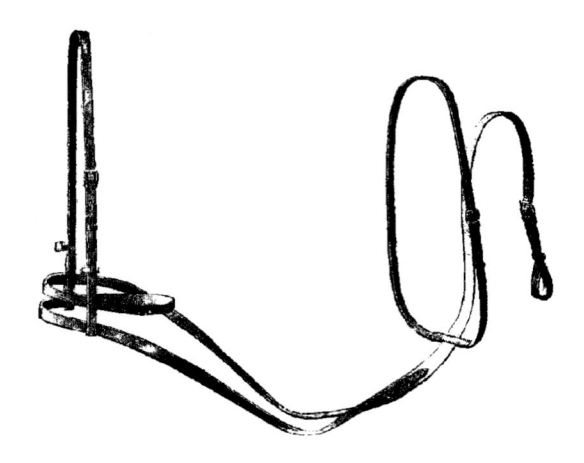

Fig. 19.2 Indian martingale.

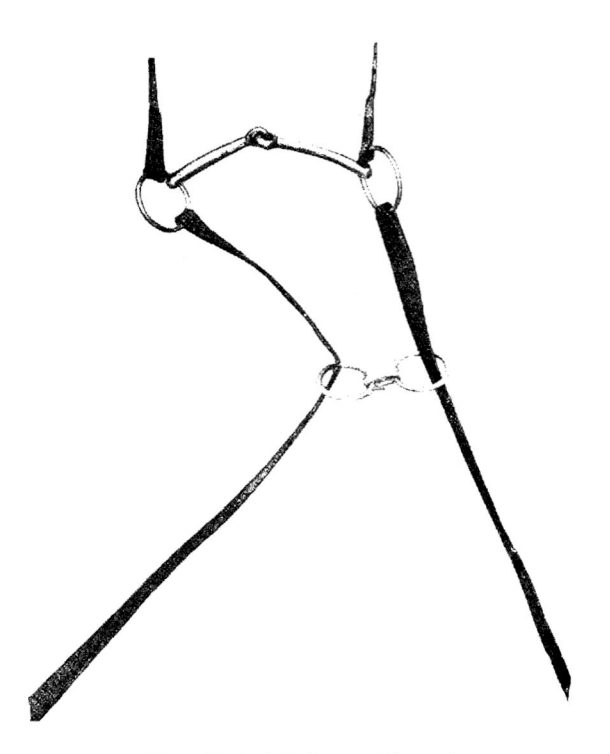

Fig. 19.3 Irish martingale.

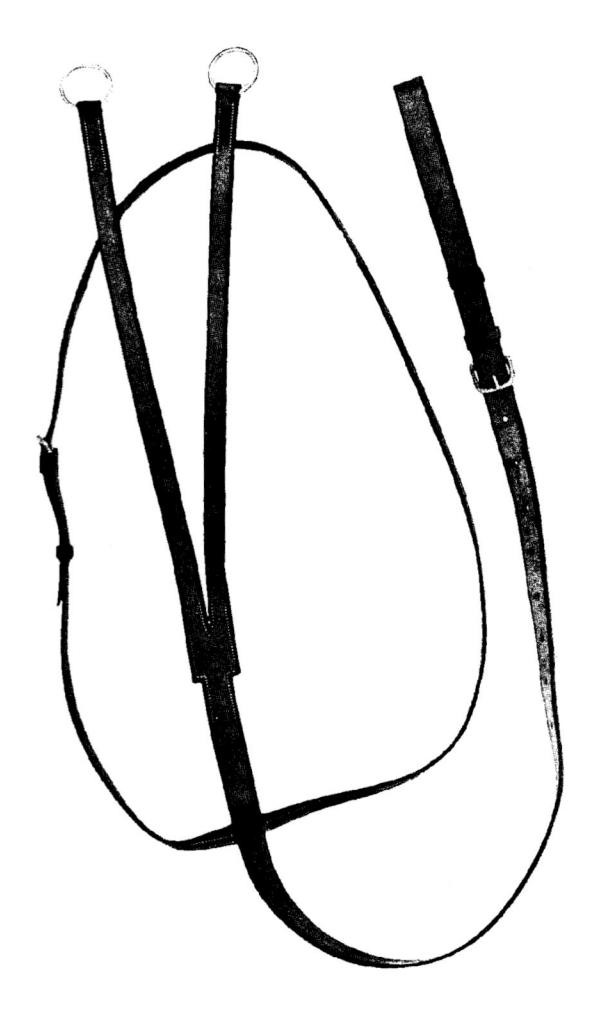

Fig. 19.4 Lord Lonsdale martingale.

Olympic Martingale: A style that is a combination of the draw rein and running martingale, with the martingale running through the snaffle rings and secured to the driving reins [Fig. 19.5].

Lord Lonsdale Martingale: A running martingale with the neck strap held tight in the structure of the running straps [Fig. 19.4].

236

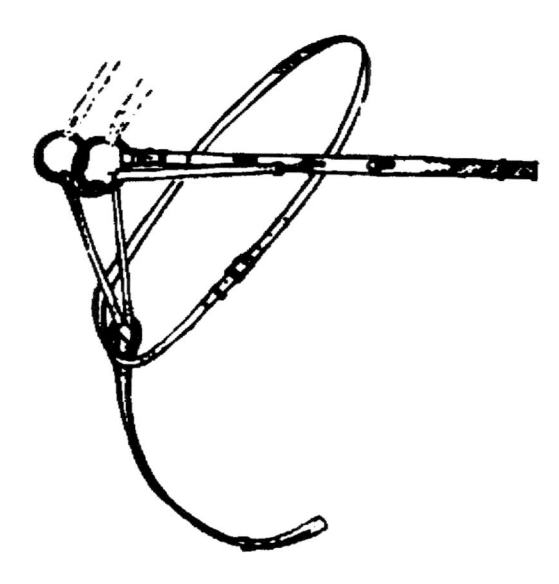

Fig. 19.5 Olympic martingale.

Round Martingale: A modern adaptation with round leather straps [Fig. 19.6].

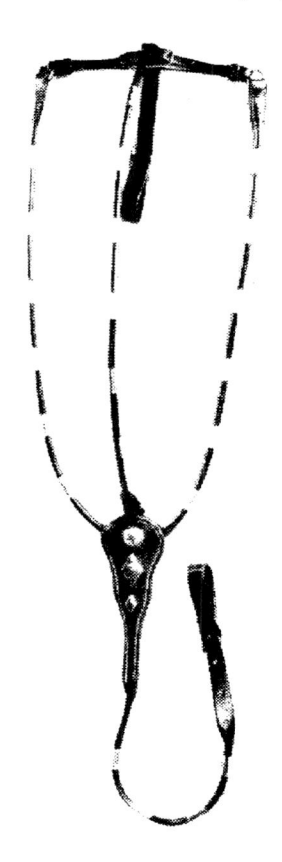

Fig. 19.6 Round leather martingale with silver ferrels.

Running Martingale: One of the two major styles of martingales [Fig. 19.7].

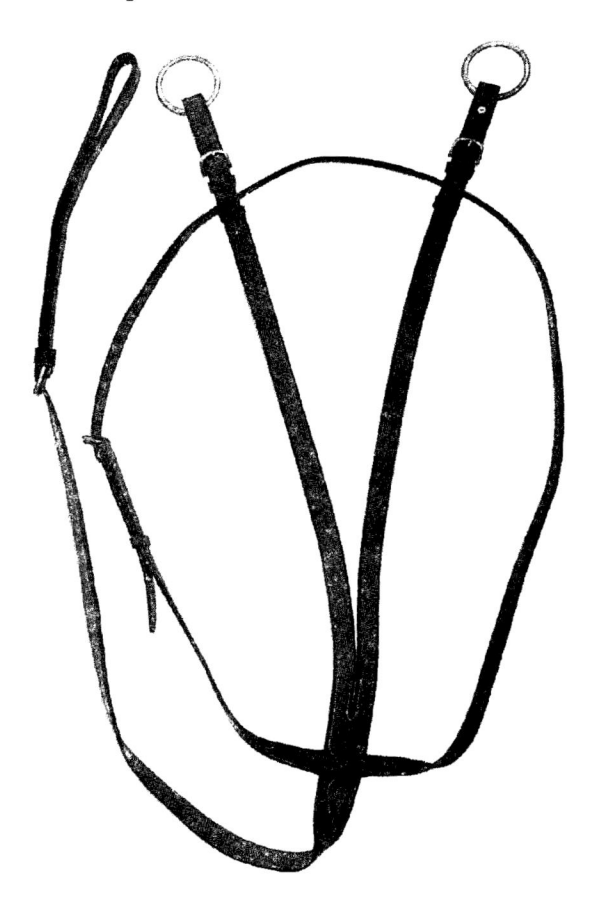

Fig. 19.7 Running martingale.

Spectacle Martingale: Connected rings for use as an Irish martingale [Fig. 19.8].

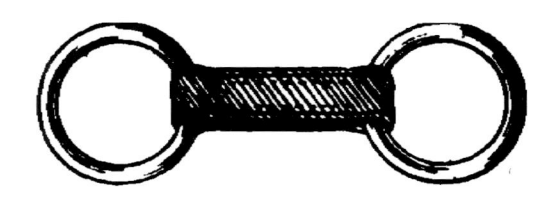

Fig. 19.8 Spectacle for Irish martingale.

Standing Martingale: One of the two major styles of martingales [Fig. 19.9].

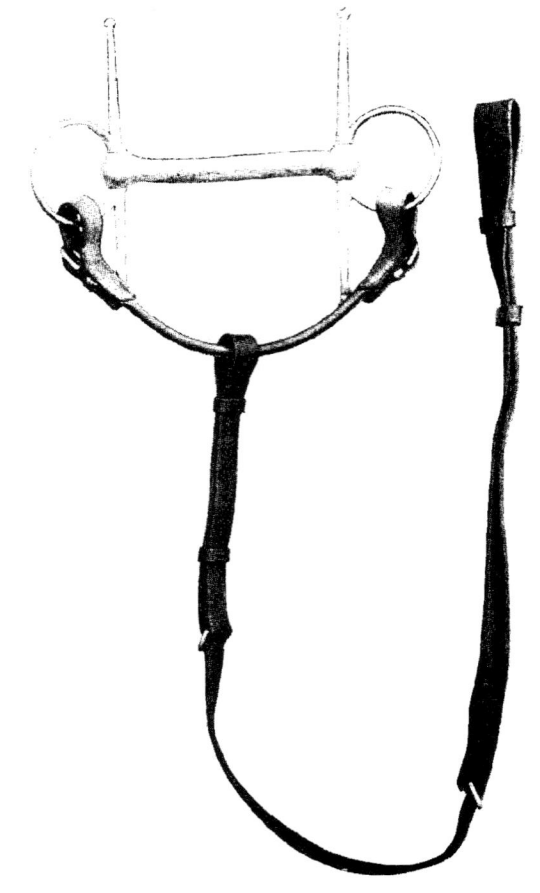

Fig. 19.9 A standing martingale.

Standing Martingale Minimum Length: Figure 19.10.

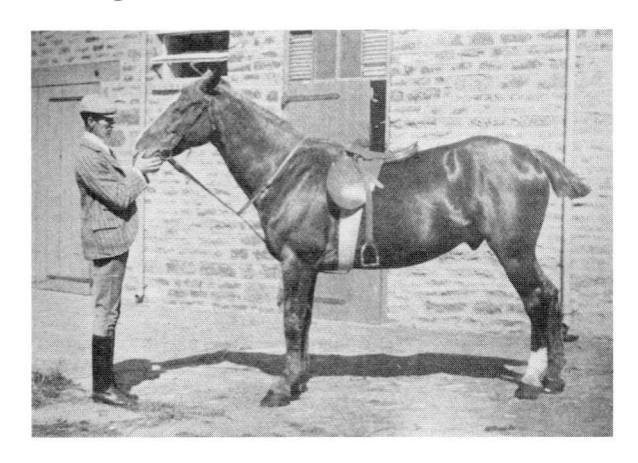

Fig. 19.10 Minimum length of standing martingale.

Standing Martingale Maximum Length: Figure 19.11.

Fig.19.11 Maximum Length of standing martingale.

Standing Martingale: Improvised a standing martingale by means of a running martingale [Fig. 19.12].

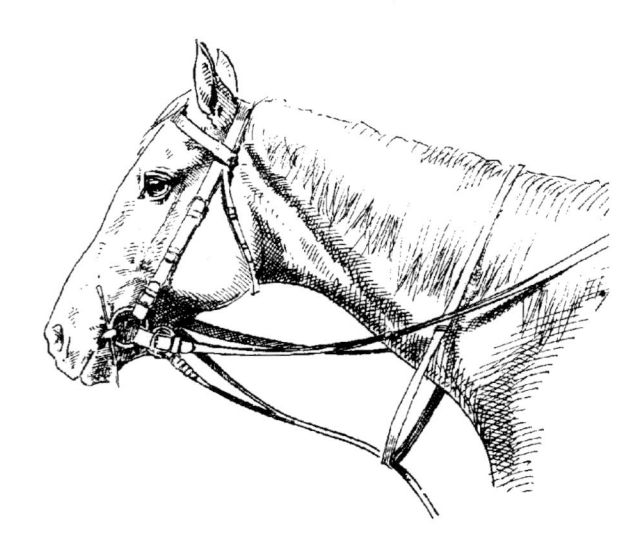

Fig. 19.12 An improvised standing martingale.

Standing Martingale with Cavesson: A standing martingale buckled to a cavesson nose band [Fig. 19.13].

Web Martingale: A running-style martingale with the two straps secured by a wide "V" shaped piece of leather sewn to the straps [Fig. 19.14].

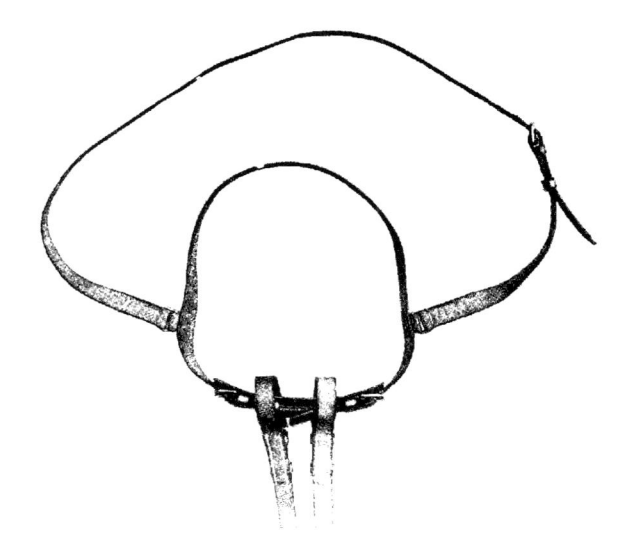

Fig,. 19.13 Standing martingale with cavesson.

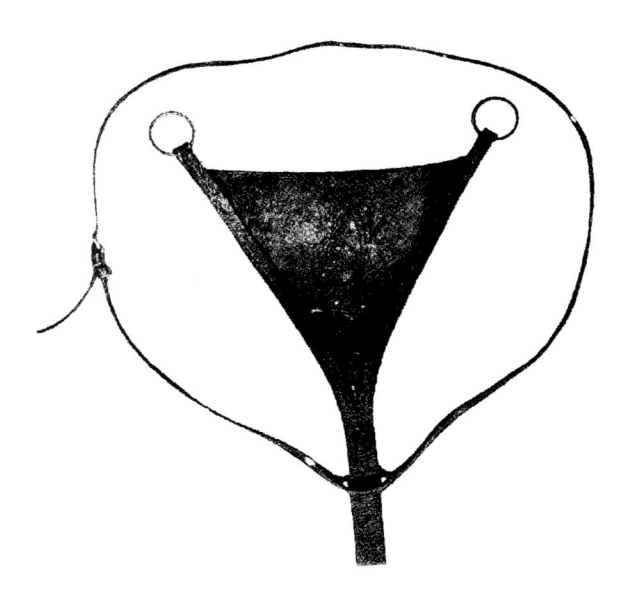

Fig. 19.14 Webb martingale.

CHAPTER TWENTY
Mason to Miklar

Mason, A. P. and Zalmon Hanford, Gowanda, NY, Patent No. 91,463, June 15, 1869 [Fig.. 20.0]. The mouth-piece has one side angular and the other rounded. The double ring at each end of the mouth-piece allows for the adjustment of the rein from one ring to the other to reverse the action of the mouth-piece.

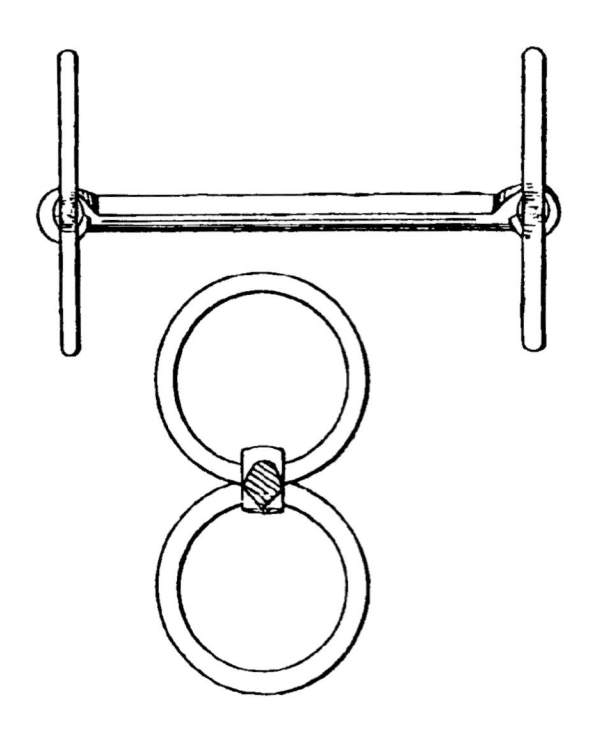

Fig. 20.0 Mason two-sided mouth-piece bit.

Mason, Arnold P., Franklinville, NY, Patent No. 115,753, June 6, 1871 [Fig. 20.1]. A hook that can be readily opened or closed for attaching the noseband of a bridle to the bit.

Mason, Arnold P. and George D. Homer, Olean, NY, Patent No. 150,696, May 18, 1874 [Fig. 20.2]. The bit consists of a leather bow or other suitable material of sufficient length to pass over the upper teeth and under the lip of the horse.

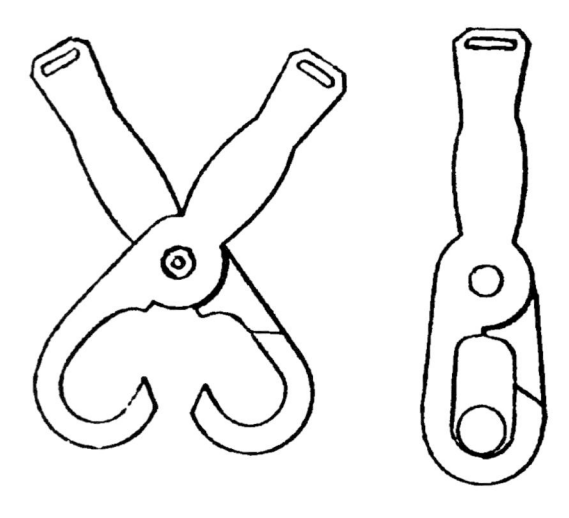

Fig. 20.1 Mason noseband hook.

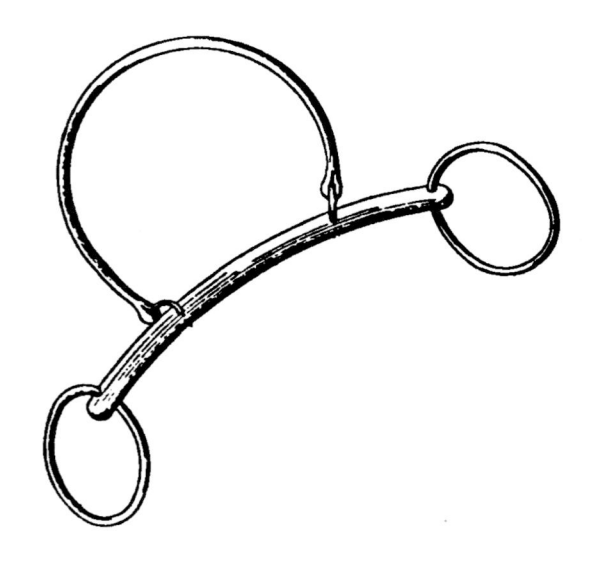

Fig. 20.2 Mason control bit.

Mason, Franklin J., Bentonsport, IA, Patent No. 65, 101, May 28, 1867 [Fig. 20.3]. The mouth-piece is a round leather strap that extends through the leather cheek-pieces and loops around the rein and headstall ring and under the chin of the horse to form a bit.

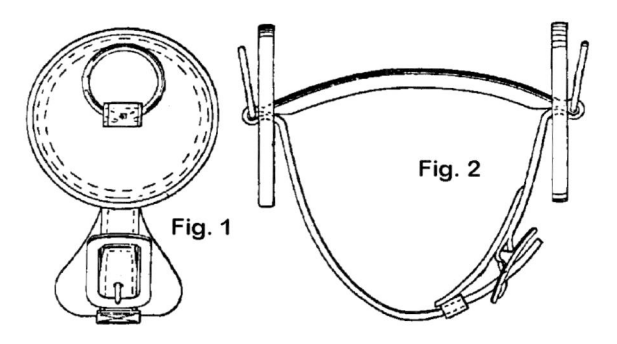

Fig. 20.3 Mason's leather-mouth bit.

MATERIAL USED TO CAST BITS: Dates indicate the approximate years the materials listed began to be in use.

Iron, Wrought Iron	up to 1890
Nickel	1900
Steel, Chrome Plate	1920
Zinc Plating, Galvanizing	1920
Aluminum	1895

Various compositions of nickel were used by different manufacturers, such as Duralex by Dewsbury, and some bits were made in different grades, such as Vicolette and Kangaroo, also by Dewsbury. After WW II the workmanship for the surface finish of English-made bits decreased, and now most English styles of bit which are still manufactured are made in Korea. Advertisements in magazines list aluminum bits as early as the mid 1890's. Crockett began making bit and spurs of "Airplane" metal in 1938.

Maxwell Overcheck: See Chapter 9, Fig. 9.10.

McCarty: Anglicized expression of the Spanish term *mecate*. See Hackamore, Chapter 13.

McCoy, Davenport C., Jacksonville, IL, Patent No. 278,576, May 29, 1883 [Fig. 20.4]. The cheek-pieces have small openings in the front of the ring to accommodate a wire cable that is placed around the teeth and under the upper lip of the horse.

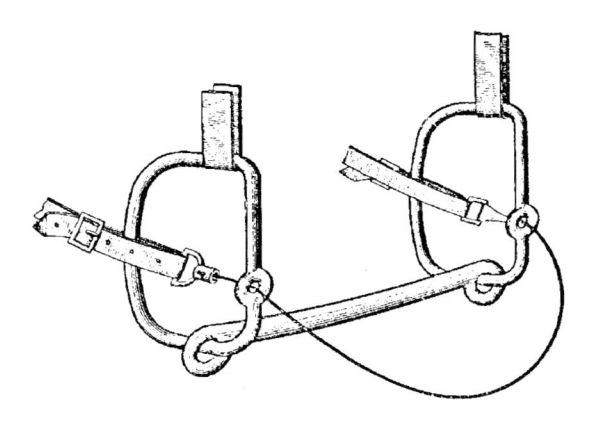

Fig. 20.4 McCoy bit with restraining cable.

McDonald, James R., Chicago, IL, Patent No. 455,049, June 30, 1891 [Fig. 20.5]. A snaffle bit with a lip-bar. The cheek-pieces swivel on the ends of the mouth-piece. The lip-bar rings have sufficient room to allow movement of the cheek-pieces.

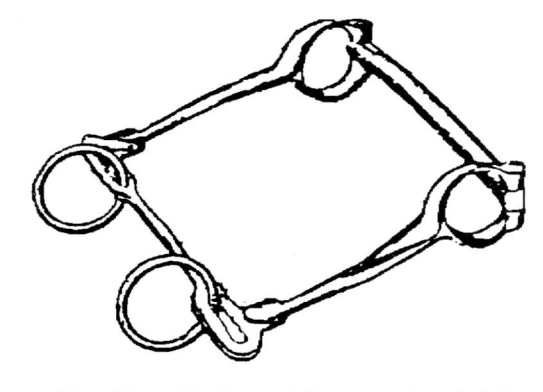

Fig. 20.5 McDonald loose-cheek bit.

McGuiness, Patrick J., New York, NY, Patent No. 78,466, June 2, 1868 [Fig.

McGuiness, Patrick J., New York, NY, Patent No. 78,466, June 2, 1868 [Fig. 20.6]. The bit consists of two pieces, hinged or pivoted together in the middle, one end of each piece connected with the reins, while the other end carries a stop near the end of the bar.

Fig. 20.6 McGuiness scissor-mouth bit.

McKenney, Joel, Boston, MA, Patent No. 402,608, May 7, 1889 [Fig. 20.7]. A snaffle bar with the two cannons joined together by a link. When the reins are pulled, the middle ends of the mouth-piece are thrust up and cause a pinching action on the bars of the horse.

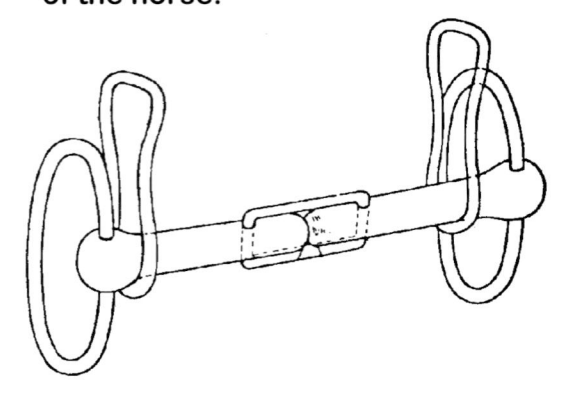

Fig. 20.7 McKenney jointed-mouth bit.

Patent No. 453,414, June 2, 1891 [Fig. 20.8]. An improvement over Patent no. 402,608, in that the two links are at right angles to each other and are used to prevent the tongue from being pinched. The actions are similar.

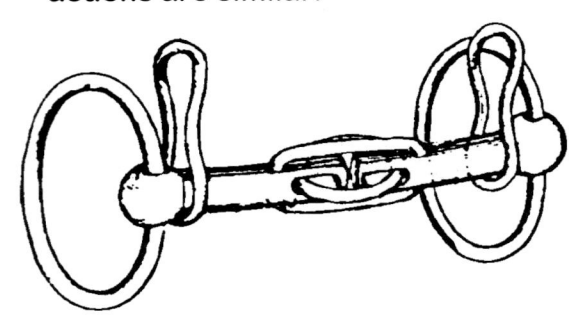

Fig. 20.8 McKenney improved snaffle.

McKerron Overcheck Bit: See Chapter 9, Fig. 9.9.

McKinley Port Bit: A style of bit sold by August Buermann Mfg. Co. in several models for single rein or double rein use. Supplied with a solid 7 inch cheek in cast steel or Star Steel Silver [Fig. 20.9].

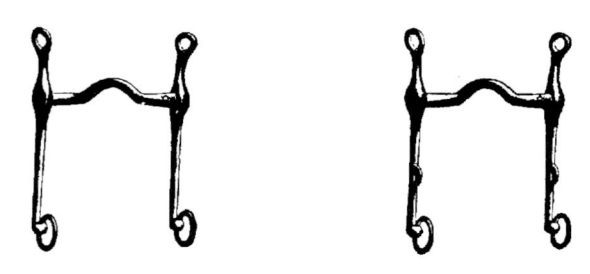

Fig. 20.9 McKinley port bits.

McKinney Port-mouth Bit: This nickel-plated wrought iron bit has the port thrown out to the front, relieving all tongue pressure [Fig. 20.10].

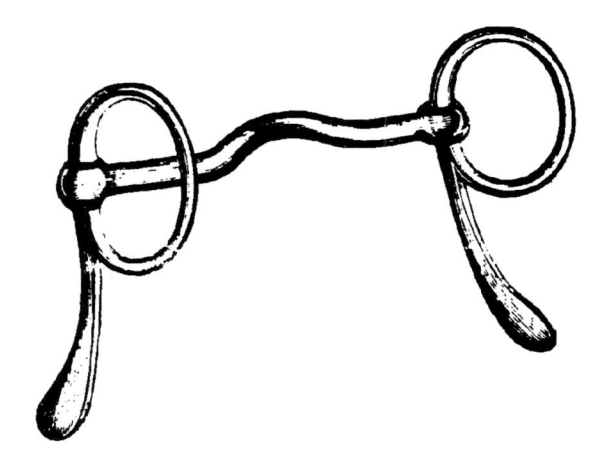

Fig. 20.10 McKinney port-mouth bit.

McNair, Jonas B., Willow Hill, IL, Patent No. 364,347, June 9, 1891 [Fig. 20.11]. The bit has a spring or yielding connection to which the reins are secured to prevent the horse's mouth from being injured by a sudden pull or stumble on the part of the horse.

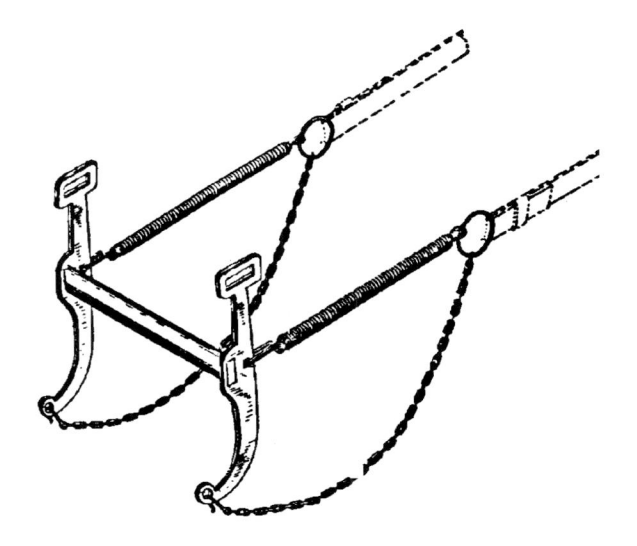

Fig. 20.11 McNair spring rein attachment.

McNalley, Michael, St. Louis, MO, Patent No. 655,508, Aug. 7, 1900 [Fig. 20.12]. This bit is designed to induce the horse to carry its head outward and away from the chest. The curb-strap and levers are projected forward and fastened to the bridle in a manner much like an overcheck bit.

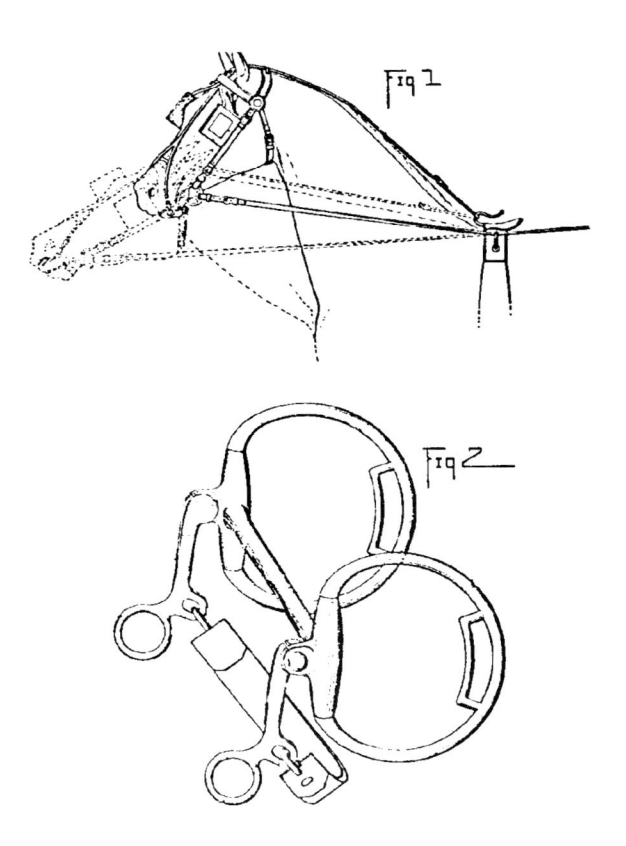

Fig. 20.12 McNalley head-control bit.

Meadow Snaffle: A snaffle bit with vertical rollers in the rear portion of the rein-ring. From *The Loriner* [Fig. 20.13].

Mealey, Johnston, Howard Lake, MN, Patent No. 591,222, Oct. 5, 1897 [Fig. 20.14]. The patent included a complete harness, collar and bridle bit. The snaffle bit has rollers on the rein-ring. The ring for the headstall is large enough to accommodate a check-rein.

Fig. 20.13 Meadow snaffle.

Fig. 20.14 Mealey snaffle bit.

Mecate: A Spanish name for a hair or maguay rope used as reins on a hackamore. See Chapter 13, Hackamore.

Medicine Bit: A bit designed to medicate an animal. The bit usually has a hollow mouth-piece or a funnel device to administer the medication.

Dr. LeGear Medicine Bit: A type of bit used to drench or give liquid medicine to horses and cattle [Figs. 20.15 and 20.16]. The bit was used in the same manner as that illustrated for the Dewsbury Drenching Bit in Fig. 20.19, with the difference being that the bottle containing the liquid was inverted into the funnel. Several different models were produced. One has the name "Dr. LeGear" embossed in the side of the funnel, another has a brass plate with the name attached to the side of the funnel and a third variety has no identification on the funnel.

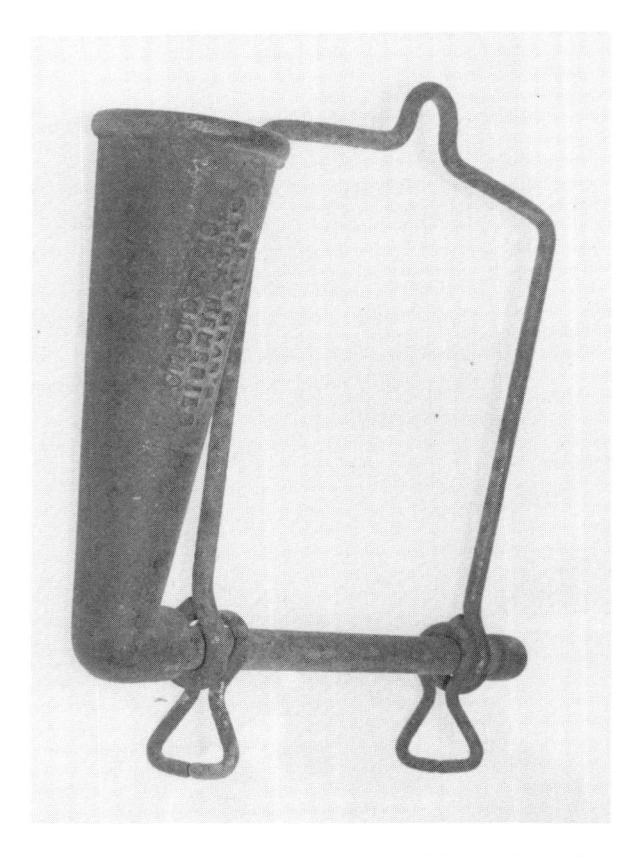

Fig. 20.15 Medicine or drenching bit made for Dr. LeGear, St. Louis, Mo.

Fig. 20.16 A variation of the Dr. LeGear-type bit with heavier and different eyes for attaching to the headstall, and the ring in the bail to lift the head of the horse.

Hansford Bit: Treated mouth-piece. See Chapter 14, Fig. 14.6.

Hartman, La Fayette and James W. Bronson, Wyoming, IA, Patent No. 174, 554, June 15, 1875 [Fig. 20.17]. The center piece of the three-piece mouth is hollow and forms a chamber of sufficient capacity to hold a dose of medicine. The opening left on the upper side for the introduction of medicine can be closed and the under side has a number of small holes which touch the tongue and through which the medicine oozes into the mouth.

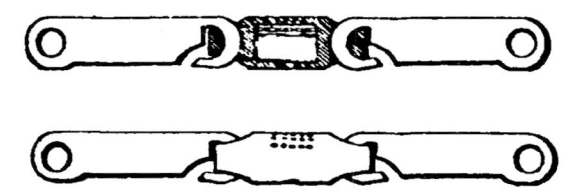

Fig. 20.17 Hartman medicine bit.

Hubner Medicine Bit: See Chapter 14, Fig. 14.36.

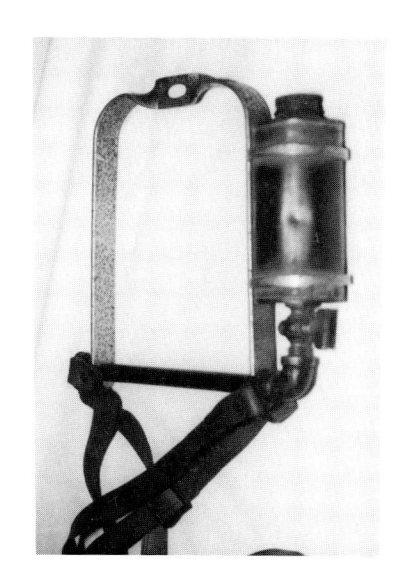

Fig. 20.18 A medicine or drenching bit with a copper cannister attached to the side and a cock-valve to release the flow of liquid medicine to flow from a center hole in the hollow tube mouth-piece. The principle is to elevate the animal's head high enough to allow the liquid to flow to the back of the horse's mouth and then forcing it to swallow.

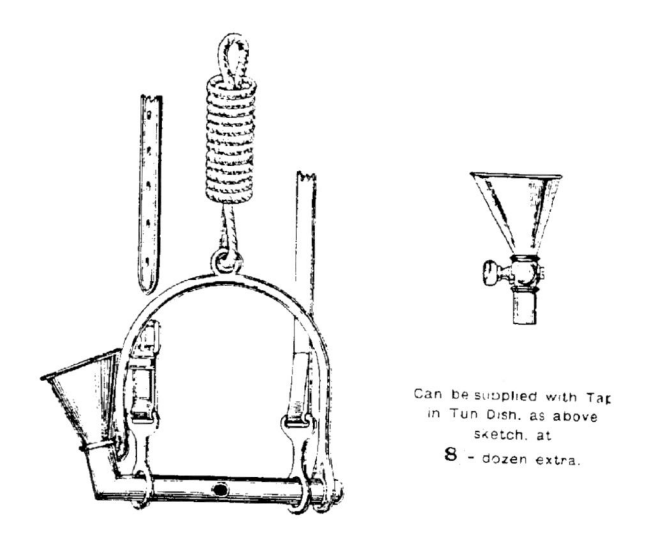

Can be supplied with Tap in Tun Dish. as above sketch. at
8 - dozen extra.

Fig. 20.19 A diagram of the medicine or drenching bit from John Dewsbury and Son, Walsall, England. The bit could be supplied with or without a tap or cock-valve in the funnel. See also Fig. 20.20 and 20.21.

MEDICINE DRENCHING BIT,

FOR HORSES AND CATTLE.

Patent No. 18647.

A NECESSITY IN EVERY STABLE.

The Bit can be taken to pieces in a few seconds, by anyone, simply by unscrewing the nut and drawing out the tube, for cleaning purposes.

Thoroughly well-made, the Rope and Head Strap being STOUT and RELIABLE, and all metal parts are heavily nickel-plated preventing rust.

Amongst the numerous advantages of this useful invention may be mentioned the following:—
1. — Administering medicine to a horse or cow in a liquid form.
2. — Administering gradually and regularly without waste.
3. — Administering stimulants preparatory to going out.
4. — Stimulating and disinfecting throat and lungs.
5. — Washing out the mouth when diseased or otherwise.

NICKEL-PLATED,

90/- DOZEN

COMPLETE WITH ROPE AND STRAP.

No. 18647.

Shewing patented arrangement for taking Bit to pieces for cleaning purposes.

Can be supplied with Tap in Tun Dish as Illustrated on opposite page.

Mouth raised above the level of windpipe

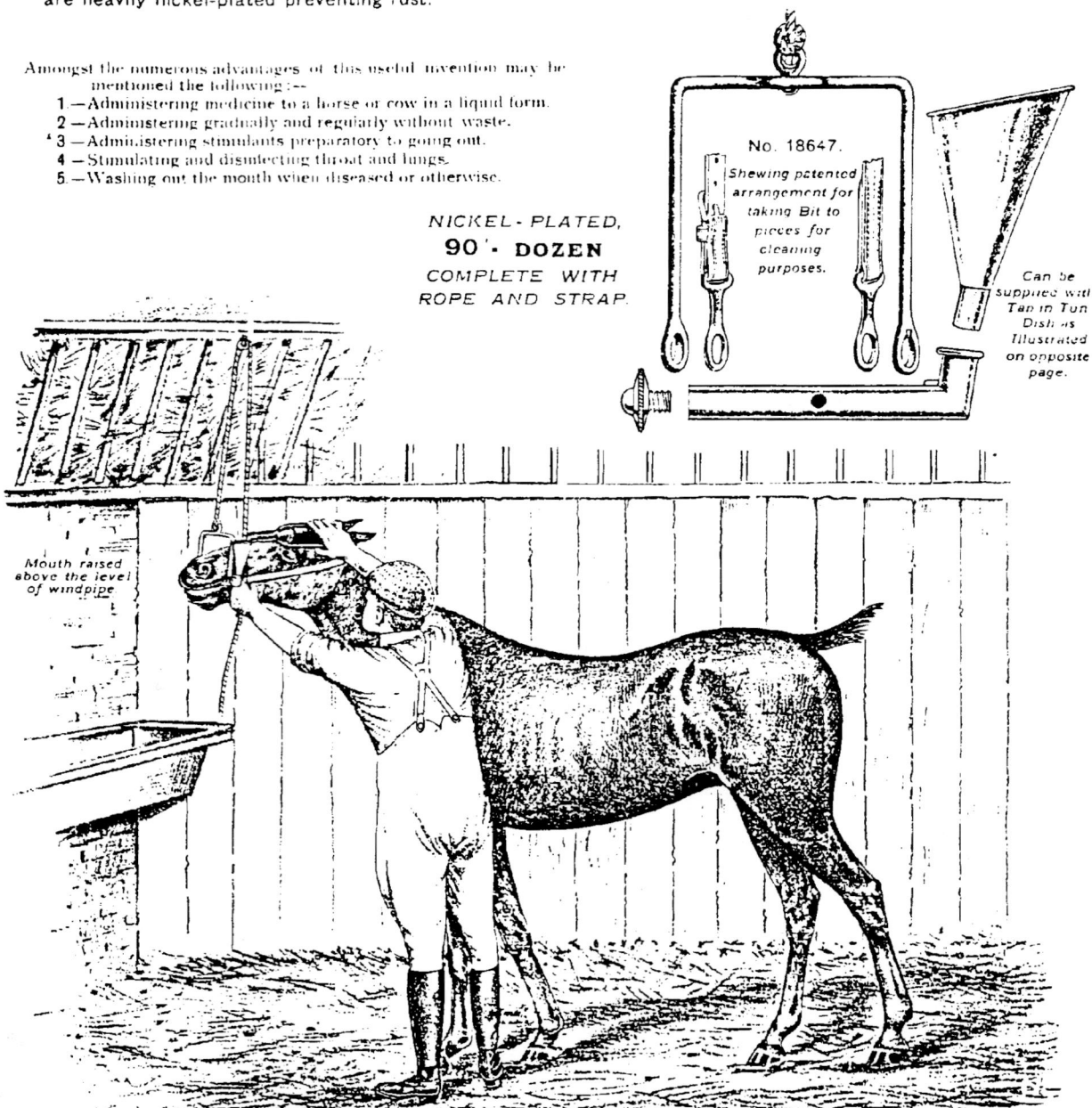

Fig. 20.20 Medicine or drenching bit from John Dewsbury and Son, Walsall England, circa 1900.

Medicine Bits: Doctoring a sick horse.

Before the common usage of the stomach tube to give horses liquid medicine by mouth, the veterinarian or owner usually resorted to the use of a "drench." The drenching of horses was a messy confrontation between horse and doctor. The procedure often resulted in the horse spitting the medication out or even worse having some of the liquid being inhaled into the trachea and subsequently the lungs. Inhalation pneumonia was a common aftermath of this type of treatment.

Dr. George A. Waterman gave some insight into the problem in his description of the technique used to drench horses. His comments, first published in *"The Practical Stock Doctor"* of 1904 are very detailed: "To administer, put the medicine in a drenching bottle or horn. A champagne or ale bottle holding about a quart, strong, clean, and smooth will answer. A horn or tin bottle is better on account of not breaking. If dose is small, the horse's head may be held up by the left while the medicine is poured by the right hand. The left thumb is placed in the angle of the lower jaw; the fingers spread out in such a way as to support the lower lip. If the dose is large, the horse ugly, or the attendant unable to support the head as directed above, then have the head held up by a loop made in a rope and slipped over the upper jaw just behind the front teeth, the free end being held up by passing through a pulley or over a beam or through a ring fastened to the ceiling. It should never be fastened, as the horse might hurt himself.

"Elevate head enough to prevent horse from throwing liquid from his mouth. The line of face should be raised a trifle more than horizontal, but not much, or it will be hard for horse to swallow. Person giving drench should stand on something in order to reach horse's mouth on a level, or little above. Introduce bottle at the side of the mouth in front of the molar teeth, in an upward direction. This will cause horse to open his mouth when base of bottle is suddenly elevated and about 4 ounces of liquid allowed to run out on the tongue as far back as possible, care being taken to keep bottle from between back teeth. Take out bottle, and if horse does not swallow encourage same by rubbing the roof of mouth with fingers or neck of bottle, occasionally removing them. Repeat when this is swallowed and continue until all is taken. If coughing occurs or if by mishap the bottle is broken, lower the head at once. Don't rub, pinch, or pound the throat, or draw out tongue. Be patient."

As you can see many problems existed. This situation stimulated horsemen and veterinarians to develop many devices to aid in their treatment procedures. Some of the devices were in the form of modified bits, speculums, gags, and drenching bottles.

The drenching bits such as Dr. LeGear's or Burton's relied on the medicine being poured in the funnel at the side of the bit. A small hole in the center of the bar allowed the medicine to flow into the horse's mouth. The theory was good, but under actual use really wasn't too satisfactory. The bit allowed the medicine to flow into the horse's mouth too far forward. As a result the horse would slobber the medication out instead of swallowing. To be swallowed, the medicine should be placed in the back of the mouth, past the base of the tongue.

Shewing Bit Complete.

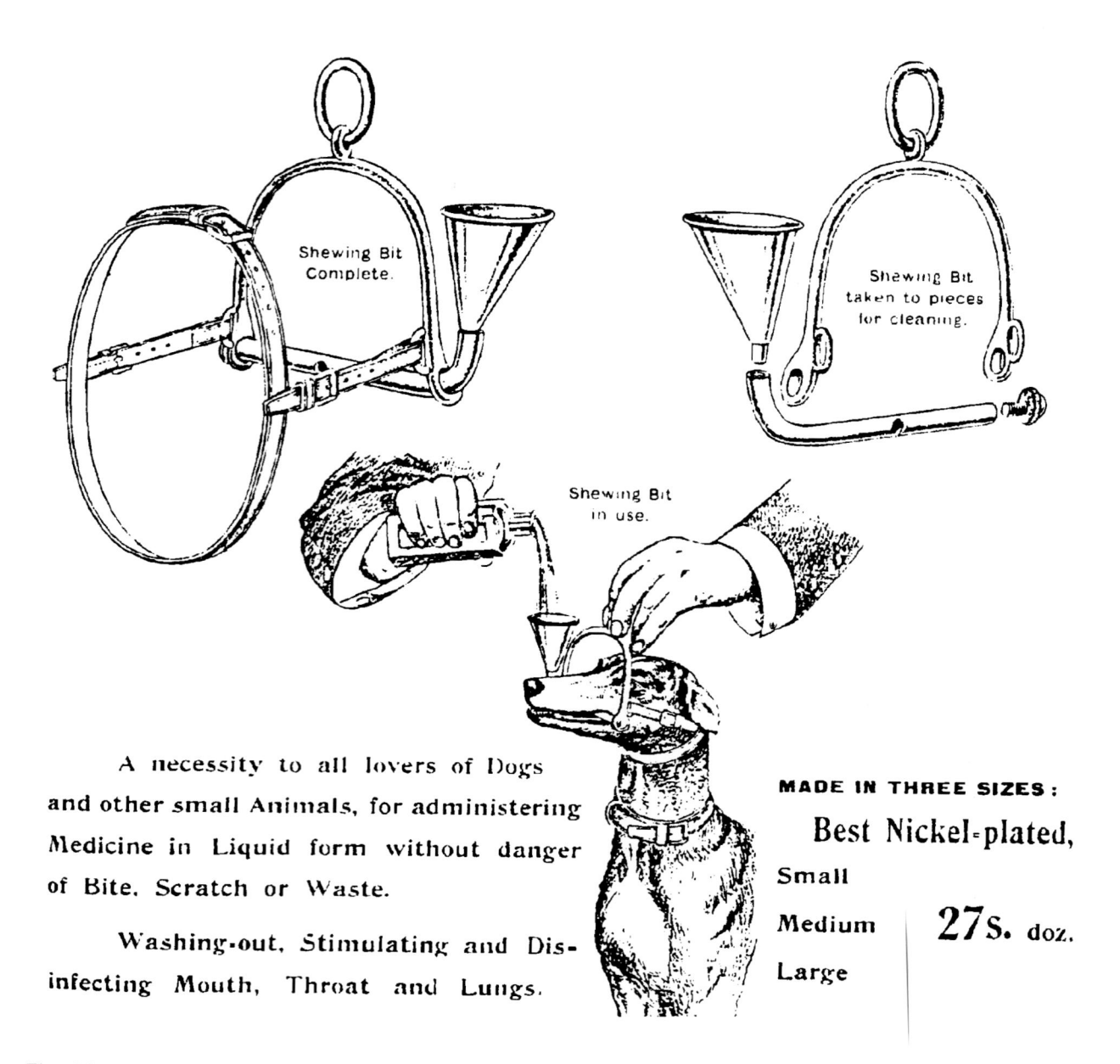

Shewing Bit taken to pieces for cleaning.

Shewing Bit in use.

A necessity to all lovers of Dogs and other small Animals, for administering Medicine in Liquid form without danger of Bite, Scratch or Waste.

Washing-out, Stimulating and Disinfecting Mouth, Throat and Lungs.

MADE IN THREE SIZES:
Best Nickel=plated,
Small
Medium — 27s. doz.
Large

Fig. 20.21 Medicine or drenching bit for dogs from John Dewsbury and Son Catalogue, Walsall, England, circa 1905.

Megargee, Stanleigh, New York, NY, Patent No. 1,875,195, Aug. 30, 1932 [Fig. 20.22]. A curb bit with the cheek-pieces able to move independently of each other.

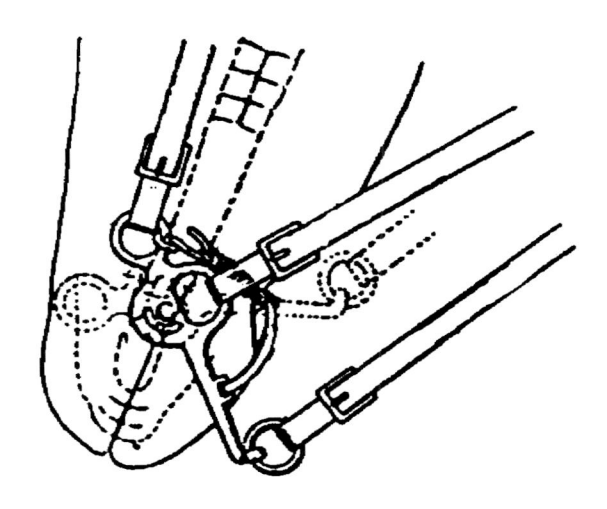

Fig. 20.22 Megargee curb bit.

Melleby, Kristian Julius, Christiania, Norway, Patent No. 774,097, Nov. 1, 1904 [Fig. 20.23]. A combined snaffle and curb bit with a three-part mouth-piece. The two outer portions swing horizontally on the middle connection portion which acts as a curved or vertical port. The bit acts as a snaffle until a curb-strap or chain is applied.

Mellor, Austin, Philadelphia, PA, Patent No. 157,340, Dec. 1, 1874 [Fig. 20.24]. A double-mouth bit with the bit being entirely made of metal or partially of wood. The lower mouth-piece is attached by the tie-bars to the upper mouth-piece and swings or moves freely within the mouth of the horse.

Merriam, Iram Z., Whitewater, WI, Patent No. 506,244, Oct. 10, 1893 [Fig. 20.25]. A pulley bit with the pully attached to the exterior and to the rear of the rein-ring.

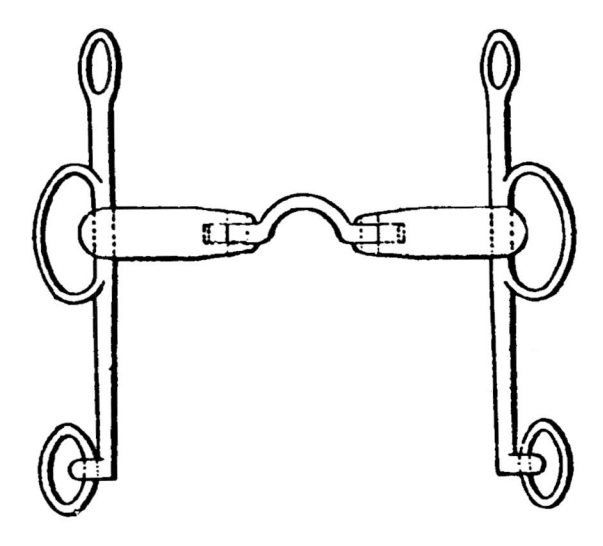

Fig. 20.23 Melleby combination bit.

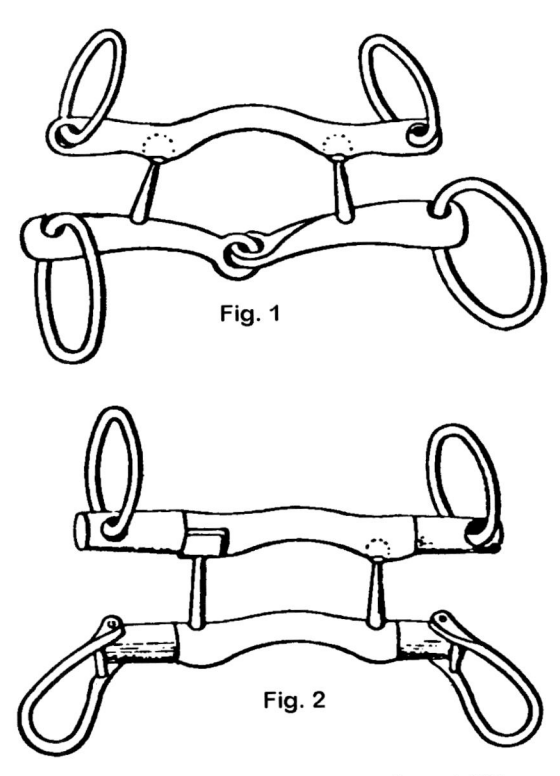

Fig. 20.24 Two styles of Mellor shifting double-mouth bit.

Metcalf, Herbert E., Boone, IN, Patent No. 636,159, Oct. 31, 1899 [Fig. 20.26]. A bit with four rings and two chains. The chain attaches to one rein-ring and the headstall ring on the opposite side and the second chain attaches in a similar manner to the opposite rings. The result is that one chain acts as a mouth-piece and the second as a curb-chain.

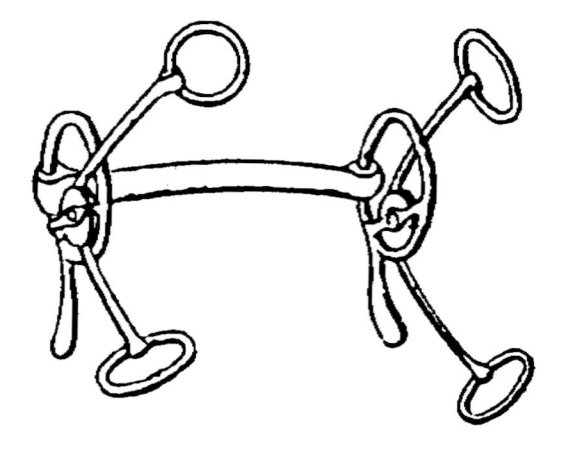

Fig. 20.25 Merriam pulley bit.

Fig. 20.26 Metcalf double-chain curb bit.

Metropolitan Bit: A snaffle bit that is sometimes referred to as a buggy bit. A wide variety of bits with ornate cheeks are named Metropolitan. Metropolitan Lead bit is another term used for this bit [Fig. 20.27 to 20.27c].

Meyer, Victor, Brooklyn, NY, Patent No. 1,796,608, Mar. 17, 1931 [Fig. 20.28]. A bit with two loosely connected sections of mouth-piece. Enlarged portions are adjacent to the point of connection. The portion of the mouth-piece extending rearward has a flattened face.

Fig. 20.27 Fancy cheek Metropolitan bit.

Fig. 20.27a Fancy cheek Metropolitan bit.

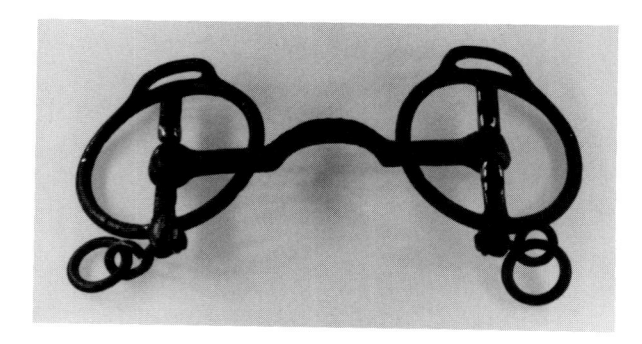

Fig. 20.27b Metropolitan bit.

250

Fig. 20.27c A buggy driving bit of the metropolitan pattern.

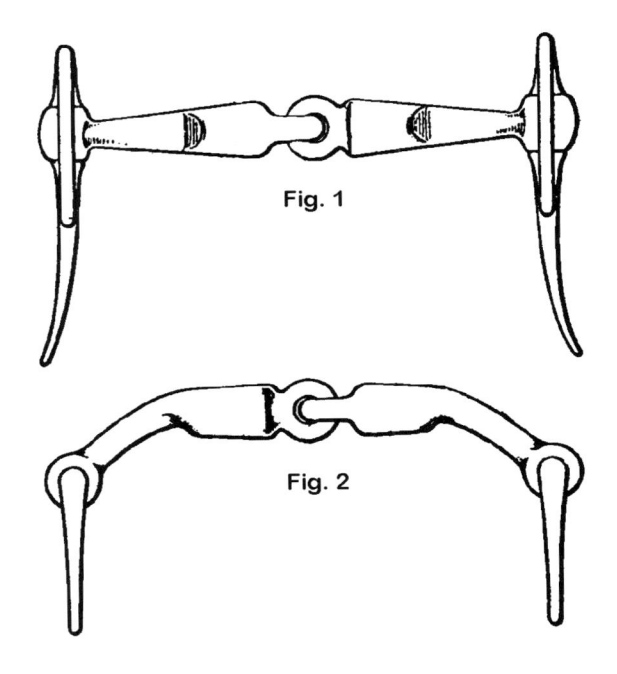

Fig. 1

Fig. 2

Fig. 20.28 Meyer snaffle bit.

Mikmar Bit: A curb bit with three points of control from the Mikmar Company, El Cajon, CA [Fig. 20.29].

Fig. 20.29 Mikmar control bit.

CHAPTER TWENTY-ONE
British and Canadian Military and Police Bits

Collectors frequently encounter British Military-style bits with a brass boss on each cheek-piece. This category of bit is sometimes incorrectly called the Order of the Garter Bit, but a more appropriate name is British Military Brass Boss Bit. Most bosses are the "Universal Pattern" (Fig. 21.0). However, many bosses are of a different pattern, being for certain cavalry regiments, police, or different corps, such as the Mounted Infantry Officers' bit

The frame of the bits is the old British Pad Cheek design (Fig. 21.1) having a vertical section for extra strength across the curve of the cheek-piece. The Regulation Cavalry bit was about 8 1/2" in height, and had a lower cross-bar between the cheek-pieces (Fig. 21.1). It was used with the pattern 1860 bridle (Fig. 21.2), and later the pattern 1885 bridle, but the style of bit was in use before 1860. The pad on each side of the bit was thin and ornate, but after about 1890 some of the bits were made in a simplified design with a larger plain vertical member and this bit, about 8' in height, was known as the "Stout Pattern."

A lighter bit about 7 1/2" in height was often used by other than cavalry, such as Mounted Infantry Officers, and these were sometimes made without a lower bar. In the 1890's another variation of bits appeared in which the pad did not extend all the way down to the lower sweep of the curved cheek-piece. This bit was used by police and different corps as opposed to cavalry.

Fig. 21.0 The Universal Pattern boss.

The bit for general officers was similar but a little more ornate, with a small steel flower attached on the curve of the cheek-piece (Fig. 21.3). Most, but not all, had the split tail in the cheek-piece at the rein-rings. All officers used a Link and Tee bradoon with their bit (Fig. 21.4) which was normally unmarked.

Fig. 21.1 Old British Pad Cheek design of the Regulation Cavalry bit.

These various British military bits were made in plain steel, but by 1890 some were nickel-plated and after 1900, they were generally cast in nickel. When a team of horses was involved, such as for artillery to pull the guns, the bits were cast with a loop in the curve of the cheek, to allow the use of extra reins (Fig. 21.5).

The "Univeral Pattern" boss consists of a crowned garter inscribed with the British motto *Honi Soit Qui Mal Y Pense*, with the centre bearing the royal cypher of the reigning monarch. During Queen Victoria's reign from 1837 to 1901, the cypher was a co-joined "VR" for Victoria Regina in script lettering, all surmounted by the St. Edward style of crown. The bosses were 2" in diameter but the Stout Pattern bit was made with a smaller "Universal Pattern" boss, 1 1/2" in diameter.

After 1901, when Edward VII came to the throne, the cypher on new bits was

Fig. 21.2 The Pattern 1860 Bridle over a halter and Universal Pattern Pad Bit and the T-bar snaffle bit.

"ER VII" for Edward VII Rex, and the Tudor crown was used.

George V reigned from 1910 to 1936, but the use of brass bosses on British military bits had substantially ended by the start of WW I in 1914. Several years after the end of WW I in 1918, the 1st and 2nd Regiments of Household Cavalry Amalgumated and together with the Royal Horse Guards adopted a sliding, revolving Banbury mouth bit, and current issues, at least, are made of stainless steel. The boss for other ranks is cast with the words "Peninsular - Waterloo" (Boss No. 3) to commemorate the victories over Napoleon in Spain, 1808 to 1814, and at the Battle of Waterloo, in 1815.

Bit bosses were almost always brass, with bosses on general officers' bits sometimes being gilt; at least some of the bosses for Royal Engineers were made in German silver or nickel and nickel was used for the universal pattern for some Yoemanry (volunteer) Cavalry. Almost all bosses are very detailed in design, but a few are encountered which are much less detailed, and perhaps these were made with a different casting process, or they may be subsequent replacements.

Fig. 21.3 British general officers bit. Kentucky Horse Park archives.

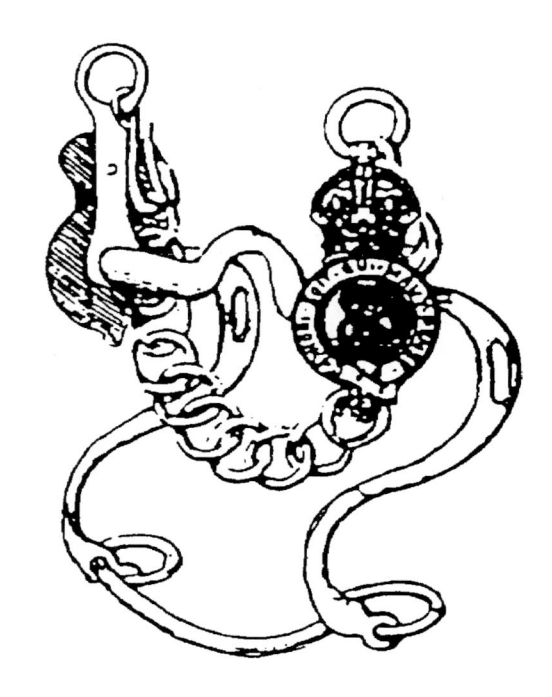

Fig. 21.5 Heavier style of bit issued to artillery units.

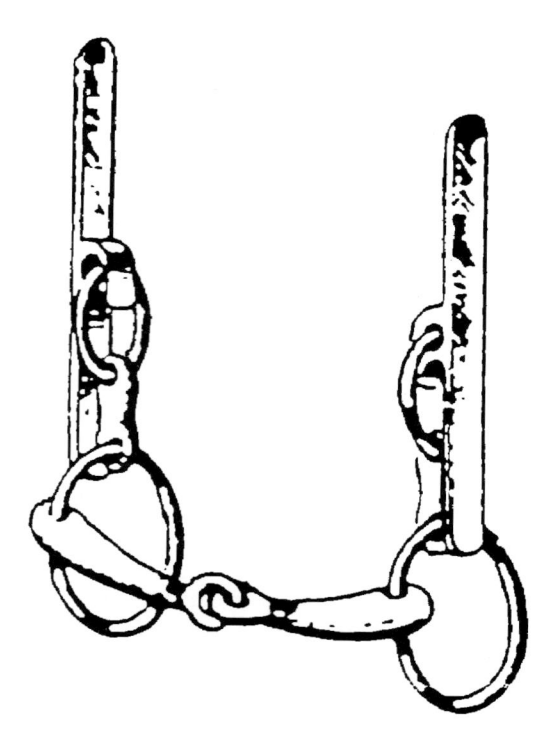

Fig. 21.4 Link and Tee bradoon used with general officers bit.

For some cavalry regiments, the specific regimental badge was used on the bosses for officers, senior warrant officers, band-masters, and sometimes for the mounted kettle drummers. Bits for the other ranks would still be issued with the "Univeral Pattern." The same boss design as on the bit was mounted on the leather of the officers' horse breastplate. A smaller boss was used on the small stirrup slide for those units which used them. It was an open-ended "box" resembling a sleeve-type matchbox used just above the stirrups to keep the stirrup leathers together. Ear bosses had the specific unit badge and were on the headstall near the attachment of the brow-band.

With all the different British and Indian cavalry units, both regular and volunteer, police for different towns, and different corps, there are a multitude of different boss designs.

Some descriptions of bosses are illustrated on the following pages.

1. 1st Life Guards, Officers, Brass.

2. Royal Horse Guards, Officers. Brass with cut-steel centre.

3. 2nd Life Guards, Officers. 1st and 2nd Life Guards and Royal Horse Guards, other ranks. Brass.

4. Universal Pattern. Brass.

5. Universal Pattern, post 1901. Brass.

6. The Queen's Bays, 2nd Dragoon Guards. Brass.

Bit Patterns: a and b, Line Cavalry; c, 2nd Life Guards and Royal Horse Guards; d, 1st Life Guards; e and f, Line Cavalry; g, 1st Life Guards; h, 2nd Life Guards and Royal Horse Guards.

7. The 4th Royal Irish Dragoon Guards, Brass.

8. 5th Dragoon Guards, Brass.

9. 6th Dragoon Guards, Brass.

10. 7th Dragoon Guards, Brass.

11. 1st Royal Dragoons, Brass.

12. 2nd Dragoons. Royal Scots Grey. Brass, white metal centre.

13. 6th Innskilling Dragoons, Brass.

14. 3rd Kings Own Hussars. Brass, white metal centre.

15. 4th Queen's Own Hussars. Brass, white metal numerals, roped edge to garter.

16. 7th Queen's Own Hussars, Brass.

17. 8th King's Royal Irish Hussars. Brass, white metal crowned harp and shamrock spray.

18. 9th Queen's Royal Lancers. Brass.

19. 10th Prince of Wales Own Hussars. Brass, white metal coronet, feathers and scroll.

20. 11th Prince Albert's Own Hussars. Brass, white metal sphinx and base.

21. 12th Prince of Wales Royal Lancers. Brass, Prince of Wales feathers white metal.

22. 13th Hussars. Brass. Roped edge to garter.

23. 14th The King's Hussars. Brass.

24. 15th The King's Hussars. Brass.

25. 17th Duke of Cambridge's Own Lancers. Brass, white metal centre.

26. 18th Hussars. Brass, white metal device. Roped edge to garter.

Bits issued to the Canadian Militia and Permanent Cavalry were the "VR" Universal Pattern. This same pattern of bit appears in military prints of British cavalry in the Victorian period, whether it be in India, Egypt, South Africa or in the British Isles. Some Canadian artillery had bit bosses cast with "Canada Dominion Artillery," with a beaver in the centre. The Toronto Police in Toronto, Ontario, have used a similar bit since being formed in 1886, with brass bosses and bits cast in steel,

256

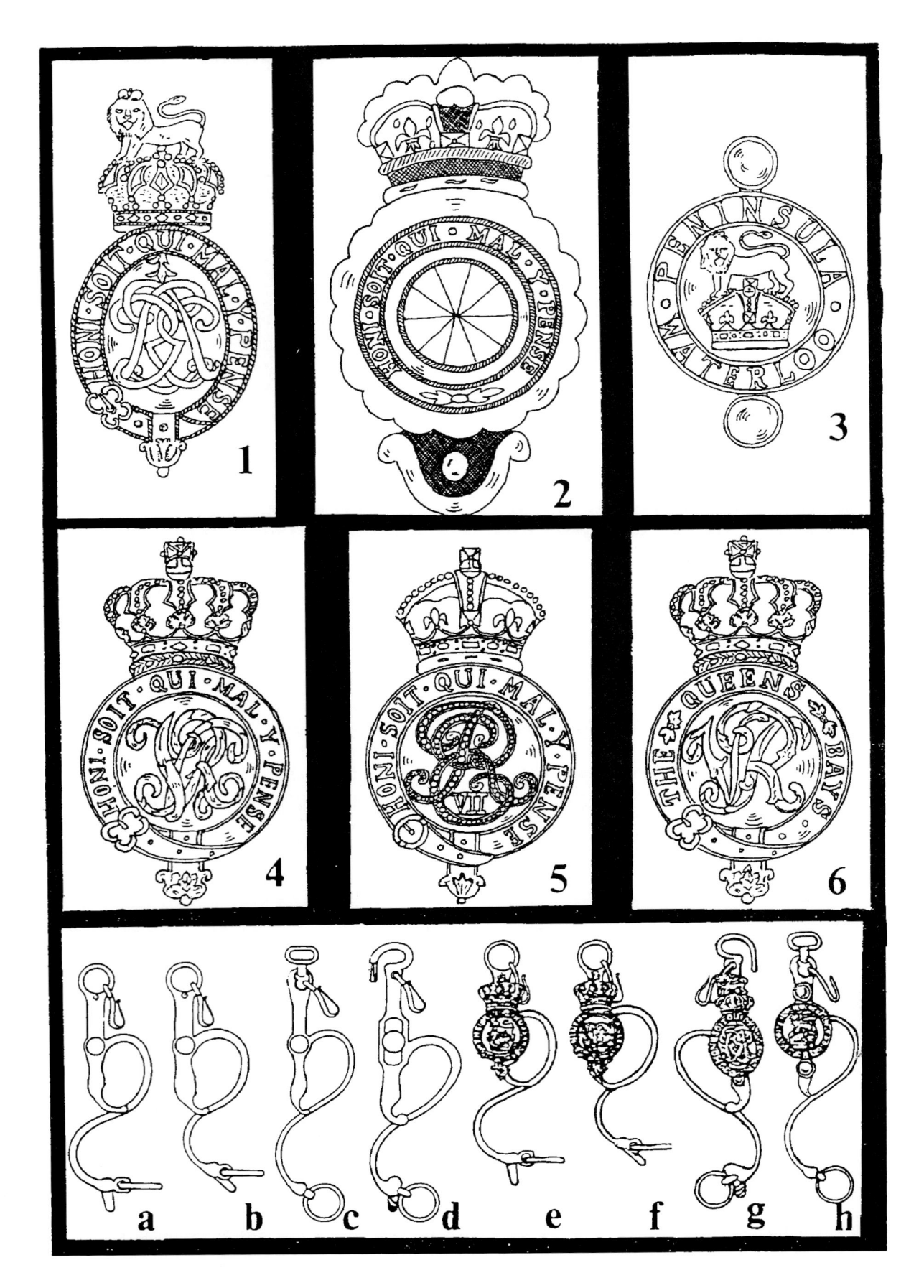

7 Royal Irish Dragoon Guards	8 Vestigia Nulla Retrorsum — 5 DG	9 Sixth Dragoon Guards
10 Princess Royal's — 7 DG	11 Spectemur Agendo	12 Nemo Me Impune Lacessit
13 Inniskilling Dragoons	14 Third King's Own Hussars	15 Queen's Own Hussars — IV

257

SEVENTH QUEEN'S OWN HUSSARS
16
PRISTINAE VIRTUTIS MEMORES
17
NINTH LANCERS
18
PRINCE OF WALES OWN HUSSARS
19
PRINCE ALBERT'S OWN HUSSARS
20
TWELFTH LANCERS
21
HONI SOIT QUI MAL Y PENSE
22
FOURTEENTH THE KING'S HUSSARS
23
THE KING'S HUSSARS
24

then nickel, and more recently in stainless steel. The boss used by the small mounted units of the Newfoundland Constabulary formed about 1906 in St. John's, Newfoundland, was a crown cast on a white metal boss.

Fig. 21.6 The 1893 Reversible Pelham.

The North West Mounted Police, which became the Royal North West Police in 1904, and is now the Royal Canadian Mounted Police, served continuously in the Canadian West, and after 1900 in many other parts of Canada. It appears that in their early years an odd assortment of English Pelham bits was used. Starting about 1880 purchases of Whitman Officers steel two ring bits were made (see Chapter 23) and these became the standard until replaced about 1920.

In 1893, British Artillery adopted a new pattern of steel bit, called the Reversible Pelham or Portsmouth Bit (Fig. 21.6) which does not have a boss.
In 1902, British Cavalry also adopted this bit for use with their new pattern 1902 bridle (Fig. 21.7). The Canadian Government placed orders in Canada in each of the years from 1903 to 1906 for a total of 3500 bits, and other purchases were made at least until 1915. The makers' name and date of

manufacture were usually stamped on these bits. The initial orders were for steel bits with steel curb-chains but most were cast in nickel. The mouth-pieces were made in small, medium and large widths, and the bits were stamped S, M or L. Mouth-pieces of the nickel bits were cast with mild serrations on one side.

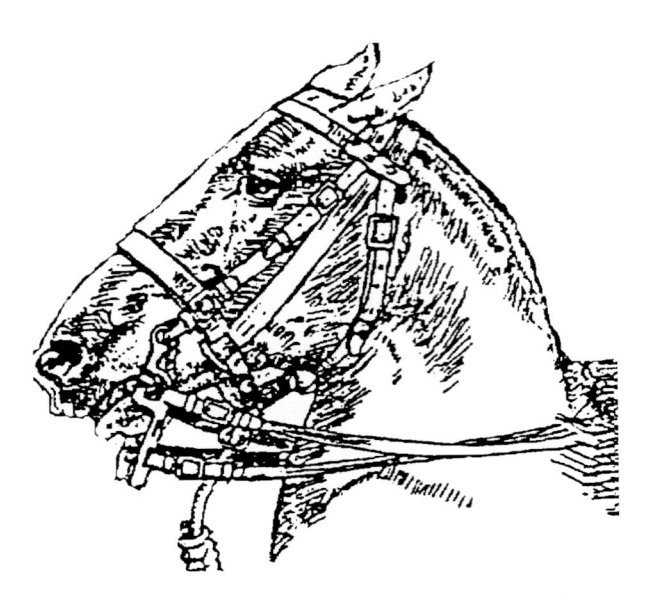

Fig. 21.7 The New Pattern 1902 British Bridle.

Canadian Field Artillery units used the same pattern 1902 bit throughout WW I, but as the war progressed bits cast in steel were purchased directly from British suppliers. Up to 1917, the bits were nickel-plated, but by 1918, plain steel was being used. Many of the bits issued to Canadian units were stamped at the time of issue to indicate the unit to which they were issued, whether it be cavalry or field artillery, and it was not uncommon to find bits marked to indicate issue to several different units during their service life. It is this reversible Pelham bit which was used by the British Cavalry Division, which included the Canadian Cavalry Brigade, in France from 1916 to 1918. British cavalry in the Middle East also used the bit during the extensive cavalry operations against the Turks, and between the wars until disbanded early in WW II.

The Royal Canadian Mounted Police also adopted these bits about 1920 but did not stamp their ownership on the bits. They subsequently replaced these with an English Pelham, a style still in use, for their spectacular Musical Ride.

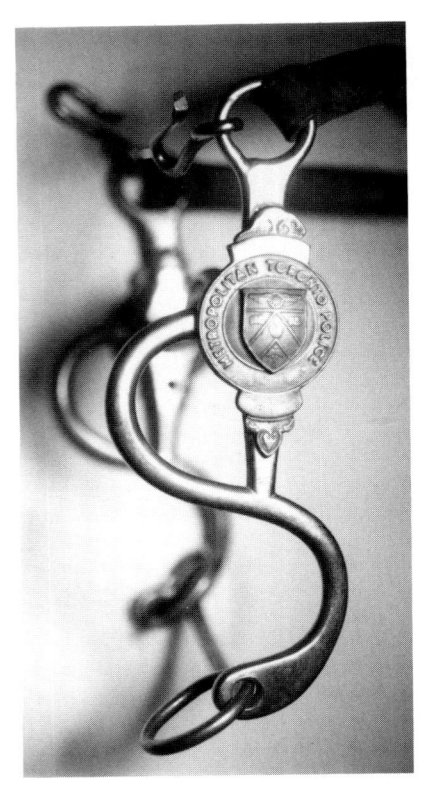

Fig. 21.8 Bridle bit and boss of the Metropolitan Toronto Police.

Illustrated examples in Chapter Twenty-one of bit bosses are from "Soldiers of the Queen" article in the publication of the *Victorian Military Society*. The remainder of the article was contributed by Hamilton May, Colborne, Ontario, Canada.

Royal Cyphers

George I, II, III 1714-1727 1727-1760 1760-1820	**George IV** 1820-1830	**William IV** 1830-1837
Victoria 1837-1901	**Edward VII** 1901-1910	**George V** 1910-1936
Edward VIII 1936	**George VI** 1936-1952	**Elizabeth II** 1952-

Royal Crowns

St. Edward's — Victorian Period

Tudor — Post Victorian Period

Fig. 21.9 Royal Cyphers and Royal Crowns as they would appear on bit bosses.

CHAPTER TWENTY-TWO
German and French Military Bits

German and French military bits are both characterized by their individual styles of mouth-pieces and by their various cheek-piece styles. A word on roles and functions of cavalry will help in understanding the different categories of mounted troops in the German Army.

The US Civil War from 1861 to 1865 introduced large-scale use of rifled muskets and rifles with greater range and accuracy for both infantry and cavalry units. The experience of this war demonstrated that cavalry used at the charge, as employed for hundreds of years before in Europe, was an out-of-date concept. From then on, mounted troops, even though they might still be called cavalry, were better trained and employed as mounted rifles. The horses were used to transport the men and their rifles, sometimes with light artillery, to the critical point of action, where the men then dismounted and fought on foot. The horses were led back behind the lines and held, to either follow up the action or for the retreat, as the case might be. US Cavalry engaged in the Indian Wars were really employed as mounted rifles, and European armies gradually and, somewhat reluctantly, adopted these concepts, led perhaps by the British, the Germans and eventually the French.

German cavalry from the time Frederick the Great reorganized the Prussian cavalry in the mid-1700's, to the First World War, 1914 to 1918, comprised two broad categories. Heavy cavalry, called Cuirassiers, including the elite Garde du Corps, were trained and employed to carry the action by the sheer force and weight of their charge, using heavy horses and much spirit by the troopers. Hussars, dragoons and lancers called ulanen, who were all more lightly armed and mounted on smaller horses, were used less at the charge and more for skirmishing and for reconnaissance.

The first German mounted rifle units, called "Jager zu Pferde" Regiments, were formed about 1895, and by 1910 there were 6 of these regiments. Regiments 7 to 13 were formed in 1913, just before the war. From about 1910 onward, all German mounted units were armed, trained and deployed, the same basically as mounted rifles, in spite of their regimental title.

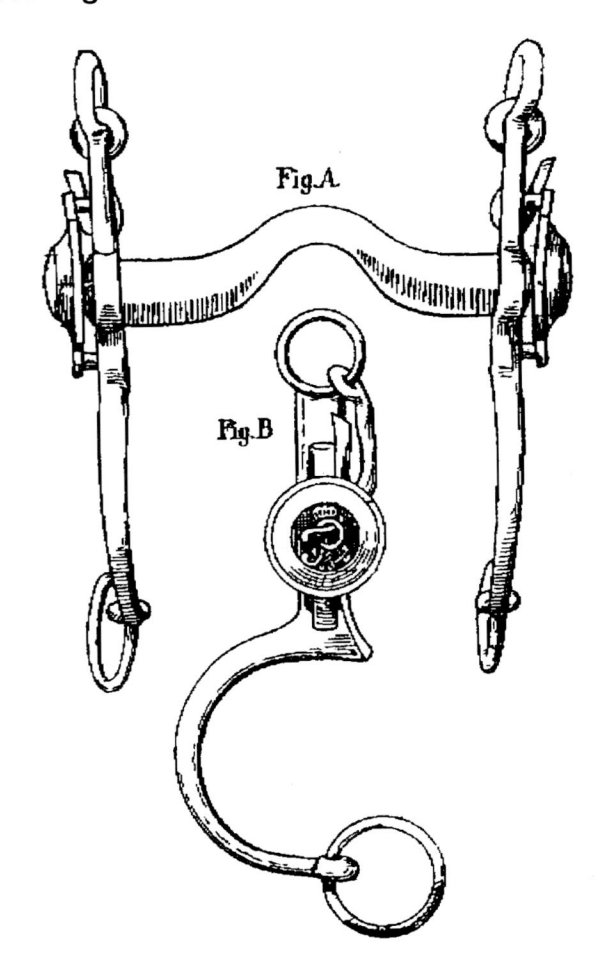

Fig. 22.0 German heavy cavalry bit.

The earliest German military bit identified is the general design issued to heavy cavalry from as early as the 1830's, and this style was in use until just before WW I. These bits had a distinct semi-circular shape forward in the cheek-piece below the mouth. A thick brass boss about 1 1/4 " in diameter was mounted on each side with initials in scroll script and the crown of Frederick the Great in a raised profile on the boss. The bits were made in several widths; the diameter of the curve in the cheek-pieces increased with the larger widths in the mouth, thus giving greater leverage. A late pattern of this bit, as shown in Fig. 22.0, is found fairly often in US collections.

Fig. 22.1 Boss detail of Fig. 22.0. Robert Maclin collection.

They appear to be machine-made as opposed to hand-made, so could date somewhere in the 1875 to 1890 period. However, some were issued as late as 1913 to mounted rifles, perhaps because there were inadequate supplies of a later pattern to equip all the units formed at that time. These bits have a large diameter mouth-piece, about 3/4" inch diameter, with a slight forward roll at the center of the mouth-piece where the diameter is smaller than at the sides. One bit examined had steel bosses instead of brass.

Usually the bits are stamped on the cheeks near the bridle ring to indicate the unit to which the bit was originally issued. The following designations for categories of regiments have been or may be encountered:

GC   Garde du Corps
GD   Garde Dragoner
D   Dragoner
GH   Garde Husaren
H   Husaren
GU   Garde Ulanen
U   Ulanen
JP   Jager zu Pferde--Mounted Rifles
SR   Schwere - Reiter
Ch   Chevaulegers
GRR   Garde - Reiter
K   Karbiner
GK   Garde -Kuassier
K   Kuassier

As an example, 8 JP with the number 125 on the top of the mouth-piece would indicate issue to horse No. 125 of the Eighth Mounted Rifles, which was raised Oct. 1, 1913, and was stationed at Trier just east of the Franco - German border.

The bits issued to hussar, lancer and dragoon regiments were a much lighter design as shown in Fig. 22.2. The mouth is similar to that on the heavy cavalry bit in Fig. 22.4, with the slight roll forward at the center. The lower side of the bridle ring has a small point at mid-point (Fig. 22.3). This bit appears in pre-WW I photos of German cavalry. Some of these bits were made with the half-moon hole in the cheek-piece as in Fig. 22.3, and some were made without it. This same style of bit was made by

Dewsbury in England, and Linden and Funke in Germany, for sale to the civilian market in Europe and the US, but these would have different manufactory marks than the military issue bits.

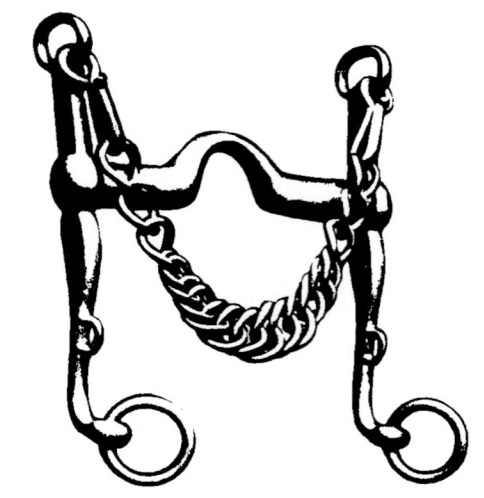

Fig. 22.2 Pre-WW I German cavalry bit.

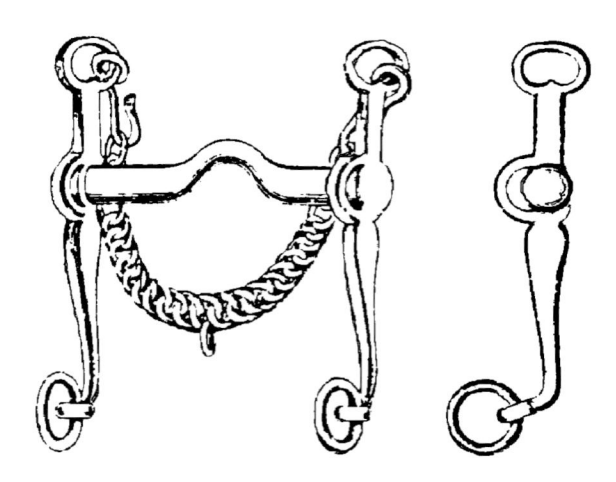

Fig. 22.3 German pattern military bit with German hook and curb. The curb is reversed from the normal position.

Another pre-WW I bit is shown in Fig. 22.3. Although the center of the mouth does not have the slight roll typical of German military bits, this style with the half moon hole in the cheek at the mouth may date much earlier, perhaps back to the 1850's. The ends of the mouth-piece are almost flat and protrude about 1/8 inch beyond the cheek-piece. The surface finish is rough on all examples seen, which could indicate declining quality towards the end of WW I. This bit could have been for artillery teams as opposed to cavalry. None of these bits examined had any manufactory marks.

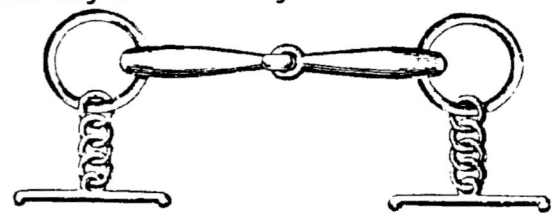

Fig. 22.3a Pre-WW I bradoon or watering snaffle bit.

The bit which almost always appears in photos of German mounted troops during WW I is shown in Fig 22.4, and is understood to be the 1912 pattern. The mouth diameter is 5/8 inch and rolls slightly forward. There is a distinct straight drop in the cheek of about 1/2 inch below the mouth, before the sharp rearward curve starts in the cheek-piece.

Fig. 22.4 German 1912 pattern bit.

All the above-mentioned bits were used by the Imperial German Army, and after the Kaiser abdicated in 1918, the WW I period bits were allowed to be used by the German cavalry by the Treaty of Versailles. However, with the rearmament of Germany which started about 1934, a new simplified style was adopted, as shown in Fig 22.7. It still had the hollow large-diameter characteristic mouth with a slight roll forward, and the cheek was similar to the 1912 pattern, except the curve started directly from the mouth, thus making the overall height slightly less than that of the model 1912 bit. Some of these WW II bits are stamped with the date of manufacture, and the earliest seen is 1935. Many photos exist showing this bit in use in France in 1940, and on the Eastern Front from 1940 to the end of the war. In both WW I and WW II, apart from the opening days of the wars, German cavalry were employed almost exclusively on the Eastern fronts.

Fig. 22.5 German military-style bit made by Linden and Funke, Hanover, Germany.

German military bits typically bear a small crest on one side of the cheek near the bridle ring to indicate the manufacturer. The bits were always used with a bradoon for the double-rein bridles. Officers' bridles seem to have had the leather ends covered with a metal tab.

Fig. 22.6 German military snaffle or bradoon bit of WW I period. Robert Maclin collection.

Most of the above styles of German military bits appear with surprising regularity in U.S. bit collections, and in excellent condition, which leads one to suspect some enterprising collector obtained a quantity of all types from a German arsenal, perhaps in the 1950's.

Fig. 22.7 German Bit of WW II Era with large hollow mouth-piece. Robert Maclin collection.

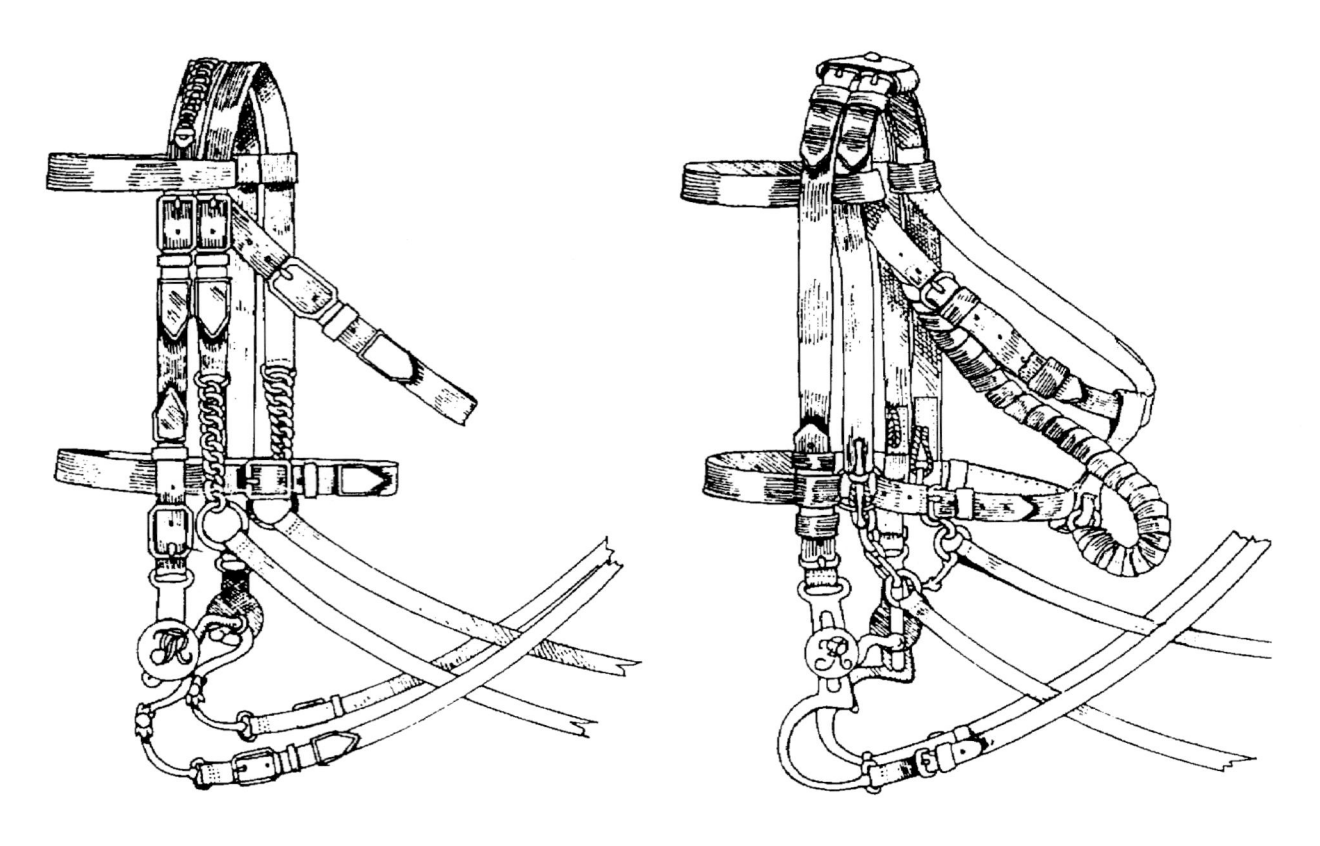

Fig. 22.8 German Officers' Pattern bridle with 1915 Pattern bridle bit, see Figure 22.4.

Fig. 22.9 NCO and Troopers Pattern with bridle of the period represented by the heavy German cavalry bit

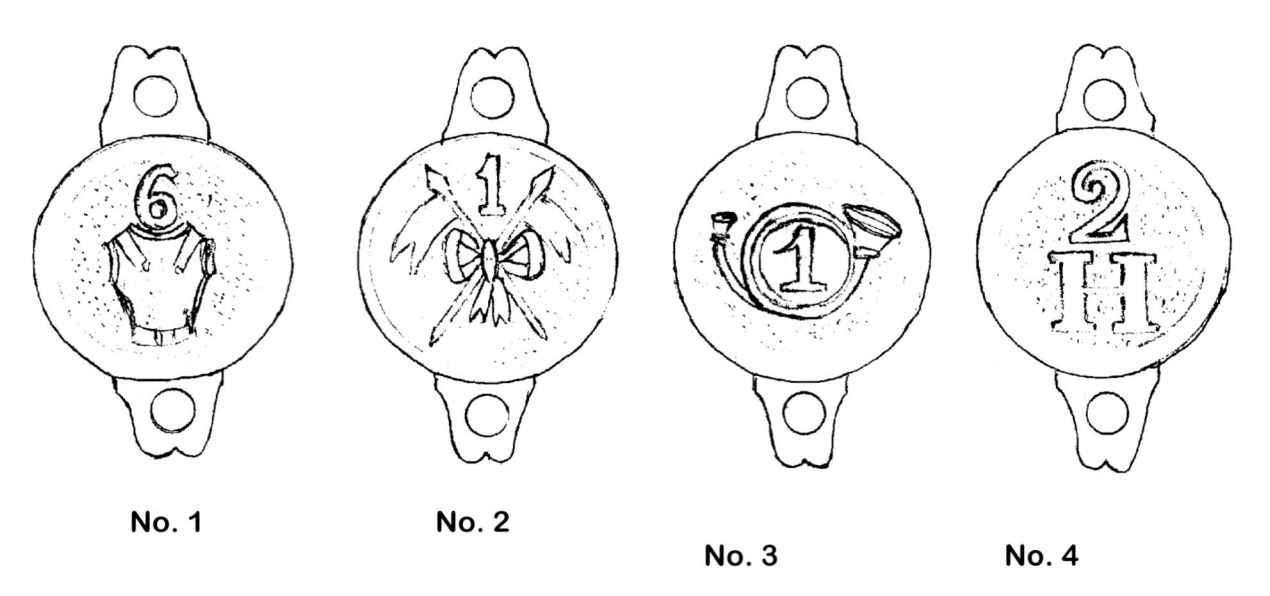

No. 1   No. 2

No. 3   No. 4

Fig. 22.10 Bosses of French cavalry used on Model 1845 Bit. No.1 6th Lancers, No. 2 1st Lancers, No. 3 1st Chasseurs a Cheval.

No. 4 2nd Hussards. From *La Cavalerie Francaise et son Harnachment*.

French cavalry and artillery bits of the 1850's followed the British practice of a brass boss on each cheek. Unlike the British bosses which were castings, some of the French bosses, if not all, were stampings in brass plate. They were about 1 1/4 inch in diameter with tabs to attach to the bit. Some were attached with proud brass rivets, and some appear to have been attached with screws. A characteristic of French cavalry and artillery bits is the oval hole for the bridle billet, and some have a small hole in the center below the oval to hold the curb-chain. The mouth-pieces are smaller in diameter than the typical German military bit, and the mild port is in line with the cheek-pieces as opposed to being tilted forward or backward.

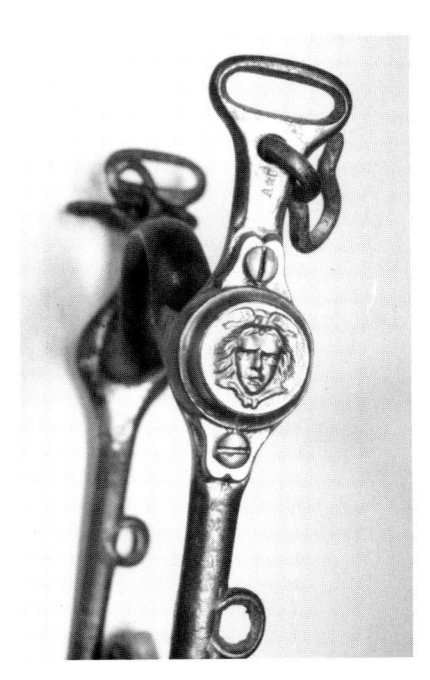

Fig. 22.11 French cavalry military Model 1845 with Medusa head boss. Robert Maclin collection.

Some mid-19th century French military bits had a broad sweep in the cheek-piece, as found on British bits of the same period, with a distinct boss mounted on each cheek. These may well have been officer's bits purchased privately, as opposed to being standard issue by the French government. In 1845, the cavalry adopted a straight-cheek bit. This model 1845 cavalry bit is shown in Figs. 22.11 and 22.12. This particular bit bears a boss with the Medusa head from Greek mythology for a particular regiment. Drawings of other patterns are shown in Figure 22.10, together with the regiment which used each boss.

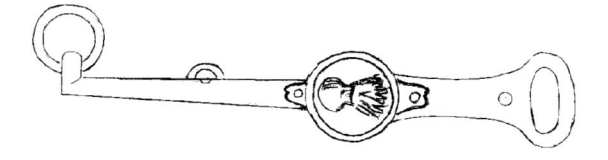

Fig 22.12 Cheek pattern drawing of 1845 French cavalry bit with ordinance boss. Compare with boss in Fig. 22.10.

The model 1853 artillery bit is shown in Figs. 22.13 and 22.14, and most have a boss with crossed cannons surmounted with a small crown. Less common are bosses with a large grenade (or ordinance) emblem. This bit saw service well beyond the Franco-Prussian War of 1870 and 1871, as it appears in a French army training manual dated 1915. Bits of late manufacture have a heavier cheek than earlier ones. The mouth widths are of the order of 6 inches, which would be required of heavier horses such as the Hanoverian or Alter-Real used by the cavalry. Some models of team bits also appear in the 1915 manual, with a pronounced rising curve in the mouth-piece, much like an exaggerated mullen mouth. Several have been found that are stamped "Paris" in small letters near the top outside of one cheek-piece. These may be French military bits, but this has yet to be confirmed.

The model 1874 French cavalry bit is similar to the model 1845, but the brass bosses were dispensed with in later years, if not from the start. Overall height of the cheek-piece varied from 6 to 7 1/4 inches, and mouth widths from 3 3/4 to 5 inches have been encountered. The larger bits would have seen service in the early years, before the greater use of cavalry as mounted infantry with resulting smaller horses. The very narrow 3 3/4 inch mouth is believed for use with the smaller breeds of horses used by the Spanish, Algerian and Morocan cavalry in French possessions of North Africa and in the Middle East. Some model 1874 bits of late manufacture were cast in nickel. The model 1874 bit continued in service until French cavalry was disbanded early in WW II.

Fig. 22.13 French artillery or ordinance bit.

Belgian cavalry, which put up such a brave fight at the start of WW I, were issued at that time a bit having a cheek-piece similar to the French model 1874

Fig. 22.14 French artillery bit boss. Photograph by Alain Eon, Montrouge, France.

bit, but the port was higher than that of the French. At least some had plain brass bosses, and some had a lip-bar and some did not. Other European countries developed their own stylish patterns in early years, or adopted bits with characteristics of the military bits in use by the leading powers at the time, namely Britain, Germany or France. As an example, Portugal, who had been allied with Britain since at least the time of the Penninsular War 1808 to 1814, might have adopted bits having the characteristics of British military bit designs. More recently, the Pelham style of bit, usually with a large diameter mouth, regularly appears in photos of European cavalry in the 1930's. During WW II, Russian Cossacks and those who later joined the German Army and fought for the

Germans used a simple snaffle. Beyond British, German and French military it is not generally possible to identify the country of origin with information available at this time.

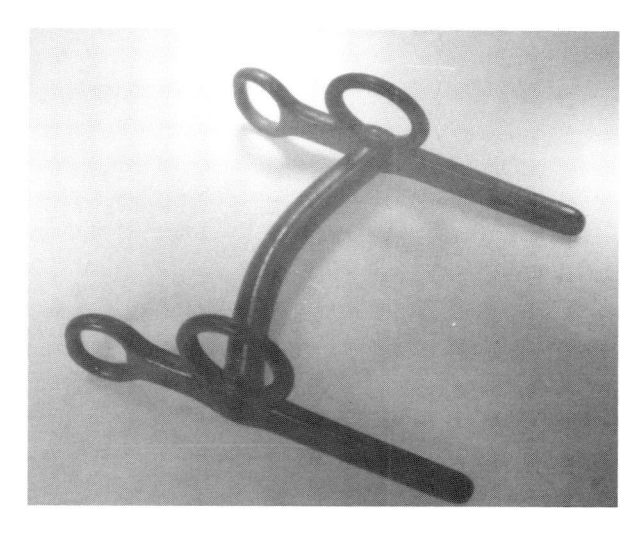

Fig. 22.15 French military team bit. Robert Maclin collection.

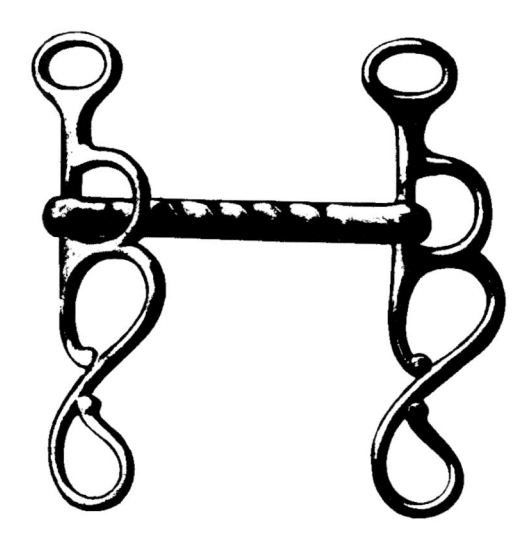

Fig. 22.16 French military bit of WW I period and before.

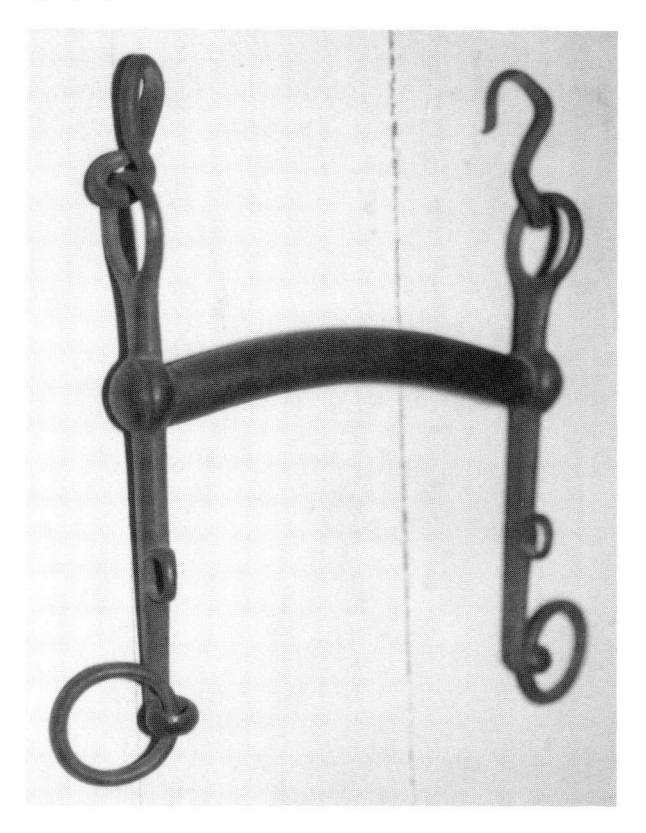

Fig. 22.17 French military team bit.

Fig. 22.18 Military bit with brass boss. Origin unknown. From Jean Gayle collection, photo by Jones Photo Co.

The text and drawings for chapter 22 contributed by Hamilton May, Colborne, Ontario, Canada.

CHAPTER TWENTY-THREE
United States Military Bits and Bridles

The new Continental Congress did not authorize mounted military organizations until the First Regiment of Continental Dragoons was formed in July of 1776.

Recruiting Orders to Elisha Sheldon, Esquire, Lieutenant Colonel and Commandant of a Cavalry Regiment to be raised: " . . . Saddles, bridles, carbines, broadswords, pistols and every other accouterment necessary (agreeable to a pattern here-with given you), you will procure as cheap as possible... Given at Headquarters, this 16th day of December, 1776. Go. Washington."

Most of the horse equipment used was of the type that was readily available to civilians or captured from British supplies. Both the civilian and military equipment was designed after the European military patterns. The bridle commonly used was the double bridle with a Pelham bit and double reins.

Following the cessation of the War with the British, Congress allowed the dissolution of the Continental Army to a mere 700 troops. Hostilities along the frontier caused a revitalization of the army and on October 20, 1786, Congress authorized a *Legionary Corps* which in part was to consist of two troops of cavalry. Little was ever accomplished and the force never developed as intended. Indian difficulties in 1791 caused the Congress to authorize a squadron of four troops of light dragoons. These were the official first regular mounted troops of the new United States Army.

No record is available as to what equipment was issued to the dragoons; in all probability it was very similar to that used during the latter part of the Revolutionary War era, the double bridle with bit and bridoon.

Contracts with civilian suppliers at the time list a double bridle with bit and bridoon as the equipment used. No additional description has survived. Several bits of the dragoons of 1812 have survived and are pictured in Figures 23.0 and 23.1.

Fig. 23.0. Dragoon officers bit of 1820-1830. Bruce Hundley collection.

The officer bridle and bit of 1812 were more ornate than those of the dragoons. The bridle was fitted with a scale of metal over the crown-piece designed to protect the horse's head from sabre cuts. The curb bit was the same type for both the officers and troopers. The officer's bit was ornamented with a decorative boss.

Ordinance General Order # 36 (1839) describes the bridle for dragoons as being of "black leather; for General and Staff officers, the bridle had a bent branch bit with gilt bosses, with the bridle front and roses being yellow. The bridle for mounted officers of artillery was of black leather, with gilt bit, stirrups and mounting for the artillery and ordinance and plated for the infantry; front and roses for the artillery, red; for the ordinance, blue; for the infantry, white."

Military insignia of 1800 to 1815 was very plain. The wings of eagles were thin and spread. Insignia of officers was made of silver, and the militia insignia was of brass.

Fig. 23.1 Close-up of Fig. 23.0 boss.

Regulation U.S. artillery curb bits for 50 years were distinct and separate from the dragoon and/or cavalry bits. The artillery bits during this period had slots on the lower branch ends in place of the loose curb rein-ring. The slots are characteristic of the Buxton or Gig driving bits usually found only on show or parade teams today. Artillery bits during this period also had a bottom bar to add strength and prevent the branches of the bit from hooking the reins of other horses of the hitch.

The following is listed as "Horse Equipment for Dragoons" from the *1841 Ordinance Manual* and referred to as the Pattern of 1841.

The leather parts of the halter and the snaffle and curb bridles are made of strong black leather. The buckles are made of wrought iron and tinned, and all the buckles have rollers. The curb bridle crown piece is 2 in. wide, split at each end into two equal parts, to fit 2 billets on the near side and 1 billet and 1 throat latch on the off side; 1 buckle and 2 loops for the throat lash, 3 loops for the spare curb chain,- the loop on the top of the crown has a button for attaching the button-hole strap on the halter; the brow band, 1 1/4 in. wide, with 2 loops at each end for the billets of the crown piece, 2 brass plates, for marking and numbering the bridle; a cheek strap, each with one buckle and one loop at the upper end, and 1 buckle, and 2 loops at the lower end;

Fig. 23.2 An early military bit with an eagle boss, circa 1840-1850.

2 bit billets, sewed to the under side of the cheek straps,- the nose band, 1 In. wide In rear, passing through openings between the cheek straps and bit billets, 1 buckle and 1 loop for ditto.

Bit, wrought iron, burnished. 2 cheeks, the upper part straight, with an eye for the bit billet and another for the curb chain; the lower part an "S" with an eye for the bridle rein, the mouth-piece dovetailed and riveted to the cheeks; the portmouth (the bar), riveted to the lower end of the cheeks; the curb chain, (tinned iron) fastened by a hook to the off side and by an S to the near cheek; 2 escutcheons (brass), riveted to the cheeks (Fig. 23.3).

The reins are 1 in. wide, made of one piece of leather, split in two; 2 bit billets with 2 buckles and 2 loops; 1 sliding loop and 1 button; the whip, of braided leather.

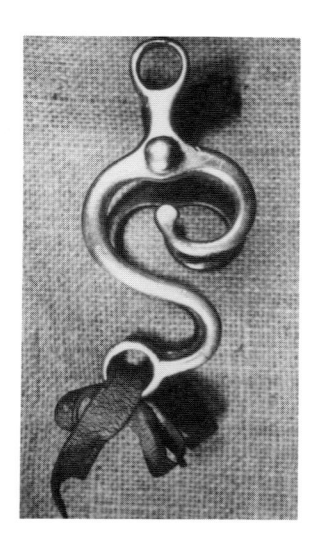

Fig. 23.3 A silver-faced bit, 1810-1815. Judy Gourley collection.

Fig. 23.4 Bit of the early 1800's. Judy Gourley collection.

Fig. 23.5 Bit of 1812-1815. Judy Gourley collection.

Fig 23.6 Bit with artillery boss. Judy Gourley collection.

Fig. 23.7 1832 U. S. artillery bit. Robert Maclin collection.

Fig. 23.9 1840's U.S. artillery bit. Robert Maclin collection.

Fig. 23.8 A bit with silver boss of 1812 to 1820. Judy Gourley collection.

The bits (1841 *Ordinance Manual*) are made of three sizes and of three varieties in the form of the portmouth and degree of severity. In large numbers, one-sixth are mild, one-sixth severe, the rest medium. One-fifth of each kind are 4.625 in. wide between the cheeks, three-fifths are 4.875 in. wide, and one fifth are 5.125 in. wide. Ralph Emerson, Jr., a cavalry history student, believes the artillery bits were issued with only one size of port.

The 1850 *Ordnance Manual* lists a change in the width of the artillery mouth-piece over the 1841 pattern to 4 7/8, 5, and 5 1/4 inches. This is an aid to determine the date of a bit.

Fig. 23.10 A military bit circa 1840. Judy Gourley collection.

Fig.23.11 Military bit l840-1850. Judy Gourley collection.

manufactured by Mr. Thornton Grimsley, St. Louis, MO. Brvt. Lieut. Col. C. A. May, 2nd Dragoons, was a member of the board.

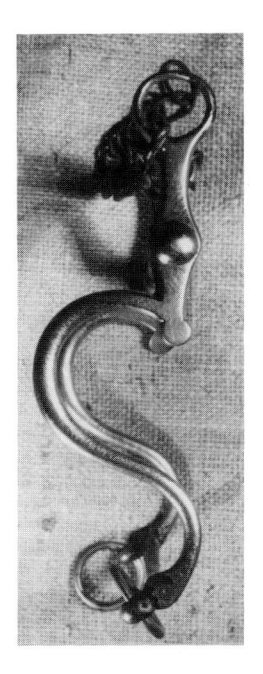

Fig.23.12 Marked with the makers name, who was in business from 1843 to 1855. Judy Gourley collection.

Prior to 1840, the available record is silent as to the official recognized type of equipment, but the "Grimsley" bit was authorized. In 1847, a board of officers recommended formally the adoption of the Grimsley equipment

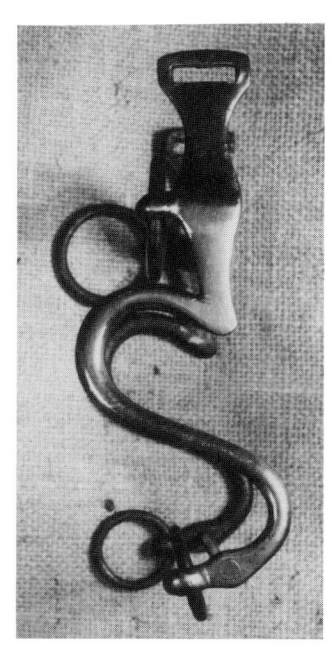

Fig. 23.13 A Grimsley bit, l845. Judy Gourley collection.

274

May later designed the smaller adapted pattern of bit referred to as the "May" bit [Fig. 23.17].

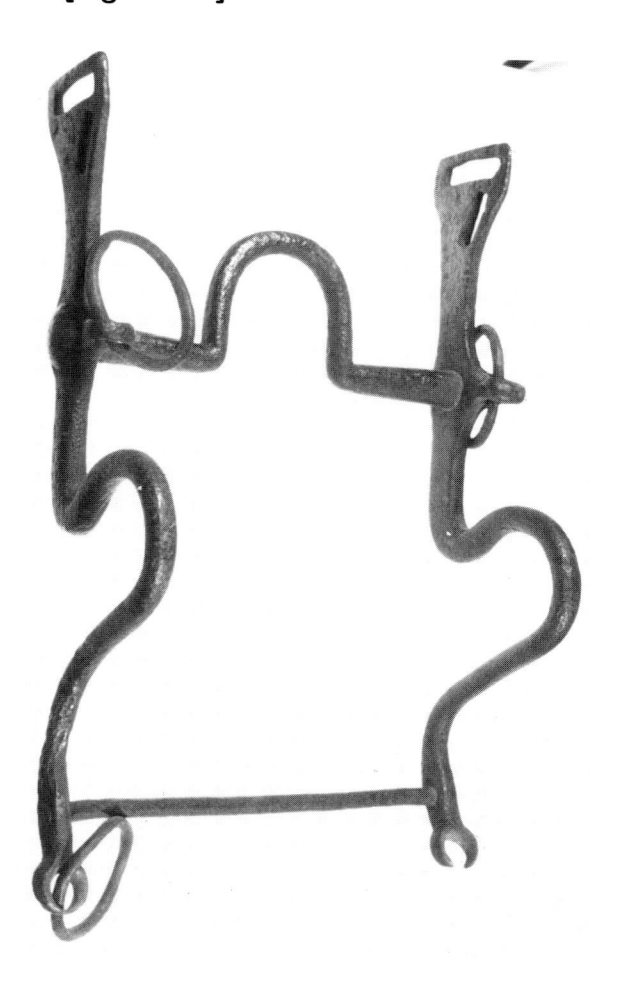

Fig. 23.14 A well-worn early version of the Grimsley bit.

The bridle selected by the board was described as: "Of the form and pattern submitted by Lieut. Col. May with an "S" bit, having a strenghening cross bar connecting the lower extremities of the branches, etc." The halter was "the same pattern as that furnished the First Dragoons in 1839, and since." Specifications indicate almost no change in the halter until 1912 (From an article in *Cavalry Journal,* Oct. 1917, by Cpt. Edward Davis).

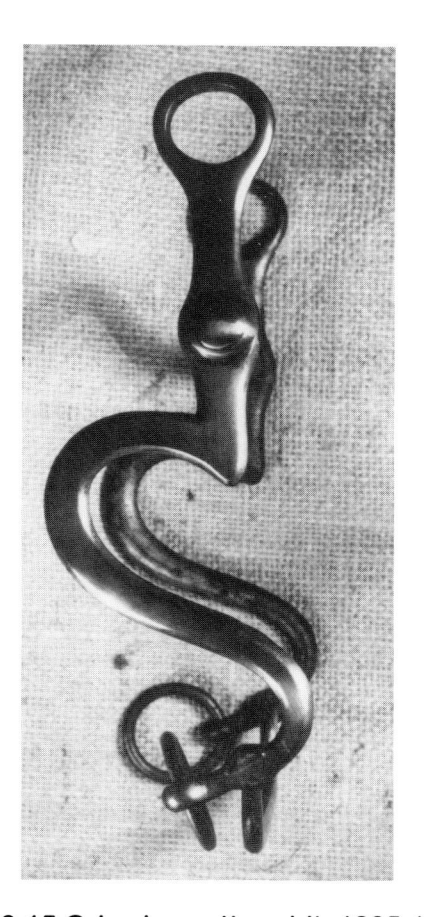

Fig. 23.15 Grimsley pattern bit, 1835-1840. Judy Gourley collection.

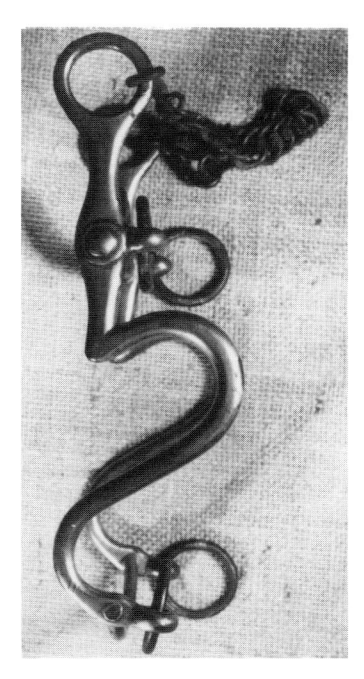

Fig. 23.16 Grimsley pattern bit, circa 1840. Judy Gourley collection.

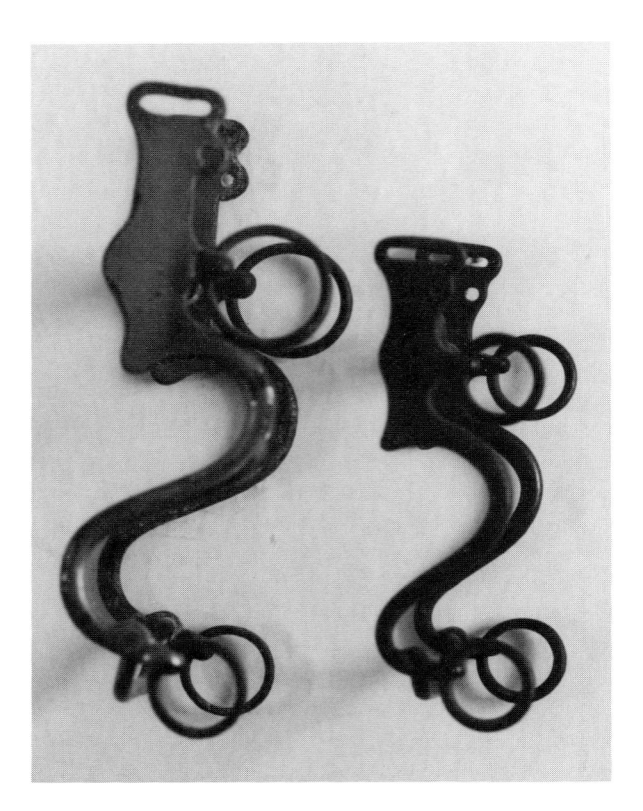

Fig. 23.17 The large and small 1844 dragoon bit referred to as the "May Bit," by Brvt. Lt. Col. C. A. May. Robert Maclin collection.

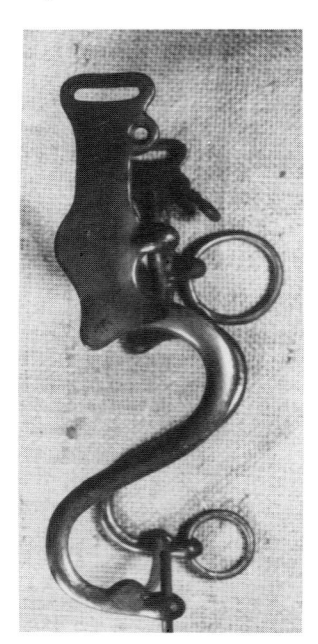

Fig. 23.18 May pattern bit, circa 1855. Judy Gourley collection.

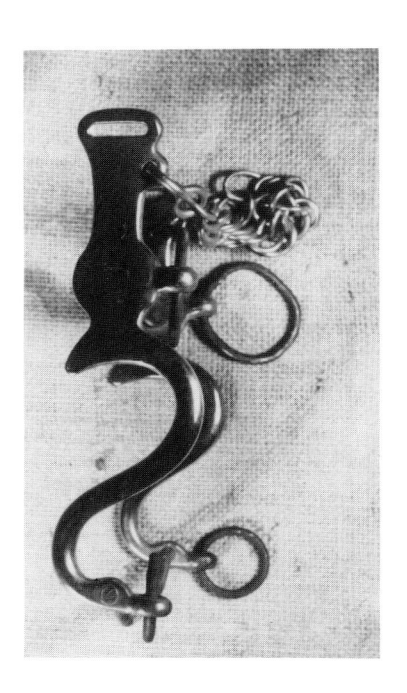

Fig. 23.19 May pattern bit, circa 1855. Judy Gourley collection.

A mouth-piece of three patterns, as prescribed in the *Cavalry Tactics,* was supplied in the proportion of 1/6 mild, 4/6 medium, 1/6 severe; branches all medium; material of bit, steel thickly plated with brass. The curb leather strap 5/8-inch wide, supplied with a brass buckle. The water-bridle had a plain-ring snaffle with a single rein and attached to the lower side-rings of the halter by short chains and attachment bars.

Fig. 23.20 1840's Ringgold dragoon bit, attributed to Major Sam Ringold. The upper cheek-ring is different from Fig. 23.17, small dragoon bit. Robert Maclin collection.

Fig. 23.21 1830-1840 large dragoon bit, referred to as the Grimsley Pattern, developed by Thornton Grimsley, St. Louis, MO., along with a saddle, bridle and stirrups. The steel bit was thickly plated with brass on the outside of the cheek-pieces. Robert Maclin collection.

Fig. 23.22 Bridle, halter and bits issued for field trial to the First and Second Cavalry, 1855. Drawing by Randy Steffen, *The Horse Soldier Vol. II*, courtesy of the U. of Oklahoma Press.

Civil War Period:

HEAD GEAR, Revised regulation, Army of the United States, 1861, described the following items.

1593. A# the leather is black bridle leather, and the buckles are malleable iron, flat, bar buckles, blued.

1594. BRIDLE--it is composed of 1 headstall, 1 bit, 1 pair of reins.

1595. HEADSTALL-1 crown piece, the ends split, forming 1 cheek strap and 1 throat lash billet on one side, and on the other, 1 cheek strap and 1 throat lash, with 1 buckle, .625 inch, 2 chases and 2 buckles, .75 inch, sewed to the ends of cheek piece to attach the bit; 1 brow band, the ends doubled and sewed, form 2 loops on each end through which the cheek-straps and throat lash and throat lash billet pass.

1596. BIT (shear steel, blued)-2 branches, 'S' shaped, pierced at top with an eye for the cheek strap billet, and with a small hole near the eye for the curb chain, terminated at the bottom by 2 buttons, into which are welded 2 rings, 1 inch, for the reins; 1 mouthpiece, curved in the middle, its ends pass through the branches and are riveted to them; 1 cross bar, riveted to the branches near the lower ends,, 2 bosses (cast brass) bearing the number and letter of the regiment and the letter of the company, riveted to the branches with 4 rivets; 1 curb-chain hook, steel wire, No. 10, fastened to the near branch, 1 curb-chain hook, steel wire, No. 11, curb-chain links 0.7 inch wide, with 1 loose ring in the middle, fastened to the off branch by a S-hook, cold-shut; 1 curb strap (leather), fastened to the curb chain by 2 standing loops.

1597 1 curb ring for bit No. 1 replaces the curb chain and curb strap. They are of two sizes: No. 1 has an interior diameter of 4 inches; No. 2, of 3.75 inches. The number is marked on the outside of the swell. No. 1 is the larger size.

1598. There are four bits, differing from each other in the arch of the mouth piece, and in the distance from the mouth-piece to the eye for the cheek strap. The branches are alike below the mouth piece. No. 1 is a Spanish bit, No. 2 is the next severest, and No. 4 is the mildest. Height of arch is 2 1/4 inches in No. 1, 2 inches in No. 2, 1 1/2 inch in No. 3, and 1 inch in No. 4. The distance between the branches is 4.5 inches in all the bits.

1599. REINS--2 reins sewed together at one end, the other ends sewed to the rings of the bit.

1600. The watering bridle is composed of 1 bit and 1 pair of reins.

1601. BIT (wrought iron, blued)--2 mouth-piece sides united in the middle by a loop hinge; their ends are pierced with 2 holes to receive 2 rings 1.7 inches in diameter for the reins. Two chains and toggles, 3 links, each 1 inch X 0.55 inch, welded into the rein rings.

1602. REINS--2 reins sewed together at one end, the other end sewed to rings of the bit.

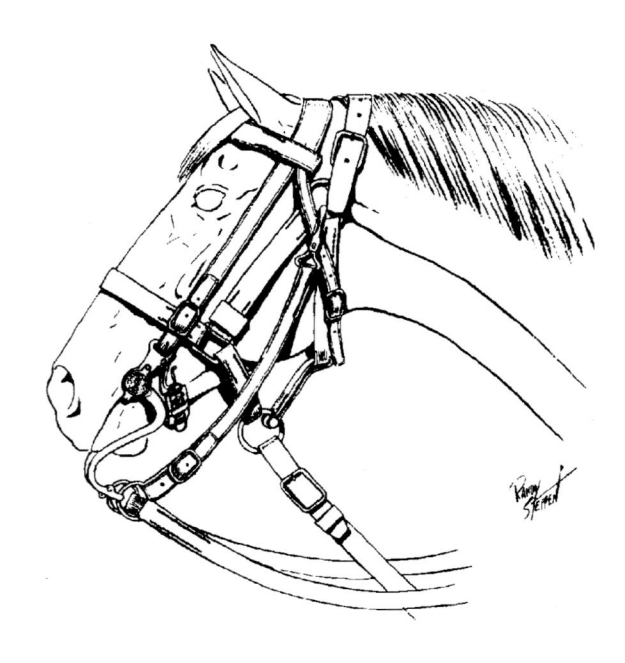

Fig. 23.23 The M-1859 Bridle with the curb bit and halter. Drawing by Randy Steffen, *The Horse Soldier Vol. II*, courtesy of the U. of Oklahoma Press.

There are four varieties of the 1859 Pattern cavalry bits; they are all alike below the mouth-piece. The basic difference is in the height of arch and opening of the arch. The specifications are:

	No. 1	No. 2	No. 3	No. 4
Height of arch	2.25	2.0	1.5	0.5
Opening of arch	0.8	1.1		
Distance of eye from axis of mouth-piece	1.5	2.25	2.25	2.25
Diameter of mouth-piece at shoulder	0.5	0.5	0.5	0.65

Distance from axis of mouth-piece to axis of cross-bar, 5 inches.
Distance from center of button to the axis of cross-bar, 0.5 inch.

Length of mouth-piece in all bits, 4.5 inches; square tenon of month piece, .35 inch.

At centre of arch, .325 inch vertical thickness, 0.45 inch horizontal. Thickness of branch at mouthpiece, 0.225 inch.

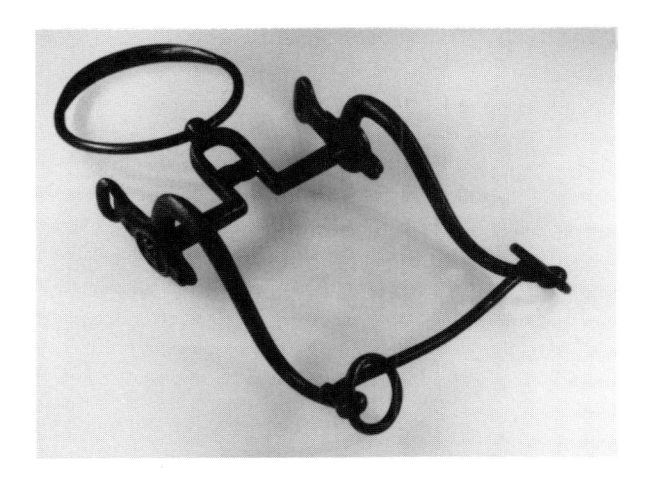

Fig. 23.24 M-1859 No. 1 or ring bit.

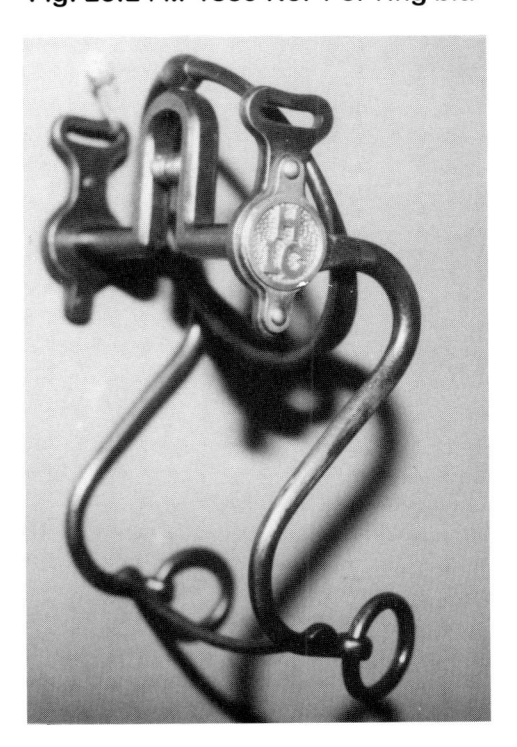

Fig. 23.25 A No. 1 M-1859 bit with the unit boss. Judy Gourley collection.

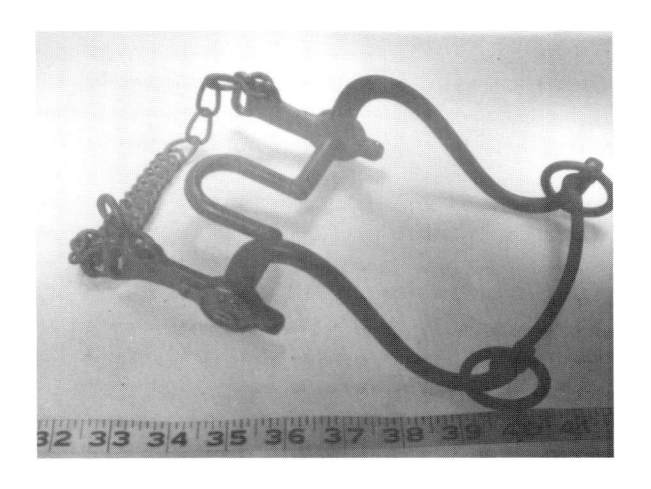

Fig. 23.26 Model 1859 No. 2 bit with curb-chain.

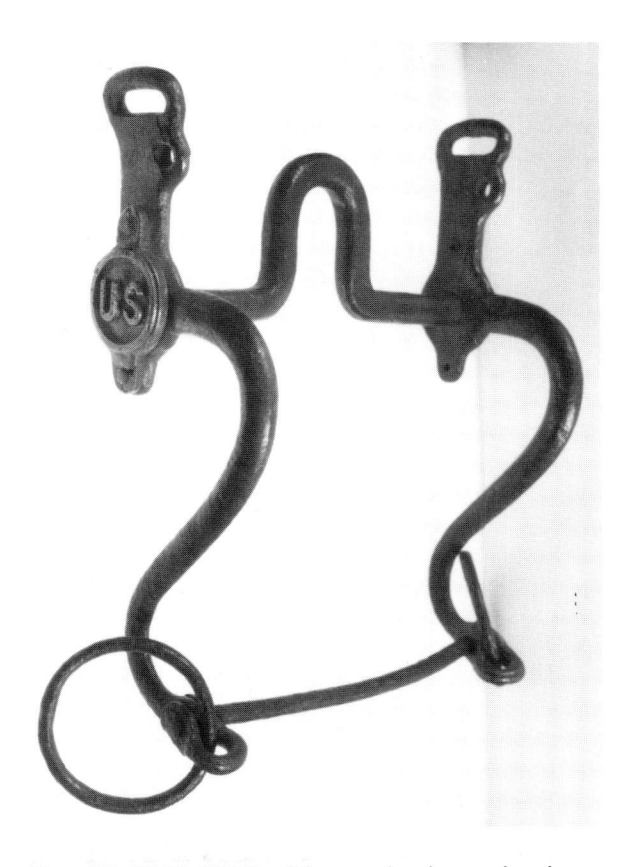

Fig. 23.27 M-1859 with a swinging rein-ring attachment and larger rein-rings.

Fig.23.28 M-1859 bit with an added set of rings to act as a Pelham bit. Judy Gourley collection.

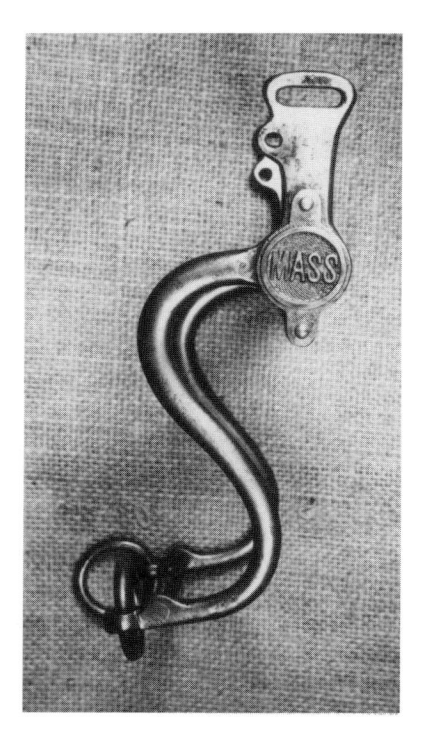

Fig. 23.30 M-1859 with the boss of the Massachusetts Militia. Judy Gourley collection.

Fig.23.29 M-1859 with a variation of the U.S. boss. Judy Gourley collection.

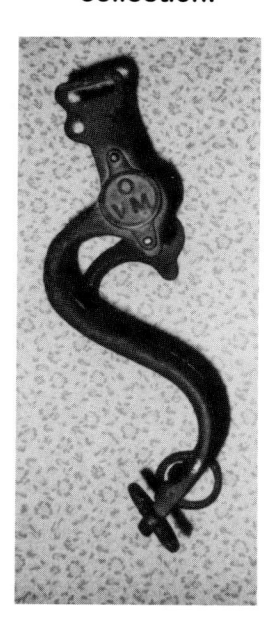

Fig.23.31 M-1859 with boss of Ohio Volunteer Militia. Judy Gourley collection.

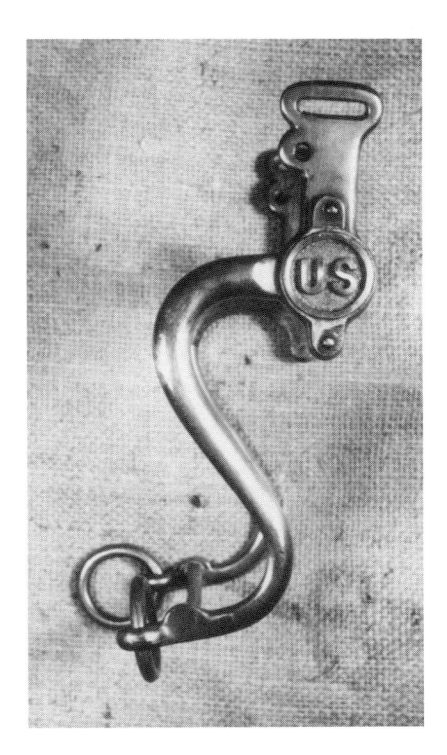

Fig.23.32 M-1859 brass-covered and gilt. Judy Gourley collection.

Fig. 23.34 A solid brass Pelham bit of the Civil War period with small raised US bosses. Judy Gourley collection.

Fig. 23.33 A Civil War period bit with the brass eagle boss upside down. Judy Gourley collection.

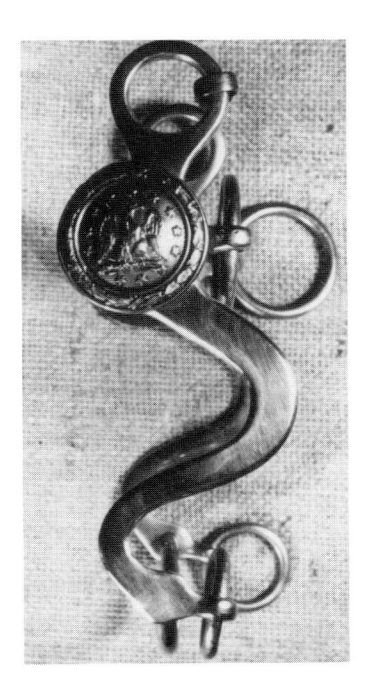

Fig. 23.35 A bit presented to Gen. Thomas Kirby Smith during the Civil War. Judy Gourley collection.

Fig. 23.36 Military bit circa 1860. Judy Gourley collection.

Fig. 23.38 M-1859 bit with the location and identification mark of maker. The mark is always on the upper cheek-piece under the rein-ring of the near side.

Fig. 23.37 A military bit with U. S. bosses and cheek pattern similar to 1800's German military. See Chapter 22, Fig. 22.9. Judy Gourley collection.

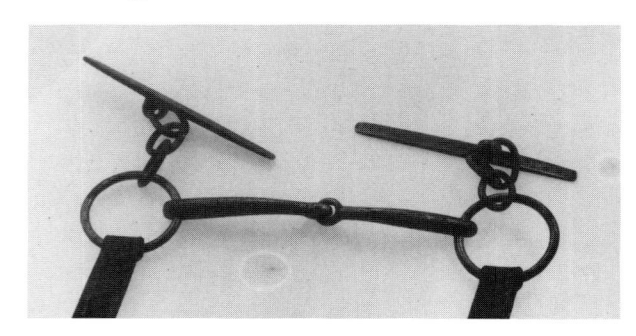

Fig. 23.39 Civil war period watering bit with toggles.

In the late 1850's, the Ordnance Department brought a design change to the artillery bit with the adaptation of the Buxton-type bit with the "S" shaped cheek-pieces [Fig. 23.15]. The 1861 *Ordinance Manual* describes the first Civil War artillery bit as:

> BIT (iron forged and brass plated)-2 cheekpieces, curved in shape of S, pierced at top with an eye to receive the cheek-billet and a hole for the curb chain, at its lower end an eye for reins, and near the mouthpiece a

282

stud. through which is inserted a ring, No. 2 for the reins; 1 mouthpiece: its ends pass through the cheekpieces, and are riveted and rounded, 1 crossbar, riveted to the cheek-pieces;...
　　　　　　　　1861 Ordinance Manual

Artillery bit inspectors kit: In archive reserve at Fort Sill Museum, Oklahoma [Figs 23.40 to 23.43].
1. Includes a 1864 (entwined USA) bit.
2. Cheek-piece pattern gauge.
3. Mouth-piece pattern gauge.
4. Mouth-piece width and upper cheek-piece flare gauge.
5. Gauge to measure thickness of mouth-piece, cheek-piece, rings and diameter and size of rings, rein slot openings and headstall slots.

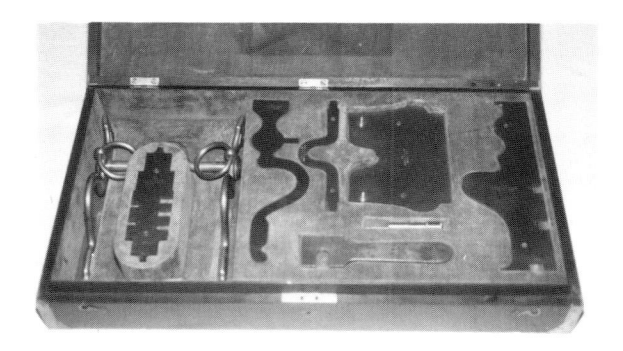

Fig. 23.40 Civil War era artillery bit inspector's kit. Complete with an 1864 artillery (USA entwined) bit. Courtesy of Fort Sill Museum, Fort Sill, Oklahoma.

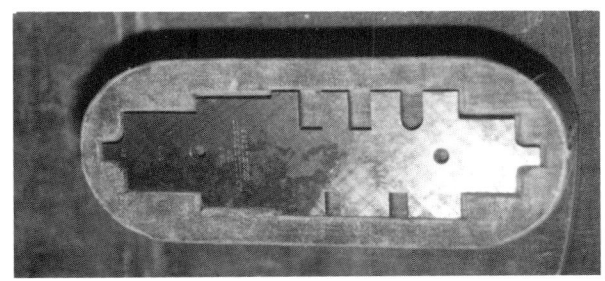

Fig. 23.41 Inspector's gauge from the kit for thickness and size of cheek-pieces, rings and rein and headstall slot openings.

Fig. 23.42 Cheek-piece and mouth-piece pattern guages of inspectors kit.

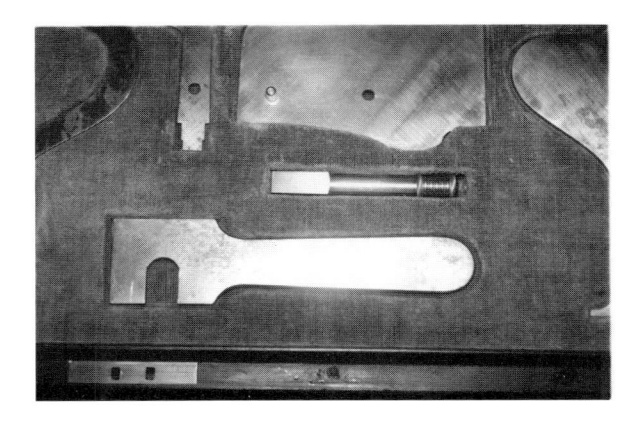

Fig. 23.43 Gauge to measure diameter of mouth-piece, from the artillery inspection kit.

Fig. 23.44 Artillery bit cheek-piece of late 1850's, the first of several changes during and right after the Civil War.

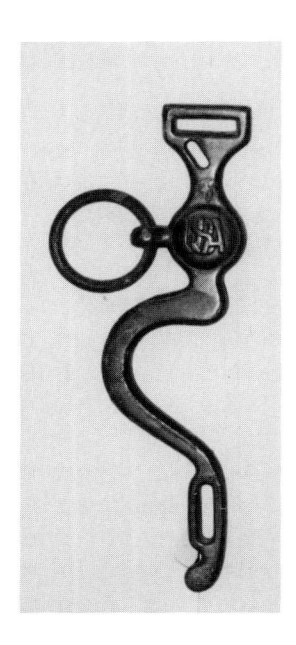

Fig. 23.46 1864 Model artillery bit. Note the change of shape and straightness of the cheek-piece and a slot for the curb in place of a hole as seen in the 1858 and 1862 Models. Shultz collection.

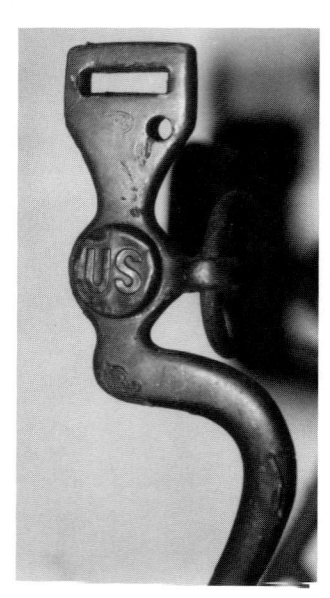

Fig. 23.45 The Model 1862 artillery bit with the small U. S. boss similar in size and character to the Shoemaker Bit of 1874.

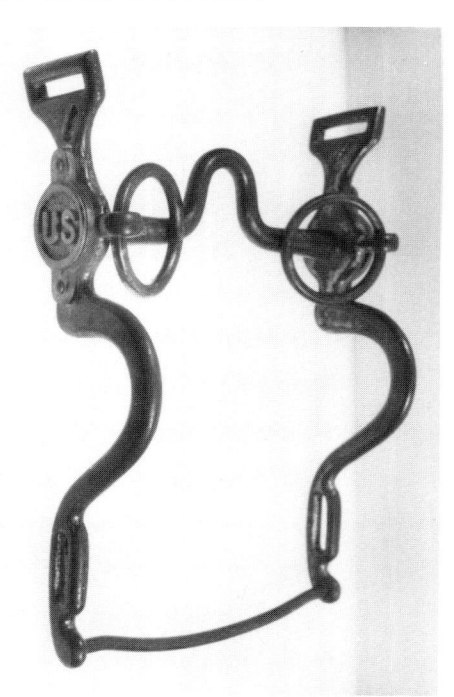

Fig. 23.47 The Model 1865 artillery bit, the last change in the cheek-piece boss design for the artillery bit until the adaptation of the Shoemaker Bit in 1885.

Fig. 23.48 Experimental two-piece mouth patterned after Patent No. 26,804 (Jan. 10, 1860) by W. F. M. Williams of Augusta, GA, with the mouth-pieces closed. The U.S. boss on this bit may not be original. It is believed that the bit was issued with unit bosses or with none. From the collection of Jean Gayle. Photo by Jones Photo Co.

Fig. 23.49 Bosses of Civil War period.

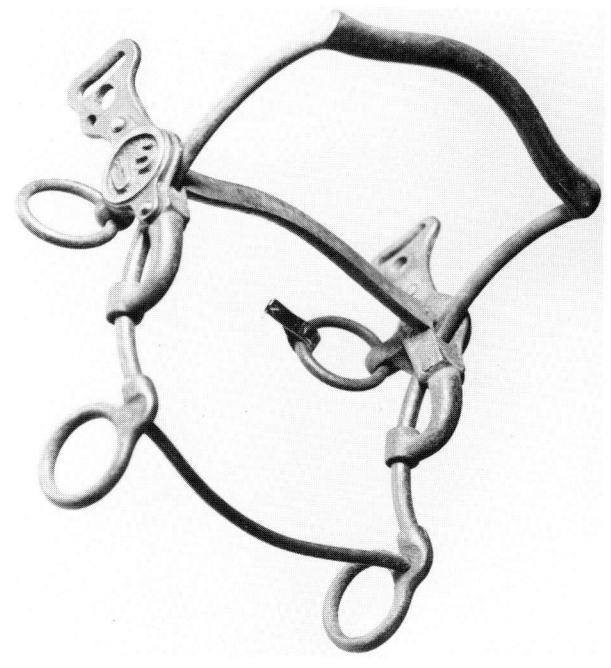

Fig. 23.50 The experimental bit with the two-piece mouth separated. From the collection of Jean Gayle. Photo by Jones Photo Co.

Fig. 23.51 Williams experimental bit without boss as they were issued. The unit boss was placed on the bit after delivery. Judy Gourley collection.

Fig. 23.52 Invented by Capt. Giov. Ciammaichella, of the Italian army and advertised in several issues of the *Cavalry Journal* in 1912 with a liberal discount to U. S. army officers. See Chapter 6, Fig. 6.21.

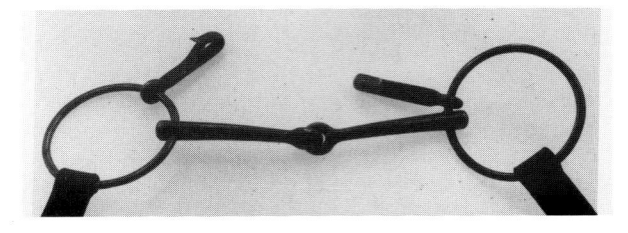

Fig. 23.53 Model 1885 watering bit with reins sewn to the rein-rings.

In the first months of the Civil War many U.S. depots and arsenals in the South were captured and occupied. The Confederate forces reclaimed issued M-1859 cavalry bits, bridles and saddles, not only in the depots, but also on the battle fields. Captured U.S. bits were repaired, which involved resetting rein-rings, re-attaching curb-chains, altering the curb mouth-piece into snaffles and in some instances shortening the "S" cheek-pieces.

The first major change in military bits after the Civil War period came with *Ordnance Memoranda No. 18* board selection in 1874, of the curb bit submitted by Capt. W. R. Shoemaker. Although the bit was used by the military for only 26 years, from 1874 until all were recalled and taken from service by *General Orders No. 103* dated August 5, 1901, it was very popular and remains a favorite bit today with some trainers.

The specifications for this bit (designated the M-1874 Curb Bit) were as follows: the Shoemaker bit was produced with three sizes of arches varying in height by half-inch increments; the No. 1 with a half-inch arch, the No. 2 a one-inch arch and the No. 3 an inch-and-a-half arch. The M-1874 mouthpiece measured 4.75 inches in width. It was issued with 20% No. 1, 70% No. 2 and 10% No. 3.

Ordinance Memoranda No. 29, 1885, brought slight change to the mouth-piece with an increase from 4.75 inches (Model 1874) to 4.9 inches in width and the issue rate was changed to 75% No. 1, 20% No. 2 and 5% No. 3. This change also brought with it the uniting of the cavalry and artillery to the use of the same bridle bit, along with other equipment for the horse and rider.

The first Shoemaker bits were made at the Watervliet Arsenal near Troy, NY. The majority of the Model 1885 were made at the Rock Island Arsenal, with the early ones marked Rock Island and then later just R.I.A. on the outside of the off-branch or cheek-piece of the bit.

The August Buermann Manufacturing Co. of Newark, NJ, and the North and Judd Manufacturing Co., New Britain, CT, the two largest manufacturers of bits in the United States, produced the Shoemaker bit in variation at least until the middle 1920's. The Buermann numbers 375, 376, and 379 were all made with a 5-inch mouth-piece, and each could be ordered blued, nickel-plated or with a burnished finish. They were all supplied in forged steel but the numbers 375 and

376 were also available in the cheaper malleable iron. They used the regulation U.S. boss on the bits with the exception of number 376, which was sold without the boss.

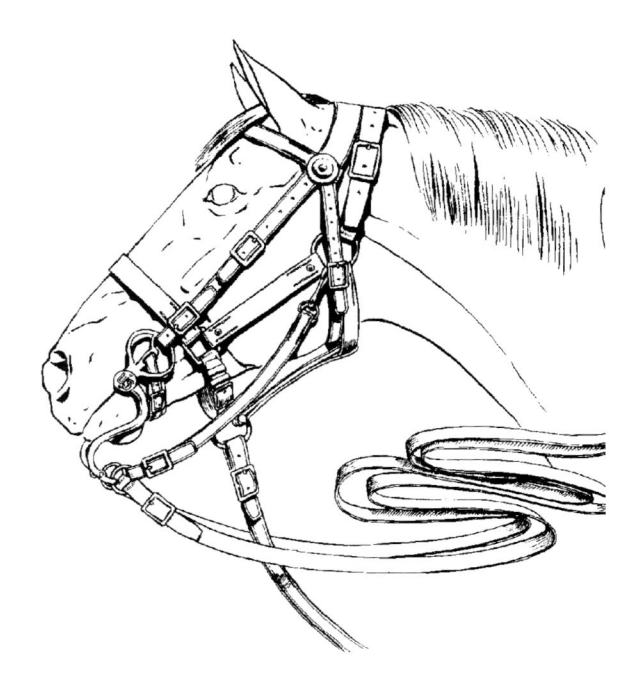

Fig. 23.54 M--1874 curb bridle and halter (with link). Drawing by Randy Steffen, *The Horse Soldier Vol II*, courtesy of the U. of Oklahoma Press, Norman, Oklahoma.

HALTER: 1874.

[Fig.23.55]

Composed of 2 cheek pieces A (made of harness leather); one end of each cheek piece is sewed to a rectangular iron loop B, and the other end sewed to an iron ring C 1 3/4 inches diameter.

The crown piece D is sewed to the off cheek ring; iron bar buckle E and chape sewed to the near ring.

Nose band F, with ends sewed to rectangular loops B.

The chin strap G, with iron bar buckle H, 2 standing and 2 sliding loops, passing loosely through rectangular loops B and halter swivel rings 1.

Throat strap J, folded on itself, making 3 thicknesses and forming at the top a loop for the throat band to pass through, and embracing in its fold at the other end a bolt which holds the ring of the halter swivel.

Throat band K passes through loop in throat strap J and is sewed to cheek rings. Ring of swivel I, 1 3/4 inches diameter. Square G, 1 1/8 inches wide, to which halter strap or lariat can be attached.

Halter strap L, with iron bar buckle without tongue sewed to one end and doubled on itself 6 inches.

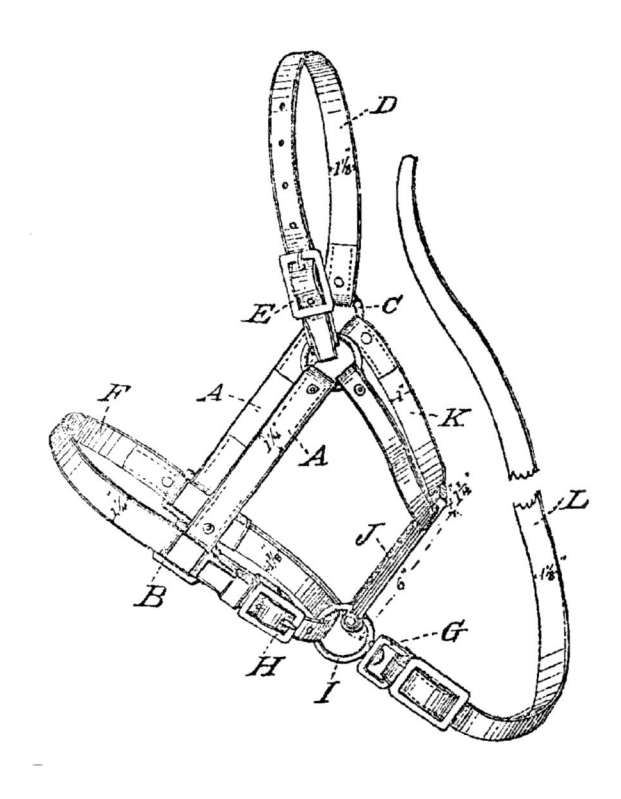

Fig. 23.55 Specifications of halter as described in *Ordinance Memoranda No. 18*, Plate VII.

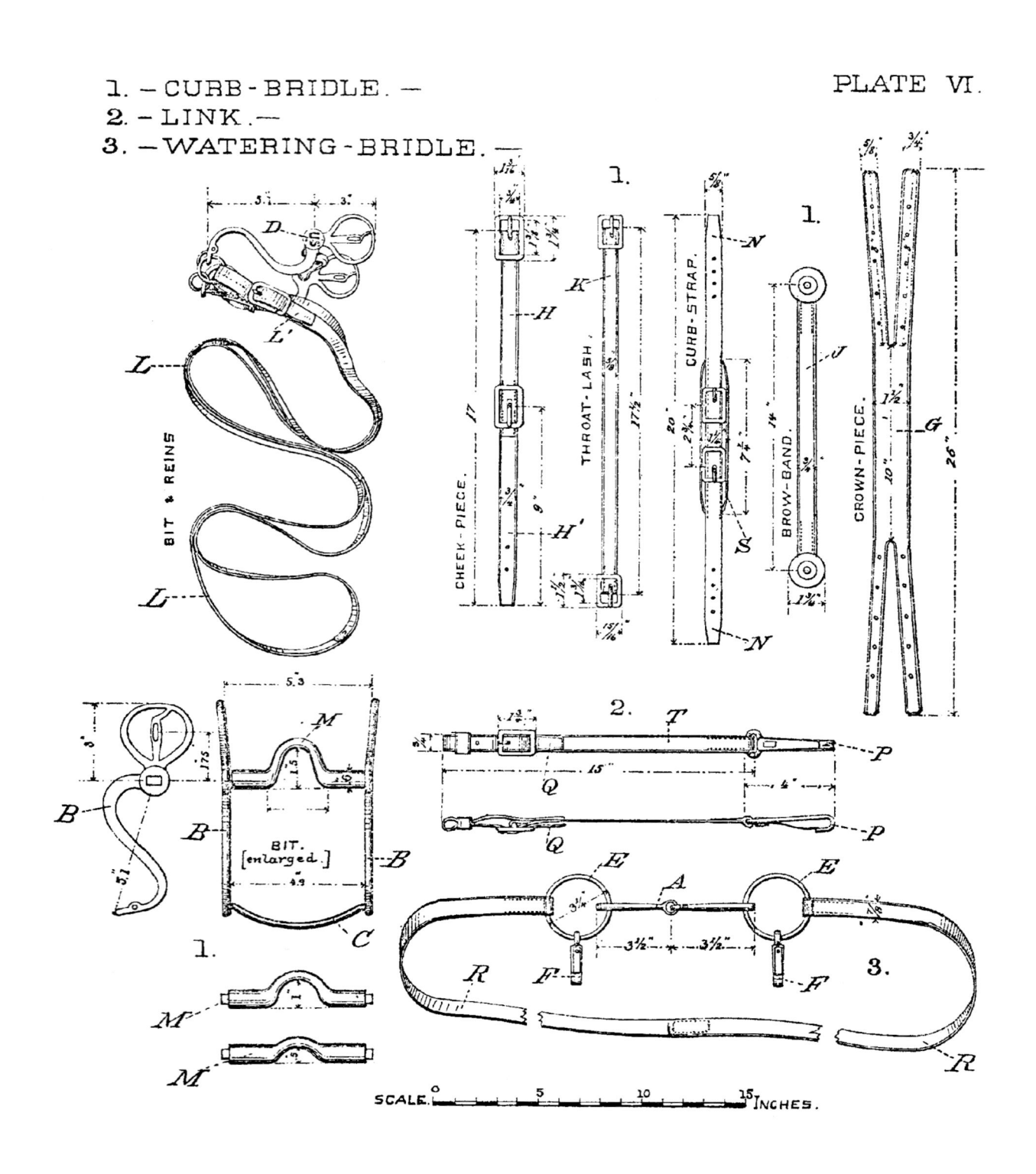

Fig. 23.56 Specifications and measurements of the Shoemaker bit specified in *Ordinance Memoranda No. 18*, 1874.

NOSE BAG: 1874
[Fig. 23.58]

Of No. 8 white cotton duck, with a flexible leather bottom M 6 1/2 inches diameter, 3 1/2 inches deep; body hemmed on top and sewed to the bottom with 2 rows of stitching; on the off side a head strap N sewed to the body and riveted to the bottom; on the near side a strap S is fastened in the same manner, with an iron roller buckle P and standing loop.

Both straps are riveted to top of body and reenforced.

The sides, through straps, are perforated with 1/4-inch holes, 1/2 inch apart; also through bottom, 1 1/2 inches from the top, 3 inches apart. The letters U. S., 1 1/2 inches long, stencilled on the body.

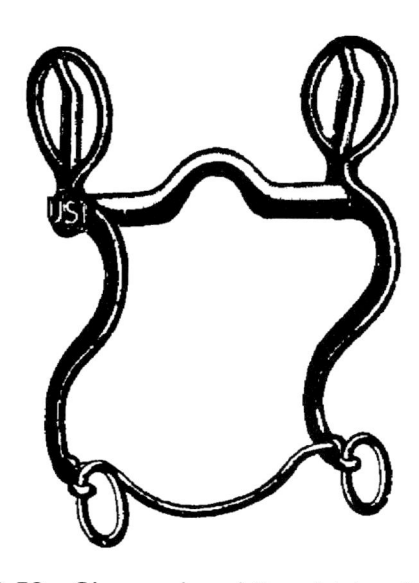

Fig. 23.59 Shoemaker bit sold by August Buermann Mfg. Co. Number 375 in Catalog No. 35.

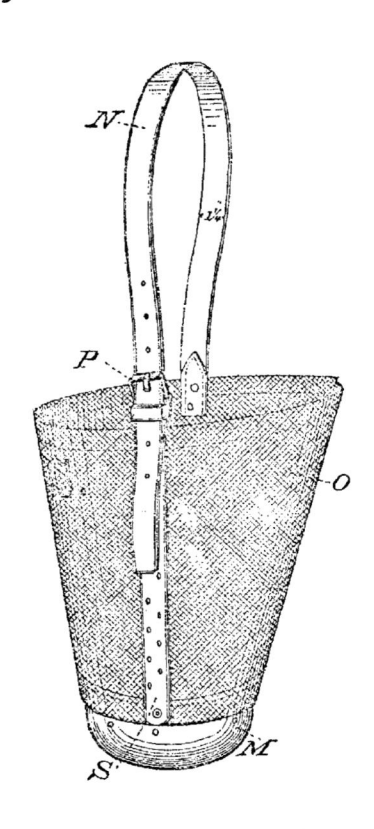

Fig. 23.58 Nosebag and specification from *Ordinance Memoranda No. 18*, 1874

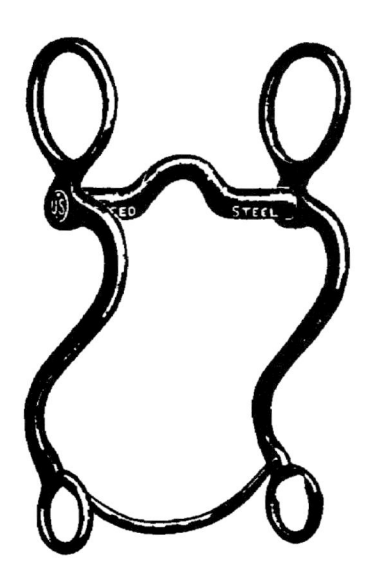

Fig. 23.60 A Shoemaker-style bit sold by August Buermann Mfg. Co. Number 379 in Catalog No.35.

The U.S. military tested several different bits and bridles during the period of the Shoemaker bit. One that received the most attention was the "Whitman" Combination Halter Bridle [Fig. 23.61]. It was a part of a package that included the saddle and other

No. 3

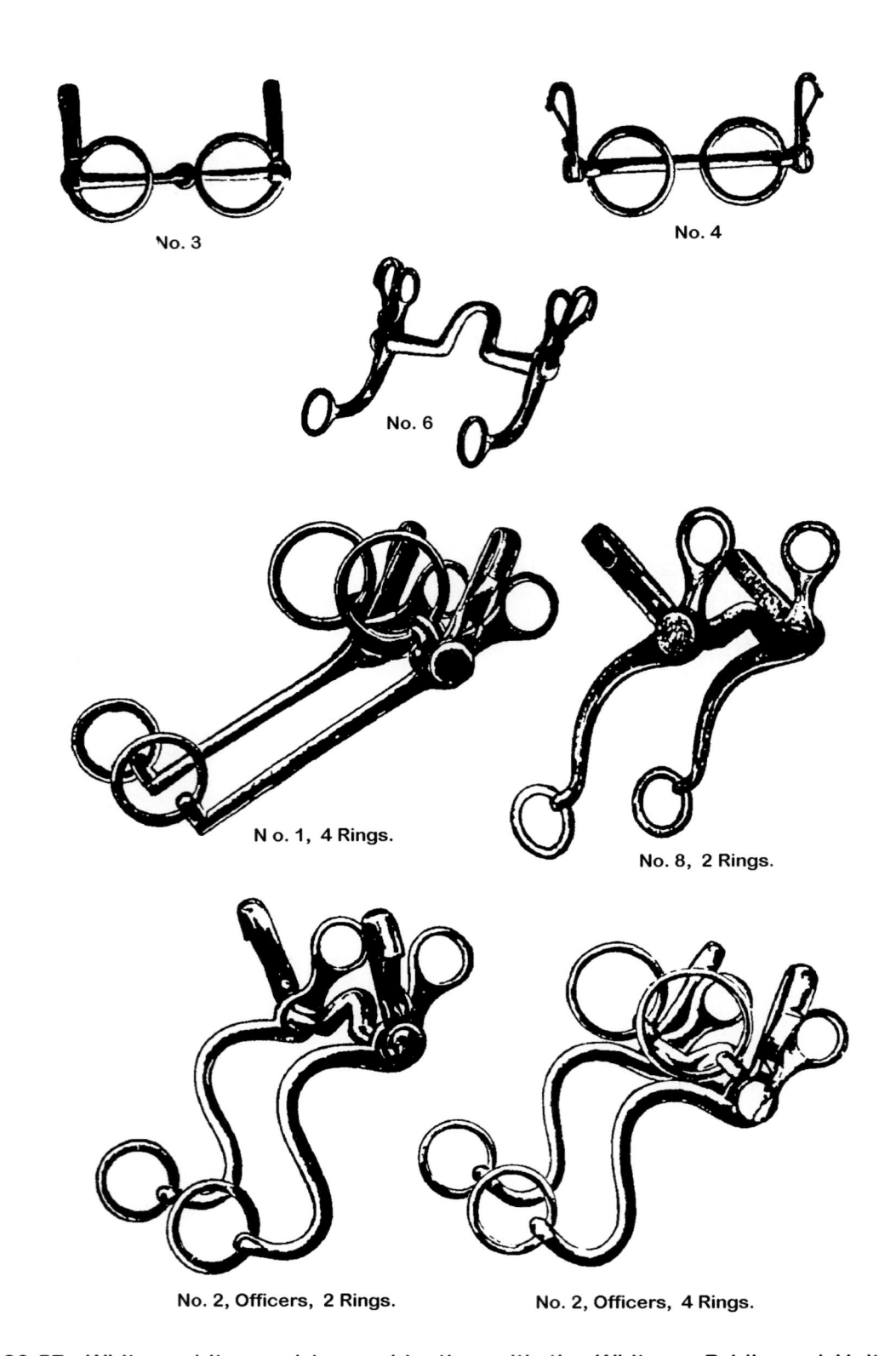

No. 4

No. 6

No. 1, 4 Rings.

No. 8, 2 Rings.

No. 2, Officers, 2 Rings.

No. 2, Officers, 4 Rings.

Fig. 23.57 Whitman bits used in combination with the Whitman Bridle and Halter on an experimental basis by the military in 1880. It was not accepted as the regulation bit.

accoutrements. It was patented by Col. Robert E. Whitman in 1860, and used by the military on an experimental basis for a brief period in the 1880's and then rejected. The Whitman Bit [Fig. 23.57] had a swivel snap attached to the outer side of the cheek-pieces at the end of the mouth-piece to facilitate the rapid attachment of the bit to the Whitman Combination Halter Bridle which was adjustable to any horse.

Fig. 23.61 The "Whitman" Combination Halter Bridle with No. 8 "Whitman" bit.

CURB BIT, Model 1892.

Capt. Whipple of the Ordinance Dept. made a commendable effort to reconcile some of the criticisms of the Shoemaker bit as being too heavy and not of the best principles of theory in bitting that had developed. He sent two bits of his design to the Ordinance Dept. to be tested. Twice modified, the last pattern seemed satisfactory to the majority of officers who tried it. The Shoemaker bit had been made in only one width of mouth-piece and the recommendation was for the Whipple bit to be made in several widths of mouth-piece.

(Appendix 12 to the *Annual Report* of the Chief of Ordinance to the Sec. of War for the year ending June 30, 1892).

The curb bit, Model of 1892, is made of best quality shear steel and has dull nickel finish. The branches are drop-forged and electrically welded to the mouth-piece, which is made of soft decarbonized steel. A loop is forged on upper part of each branch for attaching the curb-chain hook and cheek piece, and an eye on lower end of each branch into which is welded the rein ring, made of 0.203 inch decarbonized steel wire. The bits are made regularly in three sizes, which differ in length of mouth-piece, the proportions being:

No. 1	*4.5 inches*	*15%*
No. 2	*4.75 inches*	*75%*
No. 3	*5.0 inches*	*10%*

A larger size, No. 4, with mouthpiece 5.25 inches long, is occasionally made to fill special requisitions.

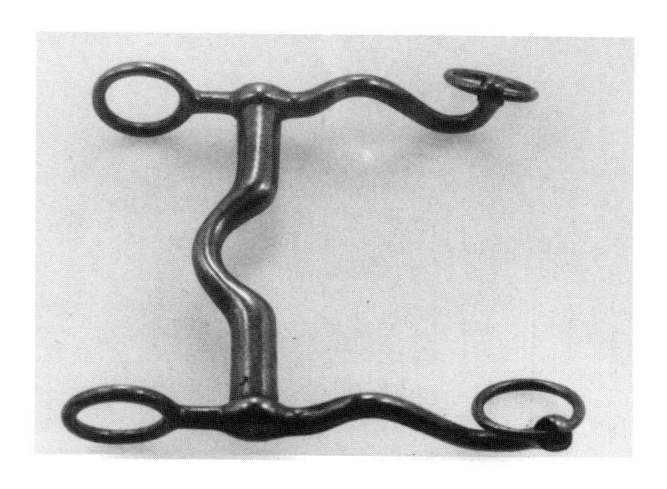

Fig. 23.62 Model 1892 regular issue.

CURB BRIDLE, Model of 1902.
 The components are:
  1 curb bit, model of 1892
  1 curb-chain, 1904
  1 rein
  Headstall--
   2 cheek-pieces
   1 crown-piece
   1 brow band

1 throat-latch
2 brow band ornaments

The curb chain, model of 1904, is a special steel chain with links and hooks finished in dull nickel.

The curb-chain hooks, Model of 1904, are made right and left, of spring-steel wire, 0.165 inch diameter, tempered, and have dull nickel finish. The left hook is formed with the eye and hook in the same plane, while the right hook has the eye twisted at a right angle to the hook. The hooks are closed so as to offer a resistance of 10 to 16 pounds to disengaging from a ring of 0.134-inch diameter wire.

All leather parts of the bridle are made from russet bridle leather weighing 9 1/2 to 10 1/2 ounces per square foot.

The reins are made of two pieces of russet bridle leather sewed together in the middle. One rein billet, with one 7/8-inch bronze center-bar buckle, is securely sewed to each end of rein.

The cheek-pieces are made of russet bridle leather. For officers' bridles they are alike, but for enlisted men they are right and left. They differ in that the right cheek-piece has a 3/4-inch bronze center-bar buckle, while the left cheek-piece has a 3/4-inch bronze "Saalbach" buckle securely sewed to upper end. This buckle has a loop at the lower end which takes the snap of the link when the link is carried on the bridle. Both cheek-pieces have billets with 3/4-inch bronze center-bar buckles securely sewed to lower end. To admit fine adjustments, the holes in the crown-piece for the cheek-piece buckles are spaced 1/2-inch apart, while those in billets are 7/8-inch.

The crown-piece is made of russet bridle leather with ends split for a distance of 8 inches and a 1/8-inch strip taken out of the center, forming a cheek and throat strap billet on each end. The brow band is made of russet bridle leather. A loop is formed on each end by doubling over and stitching the ends of the piece.

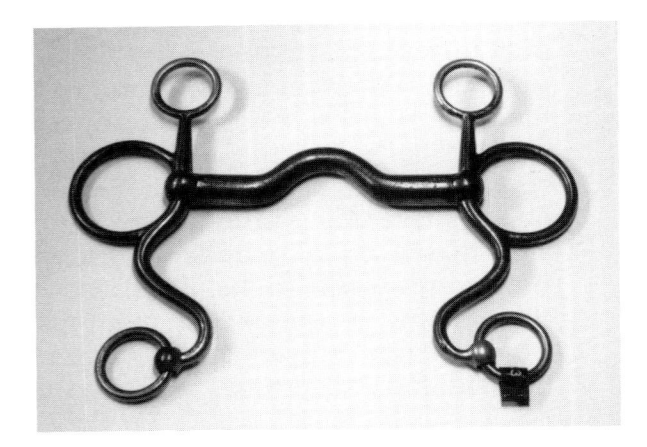

Fig. 23.63 Model 1892 "Whipple Bit" with fixed rings attached to the loose cheek-pieces to be used as a 4-rein bridle. Robert Maclin collection.

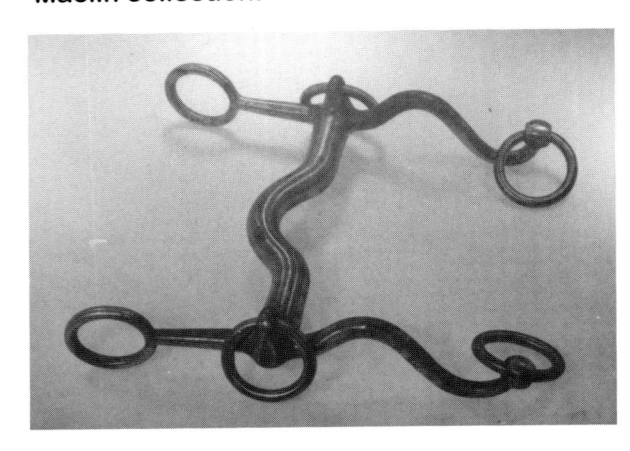

Fig. 23.64 Fixed-cheek four-ring M-1902.

The throat-latch is made of russet bridle leather and has a 5/8-inch bronze center-bar buckle securely sewed on each end.

The brow-band ornaments are made from sheet copper 0.035 inch thick for enlisted men and 0.109 inch thick for officers; both are bronzed and bear the coat of arms of the United States in relief. Loops of 0.109 inch soft brass wire, to receive the brow band, are soldered to the rear sides.

WATERING BRIDLE.

The mouthpiece is made in two parts. Each is lightly curved and tapers from 0.59 inch diameter just inside of the rein ring to 0.4 inch diameter at base *of eye, being forged from a soft decarbonized steel bar 0.625 inch in diameter. The ends of the two pieces have holes 0.34 inch in diameter and are joined together (Fig. 23.65) by having the eye in one piece cut and closed into the other. The other ends of the mouth-piece are drilled with holes 0.31 inch diameter, into which are welded the rein rings, 2.75 inches in diameter, made of 0.24 inch decarbonized steel wire.*

The reins are made of two pieces of russet bridle leather, 9 1/2 to 10 1/2 ounces per square foot, sewed together at middle. One rein billet with one 7/8-inch bronze centerbar buckle, brown Japan finish, is securely sewed to each outer end.

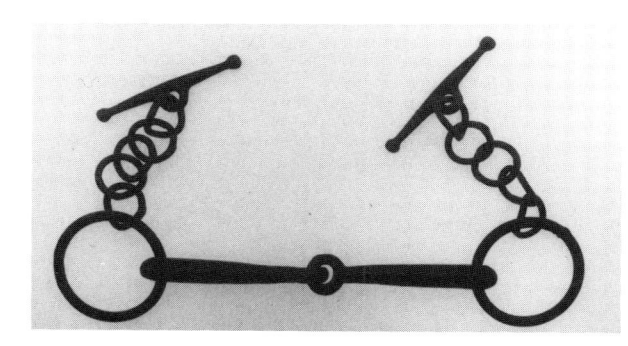

Fig. 23.65 Watering bit

Fig. 23.66 Model 1902 curb bit, an elongated version of the Model 1892.

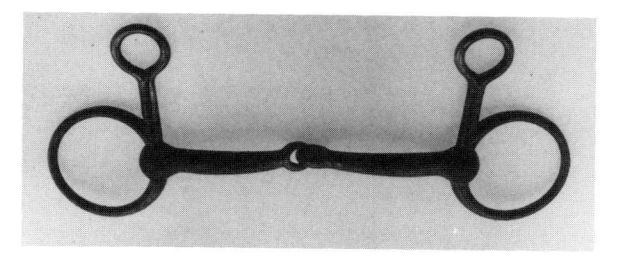

Fig. 23.67 U. S. Cavalry issue of Model 1906 Bridoon with a 5 1/2 inch mouth-piece. This bit was used with a double bridle set-up and at times as a watering bit.

The straight-branched Model 1909 [Fig. 23.68], the next change in military bits, was issued to the cavalry, and with General Orders No. 114 on 11 June 1909, was issued at the rate of 20 to each artillery regiment. The orders made the snaffle bit [Fig. 23.69] the mainstay of the artillery with the curb bit to be used only on horses the snaffle would not control.

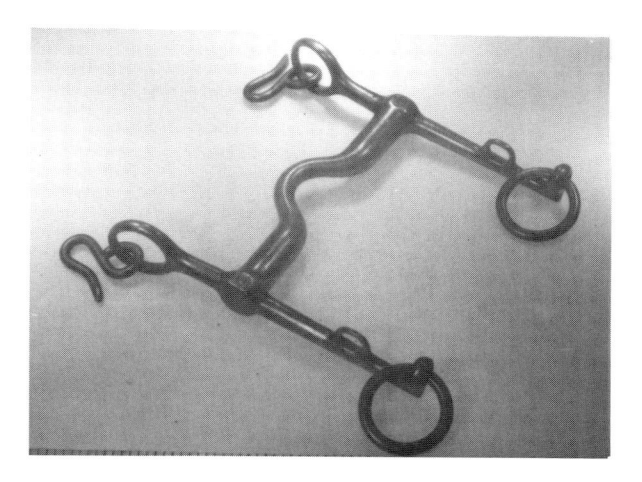

Fig. 23.68 Model 1909 curb bit.

The Model 1909 was issued in the following sizes according to the length of the mouth-piece:

    No. 1   4 1/4 inch mouth
    No. 2   4 1/2 inch mouth
    No. 3   4 3/4 inch mouth
    No. 4   5 inch mouth

The size is marked on the back of the bit at the junction of the mouth and near-side cheek-piece. The other end is marked with U. S. The manufacturer's mark is placed on the mouth-piece to the right of the size mark or on the near-side cheek-piece at the end of the mouth-piece. Some of the marks or letters seen are:

Y & T Yale and Townsend
BTC   Bridgeport Tool Co., Bridgeport, Connecticut
W.L.   White-horse LeCompte Mfg. Co., New York
RIA   Rock Island Arsenal, Rock Island, Illinois

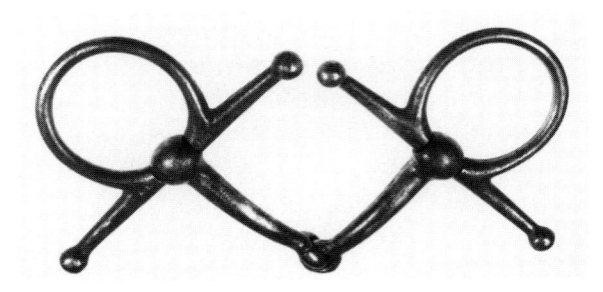

Fig. 23.69 Snaffle bit which was the main bit used by the artillery draft teams after 1909.

The Model 1909 curb bit was modified in 1914 for the artillery with the addition of short leather straps sewn to the rein-rings of the bit. The other end of the straps have snaps which were hooked to the Conway slide cheek buckles of the M-1914 artillery bridle.

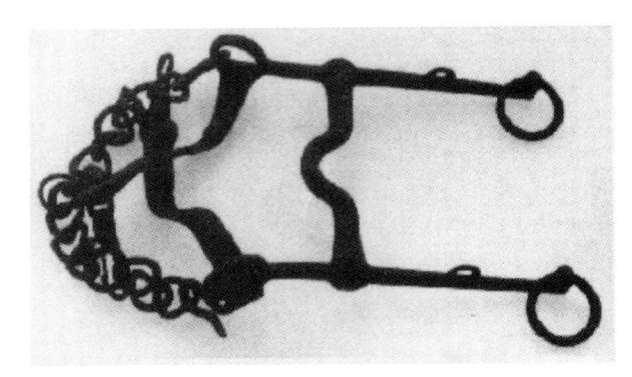

Fig. 23.70 The M-1914 artillery bit with the attached leather straps.

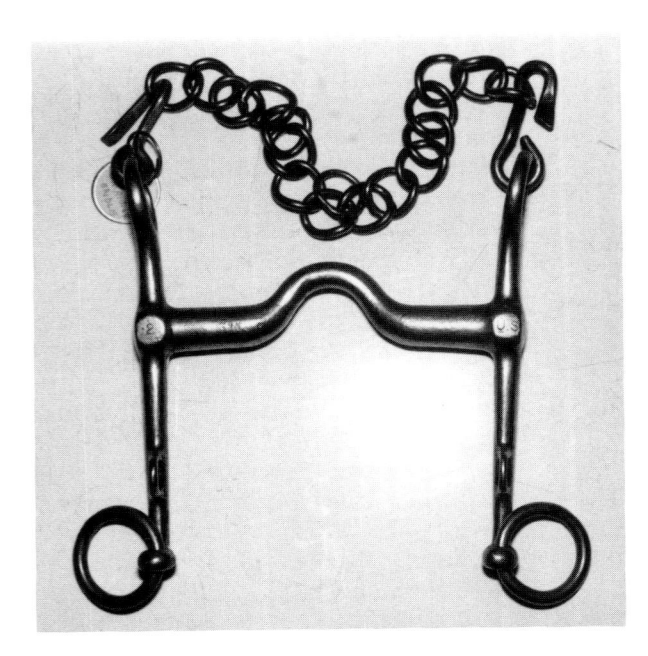

Fig. 23.71 Model 1920 cavalry curb bit was issued in four sizes of mouth-piece widths the same as M-1909. The lower cheek-piece is shorter than in the M-1909 bit. The mark of J.Q.M.D. represents the Jeffersonville (Illinois) Quartermaster Depot.

The Model 1920 cavalry curb bit was the last to be issued and was used along with the Model 1909 until the end of the horse cavalry in 1943.

Other marks or letters appear on various military bits. Some of the marks are:

A.B.   August Buermann Mfg. Co., Newark, NJ
MWW
N S   Nickel Steel
GTC
JOS. B. & CO.   Joseph Baldwin doing business with Alexander Barclay, Newark, NJ
F. B. & CO.   F. Burgess and Co., Red Bank, NJ, a reproduction for modern remount

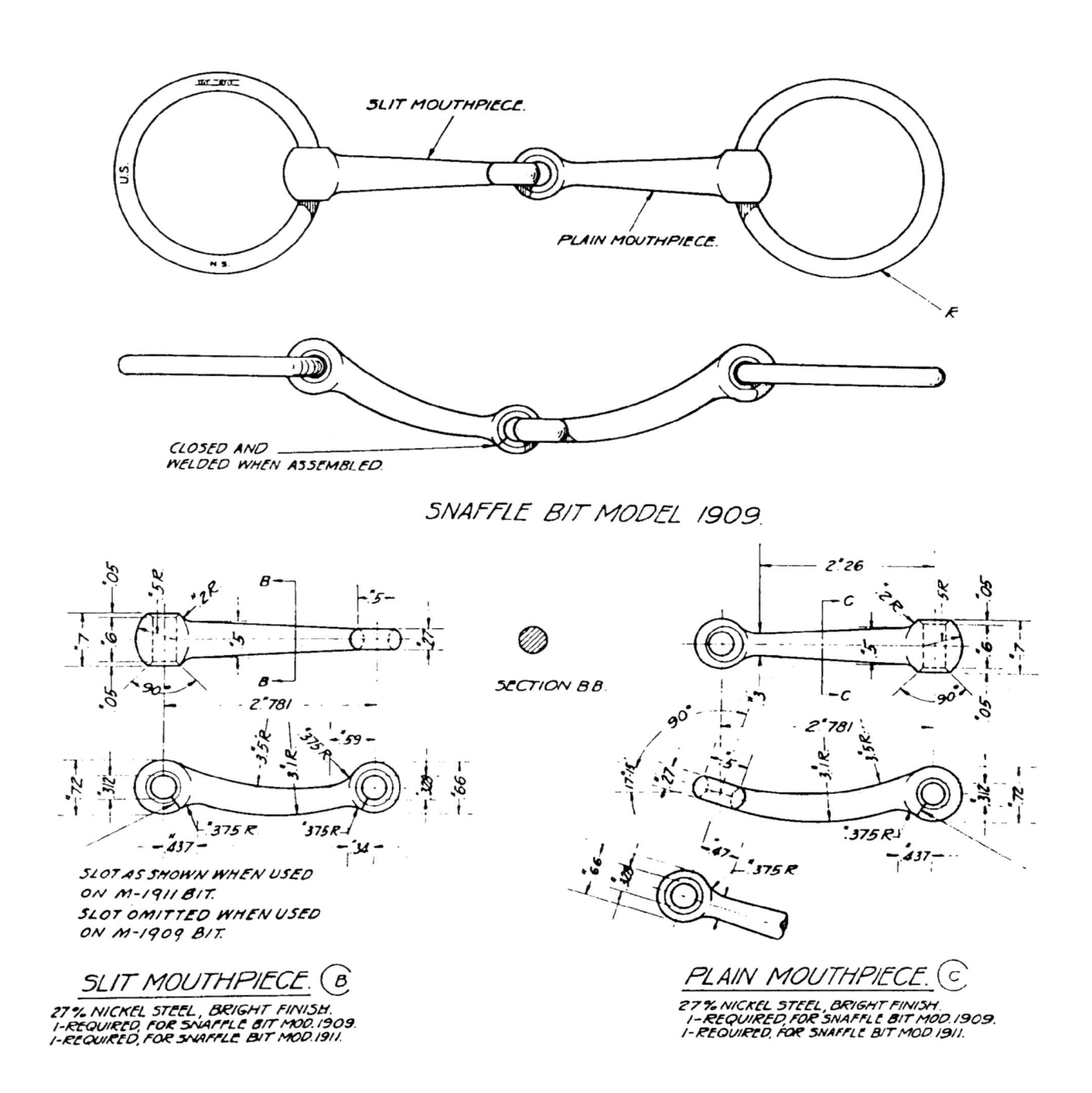

Fig. 23.72 Specifications for the M-1909 snaffle bit.

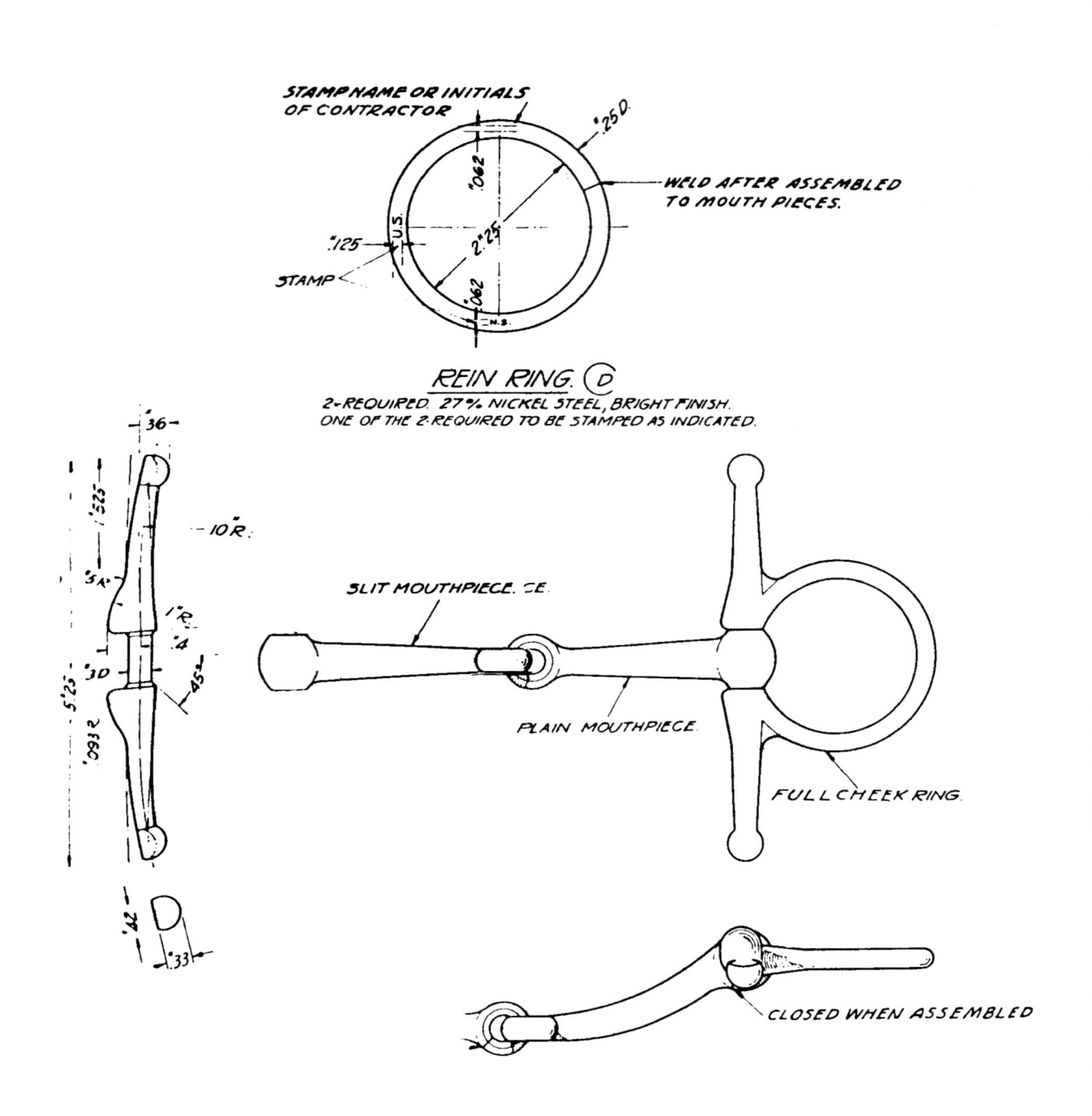

Fig. 23.73 Specifications for the M-1911 snaffle bit.

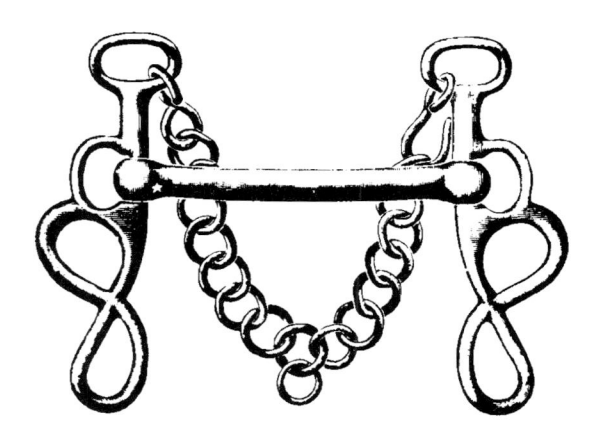

Fig. 23.74 A bit sold by August Buermann Mfg. Co. as a military bit in Catalog No. 35.

Fig. 23.75 A bit sold by August Buermann Mfg. Co. as a military bit and used by some units in the Pacific Theater during WW II.

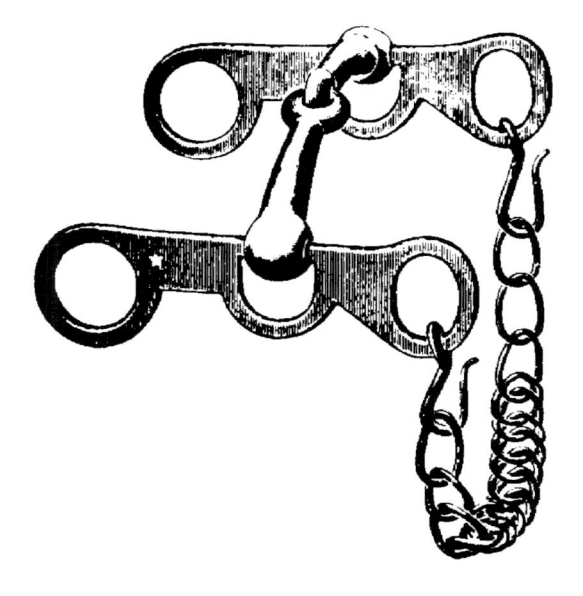

Fig. 23.76 A bridle bit sold by August Buermann Mfg. Co. as a military bit in Catalog No. 35.

CHAPTER TWENTY-FOUR
Millard to Mouth

Millard, John Austin, New York, NY, Patent No. 880,901, Mar. 3, 1908 [Fig.24.0]. A Liverpool-type bit with a spring and strap attachment to eliminate the need for a second set of reins on a bit designed for four reins.

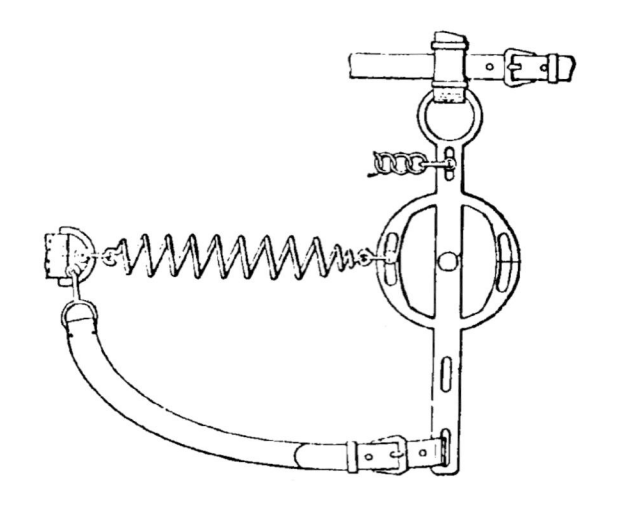

Fig. 24.0 Millard bit with rein-conversion attachment.

Miller, Basil, Coshocton, OH, Patent No. 169,718, Nov. 9, 1875 [Fig. 24.1]. A bit with a rule-joint uniting two sections of the mouth-piece. The upper-side of the mouth-piece has ears or lugs that may be removed if desired. The rein attachments have adapting hooks to secure the reins to the rein-ring.

Miller, Charles A., Buffalo, NY, Patent No. 81,395, Aug. 25, 1868 [Fig. 24.2]. The mouth-piece normally rests in the lower ends of the slots in the cheek-piece. When force is exerted, the cheek-pieces are drawn back and the mouth-piece is forced to slide up in the slot.

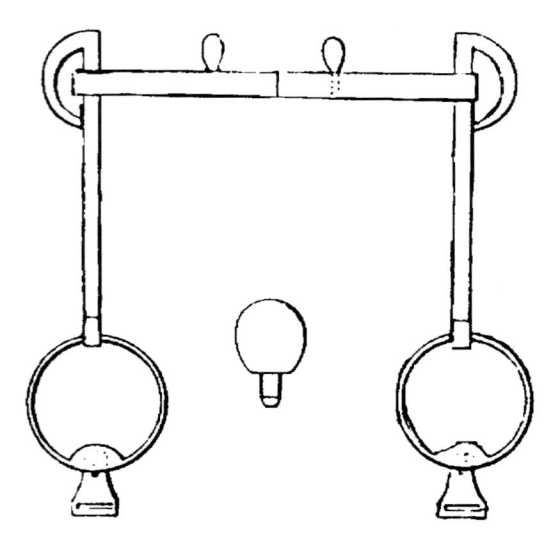

Fig. 24.1 Miller hinged mouth, loose cheek driving bit.

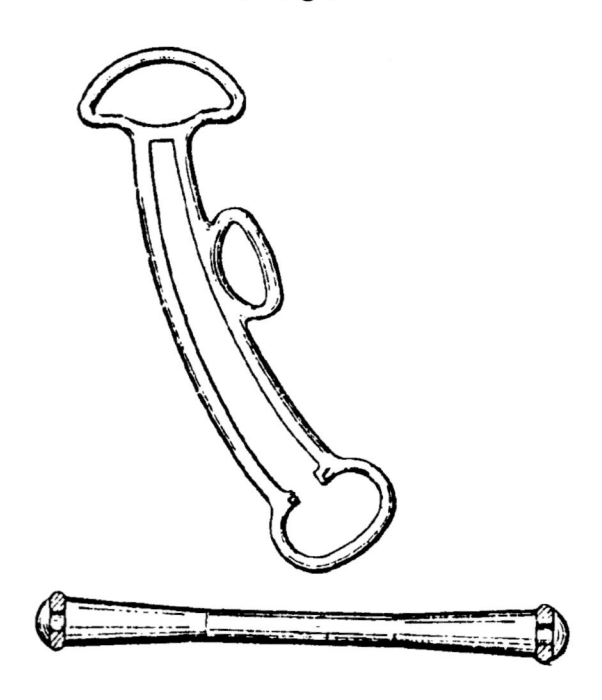

Fig. 24.2 Miller slotted-cheek bit.

Mills, Elton J., Long Pine, NE, Patent No. 1,054,593, Feb. 25, 1913 [Fig. 24.3]. A bar bit with relatively large rings to which the cheek-strap, nose-strap,

298

and reins are coupled in a normal manner. The curb-chain is attached between the rings with cold shut-links. Extra links provide an increase or decrease of the curb to correspond to the horse the bit is used on. To produce a harsher bit, the reins are attached to the smaller rings built into the cheek-rings as opposed to the position pictured.

placement of the bit and rein attachment.

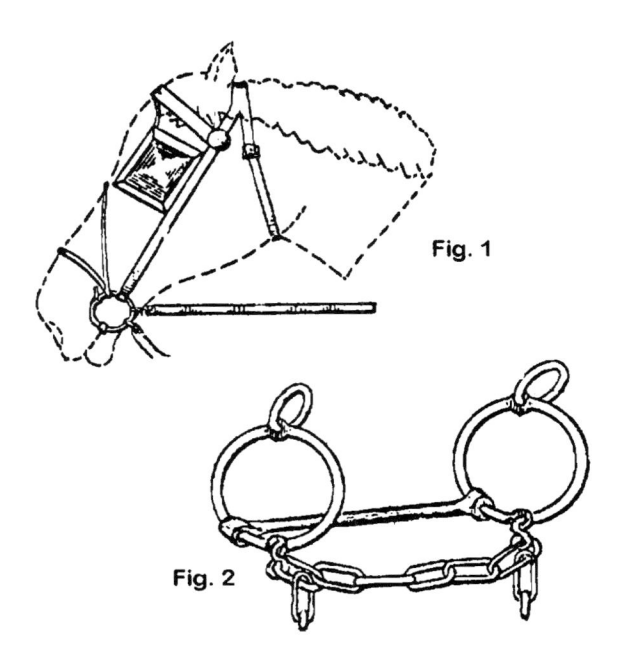

Fig. 1

Fig. 2

Fig. 24.3 Two views of Mills adjustable-curb snaffle bit.

Minnich, J. Hout, Tuscarawas, OH, Patent No. 87,864, Mar. 16, 1869 [Fig. 24.4]. The ends of the mouth-piece slide in the slots of the cheek-pieces. The reins are guided through brackets on the side of the cheek-pieces and attached to the ends of the mouth-piece. A pull of the reins causes the mouth-piece to ride up in the cheek-pieces.

Mitchell, William S., District of Columbia, Patent No. 209,911, Nov. 12, 1878 [Figs. 24.5 and 24.5a]. The fulcrum point of this bit can be over the nose or under the jaw, depending on the

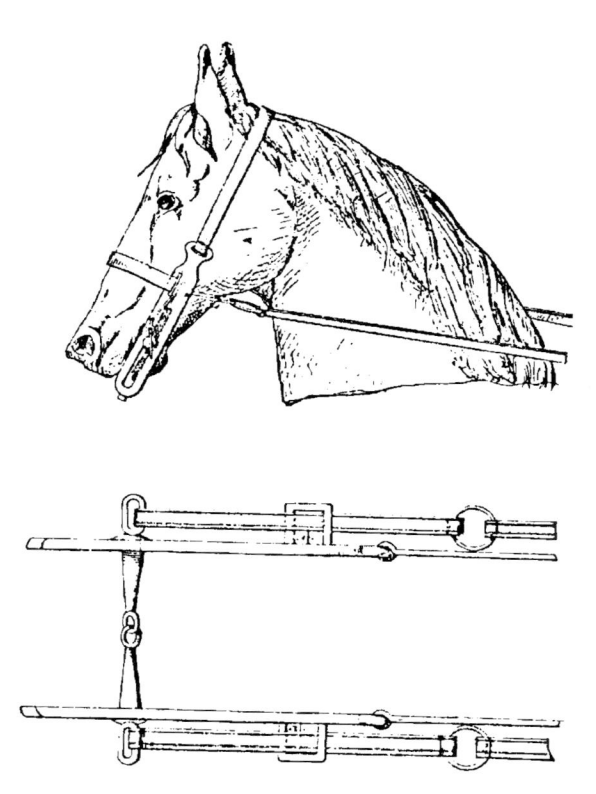

Fig. 24.4 Minnich slotted-cheek bit.

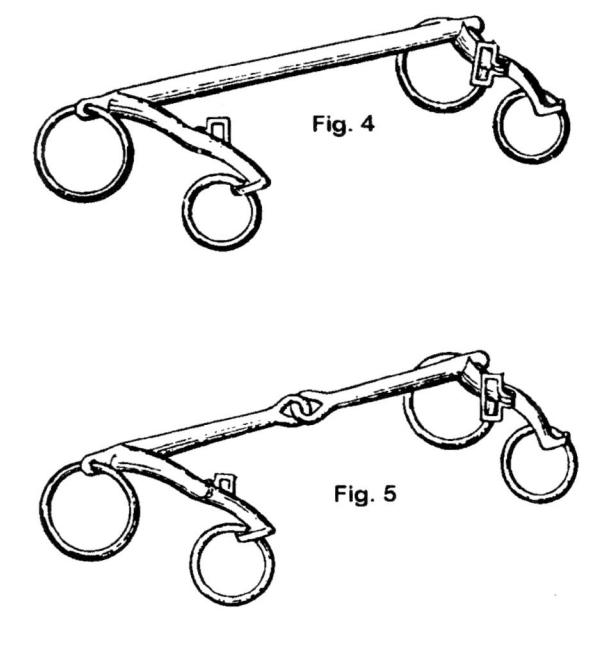

Fig. 4

Fig. 5

Fig. 24.5 Mitchell reversible curb bit.

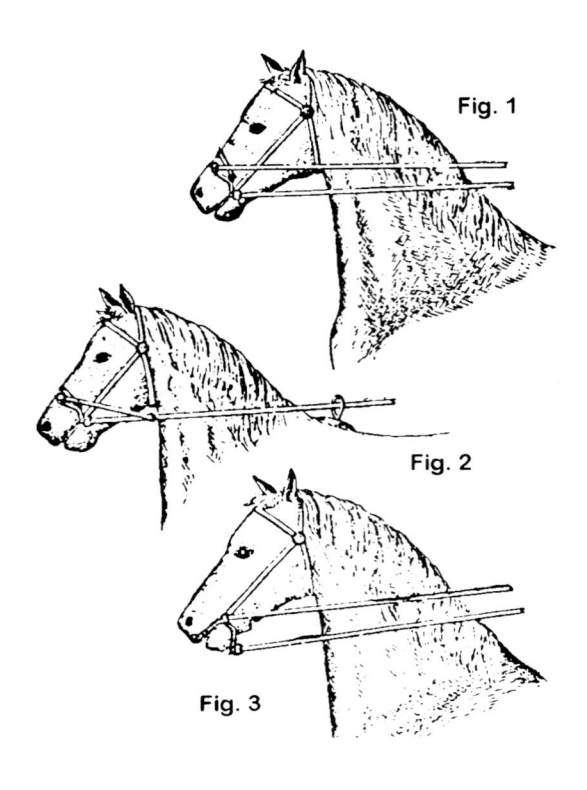

Fig. 24.5a Positions in which the Mitchell reversible bit can be used.

Mohawk Attachment: A straight bar covered with rubber-ball washers and upturned hooks on each end which fasten within the headstall rings of Pelham bits. An "S" hook fastens the Mohawk attachment to the middle of the Pelham mouth-piece [Fig. 24.6].

Monier, Fredrick, Newark, NJ, Patent No. 357,683, Feb. 27, 1887 [Fig. 24.7]. The opening in the port of the mouth-piece is designed to promote an increase in saliva to moisten the tongue of the horse.

Design Patent No. 17,158, Mar, 1, 1887 [Fig, 24.8]. Lady leg pattern adaptable to Fig. 24.7 and other bits.

Monier, Frederick C., New Britain, CT, Design Patent No. 39,664, Nov. 3, 1908 [Fig. 24.9] assigned to North and Judd Mfg. Co., Newark, NJ.

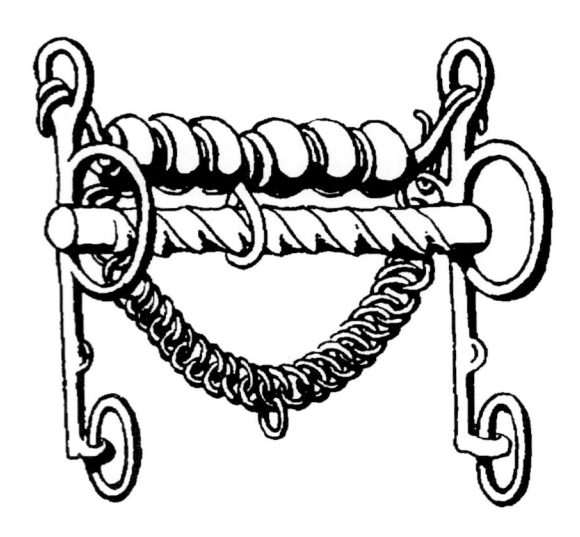

Fig. 24.6 Mohawk attachment on a Pelham bit.

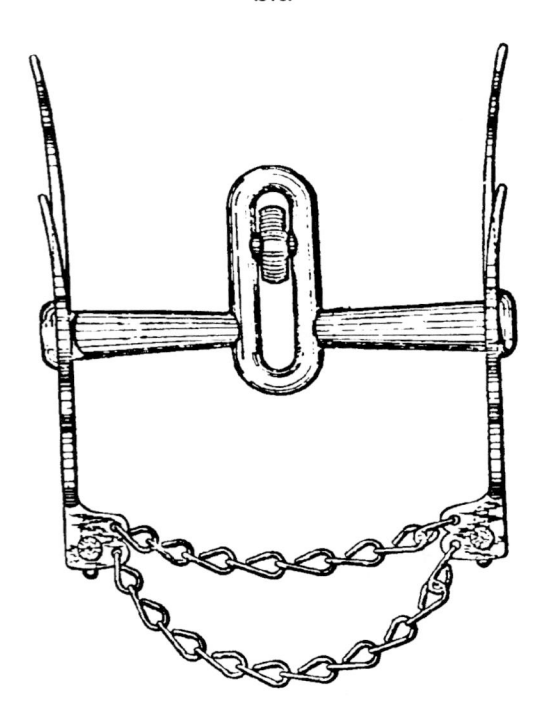

Fig. 24.7 Monier open oval-port bit.

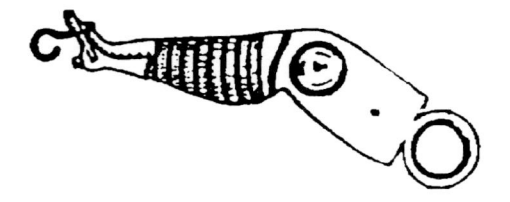

Fig. 24.8 Monier Lady Leg cheek-pattern design.

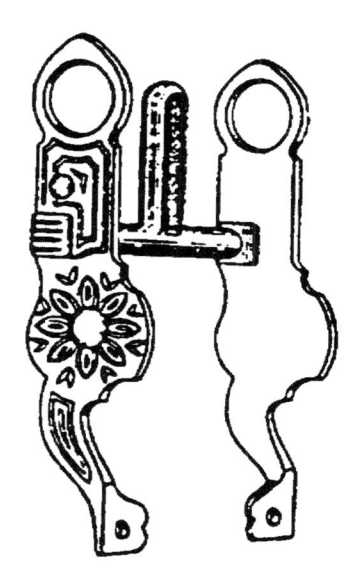

Fig. 24.9 Monier cheek-pattern design.

Design Patent No. 42,366, Mar. 26, 1912 [Fig. 24.10] assigned to North, and Judd Mfg. Co., Newark, NJ. This design is used for the basis of 5 different bosses and button adornments.

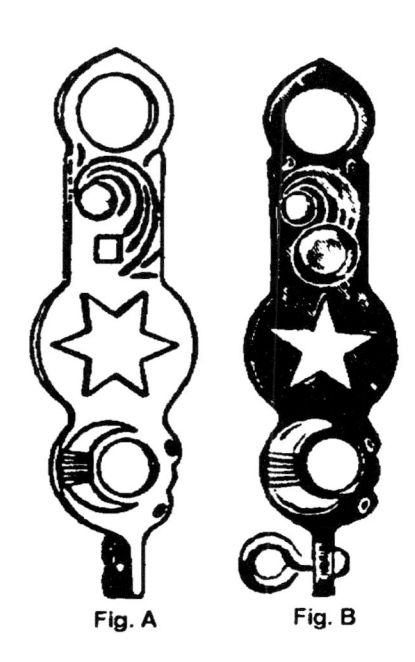

Fig. A   Fig. B

Fig. 24.10 Monier cheek-pattern design. Figure A sold by North and Judd. Fig. B sold by Buermann Mfg.Co. The major difference is the points of the star.

Design Pattern No. 44,771, Oct, 21, 1913 [Fig. 24.11] assigned to North and Judd Mfg. Co., Newark, NJ. The Indian-head boss is one of 5 patterns. A. Buermann Mfg. Co. also sold this design and style of bit.

Fig. 24.11 Monier cheek-pattern design.

Moorish Ring Bit: See Chapter 29, Ring Bits.

Morral: Spanish term for a nose-bag.

Morrey Overcheck: See Chapter 9, Fig. 9.11.

Morrisey, James, West Islip, NY, Patent No. 378,970, Mar. 6, 1888 [Fig. 24.12]. A device with a forked bit to use with an ordinary bit for only a short time. It is placed in the mouth outside of the regular snaffle, with the lower end attached to the traces or lower breast-strap or the saddle girth in riding horses.

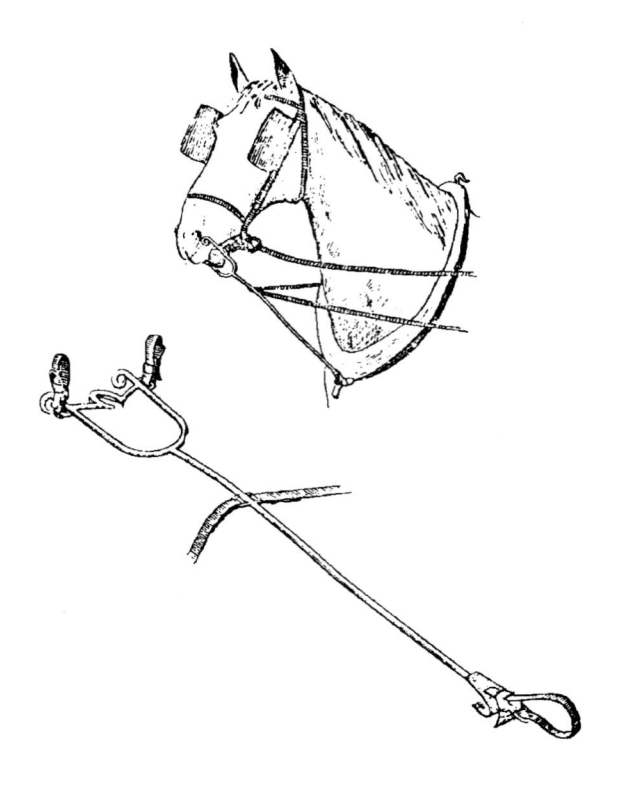

Fig. 24.12 Morrisey control device.

Moss, Martin D. and Archie Q., Elberton, GA, Patent No. 970,083, Sep. 13, 1910 [Fig. 24.13]. The twisted mouthpiece bit has two double links attached to the end of the bit and through the headstall ring on the opposite end, crossing under the chin when the bit is placed in the horse's mouth. A rein pull tightens the bit and grips the under jaw.

Mouth: Often used as a term for mouth-piece.

Mouth Cover: See Chapter 14, Fig. 14.5.

Mouth Gage: A devise used to measure the mouth of a horse to determine correct size of bit to use. See Chapter 4, Fig. 4.1.

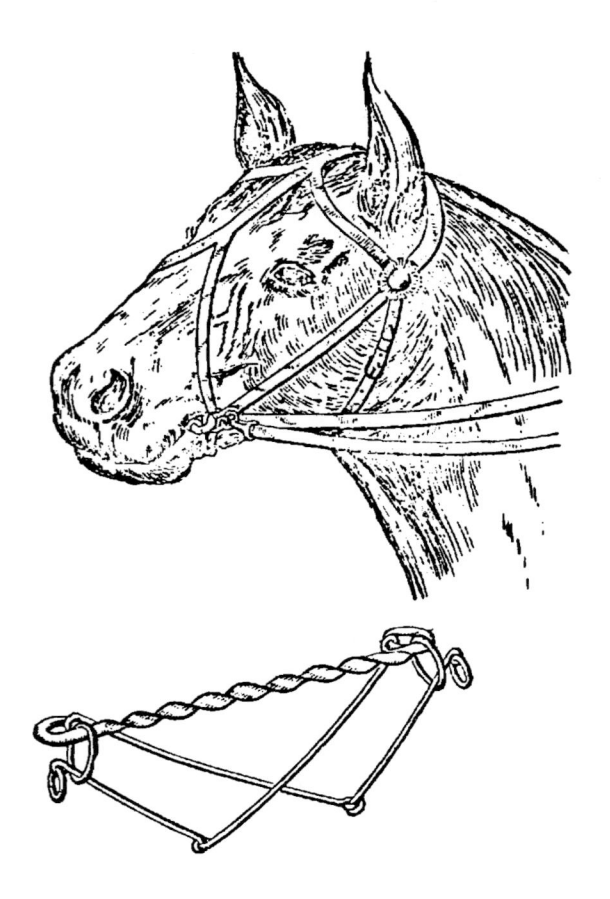

Fig. 24.13 Moss curb bit.

Mouthing Bit: A bit with a small metal object suspended from the mouthpiece to give a young horse being trained something to do with the object newly placed in its mouth and produce saliva to keep the mouth moist. A variety of shapes and designs have been used over the years. The most common are illustrated in Figs. 24.14 to 24.23. The suspended objects are usually elongated tear-shapes and are referred to as "players."

Fig. 24.14 Triple player mouthing bit.

Fig. 24.15 Triple player mouthing bit.

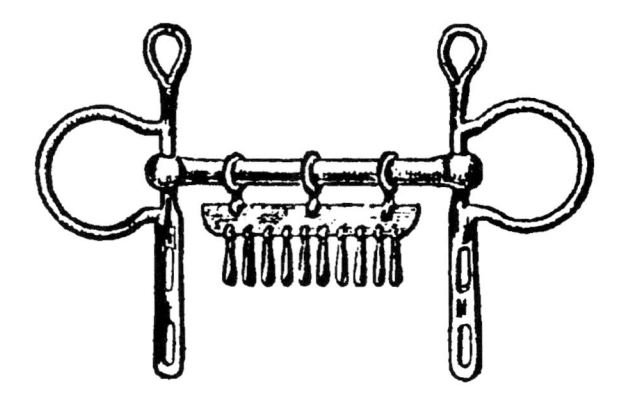

Fig. 24.16 Loose-cheek driving bit with players.

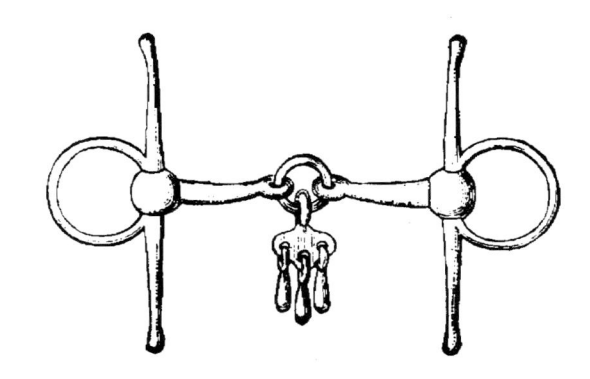

Fig. 24.17 Full-cheek broken-mouth player bit.

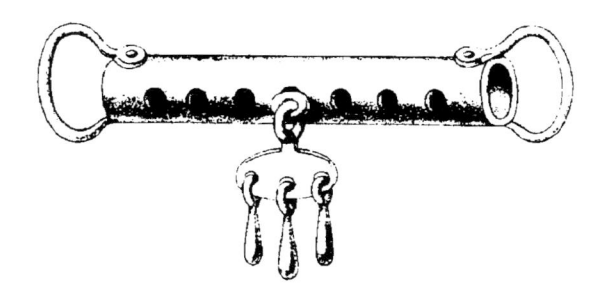

Fig. 24.18 Mouthing bit for "Wind-suckers."

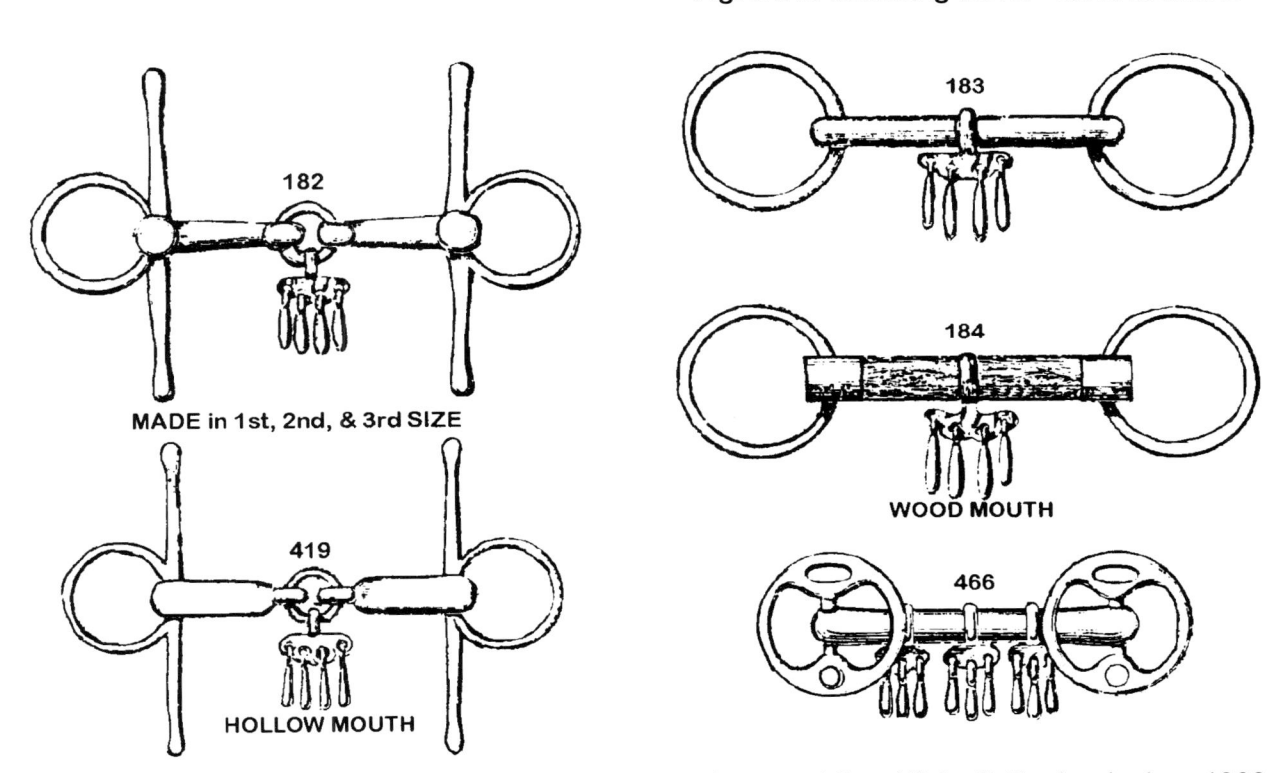

182
MADE in 1st, 2nd, & 3rd SIZE

419
HOLLOW MOUTH

183

184
WOOD MOUTH

466

Fig. 24.19 Mouthing bits with players from John Dewsbury and Son, Walsall, England, circa 1900.

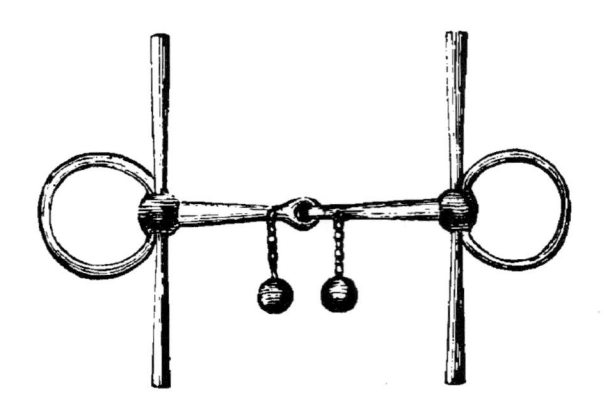

Fig. 24.20 Full-cheek broken-mouth bit with balls attached. The bit is used as a mouthing bit and as a bit to prevent tongue lolling.

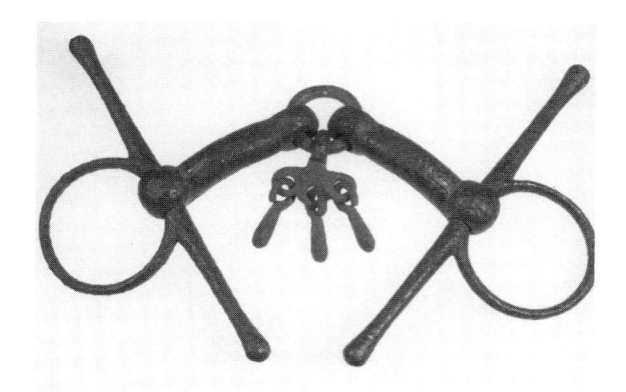

Fig. 24.21 A full-cheek mouthing bit with heavy cannons. The six-inch mouth would make it a size to use on large draft horses.

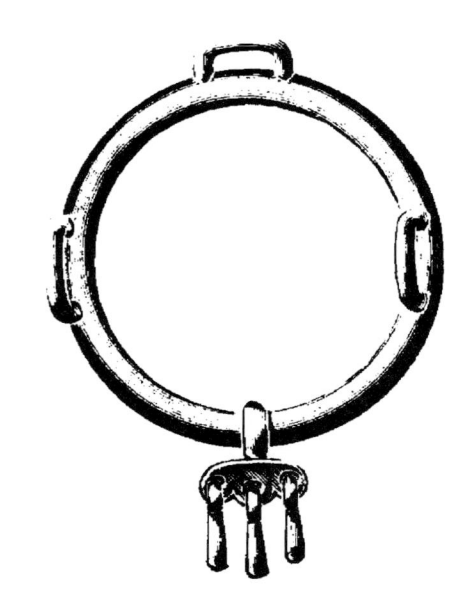

Fig. 24.23 Heavy mouthing bit with three sets of players.

CHAPTER TWENTY-FIVE
Mouth-piece

A mouth-piece is the portion of the bridle bit which is carried within the mouth of the horse. See diagram in Chapter 1.

Arch Mouth: An exaggerated upward curve to the mouth-piece [Fig. 25.0].

Fig.25.0 An Arch-mouth bit.

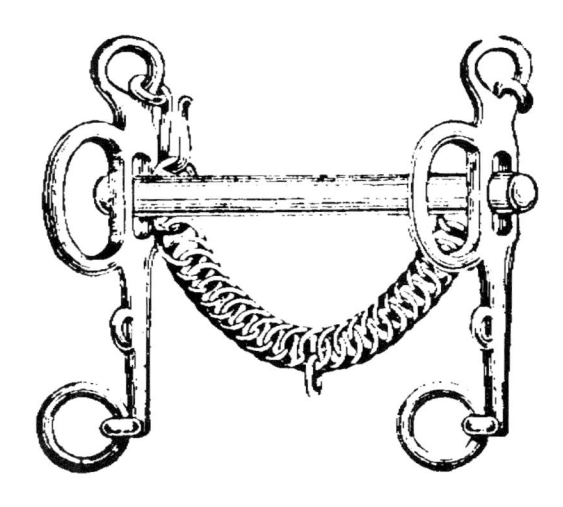

Fig. 25.1 Banbury-mouth Pelham bit.

Fig. 25.2 Bicycle-chain-mouth bit.

Fig. 25.3 A broken-mouth bit.

Banbury Mouth: The mouth-piece has the freedom to move in the short slot within the cheek-piece [Fig. 25.1].

Bar Mouth: A bit with a straight unjointed mouth-piece.

Bicycle-chain Mouth: A linked mouth-piece that resembles the links of a bicycle chain [Fig 25.2].

Broken Mouth: A mouth-piece with a joint, usually in the center [Fig. 25.3].

Butterfly Mouth: A jointed mouth with snaps on each end. Used as an overcheck bit [Fig. 25.4].

Fig. 24.4 Butterfly mouth.

Cambridge Mouth: A mouth-piece with a moderate center port that thins at the top of the port [Fig. 25.5].

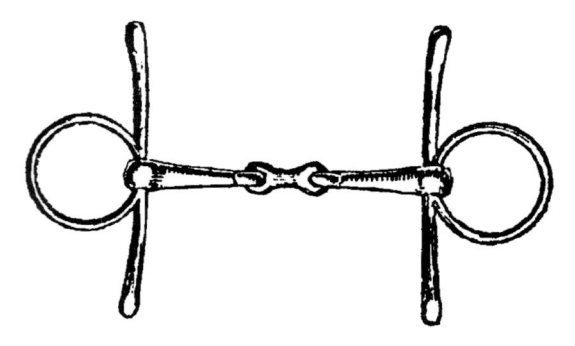

Fig. 25.6 A bit with a center link.

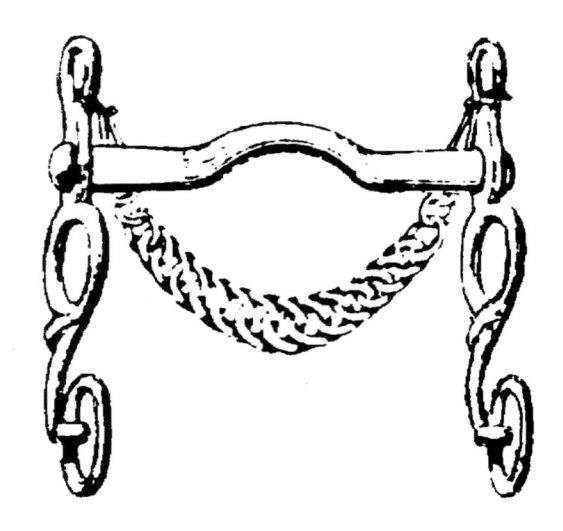

Fig. 25.5 Cambridge mouth bit.

Centaur Mouth: A flexible rubber mouth-piece associated with bits made in England [Fig. 25.7].

Center-link Mouth: A broken-mouth bit with a link or ring that combines the two cannons of the mouth-piece [Fig. 25.6].

Chain Mouth: A mouth-piece made of small chain. Made in forged steel and Star Steel Silver by A. Buermann Mfg. Co. [Fig. 25.8].

Chain-mouth Snaffle: A snaffle bit with a chain mouth [Fig. 25.9].

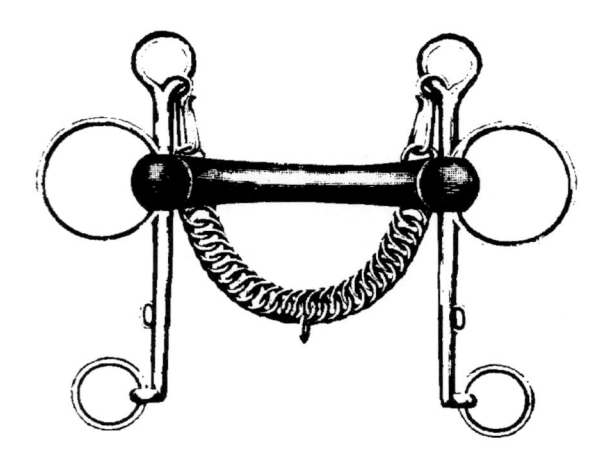

Fig. 25.7 A bit with a centaur mouth of flexible rubber.

Fig. 25.8 A chain-mouth bit.

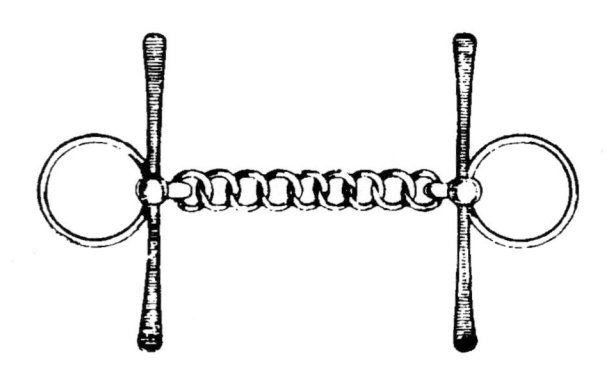

Fig. 25.9 Chain-mouth snaffle bit.

Circassian Mouth: See Chapter 6, Fig. 6.22.

Crescendo-mouth Bit: see Chapter 6. Fig. 6.54.

Cross Bar: A term for the mouth-piece.

Double Mouth: A bit with two mouth-pieces [Fig. 25.10].

Fig. 25.10 A jointed double-mouth bit.

Dr. Bristol Mouth: A mouth-piece with a flat center link [Fig. 25.11].

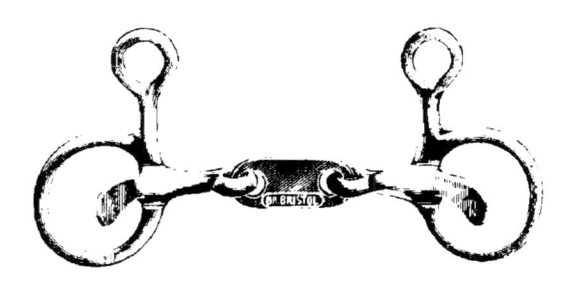

Fig. 25.11 A horned hanging-cheek snaffle with a Dr. Bristol mouth-piece.

Egg-link Mouth: A bit with an oval-shaped link in the center of the mouth-piece [Fig. 25.12].

Egg-roller Mouth: A bit with oval rollers on the cannons of the mouth-piece [Fig. 25.13].

Figure-8 Link Mouth: A mouth-piece with a figure 8 link in the center [Fig. 25.14].

Fig. 25.12 A bit with an egg-link mouth-piece.

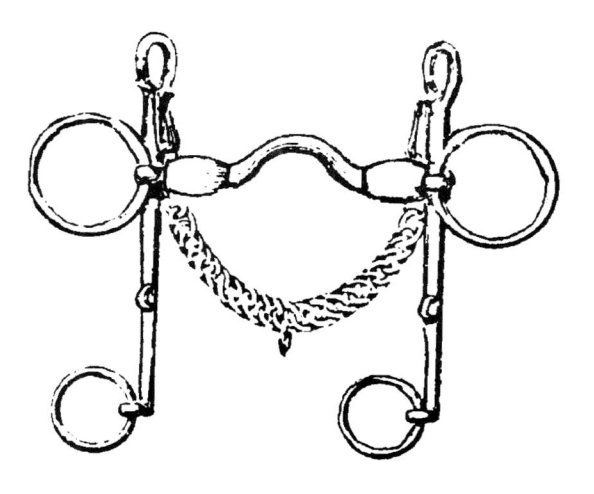

Fig. 25.13 A bit with an egg-roller mouth.

Fishback Mouth: A bit with a triangular mouth-piece which has one sharp edge. See Chapter 11, Fig. 11.17.

Fisher Mouth: A mouth-piece with three sections, each with a button or collar. See Chapter 11, Fig. 11.19.

Frog Mouth: Modern term for a Segundo mouth-piece. See Segundo.

Fig. 25.14 A bit with a figure-8 link mouth-piece.

Furlong Mouth: A design patent of a mouth-piece with enlarged grooves circling the outer portion of the mouth-piece. See Chapter 11, Fig. 11.34.

Greenwood Mouth: A mouth-piece with a wide open port. The curve of the top conforms to the palate of the horse's mouth and the open port allows for tongue room [Fig. 25.15].

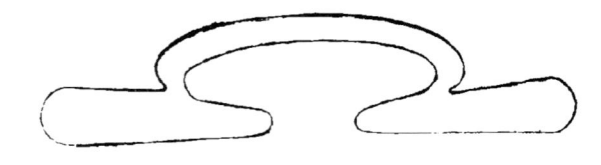

Fig. 25.15 Greenwood mouth.

Gridiron Mouth: See Chapter 5, Fig. 5.47.

Half-breed Mouth: A vertical extension from the mouth-piece usually slotted which contains a cricket or roller in the slot [Fig. 25.16].

Fig. 25.16 A bit with a half-breed mouth.

Harry Hightower Mouth: A bit with a snaffle bit linked to the arches of the ported driving bit [Fig. 25.17].

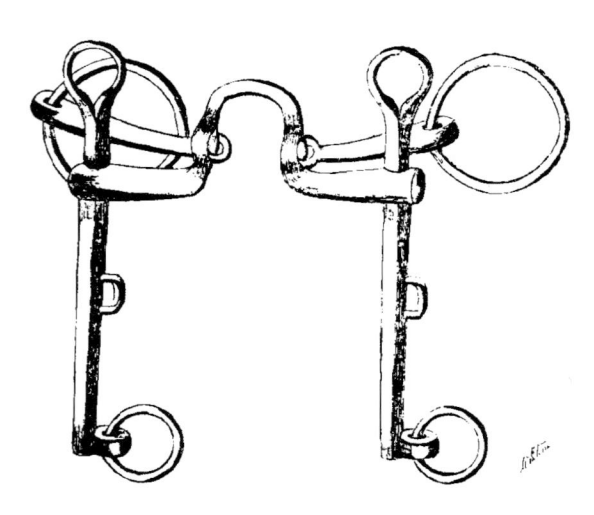

Fig. 25.17 Harry Hightower mouth-piece.

Hartwell Mouth: A mouth-piece with a small port much like a Cambridge mouth. Supplied in a variety of metals and centaur or flexible rubber mouth [Fig. 25.18].

308

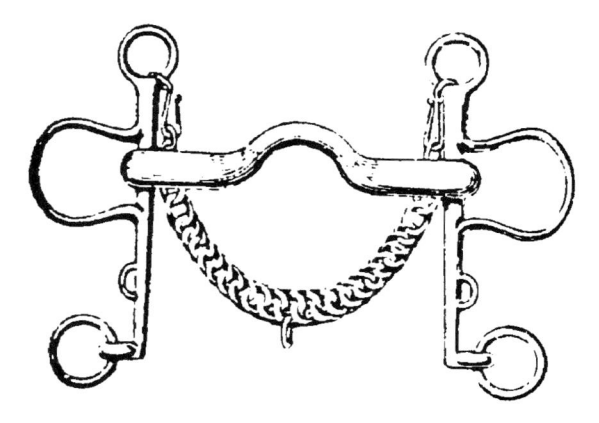

Fig. 25.18 A bit with a Hartwell mouth.

Hinged-mouth Bit: A bit with a hinged joint in the center of the mouth-piece [Fig. 25.19].

Fig. 25.19 Hinged-mouth bit. Robert Maclin collection.

Hollow Mouth: A mouth-piece built with a large diameter designed to be light in weight such as that attributed to German bits. Some bits designed to stop "wind-sucking" are hollow with holes drilled to prevent the horse from the vice of ingesting air.

Hooded Mouth: A mouth-piece with a hood or cover over the port surface nearest the roof of the horse's mouth. The hoods are usually made of copper.

Howlett Mouth: A mouth-piece with a port similar to the Cambridge mouth.

Jointed Mouth: See Figure 25.3.

Inverted Port Mouth: A bit with the mouth-piece inverted to the normal position [Fig. 25.20].

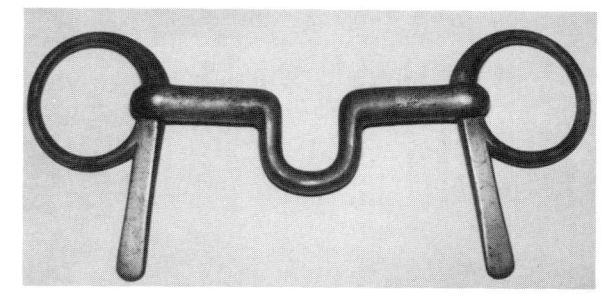

Fig. 25.20 A half-cheek snaffle with an inverted ported mouth.

Jolan Bastard Mouth: A mouth-piece designed and patented by Robert M. Hall, King City, CA [Fig. 25.21].

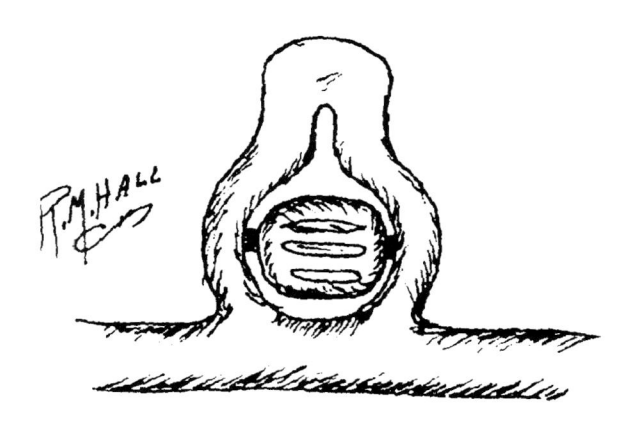

Fig. 25.21 Jolan Bastard mouth.

Kangaroo: A name for the metal used by John Dewsbury and Son and later, James Cotterell & Sons Ltd, Walsall, England, and bits made by these companies [Fig. 25.22].

Leather Mouth: A mouth-piece composed of several layers of leather sewn together to form the mouth or a wire, bar or chain mouth covered with leather. Commonly classified as a humane bit.

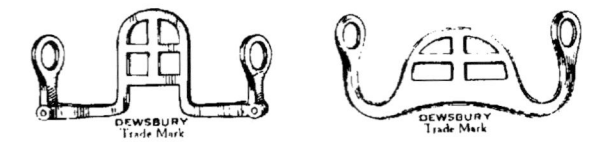

Fig. 25.22 Two mouth-pieces of Kangaroo metal.

Log Bit: A solid, large mouth-piece usually used on heavy draft horses [Fig. 25.23].

Fig. 25.23 A log bit.

Magenis Mouth: A mouth-piece designed with rollers built into each of the cannons [Fig. 25.24].

Fig. 25.24 Magenis-mouth snaffle bit.

Middle Link Mouth: See Fig. 25.6.

Mullen Mouth: A mouth-piece with a slight arch and usually thicker in horizontal diameter than vertical [Fig. 25.25].

Fig. 25.25 Mullen mouth.

Peter's Bit Mouth: A style of jointed mouth-piece of early 1800's in England [Fig. 25.26].

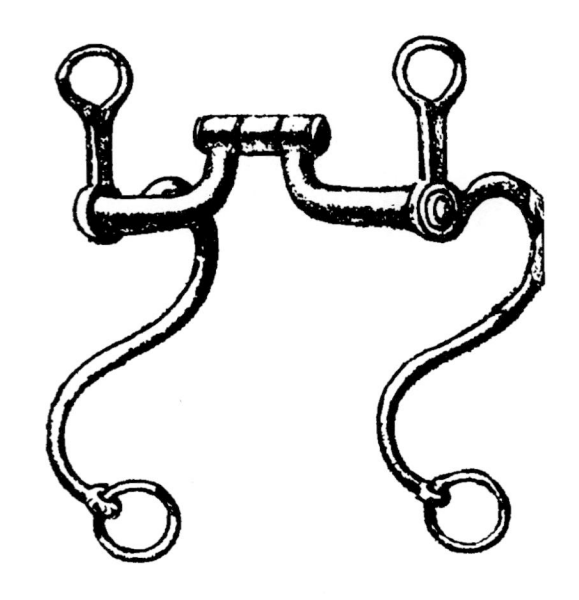

Fig. 25.26 Peter's jointed-mouth bit.

Plate Mouth: See Chapter 5, Fig. 5.21.

Reverse Arch: A mouth-piece like Fig. 25.0 except the arch is directed downward in the mouth as opposed to upward and laying on the tongue.

Roller Mouth: A mouth-piece with copper or other type of metal rollers on and around the cannons of the mouth-piece [Fig. 25.27].

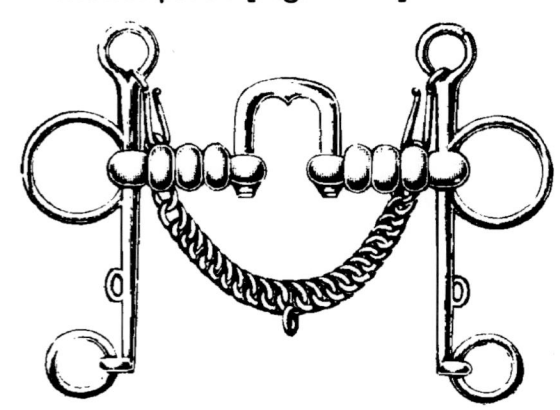

Fig. 25.27 A Hanoverian Pelham with rollers on the cannons and a swing port.

Rollers in Mouth: A mouth-piece with small wheels built into the mouth-piece [Fig. 25.28].

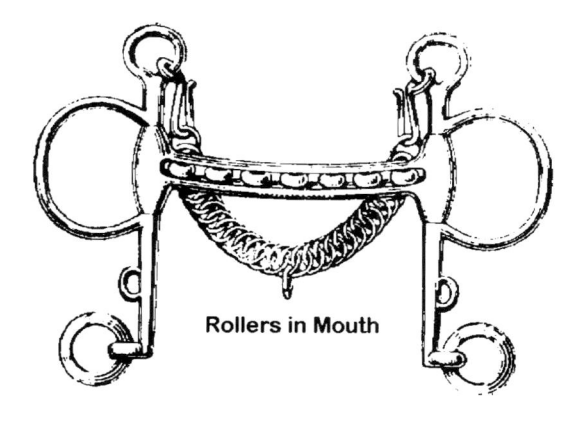

Fig. 25.28 A bit with rollers in the mouth-piece.

Roy Cooper Mouth: A series of bits with this mouth-piece named after World Champion Calf Roper Roy Cooper [Fig.25.29]. Made by Seminole Bit and Spur, Inc., Seminole, TX.

Fig. 25.29 Roy Cooper "Long Shank" bit.

Rubber Mouth: A flexible rubber or vulcanite mouth-piece that can be applied in the manufacture of most snaffle and driving bits [Fig. 25.30].

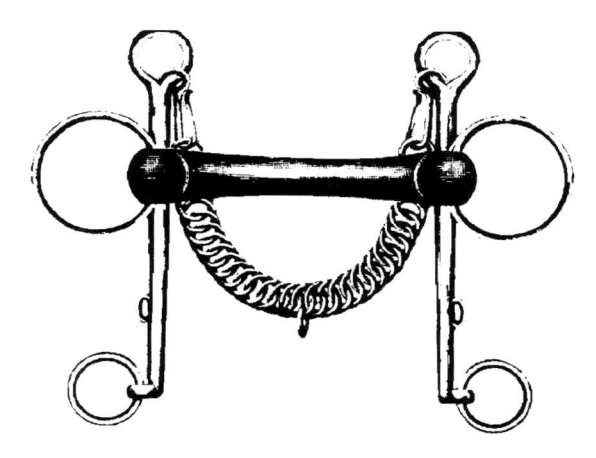

Fig. 25.30 A rubber-mouth Pelham bit.

S. M. Polo Mouth: A bit with a plate-like mouth-piece and a curb in the center of the plate. The slots in the cheek-pieces allow the cheek-pieces to move and the mouth-piece to lay flat in the mouth and never change [Fig. 25.33].

Fig. 25.31 S. M. Polo flat-mouth bit.

Scissor Mouth: See Chapter 8, Fig. 8.15.

Segundo Mouth: A mouth-piece with an oval-shaped port that tilts to the front of the bit [Fig. 25.32]. See Chapter 30, Segundo.

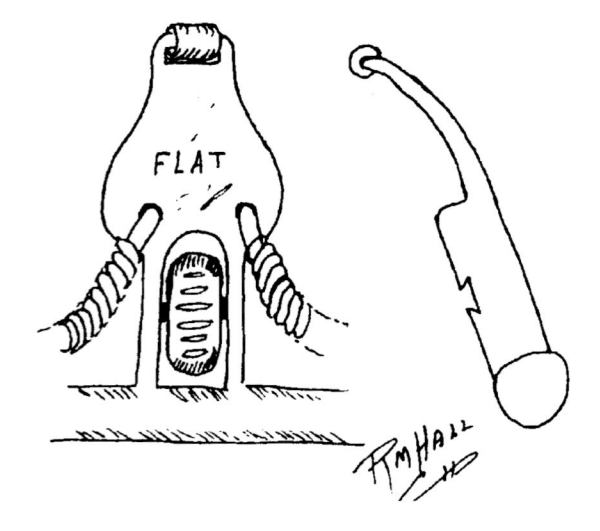

Fig. 25.33 Spade bit. Drawing by Robert Hall, Loriner, King City, CA.

Spoon Spade: A spade mouth that ends in a rounded smooth surface on the upper end of the spade [Fig. 25.34].

Fig. 25.31 A hunting bit with a Segundo mouth-piece.

Sliding Mouth: See Chapter 5, Fig. 5.25 and Chapter 6, Fig. 6.53.

Spade Mouth: A mouth-piece with a large port of three inches or more with braces on each side extending to the cheek-pieces. The spade may be copper coated or have a small copper roller in the extreme tip. Associated with western-style bits [Fig. 25.33].

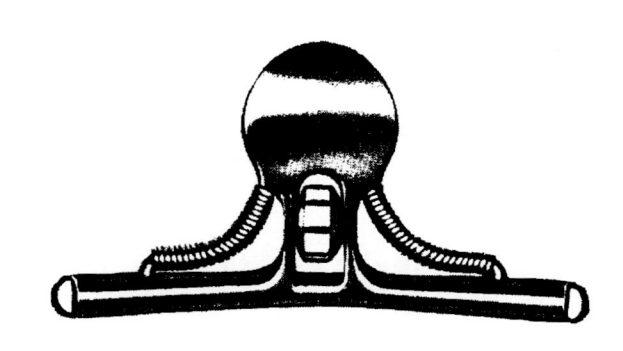

Fig. 25.34 Spoon Spade mouth.

Taper Mouth: A mouth-piece which is much larger in diameter at the cheek-pieces than at the center joint [Fig. 25.35].

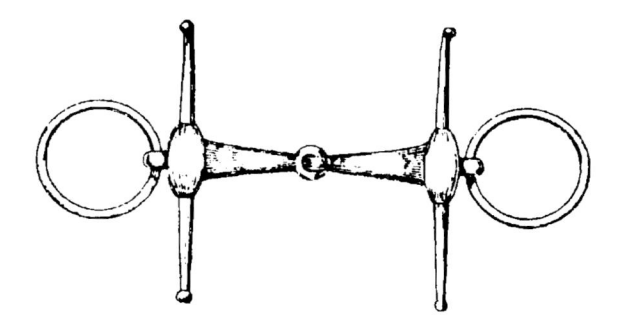

Fig. 25.35 A Taper-mouth snaffle bit.

Tongue-plate Mouth: A double plate that rotates on the solid mouth-piece [Fig. 25.36].

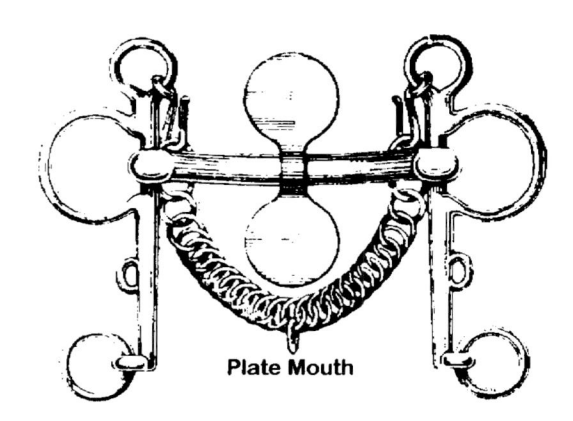

Fig. 25.36 Tongue-plate mouth.

Twisted-bar Mouth: A stiff or unbroken mouth-piece with a spiral twist to cause a roughness to the mouth-piece [Fig. 25.37].

Fig. 25.37 Twisted-mouth Wilson bit.

Twisted, Jointed Mouth: A mouth-piece that is twisted and jointed [Fig. 25.38].

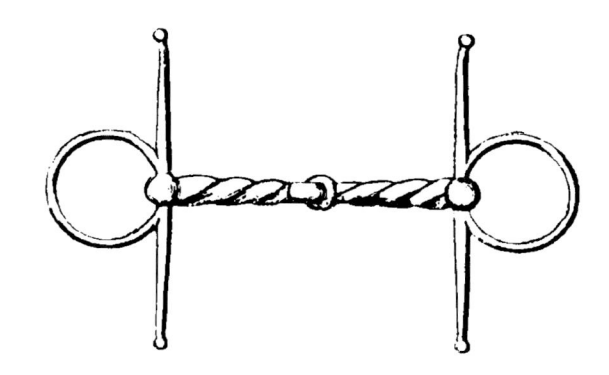

Fig. 25.38 Twisted jointed-mouth bit.

Twisted Double-jointed Mouth: Two twisted, jointed mouth-pieces, almost always with offsetting joints to give a pantograph effect on the mouth of the horse [Fig. 25.39].

Fig. 25.39 Twisted double-jointed-mouth snaffle bit.

Twisted-wire Jointed Mouth: A mouth-piece made with a heavy twisted wire and jointed [Fig. 25.40].

313

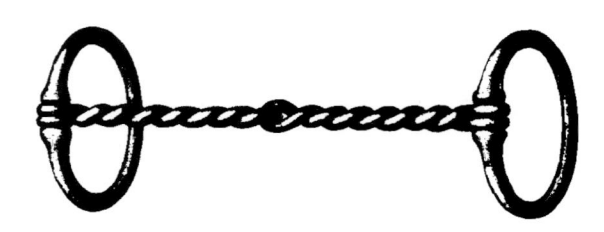

Fig. 25.40 Twisted-wire jointed mouth.

Twisted Double-wire Jointed Mouth: A mouth-piece having two twisted-wire jointed pieces [Fig. 25.41].

Fig. 25.41 Twisted double-wire jointed mouth.

Twisted-wire Bar Mouth: A straight single twisted-wire mouth-piece [Fig. 25.42].

Fig. 25.42 Twisted-wire bar mouth.

Viqueno Mouth: An old mouth-piece that originated in India. The name translates into "One Hump" [Fig. 25.43]. From *How to Make Bits and Spurs,* by Robert Hall, King City, CA.

Fig. 25.43 Viqueno mouth-piece.

Wellington Mouth: A multiple jointed mouth-piece that resembles a bicycle-chain mouth [Fig. 25.44].

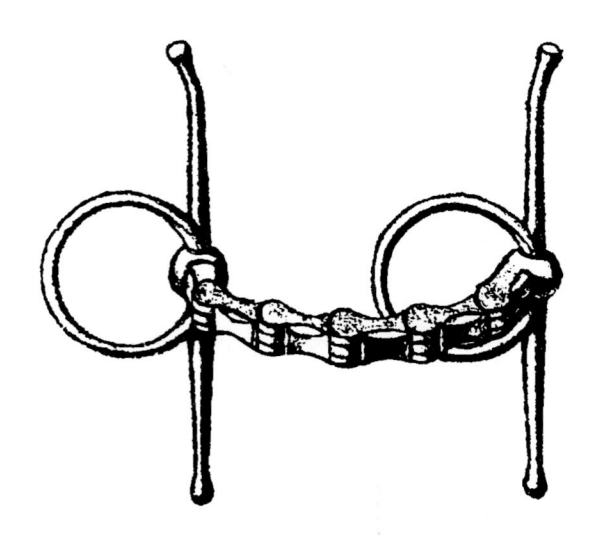

Fig. 25.44 Wellington-mouth bit.

Wood Mouth: See Chapter 27, Kerro Pattern, Fig. 27.14.

Mouth-piece Ends:

The end of the mouth-piece where it attaches to the cheek-piece. Sometimes referred to as the head of the mouth-piece.

Barrel Head End: A wide sturdy end with a loose cheek bit [Fig. 25.45].

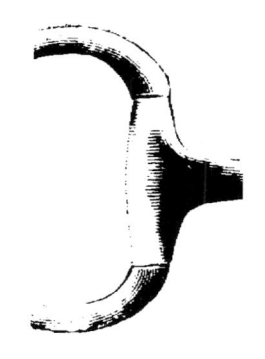

Fig. 25.45 Barrel Head end.

Closed End: A solid end into which a hole has been cast or drilled to accept the cheek-piece [Figs. 25.46 and 25.46a].

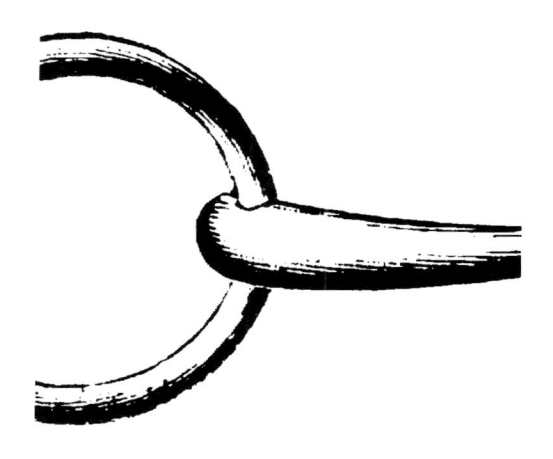

Fig. 25.46 Closed end.

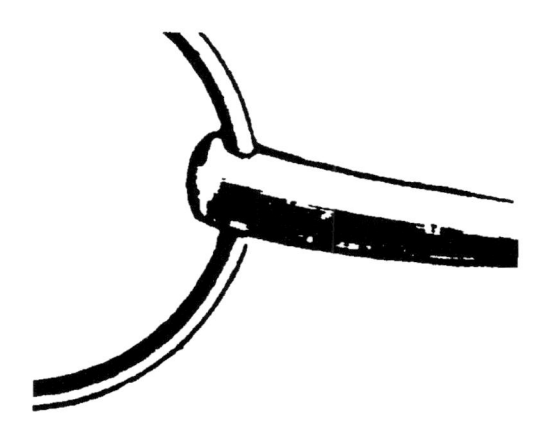

Fig. 25.46a Closed end.

Diamond Head: The end of the mouth-piece is diamond shaped [Fig. 25.47].

Fig. 25.47 Diamond head.

Egg-butt End: A wide reinforced strong end for a loose ring cheek-piece [Fig. 25.48].

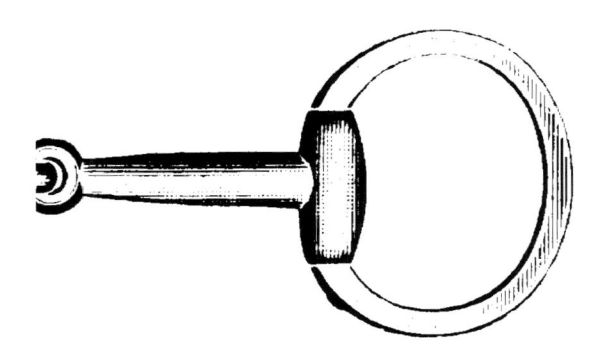

Fig. 25.48 Egg-butt end.

English Head: A small rounded end of the mouth-piece [Fig. 25.49].

Fig. 25.49 English Head.

Fish-eye End: An end that has an open space around it to prevent the cheek-piece from binding or pinching the lips [Fig. 25.50].

Fig. 25.50 Fish-eye end.

Flat End: The mouth-piece end is flattened to accommodate the cheekring [Fig. 25.51].

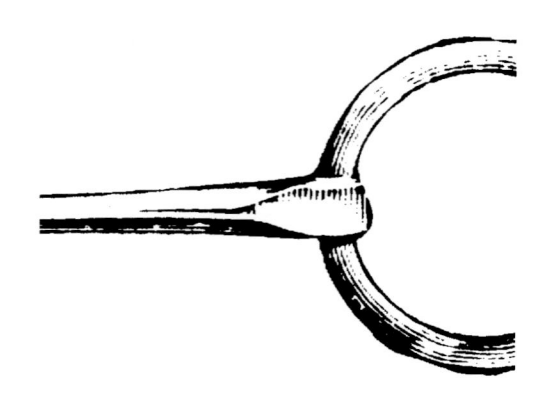

Fig. 25.51 Flat end.

Hinged End: A mouth-piece end associated with a linked or chain mouth in which the last link actually acts as a hinge [Fig. 25.52].

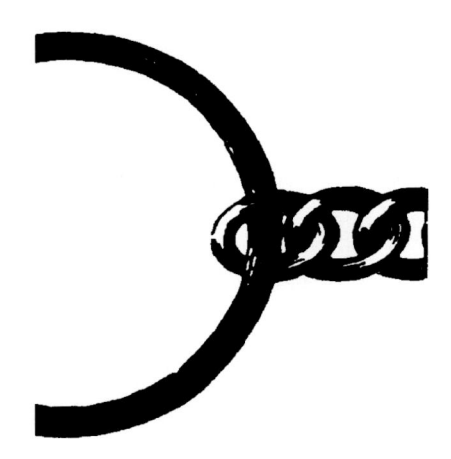

Fig. 25.52 Hinged end.

Open End: A mouth-piece end that is forged or cast with an open end which is later wrapped around the cheek-piece and closed [Fig. 25.53].

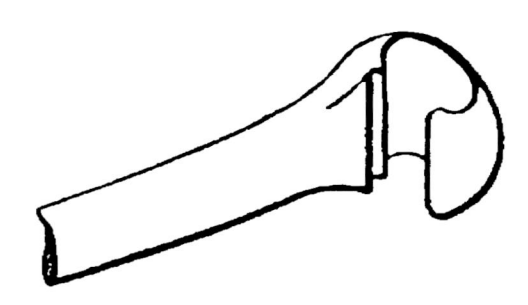

Fig. 25.53 Open end.

Round End: An enlarged version of the English Head. Seen on large diameter straight mouths such as the Log bit used on draft horses.

T-head End: A mouth-piece end that joins with the cheek-piece to form a "T" [Fig. 25.54].

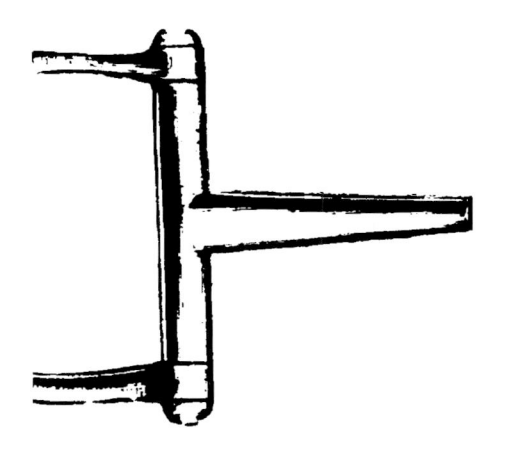

Fig. 25.54 T-head end.

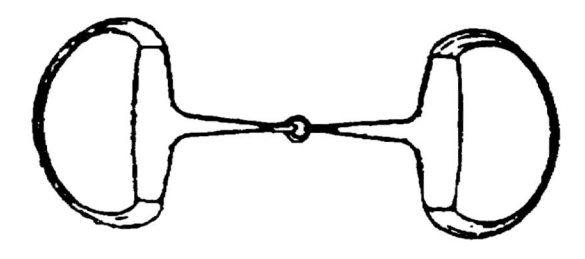

Fig. 25.55 Turton end.

Turton End: A reinforced elongated end such as used on a Fulmer full-cheek snaffle [Fig. 25.55]. Patent No. 461,514, Oct.20, 1891, by Benjamin Turton, Newark, NJ.

The Barrel Head, Egg-butt, and the Turton End are quite similar and often interchanged by some manufacturers. The Turton end is not as heavy and usually longer that the others.

The codfish lays a million eggs,
The modest hen but one,
But the codfish doesn't cackle
To inform you what she's done.
And so we spurn the codfish egg,
The helpful hen's we prize,
Which indicates to thoughful minds
it pays to advertise.

From Crockett Bit & Spur Catalog No. 12.

CHAPTER TWENTY-SIX
Mule to Pelham

Mule Port Bit: A heavy-cheeked curb bit that has been successful when used on mules [Fig. 26.0].

Fig. 26.0 Mule Port Bit.

Mule Snaffle Bit: A full-cheek snaffle bit sold by John Dewsbury and Son, Walsall, England, circa 1900 [Fig. 26.1].

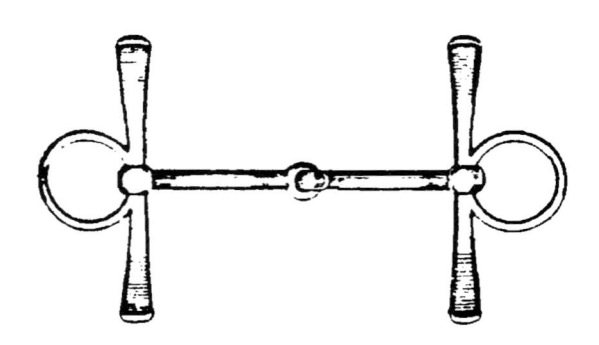

Fig. 26.1 Mule snaffle bit.

Mullen, Henry W., New Decatur, AL, Patent No. 1,107,223, Aug.11, 1914 [Fig. 26.2]. A double-mouth bit with the linked bar acting as a curb. It is placed under the chin and pivots on pins in a middle bar within the open cheek-pieces.

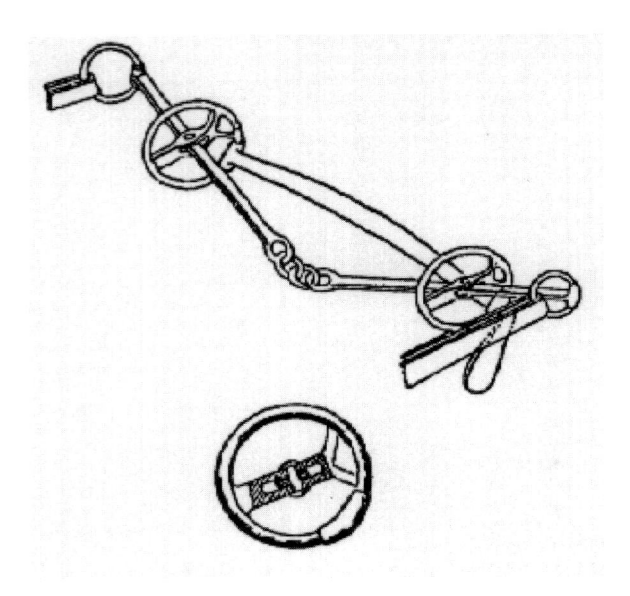

Fig. 26.2 Mullen bit with built-in curb.

Muntz, Oliver H., Pittsburg, PA, Patent No. 506,526, Oct. 10, 1893 [Fig. 26.3]. The chin strap can be attached to check-reins to hold up the horse's head.

Murphy, John, Springfield, IL, Patent No. 297,944, Apr. 29, 1884 [Fig. 26.4]. A method of uniting the cheek-piece to the mouth-piece with a screw pin. Wear on the hinged surfaces can be taken up. The hinge pin can be replaced without removing the bridle or reins from the cheek-ring.

Muscovy Bit: An anti-rear or Chifney bit used in training colts [Fig. 26.5]. See Chapter 5, Fig. 5.80.

Muzzle Bit: A bit used to prevent the horse from biting others and eating while being in the harness [Fig. 26.6]. See Chapter 30. Fig. 30.20 and Chapter 33, Fig. 33.25.

318

Fig. 1.

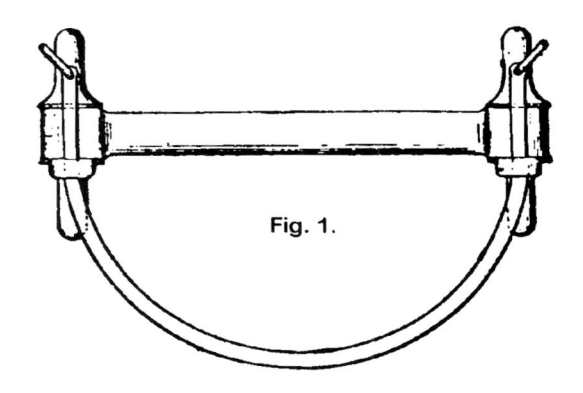

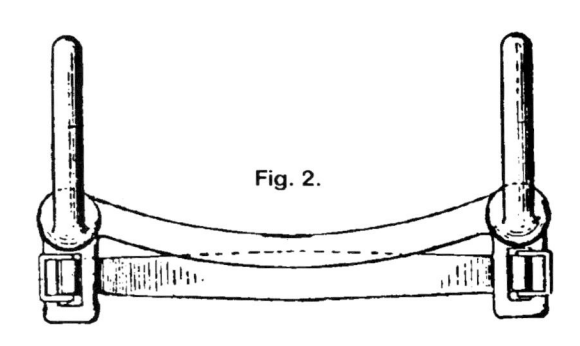

Fig. 2.

Fig. 26.3 Muntz overcheck curb bit.

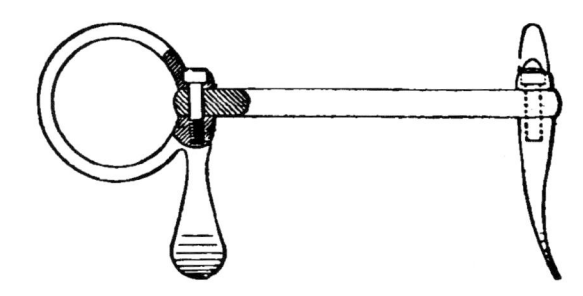

Fig. 26.4 Murphy construction method.

Fig. 26.5 Muscovy bit.

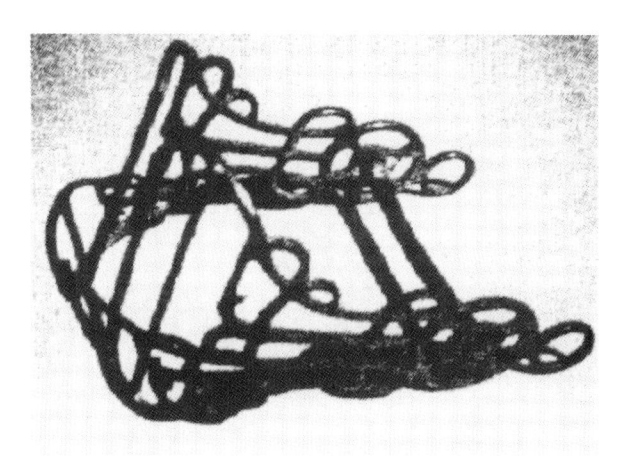

Fig. 26.6 Muzzle bit.

Fig. 26.7 Myers Dee snaffle.

Myers Dee-cheek Snaffle: A "D" cheek bit with a thin broken mouth-piece [Fig. 26.7].

Nagbut Snaffle: A tongue lolling bit with the tongue link at a 90 degree angle to the mouth-piece [Fig. 26.8].

Narrow Cheek Bit: A full-cheek bit with narrow extensions from the mouth-piece connection. See Chapter 31.

319

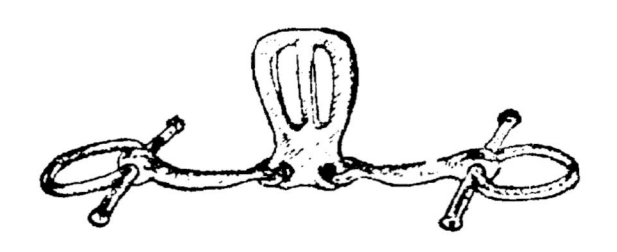

Fig, 26.8 Nagbut snaffle.

Narrow Half-cheek Snaffle: A half-cheek bit with a narrow extension of the cheek-piece. See Chapter 31.

Nash, Duane H., Millington, NJ, Patent No. 568,097, Sep, 22, 1896 [Fig. 26.9]. A pulley bit which acts as a gag bit.

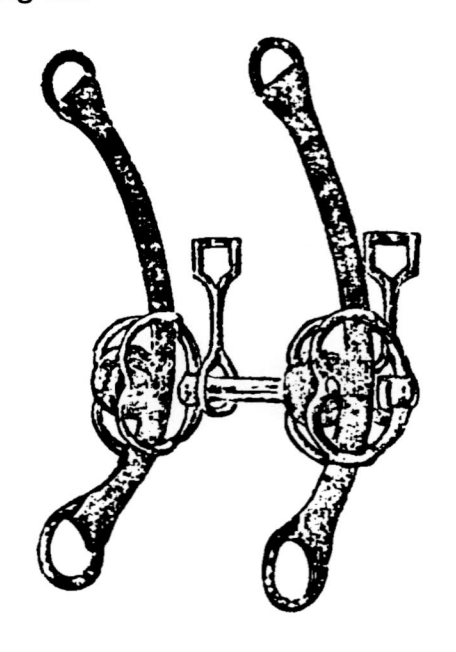

Fig. 26.9 Nash pulley bit.

Nazor, Arthur U., Shelby, OH, Patent No. 978,051, Dec. 6, 1910 [Fig. 26.10]. A bit with a mouth-piece formed of two portions swiveled together so as to have a rotary movement; a lug on each portion, and a lever on the outer ends of each portion project in an opposite direction from the lug and are adapted to receive the rein. The lug will rotate as it is raised and moves up the side of the roof of the mouth where it is uncomfortable for the horse.

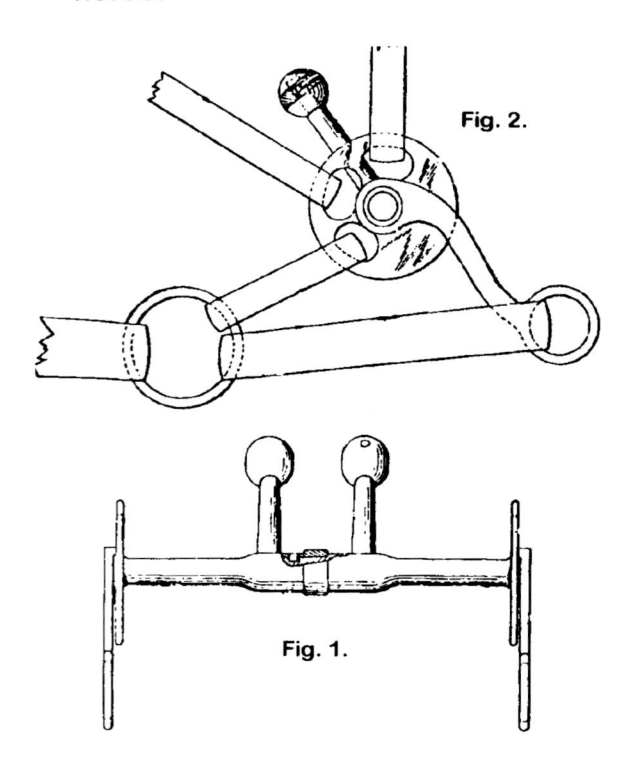

Fig. 26.10 Nazor swivel-mouth bit.

Near Side: Reference to the left side of the horse.

Neck Rein: A horse is guided by lightly laying the rein against the opposite neck of the desired direction.

Neck Rope: A small rope passing around the lariat and the horse's neck to keep the horse in line with the lariat after an animal is roped.

Nelson, Bob, Reining Horse Snaffle: The rings slide in the tube attached to the mouth-piece. The first movement of the reins causes the ring to move, giving the horse a signal to gather itself; as the pull is completed the mouth-piece raises up and turns 45 degrees to form a "V" for a more powerful and humane snaffle bit [Fig. 26.11].

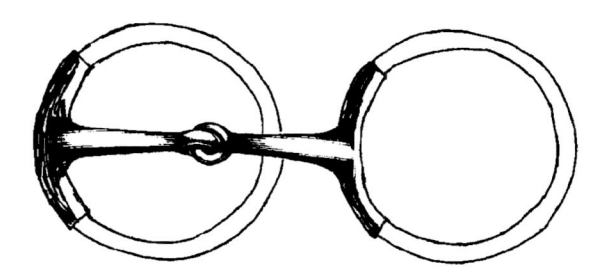

Fig. 26.11 Bob Nelson snaffle bit.

Nelson Gag Bit: See Chapter 12, Fig. 12.12.

New York Bit: A leather-mouth bit sold by A. Buermann Mfg. Co., Newark, NJ [Fig. 26.12].

Fig. 26.12 New York leather mouth bit.

New Zealand Full-spoon Bit: Figure 26.13.

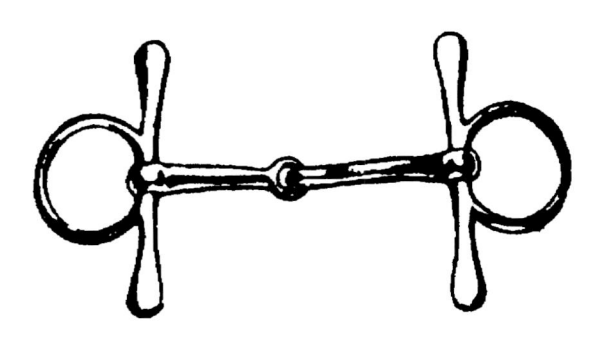

Fig. 26.13 New Zealand full-spoon bit.

New Zealand Half-cheek Spoon Bit: [Fig. 26.13a].

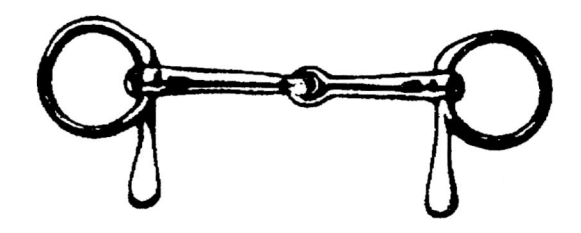

Fig. 26.13a New Zealand half-cheek spoon bit.

Newark Bit: See Stalker Patent, Chapter 32.

New Circle Curb Hook: A useful arrangement for making the curb chain lay flat against the horse's lower jaw [Fig. 26.14].

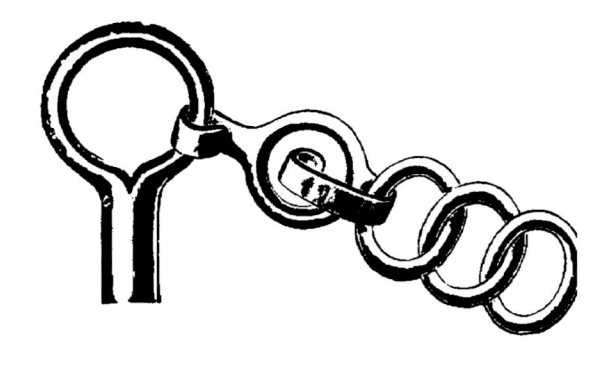

Fig. 26.14 The new circle curb hook.

Newmarket Snaffle: A short strap across a horse's nose acting as a noseband that can be attached to a snaffle bit [Fig. 26.15].

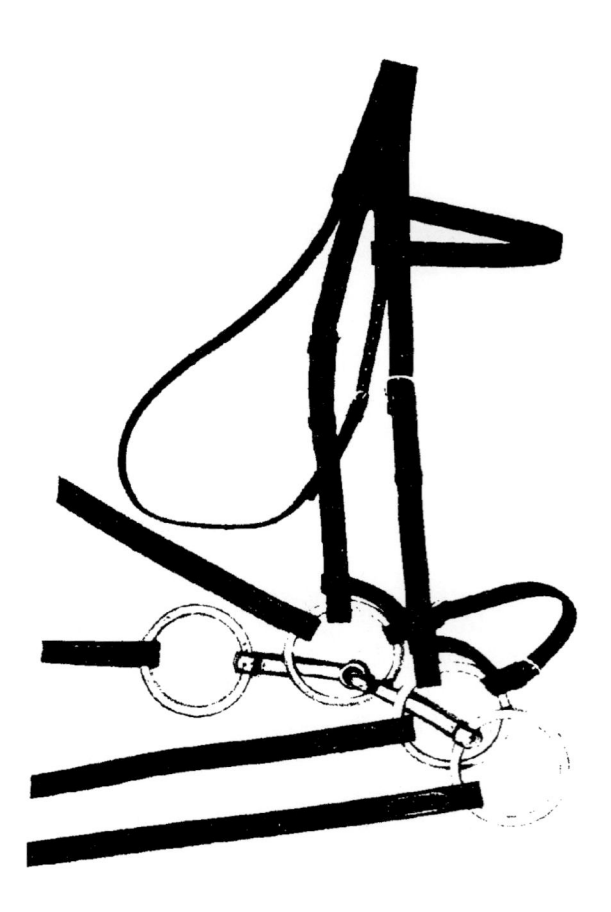

Fig. 26.15 A Newmarket snaffle bridle.

Fig. 26.16 Nichols rectangular-mouth bit.

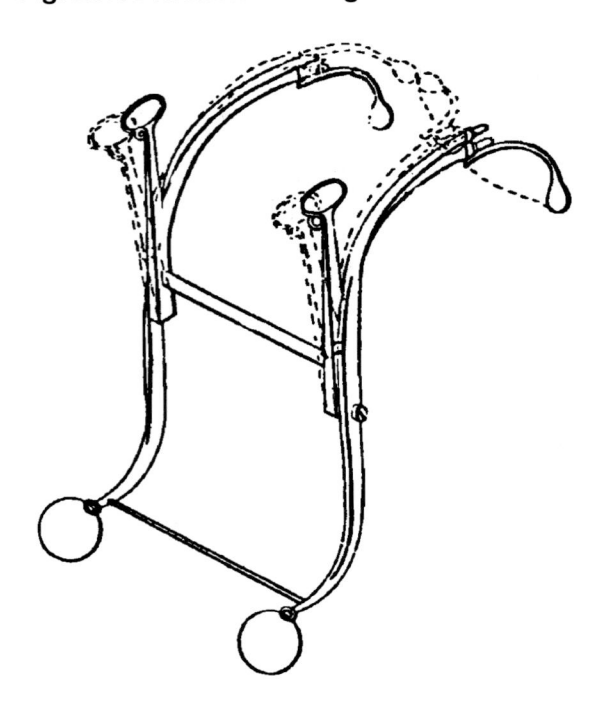

Fig. 26.17 Niel air-control bit.

Nichols, William, Ozark, AR, Patent No. 471,493, Mar. 22, 1892 [Fig. 26.16]. The rectangular bar with its diamond shaped port has the sharp edges beveled or rounded. It is designed for "unruly or vicious" horses.

Niel, Antoine, Brooklyn, NY, Patent No. 22,571, Jan. 11, 1859 [Fig. 26.17]. Gripper bars attached to an ordinary bit and operate to grip the nose of the horse at the desires of the rider or driver to check the horse.

Niemann, William H., Litchfield, IL, Patent No. 1,076,442, Oct. 21, 1913 [Fig. 26.18 and 26.18a]. A double-mouth curb bit that can operate as a gag bit.

Ninth Lancer Polo Bit: See Chapter 16, Fig. 16.3.

Nixon, Daniel M., Danville, IL, Patent No. 87,281, Feb. 23, 1869 [Fig. 26.19]. The two cannons of this bit are united by a ball and socket joint. The oblong socket is beveled on its face to permit the ball on the opposite cannon to fit closely into it.

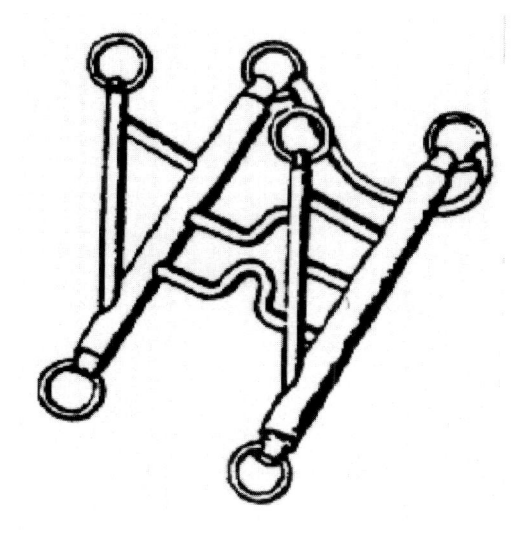

Fig. 26.18 Niemann bit patent drawing.

Fig. 26.18a Niemann bit production bit. Robert Maclin collection.

Nodine Patent: A half-cheek rubber-covered tapered mouth bit [Fig. 26.20].

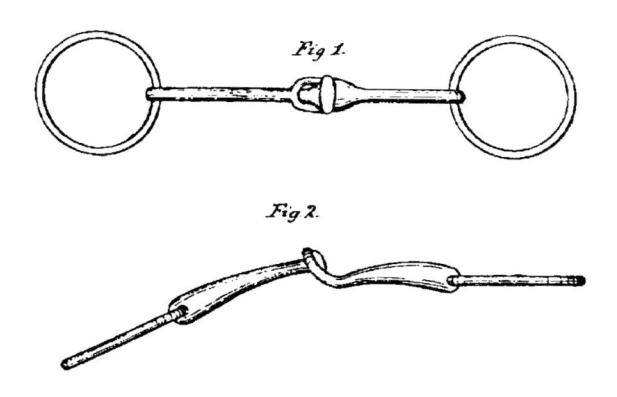

Fig. 26.19 Nixon ball-joint broken-snaffle bit.

Fig. 26.20 Nodine rubber-covered snaffle bit.

Norton, John K. Flushing, OH, Patent No. 74,122, Feb 4, 1868 [Fig. 26.21]. The bit is formed of two rigid bars attached by a central pivot so as to turn freely. Each bar has a ring in the outer end and the other end is bent at a right angle, forming a branch to receive the reins and headstall.

Norton Improved Perfection Bit: The strap shown is not a curb, but a nose-strap that is hooked to the bridle by a frontal strap [Fig. 26.22]. See Chapter 8, Fig. 8.17.

Norton Six-ring Bit: Term applies to Norton Perfection bit.

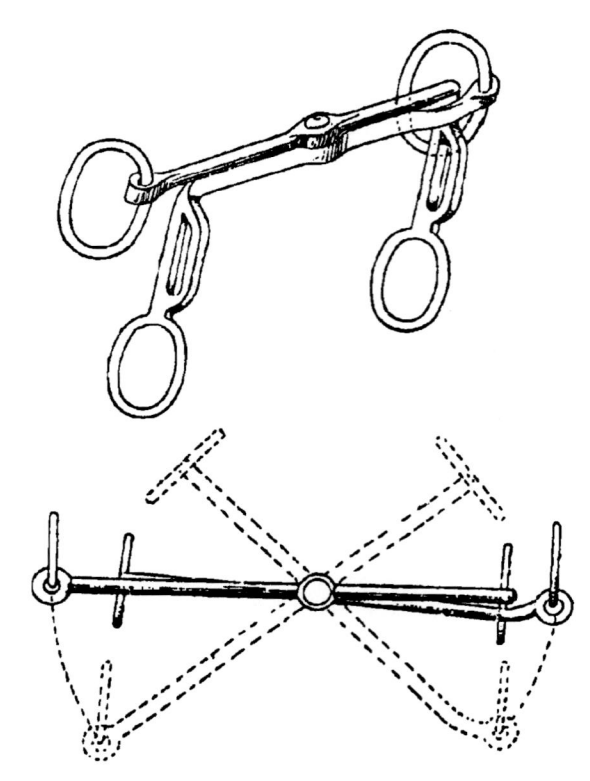

Fig. 26.21 Norton two-piece pivoting-mouth bit.

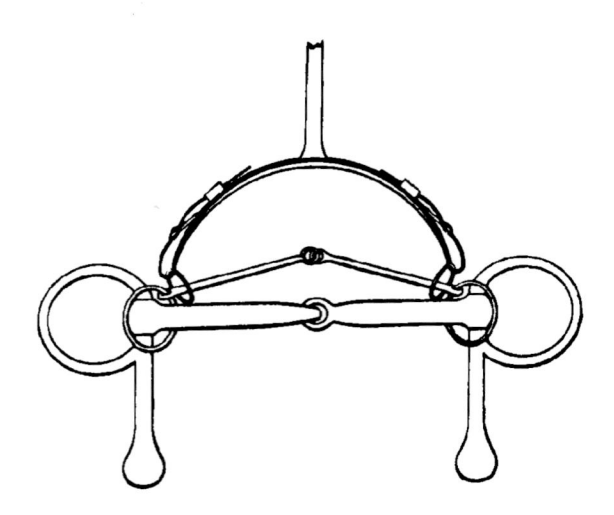

Fig. 26.22 Norton improved Perfection bit.

Nose-bag: A canvas bucket-shaped receptacle, waterproof when new, holding a day's ration of grain for a horse. Attached to the halter or by a strap over the horse's poll during feeding and often hung from the saddle when traveling. See Chapter 23, Fig. 23.59.

Nose Net: A mesh basket with rings or hooks for attachment to a halter or bridle to prevent the horse from eating [Fig. 26.23].

Fig. 26.23 A Nose Net.

Noseband: A Part of the bridle or halter passing around the face of the horse above the mouth.

Buermann, August, Newark, NJ, Patent No. 822,504, June 5, 1906 [Fig. 26.24]. A metal spring attached to metal loops that hook over the rings of most snaffle bits.

Cummings, John, New York, NY, Patent No. 909,160, Jan. 12, 1909 [Fig. 26.25]. A noseband with an open slot in the ring for easy attachment and removal.

Flynn, Oeter Harvey, New York, NY, Patent No. 821,033, May 22, 1906 [Figs. 26.26 and 26.27]. Blocks attached to the noseband can be adjusted to the size of the horse or the amount of tension desired.

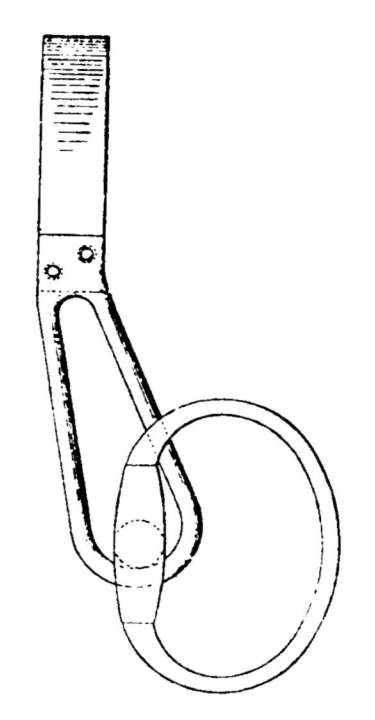

Fig. 26.24 Buermann curber and spring controller.

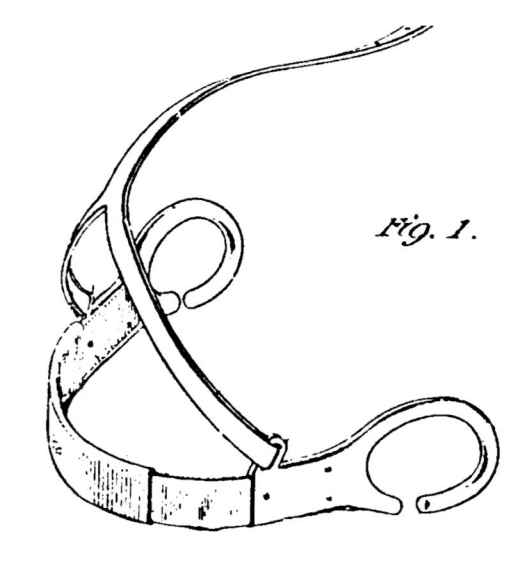

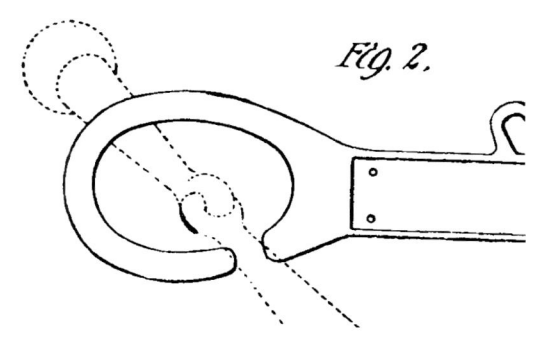

Fig. 26.25 Cummings noseband.

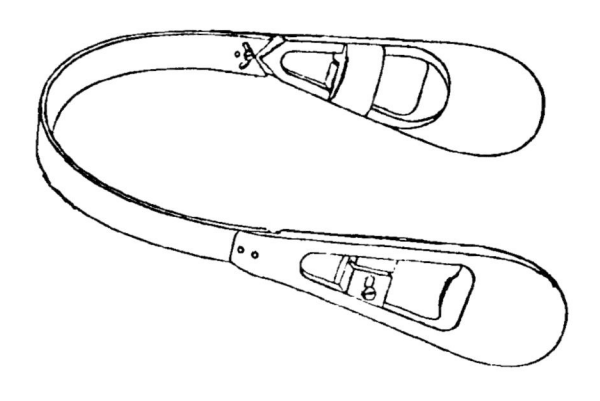

Fig. 26.26 Variation of Flynn adjustable noseband.

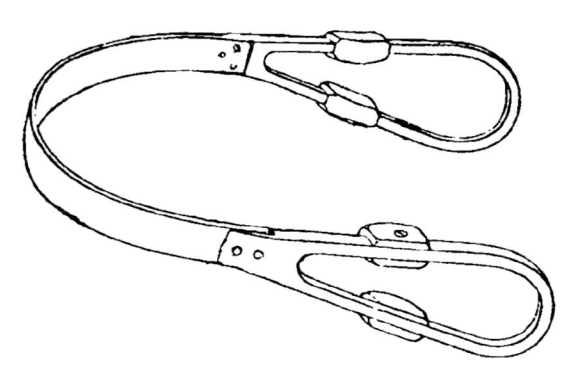

Fig. 26.27 Flynn adjustable noseband.

Fowler, Jonathan O., and George W. LeCompte, New York, NY, Patent No. 1,158,126, Oct. 26,1915 [Fig. 26.28]. A curber of spring steel and elongated openings to accept the cheek-rings of the snaffle bit.

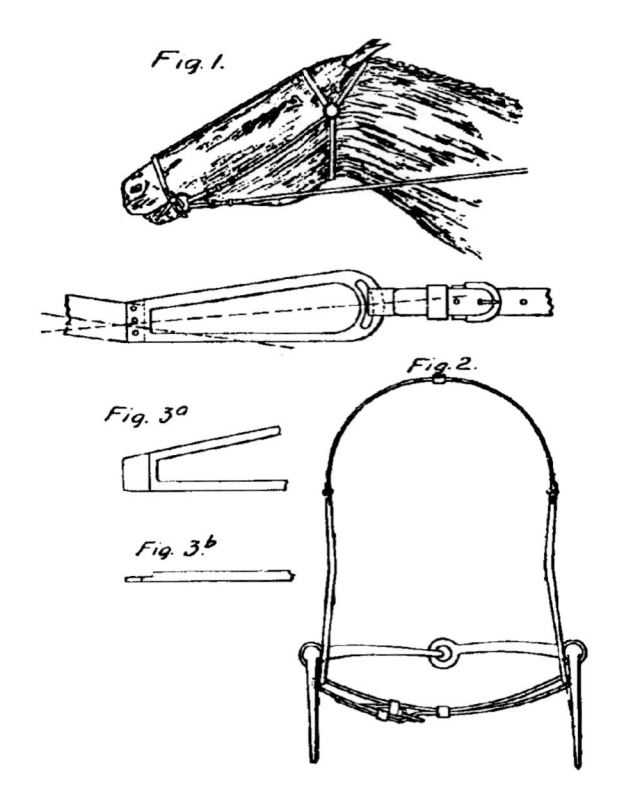

Fig. 26.28 Fowler controller noseband.

Lockard, Hiram, Newark, NJ, Patent No. 165,678, July 20, 1875 [Fig. 26.29]. A bridle bit and metal spring band. The outer one inch of the mouthpiece is square to correspond to the square hole in the cheek-plate and noseband and has a small flange to prevent the cheek-plate from pressing too far to the center.

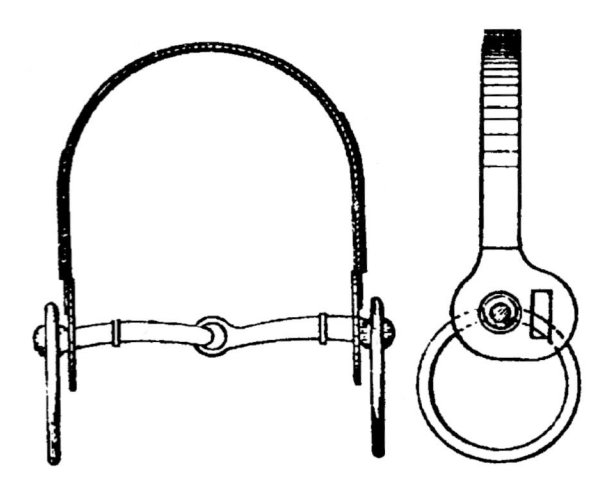

Fig. 26.29 Lockard improved controller noseband.

Lockard, Hiram and Thomas Agens, Newark, NJ, Patent No. 162,081, Apr. 13, 1875 [Fig. 26.30]. A noseband made of metal and covered with leather and connected by the cheek-pieces to the mouthpiece of any snaffle bit.

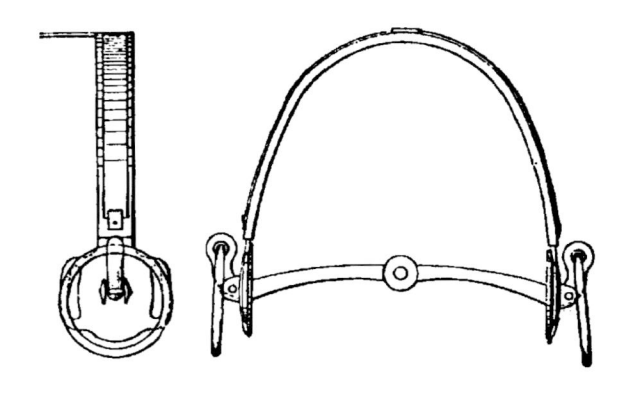

Fig. 26.30 Lockard controller noseband.

Spring Controller: A noseband similar to Buermann and Fowler patents [Fig. 26.31].

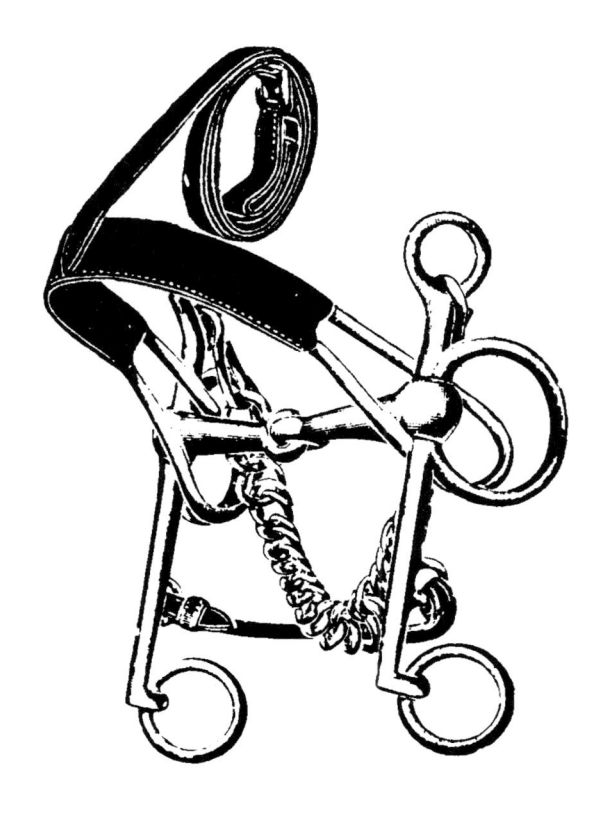

Fig. 26.31 Spring Controller noseband.

O'Donnell, James M., Forest, CA, Patent No. 2,517,338, Oct. 10, 1946 [Fig. 26.32]. A curb bit with U-shaped cheek-pieces with blocks secured to he upper ends.

O'Donnell, James M., Alleghany, CA, Patent No. 2,669,817, Feb. 23, 1954 [Fig. 26.33]. Enlarged circular end plates conceal an extension of the mouth-piece on one end. This end is turned to be in line with the port of the mouth-piece. The mouth-piece pivots within the cheek-pieces. When tension is applied to the reins, the curb-strap rotates the mouth-piece and changes the position of the port.

O'Leary, Michael J., Springville, CA, Patent No. 274,648, Mar. 27, 1883 [Fig. 26.34]. The two parts of the bit are held together by springs that operate as one when the horse is at rest or gentle but separate and operate as a double bit to open the mouth and gag the horse if necessary.

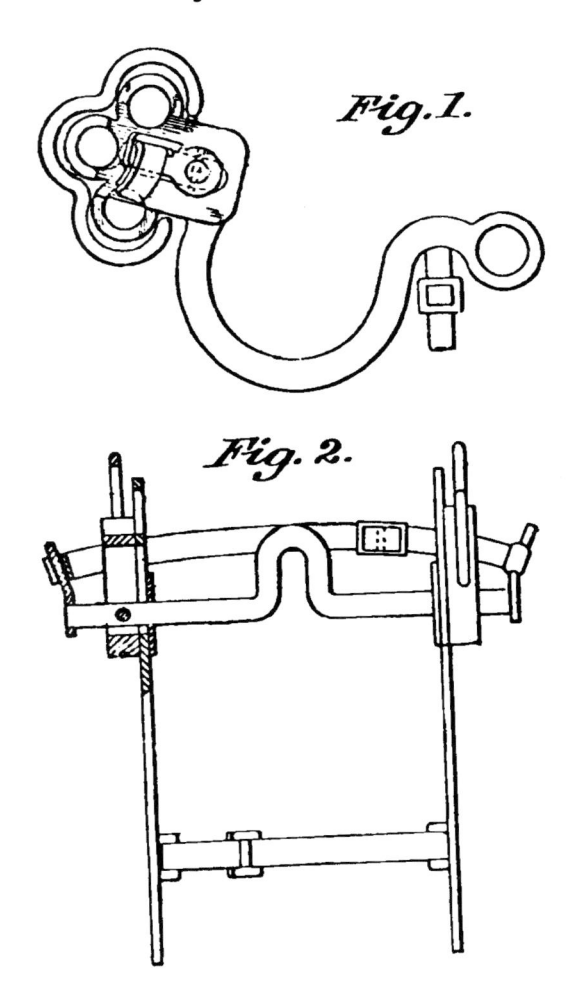

Fig. 26.32 O'Donnell bit patent.

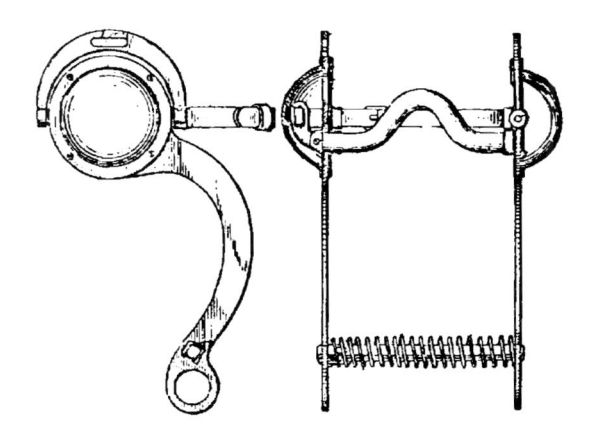

Fig. 26.33 O'Donnell rotating-mouth bit.

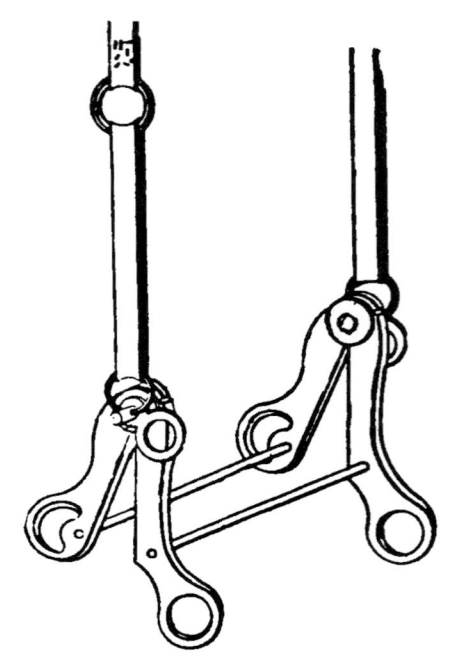

Fig. 26.34 O'Leary spring-activated double-mouth bit.

O'Neil, Phillip S., Colo, IA, Patent No. 889,396, June 2, 1908 [Fig. 26.35]. One chain acts as a mouth-piece held in place by the eyes in the cheek-rings. The second chain travels through the end rings of the first chain and under the jaw to act as a curb. A pull of the reins activates both chains to bear on bars and jaw of the horse.

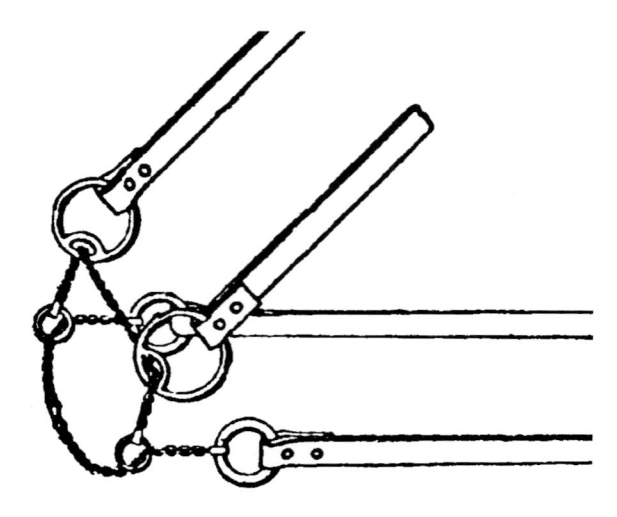

Fig. 26.35 O'Neil chain-mouth bit.

O'Neill, John H. J., New Haven, CT, Patent No. 39,165, July 7, 1863 [Fig. 26.36]. A gag bit that operates directly on the tongue.

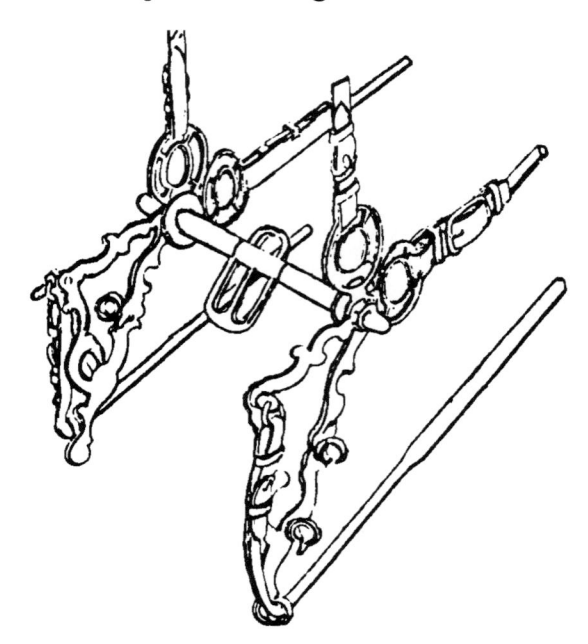

Fig. 26.36 O'Neill gag bit.

Oelkers, Henry A., Mazeppa, MN, Patent No. 1,476,999, Dec. 11, 1923 [Fig 26.37]. Designed to correct the improper position of the head of an animal. It is made in two styles, one with the jaw arm projecting from the left and the second projecting from the right side. The projecting arm in the half mouth-piece will put pressure on the jaw of a horse when its head turns in that direction.

Off-side: Reference to the right side of the horse.

Off-the-bit: In the training of a horse, the horse will maintain the position of collection and the gait and pace after the reins are relaxed.

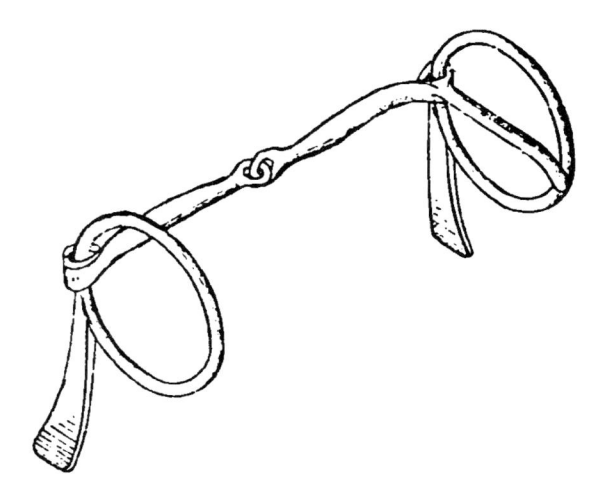

Fig. 26.37 Oelkers bit to correct head carriage.

Olin, Clarence G., Windsor, OH, Patent No. 757,954, Apr. 19, 1904 [Fig. 26.38]. Two variations of the bit are included in the patent.

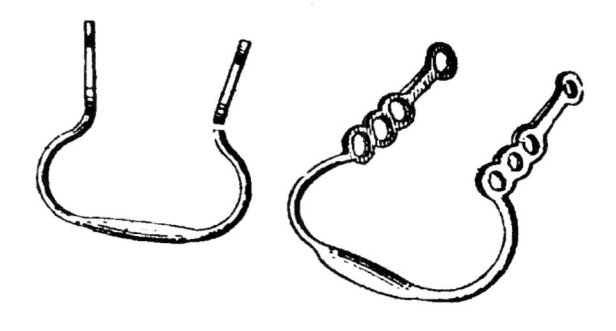

Fig. 26.38 Olin bit patent.

Omoto, Bunnosuke, Granger, WY, Patent No. 1,188,309, June 20, 1916 [Fig. 26.39]. Downward extensions from the side-pieces form a bracket to hold a removable arm that projects under the chin of the horse and acts much like a curb.

On-the-bit: A constant and light pressure applied to the bit and the horse responds as trained to any light change in pressure or movement.

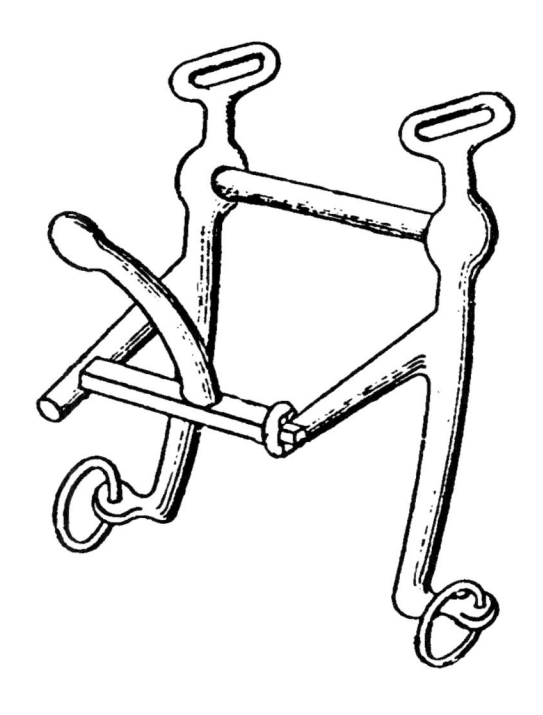

Fig. 26.39 Omoto curb bit.

One-eared Bridle: A split-eared bridle. See Chapter 35.

Open Bridle: A bridle without blinders. See Chapter 35.

Open Reins: A guiding line attached to each bit ring and not tied or fastened together.

Open Spoon: The spoon on a spade bit is open as opposed to the normal spoon shape.

Orendorff, Oliver H. and William A., Bloomington, IL, Patent No. 441,505, Nov. 25, 1890 [Fig. 26.40]. The L-shaped cheek-plates are connected by a straight mouth-piece. The cheek-plates are slotted to receive a second mouth-piece either straight or jointed. The curb-rein is attached to the opposite end of the rod with the curb-strap.

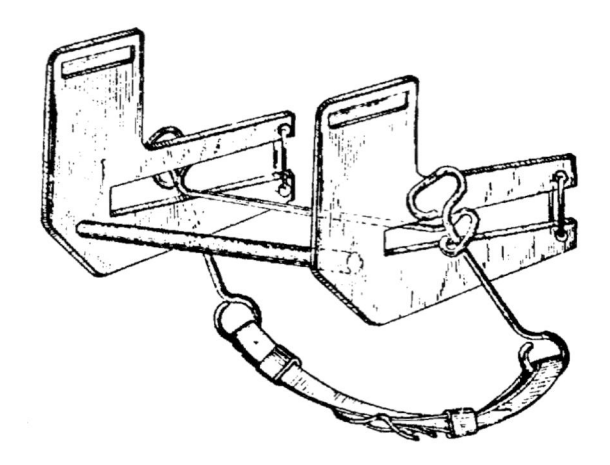

Fig. 26.40 Orendorff double-mouth bit.

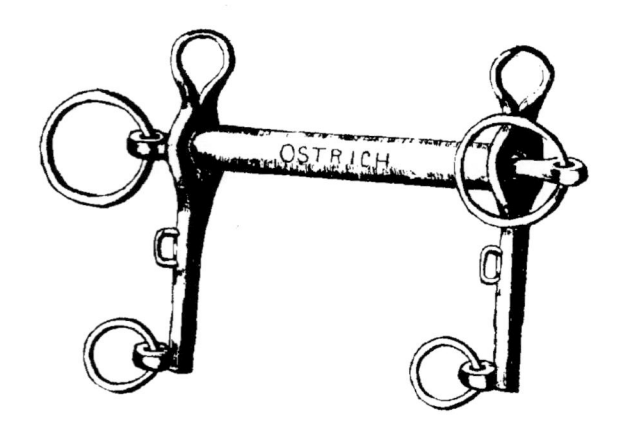

Fig. 26.42 The Ostrich Bit.

Ormsby, Henry J., Eureka, KS, Patent No. 767,117, Aug. 9, 1904 [Fig. 26.41]. The ring at each end of the mouth-piece is passed through a hole in the mouth-piece and the bridle loop extension of the cheek-piece. Designed to "prevent injury to the lips" of a horse.

Pacifier: A cricket or roller in a port.

Pair of Bits: A term used by some Texans to signify a single bit.

Panama Bit: Patented July 19, 1914, sold by A. Buermann Mfg. Co. The Diamond Head (end of mouth-piece) and the beveled edge cheek-pieces make this bit durable. Made in four styles with a half-breed mouth or a port mouth, loose or fixed rein-rings, with or without a lip-bar and with swivel rein attachments [Fig. 26.43].

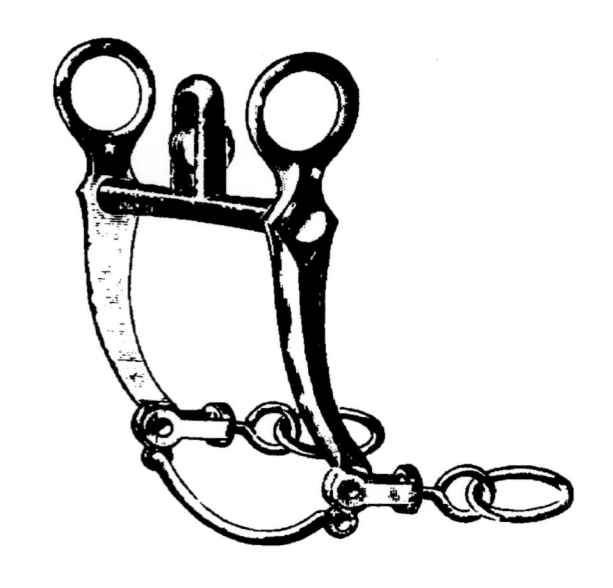

Fig. 26.41 Ormsby snaffle bit.

Ornamental Cheek Port or Curb Bit: See Chapter 8, Figs. 8.30 to 8.58.

Ostrich Bit: An 18th century bit from England. A rod which passes through the hollow mouth-piece has a ring on each end for the rein attachment [Fig. 26.42].

26.43 Panama bit.

Pancher, Freeman N., Chicago, IL, Patent No. 420,721, Feb. 4, 1890 [Fig. 26.44]. A flexible lip protector attached to bits, best made of rubber according to the designer.

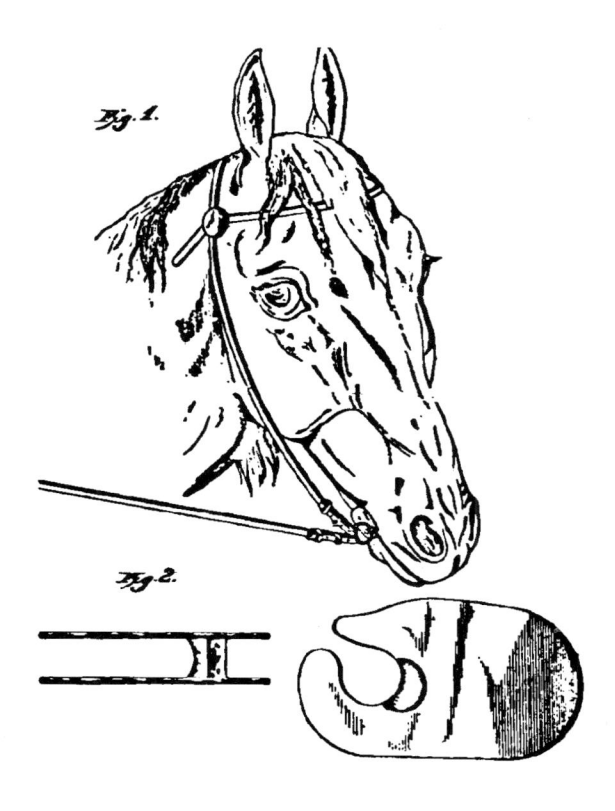

Fig. 26.44 Pancher lip protector.

Pantographic Action Snaffle: A bit with double crossing mouth-pieces [Fig. 26.45].

Fig. 26.45 Pantographic action snaffle.

Parade Bit: Term applied to any ornate curb bit, usually with silver inlay or overlay.

Parenteau, Leon, St. George de Champlain, Quebec, Canada, Patent No. 1,530,401, Mar. 17, 1925 [Fig. 26.46]. The bit is comprised of a shell adapted to enclose the mouth-piece. The cheek-pieces are attached to the ends of the mouth-piece and support the shell for movement. The horse can clench only the shell in its teeth and the mouth-piece together with the cheek-pieces are drawn inward when the reins are pulled.

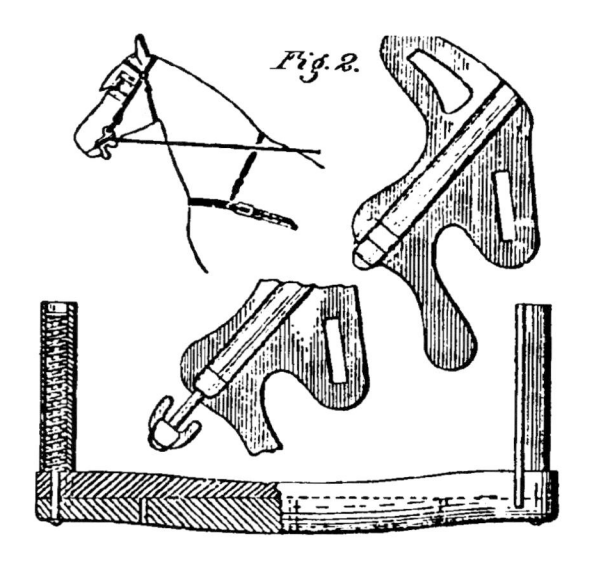

Fig. 26.46 Parenteau bit.

Park Fancy Bit: An early 1800 English bit from *The Loriner* [Fig. 26.47].

Fig. 26.47 Park Fancy Bit.

Parsons, George Sexton, Cherry Flats PA, Patent No. 477,779, June 22, 1892 [Fig. 26.48]. The action of the bit corresponds to the bridle attachment. With the bit in the position shown, the bit acts as a stable snaffle bit. When the cheekpieces are attached at a 90 degree turn, a rein pull will cause the bit to act as a pressure bit.

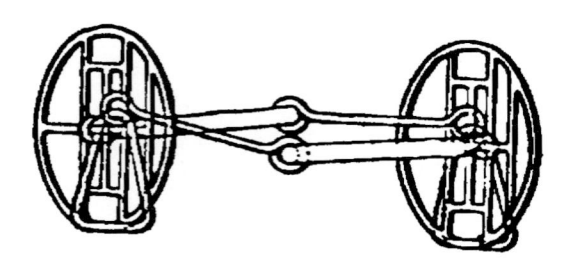

Fig. 26.48 Parsons double-mouth bit.

Payne, Elmer, New York, NY, Patent No. 623,333, Apr. 18, 1899 [Fig. 26.49]. A tubular mouth-piece with end disks provided with slots for attachment of bridle straps. A rein-bar extends through the tubular mouth-piece.

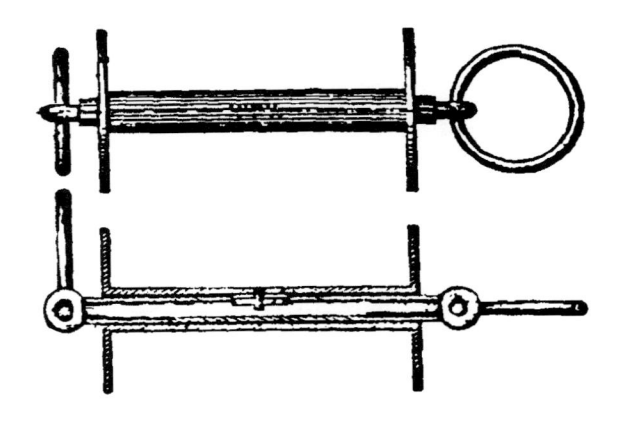

Fig. 26.49 Payne tubular-mouth bit.

Pecos Bit: Name of a curb bit made by Ricardo and several other manufacturers.

Peepers: A term for bridle blinders.

CHAPTER TWENTY-SEVEN
Pelham

American Pelham: Also called Western Pelham, compare with Figure 27.2.

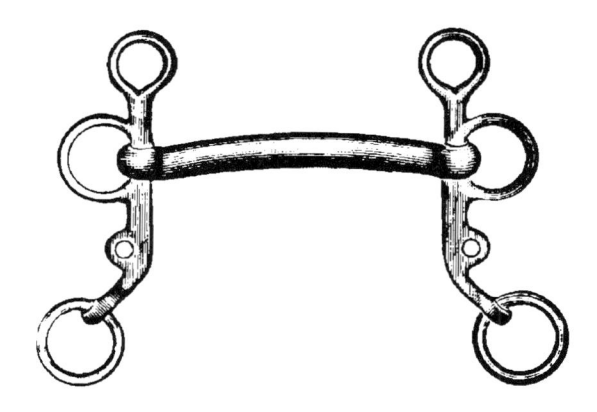

Fig. 27.0 American Pelham with mullen mouth.

Angle Cheek: See Elbow Cheek Bits, Chapter 8.

Arch-mouth Pelham: A mouth-piece with a little more curve than a mullen mouth [Fig. 27.1].

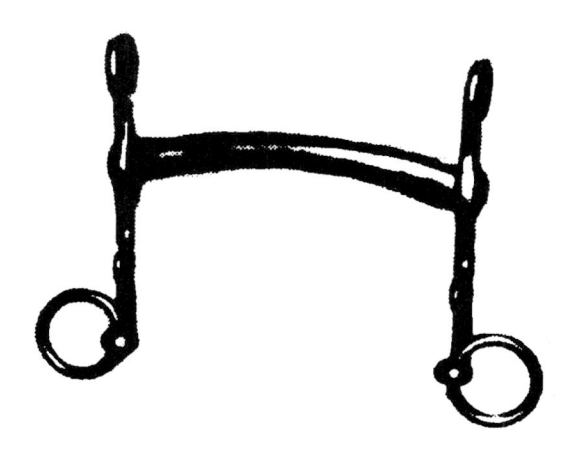

Fig. 27.1 Arch-mouth Pelham.

Argentine: The name is interchangeable with Argentine and/or Western Pelham [Fig. 27.2].

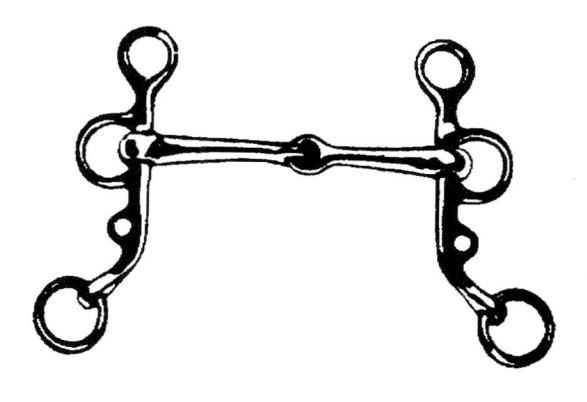

Fig. 27.2 Argentine Western Style with a jointed mouth.

Argentine Tom Thumb: See Tom Thumb, Chapter 33, Fig. 33.19.

Army Reversible Pelham: See English and Canadian Military, Chapter 21, Figure 21.6.

Banbury Polo Pelham: Refers to style of mouth-piece which floats within the cheek-piece [Figs. 27.3 and 27.4].

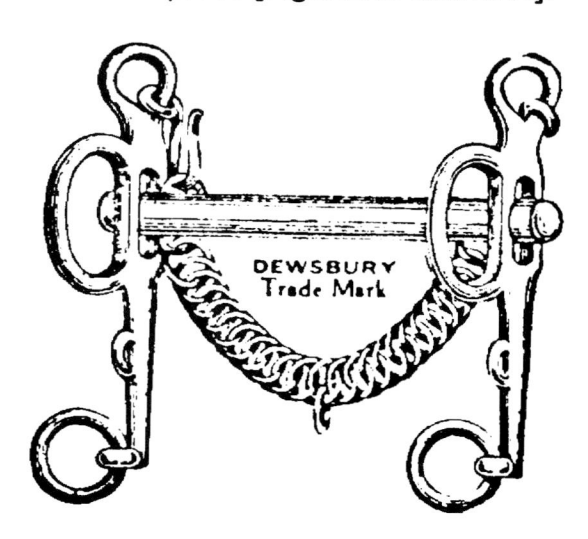

Fig. 27.3 Banbury Pelham.

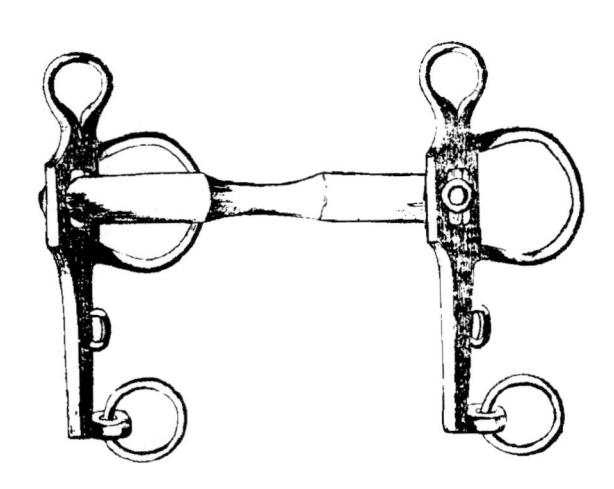

Fig. 27.4 Banbury Polo Pelham, 18th century. Drawn by W. Stone.

Bar-mouth Pelham: A Pelham bit with a straight bar mouth-piece.

Barrel-head Pelham: Refers to the end of the mouth-piece [Fig. 27.5].

Fig. 27.5 Barrel-head Pelham Bit.

Belmont Polo Pelham: Figure 27.6.

Berkley Polo Pelham: With egg-butt mullen mouth, flat rings, flat-link curb and circle hooks [Fig. 27.7].

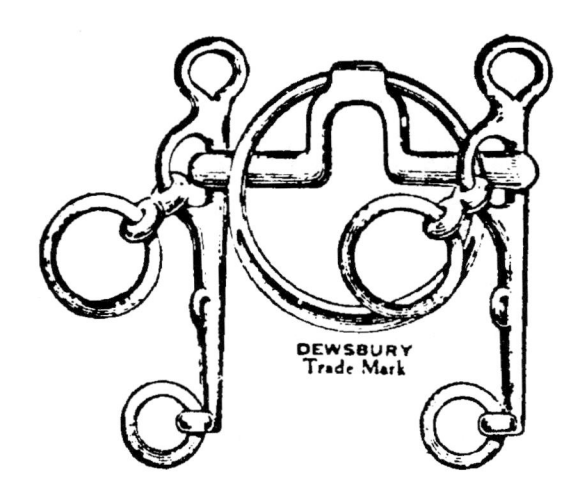

Fig. 27.6 Belmont Polo bit with flat rings.

Fig. 27.7 Berkley Polo Pelham.

Broken-mouth Pelham: A bit with a jointed mouth-piece. See Chapter 25.

Cambridge Mouth: See Kimberwick Fig. 27.20.

Cape Pelham: A bit with short side-pieces and a variety of mouth-pieces; straight, broken or ported [Fig. 27.8 and 27.8a].

334

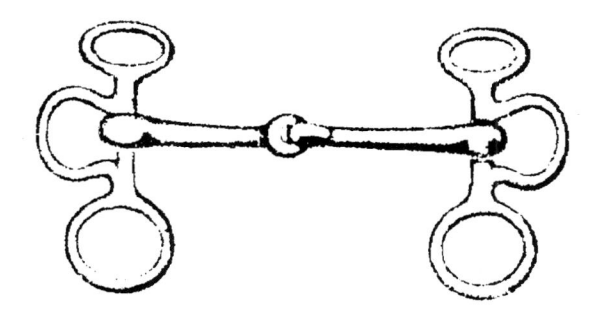

Fig. 27.8 Cape Pelham with broken mouth.

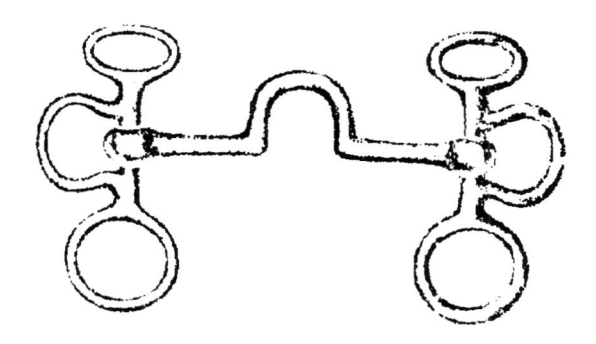

Fig. 27.8a Cape Pelham with ported mouth.

Centaur Rubber-mouth Pelham: Figure 27.9. The mouth-piece is made with flexible rubber.

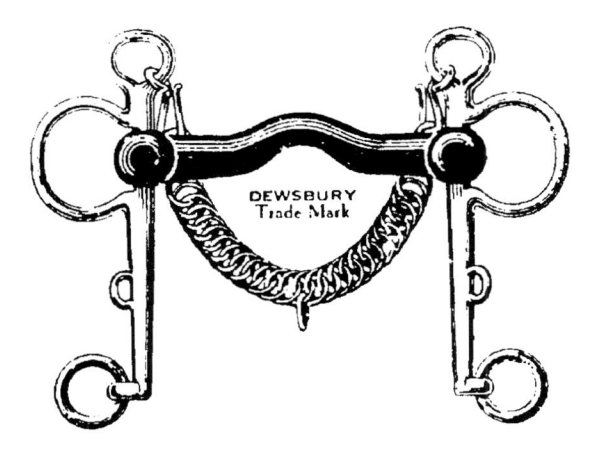

Fig. 27.9 Centaur rubber Hartwell mouth.

Combination Pelham: See Swales 3-in-1, Fig. 27.38.

Curved-cheek Pelham: Sometimes called a Saber Cheek [Fig. 27.8].

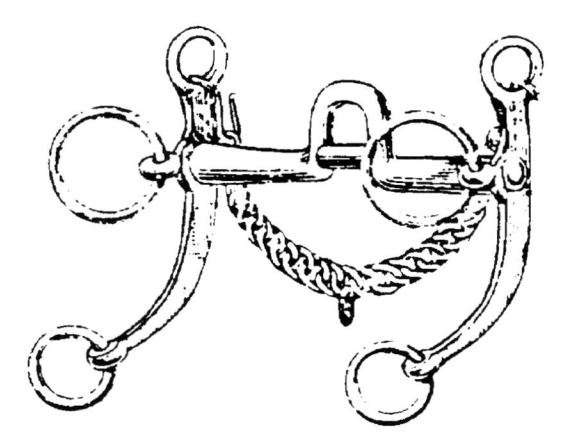

Fig. 27.10 Curved or Saber-cheek Pelham with a rollered port.

Dr. Bristol Pelham: Designates the type of mouth-piece of the bit [Fig. 27.11].

Fig. 27.11 Dr. Bristol Pelham.

Egg-butt Pelham: This bit has an egg-butt mullen mouth with flat rings, flat link curb and circle hooks, with a rubber or centaur mouth [Fig. 27.12].

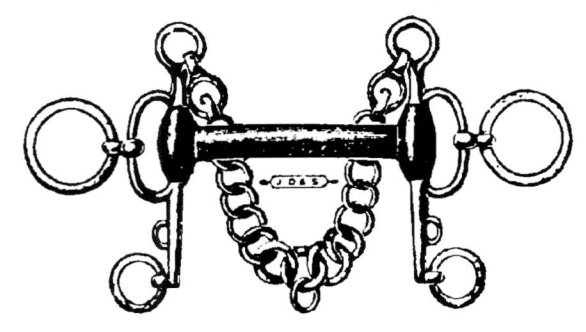

Fig. 27.12 Egg-butt Pelham.

Egg Link Mouth Pelham: The middle link of the mouth-piece is eggshaped [Fig. 27.13].

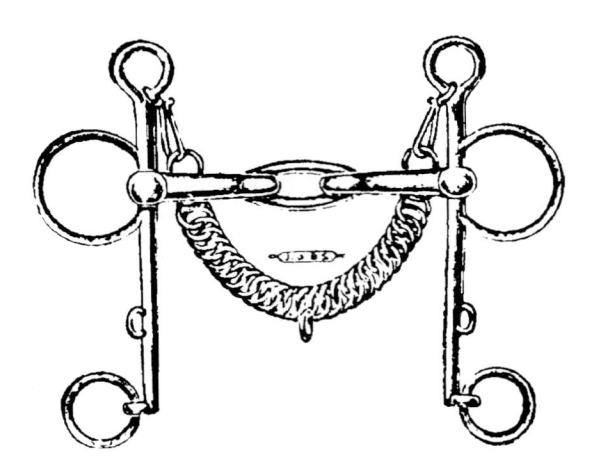

Fig. 27.13 Egg Link Mouth Pelham.

Elbow-cheek Pelham: See Elbow Bits, Chapter 8.

English Pelham: See Egg-butt Pelham Fig. 27.12.

English Polo Pelham: Figure 27.14.

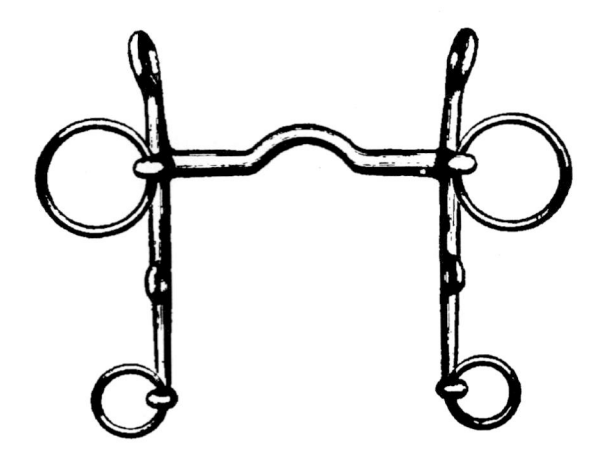

Fig. 27.14 English Polo Pelham.

Fenners Pelham: A bit sometimes called a Parallel Bit, with two mouth-pieces. The upper one slides up and down and the one at the lower end slides backward. The two mouth-pieces are joined by a rubber band at the center of the mouth [Fig. 27.15].

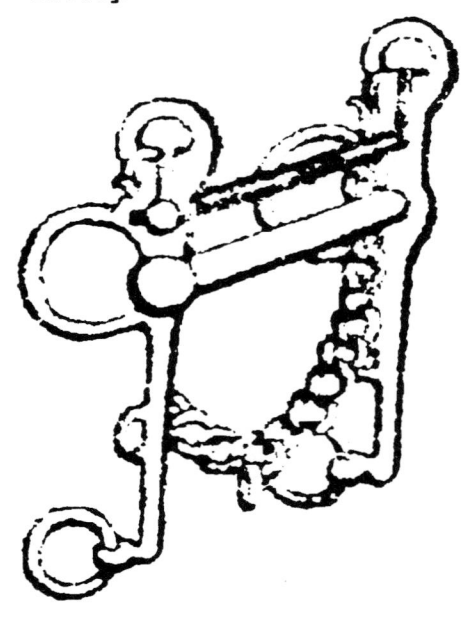

Fig. 27.15 Fenner Pelham bit.

Fixed-cheek Pelham: See Fig. 27.44.

Globe-cheek Pelham: See Nos. 473, 315 and 316 Driving Bits, Chapter 8. Fig. 8.28.

Hanoverian Pelham: Fig. 27.16.

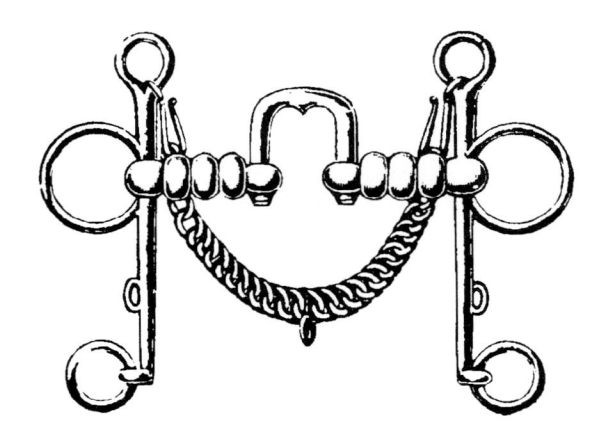

Fig. 27.16 Hanoverian Pelham bit.

Hartwell Pelham: A short-cheeked bit with a Cambridge-style mouth [Fig. 27.17].

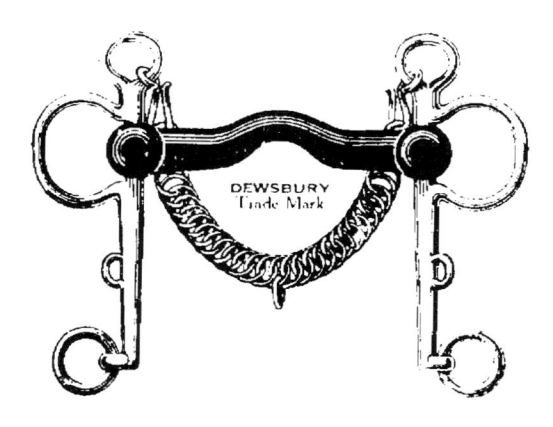

Fig. 27.17 Hartwell Pelham with rubber mouth.

Harry Hightower Pelham: An early 19th century English Pelham bit [Fig. 27.18].

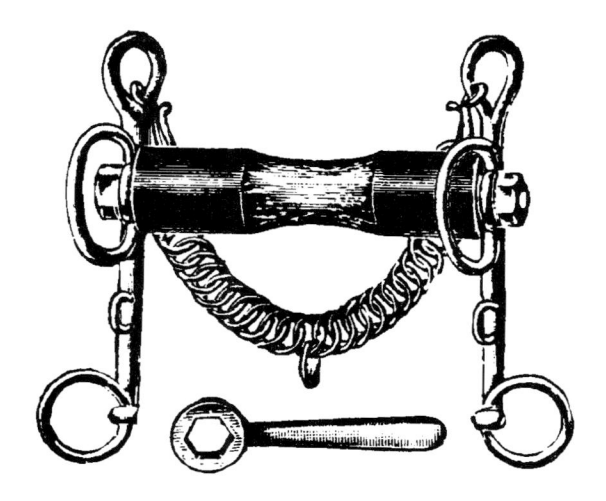

Fig. 27.19 Kerro Pattern Pelham.

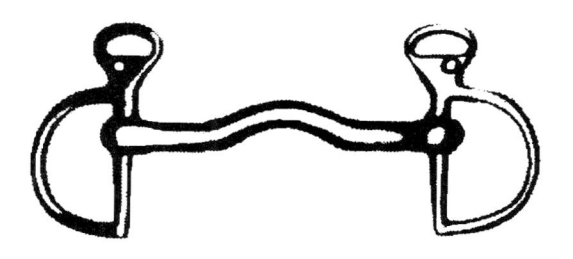

Fig. 27.20 Kimberwich Pelham. Drawing by W. Stone from Harvey Matthew.

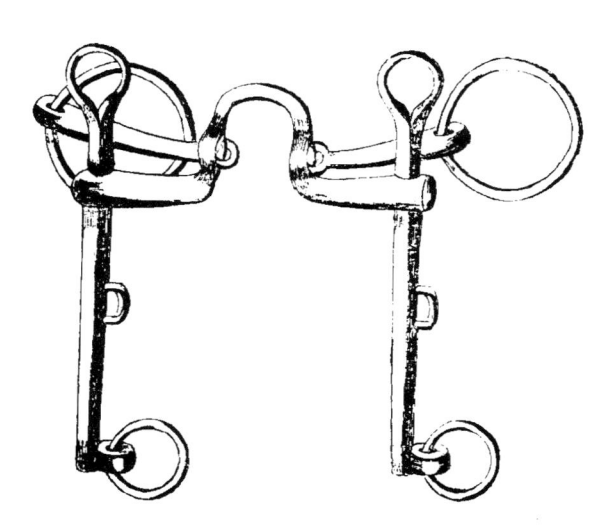

Fig. 27.18 Harry Hightower Pelham. Drawing by W. Stone from Harvey Matthew.

Jointed-mouth Pelham: See Pelhams, Figs. 27.44, and 27.45.

Kerro Pattern Pelham: A wood or rubber changeable mouth with spanner or wrench [Fig.27.19].

Kimberwick Pelham Bit: A bit widely used in England and the United States [Figs. 27.20 and 27.20a].

Fig. 27.20a Kimberwick with turn cheeks and centaur vulcanite or rubber mouth.

Kimberwicke, "Whitmore": A bit that can be used in either a snaffle or Pelham bridle. The ring at the bottom affords added leverage when needed [Fig. 27.21].

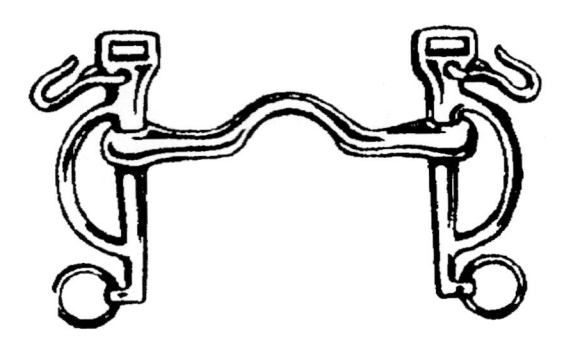

Fig. 27.21 "Whitmore" Kimberwicke bit.

Liverpool Pelham: See Chapter 25.

Loose-cheek Pelham. See Figure 27.4.

Lownde's Pelham: An 18th Century English bit with an Egg-Link mouth, [Fig. 27.22]. Compare with Fig. 27.13.

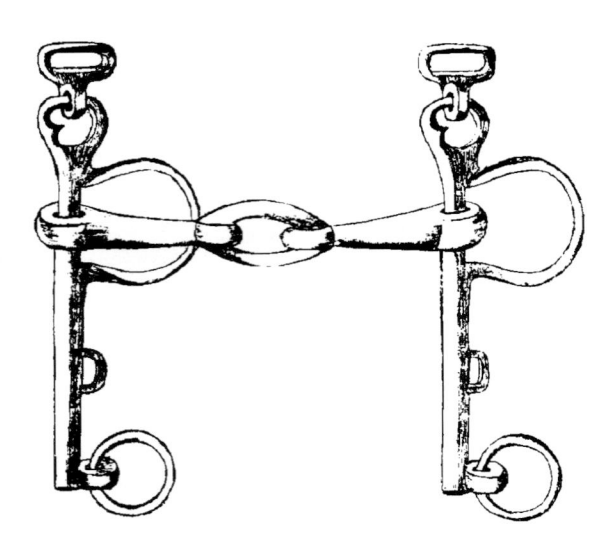

Fig. 27.22 Lownde's Pelham bit. Drawing by W. Stone from Harvey Matthew.

Mohawk Attachment for Pelham Bit: See No. 629, Fig. 27.45.

Mule Pelham Bit: See Mule Port Bit Chapter 26, Fig.26.0.

Mullen-mouth Pelham: Refers to the mouth-piece [Fig. 27.23]. See Chapter 25.

Fig. 27.23 Mullen-mouth Pelham.

Ninth Lancer Pelham: Bit used by the English military unit Ninth Lancers [Fig. 27.24].

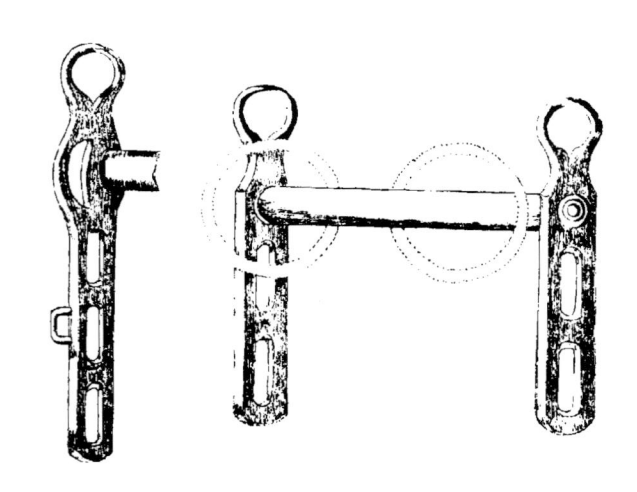

Fig. 27.24 Ninth Lancer Pelham with the United States version on the left and the original English version on the right. Rings are sometimes used. Drawing by W. Stone from Harvey Matthew.

Ordinance Pelham: See Army Reversible, Chapter 21, Fig. 21.6.

Pelham Bar-mouth: A solid straight mouth bit [Fig. 27.25].

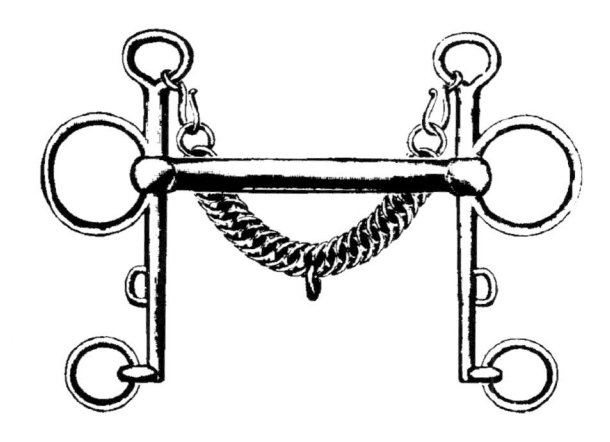

Fig. 27.25 Bar-mouth Pelham.

Pelham Jointed Mouth: See Figures 27.43 and 27.44.

Perkins Pelham: A bit with a roller in the port similar to a Half-breed mouth [Fig. 27.26].

Fig. 27.26 Perkins Pelham.

Polo Pelham: The term applies to many different Pelham bits but usually denotes a shorter cheek [Figs. 27.27 and 27.27a].

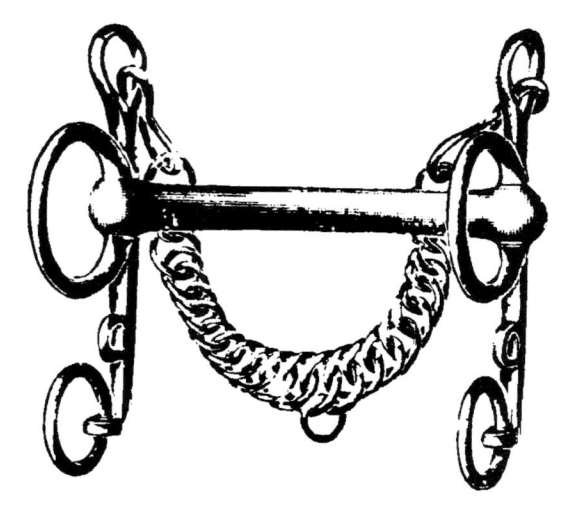

Fig. 27.27 Polo Pelham bit.

Fig. 27.27a Polo Pelham bit with loose 6 1/2 in. or 7 in. cheeks and barrel-head, a 5 in. mullen mouth of 9/16 in. diameter.

Port-mouth Pelham: A Rugby Polo Pelham with a port mouth [Fig. 27.28].

339

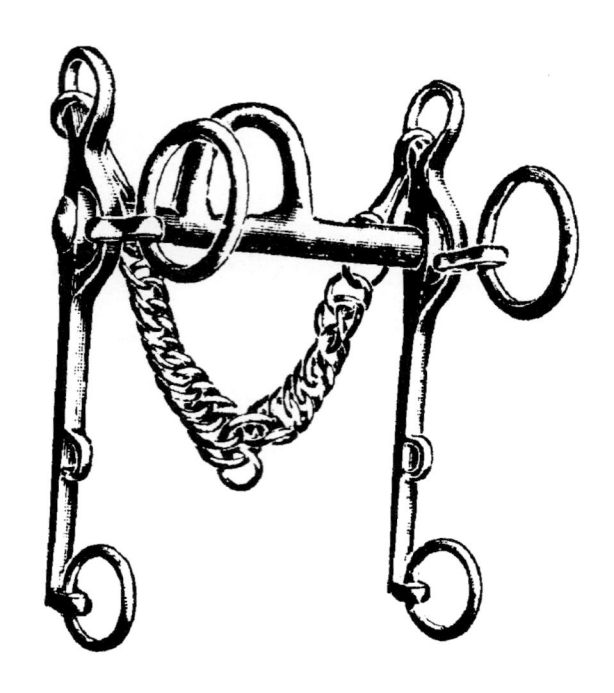

Fig. 27.28 Rugby Pelham with a port mouth.

Ramsey Pelham: Figure 27.29.

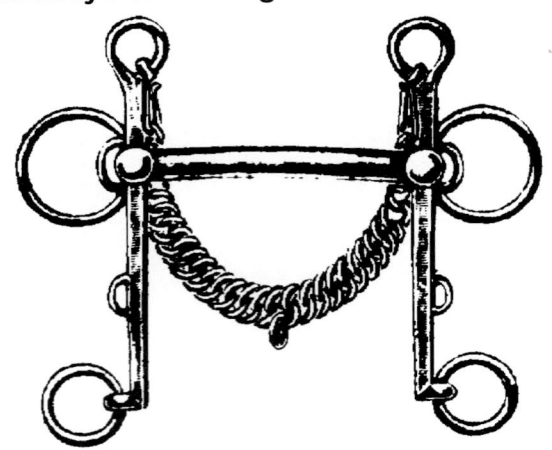

Fig. 27.29 Ramsey Pelham.

Roller-mouth Pelham: The mouth-piece has built-in rollers or small wheels [Fig. 27.30].

Rubber-mouth Pelham: A soft flexible rubber 5 in. mouth and 7 in. cheeks of Never Rust material [Fig. 27.32].

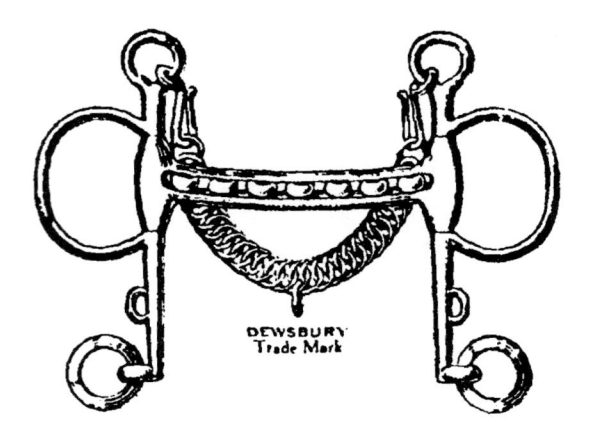

Fig. 27.30 Roller-mouth Pelham.

Rugby Pelham: Made with 6 in. cheeks and supplied with a 4 1/2, 4 3/4, or 5 in. mouth. A model with 7 in. cheeks available in 5 in. mouth only. Made of steel, polished or nickel-plated [Fig. 27.31].

Fig. 27.31 Rugby Polo Pelham.

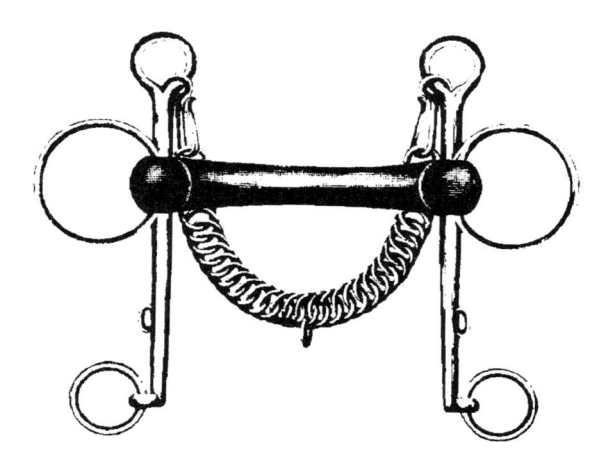

Fig. 27.32 Rubber-mouth Pelham.

Rugby Improved Pelham: Also named the United States Polo Pelham. Made in Never Rust steel, 6 in. cheeks, 4 3/4 in. Cambridge port mouth [Fig. 27.33].

Fig. 27.33 Improved Rugby Pelham.

S. M. Polo Pelham: Stanleigh Magaree Polo Pelham, Patent No. 1,875,195, Aug. 30, 1932. The position of the mouth-piece never changes in the mouth, as it works on a swivel. It is important to adjust the curb-chain tight enough to prevent the "stop" from reaching the extreme end of the slot when the curb is drawn tight. Supplied in 6, 6 1/2, and 7 in. cheeks with a 5 or 5 1/2 in. mouth of Never Rust material [Fig. 27.34].

Fig. 27.34 S. M. Polo Pelham.

Scamperdale Pelham: Figure 27.35.

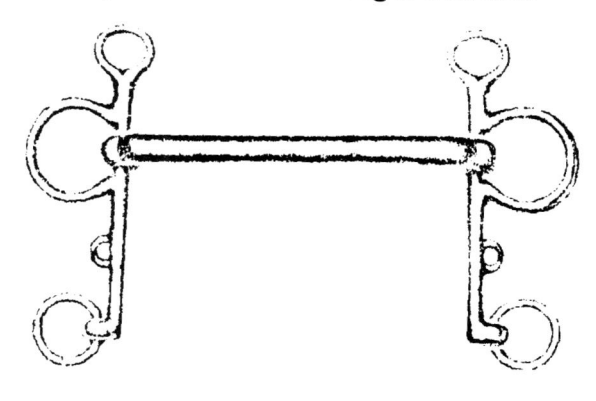

Fig. 27.35 Scamperdale Pelham.

Seften Pelham: Figure 27.36.

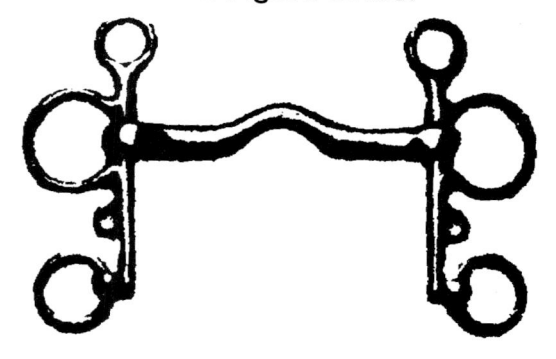

Fig. 27.36 Seften Pelham.

Solid Loose-bar Pelham: See No. 13, Fig. 27.45.

Stalker Pelham: A patented bit, leather mouth, made with six strand brass wire cable core. Solid nickel rings. The fine leather covering shapes itself to the mouth, hardens and retains its shape. Five and a half in. loose cheeks with a 4 1/2 to 5 1/2 in. mouth. Also made in 7 in. and 8 in. cheeks [Fig. 27.37].

Fig. 27.37 Stalker leather-covered mouth Pelham.

Stockton Pelham: From *The Loriner*, early 19th century bit; the bradoon-type snaffle bit fits loosely within the openings in the cheek-pieces [Fig. 27.38].

Straight-cheek Pelham: The normal style of cheek-piece for a Pelham bit.

Swales 3-in-1 Pelham: Patented by Frank Swales, East Sheen, England, No. 898,394, Sep. 8, 1908 [Fig. 27.39].

Swivel Cheek Pelham: A bit which rotates on the cheek-piece ends. See Banbury Mouth bit, Fig. 27.3.

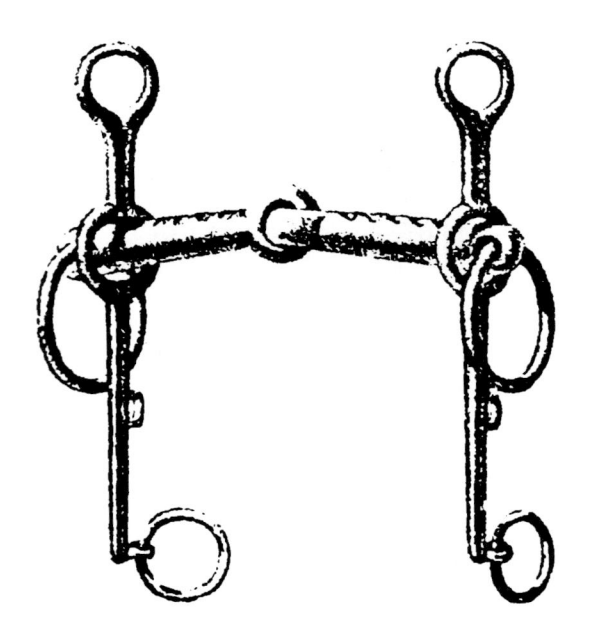

Fig. 27.38 Stockton Pelham.

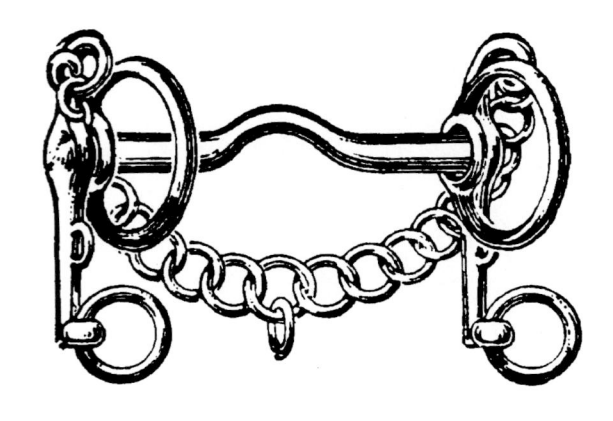

Fig. 27.39 Swales 3-in-1 Pelham.

Tom Thumb Pelham: See Tom Thumb Bit, Chapter 33, Fig. 33.19.

Tongue-plate Pelham: Figure 27.40.

United States Polo Pelham: See Fig. 27.31.

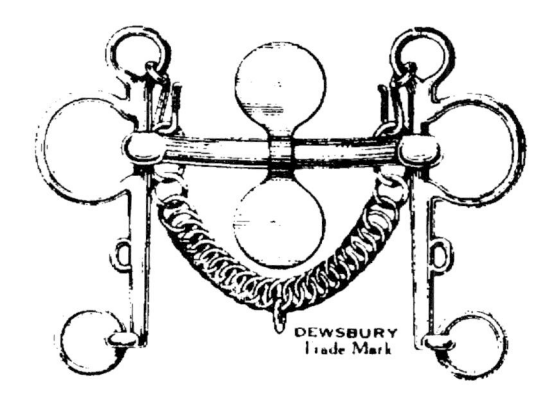

Fig. 27.40 Tongue-plate Pelham.

Washington Pelham: A rubber port is attached to the mouth-piece [Fig. 27.41]

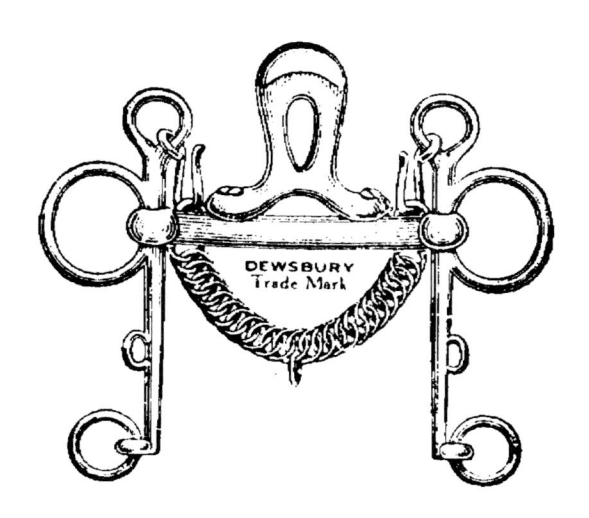

Fig. 27.41 Washington Pelham.

Western Pelham: See American or Argentine Pelham, Figs. 27.0 and 27.2.

Western Polo Pelham: Figures 27.42 and 27.42a.

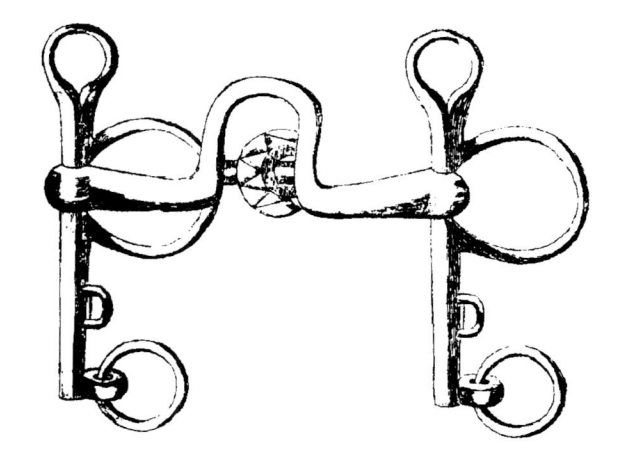

Fig. 27.42 Western Polo Pelham with echini or roller. Drawing by W. Stone from Harvey Matthew.

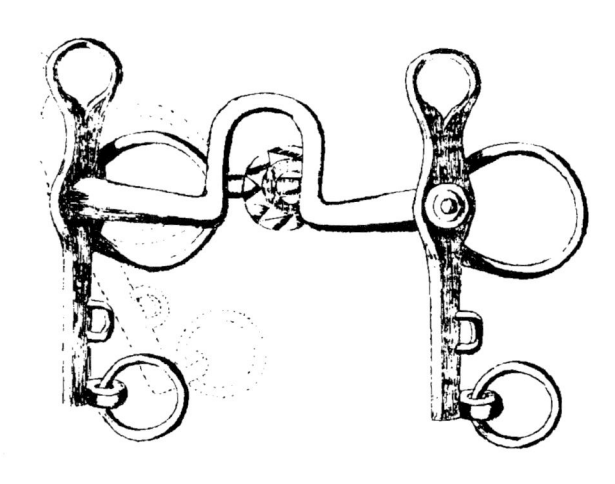

Fig. 27.42a Western polo bit with echini or roller. Mouth turns 1/3 as in the Don Juan Segundo bit. Drawn by W. Stone from Harvey Matthew.

Whitman Pelham: See Whitman Bits, Chapter 23, U.S. Military.

Pelham bits listed in John Dewsbury and Son Catalogue [Fig.27.43].

104   Loose Ring Gent's Pelham and Curb.

600   Loose Ring Gent's Pelham and Curb.

8   Loose Ring Gent's Pelham and Curb.

74   Loose Ring Egg Butt Gent's Pelham and Curb.

1064   Loose Ring Gent's Pelham and Curb.

113   Loose Ring Gent's Pelham and Curb.

11   Loose Ring Gent's Pelham and Curb.

119   Loose Ring Horse Shoe Ring Gent's Pelham and Curb.

75   Loose Ring Stout Egg Butt Gent's Pelham and Curb.

14   Loose Ring Balloon Cheek Gent's Pelham and Curb.

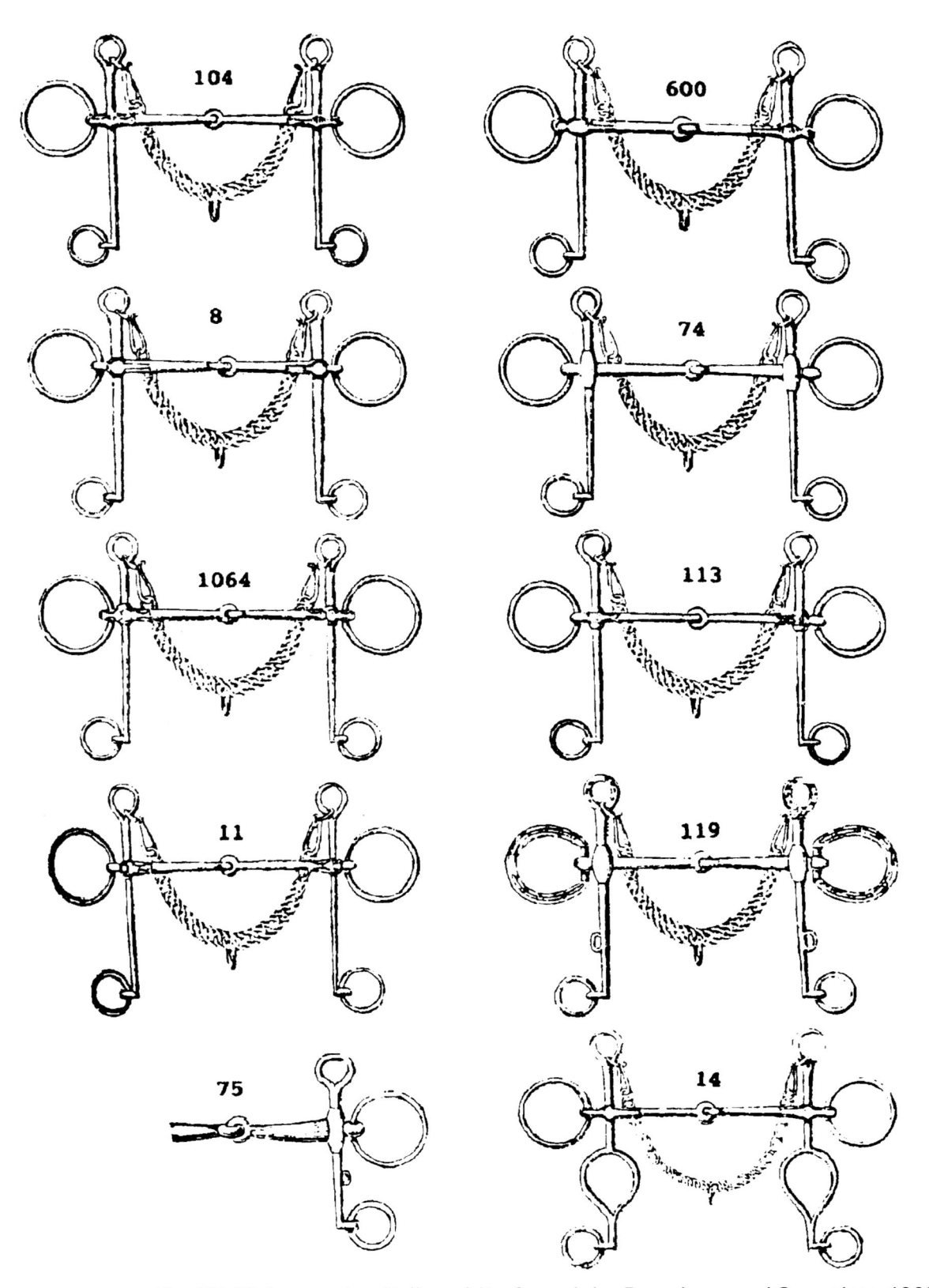

Fig. 27.43 Loose-ring Pelham bits from John Dewsbury and Son, circa 1905.

Pelham bits as listed in John Dewsbury and Son Catalogue [Fig. 27.44].

020	Fancy Scroll Cheek Loose Ring Ladies Pelham Bit and Curb.
1065	Fancy Scroll Cheek Loose Ring Ladies Pelham Bit and Curb.
1445	Fancy Scroll Cheek Loose Ring Ladies Pelham Bit and Curb, Improved Pattern.
121	Fancy Scroll Cheek Loose Ring Stout Pattern Ladies Pelham Bit and Curb.
529	Fancy Scroll Cheek Loose Ring Ladies Pelham Bit with Bosses and Curb
106	Fast Ring Scroll Cheek Ladies Pelham Bit and Curb.
1250	Fast Ring Scroll Cheek Ladies Pelham Bit and Curb, Improved Pattern.
2100	2 Straight Loop Loose Ring Buggy Driving Snaffle.
7126	2 Dee Loop Loose Ring Buggy Driving Snaffle.
290	2 Egg Loop Loose Ring Buggy Driving Snaffle.

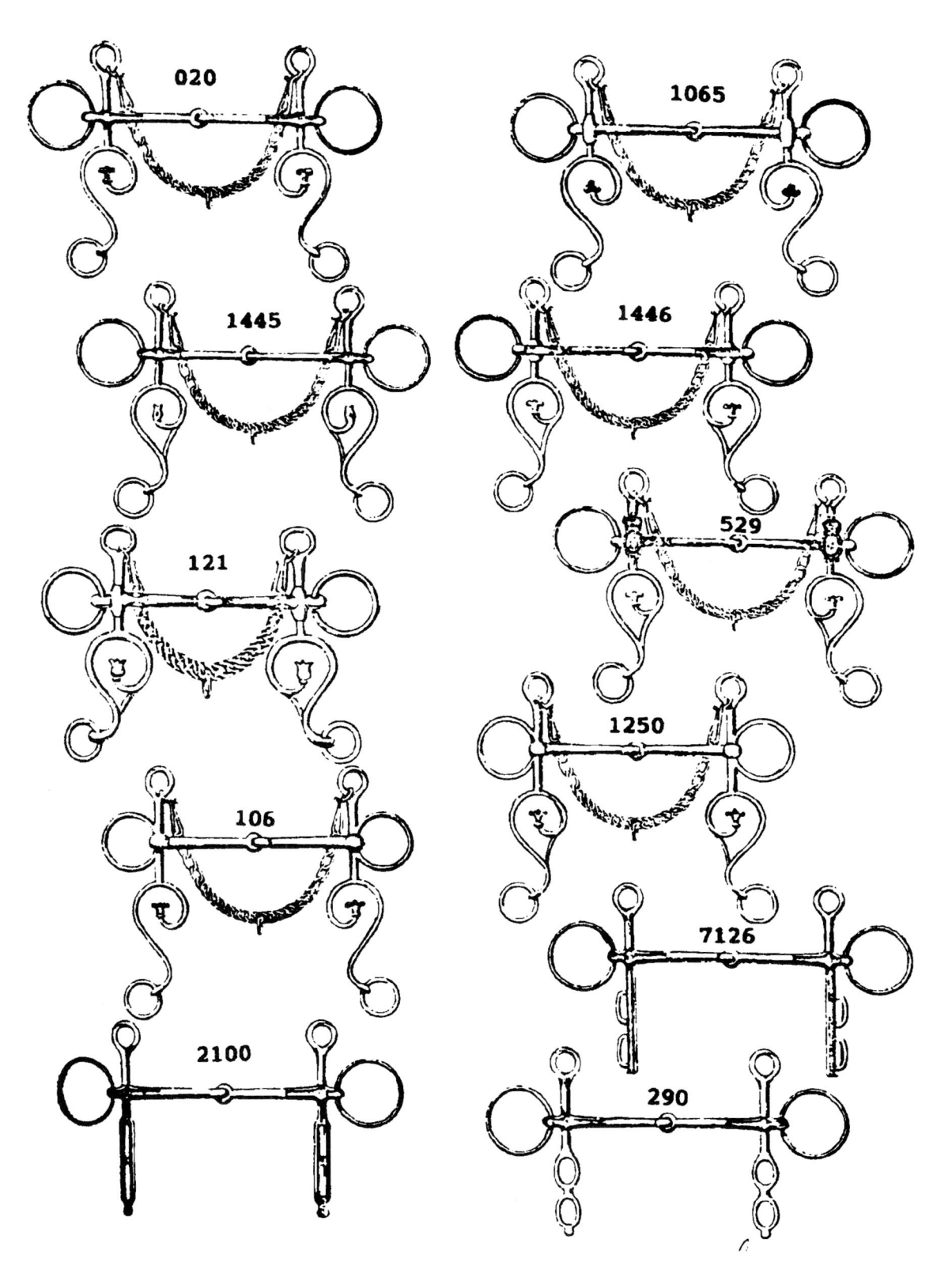

Fig. 27.44 Pelham bits from John Dewsbury and Son, Walsall, England, circa 1905.

Pelham bits listed in John Dewsbury and Son Catalogue [Fig. 27.45].

379	Sliding Half Twisted Bar Mouth Chin Loop, Stout Military Pelham and Curb.
13	Sliding Half Twisted Bar Mouth Chin Loop, Pelham and Curb.
1068	Sliding Half Twisted Bar Mouth Chin Loop, Pelham Bit and Curb with 5 in. Cheek.
278	Sliding Half Twisted Cambridge Mouth Chin Loop, Pelham and Curb.
1036	Sliding Half Twisted Cambridge Mouth Chin Loop Pelham and Curb with 4 1/2 in Cheek.
279	Plain Jointed Mouth Chin Loop 6 in. Cheek, Pelham and Curb.
147	Flat Turn Cheek, Mullen Mouth Ramsey Pelham and Curb.
200	Roller Mouth Double Ring Chin Loop Pelham and Curb.
739	Sliding Roller Barmouth Pelham and Curb with Graduated Rollers.
1045	Turn Flat Cheek Chin Loop Mullen Mouth Pelham and Curb.
629	Fast Mouth Pelham, with Swing Mouth, Rubber Rollers and Curb.
645	Rivetted Mullen Mouth Chin Loop Polo Pelham and Curb.

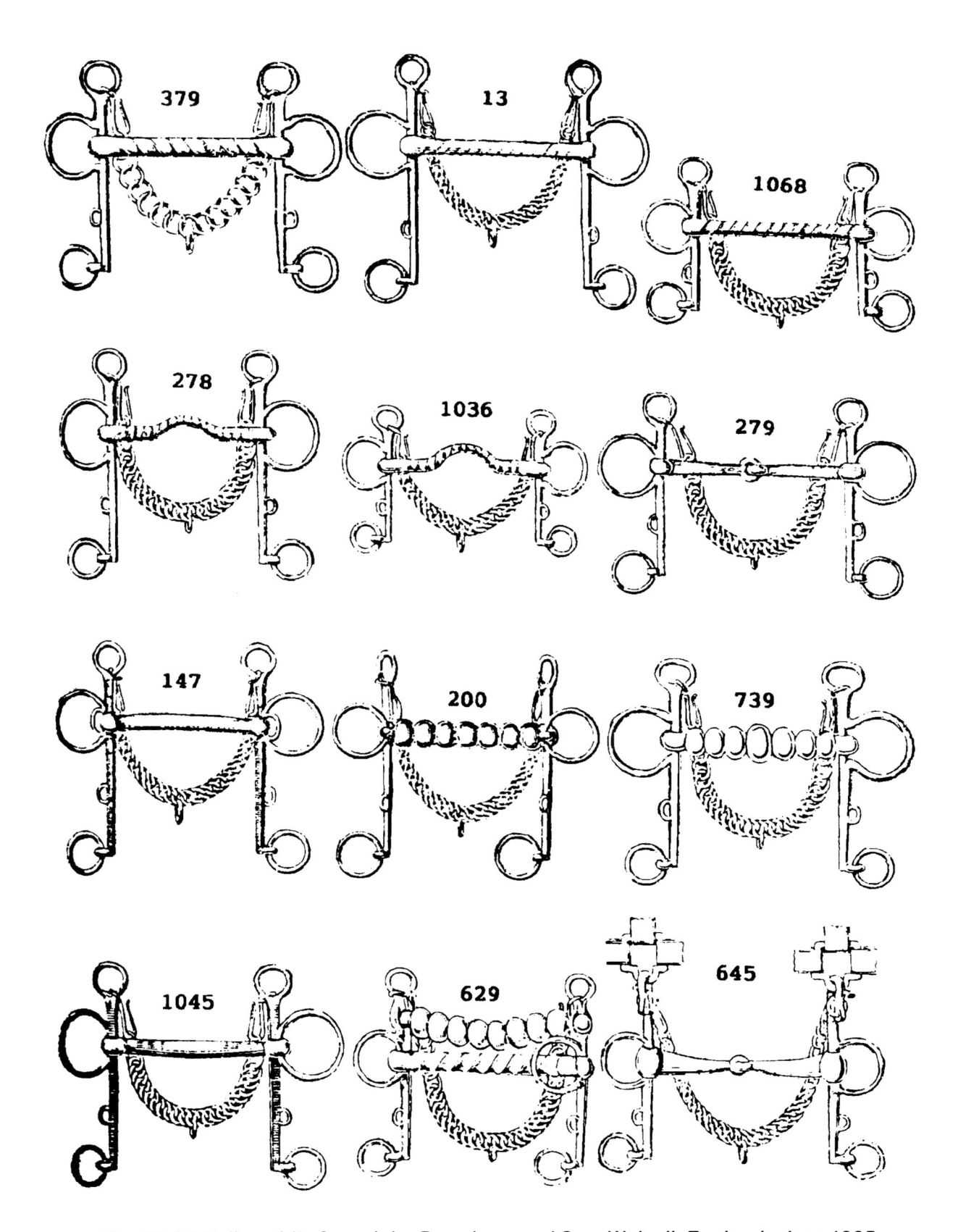

Fig. 27.45 Pelham bits from John Dewsbury and Son, Walsall, England, circa 1905.

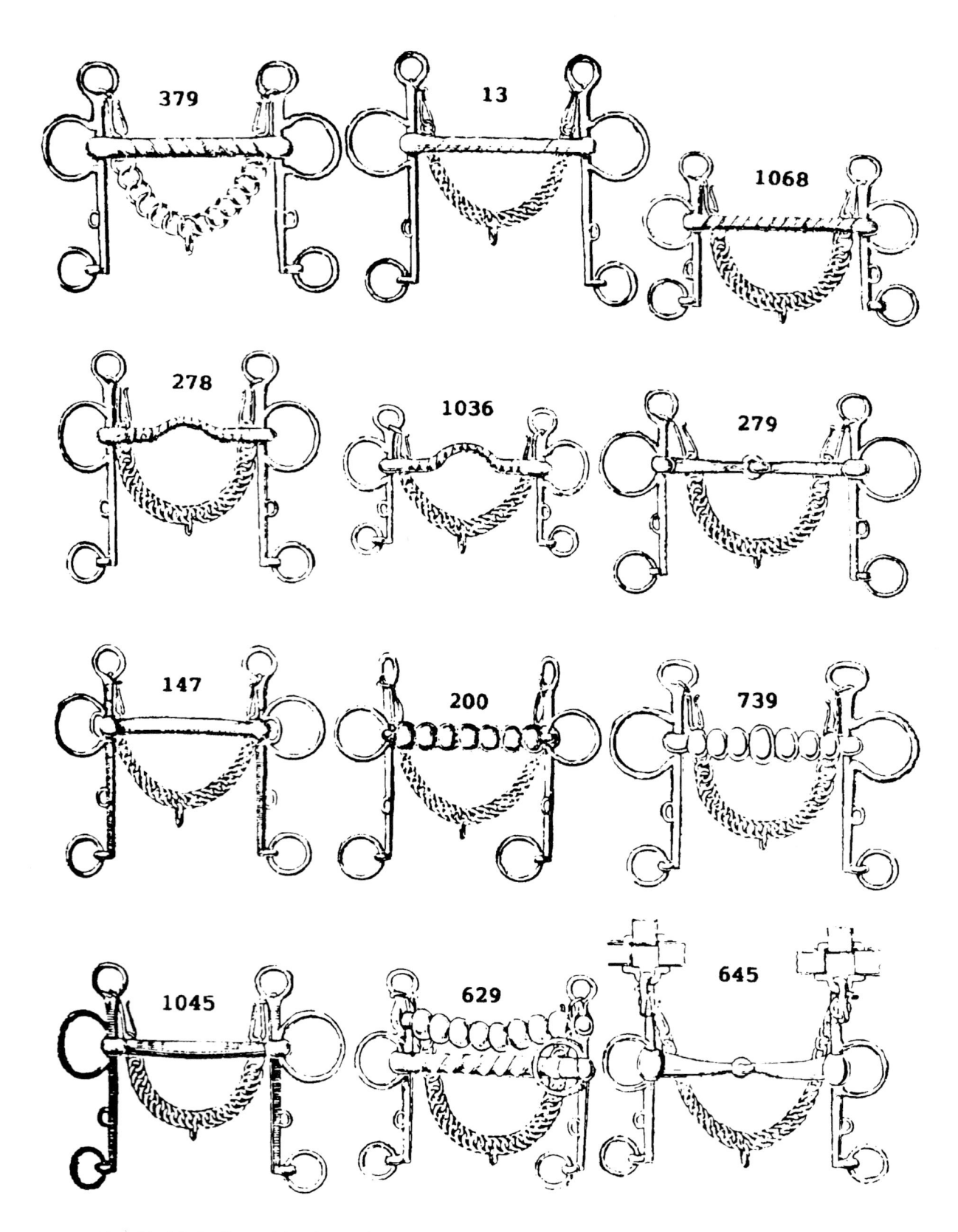

Fig. 27.45 Pelham bits from John Dewsbury and Son, Walsall, England, circa 1905.

CHAPTER TWENTY-EIGHT
Pembroke to Purcell

Pembroke Harness Bit: An early 1800's bit of England [Fig. 28.0].

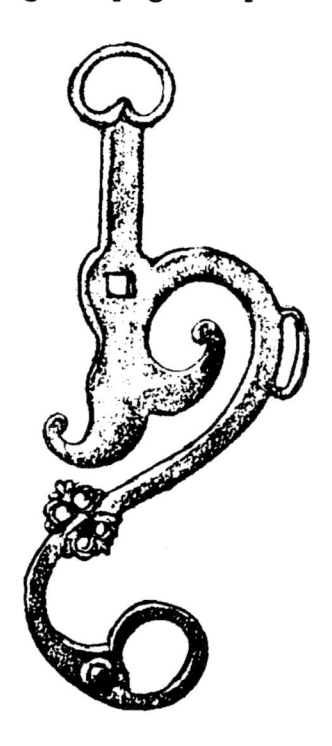

Fig. 28.0 Cheek design of Pembroke harness bit.

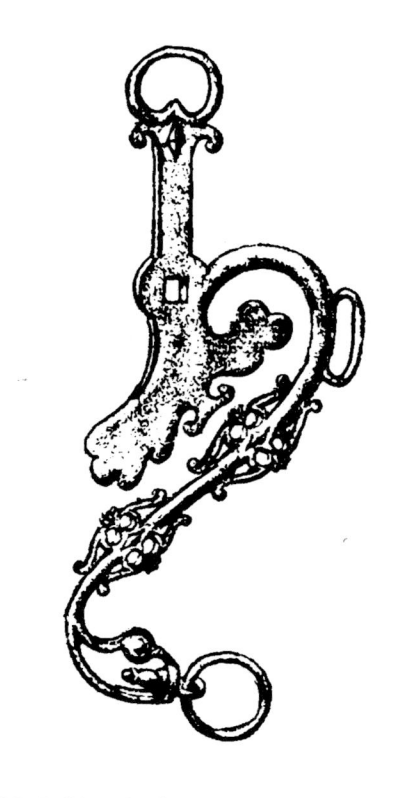

Fig. 28.1 Cheek design of Pembroke state harness bit.

Pembroke State Harness Bit: A more ornate version of the Pembroke harness bit [Fig. 28.1].

Pendleton, Albert M., Salt Lake City, UT, Patent No. 546,785, Sep. 24, 1895 [Fig. 28.2]. A curb bit with a built-in overcheck, a nose-drop and a curb-strap.

Patent No. 630,515, Aug. 8, 1899 [Fig. 28.3]. A checking device that is an improvement over the previous design.

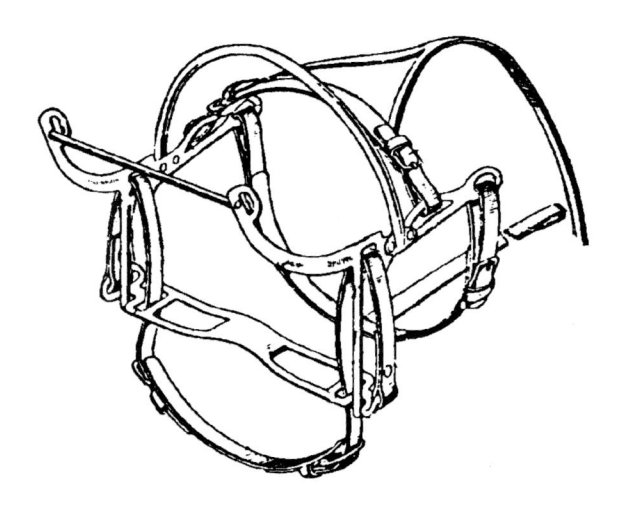

Fig. 28.3 Pendelton improved checking bit.

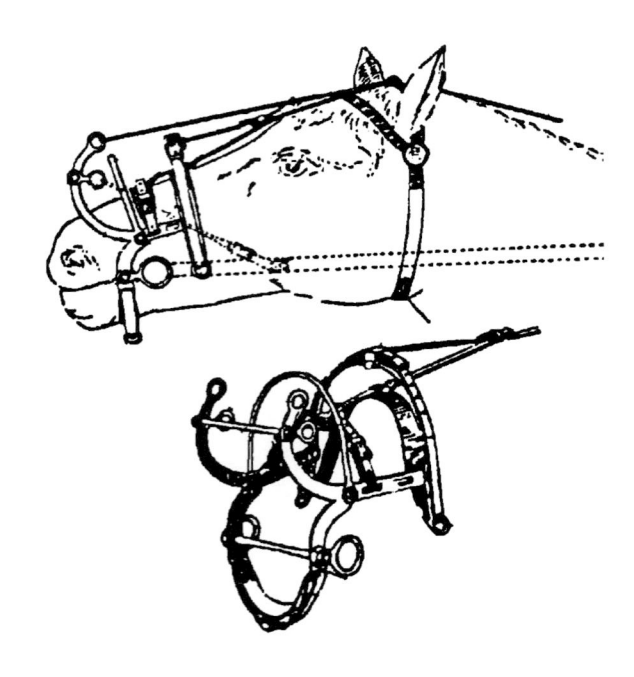

Fig. 28.2 Pendelton checking bit.

Perfection Driving Bit: The Citation bit. Patent No. 281,991, July 24, 1883 by Edwin H. Gilman, Montpelier, VT. See Chapter 8, Fig. 8.18.

Perkins Polo Pelham: See Chapter 27, Fig. 27.26.

Persian Snaffle: A snaffle bit of 19th-century England with a tapered square mouth-piece [Fig. 28.4].

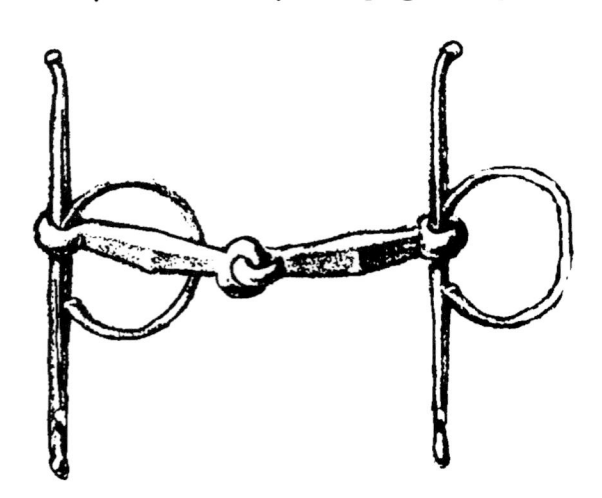

Fig. 28.4 Persian snaffle bit.

Peters, Gershom Moore, Cincinnati, OH, Patent No. 818,781, Apr. 24, 1906 [Fig. 28.5]. A compound bit with an inner and an outer portion secured together by lugs.

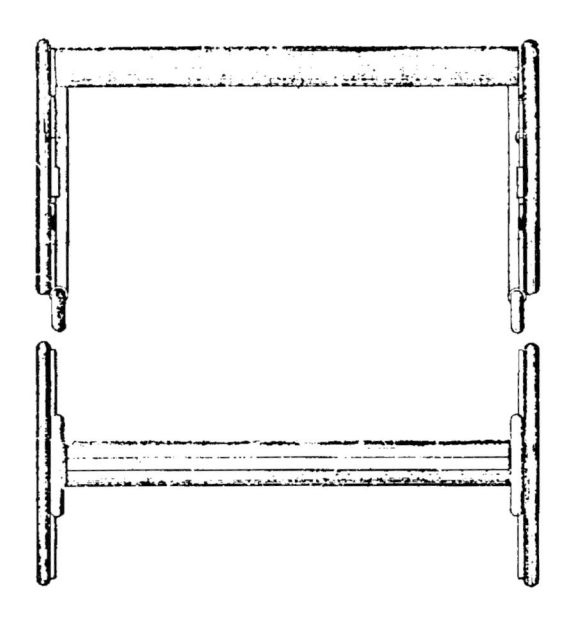

Fig. 28.5 Peters two-piece bit.

Peters Bit: See Chapter 25, Fig. 25.26.

Petersboro Bit: An early 1800's bit of England [Fig. 28.6].

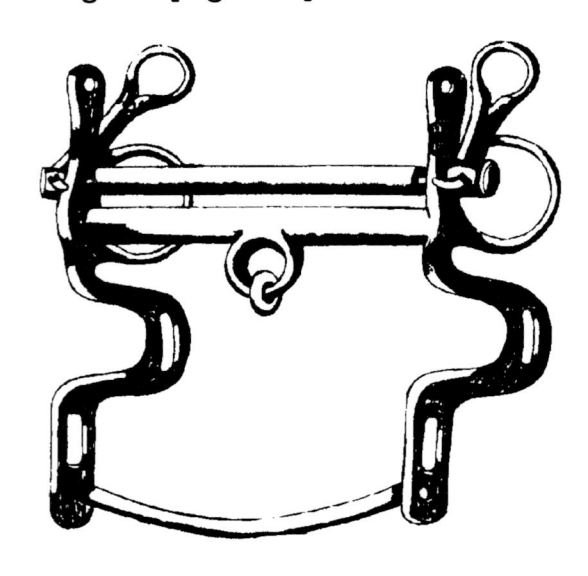

Fig. 28.6 Petersboro bit. Drawing by W. Stone from Harvey Matthew.

Petersheim, Samuel S., Upper Leacock Township, PA, Patent No. 126,231, Apr. 30, 1872 [Fig. 28.7]. A pulley gag bit.

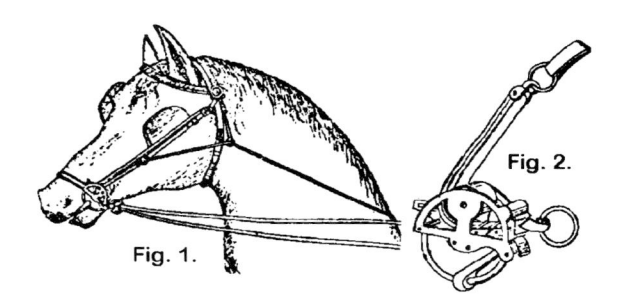

Fig. 28.7 Petersheim pulley bit.

Peterson, Jacob G., Morgantown, NC, Patent No. 164,590, June 15, 1875 [Fig. 28.8]. A bit formed of a single piece of steel wire twisted to form a strong bit.

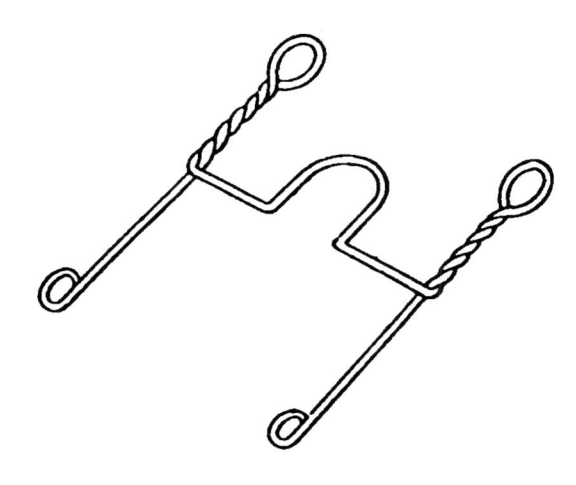

Fig. 28.8 Peterson's twisted-wire bit.

Peterson, Peter, Reels, IA, Patent No. 628,114, July 4, 1899 [Fig. 28.9]. A cheek-piece for a bit with a hook and a gravity latch.

Pfander, Heinrick, Augsburg, Germany, Patent No. 356,546, Jan. 25, 1887 [Fig. 28.10]. A bit produced with a variety of mouth-pieces. The upper rein-ring is removable to produce a two-rein curb bit.

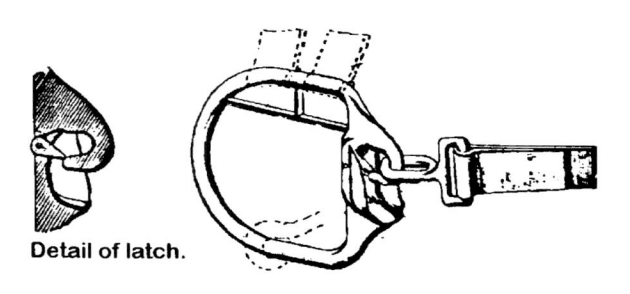

Fig. 28.9 Peterson's cheek for quick-attach reins.

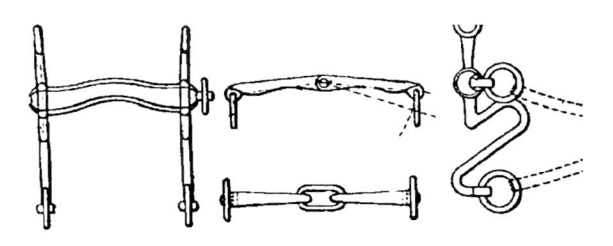

Fig. 28.10 Pfander two- or four-rein bit.

Phillips, Charles W., Omaha, NE, Patent No. 794,681, July 11, 1905 [Fig.28.11]. A built-in over-check bit attached to the main mouth-piece by a single link which can slide on the mouth-piece. Designed to prevent the horse from "grabbing" the bit in its teeth.

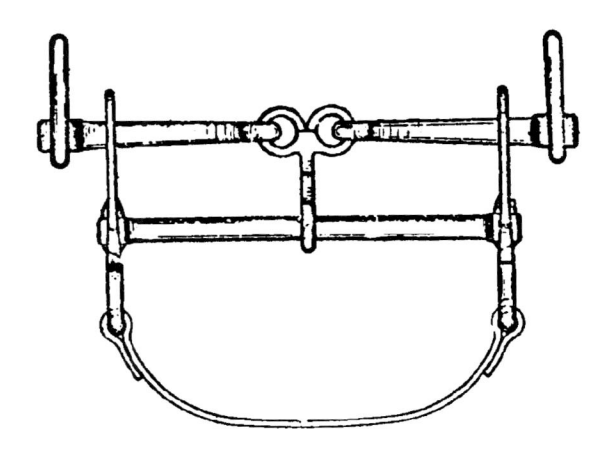

Fig. 28.11 Phillips double bit.

Phillips Safety Bit: See Chapter 8, Fig. 8.19.

Phillips, Willis E., Collbran, CO, Patent No. 1,281,203, Oct. 8, 1918 [Fig. 28.12]. The spring cheek-pieces attach to the mouth-piece by two holes in the mouth-piece ends which are forged at a 90-degree angle to the mouth-piece. A pull on the rein alters the pitch of the mouth-piece.

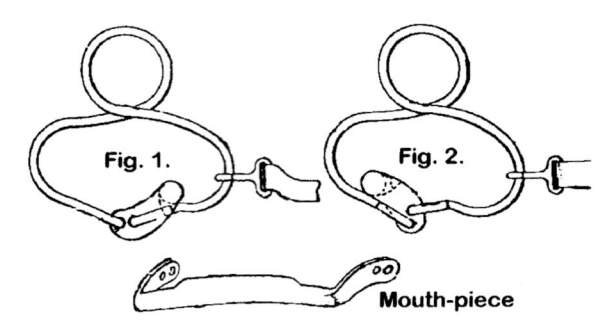

Fig. 28.12 Phillips snaffle bit.

Pierson, William A., Valley Forge, PA, Patent No. 165,863, July 20, 1875 [Fig. 28.13]. This design consists of attaching to each side of the bit a strap, which extends over the headstall to the other side, where it passes through a pulley-block secured to the bit. From there it is connected to the drive line, to a hitching strap, or to straps fitted to the legs of the horse.

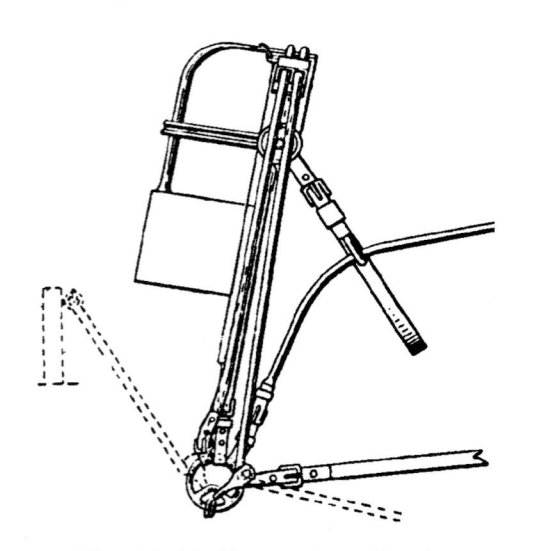

Fig. 28.13 Pierson's pulley bit.

Pistol Bit: A bit with cheek-pieces shaped as a pistol. A popular style of Buffalo Bill Cody's Wild West Shows and copied by many modern makers [Fig. 28.14].

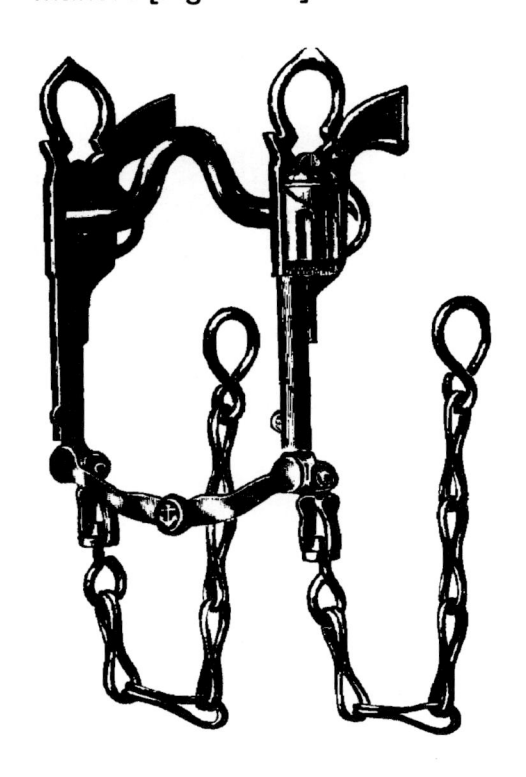

Fig. 28.14 Pistol bit by North and Judd, Newark, NJ.

Plates: A solid circular cheek-piece on a snaffle bit or a piece of metal attached to the mouth-piece of a bit to prevent tongue lolling.

Players: Small loosely hung teardrop shaped pieces of metal extending from the mouth-piece. See Chapter 26, Mouthing Bits.

Plow-lining: Lateral pulling of a rein to guide a horse.

Pneumatic Bit: A bit with a built-in air cushion in the cheek-piece to prevent chafing the horse's lips [Fig. 28.15].

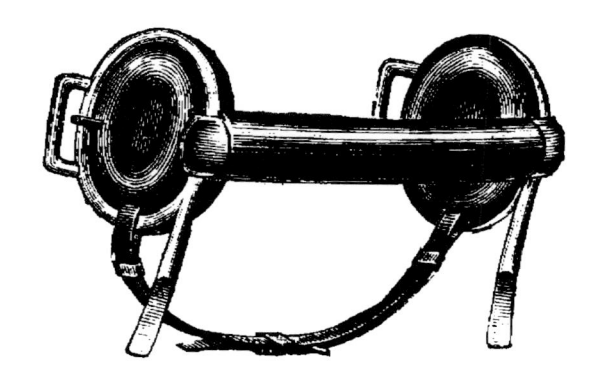

Fig. 28.15 Pneumatic bit.

Poll: The top of a horse's head directly behind the ears.

Polo Bit: A bit on a horse used to play polo. The term is applied directly to some bits.

Banbury Polo Bit: See Chapter 5, Fig. 5.28.

Belmont Polo Bit: See Chapter 27, Fig. 27.6.

Lancer Polo Bit: See Chapter 27, Fig. 27.24.

Western Polo Bit: See Chapter 27, Fig. 27.42.

Polo Bridles: See Chapter 35.

Pond, Clarke P., Olena, OH, Patent No. 416,422, Dec. 3, 1889 [Fig. 28.16]. A mouth-piece design in that one side of each half of the mouth-piece is flat and the other half is rounded.

Poole, Harold M., Medina, WA, Patent No. 2,940,238, June 14, 1960 [Fig. 28.17]. A curb bit with lever action. Rein tension does not exert a downward pressure on the bridle head-strap at the horse's poll.

Fig. 28.16 Pond mouth-piece design.

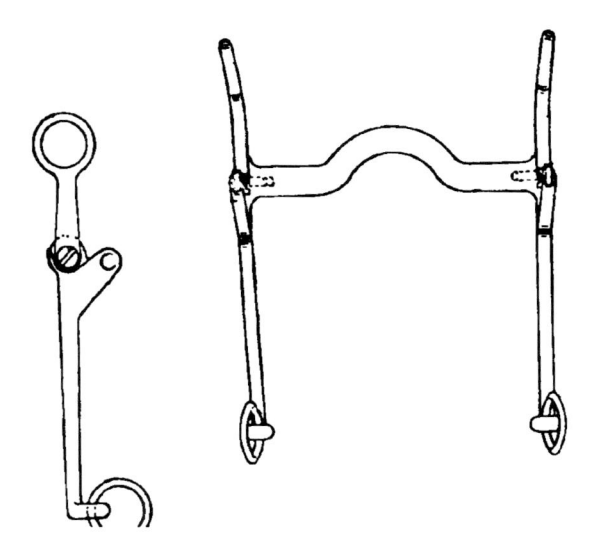

Fig. 28.17 Poole curb bit.

Pope, Alexander, Jr., Dorchester, MA, Patent No. 77,317, Apr. 28, 1866 [Fig. 28.18]. A bit that prevents a horse from dragging a tie weight. A strap connects the bridle to the weight and when the horse attempts to drag the weight, pressure is exerted to the under jaw of the horse. The snaps make it readily attached or removed from the rings of a normal bit.

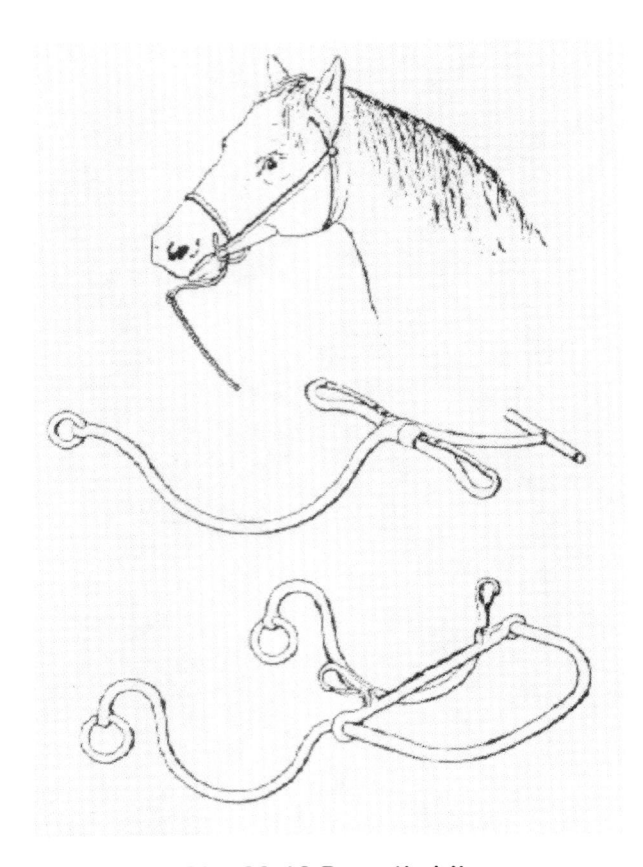

Fig. 28.18 Pope tie bit.

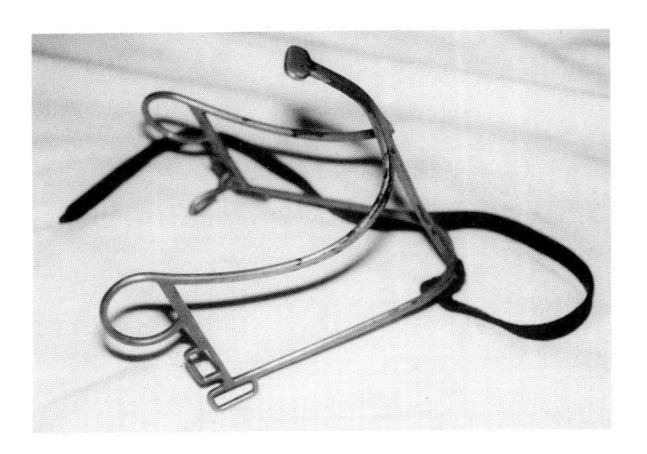

Fig. 28.19 Porter's Humane bit and bridle.

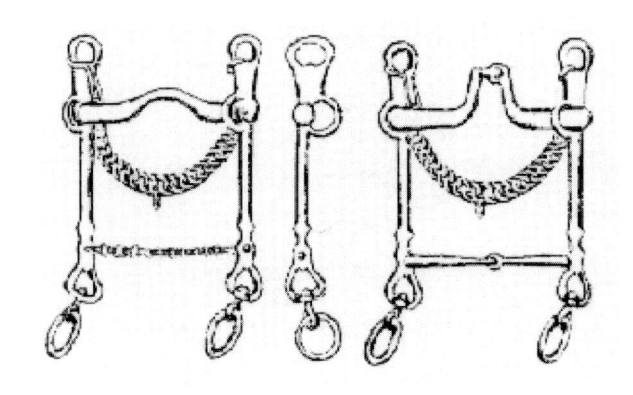

Fig. 28.20 Two variations of Portugese bits manufactured by John Dewsbury and Son, Walsall, England.

Port: A raised central portion of the mouth-piece that has parallel or even sides. See Chapter 25.

Porter's Humane Bit and Bridle: A bit without a mouth-piece that applies pressure to the nose of a horse [Fig. 28.19]. Made in nickel and enamel and supplied with straps to fit any bridle.

Port-mouth Bit: A bit with a port in the center of the mouth-piece.

Portsmouth Bit: The Universal Pattern. See Chapter 21, Fig. 21.6.

Portugese Bit and Curb: A style of curb bits manufactured by various companies for export to Portugal [Fig. 28.20].

Preece, Terence Q., Westbury, NY, Patent No. 1,678,532, July 24, 1928 [Fig. 28.21]. The copper coated mouth-piece can be move to any one of the three holes in the cheekpieces to change the fulcrum of leverage of the bit.

Price, Ebenezer N., Salem, MA, Patent No. 11,083, June 13, 1854 [Fig. 28.22]. Extending from each cannon of the bit is a nipper or jaw projecting rearward from the mouth-piece and against the side of the lower jaw. The nipper or jaws are short pieces of metal about three inches in length and may be provided with an eye or hole for a chain or leather strap. The strap will confine the jaws and, with the bit in the mouth, places pressure on the gum or bar of the horse.

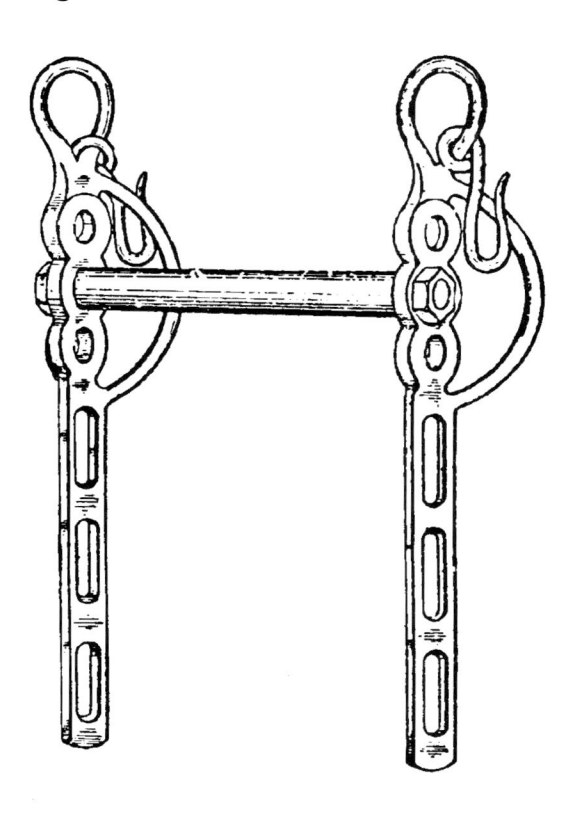

Fig. 28.21 Preece adjustable-mouth bit.

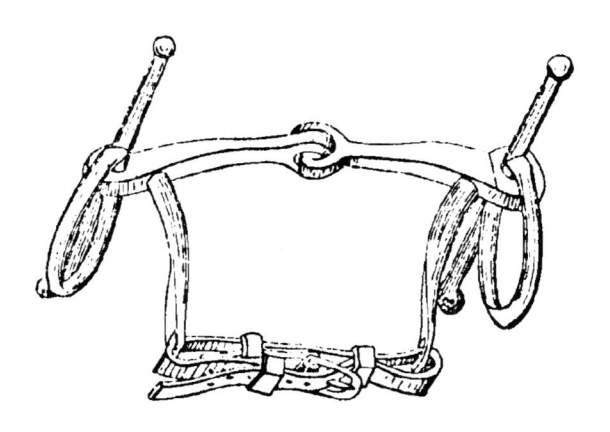

Fig. 28.22 Price jaw-pressure bit.

Price, Joshua C., New Philadelphia, OH, Patent No. 63,297, Mar. 26, 1867 [Fig. 28.23]. The cheek-pieces slide in holes in the outer ends of the square jointed mouth-piece.

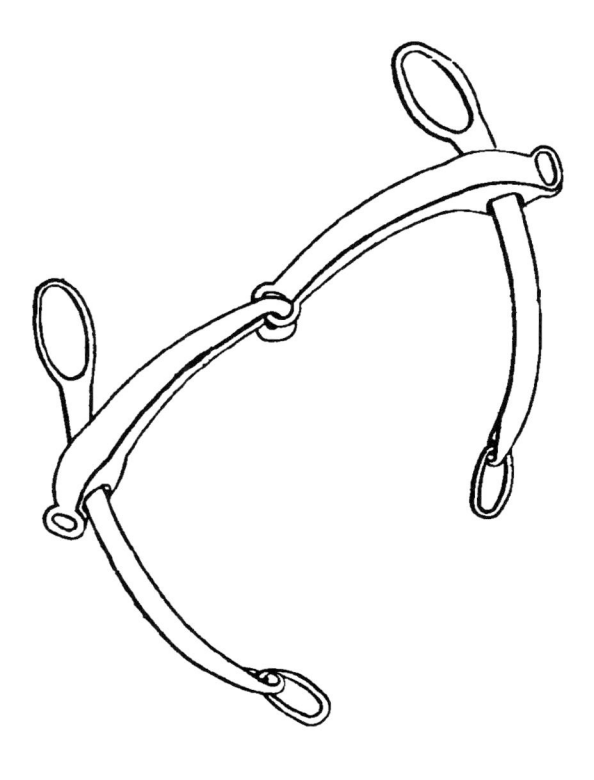

Fig. 28.23 Price loose-cheek bit.

Psalion: An ancient cavesson-type devise of two metal U-shaped straps with one around the nose and the second under the jaw.

Pulley Bit: A bit with a pulley attached to the bit or the bridle to increase mechanical advantage of the rein-pull. Some examples:

Barnes: Chapter 5, Fig. 5.31.
Binkley: Chapter 5, Fig. 5.56.
Campbell: Chapter 6, Fig. 6.5.
Clark: Chapter 6, Fig. 6.26.
Evans: Chapter 10. Fig. 10.19.
Ferry: Chapter 11, Fig. 11.10.
Jandrue: Chapter 15, Fig.15.13.
King: Chapter 15, Fig.15.35.
Nash: Chapter 26, Fig. 26.9.
Petershiem: Chapter 28, Fig. 28.7.
Roeber: Chapter 29, Fig.29.21.
Taylor: Chapter 33, Fig. 33.2.
Williams: Chapter 34, Fig. 34.30.

Purcell, James, Winona, ND, Patent No. 660,923, Oct. 30, 1900 [Fig. 28.24]. The mouth-piece and side-pieces are rigidly connected, with the upper portion of each side-piece being a hollow cylinder which houses a coil spring attached to the links for attaching the reins.

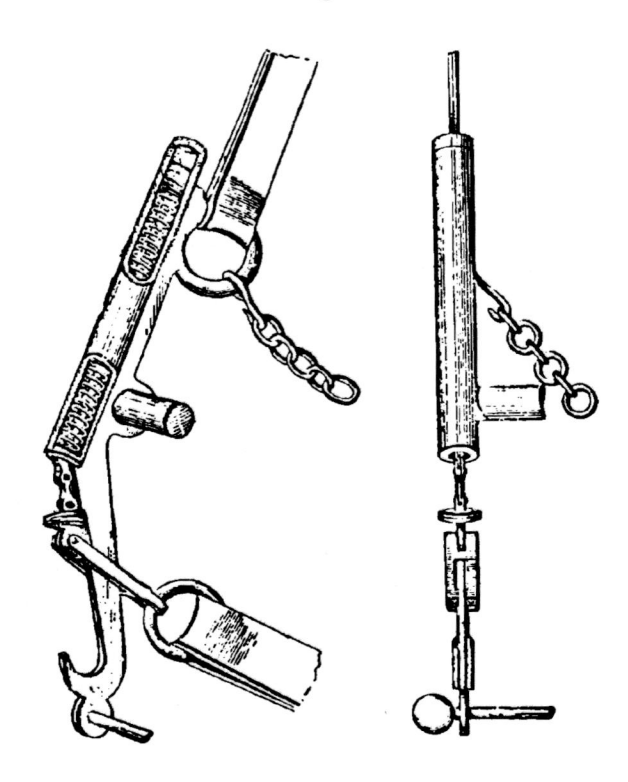

Fig. 28.24 Purcell spring-tension-rein bit.

CHAPTER TWENTY-NINE
Race to Rutledge

Race Bit: A broken snaffle bit with large cheek-rings, 3 or 4 inches or larger [Fig. 29.0].

Fig. 29.0 A Race bit.

Racine Driving Bit: See Chapter 5, Fig. 5.79.

Racking Bit: A style of bit used on gaited horses and is supplied in a variety of ported mouth-pieces [Fig. 29.1].

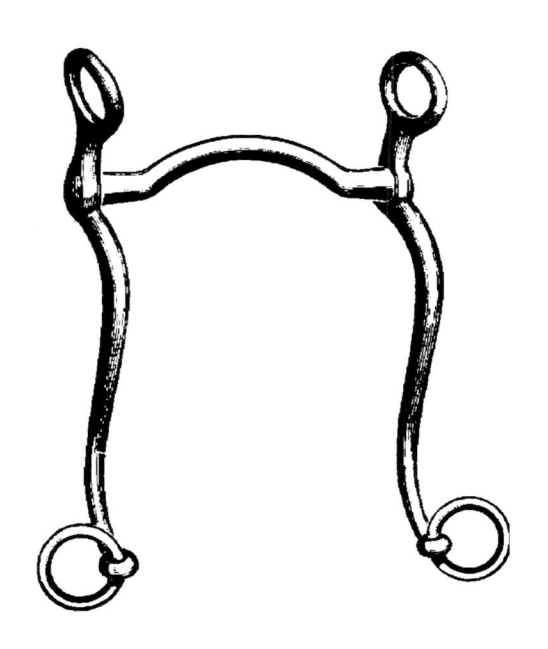

Fig. 29.1 A racking bit.

Rand, George D., Phillips and Cook, Patent No. 493,339, Mar. 14, 1893, Commonly called Phillips Safety Bit. See Chapter 8, Fig. 8.19.

Rarey Bit: John Rarey [Fig. 29.2].

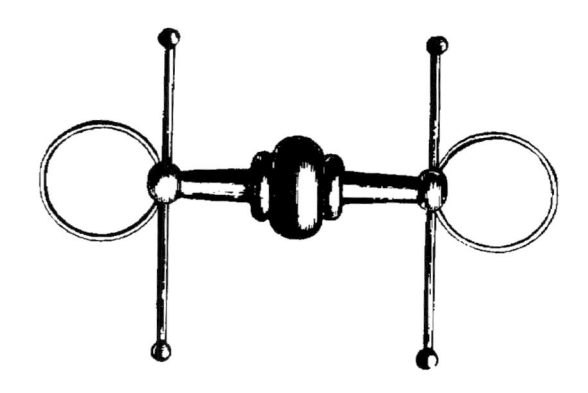

Fig. 29.2 Rarey training bit.

Ray, Frederick A., Los Angeles, CA, A hackamore bit. See Chapter 13.

Ray, Frederick A., Los Angeles, CA, Patent No. 2,494,201, Jan. 10, 1950 [Fig. 29.3]. The cheek-pieces pivot on the mouth-piece ends.

Raymond Leverage Chin Check: A checking device without a mouth-piece and works independent of a driving bit and is effective in keeping the mouth shut [Fig. 29.4].

Raymond, Liberty K., Garretsville, OH, Patent No. 670,248, Mar. 19, 1901 [Fig. 29.5]. Metal clips used to attach an overcheck bit to an ordinary snaffle bit.

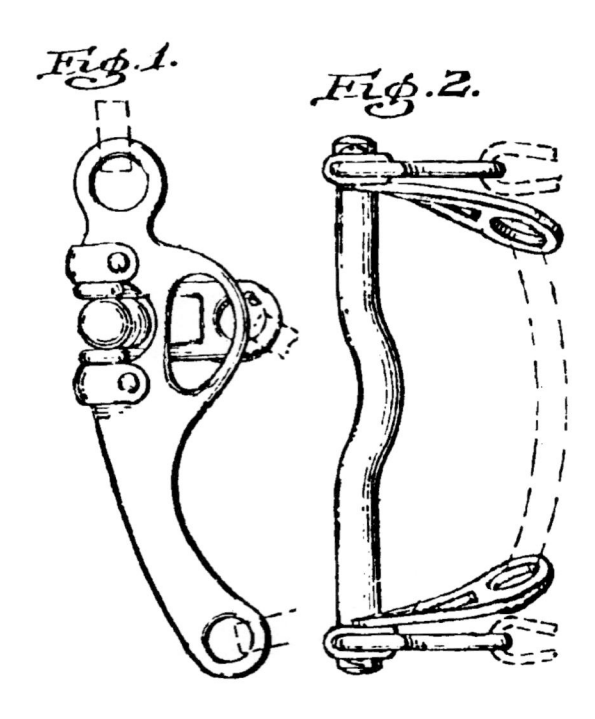

Fig. 29.3 Ray loose-cheek curb bit.

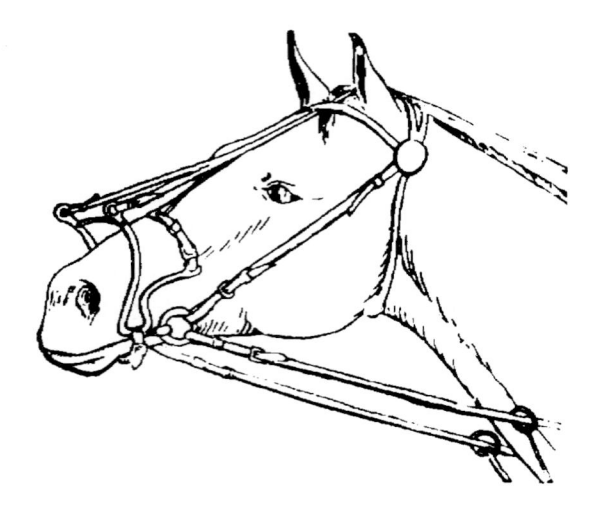

Fig. 29.4 Raymond leverage chin check.

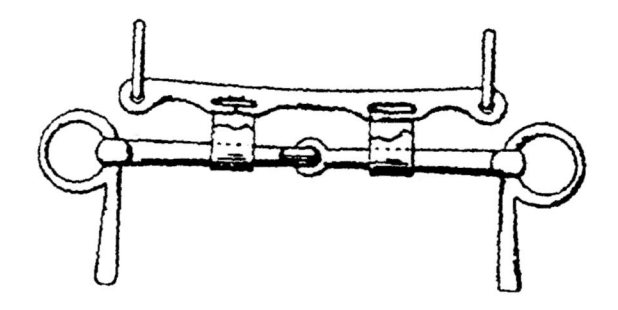

Fig. 29.5 Raymond check-bit attachment.

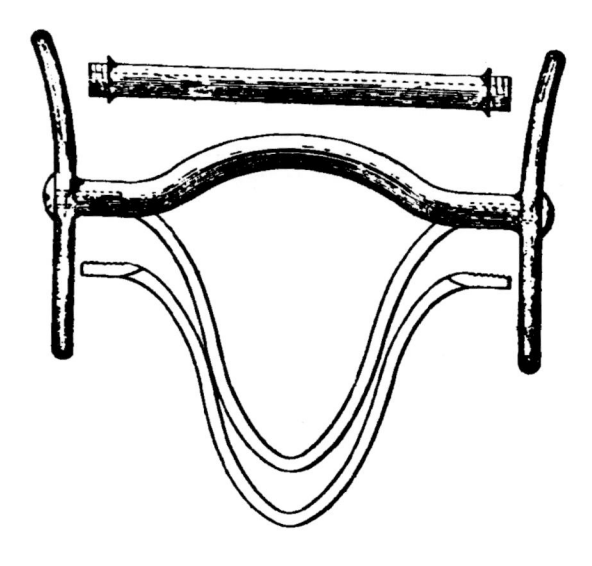

Fig. 29.6 Reade bit with a removable tongue-bar.

Reade, Charles A., Chicago, IL, Patent No. 435,189, Aug. 26, 1890 [Fig. 29.6]. A bit with a removable tongue-bar of spring steel, Large circular cheek-pieces keep the mouth-piece "out of the horse's teeth."

Rearing-horse Bit: John M. Espinosa design patent. See Chapter 10, Fig. 10.18.

Rearing-horse Bit: John G. Ridings with assignment to A. Buermann Mfg. Co., Design Patent No. 34,969, Aug. 20, 1901 [Fig. 29.7]. No. 1317 in A. Buermann Catalog No. 35.

Rearing-horse Bit: Sold by North and Judd Mfg. Co., Newark, NJ [Fig. 29.8].

Fig. 29.7 Buermann rearing-horse bit.

Fig. 29.8 Rearing-horse bit.

Regulator Bit: A bit with an extension on one side several inches past the cheek-ring with another ring in the end for rein attachment. Used for side-pulling horses and can be changed to the side desired for the effect [Fig. 29.9]. The bit is used on the track to keep racing horses from running wide on the turns.

Fig. 29.9 Regulator bit.

Reichart, John: See Chapter 8, Fig, 8.4.

Rein, Bearing: A rein running from the snaffle or bridoon to the pad or luggage saddle of the off-horse of a harness pair to keep the horse's head in the correct position.

Reinforced Bar: Braces for the spade mouth-piece of a spade bit. See drawing of Spade bit, Chapter 1.

Reins: Long leather straps used to control the horse by running from the bit in the horse's mouth to the hands of the rider or driver.

Reversed Arch Pelham: A Pelham bit with the arch directed downward to press on the tongue as opposed to the normal upward position that gives the tongue room.

Reversible Side-piece: See Chapter 31.

Reynolds, Robert F., Fisk, AL, Patent No. 644,945, Mar. 6, 1900 [Fig. 29.10]. The levered sections of the bit act as a curb and are placed under the chin of the horse.

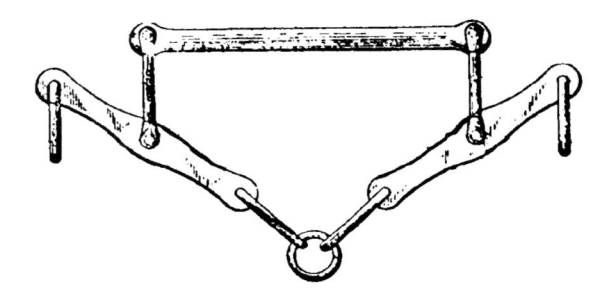

Fig. 29.10 Reynold's levered curb.

361

Richmond, Henry T., Malvern, IA, Patent No. 365,151, June 21, 1887 [Fig. 29.11 and 29.11a]. A scissor bit with square mouth-pieces.

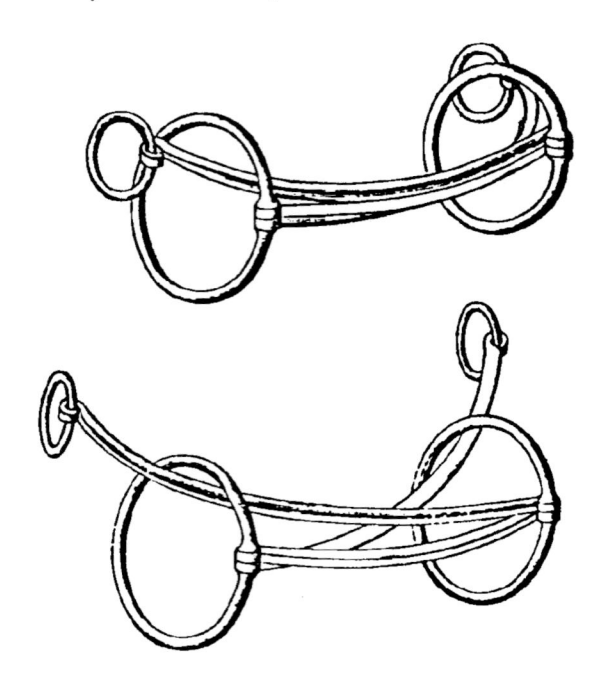

Fig. 29.11 Richmond scissor bit.

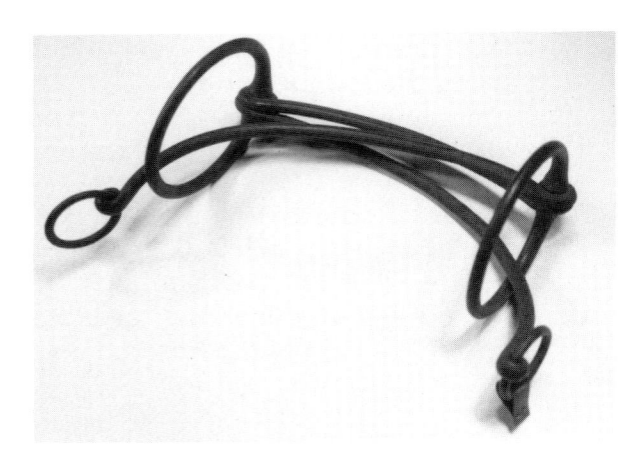

Fig. 29.11a Richmond production bit. Robert Maclin collection.

Richter, Hugo, Dresden, Germany, Patent No. 664,970, Jan. 1, 1901 [Fig. 29.12]. A combination of a shell, plungers and levers that produce a bit which does not act upon the mouth of the horse when pressure is applied to the reins. Designed for breaking or training horses.

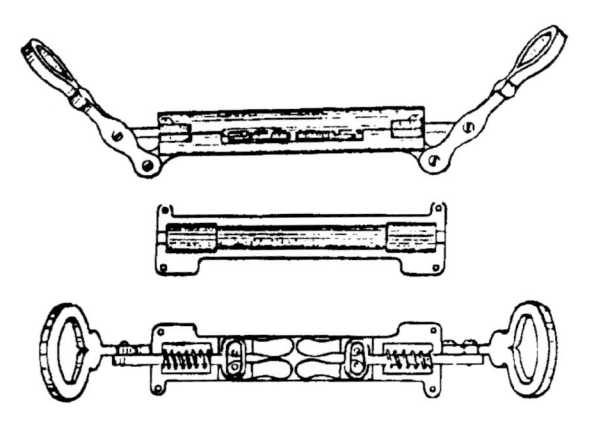

Fig. 29.12 Several views of the internal mechanism of Richter's bit.

Riding, John G.: See Rearing Horse Bit, Fig. 29.8.

Riggs, Herman L., Palmyra, NY, Patent No. 831,102, Sep. 18, 1906 [Fig. 29.13]. A bit attachment that can be adapted to most broken snaffle bits.

Rigid-mouth Snaffle: A bit with a straight stiff mouth-piece. See Chapter 25.

Ring Bit: A bit with a large ring attached to a port of 2 inches or more [Figs. 29.14 to 29.18]. The lower jaw of the horse passes through the ring which acts as a curb of a normal curb bit. See Chapter 1, diagram; Chapter 18, Fig. 18.10; Chapter 23, Fig. 23.24 and Chapter 32, Fig. 32.58.

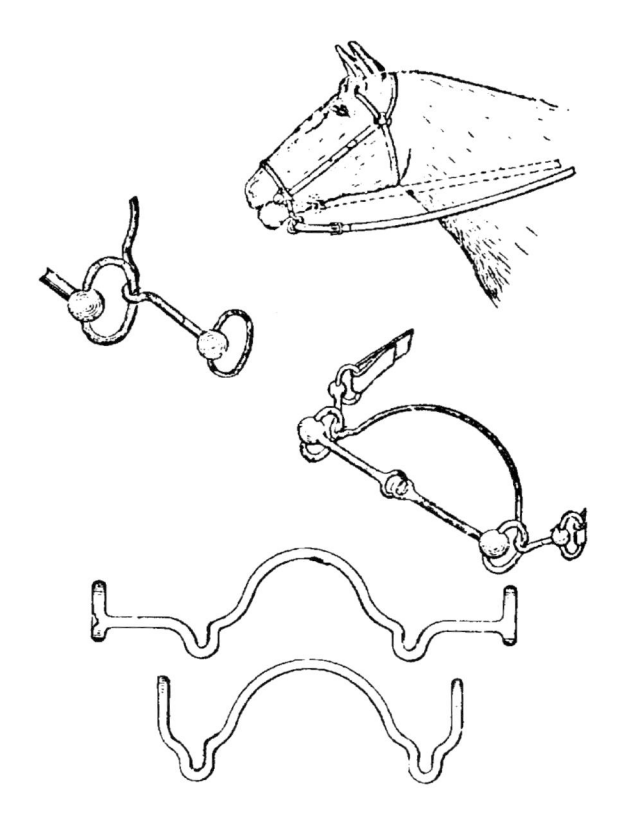

Fig. 29.13 Riggs snaffle bit attachment for side-pullers.

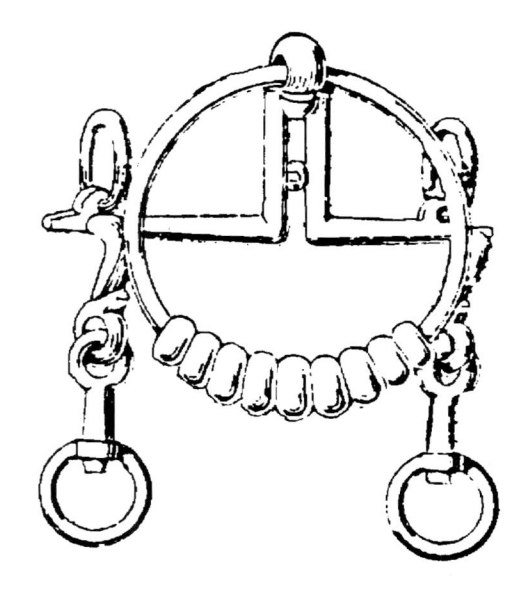

Fig. 29.14a Turkey ring bit.

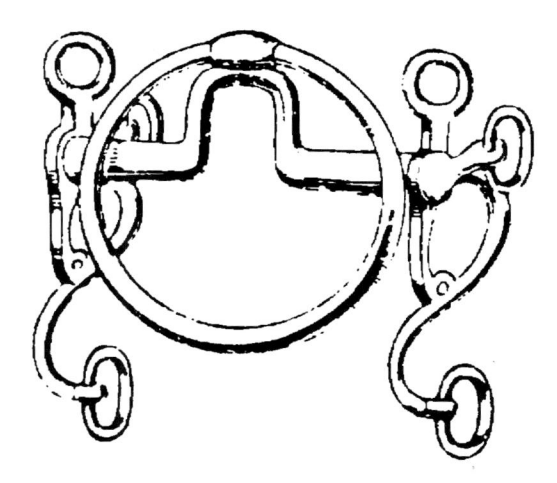

Fig. 29.15 Chilian ring bit.

Fig. 29.14 Chilian ring bit with rollers.

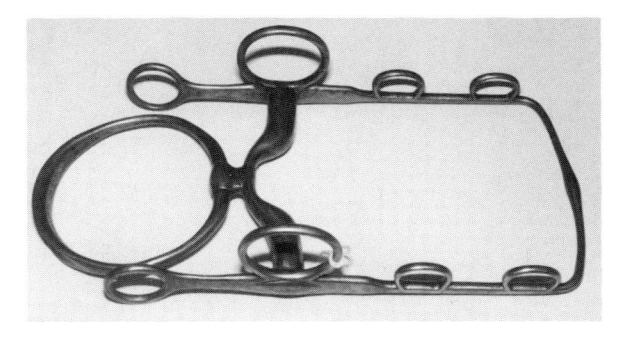

Fig. 29.16 Ring bit with a 4 1/2 inch ring and 9 inch cheeks.

Fig. 29.17 South American ring bit.

Fig. 29.18 Turkish ring bit. Robert Maclin collection.

Fig. 29.18a Robert Maclin collection.

Fig. 29.18b Turkish ring bit. Robert Maclin collection.

Ring Snaffle: A bit with wire rings for cheek-pieces. See Chapter 31.

Robbins, William S., New Bedford, MA, Patent No. 84,843, Dec. 8, 1868 [Fig. 29.19]. A double concave bit with one mouth-piece fitting snug into the other.

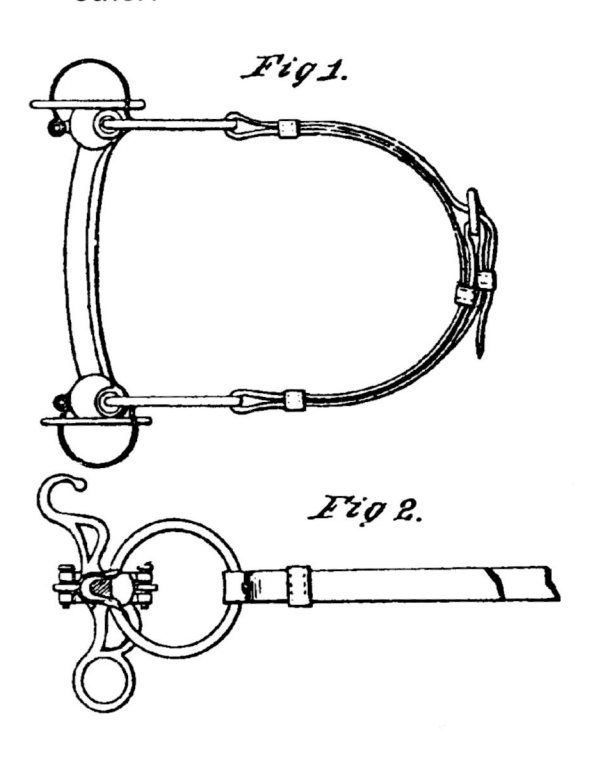

Fig. 29.19 Robbins double concave-mouth bit.

Roberds, J. M., District of Columbia, Patent No. 31,557, Feb. 26, 1861 [Fig. 29.20]. The bit has a flattened cross-piece of metal extending on each side of the mouth-piece and in the same plane as the side-pieces. It measures about one inch in width and two and one-half inches in total length. In place of a curb chain, a piece of corrugated sheet metal is attached to the bit by hooks (Fig. 2). The corrugations are made with angles in the area that comes in contact with the chin groove.

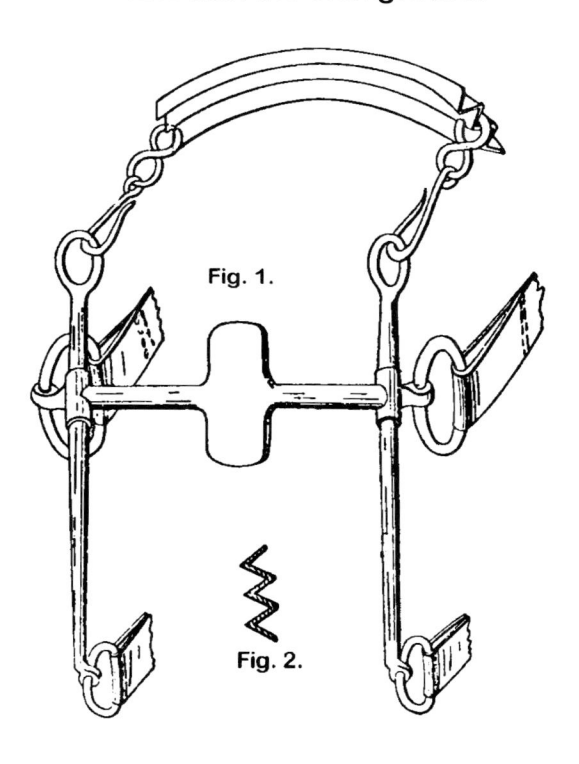

Fig. 29.20 Roberds curb bit with corrugated curb-piece.

Roberts, Benjamin P., Boston, MA Patent No. 328,975, Oct. 27, 1885 [Fig. 29.21]. The mouth-piece is constructed of a double row of small rollers. Each row is independent of the other. The rollers turn and prevent the horse from getting the bit in its teeth.

Roberts, Benjamin S. and O. B. North, New Haven, CT, Patent No. 109,145, Nov. 8, 1870 [Fig. 29.22]. A jointed bit with each portion having an arm on its outer extremity which presses hard against the jaw of the horse when the reins are pulled.

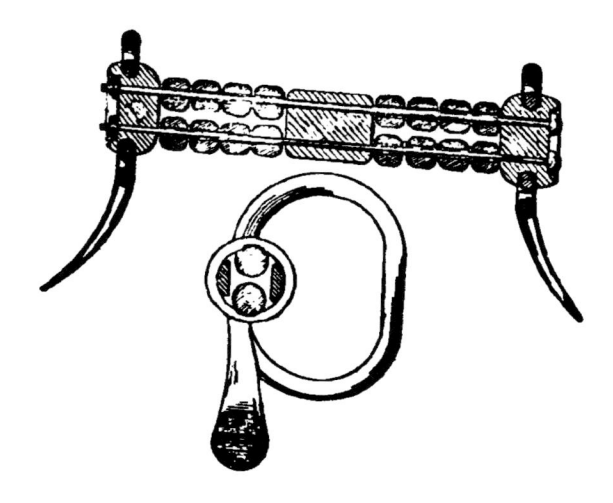

Fig. 29.21 Roberts double roller-mouth bit.

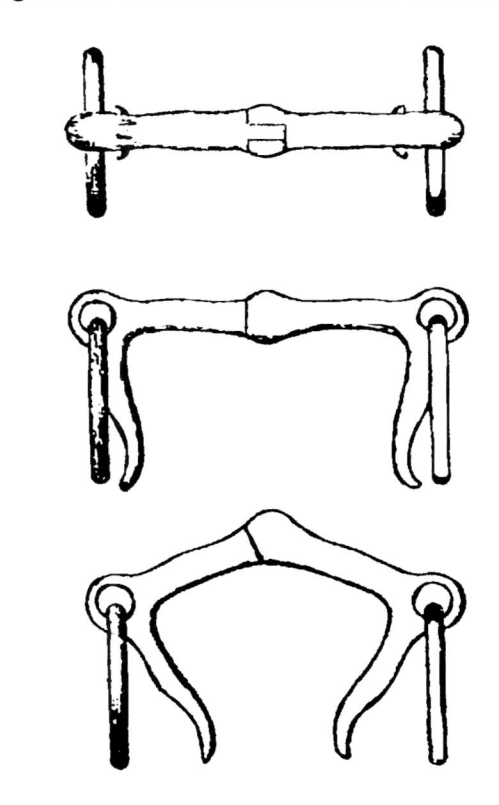

Fig. 29.22 Three views of Roberts hinged-snaffle bit.

Robinson, John H., Manchester Bridge, NY, Patent No. 202,195, Apr. 9, 1878 [Fig. 29.23]. The bit is designed to prevent a horse from shying while being driven. Side pressure of its head against one of the springs in the cheek-piece will compress the spring and cause the points to project through the slots of the springs and pierce its mouth and "after a few tries it will give up shying."

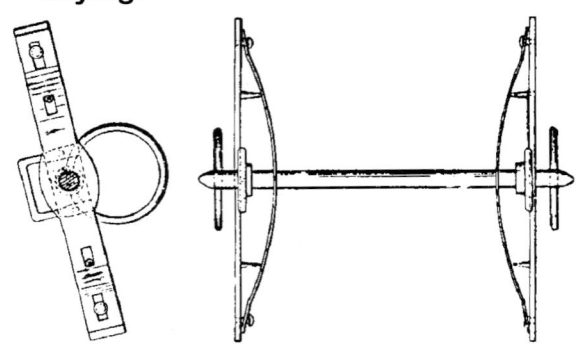

Fig. 29.23 Robinson bit.

Rockwell Driving Bit: See Chapter 8, Fig. 8.20.

Rody, Adolph E., Elmwood, Ontario, Canada, Patent No. 2,280,853, Apr. 28, 1942 [Fig. 29.24]. A medicine bit with a hollow mouth-piece and mid-portion. The opening is placed uppermost within the mouth avoiding injury to the tongue but still "dispence medication."

Roeber, Alexander, Morgan, TX, Patent No. 303,751, Aug. 19, 1884 [Fig. 29.25]. The cheek-pieces extend down and back with slides mounted to which both the check-rein and driving-rein are attached. The double attachment gives the driver added leverage and control in keeping the horse's head up.

Romal: Not a rein, but the extension of closed reins often fashioned as a quirt or whip of 3 to 4 feet in length. When dropped, cannot be lost. Incorrectly called a romal rein at times.

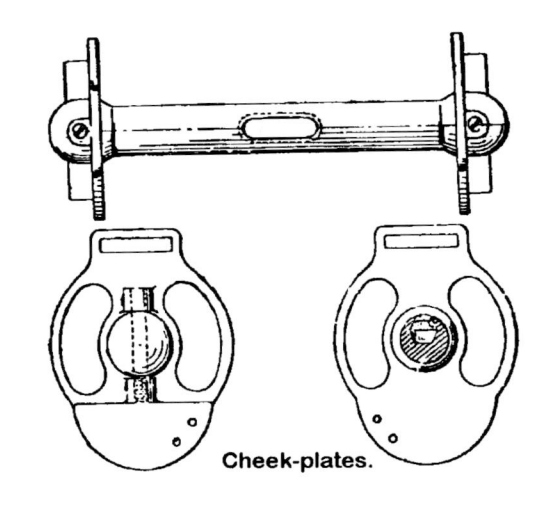

Fig. 29.24 Rody medicine bit.

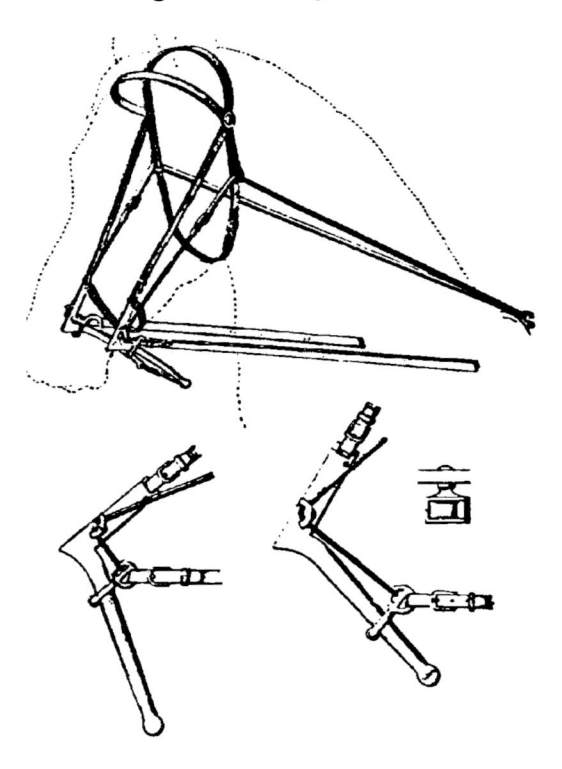

Fig. 29.25 Roeber pulley bit.

Roping Bit: A name applied to a variety of similarly designed and constructed bits [Fig. 29.26]. A roping bit by "Wallie" Boone.

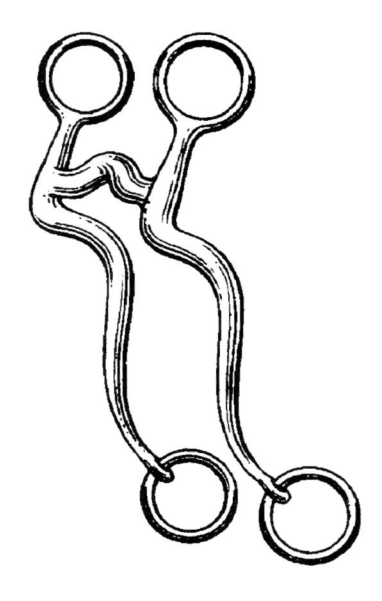

Fig. 29.26 Boone's roping bit.

Rounded-mouth Bit: A bit with a mouth-piece that is flat on one side or concave on one side and rounded on the opposite side [Fig. 29.27].

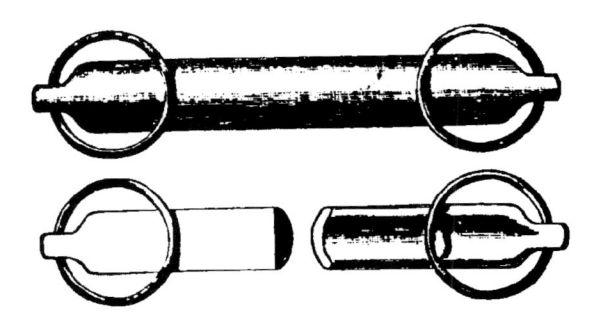

Fig. 29.27 Drawing of both sides of the rounded-mouth bit and the two styles of the flat or concave side.

Rowley, Burdett L., New Britain, CT, Patent No. 76,821, Apr. 14, 1868 [Fig. 29.28]. A flexible-mouth bit with a double-eye link used to connect the short chain of the mouth-piece. The entire mouth is covered with molded rubber or a rubber tube can be placed over the mouth-piece.

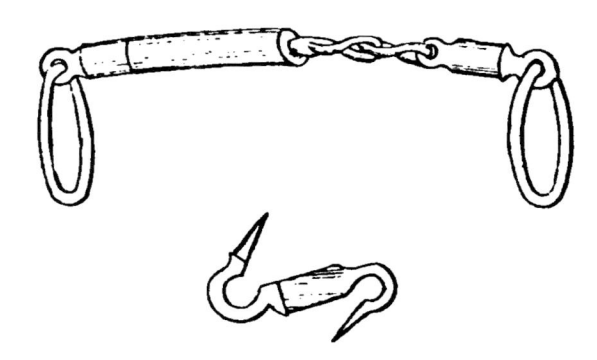

Fig. 29.28 Rowley flexible-mouth bit.

Rowley, Everett V., Alcester, SD, Patent No. 1,258,145, Mar. 5, 1918 [Fig. 29.29]. A hollow mouth-piece with an internal coil spring compresses in place and bolts at each end. The bolts can be retracted to the center of the mouth-piece to rapidly remove or replace the mouth-piece to the rein-rings. The idea is to prevent putting a cold mouth-piece in the horse's mouth.

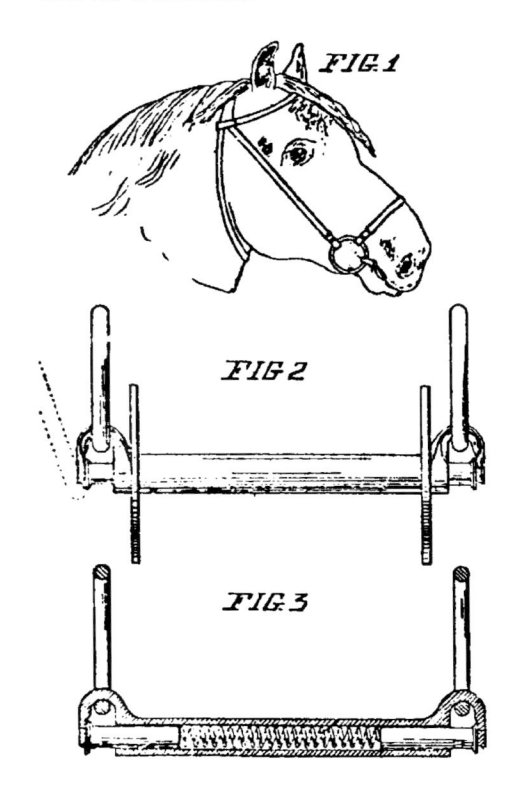

Fig. 29.29 Rowley detachable mouth-piece.

Rugby Hunt Polo: See Chapter 27, Fig. 27.31.

Ruhlow, August F., Pierce, NE, Patent No. 484,342, Oct. 11, 1892 [Fig. 29.30]. A bridle bit of two connected parts which operate as a gag bit. Each half of each cheek-piece carries half of the mouth-piece. When the driving reins are attached to the double chain the mouth-piece separates and the gag affect results. When the reins are attached to the center D-ring the bit is a normal snaffle bit.

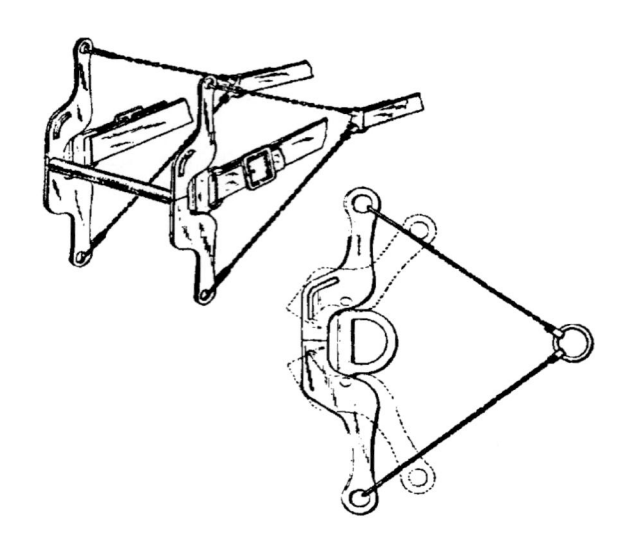

Fig. 29.30 Ruhlow gag bit.

Rule Joint Bit: See Chapter 25, Fig. 25.44.

Runaway Bit: A term for the Bicycle Chain Bit. See Chapter 5, Fig. 5.53.

Running Bit: Refers to a bit used in racing and in some areas a Runout bit.

Running Rein: See Chapter 35.

Runout Bit: See chapter 12, Fig. 12.30 and Chapter 6, Fig. 6.2.

Rupert, Lilburn L, Muskogee, OK, Patent No. 2,006,032, June 25, 1935 [Fig.29.31]. All members of this bit, including the rings, cheek-pieces and mouth-piece are of hollow metal construction.

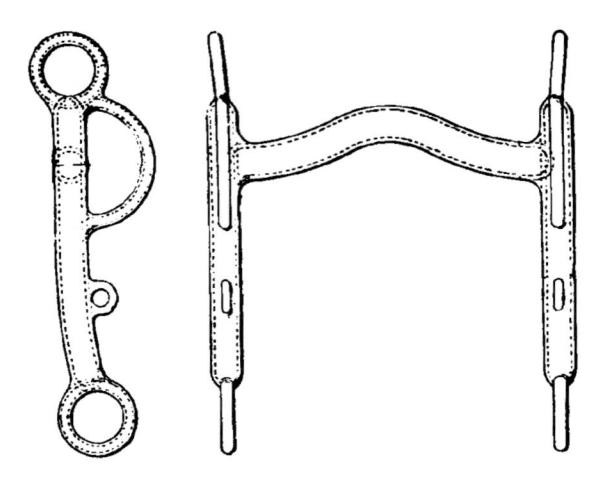

Fig. 29.31 Rupert hollow-member bit.

Russell, Arthur G., Denver, and Richard T. Hawkey, Melvin, CO, Patent No. 547,589, Oct. 8, 1895 [Fig. 29.32]. Each cheek-piece is fitted to turn independently upon the bar or mouth-piece. This enables the rider to readily turn the horse without cramping the curb-strap or chain.

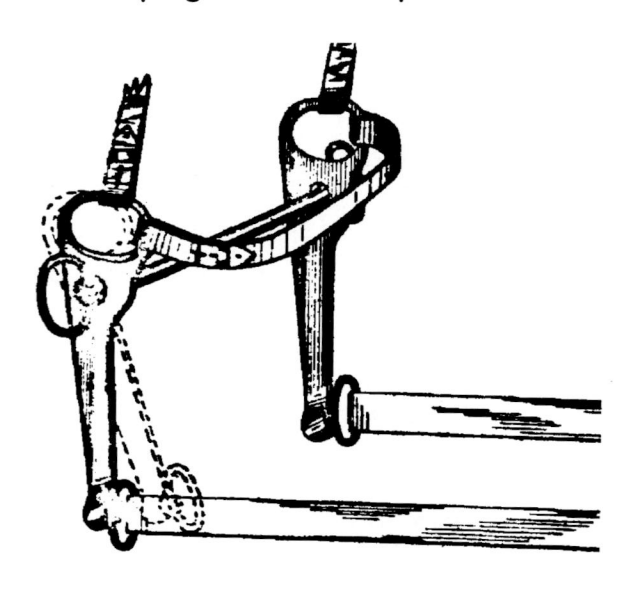

Fig. 29.32 Russel independent-cheek bit.

Rutledge Roper: A bit made by Trammell Bits, Inc. [Fig. 29.33]. A roper bit in which the cheek-pieces can pivot on the wide flat curbed mouth-piece. See Chapter 27, S. M. Pelham, Fig. 27.33.

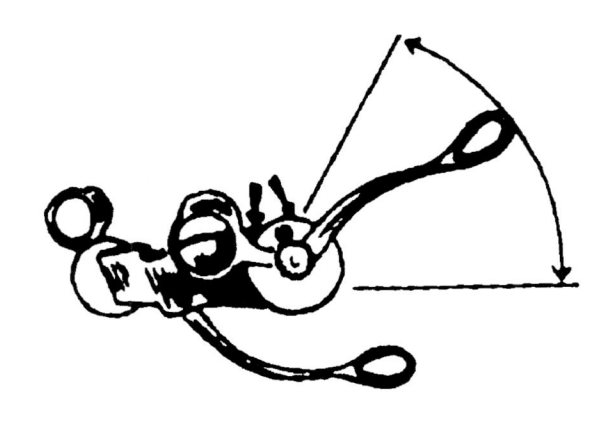

Fig. 29.33 Rutledge roper.

Saddled pony of 16th Century A.D. China.

CHAPTER THIRTY
Sabio to Side

Sabio, Simon C., Bagio, Philippine Islands, Patent No. 1,281,215, Oct. 8, 1918 [Fig. 30.0]. A ring bit with the ring loosely attached to the bit bar and arranged to pass around the lower jaw of the horse and a covered spring connecting the sides of the bit and under the jaw ring.

Fig. 30.0 Sabio ring bit.

Fig. 30.1 San Antonio bit.

Saddlery: The tack used on a horse when ridden, such as the bridle, saddle and other items used.

Safety Bit: See Phillips Safety bit, Chapter 8, Fig. 8.19.

Salisbury Gag: See Chapter 12, Fig. 12.16.

Saw-tooth Bit: See Bicycle Chain bit, Chapter 5, Fig. 5.53.

San Antonio Bit: A small Texas-style bit from Haydens and Allen, St. Louis, MO, circa 1900 [Fig. 30.1].

San Jose Bit: A small Texas-style bit from Haydens and Allen [Fig. 30.2].

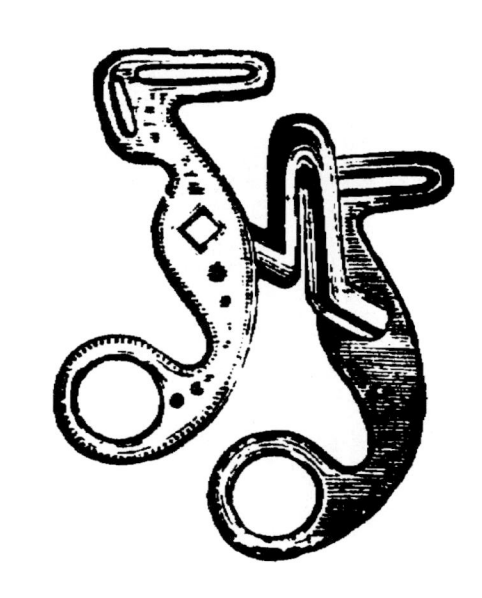

Fig. 30.2 San Jose bit.

Sanborn, William H., Rutland, VT, Patent No. 530,461, Dec. 4, 1894 [Fig. 30.3]. The bit is part of a complete bridle

370

and harness apparatus for controlling horses. A spherical or elliptical rotatable button is part of the mouth-piece center-link.

Fig. 30.3 Sanborn bit with center-button link.

Salinas Bit: A loose-cheek California-style bit designated by the design of the cheek-piece [Fig. 30.4].

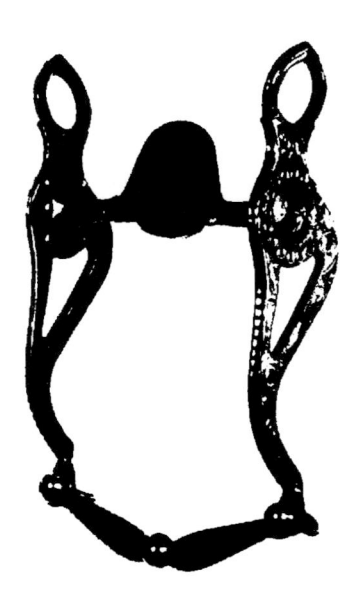

Fig. 30.4 The Salinas bit.

Santa Barbara Bit: A loose-jawed spade bit usually ornamented with silver and silver buttons on the cheek-pieces. Point of accepted origin, the Santa Barbara area of California [Fig. 30.5].

Santa Susanna Bit: A loose-cheek spade bit with snake pattern cheek-pieces.

Sargeant, E. Eugene, Newark, NJ, Patent No. 289,452, Dec. 4, 1883 [Fig. 30.6]. A construction method in which the open eye is cast (of malleable cast metal) with a core so as to leave an opening of sufficient width to admit the closed eye between the lapped parts. When the two parts are swagged or pressed together, a closed joint is made.

Fig. 30.5 Santa Barbara bit.

Fig. 30.6 Sargeant construction method.

Scamperdale Pelham: A loose-cheek, fixed ring Pelham [Fig. 30.7].

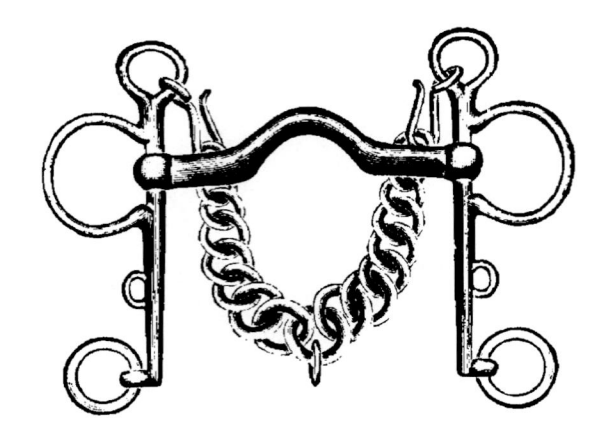

Fig. 30.7 Scamperdale Pelham.

Scherling, Conrad, Guttenburg, IA, Patent No. 290,803, Dec 25, 1883 [Fig. 30.8]. The bit is formed of short sections flexibly jointed together in such a manner that either a stiff and rigid or a yielding bit is produced by reversing the bit.

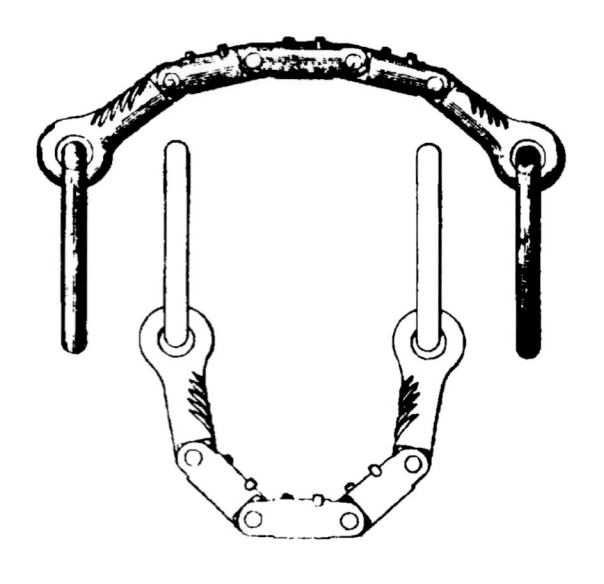

Fig. 30.8 Scherling reversible bit.

Schleuter, Henry, Scribner, NE, Patent No. 1,130,638, Mar. 2, 1915 [Fig. 30.9]. A bit that may be mounted in several different positions to be used as a snaffle bit or a curb, depending on where the headstall and bridle reins are attached. It can also be used to allow the extended ring to press against the jaw by attaching the driving reins opposite the extending ring.

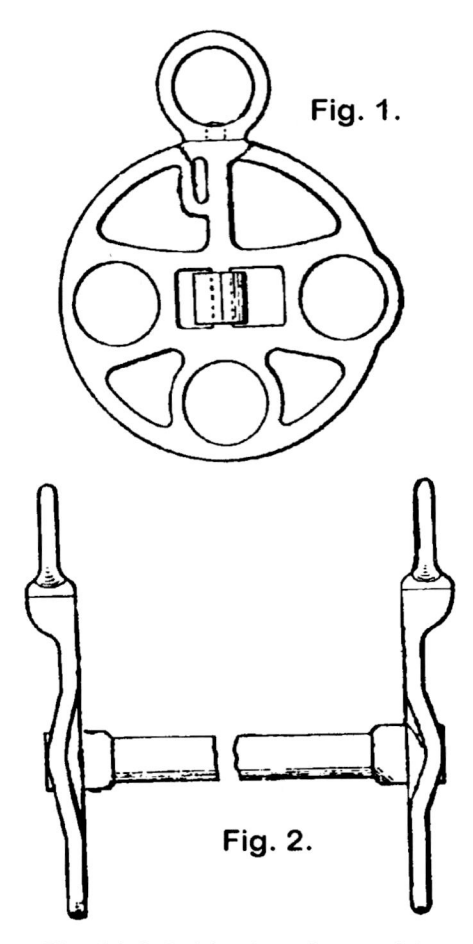

Fig. 30.9 Schleuter change bit.

Schoonmaker, Peter, New Britain, CT, Patent No. 81,510, Aug. 25, 1868 [Fig. 30.10]. The bit consists of a "japaned" ring in which the inner half of the cheek-ring is lined with German silver for beauty and durability.

Scissor Bit: A bit with a crossed double mouth-piece. Some examples:

Brown, Chapter 5, Fig. 5.81.

Campbell, Chapter 6, Fig. 6.4.
Guy, Chapter 12, Fig. 12.45.
Huckins, Chapter 14, Fig. 14.37.
Johnson, Chapter 15, Fig. 15.19
McGuinnis, Chapter 20, Fig. 20.6.
Norton, Chapter 26, Fig. 26.21.
Richmond, Chapter 29, Fig. 29.11.
Smith, Chapter 32, Fig. 32.9.
Thompson, Chapter 33, Fig. 33.9.

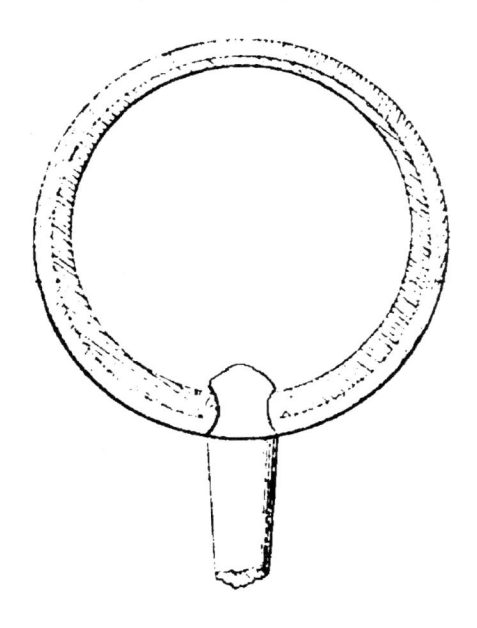

Fig. 30.10 Schoonmaker lined cheek-rings.

Scorrier Bit: A bit with check rings in slots near the end of the mouth-piece [Fig. 30.11]. The mouth-piece may be smooth or grooved.

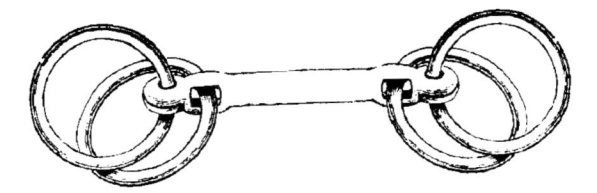

Fig. 30.11 Scorrier snaffle bit.

Sears, Robert and Lucien B. Lindsey, Spokane, WA, Patent No. 492,241, Feb. 21, 1898 [Fig. 30.12 and 30.12a]. A humane bit with a leather mouth-piece and a leather curb-strap.

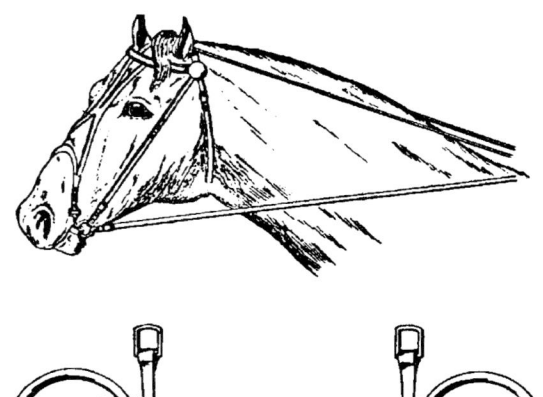

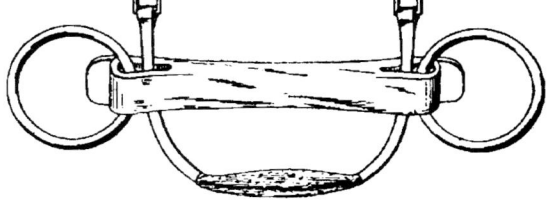

Fig. 30.12 Sears Humane bit.

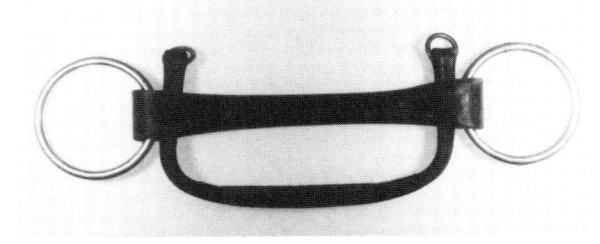

Fig. 30.12a Sears production bit.

Sears, Robert, Newark, NJ, Patent No. 514,779, Feb. 13, 1894 [Figs. 30.12, 30.13, and 30.13a]. An all leather bit commonly called a "Humane Bit" with only the rein-rings and smaller ring at the curb-strap ends (for attaching a noseband) being metal.

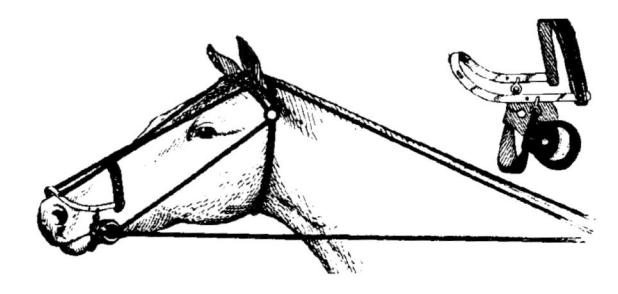

Fig. 30.13 Sears Humane bit with attachment to the bridle.

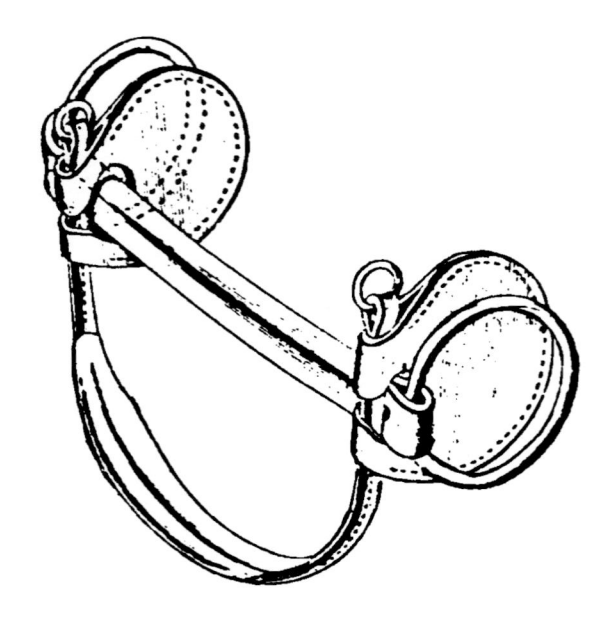

Fig. 30.13a Sears improved Humane bit.

Seeley, Hiram T., Ripon, WI, Patent No. 413,736, Oct. 29, 1869 [Fig. 30.14]. A moderate pull of the reins will cause the bit to bear only on the mouth or teeth. A greater pull will throw the two clamping arms onto the nostrils.

Segundo Bit: A bit design invented by Don Juan Segundo described in a treatise dated 1832 and published in Benjamin Latchford's *The Loriner,* dated 1871. He describes three different sizes and shapes of mouth-pieces, six different cheek-pieces and different curb-chains, all with the idea that the right combination of mouth-piece, cheek-piece and curb could control any horse. The distinctive shape of the mouth-piece is designed externally to conform to the shape of the horse's palate and internally to that of the tongue. It has the necessary width to afford the tongue the room it naturally requires between the tongue groove and the palate. He states the shape of the tongue never varies and the form of the mouth-pieces for the six bits is invarably the same for all horses.

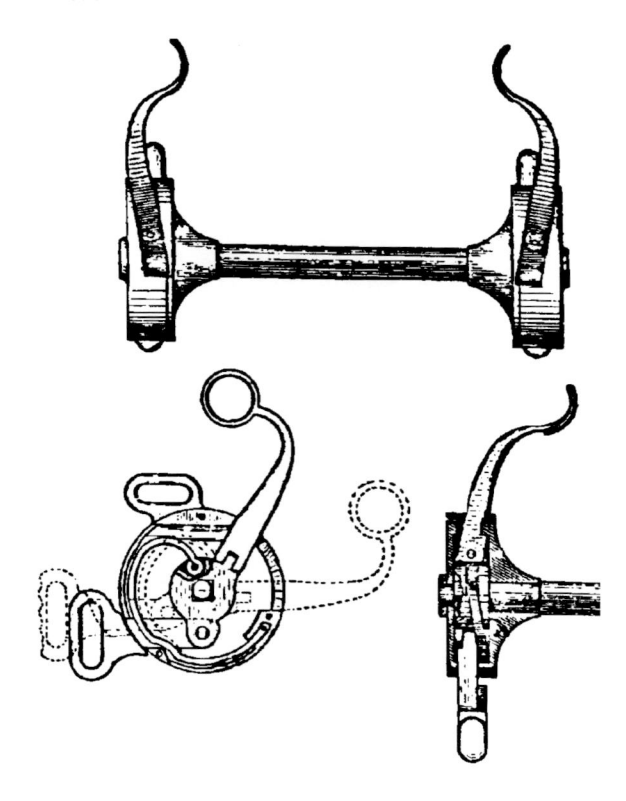

Fig. 30.14 Three views of Seeley dual-action bit.

The only difference is in the thickness of the heels (cannons) which is in proportion to the sensibility of the bars of the horse on which alone they ought to act [Figs. 30.15, 30.16 and 30.17].

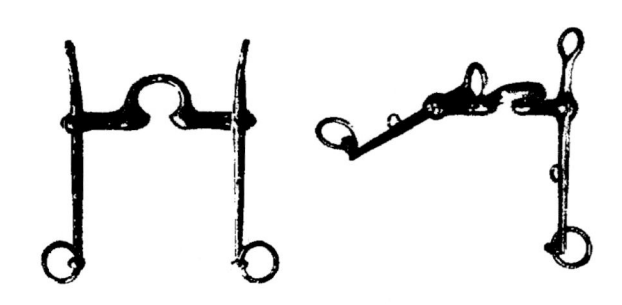

Fig. 30.15 Segundo bit with the bit in normal position and with the cheek-piece rotated showing the mouth-piece tilted forward.

374

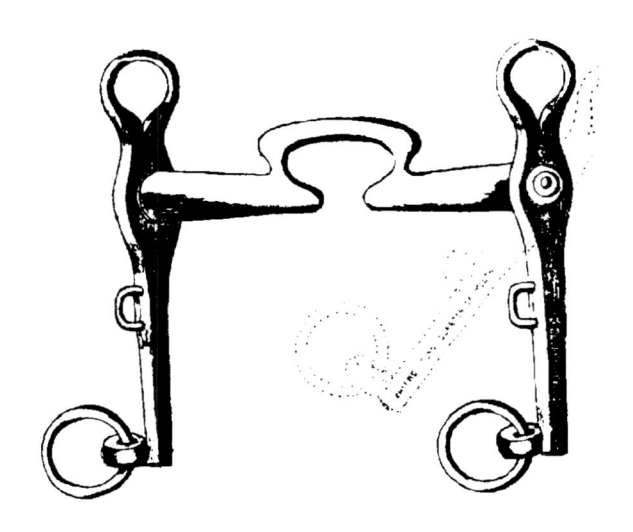

Fig. 30.16 Segundo bit of 1800's England with the cheek-pieces rotating 1/4 turn with the port of the mouth-piece tilting forward in the mouth rather than to the back of the mouth as in most curb bits.

Plan of Patent Bridle Bits shewing the new System of Bitting Horses.

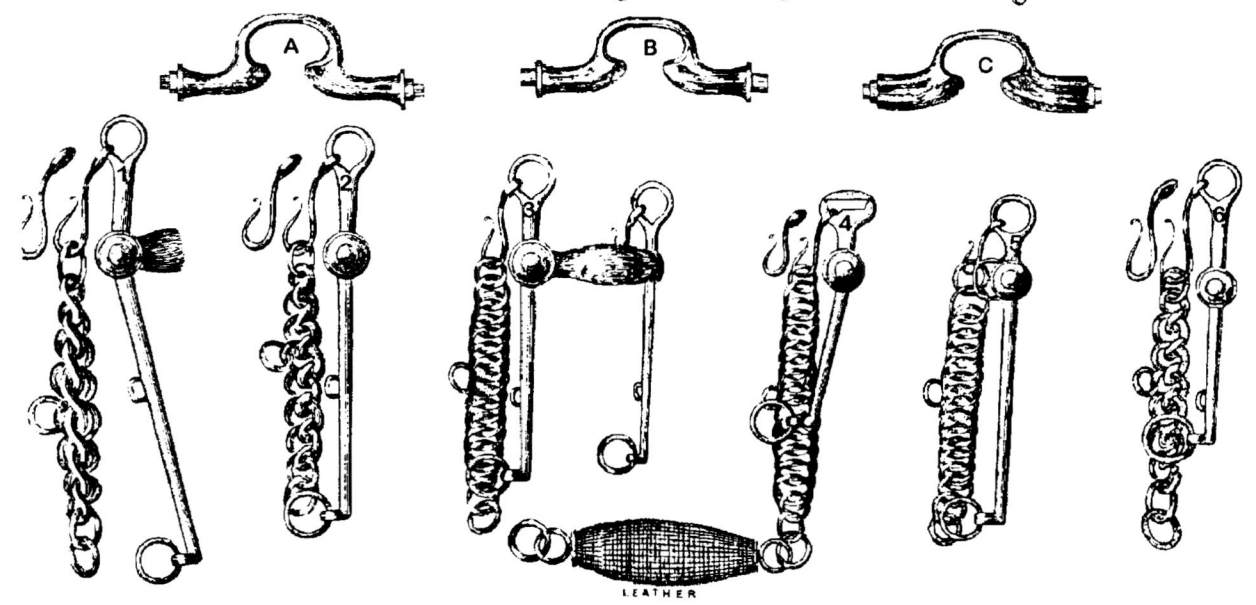

Fig. 30.17 The mouth-pieces, cheek-pieces and curb chains of Don Juan Segundo.

Shank, Grey Dillman, Philadelphia, PA, Patent No. 961,168, June 14, 1910 [Fig. 30.18]. A checking device designed to hold the horse's head up. Consists of a mouth-piece, a noseband and a curb-strap that function as a unit. The device is to be used with a bridle and bit.

Shaw, Earl, Special: See Chapter 10, Fig 10.6.

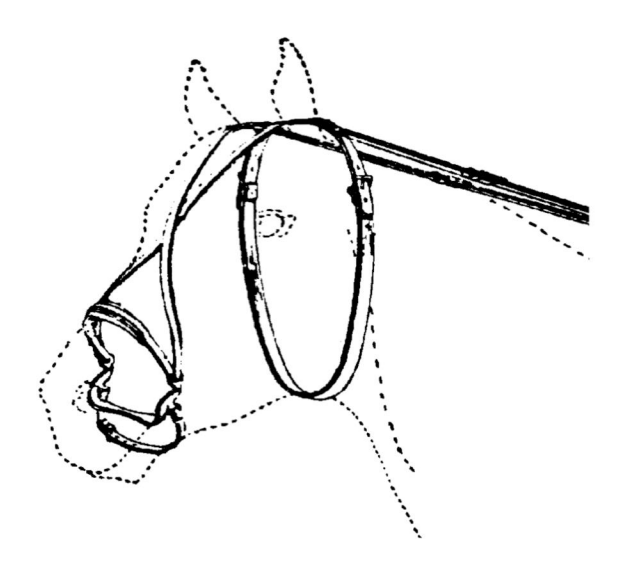

Fig. 30.18 Shank checking device.

Shields, Maxwell P., Fairfield, PA, Patent No. 216,230, June 3, 1879 [Fig. 30.19]. The L-shaped cheek-pieces which hold the rein-rings swivel in the holes at each end of the square mouth-piece. The upper extension of the L-shaped piece has a loop for the head stall.

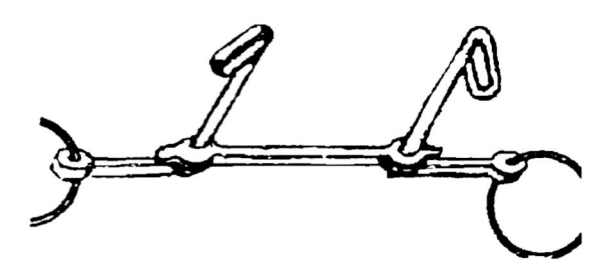

Fig. 30.19 Shields square-mouth bit.

Short, Andrew J., Gypsum, NY, Patent No. 186,371, Jan. 16, 1877 [Fig. 30.20]. A muzzle bit with an adjustable and detachable muzzle. Designed to prevent cribbing and biting of horses and mules.

Shute, Richard A., San Diego, CA, Patent No. 529,814, Nov. 27, 1894 [Fig. 30.21]. The cheek-pieces and mouth-piece are rigidly attached to each other.

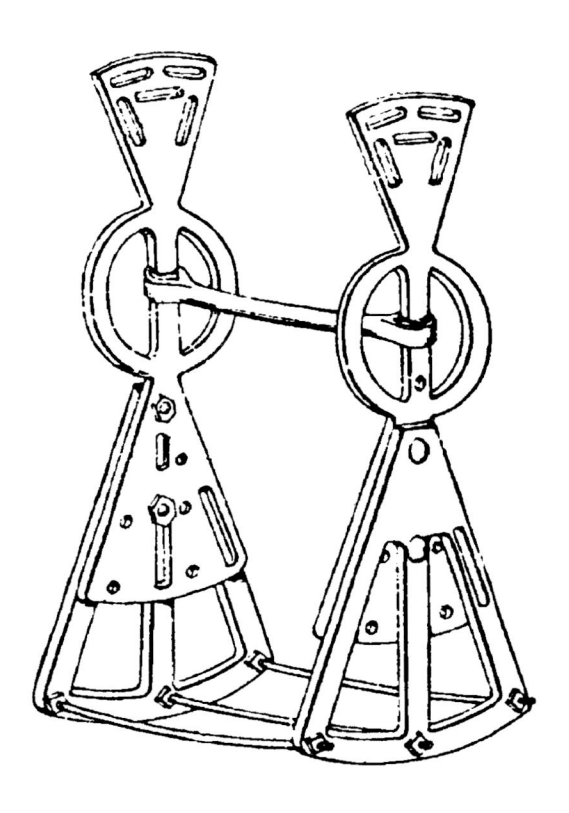

Fig. 30.20 Short muzzle bit.

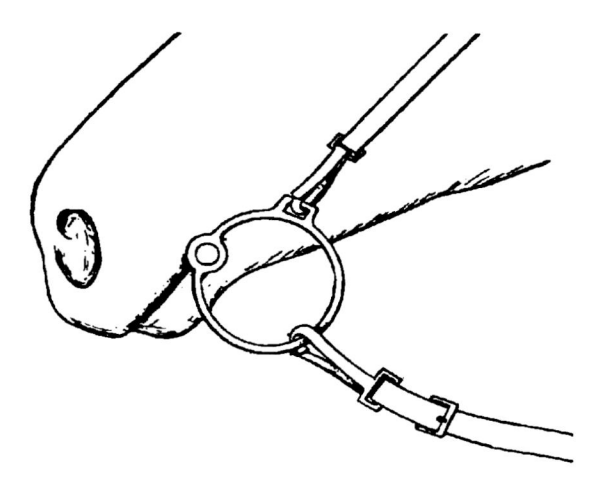

Fig. 30.21 Shute bit on the horse.

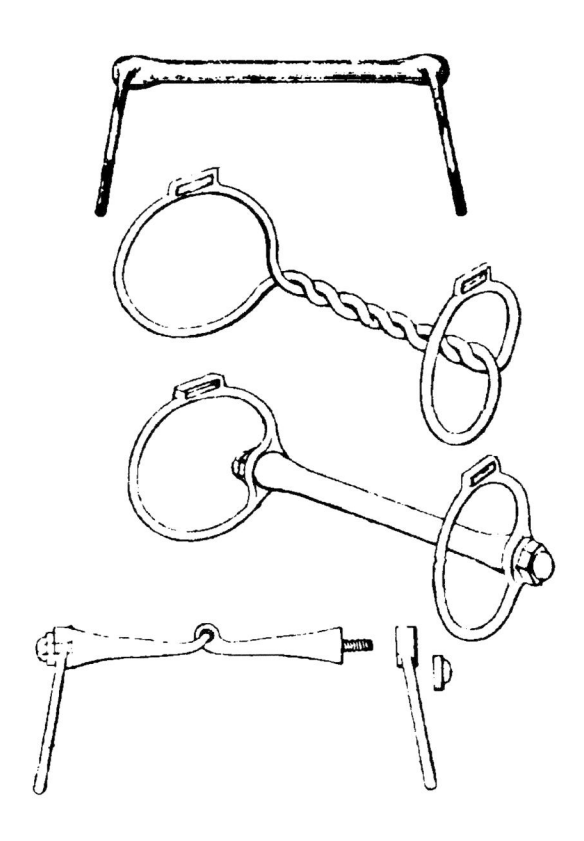

Fig. 30.22 Four variations of Shute bit.

Sibbitt, Manford R., Jet, OK, Patent No. 933,396, Sep. 7, 1909 [Fig. 30.23]. Commonly called a stud or Jack bit and adapted for leading or driving and to be used with or without a headstall. The triangular L-shaped plate is attached to the mouth-piece at the pivot of its center. A leather chin strap is attached to the plate and it can be secured in the chin groove to dispense with a bridle.

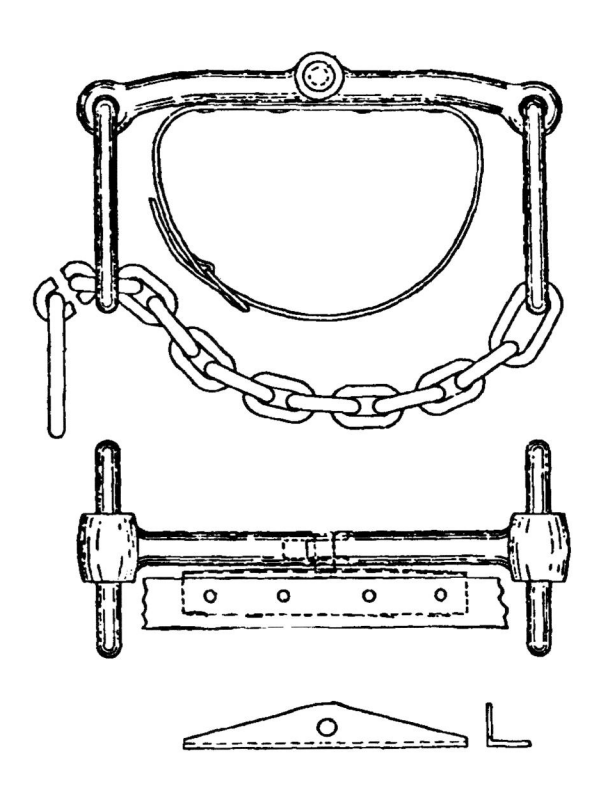

Fig. 30.23 Sibbitt Stud or Jack bit.

Side-bars: The side-pieces or cheek-pieces of a bit.

Side Claws: Sharp projections on the inside of a side-piece of a bit. See Chapter 5, Fig. 5.79.

CHAPTER THIRTY-ONE
Side-pieces

A side-piece is the portion of a bit which keeps the mouth-piece from being pulled through the mouth and to which the head-stall of the bridle and the driving reins are attached.

Angle Cheek: See Chapter 8, Figs. 8.2 and 8.26.

Banbury Cheek: Slots in the cheek-piece allow for the mouth-piece to move within the slot and the cheek-pieces to rotate on the mouth-piece ends. See Chapter 5, Fig. 5.28.

Bird Pattern Cheek: A cheek pattern used by August Buermann Mfg. Co. and several other manufacturers [Fig. 31.0].

Fig. 31.0 Bird Pattern cheek.

Boucha: See Hanging Cheek, Fig. 31.15.

Burr: A shield containing projections to irritate the corners of the mouth or cheek of the horse and placed around the mouth-piece inside of the cheek-piece. See Chapter 5, Fig. 5.57.

Buxton Cheek: A large S-shaped cheek-piece used as a coach or harness bit [Fig. 31.1].

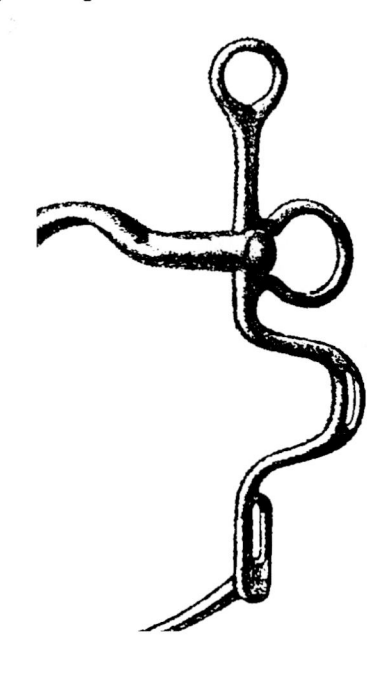

Fig. 31.1 Buxton cheek.

Collared Cheek: A cheek-piece with enlarged portions directly above and below the mouth-piece to prevent the mouth-piece from moving vertically on the cheek-piece [Fig. 31.2].

Dee Cheek: Bits with a ring in the shape of "D" [Fig. 31.3].

Dee Ring: See Dee Cheek.

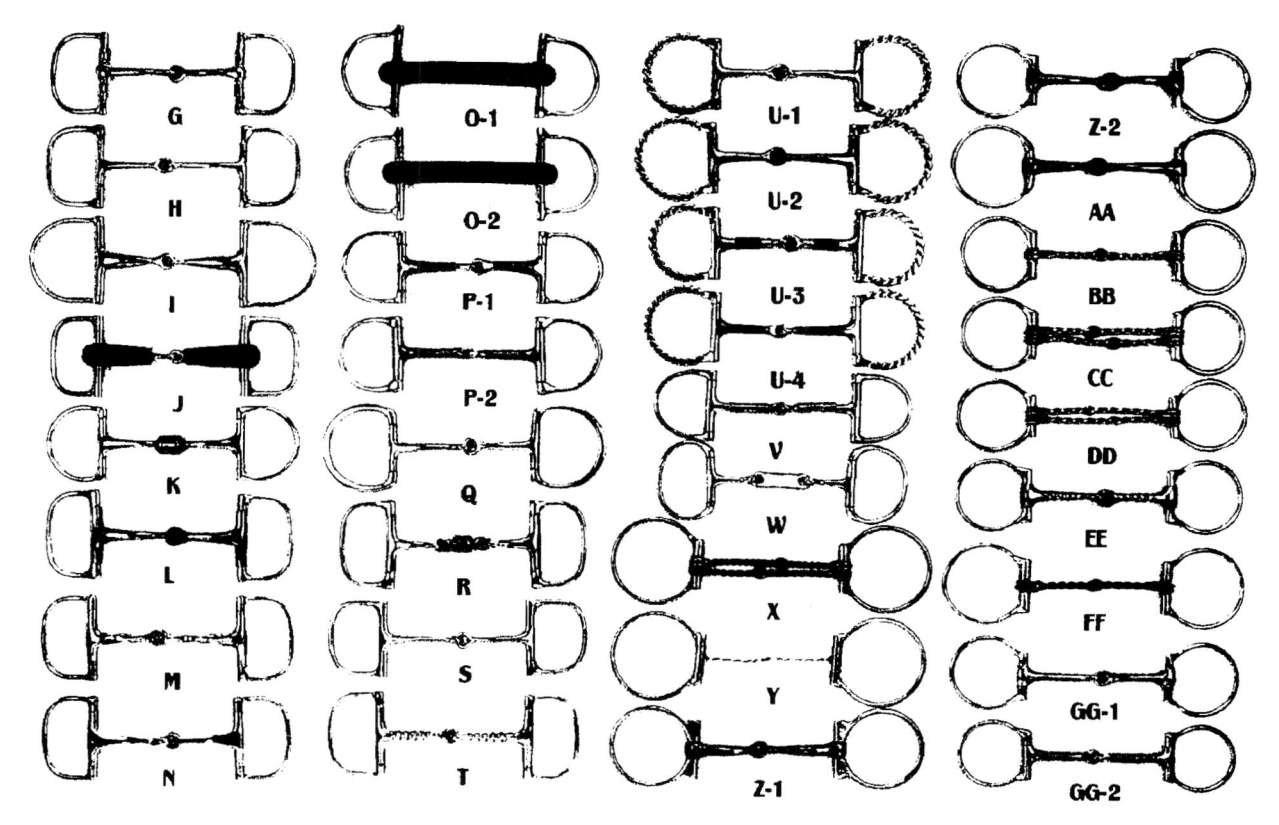

Fig. 31.3 Dee cheek snaffle bits from Libertyville Saddle Shop, Libertyville, IL.

G. Racing Dee.

H. Dee Snaffle.

I. Hollow Mouth Dee.

J. Rubber Mouth Dee.

K. Roller Mouth Dee.

L. Copper Mouth Dee.

M. Heavy Twist Dee.

N. Triangle Mouth Dee.

O. Solid Rubber Dee.

P. Wire Wrapped Dee.

Q. Show Dee.

R. Training Dee.

S. Copper Mouth Dee.

T. Cork Screw Dee.

U. Rope Cheek Dee.

V. Copper Roller Dee.

W. Dr. Bristol Dee.

X. Dee Snaffle.

Y. Fine Twisted Dee Snaffle.

Z-1 California Snaffle, Reg. Mouth.

Z-2 California Snaffle, Thin Mouth.

AA. Twisted Iron Snaffle.

BB. Twisted Wire Snaffle.

CC. Double Wire Snaffle.

DD. Double Wire Snaffle.

EE. Corkscrew Snaffle.

FF. Sweet Iron Wire Snaffle.

GG. Wire Wrapped Snaffle.

Fig. 31.2 Collared cheek.

Duke Cheek: A bit with a large sweeping curve to the cheek-piece [Fig. 31.4].

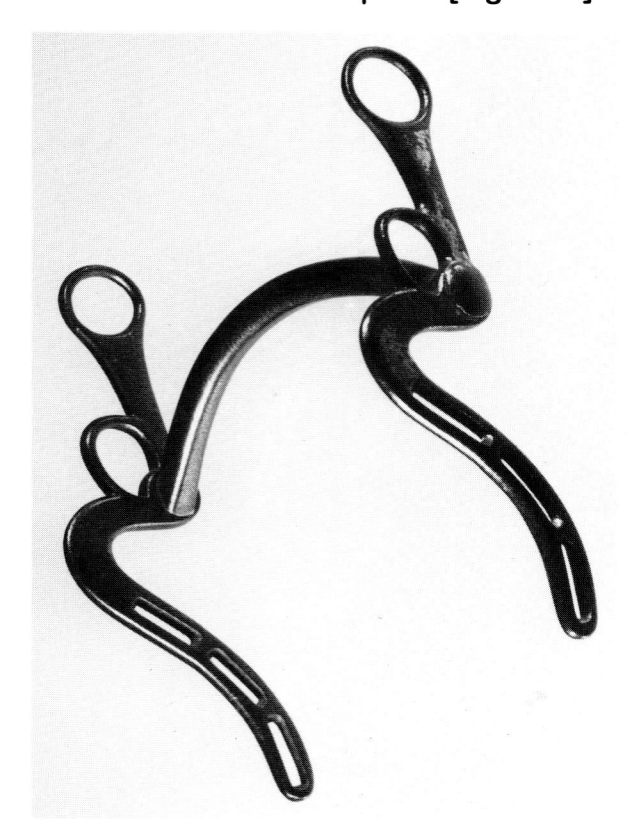

Fig. 31.4 Duke-cheek bit with an arched mouth. From Jean Gayle collection.

Elbow Cheek: A cheek-piece with two 90 degree bends [Fig. 31.5]. See Chapter 5, Fig. 5.11 and Chapter 8, Fig. 8.26.

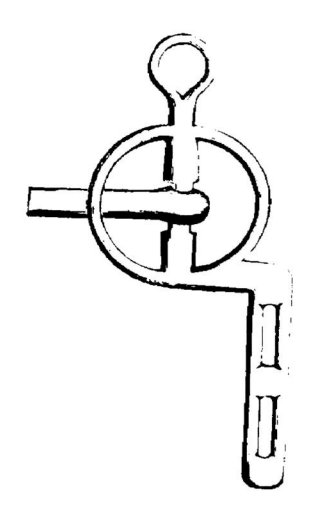

Fig. 31.5 Elbow cheek.

Fancy Cheek: An ornate cheek-piece. See Chapter 8, Figs. 8.30 to 8.58.

Fixed Cheek: The union of the cheek-piece and mouth-piece is solid and neither can turn or rotate [Fig. 31.6].

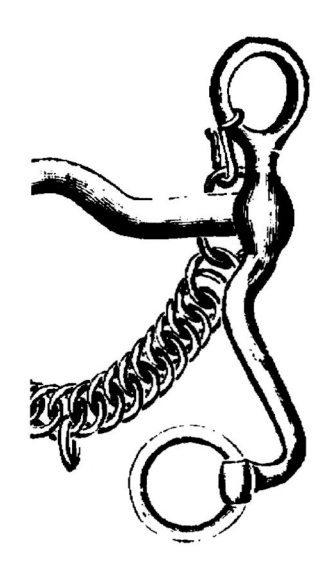

Fig. 31.6 Fixed cheek.

Flat-wire Ring: A flattened round cheek common to many snaffle bits [Fig. 31.7].

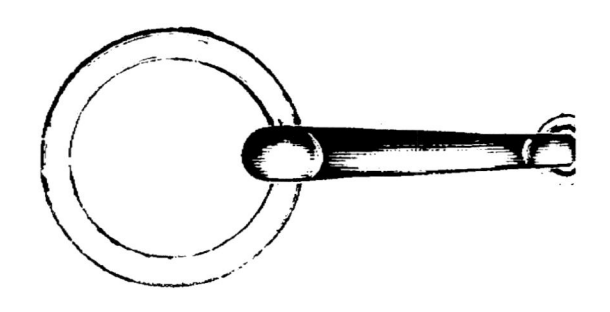

Fig. 31.7 Flat-ring cheek.

Full Cheek: A cheek with a portion of the cheek-piece extending above and below the mouth-piece [Fig. 31.8].

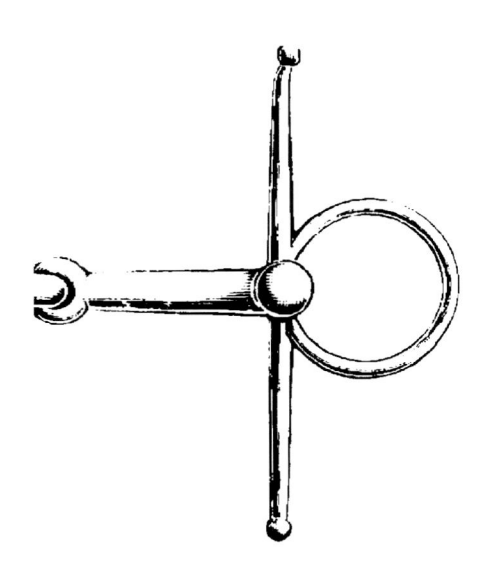

Fig. 31.8 Full cheek.

Gag Cheek: A cheek-piece with a gag action [Figs. 31.9 and 31.9a]. See Chapter 12.

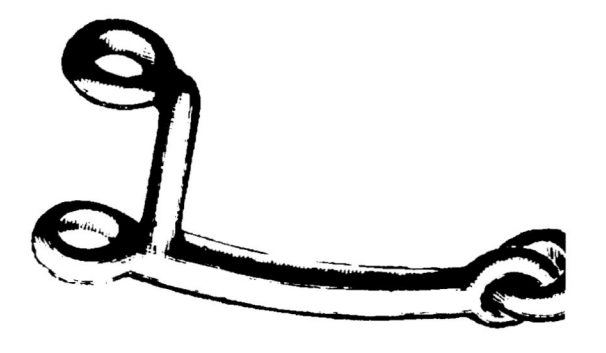

Fig. 31.9 Gag cheek.

Fig. 31.9a Gag cheek.

Gal-leg Cheek: A cheek-piece made in the shape of a woman's leg [Fig. 31.10].

Fig. 31.10 Gal-leg cheek.

Geared Cheek: A cheek-piece with gears and cogs to facilitate the

381

movement of the mouth-piece [Fig. 31.11].

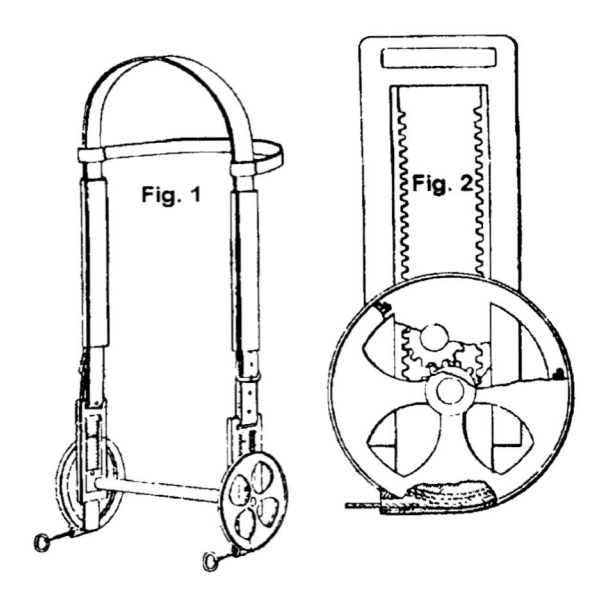

Fig. 31.11 Geared cheek.

Globe Port Cheek: A cheek-piece with a large upper bridle ring and a larger lower rein-ring [Fig.31.12].

Fig. 31.12 Globe port cheek.

Half-cheek: A cheek-piece with a downward extension from the cheek-ring [Fig. 31.13].

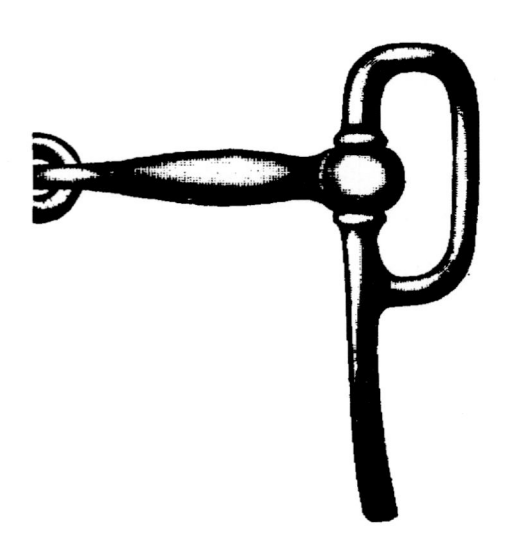

Fig. 31.13 Half-cheek.

Half-spoon: A half-cheek with an enlarged lower end to the cheek-ring extension [Fig. 31.14].

Fig. 31.14 Half-spoon cheek.

Hanging Cheek: A bit with the short half-cheek directed upward when on the horse and to which the bridle cheek-strap or an overcheck rein is attached [Fig.31.15]. A Boucha bit is a hanging cheek bit.

Fig. 31.15 Hanging cheek.

Horn Cheek: A bit with an extra extension from the mouth-piece usually as a part of the cheek-piece. [Fig. 31.16].

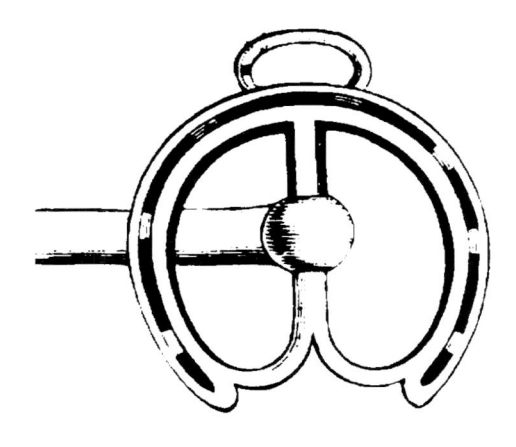

Fig. 31.17 Horseshoe cheek.

Kimberwick Cheek: A cheek-piece with the combined appearance of a hanging cheek and a Dee cheek [Fig. 31.18]. See Chapter 15, Fig. 15.29.

Fig. 31.16 Horn cheek.

Horseshoe Cheek: A cheek-piece made in the shape of a horseshoe [Fig. 31.17]. One bit of this style is named Stallion Bit.

Fig. 31.18 Kimberwick cheek.

Liverpool Cheek A common style of driving bit. See Chapter 27.

Long Cheek: A cheek-piece with an extra long lower cheek of up to 10 inches or more. Usually associated with Walking Horse bits.

Loose Cheek: A cheek-piece in which the mouth-piece has the ability to move up or down on the connection or to rotate or swivel [Fig. 31.19]. A bit of this style almost always needs a bit guard to prevent pinching of the horse's lips.

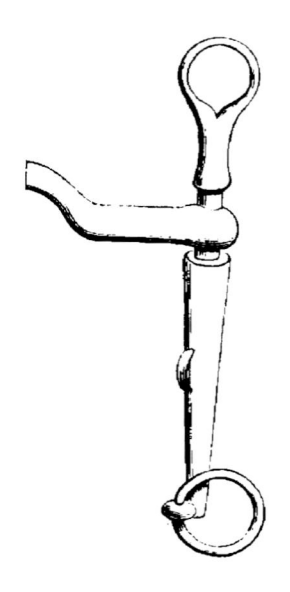

Fig. 31.19 Loose cheek.

Narrow Cheek: A cheek-piece with a narrow flat extension. May be a half-cheek or full-cheek [Fig. 31.20].

Fig. 31.20 Narrow half-cheek.

Pulley Cheek: A cheek-piece with a pulley attached to add leverage to a drive rein or used as part of a gag bridle [Fig. 31.21].

Fig. 31.21 Pulley cheek.

Rearing Horse Cheek: See Wild Horse Cheek. Fig. 31.35.

Reinforced Cheek: A long-shanked bit with a reinforcing bar attached to support the cheek-piece [Fig. 31.22].

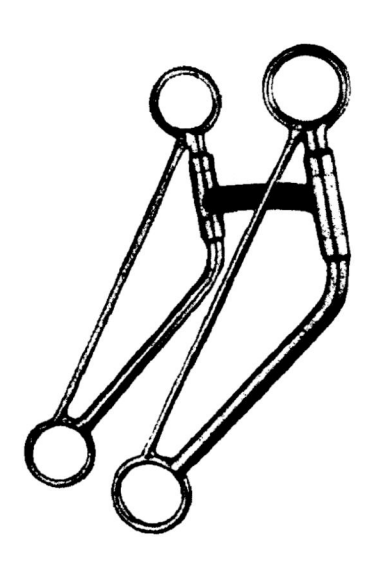

Fig.31.22 Reinforced cheek bit.

Reversible Cheek: A cheek-piece that by reversing unsually changes the mouth-piece from a smooth to a rough side [Fig. 31.23]. The Army Reversible Bit is a good example. See Chapter 21, Fig. 21.6.

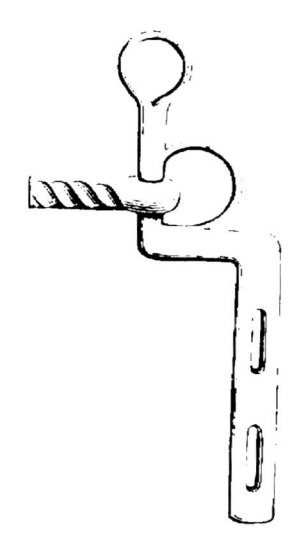

Fig. 31.23 Reversible cheek.

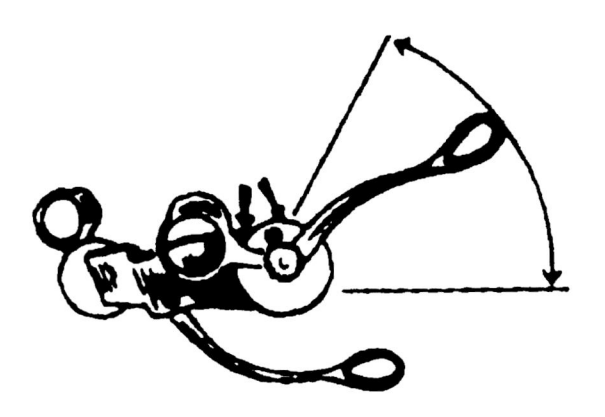

Fig. 31.25 Rotating cheek.

Rings, Wire: A round cheek-piece made of a heavy wire or small diameter steel or iron rod. Rings may be fixed or loose, flat or round, reversible, sliding or slotted.

Roller-in-cheek: A cheek-piece with a roller or pulley built into the ring. Associated with a gag bit [Fig. 31.24]. See Chapter 5, Fig. 5.56.

Rugby Cheek: A cheek-piece associated with a Pelham bit [Fig.31.26]. A link attaches the rein-ring to the cheek-piece.

Fig. 31.24 Cross-section of roller-in-cheek.

Fig.31.26 Rugby cheek.

Rotating Cheek: A cheek-piece which rotates aroung or in a partial arc on the end of the mouth-piece [Fig. 31.25].

Saber Cheek: A bit with a backward sweep of the cheek-piece [Fig. 31.27].

385

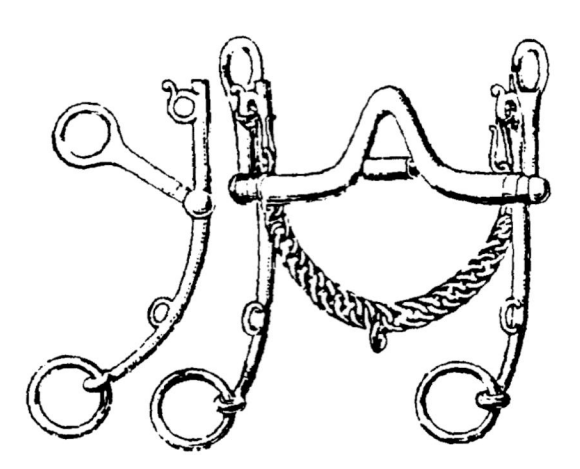

Fig. 31.27 Saber-cheek bit.

Slotted Cheek: A bit with one or more slots in the lower cheek-piece. A popular design of driving bits, such as the Buxton, Liverpool and military artillery [Fig. 31.28].

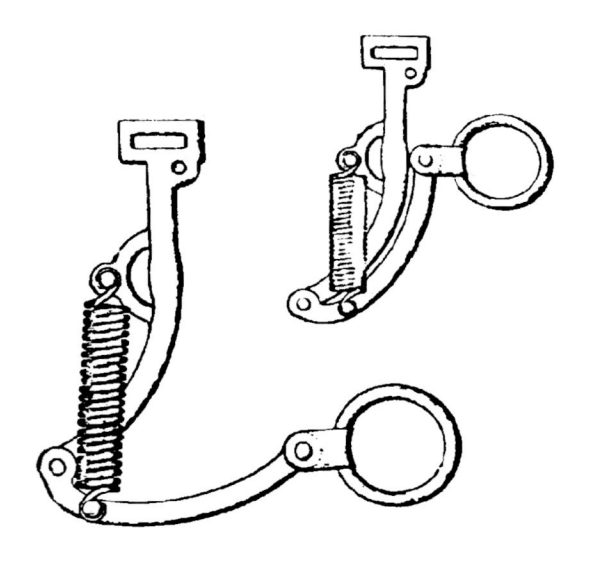

Fig. 31.29 Spring tension cheek.

Stanley-head Cheek: A Liverpool cheek with a double ring [Fig. 31.30].

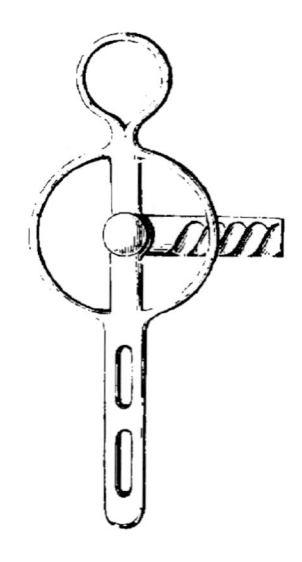

Fig. 31.28 Slotted cheek.

Spoon Cheek: the cheek-piece may be a full-spoon or half-spoon. See half-spoon Fig. 31.14.

Spring-tension Cheek: A cheek-piece with a pivot point which acts as a fulcrum and tension is maintained by a spring attached to the two arms [Fig, 31.29] or a coil spring is built into the cheek-piece. See Chapter 6, Fig. 6.14.

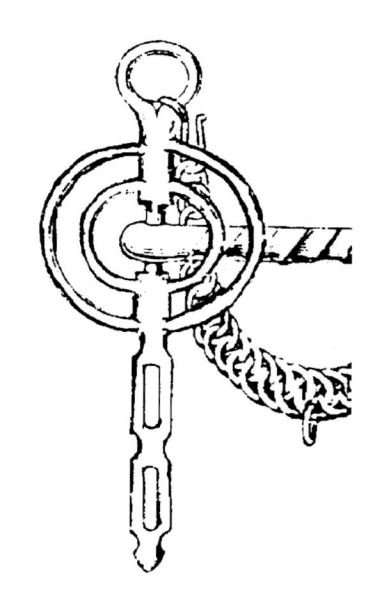

Fig. 31.30 Stanley-head cheek.

Swan Cheek: A cheek-piece with a double curve or S-shape, also called a Duke's cheek [Fig. 31.31].

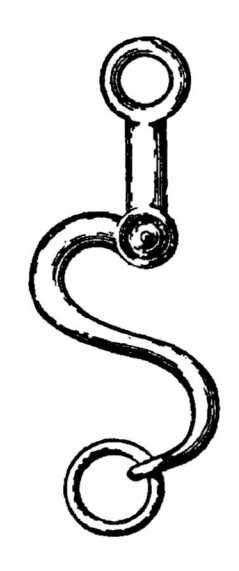

Fig. 31.31 Swan cheek.

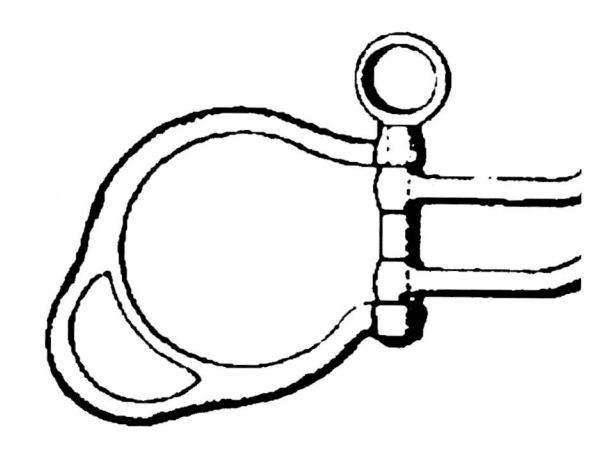

Fig. 31.33 Swivel cheek.

Swept-back Cheek: A cheek-piece used in grazing or roping bits [Fig. 31.32].

Triple-mouth Bit: A bit with three separate mouth-pieces [Fig. 31.34].

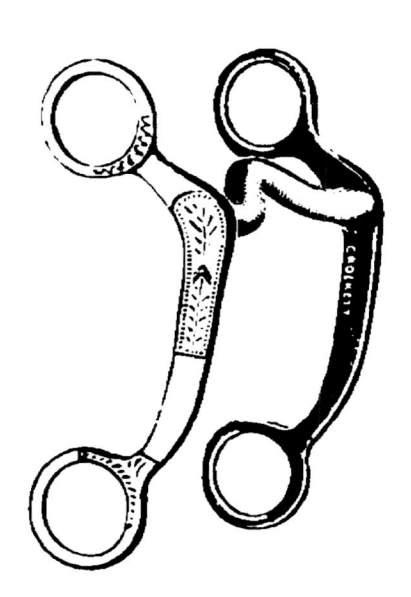

Fig. 31.32 Swept-back cheek.

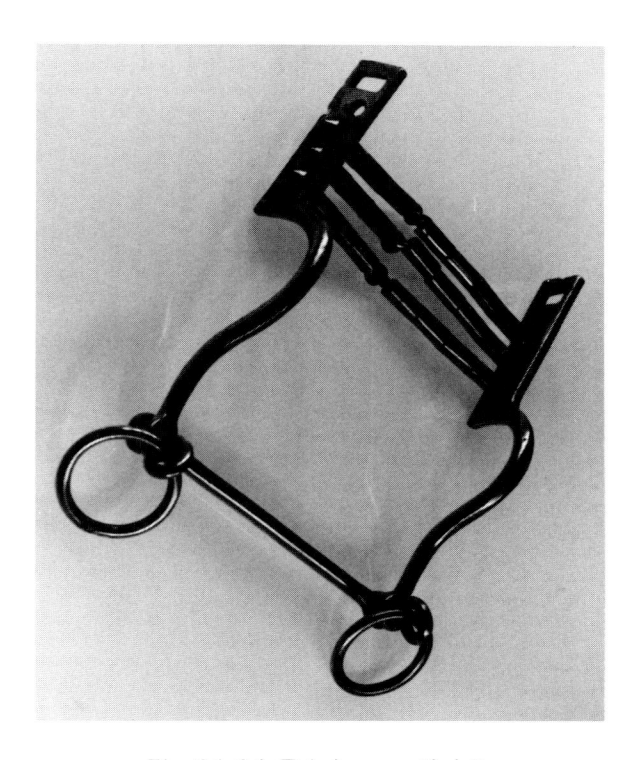

Fig. 31.34 Triple-mouth bit.

Swivel Cheek: A cheek-piece which swivels by a pin through the end of the mouth-piece and through the cheek-piece [Fig. 31.33].

Turn Cheek: Any Cheek-piece which turns, rotates or swivels on the end of the mouth-piece.

Wild Horse Cheek: A cheek in the shape of a horse, usually in a rearing position [Fig. 31.35].

Fig. 31.35 Wild horse cheek.

Percheron cart horse. *Lydekker*

CHAPTER THIRTY-TWO
Side-plates to Swartzendruber

Side-plates: A term for side-pieces.

Side Puller: A horse that pulls continually harder to one side over the other.

Side Reins: A rein attached to the saddle through the rein-ring to the rider's hands [Fig. 32.0].

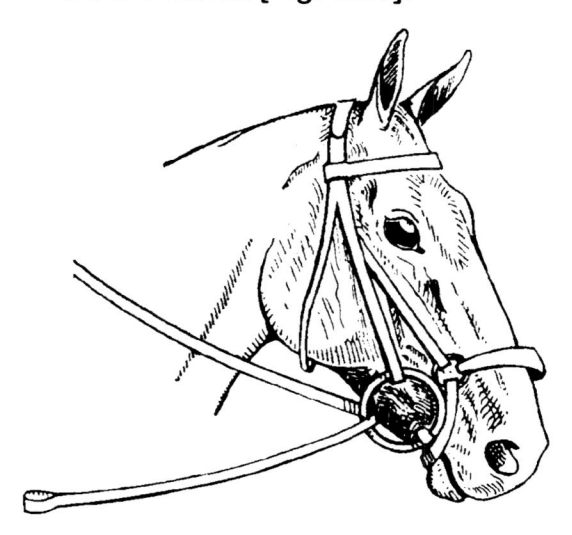

Fig. 32.0 Side rein.

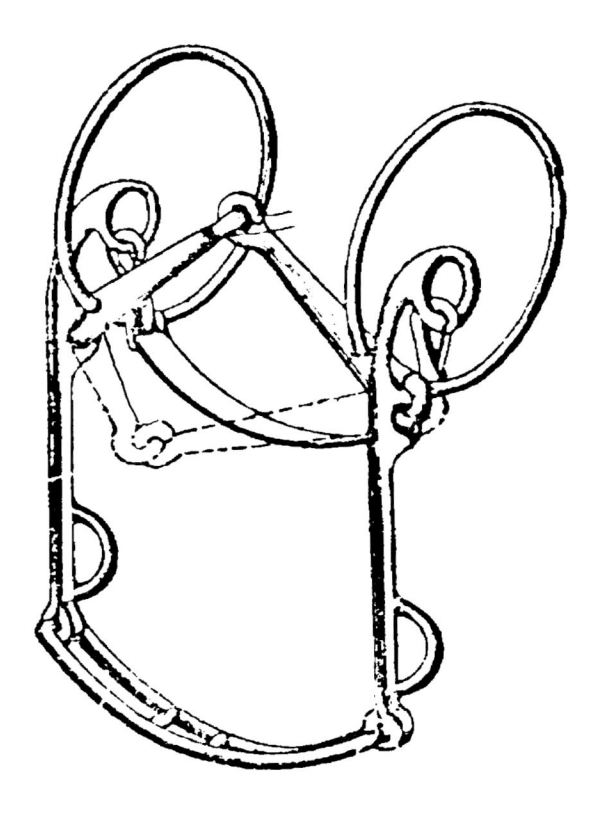

Fig. 32.1 Sievert curb bit.

Sidewinder: A term applied to tightly tying a horse to its tail so that the horse travels in a tight circle.

Sievert, Hermann A., United States Army, Patent No. 815,385, Mar. 20, 1906 [Fig. 32.1]. The bit has rearward curved upper rings for the attachment of the curb-strap with large rein-rings that are attached to the mouth-piece through holes in the mouth-piece.

Silver Bit: Designates a bit with silver ornamentation as an overlay or inlay on the cheek-piece. See Pages 390 to 394.

Silver Inlay: A strip, figure or character of silver fitted and inlaid into a channel or depression of the same shape as the silver that has been cut into the metal. The silver inlay will be even with the surface of the metal piece when finished.

Silver Overlay: A design or strip of silver is soldered to the metal surface by the use of a flux and silver solder and heated to make the bond.

Single Chain-link Mouth: A snaffle bit with a single chain as a mouth-piece [Fig. 32.3]. Produced with a wire ring, half-cheek or full-cheek.

SILVER BITS

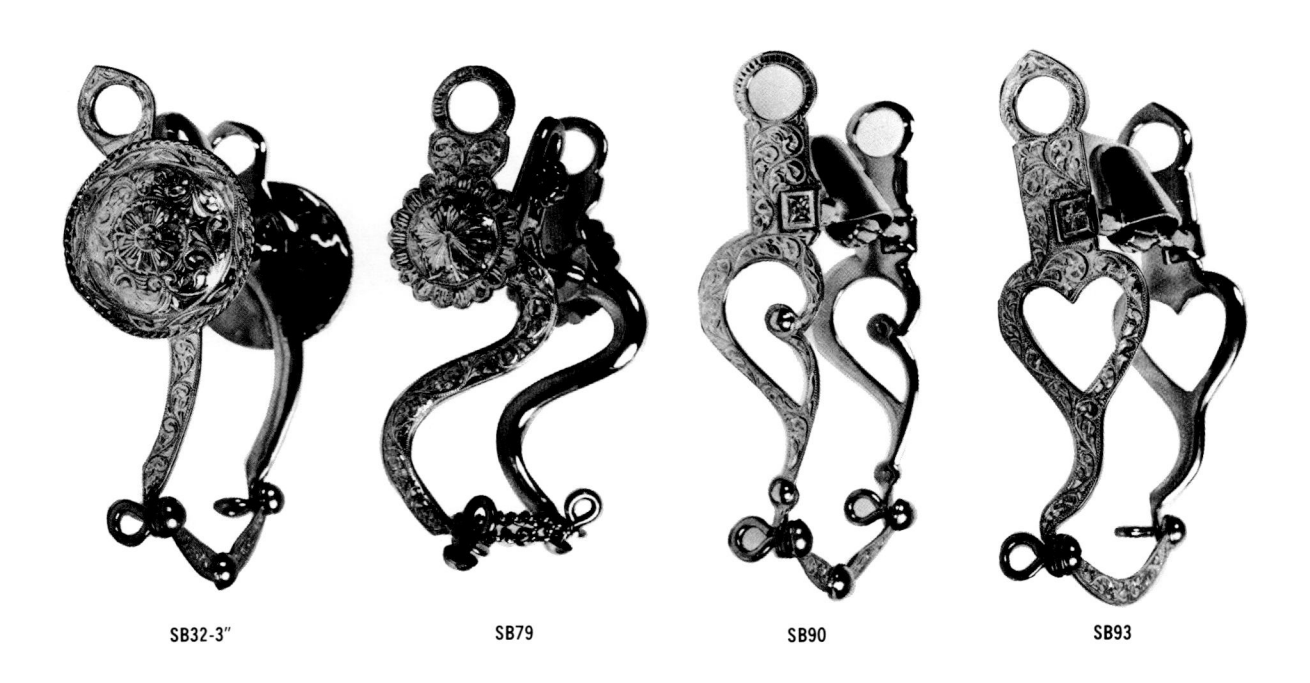

| SB32-3" | SB79 | SB90 | SB93 |

AVAILABLE IN HAND ENGRAVED GERMAN SILVER

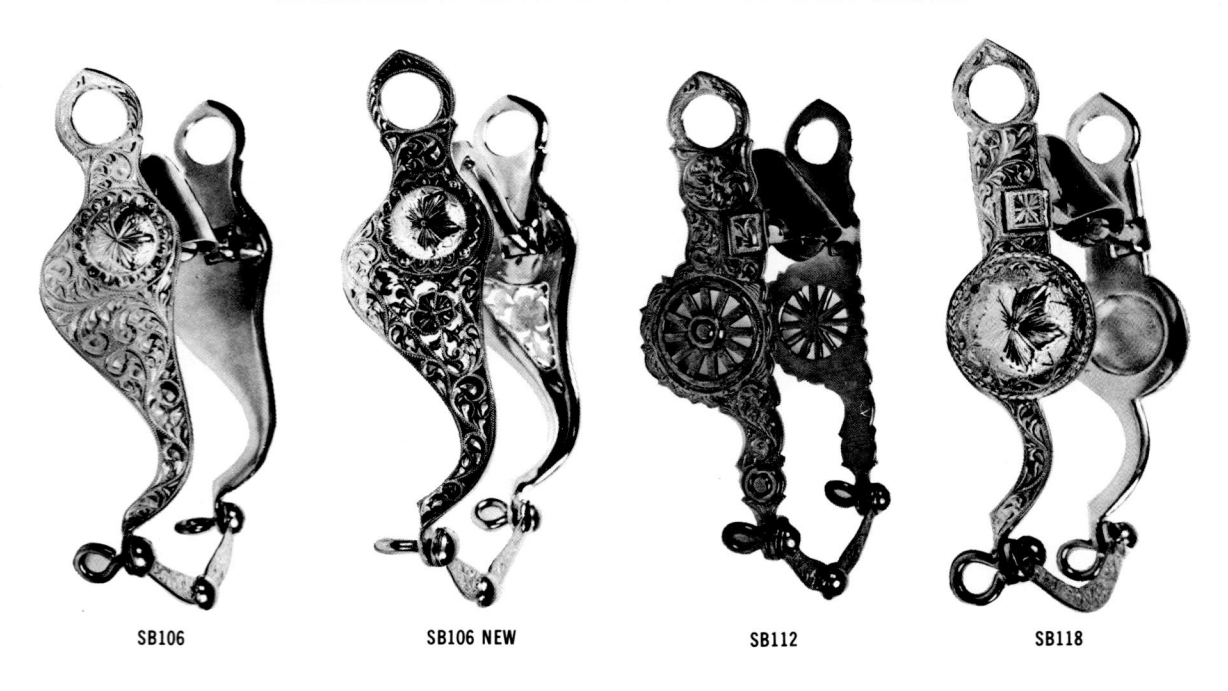

| SB106 | SB106 NEW | SB112 | SB118 |

SPECIAL MOUTHPIECES AVAILABLE ON REQUEST

SILVER BITS

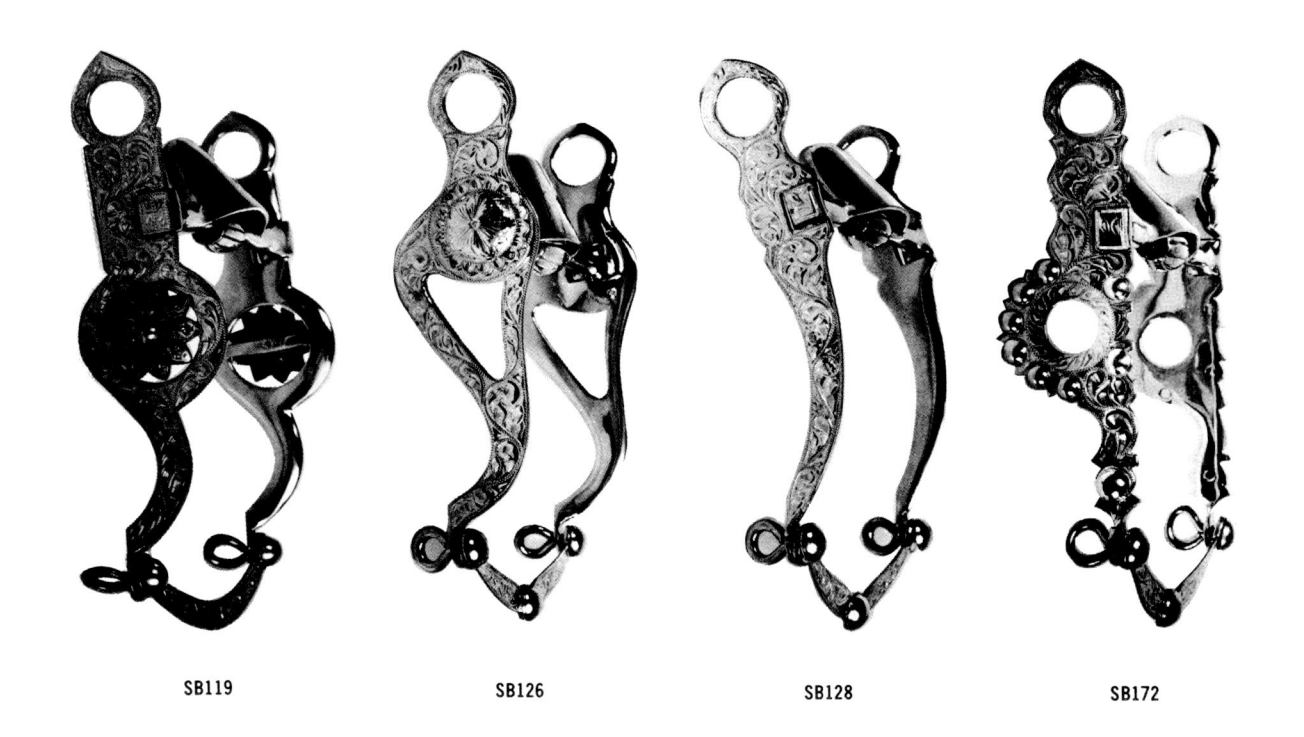

| SB119 | SB126 | SB128 | SB172 |

AVAILABLE IN HAND ENGRAVED GERMAN SILVER

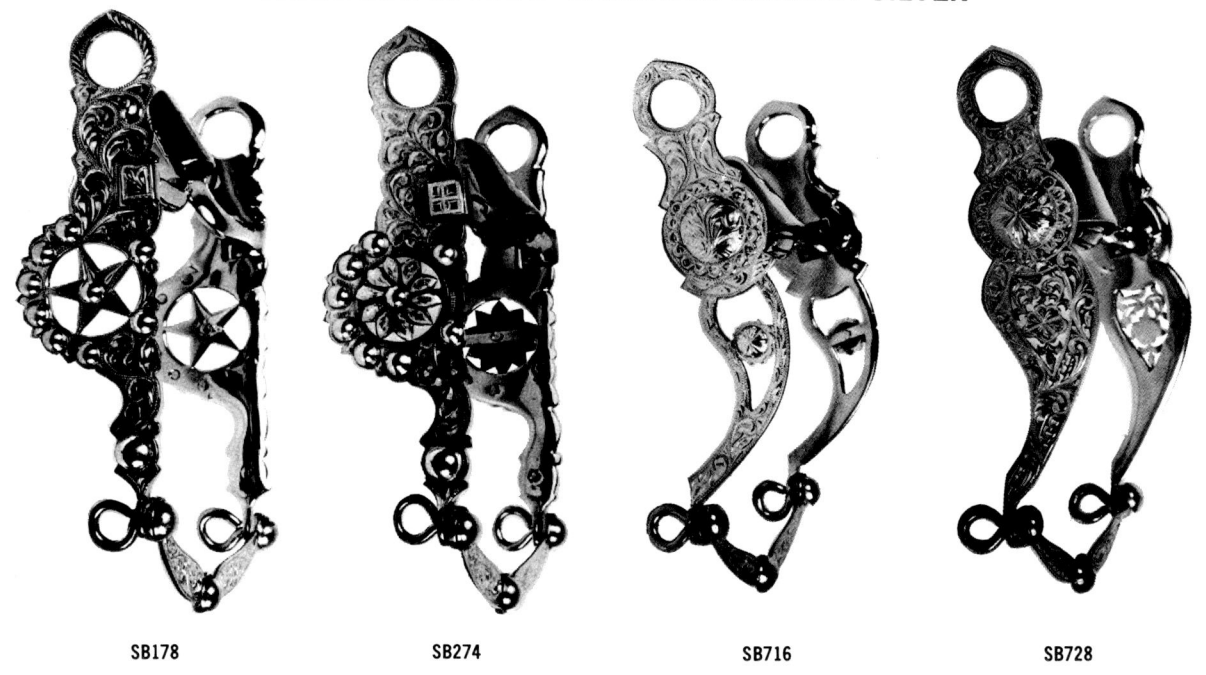

| SB178 | SB274 | SB716 | SB728 |

SPECIAL MOUTHPIECES AVAILABLE ON REQUEST

SILVER BITS

| 24 | 23 | 279 | 198 |

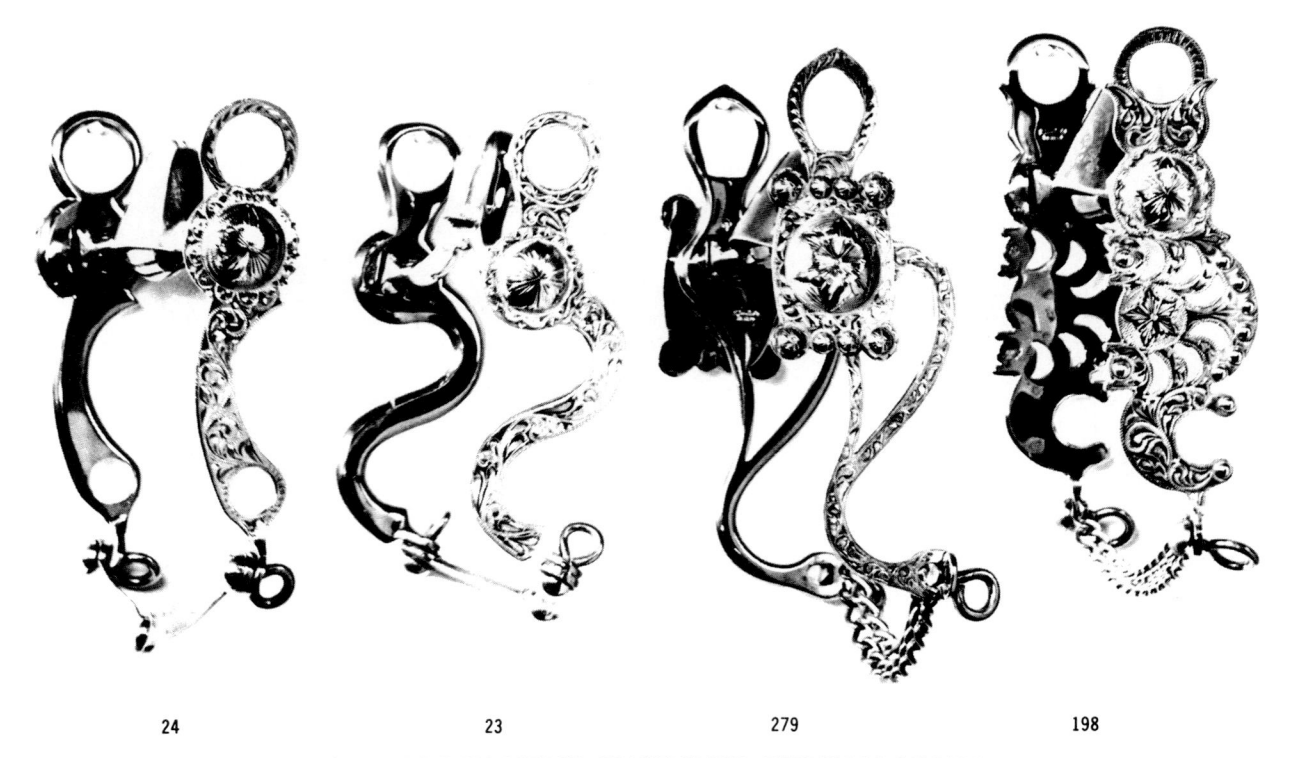

AVAILABLE IN HAND ENGRAVED GERMAN SILVER

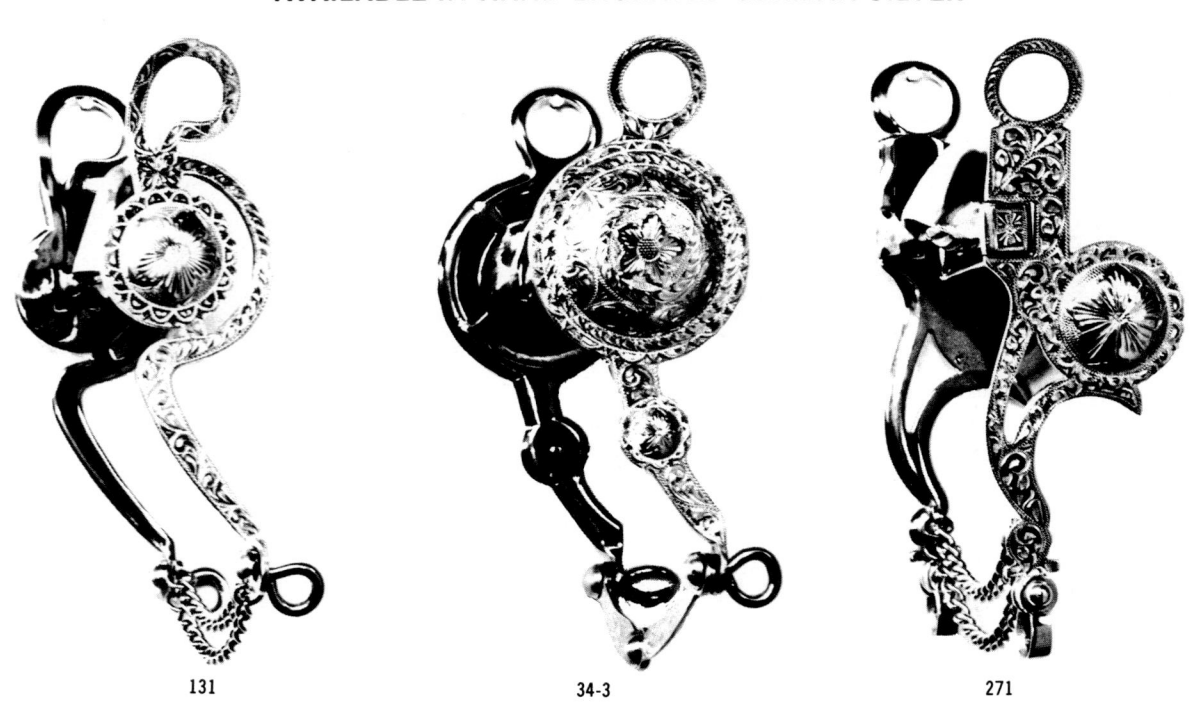

| 131 | 34-3 | 271 |

SPECIAL MOUTHPIECES AVAILABLE ON REQUEST

392

SILVER BITS

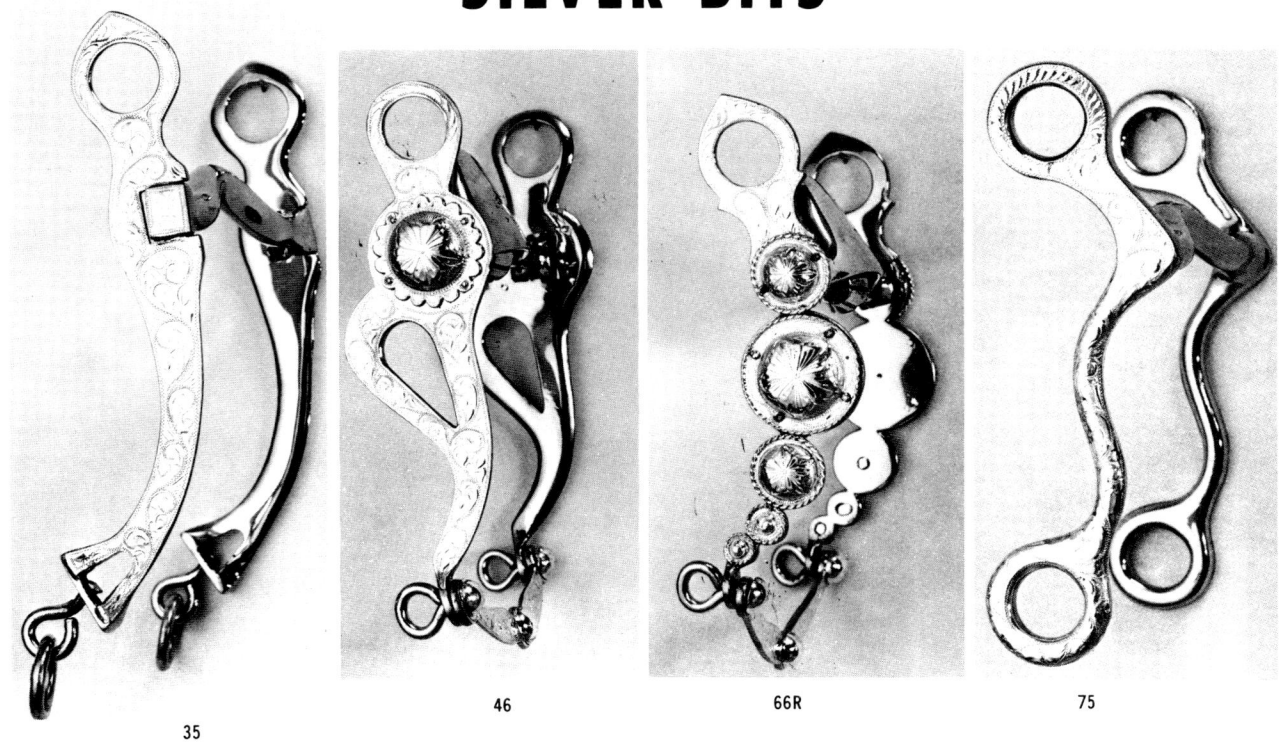

| 35 | 46 | 66R | 75 |

AVAILABLE IN HAND ENGRAVED GERMAN SILVER

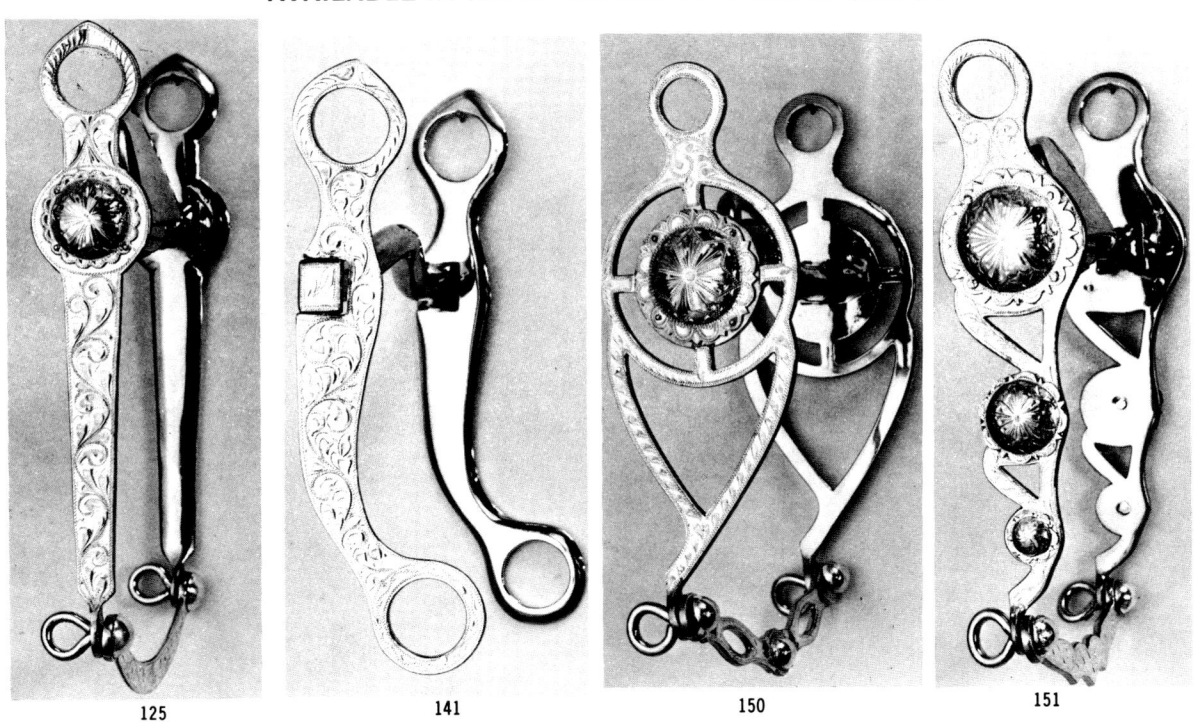

| 125 | 141 | 150 | 151 |

SILVER BITS

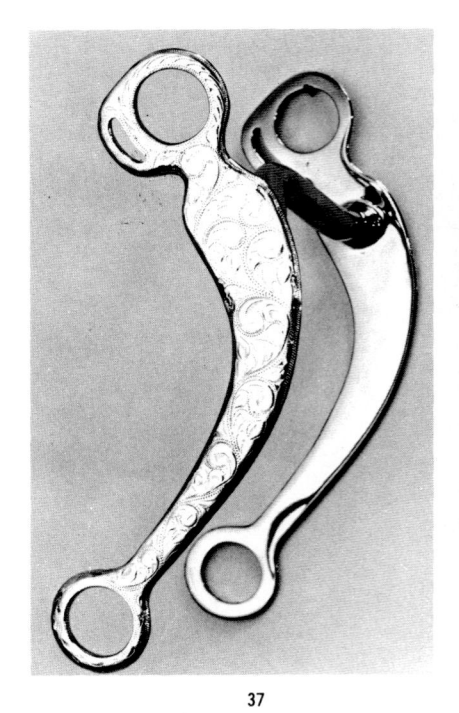

37 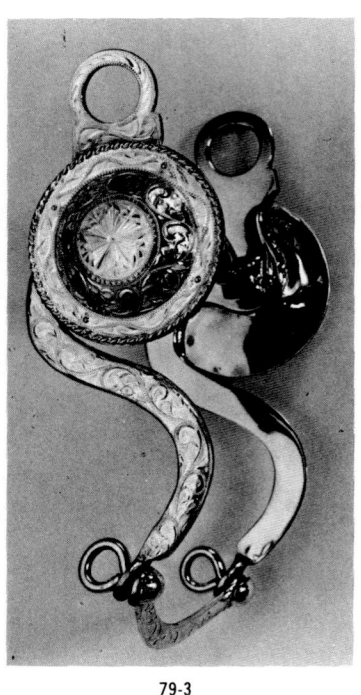 79-3 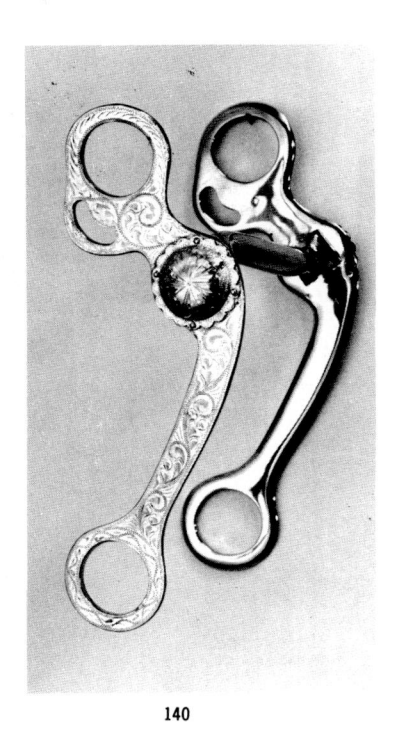 140

AVAILABLE IN HAND ENGRAVED GERMAN SILVER

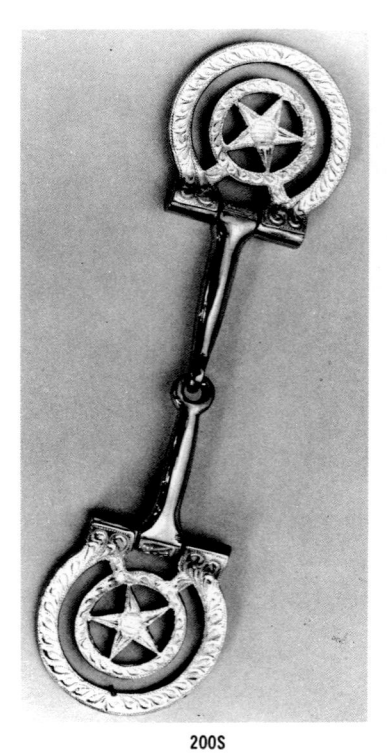

200S  201  200

394

Sims, Merrell H., Milledgeville, GA, Patent No. 655,913, Aug. 14, 1900 [Fig. 32.2]. A double mouth-piece bit with each piece passing through the slot in the cheek-piece and securely attached to the opposite cheek-piece.

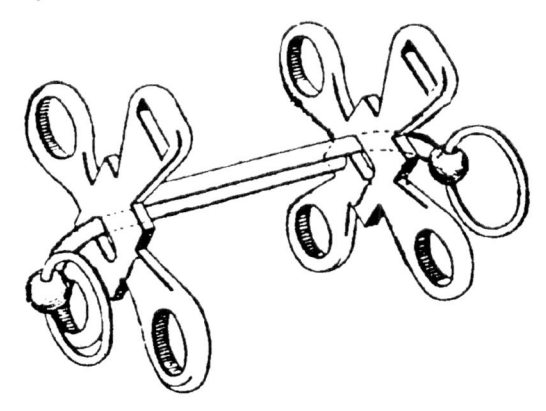

Fig. 32.2 Sims double-mouth bit.

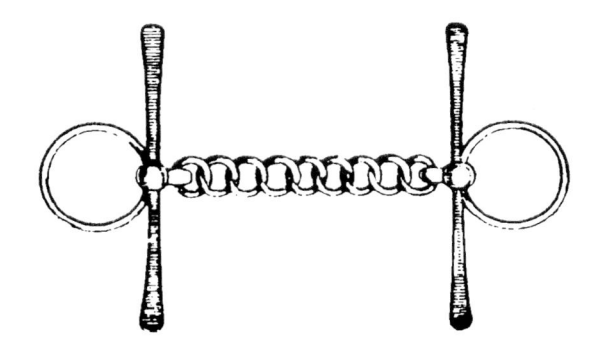

Fig. 32.3 Single chain-link-mouth snaffle.

Six-ring Snaffle: See Chapter 8, Fig. 8.17.

Slaughter, Andrew Jackson, Okolona, MS, Patent No. 150,488, May 5, 1874 [Fig. 32.4]. The bit exerts more lever power on the tongue of the horse or mule without the animal evading the pressure by opening its mouth. The mouth-piece is made with a crook, so that it will always remain on the tongue and the "upright" levers are of such a shape that a great advantage of leverage is produced.

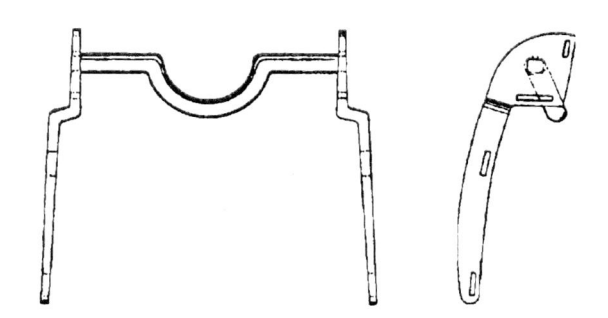

Fig. 32.4 Slaughter leverage bit.

Slawson, James Harden, Norton, Okla. Terr., Patent No. 733,601, Nov. 1, 1904 [Fig. 32.5]. Designed to produce an inexpensive, strong, light-weight bit. The plates to which the mouth-piece is attached are cast around the wire frame.

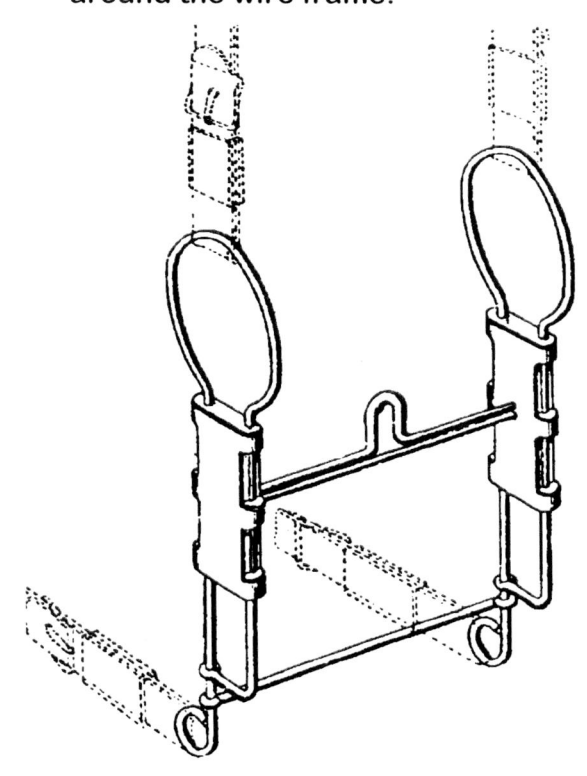

Fig. 32.5 Slawson light-weight bit.

Sliding Rein: Another term for a draw rein.

Sloat, Oliver M., Brooklyn, NY, Patent No. 435,252, Aug. 26, 1890 [Fig. 32.6]. The power of the curb is regulated by the amount of force applied to the reins. The springs offer resistance to keep the curb at a minimum when not needed.

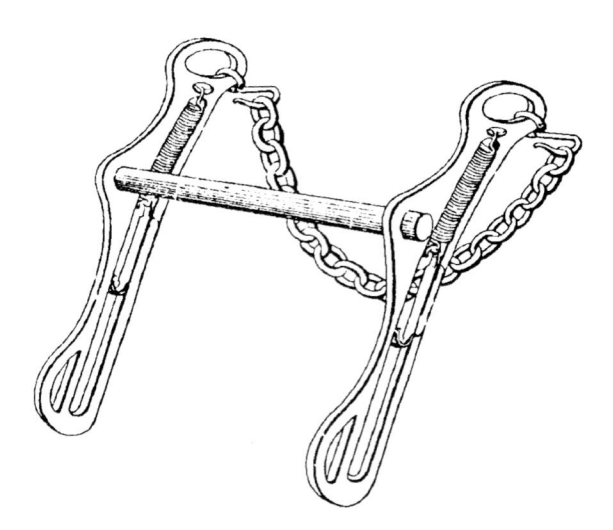

Fig. 32.6 Sloat spring-controlled curb.

Patent No. 479,670, July 26, 1892 [Fig. 32.7]. The bit has slotted cheek-pieces and a hollow mouth-piece and rein-rings that slide in the cheek-pieces with a spring through the mouth-piece with its ends attached to the rein-rings. Normally serves as a snaffle bit but as the horse begins to pull will serve as a curb bit.

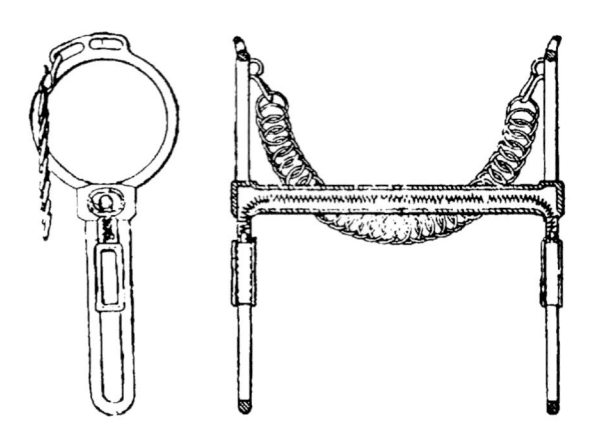

Fig. 32.7 Sloat improved bit.

Slobber Leathers: Rein covers of leather to protect rein when a horse drinks. Serves much the same purpose as rein-chains.

Small, Henry, Hartford, Ct, Patent No. 540,408, June 4, 1895 [Fig. 32.8]. A bit that is placed in the mouth of the horse under the upper lip and in front of the teeth. A strap down the center of the face is attached to a ring in the center of the bail-like bit. The pressure is placed on the upper lip to guide, stop and drive the horse without any other bit.

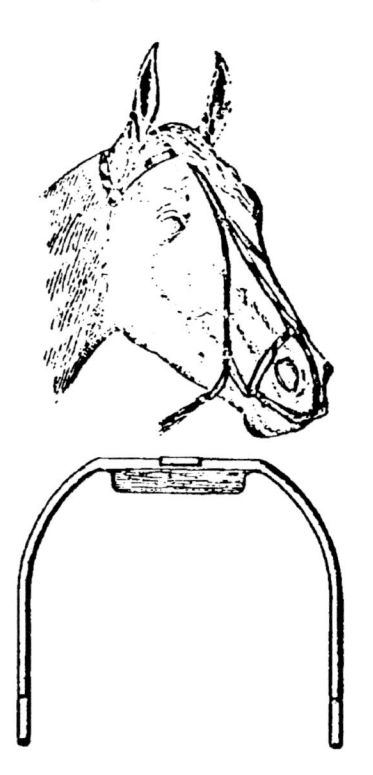

Fig. 32.8 Small lip-pressure bit.

Smith, Caleb, Sannemin, IL, Patent No. 468,309, Feb. 2, 1892 [Fig. 32.9]. The chin frame can act as a curb-bar to control the horse if necessary.

Smith, Cecil Gag: See Chapter 12, Fig. 12.1a.

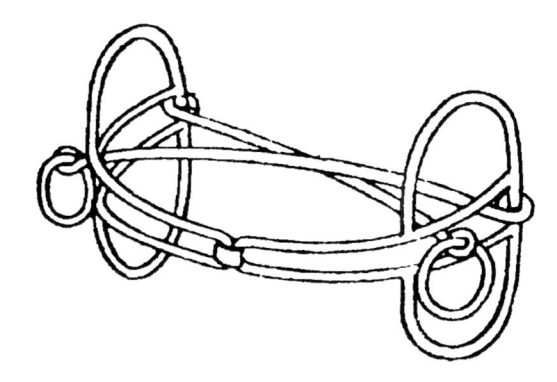

Fig. 32.9 Smith scissor bit.

Smith, Charles H., New Haven, CT, Patent No. 505,280, Sep. 19, 1893 [Fig. 32.10]. A construction method with the cheek-piece having a transverse groove and the corresponding mouth-piece end a tongue to fit into the groove.

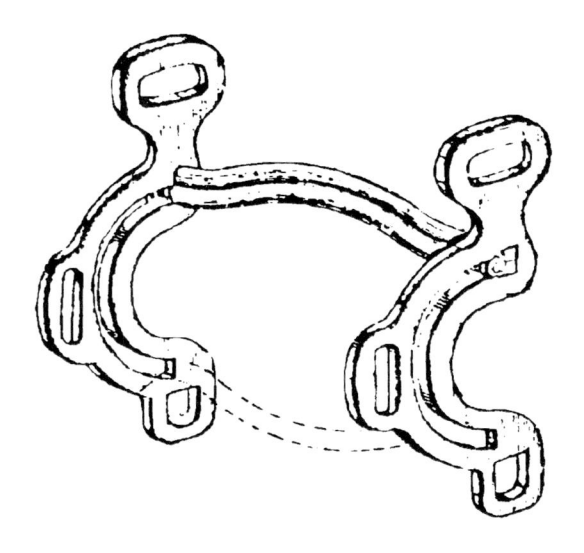

Fig.32.11 Smith double-mouth gag bit.

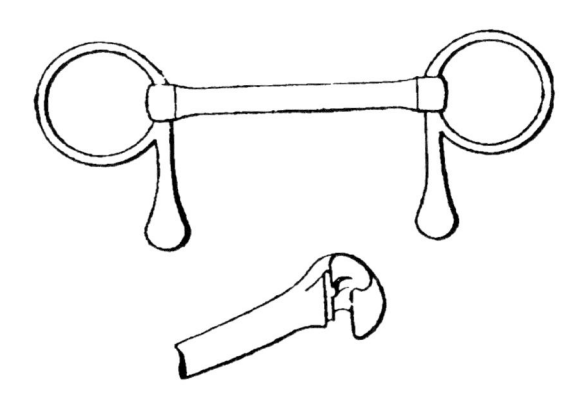

Fig. 32.10 Smith open-end construction.

Smith, George E., Buford, GA, Patent No. 637,170, Nov. 14, 1899 [Fig. 32.11] The bit has a double mouthpiece in which the lower section can be adjusted to any position in the slotted curved cheek-piece. Compare with Warfel, Chapter 34.

Smith, Henry P., Canaan, OH, Patent No. 718,539, Jan. 13, 1903 [Fig. 32.12]. A reversible bit in which the center ring of the mouth-piece may be placed up or down. The bit is designed to prevent the horse from lolling its tongue.

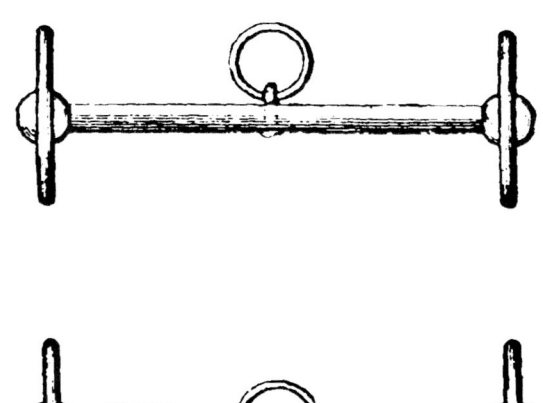

Fig. 32.12 Smith tongue-lolling bit.

Smith, Jack L., Sacramento, CA, Patent No. 2,810,250, Oct. 22, 1957 [Fig. 32.13]. This curb has a detachable port that is secured by two small screws through the bottom of the mouth-piece.

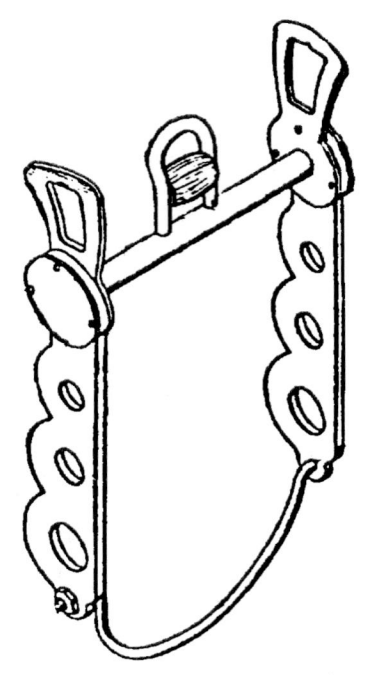

Fig. 32.13 Smith bit with detachable port.

Smith, John F. and John S. Carter, Erie, PA, Patent No. 239,567, Mar. 29, 1881 [Fig. 32.14]. The mouth-piece is formed of steel wires passing through a hole in one cheek-piece and secured to the inside of the opposite cheek-piece. A rein pull forces the cheek-pieces together, putting pressure on the sides of the horse's mouth.

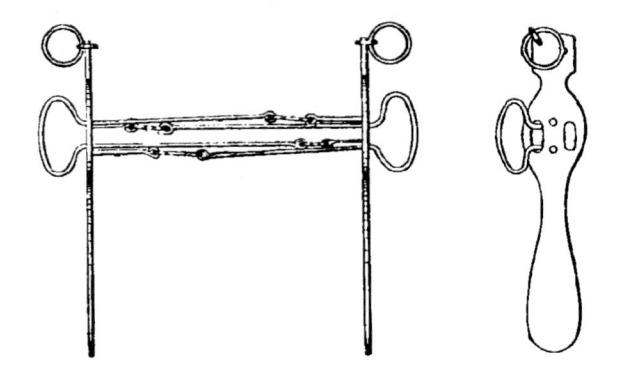

Fig. 32.14 Smith jointed wire-mouth bit.

Smith, Oscar W., Glen Haven, WI, Patent No. 981,488. Jan 10. 1911 [Fig.32.15]. The crossed bars act as a curb along with the action of the mouth-piece when the reins are used

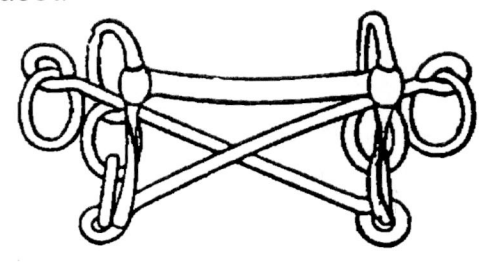

Fig. 32.15 Smith bit with curb bars.

Smith, Oscar W., Flat Rock, MI, Patent No. 1,128,631, Feb. 16, 1915 [Fig. 32.16]. The spring controlling the action of the cheek-piece is enclosed in the mouth-piece and the cheek-piece to prevent it from becoming clogged or frozen and still not interfer and pinch the lips of the horse.

Smith, William H. and Samuel D. Freeman, U.S. Army, Patent No. 511,811, Jan. 2, 1894 [Fig. 32.17]. Designed to be adjusted in width to fit varying sizes in mouth width of horses. The metal washers are of the same diameter as the mouth-piece and have a square center hole. The washers are placed on the mouth-piece inside the cheek-pieces. The screw in the end of the mouth-piece tightens to secure the new extension.

Snaffle (Bradoon): The simplest form of a bit. Usually a jointed-mouth bit with a ring on each end of the mouth for attaching the bridle head-stall and reins.

Snaffle Bars: Cheek-pieces or side-pieces on snaffle bits.

Snaffle Bridle: A bridle used in conjunction with a snaffle bit. See Chapter 35.

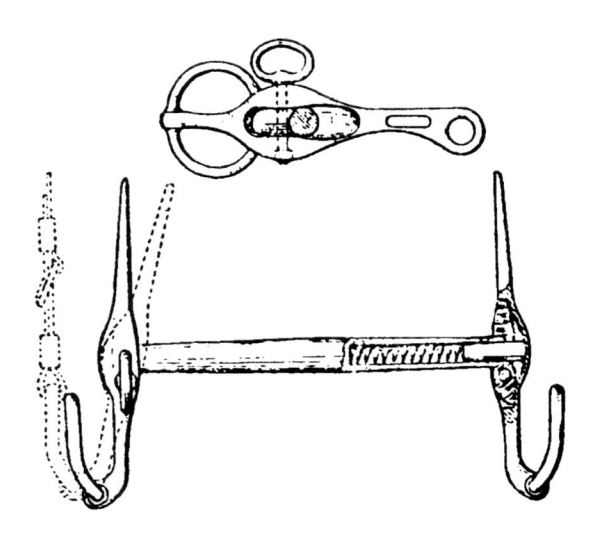

Fig. 32.16 Smith spring-controlled cheeks.

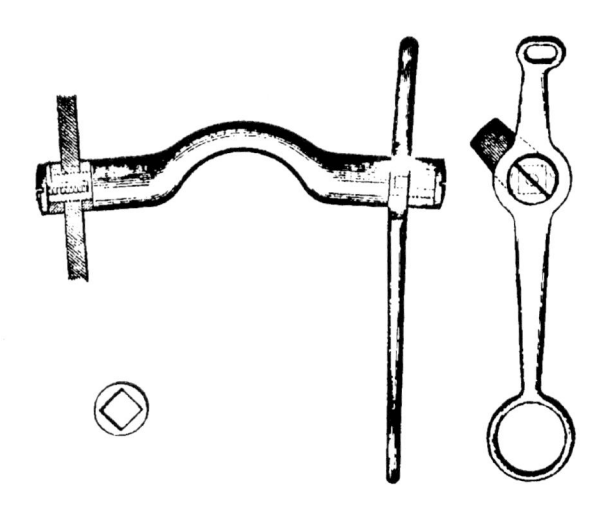

Fig. 32.17 Smith adjustable-mouth bit.

Snake Bit: A snaffle bit made with a length of chain covered by russet leather composing the entire bit. Each end of the chain has a ring which is passed through a ring of a second set used as a bridle attachment ring.

Snake Bit: A curb bit with the cheekpieces having designs in the shape of a snake [Fig. 32.18 and 32.18a].

Fig. 32.18 Snake bit made by Bob Hall, Jolan, CA.

Snubbing Post: A post to which a horse is tied for training, shoeing or other work.

Sommer, Richard, Sommerwaide, GR and Emil Polzin, Berlin, GR, Patent No. 556,564, Mar 17, 1896 [Fig. 32.19]. The top bar of the double-mouth bit pivots on the cheekpieces, while the bottom-bar movement is limited to the slots in the cheek-pieces.

Fig. 32.18a Snake bits made by McChesney.

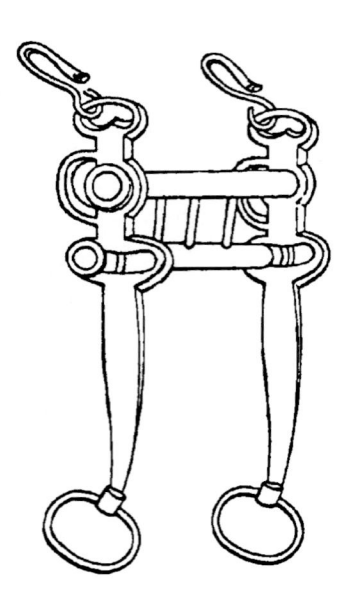

Fig,. 32.19 Sommer double-mouth bit.

Spade Bit: A bit with an elongated port that ends in a rounded curve or spoon. See Spade Bit, Chapter 1.

Spanish Cavesson: Fig. 32.20. See Chapter 6, Fig. 6.13.

Fig. 32.20 Spanish cavesson.

Spanish Jumping Bit: See Kimberwicke, Chapter 15, Fig. 15.33.

Speculum: A device used to force a horse's mouth open and keep it open for the process of dental work or to examine the mouth or tongue of a horse [Fig. 32.21 32.21a and 32.21b].

Fig. 32.21 Speculum in use.

400

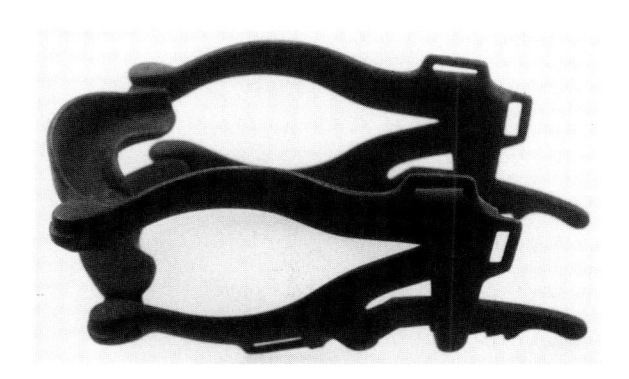

Fig 32.21a Speculum.

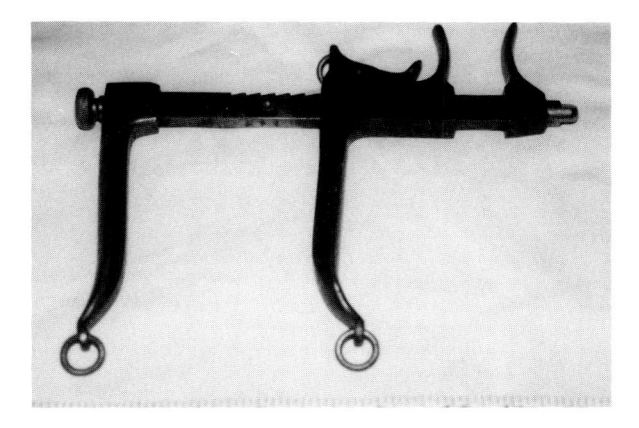

Fig. 32.21b Speculum. Robert Maclin collection.

Speedway Check: See Overcheck, Chapter 9, Fig. 9.18.

Spence, Charles A., Assumption, IL, Patent No. 635,877, Oct. 31, 1899 [Fig. 32.22]. A scissor bit with three bars comprising the mouth-piece. Two of the bars have rings attaching them to the cheek-rings and pivot near their outer ends to the end portion of the third bar.

Fig. 32.22 Spence snaffle bit.

Spohr, Peter, Giessen, GR, Patent No. 544,777, Aug. 20, 1895 [Fig.32.23]. The joint-link between the bit and head-stall to which the curb-chain is attached is designed to prevent undue twisting and injury to the jaw of the horse.

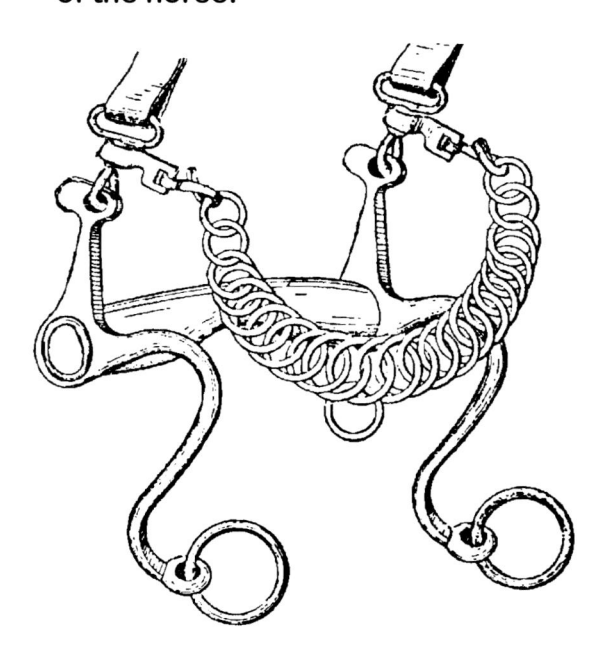

Fig. 32.23 Spohr curb bit and attachment.

Spokane Bit: A bit manufactured by the Spokane Bit Co., Spokane, WA [Fig. 32.24]. See Aughey, Chapter 5, Fig. 5.14.

Spoon: 1. The enlarged flat ends of the cheek-piece on half-cheek and full-cheek snaffle bits. 2. The upper end of the elongated port on some spade bits.

Spoonhour, Jacob, Green Township, and Samuel R. Boyd, Chambersburg, PA, Patent No. 71,806, Dec. 3, 1867 [Fig. 32.25]. The rein-ring is attached to the elliptical-shaped side-piece with a clasp which has a roller secured to the inner face of the cheek-piece. The rein-ring travels along the inner surface of the cheek-piece. The cheek-piece and ring can be attached to any solid mouth-piece.

Fig. 32.24 The Spokane bit. Jean Gayle collection. Jones Photo Co.

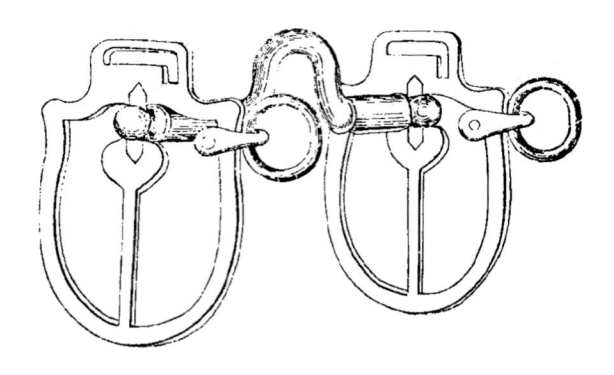

Fig. 32.25 Spoonhour snaffle bit.

Spring-mouth Snaffle: Also called a Butterfly snaffle. See Chapter 5, Fig. 5.92.

Springstein Bit: See Chapter 8, Figs. 8.22 and 8.23.

Sproul Bit: See Hackamore, Chapter 13.

Squier, Horace S., Newark, NJ, Patent No. 241,745, May 17, 1881 [Fig. 32.26]. A construction method of a flexible core for a mouth-piece with a rubber cover.

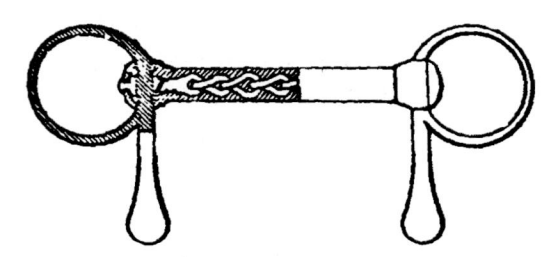

Fig. 32.26 Squier construction method.

Patent No. 248,620, Oct 25, 1881, [Fig. 32.27]. A metallic flexible core covered with rubber tubing.

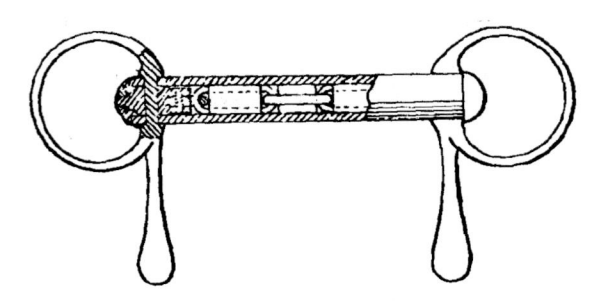

Fig. 32.27 Squier construction method.

Patent No. 255,737, Mar. 28, 1882 [Fig. 32.28]. An improvement in the mouth-piece linkage over previous patents.

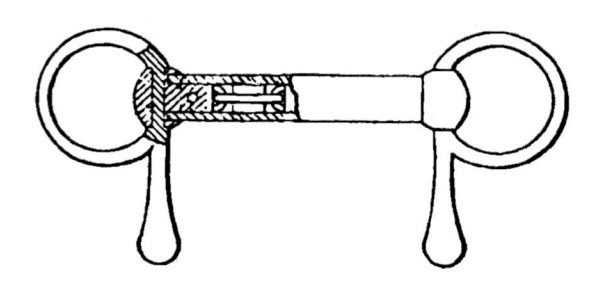

Fig. 32.28 Squier improved construction method.

Patent No. 309,660, Dec. 23, 1884 [Fig. 32.29]. A figure "8" link to which is attached an overcheck that will slide through the attachment rings.

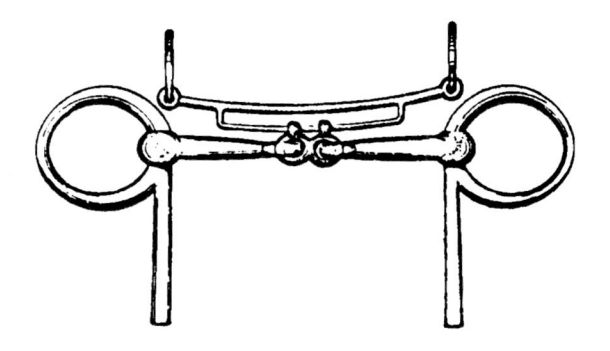

Fig. 32.29 Squier snaffle with attached overcheck.

Patent No. 312,397, Feb. 17, 1885 [Fig.32.30]. The mouth-piece and cheek-rings are made of one intregral piece of wire. The completed mouth-piece is covered with rubber, leather or other flexible material.

Fig. 32.30 Squier wire-coil mouth.

Patent No. 472,145, Apr. 5, 1892 [Fig. 32.31]. A chain mouth-piece of various types that is covered with molded rubber or other flexible material.

Stalker, Neil, Hartford, CT Patent No. 471,833, Mar. 29, 1892 [Fig. 32.32]. The rings are joined by a thick heavy strip of tough rawhide which forms the core of the mouthpiece. The rawhide is medicated or treated to make it soft. The mouthpiece is covered with tanned leather which extends to cover the inside of the cheek-rings.

Fig. 32.31 Squier covered chain-mouth bit.

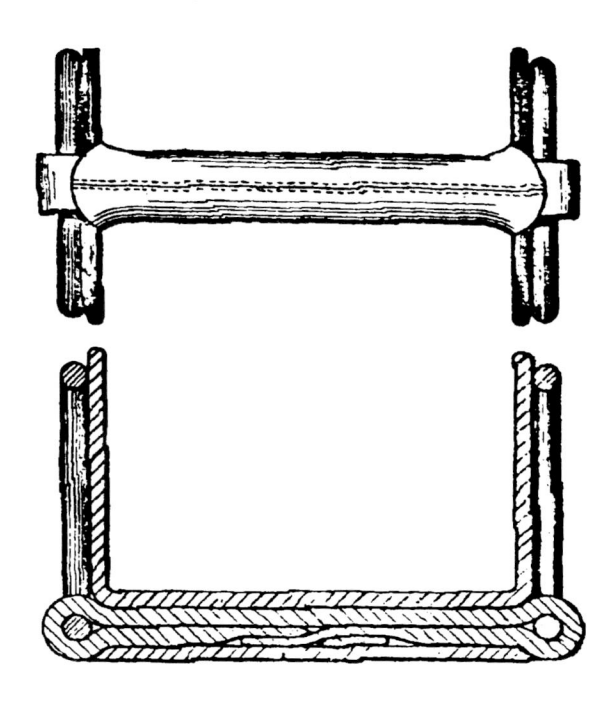

Fig.32.32 Stalker rawhide and leather mouth bit.

Patent No. 549,544, Nov. 12, 1895 [Fig.32.33]. The U-shaped portion is fitted under the upper lip of the horse in front of the top teeth. There is no control bar in the mouth in the conventional manner.

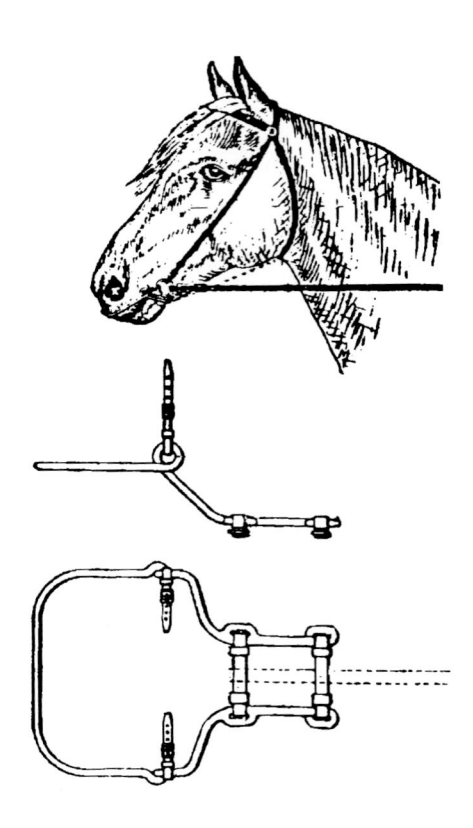

Fig. 32.33 Stalker control device.

Patent No. 549,545, Nov 12, 1895 [Fig.32.34]. A variation of the previous patent.

Patent No. 816,615, Apr. 3, 1906 [Fig. 32.35]. Construction method for a cheek-piece that is attached to a flexible-mouth bit.

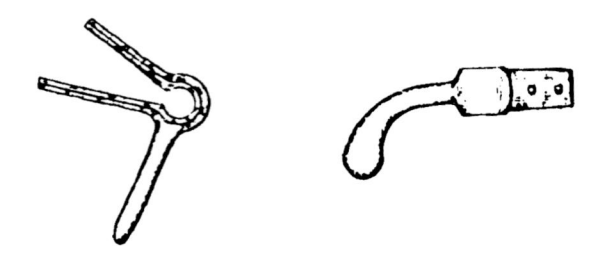

Fig. 32.35 Stalker cheek-piece construction.

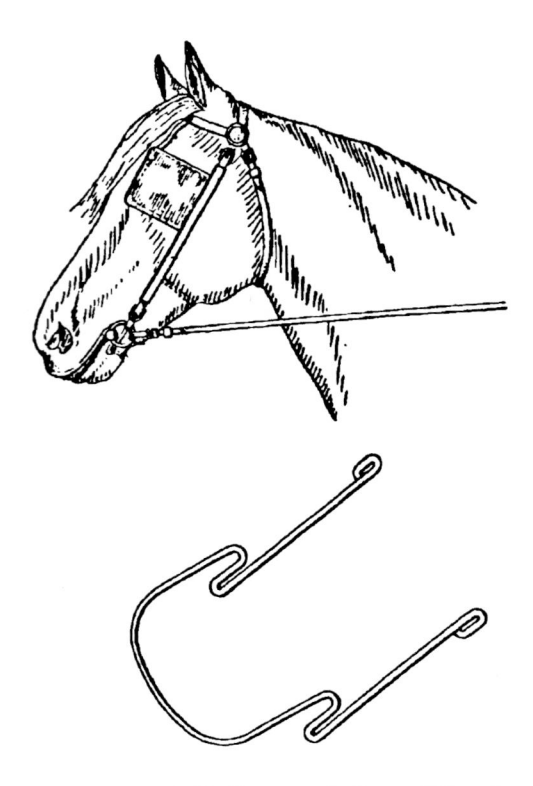

Fig. 32.34 Stalker variation of lip-check device.

Stallion Bit: A snaffle bit with horseshoe-shaped cheek-pieces [Fig. 32.36]. The horseshoe is a symbol of virility and fertility.

Fig. 32.36 Stallion bit.

Stallion Bit: A style of bit with a solid bar-type mouth and wire rings. A chain is attached to one rein-ring and passes through the other to a lead rope. A bar is often used in place of a chain with the holder of the lead rope able to exert considerable pressure on the under jaw of the horse [Fig. 32.37].

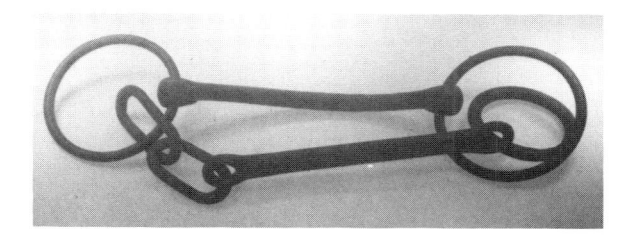

Fig. 32.37 Stallion bit.

Stanley, James, Newark, NJ, Patent No. 171,587, Dec. 28, 1875 [Fig. 32.38]. The tubular mouth-piece is removable from the cheeks and may be covered with rubber, leather, gutta-percha or celluloid.

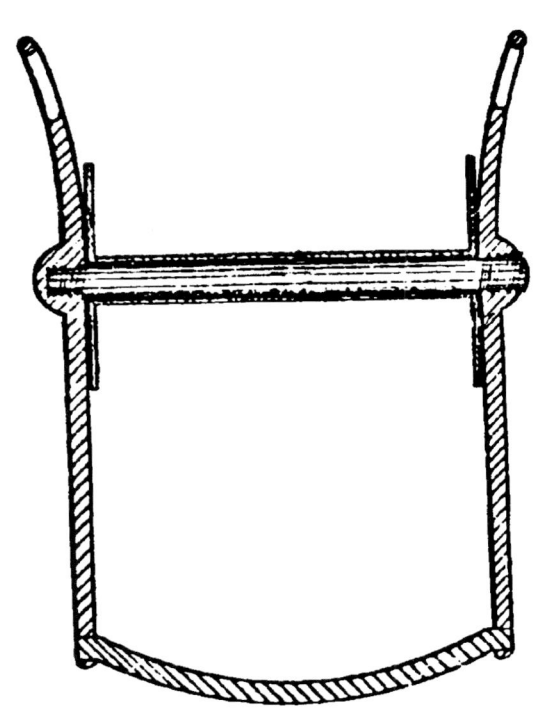

Fig. 32.38 Stanley bit with replaceable mouth-piece.

Patent No. 201,566, Mar. 19, 1878 [Fig. 32.39]. A rubber-covered jointed mouth-piece with cheek-pieces that swivel on the mouth ends and used to apply pressure to the sides of the mouth.

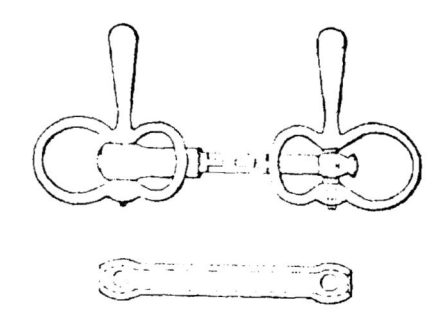

Fig. 32.39 Stanley flexible-mouth bit.

Patent No. 224.851, Feb 24, 1880 [Fig. 32.40]. The cheek-piece has a shank which is inserted into the hollow mouth-piece.

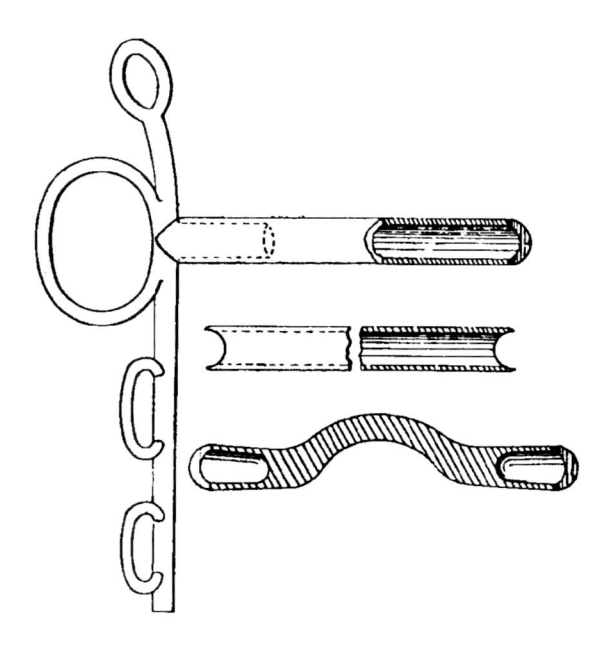

Fig. 32.40 Stanley hollow-mouth curb bit.

Patent No. 249,113, Nov. 1, 1883 [Fig.32.41]. A construction method of attaching the rubber-covered flexible mouth-piece to the cheek-piece.

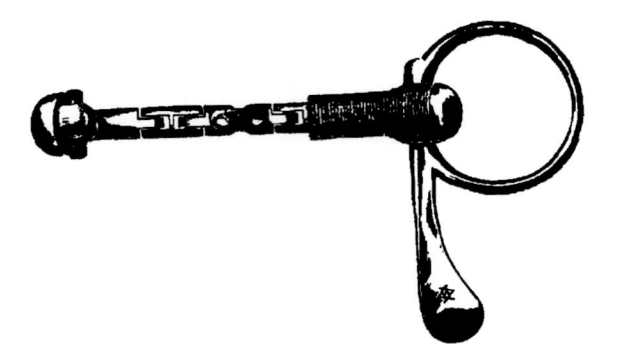

Fig. 32.41 Stanley construction detail.

Patent No. 317,034, May 5, 1885 [Fig. 32.42 and 32.43]. A bit provided with jaws directly connected by curved bars which form an eye for the reception of the head of the mouth-piece and prevent the jaws from spreading.

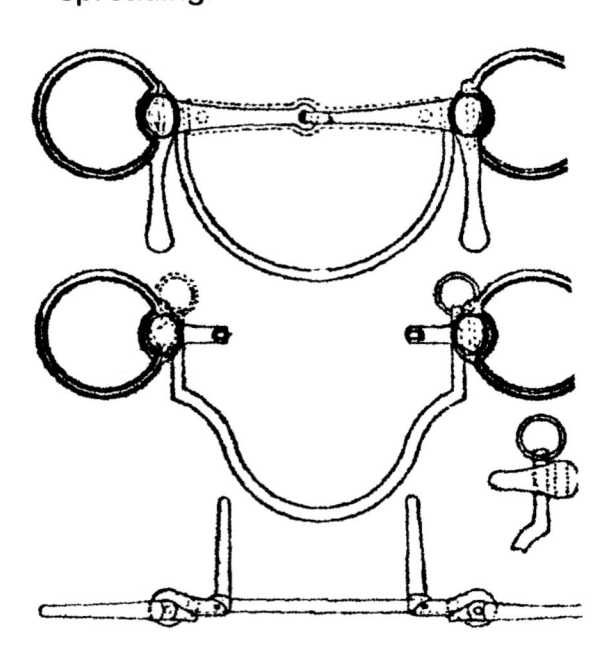

Fig. 32.42 Detail of the Fish-eye cheek-piece design.

Patent No. 346,231, July 27, 1886 [Fig. 32.44]. Construction detail for rubber-covered mouth-pieces in that the rubber covering extends around the ends of the mouth-piece.

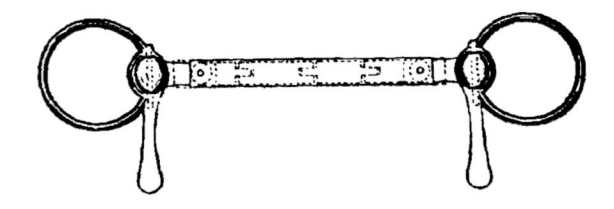

Fig. 32.43 The Fish-eye cheek on a simple snaffle bit.

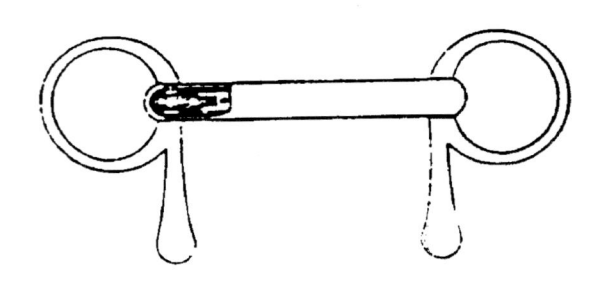

Fig. 32.44 Stanley rubber-covered mouth-piece.

Patent No. 354,263, Dec. 14, 1886 [Fig. 32.45]. A rubber covering for bits with overcheck devices attached.

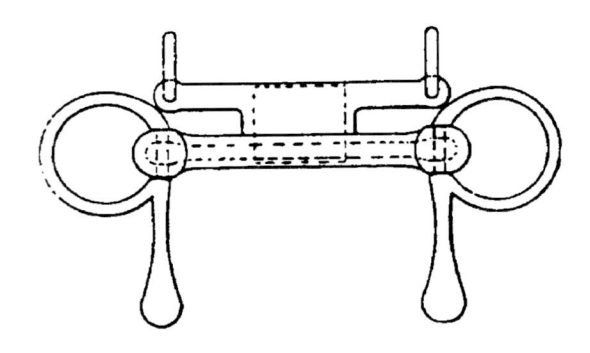

Fig. 32.45 Stanley rubber-covered-mouth design.

Patent No. 538,049, Apr. 23, 1895 [Fig. 32.46]. The leather strap marked Fig. 3 is the band going over the nose of the horse. The leather strap marked Fig. 2 is used as a chin or curb strap.

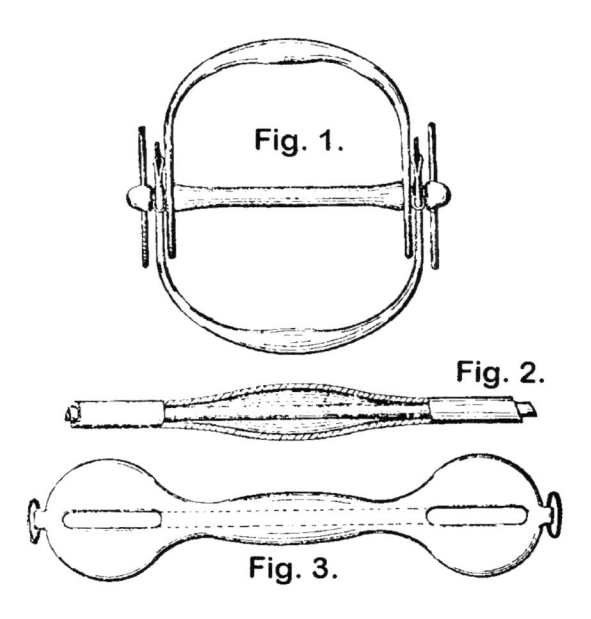

Fig. 32.46 Stanley Humane bit.

Stapleton, Matt, Stevens Point, WI, Patent No. 356,668, Jan 25, 1887 [Fig. 32.47]. The springs on the outer ends of the mouth-piece add tension to the extended end of the chin loop. The hook on the loop is a martingale attachment. Pressure is put on the bars of the horse to control the head position.

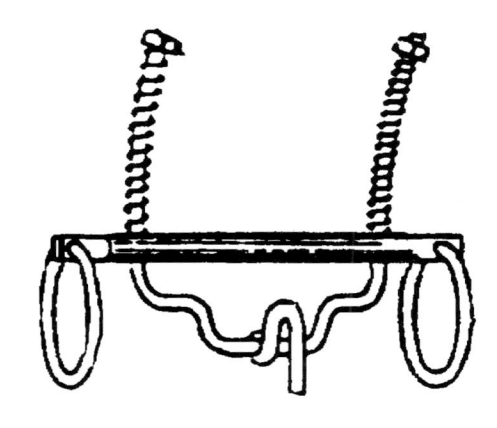

Fig. 32.47 Stapleton spring-action mouth-piece control bit.

Starcheck Double-ringed Snaffle: From *The Loriner* an early 1800's snaffle design [Fig. 32.48].

Fig. 32.48 Starcheck double-ringed snaffle.

Stevens, Nathan P., Hopkinton, NH, Patent No. 159,527, Feb. 9, 1875 [Fig. 32.49]. The center hinge of the mouth-piece to which is attached downward projecting prongs which, when the reins are pulled, can put a force on the lower jaw of the horse.

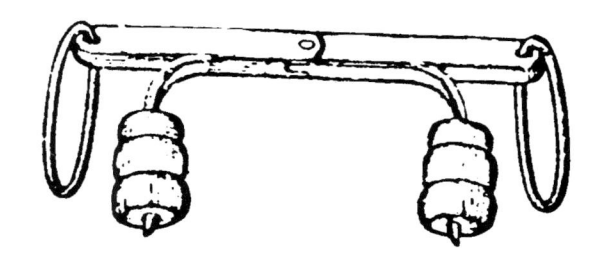

Fig. 32.49 Stevens pressure bit.

Stockder, C. E., New Haven, CT, Patent No. 39,843, Sep. 8, 1863 [Fig. 32.50]. An eye and tongue is built into the cheek-ring to which the rein is directly fastened.

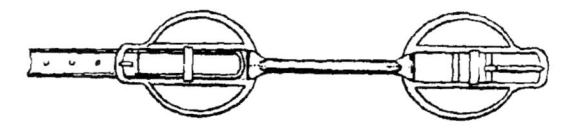

Fig. 32.50 Stockder fastener-ring bit.

Stockton Harness Bit: An early English bit with Buxton cheek-pieces with a loose broken-snaffle mouth projecting through holes in the cheek-pieces [Fig. 32.51].

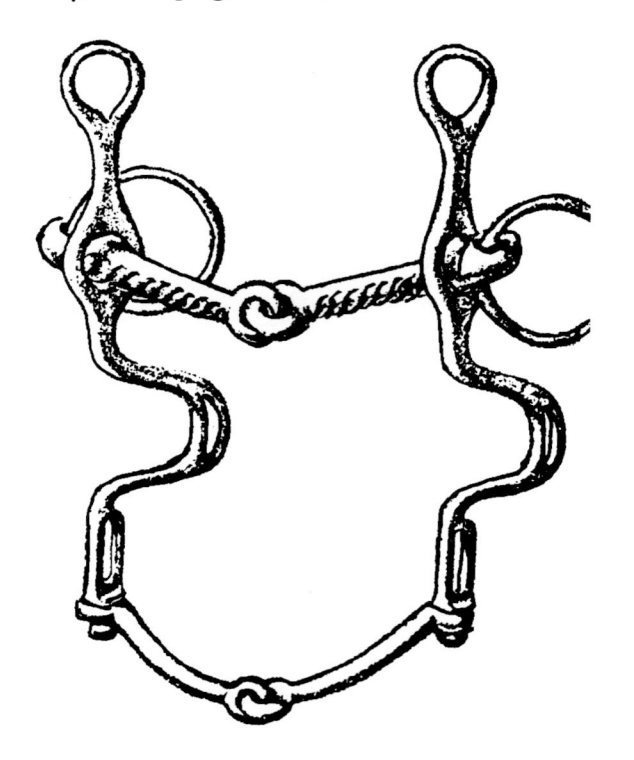

Fig. 32.51 Stockton harness bit.

Stockton Pelham: See Chapter 27, Fig. 27.31.

Stomach Pump: Term given to a spade bit in some localities.

Stone, William Bitiess Pelham: See Chapter 34, Fig. 34.32.

Stout: A term used in England to designate a bit of heavy or stouter construction.

Success Bit: See Chapter 8, Fig. 8.23.

Sulecio, Salvador A., Guatemala, Guatemala, Patent No. 1,046,897, Dec. 10, 1912 [Fig. 32.52]. A curb bit the inventor claims can be comfortably adjusted to the horse without the use of ordinary cheek and head-straps of a bridle.

Fig. 32.52 Sulecio bridleless curb bit.

Sure-win Bit Holder: A Y-shaped strap that secures an overcheck or bradoon bit and extends over the nose and up the face of the horse to attach to the bridle crown piece.

Sutton, Jessey T. and George M., Sharon, TN, Patent No. 362,591, May 10, 1887 [Fig. 32.53]. A straight-mouth bit with a buckle built into each end of the cheek-pieces.

Fig. 32.53 Sutton bit with buckles.

Swales, Frank, London, England, Patent No. 531,230, Dec. 18, 1894 [Fig. 32.54]. A mouth-piece or bradoon that can be attached by an India rubber spring to the main mouth-piece of an ordinary Liverpool or coach bit.

Fig. 32.54 Swales bit attachment.

Patent No. 760,355, May 17, 1904 [Fig. 32.55 and 32.55a]. The outer and open-ended portion of the tubular mouth-piece has eyes for attaching the bridle head-stall. The inner portion or rod to which the reins are attached is of lesser diameter and moves freely in the tubular portion.

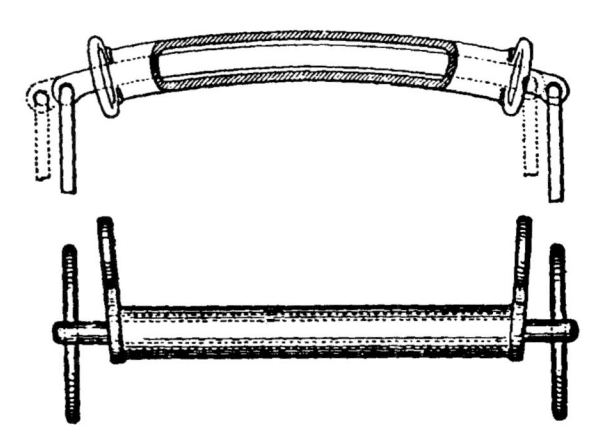

Fig. 32.55 Swales tubular-mouth bit.

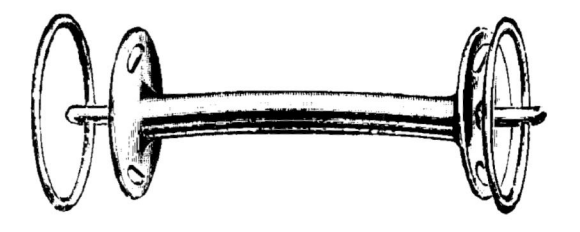

Fig. 32.55a Swales race bit.

Patent No. 898,394, Sep. 8, 1908 [Fig. 32.56]. Commonly called Swales 3-in-1.

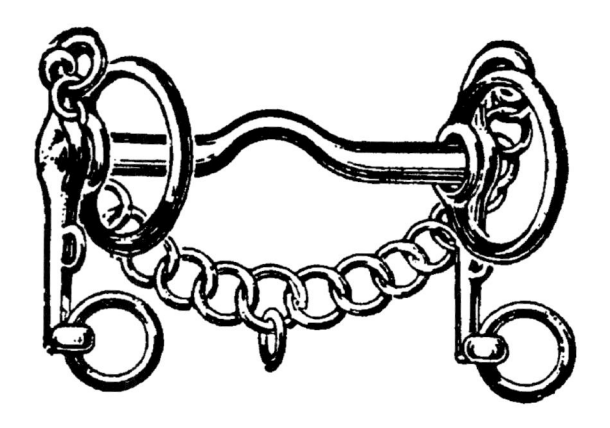

Fig. 32.56 Swales 3-in-1 bit.

Patent No. 1,076,716, Oct. 28, 1913 [Fig. 32.57]. A combined curb and snaffle with a curb hook that self-closes when the curb is in a normal position in the curb groove.

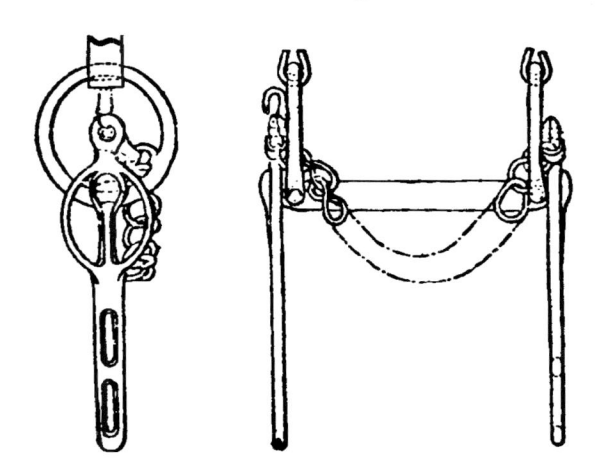

Fig. 32.57 Swales combination curb and snaffle.

Swan, Fred M., North Ansen, ME, Patent No. 103,103, May 17, 1870 [Fig. 32.58]. A snaffle bit with a copper barrel roller in the center of the mouth-piece.

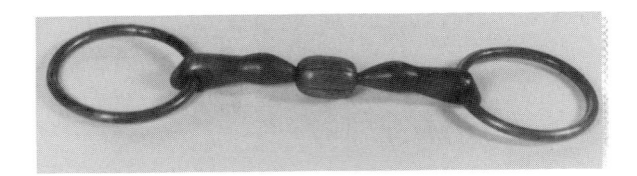

Fig. 32.58 Swan snaffle bit. Robert Maclin collection.

Swart, Fred M., Margaretville, NY, Patent No. 1,116,159, Nov. 3, 1914 [Fig.32.59]. The mouth-piece ends slide in the slots of the cheek-pieces. The springs attached to the mouth-piece allow the rider to apply pressure to the bit and the mouth of the horse by the strength of the pull.

Swartzendruber, Menno, S., Lorchester, NE, Patent No. 988,836, Apr. 4, 1911 [Fig. 32.60]. A ring bit which embraces the lower jaw.

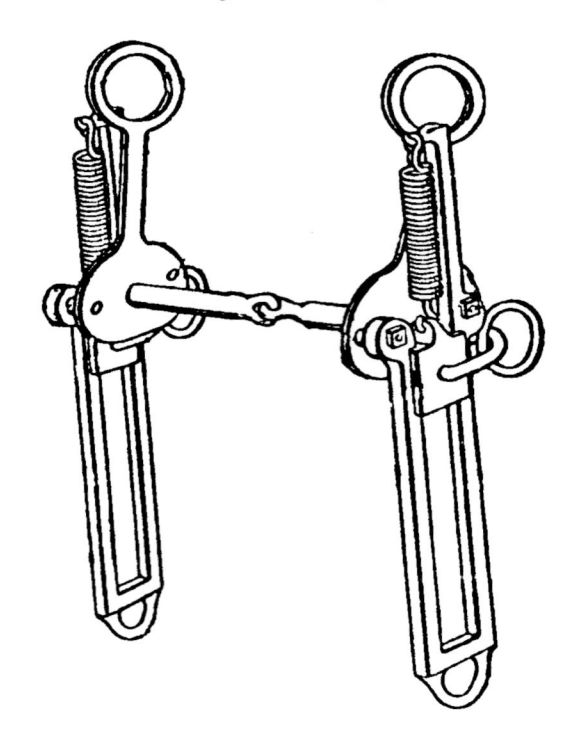

Fig. 32.59 Swart bit with spring-controlled mouth-piece.

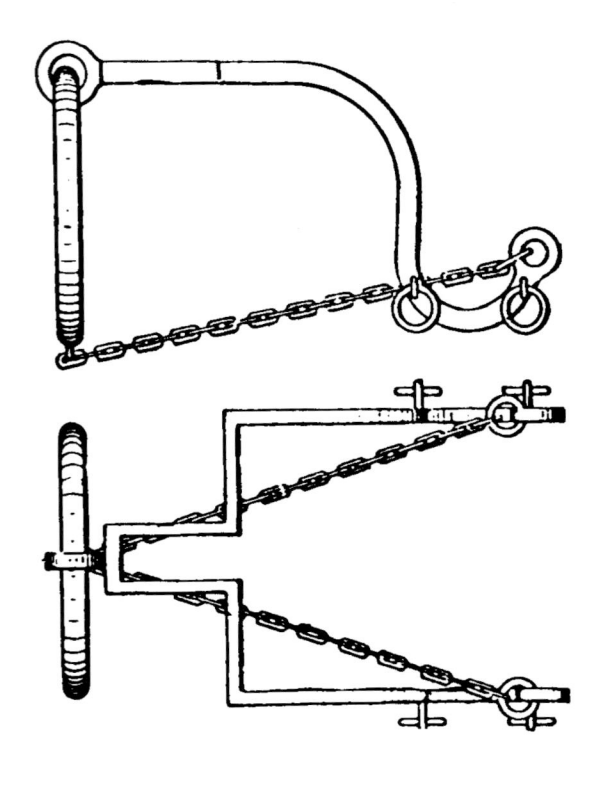

Fig. 32.60 Swartzendruber ring bit.

CHAPTER THIRTY-THREE
Tails to Typology

Tails: The lower end of a cheek-piece that accepts the rein.

Taking the Bit: The process of the horse opening its mouth and accepting the mouth-piece.

Tassels: A term sometimes applied to players on a bit.

Taster: A cricket or copper roller in the port or on the mouth-piece.

Tattersall Ring Bit: A ring bit with a small loop on each side [Fig. 33.0]. In some areas called Colt ring bit.

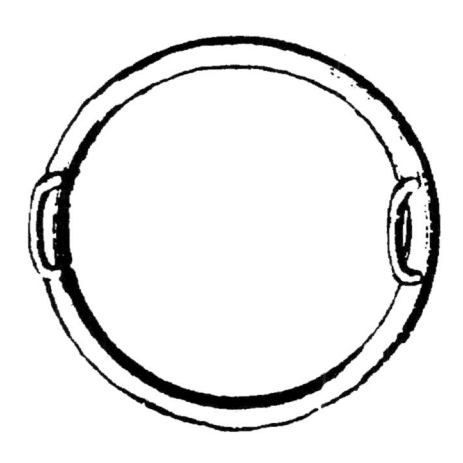

Fig. 33.0 Tattersall ring bit.

Tattersall Ring Bit with Players: A ring bit with players attached [Fig. 33.1].

Taylor, Carl E., Woodsville, NH, Patent No. 905,953, Dec. 8,1908 [Fig. 33.2]. A pulley bit with the pulley built into the outer portion of the cheek-ring. The hooks on the upper end of the round leather strap hook into the cheek-strap of the bridle. The round ring is the rein-ring.

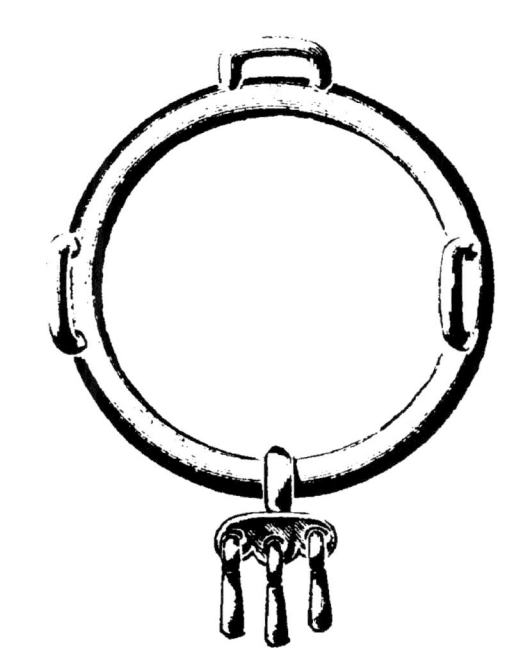

Fig. 33.1 Tattersall ring bit with heavy players.

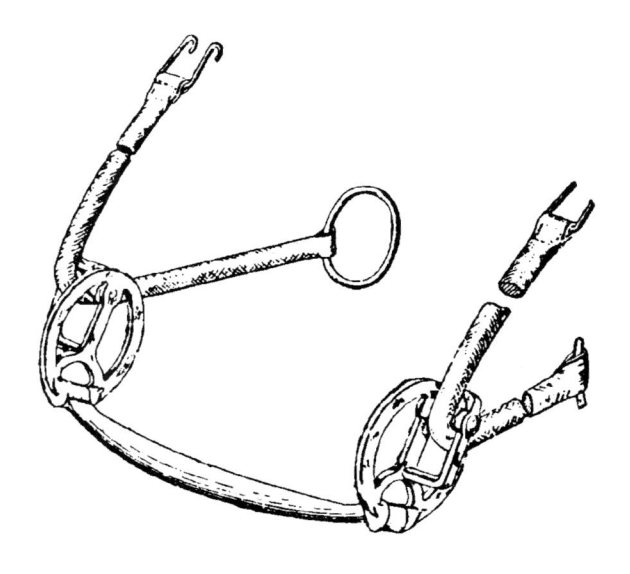

Fig. 33.2 Taylor pulley bit.

Taylor, John and Charles Taylor, Detroit, MI, Patent No. 261,278, July 18, 1882 [Fig. 33.3]. The bit has two straight bars with a ring on each end of each bar. The bits are interlocked with each other by each bit passing through one of the rings of the other. In practice both bits are placed in the mouth with the bridle attached to one set of rings and the reins to the second set.

Fig. 33.3 Taylor double-mouth bit.

Taylors Simple Bit: A bit from *The Loriner* with a clamping action that can put pressure on the lower jaw of the horse [Fig. 33.4].

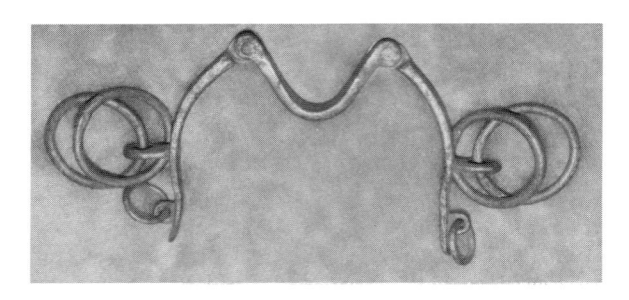

Fig. 33.4 Taylors simple bit. Harold Dawley collection.

Temple, William T., Trenton, NJ, Patent No. 733,769, July 14, 1903 [Fig. 33.5]. A jointed snaffle bit with a built in overcheck bit. The overcheck is through the cheek-ring. The drawing illustrates two different cheek-pieces.

Tepper, Thomas W., Alturas, CA, Patent No. 2,017,021, Oct 8.1935 [Fig. 33.6]. A high-ported curb bit with braces on the side of the port which give it some of the features of a half-breed bit and some of a spade bit.

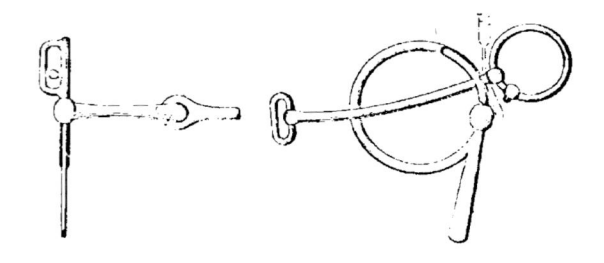

Fig. 33.5 Temple snaffle bit with overcheck.

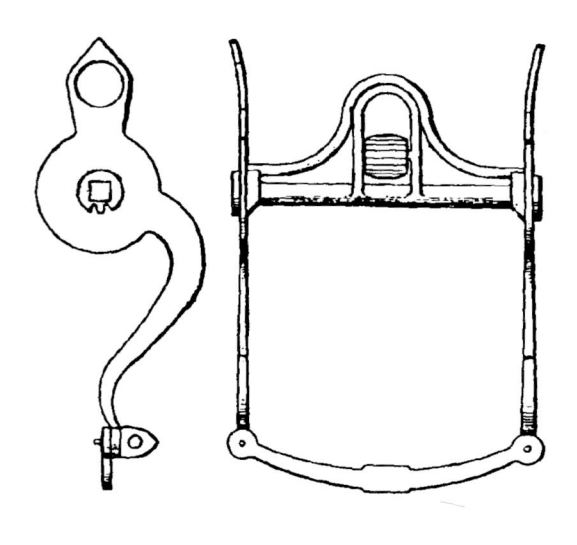

Fig. 33.6. Tepper curb bit.

Tevis, William S., Jr., San Francisco, CA, Patent No. 1,062,747, May 27, 1913 [Fig. 33.7]. A loop style bit which acts much like a war bridle when the rope used as a bridle is attached.

Texas Bit: A name given to a wide variety of short cheek-piece curb bits [Fig. 33.8]. See Chapter 30, Figs. 30.1 and 30.2.

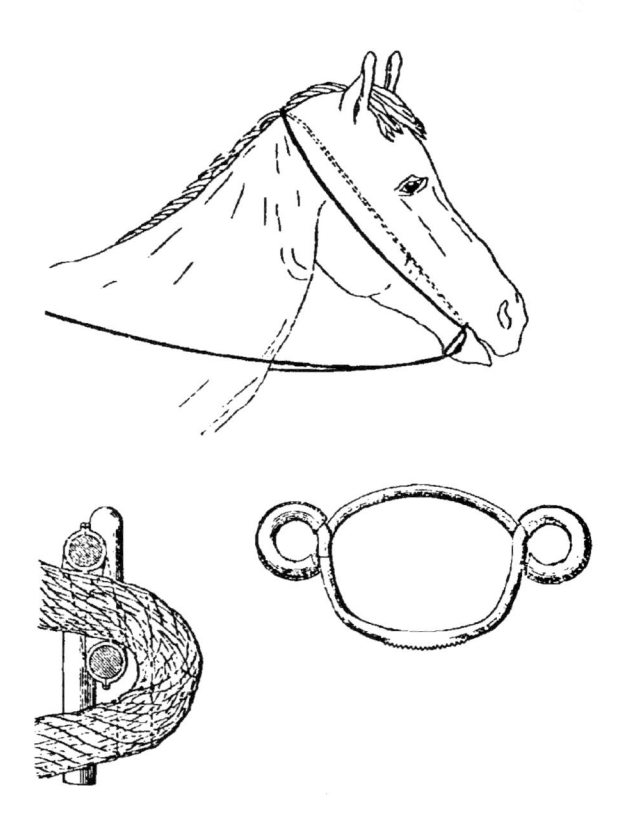

Fig. 33.7 Tevis loop bit.

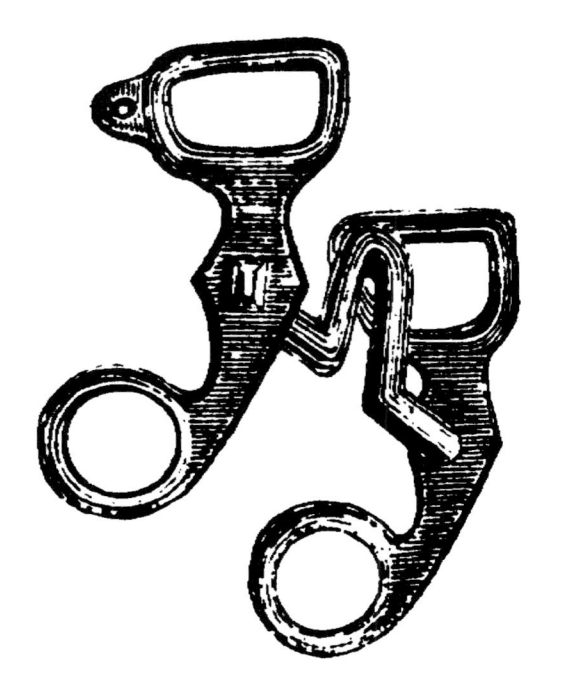

Fig. 33.8 Texas-style bit. The Indianola.

Thimbles: The portion of a cheek-piece which holds a pin to connect the mouth-piece to the cheek-piece.

Thompson, Henry C., Mount Sterling, KY, Patent No. 104,793, June 28, 1870 [Fig. 33.9]. A combination of two bits, one passing through a slot in the center of the other. They are bound together by straps in a manner that one may slide upon the other and the mouth-piece of the bit is elongated by drawing on the bridle rein-rings.

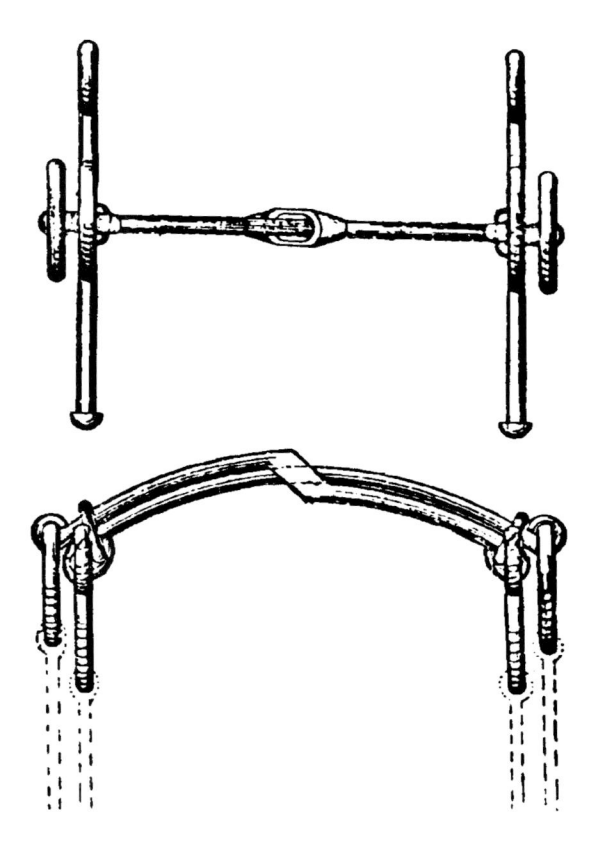

Fig. 33.9 Thompson sliding-mouth bit.

Thorn Bit: A bit from India with barbs or "thorns" on the mouth-piece [Fig. 33.10]. It is thought the severeness of the bit is needed because the average horseman there, being of slight build, is physically incapable of holding a horse with a mild bit. John L. Kipling in an article dated

1892, stated "the weakness is more moral than physical; nerve is more wanting than muscle, and reason most of all."

Fig. 33.10 Thorn bit. R. L. Emerson, Jr., collection.

Thornton, Amedee, Chelsea, England, Patent No. 314,081, Mar. 17, 1885 [Fig. 33.11]. A bit with a noseband and a two-bar mouth-piece that can move in the slots of the cheek-pieces. The wire mesh attached to the bit is designed to lay at length within the mouth when the horse is going quietly, and to be drawn to the back of the throat when the position of the bit is changed by the reins, tending to check the horse if it bolts. The noseband compresses the nostrils at the same time.

Baron Thornton Bit: A bit of 1800 England with cheek-pieces slotted for the movement of the lower mouth-piece. The upper mouth-piece is fixed [Fig. 33.12].

Thornton, James, Wellsville, NY, Patent No. 168,857, Oct. 19, 1875 [Fig. 33.13]. The mouth-piece with two arms pivots in the frame of the cheek-pieces while attached to the center of the cheek-pieces. On a loose rein the mouth-piece by gravity assumes its lowest position in the mouth of the horse.

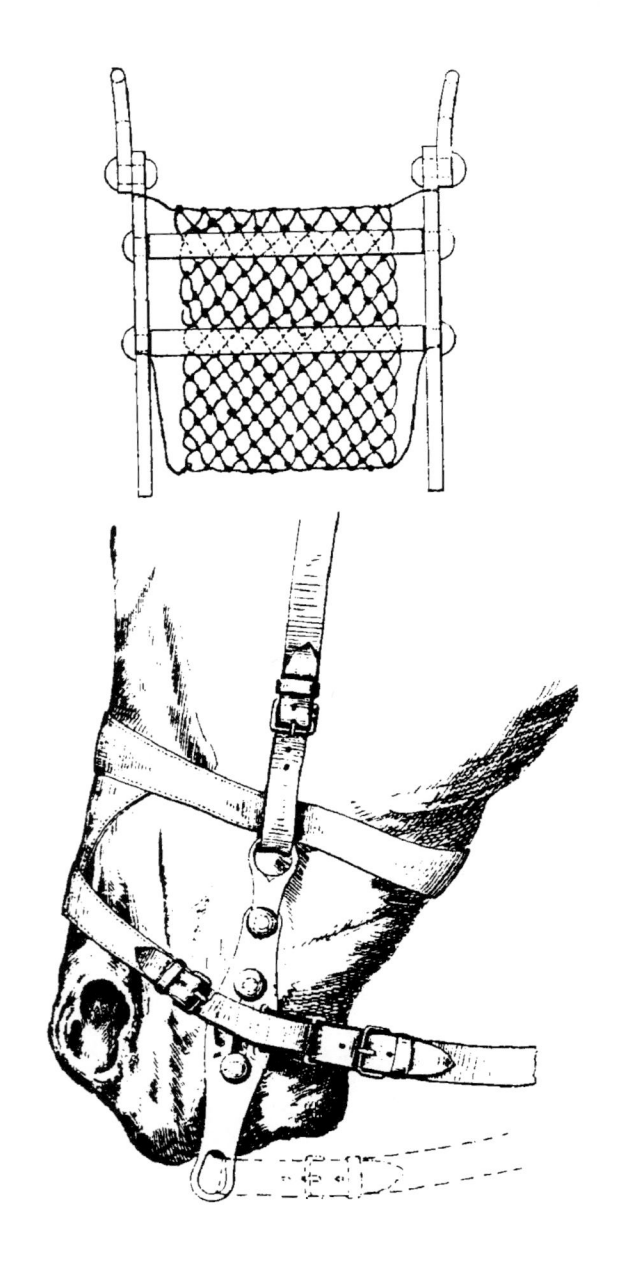

Fig. 33.11 Amedee Thornton's bit.

Thurlow Curb Bit: An 18th century bit from England. The wide head-stall loop allows for a wide and stronger bridle cheek-strap, or with a narrow cheek-strap, the bit has the ability to slide within the loop [Fig 33.14].

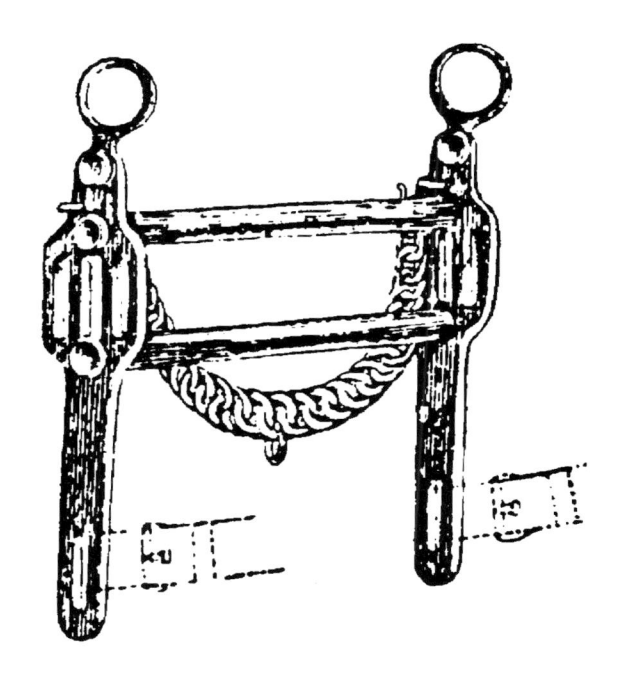

Fig. 33.12 Baron Thornton bit.

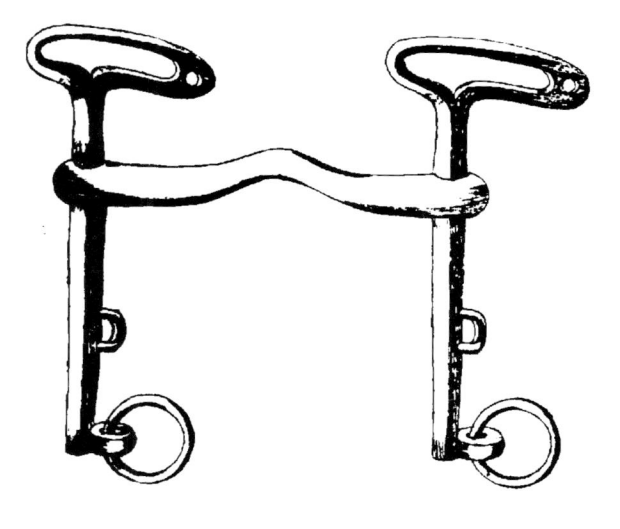

Fig. 33.14 Thurlow curb bit.

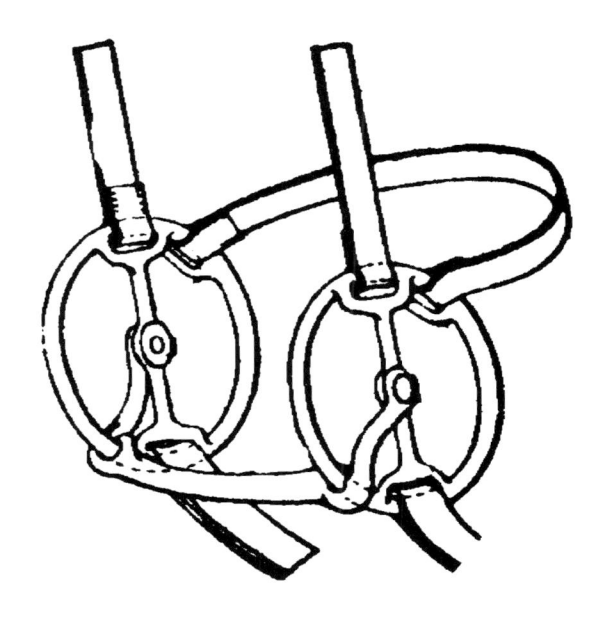

Fig. 33.13 Thornton Pivoting-mouth bit.

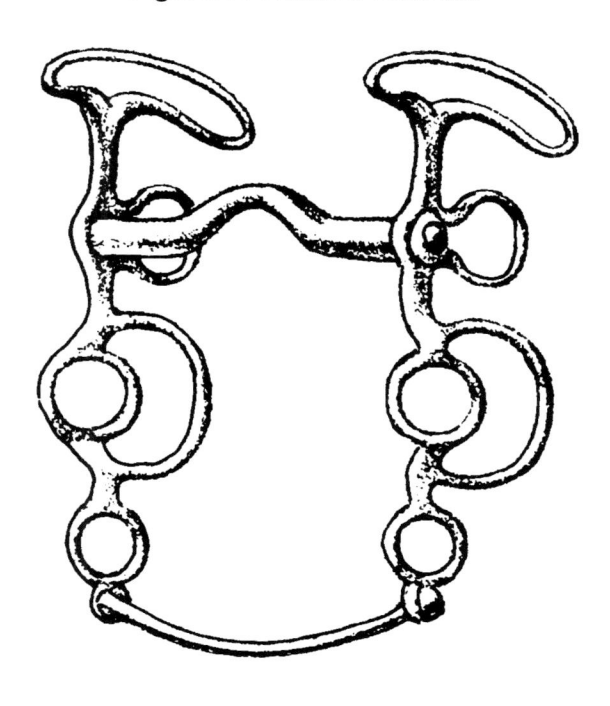

Fig 33.15 Thurlow harness bit.

Thurlow Harness Bit: A harness bit from *The Loriner* with the upper-ring feature of the Thurlow bit [Fig. 33.15].

Tichner, Arvin C., Syracuse, NY, Patent No. 190,646, May 8, 1877 [Fig. 33.16]. The hollow mouth-piece contains a flat metal spring-bar with a ring attached to each end of the spring. The spring-bar contains one or more spurs on each end and when the horse lowers or "throws its head down" the reins cause the spurs to come through holes in the mouth-piece causing the horse to immediately raise its head.

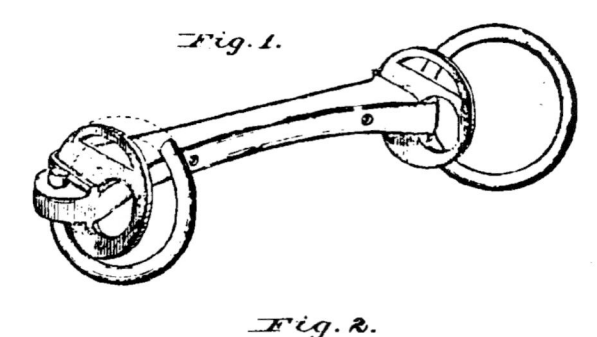

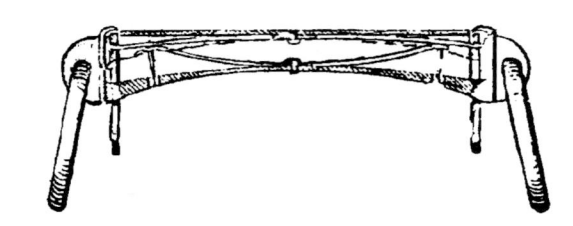

Fig. 33.16 Tichner bit.

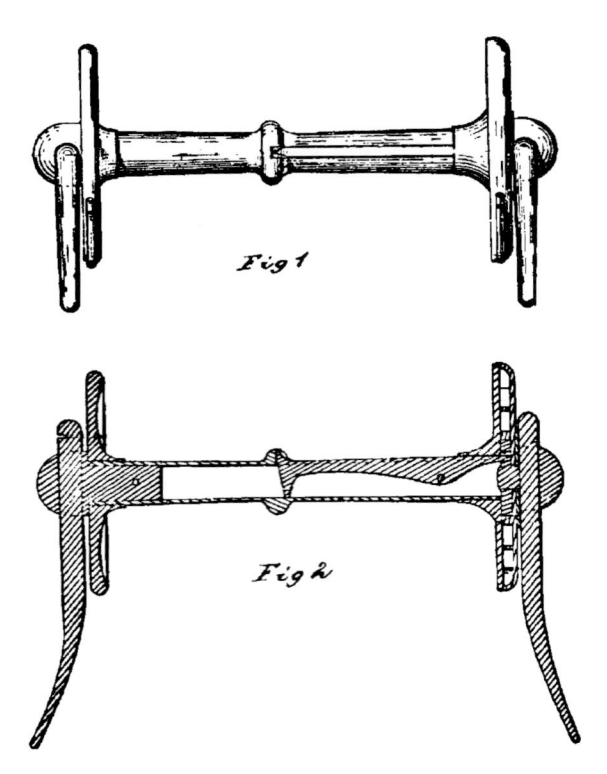

Fig. 33.17 Tichner bit.

Patent No. 351,007, Oct. 19, 1886 [Fig. 33.17]. The mouth-piece of the bit has a cam-slotted sliding plate connected to the rein. A spring in the mouth-piece holds the plate in position until the rein is pulled at which time the plate is thrust forward causing discomfort to the horse.

Tie Down: See Standing Martingale, Chapter 19.

Tilbury Bit: A bit named for John Tilbury of Pinner, Middlesex, England, a horse breeder and trainer. The bit was made during the middle 1800's [Fig. 33.18].

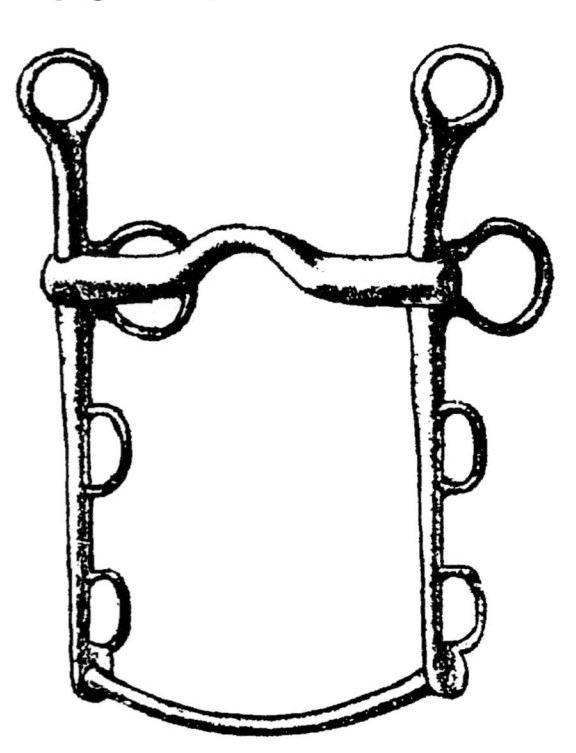

Fig. 33.18 Tilbury harness bit.

Tom Thumb: Name given to a curb bit with a small or short cheek-piece. Most often found with a mullen mouth [Fig. 33.19].

416

Fig.33.19 Tom Thumb Pelham bit with curb-chain.

Tongue Bit: Term given to a tongue-lolling bit. Its use prevents the horse from getting its tongue over the mouth-piece or hanging its tongue out the side of its mouth [Figs. 33.20 to 33.21c].

Fig. 33.20 Tongue bit.

Fig. 33.20a Tongue bit.

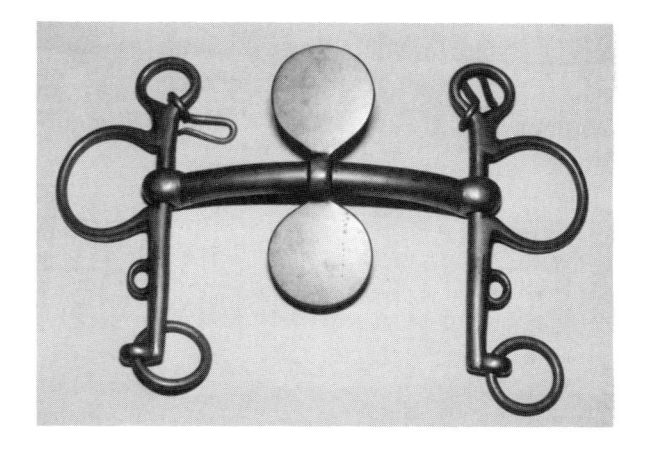

Fig. 33.21 Tongue bit.

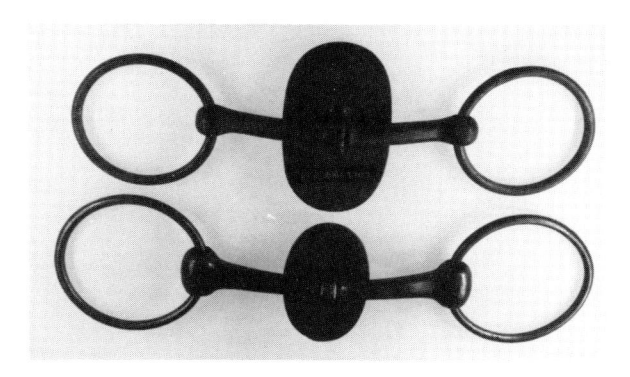

Fig. 33.21a Production tongue bits.

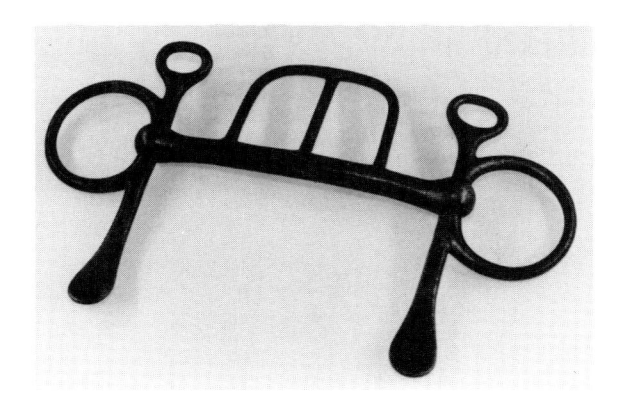

Fig. 33.21b Production tongue bit.

Tongue Bit, Hanging: A tongue bit in which the cheek-pieces are directed upward for attaching the cheek-strap [Fig.33.22].

Fig. 33.21c A variation of a tongue bit.

Fig. 33.22 Hanging-tongue bit.

Tongue Plate: A plate that is used much as an overcheck as an auxiliary bit [Fig. 33.23 and 33.23a].

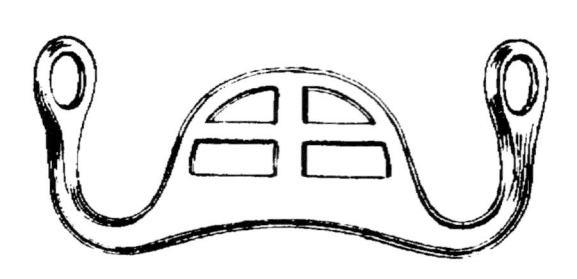

Fig. 33.23 Solid tongue plate.

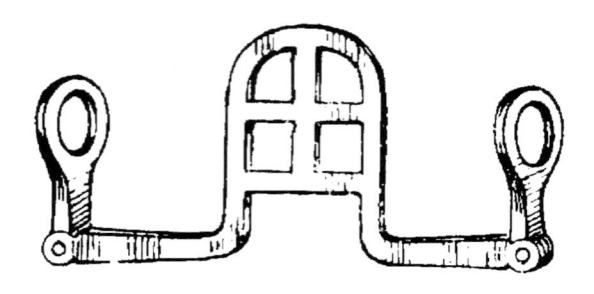

Fig. 33.23a Hinged tongue plate.

Touch Bit: A bit of 1800 England from John Dewsbury and Son Catalogue circa 1905 [Fig. 33.24].

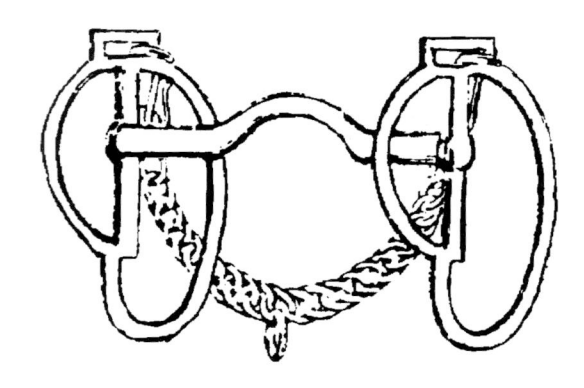

Fig. 33.24 Touch bit.

Tracy, J. D., Springfield, MA, Patent No. 30,510 Oct. 23, 1860 [Fig. 33.25]. The muzzle bit is designed to prevent the horse from biting or cribbing.

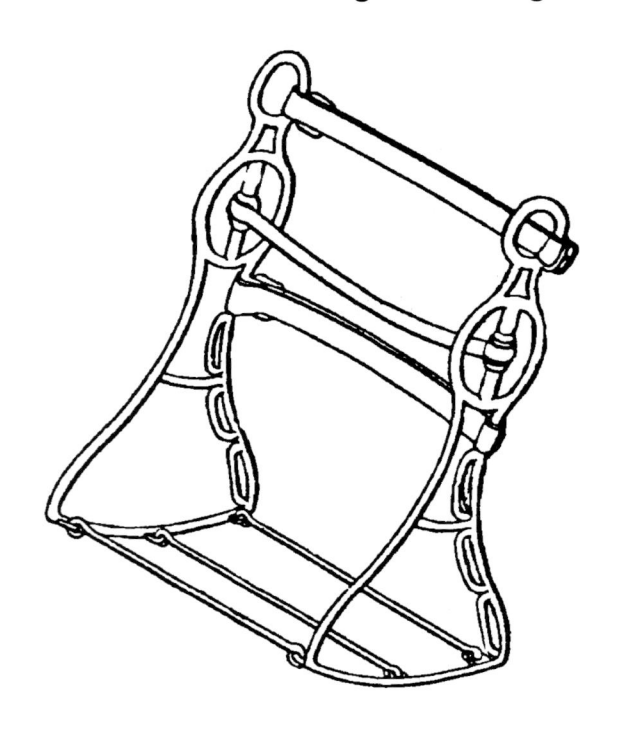

Fig. 33.25 Tracy muzzle bit.

Trademarks: A symbol, design, word or letter used by a company under which it does business. Protected by a copyright or patent.

PIMC: Pope Island Manufacturing Co., New York. The company used an outline of a whale with the letters PIMC inside the outline as a trademark.

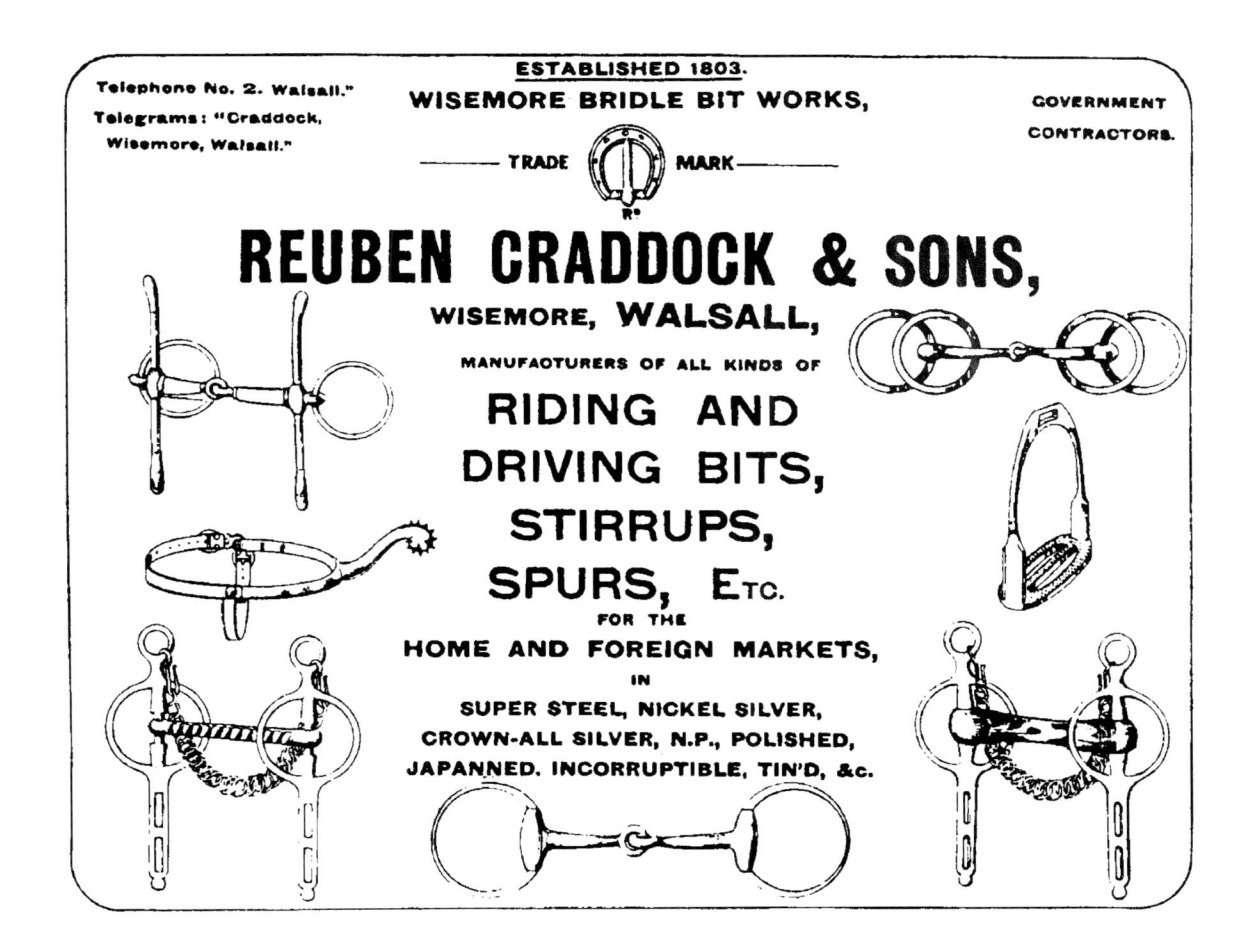

Trademark of a Walsall, England, company, circa 1916.

J. W. Chesterton & Co., Motor Car Fittings, Coach and Saddlers' Ironmongers. FIRM. Wednesbury Road, Walsall.	**Whitehouse, Cox & Co., Ltd.,** Harness, Saddlery, and Fancy Leather Goods. Marsh Street, Walsall.	**John Leckie & Co.,** Export Saddlery and Harness Manufacturers for all Markets. London Saddlery Works, Walsall.
Handford Greatrex & Co., Ltd., Tanners, Curriers, Japanners and Enamellers. TRADE MARK. Whittimore Street, Walsall.	**Walsall District Iron Company, Ltd.,** W. D. BEST, & B. B. District Ironworks, Walsall.	**John Dewsbury & Son, Ltd.,** Harness and Saddlery Furniture. Littleton Street, Walsall.
B. G. Cope & Partner, Ltd., High-grade Fancy Leather Goods, etc. Safeguard Works, Cecil Street, Walsall.	**Eyland & Sons, Ltd.,** Buckle Manufacturers. ESTD 1750. TRADE MARK. Rushall Street Works, Walsall.	**John Dewsbury & Son, Ltd.,** Harness and Saddlery Furniture. HAND BRAND. Littleton Street, Walsall.
B. Cope & Sons, Ltd., Bits, Stirrups, etc. TRADE BC MARK. Bloxwich, near Walsall.	**Job Craddock & Son, Ltd.,** For Bridle Bits, Stirrups, and Spurs. TRADE MARK. CRESCENT BRAND. Caldmore, Walsall, Eng.	**H. Frost & Co., Ltd.,** Harness Furniture. REGISTERED. TRADE MARK. Fieldgate, Walsall.
B. Cope & Sons, Ltd., Bits, Stirrups, etc. TRADE MARK. Bloxwich, near Walsall.	**Reuben Craddock & Sons,** Bridle Bits, Spurs, and Stirrups. TRADE MARK. Wisemore Bridle Bit Works, Walsall.	**C. C. Walker, Ltd.,** Manufacturers of Buckles of every description, Harness Furniture, etc. Buckle Works, Stafford Street, Walsall.

Trademarks of companies in Walsall, England, circa 1916.

Trademarks of companies in Walsall, England, circa 1916.

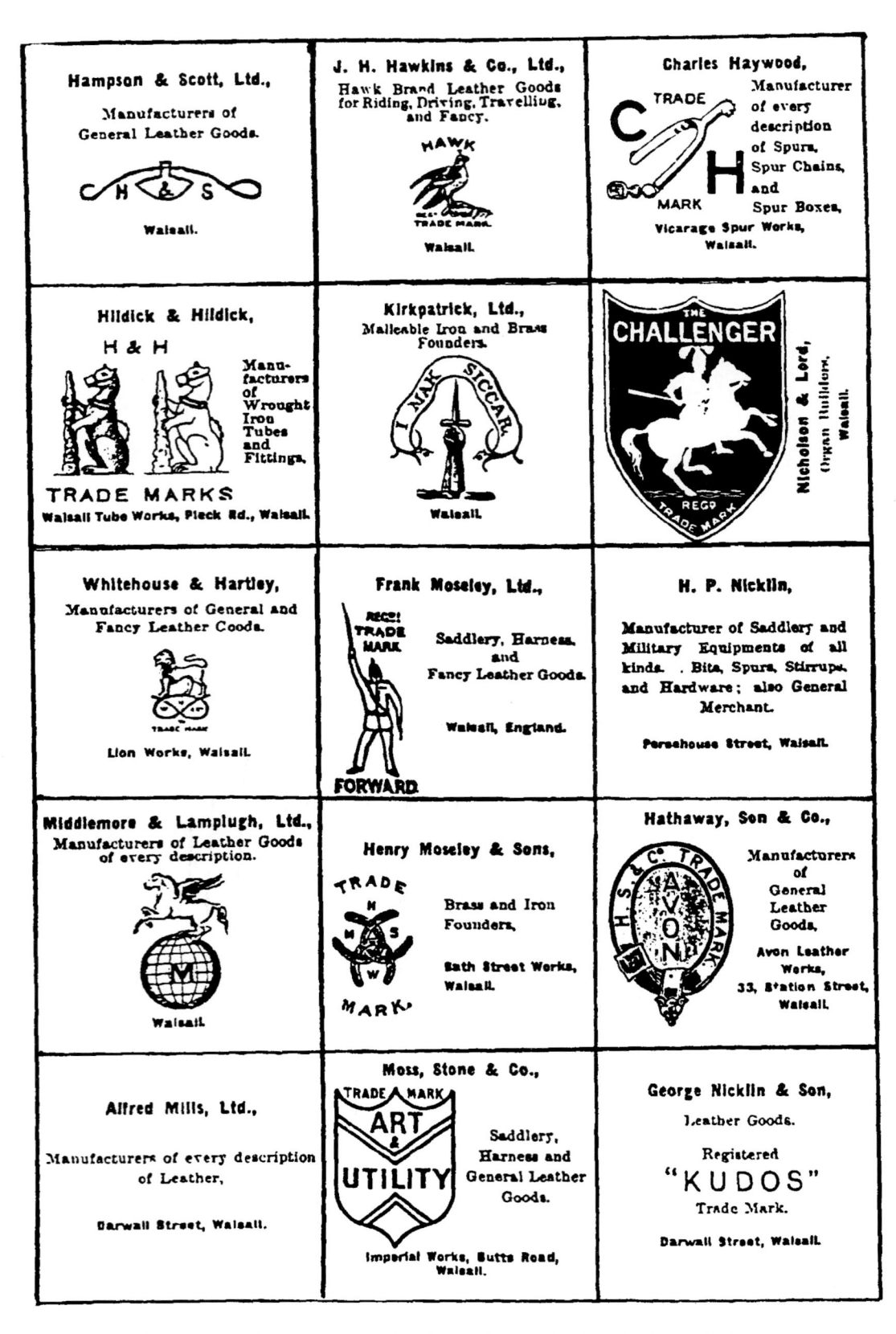

Hampson & Scott, Ltd., Manufacturers of General Leather Goods. Walsall.	**J. H. Hawkins & Co., Ltd.,** Hawk Brand Leather Goods for Riding, Driving, Travelling, and Fancy. Walsall.	**Charles Haywood,** Manufacturer of every description of Spurs, Spur Chains, and Spur Boxes. Vicarage Spur Works, Walsall.
Hildick & Hildick, H & H Manufacturers of Wrought Iron Tubes and Fittings. TRADE MARKS Walsall Tube Works, Pleck Rd., Walsall.	**Kirkpatrick, Ltd.,** Malleable Iron and Brass Founders. Walsall.	THE CHALLENGER REG^D TRADE MARK. Nicholson & Lord, Organ Builders, Walsall.
Whitehouse & Hartley, Manufacturers of General and Fancy Leather Goods. Lion Works, Walsall.	**Frank Moseley, Ltd.,** Saddlery, Harness, and Fancy Leather Goods. Walsall, England. FORWARD	**H. P. Nicklin,** Manufacturer of Saddlery and Military Equipments of all kinds. Bits, Spurs, Stirrups, and Hardware; also General Merchant. Peashouse Street, Walsall.
Middlemore & Lamplugh, Ltd., Manufacturers of Leather Goods of every description. Walsall	**Henry Moseley & Sons,** Brass and Iron Founders. Bath Street Works, Walsall.	**Hathaway, Son & Co.,** Manufacturers of General Leather Goods. Avon Leather Works, 33, Station Street, Walsall.
Alfred Mills, Ltd., Manufacturers of every description of Leather. Darwall Street, Walsall.	**Moss, Stone & Co.,** ART & UTILITY Saddlery, Harness and General Leather Goods. Imperial Works, Butts Road, Walsall.	**George Nicklin & Son,** Leather Goods. Registered "KUDOS" Trade Mark. Darwall Street, Walsall.

Trademarks of companies in Walsall, England, circa 1916.

Names encountered on English made bits, together with the bit material and the estimated approximate date of manufacture of the bit. Some of the names may refer to the saddle shop that sold the bit, as opposed to the bit maker. Adams Bros. and Lemontagne (L Ltd) were Canadian manufacturers at the turn of the century, but Adams also imported military bits. Centaur or India rubber-mouths can date as early as about 1900.

NAME	BIT MATERIAL	ESTIMATED DATE
Adonian	stainless steel	1945
Barnet	nickel	1910
Beck	steel	1900
Reuben Craddock & Sons	steel	1915
B Cope	steel, nickel	1915
Daniel	steel	1890
A Davis, 10 Strand	chrome plate	1900
John Dewsbury & Son	steel, nickel	estab. 1848
Eglentine	nickel	1910
Gibson	iron	1870
Hall & Son	steel	1870
Hampton & Scott (HS)	nickel	1910
J H Hawkins	steel	1860
Kangaroo	nickel, steel	1920
Benjamin Latchford	steel	mid-1800's
Martin and Martin	steel	early-1900's
Mason & Son	iron	1860
Merry & Co, London	steel	1880
Middlemore	steel	1890
Thomas Newton	iron	1850
Sowther & Co, Haymarket	steel	1890
Wilkinson & Kidd	steel	1900

Triumph Bit: A driving bit widely used in driving horses of the last century [Figs. 33.25 and 33.26].

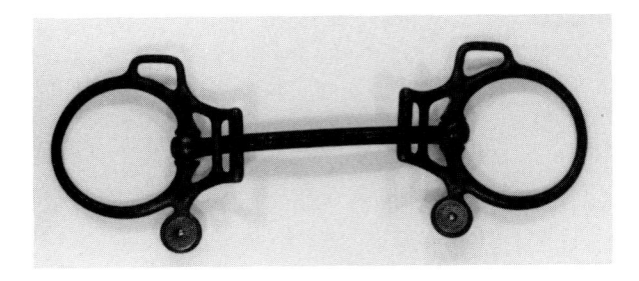

Fig. 33.25 A Triumph bit with brass bosses on the lower cheek.

Fig. 33.26 Triumph bit.

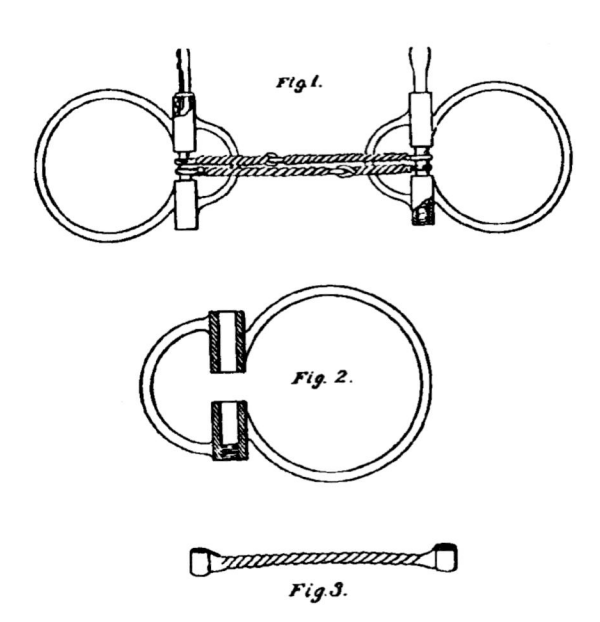

Fig. 33.27 Two designs of Truit change-mouth bit.

Truitt, Robert H., Rockfield, KY, Patent No. 187,201, Feb. 7 1877 [Fig. 33.27]. A bit with the mouth-piece replaceable or interchangable by removing the pins threaded into the vertical openings of the cheek-pieces.

Turkish Bit: A bit from *The Loriner* designated as Turkish by the Crescent Moon on the cheek-pieces [Fig. 33.28].

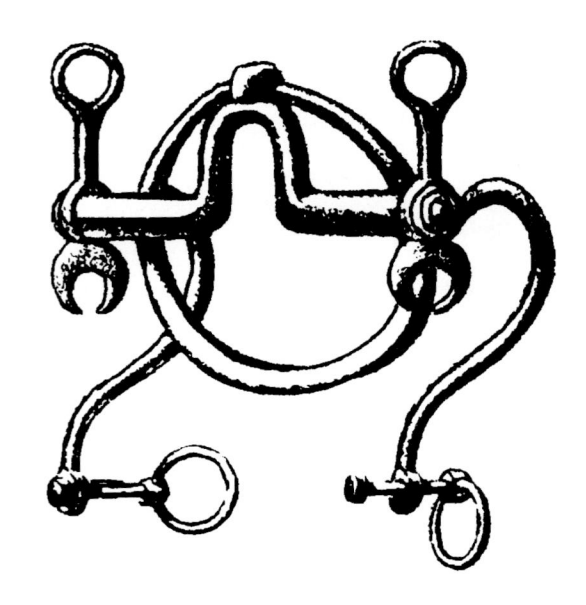

Fig. 33.28 Turkish bit.

Turton, Benjamin, Newark, NJ, Patent No. 339,716, Apr. 13, 1886 [Fig. 33.29]. A driving bit with a mouth-piece and an overcheck, the two pivotally or loosely connected together.

Twisted-wire Bit: A bit with a mouth-piece made of twisted wire and in a variety of combinations of mouth-pieces and cheek-pieces [Fig. 33.30].

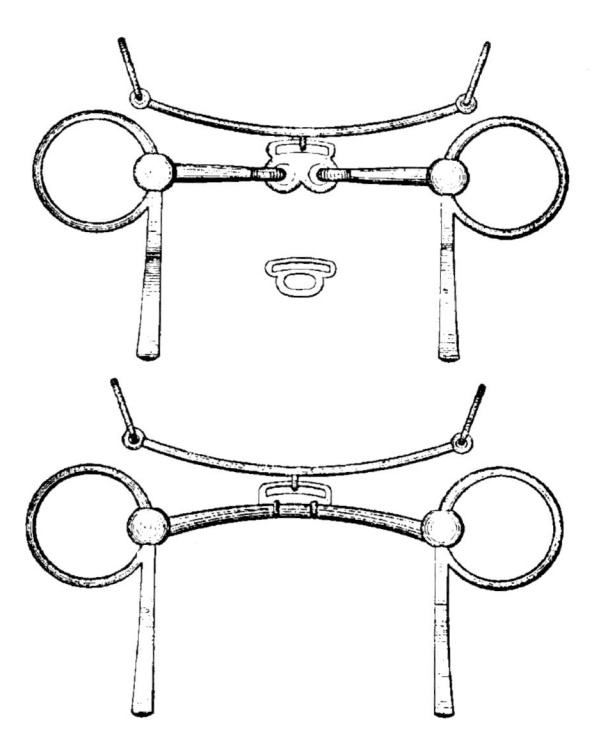

Fig. 33.29 Turton double-mouth snaffle bit.

Fig. 33.30 Twisted-wire half-cheek snaffle.

Typology: A method of dating non-carbon materials (metals) by the content or combination of metals used. This is basically the criteria used to time the origin and development of the Bronze Age, from the initial use of copper and the addition of tin (before 3000 B.C.), lead, arsenic, etc. The development of metals and alloys made trade necessary because many areas and valleys were void of metals.

Boulonais horses.

CHAPTER THIRTY-FOUR
Ulrich to Zeller

Ulrich, Eugene L., Pendelton, OR, Patent No. 2,421,123, May 27, 1947 [Figs. 34.0 and 34.1]. The headstall is buttoned to the bit in the same manner as a spur-strap is buttoned to a spur. The heavy round bar in front of the rein-rings (lip-bar) gives the bit a better balance. A small twist of the reins will engage the curb-strap. A noseband can be attached to relieve pressure on the tongue and bars of the horse and the bridle acts more like a hackamore. The outer hollow mouth-piece is a holder for the rod to which the rein-rings are attached.

Fig. 34.1 Ulrich bit with the curb strap unfastened.

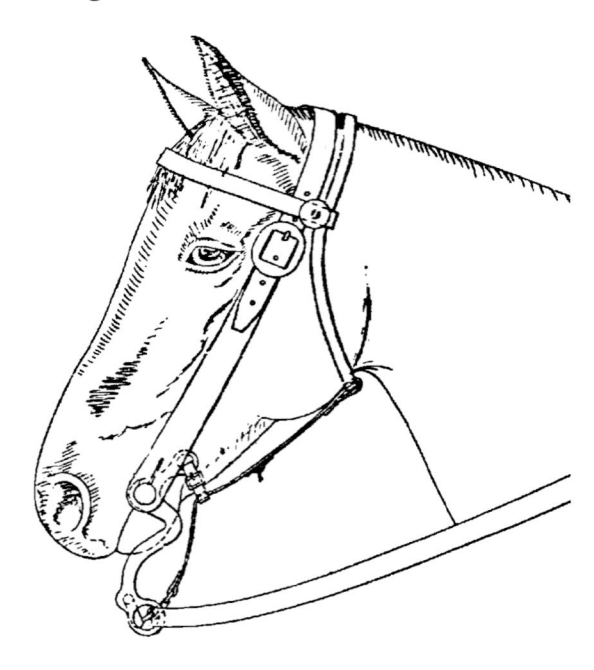

Fig. 34.0 Ulrich curb bit.

Uppingham Curb Bit: An early 1800's bit of England with a double mouthpiece each having a different angle of attachment to the side-pieces [Fig. 34.2].

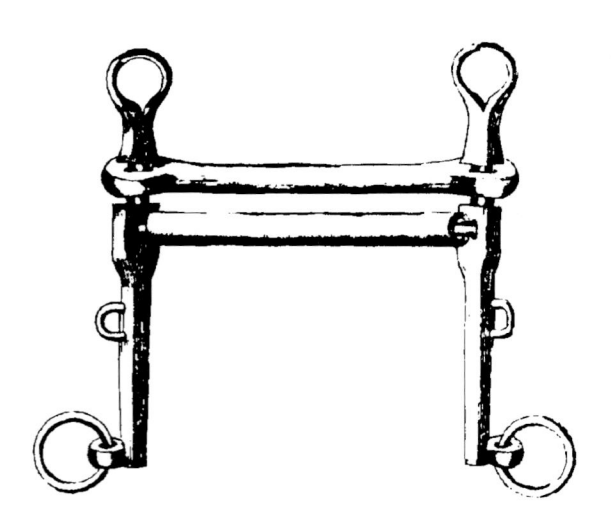

Fig. 34.2 Uppingham curb bit.

Urecht Bit: A curb bit made by John Dewsbury and Son to sell in Holland [Fig. 34.3 and 34.3a].

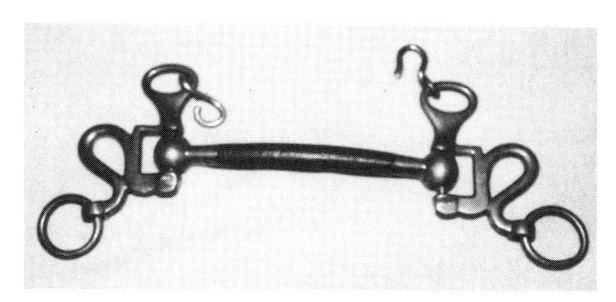

Fig. 34.3 Urecht bit.

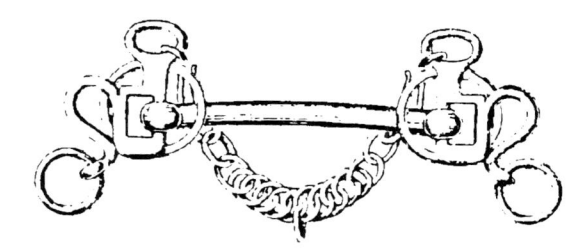

Fig. 34.3a Urecht bit with check-rings and curb-chain.

Uxeter Bit: A bit of early England designed by J. Robinson Wigan [Fig. 34.4]. Much like the Kimberwick bit and probably the origin.

Fig. 34.4 Uxeter bit.

Valencia Bit: An early bit of England from John Dewsbury and Son Catalogue circa 1905 [Fig. 34.5].

Van Arsdale, Henry, Racine, WI, Patent No. 422,469, Mar. 4, 1890 [Fig. 34.6]. A bit commonly known and sold as "The Success Bit."

Van Auken, Albert, Ludlowville, NY, Patent No. 120,913, Nov. 14, 1871 [Fig. 34.7]. A medicine bit with a hollow core and minute perforations along the mouth-piece. "A melted medicament is prepared with some bland substance as a vehicle, like lard, oil of theobroma, or other substance which melts at a low temperature. The warmth of the horse's mouth, when the bit is applied, melts the medicament, which then exudes and mingles with the saliva and flows over the diseased parts for treatment while the horse is at work."

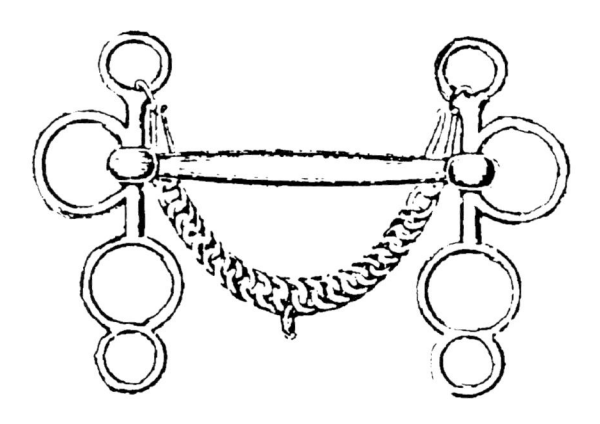

Fig. 34.5 Valencia bit.

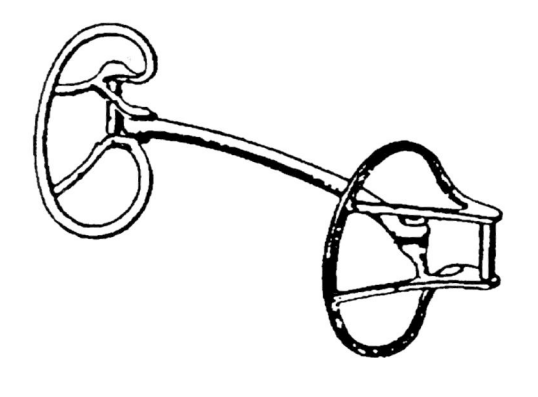

Fig. 34.6 The Success bit.

Viridet, Adren, Glasgow, KY, Patent No. 90,612, May 25, 1869 [Fig. 34.8]. The bit has no mouth-piece. The flanges on the cheek-pieces fit the lips of the horse and draw on the corners of the mouth only. The loops in the side-pieces facilitate the easy attachment and removal of the bit from the head-stall.

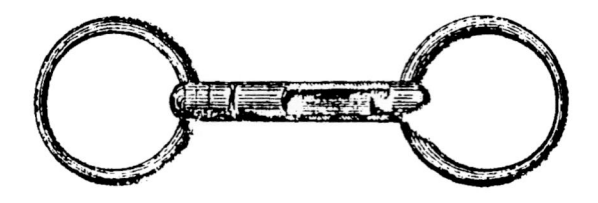

Fig. 34.7 Van Auken medicine bit.

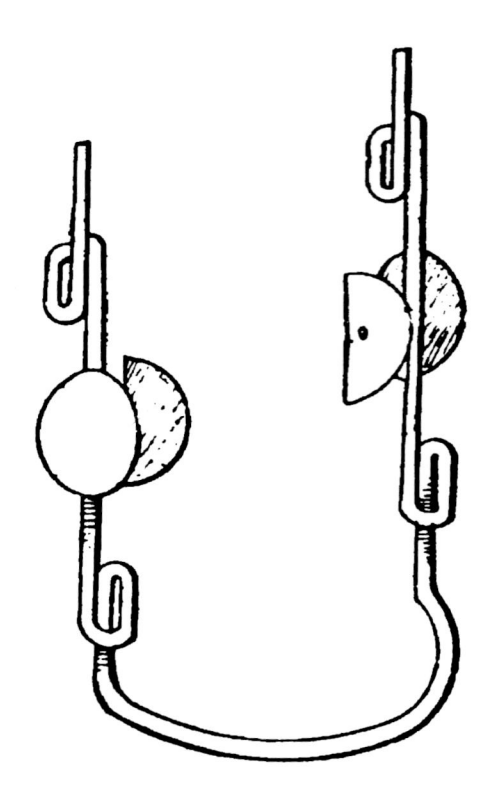

Fig. 34.8 Viridet bit.

W-mouth Bit: See Y-Mouth bit. Fig. 34.50.

Wagner, Arthur E., *et al.,* Meadville, PA, Patent No. 2,460,912, Feb. 8, 1949 [Fig. 34.9]. A unitary rigid bit moulded of polymeric plastic.

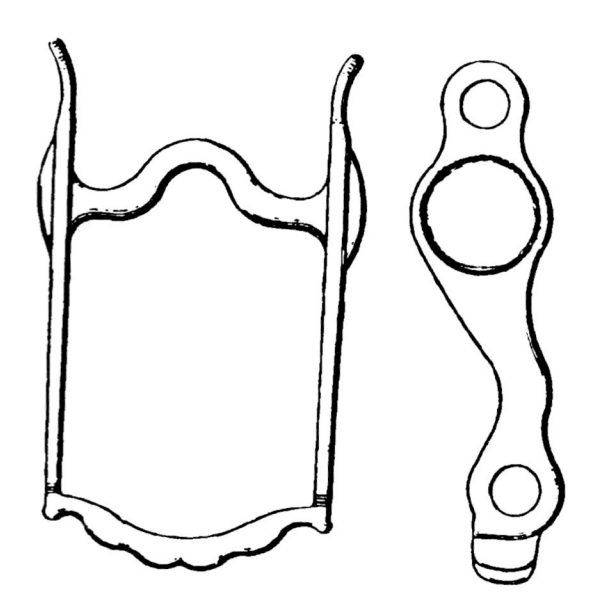

Fig. 34.9 Wagner plastic bit.

Walking Horse Bit: A curb bit with shanks or side-pieces of longer than usual lengths [Fig. 34.10 with description on preceding page].

Wallin, Charles E., Salt Lake City, UT, Patent No. 235,596, Dec. 14, 1880 [Fig. 34.11]. The snap-hooks on the upper cheek-piece swivel and are designed to attach to the bridle or a halter.

Walter, Fred R., Geneseo, IL, Patent No. 1,129,255, Feb. 23, 1915 [Fig. 34.12]. The large rings are for attachment of driving and check-reins. The small rings are for attachment to the headstall. The hooks are a continuation of the end of the mouth-piece and have a dual purpose: to keep the bit from sliding through the horse's mouth and to apply pressure to the lower jaw.

Eldonian

STAINLESS STEEL

WALKING HORSE BITS

E3.0605/RE	Round eye, fixed cheek Walking Horse Bit, with 5" mouth and 8" cheeks. Ports 1, 2, 3, 5.
E3.0605/OE	Oval eye, as above.
E3.0605/P	Round eye, fixed cheek Walking Horse Bit with 4½" or 5" mouth and 5½" cheeks. Ports 2, 3, 5.
E3.0612	Long cheek Walking Horse Bit, 10" cheeks, 5" mouths in Ports 1 or 3.
E3.0631	Heavy Walking Horse Bit, 9" cheeks, 5" mouth. Port 3.
E3.0633	Racking Bit, 5" mouth, with small loops.
E3.0641	Oval eye, braced turn cheek Walking Horse Bit with 5" mouth and 8" cheeks. Ports 1, 2, 3, 4, 5, 6, 9, 10, 12, 13.
E3.0641/A	As above but 10" cheeks.
E3.0641/P	As above but 7" cheeks and 4½" or 5" mouths. Ports 2, 3, 5.
E3.0641/J	Oval eye, braced turn cheek Walking Horse Bit with 5" plain jointed mouth and 8" cheeks.
E3.0641/A/J	As above but 10" cheeks.
E3.0641/TJ	Oval eye, braced turn cheek Walking Horse Bit with 5" twisted jointed mouth and 8" cheeks.
E3.0641/A/TJ	As above but 10" cheeks.
E3.0679	8" Change Mouth cheeks, with screws and bushes.
E3.0679/A	10" Change Mouth cheeks, with screws and bushes.
E3.0681	5" Metal Mouths with Ports 1, 2, 3, 4, 5, 6, 9, 10, 11, 12, 13, 14.
E4.0682	5" Nylon Mouth.
E4.0683	5" Rubber Mouth.
E3.0684	Spare screws and bushes.
E3.0689	5" Jointed Mouths.
E3.0690	5" Cycle Chain Mouths.
E3.0694	Twisted Wire Mouths in 4½" or 5".

Eldonian

WALKING HORSE BITS

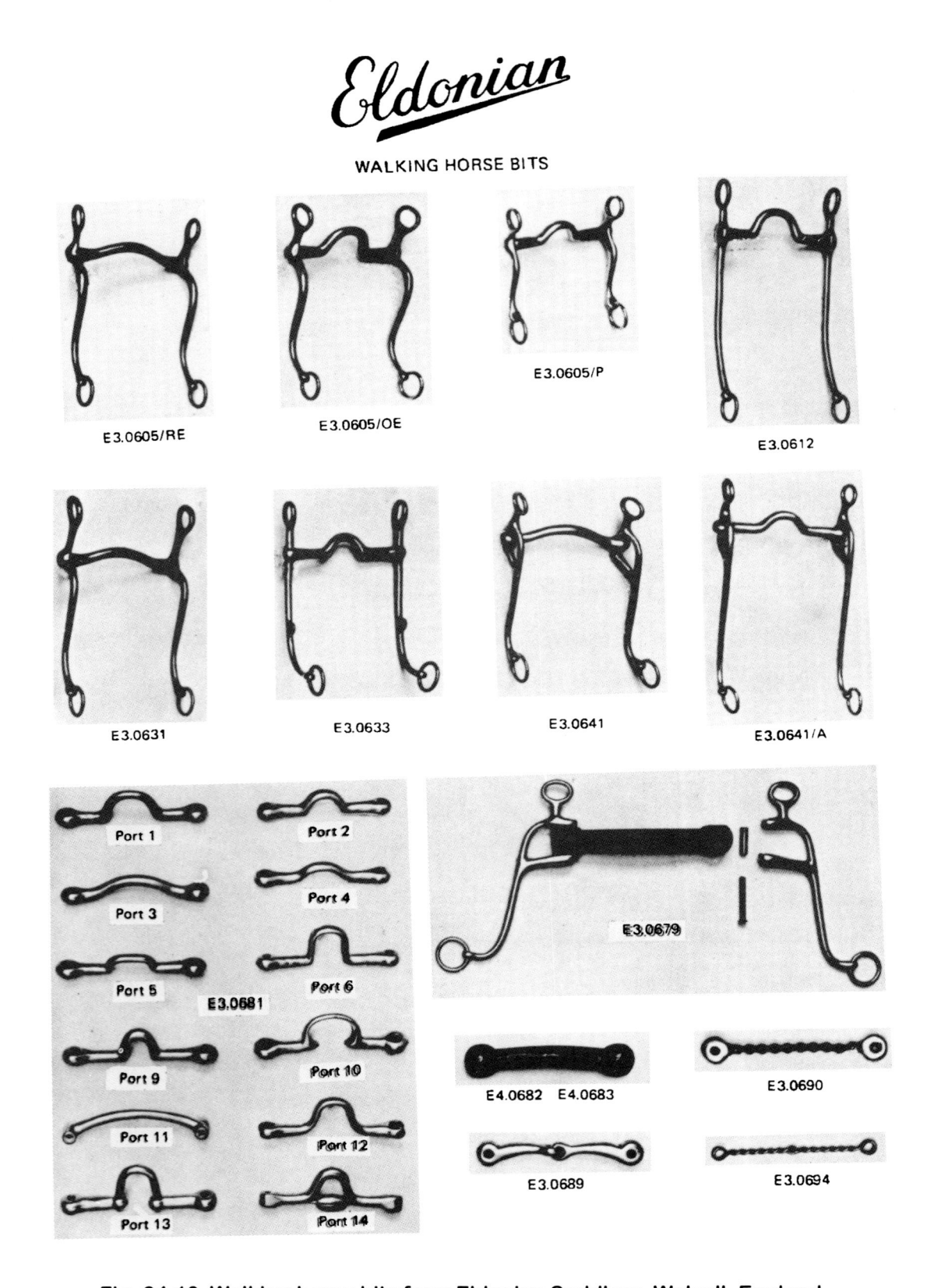

E3.0605/RE

E3.0605/OE

E3.0605/P

E3.0612

E3.0631

E3.0633

E3.0641

E3.0641/A

Port 1, Port 2, Port 3, Port 4, Port 5, Port 6, Port 9, Port 10, Port 11, Port 12, Port 13, Port 14

E3.0681

E3.0679

E4.0682 E4.0683

E3.0690

E3.0689

E3.0694

Fig. 34.10 Walking horse bits from Eldonian Saddlery, Walsall, England.

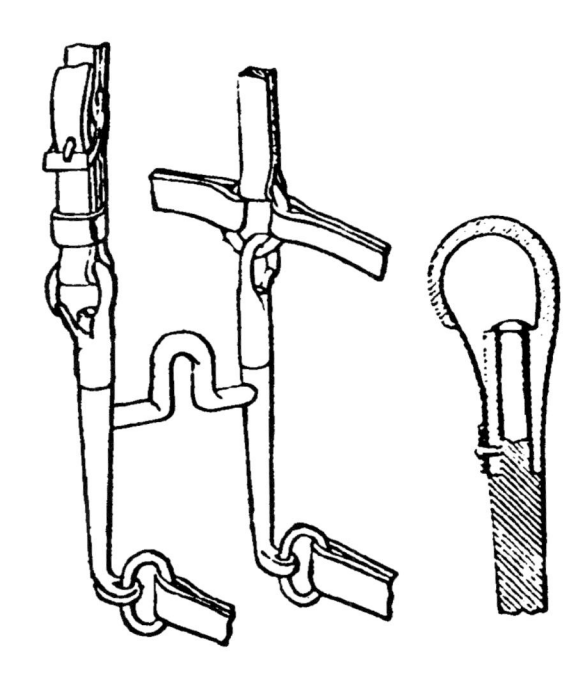

Fig. 34.11 Wallin snap-hook bit.

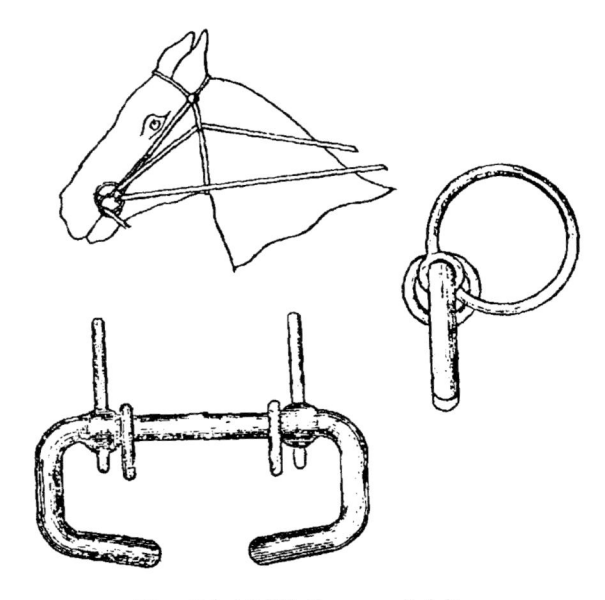

Fig. 34.12 Walter curb bit.

Wanty: An English term for a single rein to lead a horse in harness or under pack. The Royal Artillery used the term and rein as early as 1766. The artillery teams were guided by a man walking by the near lead horse.

War Bridle: A bridle made from a single piece of leather or rope that is placed over the poll of the horse and then through the mouth or around the lower jaw. See Chapter 35.

Ward, George W., St. Johnsbury, VT, Patent No. 264,496, Sep. 19, 1882 [Fig. 34.13]. The bit consists of a tongue-plate and two links or bars loosely jointed to one edge. The connection between the outer ends of the bar and the cheek-pieces may be rigid or joined.

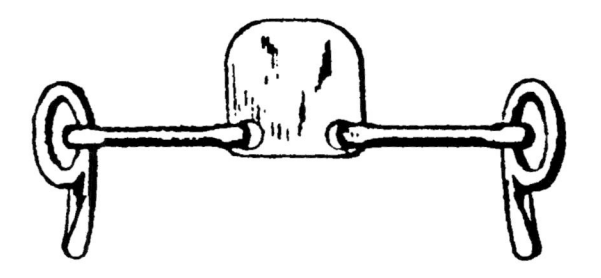

Fig. 34.13 Ward tongue bit.

Ward Union Curb Bit: A Weymouth curb bit with upper and lower cheek-pieces being of near equal proportions and a sliding mouthpiece [Fig. 34.14].

Fig. 34.14 Ward Union curb bit.

Warfel, John D., Buford, GA, Patent No. 576,502, Feb. 2, 1897 [Fig. 34.15]. The bit has a split mouth-piece in which one semi-cylindrical half is rigidly attached to the cheek-pieces and the other movable half is fitted with screw-threaded ends which can traverse the slot in the cheek-piece. The loose portion of the mouth-piece can be secured in any position on the cheek-piece by tightening the end thumb-nuts. Compare with Forrest patent, Chapter 11, Fig. 11.26.

Fig. 34.17 Large heavy four-ring watering bit with 6 1/2 inch mouth.

Fig. 34.15 Warfel split-mouth bit.

Washington Pelham: See Chapter 27, Fig. 27.41

Watering Bit: Broken snaffle, with toggles on the rings for attaching the bit to the halter or a horse [Fig. 34.17]. See Chapter 23, Military Bits.

Weathers, Franklin, Findlay, IL, Patent No. 813,337, Feb. 20, 1906 [Fig. 34.18]. The small upper rings are for the bridle cheek-strap and the small lower rings are for the reins. Check-reins are attached to the small rings on the mouth-piece.

Fig. 34.18 Weathers snaffle bit.

Webb, George, Lewiston, ME, Patent No. 73,853, Jan. 28, 1868 [Fig. 34.19]. The mouth-piece rotates within the cheek-pieces so that a pull of the reins does not change the position of the bridle or put pressure on the horse's poll.

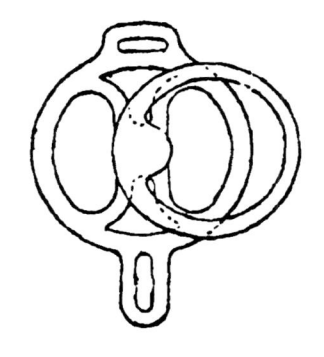

Fig. 34.19 Webb snaffle bit.

Wellington Bit: A bit of early England, at least used during the period of 1769 to 1832 [Fig. 34.20].

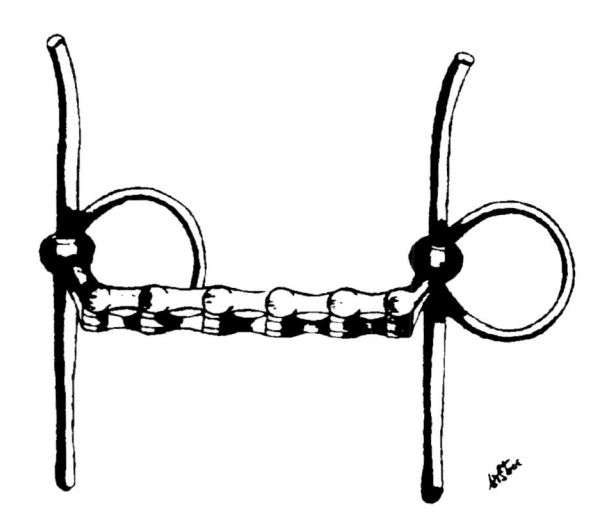

Fig. 34.20 Wellington bit. Drawing by W. Stone.

Western Polo: See Chapter 27, Fig. 27.42.

Weymouth, Aurelius L., Boston, MA, Patent No. 35,756, July 1, 1862 [Fig. 34.21]. The bit can operate as an ordinary bit, but the mouth of the horse may be distended or opened at the will of the rider or driver.

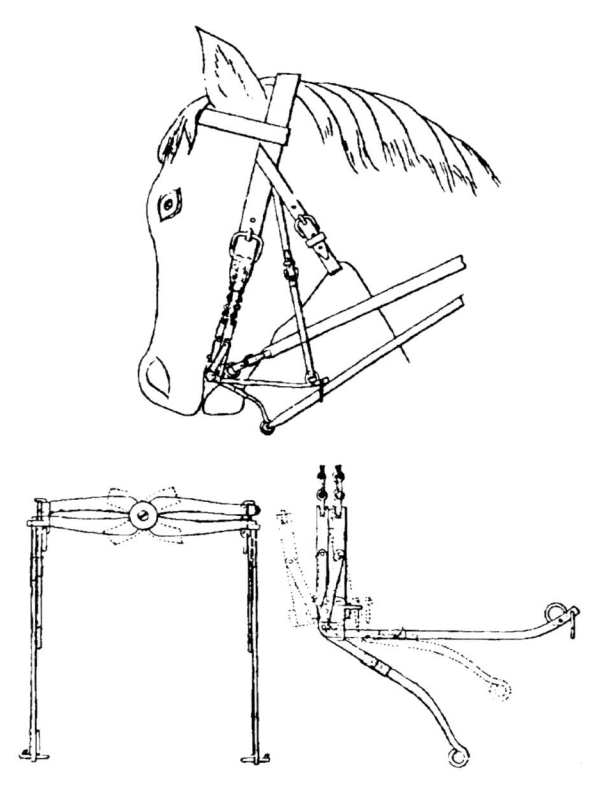

Fig. 34.21 Weymouth scissor bit.

Weymouth Bit: A curb bit with straight cheek-pieces and loops on the low cheek-piece for a lip-strap [Fig. 34.22].

Weymouth Bridle: See Chapter 3.

Wheeler, Benjamin F., Calais, VT, Patent No. 105,282, July 12, 1870 [Fig. 34.23]. This bit brings notched edges or teeth of the mouth-piece against the mouth of the horse. The hollow cylinder of the mouth-piece with the side of the cylinder toward the tongue opens nearly one-half the length of the cylinder and the edges are notched.

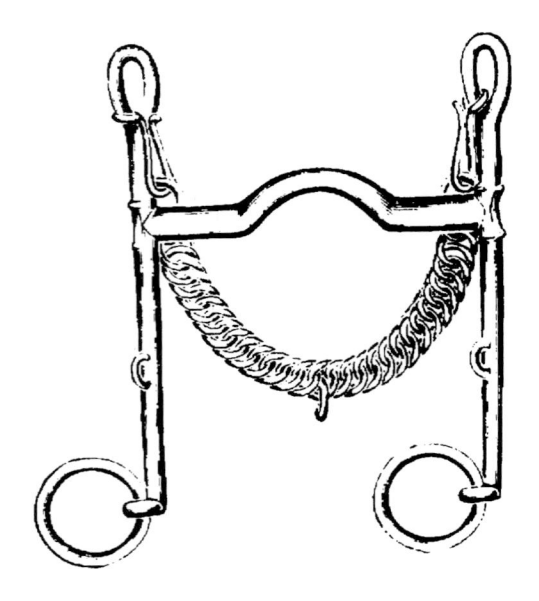

Fig. 34.22 Weymouth curb bit.

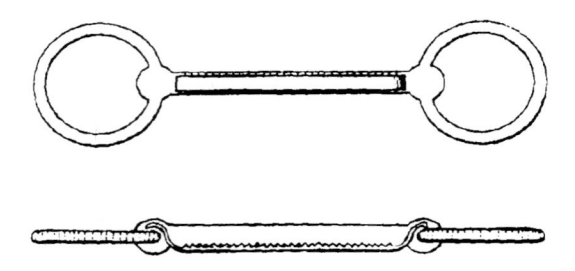

Fig. 34.23 Wheeler notched-mouth bit.

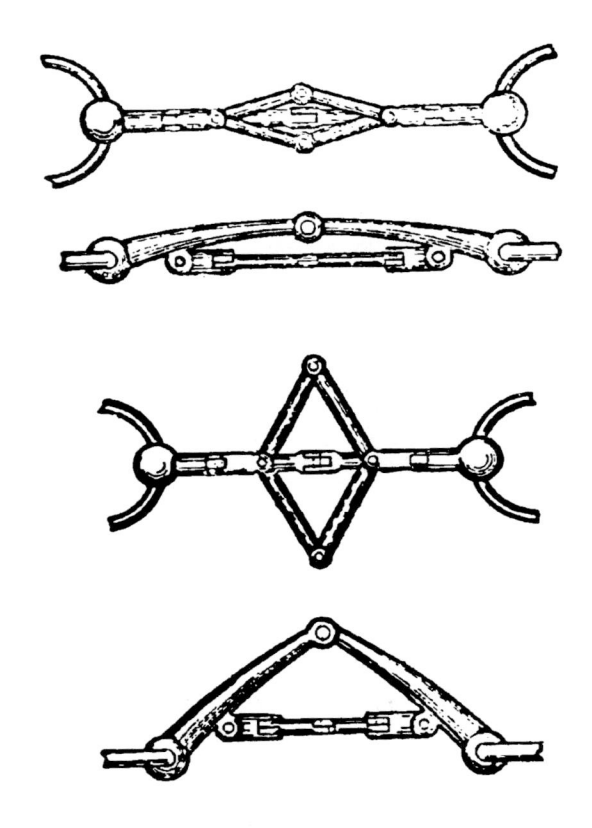

Fig. 34.24 Four views of Wheeler toggle-gag bit.

Fig. 34.25 Wheeler ported driving bit.

Wheeler, Edward E., South Bend IN, Patent No. 233,309, Oct. 12, 1880 [Fig. 34.24]. A bit known as a "double gag snaffle" bit provides a common jointed or snaffle bit with a double gag. The double gag or toggle causes the horse to throw its mouth open when the bit is brought to bear.

Wheeler, William R. M., Pinkhamton, CO, Patent No. 431,760, July 8, 1890 [Fig.34.25. A driving bit with a half-breed port with a cricket plus a roller at the top of the port.

Whelan, Richard P., Leavenworth, KS, Patent No. 79,950, Dec. 31, 1867 [Fig. 34.26]. Two large bows equal in size are placed in the center of the mouth-piece and lie on top of the tongue when the bit is in use. At right angles to the mouth-piece bows is a larger bow that rests under the upper lip of the horse. It may be covered with rubber or leather.

Fig. 34.26 Whelan curb bit.

Whitman, Royal E., Springfield, MA, Patent No. 194,202, Aug. 14, 1877 [Fig. 34.27]. The snap-hooks swivel on the outer ends of the cheek-piece. The bit is a component part of the Whitman Halter-bridle.

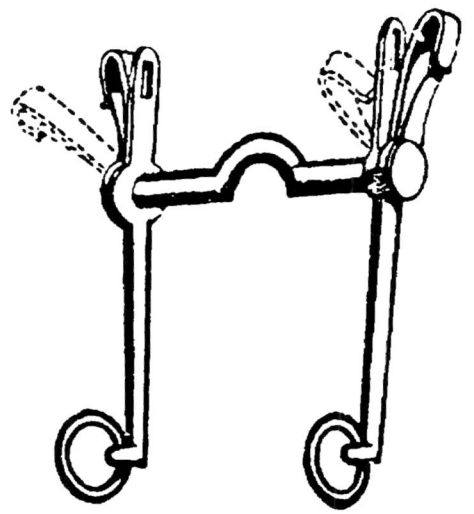

Fig. 34.27 Whitman bit.

Patent No. 221,710, Nov. 18, 1879 [Fig. 34.28]. A bit with snap-hooks that rotate on the axis of the ends of the mouth-piece. This enables the bit to be pushed into the horse's mouth from below and then the snaps swing up to be fastened to the headstall or halter. See Chapter 23.

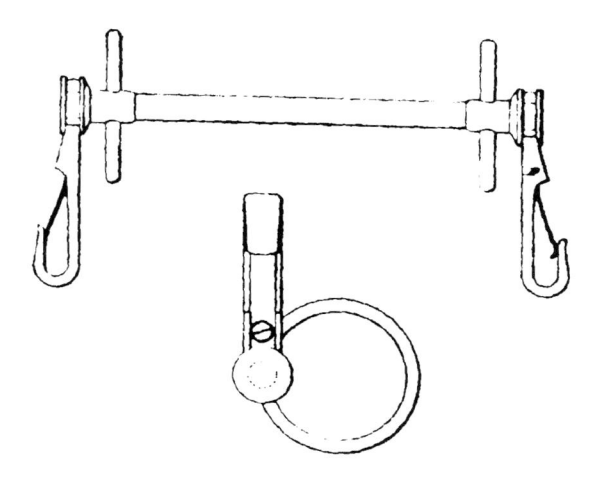

Fig. 34.28 Whitman bit.

Whoa Maker Bit: A series of bits made by Trammell Bits with a copper mouth for horses with cut tongues or injured mouths. Designed to pull down on the sides of the bars of a horse's mouth. A vicious appearing bit, but the port does not turn up in the horse's mouth [Fig.34.29].

Wiener, Oscar, Henry Coates, and Simon Wiener, Newark, NJ, Patent No. 285,717, Sep. 25, 1883 [Fig. 34.30]. The construction of a linked mouth-piece that permits a flexible strong mouth-piece that is covered by a flexible coating, preferably rubber.

Wigan, J. Robinson: See Uxeter, Fig. 34.4.

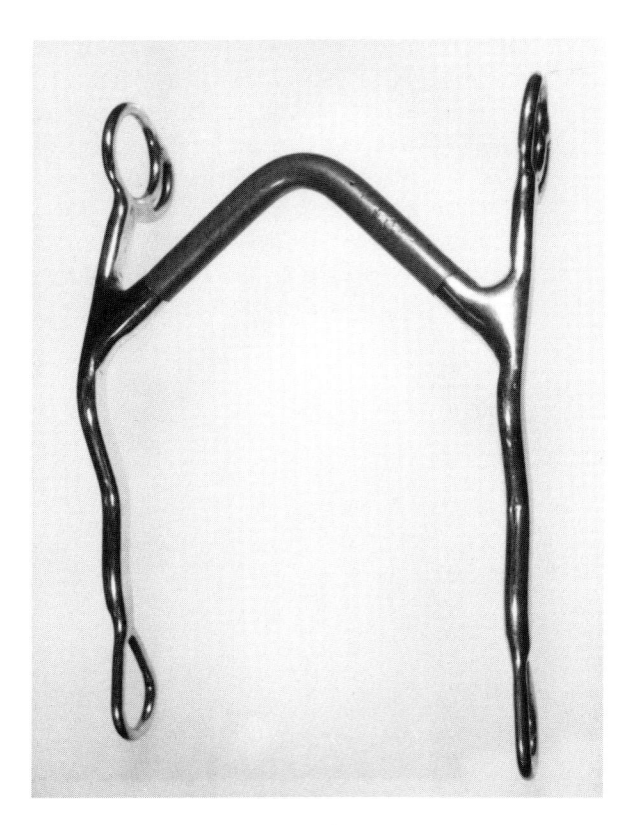

Fig. 34.29 The Whoa Maker.

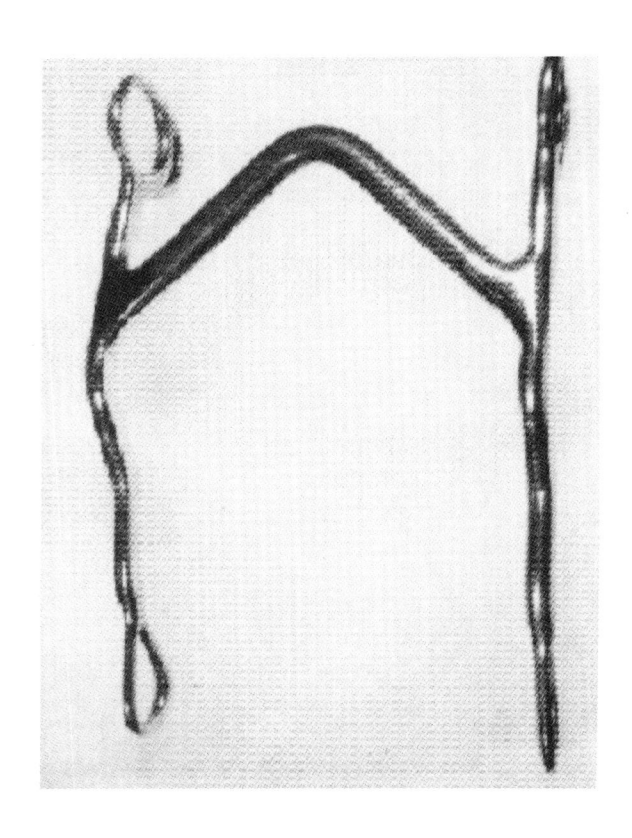

Fig. 34.30 Wiener flexible-mouth bit.

Wilder, Ezra, South Hingham, MA, Patent No. 184,026, Nov. 7, 1876 [Fig. 34.31]. A bit with a mouth-piece with a wooden shell designed for horses that have an objection to a metallic mouth-piece. "A wooden shell is cheaper than one of leather or of India rubber."

William Stone Pelham: Figure 34.32.

Williams, James B. and Albert C. Tanner, Hartford, CT, Patent No. 369,490, Sep. 6, 1887 [Fig. 34.33]. A spring-activated winding drum is on each end of the mouth-piece located outside the cheek-pieces and has straps that extend to the reins.

Williams, W. F. M., Augusta, GA, Patent No. 26,804, Jan. 10, 1860 [Fig. 34.34 and 34.34a]. A combination of levers arranged to operate on either the upper or lower jaw at the discretion of the reinsman. The two mouth-pieces are utilized with one being connected to the stationary cheek-pieces and the second connected to the sliding levers. See Chapter 23.

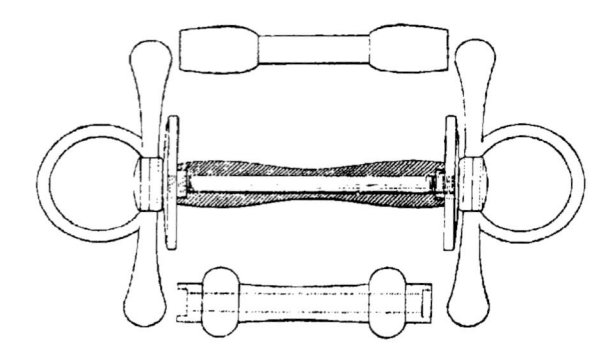

Fig. 34.31 Wilder wood-mouth bit.

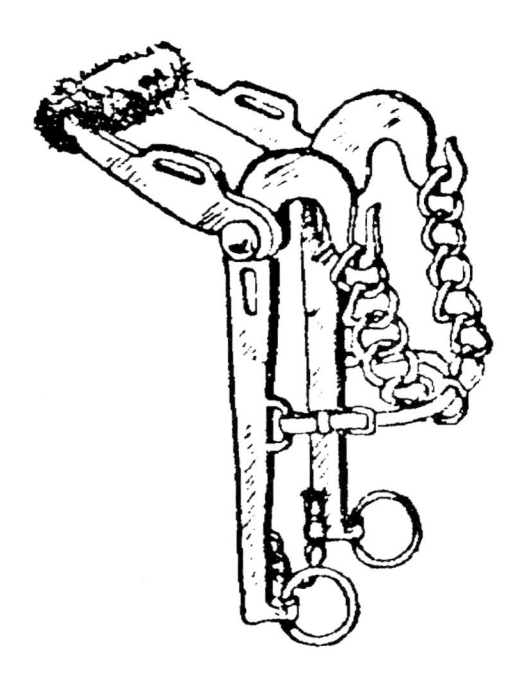

Fig. 34.32 William Stone Pelham.

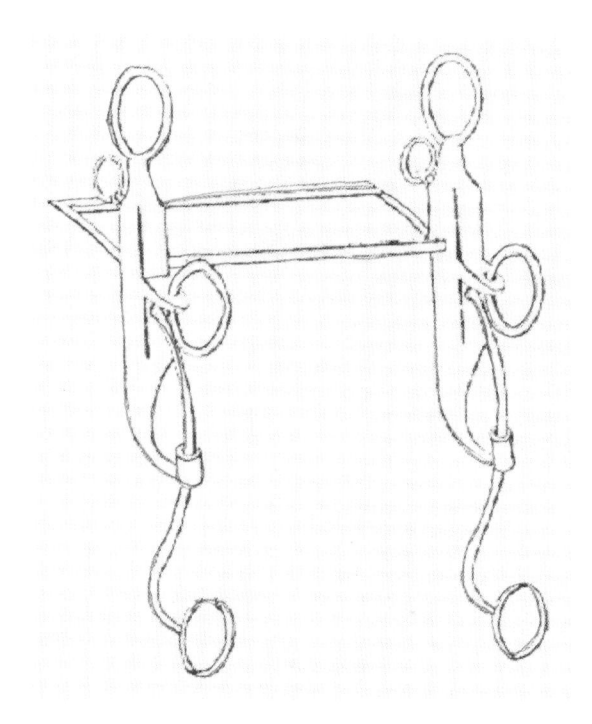

Fig. 34.34 Williams bit, patent drawing.

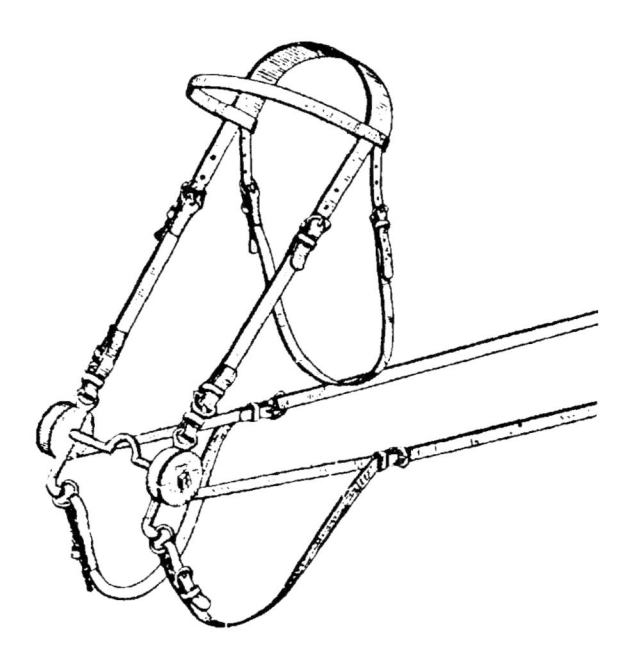

Fig. 34.33 Williams bit with spring retracted reins.

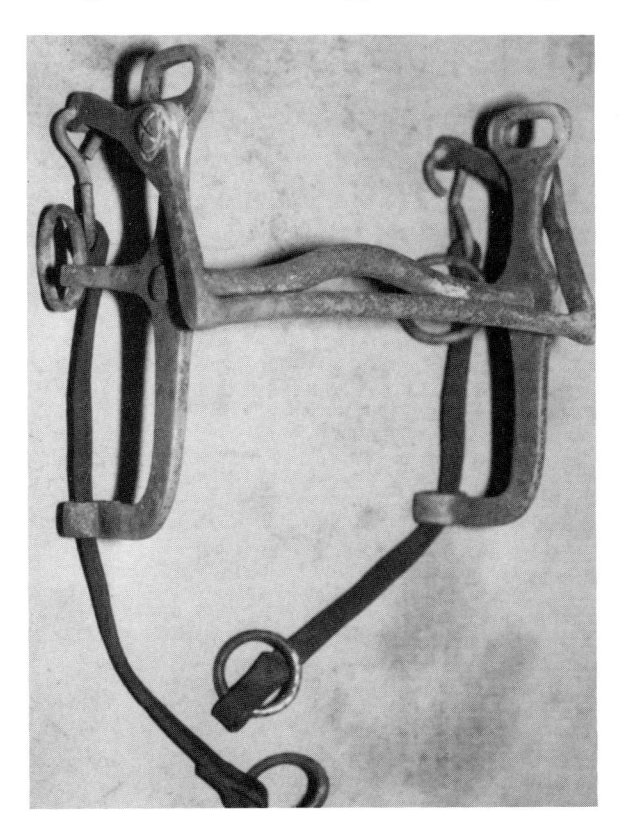

Fig. 34.34a Williams early production bit with leather straps in place of metal sleeves.

	No.	Polished	Nickel-plated	Extra Best Solid Nickel (Rustless) Registered Trade Marks V.S. NICKEL	Best Solid Nickel (Rustless) Reg. Trade Mark DEWRALEX	Solid Nickel (Rustless) Reg. Trade Mark VIGOLETTE	Steel Reg. Trade Mark	Nickel-plated Steel Reg. Trade Mark	Warranted Hard Steel Reg. Trade Mark	Nickel-plated Warranted Hard Steel Reg. Trade Mark
Plain Round Ring Wilson Snaffle	3660	3/- 3/6 4/-	5/- 5/6 6/-	—	—	—	—	—	—	—
Ditto ditto Buggy Size	37	3/6 4/- 6/-	5/6 6/- 8/-	20/-	18/-	17/-	13/-	15/-	17/-	19/-
Ditto ditto Medium Size	26	3/6 4/- 6/-	5/6 6/- 8/-	21/-	20/-	18/-	13/-	15/-	17/-	19/-
Ditto ditto Gig Size	04	4/- 5/- 8/-	6/- 7/- 10/-	26/-	23/-	21/-	15/-	17/-	19/-	21/-
Ditto ditto Cab Size	692	4/6 5/6 10/-	6/6 7/6 12/-	28/-	25/-	24/-	18/-	20/-	22/-	24/-
Ditto ditto Van Size	1055	6/6 8/- 12/-	9/- 11/- 15/-	38/-	34/-	30/-	24/-	27/-	28/-	32/-
Flat Ring Wilson Snaffle, Buggy Size	209	6/- 7/- 10/- 14/-	8/- 9/- 13/- 17/-	23/-	20/-	18/-	15/-	17/-	19/-	21/-
Ditto ditto Medium Size	210	7/- 8/- 10/- 14/-	9/- 10/- 13/- 17/-	26/-	24/-	22/-	16/-	18/-	20/-	22/-
Ditto ditto Cab Size	211	7/- 8/- 10/- 14/-	9/- 10/- 13/- 17/-	30/-	27/-	24/-	18/-	20/-	22/-	24/-
Ditto ditto Van Size	1054	9/- 11/- 13/- 16/-	11/- 13/- 16/- 20/-	38/-	34/-	32/-	26/-	30/-	30/-	34/-
Flat Ring Hollow Mouth Wilson Snaffle Ring in Mouth	175	14/- 16/- 20/-	16/- 18/- 22/-	48/-	45/-	40/-	—	—	—	—
Ditto ditto Lighter	do	14/- 16/- 20/-	16/- 18/- 22/-	38/-	34/-	30/-	—	—	—	—
Twisted Mouth Flat Ring Wilson Snaffle Stout Cab Size	174	8/- 9/- 11/- 15/-	10/- 11/- 14/- 18/-	31/-	28/-	25/-	—	—	—	—
Twisted Mouth Round ditto Gig Size	4930	5/- 7/- 9/-	7/- 9/- 12/-	27/-	24/-	22/-	—	—	22/-	24/-
Round Ring Half Twisted Bar-mouth Wilson Snaffle	172	5/- 7/- 9/-	7/- 9/- 12/-	26/-	23/-	21/-	—	—	22/-	24/-
Flat Ring Chain Mouth Wilson Snaffle	1057	10/- 12/- 15/-	12/- 15/- 19/-	30/-	27/-	24/-	—	—	—	—
Jointed Double Mouth Round Ring-Wilson Snaffle	323	8/- 12/- 16/-	11/- 15/- 19/-	36/-	32/-	30/-	—	—	—	—
Round Ring Double Mouth Wilson Snaffle	173	8/- 12/- 16/-	11/- 15/- 19/-	36/-	32/-	30/-	—	—	—	—
Broad Flat Ring Wilson Snaffle	5924	9/- 12/- 16/-	12/- 15/- 19/-	38/-	34/-	30/-	—	—	—	—
Persian Wilson Snaffle	176	8/- 10/- 15/-	11/- 13/- 18/-	40/-	36/-	32/-	—	—	—	—
Horse Shoe Pattern Wilson Snaffle	140	10/- 12/- 14/-	12/- 14/- 16/-	36/-	32/-	26/-	—	—	—	—
Plain round Ring Wilson Snaffle with Patent Hook & Drop Ring Complete with Solid Nickel or Brass Squares	639	10/- 14/- 18/-	13/- 17/- 21/-	—	—	—	—	—	—	—

Any of these patterns can be made in Best Forged Iron, Steel or Warranted Hard Steel and with any required variation in style or price.

By an improved method of manufacture, we are now able to produce all FLAT RING WILSONS with SOLID BUTTS and FORGED STEEL RINGS.

NICKEL-PLATING GUARANTEED.

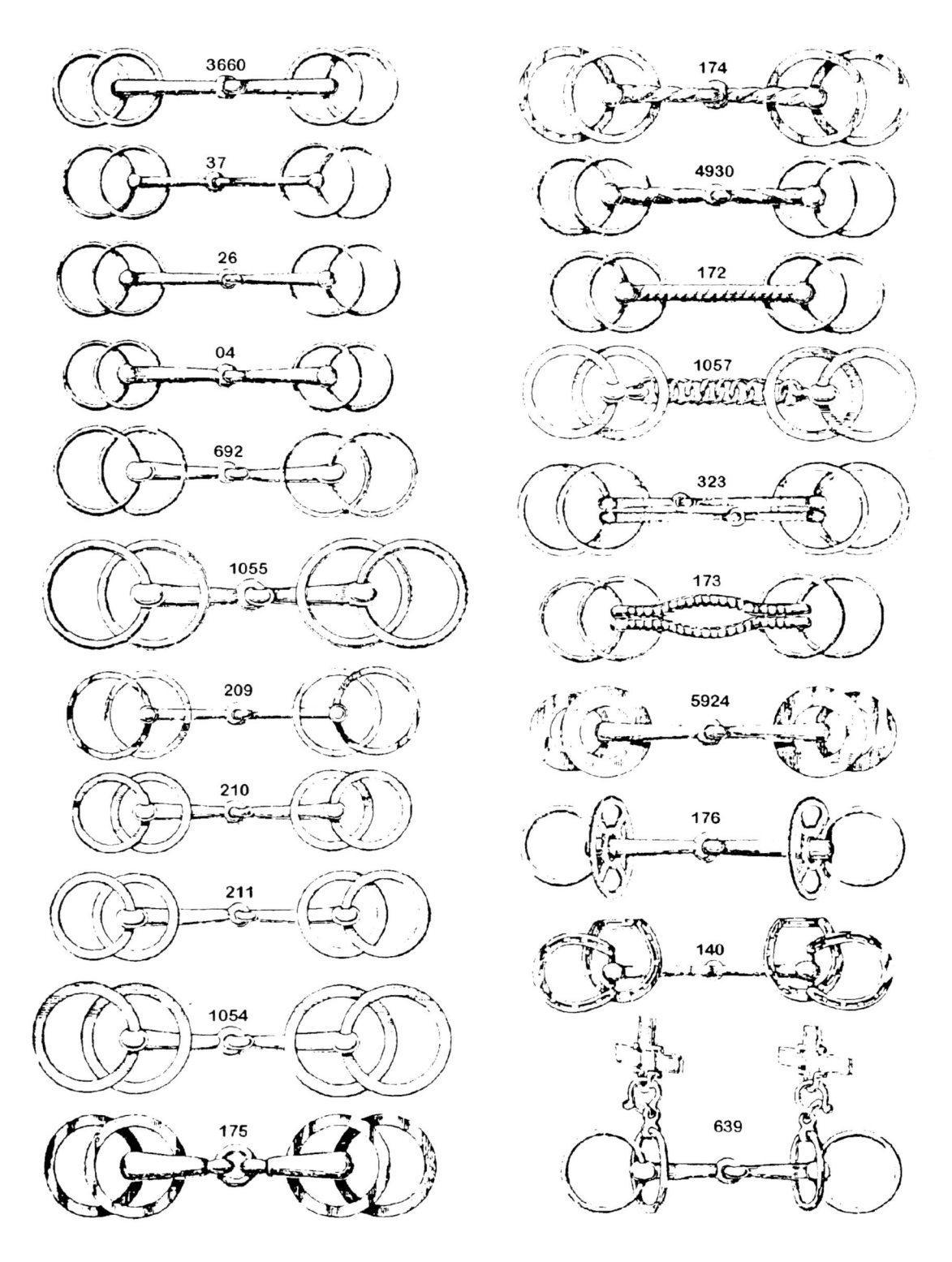

Fig. 34.38 Wilson snaffle bits from John Dewsbury and Son catalogue, circa 1905.

Williamsburg Bit: A bit associated with Williamsburg, Virginia [Fig. 34.35].

Williamsburg Bit: A bit associated with Williamsburg, Virginia [Fig. 34.35]. This particular bit is marked Reynolds and thought to have been made by Frederick Reynolds, Newark, New Jersey, a manufacturer of harness and military ornaments in 1861. In 1864-65, listed as Reynolds and Co., saddlery hardware and ornaments.

Fig. 34.35 Williamsburg bit with the bosses missing. Jean Gayle collection. Photo by Jones.

Willis Bit: An Early 1800's bit from England. Illustrated in *The Loriner* [Fig. 34.36].

Wilson Flat-ring Snaffle: A 4-ring snaffle bit with all the rings flattened [Fig. 34.37].

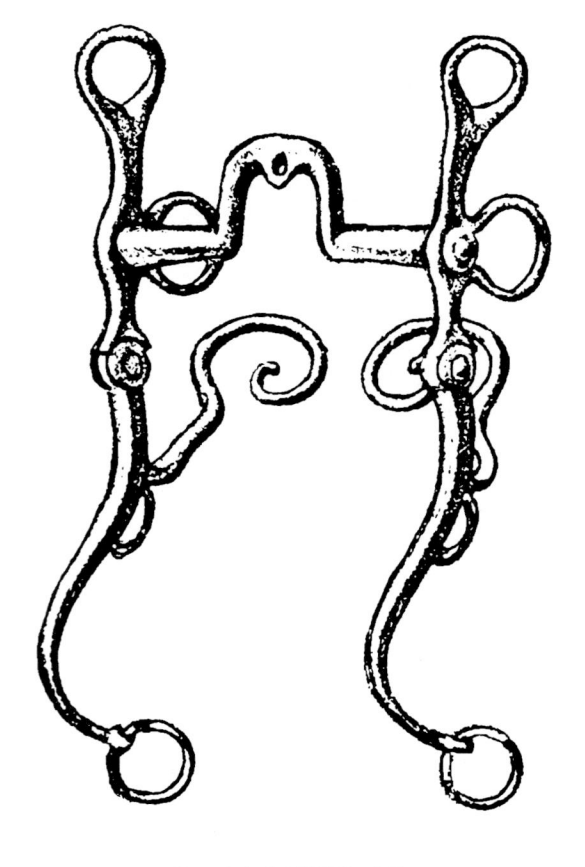

Fig. 34.36 Willis bit.

Fig. 34.37 Wilson flat ring snaffle bit.

Wilson Snaffle Bit: A series of four-ring snaffle bits made in a wide variety of mouth-pieces and sizes and shapes of cheek-rings [Fig. 34.38 with description on preceding page]. From John Dewsbury and Son catalogue circa 1905.

Wimbash Bit: An Elbow bit with exaggerated length of the lower cheek-pieces. Considered a very severe bit [Fig. 34.39].

Fig. 34.39 Wimbash bit.

Wingert, James Leonard, Randolph, NE, Patent No. 822,174, May 29, 1906 [Fig.34.40]. The bit utilizes a nose strap attached to the rings outside the bridle rings. All the rings are secure to prevent sliding on the mouth-piece.

Winkers: See Blinders or Blinkers, Chapter 5.

Withey, Ervin E., Syracuse, NY, Patent No. 523,612, July 24, 1894 [Fig. 34.41]. A metal flat bar mouth-piece covered with leather and sewn tight to exclude air and moisture from the inside with only the outer grained side of the leather exposed.

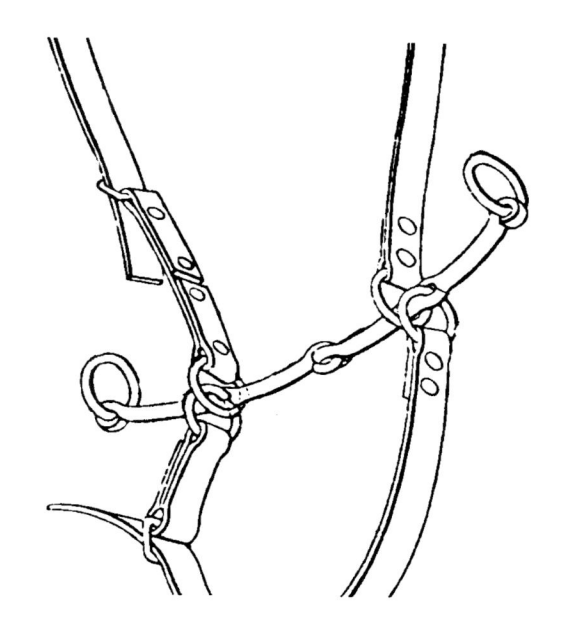

Fig. 34.40 Wingert snaffle bit.

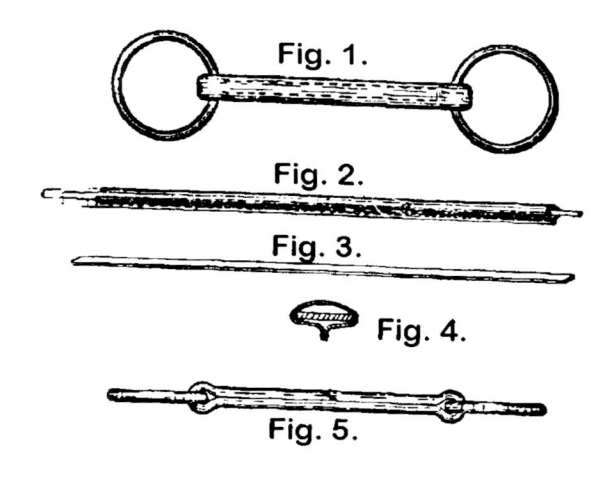

Fig. 34.41 Withey leather-covered-mouth bit.

Wittmann, Will Chris, Lincoln, NE, Patent No. 522,572, July 3, 1894 [Fig. 34.42]. A pull on the reins tightens the crossed chains against the lower jaw of the horse with the cheek-rings sliding toward each other on the mouth-bar to engage the cheeks of the horse.

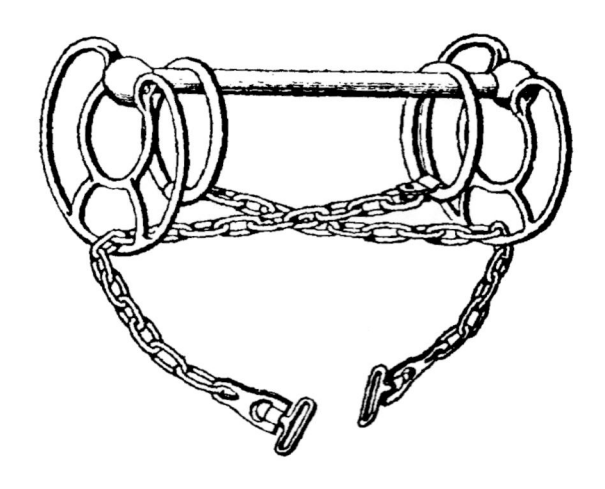

Fig. 34.42 Wittmann snaffle bit.

Wolfington, William P., Louisville, KY, 124,187, Feb. 27, 1872 [Fig. 34.43]. A curb bit with the upper portion of the cheek-piece ending in a rectangle with several horizontal bars to produce a series of slots through which the bridle cheekstraps are threaded.

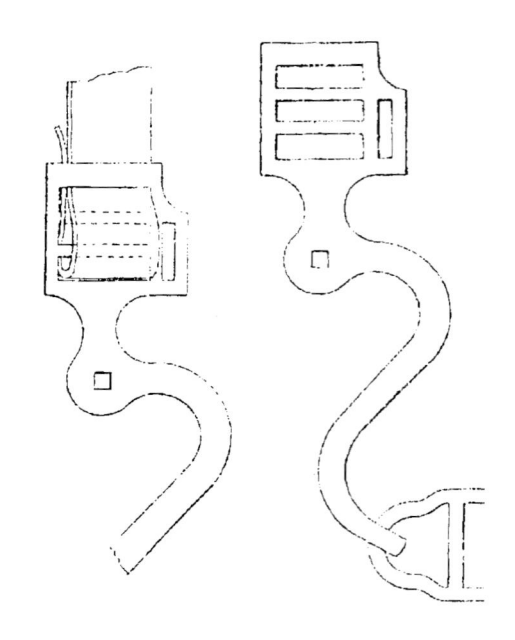

Fig. 34.43 Wolfington curb bit.

Woman Bit: Bit No. 299 in Oscar Crockett's catalog No. 11 of 1931. designed by Arthur Crockett [Fig. 34.44].

Fig. 34.44 Woman bit.

Wooden Bit: A bit with a wood mouthpiece. John S. Rarey an early 1900's horse trainer used an enormous wooden-mouth bit to "cure" biter horses [Fig. 34.45 and 34.45a].

Fig. 34.45 Rarey's wooden-mouth bit.

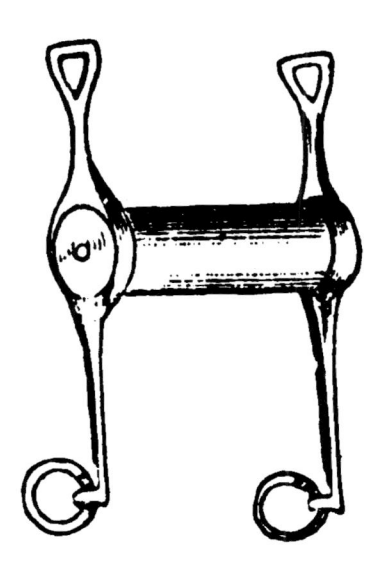

Fig. 34.45a Bit with wood mouth-piece.

Wooden-mouth Bit with Players: A bit with players or keys used in training horses [Fig. 34.46].

Fig. 34.44 Wood mouth bit with players.

Woodmansee, Lorenzo D., Dayton, OH, Patent No. 60,980. Jan. 1, 1867 [Figs. 34.47 to 34.50]. The bit consists of four bars of iron connected to the mouth-piece by small rings.

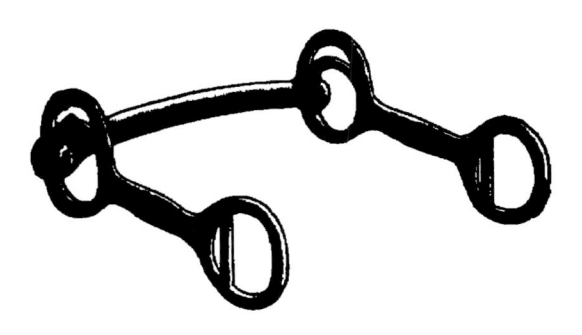

Fig. 34.47 Woodmansee production bit.

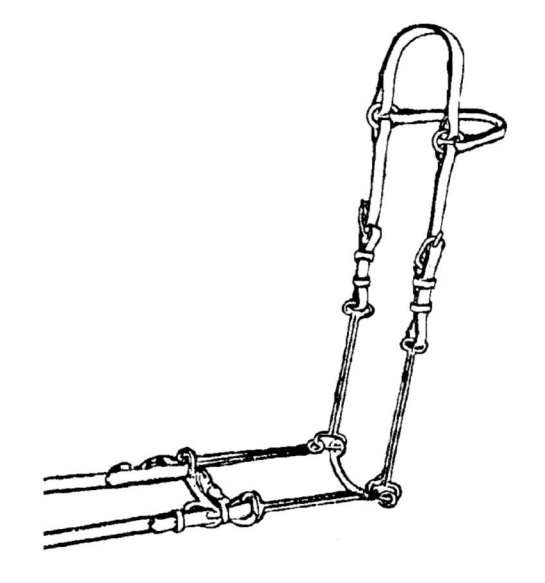

Fig. 34.48 Woodmansee bit, patent drawing.

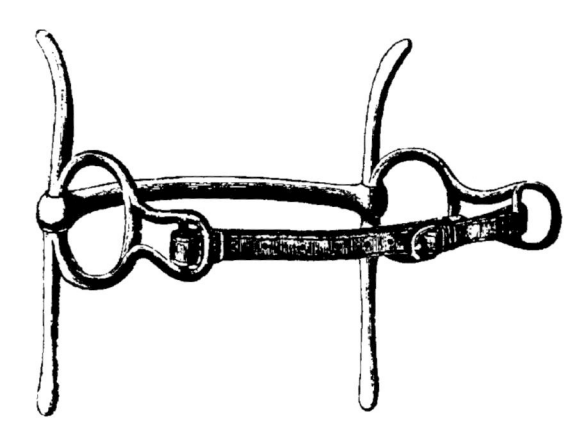

Fig. 34.49 Full-cheek production bit of Woodmansee Improved design.

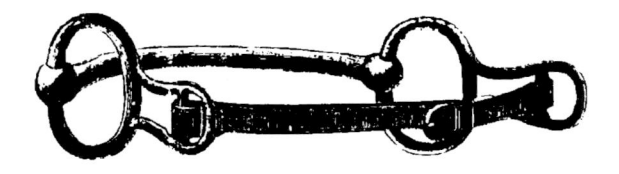

Fig. 34.50 Woodmansee snaffle bit.

Woods Snaffle: An early 1800's bit of England, from *The Loriner* [Fig. 34.51].

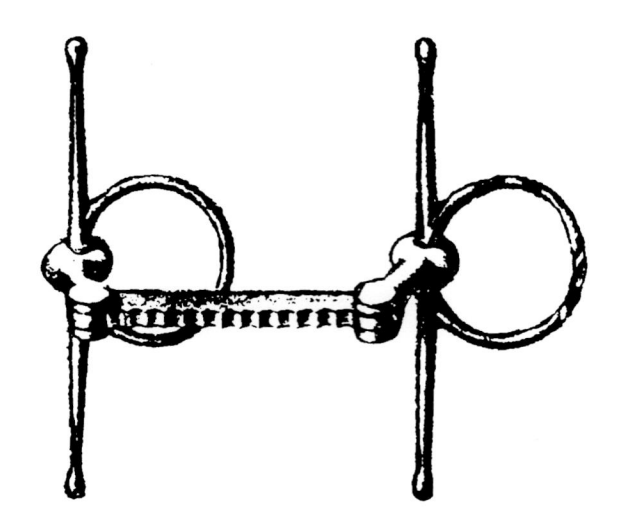

Fig. 34.51 Woods snaffle.

Wright, Jefferson G., Bit: See Chapter 8, Fig. 8.26.

Y-mouth Bit: A bit with two jointed mouth-pieces with joints offset to give a pinching action to the bars of the horse [Fig. 34.52].

Yorktown Bit: A small Texas-style bit from Haydens and Allen Catalogue [Fig. 34.53].

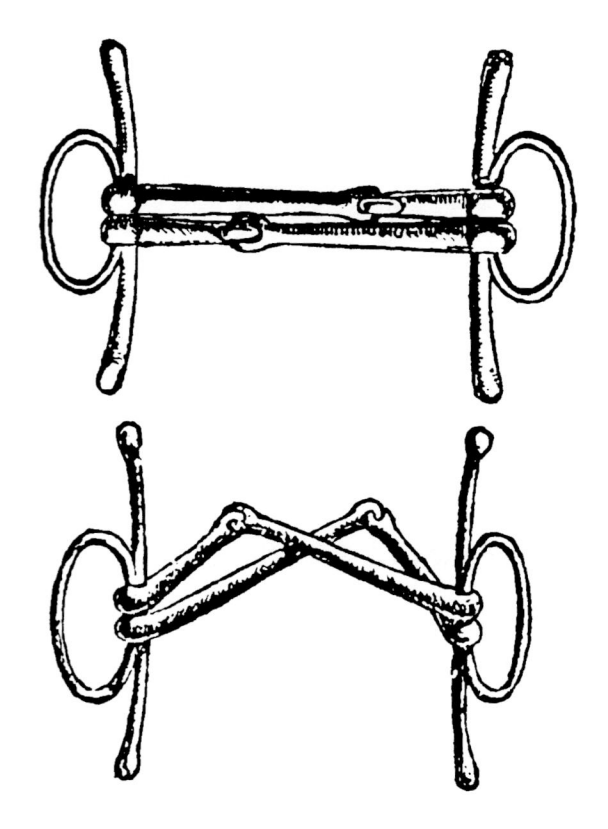

Fig. 34. 52 Y or W-mouth bit.

Zahl, Herman, Momence, IL, Patent No. 504,959, Sep. 12, 1893 [Fig. 34.54 and 34.55]. A bit comprised of two separate and independent longitudinally slotted side-links with slots for cheek-straps and a chin-strap with a mouth-piece and bit proper extending through the large elongated slots.

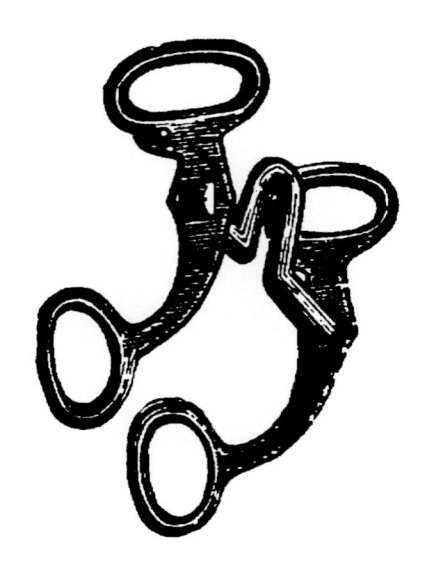

Fig. 34.53 Yorktown curb bit.

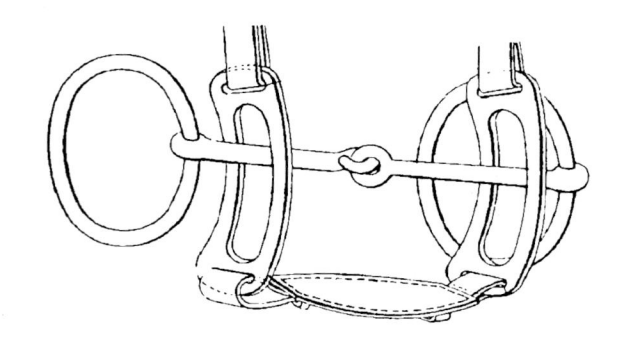

Fig. 34.54 Zahl snaffle bit with check loops.

Fig.34.55 Zahl production bit.

Zebra Bit: Name applied to a bit with bands of silver inlaid into the cheek-pieces [Fig. 34.56].

Zeller, Melancthon E., Buffton, OH, Patent No. 360,193, Mar. 29, 1887 [Fig.34.57]. A loop or strap is threaded through the cheek-piece frame and attached to the headstall. The object is to limit the downward movement of the bit and provide attachment for the reins.

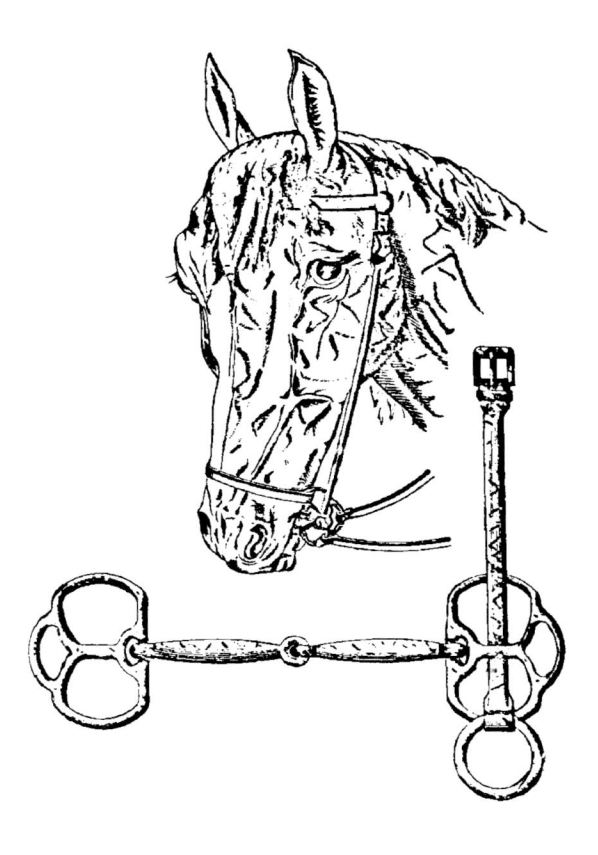

Fig. 34.57   Zeller snaffle bit.

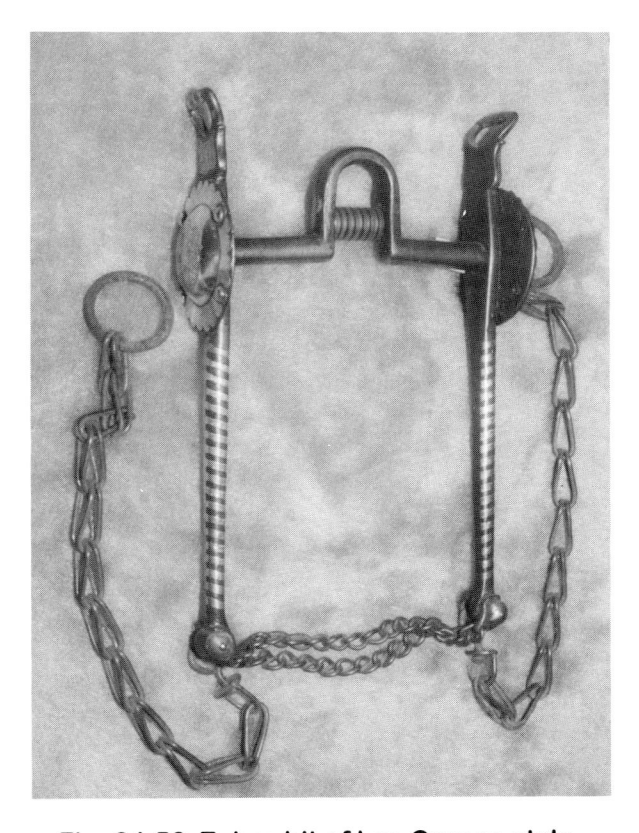

Fig. 34.56 Zebra bit of Las Cruses-style. Harold dawley collection.

445

CHAPTER THIRTY-FIVE
Bridles and Reins

A bridle is the harness which holds the bit secure in the mouth of the horse. The term usually applies to the complete piece of tack to include the headstall, the bit and the reins. But the term often applies only to the headstall. See diagram, Fig. 35.0.

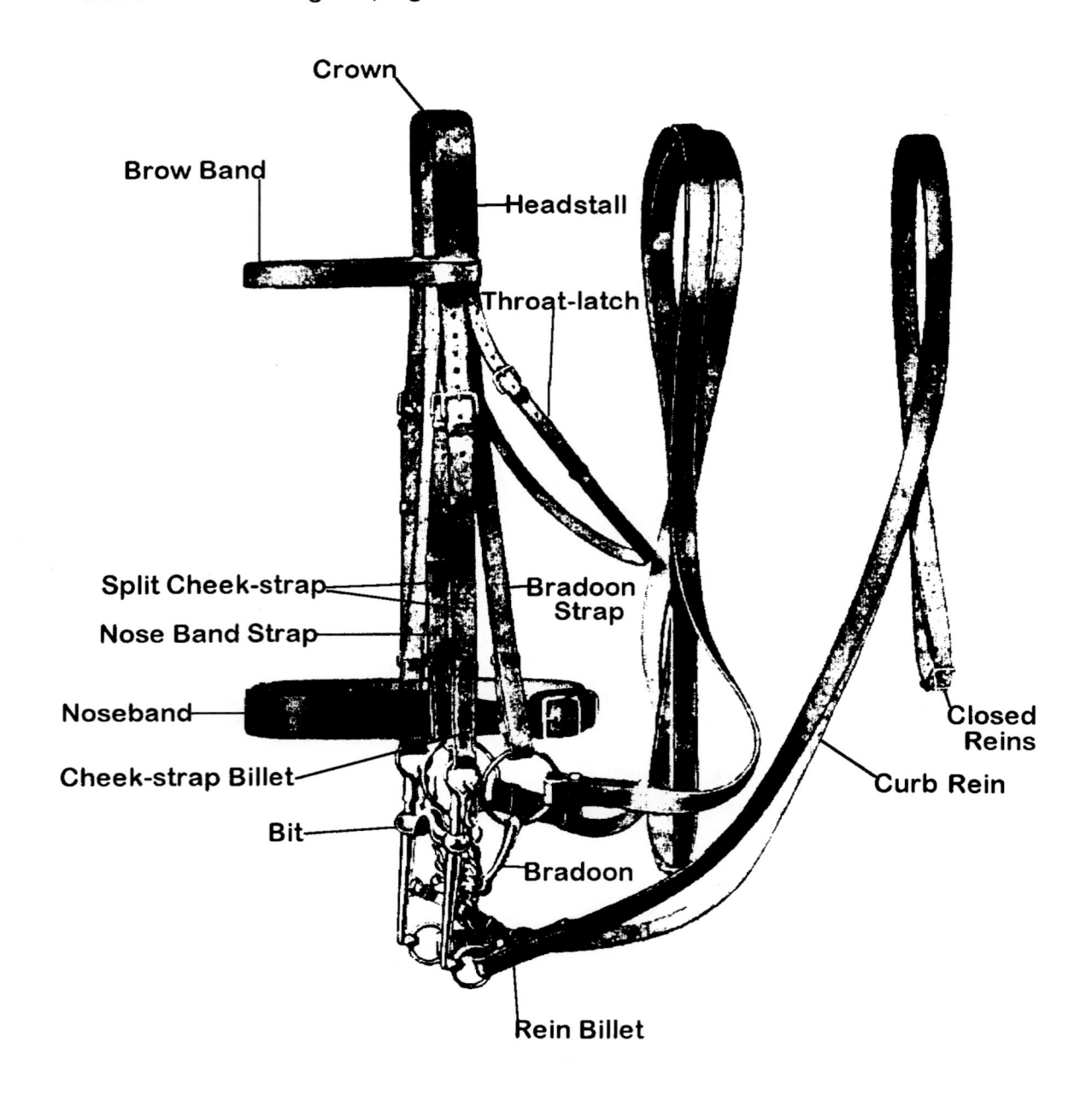

Fig. 35.0 Diagram of the parts of a Full or Double bridle.

Balding Gag Bridle: A bridle with the Balding gag bit [Fig.35.1].

Fig. 35.1 Balding gag bridle.

Beans, William R., Brownsburg, PA, Patent No. 69,983, Oct. 15, 1867 [Fig.35.2]. A combination bridle and bit with the bit having rollers in the side-pieces through which the reins travel.

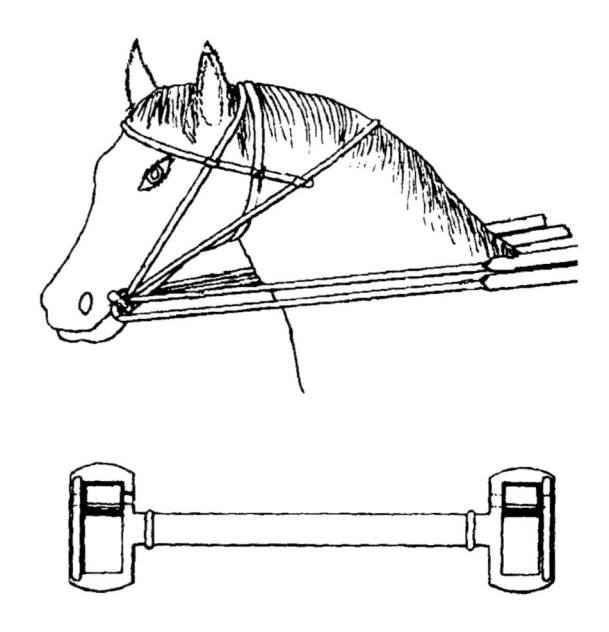

Fig. 35.2 Beans bridle.

Bearing Rein: A rein used to hold the horse's head in an unnatural position, such as a gag bit and rein or a check-rein.

Billets: The ends of reins or cheek-pieces which enter the buckles that attach the reins or cheek-pieces to the bit. There would naturally be no billets in bridles that had the reins and cheek-pieces sewn to the bit.

Bradoon Head: The headstall of the snaffle of a double bridle and consists of two straps connected by a buckle.

Bridle Chain: See Rein Chain, Figs. 35.27 and 35.28.

Bridle Ring: A metal ring on each side of a bit to which the bridle is attached.

Bridle for Tethering: A bridle for tying a horse to graze [Fig. 35.3].

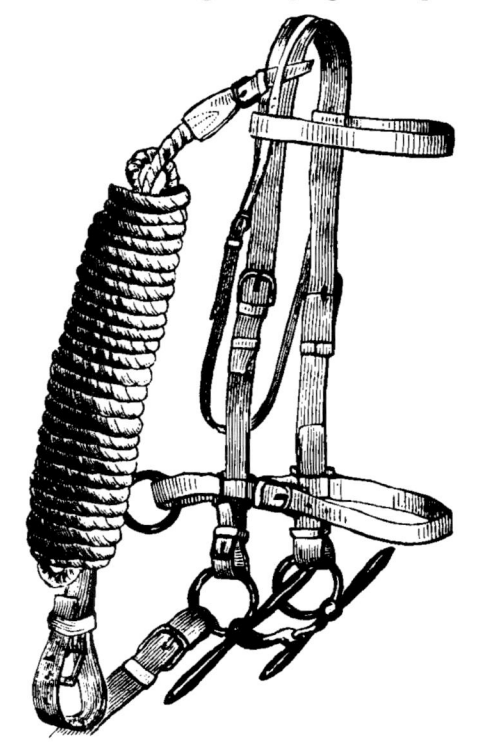

Fig. 35.3 Bridle used for tethering.

Brow-band: See Front.

California Rein: The closed reins are made with four, six, eight or twelve plaits of rawhide and decorated with plaited knots varing in number as determined by the correct weight to achieve the necessary balance between the reins and the bit [Fig. 35.4].

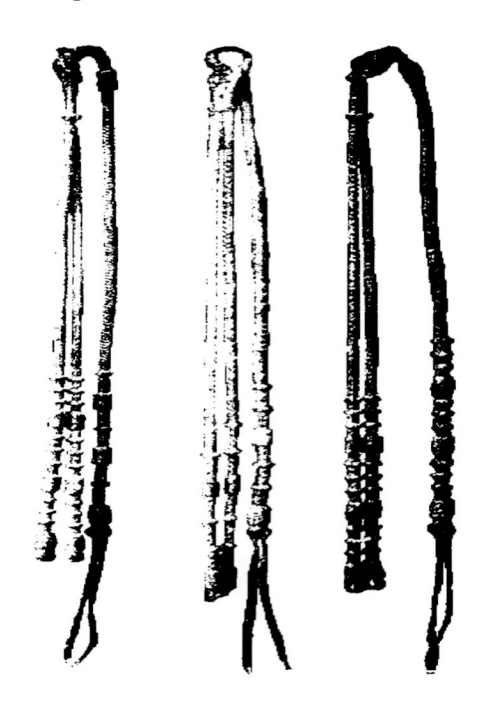

Fig. 35.4 California braided reins.

Caveson (Cavesson): A noseband attached to a headstall or strap which goes behind the ears of the horse. Rings are attached to the noseband for use with a bitting rig or longeing line [Fig. 35.5]. See Chapter 6.

Cheek Connecting Loop: A loop used to secure a double cheek snaffle and prevent tipping or rocking of the bit [Fig. 35.6].

Cheek-piece: Connects the crown-piece with the bit. See Diagram, Fig. 35.0.

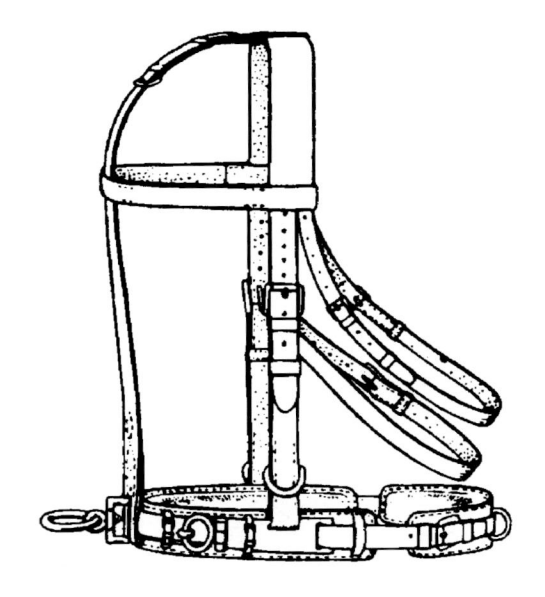

Fig. 35.5 English lunge caveson.

Closed Reins: Reins that are continuous from one bit ring to the other or are tied together. See California Reins, Fig. 35.4.

Crown-piece: The portion of the headstall that passes over the horse's poll.

Curb-rein: The reins attached to the lower bit-rings on a Pelham bit.

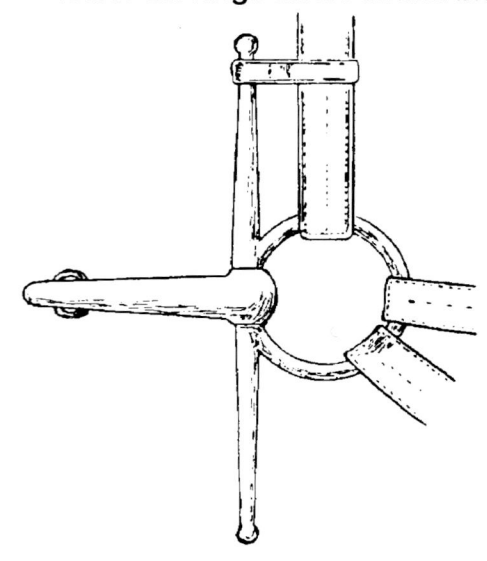

Fig. 35.6 Snaffle bit loop.

448

Diamond Swell Western Bridle: Designates the shape of the cheek-strap and may be carved or plain [Fig. 35.7].

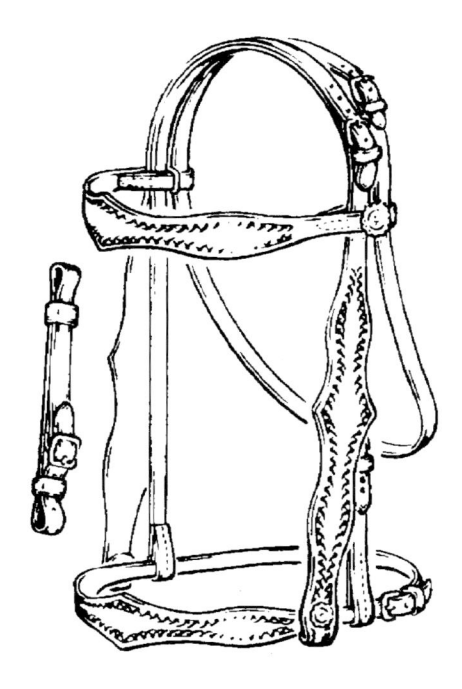

Fig. 35.7 Diamond swell western bridle.

Double-ear Rawhide Bridle: A bridle with a loop for each ear [Fig. 35.8].

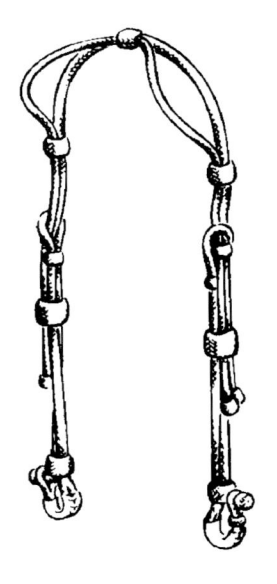

Fig. 35.8 Double-ear rawhide bridle.

Double Bridle with Martingale: Used with a curb bit and a snaffle or bradoon bit [Fig. 35.9]

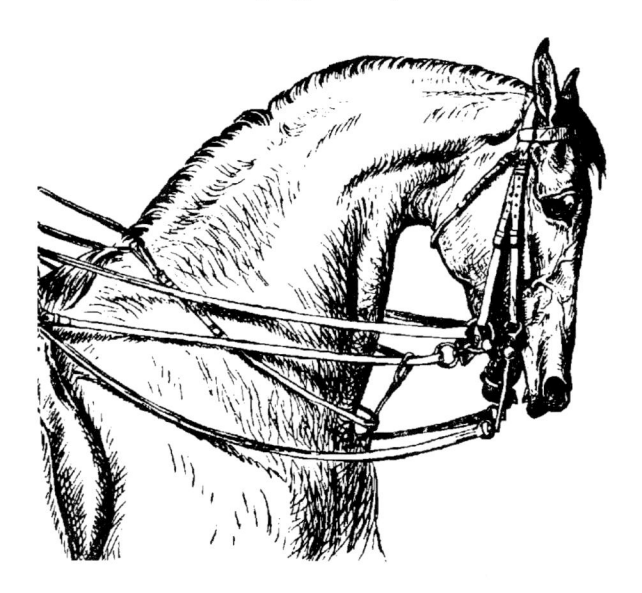

Fig. 35.9 Double bridle with martingale.

Double Hunt Bridle: A double bridle with a headstall made of heavier leather and with more width to the straps of the headstall [Fig. 35.10].

Double-ringed Snaffle Bridle: A bridle using a Wilson or four-ring bit [Fig. 35.11].

Draw Rein: A rein attached to the saddle girth or breast strap and is passed through the bit-rings to the rider. Used to train the horse to hold its head down and flex at the poll.

English Hunt Bridle: See Double Bridle, Fig. 35.10.

Ferruled Ear Bridle: A one-ear bridle headstall with round cheek-straps that have silver or stainless steel ferrules (a short tube) decorating the cheeks.

Flap Reins: reins used to secure the bit to the girth of the saddle. Normally used with children beginning to ride. [Fig. 35.12].

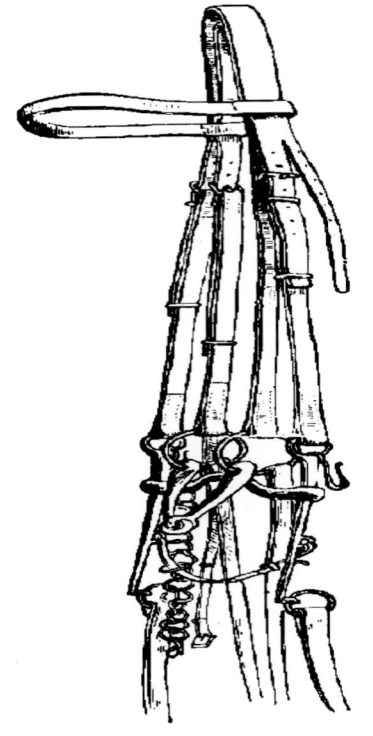

Fig. 35.10 Double Hunt bridle.

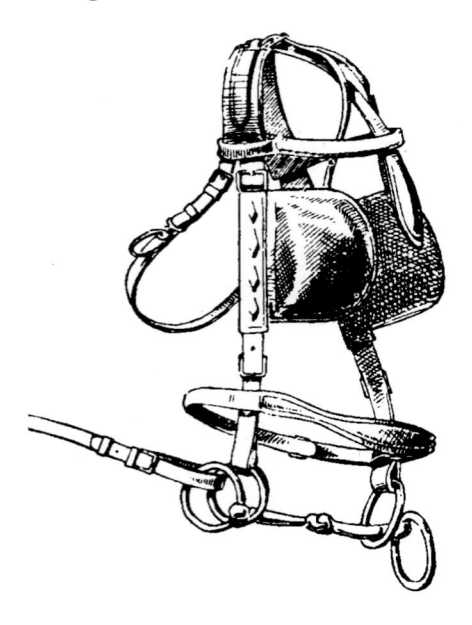

Fig. 35.11 Double-ringed snaffle bridle with blinders.

Forehead Band: See Front.

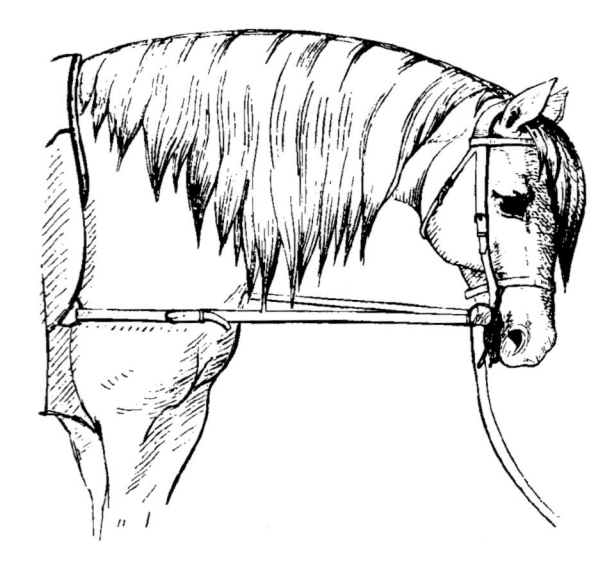

Fig. 35.12 Flap reins.

Front: The band that goes across the horse's forehead which has at each end a loop for the crown-piece to pass through.

Gag Bridle: A bridle with a gag bit [Fig. 35.13].

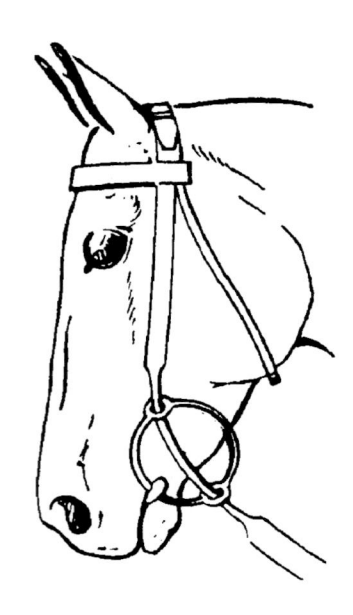

Fig. 35.13 Gag bridle.

Hackamore Bridle: A bridle that employs a bit without a mouthpiece. See Chapter 13, Hackamore.

Hale, George C., Kansas City, MO, Patent No. 505,762, Sep. 26,1893 [Fig. 35.14]. A bridle designed to use on fire horses in that the halter or headstall is left on the horse all the time, and since the bit has no mouthpiece as such, it does not irritate the horse or interfer with eating. The noseband and metal curb control the horse.

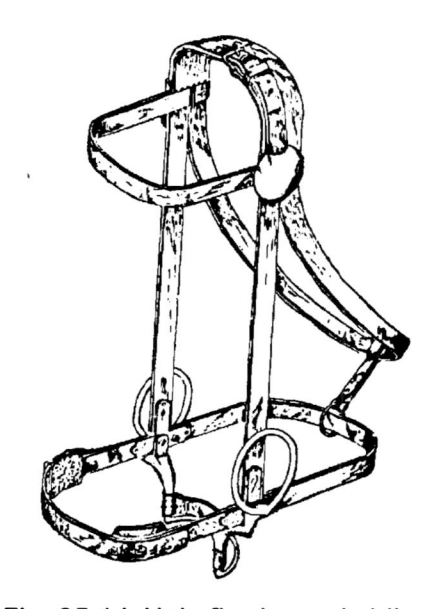

Fig. 35.14 Hale fire horse bridle.

Haskell, Franklin L., Leominster, PA, Patent No.130,994, Sep. 3,1872 [Fig. 35.15]. A bridle made specifically for the bit.

Head: See Headstall.

Headstall: The trade term for the leather work that makes up the portion of the bridle to which the bit is attached.

Hill, Harvey S., Ithaca, MI, Patent No. 505,658, Sep. 26,1893 [Fig.35.16]. A crown-piece and cheek-straps to which two short straps are attached and are placed under the upper and lower lips and in front of the teeth of the horse. The device can be used under an ordinary bridle.

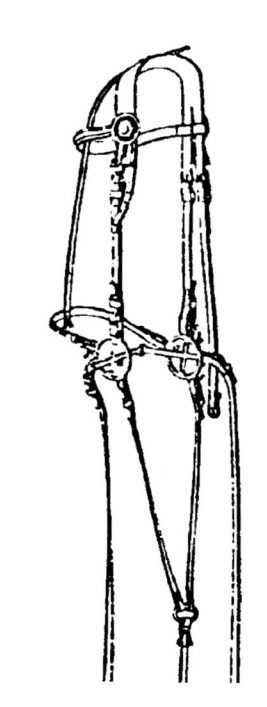

Fig. 35.15 Haskell bridle.

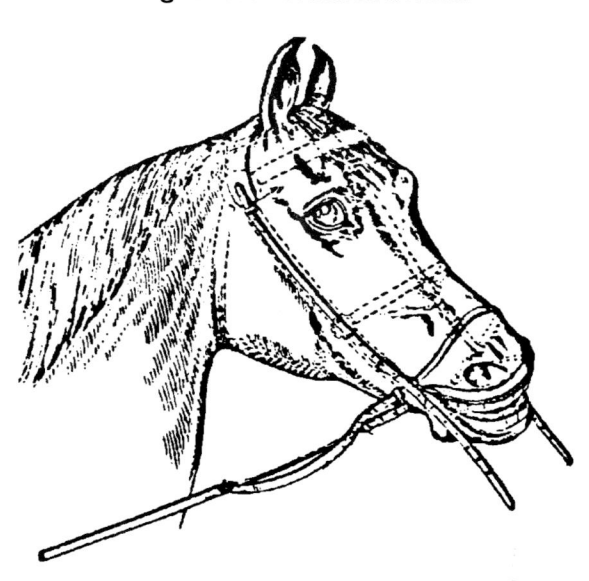

Fig. 35.16 Hill auxiliary bridle.

Hunting Snaffle Bridle: A simple heavy leather headstall with a snaffle bit [Fig. 35.17].

Keepers: See Loops.

Lewis, William A., Columbus, OH, Patent No. 515,593, Feb. 27, 1894 [Fig. 35.18]. A bridle and bit combination

451

which acts as a gag along with putting pressure on the lower jaw.

Fig. 35.17 Hunting snaffle bridle.

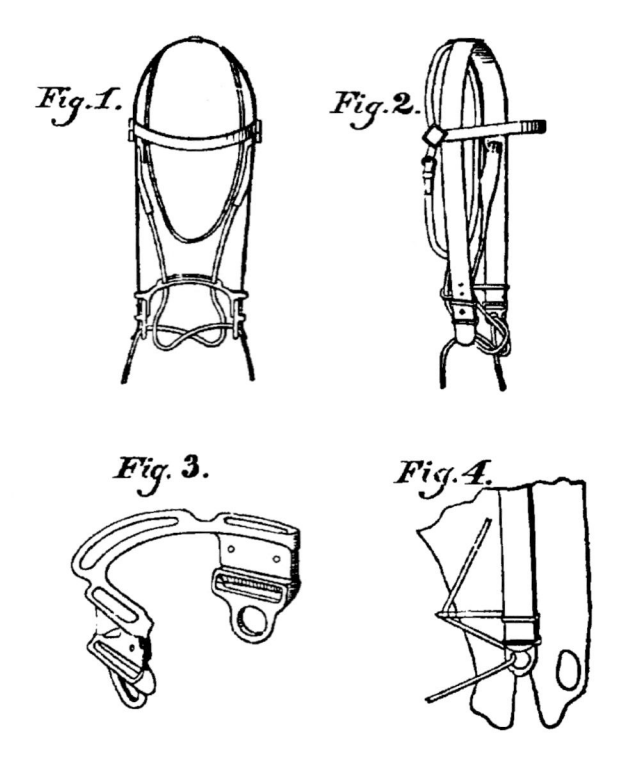

Fig. 35.18 Lewis bridle and bit.

Loops: Serve to retain the ends of the billets when billets are employed on a bridle.

Magner, Dennis, Patent No. 233,631, Oct. 26, 1880 [Fig. 35.19]. The bail on the bit is not a curb as used in the normal manner but is designed to pass around the upper incisor teeth and under the lip.

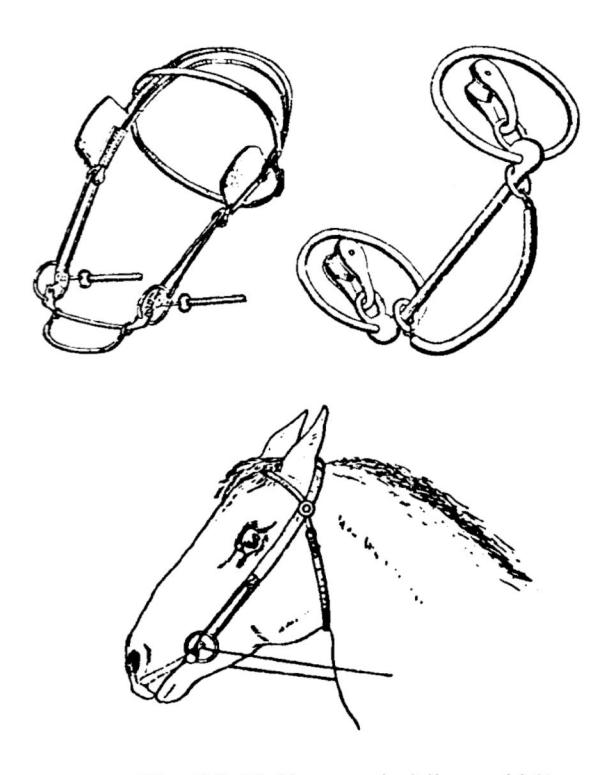

Fig. 35.19 Magner bridle and bit.

Narrow Double-stitched Bridle: A narrow-cheek bridle with a double row of stitches throughout [Fig. 35.20].

Nolan, Stephen F., Searcy, AR, Patent No. 235,643, Dec. 21, 1880 [Fig. 35.21].

Noseband: The strap that goes over the horse's nose or face between the facial crest and the nostrils [Fig. 35.22]. See Chapter 26.

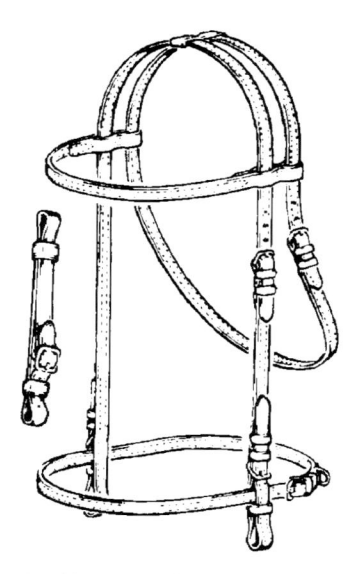

Fig. 35.20 Narrow double-stitched bridle and noseband.

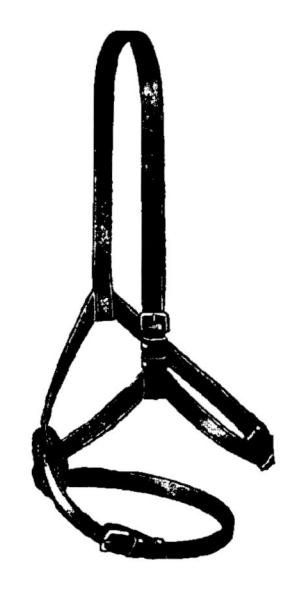

Fig. 35.22 A noseband referred to as Figure 8 or Grakle. Sometimes classified by some companies as a caveson.

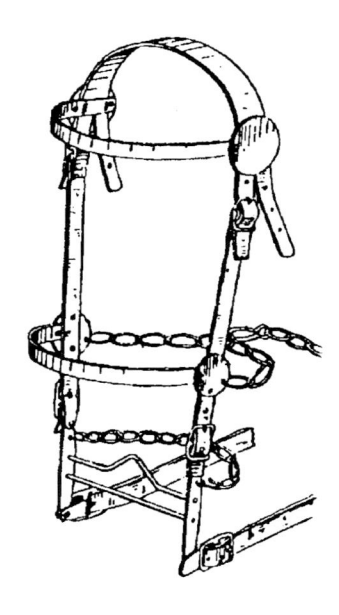

Fig. 35.21 Nolan bridle and bit.

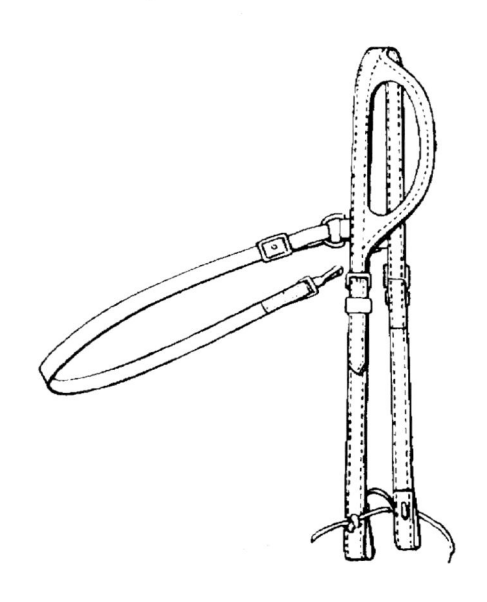

Fig. 35.23 One-eared latigo bridle.

One-eared Latigo Bridle: A bridle made of latigo leather with a loop to go over one ear [Fig. 35.23].

Open Reins: The use of a rein on each bit ring with each rein operating separately and not tied together on the end in the rider's hand.

Oval-swell Western Bridle: The shape of the cheek-strap describes the bridle. The bridle may be plain, carved or tooled [Fig 35.24].

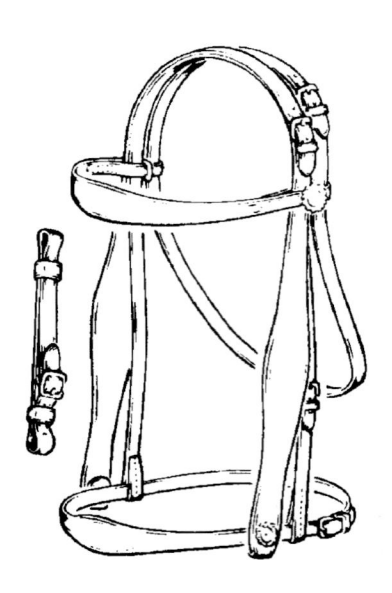

Fig. 35.24 Oval-swell western bridle.

Pelham Bridle: A bridle with a Pelham bit, a single bit used with four reins [Fig. 35.25].

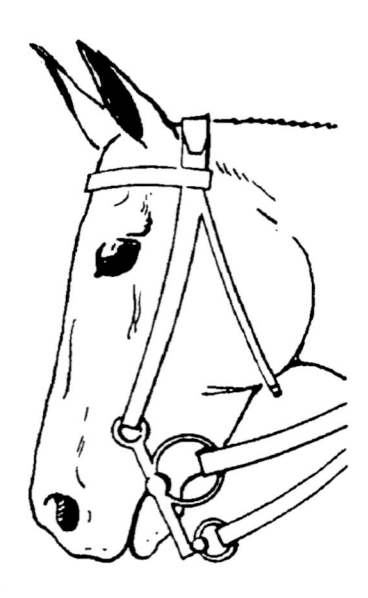

Fig. 35.25 Pelham bridle.

Plow Rein: Guiding a horse by pulling on the the rein on the side in which direction the horse is expected to turn.

Reardon, J. V., Elkton, MD, Patent No. 88,210, Mar. 11, 1869 [Fig. 35.26].

The combination dispenses with the usual headstall and throat-latch. Control is achieved by pressure on the nerves of the neck.

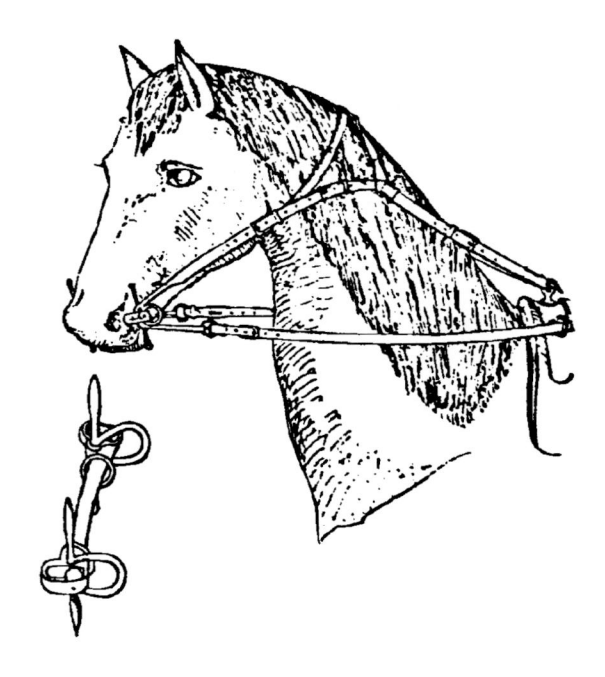

Fig. 35.26 Reardon bridle and bit.

Rein Chains: Chains used to connect the reins with the bridle rings. They prevent the leather reins from getting wet while the horse drinks water and are used to add balance to the bit which is usually a heavy California-style, Santa Barbara or Spade bit [Fig. 35.27 and 35.28).

Safety Rein Chain with Swivel and Hook.

Regular Rein Chain.

Fig. 35.27 Rein chains.

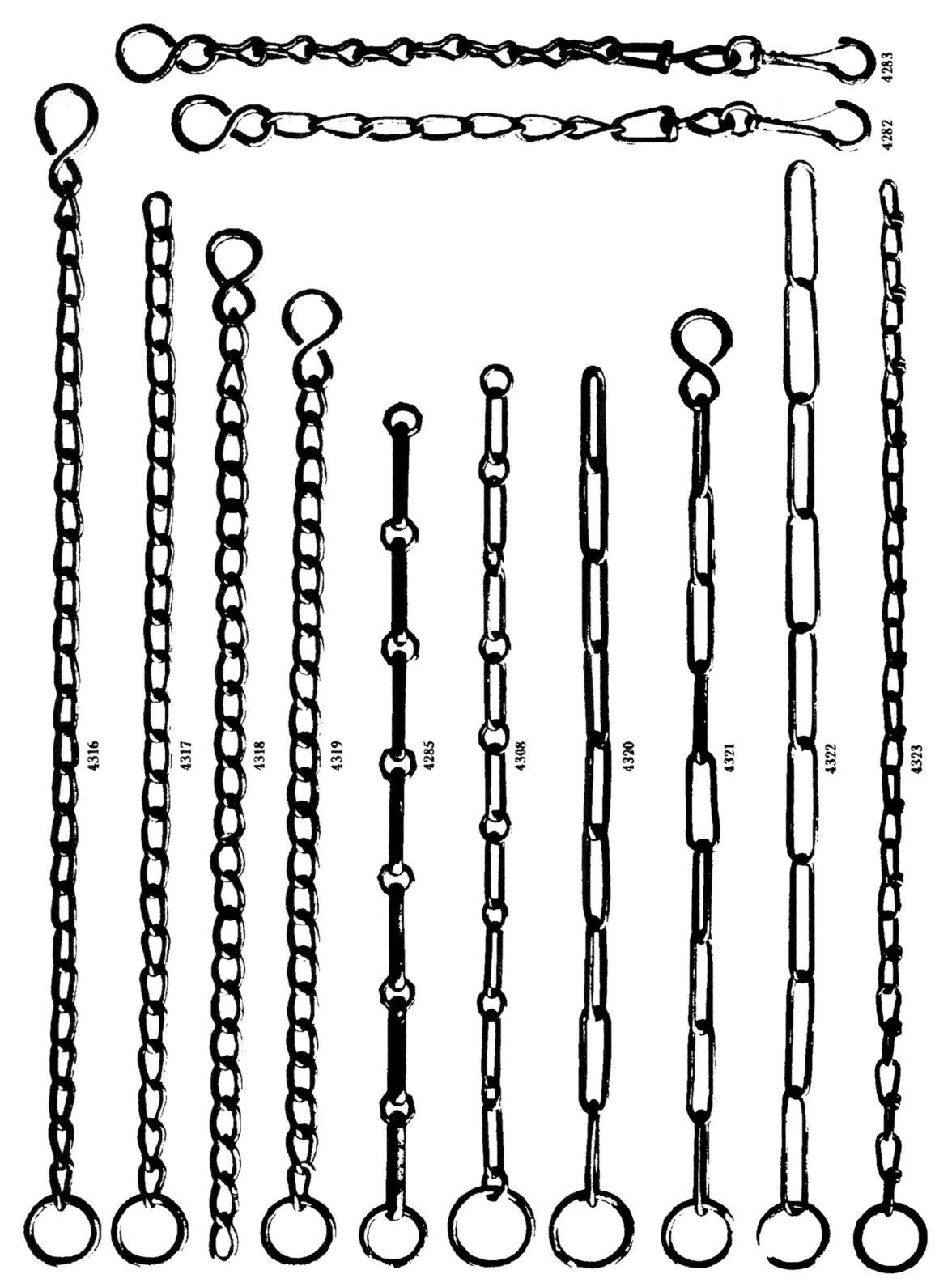

Fig. 35.28 Rein chains from Linden and Funke catalog, circa 1912.

Reins: Leather, rawhide or nylon lines that are attached to the bit of the bridle by which the rider or driver manages and guides the horse [Figs. 35.29, 35.30, 35.31 and 35.32].

Fig. 35.29 Linen reins.

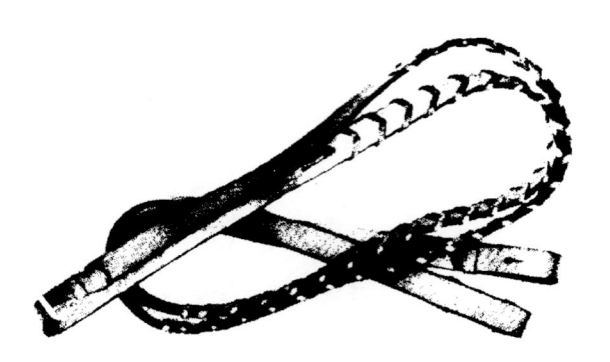

Fig.35.30 Laced reins.

Fig. 35.31 Plaited-leather reins.

Fig. 35.32 Race reins.

Round-cheek Bridle: the cheek straps are rolled and produce a round narrow cheek [Fig.35.33].

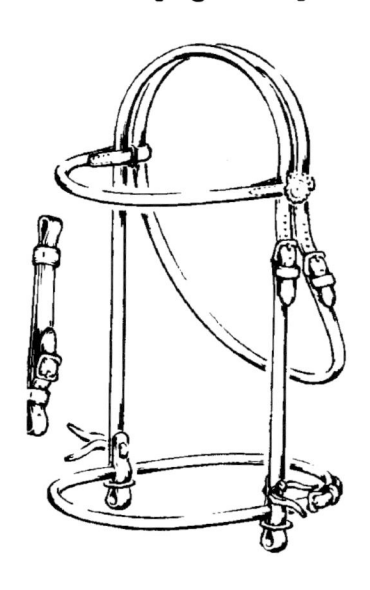

Fig. 35.33 Round-cheek bridle.

Seitz, Henry, Marietta, PA, Patent No. 5,804, Sep. 26, 1848 [Fig, 35.34]. The pulleys and arrangement of the check-rein and driving rein gives the driver the advantage of control with hard-mouth horses.

Slip-ear Bridle: A one-eared bridle in which the ear-strap will slide on the bridle [Fig. 35.35].

Stallion Bridle: A bridle used to control stallions and used more in leading than in actual driving or riding. A long lead rein is used which has a round leather disk attached to the handlers end [Fig. 35.36 and 35.36a].

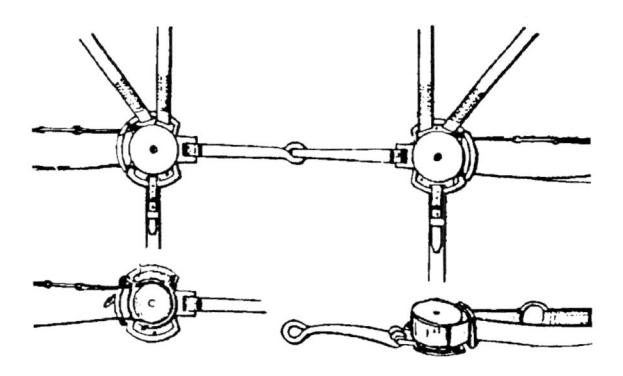

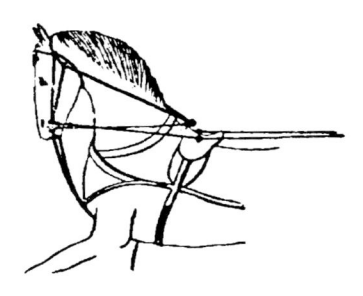

Fig. 35.34 Seitz bridle and bit.

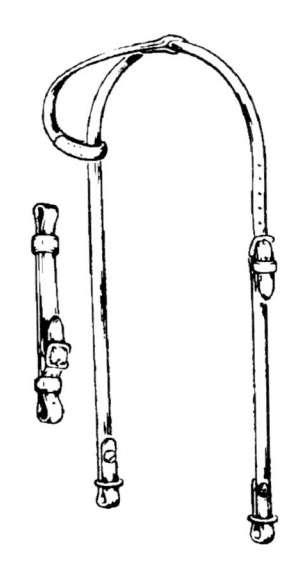

Fig. 35.35 Slip-ear bridle with noseband.

Sutton, J. T. and G. M. Terry, Sharon, TN, Patent No. 362,591, May 1887 [Fig. 35.37]. The bit is equipped with buckles for attachment of the headstall and bridle reins.

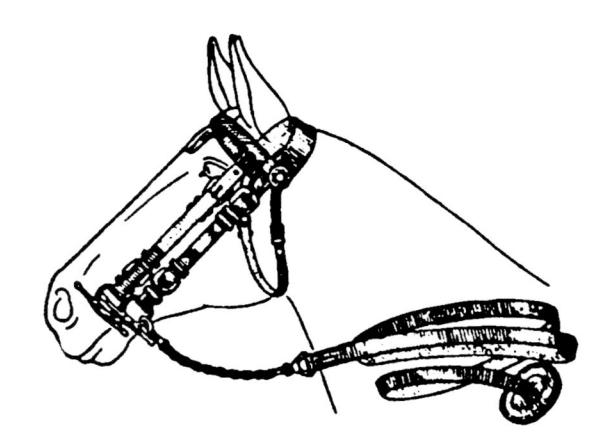

Fig. 35.36 Stallion bridle and lead.

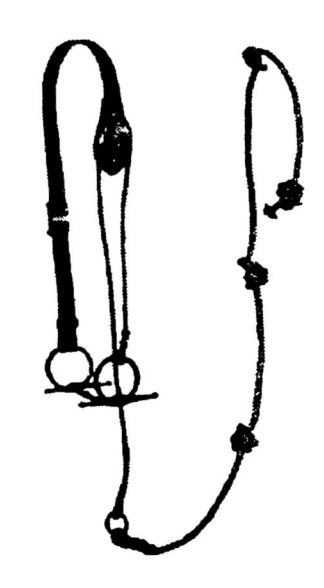

Fig. 35.36a Stallion bridle.

Tasseled Bridle: A bridle with tassels for ornamentation. This one is made of tight braided rope with the tassels added to the brow-band and to the rein ring [Fig. 35.38 and 35.38a].

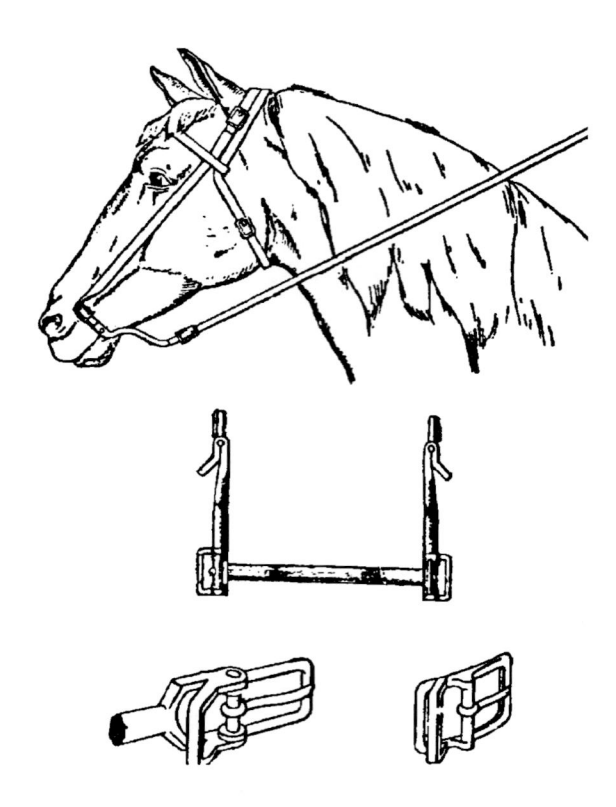

Fig. 35.37 Sutton and Terry bridle and bit.

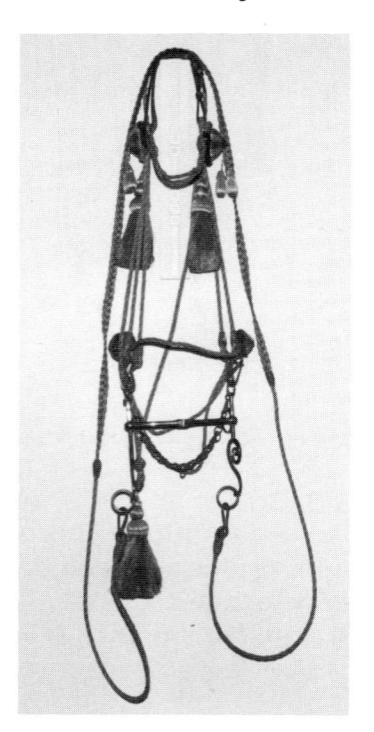

Fig. 35.38 Tasseled bridle. Hilary Harty collection.

Fig. 35.38a Detail of tasseled bridle browband.

Tooled Bridle: A bridle headstall that has been carved or tooled with a design. Most often found in western-style bridles [Figs. 35.39 and 35.40]. A tooled leather piece is imprinted by machine. A carved leather piece is carved by hand.

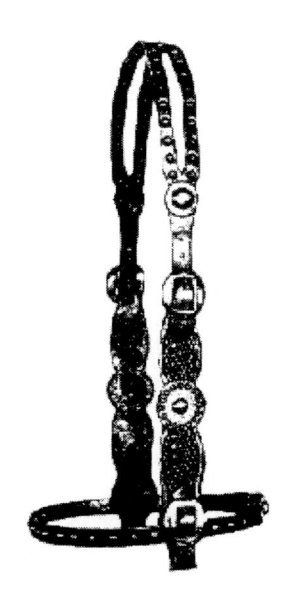

Fig. 35.39 Tooled bridle.

Fig. 35.40 Tooled bridle.

Fig. 35.42 A form of War bridle.

War Bridle: A simple bridle made with a rope and, when skillfully used, has a wonderful effect in the control of a stubborn or fractuous horse [Fig. 35.41 and 35.42].

Wilson, James H., Brentwood, TN, Patent No. 133,817, Dec. 10. 1872 [Fig. 35.43]. The bridle consists of a single strap in combination with a bridle rein and a pair of buckles so that a rein pull will draw the bit upward in the mouth of the horse.

Fig. 35.41 A form of War bridle.

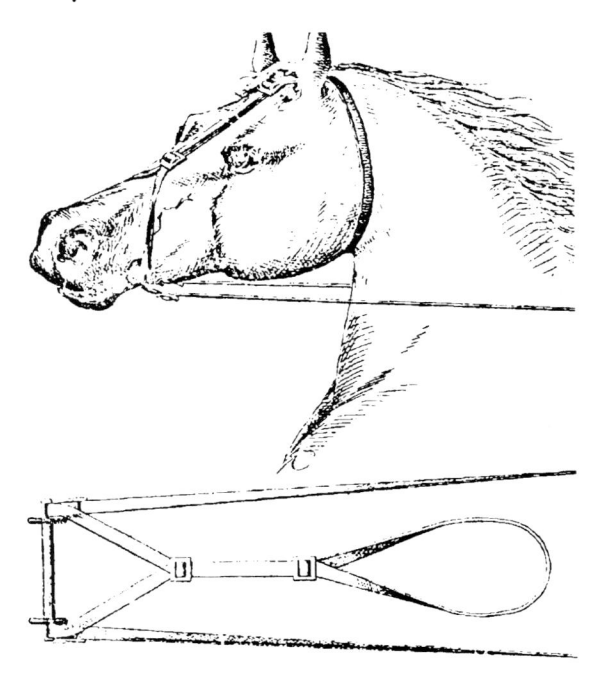

Fig. 35.43 Wilson bridle.

Weymouth Bridle: A bridle that has two bits, a curb bit and a bradoon [Fig. 35.44]. Sometimes referred to as a Full Bridle. It is the most common bridle used in finished English-style riding.

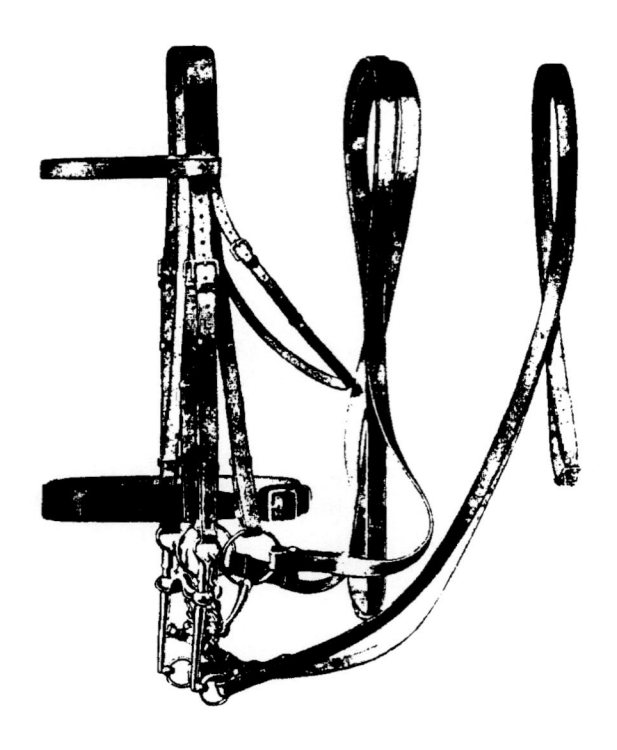

Fig. 35.44 Weymouth bridle.

NEW STYLE OPEN VIEW BLIND BRIDLES
Patented by G. A. Laub

No. 999. Front View

No. 999. Side View

No. 998.

BUGGY BLIND BRIDLE

No. 34. ⅝ inch, Nickel or Imitation Rubber, each $ 4.60
⅝ inch, Brass $ 4.70

BUGGY BLIND BRIDLE

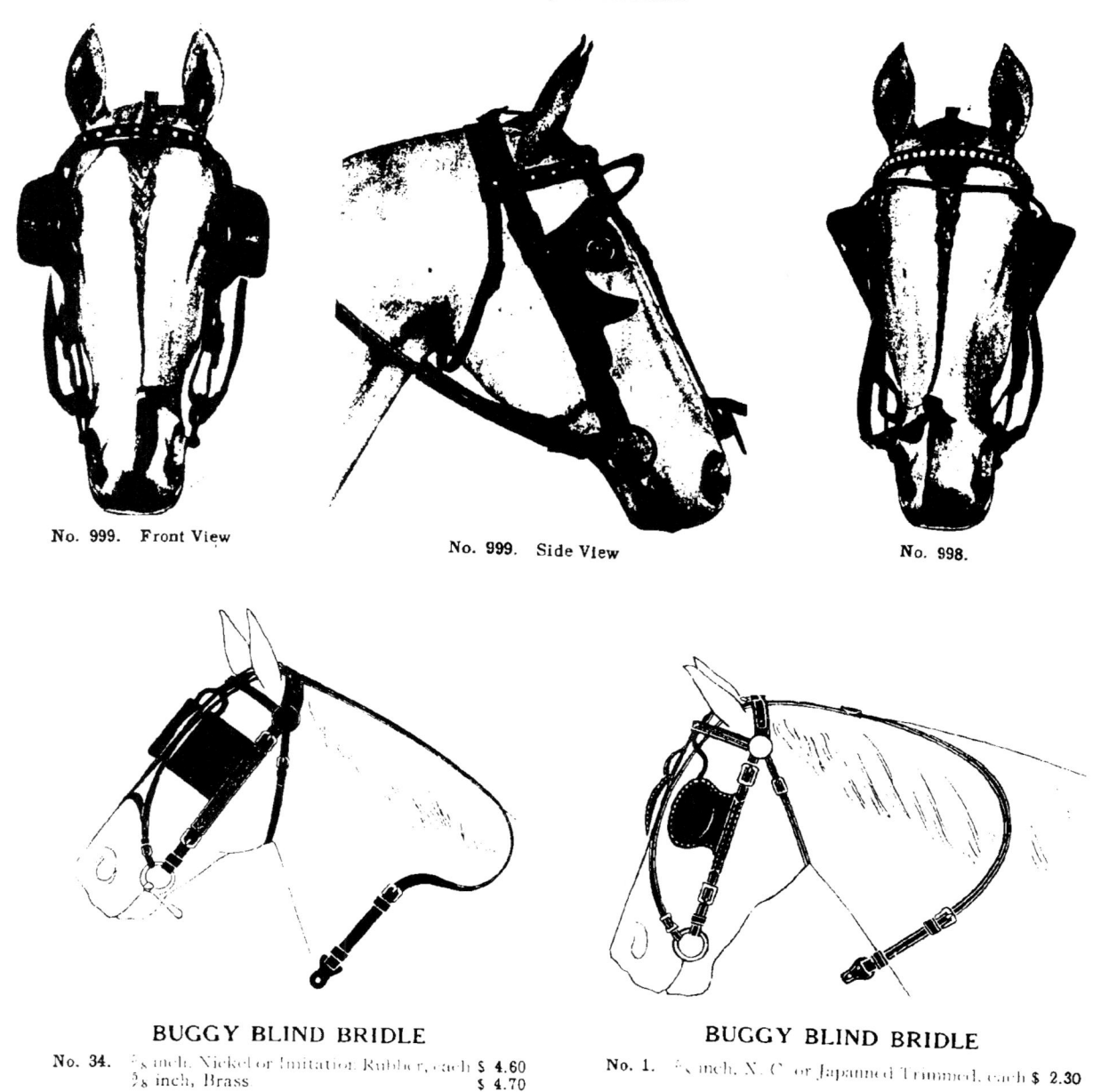

No. 1. ⅝ inch, N. C. or Japanned Trimmed, each $ 2.30

Fig. 35.45 A wide variety of bridles have been produced for use on many different types of driving and draft horses. Fig. 35.45 through Fig. 35.49 are representative of bridles manufactured by and illustrated in the catalog of Padgett Bros. Company, Dallas, Texas, circa 1900. Manufacturers of today also produce a large variety of bridles which are supplied for western-style riding.

INDIAN STOCK PORT BRIDLE

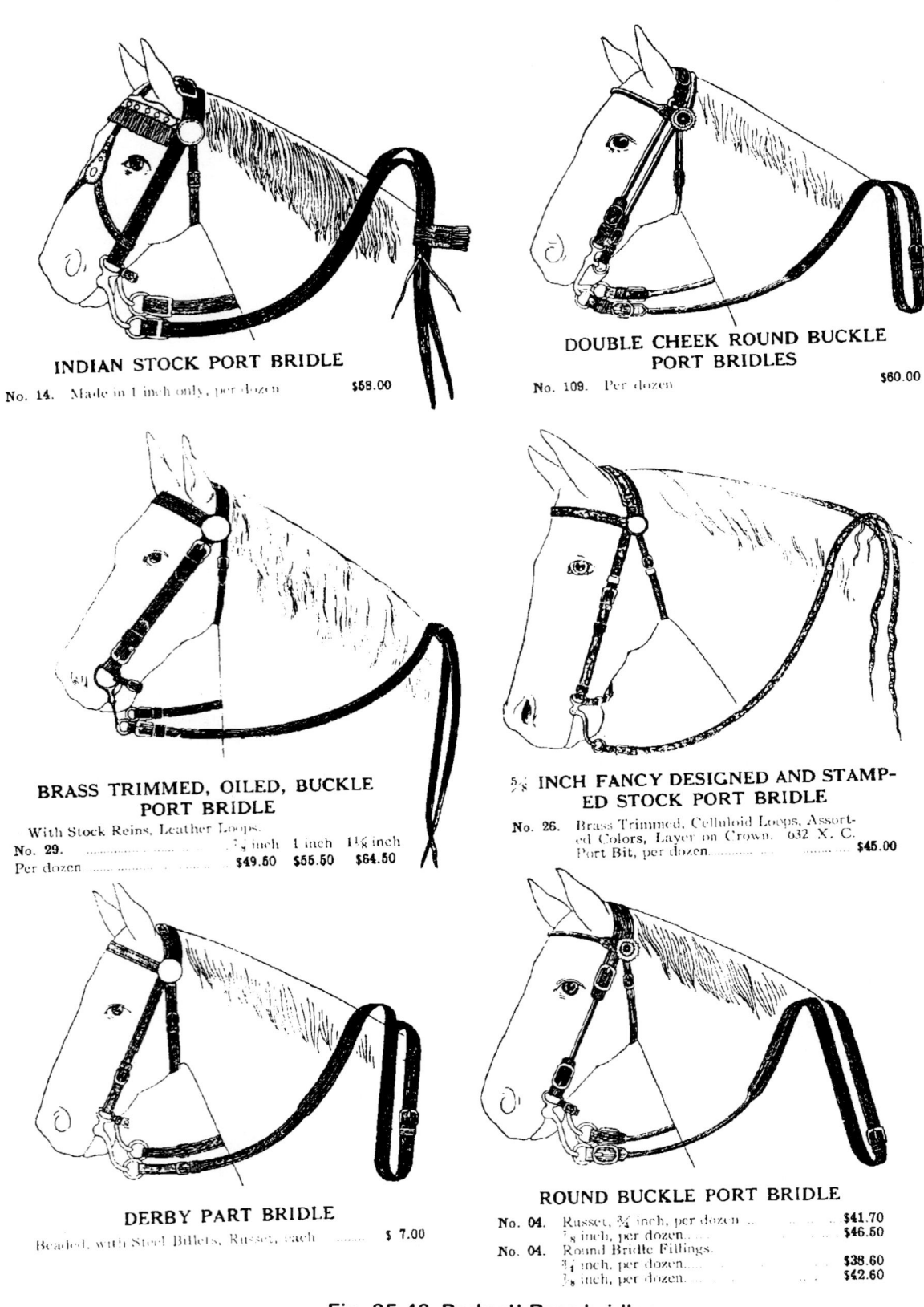

No. 14. Made in 1 inch only, per dozen $58.00

DOUBLE CHEEK ROUND BUCKLE PORT BRIDLES

No. 109. Per dozen $60.00

BRASS TRIMMED, OILED, BUCKLE PORT BRIDLE

With Stock Reins, Leather Loops.
No. 29.	⅞ inch	1 inch	1⅛ inch
Per dozen	$49.50	$55.50	$64.50

⅝ INCH FANCY DESIGNED AND STAMPED STOCK PORT BRIDLE

No. 26. Brass Trimmed, Celluloid Loops, Assorted Colors, Layer on Crown. 032 X. C. Port Bit, per dozen $45.00

DERBY PART BRIDLE

Beaded, with Steel Billets, Russet, each $7.00

ROUND BUCKLE PORT BRIDLE

No. 04. Russet, ¾ inch, per dozen $41.70
⅞ inch, per dozen $46.50
No. 04. Round Bridle Fillings.
¾ inch, per dozen $38.60
⅞ inch, per dozen $42.60

Fig. 35.46 Padgett Bros bridles.

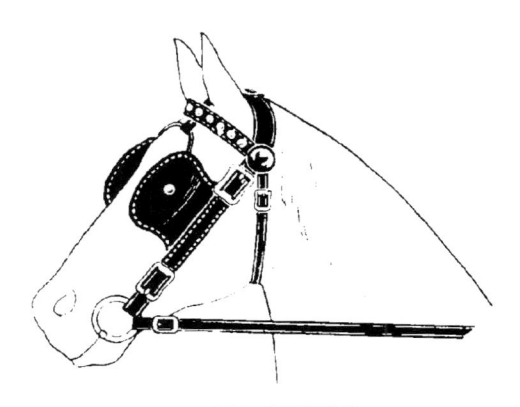

BLIND BRIDLE

No. 155. Sensible Blinds, 1¼ inch Checks, Round Winker Brace, Front Double and Stitched with Ornaments. 1¼ inch, per dozen $41.00

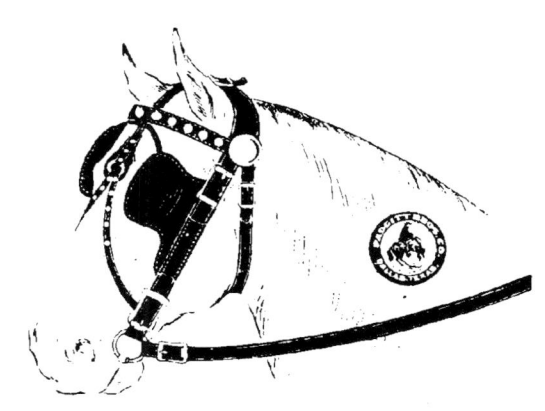

FANCY BRASS SPOTTED BLIND BRIDLE

No. 164. 1¼ inch, per dozen $44.00

NEW AND IMPROVED CUPPED BLIND BRIDLE

No. 138. Russet and Black Blinds and Fronts 1¼ inch, per dozen $46.00

Page 308

MIKE CLARK FANCY IMPROVED CUPPED BLIND BRIDLE

Russet and Black Blinds and Fronts, Spotted, 1¼ inch, per dozen $48.00

WAGON BLIND BRIDLE

No. 151. Large Bonnet Blind, Cupped, Straps with Spot, Buckle Winker Stay, 1¼ inch, per dozen $48.00

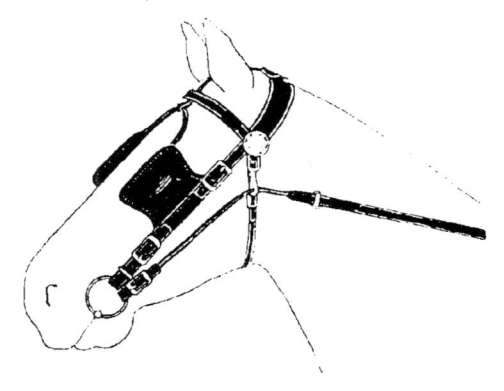

WAGON BLIND BRIDLE

No. 130. 1 inch, with Round Cup Rein, per dozen $46.00

Fig. 35.47 Padgett Bros. bridles.

CREOLE OPEN WAGON BRIDLES

o. 126. 1⅛ inch, per dozen $24.00

OPEN WAGON BRIDLES

No. 123. ¾ inch, per dozen $23.00
⅞ inch, per dozen $25.00
1 inch, per dozen $27.00
1⅛ inch, per dozen $29.50
1¼ inch, per dozen $32.00

FANCY OPEN WAGON BRIDLES

No. 127. Russet Face Piece, Front and Safe, ¾ inch Black Stock Reins. ⅞ inch only, per dozen $33.00

FANCY BRASS SPOTTED OPEN WAGON BRIDLES

No. 228. Black and Russet Cheeks. Face Piece and Front, 1⅛ inch, per dozen $36.00

FANCY BRASS SPOTTED OPEN WAGON BRIDLES

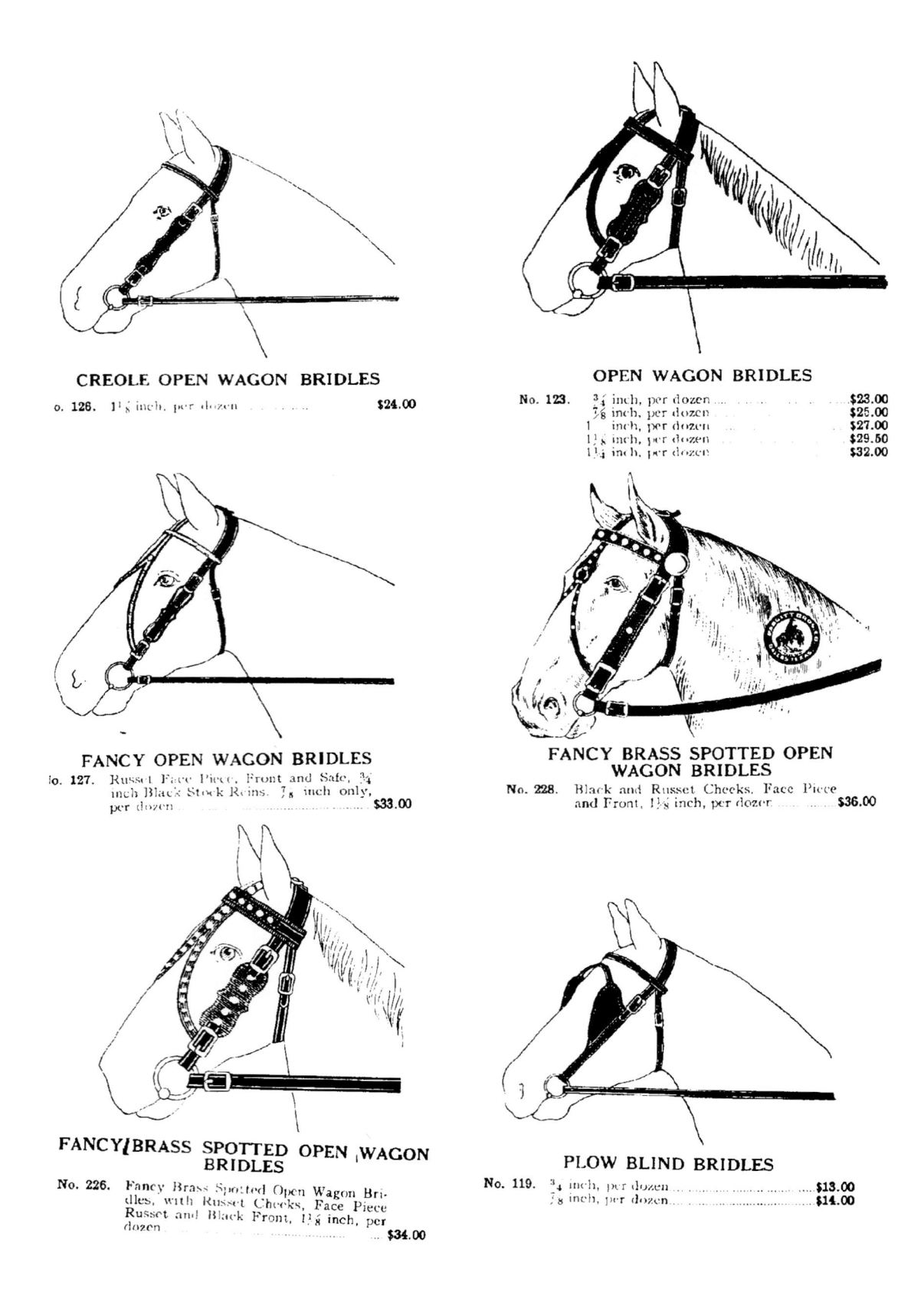

No. 226. Fancy Brass Spotted Open Wagon Bridles, with Russet Cheeks, Face Piece Russet and Black Front, 1⅛ inch, per dozen $34.00

PLOW BLIND BRIDLES

No. 119. ¾ inch, per dozen $13.00
⅞ inch, per dozen $14.00

Fig. 35.48 Padgett Bros. bridles.

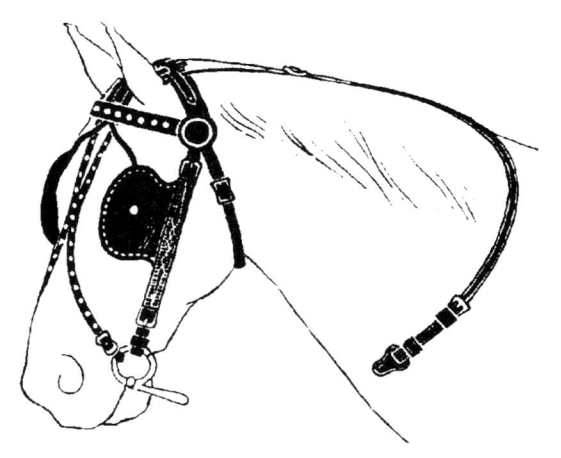

BRASS SPOTTED BUGGY BLIND BRIDLE

No. 1½S.   ⅝ inch, Japanned Buckles, each $ 3.30
           ¾ inch, Japanned Buckles, each $ 3.60

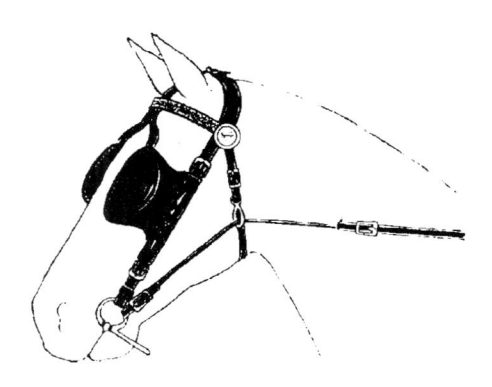

⅞ INCH EXPRESS BRIDLE

No. 40.   X. C. Trimmed, each $ 4.50

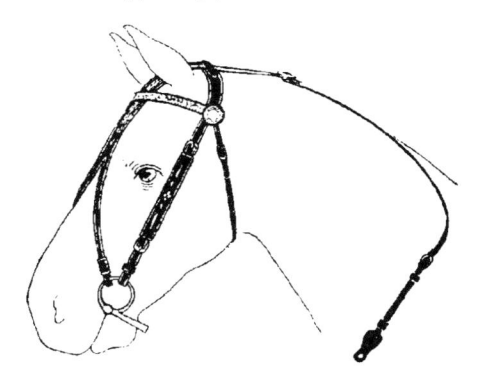

OPEN BUGGY BRIDLE

No. 1½.   ⅝ inch, X. C. or Japanned, each $ 2.70
          ⅝ inch, Nickel or Imitation Rubber, each $ 2.90
          ¾ inch, X. C. or Japanned, each $ 3.10
          ¾ inch, Nickel or Imitation Rubber, each $ 3.30

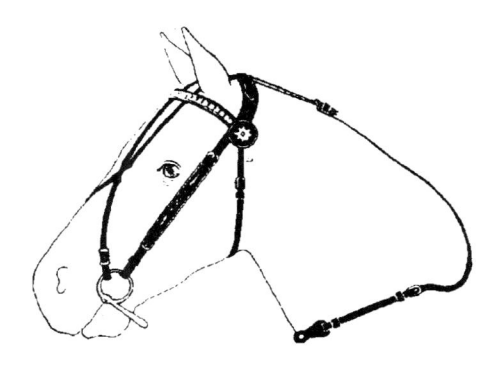

OPEN BUGGY BRIDLE

No. 32.   ⅝ inch, X. C. or Japanned, each $ 3.20
          ⅝ inch, Nickel, each $ 3.30
          ¾ inch, X. C. or Japanned, each $ 3.50
          ¾ inch, Nickel, each $ 3.60

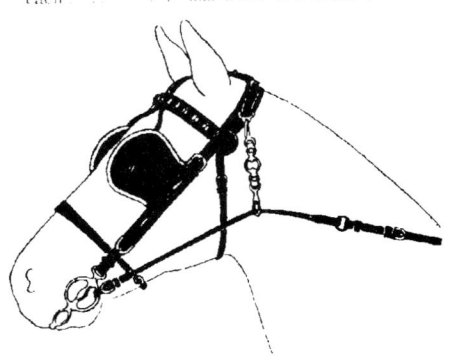

COACH BLIND BRIDLE

No. 90.   ¾ inch, Nickel or Imitation Rubber, each $ 9.50

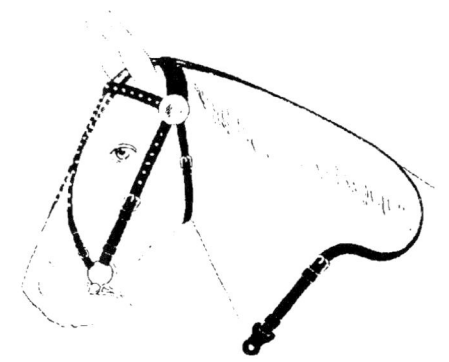

BRASS SPOTTED OPEN BUGGY BRIDLE

No. 9½S.   ⅝ inch, Imitation Rubber Buckles, each $ 2.90
           ¾ inch, Imitation Rubber Buckles, each $ 3.30

Fig. 35.49 Padgett Bros. bridles.

CHAPTER THIRTY-SIX
Loriners of the Past

Aldaco, Ruben, Elko, Nevada, maker of silver inlaid bits and spurs.

Aplan, Jens Ole (J. O.), lived in Gettysburg and Pine Ridge, South Dakota, in the 1890's. While living in Pine Ridge, he was the Indian Agency blacksmith. He lived in Ruchville, South Dakota, from 1896 to 1935.

Avila, Gary, Woodside, California, maker of silver mounted and inlaid bits and spurs.

Baldwin: Joseph Baldwin and Co., Newark, New Jersey, made bits, spurs and saddle hardware from 1871 to 1906.

Bass, James Oscar (J. O.), was born March 19, 1879, in Atlanta, Georgia. He opened his first shop in 1897, at Quitaque, Texas, and was in Tulia, Texas, from 1905 to 1925. He died February 3, 1950.

Bayers, Adolph, made all of his bits and spurs in Truscott, Texas. He started his work in the early 1930's and continued well into the 1970's. His bits were stamped with A. E. BAYERS and a style number with the odd numbers given to bits and the even numbers to spurs. He died in 1978. See pages 473 and 474.

Belknap Hardware and Mfg. Co., Louisville, Kentucky: was founded in 1840 and was a major supplier of bits, spurs and saddle and harness hardware. Their trademarks were BLUEGRASS (1940'S) and BELKNAP BLUE DIAMOND (1930'S).

Bischoff, George A., born in Emmettsville, Maryland, in 1862. He made all of his bits and spurs in Gainsville, Texas. His company was purchased by C. P. Shipley, Kansas City, Missouri, in 1915. He died in 1944. See Crockett, page 479.

Bohlin, Edward H.: Cowboy, silversmith, and saddle maker, became the outfitter of movie stars. See page 471.

Boone, Clayton, born in 1843, made some bits and spurs and taught the trade to his sons Bob, Thomas Payton (Pate), and Trent at Christoval, Texas, and Dee Boone, Henryetta, Oklahoma.

Boone, Wallie, born in 1883 and learned to make bits and spurs from his cousin Bob Boone. He stamped his work BOONE with a backward N. His shop was in San Angelo, Texas. He died in 1958. See pages 475 and 476.

Bradney, Frank, made bits and spurs in Canon City, Colorado. Before 1934, he stamped his work F. B., and from 1934 to 1964, BY F. B., and after 1964 they were numbered, since he was incarcerated that year in the Colorado State Penitentiary, Canon City, Colorado. He was later paroled and is now 81 years old.

Buermann, August, born in Germany in 1842. He came to this country in 1863, and enlisted in the Union Army in 1864. After the war he went to work for Barclay and Co. in Newark, New Jersey, and after other ventures became owner by 1880, of the company started by Barclay. He was the major manufacturer of bits and spurs in the United States from the late 1800's until the company was sold in 1926 to North and Judd following Mr. Buermann's death. Catalog No. 22 lists over 350 different bridle bits and 450 spur variations. See pages 477 and 478.

Crockett, Arthur, older brother of Oscar Crockett, was a bit and spur maker in the 1890's and early 1900's in the west Texas area. He died in an automobile accident in 1927.

Crockett, Oscar: See pages 479 to 490.

Daniels: A manufacurer of quality bridle bits in England. See pages 493 and 494.

Dewsbury, John and Son Limited: A major manufacturer of bits, spurs and stirrups in Walsall, England. Owned and doing business as James Cotterell and Sons, Limited, Walsall, England, a company established in 1831.

Easy Master Bit Co.: Their products were made of manganese bronze (yellow). Some were chrome plated over the bronze. They operated from the 1940's to 1970's.

Echavarria, J. F., San Jose, California, made silver mounted bits and spurs from 1880's to 1900.

El Gato: The company's products were stamped E. G. or QUIEN SABE (who knows).

Eldonian Saddlery Limited: A major manufacturer of bridle bits, spurs and stirrups in Walsall, England. See pages 492 to 500.

English Manufacturers and Makers: See Chapter 33, pages 416 to 420.

Estrada, Juan, Winnemucca, Nevada, and San Francisco, California, maker of silver inlaid bits and spurs from 1900 to 1920. Product stamped JE.

Field, John, Santa Barbara, California, from a family of loriners. See John Fields, IV, Chapter 37.

Figueroa, Jose, born in Sonora, Mexico, in 1880. He came to Los Angeles, California, in 1901, and in 1921, was making bits and spurs for the Los Angeles Saddlery and Finding Co. He died January 11, 1951.

Fleming Bits and Spurs: A company founded by Willard Thomas and Richard Fleming. See page 501.

Engraving detail of bridle bit by Juan Estrada. Ned Martin collection.

Garcia, Guadelupe S., born in 1864, and became famous for his saddles, bits and spurs. His shop was in Elko, Nevada, from 1897 until his sons Les and Henry took over the business in 1932. He died in 1933.

Garcia, Les and Henry moved the business to Salinas, California, in 1936. The business closed during WW II and reopened in 1946 at Salinas. Henry bought out Les' share in 1957, and Les started his own shop in Reno, Nevada, in 1960, and operated the business until he died in the late 1980's. See pages 503 to 505.

Gliem: See Crockett, page 479.

Goldberg Staunton Saddlery Co.: makers of bits and spurs in addition to saddles. Juan Estrada was one of their makers.

Grijalva, Eduardo, was a bit and spur maker for many years in southern California and Mexico. He stamped his work with E.G. and a star.

Gutierrez, Rapheal Philo; A saddle maker and loriner. See page 506.

Herrera, Alsalio, began making bits and spurs for Juan Martarel in 1868. He was working for D. E. Walker, Visalia, California, in 1880. Was affiliated with G. S. Garcia and godfather of his children. He is considered by many to be the best bit and spur maker of all time.

Hoback, Lawrence (Larry) a Ventura County, California, cowboy. Was a maker of silver inlaid California-style bits.

Hodge, Jess (J. S. or D.) was born in 1869, and lived in Ft. McKavett, Texas, where he made bits and spurs in his blacksmith shop. He died in 1953.

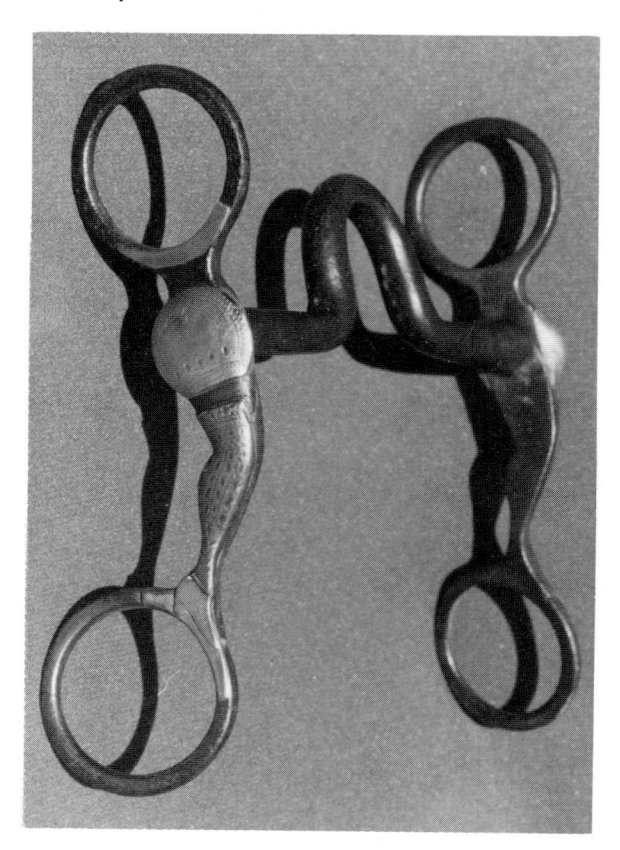

Bridle bit by Jess Hodge. Ned Martin collection.

Hunt, A. B. (Abby), made bits and spurs in Caliente and Tehachapi, California, from early to mid-1900's. His son also made bits and spurs.

Bridle bit by Abby Hunt. Ned Martin collection.

Bridle bit by Abby Hunt. Ned Martin collection

468

Huntsville Prison: Many inmates made bits and spurs during their stay in the prison. Records were not kept and most of the products were not marked.

K & C: See Crockett, Page 481.

Kelly, Pascal Moreland (P. M.), born in 1886, in Texas. Began making bits and spurs in 1903. Because he was the oldest of several boys when he began his shop in 1905, the bits and spurs were marked KELLY BROS. in anticipation of his brothers working in the shop at a future time. In 1913, he took a partner, Clyde Parker, and began marking the products KB&P or KELLY BROS. & PARKER. In 1919, he went back to KELLY BROS. His business was sold to James Renalde in 1965. See Crockett, Page 483.

Larios, A., bit maker of the late 1800's. Marked his bits and spurs with a horse head in an oval.

LeCompte Manufacturing Co., New York, NY: Advertised as United States headquarters for patent, special and staple bits, in early 1900's.

Linden and Funke: A company that manufacured bits, spurs and stirrups in three different locations in Germany. Their business office was located at Hannover, Germany. Their catalog was issued in five languages. They were the major suppliers of bits to Central and South America as well as other countries. See pages 507 to 513.

MM: See Mike Morales.

Main and Winchester: Company founded in 1848 in San Francisco. Many of their bits and spurs are marked "Patented" with a date. Records do not show that any bits were patented by Main & Winchester or that any were assigned to them.. Bits shown in catalogs are marked with M & W inside the cheek-piece.

Mardueno, Jose, Carpinteria, California, made California-syle silver inlaid bits in the 1880's and maybe before and after.

McChesney: See Pages 517 and 518.

Messing, H., San Jose, California. A bit and spur maker of the late 1800's.

Morales, Miguel (Mike), was a fine saddle maker and silversmith. He worked closely with G. S. Garcia, Elko, Nevada. He moved to Pendleton, Oregon and worked for Hamley and Company. See pages 509 and 520.

Mudro, Steve, maker of California-style bits and spurs.

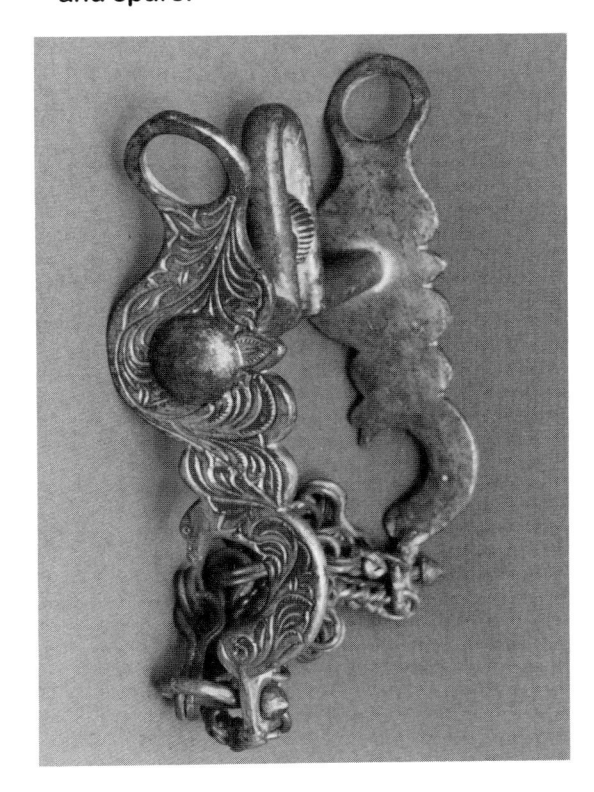

Bridle bit by J. Messing. Ned Martin collection.

Nelson, C., maker of silver inlaid California syle bits.

North and Judd Mfg. Co.: A company established in 1878 in New Britain, Connecticut. Their main products were hardware for boats with harness hardware and bits and spurs a lesser product. They used the anchor as a trademark. Only after they purchased the Buermann Mfg. Co. in 1926 did they become more involved in the manufacture of bits and spurs. They discontinued about 75% of the Buermann line but kept the most popular products doing the most volume. They discontinued all hand made bits and spurs which Buermann had made. They discontinued manufacuring all bits and spurs in 1970.

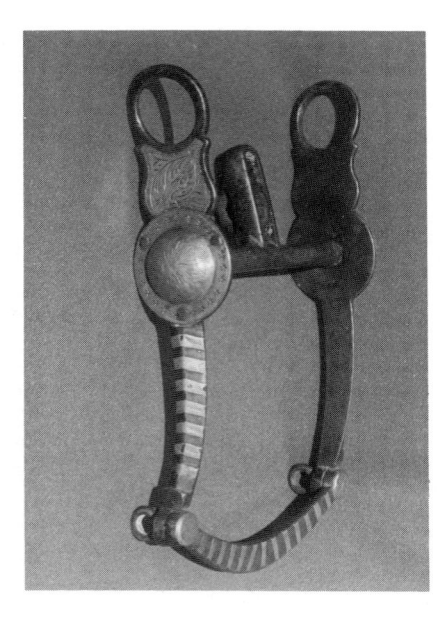

Bridle bit by M. Morales. Ned martin collection.

Overtons: makers of bits and spurs in Tyler, Texas, in the 1940's and 1950's.

Phillips and Gutierrez: W. (Bill) H. Phillips and Raphael Philo Gutierrez made bits, spurs and saddles in Cheyenne, Wyoming. The partnership lasted only one year, 1917-1918. In 1920, Gutierrez went into partnership with Juan Estrada in San Francisco, California, and continued to make products until his death in 1958.

Powder River Co., Provo, Utah: made bits and spurs that were stamped POWDER RIVER. They would buy unmarked Kelly products and put their name on them.

Prison Bits and Spurs: Most bits and spurs were not marked; some were marked with the inmates serial number and/or unit. Some were marked TPS for Texas Penitentiary System. Bits and spurs were made at Canon City, Colorado State Prison, Arizona Territory Prison, Washington State Prison at Walla Walla, Utah State Prison, Wyoming State Prison, and probably others.

Qualey, Tom, born in Idaho in 1903 and started making bits and spurs in the 1920's. His products were marked QUALEY and for a time while he worked with his brother, QUALEY BROS. JOSEPH IDAHO. He died in 1976.

Renalde, James, made bits and spurs in Denver and Boulder, Colorado. He bought the Crockett Co. in 1951, and the Kelly Co. in 1965. See Crockett, page 481.

Ricardo Metal Mfg. owned by Don Ricardo: made bits and spurs in Denver, Colorado and Victoria, Texas, from the 1930's to the 1970's. Many of his products are cast aluminum and are stamped RICARDO or Don Ricardo in script. See pages 518 to 522.

Schell, A. J., a cowboy who made bits and spurs in California and Winnimucca, Nevada, from the 1890's to the 1920's. Bits are marked A. J. SCHELL MAKER.

Bridle bit by A. J. Schell. One spade brace missing.

Shipley, Charles P., born in 1864. Began making saddles in 1885 and made bits and spurs at different times from 1915 to the 1930's. Sold McChesney and Buermann bits and spurs as well as

470

other companies. See Crockett, page 479.

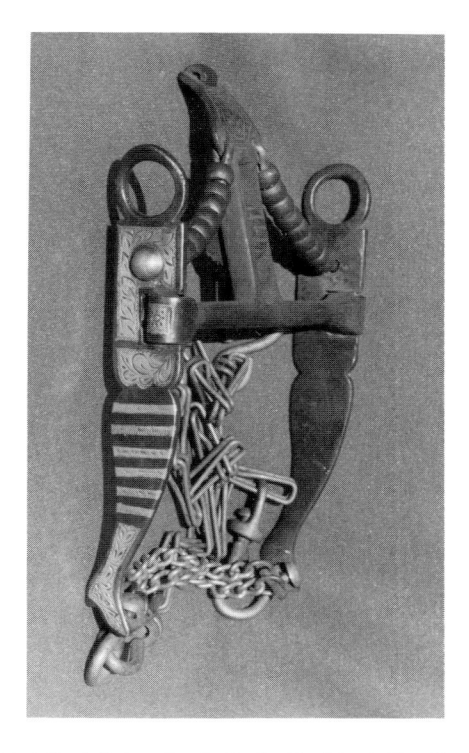

Bridle bit by A. J. Schell. Ned Martin collection.

Sliester Bit: Produced bits in Sangor and now in Auberry, California, was a major supplier of bits to Visalia Stock Saddle Company. See page 523 and 524.

Stone: The L. D. Stone company was founded in San Francisco, California, in 1852, and merged with Main and Winchester in 1905. Products were marked L. D. STONE.

Straung (Strong), Harold, started making bits and spurs in 1919. They were marked with a flying S and sometimes a date.

Tapia, Jose, Los Angeles, California, maker of silver inlaid bits and spurs from the 1880's to 1890.

Thompson Manufacturing Co., owned by J. Thompson, Waltham, Massachusetts: makers of bits and spurs for wholesale to mail order companies, including Sears and Roebuck.

Trammell Bits: A major manufacturer of bits designed and developed by Mr. Jim Trammell, a professional trainer. Produced bridle bits from the 1960's to the early 1990's at Albany and Haskell, Texas.

Visalia Stock Co.: started making bits and spurs in 1860, in Hornitas, California and then later in Visalia, California until 1897. They had many talented makers in their employ. They produced basically the California-style bits and spurs. See pages 525 to 531.

Weast, Willy N., learned the art of bit and spur making while working for J. O. Bass in Quitaque, Texas, sometime between 1897 and 1906. He marked his product MADE BY W N WEAST SILVERTON TEX.

Wimmer, John Wesley, was born on a ranch near Paso Robles, California, January 12, 1896. He started making bits and spurs in the 1920's and continued into the 1970's, marking his bits with WWW on the spade or sometimes on the inside of the left cheek-piece.

Wyatt, Charles, made bits and spurs in Maybell, Colorado, from 1906 into the 1930's. He marked his products with a quarter circle over a circle.

Bohlin:

Edward "Eddie" H. Bohlin became trusted saddlemaker for America's wealthiest men as well as for the working cowboy. He was born in Orebro, Sweden, ca. 1893. Eddie ran away from home at an early age and worked his way to America, arriving in New York City in 1910, at the age of 17. He soon migrated to Miles City, Montana, where Buffalo Bill Cody helped start him as a cowpuncher.

Always the artist at heart, Bohlin took time off from the long cattle drives to spend four months at the Art Institute of Minneapolis, where he received the foundation training for his original designs for the silver and gold products created in his shops. His abilities in trick riding and roping took him to a theater in Los Angeles where Tom Mix admired and purchased his hand-made leather jacket. The transaction inspired Eddie to open his first shop in Cody, Wyoming.

Hard work coupled with excellent quality soon rewarded him with orders from other celebrities, including Dale Evens, Roy Rogers and Gene Autry. Charter membership in the Los Angeles County Sheriff's Posse and membership in the Rancheros Vistadores, whose membership included 600 of the America's wealthiest and most powerful men, promoted his business (now located at 5760 Sunset Boulevard, in Los Angeles, California) even more.

He never abandoned his working clientel and always sought better designed equipment to benefit them. He developed a fiberglass tree which was stronger and lighter than wood. Plain leather products were readily available in his shop as well as the silver and gold-mounted speciality items.

Bohlin became semi-retired in 1972 due to ill health. He died May 28, 1980.

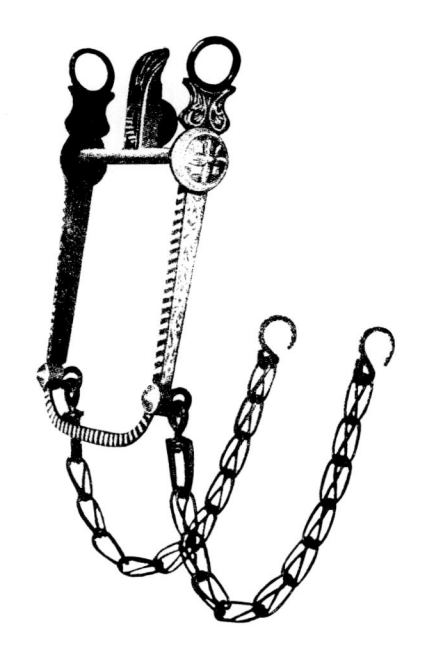

Silver inlaid bridle bits by Bohlin.

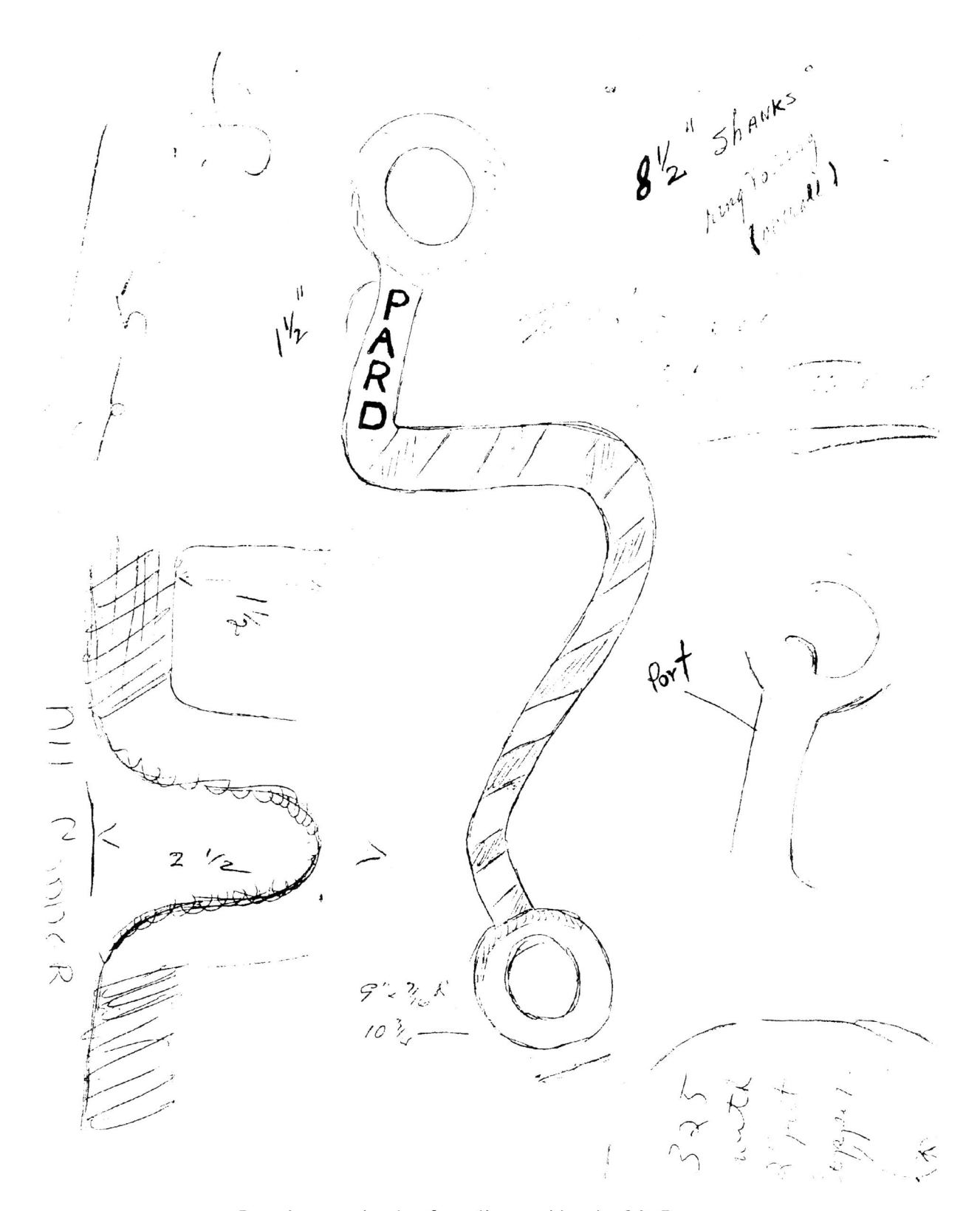

Drawings and notes from the workbook of A. Bayers.

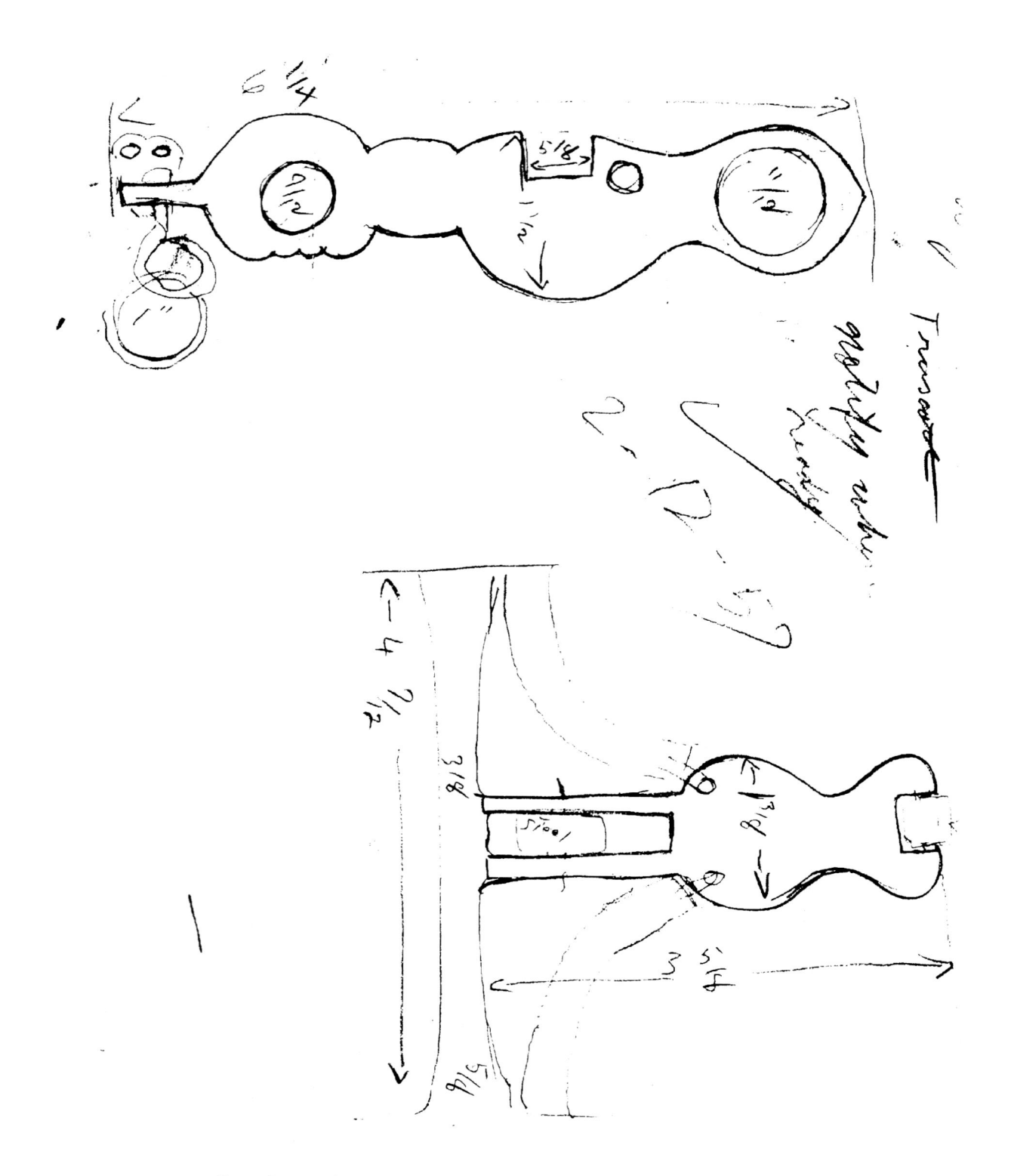

Drawing and measurements from the notebook of A. Bayers.

No. 67

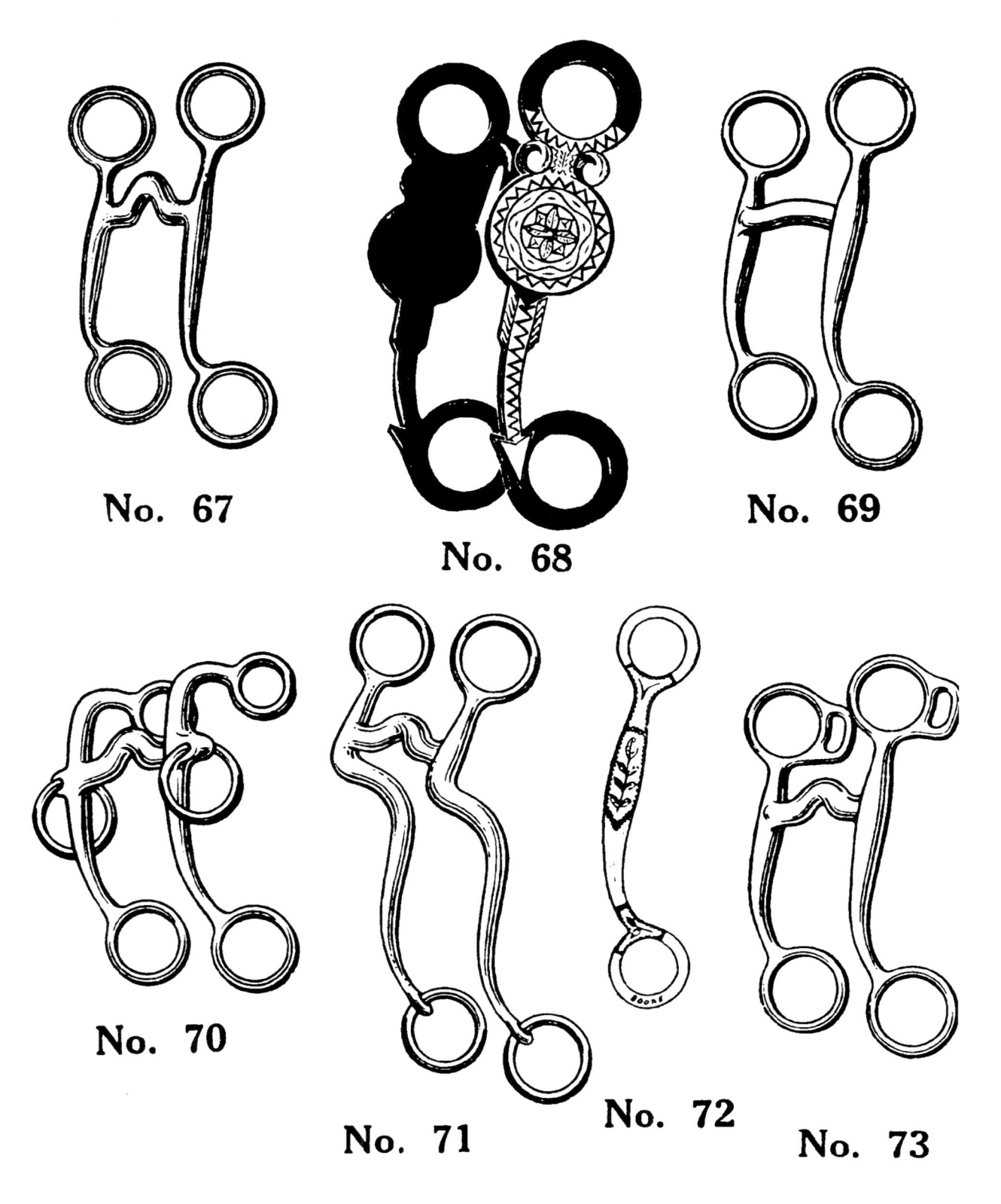

No. 68

No. 69

No. 70

No. 71

No. 72

No. 73

Bridle bits by Wallie Boone.

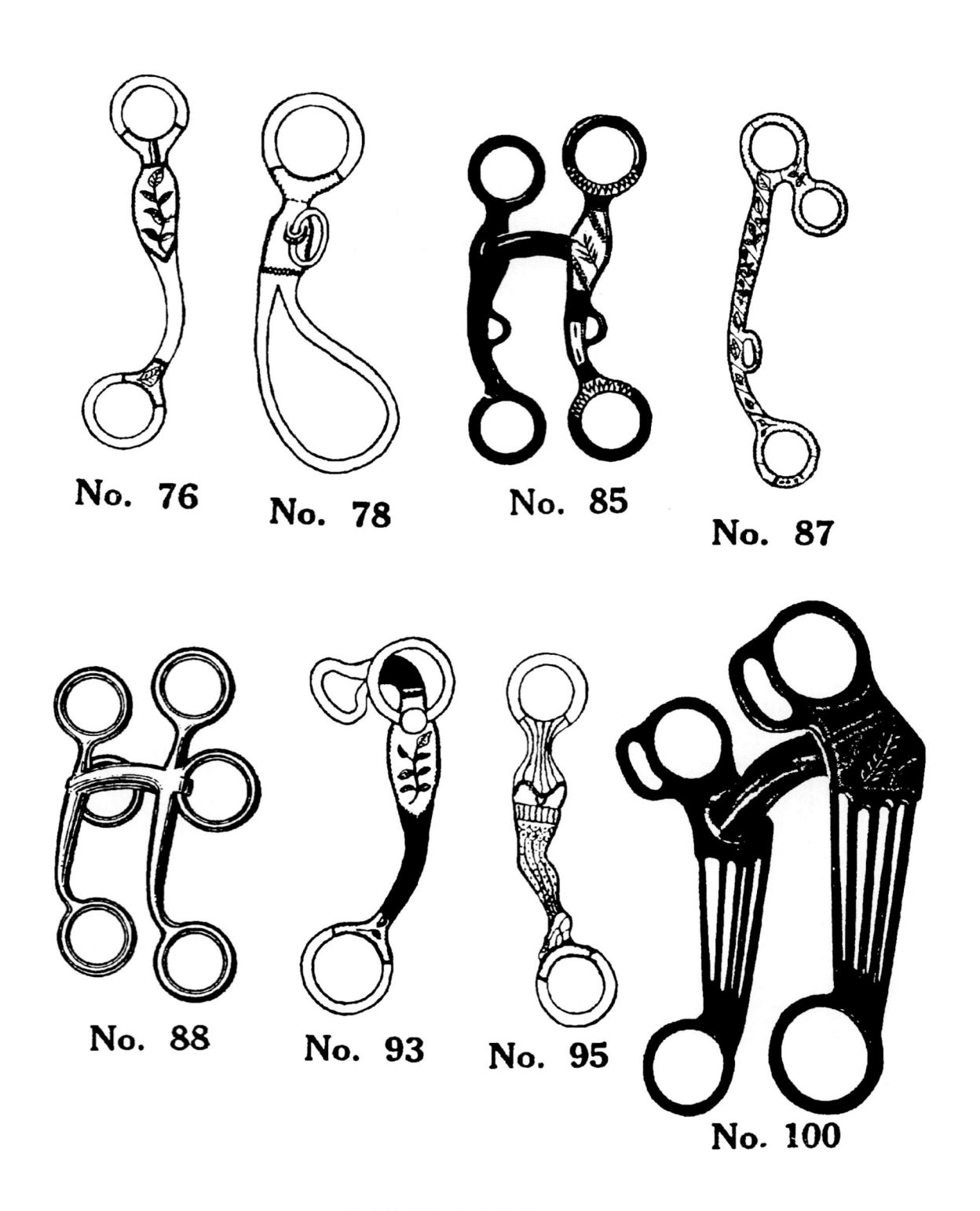

No. 76   No. 78   No. 85   No. 87

No. 88   No. 93   No. 95   No. 100

Bridle bits by Wallie Boone.

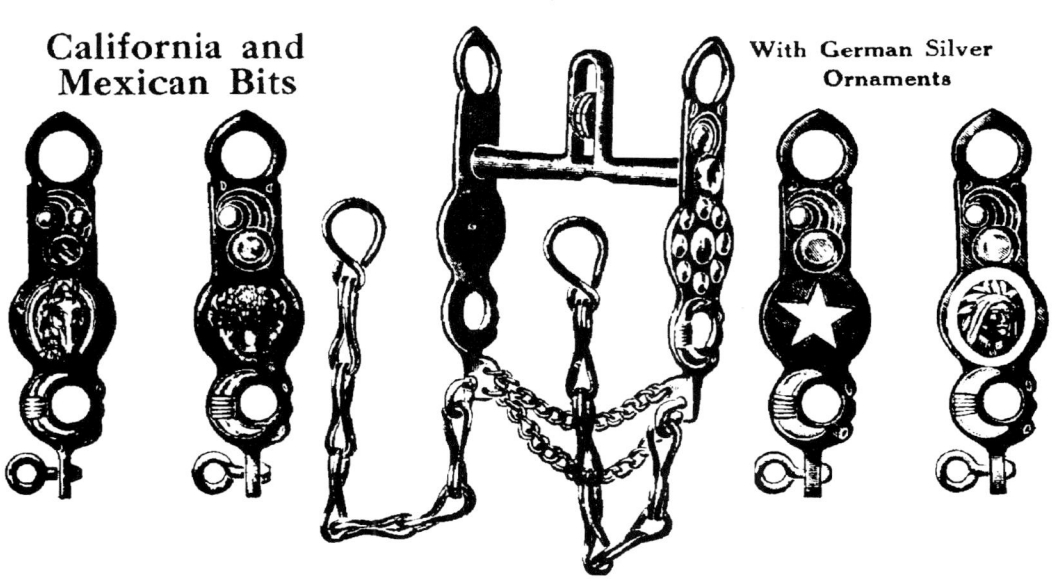

"Star 🟊 Brand"

California and Mexican Bits   **With German Silver Ornaments**

No. 1372
Horse Head

No. 1373
Buffalo Head

No. 1371—Spot
With Hercules Welded
Rein Chains

No. 1374
Star

No. 1378
"Indian Chief"

No. 1380
Horse Head

No. 1381
Buffalo Head

No. 1379—Spot
With Hercules Welded
Rein Chains

No. 1382
Star

No. 1383
"Indian Chief"

A series of five bits made by August Buermann Manufacturing Co. Matching spurs were produced along with the bits.

"Star ✯ Brand"

California and Mexican Bits — **With German Silver Ornaments**

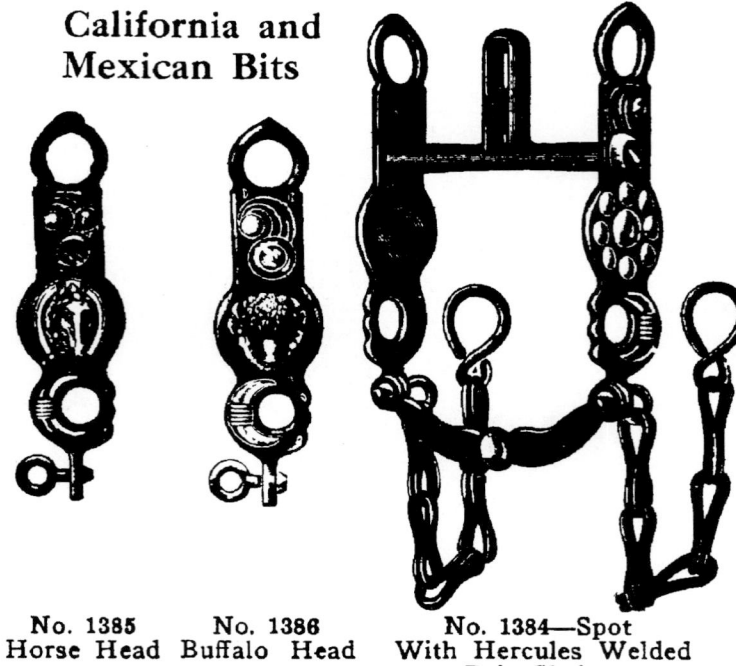

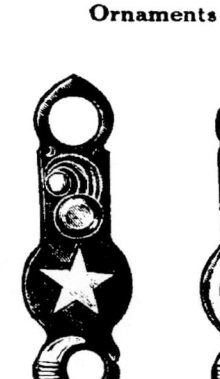

No. 1385	No. 1386	No. 1384—Spot	No. 1387	No. 1388
Horse Head	Buffalo Head	With Hercules Welded Rein Chains	Star	"Indian Chief"

No. 1390	No. 1391	No. 1389—Spot	No. 1392	No. 1393
Horse Head	Buffalo Head	With Hercules Welded Rein Chains	Star	"Indian Chief"

A set of five bits made by August Buermann Manufacturing Co. Spurs were made to match the bits.

Crockett

Oscar Crockett was born in Pecos, Texas, on November 27, 1887. He cowboyed in his youth until 1910. In that year he went with a trainload of cattle from Magdalena, N.M., to Kansas City, stayed and began working in a blacksmith shop.

It was natural for him to think of bits and spurs because in his boyhood he had watched with interest his older brother Authur make fine bits and spurs.

A relationship that needs to be clarified is that of Crockett-Shipley. When Oscar arrived in Kansas City in 1910, Shipley was impressively visible from the stockyards and had been in business for 25 years. Shipley occupied a significant amount of a large building and was a complete cowboy and ranch outfitter, a customary stopping place for cowboys arriving at the stockyards or for cattle and horse breeders attending the American Royal Stock Show. There was a buggy and wagon-making operation in the same building with Shipley. Whether this was a Shipley operation has not been verified. Oscar (from Catalogs No. 11 & 12) "made wagons during the day and worked on my own hook making bits and spurs at night."

Crockett soon encountered a party named Gliem with whom he shortly affiliated, and the two developed a small product line of C & G bits and spurs. At least a portion of their products were marked "CROCKETT & GLIEM" and "KAN CITY MO."

The Gliem connection lasted a year or two at the most because no mention is made of Gliem in the small pamphlet (circa 1915-16?) depicting the "C & G" line's five bit and ten spur designs. Rather, it is identified as "Catalogue No. 2, Oscar Crockett Bits and Spurs; 503 S.W. Boulevard, Kansas City, Mo." Nor is mention made of Gliem in mid-1916 in several news releases (fig. 36.3) showing a 'C & G' bit and spur featured in C. P. Shipley's announced entry into the bit and spur business. One issue dated July 1916 says of Shipley "They have just purchased the bit and spur business of G. A. Bischoff & Co. of Gainsville, Texas, and the machinery is being installed at this time." Further on it is stated, "Last April they purchased the plant of Oscar Crockett of Kansas City, and Mr. Crockett will have charge of this department of the business, which means that it will be a success."

Purchase of the Crockett plant presumably included the C & G line, and the C & G bits and spurs promptly appeared in Shipley's Catalog No. 16 (ca 1916) and still appeared as late as Catalog No. 35 (1935). Whether they were still producing the product or just continued to use the same picture is not known.

There is some speculation that Shipley also retained Bischoff. If so, since Bischoff was 25 years senior to Crockett, and a more refined blacksmith, Oscar became an apprentice. This probably did not last long because Oscar said in later catalogs (Nos. 11 & 12) that "soon I had enough money to open a small shop and I went to Pahuska, Okla. in 1916."

"In 1917 I went to Washington state to work for the Government and was there until November 11, 1918. Then I returned to Kansas City and in January, 1920, with my uncle, W. B. (Brice) Crockett, opened a shop there."

With Oscar's return to Kansas City it is presumed that he supervised the bit and spur operation of Shipley's until an opportunity to buy that department presented itself.

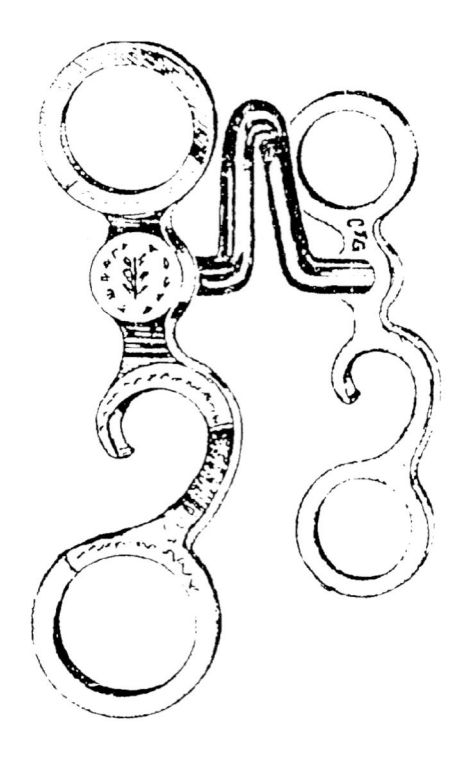

Bridle bit from a Chas. P. Shipley S. & M. Co. ad in *The Wild Bunch*, issued June, 1916, with the C & G stamp of Crockett & Gliem.

Jane Pattie in *Cowboy Spurs and Their Makers* (p.60) states that Oscar's uncle Brice financed the company. Ross Santee in *Lost Pony Tracks* (p. 57) said that "Bryce" made quite a reputation for himself in Kansas City making fancy bits and spurs. In Oscar's own words, "In 1927 I bought out my uncle, so now I am the Company." This was the same year that his older brother, Arthur Crockett, was killed in an automobile accident. The company address is given as 1525 Genesee Street in Kansas City, which would make it right next door to Shipley's (1527, 1529, 1531 Genesee). Old timers have told that Crockett's shop was across the street from Shipley's. Later dates from catalogs No. 7 (1926) through No. 11 puts the address at 1602 West 16th street, but catalog No. 12 has the company back at 1525 Genesee Street. It is doubtful that the business ever moved. He may have had a street entrance on 16th Street and used the 16th Street address to avoid confusion of people associating his business with Shipley's, which cornered on 17th and Genesee.

A catalog was produced for each year until No. 12 (1931) at which time it was becoming clear that the market crash of 1929 and the uncertainty of 1930 were not just temporary aberrations, and what was to become a depression was setting in for sure. This may have prompted the Crockett Saddle and Harness Co. that was started in 1931, maybe as competition for Shipley's leather. This also may have been one of Brice's ideas. Whatever the reason, the company was short lived, about one year. Prior to this he did not print net dealer prices; he printed list prices in the catalog and simply had a standard discount policy to dealers (25% off, postage prepaid, one free pair with every dozen ordered, additional 2% if paid in 10 days). He used Catalog No. 12 together with a supplement until 1938. A supplement "A" had aluminum colored designs worked into the pages and was used to introduce "airplane metal" bits and spurs.

Charles Shipley dabbled in bit and spur making at least twice (1916-1920 and in 1935) and maybe three times.

Shortly after Oscar's marriage to Hazel in 1932, the Crocketts bought a farm near Lenexa, Kansas, and soon moved the factory to the farm location the same year. Catalog No. 14 was produced in early 1942, and was the last to be issued from the Kansas location. There is no record of a catalog No. 13 having been produced.

Business trips to Colorado introduced the Crocketts to the eastern slope of the Rockies and on a visit to

Boulder, Colorado, they liked what they saw and within a few hours had leased a building. A short time later they moved their entire operation of plant, steel and some of the workers (10 of 18) to the Boulder location in less than two weeks and were in production by September 3, 1943. The number of employees increased from the ten or so from Lenexa, Kansas, to over 100 by the end of WW II.

Catalogs No. 16 and 17 were for 1946 and 1947 respectively after which the numbering scheme changed. Catalog No. 48 for 1948, 49 for 1949, etc.

Oscar Crockett died of a heart attack June 23, 1949, a vigorous 61 year-old who was the heart and soul of the company. The dynamo had stopped, and the company would never again be the same. His widow, Hazel, ran the business for over a year and in 1951 sold the business to James Renalde. The business continued to operate under the same name and at the same location until Renalde purchased the P. M. Kelly and Sons Company of El Paso, Texas, in 1965. At that time catalogs list the name as *Crockett and Kelly--Bits and Spurs by Renalde.* The Renalde family sold the business in 1977, to Henry Kugler who operated at the same Boulder location. In early 1980, it was sold again to the Horst family with addresses in Broomfield and Westminister, Colo., with a new name of Crockett & Kelly, Inc. A three digit number was used for catalogs: 181 for January, 1981, etc., with Catalog No. 184 the last issued. The last location was Erie, Colorado. The company discontinued the bit and spur operation in 1984, and a liquidation auction was held in January, 1985.

Several bits and spurs have surfaced with the "K & C" mark. Collectors are trying to call this a Kelly and Crockett union. I don't think this happened. The only possible time period they could have been in association with each other was during WW I. Oscar was in the Bremerton, WA, shipyards and P. M. Kelly worked for Bethlehem Steel in the Oakland, CA., shipyards. Wartime restraints on travel would have been a real problem, especially for a spurious (?) operation. I am sure that P. M. Kelly would have surely volunteered this information to Jane Pattie and Jack Thomas during their research.

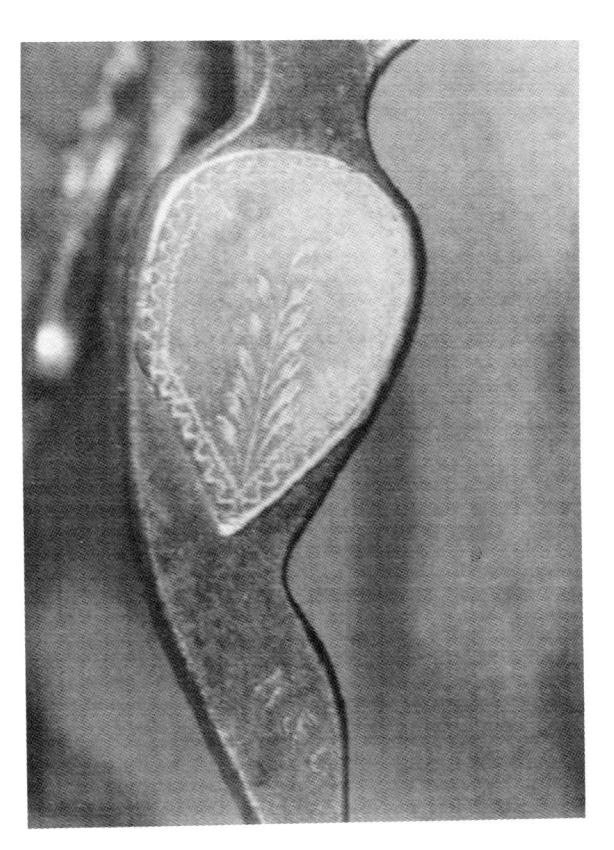

A bridle bit with the K & C mark. Courtesy Ned Martin, Nacasio, CA

CROCKETT BIT & SPUR CO., Lenexa, Kansas

Hand Forged Crockett BITS — Made from Regular TOOL STEEL or NON-RUST SILVER STEEL

No. 112 Bit 7¼" Cheeks **No. 23 Bit 7½" Cheeks** **No. 276 Bit 6½" Cheeks** **No. 120 Bit 6½" Cheeks**

No. 55 Bit 6" Cheeks **No. 128 Bit 7½" Cheeks** **No. 421 Bit 6¼" Cheeks**

No. 342 Bit 6¾" Cheeks **No. 126 Bit 6½" Cheeks** **No. 434 Bit 5½" Cheeks** **No. 418 Bit 7½" Cheeks**

CROCKETT BIT & SPUR CO., Lenexa, Kansas

Hand Forged Crockett BITS — *Made from Regular* TOOL STEEL *or* NON-RUST SILVER STEEL

No. 344 Bit
7½" Cheeks

No. 124 Bit
6" Cheeks No Coin

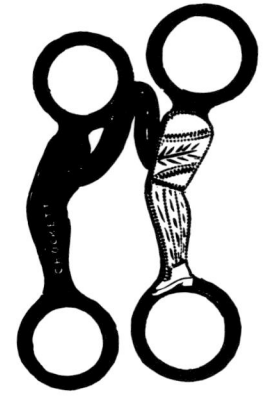

No. 108 Bit
6½" Cheeks

No. 270 Bit
7½" Cheeks

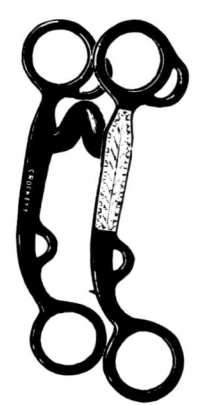

No. 447 Bit
7½" Cheeks

No. 451 Bit
6¾" Cheeks

No. 462 Bit
7¼" Cheeks

No. 282 Bit
7" Cheeks

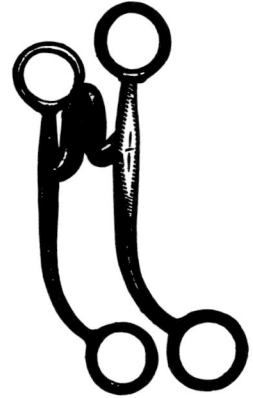

No. 280 Bit
7" Cheeks

No. 106 Bit
6" Cheeks

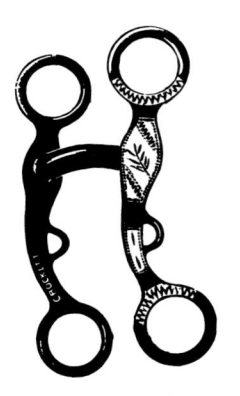

No. 140 Bit
6¼" Cheeks

No. 116 Bit
6¾" Cheeks

CROCKETT BIT & SPUR CO., Lenexa, Kansas

Hand Forged Crockett BITS
Made from Regular TOOL STEEL or NON-RUST SILVER STEEL

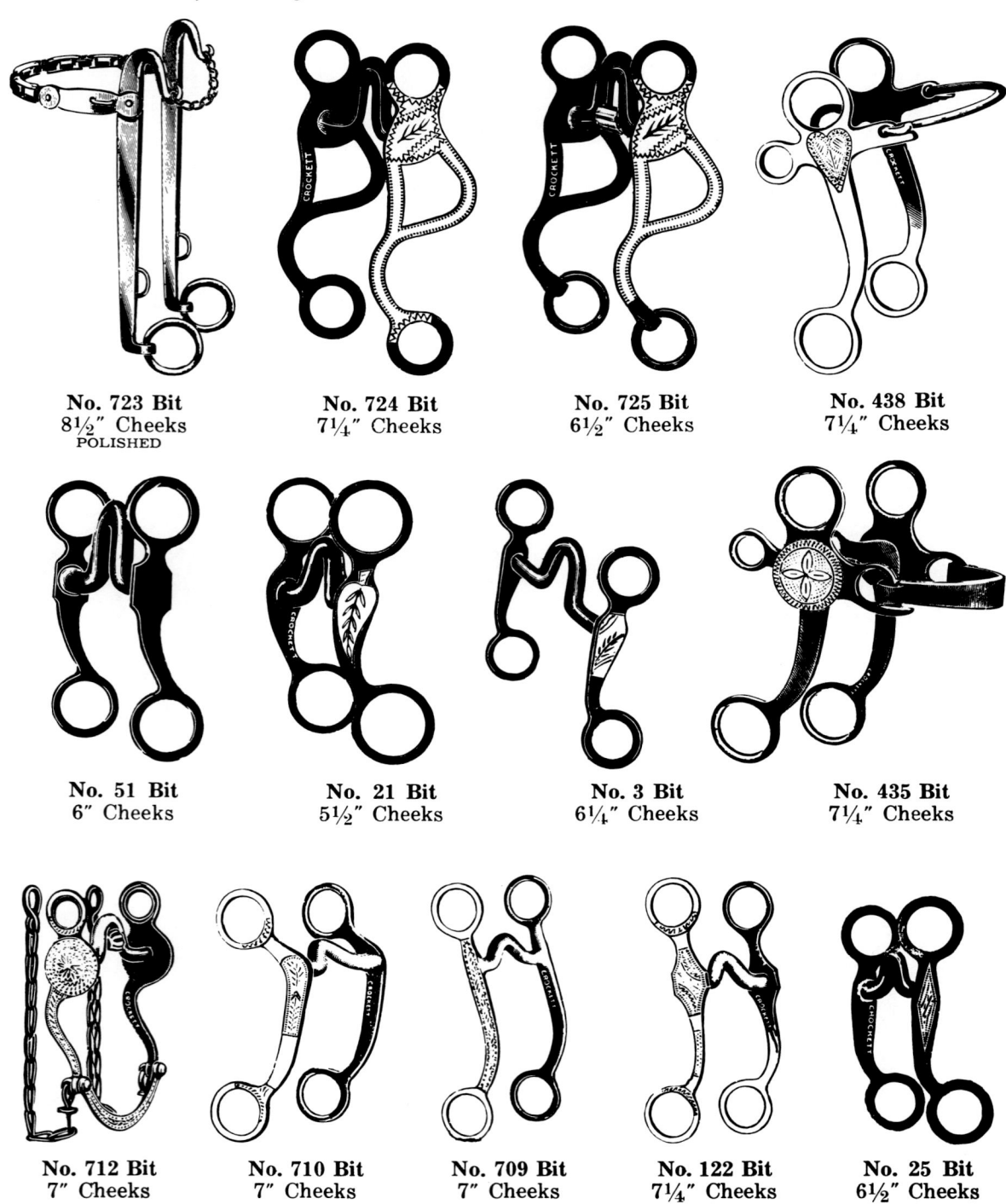

No. 723 Bit
8½" Cheeks
POLISHED

No. 724 Bit
7¼" Cheeks

No. 725 Bit
6½" Cheeks

No. 438 Bit
7¼" Cheeks

No. 51 Bit
6" Cheeks

No. 21 Bit
5½" Cheeks

No. 3 Bit
6¼" Cheeks

No. 435 Bit
7¼" Cheeks

No. 712 Bit
7" Cheeks

No. 710 Bit
7" Cheeks

No. 709 Bit
7" Cheeks

No. 122 Bit
7¼" Cheeks

No. 25 Bit
6½" Cheeks

- **Be Sure to Specify Silver Steel or Tool Steel When Ordering.**
  ALL MOUTHPIECES 5⅛" WIDE UNLESS OTHERWISE ORDERED

CROCKETT BIT & SPUR CO., Lenexa, Kansas

Hand Forged Crockett BITS — *Made from Regular TOOL STEEL or NON-RUST SILVER STEEL*

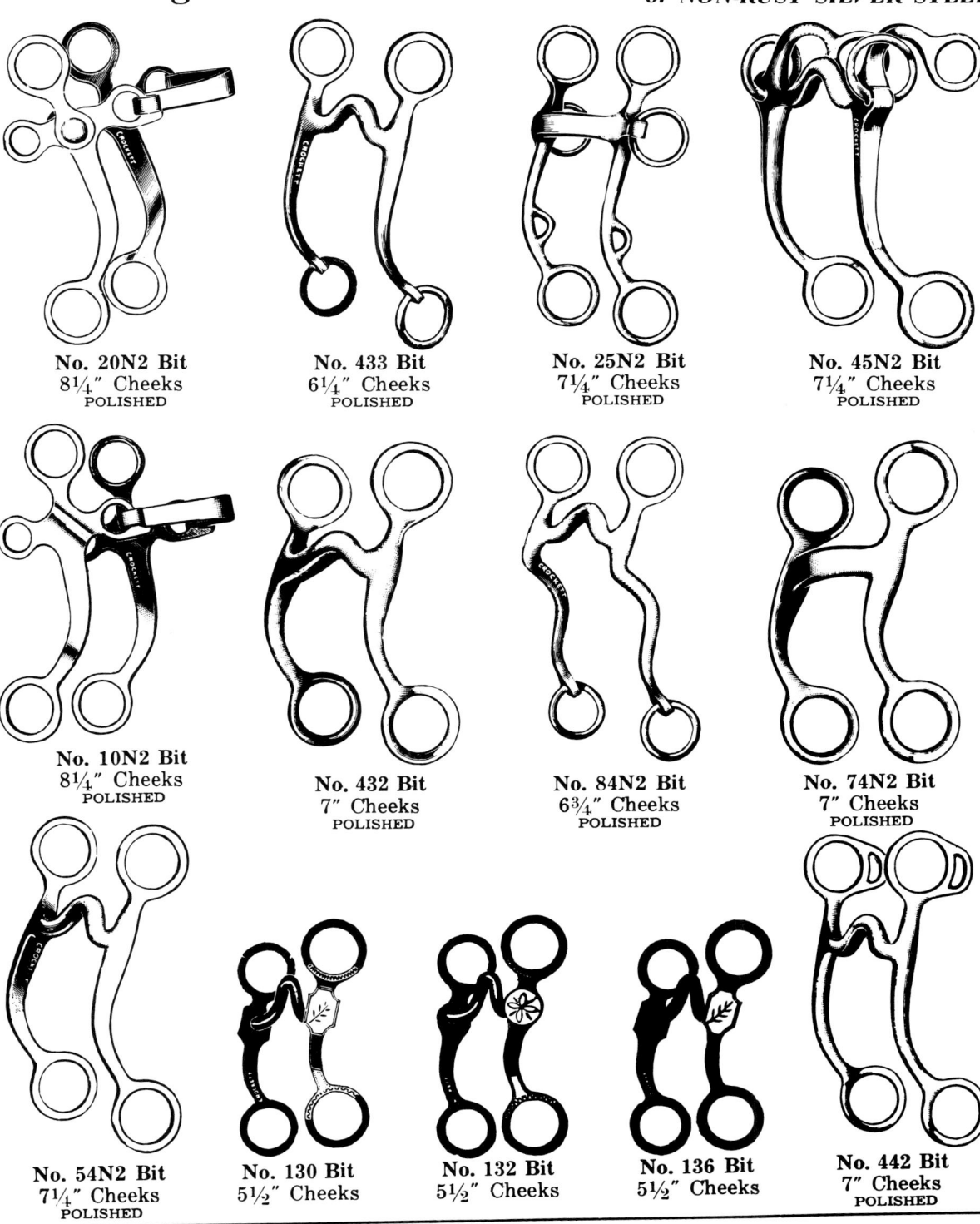

No. 20N2 Bit
8¼" Cheeks
POLISHED

No. 433 Bit
6¼" Cheeks
POLISHED

No. 25N2 Bit
7¼" Cheeks
POLISHED

No. 45N2 Bit
7¼" Cheeks
POLISHED

No. 10N2 Bit
8¼" Cheeks
POLISHED

No. 432 Bit
7" Cheeks
POLISHED

No. 84N2 Bit
6¾" Cheeks
POLISHED

No. 74N2 Bit
7" Cheeks
POLISHED

No. 54N2 Bit
7¼" Cheeks
POLISHED

No. 130 Bit
5½" Cheeks

No. 132 Bit
5½" Cheeks

No. 136 Bit
5½" Cheeks

No. 442 Bit
7" Cheeks
POLISHED

CROCKETT BIT & SPUR CO., Lenexa, Kansas

Hand Forged Crockett BITS
Made from Regular TOOL STEEL *or* NON-RUST SILVER STEEL

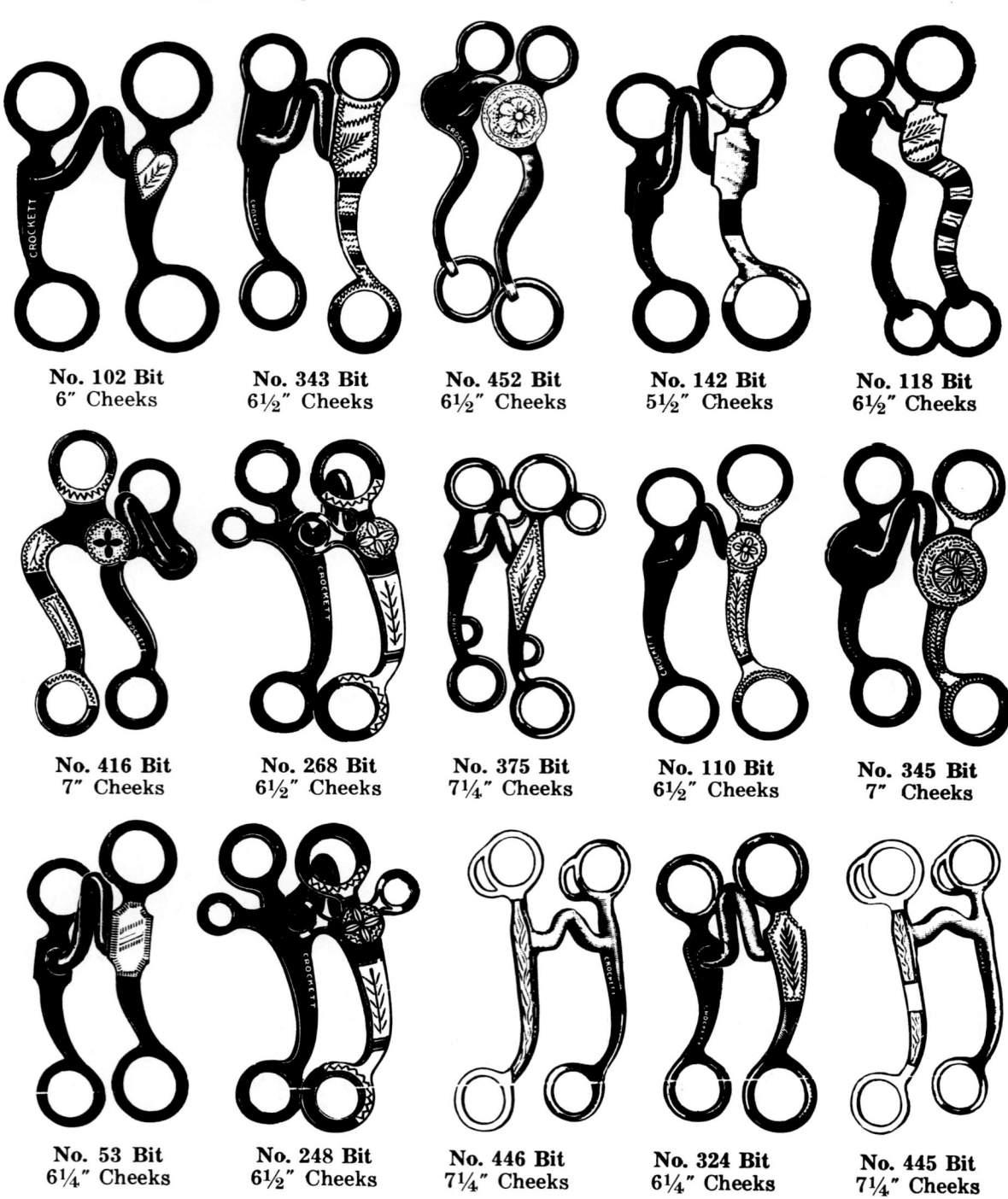

No. 102 Bit
6" Cheeks

No. 343 Bit
6½" Cheeks

No. 452 Bit
6½" Cheeks

No. 142 Bit
5½" Cheeks

No. 118 Bit
6½" Cheeks

No. 416 Bit
7" Cheeks

No. 268 Bit
6½" Cheeks

No. 375 Bit
7¼" Cheeks

No. 110 Bit
6½" Cheeks

No. 345 Bit
7" Cheeks

No. 53 Bit
6¼" Cheeks

No. 248 Bit
6½" Cheeks

No. 446 Bit
7¼" Cheeks

No. 324 Bit
6¼" Cheeks

No. 445 Bit
7¼" Cheeks

CROCKETT BIT & SPUR CO., Lenexa, Kansas

Hand Forged Crockett BITS — *Made from Regular TOOL STEEL or NON-RUST SILVER STEEL*

No. 346 Bit 7" Cheeks	**No. 410 Bit** 6½" Cheeks	**No. 459 Bit** 6¾" Cheeks	**No. 75 Bit** 7" Cheeks
No. 708 Bit 7¼" Cheeks	**No. 246 Bit** 7½" Cheeks	**No. 422 Bit** 7" Cheeks	**No. 392 Bit** 7" Cheeks
No. 420 Bit 7" Cheeks	**No. 244 Bit** 6½" Cheeks	**No. 250 Bit** 7" Cheeks	**No. 460 Bit** 6½" Cheeks

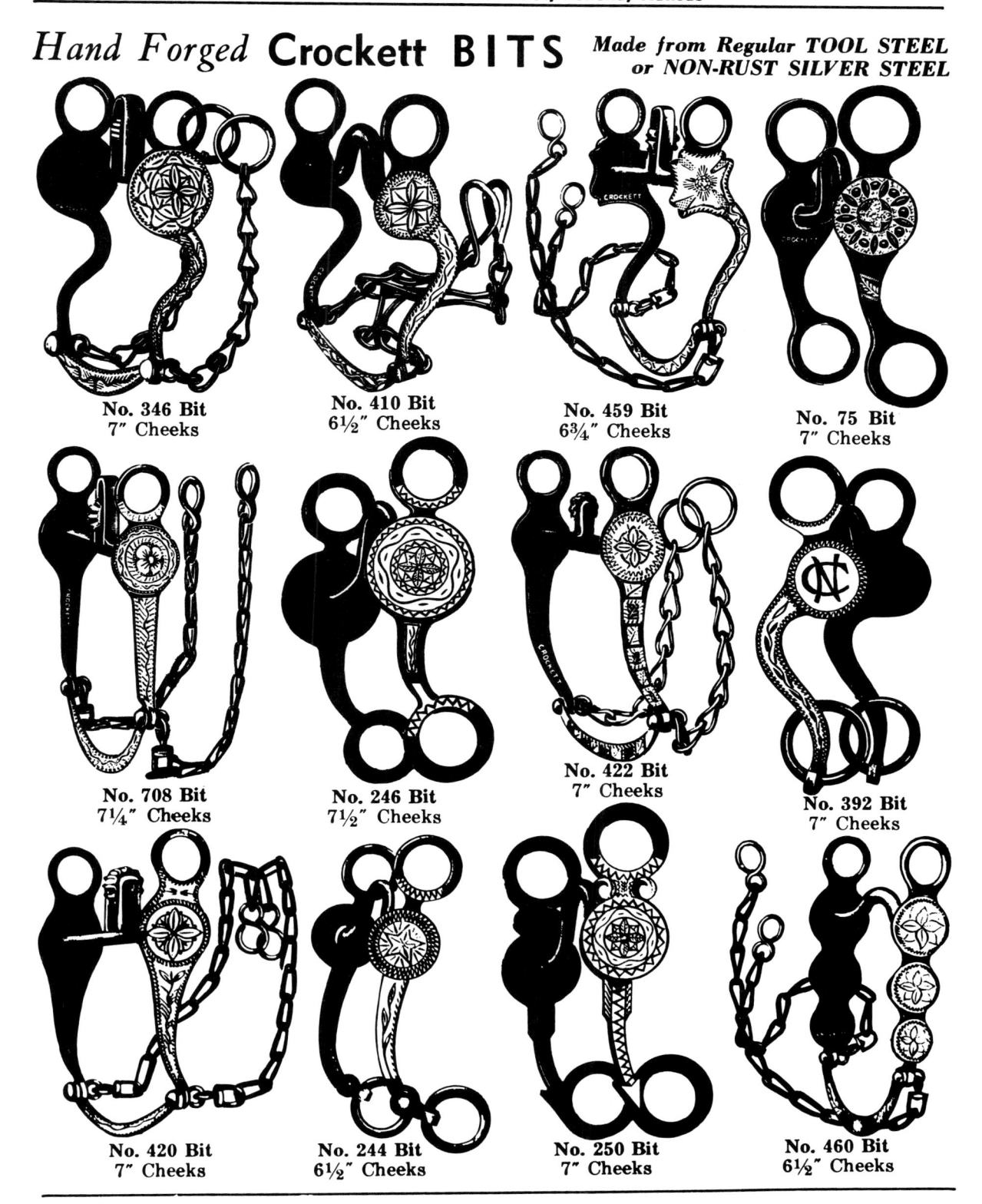

Flat & Round Cheek Bits

119-SS: Cutting Horse Bit With 8-1/4" Round Cheeks and 5LP Mouthpiece
I.C. 40-069

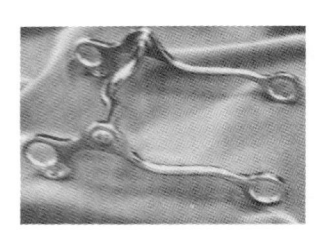

707-SS: Curb style with 8" Flat Cheeks and 7MP Mouthpiece
I.C. 40-105

721-MTD-SS: Loose Ring Cutting Horse Bit with 6-1/2" Round Cheeks and 5LP Mouthpiece
I.C. 40-120

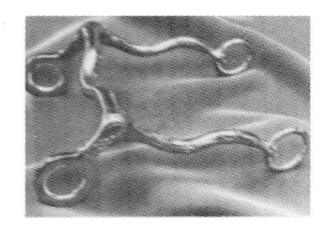

733-SS: Round Cheeks with 4MP Mouthpiece
I.C. 40-165 9" Cheeks
I.C. 40-180 6-1/2" Cheeks

749-ENG-AL: 8-3/4" Flat Cheeks and 5LP CPR Port.
I.C. 40-220

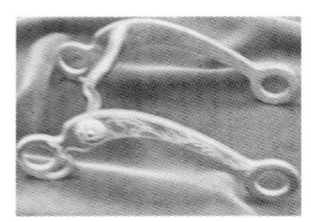

1051-ENG-AL: 8" Flat Cheeks and 6MUL CPR Port.
I.C. 40-295

1015-ENG-AL: Same as above with 5LP CPR Port.
I.C. 40-270

1258-SS: Roper with 8-1/2" Round Cheeks and 4MP Mouthpiece
I.C. 40-415

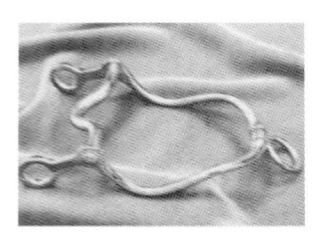

2260-SS: 9" Round Cheeks and CB Mouthpiece. Gentle but controllable
I.C. 40-630

2262-SS: 9-3/4" Round Cheeks and 10CS Mouthpiece. Tom Ferguson roper.
I.C. 40-640

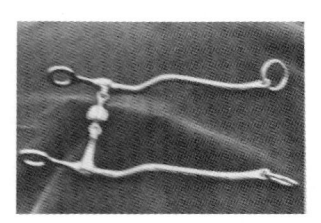

Loose Jawed Bits & Snaffles

50-CPR-SS: 9" Flat Cheeks 11 HP Mouthpiece
I.C. 40-010

50-CPR-SS: 9" Flat Cheeks 5LP Mouthpiece
I.C. 40-005

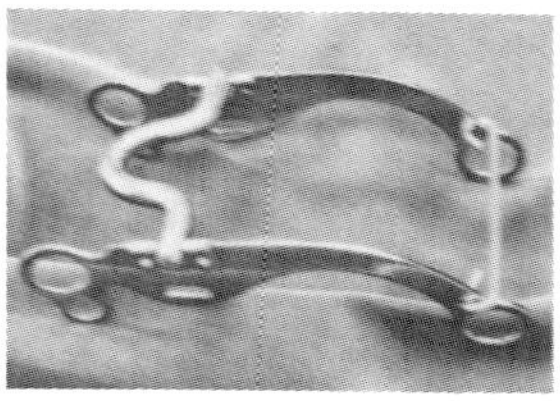

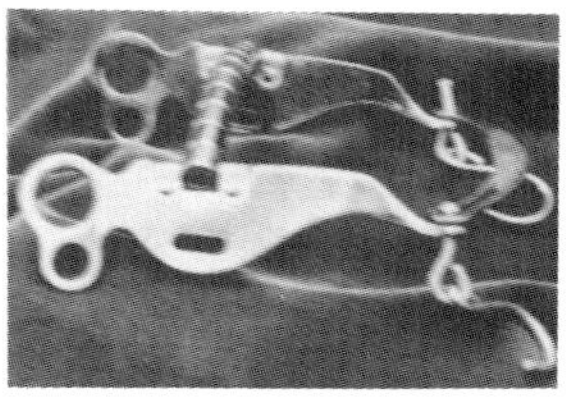

745-CPS: 2-1/2" Ring Cheek 12S Mouthpiece
I.C. 40-205

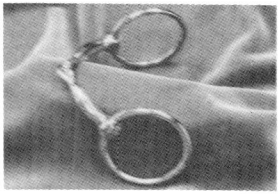

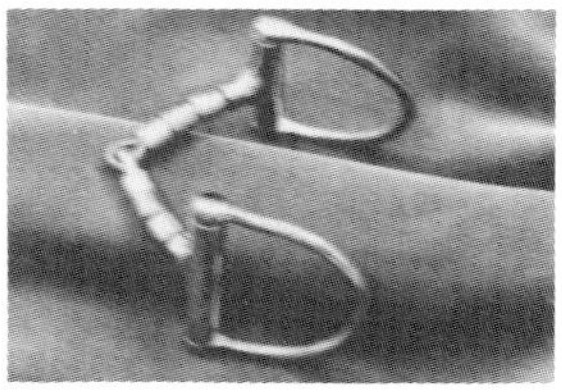

762-SS: 9" Round Cheek 10S Mouthpiece 2 or 4 Rein Use
I.C. 40-245

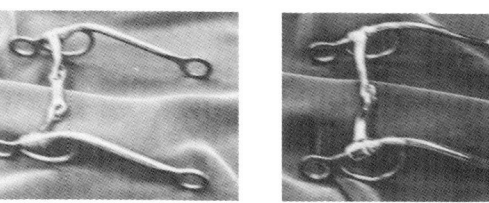

1274-SS: 3" Dee 12S Mouthpiece — Gag
I.C. 40-445

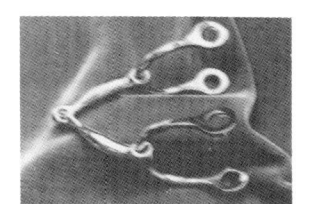

62-SS: 7" Flat Cheeks 9RP Mouthpiece, 2 or 4 Rein Use
I.C. 40-020

123-SS: 3" Dee Cheek 9RP Mouthpiece
I.C. 40-075

1241-SS: 9" Round Cheeks 12S Mouthpiece — Dual Rein
I.C. 40-350

1241-SS: 7-1/2" Round Cheeks 12S Mouthpiece — Dual Rein
I.C. 40-351

1285-SS: 6" Round Cheeks 12S Mouthpiece — Tom Thumb
I.C. 40-450

1297-CM-SS: 6" Round Cheeks 12S Mouthpiece — CPR Tom Thumb
I.C. 40-490

Mouthpieces

No. 1. Spade with Copper Winding & Brass Roller
I.C. 45-030

No. 2S. Pony Snaffle — Available in SS only
I.C. 45-031

*No. 3MP. Crickett Port
I.C. 45-035; CPS
IC. 45-040; SS
I.C. 45-045 CPR

*No. 4MP. Medium Port
I.C. 45-050; CPS
I.C. 45-055; SS
I.C. 45-060; CPR

*No. 5LP. Low Port
I.C. 45-070; CPS
I.C. 45-075; SS
I.C. 45-080; CPR

*No. 6MUL. Mullen Port
I.C. 45-090; CPS
I.C. 45-095; SS
I.C. 45-100; CPR

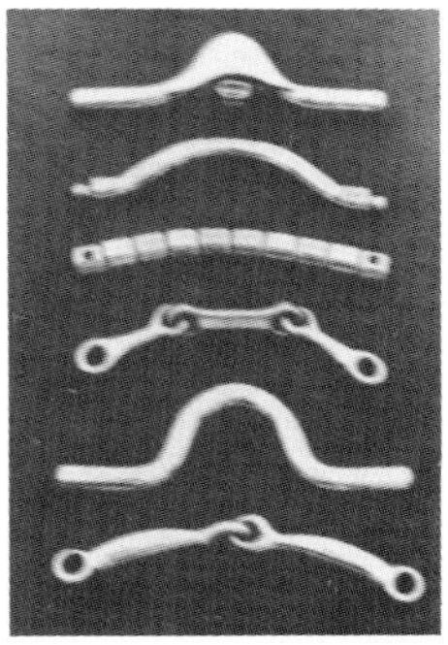

*No. 7MP. Copper Covered Crickett Port Available in SS only
I.C. 45-110

No. 8SW Sweetwater Port
I.C. 45-115; CPS
I.C. 45-120; SS
I.C. 45-125; CPR

No. 9RP. Roller Port — SS & Copper Rollers
I.C. 45-135

No. 10S. 3-Piece Snaffle with Copper Center Piece
I.C. 45-175

*No. 11HP. High Port
I.C. 45-140; CPS
I.C. 45-145; SS
I.C. 45-150; CPR

No. 12S. 2-Piece Snaffle
I.C. 45-160; CPS
I.C. 45-165; SS
I.C. 45-170; CPR

*Mouthpieces for 1293 Hackamores

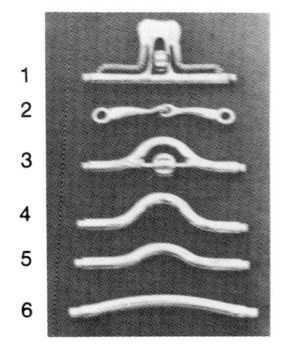

Please advise if mouthpiece is to fit Flat, Round, Loose Jawed or 1293 Hackamore.

Daniels

For a century commencing in the late 1700's, the English Daniel's Bit enjoyed the highest reputation for quality in the bridle bit market. A genuine bit stamped "Daniels" guaranteed the buyer a bit of hand-forged steel.

A bit made of "soft steel" or fine wrought iron was superior to any other that could be made. Thomas Daniel (founder of the bit business) stamped his name "Daniel" on all the first quality forged steel bits he made during the forty years he was in the business. The term "Daniel Bit" did not refer to a particular shape or pattern of bit. Thomas Daniel stamped his name on any kind or pattern of bit crafted by his company which was of finest quality forged steel. The "Daniel" stamp guaranteed the bit to be a forged steel bit.

The bits were not made under Daniel's supervision, but were forged in the shops of bit-makers in various parts of England and were stamped "Daniel" if they met the quality requirements. These bit-makers had learned the trade from their fathers, who had learned from their fathers, and so-on for generations back. Little machinery was used. The head of the family forged the bits and younger family members filed and finished the bits by hand, giving a clear polish and the process remained unchanged or upgraded for generations. The stamp "Daniel" was patented as a trade-mark, but a 6-sided star with a "D" in its center placed between the words "trade" and "mark" was an earlier trademark registered in Great Britain.

A horseman's safety often depended upon the bit. It was natural that he would purchase what he believed to be the bit of highest quality--the imported English "Daniel Bit." In America, it was sometimes assumed that an imported, stamped bit would be superior to the emerging American bits. The American bits were of forged steel, but often were made by one man with a machine, who turned out two or more to one of the English bit-maker. The American bits were of excellent quality--at least equal to the quality of the "Daniel Bit." But the horsemen clung to the idea that the stamped "Daniel Bit" was superior and would not purchase the American product and the American manufacturers were unable to compete. In order to sell bits they knew to be equal or superior to the imported bits, manufacturers began to stamp "Daniel" on their bits, thereby making them marketable to the public. It was estimated that in 1872, at least 1/2 of the bits stamped "Daniel" were imposters although of excellent quality. The stamp "Daniel" at this time in America became an indicator purely of quality and not of origin.

With the registraion of "Daniel" as an official trade mark, the rapid spread of America's reputation as bit makers, and the cost-effectiveness of the American bits, caused foreign-produced bits to be crowded out of the top of the market. The company of Jos. Baldwin and Company of Newark, NJ, was largely responsible for this consumer turn-around when it began its stamp of guarantee on superior quality articles. Many horsemen began to look to them as the "Daniel" of America.

DANIEL'S ALL FORGED GENUINE STEEL BITS
Of which we keep a full line

No. F. Ashleigh No. 18 Liverpool

Public Test of "Daniel" Bits, Oct. 10, 1896 (Lloyd's Proving House, Tipton, Staffs, England). Tested the way of the pull when in use.

- Ashleigh, 21 oz. weight, broke at 5100 lbs.
- Liverpool Bit, 24¾ oz. weight, broke at 5905 lbs.
- Dexter Snaffle, 15 oz. weight, broke at 3550 lbs.
- Half Cheek " 10 oz. weight, broke at 3500 lbs.

TRADE **D** MARK

VEIL BROTHERS
Importers of

Fine Saddlery and Saddlery Hardware

116 Chambers Street : New York

LARGE ASSORTMENT OF ENGLISH AND AMERICAN HOGSKINS FOR ALL PURPOSES

English Patent Winker, Skirting, Russet Rein and Bridle Leather
English Riding Saddles, Bridles, Halters, Rollers, Bits, Stirrups, etc.
English Patent Leather Coupe and Hansom Cab Saddles, latest style
Schomberg and Other Celebrated Makes of English Holly Whips, Crops, Riding, Jockey Whips and Whip Thongs
Currie's Waterproof Driving Coats
English Dandy, Water, Compo and all other kinds of Brushes
Dumb Jockies, Bandages, Webs and Saddle Serges

Sole Agents for North America for the renowned "**Eglentine**" Bits, Stirrups, etc., the *FINEST* and *STRONGEST* steel colored metal that will never rust or change color regardless of climate. At wholesale only.

They are UNRIVALED for strength, beauty of style, and neatness of finish, and are guaranteed.

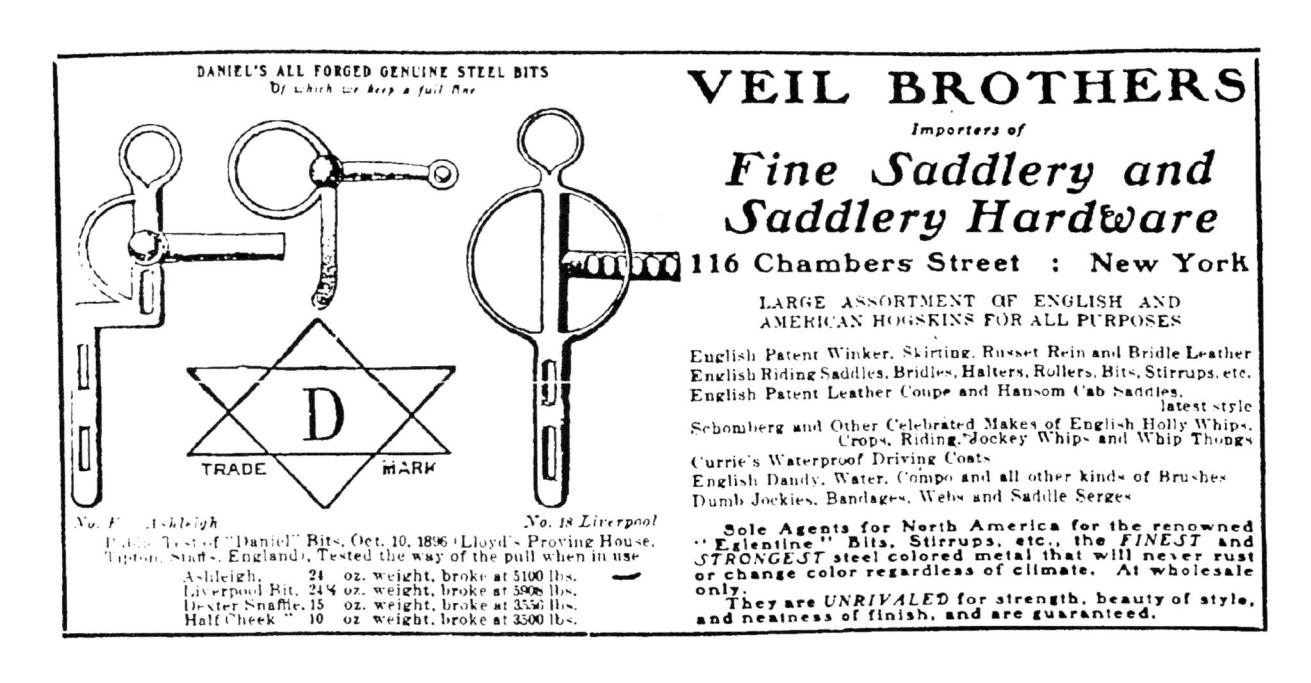

Daniels Liverpool bit and a curb bit with a cross on each cheek-piece.

Eldonian

STAINLESS STEEL
WEYMOUTHS AND PELHAMS

Code	Description						
E3.0601	Weymouth Bit, Cambridge mouth.						
		4 x 4	4 x 4½	4½ x 4	4½ x 4½	4½ x 5	5 x 4
		5 x 4½	5 x 5	5 x 5½	5½ x 4	5½ x 5	5½ x 5½
		5½ x 6	6 x 4	6 x 5½			
E3.0602	Weymouth Bit, mullen mouth.			4 x 4	4½ x 4½	5 x 5	5½ x 5½
E3.0610	Portsmouth Show Bit.			4½ x 7	4¾ x 7	5 x 7	
				4½ x 8	4¾ x 8	5 x 8	
E3.0613	Military Reversible Bit, port mouth.			5	5½	6	
E3.0617	Buxton Coaching Bit.			5	5½	6	
E3.0619	Fixed Cheek Weymouth, Cambridge mouth.			4½ x 5	5 x 5	5 x 5½	5½ x 5½
E3.0620	Spanish Jumping Bit, Cambridge mouth.						
		4½	4¾	5	5¼	5½	6
E3.0621	Dressage Weymouth, thick hollow mouth. Fitted with double curb as standard. (use with E3.0519 Bradoon).			5	5½		
E3.0622	Portsmouth Show Bit with open jointed cheeks.			4½ x 7	4¾ x 7	5 x 7	
				4½ x 7½	4¾ x 7½	5 x 7½	
				4½ x 8	4¾ x 8	5 x 8	
E3.0622/MM	Mullen Mouth Show Bit with open jointed cheeks.			4½ x 7	4¾ x 7	5 x 7	
				4½ x 7½	4¾ x 7½	5 x 7½	
				4½ x 8	4¾ x 8	5 x 8	
E3.0629	Loose Ring Show Bit with open jointed cheeks.			5 x 7			
E3.0630	Spanish Jumping Bit, jointed mouth.			4½	5	5½	6
E3.0678	Arch Mouth Weymouth.			4½ x 5	5 x 5	5 x 5½	5½ x 5½
E3.0700	Pelham Bit, T. O. S. bar mouth.			4½ x 4½	5 x 5	5½ x 5½	
E3.0701	Pelham Bit, Cambridge mouth.		4 x 4	4½ x 4	4½ x 4½	5 x 5	5½ x 5½
E3.0702	Pelham Bit, mullen mouth.	4 x 4	4½ x 4	4½ x 4½	4½ x 5	5 x 4½	
		5 x 5	5 x 5½	5¼ x 5½	5½ x 5	5½ x 5½	5½ x 6
E3.0703	Pelham Bit, nylon mullen mouth.			4½ x 4½	4½ x 5	5 x 4½	5 x 5
				5 x 5½	5½ x 5½	6 x 5½	
E3.0707	Pelham Bit, rubber mullen mouth.						
		4½ x 4½	4½ x 5	5 x 4½	5 x 5	5 x 5½	5½ x 5½
E3.0710	Pelham Bit, plain jointed mouth.			4½ x 4½	5 x 4½	5½ x 5	6 x 5½
E3.0713	Globe Cheek showing Bit, port mouth.			4½ x 4½	4¾ x 4½		
E3.0716	Globe Cheek showing Bit, mullen mouth.			4½ x 4½	5 x 4½		
E3.0723	U.S.A. Police Bit.			4½	5	5½	
E3.0724/T	Liverpool Bit, turn cheeks, T. O. S. bar mouth.			4½ x 6	5 x 6½		
E3.0726	Single Curb Chains.						
E3.0727	Double Curb Chains.						
E3.0728	Curb Hooks.						

WEYMOUTHS AND PELHAMS

E3.0601
E3.0602
E3.0610
E3.0613
E3.0617
E3.0619
E3.0620
E3.0621
E3.0622
E3.0629
E3.0630
E3.0678
E3.0700
E3.0701
E3.0702
E3.0703
E3.0707
E3.0710
E3.0713
E3.0716
E3.0723
E3.0724/T

Eldonian

STAINLESS STEEL

CHECK BITS

Code	Description	Size			
E3.0578	Lightweight walking horse gag, plain jointed mouth.	5 x 1			
E3.0579	Lightweight walking horse gag, twisted joint mouth.	5 x 1			
E3.0580	Mullen mouth check bit.	5 x 1			
E3.0581	Plain jointed check bit.	5 x 1			
E3.0582	Twisted jointed check bit.	5 x 1			
E3.0583	Critt Davis check bit.	5			
E3.0584	Speedway check bit.	5			
E3.0585	Crabb check bit.	5			
E3.0586	Burch check bit.	5			
E3.0587	Hutton check bit.	5			
E3.0588	Crabb check bit, with spoon.	5			

NYLON AND RUBBER BITS

Code	Description	Sizes					
E3.0508	Rubber Bradoon, mullen mouth, wire rings.	4½ x 3	5 x 3	5½ x 3	6 x 3½		
E3.0514	Nylon Bradoon, mullen mouth, wire rings.	4½ x 3	5 x 3	5½ x 3	6 x 3½		
E3.0516	Nylon Eggbutt Bradoon, mullen mouth, flat rings.	4½ x 2¾	5 x 3	5½ x 3¼			
E3.0522	Lightweight Nylon Eggbutt Bradoon, mullen mouth, flat rings.	4	4½	5	5½		
E3.0544	Lightweight Nylon 'D' cheek Bradoon, Mullen mouth.	4½	5				
E3.0680	Nylon Mouth Stallion Bradoon, bar mouth, 1½ wire rings.	3¾	4	4¼	4½	4¾	5
E3.0680/MM	Nylon Mouth Stallion Bradoon, mullen mouth, 1½ wire rings.	3¾	4	4¼	4½	4¾	5

TWISTED WIRE BITS
Solid Nickel Mouth

Code	Description	Sizes	
E3.0685	Single twisted wire mouth bit, jointed mouth, 1¾ wire rings.	4½	5
E3.0686	Double twisted wire mouth bit, jointed mouth, 1¾ wire rings.		5
E3.0693	Double twisted wire mouth bit, jointed mouth, ball cheeks.		5

Eldonian

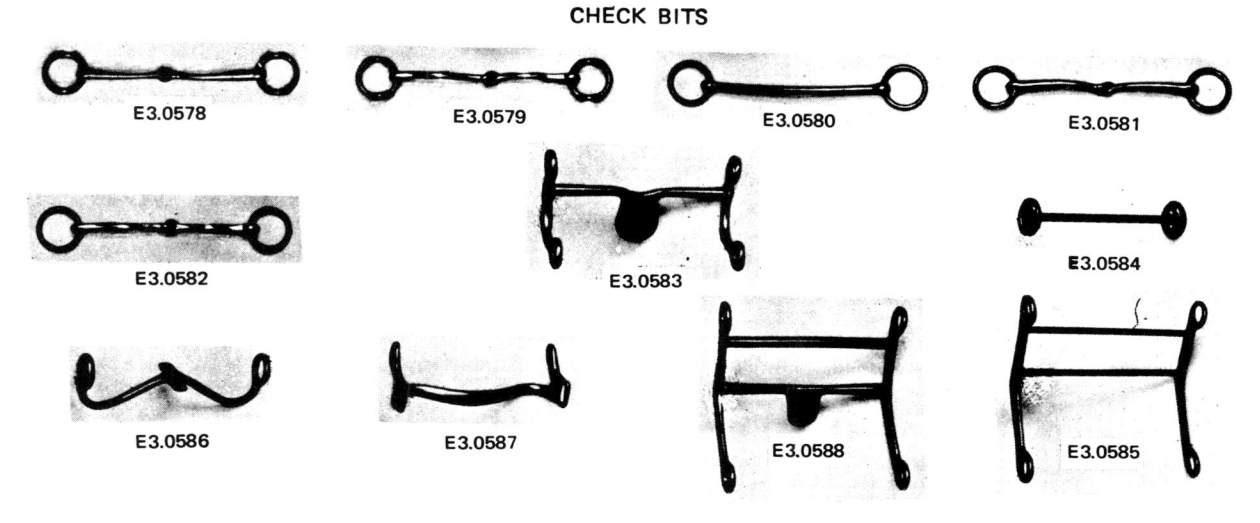

CHECK BITS

E3.0578
E3.0579
E3.0580
E3.0581
E3.0582
E3.0583
E3.0584
E3.0586
E3.0587
E3.0588
E3.0585

NYLON AND RUBBER BITS

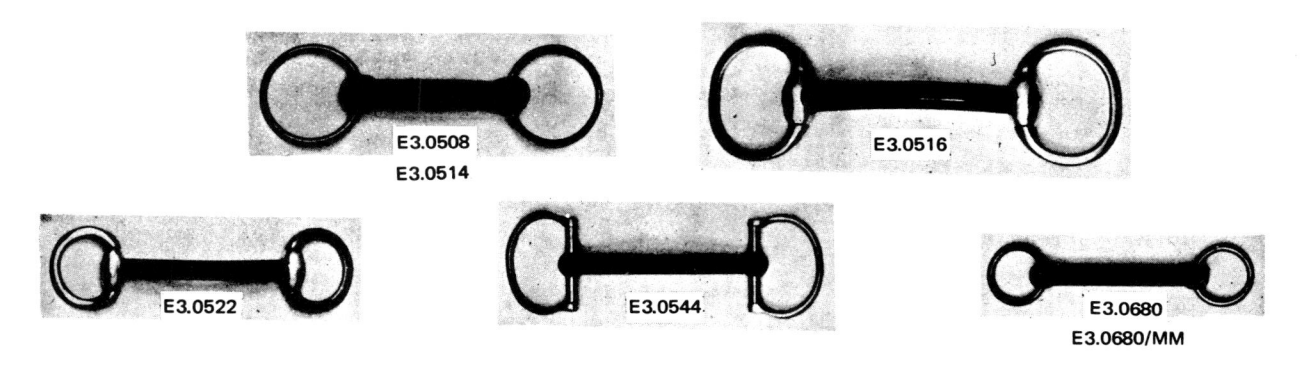

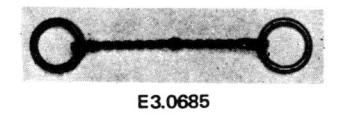

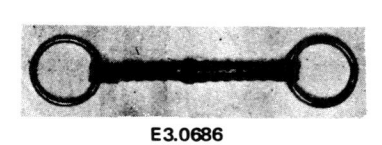

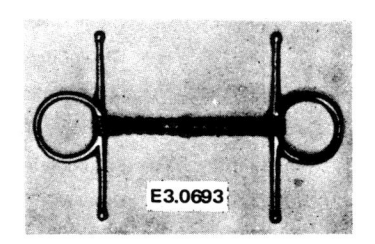

E3.0508
E3.0514
E3.0516
E3.0522
E3.0544
E3.0680
E3.0680/MM

TWISTED WIRE BITS

E3.0685
E3.0686
E3.0693

Eldonian

STAINLESS STEEL
RACE DRIVING AND LEADING BITS

Code	Description	Sizes				
E3.0523	Race Bradoon, Alum/Steel, wire rings.	6 x 3½				
E3.0524	Race Bradoon, 'D' cheek.	4½	4¾	5	5½	6
E3.0527/R	Race Bradoon, plain jointed mouth, wire rings.	6 x 3½				
E3.0527/C	Chase Bradoon, plain jointed mouth, wire rings.	6 x 3½				
E3.0528	Race Bradoon, tapered jointed mouth, wire rings.	5 x 3	5½ x 3¼	6 x 3½		
E3.0529	Race Bradoon, Alum/Steel, 'D' cheek.	4¾	5	5½	6	
E3.0536	Race Bradoon, American 'D' cheek.	4½	4¾	5		
E3.0538	Colt Lead Bit	4.3/8 inside widest part				
E3.0539	Stallion Bit, mullen mouth, horseshoe cheeks. 3¾	4	4½	4¾	5	5½
E3.0539/H	Metropolitan Bit, mullen mouth, horseshoe cheeks.	4½	5	5½		
E3.0543	American Half-spoon Driving Bit.	4¾	5			
E3.0546	Anti-rearing Bit.	4¾ inside widest part				
E3.0552	Dexter Ring Bit.	4¾				
E3.0553	Improved Norton Bit.	4¾				
E3.0557	6-ring Bit.	4¾				
E3.0559	Bar Mouth Breaking Bit with players.	4½ x 2	5 x 2	5½ x 2½		
E3.0560	Ball Cheek Breaking Bit with players.	5	5½	6		
E3.0561	New Zealand style, Full spoon Snaffle.	5¼ x 5				
E3.0562	New Zealand style, Half spoon Snaffle.	5¼ x 3½				
E3.0565	Dr. Bristol Eggbutt Snaffle.	4½	4¾	5		
E3.0566	Dr. Bristol 'D' Cheek Bit.	4½	4¾	5		
E3.0567	Cycle Chain Bit with wire rings.	5 x 1½				
E3.0570	French Bradoon with wire rings.	5 x 2½	5½ x 2½	6 x 2½		
E3.0571	French Snaffle with ball cheek.	5	5½	6		
E3.0574	French Bradoon with eggbutt rings.	5½ x 3	6 x 3			
E3.0591	Dr. Williamson Bradoon.	5	5¾			
E3.0624	Magenis Snaffle.	6 x 3¼				
E3.0625	Tattersall ring bit, with players.	4.3/8 inside widest part				
E3.0626	Tattersall ring bit, no players.	4.3/8 inside widest part				

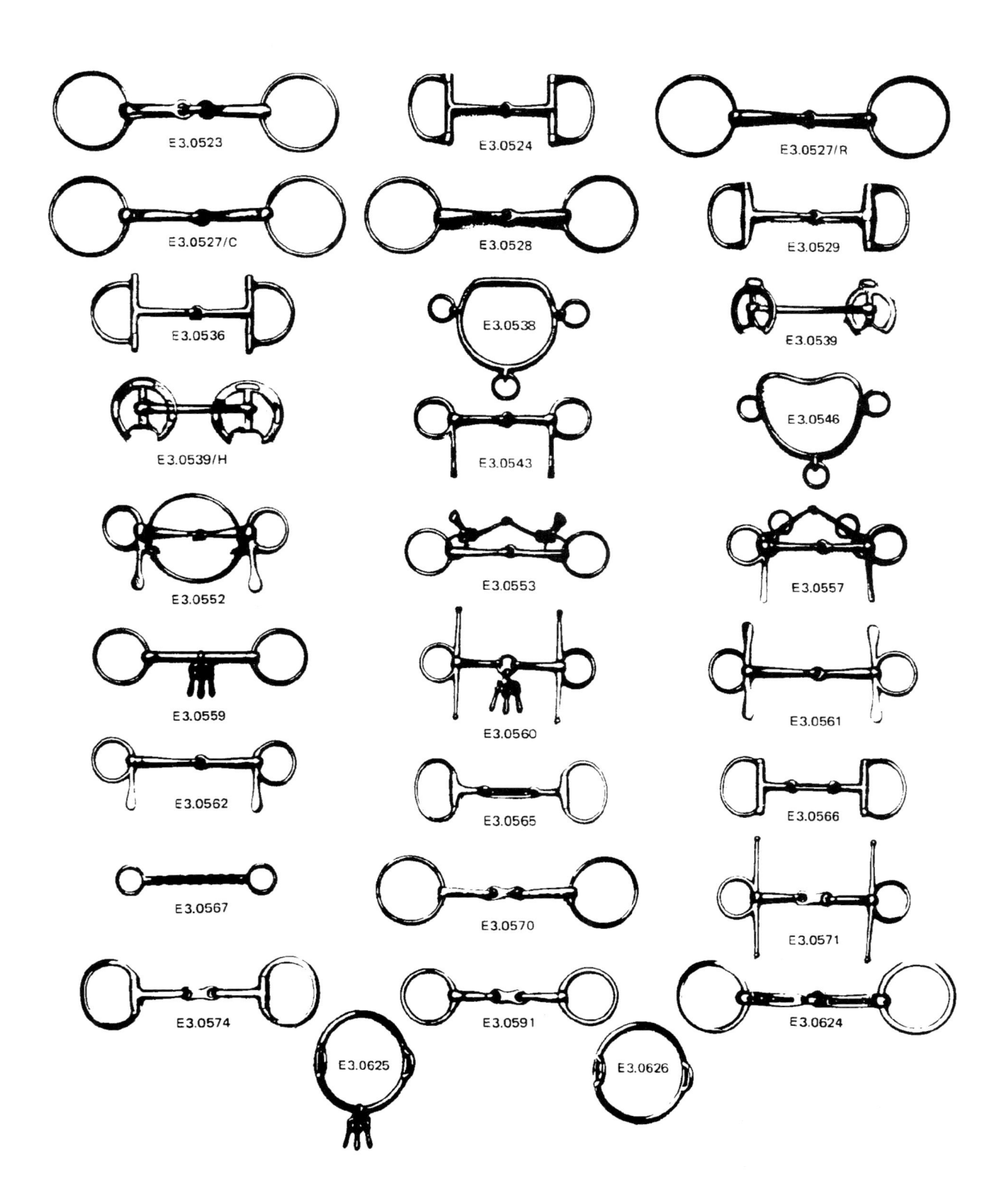

E3.0523
E3.0524
E3.0527/R
E3.0527/C
E3.0528
E3.0529
E3.0536
E3.0538
E3.0539
E3.0539/H
E3.0543
E3.0546
E3.0552
E3.0553
E3.0557
E3.0559
E3.0560
E3.0561
E3.0562
E3.0565
E3.0566
E3.0567
E3.0570
E3.0571
E3.0574
E3.0591
E3.0624
E3.0625
E3.0626

497

Eldonian

STAINLESS STEEL

BRADOONS

Code	Description				
E3.0500	Standard weight, Weymouth Bradoon, plain jointed mouth, wire rings.	5 x 1¾	5½ x 2	6 x 2¼	6½ x 2¼
E3.0502	Light weight, Weymouth Bradoon, plain jointed mouth, wire rings.	4½ x 1½	4¾ x 1½	5 x 1½	5½ x 1½
E3.0508	Rubber Bradoon, mullen mouth, wire rings.	4½ x 3	5 x 3	5½ x 3	6 x 3½
E3.0510	Irish Bradoon, plain jointed mouth, flat rings.	5 x 2¾	5½ x 3	6 x 3½	
E3.0511	Irish Bradoon, twisted jointed mouth, flat rings.	5 x 2¾	5½ x 3	6 x 3½	
E3.0514	Nylon Bradoon, mullen mouth, wire rings.	4½ x 3	5 x 3	5½ x 3	6 x 3½
E3.0515	Chain Bradoon, flat rings.	5¾ x 3	6¼ x 3¼		
E3.0519	Dressage Weymouth Bradoon (for use with E3.0621).	4½	5	5½	6
E3.0520	Eggbutt Bradoon, plain jointed mouth, flat rings.	4½ x 2¾	5 x 3	5½ x 3	6 x 3¼
E3.0520/MM	Eggbutt Bradoon, mullen mouth, flat rings.	5 x 3	5½ x 3¼	6 x 3¼	
E3.0521	Eggbutt Bradoon, twisted jointed mouth, flat rings.	5 x 2¾	5½ x 3	6 x 3¼	
E3.0525	Eggbutt Bradoon, tapered hollow jointed mouth, flat rings.	4½ x 2¾	5 x 3	5½ x 3	6 x 3¼
E3.0530	Salisbury Gag.	5 x 2½	5½ x 3	6 x 3½	
E3.0530/W	Weymouth Gag.	5 x 2¼	5½ x 2¼	6 x 2¼	
E3.0532	Eggbutt Gag.	5 x 3	5½ x 3	6 x 3½	
E3.0533	Balding Gag.	5½ x 3	5½ x 4	6 x 3½	
E3.0537	German Snaffle, hollow jointed mouth, wire rings.	5½ x 3	6 x 3	6 x 3½	
E3.0540	Light weight, Loose Ring Snaffle, jointed mouth.	4½	5	5½	6
E3.0542	Standard weight, Loose Ring Snaffle, jointed mouth.	4½	5	5½	6
E3.0545	Ball Cheek Snaffle, plain jointed mouth.	4½	5	5½	6
E3.0550	4-ring Wilson Snaffle, flat rings. Sizes as E3.0510 to special order only.				
E3.0551	Improved Wilson Snaffle, square jointed mouth.	4½	5½	6	
E3.0555	Double Mouth Snaffle, double offset jointed mouth.	5½ x 3¼	6 x 3½		
E3.0599	Bar Mouth, Stallion/Irish Bradoon, wire rings. 4½ x 2	4½ x 2½	5 x 2½	5 x 3	5½ x 3

Eldonian

STAINLESS STEEL

E3.0500	E3.0502	E3.0508
E3.0510	E3.0511	E3.0514
E3.0515	E3.0519	E3.0520
E3.0520/MM	E3.0521	E3.0525
E3.0530	E3.0530/W	E3.0532
E3.0533	E3.0537	E3.0540
E3.0542	E3.0545	E3.0550
E3.0551	E3.0555	E3.0599

SOLID NICKEL BRADOONS AND SNAFFLES

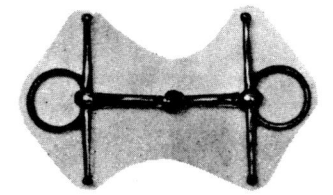

E5.2000 (7220)
Ball Cheek Snaffle
Pony, Cob, F.S.

E5.2001 (7221)
Plain Irish Bradoon with flat rings.
Shetland, Pony, Cob, F.S.

E5.2002 (7222)
Twisted Irish Bradoon with flat rings.
Pony, Cob, F.S.

E5.2003 (7224)
Stout mouth Race Exercise Bradoon,
with wire rings.
F.S.

E5.2004 (7225)
Stout hollow mouth German Bradoon,
with wire rings.
Pony, Cob, F.S.

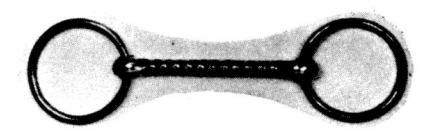

E5.2005 (7226)
Twisted one side Stallion Bradoon,
with wire rings.
Pony, Cob, F.S.

E5.2006 (7227)
Bar mouth Breaking Bradoon with
players and wire rings.
Pony, Cob, F.S.

E5.2007 (7228)
Plain Eggbutt Bradoon with flat rings.
Shetland, Pony, Cob, F.S.

E5.2008 (7229)
Twisted Eggbutt Bradoon with flat rings.
Pony, Cob, F.S.

E5.2009
Mullen mouth Bradoon,
with flat rings.
Shetland, Pony, Cob, F.S.

E5.2011 (7250)
Metropolitan Bit.
Pony, Cob, F.S.

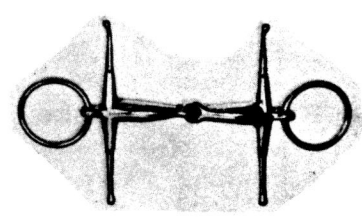

E5.2010
Fulmer Snaffle.
Pony, Cob, F.S.

E5.2022 (7300)
Kangaroo Newmarket Bradoon,
Dee cheeks.
Race, F.S.

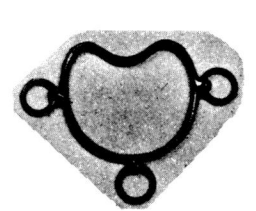

E5.2030 (7237)
Tattersalls Colt Bit with players.
Standard size.

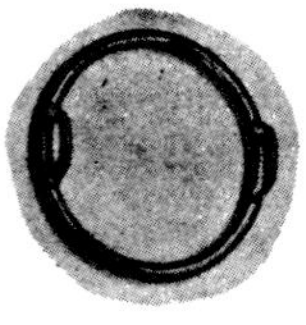

E5.2031 (7259)
Tattersalls Colt Bit no players.
Standard size.

E5.2032 (7238)
Anti-Rearing Bits.
Standard size.

E5.2033 (7260)
Colt Lead Bit.
Standard Size.

Sizes: For the jointed mouth bits on this page
Shetland mouths are 4½
Pony   ,,   ,,   5
Cob   ,,   ,,   5½
F.S.   ,,   ,,   6
For solid mouth bits, sizes are above less ½"

Fleming Bits

Willard Thomas and Richard Fleming were partners in the Saddlery Co. of Bakersfield, CA, which marketed Fleming Bits and Spurs from the late 1940's to 1978 when the company was sold to Phil Rudnick.

This information is based on two interviews with Willard Thomas in 1986, and is intended to give readers some history of his company and their bit and spur production. Keep in mind that the information is based on memory and not precisely accurate.

Mr Thomas said they started the company right after WW II, or it may have been as early as 1942 or '43. The Saddlery marketed only braided rawhide products: reins, bridles, headstalls, etc. Then after 3 or 4 years they decided to go into the bit and spur business.

Interestingly, P. M. Kelly, who had his own bit and spur company in El Paso, Texas, helped Fleming Bit and Spurs get started. Mr. Thomas headed to Mexico, because historically it has produced some of the finest makers of cowboy hardware. On his way, he stopped to visit with "P. M. - old man Kelly", in El Paso. Mr. Kelly said "I'll go with you, I know some of those bit and spur makers down there." They left together the next morning.

Amazoc is a small town about 15 miles from Puebla, which is near Mexico City. Mr. Thomas says that Amazoc has been a major bit and spur producing area for 300 years or longer. Talented craftsmen have passed this skill on from generation to generation. Of the many factories in and around Amazoc, there are at least 12 or 14 family operations.

The shops operated under very primitive conditions when they first went down there. Gradually modern equipment such as bandsaws was moved in to improve production. They came to control certain shops due to owning the equipment and these shops made exclusively for them. From using many small shops at one time, they finally wound up with three larger operations working over 40 men.

The first two or three years none of their bits and spurs were marked. "Then we began to think we'd better get our name on them so we had the Fleming stamp made." This would make the earliest marked Fleming items around 1950.

The size and depth of the stamp is no indication of age according to Mr. Thomas. Stamps would be lost, broken or misplaced. This happened several times. Different size stamps were used from the beginning and depth depended on how hard the stamp was hit or if the item had been heated first.

Some of the bit and spur makers came up to work in the Bakersfield shop so customers could see how Fleming bits and spurs were made.

The supply of good craftsmen in Amazoc is reflected by the fact that not only Fleming, but Garcia, Vogt, and C & S bits and spurs are made there. Small factories in other places, like the state of Sonora, also produce good silver inlaid bits and spurs for the United States market.

"Lester Garcia had a factory right next door to one of ours," said Mr. Thomas. "Vogt out of Turlock, California, came into the business a long time after we were in, and C & S Silver is just entering the market (1986)."

Back in 1971 or 1972, Jeff Jefferson of Fruita, Colorado, went on a 35 day trip to Mexico. His last stop was to be Amazoc to buy some silver inlaid bits and spurs.

From Mexico City, out of Puebla, he had to change buses three times to get to Amazoc. The last bus was crowded with people and their goats and chickens. Pulling into Amazoc, Jeff saw a small town where the only water supply appeared to be from a pipe sticking up in the center of the plaza. With only one hour to stay in Amazoc before he had to catch the next bus, Jeff thought, "How in the world am I going to find any bits and spurs?"

Lo and behold, right across the street from where the bus stopped was a man selling silver inlaid bits and spurs from a glass display case. There were 10 items in the display case. He was asking $50 apiece. Jeff had only $350 left for his trip and made a deal to buy all the items for $35 apiece.

Just as Jeff was getting ready to leave, the man came running up and said he forgot to ask if he wanted the items stamped. He pulled out catalogues from Vogt, Fleming, Garcia, etc., saying they made items for them. Jeff said, "No thanks," and said he was able to pay for his entire trip from the resale of the items back home.

Information supplied by Steve Rudy, Aurora, Colorado, from the Fall 1986 and Spring 1987 NBS&SCA newsletter.

Bridle bit of G. S. Garcia. Ned Martin collection.

LES GARCIA MFG. CO. • BOX 1966, RENO, NEVADA 89505

BIT No. 106

Made of highly polished non-rust Monel steel. Solid silver overlaid and finely engraved. Regular or spoon space mouthpiece, 3½" high, 5" wide. Loose jaws. 7½" cheeks. Silver overlaid bar at bottom, finely engraved. Cross chains at bottom if preferred. Non-rust rein chains. A lightweight well-balanced bit.

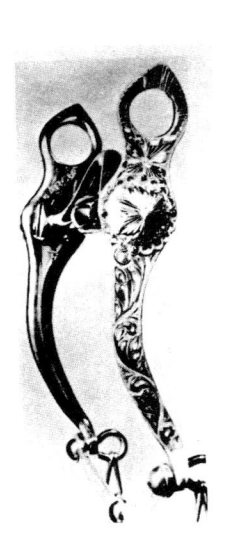

BIT No. 120

Another Garcia bit that has proven very popular. Highly polished non-rust Monel steel. Solid silver overlaid with 1⅜" conchas, finely engraved. Low port mouthpiece, 1" high with wide barrel cricket, 5" wide. Loose jaws. (Can also be made without the barrel cricket, same price.) Silver overlaid bottom bar, finely engraved. Non-rust rein chains. A lightweight beauty.

BIT No. 126

Made of highly polished non-rust Monel steel. Solid silver overlaid with 1⅝" conchas, finely engraved. New "Salinas" style mouthpiece, 1⅝" high with copper covered hood and wide barrel cricket. Mouthpiece 5" wide. Loose jaws. 7½" cheeks. Silver overlaid and engraved. Silver and engraved bottom bar. Non-rust rein chains. A fairly new style bit and one of the most popular bits we have ever made.

NEW IMPROVED BIT No. 128

Another non rust stainless steel bit. Solid silver overlaid with 1⅝" conchas, finely engraved. New Salinas mouthpiece, 1⅝" high, 5" wide. Copper covered hood with wide barrel cricket. Loose jaws, 7½" cheeks, silver overlaid and engraved bar at bottom. Open filigree design in center of cheeks. Really a beauty.

BIT No. 172

Original "SANTA BARBARA" pattern. Made of highly polished non-rust Monel steel. Solid silver overlaid, finely engraved. Regular or spoon spade mouthpiece, 3½" high, 5" wide. Loose jaws, 7½" cheeks. Silver overlaid and engraved bar at bottom or cross chains if preferred. Non-rust rein chains. An old favorite. Shown with spoon spade.

BIT No. 178

Made on the "Santa Barbara" cheek pattern with star in center. Highly polished non-rust Monel steel. Solid silver overlaid, finely engraved. Regular or spoon spade mouthpiece, 3½" high, 5" wide. Loose jaws. 7½" cheeks. Silver overlaid and engraved bar at bottom, or cross chains if preferred. Non-rust rein chains. Shown with spoon spade. One of our most popular bits.

LES GARCIA MFG. CO. • BOX 1966, RENO, NEVADA

BIT No. 925

A lightweight stainless steel bit. Loose jaws with silver overlay cheeks and bottom bar. Shown with San Joaquin mouth but can be furnished in any mouth desired.
Price $78.00

BIT No. 728

A silver overlaid bit of stainless steel with cut out filigree work in center of cheek. Loose jaws, 1-5/8" conchas. Silver overlaid bar to match, shown with Mona Lisa mouth.
Price $92.50

A new popular bit made of stainless steel, silver overlaid and finely engraved. Loose jaws. Shown with the popular Garcia San Joaquin mouthpiece but can be furnished with any mouthpiece desired.
Price $80.00

BIT No. 718

A new Garcia bit made of stainless steel on the ever popular Garcia Santa Barbara cheeks. Fully silver overlaid with inset-raised silver long horn steer head offset in a dark background. Loose jaw, silver overlaid bar.
Price $98.00

BIT No. 714

Another new Garcia bit of stainless steel made especially for the Arabian with shorter cheeks and with raised silver Arabian horse head in center. Loose jaw with overlaid cheeks and bar to match. Also made with regular cheeks and quarter horse head in center, same price. Please advise when ordering if wanted for Arabian or quarter horse.
Price $98.00

BIT No. 715

A lightweight stainless steel bit. Silver overlaid with 1-5/8" conchas, loose jaw. State mouthpiece wanted, shown with the popular Salinas Mouth.
Price $85.00

LES GARCIA MFG. CO. • BOX 1966, RENO, NEVADA

BIT No. 713

Here is a new popular lightweight bit made on the popular "Garcia Sonora" pattern with open work cheeks. Silver overlaid with cross bar to match. Finely engraved 1-5/8" silver conchas. Bit is stainless steel.   Price $78.00

BIT No. 716

Another new bit that is proving very popular made on same pattern as the "Garcia Sonora" with a 3/4" silver concha in center of open cheek. Loose jaw with cross bar to match. Stainless steel.   Price $82.50

BIT No. 712

A beautiful bit yet lightweight and perfectly balanced, made of stainless steel. Loose jaws with 4" sterling silver conchas, finely engraved. State mouthpiece wanted.   Price $110.00

BIT No. 719

Made on the same pattern as our No. 925 except a 2" silver concha with silver rope edge has been added. A beautiful bit. Loose jaw with silver overlaid bar to match.   Price $92.50

BIT No. 1

This no doubt is the most beautiful bit Garcia has ever made. Stainless steel, solid silver overlaid with 2¼" conchas. American Eagle standing on a silver engraved shield, with flying eagle cross bar to match. A beautiful job of engraving.   Price $125.00

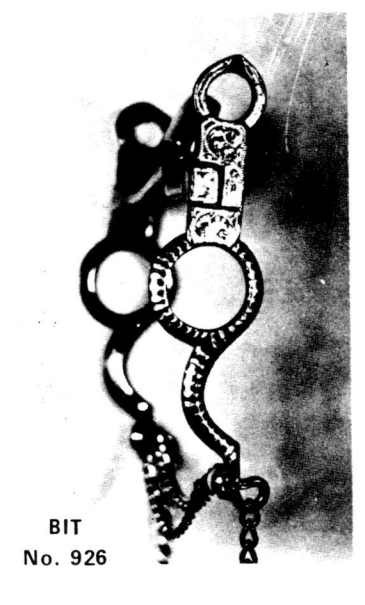

BIT No. 926

Is a silver inlaid blued steel bit on the same pattern as No. 925. Shown with cross chains instead of bar, furnished either way at same price.   Price $82.50

505

Gutierrez:

Gutierrez's life spanned almost 7 decades. In 1905, when he would have been 15 plus years of age, he was already crafting bits and spurs in Sacramento, California. The early 1900's was considered the period of time when the California bit, spur, and saddle products reached their peak, although little history of the time or its craftsmen has survived (if it was ever written). So the biographical materials re. Gutierrez is skimpy.

Raphael Philo Gutierrez was born in Northern California on Dec. 13, 1889. The next encounter we have with him was in 1905 as mentioned. Between that time and 1917 when he became partnered with Bill Phillips in Cheyenne, Wyoming, Gutierrez was learning and perfecting his bit, spur and saddle making skills from the best known companies, including the G. S. Garcia Co. of Elko, Nevada. Many of the bits and spurs created under the Garcia name were made by Gutierrez.

The Phillips-Gutierrez partnership lasted for a year or so. They stamped their products "PHILLIPS & GUT. CHEY, WYO." In 1920, Gutierrez moved to San Francisco and became partners with Juan Estrada, an arrangement which endured for 20 years. In 1940, Gutierrez ended his partnership with Estrada and worked from his home until a long illness ended his life in 1958.

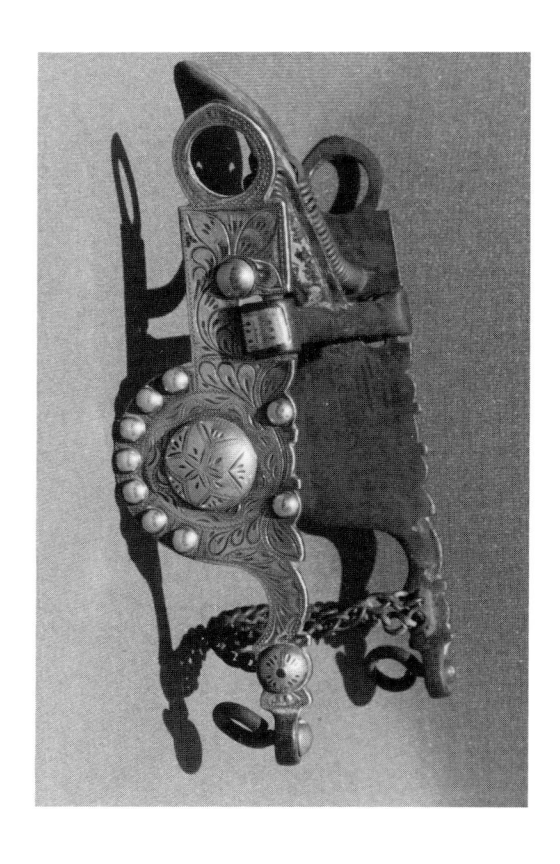

Bridle bit by Philo Gutierrez. Ned Martin collection.

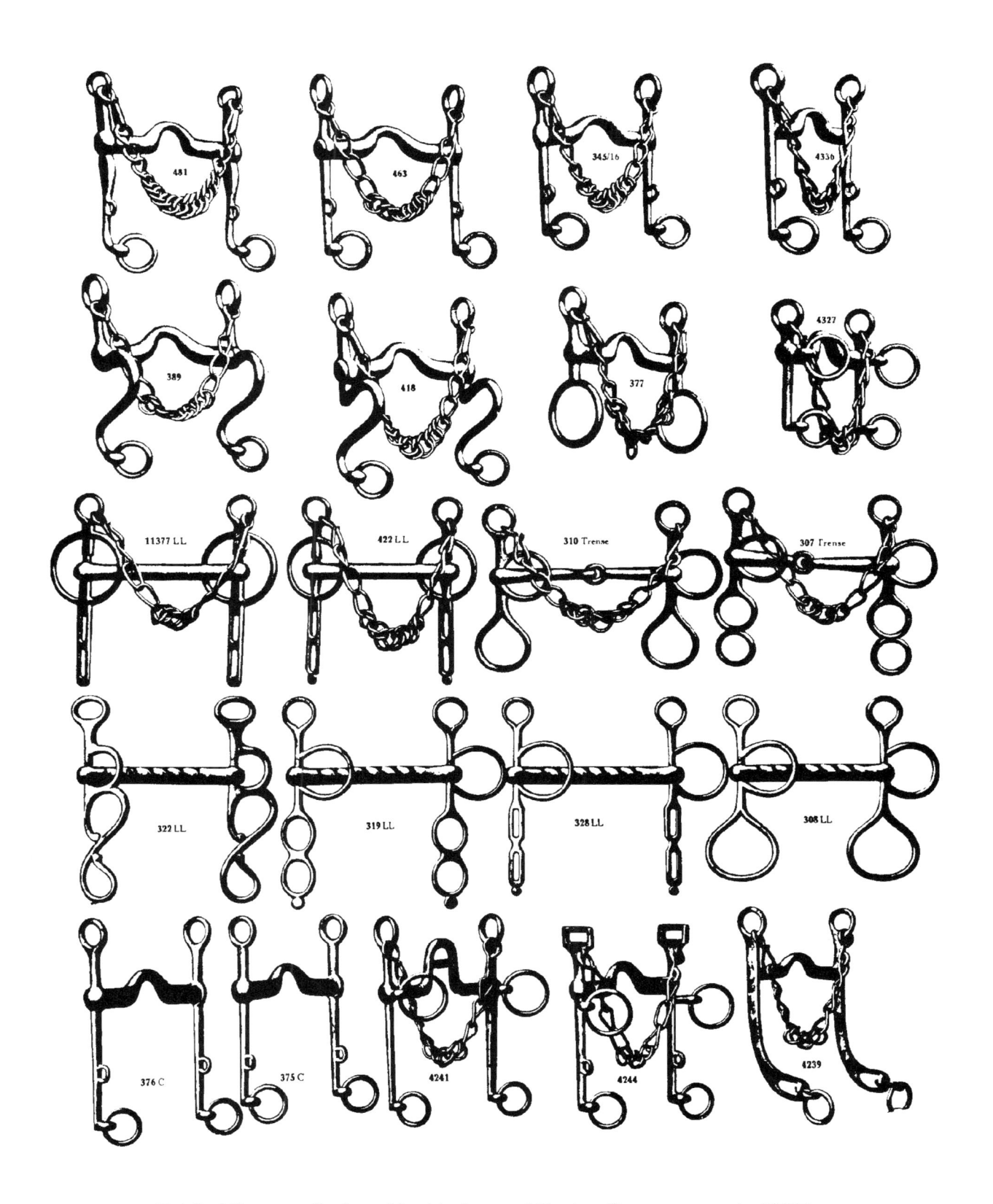

Bridle bits manufactured by Linden and Funke, Germany, early 1900's.

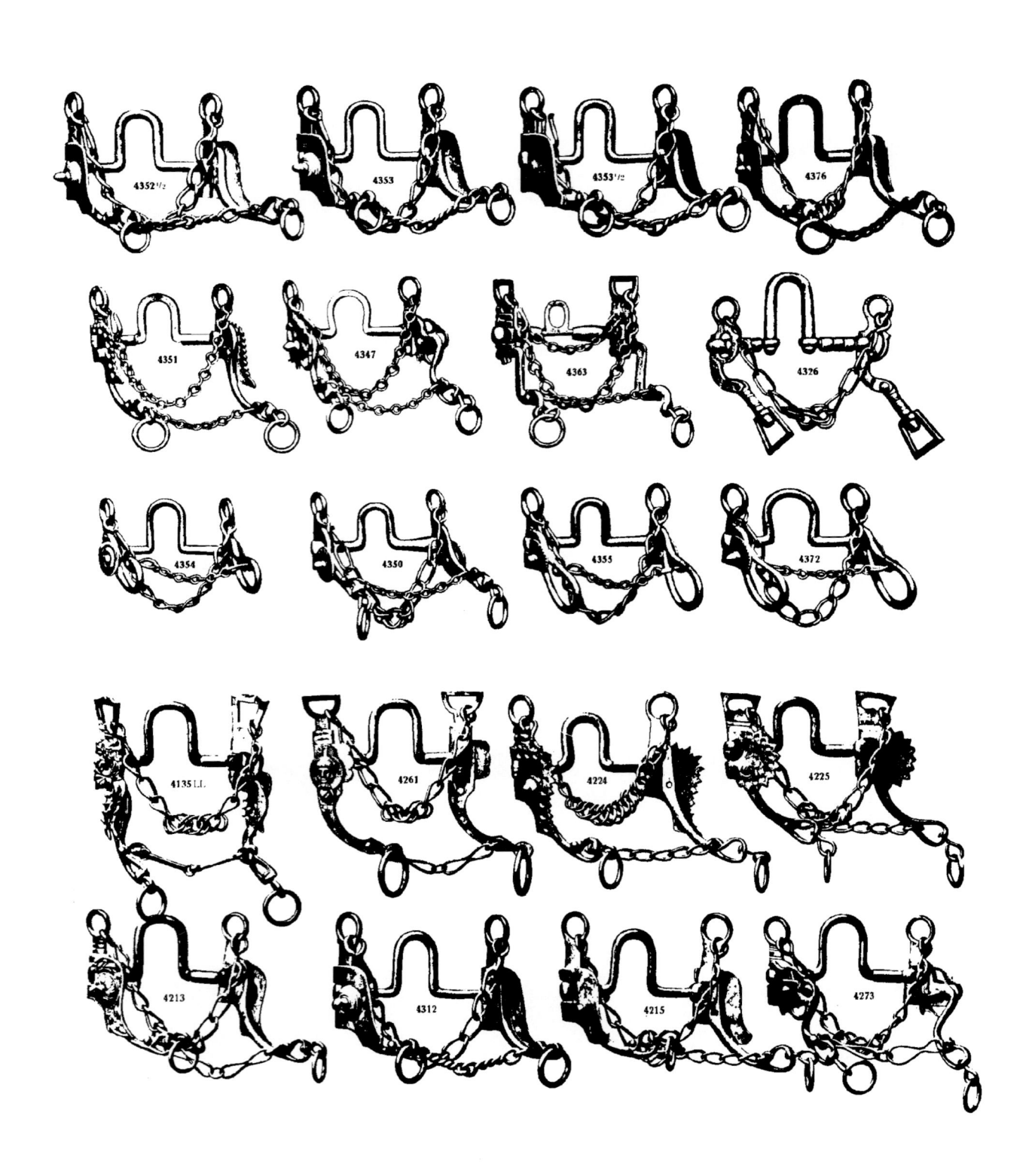

Bridle bits manufacured by Linden and Funke, Germany, early 1900's.

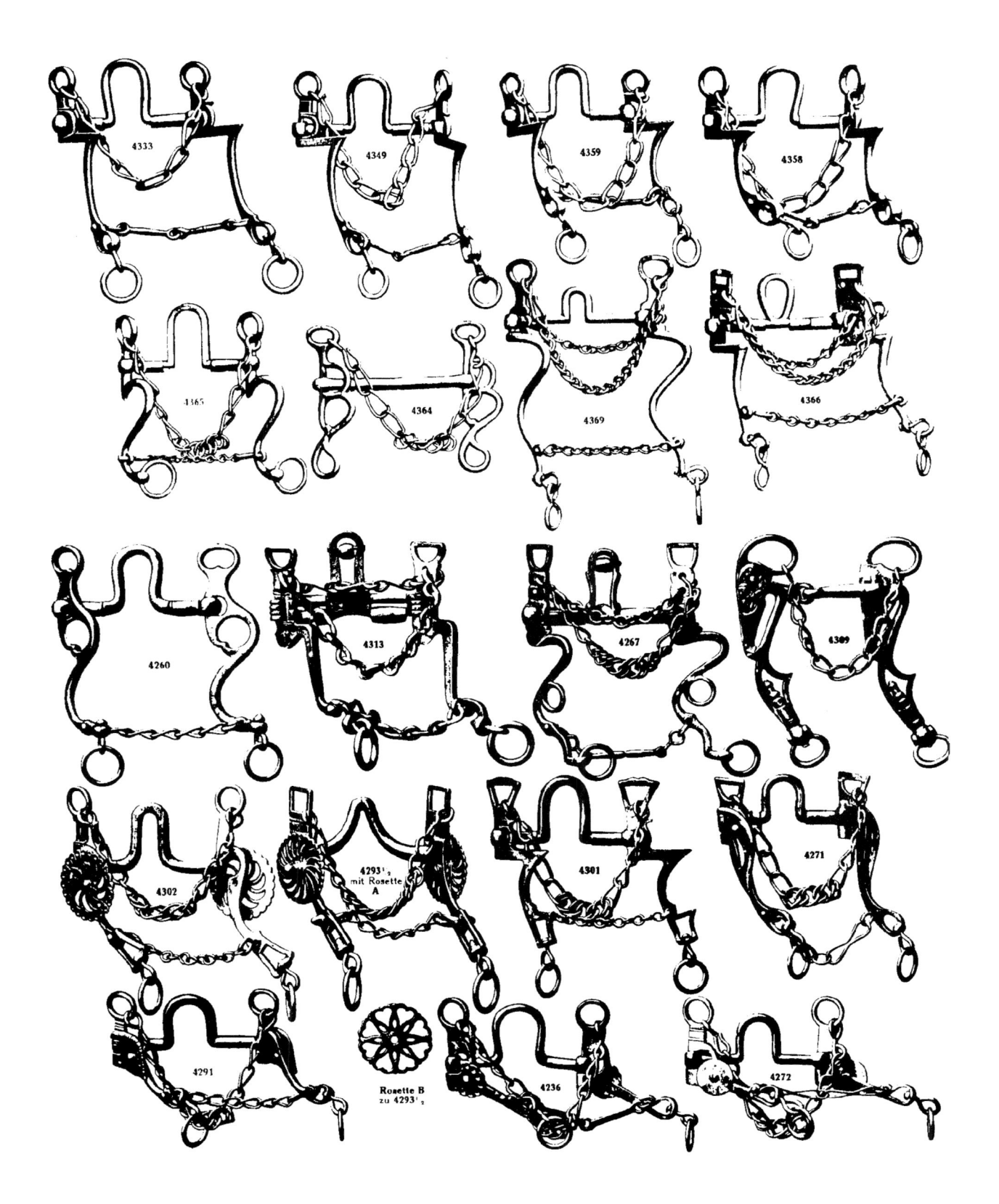

Bridle bits manufactured by Linden and Funke, Germany, early 1900's.

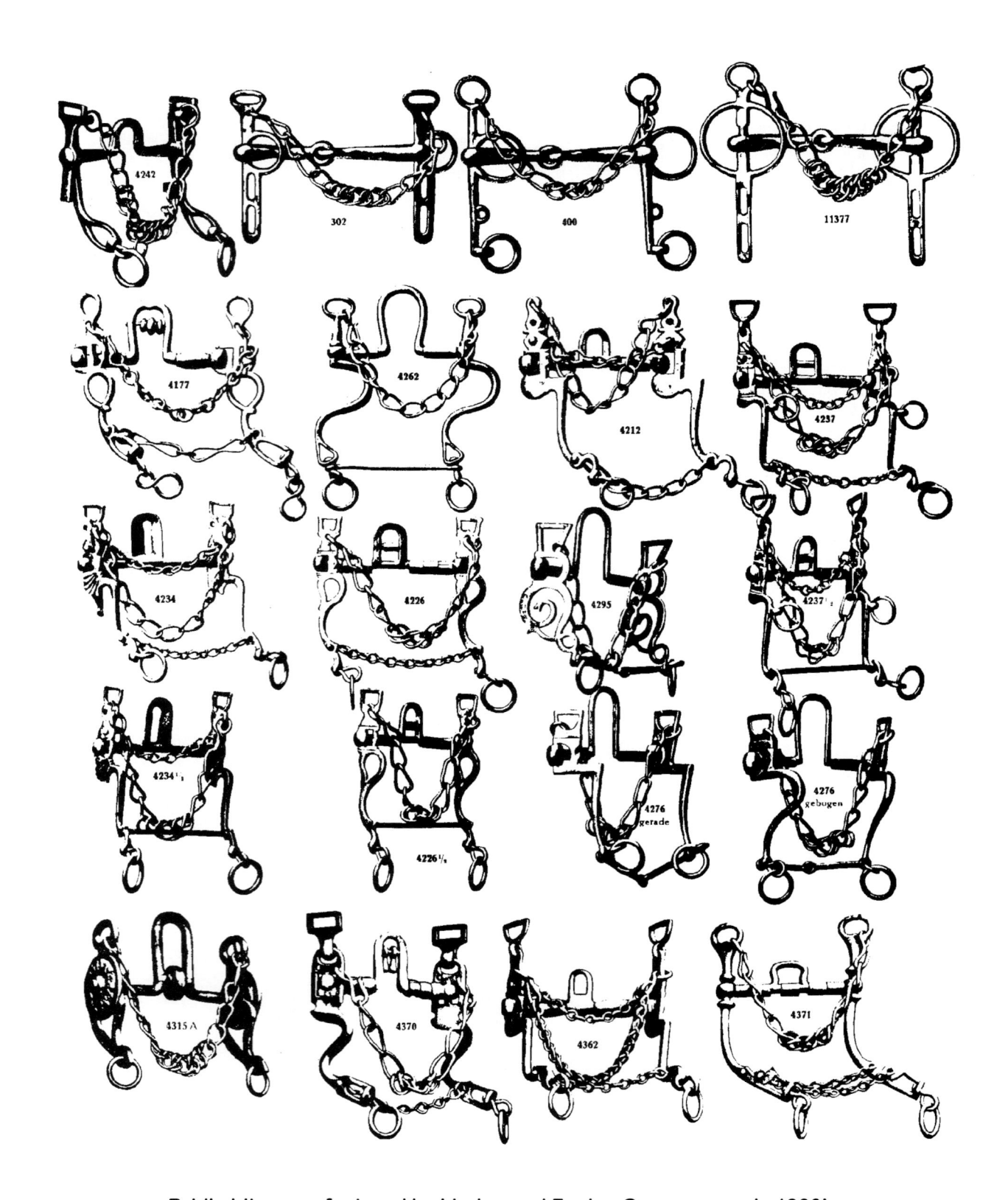

Bridle bits manufactured by Linden and Funke, Germany, early 1900's.

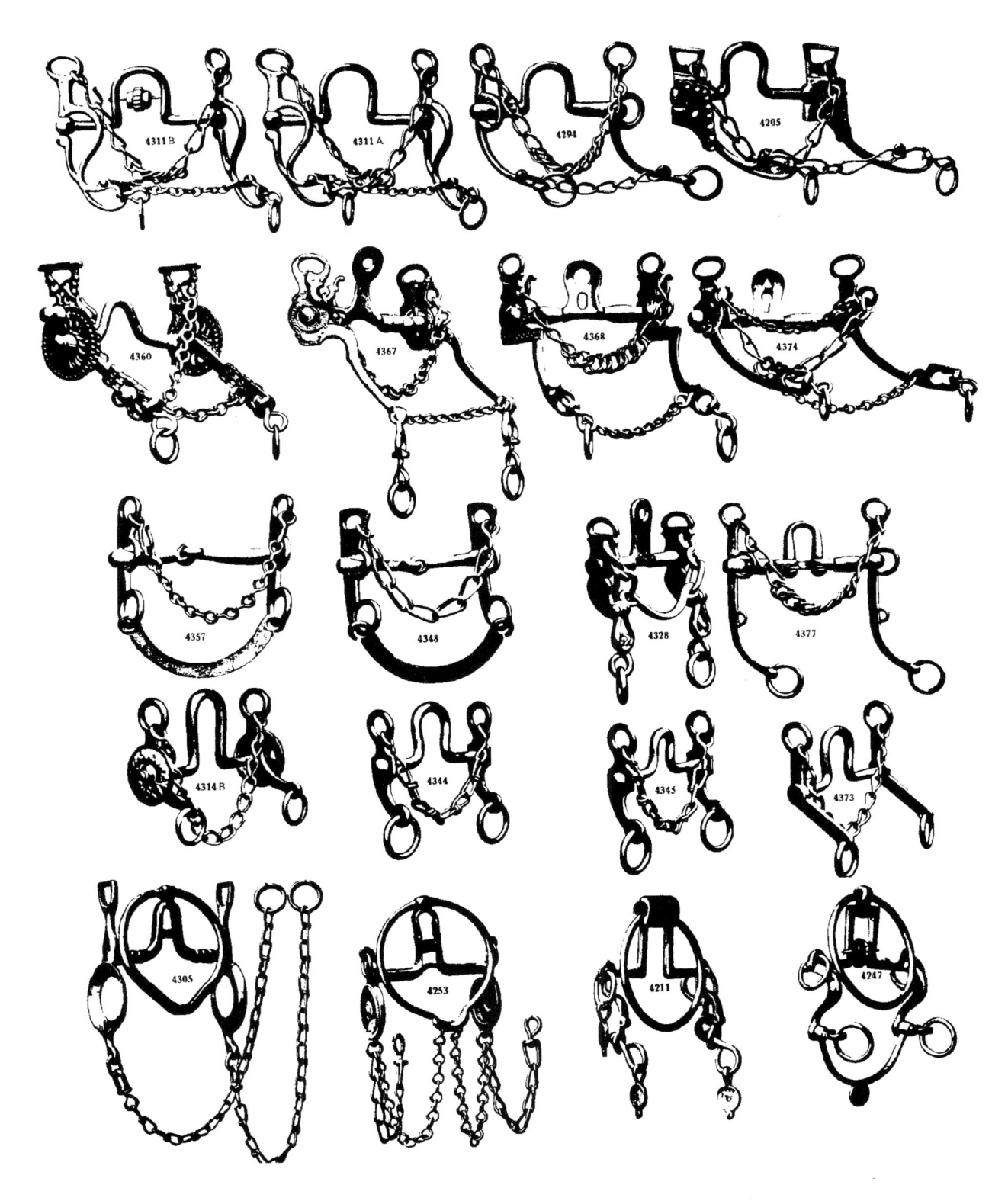

Bridle bits manufactured by Linden and Funke, Germany, early 1900's.

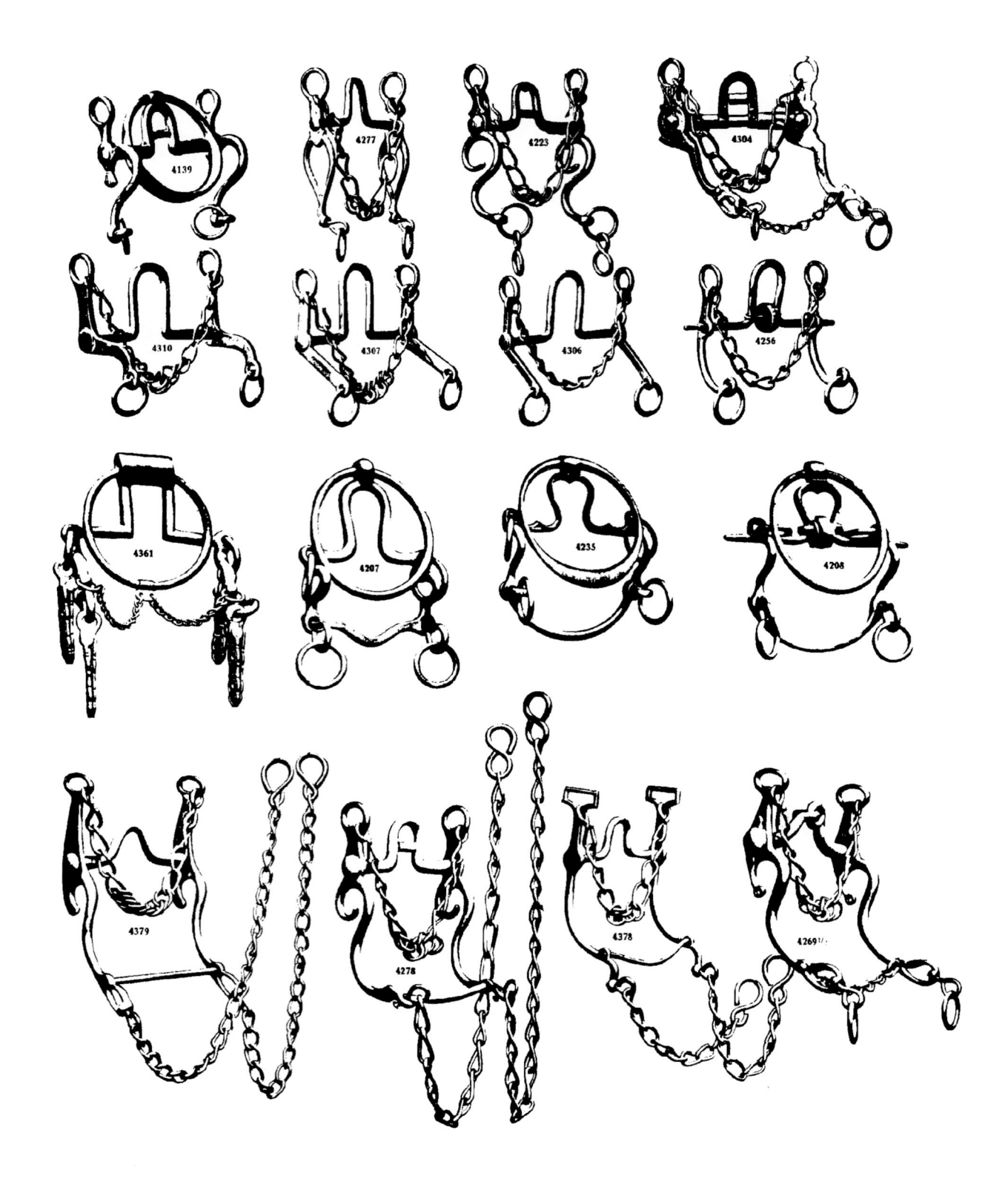

Bridle bits manufactured by Linden and Funke, Germany, early 1900's.

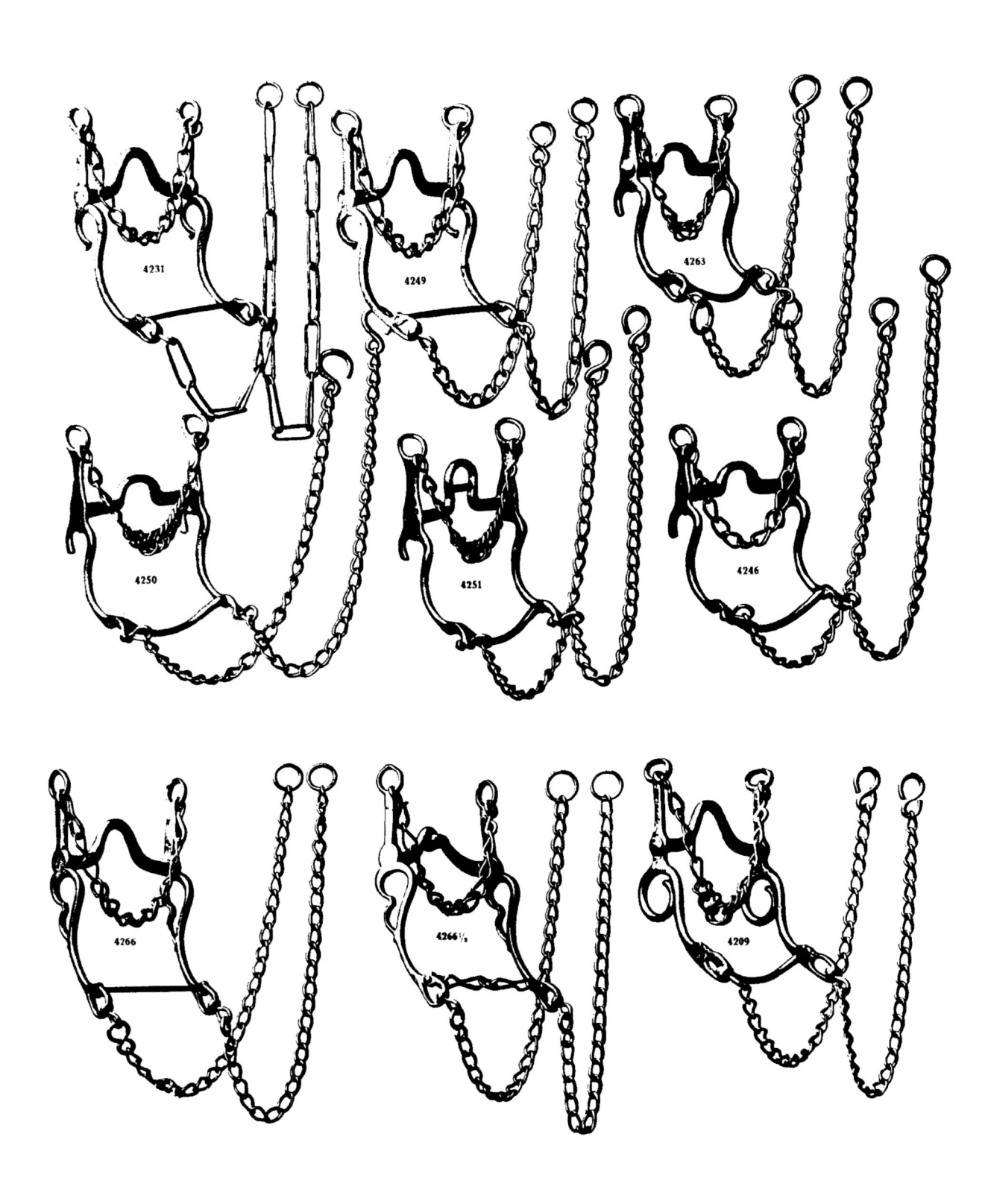

Bridle bits manufactured by Linden and Funke, Germany, early 1900's.

McChesney

John Robert McChesney was born in South Bend, Indiana, September 29, 1867. Being reared in the area, he attended Notre Dame, learning the fundamentals of the machinists trade.

In 1884, the family moved near Rogers, Arkansas. Here at the age of 19, he married and tried homesteading, but soon he was off to the frontier town of Broken Arrow, Oklahoma. In the late 1880's he made his first pair of spurs using harrow teeth as the raw material. One-piece bits and spurs were also made from hay forks.

McChesney moved from Broken Arrow to Gainsville, Texas in 1890. He worked as a ranch blacksmith until obtaining city property to open his own business in 1891. A bit and spur catalogue was produced in 1906. The Gainsville years were formative and creative bringing much attention to the unique Texas one-piece bits and spurs (offered prior to 1909). J. R. McChesney became known as 'Papa of the Texas Spur'.

After 19 years in Gainsville, he began exploring the area for relocation of the business. Pauls Valley, Oklahoma, 75 miles north, was the site selected to build the new factory in 1909-10. Large scale production and world recognition came to McChesney in Pauls Valley. During WW I the company filled army contracts, with employees working around the clock contributing to both community and the war effort.

Some of the main characteristics of McChesney products were: The bits had port mouths, no spades or half breeds, most were the grazing type bits, made plain or mounted, generally were of the lighter design but strong and functional with distinctive mountings patterned from nature themes.

During the last years at Pauls Valley he made a few patterns with heavier construction.

John Robert McChesney fostered the growth of many bit and spur makers as well as being an active communiuty leader, honored by a network of relatives and friends and "Papa" of a large family. He died suddenly in January, 1928, at the age of 60.

In 1929 Enid Justin purchased the McChesney name, machinery, remaining materials and stock and moved it to Nacona, Texas. She continued manufacturing marked McChesney bits and spurs into the early 1940's.

More can be learned about the life and product of J. R. McChesney from the book *J. R. McChesney, A Lifetime, A Legacy,* by Lee C. Jacobs.

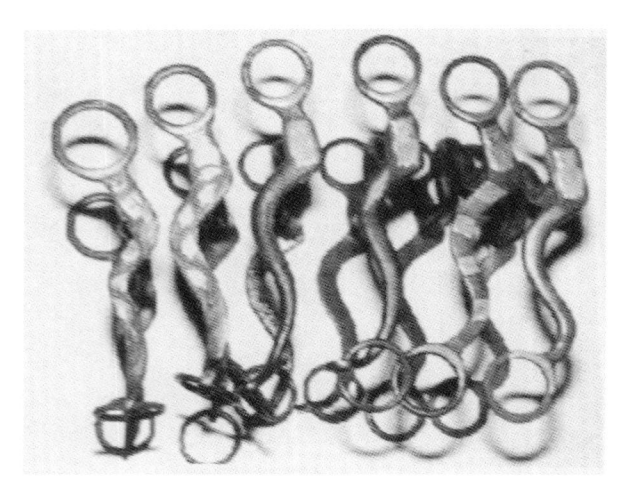

Variations of McChesney "Owl" bit. The two on the left were made early and the four to the right made in the Nacoma years.

No. 4 Bit, Leg Pattern

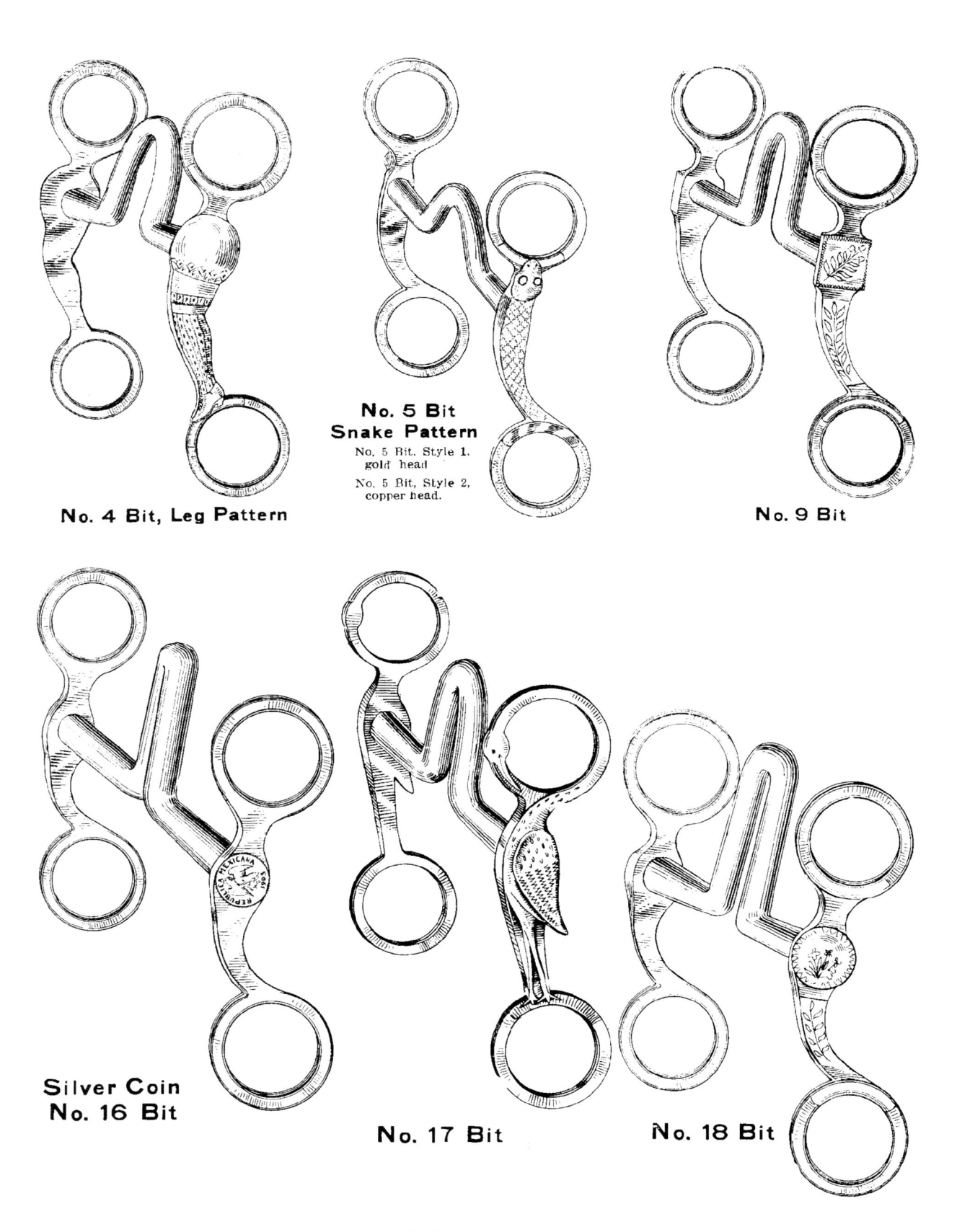

**No. 5 Bit
Snake Pattern**

No. 5 Bit, Style 1,
gold head

No. 5 Bit, Style 2,
copper head.

No. 9 Bit

**Silver Coin
No. 16 Bit**

No. 17 Bit

No. 18 Bit

McChesney bits.

M. MORALES PORTLAND, ORE.

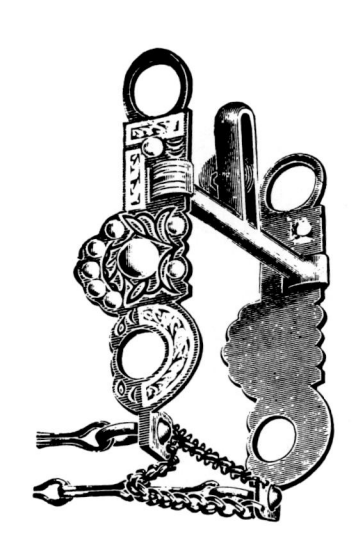

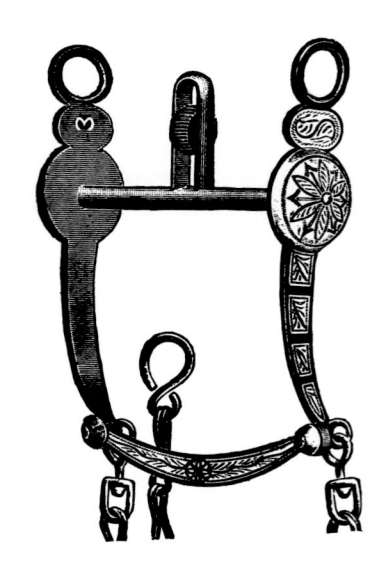

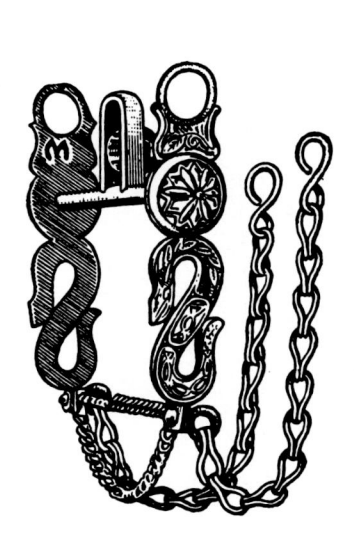

BEST MADE ON THE MARKET

516

M. MORALES   PORTLAND, ORE.

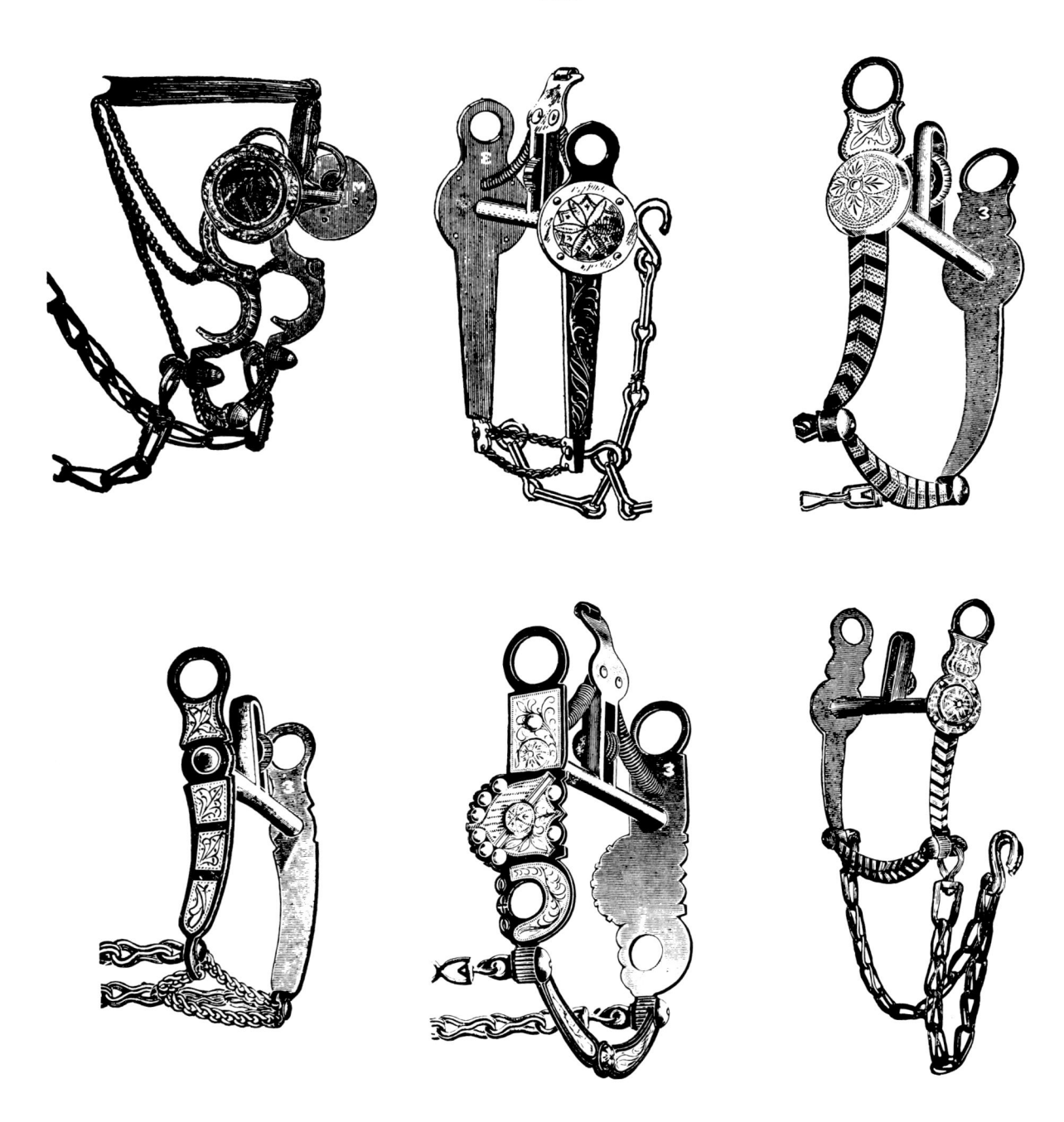

BEST MADE ON THE MARKET

517

The Finest Bits Made

CALIFORNIAN

Our California style bit is a show bit made of lasting aluminum 9-inch streamlined cheeks with heart cut out. Cross bar at bottom and nickel plated rein chains. 5⅛-inch aluminum high cricket half breed or spade mouthpiece. Specify in ordering.

No. 51—Hand engraved.
Each $10.50
No. 50—Plain. Each.......... 8.50

The BALL BEARING

RICARDO takes pride in introducing this aluminum ball bearing, loose cheek bit. The cheeks actually rotate on ball bearings. This type of assembly not only permits smooth and instantaneous action, but prevents the injuring of the tender membranes in a horse's mouth due to pinching. Loose reins rings.

No. 5—Hand engraved.
Each $16.00
No. 4—Plain. Each............ 13.50

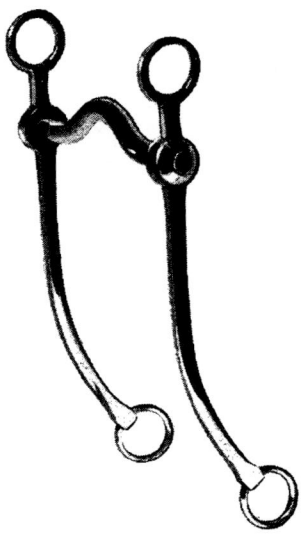

TENNESSEE-WALKER

No. 126 — Hand forged, hand shaped, Tennessee walking horse bit. Tough airplane aluminum, 10-inch round cheeks, low port, loose rings. Price, each......$7.50

The MEEKER

A short curved shank bit with curb strap slot, 5⅛-inch medium port, 6¾-inch cheeks.

No. 17—All hand engraved.
Each $4.25
No. 16—Plain. Each............ 3.25

The POLO

The aluminum cowboy polo bit, curb and string slot. Medium port, 6¾-inch cheeks.

No. 27—All hand engraved.
Each $5.25
No. 26—Plain. Each............ 4.00

The OREGON

A Western beauty, long shank, medium port, heart shaped cut-out. A real Show bit.

No. 23 — Beautifully hand engraved. Each......................$6.50
No. 22—Plain. Each............ 5.25

Ricardo METAL MANUFACTURERS, 1218 15th ST., DENVER 2, COLO.

Durable, Aluminum Bits

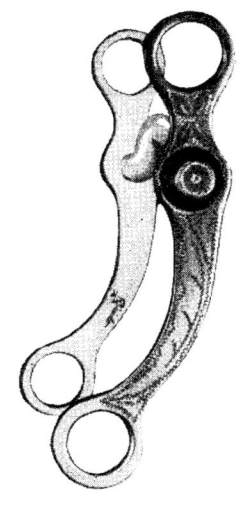

The NEVADA

A medium shank staple bit made of airplane aluminum, 7¾-inch cheeks, 5⅛-inch medium port.

No. 13—All hand engraved.
Each $4.00
No. 12—Plain. Each............ 3.00

The NAVAJO

A short shank staple bit, of airplane aluminum, 6¾-inch cheeks. 5⅛-inch medium port.

No. 11—All hand engraved.
Each $4.00
No. 10—Plain. Each............ 3.00

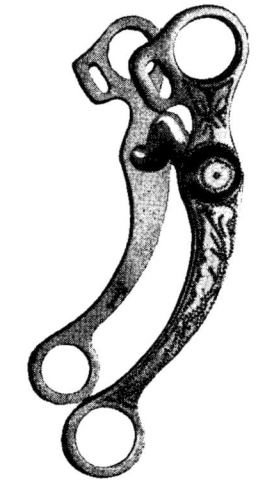

The BUTTE

An old popular bit now made with a curb slot, 7¾-inch cheeks, medium port.

No. 15—All hand engraved.
Each $4.25
No. 14—Plain. Each............ 3.25

The GLENWOOD

A beautiful bit to put on any horse, 7¾-inch cheeks, high port. Very ornamental.

No. 39 — Beautifully hand engraved. Each $5.50
No. 38—Plain. Each............ 4.00

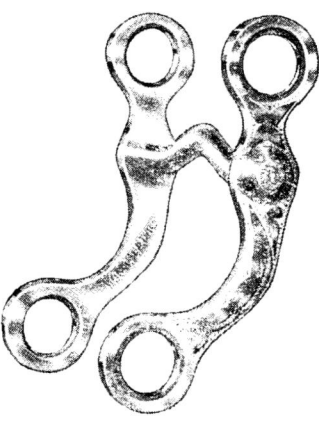

The DALLAS

Our Texas colt bit, 6¾-inch cheek pieces, 5⅛-inch low port.

No. 19—All hand engraved.
Each $4.00
No. 18—Plain. Each............ 3.00

The RANGER

The Texas grazing bit, long curved shank, curb strap slot, 8½-inch cheeks, ⅝-inch low port.

No. 25—All hand engraved.
Each $5.00
No. 24—Plain. Each............ 4.00

Ricardo METAL MANUFACTURERS, 1218 15th ST., DENVER 2, COLO.

Beautifully Designed Aluminum Bits

RICARDO offers you your choice from a fine line of quality, hand made, Airplane Aluminum bits. Durable, light and easy on the horse's mouth. Aluminum has less reaction to frost than steel—will not rust.

WALKING HORSE
Walking horse bit, low port with cross bar. Durable solid aluminum. 9¼-inch cheeks, 5⅛-inch port, 1-inch rein holes.
No. 121—Hand engraved.
Each $7.00
No. 120—Plain, each.......... 5.50

The LONGHORN
RICARDO'S new, narrow, tapering aluminum bit with longhorn steer cross bar. 10-inch cheeks, low port, 1-inch rein holes.
No. 123—Hand engraved.
Each $7.00
No. 122—Plain, each 5.50

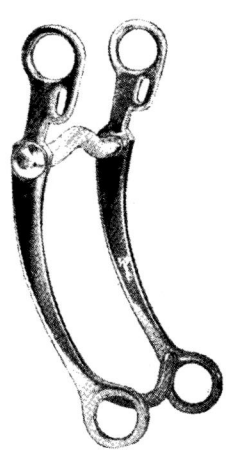

The STREAMLINER
RICARDO'S newest aluminum bit, strong and durable, light in weight, cross bar, 9¾-inch cheek pices, curb slot, 1-in. rein holes.
No. 125—Hand engraved.
Each $6.50
No. 124—Plain, each.......... 5.00

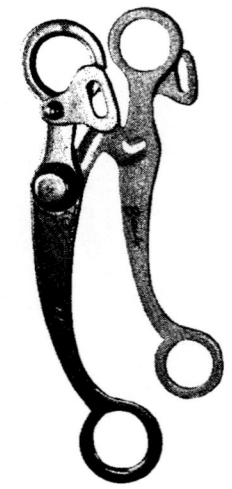

The STAN
A neat aluminum staple bit with swivel action curb strap loops that completely eliminates pinching. 8¾-inch cheeks, 5⅛-inch aluminum port.
No. 109—Hand engraved.
Each $7.50
No. 108—Plain. Each......... 6.00

The PISTOLA
No. 68—RICARD'S new pistol bit is a practical novelty made of durable solid aluminum. Each cheek is a detailed replica of a Western six-shooter. 5⅛-inch medium port, NICKEL PLATED rein chains. Each...............$25.00

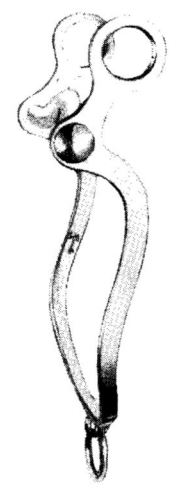

The ROPER
RICARDO'S new aluminum one-piece roping bit. Light in weight, but very strong and durable loose rein ring. 9¼-inch cheeks with 6¼-inch opening under port. 5⅛-inch aluminum medium port.
No. 6—Plain only. Each......$7.50

Ricardo METAL MANUFACTURERS, 1218 15th ST., DENVER 2, COLO.

Nickel Silver Rustless Bits

Again its the practical RICARDO combination, with parade appearance and rugged durability the partners. Note the shining beauty of the Nickel Silver cheek pieces, all hand engraved, of course; feel the sturdy strength as your mount responds to every touch. A tensile strength of approximately 7,500 pounds per square inch.

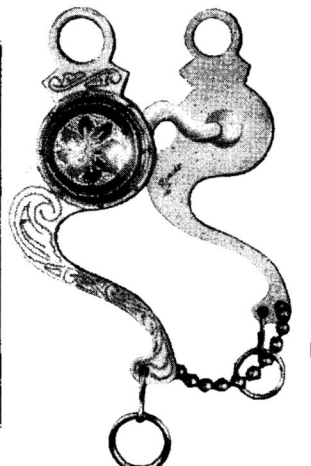

The PAGELS
No. 3000—A neat long curved shank walking horse bit with ¼-inch round crossbar constructed of highly polished NICKEL SILVER. 9-inch rounded cheeks, 5⅛-inch NICKEL SILVER low port.
Plain only. Each.............. $7.25

The BALL BEARING
RICARDO takes pride in introducing this NICKEL SILVER ball-bearing, loose check bit. The cheeks actually rotate on ball bearings. This type of assembly not only permits smooth and instantaneous action, but prevents the injuring of the tender membranes in a horse's mouth due to pinching. Loose rein rings.
No. 3005—Hand engraved.
Each $16.00
No. 3004—Plain. Each.... 13.50

The JOE DEKKER
The two discs, 2¼" in diameter, revolve easily, and where the port adjoins the rings is a ¾" ferrule that revolves on the port, giving the horse a feeling of freedom with the bit in its mouth.
The material is our never rust nickel silver. The cheeks overall measurement is 7½" and a 5¼" port.
No. 3002—Plain.
Price, each $7.50
No. 3003—Hand Engraved.
Price, each $8.75

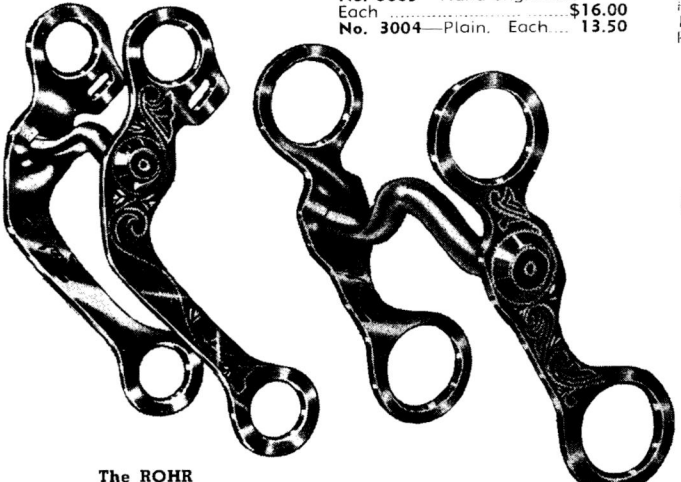

The ROHR
A beautiful Texas grazing bit with long, slender curved cheeks. Made entirely of RICARDO'S rustproof NICKEL SILVER. Handsomely engraved by experts. 8¼-inch cheeks, 5⅛-inch NICKEL SILVER low port.
No. 3025—Hand engraved.
Each $8.75
No. 3024—Plain. Each...... 6.00

The DE SOTA
Always one of the most popular bits. A short shank staple bit made of solid NICKEL SILVER. 6¾-inch cheeks. 5⅛-inch NICKEL SILVER medium port.
No. 3011—Hand engraved.
Each $7.50
No. 3010—Plain. Each...... 5.25

The ROPER
No. 3006—RICARDO'S new solid NICKEL SILVER one-piece roping bit. Light in weight, but very strong and durable loose rein ring. 9¼-inch cheeks with 6¼-inch opening under port. 5⅛-inch aluminum port.
Plain only. Each $7.50

Ricardo METAL MANUFACTURERS, 1218 15th ST., DENVER 2, COLO.

Stainless Nickel Silver Bits

NICKEL SILVER is the best of rustproof metals for bits and spurs. It has the strength of steel and finishes to the high lustre of silver. No plating to chip, peel or wear off. Engraves beautifully and with reasonable care will retain its finish indefinitely.

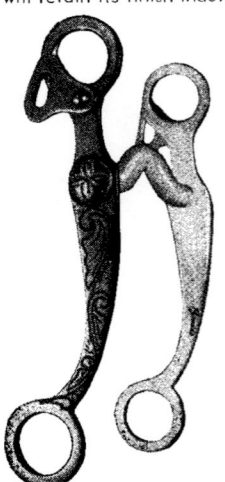

The WORSTER
A neat staple bit with swivel action curb strap loops that completely eliminates pinching. Made entirely of NICKEL SILVER. 8 3/8-inch cheek, 5 1/8-inch NICKEL SILVER medium port.
No. 3063—Hand engraved.
Each $10.00
No. 3062—Plain. Each...... 8.50

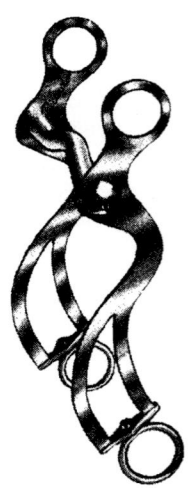

The SPLIT BIT
No. 3007 — A beautiful split cheek bit that you would be proud to own. Full swivel rein rings. Made of NICKEL SILVER with a mirror-like finish. 8 1/8-inch cheeks, 5 1/8-inch NICKEL SILVER low port.
Plain only. Each $8.50

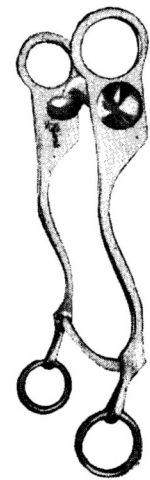

The STAN
No. 3098—An old-time favorite walking horse bit. Short, light weight rounded cheeks with 1/4-inch round crossbar. Entire bit made of NICKEL SILVER, polished to a high lustre. 7 5/8-inch cheeks, 5 1/8-inch NICKEL SILVER low port.
Plain only. Each............ $6.50

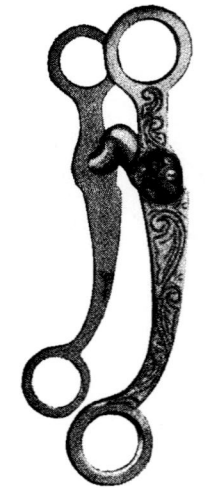

The BITNER
A good practical light weight bit. Made of RICARDO'S NICKEL SILVER. Same as No. 3062 without the curb strap loops. 8 3/8-inch cheek, 5 1/8-inch NICKEL SILVER medium port.
No. 3061—Hand engraved.
Each $7.75
No. 3060—Plain. Each 6.00

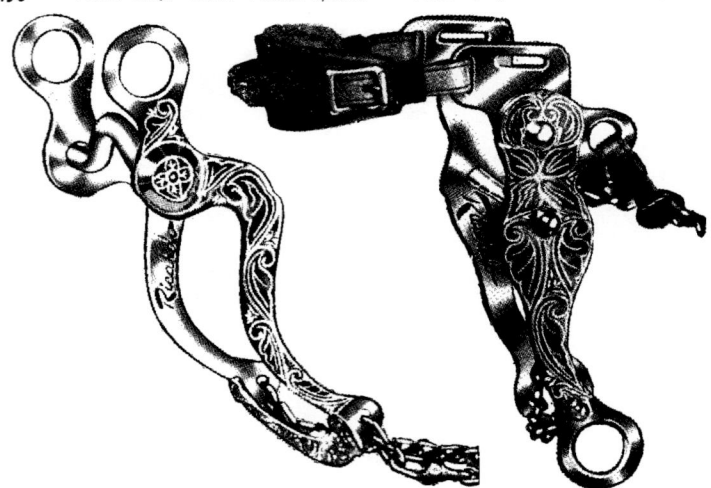

The CARLSON
A show bit that adds to any outfit. Long slenderized cheek pieces with cross bar at bottom. Made of RICARDO'S NICKEL SILVER. Beautifully hand engraved right in the metal. Furnished with solid NICKEL SILVER rein chains. 5 1/8-inch NICKEL SILVER low port.
No. 3021—Hand engraved.
Each $12.50
No. 3020—Plain. Each 10.25

The BURNETT
The ever-popular combination hackamore made of solid NICKEL SILVER. A fine bit with adjustable leverage. Removable, straight bar mouthpiece. Adjustable sheepskin-lined noseband. Curb chain.
No. 3041—Hand engraved.
Each $12.00
No. 3040—Plain. Each 9.00

Ricardo METAL MANUFACTURERS, 1218 15th ST., DENVER 2, COLO.

FRONTIER BITS BY SLIESTER

MOUTHPIECES — Available in all Bits shown

 # 01
Wide Spanish Spade
2-1/2" to top of spade 1/2" Dia.

 # 02
Half-Breed
1/2" Diameter

 # 03
Copper Covered Hi-Port
1-3/4" Tapered Port 1/2" Dia.

 # 04
Hi-Port with Cricket
1-3/4" Tapered Port 1/2" Dia.

 # 05
Hi-Port
1-3/4" Tapered Port 1/2" Dia.

 # 06
Low-Port
3/4" Port - 9/16" Dia.

 # 07
Low-Port with Cricket
1-1/4" Tapered Port 9/16" Dia.
Available in 4-1/2" - 4-3/4" -
4-7/8" - 5-1/8" Width

 # 07
Copper Covered Low-Port
with Cricket
4-1/2" - 4-3/4" - 4-7/8" -
5-1/8" Width

 # 26-348
An original patented creation by Al Ray. Nickle silver mouthpiece, tenzaloy metal shanks. Very flexible mouthpiece, will not pinch, is comfortable in a horse's mouth. Works well for starting colt, cut tongues and hard mouthed horses.

 # 25-08
Frontier Training Snaffle
5-1/2" Leverage
Highly Polished Nickel Silver. This bit is ideal for breaking, training or re-schooling the hard to handle horse.

 # 20
Frontier Hackamore
(Sliester Jackamore)
Highly polished, Aluminum Alloy. 9" Leverage, complete as shown.

 # 40
Frontier Hackamore
Highly polished nickel silver cheeks with same strength and weight as stainless steel. 9" Leverage, complete as shown.

#20 or #40 Available with Braided Rawhide Nose Band

 # 25 Series
Frontier Trainer
5-1/2" Leverage. This Bit has additional weight over the similar #22 Series.
Available in all Mouthpieces.

25-03

25-04

FRONTIER BITS BY SLIESTER

FRONTIER ARENA CHAMPION   5½" Leverage   —   Highly Polished Nickel Silver

The perfect bit for Rodeo Contestants. This bit was designed from suggestions by champion ropers and doggers. Now being used by the World's Champion Professionals.

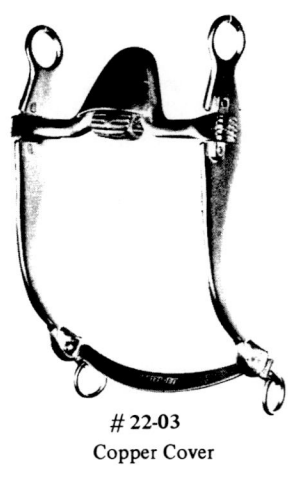

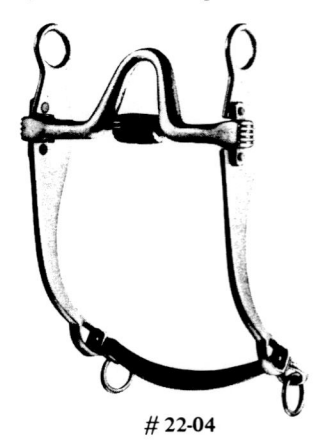

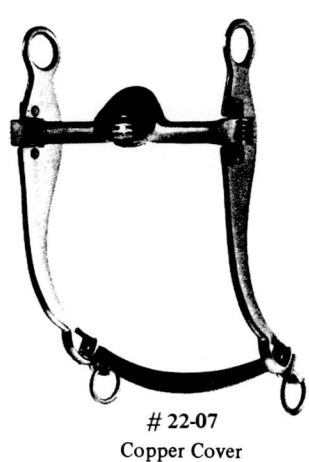

22-03
Copper Cover

22-04

22-07
Copper Cover

FRONTIER REINSMAN   5½" Leverage   —   Highly Polished Nickel Silver

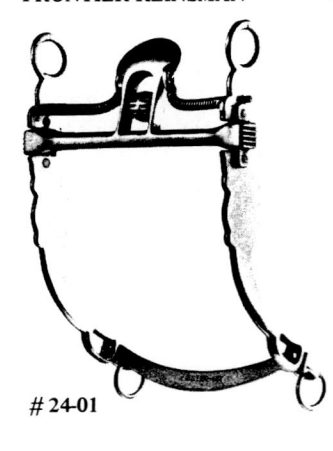

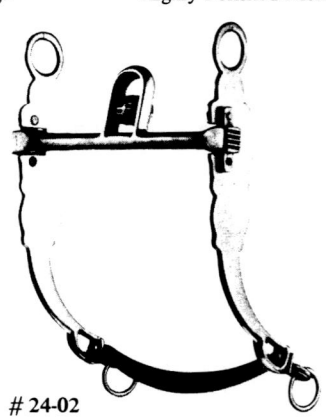

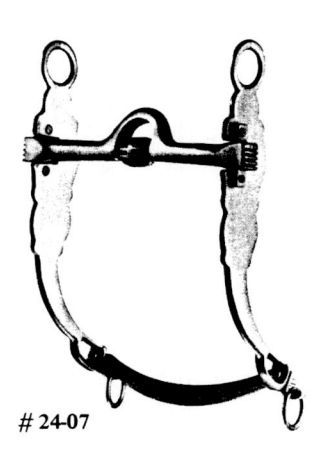

24-01

24-02

24-07

FRONTIER PLAINSMAN   4½" Leverage   —   Highly Polished Nickel Silver

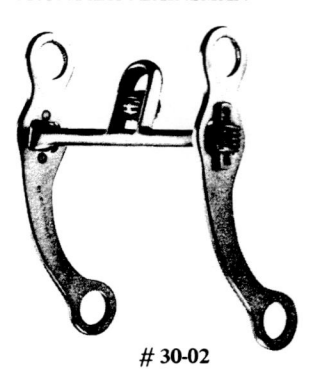

30-02

30-03

Frontier Bits feature the "square pin." This eliminates cheek pieces turning and pinching the horse's mouth, yet allows all the action required in a loose jawed bit.

History of the Visalia Stock Saddle

It is no exaggeration to state that the Visalia saddle brings into focus some eight or ten notable old-time saddlemakers, a century of West Coast history, and the involvement of men from three nations.

Following the gold rush of 1849-50, the American settlers in California turned to the ways of the old native vaqueros in first utilizing the vast rangelands as a route to fortune. Mexican cattle were plentiful; others were brought in from Texas and the eastern states. The rolling, grassy hills west of the Sierras was a natural pasture. Business was outgrowing its adolescent stage; more and more people were coming to the always summer valleys of the Bear State. Many far-seeing individuals staked their futures on an inevitable demand for western beef.

Thus, with the founding of new ranches came the need for cowboys to manage the growing herds. This, in turn, created a rising demand for saddles and assorted horseback equipment. It remained for the saddlemakers to supply the outfits necessary to a bourgeoning enterprise.

At this time, most of the state's cow work was handled with California's vaquero saddles. But progress was on the wing. The great influx of people meant a corresponding influx of new ideas. Good as the old Mexican vaquero saddles were, there still remained room for various improvements.

Juan Martarel had learned the saddler's trade in his native San Salvador. At the time of the gold rush, he had joined the migration to San Francisco by way of a sailing ship from Mazatlan. Interest in his craft, however, did not coincide with panning for gold. A few judicious inquiries persuaded him that the ranch and mining country over in Mariposa County offered the best opportunity for realizing his ambitions.

When the dust-caked stage deposited him at Hornitos, he decided that Fate had delivered him to the right spot. On the open plains to the west lay the famous Chowchilla Ranch, running some 50,000 head of cattle and employing a large force of Mexican vaqueros. To the east were the mines of Bear Valley, Coulterville and Mariposa. It was all horseback country. Long-line teams and pack strings freighted in most of the supplies. Leather goods were a most vital commodity for all concerned. Martarel promptly opened a shop and set himself up as a part of the scene.

He was just in time to take an active part in the evolution of the California stock saddle from the old Mexican type. While the native vaqueros were mostly content with their old familiar rigs, the Anglo cowboys had a predilection for Americanized designs. Like most transition periods, that of saddle development had its difficulties. Hybridization, more often than not, brought only faulty results. Many of those saddles came into Martarel's shop to have such faults corrected. It was often quite a problem.

Fortunately, Ricardo Mattle, a saddle maker from Sonora, Mexico, came along shortly after 1860, and began working in Martarel's shop. Mattle was a man with advanced ideas and had already made some improvements on the Mexican saddletree then in common use. His contention was that certain modifications of the tree would lead toward the desired results. One of the old Mexican saddles, the common stock saddle of that day, was brought into the shop for repairs. Discussion of the repair job brought the criticism from Mattley that the tree was not properly built. The two men put their heads together, eventually coming up with what was to later develop into the famous Visalia Tree. Ricardo Mattley made every tree for Visalia until 1899.

Martarel had, meanwhile, been looking for a better location in a larger place. Visalia had become the foremost cowtown in the San Joaquin Valley. Across the broad plains grazed the cattle of Yank Hazelton, Tom Fowler, Jeff James (uncle of the famous Jesse), and Lillis of the Laguna de Tache Grant. The great cattle empire of Miller and Lux was just beginning. Future prospects of a booming cattle industry seemed assured.

In 1869, Martarel moved his shop from Honitos to Visalia, taking with him Ricardo Mattle and a bit and spur maker named Alsalio Herrea. Herrea had grown up in his father's Blacksmith Shops at Robinson's Ferry on the Stanislas River and at Hornitos, where he learned to make the bits and spurs for Martarel. He also made silver-mounted bits, spurs and saddles. But it wasn't to be as easy as they had thought. Unlike the small Hornitos business, which had never known opposition, they found Visalia already supplied with a well-established and extremely popular saddle shop.

The T. Salazar firm was the only saddler in Visalia at that time, and the kingpin of the cowpuncher trade in that region. Salazar's California stock saddles were considered the best to be had. Much of the popularity was due to the skill and ingenuity of Tony Ladesma, creator of the Ladesma Tree. Ladesma was an expert saddlemaker, as well as a designer of improved trees. Long in the employ of Salazar, he directed most of his attention to saddletrees. His belief was that a fully successful saddle could be achieved only by building it on a properly constructed tree. Thus his craftsmanship was largely responsible for the popularity of Salazar saddles.

Breaking in on the Salazar trade was an uphill business, even with Mattle's new tree. After a year and a half of fighting the competition, Martarel and his associates were beginning to consider selling out, or perhaps consolidating with the opposition. Before they did anything definite, however, David E. Walker and Henry Gust Shuham came to Visalia with the intention of setting up in business. This was to be the big turning point in everyone's career.

Henry Gust Shuham was born in England in 1842. He found his way to America by way of London, Ontario. There he met David E. Walker, forming a close friendship. The two eventually decided to go to California to make their fortunes. On their arrival in San Francisco, they hired on with Main and Winchester to learn the harness and saddlemaking trade. This was in 1865.

During their tenure of employment with this firm, the two young Englishmen did well, both becoming accomplished craftsmen. In the course of events, theirs was the notable achievement of making a set of double harness for President Ulysses S. Grant. The job won them considerable praise for the artistry of their work.

Perhaps this success was the motivation which stirred Shuham and Walker to strike out on their own. Apparently, they had been considering such a venture for some time. Accounts of the thriving cowtown of Visalia had been drifting back to the Main and Winchester shop. It looked like a good place to set up a business, with the two friends as partners. The decision made, early in 1870, Shuham took the river boat up to Stockton, thence by stagecoach, via Merced and Millerton, to Visalia. He selected a location at 60 Main Street, where he was soon joined by Walker.

The new firm was not long in discovering that the two well-established saddle shops were presenting some rather serious competition. The Salazar trade was a fixture of long standing, while Martarel was doing a fair amount of business, especially with Herrea's silver-mounted bits and spurs. A few inquiries, however, revealed the fact that the Martarel firm was becoming dissatisfied with playing second fiddle. Walker's proposal for a merger of the two companies met with quick acceptance.

But even with Juan Martarel, Mattle and Herrea as part of the firm, Walker and Shuham found the competition of Salazar's Ladesma saddles hard to overcome. Use of the Mattle Tree was a help, but it wasn't enough to combat the Salazar lead. It was at this point that they learned of a saddlemaker in Bakersfield who appeared to have the ingredient they needed for a successful campaign.

Jose Rodriguez, the Bakersfield craftsman, like Ladesma, viewed improved trees as the primary secret of superior saddles. In the course of time, he had worked out a very successful tree, which he called the White River (not to be confused with the White River Tree later designed by W. R. Thompson of Rifle, Colorado). The White River Tree created by Rodriguez was based on the Chappo Tree of old Mexico, one of the best of the early Mexican trees.

Rodriguez was persuaded to come to the Walker and Shuham shop at Visalia, there to combine his talent with that of Mattle in designing a new, and more improved tree. Working on advanced ideas gleaned from the Chappo, Mattle and White River Trees, they came up with a design that was destined to make the name of Visalia famous throughout the Western cow country. So successful were these new saddles that Walker and Shuham soon surpassed Salazar as a manufacturer of California's most popular outfits. And, long after T. Salazar was all but forgotten, the renowned Visalia

Stock Saddle, carrying the D. E. Walker brand and serial number, was a favorite with the cowboy clan from Mexico to Canada.

Meanwhile, as frequently happens with partners of dissimilar natures, the Shuham and Walker Company was dissolved. Walker was the more farsighted of the two. He also believed in advertising and salesmanship, being wont to extend himself in that direction. Shuham, on the other hand, was rather conservative, shunning anything that resembled flamboyance or trying to put himself forward. It was inevitable that a rift should occur. This happened in 1877, with the dissolution of the company.

With Shuham buying Walker's interest in the firm, both went their separate ways. Walker, however, didn't go far. He simply walked across the street and opened a shop of his own. Ever the salesman, his advertising paid off. Within a very short time he had built himself up into a competitive position with his former partner. That was when the D. E. Walker brand came into being on the Visalia Stock Saddles.

Two years later, the wheel turned in the opposite direction. That summer of 1879 the Visalia region was hit by a siege of malaria; the epidemic was spreading all over the country. Henry Shuham was something of a hypochondriac by nature. Now, with illness rife in the land, his uneasiness urged him to depart. Walker, the opportunist, seized the chance to buy out his former associate, "kit and caboodle." Shop, tools and good will were all a part of the deal, as was the working personnel: Martarel, Mattle, Rodriguez and Herrea. Walker was off and running in a happy and prosperous saddle business.

With the old Shuham and Walker trademark giving way to the D. E. Walker stamp, the new firm's Visalia Stock Saddle forged ahead of all competitors. It was single-rigged, center-fire style, with rounded skirts, high fork and rather high, straight bound cantle. Most were built to fit individual riders. All this in contrast to the double-rigged Plains Saddle with its square skirts, lower fork and Cheyenne-roll cantle.

As the years went by, Walker found support and encouragement from many friends and satisfied customers. Many of the latter were notable dignitaries; among them were Senator Tom Fowler, Governor Parks of Nevada, Peter B. Kyne, and Walter Scott (Death Valley Scotty). Most of the central California cowpunchers would ride none but Dave Walker saddles.

Direct mail, handbills and catalogues were the media for advertising the Visalia product, catalogue sales forming the bulk of the business. Walker's farsighted advertising policy brought growing prosperity to the firm from most of the western states, Canada and abroad.

In 1887, another important step was taken in the development of the Visalia Stock Saddle Company. It came about through the advice of Jesse Potter, of Miller and Lux. The result of this conference found Walker going into partnership with Mr. Wade, General Manager of the Johnson Company of San Francisco, and opening a new shop in the latter city. The first location was at 111 Front Street. During the next four years, the business expanded to where they were forced to move to larger quarters at 221 California Street. This necessitated a third change in the firm's stamp, passing from D. E. Walker to Walker and Wade. Walker, however, retained his shop in Visalia as a private business.

Another change came when Henry Wegener bought Wade's interest in the company, in 1892, altering the stamp to Walker and Wegener. Soon afterward, another man joined the firm, bringing with him much that had to do with shaping the destiny of the establishment. This was a nephew of Walker, Edmond Walker Weeks, who came down from Canada to engage in the business.

Just before the turn of the century, Wegener died. Dave Walker followed him in death soon afterward. Ed Weeks, being Walker's only heir, bought Wegener's interest in the company from the latter's widow, reverting the firm once again to one-man ownership. He operated the business under the name of Visalia Stock Saddle Company.

Before his death, Walker had closed out his Visalia shop, moving everything to the Walker and Wegener place on California Street. Following the death of Wegener and Walker, Weeks added to the staff and expanded the catalogue advertising. Business continued to prosper until still larger quarters were necessary. They moved to a new location at 510 Market

Street. Following the death of Wegener and Walker, Weeks added to the staff and expanded the catalogue advertising. Business continued to prosper until still larger quarters were necessary. They moved to a new location at 510 Market Street in 1900. There they remained until the great quake and fire in 1906. Following the San Francisco catastrophe, they took up temporary quarters, with what they had been able to salvage, until moving to what was to be their permanent location for almost 50 years at 2123 Market Street.

Ed Weeks died in the early 1930's leaving the business to his stepson, Leland Bergen. Bergen managed the firm until 1945, with indifferent success. He sold it to Sheldon E. Potter in that year. Sheldon E. Potter was a grandson of the Potter who had induced Walker to move to San Francisco almost 60 years previously. He was also an ex-cowboy in his own right, as well as the son of a successful rancher. His knowledge enabled the firm to recapture most of the ranch and cowboy trade that had dwindled away under the former management. By re-establishing the old traditions of high quality products, and awareness of cow-country needs, he built the business back up to its former prosperity. Then, in the early 1950's, realizing that San Francisco was no longer a saddle town, he moved the business to new and larger quarters in Sacramento. There, after surmounting the difficulties inherent in transferring a business to a new location, the firm succeeded in rebuilding its trade in a manner reminiscent of old Dave Walker's palmy days.

The year of 1958 saw still another name added to the long and colorful list of personalities connected with the Visalia Saddles. It was in June of that year that Sheldon Potter sold his Visalia Stock Saddle Company to Kenneth Coppock, founder and owner of the Canadian Kenway Saddle and Leather Company of Calgary.

The consolidation of those two notable firms offered many advantages. Western Canada had always been a prime field for Visalia products. Coupled with Kenway's distributorships and substantial market contacts in Canada, England, France and the United States, it furnished better outlets for the benefit of horsemen and cowmen in both Canada and the United States. With the Visalia shop remaining in Sacramento and the Canadian one in Calgary, the users of saddles, harness, riding equipment and Western attire would receive a greatly increased range of products, being more or less interchangeable between the two countries.

The Canadian part of the Kenway-Visalia relationship was founded in 1949 by Kenneth R. Coppock of Calgary as the Kenway Saddle and Leather Company, Limited. He first took over the shop and personnel of Adams Brothers Harness Company, Limited. In a few years, he constructed his own building at 1418 Stampede Way, only a block north of the main entrance to the Calgary Stampede grounds. This enabled his organization of 28 dedicated personnel to operate the three divisions of the company under one roof.

It was decided that the Visalia Stock Saddle Company would continue at its old stand in Sacramento. Sheldon Potter was induced to continue his able management of the Visalia Plant. This arrangement lasted only a few years. Then came another great fire.

As in the San Francisco fire of 1906, the Visalia Shop burned to the ground; only a few hand-tools were saved from the wreckage. The reputation and great name of the old firm was about all that remained of intrinsic value. That was enough to persuade a few old employees of the San Francisco firm to buy the name, good will and what few tools were salvaged, and move to Castro Valley. The company was rebuilt in 1965 in Castro Valley and stayed there until 1972 when it was moved to Grass Valley. There under the management of Bill Rogers, a longtime saddlemaker in the Walker shop, they tackled the long, hard job of building and retooling a new saddlery for the production of the old reliable D.E. Walker Visalia Stock Saddles.

The next owner, David Stidoff, operated the company for several years.

After a ten year period of inactivity, W. C. (Bill) Cutting and his son, William, negotiated with Stidoff for the Visalia Stock Saddle Company name and logo's in January, 1983, and the company moved to Fresno, some 40 miles from where it originated in 1870. Visalia Stock Saddle Co. was once again intact!

In early 1993 William Cutting had been working with J. M. "Jack" Kendall, a master saddlemaker who learned and worked in the famous San Francisco shop. Jack worked all phases of the shop including the area where trees were made. William and Jack redesigned the famous 3B tree to fit both horse and rider of today.

Every effort is being made to replicate the quality saddles and bits made famous by the Visalia craftsmen.

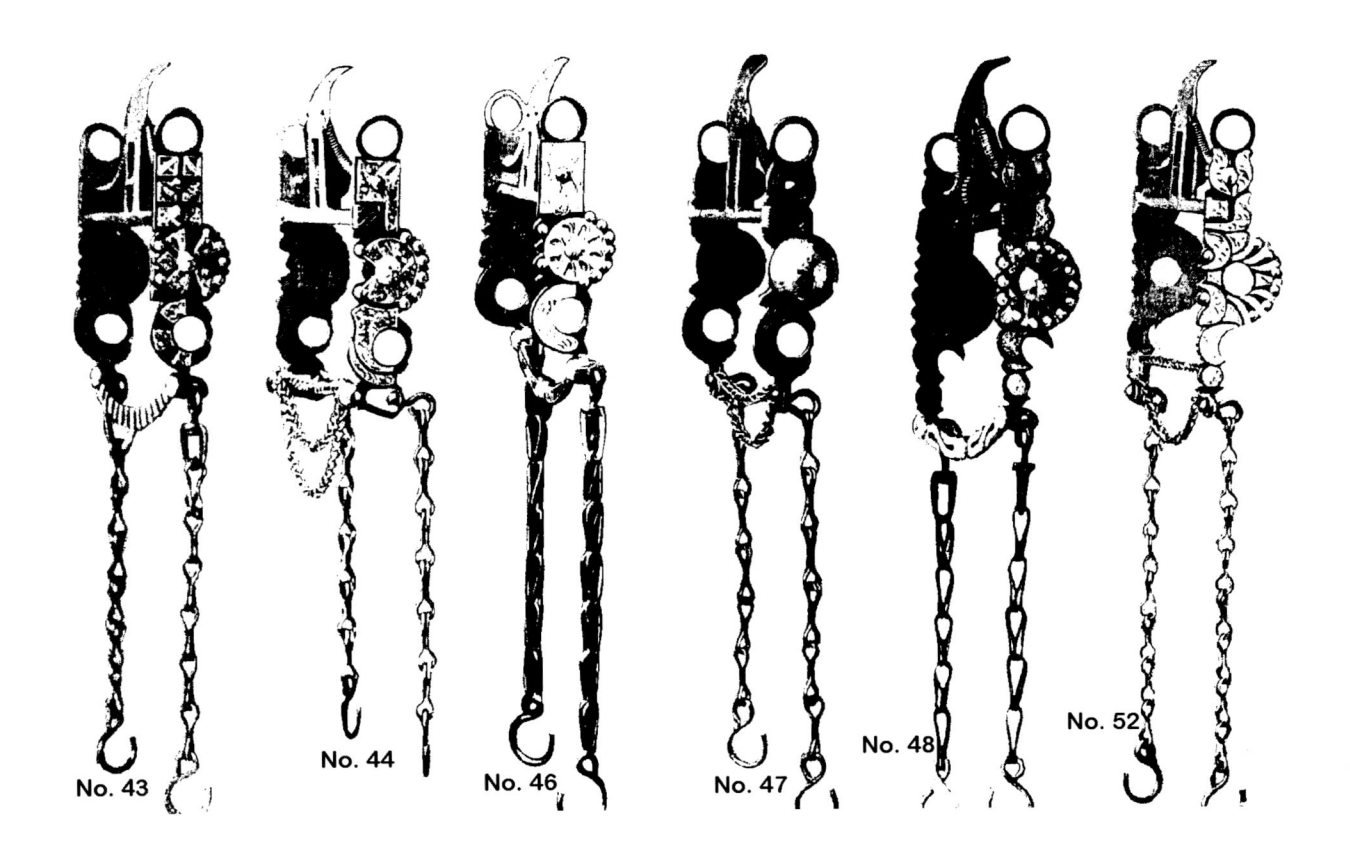

Silver bridle bits of The Visalia Stock Saddle Company of the 1920's.

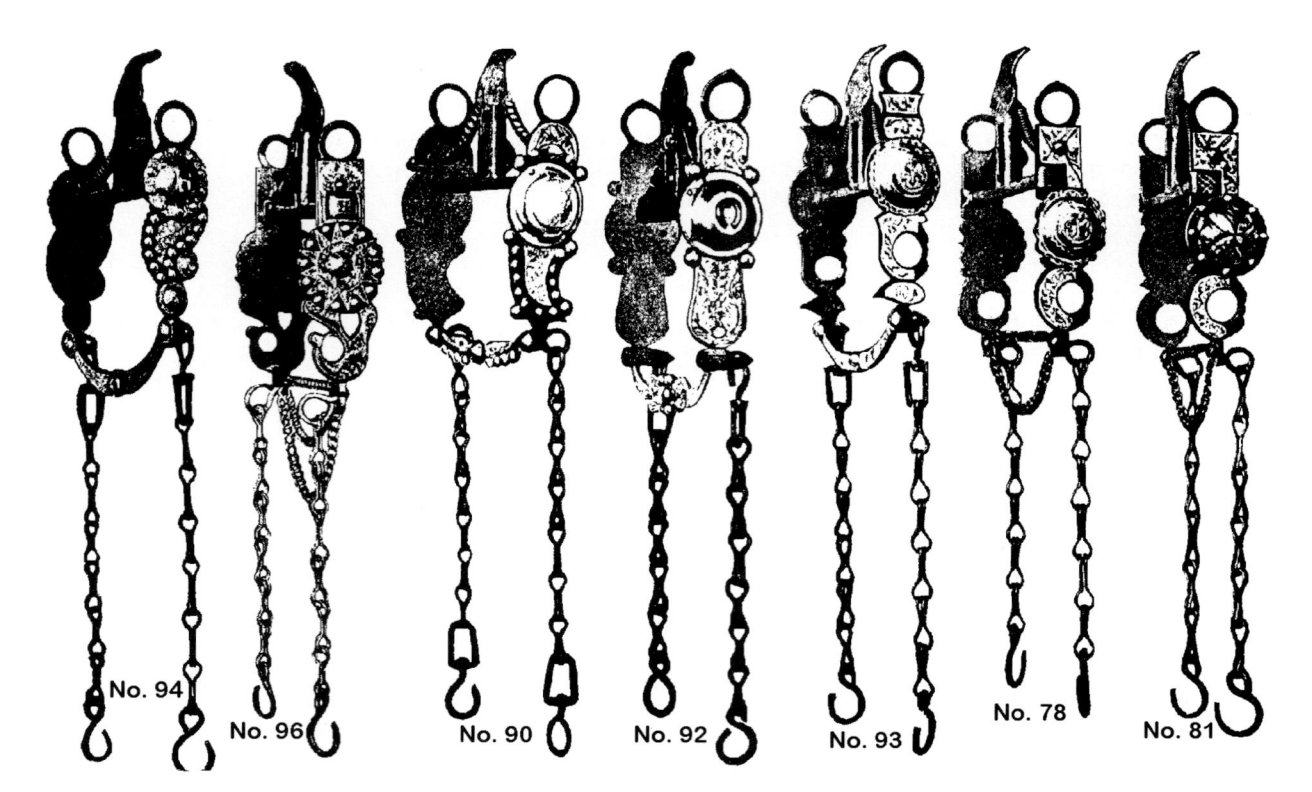

No. 94   No. 96   No. 90   No. 92   No. 93   No. 78   No. 81

Early Visalia silver mounted bits.

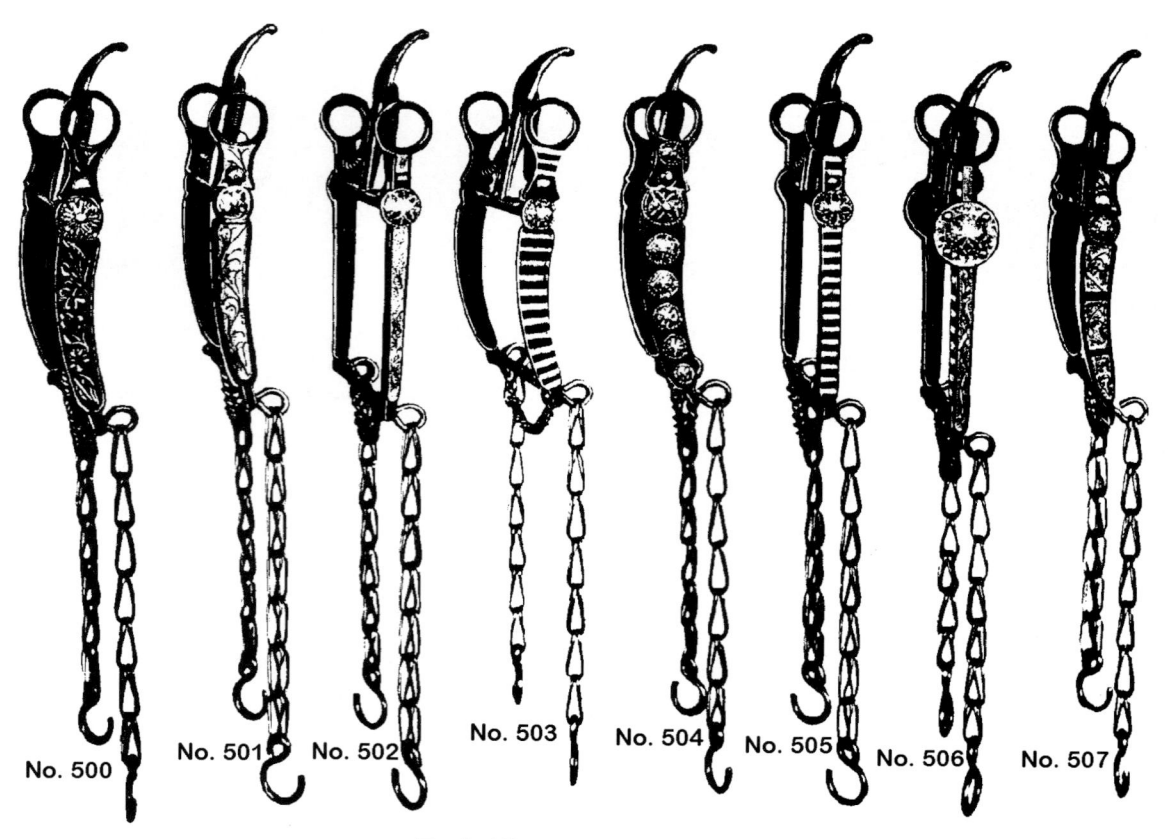

No. 500   No. 501   No. 502   No. 503   No. 504   No. 505   No. 506   No. 507

Early Visalia silver mounted bits.

CHAPTER THIRTY-SEVEN
Comtemporary Loriners

Adamson, Bill, Kersey, Colorado, has been a full-time maker of bits and spurs since 1982.

Aldrich, Ron, maker and owner of Rocky Mountain Bit and Spur, Howard, Colorado.

Alward, Tony, Dumas, Texas, maker of handmade bits, spurs and buckles.

Anderson, Ray, Weatherford, Texas. Stamps his products Ray Anderson.

Andrews, David, Joshua, Texas, maker of bits and spurs.

Apache Brand Bits and Spurs: Started in 1983, by Howdy Fowler with the product stamped APACHE.

B. E. Bits: Oswego, Kansas, maker of handmade bits and spurs.

B-H: See Harris.

Balding, Tom, Bits and Spurs, Sheridan, Wyoming, maker of basic styles with limited editions.

Billy Bits, custom-made bits by Billy Campbell, Childress, Texas.

Bits of Silver, Atascadero, California.

Bitterroot Bit and Spur: owned and operated by Frank and Vicki Schultz in Victor, Montana.

Booze, Brad, Miami, Texas, custom maker of bits, spurs, buckles and oxbow stirrups.

Brown, Charlie, Coal Creek, Colorado, handmade bits and spurs.

Burns, Kevin, Borger, Texas, made-to-order bits, spurs, conchos and saddle hardware.

Butters, Randy, Homer, Michigan, maker of overlaid bits and spurs.

C. S. Silver Bit and Spur: owned by Steve Schmidt, Caldwell, Idaho. Raised in Texas and started making spurs as a cowboy in Idaho. With the direction and instruction of Elmer Miller's Bit and Spur School, Nampa, Idaho, began making silver overlay and inlay bits and spurs. An excellent craftsman. He enjoys making one-of-a-kind items.

Campbell, Billy: See Billy Bits.

Campbell, Robert, Amarillo, Texas, all silver, brass and copper designs and figures are hand-cut. All hand-graving on bits and spurs.

Carroll, Davis G., Bishop, California, maker of early California-style bits and spurs.

Cash Loval Bit Company: Winston-Salem, North Carolina. Manufacturer of a wide variety of bridle bits.

Cates, Jerry, Amarillo, Texas, maker of bits and spurs. Used OX from 1969 to 1980 and CATES since 1980 to mark products.

Colorado Bit and Spur: Denver Colorado.

Cotterell, James and Sons Limited, Walsall, England, manufacturers of bits, spurs, and stirrups. A company established in 1831.

Crews, Duane, Pawnee, Texas, bit and spur maker.

DM: See Markel, Dennis.

Darnell, Greg, began making bits and spurs while living in Arizona, in the 1970's. He is now in Lone Oak, Texas. His work is stamped GD.

De La Ronde, Joe, Glorietta, New Mexico, maker of hand-forged Spanish colonial-style bits and spurs.

Dunning, Ken, started making bits and spurs in Wray, Colorado, in 1848. He moved to Casa Grande, Arizona, in 1983, where he is still producing hand-made bits and spurs. Items are marked KEN D.

Eichhorn: See B. E. Bits.

Field, John, IV, Santa Barbara, California, a maker of only silver inlaid bridle bits and spurs. He is a third generation loriner. His work is made by stamping the design in the same order as Indian jewelry is made, rather than by the engraving process used by most loriners.

Finchum, Jerry, Amarillo, Texas, maker of bits, spurs, and conchas.

Ford, R. F., Water Valley, Texas. His products may be marked R. F. FORD, KERMIT, TEX or SAN ANGELO TEX.

Fowler: See Apache Brand Bits and Spurs.

Freeman, E. J., Manufacuring Co., Moran, Texas, produces a series of bits with a 3/8 inch diameter mouth-piece and a variety of cheek-pieces.

Frontier Bits: See Sliester and Chapter 36, Pages 523 to 524.

GD: See Darnell.

GKJ Bit and Spur: Greg Jones, Somerville, Oregon.

Garcia and Co.: Elko, Nevada.

Garcia, E., Tecate and San Ysidro, California, marked E. Garcia. Items may be made in Amozoc, Mexico.

Gillespie, Mike, Amarillo, Texas, maker of hand-made bits.

Graham, D. Duane, Canyon, Texas, maker of contemporary bits and spurs.

Graham, Jim, Canadian, Texas, hand-made bits and spurs to the customers design.

Hakes, Gary, Sadona, Arizona, maker of bits, spurs, conchas, buckles, and trim.

Hall, Carl D., Commanche Texas. Started making bits and spurs in 1963.

Hall, Robert, King City, California, has made bits and spurs for 50 years. Born in Missouri in 1915 and moved to California in his early teens. Robert owned a saddle shop in King City, California, from 1946 to 1988. His work carried the name "Hall" until 1966, when it was changed to "JOLAN." Lately all bits are signed "RM HALL" left-side cheek and "JOLAN" on right-side cheek. He is author of the book, *How to Make Bits and Spurs.*

Hanson, Don, San Jose, California, maker of bits for Arabian horses.

Harris, Bill, San Marcos, California, began his work by studying forging from a wheelright in Escondido, California. He practiced his craft first by fulfilling his passion for swords and knives. To further his craft of knife-making he traveled and studied the whole art of sword making in Japan as well as from many other masters in the United States. He works in steel almost exclusively for the bits and spurs he has produced in the past 10 years. His work is signed "B-H." He uses silver inlay and overlay and hand engraves with a chasing hammer and push engravers--no power engraving.

Hays, Gordon, Templeton, California, began developing his craft in 1957, while still in high school. He began by making a few Spanish-style bits for himself and continued in this way until 1972. He uses only sterling silver and high grade steel to insure quality and durability in his bits.

Heisman, Bill, Tuscon, Arizona, began making bits and spurs in the early 1970's. He is an expert craftsman with very detailed ornate California bits and spurs. The past few years he has specialized in miniatures. His workmanship and items are highly prized by collectors of quality bits and spurs.

Hildreth, L., Sacramento, California, bit maker.

Jackson, James Weldon, Ft. Worh, Texas, maker of contemporaty Texas-style bits and spurs.

Jackson, John, worked for Visalia Stock Saddle Co., Castro Valley, California. Besides making bits, he repaired bits return to Visalia.

JOLAN: See Hall, Robert.

Jones, Ronnie, Hooker, Oklahoma, maker of Texas-style bits and spurs.

JP: See Pollard, Jock.

Kauffman, Jerry, Longmont, Colorado, maker of bits and spurs marked JBT.

KEN D.: See Dunning.

Kittleson, John, started at Loveland, Colorado, and recently moved to Cody, Wyoming. Bits are marked with a kettle and rising sun on the mouth-piece.

Klapper, Billy, Pampa, Texas, custom maker of bits and spurs.

Lewis, Jerry, started in 1944, in Stinnett, Texas. The bits and spurs are stamped LEWIS.

Linderman, Ted, Crownpoint, New Mexico, maker of all types of bits and spurs.

Lindley, Jerry, Weatherford, Texas, started in 1970, and stamps products LINDLEY.

Lovel, Cash: See Cash Lovel Bit Co.

Madole, Bill, Shawnee, Oklahoma, maker of several syles of cowboy bits and spurs.

Markel, D., Tuscon, Arizona, products are marked with a connected reversed DM.

Markel, Dennis, Cochise, Arizona, maker of quality hand-crafted silver-mounted bits and spurs. Products designed for the professional horseman. Son of D. Markel; products are marked the same with a connected reversed DM.

McCowen: See Montana Bit and Spur.

Meeske, Don and Ardice, Colorado Springs, Colorado, have been making bits and spurs for over 15 years.

Montana Bit and Spur: Melton McCowen, Hamilton, Montana, maker of bits and spurs.

Mosier, Floyd, Clayton, New Mexico, handmade bits, spurs and buckles.

Overton, Dennis, Whitehorse, Texas, full-time for over 24 years. Products are marked OVERTON.

Parker, Rick, Union Grove, Alabama, maker of silver overlaid bits and spurs.

Paul, Wayne, Lipscomb, Texas, makes some bits but primarialy works with spurs. Began as a knife maker.

Payne, Jeff, Bluff Dale, Texas, maker of overlaid silver bits, spurs and conchas.

Pini, Bob, Bit maker.

Pointer, Glenn, started making bits and spurs in Tuscola, Texas, in 1991. Products are markad POINTER with bits having odd and Spurs pattern an even number.

Pollard, Jock, Okmulogee, Oklahoma, started in 1987, and marks products JP.

Pollard Custom Spurs and Bits: quality handmade work in made-to-order bits and spurs by Danny D. Pollard, Fort Worth, Texas.

Ray, Leo, Sidney, Montana, raised on a ranch south of Medors in the North Dakota Badlands. His first bits and spurs were for use on the ranch and others were designed for use by neighbors and as gifts. The bits and spurs are generally overlaid with sterling or German silver. Most of his work has been done since 1979.

Roberts, Chuck, Westminster, Colorado, maker of bits only when ordered with a matching set of spurs.

Rose, John, Lingle, Wyoming, began making bits in 1985, and spurs a few years before. He specializes in lady leg bits and spurs with silver and gold. His customers are the old-time working cowboys and "buckaroos."

Scalese: See Sweetwater Silver.

Schultz, Frank and Vicki, own and operate Bitterroot Bit and Spur in Victor, Montana.

Shirley, Erlon, Memphis and Tahoka, Texas, custom-made bits and one-piece spurs.

Shirley, Murl W., Borger, Texas, custom bridle bits. Uses the brand M combined on X.

Sliester Bits, Auberry, California, manufacture bits that feature the "square pin" to keep the cheek-pieces from turning and pinching the horse's mouth. See Chapter 36, pages 523 to 524.

Smith, J. L., Cody, Wyoming, maker of bits, spurs and saddle silverwork.

Spraberry, Tommy, Anson, Texas, custom maker of bits and spurs.

Steele Bit and Spur: Oklahoma City, Oklahoma, owned and operated by Tom Steele. A maker of fine bridle bits specializing in hand-made bits on custom order for training, show and replication. Repairs and restores bridle bits and custom makes spurs.

Strait, Jim, a bit maker in Missouri. Sells his bits under the name of Sunburst Silver.

Sunburst Silver: See Jim Strait.

Sweetwater Silver: Bob and Diane Scalese started building bits and spurs for others in 1985. Bob does the metal work and Diane does the silversmithing and engraving. Products are marked SCALESE plus a production number if there is room. From 1985-1988 DILLON was added, from 1988-1991 E. GLACIER PK and from 1991 to present products are made in Big Sandy, Montana.

Trammel, Ricky, is owner and maker of the Double Bar T Custom Bits and Spurs, Graham, Texas. Products are stamped TRAMMELL.

Vaughn, Pat, North Platte, Nebraska, bit and spur maker.

Wallace, J.D., Madill, Oklahoma, maker of bits and spurs.

Walters, A. E. "Bud," San Luis Obispo, California, started making bits and spurs in 1949, in Laurel, Montana. Signs his work with his registered brand "A W." His shop is at the AAA Training Ranch, San Luis Obispo.

Welch, Dexter, McMinnville, Oregon, custom bit and spur maker. Specializes in restorations and in silver, goldsmithing and engraving.

Wilkens, Lefty, Hillsboro, New Mexico, bit maker from 1971.

Wimmer, William (Bill) S., Paso Robles, California, learned the art from his father John Wesley Wimmer. His bits are marked WSW on the left cheek-piece and/or the bottom of the mouth-piece or both.

Winbourn, Bud, Cortez, Colorado, maker of bits and spurs.

Winchester: Korean made, stamped Winchester and often have German silver leaf overlays.

Yandell, Luns, Porterville, California, maker of California-style bits and spurs.

York's Handmade Bits by Bill York, Pueblo West, Colorado, maker of silver mounted, custom-designed bits and cowboy-using bits.

BIBLIOGRAPHY

BOOKS:

Adams, Ramon F., 1968. *Western Words,* University of Oklahoma Press, Norman.

Adcock, F. E., 1957. *The Greek and Macedonian Art of War,* University of California Press, Berkeley and Los Angeles.

Ahlborn, Richard E., 1980. *Man Made Mobile,* Smithsonian Institution Press, Washington, D. C.

Alexander, David, 1963.*The History and Romance* of *the Horse,* Cooper Square Publishers, Inc., New York.

Anderson, J. K., 1961. *Ancient Greek Horsemanship,* University of California Press, Berkeley.

Apsley, Lady Viola, 1926. *Bridleways Through History,* Hutchinson and Co., London.

Auel, Jean M., 1983. *The Valley of Horses,* Crown Publishers Inc., New York.

Babcock, Gil and Frank Hilderbrand, 1972. *Bridle Bits of the West,* lst Edition, by author, Grangerville, Idaho.

Baranowski, Zdzislaw, 1955. *The International Horseman's Dictionary,* A. S. Barnes & Co., Canbury, New Jersey.

Battersby, Col. J. C., 1886. *The Bridle Bits*, 0. Judd Co., New York.

Beckman, John, 1846. *History of Inventions, Discoveries, and Origin, Vol. 1,* London.

Berjeau, Philbert Charles, 1864. *Horses of Antiquity, Middle Ages, and Renaissance from the Monuments Down to the Sixteenth Century,* Dulau & Co., London.

Bloodgood, Lida Fleitman and Piero Santini, 1964. *The Horseman's Dictionary,* E. P. Dutton & Co., Inc., New York.

Bowles, Gordon T., 1977. *The People of Asia,* Charles Scribner's Sons, New York.

Bracket, Albert G., 1965. *History of the United States Cavalry,* Argonaut Press, New York.

Brazelon, Bruce S. and William F. McGuinn, 1990. *A Directory of American Militaiy Goods Dealers and Makers 1785-1915,* by authors, printed by REF Typesetting and Publishing, Inc., Manassas, Virginia.

Broderick, A. Houghton, 1972. *Animals in Archaeology,* Praeger Publishers, New York.

Carter, Gen. William H., 1906. *Horses, Saddles, and Bridles,* Lord Baltimore Press, Baltimore, Maryland.

Cary, Pam, et al., 1987. *The Horse, A Complete Encyclopedia,* Chartwell Books, Inc., Secaucus, New Jersey.

Cavendish, William, Duke of Newcastle, 1743. *A General System of Horsemanship,* Fascimile reproduced by J. A. Allen & Co., London.

Cerum, C. W., 1947. *The Secrets of the Hittites,* Alfred A. Knoff, New York.

Chenevix-Trench, Charles, 1970. *A History of Horsemanship,* Doubleday & Co., Garden City, New York.

Cheney, Sheldon, 1962. *A New World History of Art,* Viking Press, New York.

Childe, V. Gordon, 1939. *Man Makes Himself,* Oxford University Press, New York.

    1963. *The Bronze Age,* Biblo and Tannen, New York.

Christy, E. A., 1952. *Cross Saddle and Side Saddle,* 2nd Edition, Hutchinson & Co., London.

Connell, Ed, 1964. *Reinsman of the West,* Vol. 11, Lennoche Publishers, Livermore, California.

Contenau, Geroge, 1954. *Everyday Life in Babylon and Assyria,* St. Marten's Press, Inc., New York.

Coolidge, Dane, 1939. *Old California Cowboys,* E. P. Dutton and Co., New York.

Cossar, J., and E. Prisse D'Avennes, 1967. *The Multiple Origin of Horses and Ponies and Egyptian and Arabian Horses,* Shorey Book Store, Seattle, Washington.

Cottrell, Leonard, 1964. *Digs and Diggers, a Book of World Archaeology,* The World Publishing Company, Cleveland.

Cubbitt, Col., The Hon. C. G., D.S.D., T.D., D.L., 1972. *Bits and Bitting,* The Pony Club, c/o The National Equestrian Centre, Kenilworth, Warwickshire, England.

Daumas, E., 1863. *The Horses of the Sahara and Manners of the Desert,* W. H. Allen & Co., London.

Davis, A., 1867. *A Treatise on Harness, Saddles, and Bridles: Their History and Manufacture from the Earliest Times Down to the Present Period,* Horace Cox, London.

Deacon, Alan, 1972. *Horse Sense,* Wilshire Book Co., North Hollywood, California.

Denison, George T., 1913. *A History of Cavalry,* 2nd Edition, Macmillan & Co., London.

de Pluvinel, Antoine, 1626. *Le Manege Royal,* Facsimile reproduced by J. A. Allen & Co., London.

Dent, Anthony, 1974. *The Horse Through Fifty Centuries of Civilization,* Phaidon Press, London.

Diaz del Castillo, Bernal, 1568. *The True History of the Conquest of Mexico,* Reprinted 1927, by Robert M. McBride & Co., London.

Dodge, Theodore Ayrault, 1894. *Riders of Many Lands,* Harperand Brothers, New York.

Dwyer, Francis, Major, 1886. *Seats and Saddles, Bits and Bitting,* 4th edition, Lovell, Conyell & Co., New York.

Edwards, E. Hartley, 1963. *Saddlery,* A. S. Barnes and Co., Cranbury, New Jersey.

1990. *Bitting in Theory and Practice,* J. A. Allen and Company, London.

Felton, W. Sidney, 1962. *Masters of Equitation,* J. A. Allen & Co., London.

1968. *The Literature of Equitation (One Man's Opinion),* V. S. Pony Clubs and J. A. Allen & Co., London.

Fillis, James, 1902. *Breaking and Riding,* reprinted 1963, J. A. Allen & Co., London.

Fitz-Gerald, W. N., 1875. *The Harness Makers Illustrated Manual,* by author, New York, reprinted by North River Press Inc.

Fletcher, Sydney E., 1951. *The Cowboy and His Horse,* Grosset & Dunlap, New York.

Foster, Harris, 1955. *The Look of the Old West,* Bonanza Books, New York.

Franck, Irene E. and David M. Brownstone, 1986. *The Silk Road- A History,* Facts on File Publications, New York.

Froissard, Jean, 1974. *An Expert's Guide to Basic Dressage,* Wilshire Book Co., North Hollywood, California.

Garst, Shannon, 1947. *Three Conquistadors: Cortez, Coronado, Pizzaro,* Julian Messner, New York.

Gianoli, Luigi, 1969. *Horses and Horsemanship Through the Ages,* Crown Publishers, New York.

Gilbey, Sir Walter, 1899. *The Great Horse,* Vinton and Co., New York.

Graham, R. B. Cunninghame, 1949. *The Horses of The Conquest,* University of Oklahoma Press, Norman.

Grant, Bruce, 1951. *The Cowboy Encyclopedia,* Rand McNally & Co., New York.

Green, Carol, 1978. *Tack Explained,* Arco Publishing Company, Inc., New York.

Green, Susan, 1992. *Bridle: Index of United States Patents,* by author, Leesburg, Virginia.

Griess, Thomas E. (Editor), 1984. *Ancient and Medieval Warfare,* West Point Military History Series, Avery Publishing Group, Inc., Wayne, New Jersey.

Grigson, Geoffrey, 1950. *Horse and Rider,* Thames and Hudson, New York.

Grosset, Rene, 1963. *A History of Asia,* Walker and Co., New York.

Hadingham, Evan, 1979. *Secrets of the Ice Age,* Walker and Company, New York.

Hall, Robert M., 1985. *How to Make Bits and Spurs,* Pioneer Publishing Co., Fresno, California.

Halperin, Charles J., 1985. *Russia and the Golden Horde,* Indiana University Press, Bloomington.

Hasluck, Paul Nooncree, 1962. *Saddlely and Harnessmaking,* J. A. Allen & Co., London.

Haug, LeRoy C. and Gerhard A. Malm, D.V.M., 1975. *Bible of Bridle Bits,* 1st Edition, published by author, Valley Falls, Kansas, 66088.

Holling, Holling C., 1936. *The Book of Cowboys,* Platt & Munk Co., New York.

Jacobs, Lee C., 1985. *Fancy Driving Bits and Ornamental Curbs,* by author, Colorado Springs, Colorado.

1994. *J. R. McChesney,- A Lifetime,- A Legacy,* by author, Colorado Springs, Colorado.

Jankovich, Miklos, 1971. *They Rode into Europe,* George G. Harrap and Co., London.

Jettmar, Karl, 1964. *The Art of the Steppes,* translated 1967 by Ann E. Keep. Baden-Baden: Holle Verlag.

Johnson, Swafford, 1985. *History of the United States Cavalry,* Cresent Books, Greenwich, Connecticut.

Kenrick, Vivienne, 1962. *Horses in Japan,* J. A. Allen and Co., London.

Kurten, Bjorn and Elaine Anderson, 1980. *Pleistene Mammals of North America,* Columbia University Press, New York.

Laking, Sir Guy Francis, 1920. *European Armour and Arms,* G. Bell & Co., London.

Lamb, Harold, 1930. *Gengis Kahn: Emperor of All Men,* Robert M. McBride & Co., New York.

Langdon, William G., Jr., 1989. *Bits and Bitting Manual,* Langdon Enterprises, Colbert, Washington.

Latchford, Benjamin, 1871. *The Loriner,* London.

Lattimore, Owen, 1962. *Studies in Frontier History, Collected Papers 1928-1958,* Oxford University Press, New York.

Lea, Tom, 1964. *The Hands of Cantu,* Little, Brown and Co., New York.

Le Duc, E. Viollet (Editor), 1877. *D'ictionairre raisonne due mobileir francois,* Vol 6, "Hannois," by Ernest Grund, Paris, France.

Lehmann, Johannes, 1977. *The Hittites,* Viking Press, New York.

Lepe, Jose I., 1951. *Diccionario de asuntos hipicos y ecuesestres,* Mexico City.

Littauer, Vaidimer S., 1945. *The Forward Seat*, reprinted by Hurst & Blackett., London.

　　　1945. *More About the Forward Seat,* Hurst & Blackett, London.

　　　1951. *Common Sense Horsemanship,* D. Van Norstrand Co., Princeton, New Jersey.

　　　1962. *Horsemen's Progress,* D. Van Nostrand Co., New York.

McBane, Susan, 1988. *The Horse and the Bit*, Howell Book House, Inc., New York.

McTaggart, M. F., 1925. *Mount and Man,* Country Life, Ltd., London.

Malm, Gerhard A., *et al.*, 1967. *Treasury of Bits,* by author, Valley Falls, Kansas.

Markham, Gervase, 1614. *The Complete Horseman,* reprinted in 1975 by Houghton Mifflin Co., Boston.

Matthews, W. D., 1913. *Evolution of the Horse in Nature,* American Museum of Natural History, Publication No. 36, Washington, D. C.

Mertz, Barbara, 1964. *Temples, Tombs, and Hieroglyphs,* Dodd, Mead, and Co., New York.

Miller, Dr. Robert M., 1991. *Imprint Training of the Newborn Foal,* Western Horseman, Inc., Colorado Springs, Colorado.

Mohr, Erna, 1971. *The Asiatic Wild Horse,* J. A. Allen & Co., London.

Monaghan, Jay, 1963. *The Book of the American West,* Crown Publishing, New York.

Mora, Jo, 1946. *Trail Dust and Saddle Leather,* Charles Scribner's Sons, New York. 1994 reprint Stoecklein Publishing, Ketchum, Idaho.

　　　1949. *Californios,* Doubleday & Co., Inc., New York. 1994 reprint Stoeklein Publishing, Ketchum, Idaho.

Norman, Vasey, 1964. *Arms and Armor,* G. P. Putnam's Sons, New York.

Page, Denys Lionel, 1959. *History of the Homeric Iliad,* University of California Press, Berkeley.

Perkins, J. B. Ward, 1940. *Medieval Catalogue of the London Museum,* London.

Piekalkiewicz, Janusz, 1980. *The Cavalry of World War II*, Stein and Day, New York.

Potratz, Johannes A. H., 1966. *Die Pferdetrensen des Alten Orient,* Pontificum Institutum Biblicum, Roma.

Potter, Edgar R., 1971. *Cowboy Slang,* Hangman Press, Seattle, Washington.

Powell, T. G. E., 1963. *Some Implications of Chariotry in Culture and Environment,* Essays in Honor of Sir Cyril Fox, London, pp. 153-169.

Raddatz, Diane, 1974. *Developments in Ancient Near East Cavalry in Relation to the Horse--1500 B.C. to 500 B. C.,* history thesis, University of Wisconsin, River Falls.

Rawlinson, George, 1891. *The Five Great Monarchies of the Ancient Easterm World,* Volume 1, Dodd, Mead and Co., New York.

Reynolds, James, 1947. *A World of Horses,* Creative Age Press, Inc., New York.

Rice, Lee M.. and Glenn R. Vernam, 1975. *They Saddled the West,* Cornell Maritime Press, Cambridge, Maryland.

Rice, Tamara Talbot, 1957. *The Scythians,* Frederick A. Praeger, New York.

Rojas, Arnold R., 1960. *Last of the Vaqueros,* Academy Library Guild, Fresno, California.

Rollins, Phillip Ashton, 1936. *The Cowboy,* Charles Scribner's Sons, New York.

Romaszkan, Gregor de, 1967. *Horse and Rider in Equilibrium,* Stephen Greene Press, Battleboro, Vermont.

Rudenko, Sergei I., 1970. *The Frozen Tombs of Siberia; The Pazyruk Burials of Iron Age Horsemen,* University of California Press, Berkeley.

Salaman, R. A., 1986. *Dictionary of Leatherworking Tools, circa 1700-1950,* Macmillan Publishing Co., New York.

Santini, Piero, 1933. *Riding Reflections,* Country Press, London.

1942. Learning to Ride, World Publishing Co., New York.

1967. The Caprilli Papers, J. A. Allen Co., London.

Self, Margaret Cabell, 1946. *The Horseman's Encyclopedia,* A. S. Barnes & Co., New York.

Sidney, S., 1875. *Illustrated Book of the Horse,* reprinted by Wilshire Book Co., North Hollywood, California.

Simpson, George Gaylord, 1951. *Horses.: The Story of the Horse, Sixty Million Years of History,* Oxford University Press, New York.

Smythe, R. H., 1967. *The Horse Structure and Movement,* revised edition, 1972, J. A. Allen & Co., London.

Steiner, Stan, 1981. *Dark and dashing Horsemen,* Harper and Row, Publishers, Inc., New York.

Stocking, Hobart E., 1971. *The Road to Santa Fe,* Hastings House, New York.

Stone, George Cameron, 1931. *A Glossary of the Construction, Decoration and Use of Arms and Armor,* Southworth Press, Portland, Maine.

Stone, Philip Duffield, 1939. *Horses and Americans,* Garden City Publishing Co., Garden City, New York.

Stoneridge, M. A.,1963. *A Horse of Your Own,* Doubleday and Co., Inc., Garden City, New York.

Suarez de Peralta, Juan; 1580. *Treatise of the Horseman a la dineta y de la Brida.*

Summerhays, R. S., 1975. *Summerhays' Encyclopedia for Horsemen,* 6th Edition, Frederick Warne & Co., Ltd., London.

Taylor, Louis, 1973. *Bits, Their History, Use, and Missuse,* Wilshire Book Co., North Hollywood, California.

Tozer, Basil, 1903. *The Horse in History,* Methuen & Co., London.

Trew, Cecil G., 1951. *Accoutrements of the Riding Horse,* Browning Press, Plymouth, England.

1960. The Horse Through the Ages, Roy Publishers, New York.

Tuke, Diana R., 1965. *Bit by Bit,* J. A. Allen & Co., Ltd., London.

Tylden, G., 1965. *Horses and Saddlery,* J. A. Allen & Co., London.

Van Seters, John, 1966. *The Hyksos, A New Investigation,* Yale University Press, New Haven.

Vernam, Glenn R., 1964. *Man on Horseback,* Harper & Row, New York.

Vernon, Arthur, 1939. *The History and Romance of the Horse,* Halcyon House, Garden City, New York.

Ward, Fay E., 1958. *The Cowboy At Work,* Hasting House Publishers, Inc.; paperback 1987, University of Oklahoma Press, Norman, OKlahoma.

Willoughby, David P., 1974. *The Empire of Equus,* A. S. Barnes & Co., Cranbury, New Jersey.

Xenophon; *Xenophon's Anabasis, 1962.* Edited by Maurice W. Mather and Joseph William Hewitt, University of Oklahoma Press, Norman.

1962. *The Art of Horsemanship,* translated by M. H. Morgan, J. A. Allen & Co., London.

Yadin, Yigael, 1963. *The Art of Warfare in Biblical Lands,* Volume 1, McGraw-Hill, New York.

Yetts, W. P., 1934. *The Horse, A Factor in Early Chinese History*, p. 231-255.

Young, John Richard, 1954. *The Schooling of the Western Horse.* lst Edition, University of Oklahoma Press, Norman.

Catalogs:

Arkia Village Saddlery, Emmet, Arkansas.
    1965.
August Buermann Mfg. Co., Newark, New Jersey.
    No. 35, 1922.
Bischoff, G. S. and Co., Gainsville, Texas.
    No. 1, September 1, 1911.
Bohlin, Edward H, Hollywood, California.
    1927.
    1941.
Boone, W. R. (Wallie), San Angelo, Texas.
    No. 3, 1936?.
Boyt Company, Des Moines, Iowa.
    No. 80, 1959.
Carrol Saddle Company, McNeal, Arizona.
    No. 31, 1968-70.
    No. 32, 1971-72.
Connolly Saddlery Co., Billings, Montana.
    Mid 1970's.
Crockett Bit and Spur Co.
    No. 6, Kansas City, Missouri.
    No.11, KansasCity,Missouri.
    No. 12, Kansas City, Missouri.
    No. 14, Lenexa, Kansas.
    No. 49, Boulder, Colorado.
Crockett-Kelly, Boulder, Colorado.
    No. 73, 1973, by Renalde.
    No. 184, 1984.
Dewsbury, John and Son, Walsall, England.
    Circa 1905.
English Saddler.
    1928.
    1936.
H. Kauffman and Sons Saddlery Co., New York, New York.
    No. 95A, 1974.
Kelly Bros., Mfrs.
    No. 17, Dalhart, Texas.
    No. 22, El Paso, Texas, mid 1920's
Libertyville Saddle Shop, Libertyville, Illinois.
    1976.
    1996.
Linden and Funke, Hanover, Germany.
    1912.
Nacoma Boot Company, Nacoma, Texas.
    1942.
North and Judd Mfg. Co., New Britain, Connecticut.
    No. 83.
    No. 89: 1933.
    No. 38.
    No. 43, 1968.
    No. 263, 1970.
Owenhouse, E. J., Bozeman, Montana.
    1889.
Padgett Bros. Company, Dallas, Texas.
    Circa 1905.
Perkins Campbell Company, New York, New York.
    1915.
Phillips and Gutierrez, Cheyenne, Wyoming.
    1918.
Rawhide Mfg., Inc., San Diego, California.
    1975.
    1978.
Ricardo, Denver, Colorado.
    No. 7, 1950.
Richmond Harness and Saddlery Co., Richmond, Virginia.
    1970.
    1974.
Seminole Bit and Spur, Inc., Seminole,Texas.
    1986.
Shipley Saddlery and Mercantile Co., Kansas City, Missouri.
    No.12, 1912-13.
    1953-54.
Vance, Earl and Co., Gainsville, Georgia.
    No. 26, 1940's.
Visalia Stock Saddle Co., San Francisco, California.
    No. 22, 1923.
    1940.
    1967.
    1970, Centennial Issue.
Wholesale Horse Equipment, Los Angeles, California.
    1950's, Third Edition.

Magazines:

De Yong, Joe. "The Fiador Knots." *Western Horseman* January 1950: 10-12.

"Rigging the Fiador." *The Western Horseman* May 1951: 22-23.

Bond, Marian. "Put Them in Hackamore Heaven Part I." *Horse and Rider* June 1988: 8-13.

Burk, George. "Horsehair Bridles." *Western Horseman* October 1960: 140.

Davis, Ray. "Ranch Version of a War Bridle." *The Western Horseman* December 1967: 52-53.

Edwards, Gladys Brown. "Roots of the Family Tree." *Horse and Rider* January 1972: 63-67.

"The Arabian Connection Part II." *Horse and Rider* October 1973: 44-48.

Gamble, Randy. "No Gimmick Foundation for a Good Mouth." *Horse of Course* December 1979:18-22.

Ganton, Doris. "The Driving Horse: Use of the Bitting Rig." *Horse of Course* May 1978: 54-55.

Glenn, Dick. "Mouthing the Young Horse with the Copper Technique." *The Western Horseman* May 1969: 136-137.

Goodspeed, Jess. "Try Starting With a Gag Bit." *Horseman* June 1975: 68-73.

Grant, Bruce. "That Ole Fiador Knot." *The Western Horseman* December 1954:17.

Gray, Joe. "Longe Lining the Western Horse." *The Western Horseman* August 1952:11.

Harper, Deb. "Use 'Slough' Reins for Better Control." *Horseman* January 1975: 58-59.

Henry, Stephen M. "Variations of the M1959 Cavalry Bit." *North South Trader,* March-April 1978: 9-13.

Jones, Dave. "Birth of a Bit." *Horseman* April 1974: 42-45.

"Bogus Ideas About Bits." *Horseman* July 1975: 44-48.

"The Hackamore." *Horse and Rider* Yearbook No. 13: 26-29.

Jones, Suzanne Norton. "Bits and Biting Part I." *The Western Horseman* February 1966: 50-51.

"Bits and Bitting Part II." *The Western Horseman* March 1966:18-19.

Jordon, Wayne. "Bits and How to Use Them Part II." *Horseman* June 1974:70-74.

King, Chuck. "Throw-rope Hackamore." *The Western Horseman* January 1967: 50-51.

LaVergne, J. Jose. "Headset Headaches." *Horse and Rider* October 1988: 26-29.

Lindgren, Carl H. "Snaffle and Curb Bits." *The Western Horseman* March 1956: 29.

OL' Waddy. "Bits and Spurs." *The Western Horseman* November 1952: 31.

Ortega, Luis B. "El Mecate." *The Western Horseman* April 1955:24.

Ray, Phil. "The Western Pelham." *Horse and Rider* Yearbook No. 13: 36-39.

Rickell, Walter L. "How to Tie the California Hackamore," *Horse and Rider Yearbook* No. 5: 122-123.

"The Ring Bit," *The Western Horseman* May 1969: 31.

Rodriguez, Joe. "The Spanish Spade Bit." *The Western Horseman* February 1950: 14.

Steffen, Randy. "War Horses of the Pharaohs." *The Western Horseman* January 1955: 13.

"The Ancient Assyrian." *The Western Horseman* February 1955: 23.

"The Ancient Babylonian." *The Western Horseman* March 1955:15.

"Cyrus the Great of Persia." *The Western Horseman* April 1955: 27.

"The Ancient Parthian." *The Western Horseman* May 1955: 46.

"Alexander the Great." *The Western Horseman* June 1955: 31.

"The Classic Greek." *The Western Horseman* July 1955:19.

"Atilla the Hun." *The Western Horseman* September 1955:15.

"Alaric The Goth." *The Western Horseman* October 1955: 27.

"The Franks... Founders of France." *The Western Horseman* November 1955: 33.

"Tarik the Moor... Conqueror of Spain." *The Western Horseman* December 1955: 39.

"Bits Through History." *The Western Horseman* November 1956: 28-30.

"Bits Through History Part II." *The Western Horseman* December 1956: 26-29

"Bits and Bitting." *The Horse Lovers Magazine* March-April 1969:18-20.

Thrall, Ellen. "Whatever happened to the Tarpan?" *Horseman* October 1973: 74-80.

Tollefson, Randi. "Bits of Knowledge." *Horse and Rider* Yearbook No. 5: 82-90.

"Use and Misuse of the Mechanical Hackamore." *Horse and Rider* December 1971: 54-57.

"The Pleasure of Driving." *Horse and Rider* December 1972: 28-33.

Trammell, Jim. "Develop Your Horse's Mouth." *Horseman* October 1972: 12-25.

Valentry, Duane. "Horse Gear Brings History to Life." *The Western Horseman* November 1967: 20.

Ward, Fay. "Soften 'em Up." *The Western Horseman* February 1955: 22.

Wehrman, Doris. "Which Bit for You?" *Horse of Course* February 1976: 24-26.

White, Gayle. "Build a Rope Halter." *Western Horseman* June 1995: 79-81.

Williamson, Marion. "Longeing In Luxury." *Horseman* August 1973: 66-72.

Yeates, B. F. "Fundamental Hackamore Training." *Horseman* September 1974: 22-26

Young, John Richard. "Calling a Spade Spade." *The Western Horseman* March 1950: 10-11

Index

Ace, 47
Acme driving bit, 100
Agen overcheck, 135
Aldaco, Ruben, 466
Ambrose Clark gag, 156
American half-cheek, 110
American Pelham, 333
Anderson, Prof. J. K., 13
Antler, 12
Aplan, Jens Ole (J.O.), 466
Arch mouth, 39, 305
Artillery bit, 268, 273, 283, 284
Artillery test kit, 283
Ashleigh elbow bit, 110
Auel, Jean M., 8
Avila, Gary, 466
Balancing bit, 110
Balding gag bit, 156
Balding gag bridle, 447
Baldwin, Joseph, 466
Baldwin bit, 116
Banberry cheek, 55
Banberry mouth, 305
Bar mouth, 305
Barnes pulley gag bit, 156
Barrel-head end, 314
Bass, J. O., 57, 466
Bayers, Adolph, 466, 473, 474
Beans bridle, 447
Bearing rein, 447
Beery driving bit, 111
Belknap Hardware, 466
Bentmouth overcheck, 135
Berkley polo Pelham, 334
Best Out overcheck, 135
Bicycle chain bit, 62, 135, 305
Billets, 447
Bird pattern bit, 378
Bischoff, George, 466
Blinders, 13, 64
Blinkers, 64
Bohlin, E. H., 466, 471
Boone, Clayton, 466
Boone, Wallie, 466, 475-6
Bosal, 171-3
Bosalea, 173-4
Boucha bit, 378, 383
Braden direct bit, 108
Bradney, Frank, 466
Bradoon, 446
Bradoon head, 447
Bradoon strap bridle, 446
Bridle ring, 4, 447
Bridle strap ring, 6
Bridleless curb bit, 408

Broken mouth, 111
Bronco bit, 70, 73
Brott, John R., bit, 70
Brow-band bridle, 446
Brower, William, bit, 71
Brown, Henry W., bit, 71
Brown, Lincoln F., bit, 71
Brown, William P., bit, 71
Bryden, Williamson, bit, 71
Bucheye Safety bit, 111
Buck-line, 72
Buermann, 72, 466, 477-8
Buermann noseband, 324
Buggy blind bridle, 461
Buggy snaffle bit, 72-3
Bulbs, 73
Bumper bit, 73
Burch bit, 135
Burch cheek, 135
Burgess, Richard O., bit. 73
Burns, James, bit, 73
Burr, 61, 63, 74
Butler, George P., bit, 74
Butlin, Charles H., bit, 74
Butterfly bit, 74
Buxton bit, 74-5, 83, 119
Buxton cheek, 378
Byers, Chester, bit, 74
Cahoone, Edwin R., bit, 76
Cain, James, bit, 76
Calhoun, Andrew J., bit, 76
California rein, 448
California spade bit, 4, 312
Cambridge mouth, 306
Campbell, Alonzo B., bit, 76
Campbell, Hardy W., bit, 76
Campbell, John E., bit, 77
Cannon, 1-3, 77
Canon City bit, 77
Cape, 335
Cape Pelham, 334
Carbon-14 dating, 10
Carpenter, Daniel H., bit, 77
Carpmill, John F., bit, 78
Carson, Robert A., bit, 78
Carter, Joseph, bit, 78
Case, Milton, bit, 78
Casey, Peter, bit, 79
Catlin, Arthur, bit, 79
Cavalry:
    English and Canadian, 252
    German and French, 262
    United States, 270
Cave drawings, 9
Caveson, 79, 80, 448
Cecil Smith gag bit, 156

Centaur rubber mouth, 335
Center link, 306
Centuries:
32nd	B.C.,	14
18th	B.C.,	14
17th	B.C.,	14
15th	B.C.,	14
14th	B.C.,	15
12th	B.C.,	15
9th	B.C.,	16
8th	B.C.,	16
6th	B.C.,	17
5th	B.C.,	18
4th	B.C.,	20
3rd	B.C.,	21
2nd	A.D.,	21
5th	A.D.,	21
12th	A.D.,	22
14th	A.D.,	22
15th	A.D.,	23
16th	A.D.,	23
17th	A.D.,	25
18th	A.D.,	26

Cerrata, 79
Chain mouth, 306
Chain-mouth snaffle bit, 306
Champ-Neigh bit, 111
Champing the bit, 79
Chandler, Clarence A., bit, 81
Change-mouth bit, 82
Chase bradoon bit, 81
Cheats on the bit, 81
Check bit, 135
Cheek, 81
Cheek connecting loop, 448
Cheek guard, 64
Cheek piece, 1, 81
Cheek ring, 2
Cheek strap, 446
Cheek-strap billet, 446
Cheltenham gag bit, 156
Chenault, John C., bit, 83
Cheshire martingale, 235
Chifney bit, 83
Chihuahua bit, 83
Chilean ring bit, 363
Chileno, 5, 44, 279, 362-4
Chin grove, 31, 83
Chin strap, 96
Chinese bit, 24
Christian, Dick, bit, 84
Church Window bit, 217
Ciammaichella bit, 84
Circassian bit, 84
Citation bit, 85, 157
Clamer, John, bit, 85

Clamer, Joseph, bit, 85
Clark, Frederic, bit, 85
Clark, Wilbur, bit, 85
Clemons, Hiram M., bit, 86
Clipper bit, 86
Closed bit, 86
Closed end, 315
Closed reins, 86, 446, 448
Coburn gag bit, 86
Coe reversible bit, 86
Cold blooded, 10
Cold jaw bit, 87, 171
Cole snaffle bit, 87
Collared cheek, 1, 380
Collins ground tie, 87
Collins run-out bit, 87
Colorado bit, 88
Colt curb bit, 88
Comanche bit, 88
Combs snaffle bit, 89
Conn gag bit, 89
Control bit, 89
Converter strap, 89
Cornell snaffle bit, 90
Cornish snaffle bit, 90
Corpus Christi bit, 90
Cow bit, 90
Cow Boy bit, 90
Cowboy gag bit, 157
Crab check bit, 135
Craighead bit, 91
Crane, Frederick, bit, 92
Crane bit construction method, 91
Crane snaffle bit, 92
Cratty snaffle bit, 93
Crawford sliding-mouth bit, 93
Cresendo bit, 93
Crest Strap bit, 93
Cricket, 4, 5, 94
Crit Davis bit, 102, 135
Crockett, Arthur, 442, 479
Crockett, Oscar, 94, 168, 176, 479-87
Crook gag bit, 94
Crose flat-bar bit, 94
Crown, 446
Crown pattern bit, 221, 225
Crown-piece, 95, 446
Cruger snaffle bit, 95
Cuirassiers, 262
Curb bit, 3, 40
Curb chain, 3, 41, 98, 100
Curb-chain guard, 95
Curb reins, 446
Curb ring, 4
Curved cheek, 335
Cutting, W. C. (Bill), 528
Daisy bit, 101
Daly, Henry W., bit, 101
Daly twisted-rod bit, 101

Dalziel soft-cheek bit, 101
Dan Mace snaffle bit, 102
Daniels pulley bradoon, 102
Darius I, 17
Darr swivel-mouth bit, 102
Davis, Crit, snaffle bit, 102
Day spring-tension bit, 103
Day covered mouth-piece, 103
De Wolf snaffle bit, 105
De Wolfe rotating-cheek bit, 105
Dean, John, snaffle bit, 103
Dean loose-mouth bit, 104
Dean pressure bit, 103
Dee cheek, 378
Dee-cheek bits, 379
Desert of Dzungaria, 8
Devereaux attachable bit, 105
Dewsbury, John, 467
Dexter snaffle bit, 105
di Tergolina flex-mouth bit, 105
Diamond bit, 106
Diamond head, 315
Diamond heel bit, 106
Diamond swell bridle, 449
Dick Christian bit. 106
Directum bit, 111
Disks, 106, 143
Doherty construction method, 106
Dolan snaffle bit, 106
Dolphin bit, 107
Donnelly bridleless bit, 107
Donut, 64
Double bridle, 45, 108, 446, 449
Double-ear bridle, 449
Double-gag bit, 434
Double Hunt bridle, 449
Double-jointed mouth, 307
Double-loop liverpool bit, 221
Double-ringed snaffle bridle, 449
Double-twisted wire bit, 108
Douglas flex-mouth snaffle, 108
Dr. Bristol Pelham bit, 335
Dr. Bristol snaffle bit, 108
Dr. LeGear medicine bit, 244
Dr. Thatcher Braden Direct, 109
Dragoon bit, 270, 276
Dravelling snaffle bit, 109
Draw bit, 109
Draw rein, 449
Drenching horses, 247
Dressage Weymouth, 460
Driscoll adjustable bit, 109
Driving bit, 110, 117, 119, 121, 123

Drown snaffle bit, 141
Dudley twisted-wire bit, 141
Duke cheek, 45, 380
Dumb jockey, 64
Dumpy curb bit, 141, 416
Duncan driving bit, 111
Dunks double-chain bit, 141
Dunn gag bit, 141
Dwyer, Major Francis, 32
Dwyer bit, 142
Dynastic Period, 10
Ear boss, 142
Earhart snaffle bit, 142
Earl Shaw special bit, 142
Eastwood bit, 143
Easy Master Bit Co., 467
Eberhard glass-enhanced bit, 143
Echavarria, J. F., 467
Echini, 143
Eddy pressure bit, 143
Edward VII, 253, 261
Edwards, E. Hartley, 32
Edwards adjustable-mouth bit, 143
Elbow bit, 119, 144
Eldonian Saddlery, 467, 492 500
Egg-butt end, 315
Egg-butt gag bit, 158
Egg-butt Liverpool bit, 219
Egg-link mouth, 307
Egg-link Pelham, 336
Egg-roller mouth, 307
Egypt, 10
El Gato, 467
Elk bit, 144
Elliott driving bit, 111
Ely spiral bit, 144
Emerson telescoping-mouth bit, 144
Engle pressure bit, 144
England Manufacturing Co., 423
English arched mouth, 305
English bridle, 446
Equus caballus gmelini, 7
Erickson pressure bit, 145
Escutcheon, 145
Espinosa rearing-horse bit, 145
Estrada, Juan, 467
European gag bit, 158
Evans pulley bit, 146
Eyes, 146
Fabre revolving-mouth bit, 147
Face-piece, 147
Face-strap, 147
Fairbanks construction method, 147
Falls improved bit, 148

Falls rotating-cheek bit, 148
False martingale, 235
Fancy-cheek bits, 124-134
Fancy-driving bits, 124-134
Fast rein, 149
Fate rotating-mouth bit, 149
Fenner bit, 149
Fenner Pelham bit, 336
Ferruled ear bridle, 449
Ferry pulley bit, 149
Fiador, 150, 172, 174
Field, John, 467, 531
Fields pinching bit, 150
Fiery bit, 150
Fighting-the-bit, 150
Figueroa, Jose, 467
Figure 8 link, 150
Figure-8 noseband, 453
Fillis bit, 150
Fink checking bit, 151
Finnel control bit, 151
Fish eye cheek, 406
Fish eye snaffle, 406
Fishback mouth, 307
Fishback snaffle, 151
Fisher butterfly snaffle, 152
Fisher snaffle bit, 151
FitzGibbon snaffle bit, 152
Fixed cheek, 380
Flap-reins, 152, 449
Flat-ring cheek, 381
Flat-ring snaffle, 381, 440
Fleming bits, 467, 501
Flying Trench bit, 152
Flynn noseband, 325
Fogg rubber-mouth bit, 152
Ford checking bit, 153
Ford harness bit, 153
Foreacre gag, 158
Forehead band, 450
Forget-me-not bit, 153
Forrest split-mouth bit, 153
Four-ring bit, 154, 437
Fowler noseband, 326
Fowler noseband attachment, 154
French barless bit, 154
French military, 262
Frog mouth, 308
Front, 155, 450
Frost construction detail, 155
Frozen tombs of Siberia, 18-9
Fryer socket-mouth bit, 155
Full bridle, 155
Full cheek, 2, 155, 381
Fulmer snaffle bit, 155
Furlong mouth-piece design, 155
Gag bit, 156
Gag bridle, 450
Gag cheek, 381
Gal leg cheek, 381

Gallagher overcheck bit, 161
Gallatin scissor-mouth bit, 161
Gallic bit, 161
Garcia, Guadelupe S., 467
Garcia, Les, 467, 503-5
Gardner tie-down bit, 161
Gates curb bit, 162
Geared cheek, 382
George III bit, 162
George V, 253, 261
Gerald pressure bit, 162
German martingale, 235
German mouth, 265
German snaffle, 163
Ghost cord, 163
Gig, 112
Gig bit, 163
Gilbert pressure bit, 163
Gilliam rotating-mouth bit, 163
Gillispie snaffle bit, 163
Ginkinger one-piece bit, 163
Gleason bit, 112
Gliem, 479
Gliha run-out bit, 163
Globe bit, 164-5
Globe cheek, 382
Goldberg Staunton Saddlery Co., 467
Goodyear scissor bit, 164
Gordon overdraw strap, 167
Graham adjustable bit, 167
Graham checking bit, 167
Grant plate-cheek bit, 167
Grakle noseband, 453
Graves Bronco bit, 168
Grazing bit, 168
Great migration, 7
Green snaffle bit, 168
Greenwood overcheck bit, 169
Gregory snaffle bit, 169
Gridiron bit, 112, 169
Grijalva, Eduardo, 467
Gripper bars, 169
Grooved-mouth bit, 308
Grosvenor bit, 136
Grotto of Montespan, 9
Ground tie, 169
Guard, 169
Guedez curb bit, 169
Gutierrez, Raphael Philo, 506
Gutta-Percha, 169
Guy scissor bit, 170
Hack overcheck, 158
Hackalea, 174
Hackamore, 171
Hackamore bridle, 450
Hackarie, 174
Hackma, 171
Hackney bit, 179-80

Hale fire-horse bit, 179
Hale fire-horse bridle, 451
Half-breed bit, 44, 179 308
Half-breed mouth, 309
Half cheek, 1, 382
Half-moon bit, 179
Half-spoon bit, 382
Hall, Robert, 43
Hall curb bit, 181
Halter chain, 181
Halter, military, 287
Hancock mouth cover, 181
Hand-tooled martingale, 235
Hands, 181
Hanging cheek, 181-2, 293
Hanging-tongue bit, 182
Hanoverian bit, 113
Hanoverian Pelham bit, 336
Hanscom bit, 182
Hansford medicine bit, 181
Harbec nose clamp, 182
Harmonson double-action bit, 182
Harness bit, 153, 352
Harris curb bit, 182
Harris gag, 158
Harry Hightower bit, 183
Hart combined bit, 183
Hartman curb bit, 183
Hartman medicine bit, 245
Hartwell Pelham bit, 337
Harvey pressure bit, 184
Haskell bridle, 184
Haskell toggle bit, 184
Hauser tubular bit, 184
Hayden bail bit, 185
Hayden construction design, 185
Headstall, 446
Heavenly horses, 10
Heel knot, 172, 174
Heinisch attachment, 186
Heinze mouth design, 186
Helms scissor bit, 186-7
Henry check bit, 136
Hermosillo bit, 187
Herodotus, 9
Herrara, Alsalio, 468, 526
Higman harness bit, 188
Hill auxiliary bridle, 451
Hinged hunting snaffle, 188
Hippidiam neogaem, 7
Hisley bit with snaps, 188
Hitchcock gag, 159
Hoback, Larry, 468
Hodge, Jess, 468
Hogan check bit, 137
Hogg bit connection, 189
Holland bit 426
Hollow bar, 189
Hollow bit, 368
Holm two-piece bit, 189

Horn bit, 195
Horn cheek, 383
Horner geared bit, 189
Horseshoe bit, 217, 383, 404
Hot blooded, 10
Hourglass mouth, 190-1
Hubbard construction method, 190
Hubner medicine bit, 190
Huckins toggle bit, 190
Humane bit, 190, 192
Hunt, A. B., 468
Hunting gag, 159
Hutton overcheck, 137
Hutton rotating-mouth, 191
Hypohippus miocene, 7
Iceland bit, 193
Imperial driving bit, 113
Indian Chief bit, 477-8
Indian martingale, 235
Indian stock bridle, 462
Indianola bit, 193
Ingersoll, Bobby, snaffle, 194
Initial bit, 194
Inverted port, 309
Irish flat-ring snaffle, 194
Irish martingale, 235
Iron Duke bit, 194
Ives adjustable bit, 194
J.I.C. bit, 114
Jackson bit design, 194
Jackson double-mouth bit, 194
Jager zu Pferde, 262
James curb bit, 196
James horn bit, 195
James Safety bit, 195
James side-puller, 196
Jandrue pulley bit, 196
Janes pressure bit, 197
Jankovich, Miklos, 10
Japanese bit, 197
Jaquima, 171
Jerk-line, 197
Jimenez double bit, 197
Jodhopher curb bit, 95
Johnson Humane bit, 198
Johnson pressure bit, 198
Johnson scissor bit, 198
Johnston spring bit, 200
Jointed mouth, 308, 310
Jolan bastard mouth, 309
Jones, Mrs. Suzanne Norton, 44
Jones construction method, 200
Jones removeable bit, 200
Judd construction design, 200
Jungerman curb bit, 201
Junker bit, 201
Kalkbranner split-mouth bit, 201
Kelly, Pascal M., 174, 379, 469
Kelly revolving bit, 201

Kendall, J. M. "Jack", 529
"Kentucky Belle", 229
Kerro pattern, 202, 337
Kerruish curb bit, 202
Keys, 202, 303
Kiang, 7
Kiehl split-mouth bit, 202
Kimberwick bit, 202
Kimberwick Pelham bit, 337
Kimberwick Whitmore bit, 338
Kindig flex-mouth bit, 203
King Tutankhamen, 9
King air-control bit, 203
King pulley bit, 203
Klaus pressure bit, 204
Klein double-curb bit, 204
Knight overcheck bit, 204
Knuckle bit, 205
Kochheiser reversable bit, 205
Kock floating-mouth bit, 205
Kronhein spring curb bit, 205
Kuehnhold rein hook, 206
Lady leg, 300
Lady's leg bit, 207
Lamarque curb bit, 207
Lancer polo bit, 207
Langholz reversable bit, 208
Laredo bit, 208
Larios, A., 469
Las Cruces bit, 208
Lavaca bit, 208
Le Compte bit, 114, 209
Le Compte Manufacturing Co., 469
Lead rein, 209
Leather-mouth bit, 190
Lee Alwell Special bit, 209
Lee's patent bit, 209
Leg pattern, 207
Leichester bit, 210
Leisenring double-mouth bit, 210
Lesser split-mouth bit, 210
Letchworth double bit, 211-2
Levers, 212
Lewis bridle and bit, 452
Light mouth, 212
Lilenthal insulated bit, 212
Lilly bit-bar clip, 212
Linden and Funke, 469, 507-13
Link, 213
Link "T" bradoon, 213, 254
Linville control bit, 213
Lip bar, 213
Lip loop, 3, 213
Lip strap, 3
Lip-strap loop, 3
Lipping the bit, 213
Little harness bit, 213
Liverpool bit, 215-225
Lobdell rein attachment, 226
Lockhard noseband, 326
Log bit, 310
Lolling bit, 226, 417

Long cheek, 383
Long reins, 226
Longcor double bit, 226
Longeing, 226
Loose cheek, 216, 384
Loose rein, 227
Loose-ring Pelham, 344-347
Lord Lonsdale martingale, 236
Loriner, 227
Lowbridge loose-mouth bit, 227
Lower cheek, 21, 3, 6
Lownde's Pelham bit, 338
Luristan, 15-6, 20
Lynch snaffle bit, 227
Mace, Dan, bit, 228
MacFadden, Bruce J., 7
Maddox curb bit, 228
Magenis roller-mouth bit, 310
Magner four-ring bit, 154
Magner pulley bit, 228, 452
Mameluke bit, 228
Manning spring-mouth bit, 229
Mardueno, Jose, 469
Martarel, Juan, 525
Martin long-spoon bit, 229
Mason control bit, 240
Mason hook, 240
Mason leather bit, 241
Mason two-sided-mouth bit, 240
Material for cast bits, 241
Mattle, Ricardo, 525
Maxwell check bit, 137
McCarty, 171, 241
McChesney, 517-8
McCoy cable bit, 241
McDonald bit, 241
McGuinness scissor bit, 242
McKenney jointed-mouth bit, 242
McKerron overcheck, 137
McKinley port bit, 242
McKinney port bit, 242
McNair spring-rein, 243
McNalley control bit, 243
Meadow snaffle bit, 243
Mealey snaffle bit, 243
Measuring for a bit, 36
Mecate, 171-2
Medicine bit, 244-248, 366, 427
Medicine drenching bit, 246-8
Medusa-head boss, 267
Megargee curb bit, 249
Melleby combination bit, 249
Mellor shifting bit, 249
Merriam pulley bit, 249
Metals for cast bits, 241
Metcalf double-chain bit, 249

Metropolitan bit, 250
Metropolitan Toronto Police, 260
Meyer snaffle bit, 250
Mikar control bit, 251
Military:
    Canadian, 252
    German and French, 262
    United States, 270
Millard rein conversion, 298
Miller hinged-mouth bit, 298
Miller slotted-cheek bit, 298
Mills adjustable bit, 298
Minnich slotted-cheek bit, 299
Mitchell reversible bit, 299
Model 1909, 293
Mohawk attachment, 300
Monier cheek design, 300-1
Monier oval port, 300
Mora, Joe, 43
Morales, Mike, 469, 516-7
Morrey overcheck bit, 138
Morrisey contol devise, 301
Moss curb bit, 302
Mouth gage, 37
Mouth-piece end, 1
Mouth-piece shape, 35
Mouthing bit, 302-4
Mudro, Steve, 469
Mule port bit, 318
Mule snaffle bit, 318
Mullen curb bit, 318
Mullen-mouth Pelham, 338
Muntz check bit, 318
Muscovey bit, 318
Muzzle, 23
Muzzle bit, 318, 376
Myers Dee snaffle, 319
Nagbutt snaffle, 319
Narrow cheek, 319, 384
Nash pulley bit, 320
Nazor swivel mouth, 320
Neck-rein, 320
Nelson gag, 159
Nelson snaffle bit, 320
New Circle curb hook, 321
New York bit, 321
New Zealand spoon bit, 321
Newmarket gag, 159
Newmarket snaffle bridle, 321
Nichols rectangular mouth, 322
Niel control bit, 322
Niemann double-mouth bit, 322
Ninth Lancer Pelham, 338
Nixon jointed snaffle, 322
Nodine jointed snaffle, 323
Nolan bridle and bit, 453
North and Judd Mfg. Co., 469
North West Mounted Police, 259

Northern-type horse, 10
Norton pivoting-mouth bit, 323
Norton six-ring bit, 115
Nose-bag, 289
Nose net, 324
Noseband strap, 446
Nosebands, 324-6, 446, 452
Nutcracker action, 39-40
O'Donnell curb bit, 327
O'Leary double-mouth bit, 327
O'Neil chain mouth, 328
O'Neil gag bit, 328
Oelkers horn bit, 328
Olin adjustable bit, 329
Olympic martingale, 236
Omato control bit, 329
Onager, 7, 11
One-eared bridle, 453
Open end, 316
Open reins, 329, 453
Orendorff double-mouth bit, 329
Ormsby snaffle bit, 330
Ostrich bit, 330
Oval-swell bridle, 453
Overton, Dennis, 533
PIMC, 419
Panama bit, 330
Pancher lip protector, 331
Pantographic snaffle, 331
Paranteau bit, 331
Park fancy bit, 331-2
Parson double-mouth bit, 332
Payne tubular bit, 332
Pazyryk burial burrows, 18-9
Pelham, 46, 333-50
Pelham bridle, 454
Pembroke harness bit, 351
Pendeltan checking bit, 351
Perfection driving bit, 115
Performance gag, 159
Perkins Pelham bit, 339
Persian snaffle bit, 352
Peters bit, 310
Peters two-piece bit, 352
Petersboro driving bit, 352
Petersheim pulley bit, 353
Peterson rein attachment, 353
Peterson twisted-wire bit, 353
Pfander rein attachment, 353
Phillips and Gutierrez, 470
Phillips double bit, 353
Phillips safety bit, 115
Phillips snaffle bit, 354
Pierson pulley bit, 354
Pistol bit, 354
Plate mouth, 53
Plates, 354
Playeres, 302, 354
Plow-lining, 354
Plow-rein, 454

Pluvinel, 25
Pneumatic bit, 354
Points of control, 34
Polo Pelham, 339
Pond bit design, 355
Poole curb bit, 355
Pope Island Mfg. Co., 419
Pope tie bit, 355
Port, 3, 6
Porter Humane bit, 356
Portugese bit, 356
Powder River Co., 470
Preece adjustable blt, 356
Price loose-cheek bit, 357
Price square-mouth bit, 357
Przevalski, Nicolai, 7, 8, 10
Psalion, 358
Pulley bits, 357
Pulley cheek, 384
Purcell spring-tension bit, 358
Quadragia, 12
Qualey, Tom, 470
Quick bit, 175
Race bit, 359
Racking bit, 359
Raddatz, Diane, 13
Ramses III, 15
Ramsey Pelham bit, 340
Rarey training bit, 359
Ray hackamore bit, 176
Ray loose-cheek curb, 359
Raymond leverage check, 138, 359
Reade removeable-bar bit, 360
Reardon bridle, 454
Rearing-horse bit, 360-1
Regulator bit, 361
Reichart driving bit, 111
Rein bearing, 361
Rein chains, 4, 454, 466
Rein-rings, 3
Reindeer, 9
Reinforced cheek, 384
Reins, 361, 456
Renalde, James, 481
Reverse arch, 361
Reversible cheek, 384
Reynolds levered curb, 361
Ricardo hackamore, 178
Ricardo Metal Mfg. Co., 518-22
Richmond scissor bit, 362
Richter spring-mouth bit, 362
Riggs snaffle attachment, 362
Ring bit, 379, 362-4, 370, 410, 424
Robbins double-mouth bit, 364
Roberds corrugated curb, 364
Roberts hinged snaffle, 365
Roberts roller-mouth bit, 365
Robinson "shying" bit, 366
Rockwell bit, 115
Rodriguez, Jose, 526
Rody medicine bit, 366

Roeber pulley bit, 366
Roller gag, 160
Roller-mouth Pelham, 340
Romal, 366
Roping bit, 366-7
Rotating cheek, 385
Round-cheek bridle, 456
Round martingale, 237
Rounded-mouth bit, 367
Rowley detachable bit, 367
Rowley flex-mouth bit, 367
Roy Cooper bit, 311
Rubber-ball bit, 409
Rubber mouth, 139
Rudenko, Sergei, 18-9
Rugby Pelham, 340
Ruhlow gag bit, 368
Rupert hollow bit, 368
Russell curb bit, 368
Rutledge roper, 369
S. M. Polo bit, 312, 341
Saber cheek, 385
Sabio ring bit, 370
Safety bit, 115
Salinas bit, 371
Salisbury gag, 160
San Antonio bit, 370
San Jose bit, 370
Sanborn center link, 370
Santa Barbara bit, 371
Santa Suzanna bit, 371
Sargeant construction method, 371
Sargeant overcheck, 139
Scamperdale Pelham, 341, 372
Schell, A. J., 470-1
Scherling reversible bit, 372
Schleuter change bit, 372
Schoonmaker lined rings, 372
Scissor bit, 115, 372
Scorrier snaffle bit, 373
Sears Humane bit, 373
Seeley spring-cheek bit, 374
Seften Pelham, 341
Segundo bit, 374-5
Seitz pulley bridle, 456
Sept-I of Egypt, 15
Shank checking device, 375
Shape of mouth-piece, 35
Shepard overcheck, 139
Shields square-mouth bit, 376
Shipley, Charles, 470, 479
Shoemaker bit, 287-8, 290
Short muzzle bit, 376
Shrewbury gag, 160
Shuham, Henry Gust, 526
Shute snaffle bit, 376
Sibbitt stud bit, 377
Side-arm brace, 4
Side claws, 71, 377
Side plates, 389

Side puller, 196, 389
Side rein, 389
Sidewinder, 389
Sievert curb bit, 389
Silver bits, 390-4
Silver inlay, 389
Silver overlay, 389
Simpson, Gaylord, 7
Sims double-mouth bit, 395
Single chain-link snaffle, 395
Six-ring bit, 116
Size of mouth-piece, 35
Slaugher leverage bit, 395
Slawson light-weight bit, 395
Slip-ear bridle, 456
Sloat spring bit, 396
Slobber bar, 5
Slobber chains, 4
Slobber leathers, 396
Slotted cheek, 386
Small lip controller, 396
Smith, Col. Hamilton, 8
Smith adjustable-mouth bit, 398
Smith construction method, 397
Smith curb bars, 398
Smith detachable port, 397
Smith double-mouth bit, 397
Smith scissor bit, 397
Smith spring bit, 398
Smith tongue bit, 397
Smith wire-mouth bit, 398
Snaffle bit, 1, 2, 398
Snaffle bridle, 398
Snake bit, 399, 514
Sommer double-mouth bit, 399
South Russian Tarpan, 7
Southern-type horse, 10
Spade bit, 4, 42
Spade bit mouth, 312
Spanish jumping bit, 203, 400
Spectacle martingale, 237
Speculum, 400
Speedway overcheck, 139
Spence scissor bit, 401
Split cheek-strap, 446
Spohr curb bit, 401
Spokane bit, 401
Spoon, 401
Spoon cheek, 386
Spoon-spade mouth, 312
Spoonhour snaffle bit, 401
Spring-mouth snaffle, 74
Spring-tension cheek, 386
Springstein bit, 116
Sproul hackamore bit, 176
Squire coil-mouth, 403
Squire construction method, 402-3
Squire snaffle bit, 403

Stalker control device, 404
Stalker leather-mouth bit, 403
Stalker lip-check, 404
Stalker Pelham, 342
Stallion bit, 404
Stallion bridle, 457
Standing martingale, 238
Stanley construction method, 406
Stanley curb bit, 405
Stanley head, 386
Stanley hollow mouth, 405
Stanley Humane bit, 407
Stanley rubber-covered bit, 406
Stapleton spring-action bit, 407
Star-check snaffle, 407
Stendel check bit, 139
Stevens pressure bit, 407
Stockder fastener, 407
Stockton harness bit, 408
Stockton Pelham, 342
Stout pattern, 252
Success bit, 110
Sulecio bridleless curb, 408
Sumerians, 9
Sutton bit with buckles, 408
Sutton bridle, 457
Swales 3-in-1 bit, 342, 409
Swales bit, 116, 409
Swales bit attachment, 409
Swales tubular-mouth bit, 409
Swan cheek, 386
Swan snaffle bit, 409
Swart spring-cheek bit, 410
Swartzendruber ring bit, 410
Swept-back cheek, 387
Swivel cheek, 387
Swivel gag, 160
Swivel shank, 387
Sythian tombs, 13
T-hackamore, 176
T-head, 316
Taking the bit, 411
Tannenburg, 22
Tarpon, 7
Tasseled bridle, 457-8
Tattersall ring bit, 411
Taylor, Lewis, 13
Taylor double-mouth bit, 411
Taylor pulley bit, 411
Taylor simple bit, 412
Teathering bridle, 447
Temple bit with overcheck, 412
Tepper curb bit, 412
Tevis loop bit, 412
Texas bit, 412
Thimbles, 413
Thompson sliding-mouth bit, 413
Thorn bit, 413

Thornton, Baron, bit, 414
Thornton pivoting-mouth bit, 414
Thornton two-bar bit, 414
Throat-latch, 446
Thurlow curb bit, 414
Thurlow harness bit, 415
Tichner spring-mouth bit, 415
Tight jaw, 4
Tilbury harness bit, 416
Tom Thumb bit, 416
Tongue bit, 417
Tongue bit, hanging, 418
Tongue freedom, 38
Tongue plate, 418
Tongue-plate Pelham, 343
Tongue room, 38
Tooled bridle, 458
Touch bit, 418
Tracy muzzle bit, 418
Trademarks 419-22
Trew, Cecil G., 7
Triangular bit, 106
Triple-mouth bit, 387
Triumph bit, 424
Truit change-mouth bit, 424
Tuke, Diane, 46
Turkey ring bit, 363
Turkish bit, 424
Turn cheek, 387
Turton double-mouth bit, 424
Turton end, 317
Tutankhamen, 9
Twisted-wire bit, 313-4, 425
Typology, 425
Ulrich curb bit, 426
Universal driving bit, 111
Universal Pattern, 259
United States Polo Pelham, 340
Upper cheek, 2-3, 6
Uppingham curb bit, 426
Uxeter bit, 427
Valencia bit, 427
Valley of Horses, 8
Van Arsdale driving bit, 427
Van Auken medicine bit, 427
Vernon, Arthur, Vigueno mouth, 314
Viridet no-mouth bit, 427
Wagner plastic bit, 428
Wagon blind bridle, 463
Walker, David E., 526
Walking-horse bit, 428-30
Walking-horse gag, 160
Wallin snap-hook bit, 428, 431
Walter curb bit, 428, 431
War bridle, 459
Ward hackamore, 177
Ward tongue bit, 431
Ward Union curb bit, 431
Warfel split-mouth bit, 432
Washington Pelham, 343
Watering bit, 254, 264, 286, 432
Weathers snaffle bit, 432
Webb martingale, 239
Webb snaffle bit, 432
Weeks, Ed, 527
Wegener, Henry, 527
Weight of mouth-piece, 35
Wellington bit, 314, 433
Western Pelham, 343
Weymouth bit, 433
Weymouth bridle, 460
Weymouth gag, 161
Weymouth scissor bit, 433
Wheeler double-gag bit, 434
Wheeler notched-mouth bit, 433
Wheeler ported driving bit, 434
Whelen curb bit, 435
Whitmore Kimberwick bit, 338
Whinney, 8
Whipple bit, 291
Whitman bit, 289
Whitman Pelham, 343, 435
Whoa Maker, 435
Wiener flex-mouth bit, 435
Wild-horse cheek, 388
Wilder wood-mouth bit, 436
William Stone Pelham, 437
Williams gag bit, 436-7
Williams military bit, 285
Williams spring-cheek bit, 437
Williamsburg bit, 438
Willis bit, 438
Willoughby, David P., 7,10
Wilson bridle, 459
Wilson snaffle bit, 438-40
Wimbash bit, 441
Wingert snaffle bit, 441
Withey leather-covered bit, 441
Wittmann snaffle bit, 441
Wolfington curb bit, 442
Woman bit, 442
Wood-mouth bit, 436, 442
Woodmansee bit, 443
Woods snaffle bit, 443
Wright driving bit, 117
Y-mouth bit, 444
Yorktown bit, 444
Young, John Richard, 43
Zahl snaffle bit, 444
Zebra, 7
Zebra bit, 445
Zeller snaffle bit, 445